THE WAR OF THE REVOLUTION

THE WAR OF THE REVOLUTION

CHRISTOPHER WARD

EDITED BY JOHN RICHARD ALDEN

SKYHORSE PUBLISHING

Skyhorse Publishing books may be purchased in bulk at special discounts for sales promotion, corporate gifts, fund-raising, or educational purposes. Special editions can also be created to specifications. For details, contact the Special Sales Department, Skyhorse Publishing, 307 West 36th Street, 11th Floor, New York, NY 10018 or info@skyhorsepublishing.com.

www.skyhorsepublishing.com

10 9 8 7 6 5 4 3 2 1

Library of Congress Cataloging-in-Publication Data

Ward, Christopher, 1868-1943.
    The War of the Revolution / by Christopher Ward.
        p. cm.
    Includes bibliographical references and index.
    ISBN 978-1-61608-080-8 (hardcover : alk. paper)
    1. United States–History–Revolution, 1775-1783–Campaigns. I. Title.
    E230.W34 2010
    973.3'3–dc22

                                        2010021671

Printed in Canada

The maps on pages 217, 299, 345, 367, 583, 601, 607, 727, 759, 789, 805, 819, and 829 also appear in *The Delaware Continentals, 1776–1783*, by Christopher L. Ward, copyright, 1941, by the Historical Society of Delaware.

Editor's Preface

The origins of *The War of the Revolution* are to be found in part in the late Mr. Ward's studies of the history of the Delaware Line. His volume on *The Delaware Continentals, 1776–1783*, published in 1941, contains much more than the story of one of the best units in the Continental army. Approximately one half of Mr. Ward's last work is to be found in his earlier monograph, which was put forth in a limited edition and which deserved a much wider circulation. This material, which deals with land operations in the middle and southern states after 1776, was revised by the author. To it Mr. Ward added about forty new chapters on the campaign of 1775; operations in New England, northern New York, and Canada; border conflicts; and the Yorktown campaign.

The author intended to write a history of the campaigns on land rather than a complete history of the war. He largely accomplished his purpose, although his manuscript, as submitted to the editor, contained no account of the war beyond the Alleghenies. The editor has supplied a brief description of that portion of the conflict in one chapter, emphasizing the role of George Rogers Clark.

A few words about the labors of the editor. *The War of the Revolution*, with the exception of the chapter mentioned in the preceding paragraph, has been little altered by the editor. Additions to the citations and bibliography have been inserted in order to present a few of the more important scholarly contributions concerning the War of Independence not available to the author. Some obvious errors in the text which Mr. Ward would surely have removed had they been brought to his attention have been corrected.

In so large a work, other mistakes undoubtedly remain, despite the efforts of both author and editor. The editor has also tried to perform the last minute tasks of completing citations and bibliographical entries, and similar duties. *The War of the Revolution* remains, however, the work of Mr. Ward in point of view, interpretation, emphasis, and all fundamental matters.

Relying largely upon more or less standard secondary authorities and printed source material, the author has written a detailed and accurate account of the military operations on land of the War of Independence. He has contributed a most useful work of reference. He has also added to the great store of splendid writing upon the Revolutionary period. His account of the day of Lexington and Concord thrilled even an editor who was not unfamiliar with the events of April 19, 1775.

It is not possible for the editor to express the gratitude of the author to all the persons who assisted him. Mr. Kenneth Roberts and Mr. Carl Van Doren gave him helpful advice. The editor must declare his appreciation of services performed by three assistant instructors attached to the Department of History of the University of Nebraska, Miss Lois Christensen, Mr. Carl Bader, Jr., and Mr. Philip Holmgren. Dr. John Powell, Professor G. W. Gray, and Mr. Rodman Ward gave him advice, encouragement, and help in various ways.

JOHN RICHARD ALDEN

Preface

This book is not a history of the American Revolution. It is a history of the war that was caused by the Revolution. As John Adams well said: "A history of the first war of the United States is a very different thing from a history of the American Revolution. . . . The revolution was in the minds of the people and in the union of the colonies, both of which were accomplished before hostilities commenced. This revolution and union were gradually forming from the years 1760 to 1776."

With the Revolution as thus properly described, this book is not concerned, except in the brief résumé of the causes of the war in the first chapter. Its aim is to tell the story of the war on land, the campaigns, battles, sieges, marches, encampments, bivouacs, the strategy and tactics, the hardships, and the endurance of hardship. It is purely military in its intention and scope.

The war, from the first shot at Lexington in 1775 to the cessation of hostilities in 1782, lasted nearly eight years. It was fought in a territory extending from Quebec southward to Georgia and from the Atlantic seaboard westward to the frontier settlements. Many of its campaigns, in the various regions in which they were fought, were simultaneous.

In the spring of 1776, while the American army under Arnold was still struggling to keep a foothold in Canada, a British army under Henry Clinton was on its way south to attack Charleston in South Carolina. On September 11, 1777, while Washington was fighting the Battle of the Brandywine, Burgoyne was on his way down the Hudson to Saratoga.

It will be seen, then, that an attempt to tell the tale of the various campaigns and battles in strict chronological order would involve leaping, chapter by chapter, from one campaign to another, from the North to the South and from the East to the West, and would result in hopeless confusion. Fortunately for the sake of clarity in this chronicle, the whole territory involved was fought over, by different armies, in well defined sections, in the North from Canada down to the Mason and Dixon line, in the South from Virginia down to Georgia, with practically no overlapping. It has therefore been thought best to treat the campaigns separately in the two sections, thus enabling the reader to follow the movements of the armies and the progress of the various campaigns with a minimum of confusion.

While making no pretensions to the role of a military expert, the author has ventured to express opinions as to the strategy and tactics employed in some of the operations herein recorded. In doing so, he relies upon the dictum of Baron Jomini in that eminently authoritative military treatise, *Précis de l'art de la guerre*, "The theory of the great speculative combinations of war is simple enough in itself; it only requires intelligence and attentive reflection," and upon von Moltke's statement that "strategy is the application of common sense to the conduct of war."

CHRISTOPHER WARD

Contents

VOLUME TWO

The War in the South

Maps

VOLUME ONE

VOLUME TWO

xiii

The War in the North

CHAPTER 1

The Causes of the War

Tuesday, the 17th of May, 1774, was an unpleasant day in Boston. A pelting rain, driven by a strong east wind, poured upon the town. Gutters ran full; hollows in the cobbled streets became puddles. The few of its citizens who owned umbrellas found some shelter under those newfangled, cumbrous contrivances of oiled silk or linen spread on clumsy ribs of whalebone.[1] The thousands of others who were abroad that day could only turn the brims of their hats down, the collars of their coats up, wrap their cloaks around them, and take the storm as it came, with a philosophical endurance born of habit.

But the provincial troop of horse, the Ancient and Honourable Artillery Company, the Boston Grenadier Corps, fine, tall fellows in notably handsome uniforms, and more companies of militia, drawn up in line along King Street, could not even flap their hats or turn up their collars. They had to stand stiffly at attention in their ordered ranks, while the rain beat upon their faces and dripped from their noses and chins.

The Boston Cadets, the "Governor's Own," were equally defenseless as they marched against the blast down King Street. So were "a number of His Majesty's Council, several Members of the Commons House of Assembly [and] many principal Gentlemen of the town" who followed the soldiers, in dripping discomfort.

At the Long Wharf the procession halted. The military formed its ranks, and the gentlemen following grouped themselves in proper disposition as a reception committee. All eyes, not only those of the official party but those also of the thronging multitude of common people gathered around and

3

behind them, were turned upon one of His Britannic Majesty's ships of war lying at the wharf.

There was a ruffle of drums aboard the ship; the guns on the other war vessels in the harbor and in the batteries in the town began a thunderous salute and the bells in all the steeples rang out as the expected guests, brave in scarlet coats and white breeches that glittered with gold braid, descended the gangplank and were welcomed with all due form and ceremony and with more or less sincerity according to the political principles of the individual greeters. Whether Boston liked it or not, it was indeed an occasion of moment, for these impressively arrayed military personages were none other than Lieutenant General the Honorable Thomas Gage, commander in chief of all His Majesty's forces in the American colonies and Governor of the Province of Massachusetts Bay, and his staff—his "family," in the language of the period.

The official greetings over, a procession was formed. Led by the guard of honor, the great man with his entourage and the official civilians, followed by thousands of unofficial sight-seers, proceeded up King Street. The rain, on their backs now, was no doubt less discomforting.

The troop of horse, the artillerymen, the grenadiers, and the embodied militia, all amateur soldier boys, stood stiffly at attention while their officers gave these awe-inspiring professionals their very best in the way of a military salute, which the general politely returned. They then fell in behind the procession in its march up King Street to the Town House.

In the Council Chamber, His Excellency presented his commission and was sworn in by the President of the Council. From the balcony of the State House, the High Sheriff read the new Governor's proclamation "continuing all Officers &c in their places till further orders." It was answered by "three huzzas from the concourse of the people," three volleys of musketry from the soldiers of Boston, and the discharge of the Ancient and Honourables' three three-pounder brass fieldpieces.[2]

After the Governor had "received the compliments of civil and military officers and other gentry" and reviewed the militia he was escorted to Faneuil Hall, "where an elegant entertainment was provided at the expence of the province. . . . Many loyal toasts were drank, and the strictest harmony and decorum observed." He then rode in a carriage to the Province House, his official residence.[3]

From all these sights and sounds one might have supposed that it was a day of rejoicing in Boston, that the coming of the new governor was hailed by the people as a fortunate event. But no, the flapping flags, the pealing bells, the saluting guns, all the parade and circumstance of welcome were mere matters of form; the huzzas of the populace were no more than throat-deep. The people of Boston knew what his coming meant and what his orders were; they dreaded what he had come to do. Against him and what he represented, Boston harbored strong feelings of antagonism.

Gage was no stranger in America. After about seventeen years of military service in Britain and on the continent of Europe, he had come to America in 1755 and had taken part in Braddock's disastrous expedition against the French and Indians. He had fought bravely under Braddock, and also under Abercromby in the ill-fated British attack upon Ticonderoga in 1758. Serving as governor of Montreal after the conquest of Canada, he had become commander in chief of the British army in America late in 1763, succeeding his good friend Sir Jeffrey Amherst. His wife, born Margaret Kemble, was an American and a member of a prominent New Jersey family, a cousin of Philip Schuyler and a relative of colonial Van Cortlandts and Bayards. He was a good soldier and was devoted to his duty. He was handsome and dignified, his manners were pleasing; and he was described by the historian William Smith as "a good-natured, peaceable, sociable man." With these qualities, and replacing at least temporarily the hated Governor Thomas Hutchinson, he might have been received with pleasure—would have been so received ten years earlier.

On the other hand, Bostonians had known of him as the commander of the British forces in America who had directed the activities of the four regiments sent to town in 1768, and they had not forgotten the consequent bloody affair in their streets in 1770. To be sure, the regulars had been ordered to Boston by the British cabinet, and Gage had merely executed its orders; but the memory of the "Boston Massacre" would have diminished his welcome now, even if he had come with the most amicable intentions. But he had, in fact, come under orders from his government to deprive the town and the whole province of much of their liberty, and also to close the port of Boston to commerce, which could paralyze the town's chief industries, impoverish its substantial citizens, beggar its working people, and bring them near to starvation. The whole affair of his reception, although many Bostonians sincerely welcomed him, was a triumph of good manners over deep-seated, implacable, and not unjustified resentment.[4]

To appreciate the situation, to understand the causes that gradually developed from mere muttered discontent an animosity that led to violent resistance and finally to the War which it is the purpose of this book to chronicle, one must go back a matter of a decade, to the year 1763.

For a much longer time than that the American colonies had been subject to certain restrictions imposed by the government of Great Britain. The

Navigation Acts, which restrained or rather canalized their sea-borne commerce for the benefit of the shipping interests of the mother country, the Molasses Act, which penalized the importation of molasses and sugar from other than British sources, the various acts which forbade the development of manufactures in the colonies, might seem to have been sufficient to arouse rebellious sentiments in the minds of the colonists long before the year 1763. But in fact there were certain advantages to the Americans in their operation. There were also certain extralegal methods of evasion, which served to lighten their burdensome features. So that, on the whole, there was little opposition to them on the part of the inhabitants of the colonies, and their relations with the home government were not strained. Indeed, the era preceding 1763 came in after days to be regarded by them as a golden age to which they would fain return.

In that year the Peace of Paris ended the Seven Years' War in Europe, a part of which was the French and Indian War in America. That war and three other great conflicts in the preceding seventy years had drained Great Britain's treasury and piled up a public debt of £136,000,000. To sustain this burden and to meet heavy current expenses—heavy in part because it had been decided to keep a regular army of about 6,000 men in America after 1763—she felt obliged to find new sources of income outside the kingdom; and the prosperous American colonies seemed to be the best available source. The consequence was a series of British financial measures to which the Americans strongly objected. Additional causes for American discontent lay in new restrictions placed upon their paper currency, upon westward migration, and upon their trade, and in demands that the colonists give quarters and supplies to the regular army upon certain occasions. Indeed, the very presence of the regulars in America caused great dissatisfaction when the army was stationed in the settled areas.

The Sugar Act of 1764, a successor to the Molasses Act, which had lapsed, clearly displayed the intention of the British government to secure substantial revenue from the mainland American colonies. It cut the duty on molasses in half, while raising that on sugar; and it imposed other new, though less important, duties. It did not differ greatly in form from the old act, except for one startling assertion. While the Molasses Act had been regarded as only a regulation of commerce, such small revenue as it provided being merely incidental, this new law baldly stated in its preamble that one of its purposes was to raise a revenue; in other words, it was in great part a taxing measure.[5] The British government proposed to collect threepence upon every gallon of molasses entering the colonies from the foreign West Indian islands, and shook up its collecting agencies to make certain that the colonists would pay. They had rather effectively avoided paying the duties set up in 1733.

No one had objected on principle to the Molasses Act, although the colonial merchants had flouted it. However, to the relatively new principle of the Sugar Act there was immediate and, in the minds of the Americans, well founded objection; and nowhere in the colonies was it stronger or more vocal than in this same town of Boston, where Samuel Adams became the leader of resistance. The Americans were all the more unhappy because Britain was determined not only to pass the act but to enforce it, and also to enforce the long disobeyed Acts of Navigation.

Adams declared that taxes imposed on the colonists, "without their having a legal representative where they are laid," reduced them "from the character of free subjects to the miserable condition of tributary slaves." [6] This was the answer in principle. The practical answer was a development of the technique of smuggling to such a degree that the new measures were partly nullified.

But the mother country had another rod in pickle for her refractory children, guaranteed to be proof against the tricks of the wiliest smuggler. This was the famous Stamp Act of 1765 requiring that revenue stamps be affixed to all papers in lawsuits, all commercial paper, bills of lading, ship charters, probates of wills, surveys and conveyances of land, leases, bills of sale, and a host of other legal documents, as well as newspapers, pamphlets, playing cards, and so on. The cost of the stamps ranged from a halfpenny on a small newspaper to £6 on a grant of franchise. Heavy penalties were imposed on violators of the act, and, worst of all, unstamped documents were declared void in law. [7]

As a taxing measure it was fair enough, the taxes being widely and rather equally distributed and easily collected. Nor was it a novel method of taxation, for such stamps had long been in use in England. But it could not in any sense be regarded as a regulation of commerce; it was a taxing act pure and simple, without disguise, palliation, or apology. Against it the colonists reacted even more strongly than against the Sugar Act.

In Virginia, Patrick Henry is said to have suggested to George III that he should profit by the examples of Tarquin, Caesar, and Charles I, and the House of Burgesses declared against tax laws not emanating from its own legislature. Pennsylvania and the other middle colonies passed similar resolutions. Massachusetts called for a congress of colonial representatives to take steps in the matter. The Stamp Act Congress met in New York in October, 1765, with members from nine of the thirteen colonies present.

The Congress proceeded to declare, in substance, the colonies' loyalty to

the Crown and "all due subordination" to the Parliament, but asserted that
it was essential to the freedom of a people that no taxes should be imposed
without its consent; that the colonists were not and could not be represented
in Parliament; that only their own legislatures could tax them. The Congress
added the practical argument that the stamp taxes were so heavy as to prevent them from buying English goods and so were inimical to the prosperity
of England, as well as of the colonies. An address to the King, a Memorial
to the House of Lords, and a Petition to the Commons all expressed the
unhappiness of the colonists.

Meanwhile, intense excitement prevailed throughout the colonies. The
Virginia resolutions were broadcast. Associations called Sons of Liberty
were formed in the northern provinces to resist the execution of the law.
They acted with vigor, indeed with violence. In Boston they hanged Oliver,
the stamp officer, in effigy and smashed the windows of his house. He resigned his office, but the Sons of Liberty were not appeased. They burned
the records of the vice-admiralty courts, newly empowered to enforce the
customs laws; they sacked the office of the Comptroller of Customs, and
they climaxed their vandalism by wrecking the fine mansion of Governor
Hutchinson, destroying his furniture, defacing his paintings, and casting into
the street and burning his books, historical documents and manuscripts, the
finest collection of the sort in America. Terrified stamp officers almost universally resigned their posts or refused to do their duty. When the stamps
arrived there was hardly anyone willing to receive and issue them. And when
they arrived the colonists destroyed them or secured promises from officials
that they would not be sold.

November 1, 1765, the day the act was to go into effect, was observed
throughout the colonies as a day of mourning; muffled bells were tolled,
minute guns were fired, and flags were set at half-staff. How could business
go on? How could the courts function, newspapers be issued, ships chartered or cleared, land conveyed, goods sold, without stamps? The solution
was simple. Unstamped newspapers appeared, and though for a time business was suspended it was soon largely resumed. The law was simply disregarded, and the act nullified.

But it still stood on the statute books, a menace to every American interest. To enforce its repeal, a general boycott of English goods was organized,
and a movement to encourage manufactures despite their unlawfulness was
inaugurated. The effect of these measures was impressive. Factories in
England were closed; thousands were thrown out of work; and manufac-
turers and merchants faced bankruptcy. When Parliament met in December,
it had to reconsider its action. The addresses of the Stamp Act Congress

might have been disregarded, but not the flood of petitions for repeal of the act that came from the commercial classes of Englishmen. William Pitt, the idol of the English people, declared that Parliament had no right to levy the stamp tax, and after a long and heated debate the obnoxious act was repealed.

The news of the repeal was received in America "in a transport of mingled surprise, exultation, and gratitude." Fireworks, festivities, resolutions, and addresses of thanks were evidences of the joy of the people. Moreover, there was a great outburst of loyalty to England. Statues of the King were voted in New York and Virginia. Pitt, Barré, and Conway, leaders of the movement for repeal, were honored by effigies or portraits displayed in public places. The Sons of Liberty faded away. John Adams said that the repeal "hushed into silence almost every popular clamor." Yet this was in fact but an armistice, a temporary truce and not a permanent peace between the government of Great Britain and the self-assertive colonists.

In July, 1766, there was a change in the ministry. Pitt, though disabled by physical and perhaps even mental infirmities, accepted the responsibility of leading it and then betook himself to the House of Lords as Earl of Chatham. The Duke of Grafton became prime minister in form, but exercised little influence. Leadership of the Commons was assumed by Charles Townshend, no friend of America. Unfortunately for the empire, no doubt, Pitt was too sick to control affairs, and Townshend had an opportunity to shine.

Townshend was a brash young man, whose "wonderful endowments [were] dashed with follies and indiscretions." [8] Early in 1767 he boasted that he knew the mode by which a revenue could be drawn from America without offense to the Americans.[9] His scheme was based on a distinction which had been suggested or implied by some colonists and by some Englishmen between "external taxes," that is, duties on imports, to which they did not object, and "internal taxes" such as those imposed by the Stamp Act, which they denounced. He brought in a bill to impose duties on colonial importations from Britain of glass, certain painters' materals, and tea. The proceeds were to be used to pay the salaries of the colonial governors and judges, thus freeing crown officers in America from dependence upon colonial legislatures. He coupled with this a bill to legalize writs of assistance—general search warrants to be used by the revenue officers in enforcing the new revenue law; a bill establishing new courts of vice-admiralty; and a bill creating a special Board of Commissioners of the Customs in Boston, responsible directly to the British Treasury and controlling completely a reorganized American customs service.

But, in relying on the external-internal tax distinction to procure the acquiescence of the Americans, he failed to realize that most Americans were actually opposed to external as well as internal taxes for revenue. The colonists had tasted blood in their fight against the Stamp Act. They considered that they themselves had in effect repealed that law before Parliament did. What they had once done, they felt able to do again. Moreover, there was a growing discontent with the older statutes, the Navigation Acts and those forbidding manufactures. Though long accepted without objection and, in practice, to a considerable degree nullified by simple disobedience of their provisions, these were now felt to be oppressive.

In this state of mind, the colonists cheerfully threw overboard whatever distinction between the two kinds of taxes they had formerly offered. All taxes for revenue, of whatever sort, were now equally hateful. Since 1765 they had been objecting to the standing army as an instrument of tyranny. Now they denounced the new Board of Customs, which would inconveniently interfere with the custom of smuggling. Also they wanted to pay their own governors and judges, basing the desire upon the feeling that their hold on the purse strings was a safeguard against oppression by these officers.

On more justifiable grounds, they were opposed to the writs of assistance, which would enable any customs officer to search not only any ship, but also "any House Shop Cellar Warehouse or Room or other place," [10] without showing cause for such intrusion.

With the passage of the Townshend acts, the short-lived era of good feeling among the colonists toward the mother country came to a sudden end. Massachusetts made the first move toward effective opposition to the new laws by sending a Circular Letter to the other colonies urging concerted action. The British ministry ordered the colonial governors to compel the various colonial legislatures to rescind all resolutions directed against those laws, and to dissolve the assemblies if they refused. Such steps were taken in half a dozen of the colonies, but they only poured oil on the flames of discontent.

Practical measures were taken by the Americans. The general boycott of English goods was gradually revived by new Nonimportation Agreements. The Sons of Liberty became active in their enforcement. When John Hancock's sloop *Liberty* was seized by royal officials at a wharf in Boston in June, 1768, on a charge of smuggling, a mob attacked them. The Commissioners of Customs fled in terror to Castle William, a fortress on an island in Boston harbor.

These and other acts of violent resistance could not be overlooked by the British government. General Gage was instructed to move two regiments of foot to Boston for police duty. When these regulars landed at the beginning of October, 1768, Boston declined to furnish free quarters in town and certain supplies for them, as seemingly required by an act of Parliament. Colonel Dalrymple, commander of the troops, had to rent any available lodgings for his men and for two more regiments of infantry that joined them in following months. Instead of being concentrated in barracks under firm control of their officers, the soldiers were scattered throughout the town, with unfortunate results.

Bostonians regarded them as foreign troops and accordingly hated them, ostracized them, insulted them in the streets and called them opprobrious names. They responded by swaggering, insolent, contemptuous conduct. The natural result was frequent brawls and rough encounters between the citizens and the soldiers.

On March 5, 1770, this mutual ill-feeling culminated in a serious affair. A mob of citizens pelted some of the intruders with snowballs and stones and reviled them with scurrilous language. There was a close encounter, so close that some of the mob struck at their opponents' muskets with clubs, daring them to fire, and knocked one of them down. The soldiers fired into the crowd. Eleven of the citizens fell, three of them dead, two mortally wounded. This was the famous "Boston Massacre."

Quite naturally, it caused great excitement throughout the town. Bells were rung to summon the populace. The whole town poured out into the streets. Drums were beaten to call out the militia. Several companies formed around the Town House. It looked as if the war was to begin then and there. But Governor Hutchinson succeeding in quieting the people and in obtaining Dalrymple's promise to withdraw the troops to Castle William in Boston harbor.

Meanwhile the continued boycott of British goods was seriously affecting the English economy. Exports to America shrank to half their former value, and there was nothing that the army could do about it. Confronted with this situation, several members of the ministry urged a policy of conciliation and proposed entire repeal of the Townshend taxes; but the King was firm in his demand that "there must always be one tax to keep up the right" to tax. When the others were abolished, in April, 1770, the tax on tea was retained.

At the time of the "massacre" war, at least a local civil war, had been a very near thing; but after the alteration in the tax law and after the excitement in Boston had subsided, there ensued a long period of quiet throughout the colonies. The Americans were back in the golden age of 1763, except for the tea tax. This fact, coupled with a growing weariness of the prolonged conflict, induced a spirit of nonresistance, which degenerated into apathy. The Nonimportation Agreements were violated with increasing frequency. Complaints of such violations by this colony were made by that. Such charges were met by countercharges of the same sort. Intercolonial enmities arose out of these recriminations. The partly built, ill cemented union of the colonies was falling apart. Another shock was needed to revive the fainting spirit of liberty. It came in June, 1772.

The British armed schooner *Gaspée*, while pursuing a suspected smuggling vessel, ran aground in the waters of Rhode Island. Drums beat in Providence. Eight boats full of volunteers put off, surrounded the schooner, seized it, and burned it. In the fracas the British commander was wounded. America hailed the deed as a blow against oppression; England was outraged. British investigators could not discover the names of the culprits, known to many citizens. Finally, the British authorities, perhaps loath to excite renewed animosity in the presently quiescent colonies, dropped the matter.

Distrust of the colonial courts as impartial tribunals now impelled the ministry to revive the project of paying the judges out of the royal treasury, beginning in Massachusetts. That colony astutely countered the move by offering the judges higher salaries than were to be paid by Britain, and the judges accepted the offer. Samuel Adams, who had been almost in despair over the decline of the spirit of resistance and the relaxation of the bonds of unity, saw his chance. In April, 1773, he proposed the organization of Committees of Correspondence to act as connecting links between the various Massachusetts towns. Within a few months, many such bodies appeared, some of them acting for towns, others for colonies. Soon they formed a network throughout the colonies.

Still quietude prevailed throughout America. Only a general abstention from English tea indicated the underlying spirit of opposition to Parliamentary taxation. With characteristic ineptitude the British government seized on that minor element in the contest and erected it into a major dispute.

The East India Company had been hit by the refusal of the Americans to import its tea. In the port of Philadelphia, for example, only one chest of English tea had been entered in the customhouse in five years, while an ample supply had been smuggled in from other sources. Seventeen million pounds had accumulated in the Company's English warehouses, and it was nearing bankruptcy. Government officials were largely interested in the Company. To relieve its embarrassment, an arrangement was made to reimburse the Company for the import duties it paid in England, and to allow it to export directly to its own agents in America instead of through English merchants to American merchants as theretofore. It could then sell tea in the colonies at prices less than those at which smuggled tea was sold, even though its agents paid the threepence a pound American duty to the English government; and the cantankerous colonials would get their tea, tax and all, cheaper than ever before, and even cheaper than it was being sold in England. So why should they worry about the tax? They would surely buy the Company's tea.

But they did worry. News of the scheme was like a bellows blast to the smoldering embers of resistance to "tyranny." After years of quiescence, "the whole country was in a blaze from Maine to Georgia." [11] It is said that "the transition from apathy to agitation was sudden" [12] and widespread. It was an amazing phenomenon. The duties had been legally in force for six years, and for half of that time they had been either quietly paid or tranquilly disregarded. No one was now to be forced to buy the Company's tea. So why should the colonials excite themselves about it?

It has been said that they were aroused by an attempt, at once injurious and insulting, to bribe them to surrender their rights "not to be taxed, by offering them cheaper tea." [13] A more cynical, probably less truthful, statement is that the blaze was not sudden; that it took two full months to work it up; that it was, in fact, ignited by certain Philadelphia merchants who had profited by dealing in the smuggled tea and now saw their business in peril. Be the truth as to this what it may, Philadelphia did take the lead in arousing enmity to the scheme by a series of resolutions denouncing it as "a violent attack upon the liberties of America." Committees pressed the Company's agents, consignees of the expected tea, to resign. Boston followed suit, and so did New York and Charleston. "The cry of endangered liberty once more excited an alarm from New Hampshire to Georgia." [14] Boston was "as furious as it was in the time of the Stamp Act." [15] Whatever the incitement, the resulting conflagration was genuine enough.

The announced intention of the Americans was to prevent the landing of the tea, and it was carried out. At Charleston, no consignee having appeared to pay the duty, a cargo was seized by the customs officers, stored in damp cellars, and left to rot. The captains of the tea ships bound to Philadelphia and New York saw that they could not land their cargoes and carried them back to England. But it was reserved for Boston to climax the opposition in the most spectacular manner. In December, 1773, it held a "tea party," in which an organized mob tossed overboard tea valued at £15,000.

George III, who for a long time had had Boston "on the brain," now saw red. A message from the cabinet to Parliament resulted in quick and drastic

action. Four new measures to punish that hotbed of treason were enacted.

The first, known as the Boston Port Act, closed the port of Boston to all
commerce and ordered it blockaded. Marblehead and Salem were to be the
only Massachusetts ports. The second annulled several parts of the province's charter. Its Assembly was left to function, but the upper chamber,
the Council, was to be appointed by the King. The inferior judges, the
sheriffs, and other executive officers were to be appointed by the Governor.
Juries were to be chosen by the sheriffs, who owed their appointments to
the royal chief executive. Town meetings, the very core of self-government
in Massachusetts, were to be held only with the Governor's permission,
except one each year to choose assemblymen, selectmen, and constables.
The third act provided for the removal to England or to another colony for
trial of anyone indicted for a capital offense committed in the course of a
riot or of enforcement of the revenue laws. The fourth legalized the quartering of troops on the town.

To enforce these laws, General Gage was appointed governor of the
province. Which brings us around, at last, to the point where this introduc-
tory chapter began.

C H A P T E R   2

Boston Port Closed

Boston's population numbered about 20,000, almost all of English origin, there having been but little immigration from the European continent or even from Ireland. It was, of all the colonial ports, the most active in ship-building, codfishery, whaling, and sea-borne commerce in general. It contained important American rum distilleries, which were dependent on a supply of molasses from the West Indies. As elsewhere in the colonies, so in Boston the repressive acts of Parliament had prevented the development of manufactures. The town lived on its ships, its wharves, its shipyards, ropewalks, and sail lofts. To survive, it had to have free passage for its vessels. For its food, in some part, it needed access by water to the grazing grounds on the small islands in its outer harbor, where beef cattle and sheep were pastured.

At the stroke of noon on June 1, the Port Act went into effect. From that moment, Boston harbor was sealed against the rest of the world by a tight blockade. General Gage had been instructed to compel "a full and absolute submission" to the new law. The terms of the act made it unlawful to load or receive at any wharf in the port, at any "island, creek, landing-place, bank or other place" within Massachusetts Bay, any goods whatsoever, in any vessel whatsoever, coming from or going to "any other country, province or place whatsoever." Gage construed his mandate as covering every possible movement of goods, even within the harbor. An adjacent island was a "place"; Charlestown, separated from Boston only by the Charles River, was a "place"; therefore the town was cut off not only from the sea by the blockading ships, but also from such "places." "Did a lighter attempt to land hay from the islands, or a boat to bring in sand from the neighboring hills, or a scow to freight to it lumber or iron, or a float to land sheep, or a farmer to carry marketing over in the ferry-boats, the argus-eyed fleet was ready to see it, and prompt to capture or destroy." [1]

The effect upon the town was immediate, universal, and disastrous. Although church bells had tolled, days of fasting and prayer had been observed, and badges of mourning had been displayed, nothing had availed to avert the coming catastrophe. When it came, the town was stopped dead in its tracks. The great warehouses were closed; the wharves were deserted, and the porters and stevedores were thrown out of work. The shipyards suspended operations, and the carpenters were idle. Ships were tied up at the piers, and the sailors walked the streets. Mercantile houses had no more business, and their clerks no more employment. The town was paralyzed and was like to starve. It might have starved, indeed, but for the alms bestowed upon it by other towns and the other colonies. Connecticut sent it hundreds of sheep. From elsewhere in New England came flour, cattle, fish, and other foods. The Carolinas sent stores of rice and considerable sums of money. Delaware sent money and promised more. Contributions of food and money came from all the other colonies and even from Canada; Quebec sent more than a thousand bushels of wheat. For a full year Boston lived in part on these supplies. And with them came messages of encouragement and adjurations to the Bostonians to stand by their refusal to ransom their town by paying £15,000 for the tea that had been destroyed. [2]

Gage, in accordance with instructions from the King, established the capital of the province in Salem and took up his official residence there, leaving Earl Percy, son and heir of the Duke of Northumberland, in command of several regiments of troops who were brought to Boston to support British authority in the summer of 1774.

At Salem, on June 17, the General Assembly met, under protest against the removal of the capital to that place. Gage sent his secretary with an order dissolving the session. The door was locked against him so that he could only read the order to the crowd on the stairs. The Assembly proposed a continental congress and elected five delegates to represent Massachusetts.

Thirty-six members of the Governor's Council were appointed by Gage a few weeks later. Eleven of them immediately declined to serve. The rest were so insulted, ostracized, and in every way harassed by the people that, finally, no more than sixteen remained in office, and these were forced to seek refuge in Boston under protection of its garrison.

In late August a session of the Supreme Court was to be held in Boston.

Gage came over from Salem to give it his personal support. The judges took their seats; but not a single man in the jury panel would consent to be sworn. The judges told the Governor that it was not possible to hold court even in Boston. Nor was it possible anywhere else in the province. Judges, even justices of the peace, sheriffs, and other executive officers, either voluntarily or through coercion, declined to perform their duties. In Boston the King's law, as far as it was pronounced by Parliament in the obnoxious statutes, was enforced by the military. But not even in Boston was enforcement of any other law possible. "Three hundred thousand people continued their usual avocations without a legislature or executive officers, without sheriffs, judges or justices of the peace." ³ Yet order prevailed generally. The habits of a law-abiding people prevailed, even though the machinery for law enforcement had ceased to exist. "Though the tribunals were void and silent, crime was repressed and private rights were secure, because the people were a law to themselves." ⁴

In September, Gage incautiously called the General Court, consisting of the Council and the Assembly, to meet in Salem on October 5. But, realizing that his appointees to the Council would not be allowed to take their seats, he withdrew the summons. The members of the lower house, nevertheless, gathered in Salem. After two days of intentional neglect by the Governor they adjourned to Concord and organized as a Provincial Congress—a body entirely outside the law and unknown to it—which acted thereafter as the only effective government of the province outside Boston.

In the meantime Gage had taken up residence in Boston and was steadily accumulating troops. To provide quarters for them, other than the tents on the Common and such empty warehouses as he had been able to rent, he called for workmen to build barracks. Though thousands in the town were unemployed, no one would or dared work for him. He had to send to New York and to Halifax for the necessary artificers. The people of the town countered this move by widespread sabotage. Barges transporting bricks for the barracks were sunk, wagons loaded with bricks were upset, straw for the soldiers' beds was burned. November had come and nearly gone before the soldiers could be removed from their chilly quarters on the Common to more adequate shelter.

The Continental Congress, which the Bostonians had suggested, met in Philadelphia on September 5. Twelve of the thirteen colonies sent delegates to make up the most substantial, mentally vigorous, politically powerful, and determined body of colonial representatives that had ever assembled in America. An address to the King, couched in respectful words, an address to the People of England, and a Declaration of Rights again stated the grievances of the colonies and recited thirteen Acts of Parliament to which Americans could not submit.

The addresses and the declaration made no demand for independence, nor suggestion of a resort to force to uphold the rights claimed. They were only petitions for relief from oppression, which, however, the delegates had little expectation of receiving without more pressure than such petitions alone would exert. To give them practical force, reliance was placed upon a renewal of such a boycott of English goods as had theretofore been so effective. It was therefore voted that an Association of the colonies be formed, agreeing not to import any goods from Great Britain or Ireland, nor any East India tea, nor any of certain products from the British West Indies. In addition it was agreed that consumption of British goods and exportation of goods to Britain be curtailed.

The American petitions availed nothing; neither the King nor the Parliament gave them the slightest heed. The only substantial results of the Congress were the Association and the bringing together for the first time of the leading men of the colonies to act in unison, which paved the way for the next meeting of Congress in 1775 and for united action.

Across the river from Boston, on Quarry Hill in Charlestown there was a magazine, "the powder-house," in which was kept a store of gunpowder belonging to the province and to several of the near-by towns. The towns, during August, had been removing their stocks and storing them within their own precincts, as if in readiness for use. To Gage these proceedings seemed ominous of coming trouble; he decided to take steps accordingly.

On the first of September, at dawn, a force of 260 soldiers embarked at the Long Wharf, crossed over to Charlestown and carried off 250 half-barrels, the entire remaining stock of the precious explosive. While this was going on, a detachment marched to Cambridge and confiscated two field-pieces lately procured by the militia regiment of that town. These guns and the powder were removed to Castle William. This unexpected little operation was effected peaceably, without opposition and therefore without bloodshed; but its results were far more disastrous than the withdrawal of powder by the towns had been.

News of the seizure spread swiftly throughout the province, and, as it spread, it grew in importance. By afternoon it was widely reported that the people of Charlestown had resisted the seizure, and that the troops had fired on them and killed six. By midnight this was known forty miles away in Shrewsbury. Everywhere, the rumor was received as a call to arms, and the people responded. By the next day 4,000 armed men, from all the country within thirty miles of Boston, had crowded into Cambridge; Worcester

County and Hampshire were on the march. On the 3rd, Israel Putnam, down in Pomfret, Connecticut, heard not only that the King's soldiers had shot down six of the people of Charlestown and wounded many more, but also that the King's men-of-war had bombarded Boston. By that time thousands —twenty, thirty thousand, it was said—were moving on foot toward Cambridge.[5]

On the 4th, the Committee of Correspondence of Connecticut sent the dreadful news to New York. Within a week, the Continental Congress in Philadelphia had heard of that "dreadful catastrophe." "The effect of the news we have," wrote John Adams to his wife, "both upon the Congress and the inhabitants of this city, was very great. Great indeed! Every gentleman seems to regard the bombardment of Boston as the bombardment of the capital of his own province. Our deliberations are grave and serious indeed." [6] It was, of course, an absurd idea that Gage would bombard his own town, the only place he held in the colonies. The effect upon the Congress, in unifying its members and hastening their action, was, nevertheless, decided and effective.

Many of the thousands on the march to Cambridge were turned back by word that the rumor was false; those already there were dispersed, and the excitement died down. The incident had been, however, an impressive demonstration of the inflammatory nature of the situation and of the insufficiency of the British forces in Boston to contend successfully with all New England in arms. Gage recognized his weakness and called on the home government for reinforcements: to reduce New England, a very respectable force must take the field. He recognized, also, the insecurity of his position, even in merely defensive operations, and set about strengthening it.

Boston was almost an island, being connected with the mainland by a very slim isthmus known as the Neck, at its narrowest part no wider than the causeway built across a depression that was submerged at high tide. From old times, there had been a slight fortification at the town end of this causeway. The excitement about the powder had hardly died when, on September 5, Gage ordered the erection of substantial defensive works on the mainland beyond the Neck and thereby again alarmed the people.

The selectmen of Boston protested; they apprehended an intention of shutting the town off from the rest of the province, of reducing it to the condition of a garrisoned stronghold. Gage replied that the works were merely to protect the troops and the people of Boston from attack, and that he had no intention of interrupting ordinary traffic. Although strikes and all forms of sabotage delayed the work, he succeeded in erecting a rather elaborate fortification, mounting two 24-pound cannon and eight 9-

pounders, which did nothing to allay the inflammation in the minds of the people.

The Americans did what they could to redress the balance of arms inside and outside Boston. One night they stripped a battery at Charlestown of its guns and delivered them outside the lines. Another night they brought off four cannon from the gun-house near the Common. Countrymen, returning from selling their products in the town, day after day concealed muskets, ammunition, and military gear in their wagons and carried them past the guard at the Neck. Gun running became a popular avocation. Admiral Graves, in command of the harbor blockade, could think of no way to preserve the guns in the North Battery other than spiking them, which he did.

The Provincial Congress, sitting in Concord and later in Cambridge during the latter part of 1774, appropriated what was to them the huge sums of £15,627 sterling for the purchase of twenty fieldpieces, four mortars, twenty tons of grape and round shot, ten tons of bombshells, five tons of bullets, one thousand barrels of powder, five thousand muskets and bayonets, and seventy-five thousand flints, to which the Committee of Supplies, in charge of such purchases, added three hundred fifty spades and pickaxes, one thousand wooden mess bowls, and a supply of pork, flour, dried peas, and rice. These military stores were to be deposited in Concord and Worcester. Provision was later made for securing tentage and various other kinds of munitions and supplies.

The Congress provided for the organization of regiments of "minutemen" (of whom more hereinafter) by drawing one-fourth of the men in the regular militia for that purpose. It also named Jedediah Preble, Artemas Ward, and Seth Pomeroy as general officers in command of all the forces of the province, divided into three corps: one at Charlestown, one at Roxbury, the third at Cambridge. A Committee of Safety was appointed to take charge of all the colony's affairs after the dissolution of the Congress. On December 10 it dissolved itself, having first appointed committees to notify the neighboring provinces, Connecticut, Rhode Island, and New Hampshire, of its acts and to request them to provide men to make up an army of 20,000 in all.

Gage issued a proclamation declaring the acts of the Provincial Congress to be treasonable, which, indeed, they were, and prohibiting the people from complying with its requisitions or recommendations. It had no effect whatever upon the colonials; they were busy all through the winter collecting and storing munitions of war. On every village green throughout New England, the militia were drilling more often than ever before and with more serious intent. The cannon at Fort Island in Rhode Island, six 24-pounders, eighteen 18-pounders, fourteen 6-pounders, and six 4-pounders, were seized and carried to Providence, "to prevent their falling into the hands of the King, or any of his servants." Four hundred Portsmouth, New Hampshire, men demanded the powder of that province, which was stored in the fort at New Castle. The British commander refused to give it up and fired upon them with three 4-pounders and his musketry. They "stormed" the fort, secured the captain and his garrison of five "invalid" soldiers and carried off ninety-seven barrels of powder, fifteen hundred muskets, and several pieces of artillery.[7]

On February 26, 1775, to counter the activities of the Americans in seizing powder and arms, Gage sent Colonel Leslie with 240 men to Salem to seize a few brass fieldpieces deposited there. He sailed on a transport to Marblehead, whence he had to march five miles to his destination. Salem had timely news of his approach. A large crowd, including the militia colonel, Timothy Pickering, and 40 armed men, assembled in a shipyard where carriages for the guns were being made and hoisted the drawbridge spanning a small stream that the British force would have to cross.

Leslie arrived and demanded that the bridge be replaced. He was informed that this was a private road and that no trespassing would be permitted. He turned his attention to two "gundalows," which lay in the stream. But their owners jumped into them and began to scuttle them. There was a scuffle, in which a few of the Salemites were "pricked with bayonets" but no one was seriously wounded.

Leslie had his orders, which included crossing that bridge, but he was at his wit's end as to how to execute them. At length, a Salem clergyman intervened. He told Leslie that if he crossed the stream in opposition to the Salemites he would certainly be overwhelmed by the population, but if he would pledge his word to advance no farther than thirty rods beyond the bridge to a point where the unfinished gun-carriages were, and then, if he found no guns, to return, the bridge would be let down. Leslie agreed, crossed the stream, marched the agreed distance, found no guns, faced about, and returned to Marblehead and so to Boston. In the telling, the proceeding seems farcical, but if he had not yielded Salem might have won the honors later conferred on Lexington by Major Pitcairn and his men, for the alarm had gone forth, the minutemen were responding to it, and a company from Danvers arrived on the scene just as Leslie's detachment was marching away.[8]

The news of violent opposition by the Americans did not shock the King nor, indeed, particularly displease him. "I am not sorry," he wrote, "that the line of conduct seems now chalked out. . . . The New England Governments are in a state of rebellion. Blows must decide whether they are subject to this country or independent." "He was prepared to fight and was in a hurry to begin." [9]

When the Parliament met, on November 29, the address from the throne began with notice of "a most daring spirit of resistance and disobedience to the law . . . fresh violences of a very criminal nature" in Massachusetts, and of the measures the crown had taken to restore "peace, order and good Government" there. Lords and Commons answered that "a rebellion at this time actually exists within said Province," which was not an over-statement, and besought His Majesty to "take the most effectual measures to enforce due obedience to the laws and authority of the supreme Legisla-ture." They also assured him that it was "our fixed resolution, at the hazard of our lives and properties," to stand by him—a gallant assurance, indeed, which seemed to contemplate that the coming war was to be fought against hordes of invading Yankees in the towns, villages, and fields of old England, with the King himself in the battle-front and the lords and gentlemen of the Commons in the firing line.

To avoid such an untoward event, an addition of 6,000 men to the military and naval forces was provided for, with an increase of the force in Boston to 10,000 soldiers. But this Parliament struck a still shrewder blow against the offending Americans with a statute, commonly called the Fishery Act, which restrained the New England colonies from all trade with Great Britain, Ireland, and the West Indies, and excluded them from the Newfoundland fisheries, under penalty of forfeiture of vessels engaged. The scope of the act was soon enlarged to include the other American colonies, except New York and Georgia, neither of which had yet joined in the Con-tinental Association of the colonies boycotting English goods. During the consideration of these measures the Parliament had been bombarded with petitions from the London merchants and from the mercantile and manu-facturing interest of all the other great towns, as well as with remonstrances from the colonies, urging the great importance of the American trade and the vast sums already due from the colonial merchants for goods shipped to them (estimated, for the City of London alone, at £2,000,000), which these restrictions would render impossible of payment, and praying that "healing remedies" be applied to restore the normal commerce between Great Britain and the colonies. But the "King's friends" ignored these peti-tions and voted for the new oppressive acts by such majorities as 260 to 90 in the Commons.

The restraints on ordinary commerce were felt by all the colonies, but the exclusion from the fisheries dealt a dreadful blow to New England, the prosperity of which had been built up and was still largely dependent on the capture of codfish and whales. Nantucket, for instance, had a whaling fleet of 140 vessels, which was the principal support of its 5,000 inhabitants.

At the same time that the Parliament was in session in St. Stephen's Hall, partly warmed, no doubt by good sea-coal fires, the Provincial Congress of Massachusetts was sitting in Cambridge "in a house without a fire," so cold that it was resolved "That all those Members who incline thereto may sit with their Hats on" [10] which seems in a way to symbolize the contrast in resources between the two countries at that time.

The Massachusetts Congress had met on February 1 to take steps to meet those "most speedy and effectual measures for supporting the just rights of his Crown and the two Houses of Parliament" which the King proposed to take, and for which he had asked from the Commons an augmentation of his forces. The steps taken certainly justified His Majesty's accusation of rebellion. Two additional general officers were appointed by the rebels in the persons of John Thomas and William Heath; provision was made for a commissary to receive all "Stores, Ordnance, Arms and Provisions . . . until the Constitutional Army shall take the field"; there were many other arrangements looking toward armed conflict with the King's troops, including an address to the Stockbridge Indians, welcoming and promising "a Blanket and a Red Ribbon" to each one that "enlisted in the service" of the colony; a code of rules to govern the army—usually called "Articles of War" —was adopted; delegates were chosen to visit the other New England colonies and ask them to add their quotas to the forces of Massachusetts. The Congress finally adjourned on April 15—four days before the fatal day of Lexington and Concord.

CHAPTER 3

The Two Armies

While all these events were occurring, Gage had been adding to his forces. By the beginning of 1775, he had in Boston nine regiments of British infantry and parts of two others, the 4th or King's Own, the 5th, the 10th, the 23rd or Royal Welch Fusiliers, the 38th, the 43rd, the 47th, the 52nd, the 59th, three companies of the 18th or Royal Irish, and six companies of the 65th; also five companies of the Royal Artillery. The 64th was quartered in Castle William.

The strength of each regiment was supposed to be 477 of all ranks; but there was always a considerable actual shortage, and it has been estimated that the average effective number of rank and file was about 292. The total number, including the artillery, may therefore be computed at about 4,000. In the harbor lay four ships of the line, the *Scarborough*, the *Boyne*, the *Somerset*, and the *Asia,* each carrying sixty guns or more, "besides frigates and sloops and a great number of transports," from which Gage had drawn 460 marines.[1]

These soldiers were fair samples of the personnel of the British army that was to fight in the war. Their characteristics as soldiers, their equipment, leadership, and organization, were typical of the military power against which America was to contend.

In the eighteenth century, the British army had been built up by the crown contracting with this or that distinguished soldier or gentleman of position to raise a regiment. To him as its colonel was paid so much for each man enlisted, and thereafter an annual sum sufficient to pay and clothe his men. Sometimes, instead of receiving pay for enlistments, the

24

colonel was permitted to nominate the officers, to whom he sold their commissions. A commission so acquired became the property of the holder and entitled him to receive the pay and allowances appropriate to his rank for the rest of his life, subject, however, to a reduction to half-pay if his regiment were disestablished in time of peace.[2]

As a species of property, such a commission could be sold if the holder desired to withdraw from the service; and it was by this means that promotion in the army was commonly obtained. Otherwise advancement was possible only when a vacancy in a superior rank occurred through death; and even then the hope was faint because as many as ten captains, for example, might be candidates for the commission of a dead major. The system of purchase practically restricted commissions to possessors of means.[3] The officers were almost all "men of family," that is to say, technically gentlemen. There were no military schools, except for the artillery. Raw lads of the officer class generally entered the army at the age of sixteen by favor or by purchase, learning their profession thereafter in actual service.

The common soldiers were far removed from the officers in the social scale. They were obtained by voluntary or by compulsory enlistment. The weekly pay of four shillings and sixpence was so reduced by charges for clothing, medicine, and many other impositions that they often got practically nothing in coin. Their food was "notoriously poor," their hardships severe. As a consequence, voluntary enlistment was largely confined to silly lads befooled by the glamour of the scarlet coat or to men and boys who were either desperate or drunk. Debtors released from imprisonment, criminals pardoned on the condition that they enlist, boys and men made drunk by the recruiting sergeant and persuaded to take "the King's shilling" while hardly aware of what they were doing made up a considerable part of the army.[4] "By lies they lured them, by liquor they tempted them, and when they were dead drunk they forced a shilling into their fists." [5]

Compulsory enlistment was made possible by the "Act against vagabonds," a statute authorizing impressment of "any sturdy beggar, any fortune teller, any idle, unknown or suspected fellow in a parish, that cannot give an account of himself . . . anyone who had been in gaol," or was "known as an incorrigible rogue"; poachers were fair game. But, though the recruiting officers interpreted these provisions broadly, enlistments, voluntary and involuntary taken together, were not enough to keep the ranks of the army up to the standard of strength, a condition that compelled the British government, within a short time after the war began, to employ foreign mercenaries.[6]

It would seem that the British army, so made up, would have been lacking in all the elements that go to building a force reliable in camp and on the march and effective in action; but its record in the war is all to the contrary. In the first place, it must be remembered that in conditions of economic hardship criminals are often made out of men not naturally vicious, and that under the extraordinarily severe code of criminal law then obtaining minor offenders were speedily converted into long-term felons or sentenced to death. It must also be observed that desperate men often make the best soldiers. In the second place, the effects of drill and discipline must not be overlooked. At all events, the British soldier in this war unquestionably displayed qualities of hardihood, courage, persistence, and military effectiveness that did honor to his nation.

Each regiment was composed of eight companies of ordinary foot soldiers, a company of light infantry, and one of grenadiers. These last two groups were the élite, the flower of the army, selected from the ranks for special qualities.

The light infantry were chosen for physical ability, vigor, audacity, alertness, and general fighting qualities outside ordinary service in the line of battle. Their chief duties were reconnaissance, skirmishing, outpost work and surprises, and flanking the army on the march.

The grenadiers were likewise selected troops; but they were chosen for qualities additional to those of the light infantry. They were first organized in the British army in 1678 to use a new weapon, a small iron bomb with an ignited fuse that was thrown by hand. As presumably able to throw such missiles a greater distance, the tallest and strongest men in each regiment were picked to be grenadiers. To permit slinging their muskets on either shoulder while they were engaged in such bombing, they wore brimless caps, instead of the usual broad-brimmed hats. These caps in time developed into the tall miterlike headpieces familiar in pictures of grenadiers, which added to their apparent height and gave them a more formidable appearance. The hand grenade had become practically obsolete in 1774, when the grenadiers were armed like the rest of the infantry. They were, nevertheless, retained in the army as a picked corps.

Both the light infantry and the grenadier companies remained in the regimental organization except when detached for special duty. They were known as "flank companies" because, in line of battle, they held the posts of honor at the flanks of their own regiments; they also led or flanked their regiments when in column of march. However, both the light companies and the grenadiers were frequently assembled in battalions of their own class for special operations or even as fighting units in a general battle. Some military critics deplored this practice because it skimmed the cream of the infantry and deprived the regular regiments of their best fighting men, who would have stiffened the line in defense and given it greater élan in attack. Nevertheless, it continued even to the extent of forming permanent regiments, such as the well known Grenadier Guards.

Gage had no cavalry at the beginning of 1775; but in June he did have a mounted force, a contingent of 400 men of the 17th Light Dragoons. These are to be distinguished from cavalry, whose arms were properly a heavy saber and a pair of horse pistols, and whose principal duties were to scout, to protect the flanks of the line or column, to circumvent the enemy's line, to cut communications, to pursue retreating enemies, and to act as shock troops, striking at the opposing force when it showed signs of weakness or disorder. Unlike the cavalryman, the dragoon, who was properly armed with a short musket or a carbine, a sword, and pistols, traveled on horseback but fought on foot; he was simply a mounted infantryman, and his horse, not being intended for shock tactics, was a light, wiry animal. When not engaged in battle he was usually employed for vedette work (as a mounted sentinel in advance of outposts), for orderly duty, and foraging. The distinction between the two arms (indicated in the phrase "horse, foot, and dragoons"), however, tended to diminish; dragoons were sometimes used as shock troops, as in the Battle of Monmouth in 1778 and at Camden in 1780, and the name came to be applied to pure cavalrymen,[7] as in the case of Tarleton's and William Washington's cavalry, often called dragoons.

The uniforms of the British infantrymen were modeled after those in use in Germany. They were highly ornamental, very fine for parade, but as impractical for active service as could well be imagined. The scarlet coat was lavishly decorated with colored linings, facings, and pipings, lace, and brass buttons; the waistcoat was either scarlet or white. The white breeches and the coat sleeves, also the long buttoned gaiters of some regiments, coming well above the knee, were all as tight as possible. The waist belt was broad and tight; it carried the bayonet scabbard. There was also a belt from the left shoulder to the opposite hip, carrying the cartridge box. The standing coat collars were stiff, and the movements of the head were further hampered by a high, stiff leather stock under the chin. The hats were of various types, some with broad brims cocked in the familiar, triangular form, others tall and pointed grenadier-fashion. These were often made of bearskin. None of them had a visor or brim to shield the eyes from the sun.

The hair was generally worn in a queue or club stiffened with grease and white powder, as were the tight curls in front of the ears.

Keeping all this apparatus in order—shining the brass, pipe-claying the leather, cleaning the cloth, blacking the shoes, braiding and dressing the queue, as well as polishing the arms—took from two to three hours a day. In active service, of course, much of this elaborate toilet was necessarily neglected; but the uniform and equipment were the same, so awkward, cumbersome, stiff, and constricting as greatly to hamper the movements of the soldier and to reduce his efficiency.[8]

The infantry officer was armed either with a spontoon—a sort of pike or spear with an ornamental head, which was both a badge of office and a weapon—or with a fusil, a short musket. He also wore a light dress sword.

The standard weapon of the infantry private was the musket, commonly called the brown Bess, after the first matchlock guns introduced into the British army by Queen Elizabeth, their barrels and metal fittings having been browned. By this time, however, the barrels were steel-bright. Any musket that had been inspected in the Tower of London was especially stamped, and was called a Tower musket.[9]

The brown Bess was a smoothbore gun; rifles were not yet in use in the British army. It weighed about ten pounds, was about four and a half feet long, and carried a twenty-one-inch bayonet. It had no rear sight. Its caliber was three-quarters of an inch. Because its bullet weighed more than an ounce, it had great stopping power, but the range was short: a ball fired with a regulation charge from such a gun, held horizontally at a height of five feet, fell harmlessly to the ground at about 125 yards. It was also very inaccurate, because its bore was usually untrue; but that mattered little, for the British soldier was no marksman. He had not been trained to take aim at a single object, nor even at the mass of the enemy. His instructions were to throw his gun to his shoulder in a horizontal position "point it—not sight it—toward the enemy and, at the word of command, pull the trigger."[10] As an English historian, Trevelyan, puts it: "He was taught to point his weapon horizontally, brace himself for a vicious recoil and pull a ten pound trigger till his gun went off: if, indeed, it did go off when the hammer fell." [11]

Loading involved biting the end off a cylindrical paper cartridge that contained powder and ball, shaking a little powder into the pan, closing its lid, dropping the butt of the gun on the ground, pouring the rest of the powder into the barrel, striking the gun to jar some powder into the touchhole, dropping in the ball, cramming the paper into the muzzle, and ramming it down to act as a wad. The process of firing was almost equally involved: when the trigger was pulled the cock fell, striking its flint against a piece of steel called the frizzen; from this contact, a shower of sparks (perhaps) fell on the powder in the pan; the powder flashed; there was a spurt of flame outward from the touchhole and inward into the charge, by whose explosion the bullet was projected. There was an appreciable interval of time between the pulling of the trigger and the explosion of the charge. Often, indeed, there was no explosion. The flint might be so worn as to fail to spark; the powder in the pan might be damp and so fail to ignite; the touchhole might be stopped up.[12]

In the British army the steps in loading and firing were taken in response to a series of orders by an officer. Up to a few years before the Revolution, the manual required sixteen distinct orders to put the soldier through forty-nine motions. By 1764 this had been simplified so that eight orders sufficed to effect priming and loading (but not presenting and firing) in twelve movements. The Americans reduced this to ten motions in response to a single order, "Prime and load!" It was also a part of their instructions to sight, not merely point, the musket. Two or three shots in a minute were reckoned a good rate of fire.[13]

Such delays and uncertainties and such a lack of precision made the brown Bess less useful as a gun than as a stock for a bayonet. Indeed, the "white weapon" was much the most effective British arm throughout the war. The usual practice was to advance the line to within a hundred yards or so of the enemy before firing one or more hit-or-miss volleys, and then to charge with the bayonet. Such attacks were the most dreaded by the Americans and the most often successful.

To oppose the regularly organized, fully equipped and trained British troops, Massachusetts had only its militia. That term must be understood in its true meaning. The militia included the entire potential fighting strength of the province. Every man between the ages of sixteen and sixty years was required by law to possess a gun and its proper equipment of ammunition and accessories, and to be enrolled in the company of his own township. He was supposed to turn out at certain intervals, perhaps four times a year or oftener, with the rest of his company for training; hence the common appellation, "trainbands."

The primary purpose in instituting this system in the early days of the colony had been to provide for defense against attacks by the Indians; there was no intention of sending the militia out of the province. But when, on the outbreak of the French and Indian War in 1754, it became necessary to furnish a force to operate in French territory, a new arrangement was authorized.

Service in several new regiments raised at that time was made voluntary. The officers were appointed by the governor, and each was authorized "to beat his Drums anywhere within the Province for enlisting Volunteers for His Majesty's Service in a Regiment of Foot to be forthwith raised for the Service and Defence of His Majesty's Colonies in North America." [14] This force served until the conclusion of the war in 1763, when it was disbanded, its members returning to the ranks of the militia. By their experience in the trainbands, but more especially by their service in actual war, many Massachusetts men had become familiar with the duties of a soldier. Not all of them, however, were to be useful in the coming struggle with Great Britain. Many were strong in their allegiance to the crown, in whose support they had fought.

When Gage came to Boston, the colonels of perhaps a full half of the thirty Massachusetts militia regiments were stanch Loyalists, who would in no event call out their men for action against the King's troops. The major general, the head of the entire force of militia, was a Tory. To remedy this condition, the Worcester Convention prevailed upon all the officers of that colony's three regiments to resign. It then provided for the organization of its militia in seven regiments, the towns to elect the company officers, who should choose the field officers. It went beyond this by directing the officers of each company to enlist a third of their men to be ready to act "at a minute's notice," these new companies to be made up into regiments. This was the origin of the famous minutemen.

The Worcester idea spread through the colony. Patriot officers willingly resigned, and Tories were so intimidated that they also gave up their commissions. The Provincial Congress, when assembled at Concord in October, 1774, approved the plan and directed that it be followed throughout the colony. Thus the militia of the province was rid of its Tory officers, and, as the minutemen were chosen with regard to the soundness of their political principles, the patriotism of their regiments was assured.

The minutemen have bulked large in the romance of the Revolution; but they had, in fact, a brief existence and were of little importance in the war. The formation of their regiments proceeded slowly; Woburn, for example, voted the establishment of its regiment as late as April 17, 1775, only two days before the Lexington-Concord engagements. In that same month, the Provincial Congress decided to abandon the scheme, to rely no longer upon the militia and the minutemen and to enlist, for a term of eight months, an army of 13,600 volunteers, thus reverting to the system used in the French and Indian War. It recognized the existence of the minutemen regiments by providing that their officers be given preference for commissions in the new army. Thus the minuteman passed out of existence after a career of no more than six months in the earliest companies and of a few days in the latest.[15]

There was a third class of soldiers in the Massachusetts militia scheme, the "alarm companies." These were not, as might be supposed, to be called out on the first alarm. They were, in fact, a last resort, an ultimate reserve, being composed of boys, old men, magistrates, and clergymen. Naturally, they were of little importance in the conflict.[16]

But few of these Massachusetts troops, of any class, were uniformed. The great majority came to their training days and turned out on alarms in their civilian clothes. Their guns were of any sort: brown Bess muskets surviving the French and Indian War; muskets issued in King George's War thirty years before; even perhaps a few Queen's arms, twice as old, dating from Queen Anne's War; American-made muskets of all dates; fowling pieces, blunderbusses, any kind of gun that would fire bullets or buckshot, except rifles. The rifled gun was unknown in New England, so that John Adams in Philadelphia attending the First Continental Congress wrote to his wife of "a peculiar kind of musket, called a rifle," used by "riflemen . . . from Pennsylvania, Maryland and Virginia . . . the most accurate marksmen in the world." [17]

The accouterments of the American militia were few and simple; a powder horn and a bullet pouch or a cartridge box, a bullet mold, and a bag of extra flints were the essentials. There might be added a haversack and a rolled blanket. Some of them, not many, had bayonets.[18]

CHAPTER 4

Lexington

During all the months from Gage's arrival in May of 1774 through the summer, fall, and winter, the British army lay inactive in Boston. No hostile move into the surrounding country was made, except Leslie's fruitless expedition to Salem. There were, however, a few peaceful excursions to exercise the troops, which were viewed with suspicion by the Provincial Congress. One day in February it interrupted its morning session at Concord to appoint a committee "to observe the motions of the troops said to be on their way to this town." [1] These expeditions, though harmless in themselves, did forebode more purposeful forays; Gage had not forgotten the stores of provincial munitions at Concord and Worcester. Also they put the Americans on the alert.

Late in February, Gage sent Captain Brown and Ensign De Berniere with one private to sketch the roads and test the political situation in Suffolk and Worcester counties. They were disguised, in "brown cloathes and reddish handkerchiefs" around their necks, so carefully that a Negro serving maid in the first tavern they stopped at recognized them at once as British soldiers and told their man that if they went much further "they would meet with very bad usage." At the next tavern the landlord, contrary to Yankee custom, asked them no questions at all, because "he had seen all he wanted without needing to ask." Farther on, they were overtaken by a horseman who looked them over carefully "and then rode off pretty hard." Later certain other equestrians asked them point-blank whether they were British soldiers, and at Marlborough they found the town "alive and buzzing." If they had not precipitately departed in the darkness of night from a certain Loyalist's house there, they would have been seized by the Committee of Correspondence for the town, which a few minutes later searched the house from garret to cellar. They got back to Boston thoroughly convinced that the political situation west of Boston might be very much better indeed without being too good, and that to surprise Concord invisible troops would be needed.[2]

By March, the tension in the people's minds was so great that a simple exercise march aroused the countryside; "expresses were sent to every town near," a couple of cannon were posted on the Watertown bridge, the planks were removed from the bridge at Cambridge, and the Provincial Congress voted that whenever troops of the number of 500 marched out of Boston "the Military Force of the Province ought to be assembled." [3] This nervous apprehension was nowhere more intense than among the patriots in Boston itself.

Thousands of men in that town were out of work, with nothing to do but loaf on street corners, loiter near the fortifications on the Neck, linger about the wharves, watch what was going on, and talk about what they saw. Paul Revere, silversmith, engraver, and ingenious craftsman, as well as express rider when important news was to be carried to New York or Philadelphia, had a group of watchmen "chiefly mechanics." They patrolled the streets, met secretly, exchanged the results of their observations, and reported them to Dr. Joseph Warren, who conveyed them to the Committee of Safety at Concord. Several other secret societies were similarly engaged. There was not much done in Boston that was not observed.[4]

When on April 15 the grenadiers and light infantry were ordered "off all duties 'till further orders" to learn "new evolutions," Lieutenant John Barker of the King's Own was not alone in suspecting this was "by way of a blind" and there was "something for them to do." [5] Revere's patrolmen were equally suspicious. They had an eye on the waterfront, and they had already seen the boats belonging to the transport vessels, which had been hauled up for repairs, "launched and carried under the sterns of the men of War." They too "expected something serious was to be transacted." [6] And, Yankee-fashion, they guessed, and guessed right, that an expedition was being prepared to go by boat across Back Bay to East Cambridge and so by road to Concord. Next morning Warren sent Revere to Lexington to warn John Hancock and Samuel Adams.

Returning to Boston that night, Revere arranged with "a Col. Conant & some other Gentlemen" in Charlestown "that if the British went out by water, we would shew two lanthorns in the North Church Steeple, and if by land [across the Neck] one, as a signal." This arrangement was made, not to inform Revere himself awaiting it in Charlestown booted and spurred and "impatient to mount and ride," as in Longfellow's poem, but to notify Conant and the "other Gentlemen" so that they might send word to Concord and elsewhere, Revere being "apprehensive" it would be difficult for him to cross the Charles River, "or git over Boston neck." [7]

Gage had planned a secret expedition to surprise Concord. To intercept wayfarers and prevent news of the foray from anticipating it, he sent mounted officers on the afternoon of April 18 to patrol the roads. The soldiers to be engaged in the enterprise were not to be notified until just before the time to march, when they were to be awakened "by the sergeants putting their hands on them and whispering gently to them" and "conducted by a back way out of the barracks without the knowledge of their comrades." The strictest silence was to be observed by everyone concerned.[8] But Boston's ears were cocked, and not all the British soldiers were muzzled.

One Jasper, a gunsmith, is said to have heard about the intended move in the afternoon from a British sergeant. John Ballard, a stableman, is reported to have overheard someone in the Province House say that there would be "hell to pay to-morrow." Earl Percy had been taken into Gage's confidence that evening; while crossing the Common immediately afterward, he heard one man say to another, "The British troops have marched, but they will miss their aim." "What aim?" inquired his lordship. "Why, the cannon at Concord." [9] Solomon Brown, a young man of Lexington, met the interception committee on his way home from Boston. He carried the news to William Munroe, sergeant of the Lexington minutemen, who collected eight of his company and posted them as a guard over the house where Hancock and Samuel Adams were lodging, to prevent their being kidnaped, and sent three others back toward Boston to watch the British patrol.[10]

Joseph Warren had the news before the British expedition had more than started from the barracks. He sent for Revere and William Dawes, another experienced express rider. Dawes was the first to come and was immediately dispatched to Lexington, to warn Hancock and Samuel Adams, and then to Concord. Revere arrived at Warren's house soon after Dawes. There were two main roads leading to Concord. One was by way of the Neck towards Roxbury, then around to Cambridge and Menotomy—now Arlington—and on through Lexington; it was much the longer. The other went from Charlestown to Medford and then to Menotomy, where it joined the other. Dawes managed to elude the guard at the Neck by mingling in the darkness with some soldiers passing that way, and took the first road. Revere stayed long enough to get his boots and surtout and to bid Captain John

Pulling, Jr., set the two lanterns in the Old North Church steeple. Two friends then rowed him with muffled oars across the river to Charlestown. Conant and some others, having seen the lights in the steeple, were at the wharf to meet him. A horse was furnished, and about eleven o'clock he was on his way.[11]

For this expedition, Gage had detached the grenadier and light infantry companies from his regiments, under general command of Lieutenant Colonel Francis Smith of the 10th foot. Major John Pitcairn of the marines led the light infantry, which marched in advance.[12] The number of men in the detachment is variously stated, from 600 to 800.[13]

They assembled at the foot of Boston Common at about half past ten in the evening of the 18th of April, embarked in boats on the Back Bay, and crossed to Lechmere Point, opposite the north end of the town. Because the water was too shallow to allow the boats to touch dry land, the men had to wade ashore. Lieutenant John Barker of the 4th (King's Own) regiment has described the subsequent proceedings: "After getting over the Marsh where we were wet up to the knees, we were halted in a dirty road and stood there 'till two o'clock in the morning waiting for provisions to be brought up from the boats and to be divided, and which most of the Men threw away, having carried some with 'em. At 2 oclock we began our March by wading through a very long ford up to our Middles." Thus inauspiciously began the journey to Concord.[14]

In the meantime, Dawes and Revere were speeding on their errands of alarm. Dawes met with no obstacles or interruptions, but Revere encountered a number of difficulties. He had intended to cut across from the road through Medford to Cambridge and so on to Menotomy, but he had hardly entered the crossroad before he saw two horsemen waiting in his path, British officers. "I was near enough to see their Holsters & cockades." One started toward him; but he wheeled about and "rid at full Gallop" back to the main road and so through Medford, alarming the dwellers of roadside houses as he went. At Medford he called on Captain Hull to turn out his company of minutemen. He woke up Menotomy and the houses beyond it and at last came to Lexington about midnight. At Parson Clarke's house he called on the guard to let him in. The sergeant asked him not to make so much noise, the family were asleep. "Noise!" Revere is reported to have said. "You'll have noise enough before long. The regulars are coming out!" That was enough. Hancock and Adams prepared for a hasty escape.[15]

Revere waited at Clarke's house half an hour for Dawes to come up by the longer road, and together they set out again for Concord. They were overtaken by young Dr. Samuel Prescott, who was returning home from a long evening with his sweetheart in Lexington. The three went on, alarming the houses they passed. About halfway between the two towns, they met two British officers, and two more emerged from a field beside the road. Dawes wheeled his horse about and rode hard back to Lexington. Revere and Prescott were ordered, at pistol point, to turn off the road into a pasture lot. Doing this, they immediately put spurs on their horses to escape in different directions. Prescott jumped his over a stone wall and got away. Revere struck out for a wood, but was met and taken by six other officers who had been concealed there. With them appeared three other prisoners, the men who had been sent out by Sergeant Munroe from Lexington to observe the enemy. That was the end of the Ride of Paul Revere.

He was dismounted and questioned. He told his captors that the country had been alarmed and that five hundred men were assembling at Lexington. They heard "a voley of [alarm] Guns, which appeared to alarm them very much." They took Revere's horse for one of their sergeants, gave him the small nag the sergeant had ridden, marched them all back toward Lexington, cut the bridles and girths of their captives' horses, drove them away, and rode off. Revere walked back to Clarke's house, found Hancock and Adams ready to leave, and went with them to Burlington in a chaise driven by the parson's son.[16]

Colonel Smith was so determined to preserve the secrecy of the foray that, on leaving the "dirty road" at Lechmere Point, he avoided the bridge across Willis Creek, for fear that the tramping of his men upon its planks might give the alarm, and led them through the ford mentioned by Barker. So, wet to the waist, they marched on through the cold night. Sometime after two o'clock, they halted in Somerville to let the men drink at a well. Then they went on, picking up prisoners here and there to prevent an alarm. Cambridge was next; then, at three o'clock, Menotomy, where three members of the Provincial Congress heard their tramp-tramp, fled from their beds in their nightgear, and hid in a field of corn stubble. Here six companies of light infantry, under Pitcairn, were detached and sent ahead. Now they were drawing near to Lexington.[17]

All through the night, as they passed through town after town, men awoke, dressed, took to horse, and rode away to call out the thousands who were finally to overwhelm these redcoats.

At Lexington, Revere's alarm at midnight had called out Captain Jonas Parker and his company of minutemen. One hundred and thirty of them gathered on the village green; but no more news came and the night was cold. After they had stood around cheerlessly and, as it seemed, pointlessly for an hour or so, Parker dismissed them with orders to respond again at the beating of the drum. Many went back to their near-by homes; the rest waited in Buckman's tavern close to the green.[18]

At half past four came the expected news. Riding at full gallop, Thaddeus Bowman brought it. The British were coming! They were close at hand, less than half a mile behind him! Alarm guns were fired. The minutemen in the tavern came on the run; others came from their houses. But some had no ammunition. They hurried to the meetinghouse, where the town's supply was kept. Men without guns gathered to look on. There was confusion all about the green. Finally, seventy armed men at the most were drawn up in two lines spaced somewhat apart.[19]

Lexington Green was a triangle bordered by roads. The road from Boston to Concord ran along its base.[20] Parker's men were drawn up not more than a hundred yards from this road, by which the British must march. What Parker expected to do with his three score men against Smith's six or eight hundred no one knows. He would protect the town, someone has suggested. But such an effort was hopeless, and besides Lexington was in no danger from the British. Their object, as everyone knew, was the stores at Concord. None of the towns on the way had been molested. Gallant as Parker's stand may have been, it was in effect nothing more than a challenge to the enemy which, if accepted, could only result, as it did, in futile bloodshed.[21]

It was a cold day for the season of the year, with a strong east wind; but the sky was blue, and the sun shone clear. The polished steel of ordered ranks of gun barrels and bayonets glittered brightly as Pitcairn's column came in sight, and one of the Americans saw the situation in its true proportions. "There are so few of us," he said, "it is folly to stand here." "The first man who offers to run shall be shot down," replied Parker. So there they stood, an offering for a sacrifice.[22]

Pitcairn's six light companies came on in column of march and saw the minutemen in form to oppose them. The Marine Major ordered his men into line of battle. As was customary, the rear ranks came forward at the double to line up with those in front, shouting and huzzaing as they ran. To the militia it appeared that they "rushed furiously," as if with bloody intent; but they only formed a line three deep in two sections or platoons, a little apart from each other.

Parker gave an order to his men: "Stand your ground! Don't fire unless fired upon! But if they want to have a war, let it begin here!" Some of the men, nevertheless, did drift away.

Pitcairn, with two other officers, rode to the front, within a hundred feet of Parker's lines. "Lay down your arms, you damned rebels, and disperse!"

Parker at last saw the hopelessness of the situation and ordered his men to disband and not to fire. They began to melt away, taking their muskets.

"Lay down your arms! Damn you! Why don't you lay down your arms?" shouted Pitcairn.

"Damn them! We will have them!" cried one of the officers, meaning the rebels' muskets.

Then there was a single shot, and from some one of the British officers, not Pitcairn, a command: "Fire, by God! Fire!" A volley from one platoon rang out—"They did not take sight," says a witness; the bullets went high over the Americans' heads. Pitcairn "struck his staff or Sword downward with all Earnestness as a signal to forbear or cease firing," but without avail. "The Soldiery and young Officers wanted to have at the damned Dogs, & in their impetuosity burst out into firing & continued it contrary to the Command of Pitcairn." [23] There was another volley that tore through the already retreating American ranks, answered by the feeble discharge of a scattered few, and then the Redcoats charged. Jonas Parker had fired once and had been wounded by a bullet; yet he stood his ground and was reloading his gun when he was cut down—his is a name worthy of remembrance. The rest fled, the British firing at them as long as they were within range. Eight dead men lay on the ground; ten wounded got away. Of the British, one private was slightly wounded in the leg, and Pitcairn's horse was grazed in a couple of places. The British officers had great difficulty in re-forming their men, who "were so wild they cou'd hear no orders." [24] When they were formed at last and when Smith with the main body came up, they fired a volley, gave a great cheer for their victory, "the musick struck up"—there was no hope of secrecy now—and they started off toward Concord, just as the sun rose.

That was the famous Battle of Lexington, which of course was no battle at all, not even a skirmish, for there was no contest. But who fired the first shot is a question unanswered after 165 years. The older American historians patriotically say Pitcairn. George Bancroft, for example, says so baldly and asserts further that he gave the order to fire; and so does John Fiske. For many years Pitcairn has been held in odium as a murderer of unresisting men, a "bloody butcher." But he denied it; he "insisted upon it to the day of his Death" at Bunker Hill "that the Colonists fired first: & that he commanded not to fire & endeavored to stay & stop the firing after it begun." Ezra Stiles, President of Yale College, recording this denial, believed that he was innocent, that he fired no shot and gave his men no order to fire, but that he was deceived as to the origin of the first shots. Stiles suggested, most reasonably, that these came from some of the British soldiers behind Pitcairn "as he turned to give Orders" not to fire, and regarded him as "a Man of Integrity & Honor" which, indeed, he was.[25] Pitcairn has been characterized truly as "a man whose humanity and tact had won him the love of his command, and the respect of people of all shades of opinion in the town . . . a brave and humane man." [26] His fall in battle two months later so grieved his command that their firing "slackened for some minutes many of his men echoing these words—'We have lost a father!' " [27] A certificate of character not lightly to be disregarded.

CHAPTER 5

Concord

The alarm had gone forth, not only by Revere and Dawes to Lexington, but far and wide throughout eastern Massachusetts. Conant and his friends at Charlestown took care of the country roundabout; and from town to town, as the news came, riders carried it on posthaste. Lynn, ten miles to the north, was awakened in the early morning. Billerica, seventeen miles northwest, was aroused by two in the morning, and Acton, five miles farther, soon after. So it spread by an interlacing of expresses. Woburn was out before break of day. Reading at sunrise heard the alarm guns. At Danvers bells rang and drums beat at nine o'clock. At Tewksbury, twenty miles from Boston, a hard-riding messenger awoke Captain John Trull about two o'clock, and Trull fired his gun to awaken General Varnum at Dracut across the Merrimack. Andover, twenty-five miles away, heard the alarm at sunrise; Pepperell, thirty-five miles, at nine o'clock. Before noon, a white horse, dripping with sweat and bloody from the spur, galloped into Worcester, its rider crying: "To arms! To arms! the war has begun!" and it reached the church before it fell exhausted. So the news spread. Everywhere in the counties of Middlesex, Essex, Norfolk, and Worcester bells, guns, and drums called out the minutemen. Everywhere they were afoot and on the march.[1]

To Concord young Dr. Prescott, who had escaped when Revere was captured, brought the evil tidings between one and two o'clock in the morning. The alarm bell was rung, and the first to respond, gun in hand, was the Reverend William Emerson, minister of that town. Then came the minutemen, Captain David Brown's company, Captain Charles Miles's, and Captain Nathan Barrett's. Captain George Minot's alarm company of old men and boys gathered with the rest at Wright's tavern on the town square. Uncertain as to the truth of the news, they sent a messenger back to Lexington to confirm it. Meanwhile, they set about removing and hiding the military stores.[2]

The chief depository was at Colonel James Barrett's house. After the first alarm he hurried home, and the work of concealment and removal went on. Much of the stores had been sent away the day before. Now musket balls, flints, and cartridges were put into barrels in the attic and covered with feathers. Powder was hauled into the woods and hidden. A plow was got out, furrows were struck in a near-by field; light cannon and muskets were laid in them, and other furrows covered them up. By this and that means, the movable articles were put away.[3]

The road from Lexington, as it approached Concord, swung in a curve along the base of a long, narrow ridge which rose abruptly from the plain to a height of sixty feet. Near the end of this ridge lay the principal buildings of the village, the meetinghouse, courthouse, two or three taverns, and perhaps twenty-five dwelling houses. Passing these, it swung to the right beside a similar elevation at right angles to the first, turned squarely to the left, crossed the so-called North Bridge over the Concord River, beyond which was a third eminence two hundred feet high, called Punkatasset Hill, and so went on to Colonel Barrett's place, the chief objective of the British expedition.[4]

The first reinforcements of the little Concord companies came from nearby Lincoln, Captain William Smith's company. The force assembled now made up "150 of us or more." It seemed proper to make a reconnaissance. "We thought," wrote Corporal Amos Barrett of Brown's company, "we wood go and meet the Britsch . . . We marched Down to wards L[exington] about a mild or a mild [and a] half and we see them acomming. we halted and stay[d] till they got within about 100 Rods then we was orded to the about face and march[d] before them with our Droms and fifes agoing and also the B[ritish]. we had grand musick." [5] So, with rattle of drum and squeal of fife came the war to Concord.

Captain Minot's alarm company, the Reverend William Emerson wrote in his diary, had taken post on the first ridge above the meetinghouse, where stood the Liberty Pole, as the most advantageous situation—that is to say, at the end of the first ridge overlooking the town. But, with the news that the enemy "were just upon us & that we must retreat, as their N° [number] was more than thribble ours," the old men and boys withdrew to the second ridge overlooking the bridge. The able-bodied minutemen, however, held their station on the first ridge.[6] It was now about seven o'clock in the morning.

The British came on, the light infantry in advance, followed by the grenadiers. Seeing the provincials on the height above the road, Colonel Smith threw out the light troops as flankers to clear the ridge, while the grenadiers kept to the road. Pitcairn's men "ascended the height in one line, upon which the Yankees quitted it without firing," [7] and retired to the second ridge already occupied by the alarm company.

"Scarcely had we form'd," says the clergyman's diary, "before we saw ye brittish Troops, at the Distance of a ¼ of a Mile, glittering in Arms, advancing toward [us] with ye greatest celerity. . . . Some were for making a Stand notw[ithstanding] ye Super[iority] of y^r [their] N^o but others more prudent tho't best to retreat till our Strenth sh'd be equal to ye Enemy's by Recruits from neigh^g [neighboring] towns y^t were contin[ually] coming into our Assistance." [8] Colonel James Barrett, in general command of the militia of the district, had now returned from his work of concealing the stores. He ordered all the Americans to withdraw across the bridge, take post on Punkatasset Hill, and await reinforcements.[9]

Without hindrance the British came on into the village. Three of the light companies, under Captain Laurie, were stationed to guard the North Bridge: one at its eastern end, the two others on two near-by hills. Three others, led by Captain Parsons, crossed the bridge and marched up the road to Colonel Barrett's place; and the rest, under Captain Pole, were posted about the South Bridge.

While the British superior officers refreshed themselves in the taverns, carefully paying for what they had, the grenadiers began to search the houses.[10]

The search was not very successful, nor was the loss to the Americans very severe. Two 24-pound iron cannon were found in the town and their trunnions broken off—but they were later repaired. A hundred barrels of flour were found, and some were broken open; the others were rolled into the millpond—but the outer flour swelled and waterproofed the rest, so that much of it was salvaged. Five hundred pounds of musket bullets were thrown into the millpond, but most of them were afterwards dredged up.[11] A number of gun carriages were destroyed by fire, together with a lot of trenching tools and some wooden spoons and trenchers; and the British set fire to the courthouse and a blacksmith shop, but soon extinguished the flames themselves. All in all, the rewards of this laborious and, as it proved to be, fatal expedition, were small indeed.[12]

Meanwhile, the men on Punkatasset Hill had moved down to a smaller elevation nearer the bridge. On that little mound clouds had been gathering that were soon to break into a storm. From Acton, minutemen, 38 of them under Captain Isaac Davis, and two companies of militia of unknown numbers, Simon Hunt and Joseph Robin commanding, were the first to arrive. Bedford answered the call with John Moore's and Jonathan Willson's minutemen, 79 strong. William Smith had brought 62 from Lincoln. Unattached volunteers made up a force of three or four hundred. They watched the grenadiers at work in the town, and saw smoke rising from they knew not what fires. Colonel Barrett consulted with his officers. Joseph Hosmer, adjutant, came to them with a question: "Will you let them burn the town down?" They answered with a decision "to march into the middle of the town for its defence or die in the attempt." [13] Barrett gave the order. They were to march, but not to fire until fired upon. So down the hill they marched to do battle with the flower of the King's army.

Major John Buttrick with Lieutenant Colonel John Robinson of Westford at his side led the procession. Isaac Davis's little Acton company in double column, two fifers shrilling the notes of "The White Cockade," two drums beating time to the tune followed. Miles's Concord company fell in next, and then Brown's and Barrett's. Hunt followed with his Acton militia. Bedford and Lincoln and the unattached volunteers closed the column.[14]

Captain Laurie, in command at the bridge, saw them coming and sent to Colonel Smith for reinforcements. Smith ordered two or three companies forward, "but put himself at their head by which means he stopt 'em from being [in] time enough, for being a very fat heavy Man he wou'd not have reached the Bridge in half an hour tho' it was not half a mile to it." [15]

Laurie withdrew his men to the east end of the bridge, leaving a few to take up the planks. Buttrick shouted to the men at work to stop and quickened the pace of his militia. For some unknown reason, the men lifting the planks stopped and went back to their own ranks. Laurie tried to dispose his men to resist the Americans, but "the Rebels got so near him that his people were obliged to form the best way They cou'd . . . the three companies got one behind the other so that only the front one cou'd fire: the Rebels when they got near the bridge halted and fronted, filling the road from top to bottom." [16]

The first fire came from the British, two or three "dropping shots" that splashed harmlessly in the water. But one bullet whistled by the ear of one of the captains. In utter astonishment, "God damn it! They're firing ball!" exclaimed Captain Timothy Brown. Then came a single shot from the British. The bullet struck Luther Blanchard, one of the fifers who had played them down the hill, in the side, making a slight wound. Then a volley rang out. Captain Isaac Davis, at the head of the Acton company, sprang high in the air and fell dead; Abner Hosmer, also of Acton, collapsed on the ground with a bullet through his head. Two others were wounded. Buttrick turned to his men and shouted, "Fire, fellow soldiers! For God's sake, fire!" And they did. Three British privates fell dead; four out of the eight British officers at the bridge, a sergeant and four men were wounded.[17]

The fight at the bridge was all over in two or three minutes. The British retreated in disorder towards the village, leaving their dead and one wounded man, met Smith's reinforcement of grenadiers, re-formed their ranks, and withdrew into the village. The Americans crossed the bridge and pursued the enemy, but only for a few rods. Then, undisciplined as they were, they broke ranks. A number of them went back across the bridge, picked up the bodies of Davis and Hosmer, and carried them off. About two hundred went a little farther, to the near end of the ridge on which they had taken their second position earlier in the day. Strung along behind a stone wall, they waited; but the enemy never came within range. Because of this disruption of the American force, the British light companies under Captain Parsons that had gone to Barrett's place were able to return, cross the bridge, and rejoin their comrades unscathed.[18]

Smith's grenadiers and the light companies from the bridge got back to the village about ten o'clock. An hour later, Parsons's men joined them. Another hour elapsed before they were ready for the return march. At noon they set out, having commandeered two chaises to carry their wounded.[19]

For the first mile, they marched unmolested. But then followed one of the strangest battles of the war, nearly sixteen miles long and a few hundred yards wide. It began at Meriam's Corner on the road to Lexington.

Only three to four hundred men had been in the fight at the bridge; but others had been on the way. Chelmsford sent 60 under Captain Oliver Barron and 43 under Moses Parker. Oliver Crosby, Edward Farmer, and Jonathan Stickney brought a hundred from Billerica. Framingham turned out 147 under Simon Edgett, Jesse Emes, and Micajah Gleason. The roads were black with hurrying men. Reading outnumbered the other towns with 290 men in four companies, Captains John Bacheller, Thomas Eaton, John Flint, and John Walton commanding. Woburn "turned out extraordinary" and rivaled Reading with 256 led by Samuel Belknap, Jonathan Fox, and Joshua Walker; and Sudbury's six companies, numbering 249, under Nathaniel Endworth, Aaron Haynes, Isaac Locker, John Nixon, Joseph Smith, and Moses Stone, were a good third. William Whitcomb led 81 from

Stow, while Westford added 113 under Oliver Bates, Jonathan Minot, and Joshua Parker.[20]

The men who had fought at the bridge had hurried northward across the Great Meadow to Meriam's Corner. The rest had followed or came up with them there. A few companies were gathered about the Meriam house. Smith had thrown out flanking parties parallel to the highway and at some distance from it on either side. As those on the side of the road nearer the house passed by, they wheeled suddenly and fired a harmless volley. The Americans replied, and two of the enemy fell; others were wounded. So this second battle began.[21]

Nearing a small stream, the flankers went down to the road to cross a bridge with the others. Dense groves of trees lined the road at this point; they were full of Americans, who had hurried ahead. Into the crowd pressing across the bridge, they poured a deadly fire. "A grait many Lay dead and the Road was bloddy." [22]

The British column went on. The Americans hurried to get ahead, take cover, and fire again. Parker's company from Lexington, now with full ranks, 120 strong and hot with anger, joined the hunters in Lincoln township. From Cambridge came Captain Thatcher's company, 77 men. Others from the near-by countryside flocked to them. "It seemed as if men came down from the clouds." [23] From houses and barns, from behind walls, rocks, and trees came flashes of flame and puffs of smoke, and redcoats dropped, the dead to lie where they fell, the wounded to keep on as best they could and as long as they could. To some of the British, it was a new sort of warfare, not the kind they had been drilled for, where men faced each other and shot it out, where a bayonet charge might prove decisive. It was dishonorable, this hiding and shooting at men who could not even see you. It was downright savagery. Their anger was fierce, the more bitter because it had so little vent in reprisal. "They were so concealed," said Lieutenant Barker, "there was hardly any seeing them." [24]

But it was not all one-sided. The flanking parties, well back from the road, were sometimes forgotten by the too eager Americans, who were between them and the main column. Many were shot in the back as they were drawing trigger from behind a wall or tree. The flankers took a heavy toll of their adversaries.

The British force was no longer a marching column. It was a disorderly mass of men crowding the road. Soldiers were leaving what had been ordered ranks, ransacking roadside houses and taverns for meat and drink. As they entered Lexington township, Smith halted his men and posted a rear guard to hold back the Americans while he re-formed his ranks. But there was no pursuing force to hold back. Their enemies were all around them on every side. From behind a pile of rails came a blast of fire. Smith was wounded in the leg. Pitcairn's horse plunged, threw its rider, leaped a wall, and ran directly toward the ambuscade. It was captured, and Pitcairn's pistols are now preserved in an American museum.[25]

The attempt to reorganize was not successful. The rearguard was driven in, and the rout continued. Barker reports of this time that the Americans were "increasing from all parts," while the British were "reducing from deaths, wounds and fatigue, and we were totally surrounded with such an incessant fire as it's impossible to conceive, our ammunition was likewise near expended."[26] De Berniere likewise describes the confusion of the British: "When we arrived within a mile of Lexington, our ammunition began to fail, and the light companies were so fatigued with flanking they were scarce able to act, and a great number of wounded scarce able to get forward made a great confusion . . . so that we began to run rather than retreat in order—the whole behaved with amazing bravery, but little order; we attempted to stop the men, but to no purpose, the confusion increased rather than lessened."[27]

So they passed through the village, along the edge of the green, where the conflict had begun that morning. With the least bit of organization among the Americans, Smith's force might have been stopped there, surrounded, and either taken or destroyed. But it was not an American army that so pursued and hemmed them in; it was simply a horde of angry, revengeful, individual men, each on his own, with no coherence, no concert of action. So the invaders were permitted to stumble on, fatigued to the last degree, but still able to go a little farther before they fell utterly exhausted.

There was one more effort to reduce the confusion in the British ranks. Near Lexington village "the officers got to the front and presented their bayonets, and told the men that if they advanced they should die: Upon this they began to form under a very heavy fire."[28] It was the last gasp of British discipline, before those beaten men fell on their faces under the protection of a rescue party.

When Smith had first got to Menotomy, between two and three o'clock in the morning, he had been alarmed by the increasing and seemingly hostile curiosity of the countryside about the movement of his force and had sent an express back to Boston asking for reinforcements. But Gage had already anticipated the need of relief for his Concord expedition and had given orders in the evening of the 18th for the 1st brigade and a battalion of the Royal Marines to parade at four o'clock the next morning—a reasonable precaution which was largely nullified by a series of errors.[29]

First, the brigade major was not at home when the orders were delivered to his servant. He came in late, and his man forgot to tell him about them. There was no parade at four o'clock. At five, Smith's express arrived, and the matter was looked into. At six, part of the brigade was on parade, but no marines. That stirred inquiry again, and it was found that the orders had been addressed to Pitcairn, and left at his quarters, he being then on the way to Concord. It was nine o'clock when the relief started, a delay nearly fatal to Smith's force.[30]

The relief consisted of the 4th or King's Own Regiment, the 23rd, Royal Welch Fusiliers, the 47th, less their flank companies who were with Smith, and the 1st battalion of marines with two 6-pound fieldpieces. The whole force numbered about 1,000, and was under the command of Brigadier General Earl Percy. With all their fifes and drums derisively playing "Yankee Doodle," they marched across the Neck.[31]

Percy was the son and heir of the Duke of Northumberland. There is a legend that as his force passed through Roxbury a schoolboy laughed so heartily at the tune the fifers were playing that Percy asked him the reason. He answered, "To think how you will dance by and by to Chevy Chase," the reference being to the ballad in which appears this verse:

> To drive the deer with hound and horne
> Erle Percy took his way.
> The child may rue that is unborne
> The hunting of that day! [32]

At Cambridge the planks of the bridge across the Charles had been lifted, but piled on the far side. Soldiers crossed on the stringpieces and replaced them; but the supply train of two wagons with its guard of twelve men had to wait until they could be well secured, and then proceeded far in the rear of the column. It soon fell easy prey to a dozen "old men of Menotomy," led by a half-breed Indian, who took both wagons and supplies after two of the guard had been killed and several wounded by a discharge of musketry from behind a stone wall.[33]

Percy was beyond Menotomy village when he first heard the sounds of warfare.[34] "As we advanced," Lieutenant Frederick Mackenzie of the Royal Welch Fusiliers wrote in his diary, "we heard the firing plainer and more frequent, and at half after 2, being near the Church at Lexington, and the fire encreasing, we were ordered to form the Line, which was immediately done by extending on each side of the road. The Grenadiers & Light Infantry were at this time retiring towards Lexington, fired upon by the Rebels, who took every advantage the face of the Country afforded them." But as soon as they "perceived the 1st Brigade drawn up for their support, they shouted repeatedly, and the firing ceased for a short time." [35]

It was high time for a rescue. "We had been flatter'd ever since the morning," says Barker, "with expectations of the Brigade coming out, but at this time had given up all hopes of it." [36] The wasted remnants of Smith's command hurried to the protection of Percy's line, "so much exhausted with fatigue, that they were obliged to lie down for rest on the ground, their tongues hanging out of their mouths, like those of dogs after a chase." [37]

"We could observe a Considerable number of the Rebels, but they were much scattered and not above 50 of them to be seen in a body in any place. Many lay concealed behind the Stone walls and fences. They appeared most numerous in the road near the Church and in a wood in the front and on the left flank of the line." [38] On these Percy trained his guns, harming only the church, through which he sent one ball, while the provincials retired behind a swamp. Some of his men, seeing the Americans retire, broke from their ranks in pursuit, but the swamp stopped them. They then entered the village, looted some houses, and burned one large group of farm buildings and several dwellings. [39]

All this while, the Americans were dodging here and there, creeping around the enemy's flanks, appearing and disappearing as they took cover behind trees, walls, and houses, sniping or firing small volleys, and inflicting much injury upon the massed British troops.

Percy gave the exhausted men an hour's rest. At half past three he resumed the retreat, with Smith's men in front covered by the fresh troops and strong parties on the flanks. The more impressive array of the combined forces and the vigilance of the flankers somewhat daunted the Americans, and, for a time, the British marched in comparative safety. Of necessity they proceeded slowly, and there was a fine chance to loot the roadside houses. Percy exercised no restraint on such depredations. He evidently wished to terrorize the countryside. Many of his men carried heavy burdens of household goods of all sorts. But as he neared Menotomy the aspect of affairs began to change again. The Americans were pressing more closely on his rear guard and against his passing column, and the firing from cover grew stronger and stronger, for his enemies were rapidly increasing in numbers. New companies of minutemen and militia had been hurrying to the battle from the eastern towns and now were arriving.

Brookline brought 95 men into play; Watertown, 134; Medford, 59;

Malden, 76; Roxbury, 140. Needham sent 185; Beverly, 122. Menotomy
turned out 52, and Danvers, 331. Dedham was left "almost literally without
a male inhabitant before the age of seventy and above that of sixteen"; its
337 topped all the rest.[40] There were 2,000 or more men to resume the
attack. General William Heath and Dr. Joseph Warren urged them on
against the British rear guard. Percy halted his column and turned his two
6-pounders on them, but with no effect, except to scatter his pursuers temporarily. So they went on again. The flankers kept the Americans back from
the roadside or shot down those who were too reckless in making a near
approach. They entered the houses, looted them, tried to burn them. At one
point a group of minutemen, too few to stand openly against the enemy,
had retreated into a house. Twelve were bayoneted, and the house was
plundered. "We were now," says Lieutenant Barker, "obliged to force
almost every house in the road, for the Rebels had taken possession of
them and galled us exceedingly . . . all that were found in the houses were
put to death." [41] The fury of the fight was at its height. Forty Americans fell
in Menotomy, and forty British. Many of these were killed in close personal
encounter, clubbed muskets against bayonets.

In Cambridge there was a mile and a half of continuous battle. The
sight of the burning houses and of the British soldiers loaded down with
plunder had inspired the Americans with a fierce rage. If it had been possible
to organize them into a single body, get ahead of the column, obstruct the
road with felled trees, send out detachments to waylay and destroy the
flanking troops, which were not numerically too strong, and, from the stone
walls beside the road, concentrate their fire on the main column, Percy's
troops might have been held up and destroyed. But there was no central
control over the various elements of the American forces, these township
companies. Heath at Menotomy tried to form them into regiments; but he
had no staff to carry his orders, and, if there had been one, it could not have
brought together and reduced to order those half-trained men scattered
over the country who did not even preserve their companies as units.[42]

At Cambridge, Percy, to avoid the bridge over the Charles, shrewdly
and unexpectedly changed his course from that on which he had come from
Boston and took the road to Charlestown. It was shorter as well as safer.
But in what is now Somerville he was forced to renew the fight. His fieldpieces were again in action, with no more substantial result than before.
Fire from a grove of trees cut down a number of his men. The rest hurried
on faster. At Prospect Hill there was a considerable gathering of Americans,
and many of the invaders fell. Once more Percy halted his column and
made play with the guns, and these were unlimbered again a little farther

on. In spite of the harassment of the retreating troops, the looting and destruction of property continued.[43]

The weary, almost exhausted soldiers at the head of the column, Smith's men, had expended almost all their ammunition when, after sunset, they at last crossed the little isthmus that connects Charlestown with the mainland and were free from their pursuers. In the twenty hours that they had been afoot they had marched thirty-five miles, had fought continuously for half that distance, had had little to eat, and many of them had been wounded.

The British losses that day were 73 killed, 174 wounded, 26 missing, a total of 273 casualties out of about 1,800. The Americans lost 49 killed, 41 wounded, and 5 missing, a total of 95. It has been computed that 3,763 Americans were engaged in the day's fighting at one time or another, though perhaps not much more than half that number at any one time.[44]

The fact that in so long a battle, subjected to the fire of so numerous a force, the British lost no more than 15 per cent of their men is noteworthy. If each American, in his whole day's work, had hit his mark only once, the British force would have been destroyed twice over. The militia and minutemen were supposed to carry thirty-six cartridges, or the equivalent in loose powder and bullets. If the average man fired only twenty charges (and we hear of many who fired nearly twice that number) no fewer than 75,000 shots must have been discharged at the enemy, with a total of hardly more than 247 hits. Only one bullet out of 300 found its mark. In all his day's work, only one man out of 15 hit anybody.

It is of course true that the flankers kept the roadside walls and other close cover fairly free of the Americans, compelling them to use the second line of walls at more than point-blank distance from the marching column. It is also true that those same roadside walls protected the British, in some places "almost to the height of their shoulders." [45] Nevertheless, there were many times when a heavy fire was poured upon them at short range, and the results of the entire proceeding should prove the fallaciousness of the belief so often expressed that the Yankees were superior marksmen, dead shots in fact. They were not. They could not be when armed only with the musket or fowling piece of the period. Their inaccuracy and short range have been previously noted, and the Yankees had had little practice in shooting, because of the infrequency of training days and the scarcity and expense of gunpowder.

The comments of the English officers engaged are interesting. That of Percy is noteworthy as showing a change in his opinion that the Americans were "cowards" and "timid creatures." He noted that "many of them concealed themselves in houses & advanced within 10 yds. to fire at me and other officers, tho' they were morally certain of being put to death themselves in an instant . . . nor will the insurrection here turn out so despicable as it is perhaps imagined at home. For my part, I never believed, I confess, that they wd have attacked the King's troops, or have had the perseverance I found in them yesterday." [46]

Lieutenant Barker thought the whole affair was "as ill plan'd and ill executed as it was possible to be." Especially, he complained of the "three hours on Cambridge marsh waiting for provisions that were not wanted." That delay, he thought, allowed the country people to get intelligence of the movement and gave them time to assemble. But for it, there would have been "no interruption at Lexington" and a surprise at Concord. [47]

Captain Evelyn, however, still called "the Yankeys . . . the most absolute cowards on the face of the earth," and attributed their conduct to "enthusiasm and madness." [48]

CHAPTER 6

The Siege of Boston

At ten o'clock in the morning of April 19, Israel Bissel, postrider, mounted his horse at Watertown. In his pocket was a letter:

To all Friends of AMERICAN Liberty let it be known: That this morning before break of day, a Brigade consisting of about one thousand or twelve hundred men . . . Marched to *Lexington* where they . . . Killed 6 Men and wounded 4 Others . . . another Brigade are now upon their March from Boston supposed to be about 1000. The bearer Israel Bissel is charged to alarm the Country quite to Connecticutt and all persons are desired to furnish him with fresh Horses as they may be needed. . . .

J. Palmer—one of the Com^y of S^y

At noon Bissel's horse fell dead at Worcester, thirty-six miles away. No fresh horse was immediately forthcoming, so he spent the night there; but by seven the next evening he was at New London, Connecticut, having given the tidings to Israel Putnam at Pomfret on the way. In the night he went on. Lyme had the news at one o'clock in the morning, Saybrook at four, Guildford at seven, Branford at noon, New Haven in the evening. A night there and on again. Fairfield saw him at four in the afternoon. Connecticut had been alarmed, but Israel Bissel did not stop. He was in New York on the 23rd. There the "faction," as the Loyalists called the Rebels, immediately "paraded the town with drums beating and colours flying." A sloop, loaded with provisions for the British in Boston, was unloaded. The arsenal was entered, and a thousand stand of arms were seized. "The whole city became one continued scene of riot, tumult and confusion. Troops enlisted for the service of the rebellion." So New York, hesitating and doubtful before, was aroused and began to swing into line with the other colonies.

But the furore he had excited did not stay Bissel. He was off again south-wards, riding night and day through New Jersey, New Brunswick at two in the morning, Princeton at six, Trenton at nine, then Philadelphia. A feat of endurance was that ride of Israel Bissel's.

A second dispatch, with fuller details, came to New York on the 25th and went on by relays of express riders, again riding night and day. Baltimore had it on the 27th at ten in the evening; Annapolis, at half past nine the next morning; Edenton, North Carolina, on May 4th; and finally, having been given out at every town and village the whole way, it reached Charles-ton, South Carolina, on the 10th.[1]

From every point on the road the "momentous intelligence" spread to the outlying districts and, by letters and word of mouth, reached the farthest corners of the colonies, the towns on the seaboard, the villages and farms, the backwoods settlements. Everywhere the response was a call to arms.

The veteran Colonel Israel Putnam, who was now retired to his Connecti-cut farm after having seen hard service in the French and Indian War, was "in leathern frock and apron . . . assisting hired men to build a stone wall" when Bissel brought him the news. He instantly answered the call, in his working clothes. Rousing the militia officers as he rode through the towns, "he reached Cambridge at sunrise the next morning," a hundred miles in eighteen hours on the same horse.[2]

Massachusetts men were flocking to Cambridge even before Putnam had the news. By one o'clock of the 20th, New Hampshire was afoot. Sixty men from Nottingham, joined by others on the way, made the distance to Haverhill, twenty-seven miles, by dusk, "having run rather than marched," and were in Cambridge, fifty-five miles, within twenty hours. Colonel John Stark, hardy backwoodsman, was in command of 300 of his fellow colonists at Chelsea by the morning of the 22nd. Two thousand of them were ready to come the next day.[3]

Connecticut's action was swift; thousands were on the way by the 24th. Rhode Island was on the march before Percy got back to Charlestown. Within the shortest possible time Boston was surrounded from Roxbury to Chelsea by an unorganized, undisciplined mass of men.

The minutemen had never been really organized; their officers had not even been commissioned. As separate bodies they soon ceased to exist. The militia was composed of boys and men varying in age from sixteen years to sixty. The responsibilities of many of them would prevent them from entering upon a continuous campaign. It was no army that surrounded Boston, and what force was there was soon melting away. Within four days after Concord the Massachusetts men, many of whom had departed immediately after the fighting was over, were greatly reduced in numbers, and hundreds from New Hampshire had gone home. General Artemas Ward wrote to the Congress that he was in danger of being "left all alone." [4]

The Massachusetts Provincial Congress, sitting on Sunday April 23, voted that an army of 30,000 men be "immediately raised and established," of which 13,600 were to be "raised immediately by this Province." The thousands needed to make up the full number were not provided for; but committees were sent to the other New England colonies to "request their concurrence." [5]

Rhode Island's assembly promptly voted a brigade of three regiments, 1,500 men, and appointed as brigadier general Nathanael Greene, who was "worth a thousand men" and more.[6] New Hampshire fixed 2,000 as its quota, with Nathaniel Folsom as the major general, but Colonel John Stark "the most trusty officer" in command.[7] Connecticut ordered the enlistment of 6,000, with David Wooster as the major general and Joseph Spencer and Israel Putnam as brigadiers. Of the Massachusetts forces, Artemas Ward, John Thomas, William Heath, John Whitcomb, and Joseph Warren were appointed major generals.[8] Not all the promised thousands materialized; Connecticut never sent more than half her quota; both New Hampshire and Rhode Island fell short of theirs. But, by June, there were perhaps 15,000 men encamped before Boston.

They stretched in a half-circle around Boston, from Roxbury to Chelsea. The center, at Cambridge, was held by Ward with fifteen Massachusetts regiments, Major Samuel Gridley's battalion of four companies of artillery, Putnam's own regiment and other Connecticut troops, 9,000 in all. The right wing, at Roxbury, Dorchester, and Jamaica Plains, was commanded by General Thomas. He had 4,000 Massachusetts men, Greene's Rhode Island regiments, and the greater part of General Spencer's Connecticut troops, three or four artillery companies, a total of about 5,000. On the left, there were three companies of Colonel Samuel Gerrish's Massachusetts regiment at Chelsea; Colonel John Stark's New Hampshire regiment, the largest in the army, at Medford; and the much smaller regiment under Colonel James Reed, also from New Hampshire, near Charlestown Neck, about 1,000 in all from that state.[9]

General Artemas Ward was in supreme command of the Massachusetts troops; and the New Hampshire troops had been directed to place themselves under his orders.[10] The other colonies' forces were at this time amenable only to their own commanders, though Connecticut also submitted her men to Ward's orders after Bunker Hill. Yet from the first they all seem to have cooperated in obedience to Ward.

This hastily assembled force was short of supplies of every kind—arms, ammunition, tents, blankets, provisions, and camp utensils. Of ordnance fit for siege operations, it had practically none—no more than a few large iron cannon, two or three mortars and howitzers. Sixteen fieldpieces, of which perhaps only six were fit for service, constituted their mobile artillery. Late in June, New Hampshire offered "some" 24- and 32-pounders, and the Massachusetts Committee of Safety asked for three of the smaller size.[11]

The supply of small arms was better, for generally each man brought his own firelock; yet more than a thousand men were deficient in this respect in the middle of June. Bayonets were conspicuously lacking, and uniforms almost altogether absent. The greatest shortage was in the most essential element, gunpowder. Much of Massachusetts' small stock had been seized by Gage. Late in April there were but 82 half-barrels available; on May 25 the Committee of Safety drafted 68¼ barrels from five of the eastern counties.[12]

Massachusetts had only 1,100 tents, but set about making more out of ships' sails. As many of the troops as possible were crowded into dwellings, which had been vacated by their owners removing from the combat zone. The buildings of Harvard College gave shelter to many.[13]

How to feed such an army was a problem, as it continued to be through out the war—often, indeed, almost insoluble. In the morning after the battle "all the eatables in the town of Cambridge, which could be spared, were collected for breakfast, and the college kitchen and utensils procured the cooking." Some beef intended for the Boston market was secured, and "a large quantity of ship-bread at Roxbury, said to belong to the British army, was taken." After that the Commissary General was directed to "supply the troops with provisions, in the best manner he can, without spending time on exactness"; and somehow he managed to do it.[14]

All communication between the town and the rest of the province was now cut off. But in the town there were thousands of patriots who wished to leave it, and outside it were many Loyalists who longed for the protection the British troops could afford them. After a complicated negotiation an agreement was made allowing an exchange. Gage stipulated that all the inhabitants should first deposit all their arms in Faneuil Hall, which they did to the extent of 1,778 firelocks, 634 pistols, 973 bayonets, and 38 blunderbusses. Those coming in and going out were allowed to carry their personal

effects except arms and ammunition, and the exception was soon extended
to include salable merchandise, provisions, and medicines.

Thousands took advantage of this arrangement. It has been estimated
that "near half" of the patriots went out. Wagons from outside were allowed
to enter the town, to bring in and carry out the effects of those coming and
going. Plans were made to distribute an estimated 5,000 poor refugees from
Boston in various other towns. But after a while the Tories in Boston protested against the Whigs' being allowed to go out, wishing to hold them as
hostages against an attack and, perhaps, a burning of the town. Various
obstacles and delays developed, and the system broke down.[15]

The condition of the British army, shut up in the town with no access to
the country, unable to procure fresh meat or vegetables, was unenviable.
Captain George Harris of the 5th Regiment wrote home about it: "However
we block up their port, the rebels certainly block up our town, and have cut
off our good beef and mutton. . . . At present we are completely blockaded, and subsisting almost on salt provision." He was cultivating his own
little garden of salads and greens. Lieutenant Barker wrote, "We can get no
fresh provision, but must live on our allowance of salt meat." [16]

From a military point of view, the situation was a stalemate. Boston was
blockaded on the land side, but it was not properly besieged. As long as the
fleet kept open communication by water, the Americans could not hope to
starve it out. Unless there was some definitely active move on one side or
the other, the condition might last until doomsday. But the Americans dared
not attempt to take the town. For one thing, they could not concentrate all
the available force of the four provinces against it; the seacoast towns, in fear
of attacks by the fleet, were holding their own men at home and calling for
more. There were no siege guns to batter the defenses, and the men were
not sufficiently disciplined and coordinated for storming operations. As for
the British, they had had their lesson on April 19; they knew they had not
nearly enough to try offensive operations outside the town.

There were, however, some little excursions from both sides. Gage needed
hay for his horses and the few beef cattle he had. On May 21 he sent four
sloops, with a subaltern and thirty men, to bring off a supply from Grape
Island in the harbor. General Thomas sent three companies in a lighter and
a sloop to oppose them. There was a harmless exchange of fire before the
British were driven off, with only seven or eight tons of hay; the Americans
burned all the rest, eighty tons.[17]

The Americans countered, on May 27, with an expedition against two
other harbor islands, Hog and Noddle's, on which a considerable number
of horses, cattle, and sheep were at pasture. Wading through a narrow,

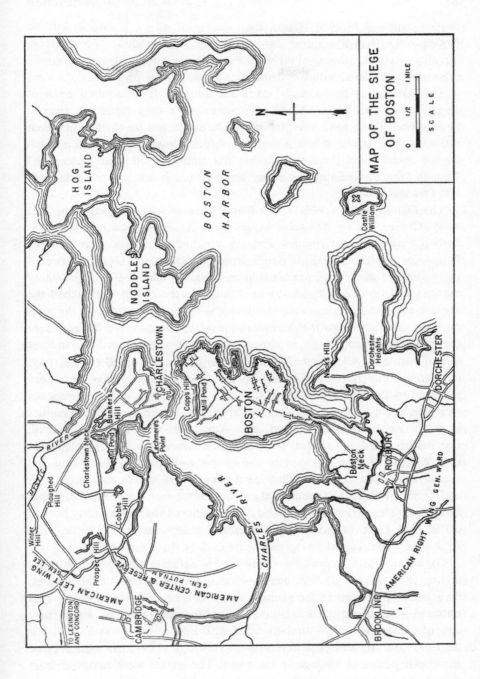

MAP OF THE SIEGE
OF BOSTON

SCALE

0   1/2   1 MILE

N

HOG ISLAND

NODDLE ISLAND

BOSTON HARBOR

Castle William

CHARLESTOWN

Bunker's Hill

Copps Hill

Mill Pond

Mill Pond

BOSTON

Charlestown Neck

Lechmere's Point

Ploughed Hill

Cobble Hill

Winter Hill

MYSTIC RIVER

Prospect Hill

CHARLES RIVER

Boston Neck

ROXBURY

Nook's Hill

Dorchester Heights

DORCHESTER

BROOKLINE

AMERICAN RIGHT WING   GEN. WARD

AMERICAN CENTER & RESERVE   GEN. PUTNAM

AMERICAN LEFT WING   GEN. LEE

CAMBRIDGE

TO LEXINGTON
AND CONCORD

shallow channel to Hog Island, they drove off all its livestock, but on Noddle's the British admiral, Samuel Graves, had landed a considerable quantity of stores. Having observed the hostile operations, he sent an armed schooner, the *Diana*, with forty marines, to protect his property.

The Americans had already taken off three or four hundred head of sheep, cattle, and horses, killed what other stock they could not remove and burned all the hay, when the enemy began to fire on them. They then retired to Hog Island, where a handful of them "squated Down in a Ditch on the marsh" and there was "a hot fiar untill the Regulars retreeted." Though "the Bauls Sung like Bees" around their heads, no one was hurt. But that was not all.[18]

The *Diana* got in trouble with adverse wind and tide and could not get away. Graves sent ten or twelve barges from the fleet to tow her, and after them the armed sloop *Britannia*. Putnam marched a thousand men with two fieldpieces to attack this little flotilla from Chelsea Neck. Graves answered by mounting three guns from his ship on Noddle's Island. Gage sent eighty marines and two 12-pounders to assist him. As the *Diana* approached the shore where the Americans stood, there was a heavy fire from all the guns on both sides and from the American musketry. Putnam led his men into the water waist-deep to get in closer range. It was growing dark, and the aim of both sides was blind. The towing barges cut loose and rowed away; the *Diana* went aground. She fell on her beam ends, and her men were taken off by the *Britannia* without waiting to save anything. The Americans swarmed aboard, looted her, and set her on fire. There were few casualties in those twelve hours of fighting; four Americans were slightly wounded, two British killed and several wounded. The Americans were pleased with their capture of four 4-pounders and twelve swivels from the *Diana* and the salvage of her ironwork. They went back to the islands three days later and carried off several hundred sheep and some cattle and horses. Other such forays stripped Pettick's Island of five hundred sheep and thirty horned cattle, and Deer Island of eight hundred sheep and more cattle. The American commissariat was greatly refreshed by these exploits.[19]

Gage anticipated a possible attack on his defenses on Boston Neck by adding to their strength. An abatis—that is to say, a row of felled trees, their butts embedded in the ground, their sharpened major limbs pointed outward—was constructed in front of one of the outer bastions, and a triple row of *chevaux-de-frise*—timbers fitted with iron spikes—was built across the road. Mortars and guns were mounted there, and batteries were erected at various points of vantage in the town. The troops were removed from their barracks to a camp on the Common, and heavy details, as many as a fifth of the whole force, were constantly on guard duty.[20] But all this was defensive, calculated merely to hold the town; there was no sign of any intention to go beyond that. The British government, however, had awakened to the fact that Gage's force was inadequate to achieve more than such a negative success; reinforcements were on the way.

Six regiments, or parts of regiments, the 35th, 49th, 63rd, 64th, 65th, and 67th, had landed in Boston in April, May, or early June, or were on the way across the ocean, also the 17th Light Dragoons, a detachment of 600 marines, and some drafts to recruit the regiments already there. With such additions Gage had, by the middle of June, a force of about 6,500 rank and file.[21]

On May 25 the frigate *Cerberus* arrived. She had on board three very distinguished gentlemen and members of Parliament: Major General William Howe, Major General Henry Clinton, and Major General John Burgoyne. They were entering upon a service from which two of them were to emerge with blasted reputations, the third with but little credit.

William Howe, not yet a knight, was in his forty-fifth year, a tall, soldierly-looking man, although his figure had been overextended and his naturally heavy features coarsened by excessive indulgence in food and drink. He was of a very dark complexion, like his brother the admiral, whose nickname was "Black Dick." He was a man of easy manners and easy morals, an inveterate gambler, a hearty drinker; his intimate relations with Mrs. Joshua Loring during his stay in America were notorious. In politics he was a Whig, and he had been opposed to coercing the Americans. When he stood for Parliament in the Whig interest at Nottingham, he promised his constituents that he would decline any command against the Americans that might be offered to him. When the King, less than a year later, assigned him to such a command, he asked whether he was to consider it as a request or as an order. He was told that it was an order and accepted it, excusing his compliance to his constituents by saying he "could not refuse without incurring the odious name of backwardness to serve my country in distress."

He had started his career as a soldier at the age of seventeen, with a cornet's commission in the Light Dragoons. After considerable military experience on the European continent, he first saw service in America as a major of infantry at the capture of Louisburg in 1758. In the next year he gained distinction for gallantry in leading the advance, a "forlorn hope" of twenty-four men, up the Heights of Abraham in Wolfe's attack on Quebec. He as always foremost in battle and conspicuously cool under fire. He became a major general in 1772.

He was a clever strategist, an able tactician; his plans were excellently

conceived and well carried out, but he was too often content with victory
in the battle itself, failing to follow up his successes as he might have done.
The fault was marked at Long Island, in the succeeding operations on Manhattan Island, and, indeed, in all his campaigns, as will be seen hereafter.
These repeated failures have been attributed by some to his Whiggish pro-
clivities, which were favorable to the Americans; by others to his naturally
sluggish temperament, which was aggravated by his dissipation; by others
again, especially when he found the Americans intrenched against him, to
memories of the slaughter of his troops at Bunker Hill. On the whole, though
he outmaneuvered Washington repeatedly and won battle after battle, his
conduct of the war in America was a failure; and he returned to England
to face a Parliamentary inquiry, which might have condemned him had it
been pushed to a conclusion.[22]

Henry Clinton, the only son of a British admiral and colonial governor
of New York, was but thirty-seven years old when he came to Boston. He
was not a man of colorful personality and, in contrast to his companion
generals, he seems rather a negative character in the drama of the Revolution. He had obtained a commission as a lieutenant in the 2nd Foot Guards
at the age of thirteen years; he was a lieutenant colonel at twenty, a major
general at thirty-four. He had seen some service in Germany between 1760
and 1763.

In his American career Clinton showed no indubitable evidence of military ability, certainly none of brilliance in his profession. He commanded
the first unsuccessful attack on Charleston, in 1776, and the second, which
resulted in its capture in 1780; and in neither did he display unusual talents.
His most able exploit was the conduct of his army in its removal from Philadelphia across New Jersey in 1778, when he reached New York without
serious losses, in spite of attacks by Washington's pursuing forces. He cannot be blamed for his failure to relieve Burgoyne at Saratoga in the circumstances then existing. His successful attacks on Forts Clinton and Montgomery in 1777 were planned with soldierly skill and carried out with
sufficient audacity; but on the whole his career in America was far from
brilliant. After his return to England, he was the object of adverse criticism
by Lord Cornwallis, with whom he engaged in a bitter controversy.[23]

In John Burgoyne we meet with a character of conspicuous interest, who
aspired to renown in such diverse fields as war, statesmanship, and literature.
It is ironical that he was defeated in that field in which he showed most
ability.

He was a scion of an ancient Lancashire family of repute and substance;
at this time he was in his fifty-third year. He was handsome in the full-fed

British style of the period, and was a wit, a playwright, a man of fashion, and a member of Parliament. He was also a good soldier, and in certain military respects was much in advance of his time. His treatise on the duties of officers urged that soldiers be treated like thinking human beings; they should not be subjected to frequent and brutal corporal punishment, and there should be no "training men like spaniels by the stick," as he called it. He insisted that the officers should read books, learn how to write accurately, know something of mathematics, and acquire a practical knowledge of the equipment of their calling; in all these points there was vast room for improvement among the British officers of the day, whose ignorance was generally of "Stygian density." Practicing his own precepts, he was popular with his men, who nicknamed him "Gentleman Johnny." "On every occasion he was the soldiers' friend."

He had entered the army in 1744 at the rather advanced age of twenty-two years, but sold out in 1747 and did not rejoin until 1756, being merely a captain at the age of thirty-four. He served on the European continent as a brigadier with considerable credit for seven years. His capitulation at Saratoga finished his military career.[24]

The arrival of the three generals produced no improvement in the situation of the British army. If any one of them had displaced Gage in supreme command, he would undoubtedly have seen, like Gage, that the pressing need was for still more troops. The army could not take the aggressive until the large forces which Gage had consistently demanded since the fall of 1774 reached America.

Burgoyne, indeed, was of no help to Gage; he was, on the contrary, a menace. He began a voluminous correspondence with some of the home authorities in which he dilated upon Gage's errors and thus i jured him in the judgment of the ministry.

In a different and well meant endeavor, he gave his chief a push down the declining path of reputation. Gage, instructed by the cabinet to proclaim martial law in Massachusetts, decided to use the proclamation as a "last effort . . . to spare the effusion of blood." Burgoyne wrote it for him, and "no manifesto was ever worse adapted to the taste of its intended readers." Its flamboyant, inflated, and verbose style widened the eyes of the simple New Englanders in sheer amazement; its accusatory and threatening substance aroused bitter resentment where it did not excite derision.

It called the people an "infatuated multitude . . . conducted by certain well known incendiaries and traitors." It warned that "those who are invested with supreme rule . . . do not bear the sword in vain," and threatened "the fulness of chastisement." It asserted that the leaders of the Americans imposed on the credulity of their followers with "the grossest forgeries, calumnies, and absurdities that ever insulted human understanding," and used "the animated language of ancient and virtuous times . . . to countenance the most abandoned violations . . . of the just rights and interests of mankind." It noted that the rebels "with a preposterous parade of military arrangement have effected to hold the Army besieged."

Proceeding to a generous offer of pardon to all persons who would lay down their arms and return to the ways of peace, except "Samuel Adams and John Hancock, whose offences are of too flagitious a nature to admit of any other consideration than that of condign punishment," it announced, of course, martial law throughout the province.[25] That from a general who dared not set his foot outside the town of Boston and could no more enforce martial law throughout the province of Massachusetts than he could throughout the empire of the Khan of Tartary.

Even in London the preposterous character of this manifesto was appreciated; its style was recognized as Burgoyne's, and much fun was made of it: "They *affect* to hold the army besieged . . . the next time you write to your friends, say in plain English that the Americans have *effected* the siege." [26]

That proclamation was issued on the 12th of June. Five days later much was to happen, but previous events in another part of the colonies must be given attention before the story of the siege of Boston is continued.

C H A P T E R   7

Ticonderoga

Fort Ticonderoga was called "the Key to the gateway to the continent," by which was meant the way from Canada to the English colonies. In a wilderness the best route is by water; from Canada southward this was furnished by the St. Lawrence River, the Richelieu, Lake Champlain, and the Hudson. At the point where Lake George discharges its waters into Champlain, the larger lake narrows to a width of half a mile, and at one point two opposite headlands leave a passage between them of less than a quarter of a mile. There on the western side, on an eminence rising a hundred feet above the water, stood the fort.[1]

The French first occupied this position in 1755. After plans by Vauban, the great military engineer, they built a fort with stone bastions surrounded by a star-shaped outer wall, the whole complete with glacis, counterscarps, covered ways, and demilunes. They called it Fort Carillon. In 1758 with a garrison of 4,000, under Montcalm, they held it against 6,000 British regulars and 10,000 provincial troops under Lieutenant General James Abercromby. In the next year, Sir Jeffrey Amherst invested it with 11,000 men; the French commander, Bourlamaque, had but 3,500. He blew up the works and retreated. The British rebuilt it in less substantial fashion and named it Ticonderoga. After the Peace of Paris in 1763, ending the French and Indian War, there was no frontier between Canada and the colonies to be guarded; the fort was manned by a skeleton garrison, used only as a supply post on the route, and allowed to fall into decay.[2]

When the relations between Britain and her American colonies became strained to the point of breaking, the New Englanders had cause to fear that

Guy Carleton, in command at Montreal, might enlarge his small force of regulars with French Canadians and Indians and attack them in the rear. To discover the inclinations of the Canadians in the contest with Britain, the Massachusetts Provincial Congress in February, 1775, sent John Brown of Pittsfield to Montreal and Quebec. His report was discouraging, and to it he added: "One thing I must mention to be kept as a profound Secret, the Fort at Tyconderogo must be seised as soon as possible should hostilities be committed by the King's Troops. The people on N. Hampshire Grants have ingaged to do this business and in my opinion they are the most proper Persons for the Jobb." Brown's information as to the New Hampshire Grants people taking on the job had been derived from one Ethan Allen whom he had met in Pittsfield.³

Ethan Allen was a true son of the backwoods, born in a log cabin in Litchfield, Connecticut, the eldest son of a substantial farmer. He had begun his schooling under a clergyman with a view to entering Yale College; but on his father's death he had to care for a family of a widow and seven other orphans. After a short tour of duty with a Connecticut regiment in the French and Indian War, he set up an iron furnace, tried lead mining, and, in 1768, removed to the New Hampshire Grants, now Vermont.

In the conflict between the settlers there and the government of New York, which claimed ownership of the Grants, Allen was a colonel of the Green Mountain Boys, defenders of their rights to land under grant of the Governor of New Hampshire. The contest was violent and tumultuous, just the sort of fight to suit such a man as he.

In 1775 he was thirty-seven years old. He was tall (he is often described as "gigantic"), broad-shouldered, lean, and straight; his bodily strength was enormous. He has been credited with "boldness, adroitness, toughness, pride, fortitude, cheerfulness and a terrific volubility in invective . . . an amplitude and appalling humor of profane swearing," also with "rough and ready humor, boundless self-confidence and a shrewdness in thought and action equal to almost any emergency." Although his schooling was brief and scanty, he was a great reader and was later to produce several pamphlets on the rights of the Green Mountain Boys, as well as a narrative of his captivity by the British, composed of "staunch, blunt, boastful, blundering, fearless words," and, rather surprisingly, a tract entitled *Reason the Only Oracle of Man,* a very cogent deistic argument.⁴

Another man had thought about Ticonderoga. When the news of Lexington and Concord came to New Haven on the 20th of April, Captain Benedict Arnold summoned his company of militia to march to Cambridge and applied to the authorities of the town for ammunition; he was thought too hasty, and his request was refused. His answer to that was that he would break in the magazine and take what he wanted. "None but Almighty God shall prevent my marching," said he. They gave him the ammunition.[5]

Arnold was familiar with the Lake Champlain and St. Lawrence country. Happening to meet Colonel Samuel Holden Parsons on the way to Cambridge and hearing him lament the lack of cannon in Ward's army, he told him that a plentiful supply could be had at Ticonderoga. Parsons went on to Hartford with this suggestion in mind.[6]

At Cambridge, Arnold broached the matter to the Committee of Safety, giving it "certain information" that there were eighty pieces of heavy cannon, twenty brass pieces, and a dozen large mortars, besides small arms and stores, at Ticonderoga, three or four more brass guns at Skenesboro near by, and that the fort was "in a ruinous condition and has not more than fifty men at the most." [7] The committeemen were interested indeed. On May 3 they gave him a colonel's commission and authorized him to enlist "not exceeding 400" men, to march to Ticonderoga and "reduce the same," taking possession of "the cannon, mortars, stores &ca." This was to be a special commission for a "secret service," and the committee reserved the right to dismiss the force to be raised "whenever they shall think proper." [8]

Benedict Arnold was at this time thirty-four years old. Though only of middle height, his appearance was commanding. He was well formed, muscular, capable of great endurance, active, graceful in his movements, and exceptionally adept in athletic exercises, such as running, fencing, boxing and skating; he was also an expert marksman with gun and pistol, and an accomplished horseman. His salient facial features were clear cut and handsome; his hair was black, his skin swarthy, his clear, bright eyes light in color.

He came of a substantial family; a collateral ancestor of the same name had been governor of Rhode Island. He had a fair common-school education, which included some Latin. As an apprenticeship to a druggist he ran away at the age of seventeen to fight in the French and Indian War. He was advertised in the newspapers in 1759 as a deserter. In any case, he returned to finish out his term. At twenty-one he set up his own drugstore and bookshop in New Haven. His business flourished, and he branched out into the West Indies, sometimes sailing his own ships. He is also said to have shipped horses between Canada and the West Indies, which gave the British a chance to belittle him as a mere "horse-jockey." By the year 1775 he was a well-to-do merchant, the "possessor of an elegant house, storehouses, wharves, and vessels."

In the Revolutionary War he had an adventurous and, as was inevitable with his disposition, a stormy career, but proved himself to be a soldier of outstanding merit. He was original in his ideas, audacious in action, quick to form his plans, and swift to execute them. Though imperious of will, arrogant, restive under orders, and possessed of a passionate belief in his own judgment and in his own superior ability as a soldier, he was a most capable commander of men. He did not merely order his troops forward, he led them; he was a fighting man, and he had, as he deserved to have, the devotion of his troops. An old soldier of his command at Saratoga said of him: "He was our fighting general, and a bloody fellow he was. He didn't care for nothing, he'd ride right on. It was 'Come on boys!' 'twarn't 'Go, boys!' He was as brave a man as ever lived."

His treason has become almost the only popularly known element of his career, overshadowing and blotting out the memory of his expedition against Quebec, his exploits on Lake Champlain, his relief of Fort Stanwix, and his services in the fighting which led to Saratoga. But for his betrayal of his charge at West Point, he would have stood out in American history as one of the great soldiers in the Revolution.[9]

Parsons, arriving at Hartford after his roadside conversation with Arnold, "undertook and projected" with four or five others the taking of Ticonderoga. They sent an express to Ethan Allen at Bennington, asking him to gather a force of Green Mountain Boys and hold them in readiness for the proposed adventure; they appointed Major Halsted, Captain Edward Mott, Captain Noah Phelps, and Bernard Romans as a committee to conduct their part of the affair, and provided them with a war chest of £300. Phelps and Romans went on in advance on the 28th, and were followed by Epaphras Bull, Captain Mott and sixteen associates the next day. At Pittsfield, Massachusetts, they met James Easton and John Brown. Easton raised between forty and fifty men, and the whole party set out for Bennington, where they met Allen with about a hundred of his Boys.[10]

A Committee of War was chosen, consisting of Easton, Phelps, and Bull, with Mott as chairman; Allen was given command by a "universal" vote, with Easton and Seth Warner as his first and second lieutenants. It was decided to send Samuel Herrick with thirty men to surprise and capture Major Philip Skene at his settlement, Skenesboro—now Whitehall—and take his boats.[11] Captain Asa Douglass was sent to Panton, also to procure boats. Other small parties were directed to secure the roads to the north, to prevent warning of the attack from reaching the fort. Gershom Beach, a backwoods blacksmith, was detailed to rouse more Green Mountain Boys; he is said to have covered sixty miles of wilderness in twenty-four hours.[12]

These proceedings in the evening of May 9 were hardly over when a very impressive gentleman in a brave uniform with a scarlet coat arrived and informed the gathering that he had come to take command of them by virtue of a commission and orders from the Massachusetts Committee of Safety. It was Benedict Arnold, who, having heard of the expedition from Pittsfield, had left recruiting officers at Stockbridge and, with one manservant, had hurried on to Castleton.[13]

The men of the little army were "extremely rejoiced" to learn that the Committee of Safety endorsed the project, but "shockingly surprised when Colonel Arnold presumed to contend for the command of those forces that we had raised, who we had assured should go under the command of their own officers." Although the leaders "generously told him our whole plan, he strenuously contended and insisted that he had a right to command them and all their officers."

But Arnold had met more than his match. His demand had "bred such a mutiny among the soldiers which had nearly frustrated our whole design, as our men were for clubbing their fire-locks and marching home." [14]

Allen was not present at this discussion; he had gone forward to Shoreham —now Orwell—two miles below the fort, where, in Hand's Cove, the forces were to assemble. The next morning, all those at Castleton followed him. Arnold renewed his contention as to the command and finally got, as he says, joint command with Allen, until he could "raise a sufficient number of men to relieve his [Allen's] people." It is doubtful, however, that he got more than the right to march beside Allen at the head of the men in the attack on the fort.[15]

Early in the morning of May 10, about two hundred men had assembled at Hand's Cove—Easton's and Allen's forces, augmented by others from the country roundabout. Between them and the fort stretched two miles of water. The moon had set, the sun not yet risen; it was dark, and squalls of wind and rain were blowing up to make the crossing more hazardous. There were no boats; those expected from Skenesboro had not come. It was near dawn when a scow appeared; it had been commandeered by two boys who had heard of the proposed attack. Soon after, Asa Douglass brought another, with a few recruits.[16]

Allen and Arnold, with eighty-three men, crowded into the two boats and landed about half a mile below the fort at daybreak. The boats were sent back for the rest, but there was no time to wait if there was to be a surprise. Allen drew the men up in three ranks and addressed them. He reminded them that, for a long time past, they had been "a scourge and a terror to arbitrary power," and that their "valor has been famed abroad." He now proposed to lead them upon "a desperate attempt, which none but the bravest of men dare undertake. . . . You that will undertake voluntarily, poise your firelocks!" Every firelock was poised.[17]

Allen and Arnold, side by side, led the advance, Arnold in his fine uniform, Allen in one of his own devising—a green coat, with large gold epaulets, and yellow breeches. Behind them went a straggling column of men in every sort of garb—buckskin, linsey-woolsey, or what not, beaver hats, felt hats, coonskin caps, buckled shoes or moccasins—armed with firelocks, pistols, swords, knives, or simple clubs, not a bayonet among them all.[18]

The main entrance in the south wall of the fort was in a ruinous condition. The leaders and their men swarmed through and over the ruins and came upon a single sentry, guarding a wicket in the curtain of the main fort. He pointed his musket at the intruders and pulled the trigger; it flashed in the pan. He turned and fled through a covered way into the middle of the fort, shouting an alarm, the attackers close behind him, yelling like Indians. Another sentry slightly wounded one of the officers with a bayonet. Allen hit him on the head with the flat of his sword and ordered him to show the way to the officers' quarters. Leaving their men drawn up in two lines, back to back, Allen and Arnold followed the sentry to a staircase in the west barracks.[19]

A door at the head of the stairs opened and disclosed an officer, Lieutenant Jocelyn Feltham, wearing coat and waistcoat, but carrying his breeches in his hand. Allen shouted at him, "Come out of there, you damned old rat," (or "skunk," or "bastard," according to different accounts), and dashed up the stairs along with Arnold and followed by others. The astonished officer asked by what authority they intruded. Allen, according to his own later account, rose to the occasion with a deathless utterance:

"In the name of the Great Jehovah and the Continental Congress!" he shouted.

It has been remarked that the officer had about as much respect for the Continental Congress as Allen had for the Great Jehovah.[20] But this astounding speech and the demands that followed for immediate surrender of "the Fort and all the effects of George the Third," with the alternative of a massacre of every man, woman, and child in the place, brought the commander, Captain William Delaplace, to terms; he handed his sword to Allen and ordered the garrison paraded without arms.

The entire force consisted of the two officers, two artillerymen, a couple of sergeants, and forty-four privates, many of them invalids; but there were also twenty-four women and children. In fact Ticonderoga, with its ruined walls, its meager garrison, its flock of women and children, was more like a backwoods village than a fort. Allen's report to the Continental Congress characteristically tells of the taking of "the Fortress of Ticonderoga by storm" and of "the resistless fury . . . of the Soldiery [who] behaved with uncommon ranker when they Leaped Into the fourt." [21]

They certainly did behave with "uncommon ranker" after the surrender. "There is here at present," Arnold reported the next day, "near one hundred men, who are in the greatest confusion and anarchy, destroying and plundering private property, committing every enormity and paying no attention to publick service." He had forbidden them to behave so riotously, but Allen had "positively insisted" that he should have no command, and he was powerless to control them.[22]

It was necessary now to dispose of the prisoners. Allen wrote to Governor Jonathan Trumbull of Connecticut of the 12th, "I make you a present of a Major, a Captain and two Lieutenants of the regular Establishment of George the Third." The major was Skene, whom, with his daughter and various dependents, Herrick had captured at Skenesboro. These prisoners were dispatched to Hartford. Lieutenant Colonel Seth Warner took a party to Crown Point, another disabled British post, and, without resistance, captured the garrison, one sergeant, eight privates, and ten women and children, also a number of cannon.[23]

Arnold's discontent with his anomalous position in the fort, where he had no recognized command and very little good-fellowship, was relieved on the 13th, when Captain John Brown and Captain Eleazer Oswald arrived in a small schooner and several bateaux, captured at Skenesboro, with fifty recruits "enlisted on the road." Arnold was a sailor; Allen was not. So there was no objection to Arnold's having command of a naval expedition against St. Johns, a frontier Canadian post on the Richelieu River, some miles beyond Lake Champlain. When he had yet thirty miles to go, the schooner was becalmed. Arnold and thirty-five men in two bateaux rowed all night and, early in the morning of the 17th, surprised the unresisting garrison, a sergeant and fourteen men, and took the post, along with a 70-ton sloop, armed with two brass 6-pounders, and its crew of seven. There were others of the King's forces at Chambly, twelve miles away, and reinforcements for St. Johns, to the number of two hundred, were hourly expected. Arnold's men took all the more valuable stores, destroyed five bateaux, and set sail with four others, the sloop, and the schooner, for Crown Point.[24]

But Allen had his ambitions for further conquest, too. He had embarked with ninety men in four bateaux and followed Arnold. The two expeditions, Allen's going, Arnold's returning, met about six miles south of St. Johns and saluted each other with three volleys apiece. Allen boarded Arnold's sloop and learned that he was too late, that St. Johns had been taken, and that its garrison was now in irons in the hold. But, though it had been taken, it had been abandoned. That did not suit Allen; he would occupy it and hold it. However, at the moment, he was in straits, "his men being in a starving condition," as Arnold put it. In fact, Allen, in his enthusiasm for conquest, had neglected the purely incidental matter of feeding his men *en route*. Arnold supplied him, and he went on in spite of warnings as to the impracticability of his venture. At St. Johns, Allen learned that the expected reinforcements were near at hand. He first decided to ambush them, placed his men accordingly, and sent out scouts. But cooler thoughts supervened; his men were tired after three days and nights with little sleep and little food. When the new forces were within two miles of him, he withdrew across the river, where his wornout men lay down to sleep. They were surprised by a volley of grapeshot from six fieldpieces ranged on the other side; the relief for the garrison had come up. They swarmed into their boats with such celerity as to leave three of their number behind, and rowed lustily away, exchanging harmless shots with the enemy as they pulled out of range.[25]

Arnold, now at Crown Point, reported to the Massachusetts Committee of Safety that he had one hundred fifty men of his own—"Colonel Allen's men are in general gone home"—and that he had determined to hold the fort at the Point until the arrival of wheels and of draught animals should enable him to remove the cannon.[26] He had armed his sloop and his schooner with "carriage guns" and swivels in anticipation of an attempt by the British to recapture the place. But the ambitions of the two leaders were not yet satisfied. They decided to send a force to Pointe au Fer and fortify it. Allen's designs went far beyond that; he was going to conquer all Canada. "I will lay my life on it," he wrote to the New York Congress, "that, with 1500 men and a proper train of artillery, I will take Montreal . . . it would be no insuperable difficulty to take Quebeck." [27] But they were stopped in their tracks by word from the Continental Congress.

The Congress had news of the taking of Ticonderoga on May 18. It at once resolved that the fort should be abandoned and all the guns and stores removed to the south end of Lake George, with a provision that an exact inventory of them be taken, "in order that they may be safely returned when the restoration of the former harmony between Great Britain and these colonies so ardently wished for by the latter shall render it prudent." [28]

But Arnold, even if he could not go any farther, had no intention of giving up the ground he had gained. On May 29 he wrote to the Continental Congress and to the Massachusetts Provincial Congress stating his surprise and alarm at the proposal, which would leave "our very extensive frontiers open to the ravages of the enemy." The same day he wrote to the Provincial Congress of New York, giving full details as to the number of men and the amount of supplies needed to hold the posts on the lake. Allen was equally averse to giving them up and even more eloquent in expressing his views to the New York Congress.[29]

These two were not alone; New England wanted the forts held; so did northern New York. Alarmed by reports that an expedition to retake the Champlain posts was contemplated in Canada, and that Guy Carleton was soliciting the Six Nations of Indians to join in such an effort, the northern colonies protested against the abandonment of Ticonderoga, the strongest position on the lake, and persuaded the Continental Congress to change its mind. On May 31 it resolved that Connecticut be requested to send strong reinforcements to Crown Point and "Ticonderogo" and that New York be requested to furnish supplies. Connecticut had already ordered four hundred men to march to the forts, with 500 pounds of its "pittance of powder," followed by a thousand more men under Colonel Benjamin Hinman. The forts were to be retained, but not with Colonel Benedict Arnold in command.[30]

A committee from Massachusetts, sent up to ascertain the needs of the forts, brought Arnold the news that he was to be second in command under Hinman. To the colonel, who had been signing his name as "Commander-in-Chief," and had just sent a long letter to the Continental Congress outlining an elaborate plan for the conquest of Canada which he was willing to undertake, and in which Hinman's regiment was to play a subordinate part, this demotion was displeasing. It was more than that, it was humiliating and altogether disgusting; "he would not be second in command to any person whomsoever." He immediately left the service under a double impulsion, his discharge by the committee and his own resignation.[31]

No exercise of military genius was involved in the taking of the Champlain posts, nor was there needed any display of valor. They fell like ripe apples from a shaken limb. Nevertheless, their capture was of vast importance to the colonies. Leaving out of consideration their subsequent value in the operations in that territory, the guns which they yielded were of inestimable value to the Americans. Many of them were found to be in such bad condition as to be useless, but no fewer than seventy-eight were serviceable, ranging from 4-pounders to 24-pounders. There were also six mortars, three howitzers, thousands of cannon balls of various sizes, nine tons of musket bullets, thirty thousand flints, and a large quantity of miscellaneous apparatus. The guns were what the army besieging Boston most needed. They were not at once removed, for lack of transport, but in the coming winter a way was found to carry them to the army.[32]

CHAPTER 8

Bunker Hill

When the frigate *Cerberus* with the three major generals was entering Boston harbor, General Burgoyne was told that "10,000 country people" surrounding the town were holding its garrison in check. "What?" he is said to have exclaimed. "Ten thousand peasants keep five thousand of the King's troops shut up? Well, let us get in, and we'll soon find elbow-room." [1] It may have been at his suggestion that Gage and his three colleagues, not long after their arrival, decided to seize and fortify Dorchester Heights on the Charles River, which, though a commanding position overlooking the town of Boston, had been neglected by both sides. This operation was to have been effected on June 18. [2]

Five days before that date, news of the intended movement was conveyed to the American command; and on June 15 the Committee of Safety decided on countermovements: that "Bunker's Hill in Charlestown be securely kept and defended, and also some one hill or hills on Dorchester Neck be likewise secured." Bunker's Hill was to be cared for at once, Dorchester being left to further consideration. [3]

Charlestown was a peninsula, roughly triangular in shape, opposite the north side of Boston. Its base was separated from Boston by the half-mile width of the Charles River. Its peak terminated in a narrow isthmus, the Neck, so low as to be often overflowed at high tide. The Mystic River washed its northeasterly side; the Charles widened into a large bay on the northwest. Its length was about a mile from north to south; its greatest width was about half a mile.

It had a rolling surface culminating at three points in low hills. The first,

73

Bunker's Hill, began at the Neck and rose gradually for 300 yards to a rounded top 110 feet high, sloping on its east and west sides to the water. This was connected by a low ridge with Breed's Hill, the second eminence, the top of which was about 600 yards distant; its height was 75 feet. The easterly and westerly slopes of this hill were steep. At the water side on the west was the village of Charlestown. Near the base of Breed's Hill, on its easterly side, the approach was broken by brick kilns, clay pits, and an area of swampy land. The third and smallest hill, Moulton's, only 35 feet high, lay at the southeast corner of the peninsula near the meeting of the Mystic and the Charles. Outside the little town the whole surface of the peninsula was divided into different holdings, separated by rail fences or stone walls and used chiefly for hay and pasture, with orchards and gardens here and there. In the middle of June, 1775, some parts had been mowed, the hay left on the ground to cure; in other places, and particularly on the sloping approach to Breed's Hill from the southeast, the grass, fully knee-high, was still standing. A narrow road ran from the Neck, passed Bunker's Hill, and encircled Breed's.[4]

At the recommendation of the Committee of Safety and on the day that it was made, General Artemas Ward assembled a council of war. The names of all the officers attending have not been ascertained; but it appears that General Putnam, Joseph Warren, lately appointed a major general but not yet commissioned, Brigadier General Seth Pomeroy, and Colonel William Prescott were there. The matter was discussed. Ward and Warren had been opposed to fortifying Bunker's Hill when it had been proposed at earlier meetings, and seem to have been reluctant now. The lack of powder—there were only eleven barrels in the whole camp—rendered rather more than doubtful the ability of the Americans to hold it, even if it should be successfully fortified. But Putnam was strong for the adventure. "The Americans," he is supposed to have said, "are not at all afraid of their heads, though very much afraid of their legs; if you cover these, they will fight forever." Pomeroy seconded him, and Prescott agreed, whereupon the others consented and the order was made, without deciding how the defenders were going to "fight forever" after their ammunition gave out.[5]

Artemas Ward, on whom the major responsibilities of American leadership were descending, was a descendant of William Ward, one of the early Puritan settlers of New England. His father was a well-to-do farmer of Worcester County. His education was that of the average country boy of the period in the short terms that "school kept" in Shrewsbury, supplemented by some home study under the supervision of the local preacher, which led to his entry into Harvard and his graduation there, followed by a later degree of A.M.

In 1755, at the age of twenty-eight, he was a major of militia, and three years later he marched with Abercromby's army against Ticonderoga. In the course of a year's service he attained a lieutenant colonelcy; but had little experience in that grade. He came home with his health impaired, and never again was a robust man. He was politically active in the civil disturbances following the Stamp Act, and was a delegate to the First and Second Provincial Congresses.

Ward was a man of medium height, "too stout for his forty-seven years," and at this time was afflicted with bladder stone, but not physically incapacitated thereby. He was precise, even elegent, in his dress. His long, sharp nose, pointed chin, and bright, knowing eyes indicated intelligence, but did not reveal his really dominant mental characteristics—slowness of thought, extreme caution, taciturnity, and inflexibility of opinion. These elements of his character were displayed in his measured speech and his habit of using biblical terms and phrases in conversation. As undistinguished as his appearance was his character, except for honesty, firm patriotism, and devotion to the American cause.

Ward was, in fact, better fitted for the council chamber or the judicial bench than for military leadership, especially in enterprises demanding forthright boldness of plan and unhesitating speed in execution.[6]

General Israel Putnam is a colorful character about whom legends have clustered so thickly as to conceal the man within. His name is still universally known, while much greater men have faded from memory since the Revolution, showing how effectively romantic adventures create reputations and embalm them.

He was a farmer, fifty-seven years of age, widely known throughout New England by the affectionate title of "Old Put." He had led the first Connecticut company sent out in 1755 in the French and Indian War, in which he saw long and hard service and was engaged in many sensational exploits. He was captured by Indians, tied to the stake to be burned, and rescued at the very last moment by a French officer. He was a prisoner at Montreal for a long time until exchanged. He led a regiment to attack Havana and was shipwrecked on the coast of Cuba. He fought the Indians again in 1764. This record, strengthened by the tradition of his victorious battle with a veritable werewolf, and by the later story of his escape from capture by the British, by riding his horse at a headlong gallop down a flight of rocky steps, has made his name a household word throughout New England. In

1775 he was believed to be not only a good soldier, but a great soldier, fit to be a major general, which he was not.

He was a rather short, broad-shouldered, burly man, with a big round head crowned by an unruly shock of gray hair. His round, open face gave evidence of the frank, generous, outspoken, jovial disposition that made him universally popular. He was courageous, enterprising, energetic, active, and persevering. As colonel of a fighting regiment, he would have been admirably placed; he would have led his men against the enemy, and they would have followed him with a cheer. Of the conduct and care of an army, of strategy in major operations, of shrewd planning of a campaign or even of a single battle, of careful preparation for the execution of plans, of the management of large bodies of men in the field, of resourcefulness in taking advantage of unexpected opportunities in battle on a large scale, or making unexpectedly necessary changes in plan, he knew nothing and should not have been expected to know anything. *Colonel* Israel Putnam he should have remained throughout the war.[7]

Colonel William Prescott, who was to lead the detachment to Bunker's Hill, was born in 1726 to a Massachusetts family of wealth and position. His early education was limited in scope, but he made up for that by his devotion to books. In person he was tall, over six feet, well set up and muscular; his features were strong and clear-cut. His disposition was kindly, his manners simple but courteous; yet he had the habit of command and the power to exact obedience from his men, whose respect he deservedly enjoyed. His customary movements were unhurried, and his coolness and self-possession in moments of danger were notable.[8]

Another important participant in the enterprise was Joseph Warren, who was but thirty-four years of age. His family dated from 1659 in Massachusetts. He was well educated with the degree of A.M. from Harvard. He had studied medicine and had acquired a large practice in Boston; his wife was Mercy Otis, the brilliant sister of James Otis. After the passage of the Stamp Act he undertook "a serious examination of the right of Parliament to tax the colonies" and, as a result, allied himself with those who resisted British measures.

His natural enthusiasm and strong impulses led him to take an active part in politics, in which he became an associate of Hancock, the Adamses, and the rest of the patriot malcontents; he was in especially close relationship with Samuel Adams. He soon became one of the leaders of the movement, to which he lent his abilities as a writer and an orator. He was the author of the Suffolk Resolves, one of the earliest and boldest declarations of refusal of obedience to the oppressive acts of Parliament. He frequently acted as presiding officer of the Provincial Congress, and was chairman of the Committee of Safety.

Though Warren had had no military experience, he was chosen to be major general, and is said to have intended to pursue a career in arms.

He was of middle height, well built, graceful in figure, active in movement, scrupulously neat in attire, and elegant in address. His fine, open countenance was indicative of his integrity, his modesty, and his gentle, friendly, and courteous disposition; yet he was courageous morally and physically, swift of thought and action, high-spirited, enthusiastic, capable of quick resentments and fiery impulses, and hot of speech in support of the cause which he had adopted. To that cause he unreservedly devoted his fine talents; indeed it had become the ruling passion of his short life. His too early death in the coming battle was universally and most feelingly lamented as an irreparable loss to his friends and to his country.[9]

Ward ordered the Massachusetts regiments of Prescott, Colonel James Frye, and Colonel Ebenezer Bridge, with a fatigue party of two hundred men drafted from Putnam's Connecticut regiment and commanded by Captain Thomas Knowlton, as well as Captain Samuel Gridley's Massachusetts artillery company, forty-nine men and two fieldpieces, to parade in the camp at Cambridge at six o'clock in the evening of June 16. They were to be equipped with packs, blankets, a day's rations, and the necessary entrenching tools. They would have made up a party of about fourteen hundred all told; but Prescott's regiment turned out only two-thirds of its paper strength, and the other two were short of their full number, so that there were between a thousand and twelve hundred actually assembled. Frye being ill with the gout, his men were led by Lieutenant Colonel James Brickett.[10]

When they were properly drawn up on the Cambridge Common, the Reverend Samuel Langdon, President of Harvard College, offered a prayer for the success of their undertaking. At about nine o'clock a column was formed, and they set out for a destination of which they were ignorant, not even the company officers having been informed of the purpose of the expedition. Colonel Prescott, preceded by two sergeants carrying dark lanterns "open in the rear," led the way; by his side marched Colonel Richard Gridley, a veteran who had seen service at Louisburg thirty years before and in many other campaigns. He was now chief engineer of the American army. Prescott wore military costume, a blue coat, "lapped and faced," and a three-cornered hat. Some of the other officers may have worn uniforms, but not the common soldiers. They were "mostly husbandmen," and they wore their ordinary clothes.[11] An eyewitness of their assemblage has left an engaging description of them:

To a man, they wore small-clothes, coming down and fastening just below the knee, and long stockings with cowhide shoes ornamented by large buckles, while not a pair of boots graced the company. The coats and waistcoats were loose and of huge dimensions, with colors as various as the barks of oak, sumach and other trees of our hills and swamps, could make them and their shirts were all made of flax, and like every other part of the dress, were home-spun. On their heads was worn a large round top and broad brimmed hat. Their arms were as various as their costume; here an old soldier carried a heavy Queen's arm, with which he had done service at the Conquest of Canada twenty years previous, while by his side walked a stripling boy with a Spanish fusee not half its weight or calibre, which his grandfather may have taken at the Havana, while not a few had old French pieces, that dated back to the reduction of Louisburg. Instead of the cartridge box, a large powder horn was slung under the arm, and occasionally a bayonet might be seen bristling in the ranks. Some of the swords of the officers had been made by our Province blacksmiths, perhaps from some farming utensil; they looked serviceable, but heavy and uncouth.[12]

At Charlestown Neck they were met by General Putnam, Major John Brooks, and some wagons loaded with fascines, gabions, empty hogsheads, and entrenching tools. Here Captain John Nutting of Prescott's regiment was detached, with his company and ten of Knowlton's men, and sent into Charlestown to watch for movements of the enemy, while the main body marched on over Bunker's Hill and to the foot of Breed's. Prescott then called the officers together, told them for the first time the purpose of the expedition, and consulted with them as to the position of the proposed entrenchment.[13]

His orders were explicit, to fortify Bunker's Hill, but there seemed to be reasons for choosing Breed's instead. It was nearer Boston. On the other hand, Bunker's was higher and nearer the Neck, their only avenue of escape if driven from their works. The matter was debated. Putnam and another general officer, whose name does not appear, were for Breed's but Putnam urged that they should first fortify Bunker's to cover a retreat, if that became necessary. The debate was prolonged; Gridley became impatient at the delay, urging a quick decision, as much valuable time was being wasted. At last it was decided first to erect the main works on Breed's, and then the auxiliary defenses on the other hill.[14]

Gridley marked out the lines of a redoubt about eight rods square. The south side, facing Charlestown, was the strongest, having near its middle a redan, or angular projection. The north side, towards Bunker's Hill, had an open entrance. There was a sally port at the southeast corner, protected by a blind.[15]

It was about midnight when the pick-and-shovel work was begun. Thoroughly used to those tools, the farmers worked steadily and swiftly to make up for the delay. They had but four hours before dawn would discover them to the enemy and expose them to attack.

Prescott detached Captain Hugh Maxwell's company of his own regiment and sent it down to patrol the shore on the Boston side of the peninsula. More than once he and Major Brooks also went down to see that there was no alarm in the enemy's camp. It was a warm, still night, dimly lit by the stars in a cloudless sky. They could see the dark outlines of the ships lying at anchor in the narrow channel of the Charles and, very near to the shore on which they stood, the *Lively* with her twenty guns, the *Falcon* sloop with sixteen, the *Symmetry,* armed transport with eighteen, the *Glasgow* with twenty-four, and the great sixty-eight-gun *Somerset.* They could hear their bells marking the half-hour and the reassuring cry of "All's well" from the British sentries. Finding everything quiet, Prescott recalled Maxwell's men a little before dawn.[16]

Soon the faint light of the coming day discovered to the watch on the *Lively* the walls of the redoubt, now six feet high. Without delay, her captain put a spring on her cable, swung her about so as to bring her guns to bear, and opened fire. The sound of her cannon aroused the British camp and the whole town of Boston. Admiral Graves signaled the *Lively* to cease firing; but about nine o'clock it was resumed by his order, and began from the other ships and the battery on Copp's Hill as well.[17]

When Prescott looked about him in the light of day, he saw his little redoubt, perched all alone on that hilltop, with no outworks, no support whatever, except the houses in Charlestown, the fences and walls on that side, and a swamp at some distance on the other. There was really nothing to prevent its being outflanked by troops marching out of musket range on either side. He prepared at once to extend his defenses on the east by running a straight line of breastworks about twenty rods long from near the southeast corner of the redoubt and parallel with its eastern face, down the slope of the hill to the swamp. The Charlestown houses, walls, and fences would have to be relied on for protection of his other flank.[18]

The ships, chiefly the *Lively, Falcon,* and *Spitfire,* and the Copp's Hill battery kept up their bombardment of the redoubt. The fire from the vessels was ineffective; their guns were too light, and they could not be elevated sufficiently to bear on their target. The battery was too far away to do much damage. The roar of the guns was terrifying to the inexperienced American soldiers; but the round shot bounced about without doing any harm, and the work on the defenses went on without interruption. At last one of the men, working on the outside of the redoubt, was hit and killed. That was a shock to them all. One of the subalterns announced the casualty to Prescott, and asked what should be done. "Bury him," said the colonel. The brusqueness of the reply shocked the questioner. "What?" said he. "Without prayers?" A clergyman present volunteered to perform a burial service. Many of the men laid down their tools and gathered about the body. Prescott ordered them back to their work, "but religious enthusiasm prevailing, the chaplain again collected his congregation," and the corpse was interred in due form.[19]

This incident worked upon the fears of some of the men. A number of them left the ground and never returned. To reassure the rest, Prescott mounted the parapet, and, thus exposed to the fire of the enemy, walked along it, encouraging his men and directing their labors. But more than fear of the big guns was working on the minds of the weary men, more than mere fatigue was exhausting their bodies.

As the sun rose in a cloudless sky, the temperature also rose; the day became one of the hottest of that summer. There was little movement of the air outside the redoubt; inside, there was none. Dust from the disturbed, dry earth hung about them in clouds; they breathed it; their lips were caked with it; their faces were grimy with sweat and dirt. Inexperienced in warfare and inefficiently organized, many of them had neglected the order to bring a day's food; now they were faint with hunger. A cannon ball smashed the two hogsheads that had held their supply of water; no more could be had except when carried in buckets from the wells in the village. "We began to be almost beat out," Peter Brown wrote to his mother after the battle, "being tired by our Labour and having no sleep the night before, but little victuals, no Drink but Rum," which though undeniably stimulating does not, when taken straight, quench thirst.[20]

All that was bad enough, but there had begun to creep into their minds doubts as to the capacity and good faith of their leaders, a suspicion that they were deserted by their comrades in Cambridge. They had been promised relief in the morning; none had come, no new men, nor any food. "The Danger we were in," wrote Brown, "made us think there was Treachery & that we were brot there to be all slain, and I must & will say that there was Treachery, Oversight & Presumption in the Conduct of our Officers." [21] It is a wonder that there was not a wholesale desertion, that the whole enterprise did not break down before any British soldier appeared in the field.

That would have been the outcome, one is forced to think, but for one man, Colonel William Prescott.

He never swerved from obedience to his orders, never faltered in the prosecution of his task. When some of his officers urged him to send to headquarters to ask for relief, for his tired men to be replaced by others, he refused. "The men who have raised these works are the best able to defend them," said he. "They have learned to despise the fire of the enemy; they have the merit of the labor, and shall have the honor of the victory." He did, however, send for supplies and reinforcements.[22]

Because of the heat he had discarded his uniform coat and put on a banian, a light linen coat. His hat and wig were laid aside; his bald head glistened with sweat, as he went about inside and outside the redoubt, encouraging his men or driving them to their labor with sharp commands, keeping them at it by the sheer power of his will, until by eleven o'clock they had finished the works, made the banquettes (or fire steps), and could rest. One veteran of the day said long afterward, "I tell ye that if it had not been for Colonel Prescott, there would have been no fight." [23]

The Neck was so raked by shot from the armed transport *Symmetry* and two gunboats that Captain Samuel Gridley refused to risk one of his artillery horses across it when Major Brooks, bearing Prescott's request to Ward for reinforcements, asked for a mount; Brooks had to go on foot. He reached headquarters in Cambridge at ten o'clock. Ward had already refused an earlier request from Putnam; he still hesitated. At the very time when courage and resolution to take risks and to dare possible dangers were most needed at headquarters, they were wanting. Ward doubted that the British would attack Prescott; he feared they would rather take this opportunity to seize his own stores of munitions and supplies at Cambridge and Watertown; and he did not wish to weaken his forces there. He referred Prescott's request to the Committee of Safety, then in session in his house. Richard Devens of Charlestown, one of its members, was so "impassioned and vehement" in urging that troops be sent that the Committee recommended their dispatch, and Ward yielded. The New Hampshire regiments of Colonel John Stark and Colonel James Reed, then at Medford, were ordered to go.[24]

All this while Putnam was not idle. His particular post was on Bunker's Hill, where he had planned to erect defenses to cover a possibly necessary retreat from Breed's. But while waiting for the completion of the redoubt, so as to get the intrenching tools, he was never idle; "burning with zeal and intrepidity," he was riding about here, there, and everywhere. He was a general and a whole general's staff at once. Twice he had ridden to Cambridge, crossing the Neck through the ships' fire there, fearless and unhurt, to demand reinforcements, which Ward refused. He was now at Breed's, now at Bunker's, now at the Neck or at any other place on the peninsula; he was seen "in so many places that he would appear to have been ubiquitous." When the works on Breed's were complete, he called on Prescott to send the tools to him at Bunker's. Prescott had only about three hundred of his Massachusetts men and Knowlton's fatigue detachment in the redoubt; he feared that any that were sent with the tools would not come back. "They shall every man return," said Putnam. Prescott yielded. "An order was never obeyed with more readiness. From every part of the line within hearing volunteers ran, and some picked up one, some two shovels, mattocks &c., and hurried over the hill." Not one of them came back.[25]

Gage had called a council of war as soon as possible after the first alarm. It was plain to all its members that the American position was bad, since it was nearly surrounded by water that was completely dominated by the King's ships. Its only communication with the other American forces for supplies and reinforcements was by way of the narrow Neck, which was exposed to the fire of the guns of some of the British ships. The only question discussed was how best to capture or destroy the provincials. Clinton, it is said, favored an immediate landing, with a force of five hundred men, on the peninsula south of the Neck and in the rear of the redoubt. Some of the ships or gondolas could then blast the Neck itself with such a concentration of fire that no aid could reach the redoubt. Cut off from either supports or retreat, the Americans must starve in their fort or come out and fight in the open between two fires, for another force could be landed at the other end of the peninsula to cooperate with the first.[26]

Gage and the majority of the council objected to this plan. It was argued that it was not good military practice to interpose a force between two bodies of the enemy—in this case, the men on the peninsula and the rest of the American army. However sound the maxim, it was not so sound as to overrule all other considerations in a particular case. A different plan was proposed and adopted. As matters then stood, it was not a bad plan. The British would land a strong force below Moulton's Point on the southeast corner of the peninsula, march it up the east side along the Mystic, out of musket shot of the redoubt, flank it, and attack it in the rear. It must be remembered that at that early hour, when the extended breastwork had not even been begun and the redoubt stood all alone, there was ample clear space for this maneuver; it might easily have succeeded, had it been promptly executed. But it was fatally delayed.[27]

"As the shore where it was judged most proper to land was very flat, the

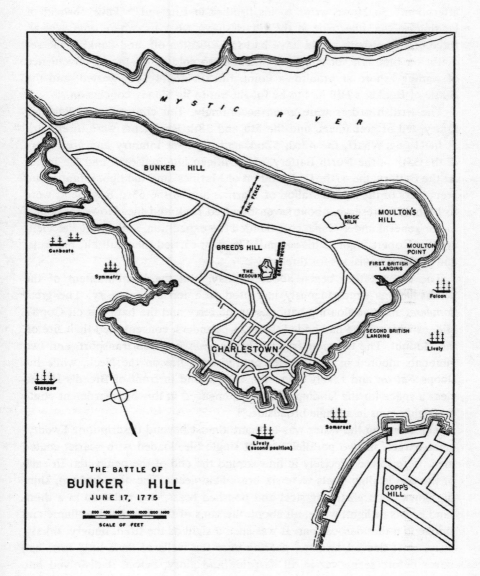

MYSTIC RIVER

BUNKER HILL

RAIL FENCE

BRICK KILN

MOULTON'S HILL

BREED'S HILL

BREASTWORKS

MOULTON POINT

Gunboats

THE REDOUBT

FIRST BRITISH LANDING

Symmetry

Falcon

SECOND BRITISH LANDING

CHARLESTOWN

Lively

Glasgow

Somerset

Lively
(second position)

THE BATTLE OF
BUNKER HILL
JUNE 17, 1775

COPP'S HILL

0 200 400 600 800 1000 1200 1400
SCALE OF FEET

landing could not be made with facility after the tide of ebb was much run off," and it was necessary to wait for "High Water at two o'clock in the afternoon." So Howe wrote to his brother in England.[28] Thus, instead of landing on the other side at the Charlestown wharves, where only a weak force of skirmishers would have had to be beaten off, and flanking the redoubt on that side, or subjecting the British soldiers to the inconvenience of wading ashore at Moulton's Point, full six hours were wasted, and the Battle of Bunker's Hill had to be fought out to its bloody conclusion.

The British orders were given accordingly. Ten companies of light infantry, ten of grenadiers, and the 5th and 38th Regiments were to embark at the Long Wharf, the 43rd, 52nd, and the light infantry and grenadiers of the 35th at the North Battery, about fifteen hundred rank and file in all. At the Battery, the 47th, 1st Battalion of Marines, and the light infantry and grenadiers of the 2nd Battalion of Marines and of the 63rd Regiment, were to be held in reserve, about seven hundred rank and file. Howe, as senior major general under Gage, commanded the expedition, with Brigadier General Sir Robert Pigot as his second. The men carried their full kit, blankets, and cooked provisions for three days.[29]

The embarkation began about midday, and the bombardment of the peninsula was simultaneously increased to a terrible intensity. The great *Somerset* and two floating batteries at the ferry and the batteries on Copp's Hill, to which Gage had added three 24-pounders, concentrated their fire on the redoubt. The *Glasgow* frigate, the *Symmetry* armed transport, and two gunboats moored in the Charles poured their fire on the Neck, while the sloops *Falcon* and *Lively* swept the low ground in front of Breed's Hill to clear a space for the landing. The ships engaged in this bombardment could fire eighty guns in a single broadside.[30]

The scene on the water was brilliant almost beyond description. Twenty-eight barges, in two parallel lines of single file, loaded with scarlet-coated men, were rowed precisely in line around the end of the peninsula. In each of the two leading boats were six brass fieldpieces. The noonday sun, shining down upon glistening steel and polished brass, was reflected in a thousand points of light, while, all about, the guns of the fleet belched flame and smoke in a thunderous roar. It was such a sight as the tired, hungry, thirsty, dirty, shirt-sleeved farmers, peering over the walls of their little fort, had never before seen, war in all its pride and glory, before it dissolved into blood and horror.[31]

The landing was made about one o'clock without resistance, and the troops were at once formed in three lines on Moulton's Hill, while Howe was examining the American works. He saw at once that the situation had changed since the early morning. Whereas then the redoubt had stood alone, with no supporting defenses, leaving a broad way around it on the east, now the breastwork extended eastward and dangerously narrowed that way. Yet it was not entirely cut off; there was still room for a flanking movement. There was, however, another matter to be considered. On Bunker's Hill there was a considerable crowd of men who had left the redoubt at various times, or who had crossed the Neck and stopped there. Putnam held them to erect his proposed covering works. But to Howe they doubtless looked like a reserve force. There was a danger that his flanking movement might land him between two American forces. Also he saw a column emerge from that formless mass of men and march toward the redoubt. The Americans there were being reinforced. He was going to need more men than he had brought. He ordered his men to break ranks and refresh themselves with the food they had brought, while he obtained his reserves and part of his main force for which there had not been room in the first embarkation.[32]

The reinforcements that Howe saw marching to the redoubt from Bunker's Hill were the New Hampshire troops under John Stark and James Reed. When they received their orders to march from Cambridge, there were no cartridges on hand. To each man were issued two flints, a gill of powder, and about a pound of lead, cut from the organ pipes of a Cambridge church. They were directed to march to their quarters and make up fifteen cartridges each. Those that had bullet molds used them; the others pounded bits of lead into slugs to fit their muskets. Few of them had cartridge boxes; the rest carried loose powder in their horns and the bullets in bags. They then started on a four-mile march to Charlestown. Stark's regiment, consisting of thirteen companies, was the largest in the army. Reed's was small.[33]

Meanwhile, the news of the landing of the British had thrown Cambridge into confusion. Bells were rung, drums were beaten, and officers ran hither and thither calling out their men to do they knew not what. Orders arrived from Putnam for the Connecticut troops to come on. Ward, with the stubbornness of his natural disposition, would not be convinced that this was the real attack; he still feared that it was a feint, and that his stores were in danger. Exactly what orders he gave is not known. It appears that some provisions, including barrels of beer, were to be sent to the peninsula; but the supply that reached the troops was tantalizingly scanty. It also appears that he reserved his own regiment, John Paterson's, Thomas Gardner's, and a part of Ebenezer Bridge's, and ordered the rest of the Massachusetts troops to Charlestown. But no one knew clearly what he was to do. Jonathan

Brewer's regiment, John Nixon's, Moses Little's, James Scammon's and Samuel Gerrish's, all Massachusetts troops, were under arms and marching about, with vague notions of what was expected of them. When Colonel Stark, leading his regiment and Reed's, approached the Neck, he found two regiments halted in the road, fearing to cross through the barrage thrown by the *Symmetry* and her attendant gunboats. Stark asked them, if they did not intend to cross, to let his men through, which they gladly did. He marched his men across the Neck at a very deliberate pace. Captain Henry Dearborn of the front company suggested "quickening the march of the regiment," that it might sooner be relieved of the cross fire. "With a look peculiar to himself," says Dearborn, "he fixed his eyes on me and observed with great composure—'Dearborn, one fresh man in action is worth ten fatigued men.' " At the top of Bunker's Hill, Stark halted to survey the scene.[34]

When Prescott saw the British forces landed at Moulton's Point and deployed as if for immediate action, against his left, he realized that the gap between the far end of the breastwork and the edge of the peninsula offered an avenue for flanking and even encircling his main position. He at once ordered Knowlton to move his Connecticut troops from the entrenchments and, with two guns, to oppose the enemy's right wing in its approach on that side.

Near the base of Bunker's Hill and about six hundred feet behind the line of the breastwork, there was a fence "half of stone and two rayles of wood." It was about two hundred yards long, running parallel with the breastwork to the river bank, and, if held, it would prevent Howe's flanking movement. Knowlton took post there. To strengthen this frail barrier, his men tore down a near-by rail fence, set it up in front of the other, with a little distance between, and stuffed this space with newly cut grass which lay all about. It seems to have been, as one of his men said, "a slight defence against musquet-ball," but it had a sufficient appearance of strength to deceive the enemy.[35]

From his place on Bunker's Hill, Stark saw that this fence was thinly held by Knowlton's men, fewer than two hundred on a two-hundred-yard length. He "harangued his regiment in a short but animated address," to which they responded with three cheers, and then led them at the double down the slope of Bunker's Hill to the fence to reinforce Knowlton. It was fortunate for the Americans that Stark came to that point, for he saw at once that, while the fence extended to the river bank, there was still a way around it. The edge of the hard ground was a bluff eight or nine feet high. Below it was a strip of beach, narrow at the near high tide then prevailing, but wide enough to permit a column to pass along it. With stones from adjacent walls, he built a breastwork across the beach clear to the water's edge. He lined this with a triple row of his best men, posting the rest and Reed's men along the fence with Knowlton.[36] One other minor element of the American defenses has been generally overlooked by historians of the battle. To cover the ground between the east end of the breastwork and the west end of the rail fence, three small flèches, V-shaped entrenchments, had been built.[37]

There were, then, four distinct elements in the fortifications: the redoubt, the breastwork, the rail fence, and the wall on the beach. When the battle began they were manned as follows: the redoubt and the breastwork by Prescott's and parts of Brewer's, Nixon's, Woodbridge's, Little's, and Ephraim Doolittle's Massachusetts regiments, the last named under Major Willard Moore; the fence by Knowlton's Connecticut troops, Reed's New Hampshire, and part of Stark's; the wall on the beach by Stark himself and part of his men.[38]

Two other unfortified positions were held by the Americans to guard Prescott's right flank on the side of the redoubt toward Charlestown. In a cartway along a fence, near the right of the redoubt a company of Little's regiment and a few other troops, including Nutting's company, which had been guarding the shore in the village, were posted. Three companies— Wheeler's of Doolittle's regiment, Crosby's of Reed's, and one from Woodbridge's—were stationed in the main street of Charlestown at the foot of Breed's Hill; these constituted the extreme American right.[39]

Before the battle began two notable volunteers appeared on the field and were greeted with cheers. One was Joseph Warren. As he had been appointed a major general, Putnam offered him command at the rail fence; he declined it. He asked only where he could be of most service as a volunteer. Putnam indicated the redoubt, where he would be under cover. Warren said he did not seek a place of safety. "Where will the attack be the hottest?" he asked. Putnam still pointed to the redoubt. "That is the enemy's object. If that can be maintained, the day is ours." At the redoubt Prescott offered to yield his command. Warren again declined, and fought in the battle as a simple soldier.[40]

The other newcomer was General Seth Pomeroy—old Seth Pomeroy, carrying his nearly seventy years as lightly as he bore the musket which he himself had made and had carried at the siege of Louisburg thirty years before. He had ridden to the Neck on a borrowed horse. As it was not his own, he would not submit it to the raking fire there, but dismounted, crossed on foot, and trudged all the way to the rail fence, where he took his place with the others amid an enthusiastic welcome.[41]

Soon after his first landing Howe had pushed forward two outposts: one of four companies of light infantry in front of his main body in a depression which sheltered it from the fire of the redoubt; the other, two battalions under Pigot, to a position farther west and just below the southern foot of Breed's Hill. This detachment became the nucleus of Pigot's wing in the attack.[42]

Pigot, in his position on the British left, was annoyed by the fire of the Americans from Charlestown on his left. Admiral Samuel Graves had come ashore to see what help the fleet could give. Pigot spoke to him about "the mischief his left wing sustained by the fire from Charlestown." Graves sent orders to burn the place. Under a shower of red-hot cannon balls and of carcasses (hollow iron balls pierced with holes and containing lighted combustibles) from the ships and the batteries on Copp's Hill, it was "instantly set on fire in many places." It had been practically deserted, except for the few American troops, who were soon driven out by this bombardment. No effort was made to extinguish the fires, and soon the entire town was in flames.[43]

The reserve ordered up by Howe landed between one and two o'clock west of Moulton's Hill below the western foot of Breed's, and near Pigot's outpost. Howe then disposed his troops for the attack. His own right wing was drawn up in three lines, the classic British battle order, the light infantry in front, the grenadiers in the second line, the 5th and 52nd Regiments in the third. Pigot had three companies of light infantry, three of grenadiers, the 38th, 43rd, and 57th Regiments, and the 1st Battalion of marines. The two divisions were about equal in number, thirty-seven companies in Pigot's, thirty-eight in Howe's; but Howe's was stronger, because he had the greater number of flank companies, picked men.[44]

Howe is said to have addressed his troops in the usual eighteenth century manner. He was happy to have the honor of commanding so fine a body of men, who, he was sure, would "behave like Englishmen, and as becometh good soldiers." He would not desire one of them "to go a step further than where I go myself at your head"—a promise he kept, for, in the good old fashion, he fought in the front ranks.[45]

Before advancing his infantry, he sent his artillery forward and opened fire on the redoubt, the breastwork, and the rail fence. Three ships, three floating batteries, and the battery on Copp's Hill, from six different directions, centered their fire on the works. Howe's fieldpieces were, however, soon silenced, not by the feeble fire from the American artillery posted in the gap between the breastwork and the rail fence, but by the discovery that their side boxes contained twelve-pound balls, instead of six-pound. Howe sent off for the proper balls, ordering the substitution of grape in the meanwhile; but the distance was too great for grape to be effective. There was a further difficulty when the guns, supported by the grenadiers of the 35th, were pushed forward to support the attack. They got into boggy ground and could not be moved. Altogether, Howe's fieldpieces were of little avail at that time, except to scare the Americans, who had an exaggerated idea of the deadliness of artillery.[46]

From the formation of Howe's line, it would have seemed that he intended to advance in the conventional three-line formation directly upon the American works, with no other plan than to make a dogged frontal attack. This, indeed, has been the story of the battle in most of the histories and pictures of the combat; but such was not the case. Howe was too able a strategist to employ such a wasteful method if a flanking movement were possible, as was to be proven more than once in this war. He still had in mind his original plan flanking and encircling the American left. Although the defenses had been so greatly extended since that plan was formed, it still seemed possible to carry it out by smashing the extreme left while appearing to lead his men to a direct attack on the works, and this he proceeded to attempt.[47]

He drew off his front line of light infantry to the right and formed them, eleven companies, in column on the beach. This left his battle line in two ranks, grenadiers in front. With these his advance began. In heavy marching order, carrying knapsacks, blankets, and all their accouterments—with their ammunition, food, and firelocks, an estimated weight of a hundred pounds for each man—the main body of redcoats marched down from Moulton's Hill, across the lowland, and up the lower slopes of Breed's toward the breastwork and rail fence. At the same time Pigot's division breasted Breed's Hill against the redoubt, which he intended to envelop.[48]

The day was hot. The unmown grass, through which they had to march, was thick and long, reaching to their knees. There were walls and fences, which they had to throw down or climb over. The brick kiln and its adjacent ponds in the hard ground between two swamps broke their ranks, which had to be re-formed. They stopped from time to time to let the artillery come up and resume its fire. Altogether, the march against the American works was as painful as it was slow. As seen from Boston, across the Charles, it was, however, a brilliant and awe-inspiring spectacle. The people thronged the river shore; they crowded the hills; they perched on rooftops and gazed at "one of the greatest scenes of war that can be conceived," as General Burgoyne wrote to a friend in England.[49]

There were those two scarlet-clad lines of men pushing forward slowly, so slowly that the suspense was heavy to bear, their gun barrels and bayonets flashing back the rays of the sun. There were the guns, the fieldpieces, the great guns on the ships and on Copp's Hill, flashing with flame, emitting clouds of white smoke in a continuous rolling of thunder. In the foreground was Charlestown, scores of houses in one great blaze, its tall church steeples flaming high in the air, ships upon the stocks burning, the crash of buildings, whole streets of buildings, falling together. From it vast, billowing clouds of smoke arose, drifted toward the central scene, now obscuring this or that element, now lifting and disclosing it again. And, in the midst of it all, that little redoubt anxiously yet grimly silent, as it awaited the shock of battle. It was, said John Burgoyne, "a picture and a complication of horror and importance beyond anything that ever came to my lot to be witness to." [50]

The plan for the attack seems to have consisted of three parts. Pigot's division was to march against the redoubt and the breastwork, not to attack them, but to engage the attention of their defenders and hold them in check. The light infantry were to storm the little position on the beach, break through, and come onto the field behind the rail fence. Then Howe's grenadiers and regulars would fall on the rail fence, which would be under the fire of the light infantry in their rear. Thus the whole American left would be shattered, and the redoubt and breastwork isolated and surrounded.

As soon, therefore, as the whole line started its slow advance, "frequently halting to give time for the artillery to fire," [51] the 11 light infantry companies formed in column of fours on the narrow beach, those from the 23rd Regiment, the famous Royal Welch Fusiliers, in the lead, followed by those from the 4th, the King's Own Regiment. They were ordered not to fire, but to take their objective with the bayonet. The beach was level and unobstructed by grass, walls, or fences. Their advance could therefore be more rapid than that of the main forces, and, as theirs was to be the first attack, they doubtless made good time.

The familiar story has it that the Americans were told not to fire until they could see the whites of the enemies' eyes, nor until the order was given, and then to aim low. Stark's men from behind their roughly piled stone wall on the beach could see the scarlet-clad column advancing steadily and swiftly upon them, coming nearer and nearer until it was almost close enough to deploy and charge. It was only 150 feet away when the order came. A blast of fire struck the Fusiliers and tore the leading ranks apart.

The column halted, recoiled, but came on again, the King's Own pushing through the broken Fusiliers. Again the Yankee muskets spoke, again men fell in heaps. The officers shouted at the men, urged them forward. Though they did re-form and try once more, it was like pushing a wax candle against a red-hot plate—the head of the column simply melted away. Ninety-six lay dead on the beach; they "lay as thick as sheep in a fold." The rest turned and ran. That part of Howe's plan had failed.[52]

But with his grenadiers and his regulars Howe had to go on. His pretty plan was wrecked. There would be no turning movement of his enemy's extreme left, no confusion and dismay behind the rail fence caused by fire on its flank and rear. He had to make a direct, frontal attack on the fence, whether he would or no. He did go on. His men marched steadily forward. They were checked and obstructed by fences and walls at the point where their bayonet charge should have begun, and there the fire from the fence broke upon them in a withering blast that shattered their lines. Every man in Howe's personal staff was either killed or wounded.

The grenadiers in front stopped, began to fire instead of charging; but they aimed too high, most of their bullets passing over the heads of the Americans, while the renewed fire from the fence still fell heavily upon them. The second line came up and "mixt with them" in disorder, and at last the whole force fell back in confusion, out of range. Meanwhile Pigot had made his attempt against the redoubt, hardly more than a feint, and had also fallen back. So ended the first attack.[53]

In the American lines there was joy and exultation. These farmers had met the famous British regulars and beaten them. At but little cost, they had strewn the ground with their enemy's dead. But Prescott knew that the battle was not yet won. The British would not give over their attack after one repulse. He mingled with his men, praising their valor, reminding them that there was yet work to be done, and encouraging them to stand to it. There were pitifully few in the redoubt now, no more than one hundred and fifty. Putnam, who had been at the fence, rode back over Bunker's Hill, where there were hundreds of men, calling on them to reinforce Prescott. He rode down to the Neck. Ward had sent men from Cambridge; but they had halted, fearing to penetrate the feeble barrage still being laid down upon that isthmus. Putnam rode through it, called on them to follow him, and rode back again, entreating them to come on. A few did, but only a few. Nor did he get many more from Bunker's Hill.[54]

Howe soon re-formed his shattered ranks. Within a quarter of an hour the second attack began, but not on the same plan. The American left, the rail fence, had proved to be too strong. His light infantry, rallied from their defeat on the beach, had rejoined his force. They were now to march against the fence to engage American attention, while Howe and Pigot threw their whole force against the redoubt and the breastwork. The artillery left behind, columns were formed and marched forward until they were within a hundred yards, where they deployed in line of battle and opened fire. The American lines were silent, until the enemy were within a hundred feet. Then came from them a blast of fire, more devastating than before. It was not merely a single volley. The Americans loaded and fired again and again, not only from the redoubt, breastwork, and fence, but also from the three little flèches, "from whence the Grenadiers received a very heavy fire," and from some buildings on Pigot's left.

Though mown down like grass under the scythe, the British struggled to advance. A bayonet charge was intended, but, against that fire, it was sheerly impossible. "An incessant stream of fire poured from the rebel lines; it seemed a continued sheet of fire for nearly thirty minutes. Our Light-infantry were served up in Companies against the grass fence, without being able to penetrate—indeed, how could we penetrate? Most of our Grenadiers and Light-infantry, the moment of presenting themselves, lost three-fourths, and many nine-tenths, of their men. Some had only eight or nine men a company left; some only three, four and five. On the left Pigot was staggered and actually retreated. Observe, our men were not driven back; they actually retreated by orders." [55] Whether they retreated by order or by the instinct of self-preservation, they did retreat, down the slope of the hill, far out of range of the American muskets, and there was a long cessation in the fighting, so long that the Americans began to think they saw a victory.[56]

Putnam had been incessant and indefatigable in his efforts to reinforce the lines from the crowd on Bunker's Hill, but with little success. Captain John Chester, who with his company had been called by Putnam from Cambridge to the scene of action about noon, describes what he found on his arrival. He had marched at the same time as three regiments. When he got to the hill "there was not a company with us in any kind of order. They were scattered, some behind rocks and hay-cocks, and thirty men, perhaps, behind an apple-tree." British bullets, flying high over the American lines, had landed among the men on the hill, and the guns on the ships had been pouring their fire on it. Some of the men there were wounded. Their solicitous comrades carried them to safety, "frequently twenty men round a wounded man, retreating, when not more than three or four could touch him with advantage. Others were retreating, seemingly without any excuse, and some said they had left the fort with leave of their officers, because they had been all night and day on fatigue, without sleep, victuals, or drink." [57]

Putnam found one of these reinforcing regiments scattered about on the safe side of Bunker's Hill. Its colonel, Samuel Gerrish, who was "unwieldy from excessive corpulence . . . prostrate on the ground," declaring that he was "completely exhausted . . . Putnam ordered them on to the lines; he entreated them, threatened them, and some of the most cowardly he knocked down with his sword, but all in vain." The adjutant, Christian Febiger, who was to distinguish himself by more than one act of valor, did rally a detachment and led it to the lines.[58] Gerrish was afterward cashiered. Two other Connecticut companies, under James Clark and William Coit, arrived in time to have some part in the battle. Colonel James Scammons marched his regiment to Lechmere Point. He was ordered to "march to the hill." He marched to Cobble Hill, about a mile from Bunker's. After a while, he went on to Bunker's, "where the shot flew very thick." "Before we got to the top of the hill, Colonel Scammons ordered a retreat," and retreat they did. Scammons was later tried by court-martial; but, on his plea that he had misunderstood his orders, was acquitted.[59]

Four hundred fresh men, the 63rd Regiment and the 2nd Battalion of marines, sent for after the first attack, had now joined Howe, and he began his preparations for another assault, in spite, it is said, of the remonstrances of some of his officers, who urged that it would be downright butchery of his men to send them again into that deadly fire. He ordered all knapsacks and other superfluous equipment laid aside. The troops were to advance in columns, without firing a shot, and take the works with the bayonet. The artillery was to be pushed forward into the gap between the east end of the breastwork and the west end of the rail fence, so as to enfilade the breastwork and drive out its defenders. Preparations were made accordingly.

Clinton, watching the scene from Copp's Hill, was not restrained by lack of orders from Gage. He crossed and, when he landed, "collected all the guards and such wounded men as could follow, which to their honour were many, and advanced in column with as much parade as possible to impress the enemy," a heroic picture. He joined Pigot's division in the attack.[60]

Within the American lines there had been little loss of men, but there was a depressing scarcity of powder; not much was left in the powder horns. The few remaining cannon cartridges were broken open, and their contents distributed. The defenses were manned with as much resolution as before, but with little hope.[61]

The British guns were brought up. Their columns were on the march again. There was to be only a slight demonstration against the rail fence, while Howe threw his division upon the breastwork, and Pigot and Clinton concentrated on the redoubt. The artillery secured its desired position and opened a raking fire on the breastwork's defenders. They were swept away, either off the field or into the redoubt. The infantry plunged forward with their bayonets advanced, and once more met a deadly fire. The Americans "rose up," wrote young Lord Rawdon, "and poured in so heavy a fire upon us that the oldest officers say they never saw a sharper action. They kept up this fire until we were within ten yards of them, nay, they even knocked down my captain . . . after we had got into the ditch of the entrenchment. . . . There are few instances of regular troops defending a redoubt till the enemy were in the very ditch of it." [62]

On Pigot's extreme left, which had curved around to the west side of the redoubt, the marines had a hard time. They were checked by that desperate fusillade, fell into confusion, and began to shoot instead of charging. Major Pitcairn, their commander, was killed, along with many others. The 47th came up and formed beside them. Under the urgent commands of their adjutant, they ceased firing, "rushed on, leaped the ditch and climbed the parapet, under a most sore and deadly fire." [63]

But that was the end. Those last volleys faded out into a sputtering finish, "like an old candle," for there was no more powder. Nor were there bayonets to meet bayonets. The British swarmed over the parapet, leaped down into the redoubt. Its defenders met them with clubbed muskets and stones. The bayonet work of the British, said Adjutant Waller of the marines, was shocking. Yet there were only thirty of the Americans killed in the redoubt. Prescott ordered a retreat. Some of his men clambered over the parapet and got away. The rest crowded toward the gateway in the rear wall, where there might have been a ghastly massacre; but the dust hung so thick in the air that the British could hardly tell friend from foe, and did not fire into the mass at the gateway. Prescott had to fight his way to it, his sword against a British bayonet.[64]

When the beaten men emerged from their fort, they found themselves between the two bodies of their enemy, which had come around opposite sides of the work. Each was afraid to fire for fear of hitting the other. But when the retreating men were clear of those two forces they were heavily fired upon. Joseph Warren, one of the last to leave the redoubt, was shot through the head; and many others fell.[65]

The defenders of the rail fence had suffered little in this last attack, which on their part of the works was but a feint. They withdrew with some degree of regularity, taking their only fieldpiece with them. Old Seth Pomeroy, grasping his veteran musket, its stock shattered by a bullet, walked away backward, still facing the foe. Chester's company, lately arrived with some others, hurried down from Bunker's Hill, posted themselves behind a stone wall, and, "by a brisk fire from our small-arms," covered the retreat as best they could.[66]

But there were others who might have helped and did not. The men behind the rail fence, Knowlton's and Stark's, might have attacked the British right wing in its rear, while it was busy with the redoubt. Unfortunately, there was no concert of effort between them and Prescott; the two wings of the Americans fought as if they had been engaged in different battles. There were many hundred, perhaps a thousand, fresh men with Putnam on Bunker's Hill no more than six hundred yards away—enough, with Stark's and Knowlton's men, to turn the tide of battle if they had come up and attacked the disorganized enemy; but they themselves were a mere mass of men without organization or unified command and they did not even fire a shot to cover the retreat. Prescott, going off the field, came upon Putnam, and asked him why he had given the fighting men no support. "I could not *drive* the dogs," Putnam answered. To which Prescott is said to have replied, "If you could not *drive* them up, you might have *led* them up." [67] The Americans had two things yet to learn, how to organize a real army, and how to stand up and fight in the open.

But the retreat was not a rout. The American rear guard kept up "a running fight from one fence or wall to another, till we entirely drove them off the peninsula." So Rawdon wrote. And Burgoyne testified that "the retreat was no flight; it was even covered with bravery and military skill." Yet it was in the retreat that the Americans suffered the heaviest losses. While the greater part of them were passing over the slopes and the top of Bunker's Hill and across the Neck, they were under continuous fire from the ships and batteries as well as from the muskets of their pursuers. More men were struck down then than in the battle itself.[68]

The defeated men withdrew to Winter Hill and Prospect Hill on the road to Cambridge, and immediately began to fortify. They worked all night under the indefatigable Putnam, and by morning had built an entrenchment on Prospect Hill a hundred feet square. Putnam's son came to him the next morning and found him "dashing about among the workmen. . . . He wore the same clothes he had on when I left him on the 16th, and said he had neither put them off, nor washed himself since, and we might well believe him." [69]

The "almost exhausted" British did not cross the Neck. With the aid of fresh troops from Boston, they threw up a line of breastworks on the northern side of Bunker's Hill, content to hold the ground they had so hardly won. This line was afterward elaborated until it became a strong fortress, well ditched, palisaded, fraised, and protected by outlying entrenchments, making such a strong post that no attack upon it was ever seriously proposed by the Americans.[70]

The losses of the British in this battle were exceedingly heavy. Out of about 2,400 engaged, including the late arrived 400, who had taken part in only the last attack, 1,054, including 92 officers, had been shot; 226 of them were killed. Howe had twelve officers in his staff on the field; every one of them was shot down. Among the light infantry and the grenadiers, who bore the brunt of the battle, the losses were staggering. Every man but four of the grenadiers of the 4th, the King's Own Regiment, was killed or wounded. Of the grenadiers of the 23rd, the Royal Welch Fusiliers, only three remained unhurt. Lord Percy wrote to his father: "My Reg*, being one of the first that entered the redoubt, is almost entirely cut to pieces: there are but 9 men left in my co, & not above 5 in one of the others." [71]

The losses of the Americans have never been accurately ascertained. Besides the original 1,200, there may have been 2,000 more on the peninsula, but it is doubtful that more than 1,500 were actually engaged in the battle at any one time. Of these, perhaps 140 were killed, 271 wounded, and 30 captured, though the figures from various sources vary somewhat. The greatest loss was in Joseph Warren's death. His devotion to the cause, his energy, ability, and personal charm were not equaled by any of the other New England leaders at that time.[72]

To the courage, energy, and unbending will of Colonel Prescott it was undoubtedly due that the redoubt and the breastwork were held after the first assault. He inspired his men in the redoubt with his own tenacity and, by force of personal example and unalterable purpose, held them to their task. Their persistence made it possible for the defenders of the rail fence to hold out.

The stories of the part played by the American artillery are as confused (even on the number of guns in action) as its service was ineffective. There were three companies led by Major Scarborough Gridley and Captains Samuel Trevett and John Callender, having two guns each. Two of them were in disgrace after the battle. Gridley led his men a short way on the road from Cambridge, halted on Cobble Hill, and opened a futile fire against the *Glasgow*. Being urged to go forward, he took his guns to the redoubt and fired a few ineffectual shots at the British batteries on Copp's Hill. Burgoyne reported that two of these cannon balls "went one hundred yards over our heads." Gridley "swang his Hat round three Times to the

Enemy and then ceased to fire." He moved to the space between the breast-work and the rail fence, where he was joined by Callender. They seem to have been with Knowlton at the fence for a time, where "Gridley's guns were soon disabled and he drew them to the rear." Callender said his cartridges were too large for his pieces, and withdrew them to Bunker's Hill. Putnam ordered him back; he went, but "soon left his post and was soon deserted by his men." Captain Ford of Bridge's regiment took the guns back to the rail fence. Trevett, against the orders of his superior, Gridley, who was then firing on the *Glasgow*, took his two guns to Bunker's Hill, where one of them was disabled. He took the other to the fence. After the battle, his one gun was the only one carried safely off. Callender and Gridley were tried by court-martial, and both were dismissed from the service. Callender, however, remained with the army as a volunteer in the ranks and at the Battle of Long Island fought "with such signal bravery" that Washington erased his sentence from the orderly book and restored his commission.[73]

The effect of this battle on the minds of the British leaders appears in a letter from Gage to Dartmouth. It was shown that the Americans were "not the despicable rabble too many have supposed them to be." He recognized in them "a military spirit . . . joined with uncommon zeal and enthusiasm. . . . The conquest of this country is not easy." [74] It has often been held by American historians, probably without good cause, that the memory of his enormous loss in this battle intimidated Howe and deterred him from future frontal attacks on fortified positions, particularly on the day after the Battle of Long Island.

By the American people in general, the battle was at first regarded as a defeat, which, of course, it technically was. The whole enterprise was denounced as rash in its conception and discreditable in its execution. "No one, for years, came forward to claim the honor of having directed it; no notice was taken of its returning anniversary." [75] With the passage of time, emphasis began to be laid on the fact that the defenders of the redoubt gave in only when their ammunition was exhausted; their bravery and their effectiveness as long as their powder held out was recognized. At last, it was held to be a virtual victory, and was so celebrated. Its final effect was, in the minds of Americans, to exalt the American raw recruit to a degree of efficiency equal to that of trained and disciplined regular soldiers—a most unfortunate result.

From a military point of view, this conflict was unnecessary, inadvisable, and without justification. There was no good reason for the Americans attempting to hold the Charlestown peninsula against the British. It could give them no advantage in the siege of Boston, unless they were able to mount there such big guns as would dominate the water route to the town and prevent ships from reaching it. They had no such guns. Again, to hold it they would have had to divide their forces, with no means of communication between them and no means of supplying the force on the peninsula except by the Neck, which would always be under fire from the ships. Success in the Americans' effort was impossible by the very nature of the situation.

As for the British attack, enough has already been said in describing their divided counsels to show that the dreadful wastage of their men was probably unnecessary. Seizure of the Neck was feasible, and the consequent surrender of the garrison would have been inevitable.

CHAPTER 9

Washington Takes Command

The Continental Congress sitting in Philadelphia did not formally, by recorded vote, accept responsibility for the army besieging Boston, or, in the phrase commonly current at the time, "adopt it," until July 25, 1775; but it had ordered powder to be bought for it as early as June 3, and practically committed itself to some degree of responsibility early in that month by other resolutions touching on "the Continental Army." The Congress had even gone so far, on the 15th, as to appoint a general "to command all the continental forces, raised or to be raised, for the defense of American liberty," George Washington.[1]

The selection of a Virginian to command an army composed exclusively of Yankees may seem strange, yet there were cogent reasons for it. The most obvious was the fact of his experience in warfare. That experience did not include large and important commands; nevertheless, his reputation as a military man was more widespread throughout the colonies than that of any other colonial. He was a rich man, an aristocrat, and therefore influential among men of his own class, too few of whom were in sympathy with the American cause. He was a southerner, and the support of the southern colonies was needed in a contest hitherto waged by New England alone. He was a moderate man, still hoping for reconciliation with England; putting him at the head of the army would be notice to other moderate men that the radicals were not to have full sway. He was a sound man in his judgments and his decisions, as everyone who came in contact with him quickly realized. He had taken little part in the debates, and so had not aroused ill feeling in the minds of any of his colleagues. Tall, of commanding appearance, reserved in manner, yet plainly capable of energetic action, he looked like a leader. He was the only one of the delegates in the Congress who wore military garb, the blue and buff uniform of a Virginia militia colonel.

Perhaps as accurate a description of Washington's appearance as may be had is that given in 1760 by Captain George Mercer, his aide-de-camp in the Braddock campaign:

He may be described as being as straight as an Indian, measuring six feet two inches in his stockings and weighing 175 pounds. . . . His frame is well padded with well-developed muscles, indicating his great strength. His bones and joints are large, as are his feet and hands.

He is wide-shouldered, but has not a deep or round chest; is neat waisted, but is broad across the hips, and has rather long legs and arms. His head is well shaped though not large, but is gracefully poised on a superb neck. A large and straight rather than prominent nose; blue-gray penetrating eyes, which are widely separated and overhung by a heavy brow. His face is long rather than broad, with high round cheek bones, and terminates in a good firm chin. He has a clear though rather a colorless pale skin, which burns with the sun. A pleasing, benevolent, though a commanding countenance, dark brown hair, which he wears in a cue.

His mouth is large and generally firmly closed, but which from time to time discloses some defective teeth. His features are regular and placid, with all the muscles of his face under perfect control, though flexible and expressive of deep feeling when moved by emotions. In conversation he looks you full in the face, is deliberate, deferential and engaging. His voice is agreeable rather than strong. His demeanor at all times composed and dignified. His movements and gestures are graceful, his walk majestic, and he is a splendid horseman.

Captain Mercer neglected to mention that his "colorless pale skin" was pitted with the scars of smallpox, as were the skins of so many of his contemporaries.

John Adams and Samuel Adams were astute enough to recognize the reasons in favor of selecting Washington to be the commanding general. John made the motion. He noted that "Mr. Washington, who happened to sit near the door, as soon as he heard me allude to him, from his usual modesty, darted into the library room." Hancock, who wanted the job, or at least the refusal of it, showed "a sudden and striking change of countenance. Mortification and resentment were expressed as forcibly as his face could exhibit them." The motion was unanimously approved, and thus, as John Adams wrote to his wife, "the modest and virtuous, the amiable, generous and brave George Washington Esquire" was made "General of the American Army." [2]

Washington's acceptance of the appointment was admirably modest and sincere. He was distressed by a consciousness that his abilities and military experience might not be equal to the task, but he yielded to the desires of the Congress and promised to exert every power he possessed in the cause. He declined payment for his services, asking only for reimbursement of his expenses.[3]

Artemas Ward, Charles Lee, Philip Schuyler, and Israel Putnam were chosen by the Congress as major generals, ranking in that order. Eight brigadier generals were elected: Seth Pomeroy, Richard Montgomery, David Wooster, William Heath, Joseph Spencer, John Thomas, John Sullivan, and Nathanael Greene. Horatio Gates was appointed adjutant, with the rank of brigadier general. Pomeroy, presumably because of his age, did not accept the offered commission. Washington appointed Thomas Mifflin his first aide-de-camp, and Joseph Reed his secretary.[4]

The commander in chief received his orders on June 20. They were in general terms suitable to the occasion, but contained one parenthetical clause which had a far-reaching and seldom salutary effect. He was authorized in all unforeseen contingencies, "or any occasions that may happen, to use your best circumspection and (advising with your council of war) to order and dispose of the said Army as may be most advantageous." [5] It soon became evident and for a long time remained evident that he took that to mean that he must not merely listen to the advice of his generals, but have their express authority before acting in any particular case. The result was that the activities of the army were sometimes dictated and directed by a majority vote of the subordinate generals rather than by the judgment of the commander in chief. This interpretation of his instructions was a consequence of his faithful adherence to the idea that he was merely an instrument of the Congress and not an independent executive. His native modesty and his distrust of his own abilities as a soldier also conduced to this subordination of himself.

Washington left Philadelphia on June 23 in a cavalcade which included Philip Schuyler, Charles Lee, and Thomas Mifflin. They were escorted with much ceremony by a number of the congressional delegates in carriages, accompanied by mounted servants, "a large troop of light horse in their uniforms; many officers of militia besides, in theirs; music playing, etc. etc.," as John Adams wrote to his wife.[6] Little John, plump as a partridge, unquestionably an indoor man, a desk man, envied the gallant soldiers, as all little men envy tall men, all civilians envy the man in uniform, all riders of ambling pads envy the man on a tall horse. "Such is the pride and pomp of war," Adams moralized. "I, poor creature, worn out with scribbling for my bread and my liberty, low in spirits and weak in health, must leave others to wear the laurels which I have sown." No doubt there recurred to his mind what he had lately written: "Oh, that I were a soldier! I will be. I am reading military books." But he never was.

New York, divided in counsel about the conflict, hesitating to take its stand definitely in one camp or the other, was embarrassed when it had to receive the rebel generals on the same day that it must welcome back from a visit to England its royal governor, William Tryon. Fortunately, they landed there several hours apart, so that "the volunteer companies raised for the express purpose of rebellion," as the loyalist judge, Thomas Jones, put it, "the members of the Provincial Congress . . . the parsons of the dissenting meetinghouses, with all the leaders and partisans of faction and rebellion," could meet the generals at four in the afternoon, and conduct them to Leonard Lispenard's house, "amidst repeated shouts and huzzas," and, at nine o'clock, "the members of his Majesty's Council, the Judges of the Supreme Court, the Attorney General . . . the Clergymen of the Church of England," and so on, all the dignified, respectable, and highly placed officials, "with a numerous train of his Majesty's loyal and well affected subjects," could meet the Governor and conduct him, "with universal shouts of applause," to the residence of Hugh Wallace, Esq. "But strange to relate . . . those very people who attended the rebel Generals in the morning . . . now, one and all, joined in the Governor's train and with the loudest acclamations . . . welcomed him back to the colony. . . . What a farce! What cursed hypocrisy!" exclaims the loyal judge.[7]

In New York, Washington detached Major General Philip Schuyler, who was to take command of all the troops in New York colony, and to occupy the posts on Lake George and Lake Champlain. Incidentally, he was to "keep a watchful eye upon Governour Tryon" and, if he attempted "directly or indirectly, any measures inimical to the common cause, [to] use every means in your power to frustrate his designs . . . if forcible measures are judged necessary." While the Continental Congress was not in session, Washington would order such measures; if it were sitting, Schuyler must get his orders from it, because "the seizing of a Governour [was] quite a new thing, and of exceeding great importance."[8]

The rest of the party went on to Cambridge, delayed somewhat on the way "by necessary attentions to the successive Civilities which accompanied me in my whole route," as Washington wrote to the Congress,[9] yet reaching their destination on July 2, only ten days from Philadelphia. He immediately assumed command of the army. Tradition has it that this was done while he stood under a tree on Cambridge Common, known thereafter as the Washington Elm, the troops being paraded before him. But there seems to be no historical basis for the legend. The army was spread over ten miles of de-

fenses, and all trustworthy indications point to his having immediately inspected them piecemeal, without any central ceremony.[10]

At Watertown, on his way, Washington had been received by the
Massachusetts Provincial Congress. Its address of welcome apologized for
the character of the army he was to command: "The greatest part of them
have not before seen service; and although naturally brave and of good
understanding, yet, for want of experience in military life have but little
knowledge of divers things most essential to the preservation of health, and
even life. The youth of America are not possessed of the absolute necessity
of cleanliness in their dress and lodging, continual exercise and strict temperance to preserve them from diseases frequently prevailing in camps," [11]
all of which Washington soon learned was true enough. "I found," he says,
"a mixed multitude of People here, under very little discipline, order, or
Government. . . . Confusion and Disorder reigned in every Department."
But he did not despair. Within three weeks of his arrival he was able to say,
"We mend every day and I flatter myself that in a little Time, we shall work
up these raw Materials into good Stuff." [12]

The army lay sprawling about Boston in a great crescent of installations.
The Reverend William Emerson, who had been so active in the Concord
fight, wrote at this time:

'Tis also very diverting to walk among yᵉ camps. They are as different in their
form as yᵉ owners are in their dress; and every tent is a portraiture of yᵉ temper
and taste of yᵉ persons that incamp in it. Some are made of boards, some of sail-
cloth, and some partly of one and partly of yᵉ other. Others are made of stone
and turf, and others again of Birch and other brush. Some are thrown up in a
hurry and look as if they could not help it—mere necessity—others are curiously wrought with doors and windows done with wreaths and withes in yᵉ
manner of a basket. Some are your proper tents and marquees and look like yᵉ
regular camp of yᵉ enemy. These are yᵉ Rhode-islanders, who are furnished with
tent equipage from among ourselves and every thing in yᵉ most exact English
taste. However, I think that yᵉ great variety of yᵉ American camp is upon yᵉ
whole rather a beauty than a blemish to yᵉ army.[13]

One particular phase of the reformation of the army, the enforcement of
proper distinction between officer and private, was fundamental in Washington's idea of an army. The "leveling spirit," the opinion that every man
was just as good as any other man and a little better, was rife in New England, and was utterly subversive of discipline in the army. The officers could
not maintain proper dignity and superiority to their men, could not give an
order and exact obedience. Instead, they must truckle to them, conduct themselves with humility, and persuade their men to do their duty. This spirit
of equality and lack of dignity was prevalent among the officers themselves.

Joseph Reed saw one of them "shaving one of his men on the parade." [14] Another officer, a colonel and the army's chief engineer, was seen carrying a large piece of beef, his rations, to his tent. He cheerfully explained that he did it "to set the officers a good example." [15]

In an army without uniforms, there was no apparent distinction between officer and private. The first step toward curing the evils of the leveling spirit would naturally be the introduction of distinctive dress. It was not possible to supply uniforms, but it was possible to distinguish the different grades by simpler methods. In one of the earliest of Washington's general orders provision was made to effect this purpose. The Commander in Chief was to wear "a light blue Ribband . . . across his breast, between his Coat and Waistcoat." Washington entered, in his expense account, an item of three shillings and fourpence, the cost of this decoration. Major generals were to wear purple; brigadiers, pink; aides-de-camp, green. The field officers were to have red or pink cockades in their hats; the captains, yellow or buff; the subalterns, green. The sergeants were to wear a shoulder knot of red cloth on the right shoulder; the corporals, a green knot.[16] These arrangements, coupled with the close attention given even to details, soon produced the desired effect. An observer noted "a great overturning in the camp as to order and regularity. New lords, new laws. The Generals Washington and Lee are upon yᵉ lines every day. . . . The strictest government is taking place, and great distinction is made between officers and soldiers. Everyone is made to know his place and keep in it." [17]

Washington felt the need of uniformity of dress among all his men. "I know of nothing," he wrote, "in a speculative view more trivial, yet which . . . would have a happier tendency to unite the men, and abolish those provincial distinctions, that lead to jealousy and dissatisfaction." He proposed to the Congress the procurement of 10,000 hunting-shirts. These were long, loose shirts, of tow cloth, either of its natural color or tanned to "the shade of a dry or fading leaf," belted at the waist and having double shoulder capes. They were worn outside the breeches like a frock. Being in common use among the American backwoodsmen, they came to be regarded, especially by the British, as the distinctive garb of the riflemen. But, though the Congress approved, and Washington canvassed several of the colonies for the necessary material, he had to give up the project, because of the scarcity of tow cloth. Except in the case of a few militia companies, such as Benedict Arnold's and Joseph Chester's, which wore blue coats faced with red, the army continued to display its motley dress.[18]

One of the first things that Washington did was to call on the adjutant of each regiment for an exact return of its men, equipment, and supplies. These, which should have been completed in half a day, owing to "the imperfect obedience which had been paid to . . . [orders] of a like nature from General Ward," were not forthcoming until after a week had elapsed. They showed a total of 16,770 men on the rolls, of which number 1,598 were on the sick list, 1,429 were absent for one reason or another, leaving 13,743 present and fit for duty.[19]

There was a prompt reorganization of the army into six brigades of six regiments each, and three divisions of two brigades each. Ward was given command of one division to constitute the right wing of the army, posted at Roxbury. Lee commanded another at Prospect Hill, the left wing; Putnam the third, in and about Cambridge, the center.[20] The need for improvement in the fortifications was apparent, and the men were put to work all along the lines. "Thousands are at work every day from four to eleven o'clock in the morning. It is surprising how much work has been done," wrote William Emerson as early as July 17.[21]

The problem of feeding thousands of men, in such a hastily assembled and completely unorganized mass as had swarmed around Boston after the day of Lexington and Concord, had been solved in a haphazard fashion during the two months before Washington took command. The first summons to arms had been sudden and unexpected. The men who hurried from their farms and homes, having no expectation of entering into a protracted service, had brought along pocketfuls of food, those from a distance relying on the inns and taverns to supply them on their march. Each Massachusetts town was, by custom, responsible for supplying its own militia in active service until the province could take over the job. Massachusetts had made provision for the collection of food, and considerable stores had been collected, which were sufficient to feed its men. Each of the other colonies had to care for its own.

Connecticut, having a patriot governor, Jonathan Trumbull, was prompt. An embargo was laid on the export of food. Joseph Trumbull was appointed commissary to collect provisions and supply them to the Connecticut forces; he did the work efficiently. Rhode Island was handicapped at first by its Loyalist governor, Joseph Wanton. But he was soon displaced, and a member of the Committee of Safety was made Chief Commissary with good results. The New Hampshire towns carried the burden for a while, each for its own men, until the province relieved them in May. Being, however, the poorest of them all in the production of foodstuffs, it was obliged to buy from the others, especially from more fertile Connecticut. On the whole, these hastily contrived measures were effective in furnishing the men a sufficient, indeed a comfortable, sustenance.[22]

When the army was adopted by the Congress, Washington was ordered "to victual at the continental expense all such volunteers as have joined or shall join the united army." [23] He appointed Joseph Trumbull commissary general. The daily ration comprised fresh beef or pork or salt fish, bread, peas, beans, or other vegetables, and milk, with a weekly addition of rice or Indian meal. Spruce beer was to be a daily drink, with molasses as a substitute. Candles and soap were also to be provided.[24]

In spite of many difficulties, particularly in the procurement of sufficient wheat flour and in recurring shortages of funds, Trumbull succeeded in his arduous tack of feeding the army during its stay before Boston. In June, 1776, Washington wrote to the Congress, "Few Armies, if any, have been better and more plentifully supplied than the Troops under Mr. Trumbull's care." [25]

In July and August there were brought into the army the first soldiers drawn from outside New England, and remarkable men they were. The Congress on June 14 had voted "That six companies of expert rifflemen, be immediately raised in Pennsylvania, two in Maryland and two in Virginia," each to consist of sixty-eight privates and the usual officers. Recruiting was promptly effected. In Pennsylvania there were so many candidates that three additional companies were authorized, and the whole nine were organized as a battalion, with William Thompson as colonel and Edward Hand second in command. Virginia turned out its share, Daniel Morgan raising his company, ninety-six men, within ten days. Maryland's first company was commanded by Michael Cresap, a veteran Indian fighter; its second, by Thomas Price.[26]

These men were drawn chiefly from the wilder, western parts of their respective colonies—Scotch-Irish many of them. They were backwoodsmen, "remarkably stout and hardy men; many of them exceeding six feet in height." Their garb was simple: round wool hats, hunting shirts, breeches, stockings, and shoes or leather leggings and moccasins, Indian style. "On the breast [of their shirts] in capital letters, is their motto 'Liberty or Death.' " They had to march from four hundred to seven hundred miles to reach the camp, bivouacking in their blankets at night. Morgan mounted his men and rode with them six hundred miles in twenty-one days. So fit were they, and so inured to exposure and physical exertion, that not a man was lost by sickness on the way. All these added 1,430 men to the army.[27]

They also added a new weapon, before that practically unknown in New England. Rifling the barrel of a gun, that is to say cutting spiral grooves inside the barrel so as to make the bullet rotate in its flight and thus increase its accuracy, was not an American invention. It was practiced in Central

Europe as early as 1500. But the so-called Kentucky rifle was evolved in the American colonies and differed greatly from the European rifled guns, which were short, heavy, clumsy, perhaps an inch in bore, and terrific in recoil. The necessities of American frontier life demanded economy in powder and lead, and therefore a small-calibered weapon of great accuracy. By immigrant expert gunsmiths, chiefly German or Swiss settled in Pennsylvania, such a gun was produced.

The rifle was slender and graceful in appearance and as much as five feet long, sometimes more, the greater length of the barrel being supposed to increase its precision. It carried a ball weighing only a half-ounce. Its range and its accuracy in the hands of an expert were extraordinary. While a musket ball dropped harmlessly to the ground at 125 yards and had little certainty of hitting a target less than man-size at half that distance, expert riflemen put ball after ball into a mark seven inches in diameter at 250 yards. Exhibitions of marksmanship and trick shooting by these men amazed and delighted the Yankees around Boston.[28]

The rifle had, however, its disadvantages. The loading was slower than with the musket. In order that the ball might have close contact with the grooves in the barrel, getting its twist and at the same time the full propulsive effect of the powder, a small disk of greased linen or buckskin was placed on the muzzle, the ball laid upon it and the whole rammed home. This took twice the time necessary to load a musket, and, besides, with its small bore and the grooves in the barrel, the rifle soon fouled and had to be swabbed out. Then, too, the lighter bullet had less stopping power against a charge. For sharpshooting and bush fighting it was a superior weapon; but in such a battle as that on Breed's Hill the musket was more useful.

These backswoodsmen proved to be difficult to deal with in the camp. They were accustomed to acting entirely on their own, and their stubborn individualism was slow to yield to army discipline and routine. The inactivity of the siege chafed them. For a while they found satisfaction in sniping sentries or other exposed men in the British lines, where their reputation for deadly accuracy was great and universal. "They are grown so terrible to the regulars," wrote Joseph Reed, "that nothing is to be seen over the breastwork but a hat." But such practices were regarded by Washington as merely a waste of the scanty supply of powder, and had to be stopped. Washington's orders irked the freeborn riflemen, and, although they were at first pampered by exemption from entrenching and general camp duties, they became unruly and troublesome.[29]

If a rifleman was confined in the guardhouse for some disdemeanor, his comrades broke open his prison and released him. On one occasion such a culprit was removed to the main guardhouse in Cambridge for safer keeping, whereupon some of Captain James Ross's Pennsylvania company, armed with loaded rifles, swore by God they would release him or lose their lives, and "set off as hard as they could run." Washington strengthened the guard to the number of five hundred men, and ordered several regiments under arms. He, with Lee and Greene, pursued the mutineers and overtook them. When he ordered them to ground their arms, they, "beginning to be frighted at their proceedings," obeyed. They were then surrounded by another Pennsylvania company and marched back to camp, where they were tried, convicted of mutiny, and fined 20 shillings each.[30]

On the whole, the riflemen were of little use in the siege. "Gen. Washington said he wished they had never come; Gen. Lee has damned them and wished them all in Boston." General Thomas wrote that the generality of them were "as Indifferent men as ever I served with, their Privates mutinous and often Deserting to the Enemy, unwilling for Duty of any kind, exceedingly vitious and I think the army here would be as well without them as with them." The whole trouble was that they were, by nature and by experience, totally unfitted for inactive life in camp. Many of them served excellently in the expedition against Quebec, and later in the war when they were in active service.[31]

Washington thought he had not enough men in his army; but, from the first, he knew he had not enough ammunition, either powder or lead. On August 4 he had but 9,940 pounds of powder, "not more than 9 Cartridges a Man." He repeatedly called on the Congress for more, on all the New England colonies, and on New York. By the 24th, with help from Philadelphia, he had built up his store to 184 barrels, equal to twenty-five rounds, and in September he got 7,000 pounds from Rhode Island. But he never had enough to allow his men to have more than twelve or fifteen rounds at a time while the British kept their soldiers always supplied with sixty cartridges apiece.[32]

To supplement their weapons during the shortage of ammunition, and particularly to make up for the lack of bayonets, several thousand iron-pointed pikes with twelve-foot shafts were procured. As missile weapons, Benjamin Franklin suggested the use of bows and arrows, supporting his recommendation with excellent philosophic reasons, which, however, did not sufficiently commend themselves to the military mind; none was employed.[33]

The shortage of ammunition alone would have prevented any major hostile movement by the Americans; but there were also other dissuasive reasons. The British losses on Breed's Hill had been more than made up by the arrival in June and July of reinforcements, so that their number of effectives was over 6,000, with 1,400 sick or wounded in hospitals.[34] Their defenses at Boston Neck had been built up and greatly strengthened, and on Bunker's Hill they had built an elaborate fortress, with a thick parapet, well ditched, fraised, and abatised, of which Washington said "Twenty thousand men could not have carried it against one thousand had that work been well defended." A large part of their army was in barracks in that fort or encamped about it. Except for the dragoons and a few of the infantry, the rest was in the defenses on Boston Neck.[35] An attempt to storm either of these two main positions, especially with an undisciplined amateur army, would have been suicidal.

On the other hand, the Bunker's Hill battle had convinced the British command of the folly of a major attempt against the fortified positions of the Americans, which stretched from Roxbury on the southeast around to Winter Hill and Prospect Hill on the northwest, and which were constantly being strengthened. The British generals knew that even a successful attack would bring no worth-while results. The two forces were therefore in an equilibrium which neither cared to disturb, and a long cessation of major hostile operations on both sides followed Bunker's Hill. There were, however, minor clashes.

In the early morning of July 8 a party of volunteers under Major Benjamin Tupper and Captain John Crane, with two fieldpieces, attacked a British advance post on Boston Neck, drove off the guard, and burnt its house. A similar attack on another post was made three days later and brought forth a harmless cannonade from the works on the Neck. Other little flurries of the same sort helped to enliven the month of July, in one of which the restless riflemen were given a chance against a post on Charlestown Neck. They crept, in true Indian style, on their hands and knees around the post, but, just as they were about to surround it, a relief for the guard arrived. There was an exchange of fire, five of the guard were killed, and two captured. There were no casualties among the Americans, except the loss of one man taken prisoner. The British retaliated by cannonading the American works on Sewall's Point, at the same time attacking and burning a tavern near Roxbury, held as an American outpost, and driving in an American advance guard of sixty men near Boston Neck. The guard was reinforced, and there was a little fight in which several of the British fell, but no Americans. Each of these affairs was noisy, and greatly alarmed the civilians in Boston, who thought a general battle was on.[36]

On the 21st an American party under Major Joseph Vose set off in whaleboats for Nantasket Point. There they drove back a British guard and destroyed the lighthouse on Great Brewster Island, a mile or so offshore. Ten days later, while the British were rebuilding it, Major Benjamin Tupper landed with three hundred Americans and killed or captured all the work party, demolishing their work. Boats from the warships were driven off after a hot little fight. In all, the British lost fifty-three men; the Americans, one killed and two or three wounded.[37]

For nearly a month after that there was little activity on either side. Then came a more important affair. Ploughed Hill was a low eminence on the road connecting Charlestown Neck with Medford, to the west of Winter Hill and Prospect Hill, the two strong points on the American left. It was of value because it was close to and commanded the Mystic River, and because it was within point-blank shot of Bunker's Hill. Washington decided to seize and fortify it.

In the night of August 26 General John Sullivan led out a fatigue party of 1,200 and a guard of 2,400, including 400 of the Pennsylvania riflemen. Work went on all night, and by daylight there was "an Intrenchment in such forwardness as to bid defiance to their Cannon." [38] Bunker's Hill, a ship, and two floating batteries bombarded it all that day. Sullivan had one nine-pounder in place, which he used so skillfully that he sank one floating battery, injured the other, and put a sloop out of commission. The next morning, a column was seen to be forming on Bunker's Hill. It seemed that a battle was imminent. A general alarm was sounded along the American lines, and 5,000 men were marched to the new post. But the enemy did not advance. For several days they continued to fire on the works. Four Americans were killed, two of them by their own folly in attempting to catch cannon balls bouncing along on the ground.[39]

Two other minor incidents occurred before the year ended. A party of 300 British light infantry raided Lechmere Point on November 9 and carried off a dozen head of cattle, despite the efforts of Thompson's Pennsylvania riflemen and parts of two other regiments to stop them. Both sides claimed a victory: the British because they got the beeves; the Americans because the raiding party left hurriedly under fire. Two weeks later a detachment under Putnam, working at night, fortified Cobble Hill, a mound south of the works on Prospect Hill, without physical objection.[40]

These little affairs accomplished nothing toward a final decision in the contest between the two armies. It was desirable for the Americans that a decisive action should be brought on under favorable conditions; but Gage showed no disposition to enter into a general engagement, nor was the condition of the American army such as to promise it a victory. There was still a deficiency in ammunition, and the army was still too uncertain a force to rely upon in an all-out attack on strongly entrenched regulars. Yet it seemed that something must be done; the existing stalemate could not last much longer.

Inactivity was demoralizing the besieging force; desertions, always a major problem among the Americans throughout the war, were much too frequent now to be ignored. The army was further weakened in September by the detachment of 1,000 men, including Morgan's riflemen, to go on the expedition against Quebec under command of Benedict Arnold. There was also to be considered the approaching dissolution of the whole army by expiration of its terms of enlistment; the Connecticut troops were engaged only to December 10, the rest to January 1. There was, also, in the army and among the people generally a growing feeling of dissatisfaction with a merely defensive policy. It was vocal "in Congress, in the newspapers and above all in the taverns." [41] "Murmurs began to be audible that the army was inactive; and that a superiority of numbers might justify an attempt against the town." [42]

Washington was harassed by the conflict among these various considerations. He could not answer the critics of his defensive policy by disclosing the condition of his powder magazines, which was known to few, and thus expose his weakness to his enemies. In this state of mind, he took refuge in the admonition of the Congress to advise with his officers. On September 8 he addressed a circular letter to the general officers, proposing the question "whether in your judgment, we cannot make a successful attack upon the Troops in Boston, by means of Boats, cooperated by an attempt upon their Lines at Roxbury." He pointed out that the coming winter would require better quarters for the men, supplies of clothing, fuel, and blankets, which could not be had. The daily wasting of the stock of powder, the coming dissolution of the army, and, "to sum up the whole . . . the expence of supporting the army will so far exceed any Idea that was form'd in Congress of it, that I do not know what will be the consequence." Yet "to avoid these evils we are not to loose sight of the difficulties, the hazard, and the loss that may accompany the attempt, nor what will be the consequences of a failure." [43]

It can hardly be said that these reasons for an attack were either cogent or compelling, nor that they indicated a conviction in the mind of the commander in chief that the suggested action should be taken. The council of war evidently did not think so; they voted, on September 11, "unanimously that it was not expedient to make the attempt at present, at least."

This result was communicated to the Congress.[44] That august body entertained the idea that it was perfectly competent to direct the operations of
the army in the field. On October 3 it voted that "General Washington may,
if he thinks proper, for the encouragement of an attack on Boston, promise,
in case of success, a month's pay to the army and to the representatives of
such of our brave countrymen as may chance to fall, and in case success
should not attend the attempt, a month's pay to the representatives of the
deceased." [45]—a half-hearted nudge to action, backed by the inducement
of a niggling, cheese-paring promise of reward. Another council met and
again disapproved the attempt.[46]

Washington had written a very long letter to the Congress on September
21, describing the condition of the army, indicating its needs for the coming winter and especially calling attention to its approching dissolution.[47]
The Congress appointed a committee, consisting of Benjamin Franklin,
Thomas Lynch, Sr., and Benjamin Harrison, to confer with the commander
in chief and with representatives of the New England colonies "touching
the most effectual method of continuing, supporting, and regulating a
continental army." [48] They were in conference in the camp for five days.
Their report resulted in congressional resolutions calling for an army of
"30,732 men, officers included," divided into twenty-six regiments (exclusive of riflemen and artillery) of 728 men each, of all ranks. It fixed their
pay and rations and the color of their uniforms, brown with distinctive
facings for the different colonies.[49]

Although this narrative concerns itself with the fortunes and misfortunes
of the American land forces only, and will not attempt to tell the story of
the naval operations, some notice must be taken of the exploits of American
seamen at this time, and the beginnings of the navy of the United States,
because these early maritime exploits were but an extension of the emerging
military power of the colonies.

They began in an effort to protect the coasts and ports of the colonies
against attacks by British vessels carried on chiefly for the purpose of foraging and seizing supplies. Rhode Island was the first of the colonies to take
steps, by chartering, in June, two armed vessels to oppose the British
frigate *Rose,* which had been annoying its coast. Massachusetts was next,
taking over a schooner and a sloop which the town of Machias in the district
of Maine had armed to protect itself against attack. Connecticut followed
by arming two similar vessels against a threatened British raid on Gardiner's
and Fisher's Islands. So far the Congress had not assumed any responsibility
for the protection of the coasts against naval aggression. On July 18 it

resolved that each colony, at its own expense, should provide for the protection of its harbors and coastal towns.[50]

All such preparations contemplated merely defensive measures; but offensive operations might greatly profit the American cause. The British army, cooped up in Boston, had to draw all its supplies from sources outside that town: fresh meats and vegetables, for instance, from the West Indies or the more southern American posts; and its other provisions, its munitions of war, clothing, and every such necessary from England. Confident of no interruption of this traffic, because there was no American naval force, the British had armed their coasting vessels lightly, with no more than small arms, while the transocean merchantmen carried no armament at all and sailed without naval convoy. It seemed to be possible, as Governor Nicholas Cooke of Rhode Island pointed out to the Massachusetts Provincial Congress on June 27, for a swift American vessel, even a small one, carrying a suitable armament, to intercept any of these ships and take her, cargo and all. Although the Massachusetts Congress took no action Washington saw the point, and after some hesitation decided to make the experiment with one vessel.[51]

His commission was in the military line only; no authority had been given him in naval matters. However, he found a way. He appointed the shipmaster Nicholson Broughton a captain in the army and ordered him to take command of a detachment of soldiers "and proceed on Board the Schooner *Hannah* . . . lately fitted out & equipp'd with Arms, Ammunition and Provisions at the Continental Expence." His orders were to cruise "against such Vessels as may be found on the High Seas or elsewhere . . . in the Service of the ministerial Army, and to take and seize all such Vessels, laden with Soldiers, Arms, Ammunition, or Provisions for or from Sd. Army." [52]

Broughton soon captured the *Unity*, a vessel laden with provisions and naval stores. Encouraged by this success, Washington sent out other ships, and the Congress took notice. Having information of the sailing from England of two unarmed brigs, "loaded with arms, powder and other stores," it authorized the General on October 5 to apply to Massachusetts for two armed vessels to go after the unprotected brigs and any other such transports. Also, it asked Connecticut and Rhode Island to send out their vessels, all to be "on the continental risque and pay." [53]

By the end of October six schooners were ready for sea, the *Lynch* commanded by Broughton, the *Franklin* by John Selman, the *Lee* by John Manley, the *Warren* by Daniel Adams, the *Washington* by Sion Martindale, and the *Harrison* by William Coit. This was the first continental fleet. It sailed under the pine-tree flag. The *Washington* was captured by the British warship *Fowey* in November, but the others had better luck; many prizes variously laden were brought in. Manley in the *Lee* was conspicuously successful. His capital prize was the ordnance brig *Nancy*, in the entrance to Boston harbor. Her cargo of 2,000 muskets, 100,000 flints, 30,000 round shot, and 30 tons of musket bullets was of immense value to the army. That was something to crow over. "Such universal joy ran through the whole camp as if each grasped victory in his hand." What chiefly excited them was a 13-inch brass mortar. "Old Put mounted on the large mortar . . . with a bottle of rum in his hand, standing parson to christen" it *Congress*. Manley made other captures: an armed ship loaded with provisions, another vessel full of military stores. "His praise was in every mouth." The little navy gave the army sorely needed supplies and equipment.[54]

During that winter "it was a miserable life inside Boston for troops who had sailed from England in the belief that they were to take part in a triumphant and leisurely progress through a series of rich and repentant provinces." [55] It was indeed, and for more reasons than one.

Everything that the British army ate, wore, or used in any way, except small supplies obtained from the West Indies and the other parts of America, had to be brought from England in slow-sailing ships, exposed to the perils of the sea and to the danger of capture by the small but active American fleet. In the cargoes of food there was a heavy loss by mildew and rot on the way. Of eighteen hundred barrels of flour in one cargo, more than eight hundred were spoiled; of six hundred in another ship, only five were edible.[56]

There was generally enough salt meat and dried peas to eat, and occasionally fish. Flour was always scarce; of potatoes, fresh vegetables, and fruits there were practically none. Most of the available milch cows had been slaughtered for beef, and milk was an extreme rarity. There were no longer any cattle or sheep on the islands in the harbor, and but a handful in any of the fields on the near-by coasts. The rejoicing over the dozen head that were taken by three hundred soldiers in the raid on Lechmere Point is an indication of the extreme need of fresh meat. Even when raids on Fisher's and Gardiner's Island in Connecticut yielded two thousand sheep and some oxen, most of them had to be devoted to their "poor sick and wounded people with whom their hospitals were crowded." [57] Scurvy, induced by the lack of vegetable food, appeared among the troops already infected with smallpox, which "raged in the streets and cantonments." [58]

Even fuel was lacking. When cold weather set in, this became serious.

The main force in the works on the Charlestown peninsula suffered severely from the cold, accentuated by the cutting winds and driving snows of an unusually severe winter. On December 12 all except a guard of six hundred were drawn in to winter quarters in Boston. Fire for warmth and for cooking was needed, but there was no store of fuel. Coal and wood were shipped from England, but many vessels with such cargoes were taken by the American cruisers. To meet this want, the unconsumed wooden buildings in Charlestown were torn down. The Old North Church, the steeple of the West Church, wharves, old ships, trees, and a hundred old houses were condemned to be broken up. The Liberty Tree, a great elm under whose shade many patriotic meetings had been held, yielded fourteen cords of wood. Still there was not enough. The soldiers demolished houses and fences indiscriminately. So frequent were such offenses that the provost was ordered to go his rounds, "attended by an executioner," and "to hang up on the spot the first man he should detect" in such depredations.[59]

To the officers, accustomed to various amusements, their stay in Boston was excessively dull and boring. There were no diversions of any sort beyond those they themselves could contrive; they did their best. To make a riding school, the pulpit and pews of the Old South Church were ripped out, and the floor was covered with tanbark. The gallery became a refreshment room, and the church library was fed into the stoves. Faneuil Hall was turned into a playhouse. An original burlesque, "The Blockade of Boston," was presented, in which Mr. Washington, an uncouth figure wearing a huge wig and a long, rusty sword, was attended by a rustic orderly armed with an absurdly long musket. Mr. Washington with an army of rustics was actually and efficiently blockading Boston at the time, so that the jest had a strong tincture of bitter irony.[60]

For the enlisted men there were no such amusements; nor was there any military activity to engage their interest and keep their spirits up except digging for new fortifications, which was not very enlivening. Idleness and boredom bred indiscipline and slovenliness, and the British regulars lost their characteristic smart appearance. Unpowdered hair, dirty linen, unbuttoned gaiters, unpolished arms were surface indications of the deterioration of the rank and file. They were even so degraded "as to borrow from the enemy that habit which was the least worthy of imitation, and chewed tobacco." [61]

And it was all so useless and so hopeless. Gage and his thousands of troops had been in possession of Boston for a year and a half, yet all he had accomplished was to ruin the business of the town and capture one hill with the loss of nearly half of his best troops, while the rest of the province and the rest of America remained in the hands of his enemies. All he could hope to do from Boston was to take more hills, without any more valuable results. There were plenty of hills: Cobble Hill and Ploughed Hill and Winter and Prospect, any one or all of which the Americans would have been glad to sell him at the price of Breed's. The occupation of Boston was entirely barren of advantage at the time, and gave no promise whatever of advantage in the future.

Gage's three colleagues, the major generals, had realized this and had "presumed . . . to offer their advice" to their chief to remove to New York. Clinton elaborated on the advantages of that town and the disadvantages of their present situation. Let victory here be "ever so compleat, it leads to nothing." [62] Burgoyne wrote home about it shortly after Bunker's Hill: "Look, my Lord, upon the country near Boston—it is all fortification. Driven from one hill, you will see the enemy continually retrenched upon the next; and every step we move must be the slow step of a siege." [63] Gage himself had long been of the same opinion. On October 1 he wrote to Dartmouth that "no offensive operations can be carried on to advantage from Boston." Even if he did drive the rebels from their entrenchments, "no advantage would be gained but reputation." It would be "more advisable to make Hudson's River the seat of war," taking New York and leaving only a defensive garrison in Boston.[64]

On August 2 Dartmouth wrote to Gage, communicating the King's order that he return to England "in order to give His Majesty exact information of everything necessary to prepare . . . for the operations of the next year," a polite way of recalling an officer in whom the British government had lost faith. Simultaneously, Howe was given command of the army in the Thirteen Colonies.[65] A month later, Dartmouth wrote to Howe that it seemed "not only advisable, but necessary, to abandon Boston before the winter, to dismantle Castle William and . . . to remove with the Troops either to New York or some other place to the Southward," affording means to "the well-disposed" Bostonians of "getting safely away with their families and effects." [66] Howe assumed the command on October 10.

Howe received Dartmouth's letter on November 9. So, by that time, all the commanding officers in Boston and the authorities at home were in agreement as to the uselessness of holding on to Boston, and orders had been issued and received directing the move to New York. But there were not enough ships. To carry away the army with its equipment and stores and the fugitives with their effects, Howe calculated, 35,172 tons of shipping would be necessary; and he had, of every sort of craft, only 23,570 tons. The army had to stay where it was until spring.[67]

To cheer up the besieged troops, great quantities of supplies were dispatched from England: 5,000 oxen, 14,000 sheep, vast numbers of hogs, 10,000 butts of strong beer, 180,000 bushels of coal, quantities of faggots, oats, beans, and hay for the horses, dried vegetables, "cured by a new process," and near half a million pounds "in Spanish and Portuguese coinage." But the transports sailed too late in the fall. Contrary winds held them back. The preserved vegetables rotted. More than half of the animals died, "and the tides carried their carcasses in thousands up and down the Channel." Nearing America, the supply ships met adverse winds. Some were driven to the West Indies. Others went ashore on the American coasts and were boarded and plundered. Not a few were picked up by the American cruisers. It was a sorry remnant that reached Boston; but what did arrive, supplemented by supplies from the more southern colonies, Nova Scotia, and the West Indies, much improved the condition of the British army.[68]

In the American camp, in November, all was going well on the surface. The 17,000 men were well fed, well housed; "the army in great order and very healthy." [69] True, there was a shortage of blankets and of fuel, but on the whole the appearance of things was promising. That it was deceitfully promising was soon to be made evident.

Underlying difficulties that were to threaten the very existence of the whole army arose out of the impending termination of its period of enlistment. By December 31 the engagement of every man in the camp would expire; the whole army would fade away. Unless the province of Massachusetts and the whole of New England were to be given over to the enemy, a new army had to be enlisted and organized before the new year.

A plan for the organization of the new army had been laid down by the Congress, as described in detail later in this book. In certain respects it differed from the system in vogue in the New England colonies. For instance, in some of them the generals were colonels as well, the colonels also captains. This was not permitted by the congressional plan; and the proposed new order, in this respect, bred dissatisfaction.[70]

The old army was composed of thirty-eight regiments varying in size, those of Massachusetts, New Hampshire, and Rhode Island numbering 590 enlisted men each, while some of Connecticut numbered 1,000, others 600. The plan of the Congress called for only twenty-eight regiments of 728 men each, including officers. To rebuild the army according to the new plan, not only would ten regiments be eliminated, with a corresponding reduction of their officers in number or in rank, but the companies in them must be either increased or diminished in size. All sorts of jealousies and objections were generated by this proposal. The custom in New England was to pay the soldiers by the lunar month, four weeks. The pay was now to be by the calendar month, thus cutting out one month's pay in a year. This was naturally displeasing to the men.[71]

Also, Washington had to contend with the ingrained localism of the New Englanders. A national spirit had not yet developed; these men were citizens of their own respective colonies, of their own respective counties and townships, not of the United Colonies as a whole. Washington wrote to Joseph Reed: "Connecticut wants no Massachusetts man in her corps; Massachusetts thinks there is no necessity for a Rhode-Islander to be introduced into hers; and New Hampshire says, it is very hard, that her valuable and experienced officers . . . should be discarded, because her own regiments, under the new establishment, cannot provide for them." John Adams upheld this contention of the colonies: "Can it be supposed that the private men will be easy to be commanded by strangers, to the exclusion of gentlemen whom they know, being their neighbors? It is, moreover, a reflection, and would be a disgrace upon that Province [Massachusetts] to send abroad [to another colony] for commanders of their own men. It would suppose that it had not men fit for officers." It was absurd, of course, but nothing could change this spirit; Washington strove against it, but had to yield to it.[72]

New Englanders had been accustomed to receiving bounties from their own provinces on enlistment. The Congress had been asked to provide for such payments, and had refused to do so. There was discontent on that account. Another thing that displeased the troops was the increase in pay of the company officers; the captains were to receive $26⅔ a month instead of $20 as before, the lieutenants $18 instead of $13⅓, and the ensigns $13⅓ instead of 10, while the privates' pay remained at $6⅔. That emphasized the distinction between officer and man, violated the new England principle of equality, and "chilled the spirits of the commonalty." [73]

Then, too, as the winter drew on, there was increasing hardship. The men's clothing, fit for summer, was now too thin and worn to keep them warm. Blankets were lacking; fuel was worse than scarce. Nathanael Greene, on the last day of the year, wrote: "We have suffered prodigiously for want of wood. Many regiments have been obliged to eat their provision raw, for want of fuel to cook it; and notwithstanding we have burnt up all the fences; and cut down all the trees for a mile round the camp, our sufferings have been inconceivable." [74] Washington told the Massachusetts Assembly that "different Regiments were upon the Point of cutting each others throats for a few Standing Locusts . . . to dress their food with." Ten thousand cords of wood were needed, he said.[75]

Underneath all these causes of discontent was plain and simple homesickness. The men were not professional soldiers, detached from civilian life. They were farmers for the most part. They had homes and families from which they had now been separated for many months. They were tired of the dreary routine of camp life, the endless round of uninteresting duties as well as the hardships. They had agreed to serve for a certain period. They had a very clear notion of the meaning of the terms of a contract. They would meet those terms, but would not go beyond them. " 'Tis the cast of the New Englanders to enlist for a certain time and, when the time is expired, to quit the service and return home, let the call for their continuance be ever so urgent." As John Adams remarked, on another aspect of the situation: "We cannot suddenly alter the temper, principles, opinions or prejudices of men." [76]

In spite of all these difficulties and discontents, it was Washington's task to disband his old army and create a new one, as far as possible out of those experienced though reluctant men, and at the same time to hold the British army where it was. "It is not in the pages of History perhaps to furnish a case like ours," he wrote to the Congress on January 4, 1776. "To maintain a post within musket shot of the Enemy for six months together, without powder, and at the same time to disband one Army and recruit another within that distance of twenty odd British regiments is more than probably ever was attempted." [77]

He could look for little assistance from his major generals. Schuyler was at Albany, in command of the troops in northern New York. Artemas Ward was ineffectual. Putnam was hopeless in matters of administration, and the eccentric Charles Lee, English by birth, could not handle such a situation. The job had to be done by Washington alone.

On November 12 the enlistment papers for an army to serve until December 31, 1776, were issued. The first week after that would test the willingness of the men to renew their engagements. It did. Out of 6,000 to 7,000 men who made up the eleven old regiments, 966 enlisted. The general officers issued an address to the troops. The struggle was not hopeless, they said. Victory was assured. The southern colonies would help. New England must not fail. And, as to the more immediate, personal considerations, they urged that never had soldiers' "pay and provision . . . been so abundant and ample." [78]

Another week passed, and the returns showed that no more than 3,500 had agreed to stay. The Connecticut troops brought the trouble to a head. Their enlistment was to end on December 10, and, in the confusion of the records, many of them believed, as Washington at one time also did, that it ended on December 1. Their officers had fancied they could be persuaded to stay at the end of the month, and had so assured Washington. Now it appeared that most of them would refuse even so short an extension of their term of service; they were going home when their time was up. Such a defection in the face of the enemy might prove fatal. The vacancies caused by their departure must be filled, temporarily at any rate. Washington called on Massachusetts for 5,000 militia and on New Hampshire for 2,000 to fill the gap until January 15, and besought the Connecticut men to stay until these should arrive. But most of them decided to leave the camp on December 1, and many did go. Charles Lee undertook to stop their premature departure.[79]

They were paraded on December 1. The men that were disinclined to stay even for four days after their enlistments expired were formed in a hollow square, and Lee addressed them. "Men," said he, "I do not know what to call you. You are the worst of all creatures." Then he "flung and curst and swore at us and said if we would not stay he would order us to go to Bunker Hill [i.e., to attack the British stronghold] and if we would not go he would order the riflemen to fire at us." They agreed to stay the four days. They got a drink of rum, and were promised another on the morrow.[80]

But they would not remain any longer than that. Washington was disgusted with them. "Such a dirty, mercenary spirit pervades the whole, that I should not be at all surprised at any disaster that may happen," he wrote to Joseph Reed. Indeed, he was almost disheartened. "I have often thought," he wrote on January 14, "how much happier I should have been, if instead of accepting a command under such circumstances, I had taken my musket on my shoulder and entered the ranks, or, if I could have justified the measure to posterity and my own conscience, had retired to the back country, and lived in a wigwam." [81]

General Sullivan wrote to the New Hampshire Committee of Safety denouncing the Connecticut troops, who "to their Eternal Infamy Demand a Bounty to Induce them to Tarry only the three weeks. This is Such an Insult to Every American that we are Determined to Release them at the Expiration of their Term at all hazards." He asked New Hampshire for 2,000 militia to serve only until January 15, 1776.[82]

New Hampshire responded nobly, as did Massachusetts. On December 11 Washington could write: "The Militia are coming fast, I am much pleased with the Alacrity which the good People of this province, as well as those of New Hampshire, have shewn upon this occasion: I expect the whole will be in this day and to Morrow, when what remains of the Connecticut Gentry, who have not inlisted, will have liberty to go to their Firesides." They left amid the jeers and hoots of their more steadfast companions; "they were horribly hissed, groaned at and pelted." [83]

On December 31, when the terms of enlistment of the rest of the army expired, "the same desire of retiring into a chimney-corner seized the troops of New Hampshire, Rhode Island and Massachusetts . . . as had worked upon those of Connecticut." Though many of them offered to stay until the new enlistments had sufficiently made up the strength of the army, they left "by hundreds and by thousands." [84]

General Orders of January 1 began thus: "This day giving commencement to the new army, which, in every point of View, is Continental, The General flatters himself, that a laudable Spirit of emulation will now take place and pervade the whole of it." [85] Then was first "hoisted the union flag in compliment to the United Colonies." There are various accounts of this flag. One describes it as the ensign of Great Britain, but with thirteen stripes, alternately red and white, instead of the superimposed crosses of St. George and St. Andrew, in the canton where are now the stars.[86] Another says that "the combined crosses of England and Scotland, which cover the British flag, on the new ensign shrank to occupy but one corner, while the larger field was crossed by thirteen alternate stripes of red and white." [87]

So the army was now the Continental Army; but a strange army it was, a medley of those old soldiers who had reenlisted, of raw recruits, and of Massachusetts and New Hampshire short-term militia. With such an uncoordinated mass of men as his only force, Washington regarded the situation as "truly Alarming and of this General Howe is well apprized . . . no doubt when he is reinforced he will avail himself of the Information." [88]

There was not only a shortage and a confusion of men; there was also a lack of arms. Few of the new men had brought muskets. Washington had tried to retain the guns of those who departed, valuing and paying for them. But so many of them were in bad condition, and so many were carried off by stealth, that, by the middle of January, he had no more than a hundred muskets with which to arm incoming recruits.[89]

Enlistments continued to lag during January. In the first two weeks no more than a thousand new men were added to the rolls. Washington wrote that the "discontented officers," displaced by the reduction of the number of regiments, "have thrown such difficulties and stumbling blocks in the way of recruiting that I no longer entertain a hope of completing the army by voluntary enlistments, and I see no move or likelihood of one, to do it by other means. . . . Our total number upon paper amounts to about ten thousand five hundred." But many of those on the lists had not come to the camp in spite of orders to do so, and there was little hope of their early coming.[90] They did, however, finally arrive in almost the full number.

January, 1776, was a quiet month. Although Howe's army had been somewhat reinforced and more men were expected, he wrote Dartmouth, "I am under the necessity of repeating to your Lordship, that the apparent strength of this army for the Spring does not flatter me with Hopes of bringing the Rebels to a decisive action." [91] It was, in fact, well settled in his mind that he would evacuate Boston as soon as sufficient transport could be gathered. Meanwhile, he had but to hold on.

The Americans were also inactive. Obviously they were in no condition to attempt the capture of the town. Their energies were sufficiently engaged in re-forming and increasing their army. One little diversion occurred on the 8th, when Major Knowlton with two hundred men crossed at night on the mill-dam to Charlestown, killed one resisting guard, captured the rest, five men, and burned eight out of fourteen still standing houses, which the enemy were daily pulling down for fuel. The flames alarmed the British, and there was much cannonading, with no harmful result to anyone, except to the audience in the Faneuil Hall playhouse, who were then enjoying the burlesque of Washington previously mentioned. They dispersed, "everyone endeavouring to get out as fast as possible, amidst fainting and shrieking among the females." [92]

Continued successes of the American attacks on British shipping cheered the army. Colonel Lord Stirling, soon to rise to the rank of brigadier general, having heard of a transport in distress off Sandy Hook, seized a pilot boat at Amboy, embarked forty men, and, with the assistance of three smaller vessels, took the prize without opposition. She was laden with coal and provisions.[93] Of greater importance, indeed of very great importance to the American cause, was a service rendered by General Knox.

Henry Knox was destined to play so great a part in the war that some special notice of him at this point is desirable. He was born in 1750, the son of a shipmaster who, meeting with financial reverses, was obliged to retire to the West Indies. Henry therefore had to leave school and go to work in a bookshop. Being a studious lad, he took the opportunity the shop provided to continue his education by reading. He became familiar with the classics in English translations and especially with Plutarch's Lives, which turned his taste toward military studies.

At the age of twenty-one he set up his own "London Book-Store" in

Cornhill, Boston, stocked with a miscellaneous shipment from London. It became "a fashionable morning lounge" and prospered. His military studies continued, and he became a member of the Ancient and Honourable Artillery Company, which gave his interest in military science a special character and determined his role in the war.

He had gained some acquaintance with engineering and his services were employed at the outbreak of the war in planning the American fortifications around Boston. After Washington took command he recommended Knox's appointment as colonel of artillery, and he was so commissioned. His subsequent services are a part of the history of the war.

Knox was a young man of large proportions, tall, broad, and thick. In spite of the hardships of the military service during the war, at its end he had attained a weight of 280 pounds. His face was large, full-cheeked, and florid; his gray eyes, rather small but brilliant. His expression was frank and kindly; he was fond of society, gayety, and laughter. His voice was noted for strength, volume, and resonance. His ability as an artillerist has not been questioned, and his integrity as a man, in addition to his technical achievements as a soldier, lent strength to the Revolutionary cause.[94]

Short as the army was of small arms, the lack of artillery was even greater. No offensive operation against Boston could be undertaken without heavy cannon. There were plenty of them at Ticonderoga and Crown Point. Because of bad roads or no roads, and no means of transport, they had lain entirely useless for six months when Washington in mid-November decided to try for them. On the 16th he ordered Knox to go after them: "The want of them is so great that no Trouble or Expence must be spared to obtain them."[95]

Knox reached Ticonderoga on December 5. There he selected for removal eight brass and six iron mortars, thirty iron and thirteen brass guns, and a howitzer. Only one of the cannon was a 24-pounder, the rest ranging from 12 to 18 pounds. Three of the iron mortars were great 13-inchers, weighing a ton each. To these he added a quantity of lead and a barrel of flints. No available wheeled vehicle being strong enough to carry such prodigious weights, they had to be transported on sledges; and Knox constructed forty-three of these. Eighty yoke of oxen to haul them were secured. He drew them to Lake George, loaded them on gondolas, flat-bottomed scows, floated them down to the head of the lake. Snow had fallen but lightly, and a thaw held him up. At last he brought them on sledges to Albany, having crossed the Hudson four times.

At Albany, one of his largest guns broke through the ice at a ferry and sank. He fished it up and went on, down to Claverack and up over the Berkshires. There the snow lay thick, and the grades were heavy; his oxen and horses had hard work. At Framingham the heavier pieces were temporarily deposited; the smaller, he brought on to the camp, where he had the pleasure of presenting to his chief what he justly called "a noble train of artillery." It soon permitted Washington to make a move that hurried the British out of Boston.[96]

Dorchester and Falmouth

As time drew on, and inactivity continued to prevail in both camps, Washington became restive. He felt that throughout the colonies there was a growing demand that his army, now much larger than that of his opponent, should force matters to a conclusion. "To have the Eyes of the whole Continent fixed, with anxious expectation of hearing of some great event, and to be restrain'd in Every Military Operation for want of the necessary means of carrying it on is not very pleasing," he wrote.[1] The lack of necessary means included both small arms and powder. Among his nearly 9,000 men 2,000 were without muskets, and powder was as always dangerously scarce. On February 8 there were no more than nine musket cartridges per man in the camp, and fewer than one hundred fifty barrels of powder in the magazines.[2] Powder from abroad, however, began to come in at New York and Philadelphia, and the promise of a supply encouraged Washington to plan an attack.[3]

On February 16 he called a council of war. The harbor was frozen over, "affording a more expanded and consequently less dangerous Approach to the Town." About half of the 7,200 militia who had been called for had come in. With the 8,797 fit for duty already in camp and 1,405 absent "on command," who might be recalled, the army would number over 13,500. There were believed to be no more than 5,000 British in Boston, which was an error. Therefore, although not much help could be expected from heavy artillery because of shortage of powder, and the principal reliance must be on small arms, yet, he thought, "a stroke, well aimed, at this critical juncture" before the British received expected reinforcements "might put a final end to the war." [4]

But the council, very wisely, demurred. They thought the King's forces in the town were much more numerous than 5,000, as indeed they were: there were about twice that many. Even if not so many, the officers said, they were well furnished with artillery and were backed by their fleet; and an assault should be preceded by a heavy and continued bombardment, which could not be had. There was, however, a practical move to be made, the seizure and fortification of Dorchester Heights "with a view of drawing out the enemy" to an attack.[5] This verdict did not please Washington. "Behold!" he wrote to Reed, "though we had been waiting all the year for this favorite event, the enterprise was thought too dangerous!" But, magnanimously he admitted, "perhaps, the irksomeness of my situation led me to undertake more than could be warranted by prudence . . . it is now at an end, and I am preparing to take post on Dorchester, to try if the enemy will be so kind as to come out to us." [6]

The extreme right of the curving American lines was somewhat beyond Roxbury, near the village of Dorchester. Beyond that a peninsula, about a mile long and half a mile wide, stretched toward the southeast, its extreme end being three-quarters of a mile from the island on which was Castle William. Dorchester Heights were two small hills in the middle of the peninsula and within 250 yards of the water. In front of them, close to the water, was another little hill. From the northern shoulder of the peninsula a sharp spur of land pointed directly at the town, with a space of water not much more than a quarter-mile wide between it and the Neck. At its extremity was another elevation, Nook's Hill.[7] It will be seen that possession of the Heights would threaten the town, the shipping, and Castle William, while heavy guns on Nook's Hill could blast the defenses on Boston Neck with a plunging fire and devastate the greater part of the town.

The fortification of Lechmere Point, close to the water at the left of the American lines, which had been under way for some time, was now complete, and some of the heavy ordnance from Ticonderoga had been mounted there. Several mortars were emplaced at Roxbury, and active preparations for the attempt on the Heights were begun.

The plan was to duplicate the surprise at Breed's Hill by completing the proposed entrenchments in a single night. But the ground was now frozen hard to a depth of eighteen inches, so that quick pick-and-shovel work as at Breed's was not possible. It had taken more than two months to complete the Lechmere's Point works. Therefore, some different method had to be adopted at Dorchester. Colonel Rufus Putnam suggested building the breastwork on the ground, instead of digging it out of the ground. His plan was to use chandeliers, heavy timber frames in which gabions, fascines, and bales of hay could be fitted, thus creating quickly a breastwork which could afterward be strengthened with earth. It was to be faced with an abatis made out of neighboring orchard trees. In front of all, there were to be placed barrels full of earth—a novel form of offensive defense, for they were to add an appearance of strength to the works but, if the British assaulted, could be rolled down the hill to break their ranks and their bones as well.[8]

This novel plan was accepted. The camp was busy in the last days of February and the first of March making chandeliers, gabions, and fascines, and baling hay. It was also busy in other preparations. Washington planned, in case the British should embark for an attack on the Heights, to send 4,000 picked men in two divisions—one under Sullivan, the other under Greene—with General Israel Putnam in general command, across the Back Bay against the undefended west side of Boston, to attack the British works on the Neck in the rear and open a way into the town for other troops. For this purpose, two floating batteries and forty-five bateaux, each to hold eighty men, were secretly collected in the Charles River. All the militia of the neighboring towns were ordered to be in readiness to join the army before the day of the attempt.[9]

To divert the enemy's attention from the real purpose, a heavy bombardment from Lechmere Point, Cobble Hill, and Roxbury was begun on the night of March 2. With a prodigal disregard of the consumption of powder, the artillery "continued in throwing in Shot and Shells 'till daylight." [10] The British replied with a heavy fire. Little harm was done to either army, except by the bursting of three 10-inch and two 13-inch mortars of the Americans, one of which was that big brass 13-incher captured by Manley on the *Nancy* and christened "Congress" with such gusto by Old Put. The cannonade was resumed on the next night and the next after that. As soon as the firing began on the third night, March 4, General Thomas, with a fatigue party of 1,200 men, led by a covering party of 800 under arms and followed by 360 oxcarts loaded with entrenching materials, marched to Dorchester Heights. To conceal from the enemy the necessary passage back and forth during the night, a screen of hay bales was placed along Dorchester Neck.[11]

The covering party was divided, one half going to Nook's Hill, the other to the extreme point toward Castle William. On the two Dorchester hills the chandeliers were placed on the lines of two small redoubts already marked out, and the fascines and bales of hay put in place. Picks and shovels were soon at work on the frozen ground, first to fill the gabions and the barrels and then to strengthen the breastwork, while axmen felled the orchard trees and made the abatis. The carts went back again and again for more materials. At three o'clock in the morning the fatigue party was relieved by a fresh force. So the work went on all through the mild night, lighted by a bright moon, but concealed from the enemy by a haze that hung over the lowland in front. The noise of the big guns drowned the sound of pick and shovel. When the Americans got below the frost line and the digging became easier, the parapets were thickened with earth piled against them. More men, including five companies of riflemen, came over to man the works. By daylight, the two little forts were ready. "Perhaps," said General Heath, "never was so much work done in so short a space of time." [12]

In the British camp the activity did not go unnoticed. At ten o'clock the night before, Lieutenant Colonel Campbell had somehow discovered and reported to Brigadier General Francis Smith "that the Rebels were at work on Dorchester heights." But this was the same General Smith that had led the march against Lexington and Concord, that "very fat and heavy man" who was so slow in coming up to the fight at the Bridge. This time he did nothing at all. The first positive news the British army had of the works was the sight of them at daybreak. It was a complete and astounding surprise. Howe viewed them through his glass, and is said to have remarked, "The rebels have done more in one night, than my whole army could do in months." [13] In a dispatch to Dartmouth he wrote that it "must have been the employment of at least twelve thousand men." [14] Lieutenant General Archibald Robertson of the Royal Engineers wrote in his diary, "A most astonishing night's work [it] must have Employ'd from 15 to 20,000 men." [15] Another officer said the works were "raised with an expedition equal to that of the Genii belonging to Aladdin's Wonderful Lamp." [16]

Surprise speedily gave place to serious consideration of a new problem. Rear Admiral Molyneux Shuldham, commanding the fleet since the recall of Graves in December, told Howe that he could not keep his ships in the harbor under the guns on the Heights, and the army in Boston was in equal danger. Either the British must evacuate the town, or they must drive the Americans from their new stronghold. Although Howe fully intended to evacuate very soon, he could not stomach an expulsion by the colonists. He tried first a bombardment, but the guns could not be elevated enough to throw their shot to the hilltops. Then he decided to attack, and immediately made his preparations.[17]

Brigadier General Jones, with 2,200 men, was to make the attempt. Five regiments were ordered to embark at the Long Wharf and proceed to Castle William. From Castle William they were to land on the extreme point of Dorchester peninsula and attack the nearer redoubt, being sheltered by it from the guns in the other. Two more regiments, with the light infantry and grenadiers, were to embark in flatboats, land on the north side of the peninsula, and join in the assault on that side. In case of success at Dorchester, these troops and certain reinforcements were to attack the lines at Roxbury. The men were to carry their blankets, a day's supply of food, and canteens filled with rum and water. No musket was to be loaded. The bayonet was to be the only weapon.[18] It is said, perhaps untruly, that the men, drawn up before embarking, looked "in general, pale and dejected" and told each other, "It will be another Bunker's-hill affair or worse." [19] So thought the inhabitants of Boston. Again they crowded the hilltops and other high places to watch the show, while the American troops continued all day long to labor at strengthening their works, and Putnam's division, ready for the attack on the town, was paraded on Cambridge common.[20]

The British attack on the Heights was to be delivered that night; but a storm arose, "A Hurrycane or terrible sudden storm," as Timothy Newell wrote in his diary.[21] Heath described it: "About midnight the wind blew almost a hurricane from the south; many windows were forced in, sheds and fences blown down and some vessels drove on shore." [22] The surf was so high on Dorchester beach that no flatboat could land. There was no attack that night, nor on the next day, for the wind continued to blow, and there was a torrential downpour of rain.[23]

That storm has been credited with preventing the planned attack. Howe, in his general orders the next morning, March 5, wrote, "The General desires the Troops may know that the intended Expedition last night was unavoidably put off by the badness of the Weather." But that was not exactly the truth. In fact, the decision to withhold the attack and to evacuate the town had been made five hours before the storm arose. There was a council of war in which some of the officers "advised the going off altogether . . . the General said it was his own Sentiments from the first, but thought the honour of the Troops Concerned." It was "agreed immediately to Embark everything." Howe's statement in the general orders was merely a face-saving device.[24]

While preparations for the evacuation of the town were afoot, the inhabitants who were to remain there became fearful that it might be destroyed, either by bombardment from the American works or by the incendiary torch of the departing army. A delegation of citizens obtained from Howe a promise that he would not burn the town unless the Americans molested his troops during their embarkation. A paper stating this promise, signed by four of the selectmen of the town, was brought to the

American lines. As it was "an unauthenticated paper . . . not obligatory upon General Howe," Washington refused to take any official notice of it. He made no agreement with Howe, but the town was nevertheless tacitly spared by both sides.[25]

While the British in Boston were hurrying their preparations to leave, the Americans went on with their Dorchester works. A party was sent in the night of the 9th to fortify Nook's Hill, the place most dangerous to Boston. Discovering it, the British bombarded the hill, and the American batteries in all the posts from Cobble Hill around to Roxbury responded. The continued thunder of the cannonade terrified all the good folk within hearing distance but, as usual, although more than eight hundred shot were fired, this long-range cannonading had little effect on either side; only five Americans were killed. But Nook's Hill was abandoned by them.[26]

In August, 1775, Dartmouth had written to Gage that if he were driven out of Boston "care must be taken that the officers and friends of the government be not left exposed to the rage and insult of the rebels, who set no bounds to their barbarity." [27] The preparations for the evacuation therefore included their transshipment to whatever destination was chosen for the army. They were to be rescued from "rage and insult," but they were forced to pay a fearful price for that rescue.

The Tories in Boston, both those whose proper residence was in that town and those who had come seeking the protection of the British troops, included many of the personally or politically outstanding people of the province, the wealthiest people, the greater landholders, the more substantial men of business, the best educated, in short the aristocrats. These had looked down on the Adamses, Warren, Otis, and the other agitators for their resistance to the crown, accusing them of various base or petty personal motives. To John Hancock, the only one of the rebel leaders who had a claim to rank in wealth and fashion with themselves, they ascribed wounded vanity as the cause of his recalcitrancy. As a class these Tory leaders were hearty free livers, free spenders, fine dressers, arrogant in their regard for social distinction, scornful of the mob. "Caste-feeling, intense, aggressive and almost universal, beyond any doubt, prevailed in the Tory society of America." [28]

The Tories very generally ridiculed the provincial military leaders raised suddenly from obscurity in the lower walks of life—Knox from his bookshop, Greene from his blacksmithing, Putnam from his tavern and his plow, Pomeroy from his gunsmith shop—to become officers pretending to rank with the gentlemen of His Majesty's army. And now, suddenly, these superior people were to be driven from their offices, their countinghouses, their houses and lands, and their churches (eighteen of them were clergymen). They must abandon their homes, their own country. They who were as firmly wedded to their native land as any other Americans, who loved it as dearly as any of those upstart rebels, they whose patriotism was indeed as strong and as pure, according to their lights, as that of any of the so-called patriots, were now to be forced to flee to the foul, ill-smelling transports and to be carried God knew where, to an exile wherever it would be, with no certainty of ever returning. It is not strange that, in Washington's words, "No Electric Shock, no sudden Clap of thunder, in a word the last trump could not have struck them with greater consternation" [29] than did Howe's order to abandon the town.

The last days of the British army in Boston were days of confusion and distress, of haste and waste, of crooked dealing and actual plundering. The first move was to bring the transports to the wharves and load them with all the ordnance, arms, and stores that could be stowed in them. The lines were stripped of their brass cannon and mortars; iron pieces replaced them. But three great brass mortars broke their lifting tackle and sank in the water; a fourth, the British tried unsuccessfully to burst and had to leave behind. There was no room for the dragoon and artillery horses. There was "a vast deal of Confusion in every Department and no settled plan of operations." [30] Great quantities of stores had to be abandoned, much of them being as nearly destroyed as was possible in the hurry of departure. [31] The soldiers misbehaved, "acting Licentiously and breaking up some stores." It was suggested by one of the officers that "it would be prudent to seize All Cloth, linnen, Shoes, Stockings, etc. in the Different stores in Town ... which the Rebel Army were very much in need of." [32] Howe directed one Crean Brush, a New York Irish adventurer, to do this. He broke open stores and storehouses and looted their contents indiscriminately to the value of many thousands of pounds, giving worthless receipts. Dwelling houses were not exempt from this thievery. His loot made a full cargo for the brigantine *Elizabeth*. Brush's labors were in vain, however, for he and his vessel, with all the stolen goods, were soon after captured by the Americans. [33]

The poor Tories had pretty much to shift for themselves. They had received vessels, but had been told they must find the sailors to man them. [34] By a liberal use of money they managed to get such portable goods as they most valued aboard and to hire enough seamen to navigate their craft; but they embarked in sad condition. One of them, Benjamin Hallowell, former Commissioner of Customs, had to take into his cabin thirty-six others, "men, women and children; parents, masters and mistresses, obliged to pig together on the floor, there being no berths." [35]

Meanwhile, Washington was becoming impatient. He had no desire to bombard the town, but he wished to hurry the evacuation; and to that end he made more threatening approaches. He threw up a redoubt on the point of the Dorchester peninsula nearest to Castle William. As a final move, "a notice to quit," he again seized Nook's Hill and in spite of a bombardment, ineffectual because only "a few old Iron Guns were left" [36] to be brought to bear on it, he fortified it. With his guns in that position, he could fire on the ships at the wharves at close range and cannonade the rear of the works on Boston Neck.

But it was now the last day of the lingering evacuation, the 17th of March. At nine o'clock in the morning all were on board, except two engineer officers and a few men, left "to fire some houses if there had appeared any Enemy in our rear, but none appeared and we went all off in the greatest order." [37] Yet there were a few minor hostilities. Castle William had not been abandoned; the 64th Regiment posted there was engaged in mining it for its destruction. Some Americans, working on fortifications on Dorchester Point, were fired upon from the Castle, and there were a few shots in reply. At nine in the evening, the fuses of the mines were lighted, and the remaining British boarded their transports, the last ever to set hostile foot on the soil of present-day Massachusetts.[38]

But Charlestown seemed yet to be held. Sentinels could be seen at their posts on Bunker Hill. Two men went over to investigate, and "found the Centinels to be Images dressed in the Soldiers Habit with Laced Hats and for a Gorget an Horse Shoe with Paper Ruffles, their Pieces Shouldered [with] fixed Bayonets, with this Inscription wrote on their Breast (viz.) Welcome Brother Jonathan." [39]

The American troops at Cambridge and Roxbury had been paraded. When the last of the enemy had left, General Ward with five hundred men crossed the Neck and entered the town. Others occupied Charlestown peninsula. On the 20th the main force was in full possession of Boston.

Still there was some apprehension as to the intentions of the enemy. The fleet had anchored in Nantasket Roads about five miles below the town—for what purpose, no one in Boston knew. Washington wrote to Trumbull on the 21st, "I cannot but suspect they are waiting for some opportunity to give us a Stroke, at a moment when they conceive us to be off guard." Three days later, he said, "It surpasses my comprehension and awakens all my suspicions." He complained that "the enemy have the best knack at puzzling people I ever met with in my life." [40] His apprehensions were groundless.

The British were only preparing for their voyage in the leisurely eighteenth century fashion, adjusting their cargoes, which had been so hurriedly shipped, taking in water, and so on. On the 27th they put out to sea, bound not for New York, as Washington thought, but for Halifax.[41]

Howe carried off 11,000 soldiers and sailors and nearly a thousand refugees, among whom were a hundred civil officials. Many of these settled in Nova Scotia, suffering the privations and hardships of pioneers. Others went to England. Few ever returned to their old homes.[42]

Although during the fall and winter of 1775–1776 the British army had lain inactive in Boston, there had been one hostile enterprise on the part of its fleet of which notice should be taken.

Vice Admiral Samuel Graves had been appointed in March, 1774, to command the British naval forces in America; he arrived in Boston harbor on July 1 to undertake the thankless job of enforcing the blockade. He had in his charge from twenty-five to thirty war vessels, ranging from the great ships of fifty to seventy guns down to sloops and cutters. The *Asia*, sixty-four guns, was stationed at New York, the *Rose,* twenty guns, and the *Scarborough*, twenty guns, were part of the time at Newport and Portsmouth respectively. Another ship was held at Halifax. Some of the smaller vessels were engaged in cruising off the coast, or from time to time stationed here and there. The rest lay in Boston harbor.[43]

Although the whole British navy at that time was in a scandalously run-down condition, Graves's fleet was of overwhelming strength as compared with the puny vessels of the Americans. But Graves himself was utterly inefficient. The Americans raided the islands in the harbor almost at will, and he could not prevent them. They gathered a fleet of three hundred whaleboats, hid them by day, and by night went about their nefarious business of burning lighthouses, foraging or whatever they would, in spite of the Admiral. He actually stood in fear that they might, by concerted action, take from him one of his capital ships.[44] Burgoyne wrote to Lord George Germain in August, 1775: "It may be asked in England, 'What is the Admiral doing?' . . . I can only say what he is *not* doing." And he went on to catalogue Graves's inactivities; he was not supplying the camp with fresh meat, not protecting the flocks and herds on the islands, not doing anything that he should do.[45]

Graves was probably nettled by the criticism in the camp and angered by his inability to find and capture, on the high seas, the American cruisers that were intercepting the supply ships. He decided to go after them in the ports and harbors where they hived. On October 6 the *Canceaux* with eight guns and forty-five men, and the schooner *Halifax* with six guns and thirty men, to which were added one hundred soldiers, sailed under command of Captain Henry Mowat. His orders were to "burn, destroy and lay waste" the seaport towns all along the northeast coast as far as Machias, and to destroy all their shipping.[46]

Mowat viewed Gloucester, and decided that the houses were so widely scattered that it would be difficult to burn the town. On the 16th he anchored at Falmouth, now Portland. He warned the people to remove "the human species within two hours, when the punishment would begin"; but, at the supplication of a committee of the townsfolk, he agreed to give them until the next day. Indeed, if they would deliver to him four cannon supposed to be there, all other arms and ammunition, and certain hostages, he would ask further instructions from headquarters. The next morning they refused to deal with him. Mowat then opened fire on the town with cannon balls and incendiary carcasses, and a landing party set additional fires among the buildings. By evening the whole town was ablaze. Two hundred houses, the church, the courthouse, the town house, the public library, the wharves and warehouses, and eleven vessels were "all laid into ashes." Four other vessels were taken. There were no casualties among the British, except two men wounded by the feeble resistance offered them. Graves was satisfied by this one outrage, and sent out no more such expeditions.[47]

CHAPTER 11

The Question of Canada

Canada had long been a word of ill omen to the American colonists, particularly to those of Massachusetts, New Hampshire, and northern New York. Time and again, the Canadian French and their Indian allies had ravaged and devastated the settlements of those colonies. Deerfield and Northampton, Saratoga and Schenectady, Keene, Exeter, Brunswick, and many another village, and countless isolated settlers' homes had succumbed to the bullet, the tomahawk, the scalping knife, and the incendiary torch. In one year alone, 1746, thirty-five bands of these marauders had ravaged the borders of the northern American provinces. When Montreal capitulated in 1760, and Canada fell into the hands of the English by the treaty of 1763, the dread of their northern neighbors departed from the minds of the colonists, only to be revived in a different form fourteen years later, when Parliament passed the Quebec Act.

To an understanding of that act in its effects upon Canada and upon the American colonies, a brief review of the character and conditions of the Canadian people may be helpful.

The inhabitants of Canada fell into four well defined classes. The habitants, who formed the first class, were the basic population. They were descendants of the first settlers, and were French in origin, Roman Catholic in religion, tenant-farmers in occupation, numbering perhaps 60,000 or more. These tractable, hard-working agriculturists held their farms under a sort of feudal tenure from the great landholders, who constituted another class, the aristocrats, seigneurs, and had been well-to-do, largely through the emoluments of office, civil or military, until the English conquest de-

prived them of official employment and ended the various feudal obligations due from the habitants except the payment of rents, which were of
small value. Most of them, including practically all the civil and military
officers, had gone back to France after the conquest; no more than 130
heads of families remained. Reduced in wealth even to comparative poverty,
their political and social influence lost, these few seigneurs were of little
importance in the affairs of the province.

Few in numbers, not more than 2,000, but having, as they thought, great
potential political importance, were the people of British origin, many of
them immigrants from the American colonies. They were commonly called
"Old Subjects" to distinguish them from the lately acquired French subjects.
The majority of them were in Montreal, engaged in the fur trade. They
were a troublesome lot. They quarreled with the military, were at odds with
the seigneurs, and contemned the habitants. As the only true-born British
subjects, they claimed privileges above the other classes, even to the extent
of demanding self-government by elective bodies of which only they would
be electors and members. They would even deny the right of the Catholic
French to sit on grand juries, an exclusion based on the then prevailing
English law, which excluded Catholics from the elective franchise and from
all political offices. James Murray, the first British governor of the province,
described them as "chiefly adventurers of mean education," all having
"their Fortunes to make and little Sollicitous ab⁺ the means." [1] Guy Carleton,
his successor, had much the same opinion of them.

The fourth class was composed of the Catholic priests. Formerly of great
importance in the government, wielding an almost unlimited and almost unrestrained power, even over the French governors and their councils, the
English conquest had brought them so low that they asked only for tolerance
in their priestly offices. They had been used to requiring the habitants to
pay legal dues to the Church. But there was no longer any basis of legality
for such requirement, and the habitants paid or did not pay, as they pleased.
The clergy, therefore, existed on sufferance only.

Thus Canada was split into incompatible parties: the seigneurs despised
both the habitants and the Old Subjects; the habitants disliked the British,
no longer respected the seigneurs, and refused to be subservient to the clergy;
the Old Subjects held the seigneurs in contempt, scorned the habitants, and
were at odds with the government; the poor priests were in good repute with
none of the others. Besides all that, the historic ill feeling between Catholics
and Protestants was in full force and vigor.

In 1763 a royal proclamation had made Canada a crown colony without
an elective assembly, promising one "as soon as the state and circumstances

of the said Colonies will admit thereof." Political power had been placed in the hands of a governor and a royally appointed council. It was the promise of an assembly in the future that gave the Old Subjects their hope of political domination, for surely, as in England, the Catholics would be excluded from voting and from sitting in the assembly.

But they were disappointed. Guy Carleton, who succeeded Murray in 1766, was an English aristocrat, a military man with all the qualities of the professional soldier of high rank. He was reserved, stern, remote from civilians, fearless, and inflexible; but he was also high-minded, incorruptible, and, at bottom, magnanimous. He looked upon the humble habitants as the real Canadian people, the solid foundation of the province, and he was emancipated from the English dread of Catholic "Popery." Partly as a result of his efforts the Parliament passed the Quebec Act in 1774.

That act put an end for the time being to any hope of an elective assembly, definitely annulling the vague promise of the proclamation of 1763. It provided for a governor and a council as lawmakers appointed by the crown. It recognized the Catholic Church, with a proper bishop, and restored its right to collect tithes and other dues. It abolished the religious "test oaths," which had disqualified all non-Protestants from holding civil office. It retained the English criminal law, but restored the French law in civil matters. It extended the boundaries of the province to include Labrador on the east and, on the west, all the land north of the Ohio River between the Allegheny Mountains and the Mississippi.

In many of its provisions the Quebec Act was an excellent law and was in advance of the philosophy of its time; but it was not well received by the Old Subjects. They wanted that promised assembly. They also wanted exclusive right to the offices of honor and emolument, and they objected strongly to the "establishment" of the Catholic Church. The Catholic priests objected to the provision requiring them to be licensed by the King only, and the Catholic laity were incensed by the compulsion to pay tithes. The French did not like the retention of English criminal law. The English disliked the restoration of the French civil law. So the cleavages in Canada's population were deepened.[2]

To the Americans the Quebec Act was anathema for several reasons, the first and most objectionable being the extension of the boundaries of Canada. Some of the colonies, notably Connecticut, Massachusetts, and Virginia, had pretensions to some parts of the western lands now given to their northern neighbor. They had seen them taken from the French by the Treaty of Paris in 1763 and, as they thought, reserved for their own settlement. Citizens of the Old Thirteen Colonies had been peering over the crest of the Alleghenies at the new lands beyond. They had even passed over the mountains and had made new settlements in the Ohio valley. They looked forward to unimpeded occupation quite to the Mississippi. This sudden reversal of conditions, by which the conquered territory was restored to Quebec, and perhaps to their old enemies, the French Canadians, was a shock to all the American colonists. Moreover, they saw themselves surrounded on the north and west by an undemocratic government whose legislature was appointed by the crown, not elected by the people, a despotic government whose power might be exerted against them at the will of the King. Also, the American colonists were Protestants in an overwhelming majority and, especially in New England, fiercely jealous of the prevalence of their religion. They had inherited fear and hatred of Catholicism from old England. Now they saw dreaded Popery practically established in all that great territory enclosing them.

There was, too, for those thinking in terms of a war of rebellion, the fact that the St. Lawrence River was a broad waterway by which troops could be carried to Montreal, where they would have access to that other waterway, Lake Champlain, Lake George, and the Hudson, which would, if held by the British, separate the New England colonies from those to the southward.

All these considerations made it desirable that Canada should be joined with the American colonies in the common cause against Britain. The Second Continental Congress in May had, rather ineptly, tried to induce the Canadians to unite "with us in the defence of our common liberty." [3]

In a letter dated May 29, 1775, and addressed "To the oppressed Inhabitants of Canada," the Congress declared that "the fate of the catholic and protestant colonies [was] strongly linked together." It was urged that "the enjoyment of your very religion . . . depends on a legislature in which you have no share and over which you have no control." [4] "The decent manner in which the religious matters were touched" [5] was received with pleasure by the Canadians. But on October 21, 1774, the First Continental Congress had addressed an appeal to the people of Great Britain, setting forth the grievances of the colonies, among which were the Quebec Act establishing in Canada "a religion fraught with sanguinary and impious tenets . . . a religion that has deluged your island in blood and dispersed impiety, bigotry, persecution, murder and rebellion through every part of the world." [6]

Unfortunately the Canadians read that appeal after they had digested the later one addressed to them, and they were not pleased with it. "They could not contain their resentment, nor express it but in broken curses." "Oh! the perfidious, double-faced Congress!" they cried. "Let us bless and obey our benevolent Prince, whose humanity is consistent, and extends to all Religions; let us abhor all who would seduce us from our loyalty, by acts that would dishonour a Jesuit; and whose Addresses, like their Resolves, are destructive of their own objects." [7]

Well then, if Canada would not willingly join, what about compulsion? What about conquest? The Second Continental Congress was at first unwilling to go so far as that. On the 1st day of June, 1775, it resolved "that no expedition or incursion ought to be undertaken or made, by any colony, or body of colonists, against or into Canada." [8]

But that vigorous and ambitious warrior Benedict Arnold was of a different opinion. On June 13 he reported to the Congress that the Indians would not assist the King's troops against the Americans; that Carleton had been unable to raise more than twenty Canadians to help him; that there were only 550 British regulars in all Canada, scattered among five posts. He proposed an attack on Montreal with 1,700 men, through St. John's and Chambly, Quebec being ripe to fall when those places had been taken. He added that "if no person appears who will undertake to carry the plan into execution . . . I will undertake it and . . . answer for the success of it." [9]

And that other vigorous and restless soul Ethan Allen was of the same opinion. When he heard of the resolution of the Congress, adopted on May 18, recommending the removal of the cannon and military stores taken at Ticonderoga to the south end of Lake George and the abandonment of the captured fort,[10] he wrote to the Congress on May 29 a letter of protest, in which he also urged an expedition against Canada: "The more vigorous the Colonies push the war against the King's Troops in Canada, the more friends we shall find in that country. . . . Should the Colonies forthwith send an army of two or three thousand men, and attack Montreal, we . . . would easily make a conquest of that place." [11] On June 2 he even more eloquently adjured the New York Provincial Congress to favor such an attack. "I wish to God," he fervently wrote, "America would, at this critical juncture, exert herself. . . . She might rise on eagles' wings and mount up to glory, freedom and immortal honour, if she did but know and exert her strength. Fame is now hovering over her head. A vast continent must now sink to slavery, poverty, horrour and bondage, or rise to unconquerable freedom, immense wealth, inexpressible felicity and immortal fame." [12]

Allen wanted his Green Mountain Boys enrolled in the Continental service. To that end, he and his lieutenant colonel, Seth Warner, presented themselves on June 23 at the door of the Congress in Philadelphia, and were admitted to the floor of the house. What he said to the Congress, whether he repeated his advice as to Canada, does not appear in the records. He did attain his chief object; his Boys were to be enlisted in a regiment of their own, under officers of their own choice.[13] It may well be that what he told the Congress then influenced it, within the next four days, to reverse its policy as to Canada, and to direct General Schuyler to proceed to Ticonderoga and Crown Point, and "if [he] finds it practicable and that it will not be disagreeable to the Canadians, he do immediately take possession of St. Johns, Montreal and any other parts of the country." [14] At all events, Ethan Allen may be credited with some of the impetus behind that resolution.

Major General Philip Schuyler was a representative of the best Dutch blood in New York, and one of its wealthiest landed proprietors. He was at this time in his forty-third year, slender yet well muscled, erect and commanding in figure, quick and energetic in movement. His face was noticeably florid and unusually expressive of his emotions, its features rather large, but not distinguished. His hair was dark brown, as were his keen, piercing eyes. His voice was clear, inclining to sharpness. His dress was always in accord with the prevailing mode. The manner of life in his mansion in Albany and his country seat at Saratoga was generous and hospitable, elegant indeed, with numerous servants, an ample stable, and a full cellar to care for his guests.

He was not lacking in intelligence, nor in kindliness, nor in courtesy to his equals, though to those of pronounced inferiority of station or of doubtful integrity he was apt to show his sense of his own superiority. In depth and breadth of mind, in stability of intention, in firm decisiveness to plan and to execute, in the ability to meet a confused situation, discern its essentials, and expend his energies upon them only, Schuyler was somewhat deficient. Thus he lacked the executive power needed to make him an effective and successful general officer; nor had his slight martial experience as a captain in the French and Indian War been sufficient to induce a habit of command. Moreover, he had not the physical vigor nor the ruggedness needed to cope with the hardships and deprivations of a wilderness campaign. This want showed itself in the outbursts of temper and exasperation which often succeeded an exhibition of uncomplaining patience on his part. He was a highminded, public-spirited gentleman and above all a patriot, wholly devoted— rather singularly among the men of his own class in New York—to the American cause. He was wrongly placed as a chief military officer; his proper place was at the council table.[15]

Brigadier General Richard Montgomery was Schuyler's second in command. Born in northern Ireland, the son of a baronet and member of

Parliament, he was well educated, and from his seventeenth year had been a soldier in the British army. He had fought under Amherst at Ticonderoga and Crown Point in 1759. At the age of twenty-six he was a captain. For ten years, he held that rank. In 1772 he resigned from the army and returned to America. In the next year he married one of the Livingstons, a family of wealth and high social position. Two years later he was commissioned a brigadier general in the Continental army. Although of studious habit, preferring the library and domestic life to the camp and the field, he was ardent for the cause of the colonies and responded to the call to arms.

He was tall, slender, of graceful address, yet strong, active, and capable of long endurance of fatigue and hardship. Forceful in command, aggressive in action, patient in adversity, cool in judgment, never negligent of duty, never avoiding danger, he was the complete soldier.[16]

With those two as aide-de-camp was Captain John Macpherson, Jr., the twenty-one-year-old son of a well-to-do Philadelphian. His portrait shows a notably handsome and refined face, and his character was in keeping with it. Bancroft has described him as a "pure-minded, youthful enthusiast for liberty . . . full of promise for war, lovely in temper, dear to the army, honored by the affection and confidence of his chief." [17]

Schuyler's instructions, when he was detached by Washington at New York City on June 25, gave him command of the New York Department. He was to occupy the several posts in the Champlain region, put them "in a fit posture to answer the End designed," and, besides keeping an eye on Governor Tryon, "watch the Movements of the Indian Agent," Colonel Guy Johnson "and prevent, as far as you can, the Effect of his Influence to our Prejudice with the Indians." "The Temper and Disposition" of the Canadians were to be investigated "that a proper line may be mark'd out to conciliate their good Opinion, or facilitate any future Operation." [18]

It will be noted that this was a cautious approach to the possible invasion of Canada, there being no definite orders or directions on the point. The Congress, however, as has been related, gave orders on June 27 for an aggressive movement if Schuyler should find it practicable and not disagreeable to the Canadians.

The Colonel Guy Johnson whom Schuyler was to watch was son-in-law and successor in office to Sir William Johnson, who had been appointed Superintendent of Indian Affairs in the northern department in 1755 and, with a rare talent for dealing with red men reinforced by his "marriage" with the sister of the Mohawk chief, had exercised a strong and generally prevailing influence over the Iroquois League, of Mohawks, Oneidas,

Onondagas, Cayugas, Senecas, and Tuscaroras, or Six Nations.[19] Besides
these, there were in Canada the Seven Nations, allies of the League, not so
numerous nor in general so warlike, yet including the Abenakis on the St.
Francis River—formerly most savage of all and most dreaded by the colonists—and the Caughnawagas, whose chiefs were all "of English extraction
Captivated in their infancy." Their superior intelligence made the Caughnawagas important, although the tribe could not muster two hundred braves.
Beyond these to the north and west were unnumbered other, unrelated
tribes, a great reservoir of potential savagery.[20] Guy Johnson as Superintendent of Indian Affairs since 1774 could cause infinite trouble to the
Americans.

There was another influence which prevailed in Canada. Louis St. Luc de
La Corne, a Frenchman, had been Superintendent of the Canadian Indians
under the French régime, and his son-in-law, Major Campbell, now held a
similar office. La Corne was hated and dreaded by the colonists as a "fiend
incarnate" and was believed to have been responsible for the massacre of
the prisoners taken at the capture of Fort William Henry in 1757.[21] He was
now on the side of the British. It was evident to the colonists that the Indian
question was one of the most important with which they had to deal in the
contemplated invasion of Canada.

Johnson, La Corne and Campbell, Joseph Brant, otherwise called
Thayendanegea, a Mohawk chief, and Colonel John Butler, Johnson's
assistant, worked assiduously to enlist the Indians under the British standard in 1775. La Corne was especially busy, giving them powder and brandy.
At a price of two johannes (about $16) a piece, he got some of the young
Caughnawagas to engage; but the older men took the money from them
and returned it to him.[22] To help Carleton break down the sales resistance
of the Indians, the home government sent a cargo of inducements, "hundreds of proved fowling-pieces, with blue barrels, walnut stocks, trimmings
of wrought brass and silver sights . . . neat, bright Indian hatchets," brass
kettles, gold laced hats, ruffled shirts, pipes, greatcoats, barrels and barrels
of gunpowder and of bullets, pots of paint for facial adornment, blue, rose,
yellow, vermilion, all to the value of £2,500.[23] Johnson had the effrontery
to deny that he was inciting the red men to fight the Americans. The charge,
he said, was manifestly absurd. It was true that he had fortified his house
in the Mohawk valley, and that it was guarded by Mohawks; but that was
only because he had heard that the New Englanders or the people from
Albany were coming in "a considerable number to seize and imprison
me." [24] But there were witnesses against him. Samuel Kirkland, missionary
among the Iroquois, testified to the contrary. Thirty Indian chiefs, on a

mission to the Congress, corroborated Kirkland's testimony. By the middle of July, it was said that Johnson was ready, with 800 or more Indians, to invade Tryon County in the province of New York.[25]

Reports as to the ultimate intentions of the Indians varied. In March, John Brown said he had word from reliable sources that the Caughnawagas, although "repeatedly applied to and requested to join the King's troops," had "peremptorily refused and still intend to refuse." [26] In June, Ethan Allen thought the Indians as a whole were attached "to our interest." He was cynical enough to believe that they acted "upon political principles and consequently are inclined to fall in with the strongest side. At present ours has the appearance of it." [27] This was immediately after Ticonderoga had been taken. But a man who had been in Montreal in the same month reported that the Caughnawagas had actually "taken up the hatchet." [28] In July another, similarly experienced, said they had refused to join Carleton though threatened with dispossession of their lands, and that the Indians were "pretty generally determined to take no part in the quarrel." [29] This was confirmed, also in July, by Captain Remember Baker, a Green Mountain Boy who had been scouting on his own hook. He said the "Seven Nations had agreed not to fight the Yankees." [30] But in August "two persons who have lately come from St. Johns" stated that Johnson had 500 Indians at Montreal "just going to join the English." [31] It was all very confusing and very disconcerting to the Americans, and it was clearly time that something was done about it.

The Continental Congress, in July, had formulated "A Speech to the Six Confederate Nations" telling them at great length about the King's oppression of the colonies and the contest to relieve it. It was couched in the language of parables. "This is a family quarrel between us and Old England," the speech said. "You Indians are not concerned in it. We don't wish you to take up the hatchet against the King's Troops. We desire you to remain at home and not join on either side, but keep the hatchet buried deep." [32]

A "council fire" was held at Albany, commencing August 23 and carried on, with great deliberation, by 700 Indians for more than a week. When they were "weary from having sat long in council," they thought it was "time for a little drink." General Schuyler, Colonel Turbott Francis, and Volkert P. Douw represented the Congress. Samuel Kirkland and James Dean, missionaries among the Indians, were also there to exert their influence. The peace pipe was passed around, which must have been a slow proceeding among 700, and then the Speech was delivered. It was a long speech, and the simple savages took three days to digest it. On the third day Little Abraham, a sachem of the Mohawks, made an elaborate reply. The essential paragraph was heralded by an injunction, "Now, therefore attend and apply your ears closely." It went on to say: "We have fully considered this matter. . . . This, then, is the determination of the Six Nations: Not to take any part, but, as it is a family affair, to sit still and see you fight it out."[33] It should be noted, however, that the Indians at the council fire were chiefly Oneidas and Mohawks of a certain canton of that nation. Most of the Mohawks, with the chief men of the Onondagas, the Cayugas, and the Senecas had gone to Montreal with Brant and Johnson. Therefore this compact was not so reassuring as it seemed on its face to be.[34] In October, however, the Caughnawagas undertook to promise for all the Seven Nations of Canadian Indians that they would not "in the least molest" the colonists.[35]

It must not be supposed that the colonists were averse to having the Indians in the war at all. Massachusetts enlisted the Stockbridge Indians in its forces immediately after the outbreak of the war. There was some excuse for that; they were at least semicivilized.[36] But its Provincial Congress sent a commissioner to the Maine Indians to enlist them and lent a willing ear to a proposal of the Abenakis to take up the hatchet for the colonists, "for which we have no immediate occasion," the Congress said.[37] Ethan Allen had had no compunctions about soliciting four tribes of the Canadian Indians "to help me fight the King's troops," offering them "money, blankets, tomahawks, knives, paint and anything there is in the army, just like brothers."[38] Some seventy or eighty of the red men joined Arnold in Canada; but otherwise very few were, in fact, employed by the colonists early in the war except as scouts, messengers, or guides.[39]

Schuyler and his companions left New York on July 4. After certain necessary delays at Albany and Saratoga, they arrived at Ticonderoga on the 18th and found a sad state of affairs.[40] At the landing place, held by a captain and a hundred men, a sentinel "quitted his post to go and awake the guard, consisting of three men, in which he had no success. I walked up and came to another, a sergeant's guard. Here the sentinel challenged, but suffered me to come up to him, the whole guard, like the first, in profoundest sleep. With a pen-knife only I could have cut off both guards and then have set fire to the block-house, destroyed the stores and starved the people there." So Schuyler reported to Washington on the night of his arrival.

This was his introduction to a post, which he soon found was "in a perfectly defenceless state," not only because "not one earthly thing has been done for offence or defence," but also because the garrison was in a wretched physical and mental condition.[41]

There were about 1,300 men in the posts on the lakes, 600 at Ticonderoga, 400 at Crown Point, 300 at Fort George. They were composed of Colonel Benjamin Hillman's Connecticut regiment, 1,000 men, part of a Massachusetts regiment under Colonel James Easton, numbering a little more than 100, 200 New Yorkers, and a few Green Mountain Boys.[42] At Ti, as the principal post was currently called, the men were "crowded in very bad barracks," insanitary to a degree; many were ill. They were largely without discipline. Those from Connecticut, especially, feeling themselves in Yankee fashion quite the equals of their officers, were insubordinate. Food was scarce: "sometimes we have no flour." The "constant cry for rum" went unappeased.[43] Schuyler found that there had been "a very considerable waste or embezzlement" of the stores.[44] Ammunition was wanting, and when it came to building boats, as the Congress had directed him to do, for an attack on St. John's, he had "not a nail, no pitch, no oakum," and no boards until he could set up a sawmill.[45]

The helpless, defenseless condition of these posts was largely due to the inefficiency of Colonel Hinman. He had come to Ti, as he said, merely to reinforce its garrison and, although he had accepted the chief command of a wilderness post far removed from any superior officer, his idea of his duty was "to wait for orders" and to do nothing until he got them.[46] He had welcomed the news that a superior was on the way to direct him. "I wait, Sir, with impatience for your arrival, as I find myself very unable to steer in this stormy situation," he plaintively wrote to Schuyler, on July 7.[47] He did not last long in the Continental army, not longer than December 20, 1775. After that, he returned to the militia.[48]

Schuyler had recognized the difficulties of his task before he came to Ticonderoga. There were under his command in the whole New York Department, present and fit for duty, no more than 2,500 men.[49] The Congress expected him to add to these the regiment of Green Mountain Boys, 500 in number, which Ethan Allen had been authorized to raise. But Allen had lost favor with the Boys. When some of "the old farmers on the New Hampshire Grants" met at Cephas Kent's tavern in Dorset, on July 27, to nominate the officers of the proposed regiment, they ignored him and elected Seth Warner lieutenant colonel, leaving the colonelcy vacant.[50] Allen came to Ticonderoga alone and solicited a place in Schuyler's force. Schuyler was "apprehensive of disagreeable consequences arising from Mr. Allen's imprudence . . . his impatience of subordination." But after he had made "a solemn promise . . . that he would demean himself properly," he was admitted as a volunteer.[51] The other 499 Boys failed to arrive.

If and when Schuyler attacked Canada with the force then in hand, he would have to use at least 200 of his men to guard the posts he already held, marching with not much more than 1,000 to take Carleton's fortified positions. The British had at least 700 regular troops, to which they might perhaps add as many Indians and a number of whites which he could not even guess at, because Hinman had obtained no information as to the probable attitude of the Canadians toward the proposed invasion.[52] Even without regard for the lack of matériel of every kind, the lack of man power was discouraging. So "with a strange and almost fatal patience," inherent in his Dutch blood perhaps, or resulting from "his patrician habit to order and not to do" or his lack of physical stamina, he lingered at Ti for more than two months, waiting for reinforcements.[53]

Not that he was idle; he got out planks for bateaux and built them, enough finally to carry 1,300 men with twenty days' provisions; he even had, on July 31, "a boat on the stocks (and nearly finished) sixty feet in length," large enough to carry "between two and three hundred men," and had started another. Also he called and called again on New York for more troops, for tents, and for equipment of all sorts from field artillery to bullet molds.[54]

In June, New York had voted to raise four regiments. On July 21 Schuyler asked for them. A week later he did "most earnestly entreat" that they should be sent up to Albany.[55] On August 14 Hinman caustically observed, "The Province of New York abounds with officers, but I have not had my curiosity gratified by the sight of one private." [56] But New York had its reasons for the delay. Its Committee of Safety had written on July 15, "Our troops can be of no service to you; they have no arms, clothes, blankets, or ammunition, the officers no commissions, our treasury no money, ourselves in debt. It is in vain to complain; we will send you soldiers, whenever the men we have raised are entitled to that name." [57]

They started at last. Colonel James Clinton arrived in Albany near the end of August with six companies. Three of these had serviceable muskets, two had guns needing repairs, the sixth had none. Lieutenant Colonel Philip Van Cortlandt got there about the same time, with four companies, "many of the men wanting shirts, shoes, stockings, underclothes," having, that is to say, no uniforms at all except coats and breeches. Three-fourths of them had no blankets, and they had no tents; but thirty men did have muskets. No barracks being available, they were kept penned up in their boats, to their great disgust. "Give us guns, blankets, tents . . . and we will fight the devil himself," they cried. "But don't keep us here in market-boats, as though we were a parcel of sheep or calves." The first of them, four companies under Lieutenant Colonel Rudolphus Ritzema, reached Ticonderoga on August 22.[58]

In his search for more men, Schuyler cast his eyes on Brigadier General Wooster's Connecticut troops sent down to help out in the defense of New York City. On July 17 the Continental Congress directed Wooster to send 1,000 men to Schuyler.[59] Colonel David Waterbury brought his full regiment. New Hampshire offered Schuyler three companies of Rangers, not part of the Continental army, under command of Colonel Timothy Bedel. They were to join him on his march to St. Johns. So, in one way and another, Schuyler gathered a little army.[60]

But, although Schuyler labored to improve the discipline of his men, they were for a long time "much inclined to a seditious and mutinous temper," partly because of their lack of good food, supplies, and equipment, and partly because of intercolonial jealousies. Major John Brown of Massachusetts thought "New York have acted a droll part, and are determined to defeat us, if in their power." [61] A Connecticut man wrote to Governor Trumbull complaining that "all the places of profit" were "filled up with men of the York Government," while Connecticut men were "obliged to do all the drudgery. . . . Commissaries' places are profitable. . . . Why should they have all the places of profit? . . . The advantage of their situation is such that it will make them rich. Are we to be wholly ruled by the Committee of New York?" [62] General Wooster, commanding the Connecticut men sent down to New York, thought it was dishonorable to his province to be subjected to the direction of a body of men—to wit, the New York Congress—when he could have "no faith in their honesty in the cause." "You know not, Sir, half their tricks," he wrote to Trumbull.[63] This distrust of New York permeated the New Englanders, and affected their relationship with their commander, Schuyler, a New Yorker himself.

In July, Schuyler had sent John Brown north to secure information about Carleton's post at St. Johns, the magazines of arms and ammunition in Montreal, and the inclinations of the Indians and Canadians in the contest. This man Brown was one of those remarkable characters that one finds hidden in the crannies of history, almost unknown even to historians. He was an educated man, a graduate of Yale and a lawyer, who had held the office of King's attorney in New York province, whence he had removed to Pittsfield, Massachusetts, to practice his profession. But he was not satisfied with such a sedentary life. He was "a strong, bold, active, fearless man . . . of noble personal appearance, genial air and chivalric manner," the best type of the gentleman adventurer.[64]

We have had a glimpse of him in February, 1775, when the Massachusetts Provincial Congress sent him on a mission to Canada, and have seen that his report recommended the seizure of Ticonderoga, in which he had afterward had a part. That journey was a severe test of his ability as a woodsman, his physical strength, and his pertinacity. It was made in the dead of winter, through deep snows, in intense cold, and over a most difficult country. On Lake Champlain amid broken ice he and his two companions, an old hunter and one who had been an Indian's captive for years, had been frozen in for two days. Thence they had gone on foot through a flooded country. It was a fortnight's journey of "almost inconceivable hardships," he said. At Montreal he talked with all sorts of people while his companions discussed matters of interest with the Caughnawagas. His report did not encourage the hope that the Canadians in general would join the colonists, but he did succeed in establishing friendly relations with some of the Old Subjects, notably one Thomas Waller, and in providing "a channel of correspondence" with them.[65]

He left Crown Point on this second errand, under Schuyler's orders, on July 24, with four companions, a Canadian and three soldiers. The journey could not be made openly as the first had been, for since the taking of Ticonderoga Canada was enemy country. Danger of captivity was now added to the difficulties of travel. After arriving in Canadian territory by boat, they "had a tedious and fatiguing march" of three days "through a vast tract of swamp." In one house where they lodged for the night, they were "surrounded by a large party of the enemy . . . escaping out of a back window,"and on their return trip they were "pursued two days." Nevertheless, they remained in Canada four days, protected by friendly inhabitants, and brought back a full and convincing report, dated August 14.

The French, he said, would not fight against the colonists. The Indians were minded to be neutral, except that they might scout for the British. St. Johns was being fortified. It was supported by two bateaux mounting nine guns each; and two sixty-foot vessels to mount twelve guns each were on the stocks. There were 700 of the King's troops in Canada, 300 of whom were at St. Johns, only 50 at Quebec, and the rest at Montreal, Chambly, and elsewhere. "Now, Sir, is the time to carry Canada. It may be done with great ease and little cost, and I have no doubt but the Canadians will join us. There is a great defection amongst them." [66] By Canadians he meant the Old Subjects.

Information from another source, coming on August 3, confirmed Brown's report except in the disposition of the King's troops, of which there were said to be 470 at St. Johns, 110 at Chambly, 80 at Quebec, and about

20 at Montreal. Samuel Mott, who got this news, urged that "we go forward now with 1500 men [rather] than with 3000 one month hence." [67]

But Schuyler lingered. There were reasons why he did, sufficient in his mind at least. He had no tents, no carriages for his fieldpieces. Many of his men were sickly—194 of them on August 14—and his expected reinforcements had not come. He was fully determined to go on, "unless your Excellency or Congress should direct otherwise," he advised Washington on August 6. As late as August 27 he wrote again to Washington, "To do it has been my determination, unless prevented by my superiours." [68] It may be unfair to Schuyler to suggest it, but that recurrent conditional clause seems to suggest a hope that he might be prevented.

On August 17 he went to Albany to attend the council fire with the Indians, leaving Montgomery in command on the lakes. That active soldier had, it seems, been tugging at the leash. On the 19th he wrote that "every intelligence from Canada evinces the necessity of a vigorous and speedy effort to crush their naval armament before it gets abroad." Now, in Schuyler's absence, he slipped the leash.

Montgomery had received a letter from John Brown, whom he had sent north on another scouting expedition, telling him of the near completion of Carleton's two vessels: "Their hulls seem to be finished . . . their masts are preparing . . . they appear of large size." He apologized for "writing in a dictatorial style," and would not have done so if it were not certain that the two vessels and their attendant bateaux "can easily sweep the lake. . . . I therefore humbly beseech that some effectual measures may be immediately entered into to keep the command of this lake." That was enough for Montgomery.[69]

He at once wrote to Schuyler that he was so much of Brown's opinion that he thought it "absolutely necessary to move down the lake with the utmost dispatch." He had therefore, without waiting for Schuyler's approval, given orders for an advance to Ile aux Noix in the Richelieu River beyond the foot of the lake, which, with the aid of two 12-pounders and a log boom, he intended to hold and so prevent Carleton's vessels from entering Champlain. He hoped Schuyler would follow him in a whaleboat, "leaving somebody to bring on the troops and artillery." He apologized for taking this step without orders, but felt that to hold back the enemy was of the utmost importance. "If I must err, let it be on the right side." [70] Schuyler was usually very touchy about his superiority in command, but he now learned "with pleasure" that Montgomery had acted in such an important matter without even consulting him. He seemed, indeed, to be glad that he had been relieved of responsibility for the venture.[71]

CHAPTER 12

Montreal

Montgomery was now about to begin the attempt against Montreal so long considered. From Ticonderoga his course lay north by way of Lake Champlain to Crown Point. Beyond that the lake widened between shores of almost unbroken wilderness, narrowed again, and emptied at the 45th parallel of latitude into a river, indifferently called the Richelieu or the Sorel, flowing nearly due north. At that point it was almost blocked by an island, the Ile aux Noix. Twenty miles farther north was St. Johns, a small settlement. Ten miles beyond that was Chambly, still smaller. At the mouth of the river, where it emptied into the St. Lawrence, was another little village, Sorel. But, at Chambly, a road led northwest to La Prairie and Longueuil, directly opposite Montreal, the main objective.[1]

In the evening of Monday August 28 the greater part of Waterbury's Connecticut Regiment, four companies of Ritzema's 4th New York, and Mott's small section of artillery, about twelve hundred men in all, embarked in the schooner *Liberty,* the sloop *Enterprise,* and a fleet of gondolas, bateaux, row-galleys, piraguas, and canoes. In the bow of each sailing vessel a 12-pounder was mounted. With a fair wind and a sufficiency of fresh and lusty oarsmen, the excursion began auspiciously, the men evincing "great cheerfulness." [2]

But at ten o'clock it began to rain heavily. They went ashore and bivouacked damply under the trees. On Tuesday they worked their way up to Crown Point. "A barbarous north wind" held them there one day, but the next morning a fair southerly breeze set in. So day by day they went on, going ashore at night to sleep, until, just beyond Isle La Motte, on a "fine, sandy beach" they disembarked to wait for Schuyler.[3]

Returning from the Albany council fire, Schuyler reached Ticonderoga on August 30, "very much indisposed . . . with a bilious fever and violent rheumatick pains"; but the next morning, after ordering forward five hundred of Hinman's regiment, three hundred of Colonel Goose Van Schaick's, and some artillery, he set out in a whaleboat to catch up with his ambitious lieutenant. In the morning of Monday September 4 he found Montgomery awaiting him and at once gave orders to move on. That evening they pitched their tents on Ile aux Noix. Hopefully, they fired three cannon shots, the signal agreed upon with their Canadian friends, who were to gather and join them. There was no response.[4]

The next day found Schuyler in rather worse condition, but he drafted an address to the Canadians telling them that "the Grand Congress" had ordered him to expel the British troops, who wished "to enslave their countrymen." The Congress, he said, "could not conceive that anything but the force of necessity could induce you tamely to bear the insult and ignominy that is daily imposed on you, or that you could calmly sit by and see those chains forging which are intended to bind you, your posterity, and ours, in one common and eternal slavery." Therefore it had ordered him "to cherish every Canadian . . . and sacredly to guard their property." [5] This document he directed Ethan Allen and John Brown to take to James Livingston, a merchant at Chambly who was well affected toward the colonists, and with whom he had been in correspondence.

On September 5 the troops embarked again, with three days' cooked provisions and their arms "in good firing Order"; their tents, baggage, and supplies were left behind under a guard. They were sailing now, all stripped for action, down the broad Richelieu between its heavily wooded shores. At three in the afternoon, they were in sight of the fort at St. Johns, two miles away. As they gazed at it, they saw white puffs of smoke break from its walls, heard the boom of its guns, and realized that they were being "kindly saluted" with round shots and bombs, though none of the missiles reached them.[6]

Half a mile farther on they went ashore "in a close, deep swamp" and started "in grounds marshy and covered with woods" towards the fort. Major Thomas Hobby and Captain Matthew Mead of the 5th Connecticut led a flanking party on the left and a little ahead of the others. They were crossing Bernier's Brook, a deep, muddy, winding stream, when they were met by a surprising blast of close fire. A hundred Indians led by Captain Tice, a New York Tory, had ambushed them. Several of the Americans fell, but the rest fired on the unseen enemy, then wheeled smartly to the left into dense thickets and for half an hour or so there was irregular bush fighting before the Indians retreated. Eight of Schuyler's men were killed or fatally wounded, and eight, including Hobby and Mead, injured less severely.[7]

They advanced no farther. As night fell, they dug "a small intrenchment" where they stood. But the enemy "kept continually throwing their bombshells" at this place, so, without tarrying long, they retreated a mile and entrenched again out of reach of the British guns.

That night there came to Schuyler "a gentleman, Mr. ————," whose name he disclosed only to Washington, begging him to erase it from his letter. This person had more effect upon the expedition than all the bombs and Indians. He told the general that the fortification at St. Johns was "complete and strong and plentifully furnished with cannon"; that the vessel there would be ready to sail in three or four days and was to carry sixteen guns; that no Canadians would join the Americans; that they had better not attack St. Johns, but rather return to Ile aux Noix.[8] Such resolution as Schuyler had was not proof against this kind of advice. He told a council of war the next morning that he considered it "absolutely necessary" to retire. The rest of its members agreed "to take measures for preventing her [the ship's] entrance into the lake," measures which, because of "the weak state of our artillery" could be effected only at Ile aux Noix, where an already prepared boom could be thrown across the channel. There they would await "intelligence touching the intentions of the Canadians" and, when reinforced, march by land against Montreal, "should the Canadians favour such a design." [9] So, instead of "expelling" the King's troops from all Canada, or even from the little fort at St. Johns, they all withdrew "without noise." If Major Preston's force at St. Johns had not been so weak that he feared to venture out of his fort, there might have been noise enough at this retirement.[10]

The news was spread abroad in Canada of their fight and flight, in which, so the tale went, 60 Indians had defeated 1,500 Americans in entrenchments, killing 40, wounding 30 more, and sending them back to their refuge at Ile aux Noix; and the victory was celebrated in Montreal by "a grand mass with a *Te Deum*." If anything were needed to ensure the abstention of the Canadians from joining Schuyler, this retreat provided it.[11]

The river was boomed, the island fortified. Now the colonials were in an excellent defensive position, very satisfactory if defense was all that was wanted. And there they received reinforcements, 300 of Hinman's Connecticut troops, 400 of the 2nd New York under Colonel Goose Van Schaick, with three pieces of cannon. Counting certain detachments sent out before that, Schuyler had altogether 1,700 men, more than twice the British regulars in all Canada. And he had five guns and three mortars.[12]

At this juncture (September 9) Schuyler received a reply to the letter he had sent by Ethan Allen and John Brown to James Livingston, the well affected merchant living at Chambly. Livingston urged him to interpose a force between St. Johns and Chambly so as to prevent Preston and his vessel from escaping to the St. Lawrence. If Schuyler would do that, Livingston promised to help him with "a considerable party of Canadians." They might even capture the vessel, loaded with "provisions and warlike supplies" and "slenderly manned." [13]

Schuyler fell in with this suggestion. He made elaborate plans. Two row-galleys, each carrying a 12-pounder, the sloop, the schooner, and ten bateaux "with 350 picked men" were to lie in the river to prevent Preston's vessel, the *Royal Savage*, from going south to the lake; and 700 men were to go again to a point near St. Johns, 200 of them to act as a covering party, protecting the boats, while 500 circumvented the fort and invested it on the north. [14]

On the 10th of September 800 men set out and landed at about ten o'clock in the evening near the first breastwork erected in the former attempt. The covering party of 300, under Montgomery, held that position, while Colonel Ritzema with 500 New Yorkers started along the shore to march around the fort. Flankers were thrown out in the woods on their left. It was dark in that forest, and the flankers, remembering the ambush on the former expedition, were nervous and apprehensive. There might be an Indian behind every tree. They drew toward the right, toward the open beach and, suddenly in the darkness, collided with the head of the main column. An instant and overpowering panic set in. They were ambushed again! They were certain of it, though only one chance shot from one of their own men had been heard. The covering party heard a noise as of many men coming in a hurry. Back they came, the whole 500, scrambling through the woods, through swamps as hard as they could go, for the boats. Ritzema was the last to come, all by himself. [15]

Montgomery took them in hand, rallied them, exhorted them "to act like men," formed them, and started them off again. They had gone a quarter of a mile, when some small shells and grapeshot from one of Preston's bateaux crashed and rattled through the trees. Half of them turned tail and ran again for the boats. But Ritzema, with the rest in a straggling band, went on to the second entrenchment of the previous excursion. A few of the enemy were holding a small house there. Ritzema had only 50 men with him. A few shots were exchanged, and two of the enemy were killed. Though 200 more of his men came up, he decided to retire. It was then three o'clock in the morning. The whole expedition spent the night at the landing place, their only satisfaction being that one of their 12-pounders had gone through that bateau of Preston's from stem to stern, torn it apart, and perhaps destroyed its crew of 35 men, or, at least had given them a ducking.[16]

In the morning another council of war decided to try again. But the officers were uncertain of the obedience of the men. They felt it necessary to call a sort of town meeting and let the privates vote on the question. The men agreed to go on. But just then Lieutenant Samuel Lockwood, who had been scouting down the river, returned and told them that the *Royal Savage* lay a little below "completely equipped." Part of Waterbury's New Yorkers at once ran to the boats, intending to get away as quickly as possible. Faced by such demoralization, fearing, too, that the schooner might come up and destroy their bateaux, the officers gave up the attempt. They embarked again for Ile aux Noix.[17]

Montgomery was not satisfied to retreat so ignominiously. After they had gone a few miles he stopped the fleet, went ashore with his officers, and called on the men to follow him on a march against St. Johns. But one of them called out that the schooner was coming. That finished it. "The Troops were hardly restrained from pushing off without their officers." So back to their haven of safety they all went, an expedition defeated by imagination.[18]

At the main camp the returning heroes were received with such jeers and upbraidings by those who had stayed safe at home, that they were "unable to bear the reproach of their late unbecoming behaviour." Schuyler, who was so ill that he could not leave his tent, concerted with Montgomery to take advantage of this state of mind. On September 13 they ordered the artillery into the boats, with the intention of carrying the whole force down the river again. The main party was to land as before, against St. Johns. The schooner and the row-galleys, manned by "determined volunteer crews and good rowers," were boldly to attack and board the *Royal Savage*. But the next day it rained, and on the next after that Ethan Allen came in to report his findings as to the disposition of the Canadians, which necessitated further consideration. That night Schuyler's "disorder reattacked . . . [him] with double violence." The 15th was again rainy, and Schuyler was so ill that "every prospect of a speedy recovery vanished." On September 16 he "was put into a covered boat and left Isle aux Noix."[19] Montgomery, of course, assumed command.

It would have been useless to call for volunteers in any event. Six hundred of the men were on the sick list, including half of Waterbury's contingent of Connecticut paladins. Sulkiness was prevalent throughout the camp, and mutiny was in the offing. One man cocked his gun and threatened to shoot an officer. Unauthorized parties wandered about the island, plundering its few inhabitants. Frequent false alarms of enemy approaches kept the camp in a turmoil. Courts-martial were of no avail, for no witnesses could be found to testify against the culprits. The officers were about ready to give up the whole expedition as a hopeless job when things took a turn for the better.[20]

Allen had helped by reporting that all the Caughnawagas had deserted Preston at St. Johns, and on the 16th the expected reinforcements began to arrive: Seth Warner and 170 of his Green Mountain Boys, "able bodied, stout, active fellows, used to the woods"; Colonel Timothy Bedel and 100 New Hampshire Rangers; and an Independent Company of Volunteers, including some Dartmouth students. These were soon followed by Captain John Lamb's Independent Company of New York Artillery—in all, something more than 400 men. Montgomery had now about 2,000 in his camp. Besides these, Easton's 200 men and the 1st New York Battalion, 125 strong, were coming from Ti.[21]

At the time Schuyler took over the command of Ticonderoga, the post at St. Johns was but a barracks, some brick buildings, and a stone house; but plans had been made to strengthen it. Two redoubts about a hundred feet square and six hundred feet apart were built of earth. One surrounded the brick buildings; the other, the stone house. A strong stockade, defended by a seven-foot ditch and fraised with pointed pickets in part and in part abatised, was drawn around the redoubts on three sides; and a moat was dug on the fourth, the river side. Cannon were mounted on the redoubts. Altogether, it was a sturdy little fort, offering a chance for a stubborn defense.[22]

Carleton's whole force of regulars was composed of 376 of the 7th Regiment, the Royal Fusiliers, and 263 of the 26th, the Cameronians.[23] Fewer than 200 men drawn from these regiments, with a few artillerymen and Indians, had garrisoned St. Johns fort at the time of Schuyler's first abortive attempt upon it. Carleton might have abandoned it and the whole Richelieu River and concentrated his forces for the defense of Montreal; but the Canadians and the Indians would have interpreted that as evidence of weakness and of fear, and would have been moved to withhold the help he so sorely needed. He had therefore decided to make a strong stand at St. Johns. To its garrison were added enough regulars to make up 500. His dire need for more men and the curiously amphibious character of the river operation appear in his withdrawing, in August, a midshipman and 12 sailors from the newly arrived armed brigantine, *Gaspé,* and sending them to the fort.

Earlier in the year, he had helped Lieutenant Colonel Allan Maclean, an old campaigner, to raise troops among the veteran Scottish soldiers who had emigrated to Canada. Maclean enlisted 70 in a company called the Royal Highland Emigrants. These went to St. Johns, and 100 Canadian volunteers with 40 artillerists and a few artificers increased the garrison to about 725 men all told. But Carleton felt he must have more.[24]

He tried the Canadians. Among the Old Subjects "damn'd rascals of Merchants, [he] met with little or no success." [25] They mostly favored the Americans. The seigneurs and the clergy used their influence among the French Canadians, but the sturdy habitants answered with armed opposition to enlistment, and with oaths on the Cross never to fight the Americans. The Indians had failed him. He had to do with what he had.[26]

On September 16 Montgomery organized his naval force, his schooner and sloop, ten bateaux, and two row-galleys (each with a 12-pounder), and 350 men, and sent them to lie in the river to prevent the *Royal Savage* from running upstream and cutting his communications with his base, Ticonderoga. He then embarked the rest of his troops and landed them at St. Johns.

He had already sent Major John Brown with 100 Americans and 30 or 40 Canadians to Chambly. Brown heard that a British supply train was on the way to the fort. He waylaid it in the night of the 17th about two miles north of its destination and captured the supplies. Expecting prompt aid from Montgomery, he entrenched. But before any help came, 100 British regulars and as many of the volunteers with two fieldpieces sallied out of the fort to attack him. Brown withdrew into the woods with his booty. There was a considerable exchange of fire until Colonel Bedel came up with 500 men and drove the enemy back to their stronghold. This new force was then posted in an entrenched camp about a mile north of St. Johns, while Brown went on with his foraging, which was quite successful. He gathered in twenty wagons laden with clothing, "rum, pork, wine &c." Montgomery sent other parties to take posts at Longueuil and La Prairie and hold those two approaches to Montreal. The rest were encamped about the fort. On the south side entrenchments were erected, and batteries of two guns and some small mortars were put in place. The siege of St. Johns was properly begun.[27]

Montgomery had promptly sent Ethan Allen on to Chambly to gather and take command of a body of Canadian volunteers. John Brown had gone to La Prairie on a similar errand. The very next day after he was dispatched, the energetic Allen wrote to his chief that he was at St. Ours, within twelve miles of Sorel, that he had 250 Canadians under arms, that, "as I march, they gather fast," and that he might be expected at St. Johns with 500 men in about three days. In a week's time, he could raise one or two thousand, he said. "I swear by the Lord I can raise three times the number of our army in Canada, provided you continue the siege; all depends on that. . . . God grant you wisdom, fortitude and every accomplishment of a victorious General . . . to fail of victory will be an eternal disgrace, but to obtain it will elevate us on the wings of fame." So wrote optimistic and eloquent Ethan to the general upon whom he was never to lay eyes again.[28]

At Longueuil, looking across the river at the twinkling lights of Montreal, Allen had a vision. He had told Trumbull in July that, if he had been given command of the Green Mountain Boys regiment, he would have advanced into Canada and invested Montreal. He was in Canada now, and there, just across the river, lay Montreal, practically defenseless. He could see victory before him and hear the rustle of the "wings of fame." Opportunity was knocking at his door.

But his Canadian recruits proved unstable; all but 80 of them drifted away. So he forgot his dream and turned back for St. Johns with his diminished force. He had gone but a little way on the road, when he met Brown, who had about 200 men. These two ambitious and daring souls agreed upon a scheme not merely to invest, but to take Montreal. Allen was to cross below the town, Brown above. Each would, as silently as possible, approach the town gate at his end. Brown's party was to give three huzzas as a signal of his arrival on the Montreal side and his readiness to attack.

Allen, having added 30 "English Americans" to his force, attempted a crossing in the night of October 24. There were so few canoes available that only one-third of his men could go at a time. They were all across before daylight, approached the town, and waited for Brown's signal. It never came. It was too late to retreat and make those three crossings again. At daybreak he would be discovered. Two-thirds of his men, left on the Montreal shore, while the first contingent crossed, would be too weak even to defend themselves. He took a good position two or three miles from the town, and waited for an attack.

News that "Ethan Allen, the Notorious New Hampshire Incendiary," was at hand threw the town "into the utmost Confusion." Carleton ordered the drums beaten. "The better sort of Citizens English & Canadian turned out under Arms." Thirty or forty soldiers, followed by about two hundred volunteers and a few Indians, issued from the Quebec Gate and advanced upon the intruders. Allen had posted his men behind trees and buildings and behind a small stream, and a smart little fight ensued. But two parties of

English and Canadians, constituting Allen's flanks, soon fled into the woods. Allen saw that he was to be surrounded. He retreated, keeping up a running fight, but was so hard pressed that he had to surrender himself and his forty remaining men.[29]

Allen's impetuosity was definitely harmful to the American cause. The complete failure of his attack heartened the loyal Canadians and disheartened those who might have joined Montgomery. The Indians now favored the winning side. "Thank God, that day's Action turned the minds of the Canadians," wrote one of them. Seth Warner wrote, "His defeat hath put the french people in to grate Constarnation." Schuyler, at Ticonderoga, reported to the President of Congress that he was "very apprehensive of disagreeable consequences arising from Mr. *Allen's* imprudence," and recalled for Hancock's benefit that he had "always dreaded" Allen's "impatience of subordination"—which was of course quite true. Carleton seized upon this turn of affairs and sent word through the province that 15 out of every 100 men must take up arms. Though the habitants in general refused to obey, Carleton did gather 900 new men to add to his force, but they began to desert "thirty or forty of a night"; he was approaching "as forlorn a State as before." [30]

The siege of St. Johns was continued, but under great difficulties. It was growing colder, and heavy rains set in. "Whenever we attempt to raise batteries, the water follows in the ditch when only two feet deep." [31] The camp was in low, swampy ground, and nothing could be kept dry. "Our men Sometimes have been Wet near Twenty Days together," said Jonathan Trumbull. "We have been like half-drowned rats crawling through a swamp," wrote Montgomery.[32] There was a vast amount of illness among the troops. Supplies of all kinds were short. Late in September the men were on a half-allowance of pork, and the flour was giving out. Powder, as always, was scanty.[33]

All this sowed seeds of dissatisfaction among the men, and they had favorable ground to grow upon. The Yorkers disliked the Yankees, and the Yankees distrusted the Yorkers. Besides, there was that ineradicable "leveling spirit" among the New Englanders, "such an equality among them, that the officers have no authority. . . . The privates are all generals," said Montgomery. He disliked, too, some of the men from his own province: "The first reg^t of Yorkers is the sweeping of the York streets." [34] The whole army was unruly, frequently near to mutiny. The men had to be coddled, their permission obtained before this or that could be done. At one time, when Montgomery wanted to erect a battery in a certain position, his field officers absolutely refused to do so. "I cannot help observing to how little purpose I am here," he wrote. "Were I not afraid the example would be too generally followed, and that the publick service might suffer, I would not stay an hour at the head of troops whose operations I cannot direct." He complained to Schuyler that it was impossible to command men "who carry the spirit of freedom into the field, and think for themselves." [35]

Schuyler, down at Ticonderoga, had found a similar condition, "a scandalous want of subordination and inattention to my orders," which had been chiefly responsible for the lack of supplies at St. Johns. He took hold, however, and in six days sent as much in the way of provisions as had before been shipped in three weeks. Conditions at the siege were immediately bettered. But he met with that same intercolonial jealousy, that disinclination of the troops from the various provinces to merge their identities so as to make a united army.[36]

It prevailed even among some of the higher officers. General David Wooster's distaste for submission to commands emanating from New York has been already mentioned. When the Continental mustermaster wanted to enroll Wooster's troops in the Continental army, he demurred "not thinking himself a Continental officer," and his men refused to sign.[37] They were sent up to Ticonderoga. Two hundred and fifty arrived in October, in advance, and Schuyler ordered them on to St. Johns. They answered that they did not "choose to move" until Wooster arrived. "Do not Choose to move! Strange language for an Army," the disgusted major general wrote to the Continental Congress. "But the irresistible force of necessity obliges me to put up with it." One of their lieutenant colonels demurred when he was directed to send a small detachment with powder and rum up to St. Johns, fearing he would be blamed by Wooster for obeying Schuyler's order. But Schuyler believed that ultimately they would "condescend to go." [38] When Wooster came, however, Schuyler found him tractable. He agreed not to dispute Montgomery's superior command at St. Johns.[39] So a regiment of the Connecticut men, 335 all told, sailed on October 22 for St. Johns, though "with the greatest reluctance," [40] and arrived on October 26. With them were 225 men of the 4th New York under Major Barnabas Tuthill.

Meanwhile, the siege had continued; and the fact that so many of the King's troops were bottled up had made some impression on the Canadians. St. Luc de La Corne found that the Indians were inclining to the Americans. He sent some Caughnawagas to Montgomery "with a string of wampum" and indefinite "proposals of an accommodation." Montgomery distrusted him but would not overlook any chance for aid. "He is a great villain and as cunning as the devil, but I have sent a *New Englander* to negotiate with him"—a left-handed compliment to the Yankee whom he sent, the ubiquitous Major John Brown. The conference came to nothing.[41]

At Chambly, down the river from St. Johns, there was a fort, an impressive, castlelike stone structure, with walls sixteen feet high and higher bastions at its corners. However, the walls were very thin and were pierced only for muskets. It was held by Major Stopford with a garrison of 88 officers and men. In the nighttime, two American bateaux carrying a few 9-pounders slipped past the guns of St. Johns and of the *Royal Savage* and landed at Chambly. James Livingston brought up 300 Canadians; Brown and Bedel brought down 50 Americans. They established batteries, and opened fire. The guns shot a couple of holes in the thin masonry and knocked down a chimney. Stopford surrendered the fort, with 10 officers, 78 privates of the Royal Fusiliers, 30 women, 51 children, 6 tons of gunpowder, 3 mortars, 150 muskets, 6,500 musket cartridges, 500 hand grenades, 300 swivel-shot, and 138 barrels of edible provisions.[42]

The investment of St. Johns was now tight above and below, but there was one thing left to bother the Americans, that armed schooner of Preston's anchored close to the fort. At last they concentrated their fire on her and on her mate, the floating battery. The *Royal Savage* and her companion both went down.[43]

Carleton had long considered a rescue. Allan Maclean had gathered a force of his countrymen. These, with 60 of the Royal Fusiliers from Montreal and a large number of Caughnawaga Indians, nearly 800 in all, assembled on an island in the St. Lawrence. On October 30, Carleton and La Corne leading part of them, they started across to Longueuil. But Seth Warner with his Green Mountain Boys and the 2nd New York was on the opposite bank. They opened fire with grapeshot from a little 4-pounder and with musketry. The boats were thrown into confusion, and the expedition turned back. Another party, led by Maclean, tried for a landing farther up the river. At the sight of a detachment of Americans posted there, they also retreated.[44]

There was by this time a strong battery on the west side of the Richelieu, with only the river and the moat, no walls, between it and the interior of St. Johns fort. Its bombardment was effective. The stone house was wrecked, the brick houses were shot through and through. There was no safe refuge anywhere in the enclosure, but still the garrison held on. It seemed evident that nothing less than an assault through a breach in its walls would take the fort.

To effect that, the position that Montgomery had before been prevented from taking by "the general dissatisfaction" of his troops, was occupied on the 25th. It was a hill on the northwest side of the fort. A battery of 12-pounders, some lighter guns, and several mortars was erected there. For about six hours all the artillery played on Preston's hold, but even this concentrated fire made no breach in the fort's earthen walls.

Then Montgomery tried other tactics. He sent one of the prisoners taken from Carleton's rescue force to tell Preston his case was hopeless, and Preston saw the point. On November 2, after holding out for fifty-five days, and with only three days' provision left in his magazines, he capitulated.[45]

The next day Montgomery drew up his troops before the fort. A motley array they were. The Yorkers were in uniform, as were Lamb's artillerymen, theirs being blue with buff facings. The Green Mountain Boys wore greatcoats of green turned up with red. But the Connecticut men, though admired for "Strength, Stature, Youth & Agility," wore any sort of clothes they happened to have. There marched out of the fort first the Royal Fusiliers in red coats faced with pale yellow, then the handful of the Royal Artillery in dark blue coats, red facings and sashes, white waistcoats and breeches, gold-laced cocked hats, and jack boots. The marines from the *Gaspé* in their short petticoats followed, with the Royal Highland Emigrants in kilts and the assorted mob of Canadians, artificers and workmen bringing up the rear. They were paraded, and Captain Lamb's artillerymen with a detachment from every regiment of the Americans marched past them and into the fort. Then Preston's men laid down their arms. One of the officers taken that day was the unfortunate John André.[46]

Montgomery treated his captives well. The officers were allowed to retain their side arms and private effects. The men were given the reserve store of clothing.[47] When this became known, "the officers of the First Regiment of Yorkers and [of Lamb's] Artillery Company were very near a mutiny . . . there was no driving it into their noddles, that the clothing was really the property of the soldier, that he had paid for it," wrote Montgomery. "I wish some method could be fallen upon of engaging *gentlemen* to serve." [48] The Canadians were allowed to go home. The regulars were to proceed to some port where they could embark for Great Britain.

Now it was necessary to proceed promptly to Montreal and to possess it. The Connecticut men were unwilling to go farther. Montgomery had "to coax them" by promising their dismissal as soon as Montreal was occupied.[49]

The march was begun on November 5, and it was most difficult. The old corduroy road had disintegrated into a succession of rotten logs and half-frozen mudholes. It snowed and rained. In places the mire was knee-deep.

The men were badly clothed and ill shod, but they pulled through to La Prairie. On the 11th, the first of them crossed to an island in the river and, on the next day, in a gale of wind, landed above Montreal.

Carleton, with something like 150 regulars and a few militia, remained in the town until the 11th; but its walls were so thin that they "could only turn Musketry," and in part had fallen down. The place was not defensible against even light artillery. He therefore put on shipboard the most valuable military stores and destroyed the rest as soon as he heard that the Americans were at La Prairie. He sailed on the 11th under fire from the American shore batteries. Montgomery spoke fairly to a deputation of Montreal citizens, and they surrendered on the 13th. At Sorel another battery threatened Carleton's little fleet. The wind was adverse. The ships turned back a few miles. Then Major Brown boarded one, under a flag, and told its commander that he had two 32-pounders in his "grand battery" at Sorel—a gross exaggeration. The *Gaspé*, two other armed vessels, and eight smaller craft were surrendered, with not only their cargoes and their crews, but also the soldiers formerly garrisoning Montreal.[50]

Carleton himself remained in the *Gaspé* until shortly before its capture. Then, "dressed like a man of the people" and accompanied by one or two of his officers, he was rowed with muffled oars down the river and by an obscure channel through the islands opposite Sorel, escaping finally to Quebec.[51]

CHAPTER 13

Arnold's March to Quebec

If one's antagonist can be forced to fight on two fronts at once, he is always at a disadvantage. While Schuyler's forces were still lingering at Ticonderoga, preparing for the advance toward Montreal, Washington in Cambridge had been pondering this strategic axiom. There was another front which might be developed: Quebec, 150 miles down the St. Lawrence from Montreal. If those two towns were attacked at the same time Carleton would be at a serious disadvantage and would be easy to overcome at one or the other, probably at both. Quebec, then, should be the object of an expedition simultaneous with that against Montreal.

The road seemed to be open—a waterway. The best, often the only possible route through a wilderness was a waterway, which permitted men to travel in boats with their provisions and supplies, escaping the hardship of a struggle through dense forests. This route had been considered in reverse by the French more than once as affording a means of attacking Boston. It had been repeatedly mapped and described, with varying degrees of correctness. It had been discussed during the French and Indian War "as a Rout by which an Army might pass, the best and shortest way, to attack Canada and Quebec." [1] In the spring of 1775 Colonel Jonathan Brewer of Massachusetts had offered to lead 500 volunteers against Quebec by this route, a project which he believed "he Could Execute With all the feility [felicity] Imaginable." [2] It is possible that Washington was made aware of this proposal.

The way led up the Kennebec River to the Great Carrying Place, where the Indians bound to Canada from New England used to leave the Kennebec

163

and take their canoes across a twelve-mile stretch of land to the Dead River. The stretch was broken into four portages by three ponds, across which boats could float, so that they had to be carried only about eight miles. After paddling about thirty miles up the Dead River, the Indians would proceed across the Height of Land about four miles to a stream emptying into Lake Megantic, from which the Chaudière River flows into the St. Lawrence within four miles of Quebec. Various portages were to be expected wherever falls or rapids on the rivers interfered with passage by water. The map of Captain John Montresor, a British army engineer, and his description made this rout seem to be quite feasible. Montresor had not told the whole tale of its difficulties and dangers; Washington, however, accepted at more than its face value the scanty information concerning it which had been conveyed to him.

On August 20, 1775, he wrote to Schuyler: "The Design of this Express is to communicate to you a Plan of an Expedition which has engaged my Thoughts for several Days. It is to penetrate into Canada by Way of Kennebeck River, and so to Quebeck. . . . I can very well spare a Detachment for this Purpose of one Thousand or twelve Hundred men, and the Land Carriage of the Rout proposed is too inconsiderable to make an objection." ³ That last sentence clearly shows how little he knew of the proposed "Rout." His thoughts about such an expedition soon crystallized into a decision to send it, and he looked about for someone to lead it. His choice of a com mander could hardly have been bettered.

After resigning on June 24 his command at Ticonderoga, Arnold went to Cambridge to settle his accounts with the Provincial Congress and secure from it the sums of money due him. He was at loose ends while this business dragged to a long deferred conclusion, because he had no office in the Continental army nor any connection with it. When Washington offered him command, as colonel, of an expedition against Quebec, he offered it to a man who still cherished the desire to invade Canada—a desire which had been frustrated at Ticonderoga. Arnold accepted with avidity.

It appears, indeed, that matters were far advanced before Washington wrote that letter to Schuyler, for on August 21 Arnold was writing to Reuben Colburn, a Kennebec boatbuilder who happened to be in Cambridge, making certain inquiries on behalf of the commander in chief. How soon could 200 light "Battoos" be procured or built at Kennebec, capable of carrying six or seven men each with their provisions, "say 100 wt. to each man," each boat to be furnished with four oars, two paddles, and two setting-poles? What would they cost? Could a quantity of fresh beef be procured at Kennebec? He also wanted information as to "the Difficulty attending an Expedition that way, in particular the Number, & length, of the Carrying Places, wheather Low, Dry land, Hills or Swamp, Also the Depth of Water in the River at this Season, wheather an easy Stream or Rapid." [4] This inquiry discloses Washington's ignorance, and Arnold's, of the nature and condition of the river they proposed to use as a road to Canada.

Colburn's reply was satisfactory as to the boats and their cost—40 shillings each with their equipment—for on September 3 Washington gave him an order for them. He also directed him to engage a company of twenty men, "Artificers, Carpenters and Guides," to go along under Colburn's command, "to bespeak all The Pork and Flour you can from the Inhabitants upon the River Kennebeck," and to notify the public there that the commissary would be in the market for sixty barrels of salted beef. [5] To get the desired information as to the route, Colburn sent Dennis Getchell and Samuel Berry to examine it and report to him.

On September 5 notice of the expedition appeared in General Orders. The detachment was to consist of two battalions of five companies each, comprising in all, with the usual battalion and company officers and musicians, 742 men; also Captain Daniel Morgan's company of Virginia riflemen and two companies of Colonel William Thompson's rifle regiment from Pennsylvania, under Captains Matthew Smith and William Hendricks, about 250 in all. To these should be added the surgeon, his mate and two assistants, two adjutants, two quartermasters, the chaplain, and six unattached volunteers, a total of 1,051. Service in the expedition was to be voluntary, and it was desired that none but "active Woodsmen" "well acquainted with batteaus" should present themselves. They were all to parade on Cambridge Common in the morning of September 6. The desire for woodsmen acquainted with bateaux was, unfortunately, not met in fact; nor does it appear that any effort was made to comply with that suggestion in the order. The men other than the riflemen were drawn chiefly from Massachusetts, Connecticut, Rhode Island, and New Hampshire Regiments, and were mostly farmers, few of them having had any experience in the wild woods or in the management of bateaux. [6]

The unattached volunteers were an interesting lot. Matthias Ogden of New Jersey, Eleazer Oswald of Connecticut, Charles Porterfield and John McGuire of Virginia, and Matthew Duncan of Pennsylvania were five, all of whom afterward became officers in the Continental army. But the sixth deserves more particular notice, because of his subsequent career.

Aaron Burr was a youth of distinguished lineage, the grandson of the great Jonathan Edwards, the son of the Reverend Aaron Burr, second president of the College of New Jersey at Princeton. Young Aaron had been ready to enter the college at the age of eleven, "a strikingly pretty boy, very fair, with beautiful black eyes and such graceful engaging ways as to render him a favorite." For want of age his admission was postponed for two years, and then he entered as a sophomore. After his graduation in 1772 at the age of sixteen he continued his residence in the college and for a while read theology. Skepticism soon undermined his hereditary beliefs, and he turned to the law. Lexington and Concord inflamed his naturally aggressive spirit. After Bunker's Hill, he called a college mate, Matthias Ogden, to the colors, and together they joined the army as independent volunteers immediately after Washington took command. Idleness fretted Burr's restless soul, actually worried him into an intermittent fever. When he heard of the proposed expedition to Quebec he got up from a bed of sickness and, despite the remonstrances of his friends, insisted on being allowed to go along.

He was nineteen years old, no more than five feet six inches tall, of slight figure and boyish countenance, but with a surprising capacity for enduring fatigue and privation. It was his indomitable will rather than his physical strength that sustained him. His intelligence was abnormally keen, his spirit unbreakable, his ambition unbounded. His subsequent career in the army was brilliant. He was in command of a regiment at the age of twenty-one, and in command of a brigade in the Battle of Monmouth at twenty-two.

He had the defects of his qualities. His overleaping ambition, his keen perception of the readiest means of bringing to pass what he desired, and his habit of ignoring conscientious scruples, resulted in the errors of conduct in civil affairs that ruined his life and blotted out the fame he won as a soldier.[7]

In the list of officers one name stands out above all the rest—Daniel Morgan of Morgan's Rifles. Although born in New Jersey to a Welsh immigrant family, Morgan was a true son of the backwoods. He ran away from home at the age of seventeen and went on foot through Pennsylvania into the wilder parts of Virginia, now West Virginia. There his character was formed and he acquired his fame as a backwoodsman.

He was first employed to run a sawmill and then became a teamster. Within two years he had set up in business with his own wagon and horse, hauling supplies to the remoter settlements. In this capacity he was employed in Braddock's expedition against Fort Duquesne. He served with distinction first as a private and then as an officer of the Virginia militia throughout the French and Indian War, in the war against Pontiac, and in "Lord Dunmore's War" with the Indians. That he was commissioned to raise a company of Virginia riflemen to join Washington's army at Cambridge has already been told.

He was a tall man, well over six feet, broad-shouldered, deep-chested, and stout of limb, weighing over two hundred pounds, all bone and muscle, yet active, even graceful, in movement. His physical and mental hardihood in endurance of fatigue under the most severe conditions matched his powerful frame. Although his usual manner of speaking was abrupt and severe and he was prone to swift angers and stern judgments, his open countenance indicated the good-humored, kindly character that lay beneath the surface and was displayed to his friends and to his men when they merited his approval. His schooling had been of the scantiest; he read with difficulty, wrote almost illegibly, and was puzzled by the simplest problems in arithmetic. But his natural genius and acquired knowledge of men and affairs, his keen intelligence, and his sound reasoning served him well in all his enterprises. His courage, daring, and resourcefulness in military affairs, added to his other characteristics, made him a great leader of men in the war upon which he was now entering.[8]

Washington's orders to Arnold were full and comprehensive, impressing upon him the necessity of discovering "the real Sentiments of the Canadians towards our Cause." If they were "averse to it and will not co-operate or at least willingly acquiesce . . . you are by no Means to prosecute the Attempt." Arnold was to restrain his men from the "Imprudence and Folly" of showing "Contempt of the Religion" of the Canadians "by ridiculing any of its Ceremonies or affronting its Ministers or Votaries . . . and to punish every Instance of it." There was to be no plundering of either friend or foe; all provisions and supplies were to be purchased and paid for. Although the expedition was to be pushed with vigor, yet, "if unforeseen Difficulties should arise or if the Weather shou'd become so severe as to render it hazardous to proceed in your own Judgment and that of your principal Officers (whom you are to consult) In that case you are to return." To the last injunction, it would seem Arnold paid little attention.[9]

In the expeditionary force the riflemen made up one corps. The musketmen were in two battalions, the first under Lieutenant Colonel Roger Enos and Major Return Jonathan Meigs, both from Connecticut, with five companies commanded by Captains Thomas Williams of Massachusetts, Henry Dearborn of New Hampshire, Oliver Hanchet of Connecticut, William Goodrich of Massachusetts, and Scott, whose first name and province of origin are unknown. The second battalion was led by Lieutenant Colonel Christopher Greene of Rhode Island and Major Timothy Bigelow of Massachusetts, with five companies under Captains Samuel Ward, Jr., of Rhode Island, Simeon Thayer, John Topham, Jonas Hubbard, and Samuel McCobb, all of Massachusetts. Isaac Senter of Rhode Island was the surgeon, Samuel Spring the chaplain. Christian Febiger was brigade major.

On September 11 the riflemen set out for Newburyport; but the musketmen, when paraded on Cambridge Common, "refused to march till we had a month's pay," says the journal of Ephraim Squier, a private. Whether it was back pay or pay in advance does not appear; but the matter seems to have been promptly adjusted, for by the 13th all had marched.[10]

By the 16th the expeditionary force had arrived in Newbury or the adjacent Newburyport, where a fleet of eleven sloops and schooners had been assembled. Three scouting vessels had been sent out to see if there were any British ships in the way. No news of such dangers having been received by the 19th, the fleet sailed, "drums beating, fifes playing and colours flying," [11] Arnold's topsail schooner in the lead. With no untoward incident on the way, except the extreme seasickness of most of these landsmen—"such a sickness, making me feel so lifeless, so indifferent whether I lived or died!" wrote Simon Fobes in his diary—the fleet made the voyage of a hundred miles to the mouth of the Kennebec in eleven hours. Sailing up the river, it reached Gardinerstown by the 22nd. There Arnold went ashore, a spruce figure in a scarlet coat, with collar, lapels, and cuffs of buff, silver-plated buttons, ruffled shirt, white linen waistcoat, breeches and stockings and black half-garters, the whole topped by a plumed cocked hat.

He inspected the bateaux provided for the expedition and found that there were 200 of them as ordered, but many were "smaller than the directions given and very badly built." [12] It was hardly Colburn's fault that they were not first-class. He had had only eighteen days to go home from Cambridge, assemble the workmen, and put through such a building program as he had never before been called upon to undertake, even with a sufficient time allowance. There was not nearly enough seasoned timber available, and so he had, perforce, used green stuff. It was unfortunate but unavoidable. Arnold could not reject them; he had to content himself with ordering twenty more.

These bateaux were of a type in common use on the Kennebec, with narrow, flat bottoms, widely flaring sides and long, pointed stems and sterns, capable of carrying heavy loads and not easily capsized. They were to be propelled by oars or paddles in still or flowing water and to be poled up rapids. They answered well on the lower Kennebec, but no one had ever tried to take them all the way up, past waterfalls, through the most difficult portages, across high, rough country, all the way to the St. Lawrence. Canoes, yes, but such heavy boats, especially when so ill built, emphatically no.

Besides the bateaux Colburn had to furnish information as to the route. The two men, Getchell and Berry, whom he had sent out had returned. Their report was not reassuring. They had gone as far as the Dead River, had met an Indian, Natanis by name, who told them he was employed by Carleton "to Watch the Motions of an Army or Spies that was daily expected from New England," and that a British officer with six men was posted on the Chaudière to look out for the Americans. Natanis declared that if the two scouts were any farther he would inform Carleton. By another Indian they had been told that a great number of Mohawks in Johnson's pay were at Sartigan, the uppermost settlement on the Chaudière. Otherwise, they said, the way was fair and was marked by blazed trees, the portages "pretty passible," the water shoal. Arnold read this report, but paid little attention to the threats of Natanis: "a noted villain," he called him in a letter to Washington, "and very little credit, I am told, is to be given his information." [13]

More helpful were a map of the route and a description of "the quick water and carrying places to and from Quebeck," furnished him by Samuel Goodwin.

By the 24th Arnold's force had reached Fort Western—now Augusta—thirty miles up the river, some in the sailing vessels, the rest in the bateaux. This "fort" was a couple of blockhouses and a magazine surrounded by a palisade, useful in the French and Indian War but no longer held as a military post. It was the real starting point for the expedition. Here Arnold detached and sent off two advance parties.

Lieutenant Archibald Steele of Smith's company of riflemen, "a man of an active, courageous, sprightly and hardy disposition," with seven men selected from the rifle companies, was ordered to reconnoiter the way to Lake Megantic, the source of the Chaudière. Steele had orders to capture or kill that "noted villain" Natanis. [14] Lieutenant Church, with a similar party and a surveyor, was to note "the exact courses and distances to the Dead River." These parties set out in canoes with guides.

The main force was then split into four divisions. The first was composed of the riflemen under command of Morgan, [15] who were to go forward as quickly as they could to clear the road, especially over the Great Carrying Place between the Kennebec and the Dead River. They departed four or five men in each bateau, the rest marching beside the river and taking turns in the boats.

The second division of three companies of musketmen left the next day, led by Lieutenant Colonel Greene and Major Bigelow. Major Meigs led the third division of four companies on the following day, and Lieutenant Colonel Enos with the fourth, three companies and Colburn's artificers, got away two days later. Arnold then started in a canoe to get to the head of the column. The bateaux of each division carried provisions estimated to be sufficient for forty-five days, although Arnold expected "to perform the march," which he figured at 180 miles, in twenty days.[16]

As the river for half a mile beyond Fort Western came against them in impassable rapids, the boats and supplies were presumably hauled by the neighboring inhabitants in wagons or on sleds to a point whence they could go by water. But even then the water was so swift that it was hard to propel the boats by oar and pole. It took them two days to make the eighteen miles to Fort Halifax, another abandoned military post. Above that, they came to Ticonic Falls, which no boat could ascend; here was their first real portage. The bulk of the cargoes was unloaded and carried to the next point of embarkation, each barrel of flour, pork, and so on being slung on two ropes, through which two poles were thrust, so that four men could take the ends on their shoulders. The bateaux were similarly carried by four men on two poles. The boats weighed 400 pounds each, and there were about 65 tons of provisions, ammunition, and general supplies, say in all 100 tons weight of the most unhandy material, to be carried in this instance a half-mile. It was a case of going back and forth until all was got over.

Not far above they came to Five Mile Falls, a series of tumultuous rapids, "very dangerous and difficult to pass."[17] They had "a scene of trouble to go through." The boatmen had often to leap overboard and struggle with their clumsy craft to keep them straight or drag them over shoals. They would be in the icy cold water to their waists, to their chins, even over their heads when they plunged into an unexpected "deep bason." "After much fatigue and a Bondance of difficulty,"[18] they got through, but not without damage.

The rocky river bottom, sunken logs, tree roots had scraped and torn the bottoms of the boats and opened their seams. They "began to leak profusely." Indeed, at least one of them, Dr. Senter's, was "in such a shattered condition" that he had to buy another from a near-by settler[19] the day before they came to Skowhegan Falls.

Even the approach to Skowhegan was difficult. The river made a sharp turn between two ledges no more than twenty-five feet apart, forming a

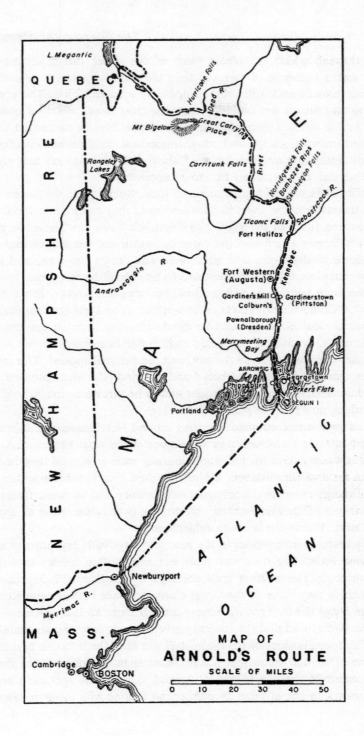

L. Megantic

QUEBEC

Hurricane Falls

Dead R.

Great Carrying Place

Mt Bigelow

Carritunk Falls

River

Rangeley Lakes

Norridgewock Falls
Bombazee Rips
Skowhegan Falls

Ticonic Falls

Sebasticook R.

Fort Halifax

Kennebec

Fort Western (Augusta)

Androscoggin R.

Gardiner's Mill
Colburn's

Gardinerstown (Pittston)

Pownalborough (Dresden)

Merrymeeting Bay

ARROWSIC

Georgetown

Phippsburg

Parker's Flats

SEGUIN I

Portland

NEW HAMPSHIRE

MAINE

ATLANTIC OCEAN

Newburyport

Merrimac R.

MASS.

Cambridge

BOSTON

MAP OF
ARNOLD'S ROUTE

SCALE OF MILES

0   10   20   30   40   50

chute through which the whole force of the water drove against them. There was a half-mile of this and then the falls themselves, divided by a towering mass of rock split in the middle by a narrow cleft. There was no going ashore for a carry on either side; the river banks were not banks but vertical rock walls. The boats and their cargoes had to be carried through that cleft, narrow, steep, and rough underfoot, and pushed through five miles of "small falls and quick water" above it.[20] The men lay that night, as often they did, in wet clothes that froze upon them.

So they went on, through Bombazee Rips, where again the banks closed in and the water came down in a torrent, until they came "face to face with the roar and foam of the great Norridgewock Falls." [21] These were three falls, a half-mile apart, and the carry around them was a mile and a half long. Some settlers appeared with two sleds drawn by oxen, and helped with the supplies, but the bateaux had to be carried by the men.

Those boats were in bad shape now, "nothing but wrecks, some stove to pieces." [22] Colburn's carpenters set to work to repair their bottoms and caulk their seams. But nothing could be done regarding supplies spoiled in the leaky boats. Quantities of dry salted codfish had been loaded loose in them. The water had washed away the salt, and the fish had spoiled. The salt beef had also gone bad. Casks of bread and of dried peas had absorbed water, swelled, and burst. All this provender had to be thrown away. Arnold's men had nothing now but salt pork and flour.

Three days were consumed in getting around Norridgewock and in repairing the boats. On October 9 they were again under way. Eleven of Arnold's estimated twenty days for the whole journey were past, and they had gone but one-third of the distance. Up to this time they had been within reach of civilization of a sort, occasional settlements and isolated farms from which they had sometimes been able to buy beef cattle. Now all that was left behind. The rest was sheer wilderness.

They made fourteen miles in the next two days with one portage around Curritunk Falls. The river was shallower and swifter, harder to work the boats through. The weather grew colder, and continuous, heavy rains fell. On the 11th they came to the Great Carrying Place between the Kennebec and the Dead River. That is, Arnold himself came to it on October 11. It must be understood that the itinerary given here is only approximately correct. The four divisions of the troops had not kept the intervals first allotted to them. This one would get ahead faster than its follower, or that one would overtake the one before it. Arnold himself was backward and forward, now with one division or another, now alone with his own canoemen.

When he reached the Great Carrying Place, Morgan's men and the second division under Greene were already there.

The first portage of the Great Carrying Place was a mere Indian trail, Morgan's men had had little time to do anything with it; the rest of the army was close upon them. It had rained so hard on the 8th that no work could be done. The ground was soaked; there was no dry place to sleep. The army had to sit up all night close to their fires.

The bateau men had to carry their unwieldy burdens, and the rest their cargoes "through a most terrible piece of woods conceivable," [23] through bogs where they sank "half-leg deep," and over rocky ledges, three and a quarter miles to the first pond. Though the pork had been removed from the barrels and strung on poles for easier carriage, seven or eight trips were necessary to get everything across. The weather was exceedingly bad, with heavy winds and snow squalls. "A prodigious number of trout" caught in the pond made a welcome addition to their narrow diet. A moose someone killed also helped out. They were three days on this carry and in crossing the pond, a distance of five miles.

The first pond having been crossed in the crazy boats, the second carry was found to be little more than half a mile, and the footing was fair. But the second pond was disappointing. "The water was quite yellow," and it was all they had to drink. They were greatly worn down by fatigue and hardship. Many of them—"a very formidable number" [24]—were ill, some of them desperately ill. This bad water sickened them so much more that a log blockhouse was built for a hospital. It was "no sooner finished than filled."

The way to the third pond was longer, about a mile and a half. It was "extremely bad, being choked with roots which we could not clear away." [25] But there were more trout in that pond.

The fourth portage was three miles long, and it was difficult. A mile up and a mile down brought them to what looked like "a beautiful plat of firm ground, covered by an elegant green moss," interspersed with groves of spruce and cedar. In fact, it was a treacherous bog. At nearly every step they sank halfway to their knees and found at the bottom sharp snags and roots that tore their shoes and bruised their feet. There was a mile and a half of this. So, stumbling along, falling now and again, dropping their burdens and recovering them again, they at last emerged, "plastered with mud from neck to heel," [26] at Bog Brook, which led into the Dead River.

While the main body was crossing the Great Carrying Place, it was met by Lieutenant Church's party of pioneers returning to report to Arnold.

Lieutenant Steele also, with two of his men but not the other five, came back to report. Steele's party had reached the Chaudière River without unusual difficulty, but their return march was another matter.

It had started in "a most severe storm of rain," which lasted a day and a night. Their provisions had run out. On the first day of the return trip on the Dead River, John Henry, one of the party, had only "a solitary biscuit and an inch of pork." He ate half his store that day. They shot a duck and divided it. His portion was one leg, another man got the head and feet. The next day Henry ate the other half of his biscuit and pork, and they made fifty miles. The day after that one of the two canoes struck a submerged snag and was ripped through its whole length, its ribs torn from its gunwales. They sewed them in place with cedar roots and patched the skin with birch bark and pitch made out of turpentine and the grease in their pork bag. They had gone five hundred yards when another snag broke the canoe in two pieces held together only by the gunwales. They mended it as before. They shot a moose, smoked its flesh, and ate it raw. They were so weak that they could not carry their canoes across the Great Carrying Place, so they abandoned them and set out on foot. Steele and two others pushed ahead to get help.

The five remaining lived wretchedly on the moose meat for four days. Half cured and without salt or bread, it sickened them. They "staggered along . . . falling every now and then, if our toes but touched a twig or tuft of grass." [27] On October 17 Morgan's pioneers sighted five scarecrows, gaunt, haggard, ghastly creatures, so weak they could scarcely stumble along. The rest of Steele's party had returned.

After Steele had reported the results of his exploration Arnold sent him and Church forward again, with twenty axmen and a surveyor, "to clear the portages and take a survey of the country." [28] He also wrote a letter to a friend in Quebec, John Mercier, telling of his approach with 2,000 men "to frustrate the arbitrary and unjust measures of the ministry and restore liberty to our brethren of Canada," [29] and dispatched it by two Indians, Eneas and Sabatis, and one John Hall, who could speak French. That letter in some way got into Carleton's hands and resulted in the arrest and imprisonment of Mercier.

Now began the trip up the Dead River, a deceptive stream that belied its name. Its black waters were deep, and so smooth that they seemed to be standing still. "A most gentle and leisurely stream" [30] it was, to all appearances. But, though it flowed like oil, its current was swift beyond all expectations. The few oars and paddles were not enough to make headway against it. The boatmen had to grasp the bushes on its precipitous banks and pull themselves along. And it meandered in such great bends and windings that, after two hours' hard work, they "seemed to have gained nothing in our course." [31] But they made thirteen miles before they camped that night. They also made a most discouraging discovery. Their food was on the point of giving out.

Although Arnold had written only a day or two before to Enos, commander of the fourth division, that the first three had provender enough for more than three weeks, Greene's division, which had got ahead, now found itself out of bread and almost out of flour. While it had been passing Morgan's riflemen they had helped themselves to Greene's supply of food without his knowledge.[32] Arnold sent Major Bigelow with three lieutenants and 100 men in twelve bateaux back to get flour from Enos, in whose division there was supposed to be a surplus. Morgan's and Meigs's divisions, somewhat better supplied, pushed ahead; but Greene had to lie in his camp for five days, awaiting Bigelow's return.

Bigelow came back with two barrels of flour, all Enos would let him have. It was a desperate situation for Greene's men. There was nothing to do but send back the least able men; the rest had to tighten belts and push on after the other divisions.

Rain began to fall gently on the 19th. It increased in volume on the next day, and by the 21st it developed into a raging tempest, driven by winds of hurricane force. Trees crashed into the river, "tumbling on all quarters" [33] and blocking the way. Floods of water drenched the men and their few supplies. Tents were few. In camp most of the men had no protection except such as could be had from hemlock boughs. The river rose and flooded the country. It overflowed its eight- or ten-foot-high banks and poured into the camp of Morgan's men during the night of the 21st. Where a campfire had burned at evening, the morning saw a lake four feet deep. Barrels of pork were swept away, and bateaux filled and sank.

About midnight the rain had ceased and stars had come out; but the wind still blew, and it grew very cold. Wet through, chilled to the bone, and hungry, the men looked out upon a strange scene that morning. The whole country was under water. The river, which had been but sixty yards wide, was now two hundred, and it was a torrent of "terrifying rapidity" and overwhelming force. "None but the most strong and active boatmen" tried to breast it. The rest started on foot, "making large circuits" to avoid the drowned land. "This was one of the most fatiguing marches we had as yet performed . . . having no path and being necessitated to climb the steepest hills and that without food." [34] But they had to go on or starve to death.

Those who took to the boats had an almost impossible task. The swift current tossed the clumsy bateaux here and there, upset them, and threw the boatmen and the precious provisions into the ungovernable flood. At last it seemed that the expedition must break down completely. A council of war was held. Arnold's unwavering determination so inspired officers and men that the council voted to go on. The men responded with more than courage. When any of them, exhausted by fatigue and hunger, were told by their comrades that they "would not be able to advance much further, they would raise up their half-bent bodies and force an animated look into their ghastly countenances, observing at the same time that they would soon be well enough." [35] But twenty-six hopeless cases were sent back to the hospital; forty-eight more soon followed them. Captain Hanchet of Meigs's division, with fifty men, undertook to hasten forward to get food in the Chaudière valley. Arnold went ahead of him with a small party. The supply in Greene's division was so low that the men were reduced to boiling some tallow candles in a gruel made of water and a little flour.

The rear division had now, October 25, come up with the second, Meigs having gone on. Arnold had ordered Greene and Enos to send back "as many of the Poorest men of their Detachment as would leave 15 days provision for the remainder." [36] Greene, Enos, and the officers of their respective companies met for a conference. Although not covered by Arnold's orders, the question was put whether the two whole divisions should go on or go back. Greene, his major, Bigelow, his three captains, and Enos voted to go on. Enos's captains, Williams, McCobb, and Scott, his adjutant, Hide, and Lieutenant Peters voted to abandon the expedition. It was six to five in favor of going on. Enos, "though [he] voted for proceeding, yet had undoubtedly pre-engaged" with his officers "to the contrary, as every action demonstrated." [37] He decided to abandon the enterprise. Greene's party then asked for a division of the food. Their "expostulations and entreaties" were in vain. Being "the weakest party," they could not compel the others "to a just division." Enos said that "his men were out of his power" and he could not enforce an order to divide. At last two and a half barrels of flour were given up, and Greene's men went back to the foremost divisions, "with a determined resolution to go through or die." Enos led his party down to Fort Western in eleven days of comparatively easy travel.

So the remains of the little army, now fewer than seven hundred men, struggled on. The boatmen in the few surviving bateaux fought the swift current through rapid after rapid. Those on shore found the country rougher than ever, full of hills and hollows, rocky ledges and bogs, ravines and dense forests. At last the expedition came to a point where it could leave the river and enter on a chain of ponds that extended to the edge of the Height of Land.

Their provisions were now virtually at an end. In all, there were only four or five pounds of flour for each man. "The riflemen were wholly destitute of meat before this for eight days." They took rawhide intended for mending their moccasins, chopped it into bits, and tried to make soup of it; but it remained only rawhide. Some of the officers, on the night of the 27th, had nothing but "the jawbone of a swine destitute of any covering." [38] They boiled it, with a little thickening of flour, and that constituted their "sumptuous eating." On such fare, after so long a period of starvation, they had to try the longest portage yet encountered, four miles and a quarter over the Height of Land, the watershed between the streams flowing north to the St. Lawrence and those flowing south to the Kennebec.

It was not, however, a portage for most of them; they had nothing to carry. The bateaux had been wrecked and lost until few were left. Morgan kept seven, the other companies only one each. The rest were abandoned. There was a trail of sorts, but it was interrupted by blowdowns, tangled heaps of fallen trees acres in extent which no man could penetrate. Several inches of snow had fallen, covering whatever trail should have been visible. There were mountains, ravines, bogs, and trackless woods to be got over or through. A broken leg, even a sprained ankle, meant death, for no man was strong enough to carry another. Perishing for want of food, worn down almost to the breaking point, they stumbled on and at last got over the divide and down into a beautiful meadow by the side of a brook known as Seven Mile Stream, that being its length from the meadow to Lake Megantic. But Seven Mile Stream was more than a hundred miles from Quebec, and it afforded no relief from marching, except to the few in the remaining bateaux. They had divided the rest of the provisions, five pints of flour and two ounces or less of pork to each man.

On they went, following the stream. The land fell away into a swamp, and the stream divided and divided again into false mouths, as the Mississippi divides and redivides in its water-logged delta. The marching men, struggling through the swamp in different companies, strayed from the stream at its first false mouth. They strayed again at its second. They were now deep in the swamps, far off the right track, hopelessly lost, but still floundering onward, desperately trying to reach Lake Megantic. "We went astray over mountains and through swamps, which could scarcely be passed by wild beasts," says one account, "waded a small river up to our waists, then marched on until night in our wet clothes. At night found ourselves within five miles of the place we started from. We marched fifteen miles in vain."

That night each man made himself a thin gruel of a gill of flour in water, or baked a little cake in the ashes, and nibbled a tiny scrap of pork. The country was the same as before, bogs and thickets and forests. At last the rest came on the tracks of the one company that had found Seven Mile Stream, and not long after they saw Lake Megantic, at which sight they gave "three huzzas." 39

The Chaudière, a swift running stream, drops 1,100 feet in 75 miles and is broken by dangerous rapids and falls. Arnold and Morgan tried it in their bateaux. In one rapid six of them crashed against rocks. The baggage, arms, and food in them were lost, and one man was drowned. There was a piece of good fortune in this disaster, however, for just below that rapid there was a waterfall unknown to them. "Had we been carried over [it, we] must inevitably have been dashed to pieces & all lost." 40 The two boats of Smith's and Goodrich's companies were wrecked and everything in them was lost.

"November the first dawned upon a famishing army," 41 lying in camps stretching over a distance of twenty-one miles. A few had a little food; many, having eaten their shares without care for the morrow, "set out weak and faint having nothing at all to eat; the ground covered with snow." They ate soap and hair grease. They boiled and roasted moccasins, shot pouches and old leather breeches, and chewed on them. "No one," says Morison, "can imagine, who has not experienced it, the sweetness of a roasted shot-pouch to the famished appetite." Goodrich's men "had been out of provisions for two days," without "a mouthful." They killed the captain's Newfoundland dog and ate all but the bones, which they kept for soup.

The next day many were so weak they could hardly get up from their beds. Some of them could not, and lay there waiting for death. The strongest "stumbled on . . . mile after mile," staggering "like drunken men," their heads hanging, eyes half closed, their brains in a stupor, dully wondering whether they could go one step farther. Men were dropping out of the straggling ranks and falling down, unable to get on their feet again.

"Never perhaps was there a more forlorn set of human beings collected together in one place," wrote Morison, "every one of us shivering from head to foot, as hungry as wolves and nothing to eat save the little flour we had left. . . . It was a dispiriting, heart-rending sight to see these men whose weakness was reduced to the lowest degree, struggling among rocks and in swamps and falling over the logs . . . falling down upon one another in the act of mutually assisting each other. . . . We had all along aided our weaker brethren. . . . These friendly offices could no longer be performed. Many of the men began to fall behind. . . . It was impossible to bring them along. . . . It was therefore given out . . . by our officers for every man to shift for himself and save his own life if possible." The "haggard looks" of those left behind, "their ghastly countenances, their emaciated bodies and their struggles to proceed with us . . . we saw with the bitterest anguish."

And then, at the very verge of their endurance, at the very last moment, the foremost party saw what they could not believe they really saw, horned cattle, driven by men on horses, coming to meet them. The glad cry "Provisions ahead!" was passed back from one group to another and so to those that had been left behind in the camps. "Echoes of gladness resounded from front to rear." [42] Two canoeloads of mutton and flour followed the beasts.

There was little ceremony about the slaughter of the first animal, or its division. The men grabbed the first bits they could lay their hands on, the entrails, and tore at them "as a hungry dog would tear a haunch of meat." [43] The rescue party took joints of the beef and rode on to those in the rear, the last stragglers being many miles behind. At the place of slaughter, two hundred of them, "an assembly of spectres rather than of men," [44] built fires, "laid our meat on the embers and for the first time for more than three weeks past were regaled with the incense of a sumptuous banquet." [45] "We sat down, eat up our rations, blessed our stars, and thought it luxury," says Dr. Senter.

On a pound of meat a day and a little oatmeal they pushed on with renewed spirits, although in sad physical condition. On moccasins worn through and broken shoes—Ogden had tied up his bursted shoes in a flour bag—they had yet sixty or seventy miles to march to the St. Lawrence.

But the wilderness was behind them. They were approaching civilization, or at least, Indian settlements, Sartigan the first. Arnold was there and had laid in a stock of provisions. "The men were furious, voracious and insatiable." In spite of the advice of the officers "to insure moderation, the men were outrageous upon the subject. . . . Boiled beef . . . potatoes, boiled and roasted, were gormandized without stint." Many of them fell ill; three of them died "by their imprudence." [46]

At this place they met that "noted villain," Natanis, whom Arnold had directed Steele to capture or kill, and found him to be a rather agreeable person. It appeared that he had hovered about the army all the way from the

Great Carrying Place, afraid to join it for fear he would be killed. Now, after Arnold had made a pacific address to a large group of Indians, Natanis and about fifty others joined the expedition and started with it down the Chaudière in their canoes.

The straggling force was brought together at the village of St. Mary, about halfway between Sartigan and the St. Lawrence. At this point they left the Chaudière and marched through snow, mud, and water knee-deep due north across the plains of Canada toward the great river.

On the 9th of November the habitants on the bank of the St. Lawrence saw, emerging from the woods, a band of scarecrows, their clothing "torn in pieces . . . hung in strings—few had any shoes but moggasons made of raw skins—many without hats, beards long and visages thin and meager. . . . So at last came to Point Levi 600, much resembling the animals which inhabit New Spain called the Ourang-Outang,"—600 out of 1,100 men who had started. Their journey had taken forty-five days, instead of twenty, as Arnold had predicted. They had traveled 350 miles, instead of 180, from Fort Western.[47]

Arnold's journey to Quebec is one of the most famous military marches recorded in history. If it had resulted in the capture of that stronghold it would have been celebrated as a great triumph. That it failed, by so little as it did, should not obscure its fame as a magnificent exploit. For sustained courage, undaunted resolution, and uncomplaining endurance of almost incredible hardships, those men who grimly persisted to the end deserved high honor and unstinted praise.[48]

CHAPTER 14

Quebec

The city of Quebec stands on a bold promontory between the St. Lawrence, which bends around it, and an affluent, the St. Charles. The blunt nose of the promontory points northeast, and its highest point, on the southeastern or St. Lawrence side, is Cape Diamond, a precipitous, rocky cliff that rises more than three hundred feet above the water. Toward the northwest, the St. Charles side, and toward the southwest the ground declines to somewhat lower levels. Along the base of the great cliff and around the point of the promontory a narrow band or fringe of lowland slopes gently to the water's edge and widens on the St. Charles side. Part of this, around the promontory's nose, was built up and was known as the Lower Town. It was defended in 1775 at its southern end by a blockhouse behind a double row of palisades just below the height of Cape Diamond. There were also timber barriers through which one might penetrate to Sault au Matelot, a narrow, crooked street, slanting upward from the base of the cliffs to an equally narrow, ladderlike passage into the Upper Town, the real city.

This Upper Town occupied the whole end of the higher level of the promontory and contained all the important buildings, including the citadel situated on the height of Cape Diamond. It was defended on the landward side by a strong wall thirty feet high and three-quarters of a mile long drawn across from one river to the other, from which six bold bastions projected, whereon were mounted heavy cannon. It was pierced by three gates, St. Louis Gate in the center, St. Johns near the northern part, and Palace Gate at the northerly approach to the Lower Town. Outside the main wall were certain built-up suburbs, the Palais toward the St. Charles River, St.

181

Roche in front of the north end of the wall, and St. Johns opposite its middle section. Beyond St. Roche and St. Johns to the west stretched the Plains of Abraham, where Wolfe had fought the great fight by which he took Quebec from the French in 1759.

Such was the fortress at which that little band of gaunt, ragged, starved Americans, shivering in the cold autumn wind, gazed with hope born of determination on the morning of November 9, 1775.[1]

They had come a long way and a hard way. They had reached the end of their march; yet a mile of water rolled between them and their grand objective. It was not an unguarded river that they had to cross. The frigate *Lizard* with twenty-six guns, the sloop-of-war *Hunter* with sixteen guns, four smaller armed vessels, and two transports lay at anchor, and small boats were constantly on patrol.

The shore on which Arnold's army stood had been cleared of every sort of craft by which a crossing might be made. It is not surprising that Matthias Ogden thought the "situation now seem'd somewhat ticklish. . . . We determined, however," he wrote in his journal, to "make a bold push for Quebec at all events." [2]

The first necessity was boats. They scoured the country for them. One party found twenty birch-bark canoes and carried them on their shoulders twenty-five miles to the camp. The Indian Natanis and his friends offered others. A dozen dugouts were discovered elsewhere and brought by night to the mouth of the Chaudière, where the little fleet was hid. Iron heads for pikes were forged in a near-by smithy and scaling ladders prepared. A supply of flour was procured from a neighboring mill. By Friday November 10 they were ready to attempt the crossing.[3]

But that night a storm arose, rain and a gale of wind which whipped the river into waves that would have swamped their canoes. In the evening of the 13th it blew itself out; and at nine o'clock, in black darkness, Arnold with as many of his men as could crowd into the boats started across. Midway in the river one of the canoes collapsed. Its crew was picked up by another, except Lieutenant Steele, who could find no room in the rescue boat. He clung to its stern and was towed the rest of the way, arriving nearly dead from the cold. They landed in a cove, the one in which Wolfe had landed to capture the city sixteen years before. In a deserted house a fire was kindled, and Steele was "restored . . . to his usual animation." The boats went back and brought another detachment, but when it had landed, at three in the morning, the tide was running so strong, and the moon was shining so brightly that it was deemed unsafe for the remaining 150 men to cross. They stayed on the opposite shore until the next night.[4]

The journal of one of the participants in the expedition asserts that Arnold, even with so few men, might have taken the city by attacking at once, as he had originally planned to do, because the keys of St. Johns Gate had been lost and it was unfastened. Others have denied that the gate was open. At all events, Arnold could not have known of this defect in the defenses that night. With only a part of his force at hand and no scaling ladders (there had not been room for them in the boats), he wisely did not attempt an assault.[5]

When all the men had been brought over they assembled and climbed to the level above, not by the goat-path that Wolfe had found, but by a slanting road since cut. They were now on the Plains of Abraham within a mile and a half of the city, near a large house that belonged to Major Caldwell, commandant of the Quebec militia. At the approach of Arnold's men, its occupants fled. The Americans crowded in and slept there.

The coming of the Americans was neither unexpected nor unobserved. A patrol boat had sighted the fire in the house in Wolfe's Cove and had been fired upon at Arnold's order. News of their actual arrival on the Quebec side of the river had been conveyed into the town, where there was considerable perturbation, with good reason. Carleton's command had originally consisted of two regiments of British regulars, the 7th and 26th. But at Ticonderoga, Crown Point, St. Johns, Chambly, and Sorel nearly all of them had been killed or captured. Remaining to him in Quebec were about seventy men of the 7th and a few artillerists.

During the storm that had delayed Arnold at the river side, the active and energetic Allan Maclean had slipped into the city with a force of Royal Highland Emigrants he had raised—Scottish veterans of former wars, brave in scarlet jackets faced with blue and laced with white, tartan kilts and hose, and blue bonnets edged with checkered white, red, and green; but they were few, not more than 80. Hector Cramahé, the governor of the city, had raised 200 British and 300 French Canadian militia. There were also 37 marines from the warships, 271 sailors from the armed ships in the harbor, and 74 from the transports. Maclean figured the total to be about 1,200.[6] But there were long walls to defend, and some of the militia were thought to be unreliable, inclined to desert. On the whole, Quebec, though well provided with munitions and food, was not strongly held. Cramahé felt that way about it. He wrote to General Howe, "There is too much Reason to apprehend the Affair will be soon over." [7]

But in Arnold's opinion 2,000 men would be needed "to carry the Town," [8] and he had not much more than a quarter of that number: nor had he cannon to breach the walls. Moreover, he was short of ammunition and even of small arms. So many cartridges had been spoiled by water that there were only five rounds for each man. Over a hundred muskets were found to be unserviceable. He had no artillery and no bayonets. All he could do at the time was to blockade the town on the land side, and that at the respectful distance of a mile and a half from its walls, where his men were quartered in houses.

There were occasional diversions. A small party of the garrison sallied out and captured an incautious rifleman on sentry duty. Arnold immediately paraded his troops and marched them "bravado-like" [9] "within 80 rods of the wall . . . in such a manner that they could not discover of what number we consisted of," [10] which must have been a difficult job of deception. Cannon were fired upon them, with no hurt. They "gave 3 huzzas" and returned to their lodgings.

In the afternoon following their arrival, Arnold had sent Matthias Ogden, with a white flag and a drum, to deliver to Cramahé a demand for surrender. Ogden was within a hundred feet of St. Johns Gate when a gun thundered and an 18-pound shot hit the ground near him. He "retreated in quick time." [11] Assuming a misunderstanding of his intentions, Arnold sent another letter the next day, with a similar result. The only course was to continue the blockade.

It was no hardship. For the first time since they set out from Newburyport, two months before, the troops had clean, warm, comfortable lodgings and plenty of good food. They would doubtless have been glad to fight it out on that line—in that manner—if it took all winter. That was also quite evidently the intention of Maclean, who had taken over the command of the city from Cramahé. He burned a part of the suburb of St. Johns and certain other houses near the walls, to prevent the Americans from using them as cover, and settled down to hold out against the siege.

But the Americans were soon routed out of their comfortable quarters. On the 18th they had news that Maclean was about to make a sortie and to attack them with 800 men. Also it was reported that a ship with 200 men was coming up the river, and that the *Lizard* had taken a station above the camp to cut off their retreat. A council of war decided to withdraw. So, at four o'clock in the morning of the 19th, "a severely dark and cold night," [12] the entire force started on a march to Pointe aux Trembles—now Neuville—twenty miles up the river. "Most of the soldiers were in constant misery during this march, as they were bare footed, and the ground was frozen and very uneven." [13] In a village at the point they were again quartered in houses. There they remained for nearly two weeks, recuperating their wasted bodies and availing themselves of an opportunity to make shoes out of the hides of the beeves they had killed for food.

It was a gloomy time. For all the effort they had made, all the hardships they had endured to get to Quebec, this period of inactivity was their only reward. The coveted city seemed as far away as when they left Fort Western. They were not even blockading it. Provisions and fuel were being smuggled into it without hindrance. On their march up the river, they had seen an armed schooner go past them, and a little later the sound of a salvo of artillery was heard. Carleton had come to take command, as they soon learned. That was bad news.

But at last good news did come. On December 2 a topsail schooner and several other craft were sighted coming down the river. In the evening a boat put off from the schooner, and, in the light of lanterns and flaring torches, there stepped ashore into a foot of snow "a gentle, polite Man, tall and slender . . . resolute, mild and of a fine Temper," [14] "well limbed, tall and handsome, though his face was much pock-marked," with "an air and manner that designated the real soldier." [15] Richard Montgomery had come from Montreal.

He had brought 300 men and, what was even more important, artillery and "a good supply of ammunition, clothing and provisions." [16] To the troops paraded in front of the little church he made an "energetic and elegant speech, the burden of which was an applause for our spirit in passing the wilderness, a hope for perseverance . . . and a promise of warm clothing. . . . A few huzzas from our freezing bodies were returned to this address of the gallant hero. Now new life was infused into the whole of the corps." [17]

The men liked Montgomery, and he liked them. He wrote to Schuyler: "I find Colonel Arnold's corps an exceeding fine one, inured to fatigue. . . . There is a style of discipline among them much superior to what I have been used to see in this campaign. He himself is active, intelligent and enterprising. . . . I must say he has brought with him many pretty young men." [18]

Montgomery had captured a year's supply of clothing of the 7th and 26th British regiments. Their winter uniforms were Canadian capotes, long, white, full-skirted overcoats of a heavy blanket material, trimmed and bound with blue, and with cape-hoods. The underjackets were of similar material, with corduroy sleeves. Leggings of heavy blue cloth, really overalls, were strapped over sealskin moccasins and reached to the waist. The caps were of red cloth, with a band of brown fur around the base, and were ornamented at the back with a fur tail.[19] These garments were now distributed in part.

Supplementary distributions were made later to the whole force. On the 5th, they marched back to Quebec, the artillery and stores following in bateaux.

The two American forces took up positions before the town: Arnold on the left, the northern side, in half-burned St. Roche, taking over the General Hospital in that suburb; Montgomery on the Plains midway between St. Roche and Cape Diamond. Now again Quebec was blockaded, but it was not Montgomery's intention to rely upon siege tactics. He well knew that they would not suffice to fulfill the desires of his superiors and of the American colonies in general. They wanted the town taken, and they expected him to take it. Schuyler wrote on November 18 that "in all probability the entire possession of Canada . . . will be [ours] soon." [20] Knox had "very little doubt" of Montgomery's success.[21] Washington on December 5 wrote to Schuyler, "I flatter myself that it will be effected when General Montgomery joins him [Arnold] and our Conquest of Canada be compleat." [22] Indeed, the commander in chief was relying on the spoils of Canada for his own troops, as he wrote to Montgomery: "I must beg . . . your attention to the Wants of the Army here, which are not few, and if they cannot in some Parts be supplied by you, I do not Know where else I can apply." Powder he wanted and arms, blankets, and clothing, of all which he understood there was "an Abundance in Canada." [23] The Congress was urgent for the possession of the town and vocal in its urgency. Clearly, Quebec must be taken by one means or another.

But a siege, without great battering guns to breach the wall, must needs be a slow, long drawn-out affair, and of time Montgomery had little to spare. He could not dig trenches to approach the town in the classic manner. He had no engineer to plan them, and they could not be dug in frozen soil. The term of enlistment of all Arnold's New England troops would expire with the year, and Montgomery had no hope of retaining them after that. It would be most difficult, if not impossible, to obtain fresh supplies of ammunition, and even of food, for Montgomery had no money except Continental paper, which would not pass in Canada. And by April, when the ice in the river broke up, British reinforcements could certainly come. A siege would not do.

Montgomery had been fully aware of all that even before he came, and had no intention of relying on a siege. He had written to Robert Livingston from Montreal giving his reasons why "to storming the place . . . we must come at last." [24] He wrote to Schuyler on the day of his arrival before Quebec that he meant "to assault the works, I believe towards the lower town, which is the weakest part." Meanwhile, he proposed "amusing Mr.

Carleton with a formal attack, erecting batteries, &c." He was sorry to have to assault, because he knew "the melancholy consequences," but saw no escape from it.[25]

First, however, he must go through the customary formality of summoning the garrison. He wrote a letter to Carleton in the usual terms. Being mindful of the manner in which Arnold's similar letters had been treated, he had recourse to a ruse. A woman carried the summons to the Palace Gate and said to the guard she had an important communication for the General. Being admitted, she told him she had a letter for him from the American General. Carleton called a drummer boy and bade him take the paper with the tongs and thrust it into the fire. He sent her back to tell Montgomery that he would receive no communication from a rebel.

Ten days later Montgomery tried again. He wrote a fierce letter, calling Carleton's attention to the weakness of his situation in the town, the great extent of his works manned only by "a motley crew of sailors, most of them our friends . . . citizens, who wish to see us within the walls, a few of the worst troops, that call themselves soldiers." He boasted of his own men "accustomed to success, confident of the righteousness of the cause they are engaged in, inured to danger and fatigue, and so highly incensed at your inhumanity . . . that it is with difficulty I restrain them, until my batteries are ready, from assaulting your works, which would give them a fair opportunity of ample vengeance and just retaliation." If Carleton persisted "in an unwarrantable defence," the consequences were to be on his head.[26] In a word, he tried to scare Carleton. But Carleton refused to take fright. When another woman smuggled this demand into the city, she was first imprisoned and then drummed out of town. As a last resort and in an effort to alarm the citizens, a flight of arrows, each bearing a copy of the letter, was shot over the walls with as little result.

Meanwhile, Montgomery was at work on those threatened batteries. Arnold's force advanced to within 150 yards of the wall, and planted five small mortars. On the heights, 700 yards from the town, in the fiercely cold night of December 10, in a heavy snowstorm driven by a northeast gale, a more formidable American battery was begun. Night by night after that gabions were set up there, filled with snow, and then drenched with water, which froze them into solid blocks of ice. In this battery five 6- and 12-pounders and a howitzer were emplaced. From these two positions a heavy fire was poured upon the walls and into the town, "with very little effect," as Montgomery admitted.[27] But Carleton's response with 13-inch shells and 32-pound balls was too much of an answer. Several men were killed, the ice-battery was shattered, and the guns were dismounted.

One more effort was made to induce Carleton to surrender. Arnold and Macpherson, with flag and drum, approached the walls. To a messenger sent to meet them they announced a desire to speak with Carleton. The reply was decisive. He would not see them. Would he receive a letter, then? He would not. They could make the best of their way off, for he would receive nothing from Mr. Montgomery.

Within the town Carleton had organized his men. The fusiliers of the 7th, the marines and Royal Scottish, 425 in all, were commanded by Maclean. Major Caldwell commanded 330 British militia. Colonel Voyer led 543 French Canadian militiamen, and Captain Hamilton the sailors and artificers from the ships, 570 of them. Thus there were over 1,800 to defend the town against Montgomery's force, no more than 800 in all. But *Audaces fortuna juvat* was Montgomery's motto.[28]

He was preparing for the attack, but he met with obstacles. The town-meeting spirit became prevalent, especially among Arnold's New Englanders —so much so that it was recognized as necessary "to have the approbation of all the officers and soldiers." That was hard to get. Everybody wanted the town taken, but not everybody wanted to take it. Many of them "appeared unwilling to attempt so daring an enterprise." [29]

The trouble seems to have originated in three of Arnold's officers, Captain Oliver Hanchet of Connecticut and Captains William Goodrich and Jonas Hubbard of Massachusetts. Hanchet, who had "incurred Colonel Arnold's displeasure by some misconduct and thereby given room for harsh language, is at the bottom of it," [30] wrote Montgomery to Schuyler on December 26. These three proposed to organize a separate corps under command of Major John Brown, who had disliked and distrusted Arnold from the time of their first meeting. Montgomery would not allow this. The three companies then appeared to be "very averse from" the proposed assault. "This dangerous party threatens the ruin of our officers," said Montgomery. But he met Arnold's officers "to compose some matters, which were happily settled." [31] He then paraded Arnold's troops, and addressed them "in a very sensible Spirited manner, which greatly animated" them.[32] "The fire of patriotism kindled in our breasts," wrote one of the Connecticut recalcitrants, "and we resolved to follow wherever he should lead." [33]

The attack was to be made in a dark and stormy night, "in the first northwester." [34] The Lower Town, the weakest in its defenses, was to be the primary objective. While a third of the troops, with ladders, feinted an escalade of the Cape Diamond bastion, another third was to attack the

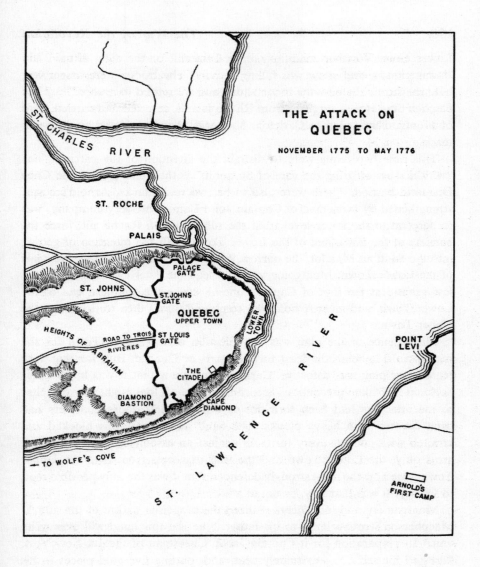

THE ATTACK ON
QUEBEC

NOVEMBER 1775 TO MAY 1776

ST. CHARLES RIVER

ST. ROCHE

PALAIS

PALACE GATE

ST. JOHNS

ST. JOHNS GATE

QUEBEC
UPPER TOWN

LOWER TOWN

HEIGHTS OF ABRAHAM

ROAD TO TROIS RIVIÈRES

ST. LOUIS GATE

THE CITADEL

POINT LEVI

DIAMOND BASTION

CAPE DIAMOND

← TO WOLFE'S COVE

ST. LAWRENCE RIVER

ARNOLD'S FIRST CAMP

Lower Town. Weather conditions seemed suitable on the night of the 27th. It was cloudy, and snow was falling heavily. The troops were assembled, but "the storm abated—the moon shone and we retired to repose." [35] Then Stephen Singleton, a sergeant from Rhode Island, deserted and carried word of Montgomery's plan to Carleton. So it was abandoned, and another was made.

This time two feints were to distract the attention of the garrison, one "with a shew of firing the gate of St. John," [36] the other against the Cape Diamond bastion. There were also to be two real attacks. Arnold's corps, strengthened by forty men of Captain John Lamb's artillery company, was to descend to the lower level from the suburb of St. Roche and force the barriers at the north end of the Lower Town, with the intention of getting into the Sault au Matelot, the narrow, crooked street that led into the heart of the Lower Town. Montgomery was to lead the 1st New York along the low ground at the foot of Cape Diamond, strike the southern end of the Lower Town, and meet Arnold, the combined forces then to drive into the Upper Town.

The essence of the plan was the selection of the Lower Town for the real assault, it being the least fortified part of Quebec. But, for that very reason, the plan was defective. Carleton well knew that it was his Achilles heel and had taken precautions accordingly. Houses that might afford shelter to the attackers had been torn down; windows and doors of others had been covered with heavy planks. The Sault au Matelot was blocked and covered with guns at every turn. As against an assault by men with small arms only, the Lower Town and the way of access from it to the Upper Town were now the most strongly defended; but it was the only possible road to victory. It was that way, or not at all.

Montgomery and his officers realized the desperate nature of the attack. Macpherson wrote a letter to his father, "the last this hand will ever write you." In preparation for it Captain Jacob Cheesman of the 1st New York "dressed himself . . . extremely neat, and, putting five gold pieces in his pocket, said that would be sufficient to bury him with decency." [37] But there was no flinching from the attempt.

The plan made and all the parts in it assigned, the Americans waited for a dark and stormy night. But the weather on Thursday the 29th and on Friday was "clear and mild." Saturday morning was fair; but in the afternoon the sky was clouded, the wind rose and brought a spit of snow. Heavy darkness came at sunset. As the night wore on the snow fell more and more heavily, "a thick small Snow" driven by an "outrageous" [38] wind into great drifts heaped and piled upon that which had fallen before, and which had already covered the earth to a depth of two to three feet. The time had come.

At two o'clock in the morning the men were assembled at their respective stations. Soon after four o'clock signal rockets were fired, and the advance began. The storm, a terrific blizzard, was at its height. The wind from the northwest drove snow mixed with hail into the faces of the men as they stumbled through six-foot drifts in the blackest darkness.

The rockets were a signal to the Americans, but they were also a signal to the town. Drums beat to arms. The great bell of the cathedral, the lesser bells of the Jesuit College, of the Recollet monastery, and of the Hôtel Dieu clanged the alarm. Officers ran through the streets shouting, "Turn out! Turn out!" The city's troops rushed to their posts. Lanterns on poles were thrust out over the top of the walls. Flaming fire balls were thrown from the ramparts to light up the ground outside. The little American mortar battery at St. Roche went into action, throwing shells into the town to divert the enemy's attention from the real points of attack. The guns on the walls roared in reply.

Amid this tumult the two feinting parties made their way toward the walls. Livingston's corps of Canadians was near St. Johns Gate, when they broke and ran. The other party, a hundred Massachusetts men led by Captain Jacob Brown, John's brother, kept up a rattling fire against the Cape Diamond bastion. Some militia were sent to reinforce the defenders there, but otherwise little attention was paid to Brown's efforts. Carleton's mind was not distracted from the Lower Town.

Meanwhile, Montgomery and Arnold had marched. Montgomery at the head of the 1st New York, about 300 men in single file, set out on the long circuit around the Diamond bastion, down the slanting road to the fringe of lowland along the river. The way down to Wolfe's Cove was a mile long, steep, narrow, and heaped with drifted snow; and the storm still raged. That part was bad almost beyond bearing. The rest was worse. On the narrow strip of land below the heights the high tides had piled "enormous and rugged masses of ice," [39] creating such obstacles that the men had to clamber up the steep slope of the cliff to get around them. They slipped, slid, and fell. Those that carried the unwieldy scaling ladders, which had been brought across the river, could hardly make way at all. There were two miles of this before they reached the first defenses of the Lower Town.

Arnold had formed his own corps of 600 men, with a forlorn hope of twenty-five men in advance led by himself and Eleazer Oswald, a volunteer. A hundred yards behind these Captain John Lamb and his forty artillerists dragged a 6-pounder on a sled. Behind them again came the riflemen, Morgan's company, followed by Smith's under command of Lieutenant Steele, and Hendricks's company. The New Englanders (except Dearborn's men, who had been late in assembling) with about forty Canadians and Indians, brought up the rear. They set out from St. Roche in Indian file and passed a two-gun battery without discovery. Hurrying on through deep snow, "deeper than in the fields" above, the van got by the Palace Gate unassailed. The main body, "covering the locks of our guns with the lappets of our coats, holding down our heads" against the driving storm, had also safely passed the Gate, when it "received a tremendous fire of musketry from the ramparts above." For a third of a mile, men falling here and there, they ran that gantlet without a possibility of a reply. "We could see nothing but the blaze from the muzzles of their muskets." [40]

At the waterside ships were moored with cables stretched to the houses. In the darkness some of the men ran into these and were thrown down violently. At last they came into a narrow street blocked by a barricade, mounting two guns.

Arnold's plan was to separate his force, right and left, and let Lamb's gun batter the barrier, while Morgan went around its end on the river ice and took it in the rear. But the 6-pounder had been abandoned in a snowdrift sometime before this. One of the guns of the barrier was fired at them with little effect. The other failed to go off. Arnold called on his men to rush the barricade. They responded, ran to it, and fired through the portholes. A bullet from one of the near-by houses hit a rock, ricocheted and hit Arnold in the leg below the knee. He still shouted encouragement to his men; but his wound was bleeding freely, and he had to be supported by two men to the rear and so to the hospital.

By general acclaim Morgan was called upon to take command instead of Lieutenant Colonel Greene. A ladder was set against the barrier, and Morgan mounted it, calling on his men to follow. As his head topped the barricade, a blaze of fire met him. Stunned, he fell backward and lay in the snow, with one bullet through his cap, another through his beard, and grains of burnt powder embedded in his face. In a moment he was on his feet. Up the ladder again he went, and over the top of the fence. His knee hit one of the cannon, and he rolled beneath it. Before any of the defenders could get at him, Charles Porterfield was over, and then the rest. The enemy, followed by the riflemen's bullets, fled into a house and out the back way. But Morgan had run around it, and he shouted to them to surrender if they wanted quarter. They all surrendered. The way into the Lower Town was open.

The Sault au Matelot lay ahead. They entered it. Two or three hundred yards up that street there was another barrier. Behind it was a platform with cannon. The gate in the barrier was open. Now was the time to break through, for the garrison was offering no resistance. Some of them, Canadians, seemed ready to welcome the Americans, shouted, *"Vive la liberté!"* and held out welcoming hands. The whole town appeared to be panic-stricken. Morgan urged his officers to push on through the gate. But there were few men with him. The rest of that long straggling line had not yet come up. He actually had more prisoners than he had of his own men. It was pitch-dark. The storm was still raging. None of the men knew the way through the crooked street and its alleyways, and they had no guide. This was the place appointed to meet Montgomery. The officers decided to stay there until their whole force came up and Montgomery joined them.

After a time the rest of the troops began to arrive, Hendricks and his riflemen, Greene, Meigs, and Bigelow with the Yankees. It was about day-break when the major part of the American force was again assembled and formed for another attack. But the town had recovered its senses. Troops had been sent to meet the Americans. A party of them sallied out through the gate in the barrier. Lieutenant Anderson, leading them, called on Morgan to surrender. Morgan shot him through the head. Anderson's men retreated, and for a while there was a pause. The spirit of fraternization again prevailed. Men from either side called to the others by name. But that was soon over, and the Americans went at the high barrier.

Mounds of snow were heaped up, ladders set on them. Morgan climbed one, Porterfield another. Humphreys, Lamb, Greene, Meigs, and yet more went up, but the houses in the street beyond were filled with fighting men. Muskets blazed from the windows. A little way up the street a double line of fusiliers presented their bayonets. No one could dare that defense. And upon the Americans and among them fell a shower of bullets. Humphreys fell, and Hendricks, and many another. Lamb and Steele, and more and more, were wounded, while their assailants were safe in the houses.

Yet, though their pieces were wet and most of them failed to fire, the Americans fought on. They tried to outflank the barricade, but it stretched from the bluff to the river. They dared the ladders again and again, even thrust one over the fence to climb down on; but to go over the top would have been sheer suicide. There was a stone house at the end of the barricade, whose gable-end windows looked down beyond the barrier. Riflemen there could shoot down on the defenders, perhaps drive them back. The Americans broke in, but the enemy had perceived the threat of the house. The ladder the Americans had left inside the barrier was set against the house, and a party of the defenders climbed it, entered through a window, came down the stairs, bayonets fixed. There was a fierce fight, in the house, but the Americans were driven out.

In the street again they were under fire of a 9-pounder hastily brought up, and of musketry as before. They retreated for a space, and the officers consulted. Some of them still looked for Montgomery and wanted to hold their position until night. The majority saw the hopelessness of the situation. It was decided to give up the attempt and withdraw.

But Carleton had moved to prevent that. He had sent Captain Laws out of the Palace Gate, with 200 men and two fieldpieces to follow the Americans' tracks down to the lower level and take them in the rear. Laws came running up the Sault au Matelot, and shouted to the Americans to surrender. They jeered at him, cried out that he was their prisoner. He looked around and saw that he was quite alone. His men had not followed as fast as he had run. Expecting them to come on at once, the Americans threw themselves into the houses along the street.

Laws's delayed party arrived, and for a while a desultory fire was maintained. But the Americans' situation was desperate. Hemmed in, front and back, the officers hastily consulted again. Morgan proposed cutting through the force in their rear. Others were for holding on until Montgomery came. But their plight was beyond hope. They were, in Carleton's words, "compleatly ruined . . . caught, as it were, in a Trap." They began to throw down their arms.

Morgan had disdained the shelter offered by the houses. He stood in the street facing his enemies. When he saw that surrender was inevitable, he set his back against a wall, and, with tears of rage and disappointment streaming down his face, defied the enemy to take his sword. They threatened to shoot him. His men implored him not to sacrifice his life. He saw a man in clerical dress in the crowd confronting him and called to him, "Are you a priest?" He was. "Then I give my sword to you. But not a scoundrel of these cowards shall take it out of my hands." [41] So ended that fight, three hours long, in the Sault au Matelot.

But where was Montgomery? His tale of disaster is soon told.

He and some of his men, having overcome the obstacles in their way, came to a barricade. Saws went to work on it. Montgomery himself took a hand, tearing down the half-sawed posts. With Macpherson and Captain Cheesman at his side, he led the forlorn hope through and was confronted by a blockhouse. No more than fifty or sixty of his men followed him. The rest were still struggling with the difficulties of their road. Montgomery and his little band advanced against the blockhouse. No shot was fired from it. They passed it, went on for a hundred yards, came to another barrier, cut through it, rounded Point Diamond, entered on a narrow road, and saw another building before them, a dwelling house. It was loopholed, armed with four small guns, 3-pounders, and held by a corporal with eight British militiamen, a captain and thirty French Canadians, a ship captain, Adam Barnsfair, and nine sailors. John Coffin, a Boston Tory, was with them. Montgomery "called to his men to Come on; they did not advance as quick as he thought they might, he Spoke to them again in the following moving Terms, saying Come on my good soldiers, your General calls you to Come on." [42]

Coffin encouraged the men in the house to withhold their fire until the Americans, indistinctly seen in the darkness and snow, should come closer. Barnsfair and his men stood by their guns with lighted matches ready. Montgomery, Macpherson, and Cheesman, with Aaron Burr, Edward Antil, a sergeant, and a dozen men pushed forward. They were within a few paces of the house, when there came from it a burst of gunfire, grapeshot and bullets. Another burst and another raked the narrow street, until not one of that forlorn hope was left standing. In the snow lay a dozen men. Montgomery was dead, shot through the head. Macpherson and Cheesman lay beside him. Burr, Antil, and one or two others got away unhurt.

That was the end of the attack on the Cape Diamond end of the Lower Town. Colonel Donald Campbell took command and ordered a retreat. What was left of Montgomery's corps struggled back through the storm. Dearborn's belated company, trying to come up with Arnold's division, was caught on the road between two fires and surrendered. Carleton sent out a small force which seized the little battery at St. Roche, picking up Lamb's 6-pounder on the way.

Carleton captured 426 men, sound or wounded, including 30 officers and 5 gentlemen volunteers. The number killed or wounded and not captured may have been 60. The British loss was 5 killed and 13 wounded.[43] There were left to Arnold perhaps 600 men, including such Canadians and Indians as had joined him. Of these, more than 100 time-expired men soon left him, and there were other defections.

Arnold withdrew his little force about a mile, erected defences of frozen snow, and sent Edward Antil to Montreal for reinforcements. But General Wooster, in command there, had only five or six hundred men with whom to hold that town, as well as Chambly and St. Johns. No help could be had from him. Antil went on to Schuyler at Albany. But everything there was in confusion and alarm, because of Tory uprisings along the Mohawk and in Tryon County. There were no reinforcements available for Arnold. Antil went on to Philadelphia, to the Congress, bearing a letter from Schuyler. The Congress, on January 19, voted to reinforce the army in Canada "with all possible despatch," called on New Hampshire, Connecticut, New York, Pennsylvania, and New Jersey for troops for that purpose, and asked Washington to detach one battalion and send it north. It also authorized Moses Hazen to raise a regiment in Canada, Antil to be lieutenant colonel.[44]

From Montreal, Wooster sent 120 men near the end of January, and himself followed later with 60 more. In February, 25 came from Massachusetts. Hard money, some $28,000, was sent to encourage Arnold, now a brigadier general by grace of the Congress. Troops were coming from here and there, but slowly. In the middle of March, Arnold had 617 rank and file, besides Livingston's not very trustworthy Canadians. But smallpox had put 400 of Arnold's men in hospital, and every sort of supplies, food as well as military equipment, was lacking in Montreal and in Arnold's camp. Yet, all this while, Carleton made no move to attack those few hundreds who were still, with some success, blockading his town. He may have had in mind the fate of Montcalm's army, when it sallied out to meet Wolfe on those same Plains of Abraham. At all events he made no hostile move, but busied himself with strengthening his defensive works.

At last, on April 2, Wooster came to the camp with troops that made up the American force to 2,000 men. He took command. Arnold, injured by a fall from his horse, withdrew to Montreal. Wooster mounted batteries on the Heights and on Pointe Lévis and bombarded the town, to which it replied vigorously and with heavier metal. He also made an unsuccessful attempt to burn the vessels in the harbor by means of a fireship.

Early in May, Wooster was superseded by General John Thomas, a more capable, more energetic officer. He found the army, which had been built up to 2,500 men, now reduced by discharges, death, and desertions to 1,900, of whom no more than 1,000, including officers, were fit for duty. The time of 300 had already expired, and 200 more were under inoculation. No more than 500 could be relied upon. A mere ghost of an army was besieging a strongly fortified town of 5,000 inhabitants, mounting 148 cannon, with a garrison of 1,600 fit to fight, besides a frigate, a sloop of war, and several smaller armed vessels as auxiliaries. It was an absurd situation, yet Carleton remained within the walls.

More men were on their way to Thomas, the 2nd New Jersey Regiment and six companies of the 2nd Pennsylvania. Some of them had already arrived when, on May 2, there came bad news from the opposite quarter. A

British fleet, fifteen ships, had entered the mouth of the St. Lawrence. On the 7th, their masts and spars could be descried. General John Burgoyne was coming, with seven Irish regiments, one English, and 2,000 hired German mercenaries. That was the end of the siege of Quebec.

A force of 900 of the garrison, with four fieldpieces, issued from the town. Thomas, with difficulty, gathered a force of 250 to oppose it; his stand was but momentary. His whole army began to retreat, and in no orderly fashion. In a panic the gunners abandoned their pieces. The men under inoculation threw away their muskets and fled. The invalids in the hospital left their beds and stumbled and staggered toward the woods. The Canadian teamsters employed in the service of the army threw up their jobs and left. Clothing, provisions, and stores, even the orderly books and records in headquarters, had to be abandoned. Bateaux loaded with invalids and such stores as could be hastily gathered pushed up the St. Lawrence. Two tons of precious gunpowder, a hundred barrels of flour, and all the hospital stores were seized by the enemy, as they were about to be loaded into boats. One of the American regiments, across the river at Pointe Lévis, was intercepted and had to scatter into the woods. The main body marching on the road by the river, deep with mud, was divided for lack of food. Parties went here and there to levy on the inhabitants, took food by force. It was a mob of muddy, hungry, tired men, wounded men, men sick with smallpox, rather than an army, that streamed westward, leaving the dead and dying in its wake. Enemy ships passed them. Marines landed to cut them off, were driven back, and the struggle westward went on.

At Deschambault, forty miles up the river, Thomas halted his shattered forces and held a council of war. A stand at that point was voted down, and the retreat was resumed, to end at last on the 17th at Sorel, at the mouth of the Richelieu, where certain troops on their way to Quebec were met. Colonel William Maxwell's 2nd New Jersey, which had been left at Trois Rivières as a rear guard, was called in. The regiment which had fled from Pointe Lévis had made its way to the main force. So now all that was left of Thomas's army was gathered together in a disorganized mass, with hardly a trace of military system, "without order or regularity, eating up provisions as fast as they were brought in," [45] a mere mob.

Thomas described it: "A retreating army, disheartened by unavoidable misfortunes, destitute of almost every necessary to render their lives comfortable or even tolerable, sick and (as they think) wholly neglected and [with] no prospect of speedy relief." He himself was ill with the smallpox. There was nothing to do except to continue to retreat. On the 2nd of June, while his men were on the march up the Richelieu to Chambly, he died.

Moses Hazen, temporarily in command at Montreal in the absence of Arnold (who had gone down to Sorel and up the Richelieu with Thomas's force) directed Colonel Timothy Bedel, with 400 men, to hold a small, fortified post at the Cedars, about thirty miles above Montreal. With 150 English and Canadians and 500 Indians, Captain Forster marched against it. Bedel, suffering with the smallpox, went back to Montreal, leaving Major Isaac Butterfield in charge. On the arrival of Forster's troops, Butterfield surrendered without any real contest. A reinforcing American regiment under Major Henry Sherburne was waylaid and, after a gallant fight, overpowered and captured. Arnold, indignant at Butterfield's cowardice, took the field, met Forster, demanded and obtained the return of the captives by promising an exchange, and returned to Montreal.

But reinforcements for Thomas's sadly battered troops were on the way. Brigadier General William Thompson, formerly colonel of one of the Pennsylvania rifle regiments at Cambridge, was coming with a brigade of four regiments dispatched by Washington, comprising 2,000 musketmen, a company of riflemen, and one of artificers. Brigadier John Sullivan led a brigade of 3,300 from New York. He had been directed to take over Thomas's command. On June 1 he arrived at St. Johns, where Thompson's troops had been lying for two weeks. With the fresh and full supplies of food, ammunition, small arms, and cannon brought by these new troops, the prospects for a reinstatement of American fortunes in Canada seemed bright. Everybody was on tiptoe for a second march against Quebec.

The primary objective was to be Trois Rivières, about halfway between Montreal and Quebec, and the coveted stronghold. It was supposed to be held by no more than 800 regulars and Canadians under Maclean. Sullivan ordered Thompson to take it with 2,000 of the best of the Americans. On June 6 they embarked in bateaux and dropped down the river to a point ten miles above Trois Rivières. In the evening of the next day they embarked again for a night attack. William Maxwell, Anthony Wayne, Arthur St. Clair, William Irvine, all men of mettle, led their respective regiments. Thompson himself was a notable fighting man.

At three in the morning of June 8 they landed about three miles above the town. Leaving 250 men to guard the boats, they marched in silence, intending to attack at four points with St. Clair, Maxwell, Irvine, and Wayne leading the several detachments. They had for a guide a habitant, one Antoine Gautier. Whether intentionally or not, he misled them. They tried to recover the right road by going across country, got into a great swamp, and were completely mired. They floundered about in the slimy mud. Shoes and even boots were sucked off their feet. It was near daybreak when they got out and found the road along the shore and close to the river.

Two or three armed vessels fired on them as they came up. For three-quarters of a mile they were under a fire that, having no artillery, they could not return. They swung away into the woods, intending to make a circuit and to return to the road. But they got into "the most Horrid swamp that ever man set foot in," [46] sank in it up to their middles.

Warning of their approach had been brought to the town. A surprise was no longer possible. But they had been told by the Congress that it was "of the highest importance that a post be taken at De Chambeaux." [47] Washington had said to Thomas, "The lower down [the river] you can maintain a stand the more advantageous it will be." He had said, too, that the Quebec "misfortune must be repaired," [48] and Trois Rivières was the first step to that end. They kept on.

For two or three hours they fought their way through the swamp and the tangled forest. At eight o'clock they saw a clearing a quarter of a mile ahead, firm ground. They had been divided, even scattered, in the swampy jungle. Wayne, with 200 men, got out first and saw a body of regulars bearing down upon him.

He threw forward a company of light infantry and one of riflemen, formed the rest, and opened fire. The enemy, twice as many as they, gave back, broke, and fled. Thompson and the rest of his force came out and saw the village lying between them and the river. But between it and themselves they also saw a line of entrenchments. Burgoyne with more than 8,000 men was on his way up the St. Lawrence, and perhaps three-quarters of them had arrived at Trois Rivières.

The Americans attacked, probably not aware of the odds they faced. A heavy fire from the ships and from the trenches converged upon them. It was impossible to advance against it. They fell back into the woods. Thompson tried to rally them for another effort, but they were scattered and disorganized. An irregular fire was kept up for a time. Then the inevitable retreat began.

A British force was landed from the ships above them to cut them off. They could not escape by the road, and another column was coming against their rear. Broken up into larger or smaller parties, each acting for itself, now making a stand and now retreating, they left the road, took to the woods. They were stalked by Indians, ambushed by Canadian irregulars. Through endless swamps and a wilderness of forest, they fled northward for two days. Major Grant held against them their only gateway of escape, the bridge across the Rivière du Loup. Carleton might have captured them

all, but he did not want them. What would he do with them? He had no
provisions to spare, nor were there any in Quebec. Let them go and tell of
his mercy to the people at home. He recalled Grant from the bridge, and
on the third day after the battle, the remains of that proud little army, 1,100
men "almost worn out with fatigue, Hunger & Difficulties scarcely to be
paralleled," [49] their faces and hands swollen by the stings of "Musketoes of
a Monstrous size and innumerable numbers" reached Sorel.

Their losses are not ascertainable. In spite of his prudent leniency Carleton found that he had 236 prisoners on his hands, men who had given themselves up rather than attempt a seemingly impossible escape. The guards of
the Americans' bateaux had escaped in their boats. About 400 in all were
killed, captured, or lost in the woods and swamps. The British lost in killed
and wounded about a dozen.

There were supposed to be 8,000 American troops in all the Champlain
and St. Lawrence regions; but, because of the inroads of the smallpox and
the results of fatigue and deprivation, not 5,000 could have been counted
as effectives, even by straining that term to the limit, before the affair at
Trois Rivières. After it, nearly half of that number, six of the freshest regiments, had been routed, cut to pieces, and completely demoralized. Supplies
of every kind, including food, were lacking, as usual. To get them up from
New York would take weeks at best. There was no money to buy provisions
in Canada. And over 8,000 hearty, well furnished British regulars were
gathering at Trois Rivières. They might march around Sorel to Chambly
and bottle up Sullivan's army on the Richelieu below, then cut off Arnold's
force at Chambly. They were, in fact, on June 13, on their way up the river
by land and in transports.

A letter from Sullivan to Schuyler describes the plight of his army. He
wanted to hold Sorel, he said, but he had only 2,500 men there and 1,000
at other posts, "most of the latter being under inoculation, and those regiments, which had not the small-pox, expecting every day to be taken down
with it." The enemy's force was reported to be "exceedingly superior to
ours," which was certainly true. "I found myself at the head of a dispirited
Army, filled with horror at the thought of seeing their enemy. . . . Smallpox, famine and disorder had rendered them almost lifeless. . . . I found
a great panick . . . among both officers and soldiers . . . no less than
40 officers begged leave to resign. . . . However strongly I might fortify
Sorel, my men would in general leave me." [50]

Even the aggressive Arnold thought there was "more honour in making
a safe retreat than in hazarding a battle against such superiority." "The junction of the Canadas is now at an end," he wrote to Schuyler. "Let us quit

them and secure our own country before it is too late." [51] There was no doubt in anyone's mind that the game was up.

It was by a close margin that the Americans got away at all. The British fleet was at Sorel within an hour after the last of Sullivan's bateaux pulled away up the Richelieu. Arnold, back at Montreal, held on to that town to the last moment. Then, with the remains of its garrison, no more than 300 men, he crossed the river to Longueuil and set out for St. Johns, with the enemy close at his heels.[52]

The two forces having been joined, the whole army, if that mob of hungry, ragged, beaten men, discouraged, disorganized, and rotten with smallpox, could still be called an "army," crowded into boats sent up by Schuyler and pushed off for Ile aux Noix. They were hardly out of musket shot when the van of their pursuers arrived on the shore.[53]

Ile aux Noix is a low, flat island, about a mile long and a quarter-mile wide. A single farm occupied a slight elevation in the middle of it. The rest was a brush-covered waste, with swamps here and there. On this unwholesome desert the 8,000 wretched fugitives disembarked. Two thousand of them were hospital cases already, smallpox cases. Within two days after they landed, a quarter of the rest were stricken with malarial fever or dysentery.

There were not tents enough to shelter even the desperately sick men. Frequent thunderstorms drenched those that lay under rude shelters thatched with brush and grass. Mosquitoes and black flies swarmed in millions, tormenting and torturing sick and well alike. There was no food except salt pork and flour, and not enough wood for fires to cook even that. Medicines gave out. The few surgeons were exhausted. The moans and groans of the sick, of the dying men tortured by the itching and burning of that most loathsome disease, smallpox, could be heard everywhere. And they died like flies. Common grave pits were opened and filled day after day with corpses wrapped in their filthy blankets.

The sights and sounds of that pest-ridden camp were unbearable. Officers, unable longer to stand them, gathered in groups and deliberately drank themselves into insensibility. To stay there was to invite complete destruction. The helplessly sick were bundled into the boats. The half-sick took to the oars. Humiliated by defeat, enfeebled by fatigue, hunger, hardship, and disease, utterly demoralized in every respect, the wreck of a once proud little army rowed away from that island of death.

In the first days of July, Crown Point saw them again, what was left of them. So they came back to that place whence Montgomery had set out, just ten months before, to conquer Canada.

CHAPTER 15

Washington in New York

Washington's uncertainty as to the destination of the British fleet and army at the evacuation of Boston on March 17, 1776, did not deter him from promptly moving to defend New York, which he thought might be next attacked by the enemy. On the 18th he dispatched to that city a Pennsylvania rifle regiment, three companies of Virginia riflemen, and General Heath's brigade. Sullivan's brigade followed on the 29th, then Greene's and Spencer's, and Knox's artillery, in quick succession. Putnam was sent down to take general command. Five regiments were left in Boston under General Artemas Ward. On April 13 Washington himself was in New York.[1]

On June 20, 1775, when Washington had been directed by the Continental Congress to take command of "the Army of the united Colonies," it was in fact an army of the four New England colonies only. Except the few hundred riflemen from Pennsylvania, Maryland, and Virginia who joined him in July and August, 1775, no troops from the other colonies came to reinforce him. When the movement against Canada was begun it was evident that additional troops would be needed. On July 25, the Congress resolved that "a body of forces not exceeding five thousand be kept up in the New York department," [2] but no specific plan for raising them was provided. That was left to the New York Provincial Congress. Not before October did the Continental Congress begin to plan for and provide a real Continental army. On the 2nd of that month it authorized a committee to go to Cambridge and consult with Washington on the subject.[3] On November 4 the report of that committee was considered, and it was resolved that "the new army intended to lie before Boston" should consist of 20,372 men, officers included, enlisted "to the last day of December, 1776." [4]

It appears that Washington had agreed to a one-year term of enlistment on the advice of a council of his general officers, who thought it would be "impossible to get the men to enlist for the continuance of the War," [5] but it also appears that the one-year term was contrary to his own judgment. In a letter to Joseph Reed dated February 1, 1776, he enlarged upon "the evils arising from short, or even any limited enlistment." It took, he said, two or three months to acquaint new men with their duty, and even a longer time to bring them into "such a subordinate way of thinking as is necessary for a soldier." By that time the end of the enlistment period is in sight, and "you are obliged to relax in your discipline, in order as it were to curry favour with them" so as to induce them to reenlist. And "with every new set you have the same trouble to encounter." The disadvantages of the one-year period were so great that it would be better "to give a bounty of 20, 30 or even 40 Dollars to every man who will Inlist for the whole time." [6]

He rehearsed this argument in a letter to the Congress dated February 9, 1776, pointing out that the apprehension of his troops leaving him on December 31 had driven Montgomery to his fatal attack on Quebec "under disadvantageous circumstances." He also referred to his own experience in having to dissolve his army at the end of 1775, the evils of which he forcefully particularized. Under such a system, he said, "you never can have a well Disciplined army." [7]

Washington's arguments were and are cogent and convincing to one with an open and unprejudiced mind, but the collective mind of the Americans of that period was not unprejudiced. In an overwhelming majority they were of British extraction. Their ancestors had, to a large extent, left England at the time when the Stuart kings were seeking to create a standing army to oppress the people and deprive them of civil and religious liberty. Cromwell had defeated the Stuarts, only to use his own troops as instruments of tyranny. By both sides of the civil conflict in England, the idea of a standing army was hated and dreaded, and that dread and hatred was an inheritance of their descendants in America. An army for the duration of the war was at this time impossible of acceptance by the general run of the colonists.

But the Congress had not awaited the report of its committee before going ahead. On October 9, 1775, it had "recommended to the Convention of New Jersey, that it immediately raise, at the expense of the Continent two Battalions, consisting of eight companies each, and each company of 68 privates." [8] Three days later a similar "recommendation" for one battalion was made to Pennsylvania, and calls were soon after made on North Carolina for six battalions, on Pennsylvania for four more, on Delaware for one, on Virginia for nine, on Rhode Island for two, on Massachusetts for six, on New Hampshire for two, on South Carolina for five, including one regiment of artillery and one of rangers, on Maryland for two, and on Georgia for one regiment of rangers. It also requested a "German battalion" of eight companies, four to be raised in Pennsylvania and four in Maryland.[9]

Slowly and gradually building up the Continental army, the Congress sought in addition to provide temporary additional reinforcements for "the army at New York." On June 3, 1776, Massachusetts, Connecticut, New York, and New Jersey were called upon for 13,800 militiamen. As a defense for "the middle colonies" a Flying Camp was to be established. Ten thousand militia were called for, 6,000 from Pennsylvania, 3,400 from Maryland, and 600 from Delaware. Perth Amboy in New Jersey was chosen as the site of the camp. Without going fully into the history of this attempt, it may be said that it was a failure. There was an insufficient response to the appeal, and the militia that did respond made but a short stay. Two Continental regiments—one from Maryland, the other from Delaware—were called upon to strengthen this force, but they remained only a few days before they were sent on to New York. By the end of the year, the Flying Camp passed out of existence.[10]

The regiments of the Continental army were to consist of eight companies of 76 privates each, with the usual officers, noncommissioned officers, drum, and fife. The pay and provisions were sufficiently generous according to the standards of the time. The pay for the officers ranged from $50 a month for a colonel to $13⅓ for an ensign. Privates were to receive $6⅔; but out of this sum there were stoppages for clothing furnished them at the rate of $1⅔ per month. Their uniforms were "as much as possible" to be brown, with different regimental facings. They were to receive "good firelocks with bayonets," each musket having a ¾ inch bore, the barrel 3 feet, 8 inches long, the bayonet 18 inches. Their rations were prescribed in detail: "1 lb. of beef, or ¾ lb. pork, or 1 lb. of salt fish . . . 1 lb. of bread or flour" daily, also a pint of milk and a quart of spruce beer or cider per day, with a weekly allowance of peas, beans, or other vegetables, rice or Indian meal, candles, and soap.[11] It needed hardly be said that these provisions for uniforms, arms, and rations, made in a hopeful spirit were seldom realized in fact.

In uniforms, there was little uniformity. Many of the regiments were supplied at the time of enlistment according to their own fancy. The soldiers of Delaware's regiment, for instance, were handsomely turned out in blue coats, faced and lined with red, white waistcoats, buckskin breeches, white woolen stockings, and black spatterdashes or gaiters. They wore small, round, blackjacked leather hats without a visor, but with a peaked front, somewhat after the fashion of the taller hats of the British grenadiers. They were armed with fine English muskets "lately imported," complete with bayonets.[12] But that regiment was said to be "the best uniformed and equipped in the army of 1776." [13] Smallwood's Maryland regiment is frequently described as arrayed in scarlet coats faced with buff; but, although that was its dress uniform at home, only the officers wore it in the Long Island battle, the privates appearing in brown hunting shirts. In the rest of the army military uniforms were rather the exception than the rule. The riflemen usually wore the conventional hunting shirt of gray or brown tow cloth, though Miles's men wore black.[14] The standards for muskets fixed by the Congress were not achieved at this time, nor were they ever in the whole course of the war. They differed in caliber, greatly to the disadvantage of the troops, since no standard size of bullets or cartridges could be maintained. Also bayonets were scarce, and continued to be so to the war's end.

Washington was impressed with the importance of holding New York against the British army. "It is the Place that we must use every Endeavour to keep from them," he wrote to Brigadier General Lord Stirling, who had been left in command there on General Charles Lee's departure for the South early in 1776. "For should they get that Town, and the Command of the North River, they can stop the Intercourse between the northern and southern Colonies, upon which depends the Safety of America." It would also give them "an easy pass into Canada." Its retention by the Americans was of "vast importance," of "infinite importance." [15] So, in spite of the great difficulty of fortifying it against "a powerful sea armament," as Lee had pointed out on his first arrival in New York, Washington concentrated most of his forces there, and busied himself exceedingly with its defensive works.

The town was small in extent, occupying about a square mile at the southern tip of Manhattan Island. Lee, who had been sent down to supervise its defenses, had planned to erect in and about it an elaborate system of forts, redoubts, batteries, entrenchments, and barricades. As they played no part in the actual battle for its possession, they need not be described here, except to note that numerous batteries were to be erected on both sides of the North and East rivers to prevent, or at least to hinder, the passage of enemy vessels to the northward of the town. Lee's opinion early in 1776 was that New York could not be indefinitely defended against the British, but that the British could be made to pay for possession of it.

He had had at first only 1,700 men to work on these extensive defenses. But before he left in March others had come in from Connecticut, New

Jersey, and the outlying districts of New York, and Stirling carried on with them. All the men of the town, white and black, were called out, and a prodigious amount of pick-and-shovel work was done by them and by the troops from Boston when they arrived. But, to defend the town, it was necessary to go beyond its limits and the limits of Manhattan Island.

Directly across the East River lay Long Island, and particularly the little village of Brooklyn and its environs. Brooklyn Heights rose a hundred feet above the water. A recollection of the domination of Boston by Dorchester Heights and of the effect of their occupation by the Americans in making that town untenable was not needed to convince Lee of the importance of these others in the scheme of defense. He had proposed to secure them by "a post or retrenched encampment" [16] for 3,000 men. This work was immediately begun.

The ground chosen was a broad, irregularly shaped peninsula facing the East River and lying between Wallabout Bay on the northeast and Gowanus Cove on the southwest. Those two bodies of water indented the sides of the peninsula, making a neck of land about a mile and a half wide. An irregularly curved zigzag line of entrenchments was drawn from the bay to Gowanus Creek. At the upper end Fort Putnam, a redoubt with five guns, was erected. From a point near the fort, the entrenchments turned at a right angle to the main line and ran to the bay. From the fort, at intervals along the main line to Gowanus Creek, there were built redoubts called, in order, Fort Greene, the Oblong Redoubt, and Fort Box. Each of these works was armed with a few guns.

Within the lines and nearer the river was Fort Stirling, armed with eight guns. On Red Hook, the extreme westerly corner of the fortified peninsula, was Fort Defiance, mounting four 18-pounders and intended to prevent the passage of ships between that point and Governor's Island. There were also two other small works of minor importance. In all they mounted twenty-nine guns, most of them of iron, old and honeycombed with rust.

These forts and the main line of earthworks were ditched and fraised with sharpened stakes set into their embankments, crossing each other and projecting outward at an angle, their points breast-high. The main line was also defended by a broad area of abatis, felled trees, their butts embedded in the ground, their pointed limbs thrust outward. The work of constructing all these defenses, in the town as well as on Long Island, was performed under the supervision of Brigadier General Lord Stirling, a vigorous and energetic officer.

William Alexander, "Earl of Stirling," was not an earl, nor was he a nobleman of any degree. His father, James Stirling, had fled to America in

1716 to escape the consequences of his activities in the cause of the Old Pretender in the year before, and had attained some eminence in his new home as a lawyer, politician, and scientist. William, his only son, was born in 1726. He had engaged in business profitably, and had served as a major of colonial forces in the French and Indian War. His father claimed to be heir to the lapsed title of James Alexander, 1st Earl of Stirling, through some degree of cousinship, but had taken no steps to assert his right on the death of that nobleman in 1737.

When his father died, in 1756, William laid legal claim to the earldom. When his case was first tried in Edinburgh, a jury found in his favor, and he was proclaimed earl at the Market Cross. The decision was reversed in the House of Lords, but he continued to assert his right to the title, and was so addressed in America throughout his life.

In person Stirling "showed a burly figure, and a fresh-coloured visage." [17] He was fond of sociability, and his detractors accused him of undue fondness for the bottle; but it does not appear that this ever lessened his efficiency in his military duties, at least not until evening. He was conspicuous for personal bravery in action. The officers on Long Island gave him "the character of as brave a man as ever lived." [18] He prided himself on his acquaintance with the technical side of his profession. Early in the war he was noted for maintaining a harsh and captious discipline. However, he "shook off the martinet, and became a practical soldier of considerable value in the field. . . . there was sure to be plenty of tough and steady fighting in the quarter towards which Stirling and his division had been ordered." [19]

At the time of Washington's arrival in New York, his army there consisted of twenty-five regiments, numbering about 9,000 rank and file. These he divided into five brigades, under Heath, Spencer, Sullivan, Greene, and Stirling. But, before the end of April, Sullivan was ordered to Canada with six regiments as has been mentioned. The rest were rearranged in four brigades, three of them posted on Manhattan Island, one on Long Island. With such of the militia as had responded to the call of the Congress on June 3, with the return of what was left of Sullivan's detachment, and with the arrival of other Continental regiments from the Flying Camp, the army had been increased to a paper strength of about 28,500 of all ranks by the late summer of 1776. Of these, about 19,000 were present and fit for duty, but the larger part of them were raw recruits, undisciplined and inexperienced in warfare, and militia, never to be assuredly relied upon.[20]

A new arrangement divided this force again into five divisions before the Battle of Long Island. James Clinton's brigade of four Massachusetts regiments, John Morin Scott's four regiments from New York, and John

Fellows's four regiments from Massachusetts made up Israel Putnam's division. The second division, under William Heath, contained Thomas Mifflin's brigade of two Pennsylvania regiments, two regiments from Massachusetts, and one from Rhode Island, also George Clinton's brigade of five New York regiments. Joseph Spencer's division included the brigade of Samuel Holden Parsons—four regiments from Connecticut and one from Massachusetts—and James Wadsworth's seven Connecticut regiments. John Sullivan, who had returned from Canada, commanded a division composed of Lord Stirling's brigade—one Maryland regiment, one from Delaware, a Pennsylvania rifle regiment, a Pennsylvania musketry battalion, and three corps of Pennsylvania militia—and Alexander McDougall's brigade, two regiments from New York, one from Connecticut, and one of artificers. Nathanael Greene had in his division John Nixon's brigade of three Massachusetts regiments, two from Rhode Island, and one from Pennsylvania, Nathaniel Heard's brigade of five New Jersey regiments, Oliver Wolcott's brigade of twelve regiments of Connecticut militia, and Nathaniel Woodhull's two regiments of Long Island militia. Colonel Henry Knox commanded the artillery.

Up to a short time before the battle, Putnam's, Spencer's, and Sullivan's divisions, with the Connecticut militiamen, say 20,000 in all, were posted in and about the city. Heath's division was separated into several parts; Mifflin's brigade of 2,400 men was on Manhattan Island at Fort Washington, and George Clinton's 1,800 were at Kingsbridge. Two regiments of Greene's division were on Governor's Island. Greene himself, with the rest, fewer than 4,000, was on Long Island.[21]

Long before Howe evacuated Boston, it became apparent even to the British government that the plans for subduing the American colonies had been conceived on too small a scale; Howe's 7,000 men were not enough to do the job. By October, 1775, the plans had been enlarged to call for a total British army of 55,000 men, and an addition of 12,000 men to the navy. Recruiting was begun in all parts of the British Isles; but, as an English historian says, there was in Britain "hardly any enthusiasm for the war among the classes from which soldiers were drawn." Ireland was combed, but the Irish were enjoying a year of unprecedented agricultural prosperity. Food was plentiful; hunger, the usual incentive to enlistment, was unknown. Scotland showed better results. There were many land-hungry Highlanders who hoped to appease their desires in the vast acres of a conquered America. But on the whole the enlistments were not enough. It was necessary to look elsewhere.[22]

The petty princes of Germany had soldiers for rent. From the Duke of Brunswick, the Landgrave of Hesse-Kassel, and the Prince of Waldeck, England hired at this time 17,775 men to be shipped to America, where they were all called by one hated name, Hessians. Others were added in the course of the war to a total number of 29,875.[23]

On June 25 three warships arrived in lower New York Bay, bringing General Howe from Halifax to the scene of his next conflict—for him, more fortunate. He hoped to use New York as a base for the conquest of the colonies. He had only a small force, but it was the forerunner of a greater soon to come. Four days later its real magnitude began to develop. Forty-five more ships hove in sight, and in another day eighty-two appeared. One hundred and thirty ships of war and transports disembarked 9,300 soldiers on Staten Island. But this was not all. Admiral Lord Howe, brother of the general, followed with a fleet of one hundred fifty sail, full of fighting men fresh from England. On July 12 they joined the others. A little later Admiral Sir Peter Parker, with nine warships and thirty transports bearing 2,500 men under General Henry Clinton and General Lord Cornwallis, came limping northward from their defeat at Charleston. Commodore Hotham brought six men-of-war and twenty-eight transports on August 12, and disembarked 2,600 of the Guards and 8,000 Hessians.[24]

In the British camp on Staten Island, across the Narrows from Long Island, there were twenty-seven regiments of the line, four battalions of light infantry, four of grenadiers, two of the Guards, three brigades of artillery, one regiment of light dragoons, and 8,000 Hessians, with Major General Howe and Generals Clinton, Lord Percy, Lord Cornwallis, and von Heister, all of them skilled in the science of war and the art of command. It was an army of 32,000 trained, disciplined, professional soldiers, completely armed, fully equipped, abundantly supplied—the greatest expeditionary force Great Britain had ever sent out from its shores. It was supported by a fleet of ten ships of the line, twenty frigates armed with 1,200 guns, and hundreds of transports, manned by more than 10,000 seamen. Britain had drawn from her war chest the staggering sum of £850,000.

To oppose this mighty force the Americans had 19,000 largely untrained, undisciplined, untried amateur soldiers, poorly armed, meagerly equipped and supplied, led by an amateur commander in chief, who was supported by amateur officers. They were backed by not a single warship nor a single transport, and their war chest was in large part a printing press in Philadelphia emitting issues of paper dollars, worth whatever one could induce another to give for them and diminishing in value day by day. To be sure they now had something very specific for which to fight, because independence had been declared early in July.

To make matters worse for the Americans, their inadequate force was divided between New York and Long Island with the broad expanse of the East River separating them, and with no means whatever of keeping open a line of communication if British warships were interposed.

In their camp the British soldiers were unseen by the Americans; but their fleet was only too visible. "Onlookers gazed with awe on a pageant such as America had never seen before—five hundred dark hulls, forests of masts, a network of spars and ropes and a gay display of flying pennants. There were ships of the line with frowning sides, three tiers of guns and high forecastles; there were graceful frigates, alert and speedy . . . tenders and galleys to land the thousands of men from the unwieldy transports." [25] It is no wonder that panic fear was in the hearts of half of New York's people, and gleams of joy were in the eyes of the other half, who were opposed to independence and who supported the British.

The first definitely threatening move was made by two warships, the *Phoenix* of forty-four guns and the *Rose* of twenty-eight. On July 12, with two tenders, they stood in toward the town. In the American camp the alarm was sounded; the troops took their posts. As the ships swept by the town on their way up the North River, the batteries there and those on Paulus Hook—now Jersey City—opened fire. The ships replied with broadsides. [26] Throughout the town there was a mad panic. Washington described its effect on the women: "When the men-of-war passed up the river, the shrieks and cries of the poor creatures, running every way with their children, were truly distressing, and I fear they will have an unhappy effect on the ears and minds of our young and inexperienced soldiery." [27]

Past battery after battery, batteries that were supposed to prevent their passage, the ships held their course to Tappan Bay, forty miles above the town. Fireships were sent against them, with no success. Six days later, they came back, running the same gantlet and anchored again in the Narrows, practically unharmed. [28]

It seems that the whole fleet, or any part of it, might have landed troops at any time on the north end of Manhattan Island and cut off the whole American army from any possible retreat, to bag it at leisure. Nothing of the sort was done, however, and, from the time of the first arrival of the British, what form the attack would take, whether against New York or against Long Island, remained an open question, puzzling and harassing to the American command. It was at last answered.

CHAPTER 16

Long Island: The Preliminaries

At dawn on the 22nd of August three British frigates, *Phoenix, Rose* and *Greyhound,* and two bomb ketches, *Carcass* and *Thunder,* took station in Gravesend Bay, Long Island, about a mile east of the Narrows. Another frigate, *Rainbow,* anchored in the Narrows off Denyse Point, the part of Long Island nearest to Staten Island. Seventy-five flatboats, eleven bateaux, and two row-galleys, built for the occasion and manned by sailors from the fleet, were assembled at Staten Island, and 15,000 soldiers, fully equipped for active service, and forty fieldpieces were drawn up before the British camp.[1]

At eight o'clock in the morning a British advance corps, consisting of four battalions of light infantry and Preston's 17th Light Dragoons, and a reserve, four battalions of grenadiers, the 33rd and the 42nd, or Black Watch Regiment, and Colonel Carl von Donop's corps of Hessian grenadiers and jägers, 4,000 men in all under the command of Clinton and Cornwallis, embarked. In ten well ordered divisions they were rowed across to Denyse Point. Under cover of the guns of the *Rainbow* they went ashore and were drawn up in military formation. The next trip of the boats brought 5,000 more men to a point below the others, which was under the guns of the three frigates and the two bomb ketches. By noon 15,000 men had been landed without opposition, mishap, or delay.[2] Three days later, on the 25th, they were joined by two brigades of Hessian grenadiers under General Philip von Heister, "a tough old soldier of the Seven Years War."[3] These were ferried over standing in the boats, "with muskets sloped and in column of march, preserving the well-considered pomp of German discipline."[4]

211

"The Soldiers & Sailors seemed as merry as in a Holiday, and regaled themselves with the fine apples, which hung everywhere upon the Trees in great abundance." [5]

There was no American opposition whatever to any of these landings. Colonel Edward Hand and 200 men of the 1st Pennsylvania Continental Regiment had been in camp in an outpost near Denyse Point. On the first alarm they marched toward New Utrecht, "to watch the movements of the enemy," who were soon discovered approaching them on the way to Flatbush. Hand turned, and marched parallel with the enemy advance guard, but at a respectful distance from it, "in the edge of the woods." Finding "it impracticable for so small a force to attack them," [6] he sent a detachment ahead to burn all the standing grain and slaughter as many cattle as possible, while his main body returned to its camp, gathered up its baggage, and after some light skirmishing, took up a position on Prospect Hill.

Cornwallis, with the reserve, ten battalions of light infantry and von Donop's Hessians, possessed the village of Flatbush and camped there.[7] The main body encamped nearer the shore, along the road running from near the bay in the vicinity of Gravesend to New Utrecht. Its camp extended from that village on the west to Flatlands village on the east.[8]

The British now occupied a broad, low plain extending from the shore northward from four to six miles and eastward a greater distance. In it lay the four villages named. Looking north from their camp, the invaders faced the most prominent feature of the terrain, which was to be their battleground.

Stretching northeast from near the waterside at Gowanus Cove nearly all the way across the island and forming a barrier between the British army and the Brooklyn defenses, ran a ridge or range of hills, varying in height from one hundred to one hundred fifty feet. It was called the Heights of Guan, or Guian. On the southerly side, fronting the British, the rugged face of the heights rose abruptly forty to eighty feet from the plain, then ascended less precipitously to the full height of the ridge. On the northerly side the ground sloped more gradually to the lower land beyond. The entire surface of the ridge was covered by dense woods and thickets penetrable only with difficulty by men on foot, entirely impassable by horse-drawn artillery or by troops in formation except at four points where roads led through natural depressions or "passes." One of the roads circumvented the westerly end of the main ridge; the others went through at different points toward the east.[9]

The first road, to the left of the British, starting at Gravesend ran westerly through New Utrecht to a point near the shore of the Narrows, then turned north parallel with the shore, finally quite close to the edge of Gowanus Cove, and so around the westerly end of the ridge on its way to Brooklyn. It was called the Gowanus Road. The second ran from Flatbush almost due north, through Flatbush Pass, then split in two, both branches coming finally to Brooklyn. The third road took off from the second just before Flatbush Pass, swung to the east, then to the north, and ran through Bedford Pass to the village of Bedford, whence a straight road ran to Brooklyn. These three roads accounted for more than three miles of the length of the ridge between the westerly and easterly passes. The fourth ran northeast from Flatlands to Jamaica Pass, nearly three miles east of Bedford Pass.[10] These four passes, with their respective roads, were obviously to be defended in force if any attempt was made to hold the ridge against an advance from the south.

After the arrival of the British on Staten Island there were changes in the command of the American troops on Long Island. Major General Nathanael Greene fell ill of a fever and took to his bed in New York. On August 20 Washington turned the command of the troops about Brooklyn over to Major General John Sullivan. This change was unfortunate, because Greene, a much abler general officer, had a thorough knowledge of the Long Island terrain, while Sullivan knew little of the lay of the land. Still more unfortunate was another change, made on the 24th, by which Major General Israel Putnam superseded Sullivan in general command on Long Island, Sullivan being retained there as a subordinate.[11] Putnam, who knew practically nothing of the topography of the island, was for other reasons totally unfit for the controlling position into which he had been put.[12]

There were changes in the forces defending the Brooklyn position as well. Immediately on receiving news in New York of the landing of the British on the 22nd, Washington sent over Miles's Pennsylvania riflemen, Atlee's Pennsylvania musketry battalion, Chester's and Silliman's newly raised Connecticut regiments, Lasher's New York Independent companies, and Drake's New York minutemen, about 1,800 men in all.[13] There were consequently about 5,800 men in and about the Brooklyn lines; but more than two-thirds of these were militia, not dependable even behind entrenchments and totally unreliable in a stand-up fight in an open field. Even the loyalty of the New York and Long Island contingents was seriously suspected.[14]

Although Washington knew of the landing of some of the enemy on Long Island, he was led to think, even as late as the 24th, that they amounted to no more than eight or nine thousand, a minor part of the whole force. Therefore, expecting an attack on "our works on the Island and this city at the same time," [15] he retained three-quarters of his whole army on the New York side, including many of the better regiments. Any respectable intelligence service, of which he had at this time almost none, could have told him that the major part of the British army and all its best general officers were on Long Island, and that without doubt the grand attack, the only immediate attack, was to be made on Brooklyn. Nevertheless he did send over other reinforcements, Parsons's Connecticut Continentals, Lutz's Berks County (Pennsylvania) militia, Hay's militia from Lancaster County, and Kachlein's Berks riflemen, perhaps fewer than 2,000 in all. These Pennsylvania militiamen were about half of Stirling's brigade, and Stirling crossed with them, leaving his best two, his only thoroughly dependable regiments, Smallwood's Maryland and Haslet's Delaware Continentals, in camp on the Manhattan side.[16]

Washington expected an immediate attack after the British had settled themselves on Long Island; but Howe was in no hurry. There was brisk skirmishing in front of Flatbush Pass on the 23rd. At the same time von Donop's Hessians made a move against Bedford Pass, evidently to try it out; but they met a sharp fire from Hand's corps, which advanced to meet the enemy, drove them back, and burned some houses they had held. They returned in force and regained their former position, the Americans retiring to their post on the ridge. From the ridge on the following day the Americans harassed the Flatbush camp with round shot and grape from their fieldpieces. But the heavier artillery of the Hessians soon silenced them. There were few casualties on either side.[17]

In the afternoon of the 26th Cornwallis, leaving the Black Watch and the Hessians in the Flatbush camp, moved the rest of his troops to Flatlands village, where the British headquarters had been established. The Hessian General von Heister, who had landed the day before with two brigades, took over the command at Flatbush.[18] This movement to Flatlands might have indicated to an intelligent observer that neither the Flatbush nor the Bedford Pass was to be the scene of the main attack, because it shifted the weight of the British force away from them; but none of the Americans on the ridge seems to have understood its meaning.

By this time, however, Washington had come over from New York. At last he realized that the strength of the British was on Long Island, and that "the grand push" was to be against Brooklyn.[19] He ordered more men over, Lieutenant Colonel Thomas Knowlton with 100 Connecticut Continentals, two or three independent companies from Maryland, and, most important, Smallwood's Maryland and Haslet's Delaware Continental regiments, the best equipped and (the Delawares) the largest in the army. By a singular coincidence the Smallwood and Haslet regiments arrived under command of their majors, Mordecai Gist for Maryland and Thomas McDonough for Delaware; their colonels and lieutenant colonels had been detailed to sit in a court-martial in New York on that day. Now Stirling's brigade was complete in its camp outside the Brooklyn lines. By these additions, Putnam's command on Long Island was built up to about 7,000 men fit for duty.[20] On the evening of the 26th the coast, or Gowanus, road was guarded by Hand's 200 of the 1st Pennsylvania Regiment, half of Atlee's Pennsylvania musketry battalion, some part of Lutz's Pennsylvanians, and certain detachments of New York troops, perhaps 550 in all. On their left, more than a mile and a half distant at the Flatbush Pass, the center of the line, were Daniel Hitchcock's Rhode Island and Moses Little's Massachusetts Continental regiments, commanded, respectively, by their lieutenant colonels, Elias Cornell and William Henshaw, and Knowlton's detachment of Connecticut Continentals, perhaps fewer than 1,000 in all. They held a rude fortification of felled trees, mounting three guns and one howitzer.

At the Bedford Pass about a mile to the east were stationed Colonel Samuel Wyllys and his Connecticut Continentals and Colonel John Chester's Connecticut State Regiment, under command of Lieutenant Colonel Solomon Wills, about 800 men, with three guns and a fortification like that at Flatbush Pass; also Colonel Samuel Miles with about 400 Pennsylvania riflemen. Thus there were probably fewer than 2,800 men in all posted along more than three miles of the densely wooded ridge in separate detachments, with no communication between them except by sentinels stationed at intervals. It was a long line and a thin line; pierced at any point, it must give way. Facing them on the plain below were seven times their number; in military efficiency, man for man, one might say fifteen times their number.

But what about Jamaica Pass, three miles to the east of the Bedford road? It was guarded, too—by a mounted patrol of five young militia officers. While the right of this long line rested on Gowanus Cove, its left was in the air.[21]

CHAPTER 17

Long Island: The Battle

At about midnight on the 26th of August, Hand's Pennsylvanians, who had been on constant duty for four days picketing the American right, were relieved by a detail of Kachlein's and Hay's troops under Major Edward Burd. Hand's men, "not having lain down the whole time and almost dead with fatigue," [1] retired to the fortified lines to rest. Now all was quiet along the American front; but on the British side something was happening.

At the far left of the British positions, near the Narrows, lay Major General James Grant with his two brigades, 5,000 strong.[2] In the center von Heister's Hessians and the Scottish Black Watch still occupied Flatbush. But the main body of the British army had been massed at Flatlands. All these were astir that night.

At nine o'clock in the evening a column of march was formed at the principal post at Flatlands. General Henry Clinton led the van, made up of the 17th Light Dragoons and a brigade of light infantry. General Lord Cornwallis came next with the reserve—that is to say, the 1st Brigade of four battalions of grenadiers, two regiments of foot, and the 71st (Fraser's Highlanders), with fourteen pieces of field artillery. After them fell in General William Howe and General Lord Percy with the main body—the Guards and three brigades of infantry comprising twelve regiments, with ten guns. Bringing up the rear were one regiment and the baggage train with its guard and four guns. In this column were 10,000 soldiers and twenty-eight pieces of artillery.[3]

Led by three Tories from Flatbush, this formidable array set out on the road to the Jamaica Pass. Proceeding with the utmost caution, it left the

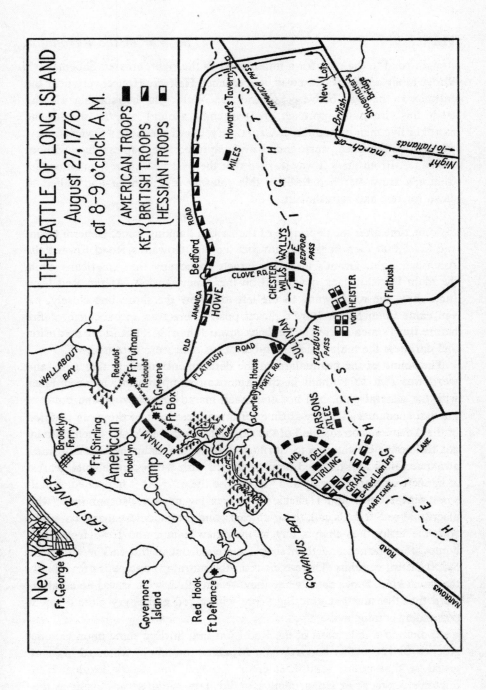

THE BATTLE OF LONG ISLAND
August 27, 1776
at 8-9 o'clock A.M.

KEY { AMERICAN TROOPS / BRITISH TROOPS / HESSIAN TROOPS }

straight road to the pass for a minor road to the right, crossed Shoemaker's Bridge along a narrow causeway, and reached Halfway House, very near the entrance to the pass, between two and three o'clock in the morning. Having made this circuitous approach, the van came around into the rear of the patrol of five men posted there. Captain Evelyn of the King's Own infantry, leading the advance, surrounded and captured the hapless five without resistance. From them it was learned that the pass was entirely undefended. Clinton's army marched through this gateway in the ridge and halted at dawn for rest and refreshment.[4]

Some time after the departure of the British flanking force, General Grant and his 5,000 men began an advance up the Gowanus Road toward the American right. Grant's task was largely to occupy the Americans while the main British attack developed on the American left. At the Red Lion Inn, where the road swung to the left to follow the shore line closely, his van came upon Major Burd's picket post. There was an exchange of fire before Burd's men started to fall back toward the ridge; but in the confusion and darkness the major and a number of his men were captured.[5]

The sound of the firing alarmed the detachment guarding that pass, and word was sent to Putnam in the American camp. Grant, in accordance with the general plan, had not continued his advance beyond the point of the first encounter. There was time for a reinforcement of the main position of the Americans on that end of the ridge. It was three o'clock when Putnam got the news. He hurried to Stirling's tent in the camp outside the lines, awakened him, and directed him "to march with the two regiments nearest at hand" to meet the enemy and "to repulse them."[6] As it happened, Smallwood's Marylands and Haslet's Delawares lay nearest. Responding "with alacrity"[7] to Stirling's call, these untried young soldiers less than two weeks with the army, less than a day in their new camp, and fresh from their homes, their farms, and their shops, marched out in the darkness to meet 5,000 British veterans. Three-o'clock-in-the-morning courage is proverbially the rarest kind. Dawn came while they were on their way. It was noted afterward that the sun that morning "rose with a red and angry glare,"[8] as if portending coming evils.

About half a mile short of the Red Lion Inn, Stirling came upon Colonel Atlee with 120 of his Pennsylvania Musketry battalion, who had been on guard at that point,[9] and Lieutenant Colonel Joel Clark leading Huntington's regiment of Connecticut Continentals. Grant's van, again in motion, was in sight, marching directly toward them. Stirling ordered Atlee forward to hold the enemy until he could form his troops on the ridge.[10]

Atlee took a position in an orchard beside the road at the foot of the west end of the ridge. Although his men had never before faced an enemy in battle, they held their ground and exchanged fire with Grant's advance until Stirling had selected his ground and drawn up his troops. Then they retired to join him.

The ground chosen was on a slope running up from the Gowanus Road to a wood at the top of that end of the ridge. Because of the lay of the land and the position of the road, Stirling's line was most peculiarly shaped like a V. On the right branch, as viewed from behind, the Marylanders were drawn up; on the left, Haslet's Delaware regiment.[11]

The right wing of the line rested on a marsh at the foot of the hill; the left had no support. The two parts of Atlee's regiment—the men originally on guard there and those now newly arrived—having been joined together, Stirling posted them and Huntington's regiment in the woods on his unprotected left. Kachlein's Pennsylvania riflemen had now come up, and he divided them, placing half behind a hedge in front of his right and the rest in front of the woods near Atlee.[12] This extreme left, somewhat separated from Stirling's own troops, was put under command of Brigadier General Samuel Holden Parsons of Connecticut, who was early on the scene.

The shape of Stirling's line created a singular condition, in that his extreme left was nearer his extreme right than either was to his center. Because of this anomaly, a part of the Delaware battalion, held in reserve on the end of one wing, was called upon in the course of the fighting to meet and repulse the advance of the 2nd British Grenadiers attacking the end of the other wing.

Another remarkable thing about Stirling's formation was that, instead of letting his men break ranks and take cover, he drew them up in the open in formal order, and, in the words of one of them, offered the British "battle in the true English taste." [13] So in line they stood, to quote Haslet, "upwards of four hours, with a firm, determined countenance, in close array, their colors flying, the enemy's artillery playing on them all the time." [14]

Their position was precarious. In their rear was a marsh bordering Gowanus Creek. They had no connecting support on the left except Parson's command at some distance, and beyond that none at all. On their far right was the bay commanded by the British fleet, and in front was Grant's division outnumbering them four to one, for Grant soon brought up the 42nd Highlanders, drawn from von Heister's corps at Flatbush, and two companies of American Loyalists. He had then about 7,000 men facing not more than 1,600 Americans. In reply to the American challenge, he drew up his troops as if for immediate attack. One brigade was extended in a double line in front of the Americans' right, the rest in a single line against their left. The extent of this latter line threatened to overlap the Americans. Stirling accordingly desired Parsons to move Atlee's and Huntington's regiments to a point in the woods farther to the left, leaving Kachlein's riflemen nearer at hand. This shift, though necessary to meet Grant's tactics, separated the two bodies by a considerable distance, and left Stirling, with not much more than a thousand men, to oppose Grant.[15]

Parsons's troops, filing off to the left, saw before them "a hill of clear ground," which seemed to be a desirable position from which to watch the enemy's movements. As they were approaching within forty yards of its top, they were surprised by a volley of musketry from the 23rd and 44th British regiments and a part of the 17th Light Dragoons, who had penetrated the woods. They wavered and fell back in some confusion; but most of them were soon rallied, and they advanced again with somewhat surprising coolness. Their fire was so effective that the enemy retired, leaving twelve dead and five wounded. The American loss in this preliminary encounter included Atlee's lieutenant colonel, Caleb Parry, and a few minor casualties. Parsons's contingent held the hill.[16]

Within half an hour this detachment was again attacked by the same British regiments; but, partly under cover of trees and fences, partly in the open, it delivered such a heavy fire that again the enemy were repulsed. In the engagement the British Lieutenant Colonel Grant was killed. Parsons's men exhausted their ammunition, and would have been obliged to retreat but for the timely arrival of a new supply.[17] A third attack was threatened, but the enemy did not carry it out, contenting themselves with holding the Americans' attention at a safe distance. As a matter of fact the strategy of the whole battle did not call for a full-scale assault upon the American right at this time. These several little engagements, though hot, were intended merely to hold the Americans' attention while the larger plan for the battle was being worked out.

Returning now to Stirling, and going back somewhat in time, we find his men in ordered line of battle as first drawn up, and Stirling addressing them. Recalling that he had chanced to be in the gallery of the House of Commons when General Grant, then a member, had made his famous boast that, with 5,000 men, he could march from one end of the American continent to the other, Stirling told his men: "He may have 5,000 with him now. We are not so many. But I think we are enough to prevent his advancing further on his march over the continent than that mill-pond." [18]

It is noteworthy that this was the first time that American and British forces ever met in formal array in the open field. It may also be remarked that Stirling's formation was the only one on the American side that was preserved throughout the battle.

Grant's next move was to advance a small body of light infantry within 150 yards of Stirling's right. Protected by the trees and hedges of an orchard, they opened fire, to which the Americans briskly replied. This exchange continued about two hours, after which the light infantry withdrew to the main line. A two-gun battery under Captain Benajah Carpenter of Rhode Island had come from the American lines and was posted to command the road. It opened upon the enemy. To answer it, Grant posted one howitzer about 300 yards from Stirling's right, and another 600 yards from his left.[19] There followed sustained and vigorous cannonading from both sides. Except for the body of light infantry while they were in the orchard, it does not appear that any part of the two forces was within musket shot of the enemy. The few American accounts of this stage of the battle dwell on the "heavy fire from their cannon and mortars." "The balls and shells flew very fast," yet did little damage.

The plain fact again was that Grant did not intend to drive Stirling from his position until the proper time according to the plan of the high command. But Stirling's men did not know this. At every moment of the four hours of the cannonading they seemed to face the possibility of attack by the overwhelming number of their opponents. That they, raw recruits as they were, stood firmly in line under the fire of heavy guns—always formidable to untried soldiers—while awaiting that assault, redounds greatly to their credit, especially so since all the time their ears were assailed by the guns of the warship *Roebuck* bombarding the fort at Red Hook, and the fort's batteries replying.

Admiral Lord Howe had tried to bring five other warships up the East River within supporting distance of the land forces. But a strong north wind and a swiftly ebbing tide kept back all save the *Roebuck,* which itself could not sail above Red Hook. Had the attempt succeeded, he could have poured terrible broadsides on Stirling's troops and on the Brooklyn fortifications. Thus bombarded, and at the same time cut off from retreat to New York, the Americans must have been overwhelmed; Washington, Putnam, Stirling, Sullivan, and all the Long Island army would have been killed or captured, and the Revolution might have ended then and there.[20]

At nine o'clock in the morning, after four hours of all this cannon fire, Stirling heard two heavy guns far in his rear—sounds more ominous than the thunder of Grant's guns or the roar of the *Roebuck*'s broadsides. But

no interpretation came to him from headquarters or elsewhere, no orders
to withdraw. He could only surmise some danger behind him, wonder what
it was, and continue to hold his ground.

Up to this time General von Heister's Hessians had contented themselves
with cannonading the American center in the Flatbush Pass, varying it with
a sufficient show of advancing to keep the defenders in constant apprehension of an assault. About nine o'clock, General Sullivan rode out from the
Brooklyn lines and took command of the posts at the two middle passes,
Flatbush and Bedford. He remained at the Flatbush post, with the troops
of Hitchcock, Little, and Knowlton. The post at the Bedford road was about
a mile distant, separated by rugged, broken country.[21]

It may seem impossible that anyone could further stretch and weaken the
already attenuated and feeble American line; but Colonel Miles did just
that. At about seven o'clock, he says, he became convinced that "the main
body of the enemy would take the Jamaica Road." Accordingly he thought
best to get into that position first.[22] It was a good guess, except that it was
made about four hours too late. However, he marched his Pennsylvania
riflemen through the woods toward the Jamaica Pass and away from Wyllys
and Wills, nearly two miles. He was still proceeding at eight o'clock when
he disconcertingly came into contact with the enemy's army—not with its
van, but actually with its baggage and rear guard.

The British, after breakfasting just beyond the Jamaica Pass, had taken
a straight road toward Bedford. Their column of 10,000 men, almost two
miles long, with horse, artillery, and wagons, had been marching five or six
hours over that road in the rear of the American lines, parallel with Miles's
line of march but in an opposite direction and within half a mile of him
without his having observed them.

Their entire movement was a masterpiece of secrecy and silence. Where
it was necessary to cut down young trees to clear the way for the artillery
and wagons, these were sawed instead of chopped for fear that the Americans might hear ax strokes and be alarmed. They had marched nine miles.[23]
Their van had by this time almost reached the village of Bedford, without
any of the Americans even suspecting its presence in the rear of the ridge.

Miles was completely cut off from a retreat to the lines. His 400 men
could do little against the foe. After two or three slight encounters he and
half of his men surrendered. The rest scattered in the woods, found their
way to the American camp, and gave Putnam the first news of the encircling
march of the British.[24] There was still time to send word to Stirling and to
the Flathush, if not the Bedford, post to withdraw from a position that had

become untenable and concentrate in the fortification. Putnam sent no such word, nor did anyone else. Nothing whatever was done to avert coming disaster.

At nine o'clock, in the village of Bedford, the British fired two heavy guns, the signal for action. Wyllys and Wills at the Bedford Pass heard them. Already alarmed by the firing on their left, between the enemy and Miles's men, they realized their danger and immediately started for the fortified lines.[25] Sullivan, at the Flatbush post, heard the guns, too, and knew the enemy was behind him. Leaving pickets and outposts to delay an attack by the Hessians in front, he fell back, only to meet the British light infantry and dragoons pouring down upon him from Bedford. His men turned their three fieldpieces on these unexpected foemen. But four companies of the Guards overwhelmed the gunners. The Americans recoiled, turned about, and met von Donop's Hessian jägers coming up over the ridge.[26]

In anticipation of the signal von Heister had formed his troops on the plain below the pass, dressing their lines as if on parade, with von Donop's jägers on the right and left flanks, his artillery meanwhile playing on the American position. At the expected sound of the guns he had given von Donop the word. The jägers had dashed forward, reached the top of the wooded ridge, taken cover as they had been trained to do, and advanced from one protected point to another, driving back the American outposts.[27] After them came the Hessian grenadiers. Muskets at shoulder, bayonets gleaming, halting at intervals to re-dress their lines, they advanced "with colors flying, to the music of drums and hautboys, as if they were marching across Friedrich's Platz at Cassel on the Landgrave's birthday. They did not fire a shot, but pressed steadily forward until they could employ their bayonets." [28]

At the top of the ridge the Hessians deployed and fell upon Sullivan's men thrown back by the British. The rifles in the hands of the Americans were good for only a few shots before bayonets were at the breasts of the riflemen, and a clubbed rifle is a weak weapon against half a dozen bayonets. Driven back and forth between the British and the Hessians, the Americans fought as long as they could, and then, along with what was left of Miles's men and Wyllys's and Wills's and the rest, they fled. Through the woods, down the slopes, across the fields, singly, in groups, in companies, they fled. Meeting here and there light infantry, dragoons, and grenadiers who fired at them, they ran for the fortified camp. Many of them reached it, but many were killed and many captured, among them Sullivan. It was in these ragged encounters that most of the American casualties occurred.

The wave of attacks swept westward. Detachments of von Heister's grenadiers, swinging to their left, struck at Parsons's command, Atlee's regiment, Huntington's contingent, and Kachlein's riflemen. There was no possibility of successful resistance; they retreated in broken groups, only to meet the British grenadiers in their rear. Atlee's journal says: "We kept up a close fire until the grenadiers retired. Then not being able, through the weakness of my party, already greatly fatigued and . . . destitute of ammunition, to break through the enemy . . . I filed off to the right [towards the camp] to endeavor, if possible, to escape." He soon fell in with Parsons "and a small number by him." They decided to try to break through the enemy. "I then pushed off," he continues, "with such of the officers and men that were willing to run the hazard."

Almost immediately they came upon a party of Highlanders, from whom they retreated, receiving in their flight "the fire of this party and sundry others, through which we were obliged to run for near two miles." With a handful of men Atlee tried to find a way to the north, toward Hell Gate, but at last had to surrender to a Scottish battalion.[29]

By eleven o'clock the British, as a result of their skillfully planned and perfectly executed strategy, had established themselves within two miles of the American camp, and had swept the ridge clear of their enemy—of all but Stirling's two regiments. These were still holding their ground, "ranks full, their uniforms smart, their weapons the best that money could purchase, their courage high." [30]

Up to this time Grant had made no move against Stirling's position. He had heard the signal guns, but, possibly because he had run short of ammunition, he had not acted as quickly as the other British and Hessian commanders. He had sent to the fleet for more powder and shot. Admiral Howe had sent him not only the desired supply, but also 2,000 marines, a scarcely needed reinforcement of his 7,000 men against Stirling's men. When they arrived, the real attack on Stirling began.

Grant's full force struck at Stirling's center. Unable to withstand the blow, the American line recoiled. The 33rd foot and a detachment of grenadiers swept down from the rear to join Grant. With a party of von Heister's Hessians they attacked the American left. Stirling called up some of Haslet's men, held in reserve, to strengthen his line. They came up and opened fire. The colonel of the 2nd British Grenadiers, whose men were under fire, saw that his assailants, the Delawares, wore uniforms of blue faced with red—the Hessians' colors. They were Hessians, of course, firing on their British comrades in arms by mistake! He sent Lieutenant Wragg of the marines forward with a sergeant, a corporal, and twenty men, to tell them to stop. The unfortunate Wragg was so close to the Delawares when he discovered the mistake that he could not withdraw. He and his entire party were taken by Haslet's men and sent across the Gowanus marsh and creek to the lines.[31]

But this was merely a momentary diversion. Grant's 7,000 and those others that had come to help him would not be denied by Stirling's 950. It was clear that the American position could not be held much longer. Nor was the direct way of retreat to the rear open. Cornwallis was there with the 71st Regiment. The 2nd Grenadiers also overlapped Stirling's left and rear.

Cut off from their natural line of retreat, Stirling's men had only one possible avenue of escape; and that was but barely possible. On their right rear was Gowanus Creek at its widest, and not only that stream, but also the broad marshes lining both its shores. The creek and its swamps were usually considered impassable, but the detachment with the prisoners had crossed them, and there was no other way.

To attempt such a crossing with his whole force in retreat, under the fire of the musketry and cannon of the British before and behind him, was to court and probably to suffer complete disaster. But Stirling met the emergency with characteristic resolution and courage. He detached Major Gist and about 250 men of Smallwood's Maryland regiment. He then ordered Major McDonough with the Delawares and the rest of the Marylands to retreat across the creek. They faced about and, "in perfect order," their shot-torn colors flying, marched away.[32]

Gist's 250 Marylanders, Stirling leading, set out up the Gowanus Road to meet the enemy. If possible, Stirling meant to cut his way through the British. If not, he might be able to engage them and hold them off until the remainder of his command crossed to safety. His plan was born of desperation, a forlorn hope.

Cornwallis in person commanded the British right wing pressing against what had been Stirling's rear. He had established himself in and about the Cortelyou House on the Gowanus Road. Against this position Stirling led his men. When within gunshot, he opened fire and received the enemy's reply which came not only from their musketry, but also from two field-pieces. The British artillery added grape and canister to the rain of bullets.

The little American column halted and fell back, only to advance once more. Again and again and again, five times, the Americans were driven back, and five times returned to the fight. Stirling "encouraged and animated our young soldiers," wrote Major Gist, "with almost invincible resolution."

"General Lord Stirling fought like a wolf," wrote another participant.[33] It seemed at last that they would force Cornwallis to retire and let them through. A sixth time they advanced, but Cornwallis had now been reinforced. For the last time the brave young Marylanders were thrown back, this time "with much precipitation and confusion." They had done all they could, but they could not win through. They broke up, and in small, scattered parties tried to find a way to the American entrenchments; but only Major Gist and nine others succeeded. The rest, all that had not fallen in the fight, were captured, and 256 were either killed or taken prisoner. Stirling alone tried to find a way out, but the enemy, before and behind and on both sides, kept up a "constant firing" on him. He made his way around "the point of a hill" that covered him from their fire, then sought out General von Heister and surrendered his sword.[34]

It was reported at the time that Washington was on a hill within the lines, whence, with a glass, he watched Stirling's fight, and that he displayed great emotion, exclaiming: "Good God! What brave fellows I must this day lose!" [35]

Meanwhile, still in good order, in column of march (so the historians say, though it may be doubted that there was no confusion), McDonough's Delawares and Marylands were retreating. They had made no more than a quarter of a mile when they met a party of the enemy and were fired upon. The artillery in their rear also still played upon them. Apparently with no thought of surrender, they replied to the enemy in front and forced him to give way. Through an opening thus created they got down to the edge of the marsh, and started across the creek.[36]

At that point, Gowanus Creek was eighty yards wide, deep and swift with the inflowing tide. The retreating Americans waded in knee-deep, waist-deep, neck-deep, here and there over their depth; some of them had to swim. Four fieldpieces were firing upon them, and an unknown number of muskets. Fortunately, Smallwood had come over from New York early that morning, too late to join his regiment in the battle. He had foreseen that the retreat must be made at that point if at all. He had secured from Washington "a New England regiment and Captain Thomas's company," and had posted them with two guns to cover the crossing. Their fire dislodged the enemy guns that were firing on the fugitives. Except for half a dozen men either shot down or drowned, the fleeing Americans came safely "out of the water and mud, looking like water-rats." [37]

Howe claimed that the Americans lost 3,200 men in this battle, but the American returns on October 8 showed 1,012 casualties of whom probably

200 were killed, the rest captured. The British casualties were 392 killed, wounded, and taken prisoner.[38]

The Battle of Long Island, as the first in which the American and British forces met in the open field in formal battle array, was of very great importance as an indication of what was to be expected in such encounters thereafter. The disastrous defeat of the Americans boded ill for their future. Consequently, it was extremely desirable to ascertain wherein their army was at fault, and whether the blame for their discomfiture should rest upon the rank and file or upon the leaders. There was much discussion of the question at the time, and it has continued among historians ever since.

Sullivan has been blamed because, being in command of the troops outside the lines, he failed properly to guard the Jamaica Pass; but he denied that he held that command, asserting that it belonged to Stirling and his own function was to command within the lines as subordinate to Putnam.[39] He is credited with having posted the captured patrol at the Jamaica Pass; but, if that be true, it boomerangs upon him because it shows that, in spite of his disclaimer of authority outside the lines, he did in fact exercise such authority. In which case, the pitiful weakness of the post he thus established reflects discredit upon him.

Putnam has been blamed because, having reconnoitered the enemy's positions on the 26th, he should have concluded from the concentration of their forces that they intended to launch their main attack against the Jamaica Pass, and should have arranged for an adequate defense.[40] The fact that Washington, Sullivan, "and others" were with him on that reconnaissance cannot exculpate him, though it may prove them equally blind.

Putnam has been censured also because, having received news, "early in the morning," of the British advance along the road to Bedford, he failed to inform Washington or to order Stirling and the others on the ridge to withdraw while there was yet time.[41] It is true that the news was brought to him first only by one or more fugitives in the rout of Miles's battalion; and doubtless it was long delayed by the distance it had to be brought through the woods. Nevertheless, it does seem that he received it in time to recall Stirling and the others.

George Bancroft blames "the incapacity of Israel Putnam" for "the extent of the disasters of the day," specifically because, "having sent Stirling and the flower of the American army into the most dangerous position," he "neglected to countermand his orders." [42] "The Militia are most indifferent troops." They "will do for the interior Works, whilst your best Men should at all hazards prevent the Enemy's passing the Wood, and approaching your Works." [43] Clearly, if there was error in disposing the American forces, it cannot be ascribed to Putnam alone.

The most all-inclusive charge is made by General Francis V. Greene, who says: "No one exercised general command," although it had been conferred on Putnam. "Putnam did practically nothing as a commanding general." [44] And it is certainly true that, having sent his "best men" out to defend the ridge, he did none of the things proper and necessary to save them from disaster. Even Washington's orders were no warrant to him for leaving them to be surrounded and captured by the British turning movement, which Washington certainly did not expect when he gave the orders.

Washington has been blamed for the defeat, because, though he was familiar with the ground and had arrived within the lines on the 26th, thus certainly putting himself in command superior to Putnam, he did not alter Putnam's dispositions and allowed a manifestly inadequate force, strung out along six miles of the ridge, to attempt to defend it, instead of "keeping his men in the redoubts and repeating the performance of Bunker Hill." [45] He has been censured, too, for not having any cavalry to patrol between the various passes, so that word of the flanking movement could be brought to the camp in time to withdraw the troops from the ridge before they were hopelessly enveloped. Washington Irving says the flanking of the Americans "might have been thwarted had the army been provided with a few troops of light-horse to serve as videttes." [46]

There was no cavalry in the American army. None had been provided by the Congress. Washington had not called for any, nor made a move to organize any on his own. Charles Francis Adams says he "apparently had no conception of the use to be made of cavalry, or mounted men, in warfare," [47] and develops that thesis at length. Yet, strange to say, there was available to him at the time a mounted force which could have provided the patrols so needed. He refused to use it.

There had come over from Connecticut, on the 8th of July, a regiment of four or five hundred volunteers called rather absurdly "Light Dragoons"— mostly farmers mounted on "rough, country horses" and armed with muskets, fowling pieces, or whatever sort of guns they owned. They were not a stylish lot. Dapper, or at least dapper-minded, Captain Alexander Graydon of Philadelphia made great fun of them in his memoirs.[48] Washington received these cavaliers rather cavalierly. He said they could not remain in New York because forage for their horses could not be furnished, "and, if it could be, it would only be at great expense, without a single advantage arising from it." [49] They were discharged, and went home.

Sir George Trevelyan comments that Washington "surveyed that quaint procession too much in the spirit of a country gentleman who rode to hounds. There was plenty of capability and some youth" among them. Two hundred of the best might have been chosen and trained in the next six weeks. "Captain Henry Lee or Captain William Washington would have got a small body of cavalry into shape soon enough. . . . On the 27th of August, 1776, a couple of troops of yeomanry posted and handled by two such officers would have saved many hundred Americans from capture." [50]

One of these horsemen, lingering on the scene, was picked up by the British. Captain Graydon reports, "On being asked what had been his duty in the rebel army, he answered that it was *'to flank a little and carry tidings.'* " No one could have put in fewer or more apt words just what Washington needed on Long Island—someone "to flank a little and carry tidings."

On the whole, it seems impossible to avoid placing the bulk of the responsibility for the mismanagement of affairs on Long Island upon the shoulders of the commander in chief, George Washington. Such has been the verdict of the later and more judicious historians of the war. "There was no excuse for the local dispositions of the defense," says Thomas G. Frothingham.[51] And those dispositions had been made in accordance with Washington's specific orders. Claude H. Van Tyne refers to Washington's "almost fatal errors in both strategy and tactics." [52]

Most of these criticisms of the conduct of the affair on Long Island are directed at the tactics employed there. The fundamental fault lay deeper, in the strategy of the campaign, the attempt to hold New York. That city could not be held without holding Brooklyn Heights. Those Heights could not be held without dividing an army far too weak, even as a whole, successfully to oppose the British. To divide it was to expose the two parts to the danger of being held apart by the British fleet and of being separately and successively overcome by the British army.

Even if Brooklyn Heights had not been there to bring about this unfortunate result, the Americans could not have held New York, for the British armada commanded the waters environing the town. Indeed, New York could easily have been a fatal trap for the American army, since it had only one readily available exit to the mainland: Kingsbridge.

It has been said that the attempt to hold it was based upon political instead of military considerations, that the Congress wanted it held, that the attempt to hold it was necessary to fortify the American spirit of resistance.[53] But if a commanding general sees that a task is impossible of accomplishment, though he may risk and sacrifice an expendable detachment in the attempt, how far is he justified in risking his whole army, the whole army of his country, and with it his country's cause? If on the other hand he fails to perceive the obvious impossibility of the task, how can he be allowed merit as a military leader? And Washington did not perceive the impossibility of holding New York before he attempted it, not even after the defeat on Long Island. As late as September 2 he wrote to the Congress, "Till of late I had no doubt in my mind of defending the place [New York], nor should I have yet, if the men would do their duty." [54]

The truth is, in Van Tyne's words, that Washington had "little genius and not much natural aptitude for war." [55] Or, as the English military historian Sir John Fortescue, a most generous critic of the American commander in chief, puts it, "Though every Englishman must admire him as a very great man and a brave and skilful soldier, it is, I think, doubtful whether he has any claim to be regarded as a really great commander in the field." [56] As Van Tyne says: "It was courage, noble character, the gift of inspiring confidence, and the ability to learn by experience" rather than military genius that were "to place him in the forefront among the leaders of men, safe and competent as a commander-in-chief. Even in the midst of his worst errors, his greatness and his magnanimity surmounts everything." [57] And Fortescue, after commenting on the "very grave flaws in the campaign of 1776 about New York" and in the campaign against Howe about Philadelphia, in 1777, culminating in the Brandywine disaster, recognizes "his constancy, his courage and his inexhaustible patience" as his "finest qualities." [58]

Long Island: The Retreat

By noon of August 27 all the Americans that had escaped death or capture were within the fortified lines on Long Island, expecting with anxiety a concentrated attack. But it did not come. The British grenadiers and the 33rd Regiment had pursued the fugitives to within musket shot of the lines. Hot with the ardor of battle, they were eager to storm the entrenchments, so eager that, in Howe's own words, "it required repeated orders to prevail on them to desist from this attempt." He "would not risk the loss that might have been sustained in the assault," it being, as he is reported to have said, "apparent that the lines must have been ours at a very cheap rate by regular approaches." He therefore withdrew his men to a safe distance.[1]

Astonishingly enough, not recognizing the peril of his position, Washington called for reinforcements from New York; and early the next morning Colonel John Shee's 3rd Pennsylvania Regiment and Colonel Robert Magaw's 5th, also Colonel John Glover's Massachusetts Continentals, came over. There were then within the works perhaps 9,500 men.[2]

For two days following the battle the Americans held their lines, while within a mile or so and in plain sight lay the British camp. There was skirmishing throughout the 28th, "pretty smart" skirmishing, Washington called it.[3] To present a bold face to the enemy, he encouraged the riflemen to keep up their fire, thus not only maintaining a show of resistance, but also sustaining the morale of his men.[4]

Pickets and riflemen were thrown out by the Americans about a hundred rods in front of the lines. About sunset of the 28th the enemy made a push to drive them in. "The fire was very hot," Colonel Moses Little of Massachusetts wrote. "The enemy gave way & our people recovered the ground. The firing ceased, our people retired to the fort." By the next morning the British not only possessed the disputed ground, but had dug trenches and built a breastwork within 150 rods of Fort Putnam. Howe's "approaches" had begun. This first breastwork was a menace of disaster nearing the Americans.[5]

On that same day a northeasterly storm blew up, and a downpour of rain began. It had one immense advantage for the Americans: it prevented Admiral Howe from sending ships up the East River to lie between Brooklyn and New York and thus to cut off their only line of retreat. Otherwise it was exceedingly distressing to them. "We had no tents to screen us from its pitiless pelting," wrote Captain Alexander Graydon of Shee's regiment in his memoirs; "nor, if we had had them, would it have comported with the incessant vigilance required to have availed ourselves of them, as, in fact, it might be said, that we lay upon our arms during our whole stay on the island." [6] In food also they were badly off. They had only hard biscuits and pickled pork, which must be eaten raw, for cook fires were impossible in that downpour.

The rain continued all the next day and the day after that. The camp became a morass and worse. Water lay "ankle deep in the fort"; and in some parts of the trenches the men stood waist-deep in water. Not only was the clothing of the troops soaked, the ammunition of nearly all of them was saturated. But even those who managed to keep a few dry cartridges could not use them, for their muskets were practically valueless, as are all flintlock guns when the flints, the priming pans, and the touchholes become wet.

Howe's reluctance to storm the works immediately after the retreat of the Americans has been attributed to the memory of Bunker's Hill, to the lesson he there learned of the steadfastness and the deadly fire of the Americans, even the militia when behind breastworks. Trevelyan says that the minutemen who defended the redoubt on Breed's Hill saved the American lines on Long Island. But that lesson should have been no deterrent to an assault on the second day or the third day after this battle. No overwhelming fire such as had met him in that former battle could have been delivered against him now. British bayonets would have been met by few American bayonets—the Americans had but few. It is difficult to believe that a determined assault upon those entrenchments would have failed against their tired and hungry defenders, discouraged by defeat and disorganized by the loss of so many officers.[7] Howe may have assumed that his brother's fleet could prevent an American retreat, and that an expensive frontal assault was unnecessary. A veritable Caesar on the battlefield, Howe was commonly sluggish before and after the fighting.

It was an extraordinary situation. "Nine thousand disheartened soldiers, the last hope of their country," says Trevelyan, "were penned up, with the sea behind them and a triumphant enemy in front, shelterless and famished on a square mile of open ground swept by a fierce and cold northeasterly gale. . . . If Howe's infantry had been led to the assault, they would have walked over the intrenchments behind which the beaten army was now gathered." [8] It would have been more than a victory in a battle. Washington was there, with three or four of his ablest generals and the best of his whole army. By their capture the British might have won the war then and there. But Washington *was* there, and he finally saved the day.

On the morning of the 29th he sent orders to General William Heath at Kingsbridge and to Hugh Hughes, Assistant Quartermaster General in New York, to gather every boat of every sort fit for transporting troops and to assemble them on the New York side by dark. Was he planning a retreat? He did not say so. On the contrary his orders to Heath intimated a reinforcement of his lines.[9] But late in that day a council of his general officers agreed that it was "eligible to remove the Army to New York" for eight severally stated reasons, any one of which seemed to be sufficient in itself.[10]

So there was to be a retreat—if it could be accomplished. But the troops were not informed until the last moment. If the truth had been known among the militia and volunteers a panic desire to get out in the first boats might have resulted in riotous confusion. Accordingly general orders were issued in the following terms: "As the sick are an encumbrance to the Army & Troops are expected from the flying camp in New Jersey, under General Mercer, who is himself arrived & cover is wanted for the [new] troops, the commanding Officers of Regt's are immediately to have such sick men removed. . . . As the above Forces under Gen'l Mercer are expected this afternoon, the General [Washington] proposes to relieve a proportionate Number of Regiments & make a change in the situation of them. The Commanding Officers of Regiments are therefore to parade their men with their Arms, Accoutrements and Knapsacks, at 7 o'Clock at the Head of their Encampments & there wait for Orders." [11] Washington could tell a lie when it was needed. He told half a dozen in that one order.

It was obviously necessary that the lines should be manned while the removal of the great body of the troops was in progress, so as to prevent the enemy from discovering the movement and assaulting while the camp was in disorder. To this honorable and dangerous duty Haslet's Delaware regiment was assigned, along with Shee's and Magaw's Pennsylvanians, Chester's

Connecticut battalion, and the remains of Smallwood's Marylanders. This detachment, the pick of the army, was commanded by General Thomas Mifflin.[12] The post of greatest danger, at Fort Putnam, within 250 yards of the enemy's approaches, was taken by Smallwood's and Haslet's men. When Glover's Marbleheaders were withdrawn from their left to help man the boats, the Delaware and Maryland men were exposed to a flank attack which would have been impossible to stem.

At dusk the boats began to arrive. The two amphibious regiments, Glover's from Marblehead and Hutchinson's from Salem, all fishermen or sailors, took them in charge. Between nine and ten o'clock the regiments on parade were drawn off one by one, the volunteers and militia first. With their baggage and equipment on their backs they marched to the ferry landing to embark. Other regiments were marched into their places or extended to right or left to fill the gaps and keep up an appearance of completeness in the line. The utmost quiet and orderliness were preserved; no unusual lights were shown. In fact, the embarkation was begun in almost complete darkness.

The first detachments were ready to embark and the next were on their way to the landing when the elements, which had so far befriended the Americans by preventing Admiral Howe's ships from coming up the river, made trouble. The northeasterly wind so increased in force and the ebb tide began to run so strongly that even the practiced sailors manning the sloops and other sailboats could not make the crossing. There were not enough rowboats to take all the men across in one night. It seemed that the attempt to withdraw must end in disaster. But the wind lessened about eleven o'clock and shifted to the southwest, favoring the sailing craft.

The work went on. Stores of ammunition, supplies, and provisions were brought to the landing. All the artillery was assembled there except five heavy cannon, old and worn and of little value. They were spiked and abandoned.

At two o'clock in the morning, when everything seemed to be going well, an error occurred that might have been fatal. Major Alexander Scammell, acting aide-de-camp to Washington, came to General Mifflin and told him that the boats for the covering party were waiting and he was to march his men to the landing at once. In spite of a protest that there must be some mistake, Scammell insisted that there was none. Accordingly the sentinels and advanced posts were called in. The entire detachment abandoned the lines and marched toward the landing. They were well on their way when they met Washington. He was aghast at this seeming desertion of their duty.

"Good God!" he exclaimed. "General Mifflin, I am afraid you have ruined us by unseasonably withdrawing the troops from the lines." "I did it by your order," Mifflin answered hotly. Washington said that could not be so. "By God, I did!" said Mifflin. Washington replied that it was a dreadful mistake, that there was confusion at the ferry, and that unless the covering party could resume their posts before the enemy discovered their abandonment "the most disagreeable consequences would follow"—surely a masterpiece of understatement. The troops were faced about and their posts, unguarded for nearly an hour, were again occupied.[13] Major General Heath characterizes the immediate return of these men to their posts as "an instance of discipline and true fortitude." "Whoever," he says, "has seen troops in a similar situation, or duly contemplated the human heart in such trials, will know how to appreciate the conduct of these brave men on this occasion." [14]

To the troops holding the lines within sound of the thudding pickaxes and the scraping shovels of the British working on a new and nearer approach, that night must have seemed interminable. Would the hour of their relief come before daylight and certain discovery of the retreat by the enemy? Would they, a few hundreds, be compelled to face an attack by thousands? It was daylight when the order to embark came, and those steadfast battalions marched away.

It was full time they did, for British reconnoitering parties, suspicious of the unnatural silence within the American lines, were already creeping up to spy on the camp. Before daybreak a corporal's guard pushed cautiously through the abatis. At four o'clock the British were peering over the breastworks. Thirty minutes later the British pickets were inside. There was still time to catch the rear guard at the landing, but freakish Nature again favored the Americans. A dense fog settled down. Even at a little distance nothing could be seen. Under its cover the last boats with the last regiments and Washington himself pushed off.

Through six hours of that night, "the hardy, adroit, weather-proof" [15] Marblehead fishermen of Glover's regiment and Hutchinson's skilled Salem fishermen had rowed and sailed from shore to shore. By seven o'clock in the morning 9,500 men and all their baggage, field guns, and horses, equipment, stores, and provisions, "even the biscuits which had not been and the raw pork which could not be eaten," [16] were safe in New York. Howe captured three stragglers, who had stayed behind to plunder.

Both the contemporary and the later historians have praised this successful retreat. Charles Stedman, an officer in the British army at that time, called it "particularly glorious." Alexander Botta wrote, "No military opera-

tion was ever conducted by a great captain with more ability and prudence."
Irving calls it "one of the most signal achievements of the war." Trevelyan
says it was "a master stroke of energy, dexterity and caution, by which
Washington saved his army and his country." Frothingham describes it as
"a feat that seemed impossible." General Francis Vinton Greene, a military
critic of distinction, says, "A more skilful operation of this kind was never
conducted." Any number of others might be quoted in similar terms.[17]

The credit for the achievement must unhesitatingly be accorded to Washington, who not only conceived and planned it but personally supervised its
effective accomplishment throughout the night. Although, as he wrote to the
Congress, he had hardly been off his horse and never had closed his eyes in
the forty-eight hours preceding the retreat, all night long he rode his gray
charger to and fro watching the movements of his men, or stood by the landing to superintend the embarkation. He seemed to be everywhere at once;
and everywhere he cheered, calmed, and encouraged his troops through one
of the most difficult trials a soldier has to endure. He was the last man to
step into the last boat that left the island.

Both Howe's attack and Washington's retreat were masterpieces of planning and execution, and each was successful because of the mistakes of the
other principal. Washington exposed an inadequate force on the ridge and
neglected the Jamaica Pass, thus permitting Howe to encircle his army and
defeat it; Howe failed to follow up his first success by assaulting the American lines, thus giving Washington a chance to withdraw to New York.
Both of them were destined to repeat the same errors in a future battle with
similar results, which throws light upon their respective abilities as military
leaders.

The results of this battle created a great sensation on both sides of the
Atlantic. The surrender of Boston had depressed England, and news of
succeeding events in America was anxiously awaited. Howe's report of the
battle, greatly exaggerating both the number of American troops engaged
and their losses, reached London on October 10. Immediately the court
was "filled with an extravagance of joy." The King conferred the Order of
the Bath on the victorious general. In various towns throughout the kingdom
bells were rung, windows were lighted, cannon were fired, and bonfires
blazed. The English Tories thought the war practically finished. British
stocks rose in Amsterdam. The American agent Silas Deane wrote from
Paris, "The last check on Long Island has sunk our credit to nothing." [18]

In America disappointment and gloom were widespread. General Greene
wrote to Washington, "The country is struck with a panic." [19] Washington
wrote to the Congress that the defeat had "dispirited too great a proportion

of our troops and filled their minds with apprehension and dispair. The militia . . . are dismayed, intractable and impatient to return" to their homes. "Great numbers of them have gone off; in some instances, almost by whole regiments . . . their example has infected another part of the army. I am obliged to confess my want of confidence in the generality of the troops." He urged the Congress to put no dependence "in a militia or other troops than those enlisted and embodied" for longer periods than were then in vogue, and declared his conviction that "our liberties" might be lost "if their defence is left to any but a permanent standing army; I mean, one to exist during the war." [20] The Congress overcame its dread of "standing armies" and resolved on September 16 that eighty-eight battalions be enlisted "as soon as possible to serve during the present war." [21]

CHAPTER 19

Kip's Bay

"On this 30th of August, 1776, Washington was probably the most astonished man in America. He had snatched a beaten army from the very jaws of a victorious force, and practically under the nose of the greatest armada ever seen in American waters." [1] He may have been astonished at his successful retreat; he was certainly perplexed as to his next move. He had his army in New York, but what to do with either the army or New York was a puzzle whose solution was far from obvious.

The army was in a deplorable condition, mentally and physically. Dispirited by its recent defeat, dejected by its hardships, dismayed at the prospect of the future, the militia was in the condition described by Washington in his letter to the Congress of September 2. The Continentals were similarly affected, though in a lesser degree. Such discipline as had been achieved in that hastily gathered army of practically raw recruits was greatly relaxed. Their commander in chief took notice of the resultant disorder in general orders on September 4. He expressed his "amazement and concern . . . that the men of every regiment are suffer'd to be continually rambling about, and at such distances from their respective quarters and encampments, as not to be able to oppose the enemy in any sudden approach." He therefore not only commanded but earnestly exhorted "the officers to remedy this fault." Two days later he expressed his purpose "to put a stop to plundering . . . either public, or private property" and threatened to break "with Infamy" any officer who connived at it by inaction.[2]

A more fundamental evil was a growing distrust of Washington himself— not of his character as a man, but of his ability as a general, or at least of the plans for the campaign made by him and his associates in the high command. This feeling was not uncommon among the regimental officers. Colonel John Haslet of the Delaware Regiment, an officer of proven sagacity and sound judgment, expressed it in a letter to Caesar Rodney on September 4 in the words: "The Genl I revere, his Character for Disinterestedness, Patience and fortitude will be had in Everlasting Remembrance, but the Vast Burthen appears to be too much his own. Beardless youth and Inexperience Regimentated are too much about him. . . . W'd to Heaven Genl Lee were here is the Language of officers and men." [3]

Physically, too, everything was in sad condition. The men were tired, soaked to the skin, hungry, and in some part leaderless, by reason of the loss of officers. Their disorganization showed itself in the wet clothing, accouterments, and tents spread about in complete confusion to dry in front of the houses and in the streets.[4]

Desertion was consequently rife, especially among the militia. They went off in whole companies, in whole regiments.[5] Within a few days the Connecticut militia dwindled from 8,000 to 2,000 men. "The impulse for going home," wrote Washington, "was so irrisistable, it answered no purpose to oppose it, tho' I could not discharge, I have been obliged to acquiesce." [6]

The prime necessity, if order was to be restored, was obviously a reorganization of the army. Three grand divisions were made up. Major General Putnam commanded one, composed of Parsons's brigade of Connecticut and Massachusetts regiments, James Clinton's and Fellows's brigades from Massachusetts, Scott's from New York, and Silliman's from Connecticut. Spencer was to command another, until Greene should recover from his illness. It included Nixon's brigade, composed of Hand's Pennsylvania riflemen, Varnum's and Hitchcock's brigades from Rhode Island and Prescott's, Little's, and "Late Nixon's" brigades from Massachusetts. The third division, under Heath, consisted of George Clinton's brigade from New York and Mifflin's brigades comprising Magaw's and Shee's Pennsylvanians, Hutchinson's, Sargent's, and Andrew Ward's brigades from Connecticut, Haslet's Delawares, and Smallwood's remnant from Maryland.[7]

Before these divisions could receive their respective posts, the great question had to be answered: Should New York be held or abandoned? And, if abandoned, should it be left intact and unscathed to the enemy? There were differences of opinion.

Greene's answers were given in a letter to Washington. The city could not be held in the face of an enemy that could land on both sides of the island in its middle section and cut in two the American forces to the north and the south. "The City and Island of New-York are no objects for us . . .

in competition of the general interests of America. Part of the army already
has met with a defeat; the country is struck with a panick; any capital loss
at this time may ruin the cause. . . . A general and speedy retreat is
absolutely necessary. . . . I would burn the city and suburbs" because, "if
the enemy gets possession of the city, we can never recover the possession
without a superiour naval force. . . . It will deprive the enemy of an op-
portunty of barracking their whole army together, which, if they could do,
would be a very great security. . . . Not one benefit can arise to us from
its preservation." Anyhow, "two-thirds of the city of New-York and the
suburbs belongs to the Tories," so why worry about its loss by burning? [8]
Colonel Joseph Reed, the adjutant general of the army, agreed that it
should be burned. Colonel Rufus Putnam, the army's chief engineer, and
John Jay, one of the largest propertyholders in the town, likewise urged its
destruction.[9]

Washington had already put the question up to the Congress on September 2, before Greene's letter was written: "If we should be obliged to abandon the Town, ought it to stand as Winter Quarters for the Enemy?" And
the Congress answered on the 3rd that no damage should be done to it, if
abandoned.[10] So that settled that. But the question of evacuation was still
open.

Washington himself was in two minds about it. He acknowledged the obvious danger to his whole army, if the enemy should "enclose us . . . by
taking post in our rear" and "oblige us to fight them on their own Terms, or
surrender at discretion." Yet he still debated whether he should not try to
hold the town, because giving it up would "dispirit the Troops and enfeeble
our Cause." [11] He put the matter up to a council of war on September 7.

It was generally admitted by the members of the council that the town
was untenable, but the majority could not face the logical consequences of
their own opinions. The decision was a compromise. Putnam's division,
5,000 men, was to remain in New York. Heath with 9,000 was to hold the
ground from Harlem up to Kingsbridge. Greene with five brigades, mostly
militia, posted along the East River chiefly in the neighborhood of Turtle
Bay and Kip's Bay, at the end of what is now Thirty-fourth Street, was to
hold the intervening space.[12] As is the case with most compromises, this
one served neither purpose; it was not effective to secure the city, nor to save
the army. In fact, as one military historian has said, it was, "of course,
fatuous." [13] It strung the army out in three divisions widely spaced over a
length of sixteen miles, with its weakest element midway between the two
ends, and so invited the enemy to cut it in two and defeat the ends sepa-

rately—a chance which was not overlooked by the British. Nevertheless, the troops were posted in that manner.

In his letter to the Congress, September 8, telling of the decision of the council of war, Washington said that some of the officers had been not "a little influenced in their Opinion" by their belief that Congress wished the defense of the town "to be maintained at every hazard." [14] To this the Congress replied on the 10th that "it was by no means the sense" of their resolution of the 3rd against destroying the town "that the army, or any part of it, should remain in that city a moment longer than he [Washington] shall think it proper." [15]

Greene was much disturbed in mind by the council's decision disposing the troops in that "so critical and dangerous" manner. Before he heard of this last resolution of the Congress he and five other officers asked Washington to call another council to consider the matter.[16] That council was held on the 12th, and ten of its thirteen members voted "to reconsider" the former decision, that is to say, voted to withdraw from the city.[17] In this decision Washington concurred. "We are now," he wrote to the Congress on September 14, "taking every Method in our Power to remove the Stores &ca. in which we find almost insuperable difficulties; They are so great and so numerous, that I fear we shall not effect the whole before we shall meet with some Interruption." [18]

Lack of transport was the difficulty. Although all the horses and wagons found in the town were impressed and cargoes were shipped up the Hudson in boats, both methods of carriage were too little and too late.

It was not Howe's fault that Washington was pressed for time in reassembling his forces and removing his cannon and stores. The British army lay inactive on Long Island in camps stretching from Brooklyn to Flushing for more than two weeks while Washington was tying and untying the apron strings of the Congress and finally making the proper decision.[19]

There had, indeed, been hostile demonstrations by the navy. On September 3 the thirty-two-gun frigate *Rose* sailed up the East River towing thirty flatboats and anchored in Wallabout Bay above the city. She was fired upon by the batteries on the New York side, and after suffering "a good deal of damage" [20] she retired with her tow to a safer position in the mouth of Newtown Creek. On the 13th, four frigates, the *Phoenix* and the *Roebuck* of 44 guns each, the *Orpheus* of 32, and the *Carysfort* of 28, passed up, and "in supreme Contempt of the Rebels and their Works, did not fire a Gun." The next day, another warship and six transports joined them. The *Renown* of 50 guns, the *Repulse* and the *Pearl*, 32 guns each, with an armed schooner, also went up the Hudson, daring the American batteries, which cannonaded them "as furiously as they could," but with little effect. They anchored above the American works, and thus prevented the further removal of stores from the city by water.[21] The stage was now set for the next act. Howe was ready to attack Manhattan.

The sun rose in a clear, blue sky on Sunday September 15, with a fresh breeze blowing. Early in the morning five warships took stations in the East River, in a line from Kip's Bay towards the south at about two hundred yards from the shore and broadside to it. At ten o'clock eighty-four flatboats laden with British soldiers put out in four divisions from the Long Island shore. At a little before eleven, the ships opened fire on the entrenchments along the New York side of the river, "such a fire as nothing could withstand." [22] "About 70 large pieces of Cannon were in Play, together with Swivels & small arms," making "so terrible and so incessant a Roar of Guns few even in the Army & Navy had ever heard before." [23] And all this fire was poured upon a line of entrenchments at Kip's Bay held by Captain William Douglas with a brigade of Connecticut militia. "Entrenchments," they were called; but in fact "they were nothing more than a ditch dug along the bank of the river, with the dirt thrown out towards the water." [24]

The boats came up with the line of ships. The fire ceased, but the boats came on, crowded with redcoats and looking like "a clover field in full bloom." They reached the shore at Kip's Bay. The light infantry leaped from them, clambered up "the steep and just accessible rocks" [25]—and found no one to oppose them. Douglas's troops, their frail defensive works already beaten down by the gunfire, had fled "with the utmost precipitation." [26] Wadsworth's brigade, next below them, followed.[27] Parsons's and Scott's militia, farther south, took notice and retreated up the Bowery Road.[28]

Washington, at Harlem when he heard the sound of the bombardment, took horse and rode at full speed to the scene of action. On the Post Road, now Lexington Avenue, about where Forty-second Street crosses it, he met Douglas's men, still retreating precipitately and in confusion. "The demons of fear and disorder seemed to take full possession of all and everything that day," one of them said.[29] Parsons's brigade, also in complete disarray, hurrying north for safety's sake had come up with them.

Washington tried to halt them, to rally them. "Take the walls!" he cried. "Take the cornfield!" Some of them ran to the walls, some into the cornfield. With Putnam and several other officers he tried to form them behind the walls, but there was no controlling them. Washington's anger was spectacular. "He dashed his hat upon the ground in a transport of rage," crying out, "Are these the men with whom I am to defend America?" He snapped a pistol at them. With his riding cane, "he flogged not only private soldiers, but officers as well," a colonel, even a brigadier general.[30] But nothing would do. At the sight of sixty or seventy Hessians coming at them they broke, flung away muskets, knapsacks, even coats and hats, and ran "as if the Devil was in them." "The ground was literally covered" with such discarded encumbrances.[31] And they left Washington almost alone within eighty yards of the oncoming Hessians. Blinded with rage— or with despair—he sat his horse, taking no heed of his imminent danger. He would have been shot or captured had not an aide-de-camp seized his bridle and "absolutely hurried him away." [32]

Putnam, seeing that no stand could be made there, galloped south through Wadsworth's and Scott's brigades coming up in full retreat, to attempt the rescue of Sullivan's brigade, Knox's artillery, and the others still in the town before the British could stretch across the island and hem them in.[33]

He gathered the troops in the city, abandoned the heavy guns and the remaining military stores, and started north. But he knew as little of the geography of Manhattan as he had known of the terrain on Long Island. The Post Road on the easterly side, the main artery leading north and the only one he knew, was held by the enemy. He would have found himself hopelessly entrapped, had not young Aaron Burr, his aide-de-camp, guided him to an unfrequented road along the west side, close to the Hudson.[34]

The day had become intensely hot. Dust hung in stifling clouds over the troops. The water in their canteens was soon exhausted. With dust in their parched throats, sweat streaming from their faces, they slogged along dejectedly. It was hard to keep them going at a reasonable speed. But Putnam now displayed his best native qualities, courage and energy. He rode up and down the two-mile-long column, heartening his men, hurrying them along. They met a detachment of the enemy, beat it off, and at last after dark ended their twelve-mile exhausting march in the main camp at Harlem, where the rest of the army was now collected.[35]

The first division of the British army was led by Howe, Clinton, Cornwallis, Vaughan, Matthews, Leslie, and von Donop. It comprised three battalions of light infantry, four battalions of British grenadiers, three of Hessian grenadiers, the Hessian jägers, and the brigade of British Guards, about 4,000 in all. Immediately on landing, Leslie and the light infantry swung to the right. Von Donop's Hessian grenadiers turned left, met Wadsworth's retreating New York militia, and after a short engagement captured three or four hundred of them. Howe and the rest advanced to Incleberg, otherwise called Murray Hill—a height of land lying between the present Fourth and Sixth avenues and Thirty-fifth and Fortieth streets. There they halted to await the arrival of the second division for which the boats had been sent back.

Repeated trips of the boats brought this division to land about five o'clock. It comprised five brigades and two regiments of British regulars, one brigade of Hessians, and the artillery, about 9,000 men. One brigade was then sent south, and its men were billeted in houses and barns along the Post Road all the way down to the town.

With the main army Howe marched north to McGowan's Pass and rested there for the night.[36] On the way up the Post Road they marched for a time parallel with Putnam's sweating militiamen, separated from them by no greater distance than the width of the present Central Park; but neither force was aware of the other's proximity.[37]

During the afternoon detachments of the British force had ranged about, picking up prisoners here and there, singly or in groups. The Americans lost 17 officers and 350 men that day, nearly all captives; very few were killed. But fifty or sixty cannon and a very considerable amount of ammunition, stores and baggage had been left behind in the town.[38]

That night the British rested, presumably in comfort, in their billets in New York and in the tents of their camp, which stretched across the island from Bloomingdale on the Hudson to Horn's Hook on the East River. Not so the Americans within the hastily entrenched lines on Harlem Heights. "Our soldiers," wrote Colonel David Humphrey, "excessively fatigued by the sultry march of the day, their clothes wet by a severe shower of rain that succeeded towards the evening, their blood chilled by the cold wind . . . and their hearts sunk within them by the loss of baggage, artillery and works in which they had been taught to put great confidence, lay upon their arms, covered only by the clouds of an uncomfortable sky."

That wild flight from Kip's Bay was a sad exhibition. Washington called it "disgraceful and dastardly," but such strong epithets were hardly merited. Douglas's men were not trained, experienced, disciplined soldiers; they were raw militia. With their slight defenses battered down and in the face of an advancing foe of overwhelming numbers, it was natural, indeed it was proper, that this thin line of men should leave their indefensible positions. After that withdrawal they might have rallied, as Washington called on them to do, and annoyed the oncoming enemy for a while. But to what end? They could not possibly have held those stone walls. They would have been enveloped and swallowed up with little delay. A retreat was the only sensible move, though, of course, it ought to have been made in good order.

That is not to say that they reasoned this out. After that withdrawal from their trenches the simple fact is that they were panic-stricken. Panics are often inexplicable in their origin and usually ungovernable in their course. Crowds of people are infected by them without knowing how or where they started. They grow by what they feed upon, ignorance of the reason for their existence. Yielding to them does not prove a lack of personal courage. Habits of discipline, well drilled into men so that they automatically obey orders without questioning the reasons for them, are the only safeguard against such occurrences as this in any army at any time. The militia at Kip's Bay had never had even a chance to acquire such habits.

CHAPTER 20

Harlem Heights

The position to which the Americans retreated from New York was on the narrow neck of land that lies between the Harlem River and the Hudson and is the upper part of Manhattan Island. A plateau called Harlem Heights, occupying the full width of the neck, was bordered on the south and on the two river sides by rocky heights, making it a good defensive position. On this plateau Washington had planned a series of three fortified lines, each extending its full width.

On the first line, about a mile back from the southerly edge of the plateau, three small redoubts had been built at the time of the retreat. The connecting entrenchments were now pushed to completion. The second line with four redoubts, about three-quarters of a mile behind the first, and the third line perhaps a half mile behind the second, were to be built later. The plan, therefore, provided for a defense in depth from the rugged edge of the plateau north for nearly four miles.[1]

The returns of the American army under Washington, dated September 21, show a paper strength of 27,273 infantry rank and file, 104 horse, and 543 artillery. Of this number, 16,124 are listed as "present, fit for duty."[2] But to man the Heights there were probably not more than 10,000, the rest being posted farther north at and about Kingsbridge, where the Harlem River turned west to join the Hudson.

The various elements of the force on the Heights were disposed in depth as follows: Greene's division, comprising Nixon's, Sargent's, and Beall's brigades, 3,300 strong, along the southern edge of the plateau; Putnam's division of James Clinton's, Heard's, and Douglas's brigades, 2,500

246

men, about halfway between Greene's division and the first fortified line; Spencer's division of Fellows's, Silliman's, Wadsworth's, and Mifflin's brigades, 4,200 men, within the first lines.[3]

Facing this plateau on the south was another, the northern edge of which ran very irregularly across the much broader part of the island. Its nearest approach was on the westerly side, where it extended in a sort of peninsula or tongue of land of about the same width as the northern plateau. At this point the two elevations were separated by a narrow depression, perhaps three-quarters of a mile at its widest, a quarter at its narrowest, called the Hollow Way. At its easterly end it widened to an extensive plain with Harlem village at its eastern side.[4]

The British army encamped on the evening of the 15th on the southerly plateau in lines extending on a two-mile front from Horn's Hook on the East River to Bloomingdale on the Hudson. Its front line was thus two miles or less from the front line of the Americans. Two brigades, including the Guards, lay more than a mile in the rear of the lowest line of the main camp and so about three miles back from the American front line.[5]

In the heights at the northern edge of the southern plateau was a gap called McGowan's Pass, through which ran the only road connecting Harlem Plains and the southern parts of the island. It was held by the British.

Washington had much confidence in the strength of his position, but not in the steadfastness of his troops. In the early morning of the 16th he wrote to the Congress: "We are now Encamped with the Main body of the Army on the Heights of Harlem, where I should hope the Enemy would meet with a defeat in case of an Attack, if the generality of our Troops would behave with tolerable resolution. But, experience, to my Extreme affliction, has convinced me that this is rather to be wished for than expected." [6] His confidence in the strength of his position was justified provided Howe made a frontal attack. His apprehensions as to the behavior of his men, engendered by the rout of the militia at Kip's Bay, were almost immediately dispelled.

The great question in the minds of the American command the night of the 15th was whether Howe would follow up his success by an immediate attack. From the American lines, because of the dense woods on the heights to the south of the Hollow Way, nothing could be seen of the enemy's camp in that quarter. Hence there could be no knowledge of preparations for attack, nor of its launching, until the van of the attacking force emerged from the woods into the Hollow Way. To obtain such information a reconnaissance was necessary.

There was in the army a corps of Rangers, about 120 volunteers chosen chiefly from the Connecticut regiments for detached duty, scouting, and the like. They were commanded by Captain Thomas Knowlton, a figure of note. "Six feet high, erect and elegant in figure and formed more for activity than strength," cool and courageous in battle, "courteous and affable in manners . . . the favorite of superior officers, the idol of his soldiers," he had already achieved reputation at Bunker Hill and on Long Island. To him and his corps Washington looked for information as to Howe's intentions.[7]

Before dawn on the 16th Knowlton led his men down from the American position, across the Hollow Way, and up through the woods on the opposite heights behind which lay the British left. They came at length upon a stone house considerably in advance of the main body of the enemy, and at the same time upon the pickets of two battalions of British light infantry under General Leslie holding an advanced post.

At the alarm the light infantry, about 400 strong, advanced. The Rangers took a position behind a stone wall and opened fire. A brisk skirmish ensued. The Americans had fired eight rounds when they discovered the 42nd Highlanders, the Black Watch, coming up on their left and threatening to flank them. Ten of Knowlton's men having fallen, he gave the order to retreat. The British light infantry pushed forward after them through the woods, but the Rangers got away in good order.[8]

The sound of the firing put both armies on the alert. In the American camp the advancing light infantry could be seen emerging from the woods on the opposite height. It might prove to be the beginning of an attack.

The Americans were ordered under arms, but the enemy halted at the edge of their plateau. Pleased by the sight of the Rangers in retreat, the British "in the most insulting manner sounded their bugle-horns as is usual after a Fox-chase. I never felt such a sensation before—it seemed to crown our disgrace." So Colonel Joseph Reed wrote to his wife.[9] Washington, that old fox hunter, must have recognized the taunting notes of the horns as the customary signal of a fox gone to earth. On top of yesterday's affair at Kip's Bay it was too much. Something must be done to wipe out that disgrace and arouse the spirits of his men.[10] He planned a frontal feint with a small force to draw the British light infantry down to the open ground of the Hollow Way, so that a stronger detachment could encircle their right flank and cut them off. For the feint he ordered out 150 volunteers from Nixon's brigade, led by Lieutenant Colonel Archibald Crary of Rhode Island. Knowlton's Rangers and three companies of riflemen from Weedon's 3rd Virginia Regiment, under command of Major Andrew Leitch, were to be the flanking party, about 230 in number.

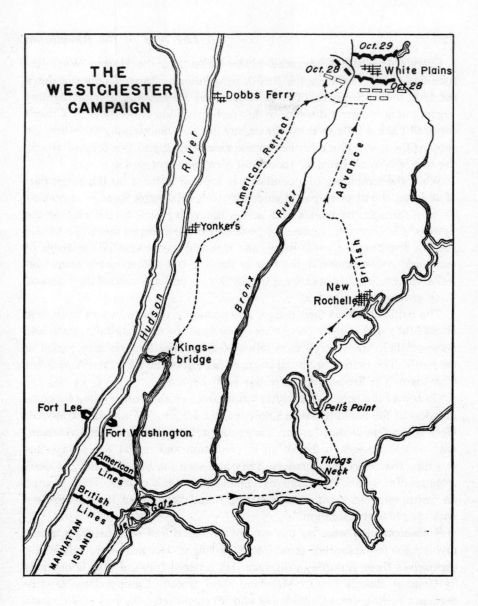

THE
WESTCHESTER
CAMPAIGN

Oct. 29
Oct. 28   White Plains
Oct. 28

Dobbs Ferry

Hudson River

Bronx River

American Retreat

Advance

British

Yonkers

New Rochelle

Kings-
bridge

Pell's Point

Fort Lee

Fort Washington

Throgs
Neck

American
Lines

British
Lines

Hell Gate

MANHATTAN
ISLAND

Crary's detachment advanced boldly down into the Hollow Way. Responding to this challenge the British light infantry "immediately ran down the Hill, took possession of some fences and Bushes and a smart fighting began, but at too great distance to do much execution either side." [11] Crary's men fell back a little to draw the enemy on, still maintaining their fire. To support them and give a further appearance of reality to this feigned attack, the rest of Nixon's brigade, about 800 men, was sent down.

While the semblance of a conflict was kept up in front for the better part of an hour, the flanking party, guided by Colonel Joseph Reed, was making its way through the woods and across the valley well to the east of the fighters. Unobserved, it gained a position on the enemy's flank. So far, so good; a few hundred yards more, and it would have mounted the ledge of rocks and swept around in the rear of the foe. But unfortunately some "inferior officers" could not restrain their ardor, or perhaps control their nerves. They gave an order to fire.

The British realized their danger and promptly withdrew to an open field about 200 yards in their rear, where they again formed behind a fence and resumed their fire. Crary's men followed them. The flankers also joined in the battle. The British again fell back, to the top of the ridge, the Americans after them. The fire on both sides was hotly kept up.

On top of the height and within ten minutes of each other, the two commanders of the flanking party, Knowlton and Leitch, fell mortally wounded. Here was a fine chance for the Yankee Rangers and the Virginia riflemen, both now leaderless, to break up in confusion and repeat Kip's Bay. But this time they were the pursuers. They had seen the backs of the redcoats, a stimulating sight. The company commanders took charge. They pressed on "with splendid spirit and animation," and "continued the engagement with the greatest resolution."

Reinforcements were on the way. Washington had seen his little affair, involving a few hundred, grow into a real fight. His men were redeeming themselves from yesterday's disgrace. He ordered forward nine companies of General Reazin Beall's Maryland state troops, Colonel Paul Dudley Sargent's brigade from Connecticut and Massachusetts, the rest of Weedon's Virginians, and, most important for the morale of the army, Douglas's regiment, the one disgraced at Kip's Bay. That old warhorse, Israel Putnam, hurried to the fray, along with General Nathanael Greene, General George Clinton, and two field guns. Meanwhile, the first British contingents had retired into a buckwheat field, the American light artillery having "put them to flight with two discharges." [12] There they were reinforced by additional light infantry and by the Black Watch.

The fighting grew hotter, the Americans firing steadily and the British stubbornly holding their ground. As the American reinforcements came on, Leslie called on the British reserve in that quarter for more troops. From their post three miles in the rear, on the run, "without a halt to draw breath," [13] came British grenadiers, the 33rd Regiment, a battalion of Hessian grenadiers, and a company of jägers, with two fieldpieces hauled by men. This addition brought the number of British engaged up to 5,000.

The jägers and the Highlanders with the two field guns got there first. For two hours, from noon to two o'clock, the combat was spirited. The British guns fired sixty rounds. Then the Hessians and the Scotsmen, their ammunition running low, retreated. The Americans followed them in hot pursuit, back into an orchard, down a slope, and up another hill. The Hessian grenadiers came up to them. The rest of the British reserve was near at hand, when Washington, seeing that the affair was developing into a general engagement in full force, which he by no means desired, sent an aide, Tench Tilghman, with orders to his troops to withdraw. "The pursuit of a flying enemy was so new a scene that it was with difficulty our men could be brought to retire," but they "gave a Hurra! and left the field in good order." [14]

The losses on both sides were, as usual, variously reported, each side minimizing its own and exaggerating the other's casualties. Howe reported for the British 14 killed and about 78 wounded,[15] but Major Baurmeister, a Hessian, said there were 70 dead and 200 wounded.[16] Washington said his loss was "about sixty"; [17] but more probably there were 30 killed and something less than 100 wounded and missing.[18] In the deaths of Knowlton and Leitch the Americans suffered their severest loss. Knowlton was, in Washington's words, "a valuable and gallant officer." [19] Leitch had arrived in camp with Weedon's Virginians but a few days before the battle. He was a brave soldier of great promise.

Though gallantly fought on both sides, it was a small affair. Yet its effects in both camps were immediate and important. Among the Americans the depression engendered by the recent succession of defeats and retreats was dispelled. Many of the soldiers who had fled from Kip's Bay without firing a shot had now helped to drive the British and Hessian regulars back more than a mile, had fought them in the open field at forty yards range for more than an hour, and had withdrawn in good order to their own lines only when commanded to do so, without being pursued. That was good news for the whole army. Caesar Rodney wrote to his brother about it: "That New England men placed to defend the landing-place [Kip's

Bay], behaved in a most dastardly, cowardly, scandalous manner, is most certain; but that courage is not always to be found the same, even in the same person, is equally true, and verified in the very same men; for some of them the day following were in the other engagement and behaved with great bravery." [20]

Moreover the "Southern" and New England troops had fought side by side with equal courage; neither could criticize the other. To be sure, both claimed the honors of the day. Captain John Gooch of Rhode Island gave "the first Lawrells" to the Yankees, while Lieutenant Tench Tilghman of Maryland wrote, "The Virginia and Maryland Troops bear the palm"; [21] but that was only human. As a whole the army had recovered its self-respect and gained greatly in morale. "You can hardly conceive the change it has made in our army," wrote Colonel Joseph Reed. "The men have recovered their spirits and feel a confidence which before they had quite lost." With some suggestion of doubt he added, "I hope the effects will be lasting." [22]

To the British this affair was an eye-opener. The rebels could stand up and fight bravely against the best of the British and Hessian regulars. The campaign was not going to be an easy succession of Kip's Bays. In the light of this discovery, some thought must be given to the next move. So, for nearly four weeks, Howe contented himself with fortifying his lines, forgoing further offensive movements until what he had gained had been secured.

CHAPTER 21

Throg's Neck and Pelham

While the two armies sat facing each other in their respective fortified positions, there was much speculation in the American camp as to Howe's next move. "The General Officers," says Heath in his memoirs, "were divided in opinion." Some of them expected an effort by Howe to make himself master of the whole island, and thought that the reduction of Fort Washington would be first attempted. That stronghold, upon a height overlooking the Hudson, was a mile or more in the rear of the American lines on Harlem Heights, and it is not clear what plan for its conquest was attributed to Howe that did not involve first a frontal attack on Washington's entrenchments. Others looked for a landing at some point on Long Island Sound in a line with or in the rear of the Americans' more northerly defenses, so that they could be flanked.

With this difference of opinion prevailing, it was "determined in council to guard against both." Ten thousand men were to be held on the Manhattan Island "at or near Fort Washington," that is to say, within the existing lines. Heath, with ten thousand, was to hold the Kingsbridge sector at the upper end of the Harlem River, a floating bridge being thrown across that water so that communication with the first body could be maintained. Greene was to command five thousand on the other side of the Hudson at or near Fort Constitution, which was directly opposite Fort Washington.[1]

Washington had 25,000 troops on paper, but only on paper. As has been said, no more than about 16,000 were present and fit for duty, and of these a large proportion were militia, no more to be depended upon than "a broken staff," as Washington put it.[2] The success of this ambitious plan, therefore, would appear more to be desired than expected.

Washington fully realized his difficulties. "It is not in the power of words," he wrote to his brother on September 22, "to describe the task I have to perform. Fifty thousand pounds would not induce me again to undergo what I have done." And to his cousin: "Such is my situation that if I were to wish the bitterest curse to an enemy on this side of the grave, I should put him in my stead with my feelings." [3]

It was not only that he had too few men to defend all the threatened positions, but also that those he did have were not of the best quality. Although the troops engaged in the recent affair at Harlem Heights had proved themselves good soldiers, the American army was not entirely composed of heroes. The present, too long period of inactivity was undermining the army's morale and sapping its discipline. "A spirit of desertion, cowardice, plunder and shrinking from duty, when attended with fatigue or danger, prevailed too generally throughout the whole army," Colonel Joseph Reed wrote of this period.[4]

Courts-martial sat day after day trying cases of insubordination, mutiny, theft, cowardice in the face of the enemy, desertion, and other offenses. Such crimes and misdemeanors are, of course, common in all armies, but in this they were far too prevalent. Washington wrote to the Congress: "Such a spirit has gone forth . . . that neither publick or private property is secure. Every hour brings the most distressing complaints of the Ravages of our own Troops who are become infinitely more formidable to the poor Farmers and Inhabitants than the common Enemy. . . . The Baggage of Officers and the Hospital Stores, even the Quarters of the General Officers are not exempt from Rapine." [5]

Besides these defects in its personnel, the army as a whole was "in want of almost every necessary; Tents, Camp Kettles, Blankets and Clothes of all Kinds." Reinforcements from New England were coming in "without a single Tent nor a necessary of any kind . . . not a pan or a kettle," [6] and winter was on its way. Even now it was cold at night on Harlem Heights.

All this was bad enough, but the prospect for the near future was worse. The entire army could look forward to its dissolution and complete disappearance within the next two or three months, when its term of enlistment would expire. It was true that the Congress had at last, on September 16, overcome its "jealousy of a standing army," [7] and voted for a new army of eighty-eight battalions "to serve during the present war." [8] But who could foretell when that projected force would be an army in being?

Howe remained inactive for twenty-six days while with characteristic deliberation and with equally characteristic sagacity he made his plans. The

American lines were too strong to invite a frontal attack. Nor was that Howe's favored strategy. Circumvention was less costly and more nearly certain of good results.

There was a small peninsula sticking out into the Sound from the mainland almost due east of the American lines, Throg's Neck—originally Throckmorton's, hence Throck's and Throg's, but also Frog's Neck or Point. And there was a road running northwest from that point to Kingsbridge, well in the rear of the main fortified position of the Americans. Howe finally decided to use that road in the hope that he could sweep the American left flank and possibly pin the American army against the Hudson.

Leaving Lord Percy to hold his lines with three brigades, Howe embarked his main army in the evening of October 12 in eighty vessels of all sorts, passed through Hell Gate under cover of a fog and landed an advance force of 4,000 on Throg's Neck. But it was not a neck, a peninsula; it was, in effect, an island, separated from the mainland by a creek with marshy borders. There were but two approaches from it to the main, a causeway and bridge at the lower end, a ford at the upper, and those approaches were not unguarded. Had Howe landed his men farther to the east, his flanking movement would have had much greater chances of success.

General Heath had posted Colonel Edward Hand with a small detachment of his 1st Pennsylvania rifle regiment at the causeway. The riflemen had removed the planks of the bridge and concealed themselves behind a long pile of cordwood beside its western end. When the van of the enemy approached the gap, it was met by a sudden well aimed fire. The surprised troops were thrown into confusion and fell back to the top of the nearest elevation. No further effort was made to pass that way. Twenty-five American riflemen behind a woodpile had stopped the British army. Another British detachment had headed for the ford, but it too was checked, by a guard posted there. Both of these outposts were promptly reinforced. Colonel William Prescott's Massachusetts Continental regiment and Captain-Lieutenant David Bryant with a 6-pounder and its crew went to Hand's aid. Captain John Graham led a New York regiment of Continentals, together with Captain Daniel Jackson and his fieldpiece, to the post at the ford. The defenders then numbered about 1,800 men. Both sides now began to dig in at their respective positions, the riflemen and the jägers keeping up "a scattered popping at each other across the marsh."

The rest of Howe's force arrived in the afternoon, and the bulk of the British army was at the Neck. But Howe saw that the creek and the marshes were not easily to be crossed against such determined opposition. His men went into camp and lay there for six days while their baggage and supplies were brought up from New York.[9]

Howe had got off to a bad start, but his course was not yet run. Throg's Neck was not the only available landing place. There was Pell's Point, only three miles to the east, which was part of the mainland. It offered the Americans no narrow way to defend.

Howe's flanking move placed the American army in great peril, and a council of war assembled at Washington's headquarters on October 16 to consider the situation. General Charles Lee, who had just rejoined the main army after winning laurels by a successful defense of Charleston in South Carolina, vehemently urged a general retreat to safer positions. However, Congress had resolved on October 11 that Washington be "desired, if it be practicable, by every art and whatever expence, to obstruct effectually the navigation of the North River, between Fort Washington and Mount Constitution." [10] That meant that the line of sunken hulks and the "chevaux-de-frise" stretching across the river from Fort Washington to Fort Constitution, which line had already been found to be easily penetrable by British ships, should be maintained, if "practicable." If the chevaux-de-frise was to be maintained, the two forts had to be defended. Since the barrier had already been proved to be useless, the council of war need not have been concerned about this resolution. Accordingly there was no need to hold Fort Washington. However, the generals decided that, as "the enemy's whole force is in our rear at Frog's Point," it was not possible to hold the present positions on the Heights, and at the same time "that Fort Washington be retained as long as possible." [11]

The proposed withdrawal was to go as far as White Plains, leaving Fort Washington, with its garrison of 2,000, fifteen miles away and completely isolated in a country entirely held by the enemy, with no possibility of succor or supplies except from Fort Constitution across the Hudson. Yet it was to be held. A worse military decision has not often been made. The cost incurred was to be frightful.

Stirling's brigade was hurried northward to seize and hold the desired position at White Plains until the main army should arrive. It made the march in about four hours. The movement of the main army northward was begun on the 18th. Over Kingsbridge, which crossed the Harlem River, and along the west bank of the Bronx River, the American column, 13,000 men with artillery, baggage, and supplies, made its slow and toilsome way— slow and toilsome because of the lack of horses and wagons. After a day's journey, the wagons would dump their loads by the wayside and return for more. The artillery was dragged by hand. Thus, by starts and stops and with infinite labor, a day's journey was accomplished in four.[12]

Meanwhile, entrenched posts were established at intervals along the heights on the west side of the Bronx River to protect the movement of the troops on the road farther west and close to the Hudson. Spencer's division held that line until the main American army had reached White Plains.

Howe finally found that more favorable landing place at Pell's Point. On the same day that the Americans started their northward trek, he embarked his army at Throg's Neck and landed it on the Point.

Colonel John Glover, of the amphibious Marblehead regiment, was then commanding a small brigade made up of four skeleton Massachusetts regiments—his own, Colonel Joseph Read's, Colonel William Shepard's, and Colonel Loammi Baldwin's—in all about seven hundred fifty men with three fieldpieces. He had been but lately posted near the little village of Eastchester to guard the roads from Pell's Point towards the American rear. Early in the morning of the 18th he ascended a near-by hill with his glass and discovered in Eastchester Bay, beside the Point, "upwards of two hundred [boats] . . . all manned and formed in four grand divisions." He turned out his men and marched to meet the landing force.

Glover took a position on the road about a mile from the Point. His own regiment was stationed in the rear as a reserve. The others were strung along behind stone walls lining the road, Read's at the front end or left of the line, Shepard's next, and then Baldwin's. A captain and 40 men were detached and sent forward. They met the enemy's advance guard and, at 50 yards distance, received their fire without loss. Their own reply struck down four men. Five rounds were exchanged in which two Americans were killed and several wounded. When the enemy were "not more than thirty yards distant," Glover ordered his little party to fall back, "which was masterly well done." "The enemy gave a shout and advanced." When they were within a hundred feet, Read's men, lying undiscovered behind their stone wall, "rose up and gave them the whole charge; the enemy broke and retreated for the main body to come up."

For an hour and a half there was no further conflict. Then the whole advance unit of the British, 4,000 men with seven guns, came on. At fifty yards distance Read's men again arose and delivered a volley. The British replied with musketry and fieldpieces. Seven rounds were fired by this regiment before it retreated to take a position behind the wall beyond Shepard's battalion. Again the enemy "shouted and pushed on till they came to Shepard, posted behind a fine, double stone-wall." His men fired by platoons seventeen rounds, "causing them to retreat several times."

Another backward movement of the Americans carried Shepard and Read behind Baldwin. Then Glover ordered his brigade off the field, across a creek, and to a position in his rear on a hill. "The enemy halted and played away their artillery at us and we at them, till night, without any damage on our side and but little on theirs," says Glover. After dark the Americans marched away, about three miles, and encamped, "after fighting all day without victuals or drink, laying as a picket all night, the heavens over us and the earth under us." [13]

Glover lost eight killed and thirteen wounded. Howe reported three killed and twenty wounded; but the chief of the attacking force were Hessians, and their losses were not always included in the British official reports. The Americans thought the Hessian losses were very heavy.[14]

Another interesting little affair occurred on October 22. Major Robert Rogers, noted for audacity and ruthlessness in the French and Indian War, commanded a corps of Tories called "The Queen's American Rangers," about five hundred strong. Looked upon as renegades, he and his men were especially detested by the American troops. Moreover they had been aggressively active, attacking and defeating militia companies and capturing quantities of army stores. They were now in a detached camp at Mamaroneck not far from the right wing of the main body of the British. It was decided to try to cut them off.

"The redoubtable Colonel Haslet" was chosen to conduct this enterprise, with his Delaware regiment,[15] "which since the bravery exhibited on Long Island . . . seems to have been chosen for all feats of peculiar danger." [16] Reinforced by certain Virginia and Maryland companies, his force was made up to seven hundred fifty men.

Late in the night of Tuesday the 22nd, Haslet's force set out on the road from White Plains to Mamaroneck, about five miles. It led them so close to the British right that the most profound silence was necessary to avoid discovery. Having accurate knowledge of the usual disposition of Rogers's men, they approached his camp at a point where but a single sentinel was posted. They seized and silenced him. The way seemed open for a surprise attack on the whole camp, but the astute Rogers had that day concluded his encampment was insufficiently guarded and had posted Captain Eagles and sixty men between the lone sentinel and the main position.

Haslet's vanguard came upon their bivouac, fairly stumbling over the sleepers in the darkness. The rest of his force came up on the run, and there ensued a hurly-burly of a fight. To deceive their assailants, the Rangers echoed the Americans' cry: "Surrender, you Tory dogs! Surrender!" In the darkness friend and foe could not be distinguished. There was a hopeless tangle, Rangers and Haslet's men grappling each other indiscriminately. In the turmoil Eagles and about a third of his men slipped away. The rest were subdued and captured.

Haslet then pushed on toward the main camp. Rogers's troops, thoroughly alarmed, had turned out. There was an exchange of fire, but the advantage of a surprise had been lost. Haslet, contenting himself with a partial success, called off his men and marched back to White Plains with thirty-six prisoners, a pair of colors, sixty muskets, and as many highly prized blankets. He had lost three killed and twelve wounded. The Rangers' loss, besides the prisoners, remains unrecorded. General Heath praised it as "a pretty affair . . . conducted with good address." [17] Like Glover's little fight, this enterprise was chiefly valuable as a stimulus to the fighting spirit of the Americans.

CHAPTER 22

White Plains

Before Howe moved in force against the American position at White Plains the American army was again reorganized. Charles Lee was again with the main army, and also Sullivan and Stirling. Sullivan had been released from captivity in exchange for General Richard Prescott, taken by Montgomery when he captured the British ships at Montreal. Stirling had also been freed, in a trade for Montfort Browne, former royal governor of West Florida. Seven divisions were formed, under the command respectively of Generals Greene, Lee, Heath, Sullivan, Putnam, Spencer, and Benjamin Lincoln. Greene, with about 3,500 men, held the fort across the Hudson from Fort Washington formerly named Constitution but now called Lee in honor of that much respected soldier. About 1,500 men under Colonel Robert Magaw occupied Fort Washington. The main army under Washington numbered about 14,500 present and fit.[1]

Washington had chosen a position on a series of hills overlooking the White Plains. Putnam's division was posted at the right on Purdy Hill, Heath's at the left on Hatfield Hill. Washington himself held the centre at White Plains village. Two lines of defensive works were thrown up, in a shallow curve from the Bronx River on the right to a millpond on the left. The ends of the lines were drawn back so as to defend the flanks.[2]

On October 19, when Howe left his camp at Eastchester, the American retreat from Harlem Heights to White Plains was only well begun. If he had seized his chance then or on the next day and sent his light infantry, grenadiers, and jägers, 4,000 strong, across by the straight road to Kingsbridge, only six miles away, in a swift attack upon the long, straggling line

260

of Washington's army in the confusion of its movement, there could hardly have been any other result than a complete rout of the Americans. Instead he lay at New Rochelle for three days, and then only moved to Mamaroneck, two or three miles. There he encamped for four days. It was not until the 28th that he arrived before Washington's position at White Plains. He had advanced about seventeen miles in ten days.[3] Why Howe executed his flanking movement so slowly is not known.

"The sun had set and risen more than forty times," wrote Trevelyan, the English historian, in acid comment on the progress of the British army, "since General Howe broke up his Summer cantonments on Staten Island. In seven weeks—with an irresistible army and a fleet which there was nothing to resist—he had traversed, from point to point, a distance of exactly thirty-five miles." [4] Trevelyan's judgment of Howe is perhaps too harsh, on this and other occasions.

Meanwhile the British general had received reinforcements, in any event. On the day he landed at Pell's Point there came into New York harbor 120 sail bringing the second grand division of German mercenaries, 3,997 Hessians, 670 Waldeckers, and a company of jägers, all under command of Lieutenant General Wilhelm von Knyphausen, also about 3,400 British recruits. The Germans were at once dispatched by water to New Rochelle to hold that position while Howe proceeded toward White Plains.[5]

The opposing armies clashed again in the morning of the 28th. Spencer, with a half-dozen New England regiments from Lee's division, about 1,500 men, had been sent out to meet the British advance. They took a position behind stone walls about a mile and a half below the American lines and held their fire until the British van was within one hundred feet. Then they delivered a volley that halted it and threw it back. But when Colonel Rall's regiment of Hessians was about to turn their left, the Americans retreated to another wall and after that to another, holding each position until nearly outflanked. At one time a general volley delivered at close range scattered an attacking party of Hessian grenadiers "like leaves in a whirlwind; and they ran off so far that some of the Americans ran out to the ground where they were and brought off their arms and accoutrements and rum that the men who fell had with them, which we had time to drink rounds with before they came on again." So wrote one of the American officers.[6]

But the Hessians did come on again and drove Spencer's troops back across the Bronx River and to Chatterton's Hill, which two militia regiments were engaged in fortifying under the direction of Colonel Rufus Putnam. Rall's regiment, checked by the fire from that elevation, retired to a small hill just south of Chatterton's. The loss of the Americans in this series of encounters was 12 killed, 23 wounded, and 2 missing.[7]

Chatterton's Hill was about half a mile from the right of the main American lines, separated from it by the narrow valley of the Bronx River. It was a ridge three-quarters of a mile long in a north and south direction, rising one hundred eighty feet above the river, which ran along its eastern foot. That side of the hill was steep and heavily wooded. The gently rounded top was divided by stone walls into cultivated fields. Because the hill was a menace to the westerly end of the American lines a belated effort to fortify it was now being made.[8]

After the retreat of Spencer's corps Washington ordered Colonel Haslet with his Delaware regiment to reinforce the men entrenching there. Haslet took post a little below the top of the hill on its eastern side. Later General Alexander McDougall's brigade was also sent there. It was composed of McDougall's own regiment, the 1st New York, Ritzema's 3rd New York, Smallwood's regiment of Marylanders, lately strengthened after its disaster at Long Island, Webb's from Connecticut, and two fieldpieces. These, with Haslet's men, made up a force of about 1,250 rank and file. With the militia already there, the American detachment numbered about 1,600.[9] As senior officer McDougall took command.

Before he arrived several enemy fieldpieces had opened fire on the hill and had hit one of Colonel Putnam's militiamen. "The whole regiment broke and fled immediately and were not rallied without much difficulty." [10] On McDougall's arrival the two militia regiments, Brooks's from Massachusetts and Graham's from New York, were stationed on the right behind a stone wall, at Haslet's suggestion. Smallwood and Haslet held the centre, from which McDougall's, Ritzema's, and Webb's regiments extended to the left.[11]

The whole British army was now coming on in the plain below. It halted, and its general officers gathered in a wheat field for consultation. To the Americans on Chatterton's Hill and in their fortified lines, it presented a brilliant, though formidable, spectacle. "The sun shone bright, their arms glittered, and perhaps troops never were shewn to more advantage than those now appeared," wrote General Heath in his memoirs.[12] An officer in Webb's regiment even more eloquently described the scene: "Its appearance was truly magnificent. A bright autumnal sun shed its lustre on the polished arms; and the rich array of dress and military equipage gave an imposing grandeur to the scene as they advanced in all the pomp and circumstance of war." [13]

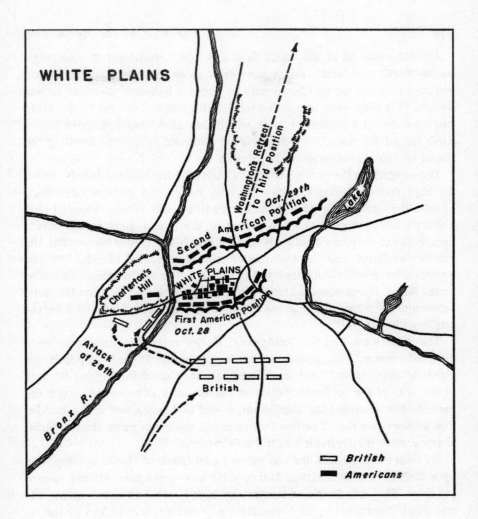

WHITE PLAINS

Washington's Retreat
to Third Position
Oct. 29th

Lake

Second American Position

WHITE PLAINS

Chatterton's Hill

First American Position
Oct. 28

Attack
of 28th

Bronx R.

British

☐ British
■ Americans

After the council in the wheat field a British detachment of eight regiments, 4,000 men, and a dozen guns drew away from the main body and marched to a hill facing Chatterton's at about a half-mile distance. It was obvious that they were to attack McDougall's force. The rest of the army "all sat down in the same order in which they stood, no one appearing to move out of his place," [14] a professional audience of 10,000 awaiting the rise of the curtain on an interesting drama.

The overture to the performance was played by the British artillery. From the high ground facing Chatterton's Hill, it began a furious cannonade against the little force of Americans awaiting the attack. General von Heister's adjutant general afterwards said that these guns made such a thunderstorm that one could neither see nor hear. Haslet wrote that the enemy's artillery "kept up a continual peal of reiterated thunder." [15] The attacking force meanwhile deployed in line of battle on the other side of the Bronx River. It was obscured from the Americans by the woods on the slope below and by the smoke of a fire among the trees, probably ignited by the artillery discharges.[16]

The Americans had two fieldpieces. Haslet urged McDougall to bring them into action. The general ordered one forward. It was "so poorly appointed," says Haslet, "that myself was forced to assist in dragging it along in the rear of the regiment. While so employed, a cannon-ball struck the carriage and scattered the shot about, a wad of blazing tow in the middle. The artillerymen fled. The few that returned made not more than two discharges when they retreated with the field-piece." [17]

As soon as the British line was formed a battalion of Hessians, supported by a British brigade and von Donop's Hessian grenadiers, started toward the river. The little Bronx was unusually high because of recent rains, and was much obstructed by an accumulation of old tree trunks and by the remains of ancient beaver-dams. The Hessians declined to try to cross it. It was therefore necessary to construct a rough bridge by felling trees and laying fence rails across them. While the bridge building was in progress, Smallwood's Marylanders and Ritzema's 3rd New York came more than halfway down the hill and opened fire, throwing the Hessians into disorder.

The British General Leslie was then informed of a ford a short distance downstream. He called on the 28th and 35th British regiments to show the Hessians what true British courage could do. Cheering lustily they followed him to the ford and across it. Immediately he ordered a charge with the bayonet; but the hill was steep, the trees thick, and the fire of the Americans heavy. The attackers were thrown back upon the 5th and 49th regiments and the Hessians, who were hurrying to their support.

The whole attacking force had now crossed the stream, either by the bridge or through the ford. It formed in column, marched north along the base of the hill, faced into line parallel with the Americans, and started up the steep slope. Ritzema and Smallwood contested the advance with great gallantry. A detachment of British light infantry tried to turn the Americans' left flank. Webb's Connecticut regiment moved to the left, met the detachment and drove it back.

The British cannonade was now imperiling the attack well advanced up the hill. It was silenced, and orders were sent for attack from another quarter.

Rall's Hessian regiment, unobserved by the defenders since it had betaken itself to the hill on their right after driving back Spencer's force, now went into action. Suddenly, it swept down the slope, across a little intervening valley, and charged up Chatterton's Hill against the New York and Massachusetts militia regiments of Brooks and Graham. They changed front to face the attack, and fired a good volley. But then Birch's British light dragoons came into view, kettledrums beating, trumpets sounding a charge. The galloping horses and the flashing sabers struck terror into the hearts of the green militiamen, who had never seen cavalry in action. They broke and fled in the utmost disorder. The horsemen pursued them, cut off their retreat to the camp, fell upon them in scattered groups, killing and wounding many. For half a mile this rout continued. Then a hundred of the fleeing men rallied and tried to resist, but in vain. Some of them escaped into the woods. The rest surrendered.

The flight of the militia had uncovered the right flank, had left the Delaware regiment unsupported on that side. Haslet drew his men back toward the north, but Rall's Hessians fell upon them in full force. A part of the first three Delaware companies broke and were driven from the field, but Haslet held the rest, lined them up behind a fence, and "twice repulsed the Light Troops and Horse of the enemy." [18]

"During the struggle thus made by the heroic Haslet," [19] the frontal attack had continued. The New York and Maryland troops were driven back. Smallwood's men fought desperately. Smallwood himself was twice wounded, and at last his regiment was thrown into confusion. Ritzema's New Yorkers made an equally gallant effort, but the weight of the onslaught was too heavy. McDougall saw that further resistance was hopeless. He retreated with the New York and Maryland troops to a road leading to the American camp and held them there to protect the withdrawal of the Delawares, standing alone on the field.

Now the dragoons were returning from their chase and forming for a charge on the Delawares, along with all the rest of the attacking force. "Seeing ourselves deserted on all hands," says Haslet, "and the continued column of the enemy advancing, we also retired." [20] "In a great body, neither running nor observing the best of order," they were the last to leave the field, and they brought off the one remaining American gun.[21]

Trevelyan says, "The Delaware regiment, which had learned at Long Island that prisoners are not easily made, unless they make themselves, brought up the rear and fought sullenly and composedly while any of the assailants followed them within shooting range." [22]

The retreating troops were met by a detachment from the main body coming too late to help them in the fight. Haslet then re-formed his men and "marched into camp in the rear of the body sent to reinforce us." "The British ascended the hill very slowly; and, when arrived at its summit, formed and dressed their line without the least attempt to pursue the Americans." [23]

The loss of the Americans is variously reported. Bancroft says fewer than a hundred killed and wounded. Irving says three to four hundred, including prisoners taken. Whitton, citing an English account, says very definitely 313. Hufeland, citing regimental returns, says 175.[24] On the other side, as officially reported, there were 28 killed, including 5 officers, and 126 wounded, also including 5 officers. Among the Hessians there were about 77 casualties.[25]

This battle, measured by the numbers engaged, was a small affair, but it had important results. The check Howe received changed the course of events, as will be seen.

CHAPTER 23

Fort Washington

The British army dug in on Chatterton's Hill, establishing in that position the left wing of a line of entrenchments that extended eastward in a curve threatening both flanks of the American lines. Anticipating further British attacks, Washington prudently had his sick and wounded removed to a safer place in the rear and, even while the battle on the hill was in progress, transferred much of his baggage and equipment to a stronger position on the heights of North Castle.

The results were uncomfortable to the Americans who had been engaged in the fight. When they got back to camp they found that their baggage had been removed. For three or four nights they slept in the woods without even blankets, covered only by the snow that fell upon them.[1] In the night of October 31 the American army slipped away to the North Castle heights, leaving Stirling's brigade to hold the old position temporarily. The garrison at Fort Washington was not moved.

Howe, reinforced by two brigades from Percy's force on Manhattan, now had about 20,000 men. He took possession of the old American lines but made no other hostile move for the next four days except a brief and unimportant artillery engagement with Heath's division on November 1.[2]

Washington busied himself with his entrenchments. Three redoubts, with a line of earthworks in front, were erected with what must have appeared to the enemy to be magical swiftness. Indeed, there was something of magic about them, that is to say of illusion, for that line of earthworks was, in fact, largely made up of cornstalks pulled from near-by fields, with lumps of earth clinging to their roots. They were piled, tops inward, clods outward, and covered with loose earth.[3]

Considering these apparently formidable defenses, Howe altered his plans. During the night of November 4, the sentinels at the American outposts heard sounds like the rumbling of heavy wagons in the British camp. In the morning it was seen that their advanced sentinels had been withdrawn. Some hostile movement of their army was apprehended, and the Americans were ordered under arms. But before long it appeared that the enemy forces were on the march towards the southwest. They were, in fact, on the way to Dobbs Ferry.

A cheering sight to the Americans was this withdrawal. They were again feeling satisfied, in spite of Chatterton's Hill, having "good flour, beef and pork in plenty, with grog to wash it down." They had been retreating and retreating. But now it appeared that they had balked Howe's repeated efforts to get behind them and hem them in. He had given up and was decamping. Contented with the results of the strategy of their generals, warworn and ragged though they were, soldiers and officers were "in high spirits, loath to give an inch to their enemies." [4]

But where were their enemies going right now? That was, as Washington wrote to the Congress, "a matter of much conjecture and speculation." His own belief was that Howe would "make a descent with a part of his troops into New Jersey, and with another part invest Fort Washington." [5]

A council of war was held on November 6. It was decided that, "supposing the enemy to be retreating towards New-York," it would be "proper to throw a body of troops into New Jersey immediately," and that 3,000 men should take post at Peekskill and the passes of the Highlands.[6] But no serious consideration seems to have been given to abandoning Fort Washington, against which, as soon after appeared, Howe was now actually marching.

The northernmost part of Manhattan Island, extending from Washington's old lines on Harlem Heights to Spuyten Duyvil Creek, a distance of about four miles, is a narrow tongue of high land lying between the Harlem River and the Hudson, its width about three-quarters of a mile. It is bordered on both rivers by precipitous rocky cliffs a hundred feet high. These flank a plateau which rises close to the Hudson, to a narrow hill one mile long and 230 feet high above the water. This hill, called Mount Washington in 1776, is now known as Washington Heights. On the Harlem River side was Laurel Hill, nearly as high. Between the two there was a narrow valley, a gorge through which a road led to Kingsbridge beyond the Harlem. The sides of these two eminences were steep, rocky, and rugged. They and most of the whole tongue of land were densely wooded.[7]

On Mount Washington Colonel Rufus Putnam, the American army's chief engineer, had laid out the lines of a fort which the 3rd and 5th Pennsylvania regiments had erected in July under the command of Colonels John Shee and Robert Magaw.

The fort was a pentagonal earthwork with five bastions. It covered about four acres of ground, but it was a simple, open earthwork with a surrounding abatis and no ditch worth mentioning. It had no casemates, no bombproofs, no barracks, no buildings of any sort except "a wooden magazine and some offices," [8] no fuel, and no water. There was no well, nor any interior water supply whatever. In case of a siege water could be got only from the Hudson, 230 feet below. It had no outworks except "an incipient one at the north, nor any of those exterior, multiplied obstacles and defences, that . . . could entitle it to the name of fortress, in any degree capable of withstanding a siege," wrote Captain Alexander Graydon in his *Memoirs*.[9]

The function of the fort, its only important function at least, was to defend the eastern end of a line of sunken hulks and a chevaux de frise stretching across the Hudson. The purpose of these was to prevent the passage of British ships up the river. The western end of the line was similarly supported by Fort Lee on the New Jersey shore. That anyone should have seriously considered trying to hold such a fort against Howe's whole army of more than 20,000 completely equipped soldiers, operating freely both by land and by water, seems incredible. That such an attempt should have been persisted in after November 7, when the passage of three British ships around those obstructions had proved them to be ineffective and, by the same token, demonstrated the uselessness of both forts, is still more unbelievable. Yet such was the case.

Israel Putnam, with his characteristic exuberant optimism, had "an overweening confidence" [10] in the impregnability of Fort Washington. Colonel Magaw, its commandant, said he could hold it "till the end of December," and that, "should matters grow desperate," [11] he could carry off the garrison and even the stores to the New Jersey side. Strangest of all, Nathanael Greene, one of the most competent general officers in the army, entertained a similar delusion. He could not "conceive the garrison to be in any great danger." He was sure that it could be "brought off at any time." [12] Washington, however, doubted.

On November 8 Washington wrote to Greene, who commanded the troops in both forts: "The late passage of the 3 Vessels up the North River . . . is so plain a Proof of the Inefficacy of all the Obstructions we have thrown into it, that I cannot but think, it will fully Justify a Change in the disposition which has been made. If we cannot prevent Vessels passing up, and the Enemy are possessed of the surrounding Country, what valuable purpose can it answer to attempt to hold a Post of which the expected Benefit cannot be had; I am therefore inclined to think it will not be prudent to hazard the men and Stores at Mount Washington, but as you are on the Spot leave it to you to give such Orders as to evacuating Mount Washington as you Judge best." [13]

Four days later the commander in chief crossed the Hudson and rode down to Greene's camp at Fort Lee. The matter was discussed, "but finally nothing concluded upon." That the failure to give Greene positive orders to evacuate the fort was an instance of the indecision that so often throughout the war beset Washington's mind is proved by his own words. Three years later he wrote to Joseph Reed that Greene's opinion, the wishes of the Congress, and various other conflicting considerations "caused that warfare in my mind, and hesitation which ended in the loss of the garrison." [14] It is somewhat difficult, however, to find fault with Congress in this connection.

Two days after his visit to Greene, Washington made another, and was rowed with Greene, Putnam, and Mercer to Fort Washington early in the morning, "to determine what was best to be done." They were just in time to hear the beginning of Howe's attack on the fort, "a severe cannonade." It was too late to determine anything, except that it was too late. They went back to Fort Lee.

The decision of the council of war to maintain the post having been left standing, the question had arisen whether the Americans should try to hold, in addition to the fort, "all the ground from King's Bridge to the lower lines," that is to say the old American lines on Harlem Heights. On October 31 Greene had asked for Washington's opinion. "If we attempt to hold the ground, the garrison must still be reinforced, but if the garrison is only to draw into Mount Washington and keep that, the number of troops is too large." [15] To this Washington's secretary, replying for him on November 5, wrote that "the holding or not holding the grounds between Kingsbridge and the lower lines depends upon so many circumstances that it is impossible for him to determine the point. He submits it entirely to your discretion." [16]

Magaw's original force in the fort was made up of his own and Shee's regiments, numbering about 700 of all ranks, including those on the sick list.[17] Various additions had been made from time to time. While waiting for Washington's reply Greene had sent Colonel Moses Rawlings from Fort Lee with his regiment of 250 Maryland and Virginia riflemen and Colonel Baxter with 200 Bucks County, Pennsylvania, militiamen. Magaw's troops had thus been raised to 2,800 or 2,900 too many, as Greene himself had said, merely to hold Fort Washington. Greene's intention, therefore, may have been to try to hold all the ground between Harlem Heights and Kingsbridge, although the council of war on September 12 had declared that 8,000 men would be needed for that task.[18]

In pursuance of this hopeless plan Magaw disposed his force. At the northern end of Mount Washington, half a mile from the fort, Rawlings and his riflemen held a small redoubt and a battery of three guns. In a couple of flèches on Laurel Hill near the Harlem River, Colonel Baxter and his militiamen were posted. Two miles to the south, Lieutenant Colonel Lambert Cadwalader had Magaw's and Shee's Pennsylvanians, a part of Miles's, the Rangers, and some others, about 800 men. They occupied the front line of the old entrenchments on Harlem Heights. Minor detachments were posted at other points, leaving Magaw himself, with a small party, in the fort.[19] It was an ambitious plan, an attempt to hold a circuit of four or five miles with such small detachments posted at such distances from each other.

Howe devoted about 8,000 of his men to simultaneous attacks upon these three points. Lord Percy was to go from New York with a brigade of Hessians and nine British battalions [20] against Cadwalader. General Matthews with two battalions of light infantry and two of the Guards, supported by two battalions of grenadiers and the 33rd Regiment under Lord Cornwallis, perhaps 3,000 men, was to cross the Harlem River and take on Baxter's militia. General Wilhelm von Knyphausen had claimed the honor of making the main attack with German troops alone. Rawlings's position was therefore assigned to him, his force to number 3,000 Hessians and Waldeckers. Besides these three real attacks there was to be a feint by the 42nd Highlanders under Colonel Sterling from the Harlem side at a point between Cadwalader's position and the fort, to confuse the Americans.[21]

Operations began on the night of November 14, when thirty British flatboats were sent up the Hudson, through Spuyten Duyvil Creek, and so into the Harlem River, entirely unobserved by the Americans. The next morning, the British Lieutenant Colonel Patterson with flag and drum approached the fort and demanded a surrender, making the usual threat that the entire garrison might be put to the sword if the fort had to be stormed. Magaw declined with the customary assurance of his determination "to defend this post to the last extremity." [22]

At a little after seven the next morning the battle began. Twenty-one guns in British batteries on the eastern side of the Harlem, and those of the

frigate *Pearl,* stationed in the Hudson between the fort and Rawlings's position, opened fire on all the American positions and kept up a heavy cannonade for two hours or more. At ten o'clock, Percy advanced against Cadwalader. His field artillery having driven in a small outpost, he crossed the
Hollow Way, gained the heights above it, and approached the lines marching in column. At a proper distance, his fieldpieces and a howitzer opened
fire. Cadwalader replied with his lone 6-pounder. Thereupon, to the surprise
of the Americans, Percy's column inclined to the left and halted behind a
piece of woods, where it remained inactive for an hour and a half. The
reason for this seemingly peculiar behavior was that the detachments under
Matthews and Cornwallis had been delayed in crossing the Harlem by an
adverse condition of the tide and by "some neglect not foreseen before," [23]
and the plan for simultaneous attacks compelled Percy to wait.

About noon Matthews and his light infantry crossed the Harlem in the
thirty flatboats and landed below Baxter's position. While crossing and on
landing they were under a galling American fire, but they came on and, with
characteristic gallantry and dash, swarmed up the steep, wooded sides of
Laurel Hill. Cornwallis, with the Guards, the grenadiers, and the 33rd,
crossed without injury and followed the light infantry. Colonel Baxter was
shot down. Leaderless, his militia fled to the fort.

Knyphausen had started his troops from their camp on the mainland
side of the Harlem early in the morning. By seven o'clock he had crossed
Kingsbridge. In two columns, that on the right led by Colonel Johann Rall,
the other by Major General Martin Schmidt, his troops came down into the
ground below Rawlings's position; but there, because of Cornwallis's delay,
they had to halt. About ten o'clock they got word to advance. They pushed
forward eight or ten fieldpieces in the ground below Rawlings and opened
fire. Rall led his column to the right through a break in the wooded hills
along the Hudson and toward the north end of Mount Washington. Knyphausen, with Schmidt's column, kept to the left and "made a Demonstration . . . as if he intended to attack" [24] the easterly side of that elevation.
His men had to wade through a swamp and break through a triple abatis of
trees felled by the Americans on their retreat from Kingsbridge on November 2.

Rall's men had "an Excessive Thick Wood" to get through and "Steep
Rocks to get up." Struggling up the long, steep, rugged height, grasping
bushes to pull themselves up the almost precipitous slope, they came under
the fire of the American guns. Grape and round shot were hurled upon
them; then came a shower of bullets. The riflemen, in the redoubt and from

behind rocks and trees outside, poured a well aimed and deadly fire on their foes. But the persistent Hessians pressed on with great gallantry against the unseen defenders of the height.

When Rall had come near to the top, Knyphausen "made a sudden face to the Right" against the side of the hill assigned to his force and met the same difficulties, the same fire. For nearly two hours these courageous assaults and this stubborn defense continued. But the rifles of the Americans became fouled by the frequent and long continued discharges. Man after man found that he could not drive home a bullet in the clogged barrel of his gun. The fire of the defenders waned and at last was too feeble to hold back the enemy, now nearing the top of the ascent. They had no bayonets to repel a charge with that weapon. A retreat was inevitable. Rawlings drew them back toward the fort. They gained it ahead of their pursuers. This was the hottest fight of the day and the longest.

While all this was going on Percy emerged from his cover and with his two brigades—one English, the other Hessian under Major General Johann Stirn—assailed Cadwalader's lines. An outwork fell to him. He extended his front across to the North River, temporarily desisting from further attack.

After his success against Baxter's small force Cornwallis, foreseeing a necessary retreat by Cadwalader's men, also saw that the proposed feint by the men of the 42nd could be turned into an actual participation in the fight. He ordered Sterling, their commander, to join two battalions of the 2nd Brigade with his Highlanders and come over the Harlem River so that he could strike across Manhattan Island and intercept Cadwalader's withdrawal.

Cadwalader had news of Sterling's embarkation and sent Captains David Lennox, George Tudor, and Evan Edwards of the 3rd Pennsylvania with 150 men to oppose the landing. Magaw sent one hundred men from the fort. They acted with spirit. From an 18-pounder and their rifles and muskets they poured a heavy fire on the boats. But the Highlanders and British were not to be denied. In spite of a loss of 90 men, they made their landing, clambered up the high, steep, rocky ascent from the river, and assailed the Americans with such speed and dash that they actually captured 170 of them.

Percy, hearing the fire from that quarter, pressed hard on Cadwalader. Alarmed by the sounds in his rear and fearing to be caught between two fires, Cadwalader precipitately retreated. He was closely pursued. Near the fort he halted his men in a small wood and delivered a heavy fire, which for a moment checked the enemy. But the 42nd had come across. They

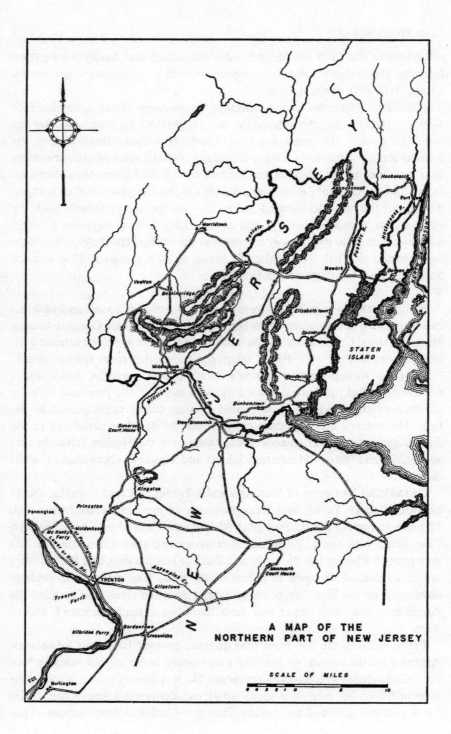

A MAP OF THE
NORTHERN PART OF NEW JERSEY

SCALE OF MILES

8 6 3 2 1 0   5   10

CHAPTER 24

The Retreat Through the Jerseys

After the fall of Fort Washington the main American army was still divided into three parts. General Lee was in command of the position at North Castle with three divisions—his own and those of Generals Sullivan and Spencer, each composed of two brigades. His paper strength was about 10,000 rank and file, but 4,000 men were absent, either on command or sick. Of those present 1,200 were on the sick list. His effectives numbered only 5,500.[1] General Heath had four brigades at and about Peekskill. There was a similar discrepancy between his paper strength and those actually present and fit, 5,400 on paper, 3,200 effective. Washington had the rest, 5,400, including Greene's men at Fort Lee.[2]

Thus there would seem to have been 14,000 able-bodied private soldiers to be relied upon for the rest of the campaign, a substantial force. But the number was rapidly dwindling. For a time after the affair at White Plains, while they were idle at North Castle with plenty to eat and drink, the men were cheerful and hopeful. But the catastrophe at Fort Washington had been enough to chill the ardor of a far more experienced, better disciplined, and more comfortably equipped army than this one.

Winter was coming on. The nights were already frosty. November rains were frequent and chilling.[3] Tents were lacking, blankets scarce, and the men's clothing was too meager and too ragged to keep them even passably warm. An English officer noted in his diary on November 5 that "many of the Rebels who were killed in the late affairs, were without shoes or Stockings, & Several were observed to have only linen drawers on, with a Rifle or Hunting shirt, without any proper shirt or Waistcoat. They are also in great want of blankets." The weather before that, he noted, had been mild, "but in less than a month they must suffer extremely." [4]

No one knew that better than the men themselves. Their terms of enlistment were soon to expire. The time of 2,060 of Washington's own force would be up on December 1, and all the rest, not only of his contingent, but of the whole army, would be free by the 1st of January.[5]

Under these conditions it is not surprising that "the contagion of desertion, which had been epidemic in his [Washington's] cantonments, now raged after the manner of a plague." [6] On November 9 Washington wrote that many of the Connecticut militia regiments had been reduced "to little more than a large company." On November 30 he said that the Pennsylvania militia of General Ewing's brigade, though enlisted to January 1, were "deserting in great numbers." [7] The prospect of any success in the rest of the campaign of 1776 was slight.

A few days before the fall of Fort Washington the American commander in chief moved westward with the force mentioned above, leaving General Lee and his detachment to protect New England. Washington detached Stirling's brigade to find a suitable crossing over the Hudson and to act as advance guard. Stirling crossed from Peekskill to Haverstraw on the 9th, found a gap in the Palisades through which passed a road to the west, posted a hundred men to hold it, and sent scouts to spy out the country beyond.[8] Washington followed on the 10th, marched through the gap, called the Clove, and encamped at Hackensack. From that point he rode down to Fort Lee and became a spectator of the disaster at Fort Washington. The surrender completely upset his plans. Instead of detaining the British army for months in a siege, the fort had fallen in a few hours. Howe was free to move any force he pleased into the Jerseys at once.

On the day Fort Washington was surrendered, the commander in chief wrote to the Congress that he hoped to hold Fort Lee. But three days later he had convinced himself that the fort was "only necessary in conjunction with that on the other side of the river" and was now "of no importance." He proposed to evacuate it and remove his stores. He was a day too late in reaching that conclusion, for Howe had taken prompt advantage of his freedom of movement and was preparing that very night for an attack to be launched on the morrow.[9]

At nine o'clock in the "very rainy" evening of the 19th, the 1st and 2nd battalions of British light infantry, two of British and two of Hessian grenadiers, two of the Guards, two companies of Hessian jägers, and the 33rd and 42nd British regiments, about 4,000 in all, struck their tents. By daylight, under the leadership of Cornwallis, they landed on the Jersey side of the Hudson at Closter, five or six miles above Fort Lee, and marched down the river, intending to cut off its garrison from retreat to Washington's army at Hackensack and pen it up between the Hackensack River and the Hudson.[10] Fortunately an American officer on patrol discovered their advance, rode down to the fort, got Greene out of bed, and told him about it. Greene relayed the news to Washington, ordered his men under arms and out of the fort, and hurried them away, in flight rather than in retreat, to the head of a small stream in his rear, thus gaining the road to the bridge over the Hackensack. Here he assembled as many as possible of his confused and disordered men, left them in charge of Washington, and galloped back on the road to the fort to round up three hundred stragglers and bring them off. But the British force was so hot on his heels that one hundred and five Americans were captured and eight or ten were killed.[11]

When the British arrived at the fort there was no one to oppose them. Three hundred precious tents had been left standing, all the blankets were there, and the breakfast camp kettles were boiling over the fires.[12] Besides the cannon already mentioned in the account of Fort Washington, a thousand barrels of flour fell into the enemy's hands. Fortunately the store of gunpowder had been got away a day or two before.[13]

While there was still doubt as to Howe's intentions, Lee's division had been left at North Castle to oppose him if he moved north. Washington in his instructions to Lee had said that, if the enemy moved westward into New Jersey, "I have no doubt of your following with all possible dispatch." [14] There was no longer any doubt that Howe was throwing large forces into New Jersey. He had actually sent over Cornwallis. It seemed to be time for Lee with his 5,000 effectives to come to the aid of Washington "with all possible dispatch." Colonel William Grayson, one of Washington's aides-de-camp, wrote Lee on the day Fort Lee fell, "His Excellency thinks it would be advisable in you to remove the troops under your command on this side of the North River." [15] Washington wrote the next day, "I am of opinion . . . that the publick interest requires your coming over to this side." [16]

These letters were not couched in the terms of a positive order. Lee did not move immediately, suggesting that part of Howe's army might still move against New England. He wrote to Colonel Joseph Reed, Washington's adjutant general: "His Excellency recommends me to move . . . to the other side of the river . . . but we could not be there in time to answer any purpose." [17]

Lee was vain, as he himself admitted, and his vanity had been fed to bursting by the admiration and adulation which had been his from the moment he joined the army. At a time when the Congress was making generals out of blacksmiths and booksellers, farmers and lawyers, whose military knowledge and experience were of the most meager sort, the appointment of Charles Lee as second in command under Washington was hailed with enthusiasm. Here was a professional soldier who from the age of fifteen had worn a military coat and had flashed a gleaming sword on many a battlefield in Europe and America. His homespun colleagues listened with awe and with but little understanding to his talk of redans and redoubts, ravelins and counterscarps. Simple provincials as they were, they looked upon him as the very epitome of the arts of war in the grand manner and valued him accordingly.

Lee, always ambitious, tended from now on, with his own division separated from that of the commander in chief, to use his own judgment rather than follow Washington's recommendations; and at this crucial time in his career Colonel Reed, Washington's adjutant general, encouraged him to act independently.

On November 21 Reed wrote to Lee in most fulsome adulation: "I do not mean to flatter or praise you at the expense of any other, but I confess I do think it is entirely owing to you that this army, and the liberties of America . . . are not entirely cut off. You have decision, a quality often wanted in minds otherwise valuable." Washington's for one, of course. Reed wanted him to join Washington's army, where his judgment and experience were "so likely to be necessary." He assured Lee of the confidence in him of every member of Washington's staff and of the officers and soldiers generally. Of Washington's part in the retention of Fort Washington he exclaimed: "Oh! General, an indecisive mind is one of the greatest misfortunes that can befall an army; how often have I lamented it in this campaign . . . We are in a very awful and alarming situation—one that requires the utmost wisdom and firmness of mind." Lee's and Reed's to be sure.[18]

Lee answered on the 14th that he too lamented "that fatal indecision of mind which in war is a much greater disqualification than stupidity." Acknowledging that Washington had recommended his crossing over to New Jersey "in so pressing a manner as almost to amount to an order," he had various reasons for not coming at once. He would, however, soon come, "for to confess a truth, I really think our Chief will do better with me than without me." [19]

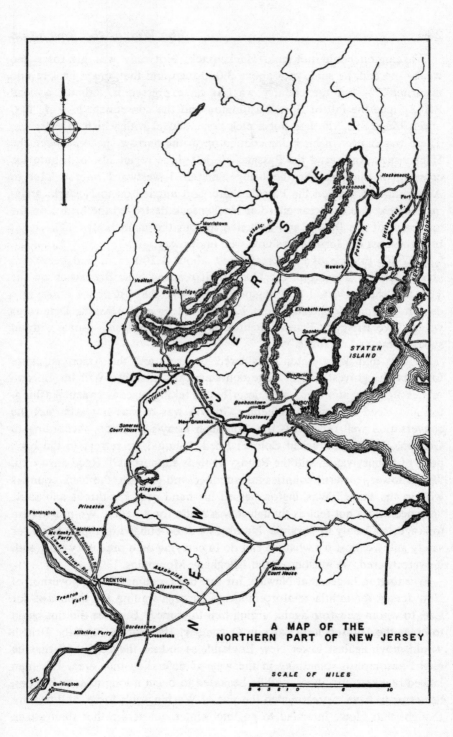

A MAP OF THE
NORTHERN PART OF NEW JERSEY

SCALE OF MILES

5 4 3 2 1 0   5   10

Washington could not hold Hackensack. Not only was his force too weak—he had, he said, "not above 3,000 men and they much broken and dispirited" [20]—but the country was, as he expressed it, "almost a dead Flat." Since the fall of Fort Washington and the consequent loss of "500 intrenching tools," he had not a pick nor a shovel with which to entrench. There was danger of his being cooped up in the narrow space between the Hackensack River and the Passaic. He left three regiments to dispute the crossing of the river by the bridge, marched westward on the 21st to Aquackanock, crossed the Passaic there, and hurried on to Newark, arriving the next day. His rear guard at Hackensack destroyed the bridge on the approach of the British and hastened to join the main body.[21] The great retreat across the Jerseys was now well under way.

Stirling's brigade of eight regiments, about 1,200 men, had been sent ahead after its crossing of the Hudson. It reached New Brunswick on the 17th and there awaited Washington. It was, like the rest of the army, in a deplorable condition. Lieutenant Enoch Anderson of Haslet's Delawares wrote: "We arrived at Brunswick broken down and fatigued—some without shoes, some had no shirts."

At that time Washington considered his army and the American cause to be in the gravest danger. The contemporary historian William Gordon relates a conversation which he describes as taking place between Washington and Reed at Newark. Whether Gordon was or was not accurate, the conversation well represents the American army's situation. According to Gordon, Washington asked Colonel Reed, "Should we retreat to the back parts of Pennsylvania, will the Pennsylvanians support us?" Reed answered, "If the lower [eastern] counties are subdued and give up, the back counties will do the same." Washington passed his hand over his throat and said: "My neck does not feel as though it was made for a halter. We must retire to Augusta County in Virginia. Numbers will be obliged to repair to us for safety and we must try what we can do in carrying on a predatory war, and, if overpowered, we must cross the Allegheny Mountains." [22]

Washington lingered at Newark for five days, calling on the governor of New Jersey for militia reinforcements.[23] He was waiting for them and for Lee, to whom he wrote again, urging him to come.[24] But Lee did not begin to cross the Hudson until early in December. He believed that the British would move against lower New England, as indeed they did, and that he might accomplish something in the way of defending that area. His men lacked blankets and shoes, and he hesitated to begin a long march. Besides, he seems to have overestimated the size of Washington's force, and to have thought that Howe intended to go into winter quarters rather than attack

Washington. Lee continued for many days to follow his own judgment rather than the recommendations of the commander in chief. Perhaps Washington did not trust *his* own judgment, since he did not send Lee explicit orders.

Dispirited by a succession of defeats, wearied with marching day after day, lacking tentage, blankets, clothing, and even shoes, Washington's force was indeed, as Reed described it, "the wretched remains of a broken army." [25] It is not surprising that British officers were writing home, "Peace must soon be the consequence of our success." Howe was so confident of his ability to finish off his staggering opponent that he divided his army and sent Clinton, with more than 6,000 men, to possess Rhode Island and winter there. Clinton took Rhode Island without opposition. His troops remained in and about Newport three years. Trevelyan says, "For any effect which they produced upon the general result of the war, they might have been as usefully, and much more agreeably, billeted in the town of the same name in the Isle of Wight." [26]

Washington had called on the Congress and on the governor of New Jersey for more men.[27] The Congress called on the Philadelphia Associators, a volunteer organization, to march. They were coming, but had not yet arrived. The New Jersey militia failed to respond to Washington's call.[28] On the 28th the van of Cornwallis's troops, in their inexorable pursuit of their quarry, marched into Newark as Washington's rear guard was marching out to join Stirling at New Brunswick.[29] November 30 came and went, and with it went the Maryland and New Jersey militia brigades of General Reazin Beall and General Nathaniel Heard, the 2,000 time-expired men: "being applied to they refused to continue longer in service." [30] "But what is still worse," Washington wrote, "Altho' most of the Pennsylvanians are inlisted till the first of January, I am informed that they are deserting in great numbers." [31]

There was a postscript to Washington's letter of December 1, from New Brunswick to the Congress: "½ after 1 o'clock P. M. The Enemy are fast advancing, some of 'em in sight now." At seven o'clock he wrote: "We had a smart cannonade [across the Raritan] whilst we were parading our Men, but without any or but little loss on either side. It being impossible to oppose them with our present force with the least prospect of success we shall retreat to the West side of Delaware [River] and have advanced about Eight miles." [32] At Princeton he did not stop. Pushing on in full flight he came to Trenton the next day. Safety was now his only aim, and the other side of the Delaware offered that.

He had hurriedly ordered the collection or destruction of all the boats on the river for a space of seventy miles above Philadelphia. In such as had arrived at Trenton he immediately began the transportation of his stores and baggage, his sick and wounded men.[33]

At New Brunswick, Stirling's brigade—five Virginia regiments and one from Delaware, about 1,200 men, "the flower of the army, though a faded flower it was" [34]—had joined in the retreat, first burning a hundred of their precious tents, which they had no wagons to carry off. "When we saw them reduced to ashes," wrote Lieutenant Enoch Anderson of Haslet's Delaware Regiment, who was detailed for that purpose, "it was night. We made a double quick-step and came up with the army about eight o'clock. We encamped in the woods, with no victuals, no tents, no blankets. The night was cold and we all suffered much, especially those who had no shoes." [35]

While the rest pushed on to Trenton, Washington left Stirling's brigade at Princeton to hold back the enemy. There it found a welcome though temporary relief from the hardship it had endured. "We had comfortable lodgings in the College," says Anderson.

But Stirling's men were not put to the expected test of holding back Cornwallis, for a most surprising thing had happened. Cornwallis was an energetic, swift-moving soldier. To overtake Washington at New Brunswick he had marched his men twenty miles through a heavy rain, over the most wretched roads deep with mud, in a single day. Washington had destroyed the bridge there, but the Raritan was easily fordable, "in a variety of places, knee deep only." [36] Cornwallis might have crossed it and caught up with the retreating army to its destruction. Instead, he halted his men, and did not move again for four days; meanwhile Washington made good his escape across the river. It was not Cornwallis's fault. He was under orders to remain there until Howe came up with the main army.

Charles, second Earl Cornwallis, was born of an ancient family on December 31, 1738. He began his military career as an ensign of the Grenadier Guards at the age of eighteen. He served in the Seven Years' War on the continent of Europe, was a captain at twenty-one, lieutenant colonel at twenty-three, a colonel of the 33rd Regiment of Foot at twenty-eight. Although he was a Whig and had stood in the House of Lords with Lord Camden and a few others in opposing the taxation of the American colonists, the King made him a major general in 1775 and sent him to America in 1776. Two years later he was made a lieutenant general. Trevelyan has described him as "an English aristocrat of the finest type . . . a man of immense and varied experience; careful and industrious; modest in success and equable in adversity; enlightened, tolerant and humane; contemptuous of money and indifferent to the outward badges of honour . . . he presented . . . a living and most attractive example of antique and single-minded patriotism."

As a soldier, Cornwallis was personally courageous; as a general, he was vigorous, active, and enterprising. Trevelyan contends that "the energy and enterprise, which . . . marked his two campaigns in the Carolinas, revived the dying credit of our natural generalship"; but this is overgenerous praise, for though his notable energy was in strong contrast to the habitual sloth of Howe, and though he is rated by Fortescue as "a good skilful and gallant soldier," it may be doubted that he was a military leader of exceptional genius. Certainly he was outgeneraled in the Carolina campaigns by Greene, who drove him to his final defeat at Yorktown.

In person, Cornwallis was a figure of distinction, thirty-eight years old, tall, erect, and handsome in the full-fed, well fleshed, portly fashion of the period. His features were bold, his nose well shaped, his full lips curved in an agreeable, rather humorous expression, his chin strong and deeply cleft, his face marred by an injured eye, the result of colliding in a hockey game with a future bishop of Durham while they were schoolboys at Eton.

He distinguished himself after the war in America by his services as Governor General of India and commander in chief of the British forces there.

By the 5th of December, Washington was strengthened by the arrival of some of the Pennsylvania Associators and part of Colonel Nicholas Haussegger's regiment of Pennsylvania and Maryland Germans.[37] Having to cross the river and lacking information as to the movements of the enemy at New Brunswick, he decided to "face about with such Troops as are here [Trenton] fit for Service and March back to Princeton and there govern myself by Circumstances and the movements of General Lee." [38] On the 7th he set out with 1,200 men. But when he was within a few miles of the college town he met Stirling in full retreat. Howe had arrived at New Brunswick the day before and had sent Cornwallis forward.[39] While Washington was marching, Cornwallis was on his way to the same destination. Washington turned back.[40]

Haslet's Delawares were the rear guards in that final retreat. Lieutenant Anderson of the regiment has left a lively picture of the commander in chief's personal activities during the withdrawal: "We continued in our retreat—our Regiment in the rear and I, with thirty men in the rear of the Regiment and General Washington in my rear with pioneers—tearing up bridges and cutting down trees to impede the march of the enemy. I was to go no faster than General Washington and his pioneers. It was dusk before we got to Trenton. Here we stayed all night." [41]

Cornwallis had marched slowly and cautiously, with flankers thrown out on both sides to scour the woodlands and look out for ambushes. The broken-down bridges and other obstacles also delayed him. His vanguard reached Trenton about two o'clock the next afternoon, just as the last of the Americans were putting off for the Pennsylvania shore. His light infantry and jägers were greeted by the fire of American batteries across the river and put to flight, with the loss of thirteen men. [42] The British responded, "but," says Anderson, "we were in the woods and bushes and none were wounded that I heard of. . . . That night we lay amongst the leaves without tents or blankets, laying down with our feet to the fire. We had nothing to cook with, but our ramrods, which we run through a piece of meat and roasted it over the fire, and to hungry soldiers it tasted sweet."

The British ranged up and down the river, looking for boats, but found none. Washington had them all on the other side.

The next morning, Washington posted Stirling's brigade in detachments at different landing places up the river to "prevent them from Stealing a March upon us from up above." [43] Howe gave up the idea of crossing and distributed his troops in various posts, at Pennington, New Brunswick, Trenton, and Bordentown. Now, for some little time, all was quiet along the Delaware. Howe seems to have assumed that the campaign of 1776 was ended, and that there would be no further major military activity until spring.

CHAPTER 25

The Crisis

"A thick cloud of darkness and gloom covered the land and despair was seen in almost every countenance," wrote one of the American officers of that period.[1] Said another, "Such is now the gloomy aspect of our affairs that . . . strong apprehensions are entertained that the British will soon have it in their power to vanquish the whole remains of the continental army." [2]

It was indeed the darkest hour of the war. Newport and New York were already held by the enemy. Philadelphia, the largest and finest American city, the seat of such government as the infant republic had, was unfortified, virtually ungarrisoned, open to attack on all sides. Only thirty miles away lay an army of 10,000 British and Hessian soldiers flushed with repeated victories, confident of their strength, and eager for rest and refreshment in such pleasant winter quarters as Philadelphia afforded. There was nothing to hinder a descent upon that apparently doomed town but the Delaware River, Washington's little force "crouching in the bushes" [3] on its western side, and possibly the weather.

The river was no substantial barrier. It could easily be crossed in boats and barges. The material to construct them was at hand in lumber yards in Trenton and, if more was needed, in the wood of its houses. Or the ice might within a few days be thick enough and strong enough to bear the weight of marching men, their horses, wagons, and artillery. The river offered little hope of enduring protection.

Nor did Washington's army seem to offer much more. It numbered no more than 5,000 men "daily decreasing by sickness and other causes," half of them militia or raw recruits, most of them clad like scarecrows in worn and ragged garments, shod like tramps, if shod at all, "many of 'em being entirely naked," said Washington, "and most so thinly clad as to be unfit for service." [4] Shivering in their unprotected posts or in their blanketless, restless sleep, these wretches were trying to cover thirty miles of the western shore of the river against an enemy that might strike at any time, at any place, or at several places at once. Washington was forced to say that he could see no means of preventing the British from passing the Delaware. "Happy should I be," he wrote to the Congress, "if I could see the means of preventing them. At present I confess I do not." [5] He told his nephew that, without reinforcements, "I think the game is pretty near up." [6]

The Howe brothers were ready to take full advantage of America's extremities. They had come to America not only as military commanders, but also as peace negotiators, bearing the King's commission "for restoring peace to his Majesty's Colonies and Plantations in North America." In New York, Admiral Lord Howe issued a proclamation, signed also by Sir William, offering "a free and general pardon" to all who would return to "their just allegiance" and take oath accordingly.[7] The effect of this announcement on the inhabitants of New Jersey was instantaneous. Already disaffected to the American cause by reason of their desire to rank as tranquil and obscure supporters of the winning side, which the American side no longer appeared to be, large numbers of them flocked to the British to take the oath and receive protection papers. Washington was disgusted by this desertion of the cause. "The Conduct of the Jerseys," he wrote, "has been most Infamous. Instead of turning out to defend the Country and affording aid to our Army, they are making their submissions as fast as they can." [8]

Philadelphia took notice. Estimating its chances of continued liberty at their apparent value—not much—its inhabitants in droves sought an asylum in the country. An observer there noted in his diary, "Numbers of families loading wagons with their furniture &c., taking them out of town. . . . Great numbers [of] people moving. . . . All shops ordered to be shut. . . . Our people in confusion, of all ranks, sending their goods out of town." The city was "amazingly depopulated." [9]

The fear of final defeat of the American cause and of the consequent ill fortune of its adherents smoked out many of the more faint-hearted Americans in high places. The wealthy and respected Allens of Philadelphia—John, a former member of the Committee on Observation, Andrew, a member of the Congress, and William, a lieutenant colonel of the 2nd Pennsylvania—went over to the enemy and joined Howe at Trenton. So did Joseph Galloway, a leader of the bar and a talented member of the First Continental Congress.[10]

Even John Dickinson, so prominent in the early efforts for liberty and whose *Letters of a Farmer in Pennsylvania* had done so much to arouse the country, now was said to have "discovered sentiments inimical to the freedom and independence of the American states." When elected a delegate from Delaware to the Congress, in January, 1777, he declined the office on the ground that he was "in a very low state of health . . . forced to attend my wife and child in the country." He retired to his farm in Kent County, whence he wrote urging George Read to exert himself for peace "before we suffer indescribable calamities." [11] Dickinson was discouraged, though hardly disloyal to the patriot cause.

In contrast with Dickinson's conduct was that of another pamphleteer, whose *Common Sense* was also a popular and potent force in the Revolution. Thomas Paine had joined Greene at Fort Lee as a volunteer aide-de-camp. Musket on shoulder, he had tramped day by day, all day long, in the weary retreat. At Newark, however, he began to fight with his proper weapon, the pen, with a drumhead for a desk.

In the middle of December, Paine published in Philadelphia a new pamphlet, *The Crisis*. It began with the eloquent words known ever since to many a schoolboy:

These are the times that try men's souls: The summer soldier and the sunshine patriot will, in this crisis, shrink from the service of his country; but he that stands it Now, deserves the love and thanks of man and woman. Tyranny, like hell, is not easily conquered; yet we have this consolation with us, that the harder the conflict, the more glorious the triumph.[12]

This little book "flew like wildfire through all the towns and villages." The privates in the army were called together in small groups to hear it read. It animated them to endure their hardships and renewed their determination to prove themselves all-season soldiers and all-weather patriots.

Apprehension of oncoming disaster induced the Congress to order the removal of all the principal military stores from Philadelphia down to Christiana Bridge in Delaware. Then, on December 12, it abandoned completely its control of the operations of the army by conferring on Washington "full power to order and direct all things relative to the [military] department and to the operations of war until otherwise ordered. Having thus prudently shifted to his shoulders additional responsibility for the conduct of a desperate war, it adjourned to Baltimore "amid the jeers of tories and the maledictions of patriots." [13] No doubt Congress was wise to remove to Baltimore and also to vest larger powers temporarily in the commander in chief.

On the very next day after this adjournment, two events occurred which later led the English historian George Trevelyan to remark that the Americans, "a people observant of anniversaries . . . might well have marked the thirteenth of December with a white stone in their calendar," and that these two events "must have presented every appearance of special providences." [14]

The first was Howe's decision, disclosed that day, to suspend military operations until spring and to retire with the greater part of his army into winter quarters in New York, leaving only a chain of military outposts to hold New Jersey. Boats were not to be built to cross the Delaware, and there was to be no crossing on the ice. The pressure on the Americans holding the river was lifted. The patriots in Philadelphia took heart; the Tories were correspondingly downcast.

The second event characterized by Trevelyan as fortunate for the Americans had to do with General Charles Lee. Washington had continued to write to him at every stage of the retreat, from Newark, from New Brunswick, urging him and almost entreating him to come over to the Jerseys. Lee was fertile in excuses for not joining his superior. He wrote Heath that he had "received a recommendation—not a positive order—from the General to move the corps under my command to the other side of the river," and asked Heath instead to send 2,000 of his men to Washington. Heath, being under orders to stay where he was, refused and stuck to his refusal, in spite of efforts to make him comply. Lee then tried to get the 2,000 men from Heath to join his own, Heath's men to be replaced from Lee's forces coming up to the Hudson. "I am going into the Jerseys," he said, "for the salvation of America." Heath again refused, and at last, on December 2, Lee started over the river with part of his original force, the remainder having served out their time, deserted, or fallen ill.[15]

But even then Lee had no intention of joining Washington and giving up his independent command. He thought it would be better for him to act in the rear of the enemy, "beating up and harassing their detached parties." To be sure, he did have an excellent chance to assail the long line of British communications across New Jersey. He was "in hopes . . . to reconquer the Jerseys" on his own hook. New Jersey, he wrote, "was really in the hands of the enemy before my arrival." [16]

Lee's progress southward seems to have been slow beyond any reason or excuse. He marched at an average rate of three miles a day. At Morristown he rested two days. The day after that rest, he made only eight miles, to Vealtown.

In the evening of the 12th he left his army at Vealtown in Sullivan's care, and with a small guard rode off about three miles to a tavern in Basking Ridge to spend the night, indulging in that "folly and imprudence . . . for the sake of a little better lodging," as Washington caustically observed.[17] He breakfasted the next morning and then employed his leisure in writing a letter to his friend General Horatio Gates, in which he characterized Washington as "most damnably deficient." [18] He had not even sent the letter when British cavalrymen surrounded the tavern.

Colonel William Harcourt, with thirty horsemen, had been scouting in the neighborhood under orders from Cornwallis to find Lee's army. He learned of Lee's presence in the tavern. His men surrounded the house and let fly a shower of bullets. Lee's guard, surprised, fled. Within a few minutes Lee was forced to surrender. He was carried off and was locked up in New Brunswick before twenty-four hours had passed. The crowning irony of his capture was that the dragoons, his captors, were of a regiment which he had led in a notable feat of his European military career, a dashing raid across the Tagus against the Spanish in Portugal in 1762.

The news of Lee's capture was a dreadful shock to the Americans; many of them had looked upon him as their most capable leader. To some his capture seemed the last straw. "His loss was almost universally bewailed as one of the greatest calamities which had befallen the American arms." Washington wrote, "Our cause has also received a severe blow in the captivity of Gen. Lee." [19]

Events were soon to prove that the American cause was not dependent upon Lee's services. General John Sullivan, Lee's second in command, promptly marched his troops into Washington's camp on December 20, though there were only 2,000 of them, instead of the 5,000 Lee had led across the Hudson. Gates came from the north with what were called seven regiments, though they numbered only 500 men. A thousand Philadelphia Associators under Colonel John Cadwalader also came in, as did the rest of the German Regiment. There were with Washington by Christmas time about 6,000 men listed as "fit for duty." [20] Something like an American counteroffensive could be undertaken, since Howe's forces were divided and going into winter quarters.

But the condition of these new recruits, except for the Associators and the Germans fresh from home, was no better than that of the men who had retreated across the Jerseys. Sullivan's 2,000 were "in a miserable plight; destitute of almost everything, many of them fit only for the hospital."

Gates's 500 were in no better shape. "Fit for duty" seems to have been a term reeking with optimism. And this army, such as it was, had only about ten days more of life. The enlistments of so many were to expire on December 31 that no more than 1,400 would be left.

To guard "every suspicious part of the river" Washington divided his force into three separate corps. The brigades of Generals Stirling, Mercer, Stephen, and Roche de Fermoy, about 2,000 men, were posted along the stretch from Yardley up to Coryell's Ferry. General Ewing had about 550 along the river from Yardley down to the ferry to Bordentown. Cadwalader, given the temporary rank of a brigadier general, with 1,800 took over the ground south of Ewing down to Dunk's Ferry, with headquarters at Bristol. There were no fewer than nine ferries to be guarded; at each of them a small earthwork was thrown up, and a few guns mounted. There being a great scarcity, almost a total lack, of tents, the men built themselves rude huts. So the army settled down, as it seemed to many, for the winter.[21]

CHAPTER 26

Trenton

"Headquarters, December 14, 1776. The Campaign having closed with the Pursuit of the Enemies Army near ninety Miles by Lieut. Gen. Cornwallis's Corps, much to the honor of his Lordship and the Officers and Soldiers under his Command, the Approach of Winter putting a Stop to any further Progress, the Troops will immediately march into Quarters and hold themselves in readiness to assemble on the shortest Notice." [1] In those words General Howe officially closed the campaign of 1776 in New Jersey —officially, but not effectively.

For "the Protection of Inhabitants and their Property," much of which had already been taken into permanent protective custody by his marauding troops, he established a chain of posts on a line from Staten Island to Princeton. There was one at Amboy, one at New Brunswick, and one at Princeton. Along the Delaware, from Bordentown to Burlington, the Hessian Colonel von Donop was in command of about 3,000 men, Hessian grenadiers, jägers, and the 42nd Highlanders. Half of these were based at Trenton and half at Bordentown, the distance between the two being six miles.

The line was eighty miles long, "rather too extensive" as Howe admitted.[2] The distances between the various posts invited trouble. But who was there to trouble them? Six thousand or so American soldiers,[3] a large part of them untried militia, the rest ragged, war-worn, discouraged Continentals, lay on the other side of the Delaware, whose ice-laden waters seemed impassable. And three-quarters of the whole force would be leaving for home in two weeks or less. Howe had good reason for his trust in "the strength of the corps placed in the advanced posts" and for his belief that "the troops will be in perfect security." [4] For himself there were the comfort and the pleasures of life at headquarters in New York. For Cornwallis there was leave to return to England for the winter. So everything was arranged to the satisfaction of everybody, including the Americans.

On no day, from the time his thin line of posts had been strung along the river, was Washington free from apprehension that an attack on that line was planned, to be carried out in boats especially built for it, or on the solid ice when it should form. He knew well enough that such an attack, properly organized and carried out, could not be effectively resisted, that it would be fatal to his army and perhaps even to his cause. And there was the 31st day of December coming so soon, when his army would practically disappear on one day; he would have left but 1,400 men, sick and well. Before he could be reinforced by newly enlisted troops even a small fraction of his foes, say the three thousand Hessians already on the other shore, might cross and march against Philadelphia.

Here was food for thought. If no adequate defense to an attack launched at some unexpected point were possible, could anything be done to forestall it? Could he possibly, with such a force as he had, reverse the situation, attack instead of being attacked? It was a desperate idea, but his situation was desperate.

Washington had begun to think as early as December 8 that audacious counterattacks upon British detachments might pay. On December 14 he expressed in three letters the same hope, that, if he were reinforced by Lee's troops, he might "under the smiles of Providence, effect an important stroke." [5] The news of the withdrawal of Howe's main force to New York and of the straggling disposition of the troops left to hold the river territory was vastly encouraging; but there was yet the fateful decision to be made, a definite plan to be evolved. One who came with Lee's troops under Sullivan on the 20th observed him in the last stages of his cogitation. "I saw him in that gloomy period," reports the erratic James Wilkinson, "and attentively marked his aspect; always grave and thoughtful, he appeared at that time pensive and solemn in the extreme." [6] And well he might, for it was no ordinary expedition that he was planning, no affair of an American detachment whose defeat would be merely a regrettable incident of the war. His whole army was to be risked. If the attempt failed, it would be cut off from retreat by the river behind it. There could be no hope of another unmolested crossing. It was, indeed, a desperate venture, and Washington knew it to be so; "but necessity, dire necessity, will, nay must, justify my attack," he wrote to Colonel Reed on the 23rd. [7] The next evening, at a meeting with

Generals Greene, Sullivan, Mercer, Stirling, Roche de Fermoy, and St. Clair and several colonels, including John Glover, the plan was discussed and adopted.

The principal objective was to be Trenton. The river was to be crossed at three places by three separate divisions. Lieutenant Colonel John Cadwalader as a temporary brigadier general was to command one, composed of about 900 men from Hitchcock's Rhode Island Continentals, 1,000 Philadelphia Associators, Captain Thomas Rodney's little Delaware militia company from Dover, and two artillery companies, each with one 6-pounder. This division was to cross the river at or near Bristol and engage Donop's forces at Mount Holly so as to divert their attention from the principal attack.

The second division, under Brigadier General James Ewing, was made up chiefly of Pennsylvania militia, with a few from New Jersey, about 700 in all. It was to cross at Trenton Ferry, take up a position south of Assunpink Creek and hold a bridge over that stream so as to close that avenue of escape of the Hessians in Trenton after the attack on the town from the north by the principal division.

The third and principal division was to be commanded by Washington. It was to be made up of about 2,400 men selected from the brigades of Stephen, Mercer, Stirling, St. Clair, Glover, Sargent, and Roche de Fermoy, each of whom was to lead his own men. It was to be divided into two corps under Greene and Sullivan respectively. Colonel Henry Knox was to be in charge of the artillery, 18 fieldpieces in all. Each man was to carry his blanket, cooked rations for three days, and forty rounds of ammunition. This division was to cross at McKonkey's Ferry, about nine miles above Trenton, and take the roads leading down to that town.

When his own and Ewing's division had converged upon and taken Trenton, and after Cadwalader had driven Donop from his cantonments, Washington planned that the three bodies should join and, if circumstances favored, should push on against the British posts at Princeton and New Brunswick.

Provided and equipped as ordered, the various elements of the main division were paraded in the valley behind the hill at McKonkey's Ferry, out of sight of the opposite shore, in the afternoon of Christmas Day. By three o'clock they were on the march toward the river, where the boats had been assembled.

These vessels were for the most part of a kind peculiar to the Delaware. They were called Durham boats from their first builder, Robert Durham, who had been turning them out since 1750. They were from forty to sixty feet long, eight feet wide, and two feet deep, and were provided with keels. Pointed at both ends, they could travel in either direction, the heavy steering sweep fitting either end. Each carried a mast with two sails, useful when the wind served. At other times its crew of four, exclusive of the steersman, used setting poles, two on each side. Thrusting them against the river bottom at the bow, the four walked aft on running boards built along each side, thus pushing the boat forward its full length, and then returned to the bow to repeat the operation. As the larger boats could carry fifteen tons while drawing only twenty inches, they could easily convey artillery, horses, and many men.[8] For this expedition these boats were manned by the amphibious Marbleheaders of Glover's regiment, the same men who had rescued the army after the defeat on Long Island.

At dark the embarkation began. The Virginia Continentals of Stephen's brigade, the advance party, were the first to enter the boats and push off for the opposite shore. The river was full of cakes of ice, so that the crossing was slow and exceedingly difficult even for those hardy and veteran crews. The second section to cross was Mercer's, composed of men from Connecticut, Maryland, and Massachusetts, chiefly Continentals. Stirling followed with his men, drawn from two regiments of Virginia Continentals, Haslet's Delawares, and a Pennsylvania rifle regiment. These three corps constituted the left wing of the expedition, under command of Greene, Stirling's forming the reserve.

Roche de Fermoy followed with men chosen from the German Regiment and from one of Pennsylvania, and then Sullivan's division, drawn from the brigades of St. Clair, Glover, and Sargent—New Hampshire, Massachusetts, Connecticut, and New York troops. This was the right wing, Sullivan commanding, Roche de Fermoy in advance, St. Clair in reserve.

The moon was full, but the sky was so shrouded by dense clouds that darkness covered everything. In this respect the night was most suitable for a secret adventure; but it was a dreadful night indeed for the men engaged. It was bitterly cold, the current was swift, and the floating ice prolonged the passage. About eleven o'clock hail and sleet, driven by a high wind, broke upon them, doubling the difficulties of the boatmen and making the soldiers in the boats or on shore acutely miserable. Captain Thomas Rodney wrote, "It was as severe a night as ever I saw . . . [with this] storm of wind, hail, rain and snow." [9]

It had been expected that the entire division would be over the river by midnight and that it would have five hours before daybreak in which to cover the nine miles to Trenton. But it was past three o'clock when the last man got ashore, and nearly four o'clock when the army formed and began to march.

None of these men were warmly clad; many of them wore threadbare summer clothing. Few were properly shod, and many were not shod at all. Slogging along on the rough, frozen road made slippery by ice and snow, buffeted now by hailstones, now by rain that froze upon their hair and their clothes, they underwent a prolonged and continuous torture. The story of ragged, shoeless men leaving bloody footprints in the snow has been told so often that it has become commonplace, and often fails to impress the reader as it should. But to one of Washington's staff, as to every other man on that march, it was sufficiently real. He made an entry in his diary before the embarkation. "Christmas, 6 p.m. . . . It is fearfully cold and raw and a snow-storm setting in. The wind is northeast and beats in the faces of the men. It will be a terrible night for the soldiers who have no shoes. Some of them have tied old rags around their feet, but I have not heard a man complain." [10]

Added to these physical tortures was the mental stress of the knowledge that they were three or four hours behind time and could not now hope to surprise the enemy at daybreak. It would be broad day before the attack could be launched, and that might make all the difference between victory and defeat, a defeat that might develop into a catastrophe fatal to the American cause.

Such forebodings were, of course, still more depressing to the officers, who were familiar with the details of the plan. Even while crossing the river many of them, well knowing what a touch-and-go affair it was, were despondent.[11] How much more so, then, were they when they realized how sadly the timing of the plan had gone awry. But Washington kept his poise and never faltered. The same officer who wrote about the shoeless soldiers also wrote: "I have never seen Washington so determined as he is now. He stands on the bank of the stream, wrapped in his cloak, superintending the landing of his troops. He is calm and collected, but very determined. The storm is changing to sleet and cuts like a knife." When on the march a man came to Washington with a message from General Sullivan that the storm was wetting the muskets and rendering them unfit for service his answer was: "Tell General Sullivan to use the bayonet. I am resolved to take Trenton." That resolve, that unbending will carried the army to Trenton in spite of everything.

At Birmingham, about four miles from the landing, the column halted for a meal of the prepared rations. When the order to march was given many of the men were found asleep by the roadside and were roused with difficulty.

Two roads led from Birmingham to Trenton. The right-hand road ran roughly parallel to the curve of the river and entered the town at its south or lower end. The other, the Pennington road, swung left in a similar shallow curve and came into Trenton at its upper end. They were about equal in length.

Stephen's advance, followed by Mercer's and Stirling's corps and a small troop of Philadelphia light horse, all under Greene, with four guns, took the Pennington road. Washington rode with this division. Roche de Fermoy followed, with orders to break off to the left and interpose his men between the Trenton garrison and the troops at Princeton. Sullivan, with St. Clair's, Glover's, and Sargent's troops and four guns, set out on the river road.

The garrison in Trenton consisted of three regiments of Hessians, known by the names of Rall, Knyphausen, and Lossberg, 50 Hessian jägers, and 20 light dragoons of the 16th British regiment, about 1,400 in all, with six 3-pounder fieldpieces. Colonel Johann Gottlieb Rall was in command, the officer who had led the flank attack against Chatterton's Hill and had summoned Fort Washington to surrender.

The town had two nearly parallel main streets, King and Queen, running in a north and south direction, but coming together at the north end so as to form a long, narrow wedge. These were crossed near their lower ends by Front, Second, and Third streets. At the south end of Queen Street a bridge crossed Assunpink Creek to the road for Bordentown. The town was largely depleted of its usual residents, whose houses, the jail, the taverns, the churches, and other buildings, mostly along the main streets, now furnished quarters for the soldiers. One company was in an outlying position north of the town, and another south of the creek. Rall had his headquarters in the middle of the town on King Street.

There were no natural defenses against attack from any quarter, except the Delaware River on the west side; the town was approachable over a flat country by many roads from every other direction. Several of Rall's officers had urged him to fortify the approaches, and Colonel von Donop, in command of the district, had actually instructed him to do so. But, although two positions for redoubts were chosen and even approved by Rall, nothing was done. He scoffed at the idea that the miserable rabble on the other side of the river, "nothing but a lot of farmers," were capable of an attack in force sufficient to endanger him. "Let them come!" he said. "We want no trenches. We'll at them with the bayonet!" In this attitude he was supported by General James Grant, who commanded all the British forces in New Jersey. Grant went even further in his contempt of the rebels. When Rall suggested that it would be well to have more troops to keep open his communications with Princton and New Brunswick, Grant is said to have replied to the messenger: "Tell the Colonel he is safe; I will undertake to keep the peace in New Jersey with a corporal's guard." This was the same Grant that had boasted before the war that he could march through all the colonies with 5,000 men.

Christmas Eve and Christmas Day were high holidays in Trenton, celebrated with much feasting and drinking in the hearty German fashion. The merrymaking and revelry were kept up all day and late into the night, interrupted only for a short time in the early evening by an attack on one of the pickets by about thirty Americans, who, without Washington's knowledge, had been scouting in the neighborhood. They had shot up the picket guard as a mere adventure. After an exchange of fire in which six Hessians were wounded the Americans quickly withdrew, carrying off six muskets as trophies. The troops in the town had been called to arms; but the affair was over in a few minutes, and they returned to their quarters.

Rall had then dropped in on a supper party in the house of a wealthy merchant of the town, who seems to have been a political trimmer. The attractions of wine and cards kept the party going all night. Near the middle of the night there came a knock at the door; a visitor wanted to see the colonel. The servant refused to let him in. The caller then wrote a note, which the servant delivered to Rall. It contained the information that the American army was on the march against the town. Rall thrust it into his pocket unread. Perhaps he never read it; it was found in his pocket after his death two days later.

The pickets had been posted as usual. On the Pennington road, by which Greene's column, with Washington, was approaching, there was an outlying post of a lieutenant, a corporal, and twenty-four men at some distance from the town. About halfway between that and the town, Captain von Altenbockum's company of the Lossberg Regiment was posted. On the river road, the route of Sullivan's division, there was a guard of a captain and fifty jägers about half a mile from the town. Other posts were at the Assunpink bridge, on the road to Maidenhead (now Lawrenceville), on the road to the ferry landing, and on the road to Crosswicks, these four being away from the direction of the American attack.

At about quarter to eight in the morning of the 26th, Lieutenant Andreas Wiederhold, in charge of the picket post on the Pennington road, stepped out of the "alarm house," the center of his guard, and saw a small body of men about two hundred yards distant coming toward him from the northwest, the advance guard of Stephen's corps. At the same time his sentinels came running toward him, shouting: "Der Feind! Heraus! Heraus!" (The enemy! Turn out! Turn out!) There was a brief exchange of fire, and the picket turned and fled to Captain von Altenbockum's post in their rear. The company there had turned out on the alarm. It fired one volley, but Stephen's men, backed by Mercer's, charged it with such spirit that the Hessians retreated in haste toward the town, the Americans following and firing as they came. At almost the same moment, the advance guard of Sullivan's division fell upon the picket of jägers on the river road and drove it pellmell back into the town. So far the plan of simultaneous attack at the two ends of the town had been perfectly executed.

Lieutenant Jacob Piel, hearing the musket shots, ran to Rall's house and aroused him by hammering on his door. Rall, in his nightclothes, appeared at an upper window. Piel asked him if he hadn't heard the firing. In a very few minutes Rall was out and on his horse. His own regiment formed in the lower part of King Street. The Lossbergs hurriedly paraded in a cross street with orders to clear Queen. Dechow's battalion of Lossbergs was in the rear at a right angle to the rest, to face Sullivan's men in the lower part of the town. The Knyphausen regiment was held in reserve at Second and King streets.

Meanwhile Stephen's and Fermoy's corps had left Greene's division, swung to the left past the upper part of the town, and drawn a line around it from the Princeton road to Assunpink Creek. Mercer's had turned to the right to the west of the town and down toward the river until it got in touch with Sullivan at the lower end. Stirling, in the rear of the column, had marched straight to the junction of King and Queen streets at the upper end. At that point, from which artillery fire could command the whole length of the town, four fieldpieces under Captain Thomas Forrest were trained down Queen Street and two under Captain Alexander Hamilton pointed down King. Both immediately opened fire.

Rall's regiment and a part of Lossberg's advanced up King Street. Hamilton's shot tore into their ranks. Mercer's corps, coming in on their left, fired upon their flank. The Hessians gave two volleys and then fell back in disorder, throwing the rest of the Lossbergs into confusion. Two Hessian guns that had been brought up opened fire, but the gunners fell under the fire of the Americans. Stirling's troops charged down both streets, Weedon's

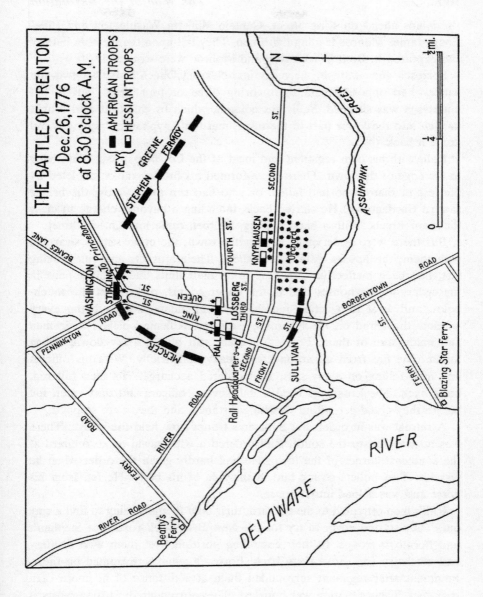

THE BATTLE OF TRENTON
Dec.26,1776
at 8.30 o'clock A.M.

KEY {
■ AMERICAN TROOPS
□ HESSIAN TROOPS
}

Virginians ahead on King Street, Captain William Washington and Lieutenant James Monroe leading their men. They fell upon the Hessian battery
and captured it. Both Washington and Monroe were wounded.

Forrest's guns were in the meantime clearing Queen Street. A two-gun
battery had opposed them there, firing three or four times; but in ten
minutes it was silenced. Sullivan's column, which by this time had fought
its way into the lower part of the town, met the Knyphausen regiment and
drove it back.

Rall, with his own regiment and most of the Lossbergs, had fallen back
to the edge of the town. There he re-formed his broken ranks, depleted by
the loss of many who had fallen, or who had run away across the bridge
toward Bordentown. He started back, intending a bayonet charge to clear
the main streets. With a band playing, his men came into Queen Street.

But there were Americans all over the town; the cross streets swarmed
with them; the houses were full of them. Their muskets and rifles, being
wet, had been ineffective. But they dried their flints and priming pans in
the cellars of the houses and in the upper rooms, picked out the touchholes, and went into action individually and independently. From every
window they fired on the returning Hessians. Riflemen picked their men
and made sure of them. Forrest's battery still blazed away down Queen
Street. The fire from all around was heavy and deadly. With his officers
and men falling on every side, Rall ordered a charge. His men faltered,
hung back. The Lossbergs tried it, but several officers and thirty men fell
before they could get within thrusting distance, and they were stopped.

A retreat was in order, but Sullivan's troops now held the bridge. There
was no way out to the south. Rall ordered a withdrawal to an orchard at
the southeast corner of the town. He had hardly given the order when he
was hit. Two bullets struck him in the side of his body. He fell from his
horse and was helped into a house.

Rall's men retreated to the orchard, their only thought being to find a way
out. They started north to try for the New Brunswick road; but Stephen's
and Fermoy's troops, in their encircling position, met them with artillery
and musketry and drove them back. Forrest's guns were trained on them.
Regiment after regiment surrounded them at a distance of no more than
sixty feet. Their situation was hopeless. They surrendered. Stirling received
the swords of their officers.

Meanwhile Sullivan's division was taking care of the Knyphausen regiment and a battalion of the Lossbergs under Major von Dechow at the
lower end of the town. Colonel John Stark of New Hampshire, shouting to

his men to come on, led them in a charge that drove back the Hessians. Dechow was mortally wounded and gave himself up. His men tried to retreat by the bridge, but it was too strongly held. They tried for a ford above it, but found none. Their two guns were bogged down in a marsh. They left them and made a desperate effort to cross the creek through deep water. Some of them got through, only to meet St. Clair's corps drawn up on the other side ready to mow them down. Amid a shrieking crowd of camp followers, men and women milling about in helpless terror, they lowered their colors and grounded their muskets, while their officers raised their hats on the points of their swords in token of submission. The Americans tossed *their* hats in the air and shouted so loud that they were heard throughout the town. It was nine o'clock, and the battle was over.

That is a description of the Trenton fight in its essentials; in detail it is indescribable. From the beginning to the end, the little town was the scene of a hurly-burly of 4,000 fighting men moving here and there by regiments, by companies, and in smaller groups. Single men fired on their enemies in the streets, from inside the houses, from behind houses and fences. The usual chaos of street fighting was made worse by the fog of gunpowder smoke that hung over the town and by the hail, snow, and sleet that continued to beat upon the fighters. It was a grand mêlée, a great, informal "battle royal."

One outstanding feature of the fight was the comparative lack of musketry fire. The Americans had done the best they could to keep their flints and the pans of their flintlocks dry during that long march through the rain and sleet, by wrapping them in greased rags and covering them with their blankets and the skirts of their coats. The Hessians, emerging from their dry quarters, had their muskets in firing condition. But the rain soon drenched the weapons of both sides. The flints would not strike a spark; the priming charges would not flash; the touchholes were clogged with wet powder. Men on both sides could be seen chipping their flints, pulling their triggers again and again without effect. Those that got into the houses dried their gunlocks and could fire toward the end of the battle. Otherwise, it was mostly an affair of artillery, bayonet, sword, and spontoon.

But there was noise enough. The roar of the fieldpieces, the yells of both sides in their bayonet charges, the vociferous words of command or of encouragement of the officers, the indescribable general tumult filled the little town with a howling pandemonium of sound, even when the musketry fire slackened.

It was a great victory for the Americans, the more important because it was won at such a crucial time. But it was not so complete as Washington had planned and hoped. General Ewing's division was not in its appointed place, south of the Assunpink Bridge to cut off the fugitives. Many escaped that way—the picket of fifty jägers on the river road, the guards at the bridge, the guards at Trenton landing and other outposts, various groups from the regiments engaged and the detachment of twenty British dragoons, who galloped away soon after the first attack. In all about 500 escaped.

Nevertheless, the bag was substantial. Of the Hessians 22 were killed and 92 wounded. Prisoners were taken to the number of 948, including 32 commissioned officers. Of spoils there were six brass fieldpieces; six wagons; 40 horses; 1,000 muskets and rifles with bayonets and accouterments; 15 regimental and company colors; 14 drums; all the trumpets, clarionets, and hautboys of two bands; and 40 hogsheads of rum, which Washington ordered staved in and the liquor spilt on the ground, though perhaps not before his cold and tired men had had at least one drink. The casualties on the American side were two officers and two privates wounded.[12]

The failure of support of Ewing's and Cadwalader's divisions, neither of which had fulfilled its allotted task, made it impossible to proceed with the original plan of pushing on to attack the stations at Princeton and New Brunswick. But it is more than doubtful, considering the hardships and fatigues suffered by Washington's force and the necessity of caring for nearly a thousand prisoners, that that plan could have been carried out even if Ewing and Cadwalader had been at hand. With Donop's troops so near at Bordentown, aroused by the news of the battle brought by the escaped Hessians, it was manifestly inadvisable to linger in Trenton. Safety and rest on the other side of the river were plainly indicated.

Twenty-eight of the badly wounded Hessians were paroled to be left there, including Rall and Dechow, both of whom died of their wounds within two days. The rest of the prisoners were committed to the care of Stirling's corps, and the toilsome march back to the boats was begun soon after noon.

The storm had not abated. The northeast wind still drove the snow and hail against their faces. The road was no better than in the morning. Crossing the river proved even more difficult than before. It is said that three of the American privates were frozen to death in the boats. It was night before they all got across, and it was morning again before all got back to their huts. Some of the most remotely posted did not reach their camps before noon.

These men had marched and fought continuously for thirty-six, forty, and even fifty hours. Some of them had covered more than forty miles, in the bitterest cold and a driving storm, with no more than two or three hours' cessation of the most arduous labor. It is not surprising that more than a thousand were reported the next day as unfit for duty. "This was a long and a severe ordeal, and yet it may be doubted whether so small a number of men ever employed so short a space of time with greater or more lasting results upon the history of the world." [13]

Now it may be asked why Ewing's force was not on hand south of the bridge as ordered, and what Cadwalader's troops were about that night that they did not appear where they were expected. The answer to the first question is short. General Ewing, having seen the condition of the river, thought a crossing impossible. He did not even try it. Concerning the other, there is more to be said.

Cadwalader took a look at the floating ice above Bristol. It seemed to him too great an obstacle. He marched his men from the Neshaminy Ferry a few miles down to Dunk's Ferry. There four companies of Philadelphia militia and Captain Thomas Rodney's Dover company, acting as light infantry, embarked in five large bateaux and three scows about eight o'clock in the evening. They were to land on the Jersey shore and cover the subsequent disembarkation of the rest. They did land, "with great difficulty through the ice," having to walk on it a hundred yards before they got ashore. About two hundred yards from the river's edge, they formed and awaited the others.[14]

About nine o'clock the 1st and 3rd battalions of the Philadelphia Associators, with two fieldpieces, started across. They got no nearer to land than the advance party, but they all scrambled ashore, 600 of them. But Cadwalader did not see how he could land the fieldpieces.[15] The former colonel of the Philadelphia Silk Stocking Regiment therefore gave up and ordered his men back to the Pennsylvania side.[16] Rodney described the scene in a letter to his brother, Caesar: "We had to stand six hours under arms—first, to cover the landing, and till all the rest had retreated again; and by this time, the storm of wind, hail, rain and snow was so bad that some of the Infantry could not get back until the next day." [17] So that part of Washington's plan failed entirely of execution.

Rodney wrote in his diary that the order to retreat "greatly irritated the troops that had crossed the River and they proposed making an attack without both the Generals and the artillery"; but they were dissuaded from the attempt by the argument that, "if Gen. Washington should be unsuccessful and we also, the cause would be lost, but, if our force remained intact, it would still keep up the spirit of America." Washington's plan and his orders involved risking the whole army on the success of the combined attack, so that that reasoning seems to be altogether specious. Rodney expressed the opinion that "if our Generals had been in earnest, we could have taken Burlington with the light troops alone." He concluded that Washington meant these secondary expeditions under Ewing and Cadwalader "only as feints." [18] In this conclusion he was in error. Washington fully intended that those two forces should cooperate with his in reality, the one to hold the Assunpink against Rall's retreat, the other to attack Donop and at best defeat him, but at least to keep him from going to the aid of Rall. Even without those two little fieldpieces, a vigorous and bold commander could have done that much.

That Washington desired such an effort made, under any and all conditions, he had made plain to Cadwalader in a letter written at six o'clock that very evening: "Notwithstanding the discouraging Accounts . . . of what might be expected from the Operations below, I am determined, as the Night is favourable, to cross the River and make the attack upon Trenton in the Morning. If you can do nothing real, at least create as great a diversion as possible." [19]

Cadwalader could have put 1,900 men ashore as easily as 600. Colonel Reed and one other officer got their horses ashore. It would seem that, with the proper amount of courage and dogged determination, even the two 6-pounders could have been landed. Guns have been got over worse terrain than ice which a horse could negotiate. But, with 1,000 well clothed and equipped men, as were these Philadelphia Associators, fresh from home, and even without the guns, Cadwalader could have made "as great a diversion as possible," and held, if not actually defeated, Donop's force. If Washington's victory at Trenton had not been so swift and so complete, he might have had to fight all Donop's troops as well as Rall's to a disastrous finish. One can only conclude that it took a Washington to cross the river that night, and a Ewing and a Cadwalader to funk a crossing.

Washington's prisoners were immediately marched to Newtown in Pennsylvania and thence on December 30 to Philadelphia, where, with the captured colors, they were paraded through the streets. In their handsome uniforms, dark blue for Rall's regiment, scarlet for the Lossbergs, black for the Knyphausens, and dark blue coats with crimson lapels for the artillerymen, they made a fine show. An eyewitness gave an account of this display. "They made a long line—all fine hearty looking men and well clad, with knapsacks, spatterdashes on legs, their looks were *satisfied*. On each side in single file, were their guards, mostly in light, summer dress and some without shoes, but stepping light and cheerful." [20] They were finally sent, by way of Lancaster, to the western counties of Pennsylvania and into Virginia, where they proved to be the most docile of prisoners.

The effect of the battle on the disposition of the enemy near the Delaware was instantaneous and drastic. Donop immediately withdrew from Mount Holly to Allentown and ordered the Hessians at Bordentown to join him at once. Burlington was evacuated, part of its garrison going to Princeton, the rest to New Brunswick. Within the shortest possible time for the movement of troops, every post in the Delaware River territory was cleared of the enemy.[21]

Howe was staggered by the news. "That three old established regiments of a people, who made war a profession, should lay down their arms to a ragged and undisciplined militia" [22] was simply stupefying. He stopped Cornwallis, who was on the point of embarking for England, and sent him to take command in New Jersey. He himself set out with reinforcements for the scene of trouble.

The effect upon the American people was as instantaneous, but different. From the depth of despair they rose to new confidence. From every direction came news of militiamen on the march to serve for two months, while the new Continental army was being organized.

Washington's reputation as a military leader had been on the wane ever since Long Island. Successive defeats and retreats had cumulatively discredited the commander in chief. But Trenton wiped out all that. "The country awakened to the belief that its general was a genius." [23] The Congress at Baltimore gave him full support. On December 27 it adopted a resolution vesting in Washington "full, ample and complete powers" to raise more battalions, infantry, light horse, artillery, and engineers, to appoint all officers under the rank of brigadier general and to displace them at will, to fix their pay, to commandeer "whatever he may want for the use of the army," and to arrest the disaffected. In short, he was to be something of a military dictator—for a period of six months.[24]

CHAPTER 27

Princeton

In the morning of December 26 Cadwalader, presumably dry and un-fatigued in his quarters at Bristol, wrote a letter to Washington, telling him why he did not get his corps across the river. "I imagine the badness of the night must have prevented your passing as you intended." [1] Then he heard the thunder of the guns at Trenton, but could hardly believe his ears. The firing, he thought, must be on the west side of the river. Two or three hours later Ewing disabused his mind with news of the victory. "Such was the exhilaration produced by this intelligence" [2] that he ordered his men to be prepared to cross at sunrise the next day.

About ten o'clock Cadwalader's men began to embark at the ferry above Bristol, the exact point of departure fixed for him in Washington's orders for the night of the 25th, which he had not tried. The condition of the ice in the river could not have changed greatly, but now he was sufficiently "exhilarated" by the news of the victory to try it. He had got nearly all his men and his guns across when he received a reply from Washington to his letter. It politely regretted his failure to cross on the 25th, also Ewing's, which had prevented complete success: "The whole of the Enemy must have fallen into our hands," if Ewing had been at the bridge. Also it announced the return of the army to the west side of the river.[3]

Here was a pretty situation! Cadwalader and his 1,800 men were alone in New Jersey, facing he knew not what force of an aroused and revenge-ful enemy. There was Donop at Mount Holly, he thought, with perhaps 1,500 Hessians and the 42nd Highlanders, besides 500 of Rall's men who had escaped from Trenton. And Mount Holly was less than ten miles distant. Donop might even have advanced to Bordentown, six or seven miles away. Who could tell and what was one to do? He was "in a dilemma." [4] Among his officers there was "much perplexity and a great variety of opinions." It was urged by some that, as Washington was now back in Pennsylvania, the whole purpose of the expedition had failed. They had no support; Donop was a dangerous menace; if he came up, it would be impossible safely to retreat across the river; they had better go back at once. Cadwalader agreed with this opinion.

Colonel Reed, on the contrary, urged that the militia wanted action without any more fooling. They had crossed that damned river three times, and, if this present movement proved to be a fiasco, they would all go home in disgust. What was needed was enterprise. Follow up Washington's success by attacking a demoralized enemy. "On to glory!" was his watchword. But the majority was against him. At last, as a compromise, it was agreed to march to Burlington, where they were pretty sure no Hessians would be found. The bewildered temporary brigadier general gave orders accordingly. [5]

Cadwalader's men reached Burlington by nine o'clock in the evening and found no enemy there. Reed had been ahead, scouting. He brought word that Bordentown had been cleared of the foe. At four in the morning they marched toward that town through a "scene of devastation. Neither Hay, Straw, Grain, or any live stock or poultry to be seen." The Hessians had swept the area clean. Half a mile from the town they got word that the enemy was only five miles away and "were disposed to return." They lingered for an hour in a cornfield, then heard that "the enemy were flying with all speed." They marched in and "took possession of a large quantity of stores" left by the fleeing Hessians, whom they followed as far as Crosswicks. [6]

Colonel Reed had pursued his scouting activities to Trenton. Finding it entirely devoid of soldiers of either army, he so informed Washington and urged him to come over and follow up his victory. Washington had already planned a return to the Jerseys "for the purpose of attempting a recovery of that country from the enemy." [7] On the 29th his army started to cross the river, but it took two days to get them all across and into Trenton. There he learned that Cornwallis and Grant, with 8,000 men and a powerful train of artillery, were at Princeton, no more than a dozen miles distant, and that their advance troops were already feeling their way toward Trenton. Why Washington ventured to place the river at his back when it was likely that the British would appear in major force is not easy to explain. It would seem that prudence dictated remaining on the west side of the Delaware.

Washington's situation was critical. The hardships suffered by his men in those recent marches to and from Trenton had incapacitated many of them for immediate active service. He had left guards in the camps on the other side of the river. His present force numbered no more than 1,500. Clearly he could not hope to withstand his approaching enemy with so few. He might again retreat to Pennsylvania, but that would dash the hopes raised by his late exploit and depress the morale of his whole army. However, some reinforcements were near. General Mifflin's eloquence had raised 1,600 militia in Philadelphia. They were now at Bordentown. He sent for them and for Cadwalader's troops at Crosswicks, 2,100 men.

But there was still the fact that the enlistment of most of his Continentals would expire on the 31st. Knox and Mifflin addressed them, offering a bounty of ten dollars for six weeks' additional service, which many of the New England men accepted.[8] It was easy enough to promise a bounty, but what about paying it? The military chest was empty. Washington wrote to Robert Morris in Philadelphia: "If it be possible to give us Assistance, do it; borrow Money where it can be done, we are doing it on our private Credit; every man of Interest and every Lover of his Country must strain his Credit upon such an Occasion. No Time, my dear Sir, is to be lost." [9] Morris raised $50,000, paper money, on his own credit and sent it to him.

By the addition of the Pennsylvania militia and Cadwalader's troops, Washington had now 5,000 men and forty pieces of artillery. But many of the men were not merely militia, they were untrained, inexperienced militia, farmers, mechanics, men fresh from offices and shops who knew nothing of war, nothing whatever of the duties of a soldier. Fresh from home, they were doubtless sufficiently clad, properly shod, and in a fairly well fed condition. But the old Continentals, the backbone of the army, on whom alone the General could rely in action, were almost at the ends of their tethers. Ragged, gaunt, footsore, fatigued by their recent exertions, and worn almost to exhaustion by lack of sleep, that "flock of animated scarecrows" [10] was more fit for a hospital than for active service. It seems that they must have carried on rather by force of habit than by their own volition. Against these Cornwallis had 8,000 of the flower of the British army, presumably reasonably fresh.

Cornwallis left three regiments of the 4th Brigade, 1,200 men, under Lieutenant Colonel Charles Mawhood as a rear guard at Princeton, the 2nd Brigade, about as many, under General Leslie at Maidenhead (now Lawrenceville), and with the rest, 5,500 strong, set out for Trenton on January 2 accompanied by twenty-eight guns of various calibers up to 12-pounders.

Washington had sent forward, on January 1, General Roche de Fermoy, with his own brigade, Colonel Hand's Pennsylvania riflemen, Colonel Haussegger's new German battalion, Colonel Charles Scott's Virginia Continentals, and Captain Forrest's two-gun battery. They had taken a position a short distance south of Maidenhead.

It rained heavily that night and, the temperature being high for January, the roads were deep with mud. Cornwallis's troops in three columns had no easy going. His advance came upon the American vedettes about ten o'clock and drove them in. General Fermoy had left his troops and had returned to Trenton "in a very questionable manner." [11] Hand took charge of the detachment and ordered a slow retreat. At every point where they could find a good position, the Americans disputed the advance of the enemy. In the woods beside Shabbakonk Creek they made a stand, and there was a smart skirmish. The Americans' fire was so heavy and so well aimed that the British advance was confused, and two Hessian battalions were drawn up in battle order expecting a general engagement. For full three hours the Americans held this position. Again at the northern end of Trenton, where some little earthworks had been thrown up and four guns placed, they held off the enemy. A British battery was brought up, and an hour was consumed in forcing this point.

Following on the renewed retreat the British advance party, about 1,500 men, entered the town to meet an irregular fire from behind houses and fences and from American batteries posted on the south side of Assunpink Creek, to which the retreating Americans had retired. The main body of the British army, delayed by the condition of the roads, had not yet come up.

Washington had taken a position on a ridge along the south bank of Assunpink Creek, his line extending nearly three miles. Earthworks had been thrown up. Mercer's brigade was in the front line on the extreme left, Cadwalader's in the center, and St. Clair's next. Behind these there was a line of reserves.

It was five o'clock in the afternoon of the 2nd when the British advance neared the creek. They made three attempts to force a bridge. The failing light made the American fire uncertain, but it was heavy enough to hold the bridge. A party of Hessians tried to cross at a ford, but Hitchcock's Rhode Island Continentals dissuaded them from the attempt. For some time there was cannonading from both sides, which gradually died down.

When Cornwallis came up with his main army he consulted with his generals. Sir William Erskine urged an immediate attack in spite of the darkness. "If Washington is the general I take him to be," he is reported to have said, "he will not be found there in the morning." But the others saw the Americans caught with the Delaware River behind them and no way out. Cornwallis decided that he had Washington in a trap, and that he could easily "bag him" in the morning. So the British and Hessians withdrew to the upper part of the town. The Americans lighted their campfires along the ridge, and both armies settled down for the night.

Washington's plans for the "recovery" of the Jerseys seem not to have been disclosed to anyone. Howe's forces in that state, even after the withdrawal from the Delaware River territory, were strung out in a long line of posts from Amboy through New Brunswick to Princeton. The line would include Trenton if and when he recovered it. The main highway from New York to Philadelphia, the main artery of his supply line, ran through those towns. If the Americans cut it at any point, the posts below would be left.in desperate straits. It seems probable that Washington intended to do that. Trenton was not of first importance, since it was at the end of the string. New Brunswick was, both because its possession by the Americans would leave Princeton out on a limb, and because it was the principal depot of British military stores in New Jersey. Trenton was merely the first station on the road to New Brunswick.

But Washington had not taken into consideration certain traits absent in Howe, but conspicuously present in Cornwallis's make-up; namely, energy and swiftness of action. Instead of having time to go on to New Brunswick before his foes could be got into the field to oppose him Washington found himself at the very threshold of his adventure face to face with Cornwallis in force. For the moment the British had been held off, or perhaps one should say they had held off. But the morrow was on its way. In a few hours the attack would be renewed in full strength, and Washington had neither the strength of men nor that of position to repel his enemy indefinitely.

His position was only apparently strong. The Assunpink was there, and its only bridge might be held. But it was after all a very small stream, and there were several fords a few miles above the bridge. If Cornwallis threw a body of troops across there, he would be "bagged" indeed, with the Delaware River in his rear, and neither the time nor the means to cross it. It was evident that some plan to extricate the army must be devised.

An American council of war was held. Should they fight it out there, or retreat down the river and try to get across at some lower point? Both attempts would be hazardous in the extreme—a battle because of their obvious weakness, and a retreat because the enemy hot on their heels would make it a disastrous rout and there were no boats below to rescue even a remnant. Then someone made an audacious suggestion. Who made it, no one knows; it has been claimed for several, but it is quite possible that Washington himself proposed it.[12]

The plan was to withdraw in the middle of the night, but not down the river. Instead, the army was to march around the left flank of the enemy, avoid the British post at Maidenhead, strike the British rear guard at Princeton, some twelve miles away, defeat it, and go on to New Brunswick. The very audacity of the plan seized the imagination, and it was adopted.

One obstacle in the way of success was removed while the council was in session. "A providential change of weather" occurred. A cold northwest wind sprang up, the temperature fell, and the roads froze hard.[13]

Preparations for the move began at once. The campfires were heaped high with fence rails. A party of 400 men was detailed to work on entrenchments at certain points whence the sound of pick and spade would be heard in the British camp. They were also to keep the fires going and to make a show of patrolling at the bridge and elsewhere. Finally they were to steal away at daybreak and follow the army as speedily as possible.

The baggage, stores, and three heaviest guns were started for Burlington under a strong guard. The wheels of the other gun carriages were wrapped with rags to deaden their sound on the frozen roads. At one o'clock in the morning of January 3 the march began, no one under the rank of a brigadier general having any knowledge of its destination or purpose.[14]

The Dover light infantry and the Red Feather Company of Philadelphia militia led the van, followed by Mercer's brigade. Beside Mercer's horse Colonel John Haslet, whose Delaware regiment of time-expired men had gone home, trudged along on foot. St. Clair's brigade, with Washington and his staff, came next, and then the rest of the army. Captain Henry, with the other three companies of the Philadelphia light infantry militia, brought up the rear. Orders were given in whispers; the muskets were carefully handled, and every care was taken to maintain silence. So the army passed along the front of the enemy's lines and took the road to Sandtown. That road ran through dense woods and had been lately made. It was rugged and rutted. Stumps had been left standing, which "stopped the movement of some of the guns and caused many a fall and severe bruise to some of the overweary, sleepy soldiers." [15] At Sandtown, they took the road to Quaker Bridge. At some time on this part of the march, "great confusion happened in the rear" among Henry's Philadelphia militia. "There was a cry that they were surrounded by Hessians, and several corps of Militia broke and fled towards Bordentown, but the rest of the column remained firm and pursued their march without disorder." [16]

At Quaker Bridge, the column swung toward the northwest on a road leading directly to Princeton. Two miles from that town it came to Stony Brook. It was then daylight. "The sun rose as we crossed the brook on a clear frosty morning." [17] Here the army was divided. Mercer's brigade of 350 tired, sleepy, hungry men, with Cadwalader's Associators, was split off to the left to secure a stone bridge on the direct road to Trenton, so that, if Cornwallis were pursuing, he could be held or at least delayed there. Sullivan, with three brigades, took a road to the right to enter Princeton on the east.

The British force in Princeton consisted of three regiments, the 17th, 40th, and 55th, with three troops of light dragoons. Lieutenant Colonel Charles Mawhood, the commander, was under orders to march the bulk of these, join General Leslie at Maidenhead, and then push on to Trenton that morning, leaving the 40th as a guard for the stores in Princeton. At about dawn Mawhood set out. He rode a brown pony, and his two favorite spaniels trotted by his side. The 17th, a part of the 55th, and a troop of the 16th light dragoons were with him. The rest of the 55th followed at a short distance. Mawhood had crossed Stony Brook bridge and was at the top of a small hill on the Trenton road when his eye caught the glitter of the sun's level rays reflected from bright metal at some little distance on his left. A searching look disclosed a motley band of armed men just emerging from a wood. It was the vanguard of Mercer's troops on its way to the bridge.

Having no thought of an attack in that vicinity, Mawhood supposed this was some part of the American army fleeing from a defeat by Cornwallis. He sent two mounted officers to reconnoiter the approaching body. As a measure of precaution, in order to intercept the Americans, if indeed they were bound for Princeton, he withdrew his force across the bridge to take up a position in an orchard and some farm buildings on a piece of rising ground on the other side of the stream. He led his men at the double in a dash for the orchard, but the Americans were nearer to it. With equal speed they gained it first and formed behind a hedge facing the British in an open field below.

Mawhood quickly deployed his men in line of battle at a distance of forty yards. Both sides at once opened fire, each having two fieldpieces in play. Mercer's horse was hit in one leg. He dismounted to fight on foot.

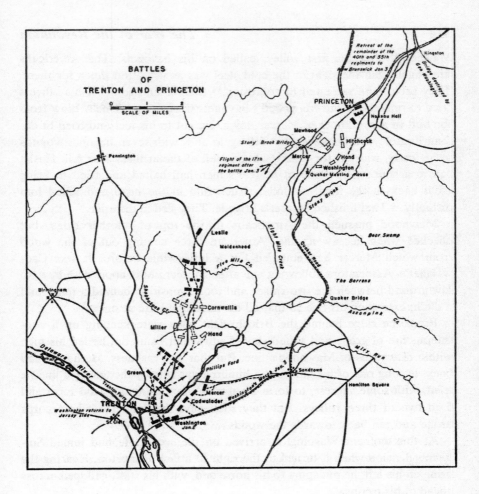

BATTLES
OF
TRENTON AND PRINCETON

0   1   2
SCALE OF MILES

PRINCETON

Kingston

Bridge destroyed by Gen Washington

Retreat of the remainder of the 40th and 55th regiments to New Brunswick Jan 3

Nassau Hall

Mawhood

Stony Brook Bridge

Hitchcock

Mercer

Hand

Pennington

Flight of the 17th regiment after the battle Jan. 3

Washington

Quaker Meeting House

Stony Brook

Leslie

Maidenhead

Bear Swamp

Five Mile Cr.

Eight Mile Creek

The Barrens

Birmingham

Shabakonk Cr.

Quaker Bridge

Cornwallis

Assanpink Cr.

Miller

Hand

Miry Run

Delaware River

Phillips Ford

Sandtown

Greene

Washington's March Jan. 3

Trenton Ferry

Mercer

Cadwalader

Hamilton Square

TRENTON

Washington returns to Jersey side

St Clair

Washington Jan. 2

Mawhood, after his first volley, called on his bayonets. The Americans fired again, but the sight of the cold steel was as usual too much for them. They broke and retreated in confusion.[18] Mercer and some of his officers tried to rally them, but Mawhood's bayonets were upon them. A blow from the butt of a gun knocked Mercer down. He got to his feet and tried to defend himself with his sword but fell again and, with seven bayonet wounds in his body, was left for dead. Captain Neil of the artillery also fell. Haslet ran to a spot where some of Mercer's men had halted and tried to bring them back to the fight. A bullet struck him in the head and killed him instantly.[19] That finished Mercer's brigade. They fled in disorder.

Mawhood pursued the Americans to the top of another ridge, but checked when he saw another American force coming out of the wood from which Mercer had emerged but a little while before. It was Cadwalader's Associators following on after Mercer. Mawhood withdrew to low ground between the two ridges and took a position behind a fence and a ditch, extending his line so that all his men could fire at once.[20]

From the ridge behind the British eight guns were keeping up a continuous fire of grape and round shot. Cadwalader came on; he led his men within fifty yards of Mawhood's line. But that was rashness. He had to fall back, leaving one of his guns. At a hundred yards from the enemy's line he tried, with some success, to form his men. A few companies did form and fired two or three volleys. But they soon gave way and the whole corps broke and ran back towards the woods.

At this moment Washington arrived on the scene. He had joined Sullivan's division when it turned to the right to attack Princeton. Hearing the firing on his left, he put spurs to his horse and, with his staff, galloped across ahead of his troops.

He came upon a scene of desperate confusion, Mercer's men and Cadwalader's in disorganized retreat. Waving his hat to the huddled groups as he passed, and calling on them to stand their ground, he dashed to the front, into the hottest fire and within thirty paces of Mawhood's line, to encourage his troops by the force of his own example.

The British soldiers were amazed at the sight of this big man on a great white horse so recklessly exposing himself. One of his aides thought to see him fall and covered his eyes to shut out the sight. A volley rang out from the enemy's line. The smoke from it shrouded Washington from all eyes. But when it blew away there he was, unhurt and still calling his men to come on.

They did not respond. It seemed that they were completely beaten. Then Hitchcock's Rhode Island Continentals, Hand's Pennsylvania riflemen, and the 7th Virginia came hurrying over from Sullivan's division. The defeated men took heart. Cadwalader's men rallied, and a part of Mercer's.

Meanwhile Captain Joseph Moulder's two-gun battery in the farmyard on the ridge, which had been first occupied by Mercer's men, had held its position and continued to pour grape on the enemy. While the Americans were re-forming for an advance Captain Thomas Rodney brought his handful of men and a few of the Philadelphia Associators to support Moulder. From behind strawstacks and buildings they kept up a good fire, deceiving the enemy as to their numbers by its continuity and rapidity.

At last the retreating troops were re-formed and, led by the Virginians yelling lustily, they came up to the battery's post, firing by platoons as they advanced.[21] Hand's riflemen went against Mawhood's right, and St. Clair's corps attacked the rest of the British 55th, now coming up to support the part of their regiment that had marched with Mawhood. They gave way and retreated across the fields and then along the road to New Brunswick. Mawhood was now almost surrounded, but his men fought on with great bravery. The action increased in intensity. The Americans' fire was hot and was delivered at such close range that they could hear the cries of its victims; they "screamed as if so many devils had got hold of them."

The 40th Regiment, cut off from the fight by St. Clair's brigade, had not come up from Princeton. But gallant Mawhood had no thought of surrender. He ordered a charge with the bayonet, broke through the swarm of Americans on the main road, crossed the bridge, and began a rapid retreat to Trenton, the dragoons covering his rear.

Washington with a troop of Philadelphia light horse led the pursuit, followed by many of his men on foot. The retreating British at first maintained good order, but finally broke and scattered away from the road with the American infantry after them. Many were shot down, 50 were captured. The fields were littered with their muskets and accouterments thrown away in their flight.[22] The pursuit continued until the British dragoons halted and made a determined stand to let such as still followed the road get away. Then it was called off.

Meanwhile the 40th Regiment and the men of the 55th who had not joined Mawhood had been driven back to Princeton. A part of them fled towards New Brunswick, the rest took refuge in Nassau Hall. It was surrounded. Captain Alexander Hamilton fired one ball from his fieldpiece into it, and a party of Jerseymen entered it. A surrender was inevitable; 194 prisoners were taken there.

The actual battle near the bridge had lasted only fifteen minutes; but it had been a very hot combat, fought at close quarters. In that short time 40 Americans were killed or wounded. Among the dead were General Mercer, who succumbed to his wounds, and Colonel Haslet—both of them officers of great merit and promise—Captain Daniel Neil of New Jersey, Captain William Shippen and Ensign Anthony Morris, Jr., of Philadelphia, and Captain John Fleming and Lieutenant Bartholomew Yeates of Virginia.

Washington estimated that the British lost 400, of whom 100 lay dead on the field;[23] but Howe's official report showed 18 killed (to which must be added 10 artillerymen not included in the return), 58 wounded, and 187 missing. As usual, the two claims cannot be reconciled. The Americans took two brass guns, which, for want of horses, could not be carried away, and some blankets and shoes, whose transportation was not difficult.

This victory, like that of Trenton, had an effect on the American cause entirely disproportionate to the number of men engaged. It heartened the people of all the states with hopes of ultimate complete success. Moreover, it strengthened Washington's military reputation at home and abroad, with a corresponding increase of his authority. "From Trenton onwards," says Trevelyan, "Washington was recognized as a far sighted and able general all Europe over—by the great military nobles in the Empress Catherine's court, by the French Marshals and Ministers, in the King's cabinet at Potsdam, at Madrid, at Vienna and in London. He had shown himself (says Horace Walpole) both a Fabius and a Camillus, and his march through the British lines was allowed to be a prodigy of leadership."[24]

A stroke at New Brunswick had been part of Washington's plan; but his men had been under arms for forty continuous hours of bitter winter weather, with no interval to rest or to cook a meal. They had made a most difficult march of sixteen miles over the roughest of roads in the darkness of night, and had then fought a hotly contested battle. They were so spent that there was hardly anything left in them. They were actually falling asleep on the frozen ground, and New Brunswick was eighteen miles away. Moreover, Cornwallis was surely now on the march against them with his much stronger army, and would be deeply interested in his stores at New Brunswick. Also, General Leslie at Maidenhead was only six miles distant.

Halting the pursuit of Mawhood's troops at Kingston after a three-mile chase, Washington held a council of war on horseback and put the question of his next move to his officers. It was agreed that they should give up New Brunswick and push off at once for the hills and the broken, heavily wooded country about Morristown, where a northern base for the army had been already established.

Washington confirmed this inevitable decision with much regret. He wrote to the Congress on January 5 that in his judgment "six or seven hundred fresh troops, upon a forced march, would have destroyed all their stores and magazines" at New Brunswick, "taken (as we have since learned) their military chest, containing seventy thousand pounds, and put an end to the war." [25] If his men had known £70,000 was to be had at New Brunswick, they might have summoned the strength to go and get it, despite their officers' judgment as to their incapability.

The army was on the move none too soon. Cornwallis, when he awoke that morning and overcame his astonishment at the discovery that the American army was not on the ridge across the Assunpink, was informed by the distant sound of guns that it was fighting elsewhere. He broke camp and marched for Princeton with haste and, coming to the bridge over Stony Brook which the Americans had broken down to delay his advance, did not pause, but drove his troops through the breast-deep stream. His speed was so great that his van, when it entered Princeton, was within sight of the American rearguard quitting the town.

Cornwallis was now convinced that Washington was headed for New Brunswick and its treasures. He followed on, but when the Americans took a left-hand road along Millstone River at Rocky Hill he took the right-hand road leading straight to New Brunswick. For how could he tell that the elusive Washington was not making a roundabout march to that valuable objective, in order to deceive his pursuers?

The van of the Americans reached Somerset Courthouse at dusk, but not all were in before eleven o'clock. There they encamped, if sleeping on the frozen ground without blankets, as many of them did, can be called "camping." "Our army was now extremely fatigued," wrote Captain Rodney, "not having any refreshment since yesterday morning." But they were up at daybreak and on the road again. At Pluckemin they halted to "await the coming up of nearly 1,000 men, who were not able through fatigue and hunger to keep up with the main body, for they had not had any refreshment for two days past" and had been "obliged to encamp on the bleak mountains, whose tops were covered with snow, without even blankets to cover them." They rested there for two days and were "pretty well supplied with provision." On the 6th the army went on to Morristown, where it was safe from sudden attack.

Meanwhile American contingents captured Hackensack and Elizabeth-Town, on January 6. Washington had swept the Jerseys clear of the enemy, except at Amboy and New Brunswick, which Howe still held with a force of 5,000 each. They were harmless posts, offering no opportunity for a blow against the Americans. This considerable feat had been accomplished by an army of fewer than 5,000 ragged, shoeless, ill fed, poorly equipped, often defeated amateur soldiers, mostly militia, operating against twice that number of veteran professionals, abundantly supplied with all martial equipment, and within a space of eleven days in the depth of winter.[26]

So ended the New Jersey campaign of 1776, which had ignored the calendar and lapped over a few days into 1777.

CHAPTER 28

Morristown

Morristown was a village of a church, a tavern, and about fifty houses of the better sort, set in an excellent defensive position on a high triangular plateau, with steep declivities on two sides and the bold ridge of Thimble Mountain at its back. It was approachable from the east only through rugged defiles in a chain of hills, while various passes to the west afforded access to a rich country for supplies, as well as ways for retreat, if necessary. For offensive operations it threatened Howe's flank if he should move either towards Philadelphia or up the Hudson.

In Freeman's Tavern on the village green Washington set up his head-quarters. The troops were lodged in log huts in and about the village and outlying posts.[1] He had come there, as he said, "to draw the force on this side of the North River together . . . watch the motions of the Enemy and avail Myself of Every favourable Circumstance," [2] expecting to remain a few days. He lay there for nearly five months.

Whatever activities Washington may have had in mind, in the event of favorable circumstances, the condition of his army enforced a winter of inactivity. Depleted by expiration of enlistments and by the usual desertions, worn down by its recent severe service, it was at its lowest ebb in numbers, in physical condition, and in equipment.

On January 29, 1777, Washington wrote to the Congress that, unless speedily reenforced, he would be reduced "to the Situation . . . of scarce having any army at all." [3] By March 14 he had fewer than 3,000 men, of whom two-thirds were militia enlisted only to the end of the month.[4] At times, he was put to it to find men to mount the ordinary guards.[5] Yet

319

with this handful he had to "keep up Appearances" before the enemy. "How I am going to oppose them, God knows," he wrote on April 3, "for except a few hundred from Jersey, Pennsylvania and Virginia I have not yet received a Man of the new Continental levies." [6]

The army was not only small; it was also destitute, "absolutely perishing for want of clothes," many of the men "quite bearfoot," so the General said. An ill organized commissariat failed to supply food. He wrote angrily to one of the commissaries: "The Cry of want of Provisions comes to me from every Quarter. . . . What, sir, is the meaning of this? . . . Consider, I beseech you, the consequences of this neglect and exert yourself to remedy this Evil." [7] He had to use the plenary powers granted him by the Congress in December, 1776, and order that "all the Beef, Pork, Flour, Spirituous Liquors &C &C, not necessary for the Subsistence of the Inhabitants" of lower East Jersey, should be commandeered.[8]

To crown the misfortunes of the army, smallpox ravaged the camp. The commander in chief took vigorous steps to combat it,[9] quartering the troops in small parties in the houses in Morristown and the near-by villages and ordering the inoculation of soldiers and citizens alike. Despite the protests of the dismayed civilians, this was done "with amazing success," [10] although at one time a third of his army was ill from the treatment.[11]

In addition to calling on the states in September, 1776, to raise eighty-eight battalions, Congress had authorized Washington on December 27 to raise sixteen Additional Battalions of infantry, 3,000 light horse, three artillery regiments, and a corps of engineers,[12] a grand total of 75,000 men —on paper, never to be realized in fact.

Recruiting lagged painfully. The soldiers of the old army were loath to reenlist. They had had enough of hardship, enough of cold and hunger, enough of barefoot marching in winter, enough of the dreadful squalor and filth of the "hospitals," where men merely lingered awhile in misery and wretchedness on their way to the grave. They told their tales of woe in the taverns and market places and so discouraged others that might have been ambitious to go a-soldiering.

The bounty system also acted against enlistment in the forces to be raised. The Congress offered $20 to each recruit enlisting for three years or the duration of the war and promised each man who served his full term a hundred acres of land.[13] In their efforts to fill their quotas of the original eighty-eight battalions, some of the New England states began to offer an additional bonus of $33.33. To the men whom Washington tried to enlist in the sixteen Additional Battalions $53.33 in hand looked better than $20 and a hundred acres, if they survived the war. He protested that the colonels appointed to raise the sixteen could not "get Men for 20 dollars when the state allows 53⅓." [14] Massachusetts answered by doubling its offer, making the total bounty $86.66; other states fell in line and went even higher.[15]

Some of the states made difficulties for themselves by raising regiments exclusively for home duty, while their quotas for the eighty-eight Continental battalions were yet unfilled, and paying these home guards £3 a month for "easy and secure duty at, or near their own firesides," against Continental wages of 40 shillings "for hard and dangerous service, far distant from home," as Washington put it in a protest to the executive officials of Massachusetts.[16]

On December 27, 1776, the Congress had called upon the new levies in the states from Pennsylvania down to Virginia "to march by companies or parts of companies, as far as they shall be raised, and join the army under General Washington with the utmost dispatch." [17] A month later Washington wrote, "They are so extremely averse to turning out of comfortable Quarters, that I cannot get a man to come near me." [18] And all through the spring and early summer, he kept repeating his call for more men.

There was a bit of good news in March; a ship from France came in with a useful cargo: nearly 12,000 muskets, 1,000 barrels of powder, 11,000 gun flints, and an assortment of clothes and incidentals, such as "1 case of needles and silk neck-cloths." [19] In its wake came another with 10,000 muskets. Guns and ammunition in plenty, but where were the men to use them?

They came at last. The thin trickle of recruits became a rivulet, then a clear stream, though never a flood. By the middle of May, forty-three of the new Continental regiments had arrived at Morristown, but not in full strength; they averaged 200 each, officers and men. Still, an army of 8,738 soldiers was something to be thankful for, even if only two-thirds of them were actually present and fit for duty. This force was organized in five divisions under Major Generals Greene, Stephen, Sullivan, Lincoln, and Stirling. Optimism returned; Congress moved back to Philadelphia.

Howe had learned the lesson of Trenton and Princeton; outlying posts, even if fairly strong, were not safe from those night-prowling Americans. By January 10 he had withdrawn all his troops to New Brunswick and Amboy. His own winter quarters were in New York, where he diverted himself in "feasting, gaming and banqueting" and in dalliance with his mistress, Mrs. Joshua Loring.[20] His troops were not so well off. Fourteen thousands of them were cantoned at Amboy and New Brunswick and the villages of that district in every sort of makeshift quarters. An entire company was crowded into two rooms; a regiment, in a church. Stables were filled with them. Open sheds were boarded up for them to freeze in. Many lay in the open. And it was not only overcrowding and the cold that made their lot hard. They were hungry, too. Food, as well as fuel and forage, was scarce, for "Amboy and Brunswick were, in a manner, besieged." [21]

The Americans were constantly on the alert to prevent the British from drawing subsistence from the countryside. No British foraging party could venture out of the lines with impunity. Attacks on such parties were frequent, and usually successful. The depredations and ravages committed, by the Hessians especially, but also by the British soldiers, had so angered the populace that they became fervent patriots, spied on the enemy, and kept Washington informed of their every move. The militia turned out in great numbers and aided the Continentals in harassing the foe. General Philemon Dickinson, with 400 militia and 50 Pennsylvania riflemen, fell upon a British foraging party of about the same strength, defeated it, and recaptured 40 wagonloads of plunder, 100 horses, and many cattle and sheep. Even 4,000 men in another party were not safe from attack. Washington kept his own men busy in such affairs and in "incessantly insulting, surprising and cutting off their pickets and advanced guards." [22]

But, except for such sporadic skirmishes, there was no military activity in the Jerseys that winter. Howe was now thinking of Philadelphia as his next major objective, but did nothing to achieve it. There is no doubt that the British army of 27,000 of the best professional soldiers, directed by Howe's military genius, led by the active and vigorous Cornwallis, and opposed only by Washington's meager 4,000, could have attained its object at any time in the first four months of 1777. Washington's position at Morristown could have been circumvented; and if he had seen fit to come down and attack the British on the march Howe would have had his opportunity for a decisive battle in the open field, in which his troops would have had every advantage.

Whether it was Howe's naturally sluggish temperament, or his adherence to the classic tradition that winter was a season for quarters and not for a campaign, or an exaggerated estimate of Washington's total strength, or an imagination of "hordes of Americans" ready to fall on his army if he advanced through the Jerseys, that caused him to waste those winter months and even the whole spring, no one can tell. But waste them he certainly did, while Washington's army grew stronger and stronger and his own job grew more and more difficult.[23]

There was, however, some activity elsewhere. It will be remembered that in November, 1776, when Washington withdrew from North Castle, he left Heath with four brigades, about 3,300 men, at Peekskill to guard the Highlands of the Hudson. Although a very large quantity of military stores had since been accumulated in magazines the troops had been drawn away for one reason or another until few remained. Washington had urged Massachusetts to send eight regiments to hold that post, but without result. In March, 1777, General Alexander McDougall, an inexperienced officer, was there, with but 250 men. The situation invited attention by the British. At midday of March 23 nine or ten British vessels arrived before Peekskill and disembarked 500 men. McDougall attempted to remove some of the stores, with little success. He then retired from the town, having first appealed for aid to Colonel Marinus Willett in Fort Montgomery on the other side of the river. Willett, a capable officer who was to prove his military efficiency a few months later at Fort Stanwix, crossed with 80 men, but the British had already been effectively busy burning the barracks and firing the magazines. He urged McDougall to attack, without avail. However, he obtained permission to try his luck. After firing one or two volleys he charged the British advance guard with the bayonet and drove it back on the main body, which at once took to its boats and withdrew to the ships.

The British had, however, accomplished their purpose, having practically destroyed the town by fire and burned great quantities of provisions, including 400 hogsheads of rum, 150 new wagons, several sloops and boats, and a quantity of entrenching tools. They carried off other stores of food, arms, artillery equipment, and munitions. They boasted that "the destruction was complete and effectual, scarce anything escaping that could be of use," which was no more than the truth. McDougall was relieved of his command and replaced by General Putnam, who held the post seven months before he too proved his incapacity and was removed.[24]

There was a similar British foray against Danbury, Connecticut, in the following month, which will be treated in connection with the northern campaign of 1777.

The Americans had their turn in May. A British foraging party was sent from New York to Sag Harbor near the eastern end of Long Island in twelve vessels protected by an armed schooner carrying 40 men and 12 guns and by a company of 70 men from Lieutenant Colonel Stephen De Lancey's Tory battalion. Colonel Return Jonathan Meigs with one of the Additional Battalions heard of this incursion. He embarked 170 men in whaleboats at Guilford in Connecticut in the evening of May 23, crossed Long Island Sound, which was "full of British cruisers," and landed at Sag Harbor at two o'clock the next morning. Taking De Lancey's troops by surprise, he killed six of them and captured all the rest, burnt all their vessels, except the schooner, also a large quantity of provisions and forage, and was back at Guilford by noon, having covered a distance of nearly 100 miles in eighteen hours. For this feat, the Congress voted him "an elegant sword." [25]

Maneuvers in New Jersey

Winter had gone, spring had come and had nearly gone before the first move was made in the game played by Washington and Howe with Philadelphia and perhaps American independence as the stakes. On May 29 Washington made it.

Fearing that Howe might make a swift march from New Brunswick straight to Princeton and so to Trenton, passing some thirty miles below the American position, Washington marched twenty miles south to Middlebrook, near Bound Brook and about eight miles from New Brunswick. His new position, at which he hoped to intercept Howe, was in the first range of the Watchung Mountains behind certain commanding heights from which the country between Amboy and New Brunswick and the road to Philadelphia could be watched. It was strengthened by entrenchments and artillery posts.[1] At Princeton, he placed Smallwood's Maryland and Delaware brigade and Hazen's "2nd Canadian Regiment," under Sullivan.[2]

It was now Howe's turn. He wanted to get the Americans down on open ground, for a fair stand-up fight in which his trained army might beat them and so open the way to the American capital. To this end he made a series of three maneuvers.[3]

The first began on June 12. The British forces operating in New Jersey had been assembled at Amboy, 18,000 rank and file.[4] They marched to New Brunswick and thence in two columns: one, led by Cornwallis, to Somerset; the other, under von Heister, to Middlebush near Somerset.[5] They hoped not only to entice Washington down from Middlebrook, but also to cut Sullivan off from the main American army. Washington saw Sullivan's danger and ordered him to retire to Rocky Hill, where he could cover the road from that point to Pennington and also have a way of retreat open to the main army. While there he was to "harrass the Enemy by incessant parties when they attempt to march thro the country" but "by no means to risk a General Engagement." [6] A few days later Sullivan was shifted to Flemington on the enemy's right flank. Howe was also foiled in his other purpose. Washington refused to be drawn down from his stronghold.

Washington knew that Howe was "marching light," that is to say, that he had left at New Brunswick all his heavy baggage, his bateaux, and the portable bridge intended for crossing the Delaware. He knew, too, that if Howe really had intended now to march for the Delaware he would have pushed on with speed and would not have halted at Somerset or Middlebush and entrenched there.[7] As Stedman says, the American general "easily penetrated into the designs" of Howe "and eluded them by his cool and prudent conduct." [8] To strengthen his right, his most vulnerable point, Washington called on Sullivan to send him 1,000 Continentals and an equal number of the militia which had joined him and posted them at Steel's Gap in the Sourland Mountain, about two miles from Middlebrook.

Howe was now in an embarrassing position. He could not go on to the Delaware without his baggage, boats, and bridge, and, even if he brought them up, the American army still threatened his flank. Also there was a considerable force of Continentals and militia on the opposite side of the Delaware to oppose his crossing.[9] With Washington in his rear, he would be between two fires. There was, too, an ominously increasing number of Jersey militiamen hovering about his camp like a cloud of mosquitoes, picking up any men that strayed outside and promising more material aid to Washington when it was needed.[10]

But the British general had not yet exhausted his store of artful devices to lure Washington from his position. In the night of the 19th of June, he suddenly and secretly retreated from Middlebush and Somerset towards New Brunswick "with marks of seeming precipitation." [11] This time he was partially successful. Washington was deceived into thinking the movement was a final retreat. He sent Greene with his division of three brigades, reinforced by Wayne's brigade and Daniel Morgan's riflemen, to fall on the rear of the enemy. Orders were sent to Sullivan and Maxwell to cooperate with Greene.

Morgan led the advance along the right bank of the Raritan. At dawn he came upon Howe's Hessian picket guard at the New Brunswick bridge. The picket fled, hotly pursued by Morgan, until it came to the British rear guard. Greene and Wayne came up and charged upon the enemy, driving them through the town and across the bridge to their redoubts on the east side of the river. The Americans pushed them from these works and pursued them as far as Piscataway. But Sullivan had received his orders too late to come up with the pursuit, and Maxwell never got his. So Greene gave over the chase. The main body of the British went on its way towards Amboy, burning houses and barns along the road.[12] An English civilian, who accompanied the army, described this feature of the retreat: "All the Country houses were in flames as far as we could see. The Soldiers are so much enraged" at being called upon to retreat "that they will set them on fire in spite of all the Officers can do to prevent it." [13]

The Americans accomplished little by this affair, but Howe gained a point in the game. Deluded by him Washington came down from the hills to Quibbletown (now New Market) and encamped there, so as to be "nearer the enemy" and "act according to circumstances." [14] He sent Stirling with a strong detachment to the Short Hills in the neighborhood of Metuchen.

Howe's second maneuver having so far succeeded, he grasped at the chance to bring on a general engagement by a third movement. At one o'clock in the morning of the 26th his army moved out of Amboy in two columns. Cornwallis led one towards Woodbridge; Vaughan, the other towards Bonhamton. Howe accompanied Vaughan. Marching on parallel lines, they intended to pinch Stirling between them and to seize the passes back to Middlebrook, thus cutting Washington off from a retreat to the heights and compelling him to fight where he was.

They were long hours on the road. The weather was exceedingly hot. As the sun rose and climbed the sky the heat became increasingly intense. The marching men, especially the more heavily clad and equipped Hessians, suffered almost as much loss from sunstroke as from the bullets of snipers along the way.

The two columns joined before they came to Lord Stirling's camp, "strongly situated and well provided with artillery." [15] They attacked furiously. "His lordship was in no hurry to retreat, but preferred engaging for a while, wherein he made a wrong choice, for he had been nearly cut off by the right column under Lord Cornwallis." [16] He was driven from his position and pursued as far as Westfield where, "on account of the intense heat of the day," Cornwallis halted his men. The losses in this affair are impossible to reckon with certainty. The British claimed 100 Americans killed or wounded and 70 taken captive. They admitted 70 casualties on their side. These figures are all doubtful, but the Americans certainly did lose three small but valuable French brass guns.[17]

Near Woodbridge the British had fallen in with a party of American riflemen. Washington heard their fire, retired at once to the Middlebrook passes, and regained the heights before the enemy cut him off. So there the two armies were again in the same old positions.[18] Howe's third attempt had failed. "Sir William Howe," says Stedman, "being now sensible that every scheme of bringing the Americans to an engagement would be unattended by success, resolved to retire from the Jerseys." [19] He withdrew all his troops to Amboy and thence to Staten Island. By June 30 "the Province of New Jersey was entirely evacuated by the King's Troops." [20]

Now ensued a period of inactivity for both armies. For Washington, however, it was a time of increasing doubt and anxiety as to Howe's next move. General John Burgoyne had arrived in Quebec early in May, intending, as was well known, an expedition southward by way of Lake Champlain and the Hudson to Albany. He had now set out with a force of 8,000 British, Brunswickers, Canadians, and Indians. To Washington it seemed "almost certain" that Howe would go to meet him in Albany. That would mean that the great fleet, which Howe had been assembling for two months in New York waters, would sail up the Hudson.[21]

But there were other possible destinations—Philadelphia, for instance, by way of the Delaware River or Chespeake Bay, or even Charleston in South Carolina. With such a crafty strategist as Howe you never could tell. Then came news of Burgoyne's approach to Ticonderoga. Washington was surer than ever that Albany was Howe's objective.[22] In that case the American forces on the Hudson should be strengthened.

But not too indiscreetly or prematurely. If Washington's army went up there, Howe could make a swift and easy march to Philadelphia, take that city, and still have time for the Hudson River enterprise. Only Varnum's and Poor's brigades were sent to Peekskill, and Sullivan's as far as Pompton "till the intentions of the enemy are more clearly and fully known." In order to be "more conveniently situated for Succouring Peekskill," and yet "near enough to oppose any design upon Philadelphia," Washington transferred his main army to Morristown.[23]

When he received information as to the fitments of Howe's transports for carrying horses and the amount of "Provender taken in"—enough for a month's voyage—he began to doubt that the fleet would go up to Albany and to think of Charleston as its destination.[24] He was puzzled. Nevertheless, he ordered Sullivan farther north, to the Clove in the Ramapo Mountains, a rugged defile through the Highlands on the west side of the river.[25]

Howe began to embark his troops on July 8, but did not immediately sail. For nearly two weeks "both foot and Cavalry remained pent up in the hottest season of the year in the holds of the vessels." [26] The day after the embarkation, Washington learned to his "Chagrine and Surprise" that General Arthur St. Clair, with 3,500 men, had evacuated Ticonderoga, without firing a shot in its defense and that Burgoyne was rapidly advancing towards Albany.[27] He could not believe that Howe would not go up to meet him, and wrote on July 12, "His designs I think are most unquestionably against the Highlands." Washington therefore decided to march "towards the North River and cross or not as shall appear necessary from the circumstances." On his arrival in the Clove he sent Sullivan and after him Stirling across the river to a position behind Peekskill.[28]

On July 23 Howe's fleet of more than 260 warships and transports, laden with fifteen to eighteen thousand soldiers, innumerable horses, field-pieces and small arms, quantities of ammunition, provisions, and military equipment of every sort, set sail from Sandy Hook. It was an impressive armada. A little below, the transports formed in two divisions. The flagship *Eagle*, 64 guns, and the frigate *Liverpool*, 32 guns, led the convoy. After them and on both sides of the transports came the warships *Augusta*, 64 guns, and *Isis*, 50 guns. In the rear were the *Nonsuch*, 64 guns, with its "couriers" the armed schooners *Swift* and *Dispatch*, 16 guns each. Nine frigates "sailed around the fleet at some distance." So they left the Hook bound for—no one on the American side knew where.[29]

Washington, up in the Clove, got the news the next day and perceived that he had guessed wrong. He ordered Sullivan, Stirling, Stephen, and Lincoln, with their divisions, Morgan's riflemen, and the squadrons of horse led by Sheldon, Moylan, and Bland to proceed immediately to Philadelphia. He detached Wayne from his brigade and sent him to Chester in Pennsylvania to command the militia there. With the rest of his army he started southward.[30]

When he gave those orders he was sure Howe was for Philadelphia by way of the Delaware River; but by the time he himself got to that river, on the 29th, he began again to doubt. Howe had then been six days at sea, yet had not appeared at the Delaware capes. Perhaps after all his start southward from New York was merely a ruse to draw the American army away from the Hudson. That fleet might have turned about and be now on its way back to join Burgoyne. He decided to hold his troops on the Jersey side of the Delaware, at Trenton, Coryell's Ferry, and Howell's Ferry. He halted Sullivan at Morristown until further orders.[31]

But the very next day Henry Fisher, a pilot at Lewes, at the mouth of the Delaware Bay, sent an express to Philadelphia telling that the fleet was in sight. Washington got the news at Coryell's Ferry, 150 miles from Lewes, at ten o'clock in the morning of the 31st—in twenty-four hours, a creditable performance for men and horses.[32]

Washington immediately ordered his troops across the Delaware and to Philadelphia, called on Sullivan to come on, and himself took horse for Chester "to look out for a proper place to arrange the army."[33] But on August 2 Fisher wrote that the fleet had left: "A large ship which we took to be the Admiral fired a gun and immediately the whole Fleet backed and stood off . . . to the eastward . . . about four o'clock P.M. they were ought of sight; whether they were bound to New York or Virginia is not in my power to tell."[34]

Nor was it in Washington's power; but he guessed—and guessed wrong again. It seemed to him, he said, that Howe had been "practising a deep feint, merely to draw our attention and whole force to this point." "There is the strongest reason to believe that the North River is their object." "This unexpected event makes it necessary to reverse our disposition." "I shall return again with the utmost expedition to the North River." So he wrote to this and that one of his generals, with orders to hasten back to Peekskill.[35]

But on more sober thought he decided on August 3 to wait until he had sure intelligence that the fleet was back at Sandy Hook before he returned to Peekskill. So he halted Sullivan at Hanover in New Jersey and held his main army at the Falls of Schuylkill near Germantown in Pennsylvania.

Yet again, on the 8th, his fears of Howe's strategy prompted him to move back to Coryell's Ferry; and he was actually on the march when, on the 10th, another flash came from the south. The fleet had been seen off Sinepuxent Inlet in Maryland, thirty miles below the Delaware capes, and was headed south. He halted his army and went into camp beside Neshaminy Creek, thirty miles north of Philadelphia.[36]

Still, he was "puzzled . . . being unable to account upon any plausible Plan . . . why he [Howe] should go to the southward rather than co-operate with Mr. Burgoyne."[37] Even as late as the 21st of August he still thought Howe was making a feint and would return either to the Delaware or to the Hudson, for, "had Chesapeake Bay been his Object, he would have been there long since." A council of war held that day decided unanimously that Charleston in South Carolina was Howe's most probable destination. So sure were the American generals that it was decided to move "to-morrow morning towards Hudson's River," and orders were given accordingly.[38] But on the next day came an express: the fleet was in the Chesapeake, "high up in the North East part of it." [39] The orders were canceled.

Why Admiral Lord Howe, in command of the fleet, and his brother, Sir William, in command of the army, after reaching the Delaware capes, failed to attempt a landing near Philadelphia and instead made the long voyage south, around Cape Charles, and up the Chesapeake, has puzzled many able historians and they still continue to debate the question. Yet the facts seem to give a plain answer.

The fleet had sailed from Sandy Hook on July 23, 1777. Meeting variable weather and winds, it made the Delaware capes on the 29th. After tacking to and fro for a whole day, it was joined by the *Roebuck*, which had long been stationed in Delaware waters under command of Captain Sir Andrew Snape Hamond. Captain Hamond boarded the flagship and gave the Admiral such a report of conditions in the bay and river that it was decided to draw off and make for the Chesapeake.

The first question debated by the historians is whether it was General Howe's intention, when he planned the excursion, to go up the Delaware or the Chesapeake. But that question is certainly easily answered. He planned at first to enter the Chesapeake. However, he wrote to Germain July 6, 1777, "I propose going up the Delaware." The second question is why he changed his mind. That is answered in a letter to Germain dated August 30: "Arrived off the Capes of the Delaware . . . when from information, I thought it most advisable to proceed to Chesapeake Bay." Hamond gave him reasons that quite properly seemed sufficient to make him change his plans.[40] Lieutenant William John Hall of the 45th regiment makes this point clear in a letter dated December 26, 1777: "In our appearance off the capes of Delaware, the *Roebuck* came out and Capt. Hamond going on board the Admiral produced a chimerical draught of fortifications that were never erected and Chevaux de Frise that were never sunk. This intelligence caused us to bear away for the Chesapeake." [41] What was even more important in the situation was that Howe hit upon the idea of using the Delaware because he feared Washington was about to go to the assistance of the American army in northern New York and because he could follow Washington much more readily from the Delaware. When he learned that the American commander in chief was not moving northward, he was able to pursue his original plan.

One may ask two more questions: Was Hamond's advice justified by conditions in the Delaware? Was the decision unfortunate in fact?

The substance of Hamond's objections to going up the Delaware was the condition of the river itself and the condition of its defenses. Of the river itself he said that its navigation was intricate and hazardous; that large ships could pass certain places only at particular times of the tide; that its shores from Henlopen to Reedy Island were marshy and full of creeks; that from Reedy Island to Chester the channel was so narrow as to require four miles of anchorage for the fleet, which must lie within cannon-shot of the shore; that the tidal current ran at three to four miles an hour.[42]

In answer one might urge that the navigation was not too difficult, nor the tidal current too strong to prevent the flagship and twelve other ships from going up in October as far as Chester. As to anchorage, in November there were 100 vessels anchored between Reedy Island and New Castle; although much of the shore was marshy, both New Castle and Chester afforded good landing places, New Castle being a port much used by overseas vessels. On this point Hamond's advice was clearly unjustified.

Of the river's defenses, he said that the Americans had a fleet of one frigate, two xebecs, one brig, and two floating batteries, and that there were numerous channel obstructions.[43] Certainly that little American fleet could offer no substantial opposition to Howe's great warships, and there were no forts and no "channel obstructions" even as far down as Chester. Hamond's advice was bad on all those points, too.

That the decision was unfortunate in fact is equally certain. From the 31st of July, when the fleet left the Delaware capes, to the 14th of August, when it sighted Cape Charles, it fought adverse winds and endured calms. It took eleven more days to reach its landing at the Head of Elk—thirty-two days out from Sandy Hook—having sailed three hundred and fifty miles from Henlopen to land only fifteen miles from New Castle, which it might have reached in less than ninety miles from Henlopen. In all that long voyage men and horses suffered greatly from the rough sea, the heat, the shortage of fresh provisions, fresh water, and forage. Many of the horses, dead or dying, were thrown overboard; those that survived were "mere carrion."

As against Head of Elk, New Castle would have been a much more favorable landing place. From Head of Elk the army had to march fifty miles to Philadelphia. From New Castle, the distance is but thirty-three miles. Better still would have been Chester, only fifteen miles from Philadelphia with no such defensible river to cross as the Brandywine, until they came to the Schuylkill at Philadelphia itself.

As Trevelyan points out, after all that delay and all those hardships, the army at Head of Elk was ten miles farther from Philadelphia than it had been the previous December at Amboy. And it had the same army, but much larger in numbers, to contend with in August as in the previous December.

Altogether the decision to go to the Chesapeake was undeniably unfortunate. But that the fault lay with Howe, because he took advice that sounded convincing from a sea captain who should have been well informed, is probably not true. Howe chose the Chesapeake route in the beginning with a rather vague idea that he could more or less cut off communication between the middle and southern colonies and at the same time possibly force Washington to fight at a disadvantage somewhere east of the Susquehanna River. No doubt he also calculated that he could later open up the Delaware as a safe supply route.

Whatever Howe may have planned, Washington's suspense and anxiety were now at an end. Orders went to Sullivan to join the army "with all convenient speed"; to General Nash to hasten with his brigade and Proctor's artillery to Chester; and for all the troops to march "to-morrow morning very early towards Philadelphia and onwards." [44] News of the American victory at Bennington was given out and greatly cheered the soldiers.

CHAPTER 30

Head of Elk

Washington started southward from his camp on the Neshaminy on August 23, at four o'clock in the morning. That evening he camped near Germantown, and the next morning he formed his troops for the march through Philadelphia in such manner as to impress the strong Tory element there, including the Quakers. His preparations and directions for this display of strength were "pathetically minute." [1]

The army was to march in one column "First—A Sub. and twelve light horse, 200 Yards in their rear a complete troop," then a space of 100 yards, and "a company of pioneers with their axes in &c in proper order." At another hundred yards distance, a regiment of Muhlenberg's brigade, followed by field artillery, then Weedon's, Woodford's, and Scott's brigades, Lincoln's and Stirling's divisions, the artillery, and the cavalry, winding up with a troop of horse 150 yards in the rear of all the rest. The men were to be "made to appear as decent as possible" and to "carry their arms well"; any man who dared "to quit his ranks" was to receive thirty-nine lashes at the next halting place. The drums and fifes were to play "a tune for the quick step . . . but with such moderation that the men may step to it with ease; and without dancing along." To give them some appearance of uniformity in default of uniform dress, they were to wear sprigs of green leaves in their hats.[2]

So, with Washington riding at the head, the Marquis de Lafayette at his side and his mounted staff following, the long column of 16,000 men marched down Front Street and up Chestnut to the awe of the disaffected and the delight of the patriots. John Adams watched the procession. "They marched twelve deep," he wrote to his wife, "and yet took up above two hours in passing by." They were "extremely well armed, pretty well clothed and tolerably disciplined," yet had not "quite the air of soldiers. They don't step exactly in time. They don't hold up their heads quite erect, nor turn out their toes exactly as they ought. They don't all of them cock their hats; and such as do, don't all wear them the same way." [3] Another observer, a military gentleman, Alexander Graydon, who was inclined to be critical, noted that "though indifferently dressed, [they] held well burnished arms and carried them like soldiers, and looked, in short, as if they might have faced an equal number with a reasonable prospect of success." [4]

They marched to Darby that day, and moved on to Naaman's Creek on the next, under orders to "encamp in the first good ground beyond it." The horsemen, however, were to keep on to Wilmington before encamping. Washington himself with his staff also kept on, entered Wilmington, and set up his headquarters in a house on Quaker Hill. Here he learned that the enemy had begun to land that morning "about Six Miles below the Head of Elk opposite to Cecil Court House." He set about gathering in all available troops, called on Armstrong to send on "every Man of the Militia under your command" at Chester and Marcus Hook "that is properly armed, as quick as possible," to march them, indeed, that very night. He called on Baylor to bring "Such Men as you have ready," on Greene's division and Stephen's, also on Sullivan's; but Sullivan was not to press his men "too hard in their march," as they "must no doubt have been greatly harassed" in a futile expedition against Staten Island he had undertaken while at Hanover.[5] Washington had already detached General Smallwood and Colonel Mordecai Gist from their commands in Sullivan's division and sent them to Maryland to take over the militia of that state, called out to the number of 2,000 in accordance with a resolution of the Congress.[6]

On the following morning Washington, accompanied by Greene, Lafayette, his aides, and a strong troop of horse, rode southward on a scouting expedition. From the summits of Iron Hill and Gray's Hill they scanned the country below. Although Gray's Hill was within two miles of the enemy's camp and they could see their tents, they could not form a satisfactory estimate of their numbers. After spending the rest of the day in surveying the surrounding country, they were overtaken by a severe storm. Having taken refuge in a farmhouse Washington showed no inclination to go out into the tempestuous night. His companions urged upon him the danger of capture, perhaps citing the fate of Charles Lee in similar circumstances, but he chose to remain until daybreak. The owner of the house was a Tory; he might have sent word to the British camp of the archrebel's presence and so led to a coup disastrous to the Americans, if Washington's escort had not surrounded the house and guarded against that danger. Washington himself afterwards acknowledged his imprudence at this time.[7]

It was on a Monday morning, August 25, "a distressingly hot, close morning," that the van of the British fleet dropped anchor in the Elk River opposite Cecil County Courthouse and the debarkation began. Two regiments of British light infantry, two of British grenadiers, and the Hessian and Anspach jägers in flat-bottomed boats were the first ashore on the courthouse side and the first to come in contact with the Americans—four companies of militia stationed there, who "fled without firing a shot." The light infantry at once advanced to a post about four miles towards the Head of Elk. The rest of the army landed that day, all except the light dragoons, who came ashore with their horses on the morrow. The troops were ordered to hut themselves with fence rails and cornstalks, which could have afforded little protection from the "heavy storm of Rain, Lightning and Thunder" that broke upon them that night.[8]

Orders were given by Howe to march at three o'clock in the morning, but were countermanded because of another heavy storm that lasted all night and part of the third day. In spite of the rain and the hanging of two soldiers and the severe whipping of five others as a punishment for plundering, the troops indulged in extensive looting of houses and farms. The inhabitants were not to be seen "having deserted their houses and drove off their stock." Not all of it, however, for "the soldiers slaughtered a great deal of cattle clandestinely." [9]

There were other reasons for the British delay than the storm; the troops were not yet sufficiently refreshed from their long confinement in the transports, and the "miserably emaciated" horses—those that had survived—were in no shape to be used. On the 28th, however, the weather being "extremely fine" and the roads somewhat dried, the van of the army marched to Elkton, a town of "about 40 well built brick and stone houses," from which "one thousand men under a Colonel Patterson and the Philadelphia Light Horse" fled to Gray's Hill. They fled again when the British advance guard came up. In Elkton the invaders found "Storehouses full, consisting of molasses, Indian Corn, Tobacco, Pitch, Tar and some Cordage and Flour," which the American troops had failed to remove.[10]

The British army was in two grand divisions. It was the one commanded by Cornwallis that had moved on Elkton; the other, under the Hessian general, Wilhelm von Knyphausen, had crossed the Elk and encamped at Cecil Courthouse. This arrangement was designed to permit an advance up

Schuylkill R.

Valley Forge

#Whitemarsh

HOWE

Germantown

Philadelphia

Chadd's Ford

CORNWALLIS

Chester

Fort Mercer

Brandywine Creek

Wilmington

Delaware River

Chesapeake Bay

Head of Elk

THE
PHILADELPHIA
CAMPAIGN

----------- British Advance
+-+-+-+-+-+-+ American Retreat

both sides of the Elk, the two bodies to join at a point seven or eight miles south of the Christina River.[11]

They lay in those camps for the next five days. There were unimportant skirmishes with small bodies of Americans. On the 29th "the Chasseurs [jägers] encountered a body of the rebel infantry" and on the 30th "the Welch fusileers fired a few Platoons into a body of rebel cavalry of about 200." But there was organized foraging on a grand scale. On the 31st Knyphausen with a large detachment made a foray "thro Bohemiah Mannor" and rounded up "261 head of horned Cattle and 568 sheep and 100 horses." [12] Another party got 350 sheep, 55 horned cattle, and 204 horses or mules. There was great need of horses, over 300 having died on the voyage or been rendered unfit for duty.[13] There was also a great hunger for fresh meat. "Some Hessians . . . demolished a whole flock of sheep which the owners were voluntarily driving to us." [14] On September 1 Wemyss's corps of rangers attacked an American outpost and took the commanding officer, "his lieutenant and 3 privates—killed 2 and wounded 1—the rest consisting of 100 fled—this was effected without any loss on our side." [15]

While Washington was encamped on the Neshaminy and was still in doubt as to Howe's purposes he had sent Colonel Daniel Morgan and his corps of riflemen to join Putnam at Peekskill and to go thence to reenforce the Northern American army facing Burgoyne. To provide a corps of light infantry in place of Morgan's men, a hundred good soldiers were selected from each of six brigades and placed under command of Brigadier General William Maxwell of New Jersey. With two captains, six subalterns, and the appropriate number of noncommissioned officers, they numbered about 720 in all. They were to be "constantly near the Enemy and to give them every possible annoyance." Maxwell posted his corps in the neighborhood of Cooch's Bridge on the upper waters of the Christina River. On September 2 Washington warned him of the intention of the enemy to march next day and begged him "to be prepared to give them as much trouble as you possibly can." [16]

The British army had, indeed, begun its movement that very day. Knyphausen, commanding one of the two grand divisions, marched from his camp at Cecil Courthouse and encamped that night at the Buck Tavern, otherwise called Carson's, just below the present Delaware and Chesapeake Canal.[17] At daybreak on the following morning Cornwallis with the other column, Howe accompanying him, took "the lower road to Christeen by way of Rikin's [Aiken's] Tavern in order to avoid Iron Hill." They had expected to join Knyphausen at the tavern (now the town of Glasgow) "but did not perceive them." They pushed on through a "close" country, "the woods within shot of the road frequently in front and flank and in projecting points towards the Road." [18] Evidently it was the kind of country disliked by the regulars, who preferred combat in the open in regular battle formation.

Along this unpleasant road at about nine o'clock in the morning the van of the column, Hessian and Anspach jägers, under Lieutenant Colonel Ludwig von Wurmb, followed by British light infantry with two small fieldpieces, was making its way—cautiously, no doubt—when it met a sudden fire from Maxwell's men posted among the trees by the roadside. Wurmb formed his men, and there was a hot fire from both sides. The fieldpieces were brought into play; a detachment of Hessians shifted to the woods and attacked Maxwell's right flank; Wurmb charged with the bayonet. The Americans retreated up the road, took a new position under cover, and renewed their fire. Again they were driven back to another stand. The British light infantry entered the engagement; the Americans again retreated, keeping up a running fight. At one point "a body of Riflemen formed a kind of Ambuscade" and gave the British "several close, well-directed Fires." An attempt at getting into the American rear failed because "an unpassable swamp" intervened, "which prevented this spirited, little affair becoming so decisive" as it might have been. But Maxwell's men were now pretty well disorganized. Their retreat became a flight. They were pursued for some distance, but finally made their way to the main army on the White Clay Creek.[19] The casualties were perhaps thirty killed on the American side and about as many killed or wounded on the other.[20]

Knyphausen's column came up to Aiken's Tavern just after this affair, and both columns encamped between Iron Hill and the tavern. They had moved slowly, having to drive a herd of cattle with them and to keep pace with two detachments flanking Knyphausen's column sent out to comb the country for livestock. These brought in "500 Head of Horned Cattle, 1000 Sheep and 100 horses, but not above forty of these Horses were fit for draught." [21]

The next four days the British spent in reconnoitering the country, bringing up provisions from the fleet, and sending back the sick and wounded. Grant, with two brigades left at Elkton, came up on the 6th. All communication with the fleet was then abandoned, and it withdrew down the bay.

On August 28 Greene's and Stephen's divisions, mostly Virginia Continentals, under Brigadiers Muhlenberg, Weedon, Woodford, and Scott, with

Sheldon's horse, were advanced to the White Clay Creek.[22] But an American council of war decided to concentrate the army on the northerly side of the Red Clay Creek near Newport, on the main road to Philadelphia. To that position it was moved on September 6,[23] Maxwell's corps remaining in advance on the White Clay. Washington, having learned that the British had disencumbered themselves of their baggage and tents, indicating "a speedy and rapid movement," ordered his troops similarly relieved. Both officers and men were to retain only their greatcoats, if they had any, and their blankets. Everything else was to be sent north of the Brandywine.[24] Thus stripped for action they awaited the enemy's next move.

It began on the 8th two hours before daybreak when the whole British army advanced by the light of "a remarkable borealis." Washington had expected a movement against his position on the Red Clay and seems to have been desirous of bringing on an engagement there. Howe fostered this delusion by sending a detachment to a point opposite the American position [25] but marched his main army northward. This was construed by Washington as a flanking movement to carry the enemy around his right to his rear and so on to Philadelphia. To prevent this he withdrew his force at two o'clock in the morning of the 9th to Chad's Ford on the Brandywine and on the more northerly Philadelphia road. But Howe was proceeding in good faith to Kennett Square in Pennsylvania. Early in the morning of the 10th the whole British force was collected at that place on the road which Washington held at Chad's Ford.[26]

CHAPTER 31

Brandywine

The Brandywine proper begins at the confluence of two streams, known as the east and west branches, which meet at a place called the Forks about six miles northwest of Chad's Ford. It flows in a valley, now very narrow and again somewhat wider, where meadows border the stream, between hills rising to a height of 200 feet or more three-quarters of a mile from the river edge. In places these hills slope gradually down to the river; in others they drop steeply, 200 feet in a half-mile or even in a quarter-mile. The uplands back of the hilltops were largely cultivated, but the slopes were densely forested. Between the Forks and the Ford the river receives little streams coming down small valleys.

Along the valley ran roads to find shallow crossings. These several roads and fords played an important part in the battle and must be distinguished by name.

The Nottingham Road (now the Baltimore Pike), running eastwards through Kennett Square on its way to Chester and Philadelphia, came to the river at Chad's Ford. Just before it reached the stream, it forked and crossed by two fords, one about 300 feet north of the present bridge, the other about 150 feet below the bridge. At this point the shallow but swift stream was about 150 feet wide.[1]

About a mile upstream, another road crossed at Brinton's Ford. Two miles above that, the Street Road ran to Painter's Ford. A branch of that road used Wistar's Ford, an equal distance farther up. Again there was a two-mile interval to Buffington's Ford, where a road running roughly parallel to the stream on its east side swung to the west to cross the East Branch a

341

little above the Forks. A mile above that Jefferis Ford crossed the East Branch and, opposite it, Trimble's Ford crossed the West Branch. The width of the tongue of land between them was about two miles. About a mile and half below Chad's was Pyle's Ford.[2]

The American army arrived at Chad's Ford in the morning of September 9 and established its center there, Wayne's brigade of Pennsylvania Continentals being posted on the brow of an eminence near Chad's house a little above the Ford, and Weedon's and Muhlenberg's brigades of Virginia Continentals directly east of the Ford. Proctor's Pennsylvania artillery was with Wayne. Greene commanded the center. Light earthworks and a redoubt were erected for Wayne and Proctor as a front line, the Virginians being in reserve.

The right wing was composed of three divisions of two brigades each posted along the east bank of the river, covering Brinton's Ford and running up some distance below Painter's. Stirling held the extreme right; Stephen was next below him; and Sullivan was nearest the center, he being in general command of the wing.

The left wing was posted at Pyle's Ford, where the heights on the east side were steep and rugged and there was little apprehension of a crossing. Its defense was entrusted to a thousand Pennsylvania militia under Armstrong.

To guard the forces above the right wing, Sullivan detached the Delaware Regiment to Painter's Ford, one battalion from Hazen's "Canadian Regiment" to Wistar's and another to Buffington's.[3]

Maxwell's light infantry took a position west of the river on high ground on both sides of the main road. Picket guards were thrown across the upper part of the stream. Colonel Theodorick Bland with the 1st Dragoons, one of Washington's few cavalry corps, which were all commanded by Count Pulaski, was stationed about opposite Painter's Ford. Major James Spear, with a body of Pennsylvania militia, picketed the ground above the Forks near Buffington's Ford. Washington established his headquarters in a house about a mile back of Chad's Ford, and Lafayette set up his a half mile farther back.[4]

September 11, 1777, began with a foggy morning, but ripened to a noon of blazing sunshine and sweltering heat. Before daybreak Maxwell's corps, with three small detachments from the Virginia line, was sent back along the main road towards Kennett Square to feel out the enemy and delay their approach. Maxwell marched as far as Kennett meetinghouse, about three miles from the Ford, and sent a party of mounted vedettes farther forward.

They stopped at Welch's Tavern a mile or so beyond, tied their horses to a rail, and gathered at the bar, waiting for something to turn up. About nine o'clock, one of them espied through a window uniformed men coming down the road and not more than a few rods away. It was Major Patrick Ferguson's Riflemen and the Queen's Rangers, Tory troops, the point of the vanguard of Knyphausen's columns. The vedettes fired a single harmless volley and fled through the back door, leaving their horses.[5]

The Riflemen and Rangers were followed by two British brigades under General Grant, Stirn's brigade of three Hessian regiments, half of the 16th Dragoons, and two brigades of heavy artillery. Behind them the rest of the artillery, the provision train, the baggage and cattle dragged along, followed by the rear guard of one battalion of the 71st Regiment of Highlanders, two others marching beside the train as flankers. There were about 5,000 men in all in this column.[6] They had left Kennett early in the morning and advanced so far without the Americans even knowing that they were on the march.

After dispersing the little band at Welch's Tavern, the column kept on to the Meetinghouse. There it met with a surprise. A sudden burst of fire from Maxwell's corps posted behind the graveyard wall checked the van and threw it into confusion. It rallied and returned the fire. Maxwell fell back slowly down the road, taking cover from time to time and keeping up his fire until he reached the Ford. There he was reinforced. He turned back to high ground above the road and again engaged the enemy. The vanguard was not strong enough to dislodge him, and the British deployed. Ferguson's Riflemen supported by a hundred Hessians were thrown out to the right. But in the meantime Porterfield's and Waggoner's Virginians had crossed the stream to Maxwell's aid. They drove the Riflemen and Hessians back to the shelter of a stone house. The British 49th Regiment, with two heavy guns and two three-pounders, taking a position on an elevation behind Ferguson, backed him up and opened fire on the Americans. The Queen's Rangers, led by Captain Wemyss, and the 23rd Regiment filed off to their left and flanked Maxwell, whose men "had been shouting Hurrah! and firing briskly." The 28th Regiment also went into action, and Maxwell was driven out of the woods and back across the upper branch of the Ford. The Rangers then joined the Riflemen and Hessians at the stone house, swept down on Porterfield and Waggoner and drove them back by the lower ford to the other side.[7]

While all this was going on Porter's artillery was cannonading from its position on the east side; but "though the balls and grapeshot were well aimed and fell right among us," says Captain Baurmeister of the Hessian

Regiment von Mirbach, "the cannonade had but little effect—partly because the battery was placed too low." [8]

Under the covering fire of their guns, mounted hastily in strategic places and on the high ground west of the river, the 28th, 23rd, 55th, and 40th British regiments and the Leib and Mirbach Hessian regiments formed a line on the heights overlooking the Ford; the Combined Battalion and Donop's Hessians held the road; and the 4th, 5th, 27th, and 49th British regiments took position on the slope from the heights down to the lowland along the river. The light troops and outposts were pushed forward close to the stream. The lines were straightened in formal fashion, and one battalion of the 71st, with the 16th (or Queen's Own) Regiment of light dragoons, was posted on the right flank, while two other battalions of the 71st guarded the baggage in the rear. These dispositions were completed by half-past ten. Then things quieted down; the musketry ceased; the artillery fired only occasionally, and was similarly answered by the Americans. [9]

One might suppose that this cessation of activity on the part of the enemy, this desultory firing with no attempt to advance, would have brought to Washington and his officers memories of an exactly similar situation at Long Island a year before, when Grant held Stirling by the same tactics while the main British army was about its business elsewhere; but the same bland confidence that Howe intended a frontal attack seems to have persisted in the minds of all. Washington and Greene spent most of the morning at headquarters, a mile back from the Ford. [10] At the front the hours passed in watchful waiting for the enemy to launch their attack.

This confidence was first disturbed after nine o'clock when word came to headquarters from Colonel Hazen that a body of the enemy had been seen marching up the Great Valley Road, parallel with the river on its western side and leading to Trimble's Ford on the west branch a mile above the Forks. Washington sent a note to Colonel Bland, who was on the west side of the stream opposite Painter's Ford, earnestly entreating "a continuance of your vigilant attention to the movements of the enemy" and calling for reports of such movements, of their numbers "and of the course they are pursuing." "In a particular manner," he wrote, "I wish you to gain satisfactory information of a body confidently reported to have gone up to a ford seven or eight miles above this. You will send an intelligent, sensible officer immediately with a party to find out the truth." [11] Bland reported that he had seen a body of the enemy advancing on "the valley road" towards Trimble's Ford. [12]

On top of this came a dispatch forwarded by Sullivan, from Lieutenant

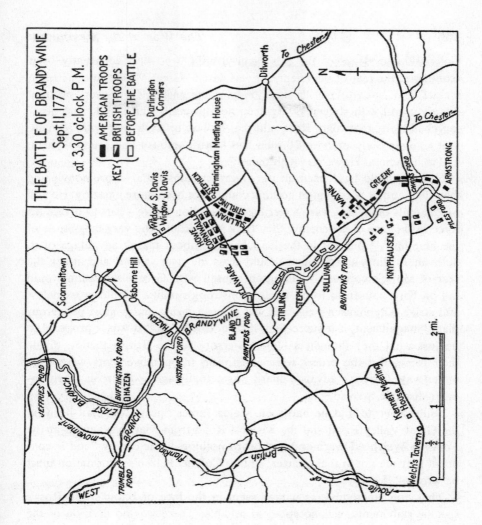

THE BATTLE OF BRANDYWINE
Sept. 11, 1777
at 3.30 o'clock P.M.

KEY
■ AMERICAN TROOPS
▨ BRITISH TROOPS
☐ BEFORE THE BATTLE

To Chester

To Chester

N

Dilworth

Darlington Corners

Birmingham Meeting House

STEPHEN

Widow S. Davis
Widow J. Davis

STIRLING
SULLIVAN

HOWE
CORNWALLIS

WAYNE

GREENE

CHADD'S FORD

ARMSTRONG

PILE'S FORD

KNYPHAUSEN

Sconnetown

Osborne Hill

DELAWARE

BLAND

BRANDYWINE

PAINTER'S FORD

STIRLING

STEPHEN

SULLIVAN

BRINTON'S FORD

HAZEN

WISTAR'S FORD

JEFFRIES' FORD

EAST BRANCH

Buffington's Ford
☐ HAZEN

MOVEMENT

WEST BRANCH

TRIMBLE'S FORD

Flanking

British

Kennett Meeting House

Route

Welch's Tavern

0   ½   1   2 mi.

Colonel James Ross of the 8th Pennsylvania, who had apparently been scouting in the rear of the enemy. It was dated "Great Valley Road, Eleven o'clock A.M." and told of "a large body of the enemy, from every account five thousand with sixteen or eighteen field-pieces," which had "just now" marched along that rôad. Ross said that he was on their rear with 70 men, that Captain Simpson with 20 men had lain in ambush and fired on them, and that General Howe was with them.[13]

Nothing could have been clearer, more circumstantial, more convincing than that, and to Washington nothing could have been more amazing. He and his generals thought it was "a terrible blunder" on Howe's part to divide his force in the face of his enemy; they were puzzled by "the very magnitude of the blunder," [14] but not in the least hesitant about taking advantage of it. Sullivan, Stirling, and Stephen should cross the river at once and attack the rear of Howe's column. Washington himself with Greene's division would fall on Knyphausen in front, while Armstrong's militia should cross below and strike Knyphausen's right. It was a most daring and a most dangerous plan, "magnificent, if it succeeded, insane, if it failed." It was a proposal to do just what they thought a "terrible error" in the British tactics, divide their force. But the orders were given, and troop movements were soon under way. Greene's advance guard was actually across the river when another dispatch arrived.[15]

Sullivan wrote that he had seen Major James Spear, who had been on the Great Valley Road and the Kennett Road from Martin's Tavern at the Forks to Welch's Tavern and had heard nothing of the enemy "and is confident they are not in that quarter; so that Colonel Hazen's information must be wrong." [16]

That note, incredible as it may seem in the face of Bland's and Ross's specific statements, was accepted as reliable. There *was* no division of the British army, no force threatened the American right wing; all the enemy were in front. The orders to cross were canceled; Greene's advance was withdrawn. The army settled down to await a frontal attack. Time passed. Knyphausen made no move. Only his intermittent cannonading declared him an enemy. And still no one remembered Long Island. Two o'clock came; no change. Then there was a sudden commotion.

A sweating horseman, a hatless, coatless, barelegged farmer, dashed into Sullivan's lines. He must see the General—Washington—at once. Sullivan couldn't allow that; the General mustn't be disturbed by such an uncouth person. But the man *must* see him; he was Thomas Cheyney, a good patriot, one of the few about there, and he had important news. What was it? He told it. He had been watching the movement of the armies, and had got up that morning early to do a bit of scouting, dressed in a hurry without bothering to put on his stockings. He rode to the top of a hill, and there the British were, not a hundred yards away. He turned his horse and fled. They followed, fired on him, but his horse was fast. He got away, and here he was. They were across the creek and coming down this way. Wasn't that important? It seemed so. He was taken to the commander in chief.

Cheyney told his tale again. Washington was incredulous. He had had that Spear report to the contrary. Probably he thought the man was a Tory, trying to mislead him; they were all Tories, these Chester Countians. The staff smiled and shook their heads. Cheyney turned on them. "I'd have you know I have this day's work as much at heart as e'er a blood of ye!" Then to Washington: "If Anthony Wayne or Perse Frazer was here, they'd know whether I'm to be believed." He dropped on one knee, drew in the dust with his finger a map, the roads, the fords, marked the place where he had seen the enemy. Still Washington disbelieved. "You're mistaken, General," cried the exasperated man. "My life for it you're mistaken. By hell! it's so. Put me under guard till you can find out it's so!" [17]

What to do? It might be so. Those conflicting reports? Then came the thunderclap that cleared the air, banished all doubt, a courier with a dispatch enclosing another:

Dear General;
    Col⁰ Bland has this moment Sent me word, that the enemy are in the Rear of my Right about two miles Coming Down, there is, he says about two Brigades of them. 2 of Clock PM he also says he Saw a Dust Rise back in the Country for above an hour.
                              I am &c   JOHN SULLIVAN

    The enclosure read:

                                            A quarter past One o'clock.
Sir:
    I have discovered a party of the enemy on the heights, just on the right of the two Widow Davis's who live close together on the road called the Fork Road, about half a mile to the right of the [Birmingham] Meeting House. There is a higher hill in front.
                                            THEODORICK BLAND [18]

There at last was the indubitable truth. At four o'clock that morning, a full hour before Knyphausen had started, Howe and Cornwallis had left Kennett Square with the Hessian jägers, the 1st and 2nd battalions of grenadiers, the Guards, two squadrons of light dragoons, one of dismounted dragoons, and the 3rd and 4th brigades of infantry. They had kept to the

main road until within a mile and a half of Welch's Tavern. There they
had taken a left fork and so had come into the Great Valley Road, which
led to Trimble's Ford on the west branch, crossed the two-mile interval to
Jefferis's Ford on the east branch, crossed that, turned south past Sconneltown, and come out into the open at Osborne's Hill, a mile and a half east
of the Brandywine, in the rear of the American line and within two miles of
their extreme outposts on the right.[19]

Hazen picked up his two battalions at Buffington's Ford—the outpost
nearest the enemy crossing at Jefferis's Ford—and at Wistar's, and the
Delaware Regiment at Painter's Ford, and started south towards the main
army.

The van of the British column had halted at Sconneltown, just beyond
Jefferis's Ford, to let the rear catch up and then had gone on to Osborne's
Hill. It was now half after two. The soldiers had been afoot since four in
the morning, marching fifteen miles on a swelteringly hot day. Food and
rest were needed; they took both sprawling on the grass, and the countryside turned out to see them.

Joseph Townsend, a Quaker youth of twenty who saw them first when
they came out of the woods, wrote afterward: "In a few minutes the fields
were literally covered with them. . . . Their arms and bayonets being
raised shone as bright as silver, there being a clear sky and the day exceedingly warm." He saw Cornwallis: "He was on horseback, appeared tall and
sat very erect. His rich scarlet clothing loaded with gold lace, epaulets &c.,
occasioned him to make a brilliant and martial appearance." Most of the
officers were "rather short, portly men, well dressed and of genteel appearance, and did not look as if they had ever been exposed to any hardship,
their skins being as white and delicate as is customary for females who were
brought up in large cities and towns." The Hessians interested him: "Many
of them wore their beards on their upper lips, which was a novelty in that
part of the country." General Howe was "mounted on a large English horse,
much reduced in flesh. . . . The general was a large, portly man, of coarse
features. He appeared to have lost his teeth, as his mouth had fallen in." [20]

Meanwhile, the Americans had been astir. Washington ordered the whole
right wing—Sullivan's, Stephen's, and Stirling's divisions, all under Sullivan
—to shift from their position along the river and oppose the approaching
enemy. Wayne's brigade of Pennsylvanians, Maxwell's light infantry, and
Proctor's artillery were to continue to hold the Chad's Ford position against
Knyphausen. Greene's division of two brigades—Weedon's and Muhlenberg's Virginians—was to remain in reserve to help Sullivan or Wayne as
needed. Washington remained with Greene.[21]

There was some delay in starting the march of one of Sullivan's own two brigades. Stirling's and Stephen's divisions and even one brigade of Sullivan's, under General Prudhomme de Borré, got away before Sullivan did with the other. When he moved with that other he met Hazen with the "Canadians" and the Delawares on the march down to the main army. Hazen told him that "the Enemy were Close upon his Heels." While these two were talking together, the soldiers still moving on, "the Enemy headed us [Sullivan's men] in the Road about forty Rods from our Advance Guard." This was probably one of two small detachments thrown out to the right of Cornwallis's column to cross at Wistar's Ford or Painter's. To avoid them, Sullivan swung his column to the right and got away without a fight. Soon after that he discovered Stirling's and Stephen's divisions already "Drawn up on an Eminence, both in the Rear & to the Right of the place" where his men were and facing the British force on the opposite hill to the north of them, that is to say on Osborne's Hill. Sullivan had simply overshot his mark by coming up too near the enemy and undershot it by not being near enough to his colleagues. He was separated from them by an undefended space of half a mile.[22]

Sullivan now ordered Hazen's regiment and the Delawares to pass a slight depression between two hills, "File off to the Right & face to Cover the Artillery," thus separating them from his own brigade. With the rest of his troops he fell back and formed them "on an advantageous Height, in a Line with the other divisions," but with that half-mile still open between him and the others. He then rode off to consult with Stirling and Stephen. They told him that the enemy, now advancing down the slope of Osborne's Hill, were aiming to outflank the American position on the right, wherefore his troops should be brought up to join theirs, and "that the whole Should incline further to the Right," to prevent being outflanked. Sullivan went back to his men to bring them up.

The American line was formed on the northern slope of a round hill a hundred rods southeast of Birmingham Meetinghouse and facing Osborne's, with an interval of a mile and a half between their summits. Northeasterly through this valley ran the Street Road from Painter's Ford. The line curved around the face of the hill. De Borré's brigade held the right; Stephen's division was next; and then came Stirling's, these two composing the center. Sullivan was to hold the left. The artillery, four pieces, was "judiciously placed," and several outposts were thrown out in front of the line. "This position," says Captain John Montresor, chief engineer of the British forces in America, "was remarkably strong, having a large body advanced, small bodies still further advanced and their rear covered by a wood wherein their main body was posted, with a natural glacis for ¾ of a mile." The flanks also rested on woods.[23] Cornwallis, watching from the top of Osborne's Hill the arrangement of the Americans, remarked, "The damn rebels form well." [24]

By about half-past three the British army had formed in three divisions on Osborne's Hill. On the right were the Guards; the British grenadiers composed the center; the left was made up of the light infantry and the Hessian and Anspach jägers. The support, from right to left, was the Hessian grenadiers and the 4th Brigade. The 3rd Brigade, under Major General Charles Grey, was held in reserve.[25] A little after four o'clock the advance began in style. The uniforms were gay in their various colors, the muskets and bayonets "shining like silver," the bands playing "The British Grenadiers." So the exactly formed columns marched down the slope of Osborne's Hill and across the vale. There was no irregularity, no hurry. They came on with the arrogant assurance that marked the disciplined troops of that period of formal, dress-parade warfare.

The advance guard almost reached the Street Road. No shot had yet been fired. Then suddenly the jägers, on the left of their line, met a blaze of musketry from an American outpost in an orchard beside the road. They "stepped up" the roadside bank to the orchard fence, rested their muskets on it, and fired a volley. The artillery on both sides opened up, and the battle was on.[26]

The British light infantry and the Hessian and Anspach jägers were the first up the hill. They fell upon the American right, De Borré's brigade of three Maryland regiments, and met little resistance. The brigade broke and fled into the woods behind, exposing Stephen's right flank. The British Guards and grenadiers fired no shot, but advanced up the hill, their bayonets their only weapons.[27] Sullivan's men were on the way to close the gap that separated them from Stirling's left. In a column that straggled irregularly because of excitement and lack of training, they marched right across the front of the oncoming Guards and grenadiers, both British and Hessian. They had hardly formed a ragged line facing the enemy when the bayonets were upon them. Few of the American troops in that war could ever stand against the cold steel of the bayonet. These were unready for battle; Sullivan, their leader, had left them, gone to the center to direct the artillery. They fell back in confusion. Sullivan sent his aides to rally them and re-form them in the rear. He went back himself, "but all in vain," he says; "no Sooner did I form one party than that which I had before formed would Run off." He went back to the artillery, "left them to be Rallied if possible by their own officers and my aid De Camp." It was not possible. The entire left of the American line was swept away. Shorn of its wings, the center of Stirling's and Stephen's divisions with Hazen's "Canadians" and the Delawares now held the field alone.[28]

Miles in the rear with Greene and the reserve, Washington had been awaiting news of the grand attack, either at the Ford or at Birmingham. It came at half past four, in "a sudden burst of cannon from the northwestward," so loud that it was heard in Philadelphia. The grand attack was on up there at Birmingham. It was a signal for Knyphausen; he got ready to cross the Ford. The battle was to be fought on two fronts.

There must have been some hesitation in Washington's mind about the use of the reserve, whether at the Ford or at Birmingham, for about five o'clock his aide, Lieutenant Colonel Robert H. Harrison, was writing to the Congress about the attack at the north: "The Action has been very violent ever since. . . . It still continues." Knyphausen was preparing his attack. "A very severe cannonade has begun here too and I suppose we shall have a very hot evening." [29]

But at last the decision was made. The Ford must be left to Wayne, Maxwell, and Proctor. Greene with the reserve must go north to back up the troops on the hill and hold that road to Philadelphia. Washington himself wanted to be at that scene of action, but he did not know the way to it. Among the country people standing about was an old man, Joseph Brown. Washington asked him to lead the way by the shortest road. Brown demurred; Washington insisted. One of his aides dismounted, threatened the old man with his sword, hoisted him into the saddle. Across country they went; three miles as the crow flies, Washington continually crying, "Push along, old man! Push along!" His staff trailed behind. They came out on the road leading to Philadelphia, half a mile west of Dilworth.[30] Greene was coming along, with Weedon's brigade in advance, Muhlenberg's following. They arrived with speed. Weedon covered nearly four miles in less than 45 minutes.[31]

On the hill there had been hot fighting. Sullivan, Stirling, Stephen, and Thomas Conway the French-Irishman, one of Stirling's aides, encouraged the 3,000 Americans still there to repel the repeated attacks of twice their number of the best soldiers of Britain and Germany. They were seconded by Lafayette, who, ardent for battle, had galloped to the fight ahead of Washington and Greene. On the left Hazen's men and the Delawares with Dayton and Ogden of Stirling's division stood firm, although that flank had been exposed by the flight of Sullivan's brigade.

Cornwallis was edging his troops towards the Americans' extreme right and towards Dilworth, which was the key of the situation because it was on the Philadelphia road. The Americans had to shift and shift again in order to avoid being outflanked.[32]

For an hour and forty minutes, under fire of Cornwallis's artillery, four 12-pounders, the Americans on the hill disputed the way of the enemy. For fifty minutes of that time they fought "almost Muzzle to Muzzle, in such a manner that General Conway, who has Seen much Service, says he never Saw So Close & Severe a fire." A captain of the Delawares describes it: "Cannon balls flew thick and many and small arms roared like the rolling of a drum." Five times the Americans were driven back, and five times they surged forward to their old position. But the odds against them were too great. Stephen's division on the right, upon which the fire had been especially heavy, retreated. Stirling and the rest could no longer resist. The order to withdraw was given.

They were pursued by the British and Hessians, except the British Guards and the British and Hessian Grenadiers, who when they followed Sullivan's retreating brigade had "got entangled in a very thick woods" and "were no further engaged" until near the end of the battle.[33]

The American retreat was developing into a stampede when the fugitives met the head of Greene's column. He opened his ranks, let them through to rally and re-form in his rear, closed again, and stood against the pursuers, turning his artillery upon them. But the pressure was too great. Retreating slowly and in good order, keeping up their fire, Greene's troops at last made another stand in the road from Dilworth about a mile from the Meetinghouse, in a place called Sandy Hollow, "a narrow defile flanked on both sides by woods and commanding the road." [34] Weedon's men were posted in the defile, Muhlenberg's on the side of the road.

The enemy came on and there was hot fighting. The musket fire on the Americans was heavy, and there were repeated bayonet charges. The fighting was so close that some of the Anspach jägers recognized Muhlenberg, who had served in the ranks in Germany in his youth, and greeted him with his old nickname, "Hier kommt Teufel Piet!" (Here comes Devil Pete!) Weedon's brigade, especially the 10th Virginia under Colonel Stephens and Colonel Walter Stewart's Pennsylvania state regiment, which had never before been in action, bore the brunt of the attack. For forty-five minutes, until the sun went down, they held the pass.[35]

At last, again overborne, Weedon's force retired, but in good order. They retreated to the rear of Muhlenberg's brigade, and Greene drew off his whole division. The tired British and Hessians made no attempt to follow.[36]

Meanwhile, there had been desperate fighting at the Ford. The sound of Cornwallis's gunfire was the signal to Knyphausen that his function of "amusing" the Americans, while the flanking march was made, was now fully performed. He first opened fire with all his guns, six 12-pounders, four howitzers, and the light artillery, bombarding the positions held by Wayne, Maxwell's light infantry, and Proctor's batteries, while he formed his troops. After severely blasting the American defenses he launched his attack. A battalion of the 71st Highlanders led the van; the Riflemen and Queen's Rangers with the British 4th Regiment and Knyphausen in person followed. Then came the rest, Stirn's Hessians last. In the face of the American artillery and musketry they advanced to the lower of the two fords, waded in, and gained the opposite bank. Forming again, they attacked "furiously." The American left gave back and lost the battery near the river, three field-pieces and a howitzer.

The British Guards and the grenadiers of Cornwallis's column, who had got lost in the forest while pursuing Sullivan's brigade, now "came blundering through the woods—accidentally, but most opportunely—upon the uncovered flank of the American centre," and the whole American line fell back.

The British followed, "gained one height after another as the enemy withdrew." There was a check, says Baurmeister, when the Americans or some of them made a stand "behind some houses and ditches" and for a time "withstood one more rather severe attack. Finally we saw the entire enemy line and four guns, which fired frequently, drawn up on another height in front of a dense forest, their right wing resting on the Chester road." [37] "Darkness coming on before Lieutenant General Knyphausen's corps could reach the heights, there was no further action." [38]

The battle was over except for one last flare-up. Two battalions of British grenadiers were ordered to occupy a cluster of houses beyond Dilworth. "They marched carelessly, the officers with sheathed swords. At fifty paces from the first houses, they were surprised by a deadly fire from Maxwell's corps, which lay in ambush to cover the American retreat. The British officers sent for help, but were nearly routed before General Agnew could bring relief. The Americans then withdrew, and darkness ended the contest." [39]

It had been a fierce and many-sided fight, but the losses on both sides were less than might have been supposed. Howe reported 90 killed, 480 wounded, and 6 missing. The American casualties were never definitely ascertained. Howe estimated them at 300 killed, 600 wounded, and "near 400" made prisoners.[40] But his figures are properly subject to some discount, because of his customary exaggeration of enemy losses and because the numbers of wounded and captured to a considerable extent duplicated each other. The Americans had to leave many of their wounded on the field, so that they were taken by the enemy; but not many unwounded men were taken prisoner. Among the American wounded was Lafayette, who received a bullet in his leg, but was able to escape capture. One howitzer and ten fieldpieces were lost by the Americans, among them two brass guns captured at Trenton.[41]

The whole American army was in retreat towards Chester. Except for a few regiments and companies that withdrew in good order, its units were completely disorganized. There was no coherence of divisions, of brigades, of regiments, or even of companies. Thousands of beaten men, already dispersed before the final retreat began and now uncontrolled by any sort of military discipline, thronged the road in utter confusion. Darkness added to their bewilderment. All any man knew was that he must hurry forward with the crowd before him and the crowd behind. Twelve miles of this chaos brought them to a bridge across Chester Creek and found at last someone in command of the situation. Lafayette, with an improvised bandage about his wounded leg, had set a guard there to stop the passage of the mob. Washington and Greene (with his division unbroken) soon arrived and aided in restoring order. They all encamped "behind Chester."

And yet, though they had been as badly beaten as any army could be without being entirely destroyed, there had been no panic; there was no suggestion of despair. The American Captain Anderson wrote: "I saw not a despairing look, nor did I hear a despairing word. We had our solacing words already for each other—'Come, boys, we shall do better another time'—sounded throughout our little army." That this was true of the army in general was proven by their ready reorganization the next day and by the spirit in which the campaign was so soon and so courageously resumed.

CHAPTER 32

Philadelphia

Howe's army encamped on the battlefield. But first he sent the 71st Regiment, Fraser's Highlanders, to take possession of Wilmington. They also took possession of John McKinly, President and commander in chief of Delaware, and confined him on the frigate *Solebay,* lying in the river off the town.[1]

At midnight of September 11–12 Washington sent a dispatch to the Congress, informing it of the result of the battle and adding, "Notwithstanding the misfortune of the day, I am happy to find the troops in good spirits." [2] Congress was, as John Adams expressed it, "yet in Philadelphia, that mass of cowardice and Toryism." John Hancock received the dispatch at four o'clock in the morning. The delegates to the Congress were routed out of their beds to meet at six and hear the news. At ten they reassembled, called on Putnam at Peekskill to send down 1,500 Continentals at once, on Philemon Dickinson in New Jersey and on Smallwood and Gist in Maryland to send their militia, and on the Pennsylvania militia generally to join Washington. Aid from Virginia was also solicited. To the soldiers of the army, thirty hogsheads of rum were donated "in compliment . . . for their gallant behaviour," each man to receive "one gill per day, while it lasts." [3]

Washington marched from Chester in the morning of the 12th to the Falls of the Schuylkill and encamped there on the edge of Germantown. Notwithstanding his defeat at the Brandywine, his army was still between Howe and Philadelphia, and his maneuvers were directed toward holding that advantage. He guessed that the British would try to turn his right flank, cut off a retreat to the west, and force him into the pocket beween the

Schuylkill and the Delaware. To prevent that, he broke camp on the morning of the 14th and marched west to the neighborhood of the Warren Tavern and the White Horse Tavern, thus, "with a firm intent of giving the Enemy Battle," [4] interposing his army between the British and Swede's Ford across the Schuylkill, at which point he thought they would try to cross.

On the 16th Howe marched from Chad's Ford in two columns. Cornwallis led one towards the White Horse Tavern, Knyphausen the other towards the Boot Tavern.[5] Early in the morning Washington had news of their approach. Howe heard that the Americans were "advancing upon the Lancaster Road and were within five miles of Goshen Meeting House." He decided to "push forward the two Columns and attack them." [6] Thus, with one intention, the two armies approached each other.

Washington sent Count Casimir Pulaski, newly appointed "commander of the horse" ranking as a brigadier, with the cavalry and 300 infantry to retard the advance of the enemy; but the foot soldiers "shamefully fled at the first fire" and delayed the enemy not at all.[7]

The first real encounter came when Wayne and Maxwell, who had been detached forward to observe the enemy's movements on the Chester-Dilworth road, met Knyphausen's column near the Boot Tavern. Colonel von Donop, with a part of the Hessian jägers, was reconnoitering the road ahead of that column when Wayne and Maxwell suddenly came upon him. He "was almost cut off, but joined the vanguard again with all possible speed, after skilfully executing some manoeuvres to his left." [8] The Hessian jägers and grenadiers immediately formed and advanced in line against Wayne and Maxwell, who had taken a position "on high ground covered with a cornfield and orchards." The jägers delighted in displaying the results of their training and experience in irregular fighting; "ducking behind fences around the fields and woods, [they] had an opportunity to demonstrate to the enemy their superior marksmanship and their skill with the amusettes." There was a considerable exchange of fire before the Americans "retired to a dense forest," leaving behind a number of killed and wounded.[9]

Howe was ahead in the choice of ground; he seized an eminence near the White Horse. Washington started to form his troops in an inferior position, with "a valley of soft wet ground, impassable for artillery" behind his center and left, but was persuaded to withdraw to "high ground on the other side of the valley." [10] A real battle seemed to be in the making when Nature took a hand. The extreme heat of the day at the Brandywine had been dispelled on the 13th by "a hard North West wind," which continued to blow colder and colder. On the 15th it shifted to the northeast and increased in violence; the sky was heavily overcast with clouds. Now the gathering storm broke.

Major Baurmeister had never seen the like of that cloudburst. "I wish I could give you a description of the downpour," he wrote to the "Right Honourable Lord, Gracious and Mighty Colonel von Jungkenn" in Hesse-Kassel. "It came down so hard that in a few minutes we were drenched and sank in mud up to our calves." [11]

That deluge fell upon the two armies in line of battle and about to engage. It soaked their clothes, wet their muskets inside and out, and drenched their ammunition, ruining 400,000 of the Americans' cartridges—"a most terrible stroke to us," said Henry Knox. No flint would flash, no charge ignite.[12] So there the two armies stood, face to face and unable to fire a shot. The British might still have used a favorite weapon that worked wet or dry—the bayonet; but a wind of great force was driving the rain directly into their faces, and the low ground between the armies was a treacherous quagmire. There was simply no fighting to be done by either side.

"At first," Washington wrote to the Congress, "I expected that the loss [of ammunition] was by no means so considerable and intended [only] to file off with the Troops a few Miles to replace it and clean their arms"; but, finding it completely ruined with no other supply at hand, he had to march "as far as Reading Furnace" to refit.[13] So, under the heavy rain driven by the howling northeast wind, the blanketless men, "nearly a thousand of them actually barefooted," slogged along through the mud the rest of that day and much of the night eleven miles to Yellow Springs, and "there Stay'd all night on the Brow of a hill without tents." [14]

At Yellow Springs, Washington discovered the true state of his ammunition supply and realized that he must go at once to a more secure position at Reading (Warwick) Furnace to await a new supply from the magazines. So on the Americans went—it was still raining—nine miles and camped, again without tents. Then up at three in the morning and on, twelve miles more, to the Furnace. Presumably the new ammunition was supplied there, for the third day they were on the march back to Yellow Springs, twelve miles, crossed the Schuylkill at Parker's Ford, through rapid water breast-deep [15]—they were all night at it—marched seven miles towards Swede's Ford and then ten miles to Richardson's Ford, twenty-nine miles in all,[16] and certainly a great feat of endurance in their distressed physical condition. But they were again east of the Schuylkill and between Howe and Philadelphia, their camp being along Perkiomen Creek.

The movement of Howe's army from Goshen was a mere saunter, in comparison. It lay on the field the day after that aborted battle and "suffered much from the weather." On the 18th Knyphausen marched three

miles to White Horse, where he joined Cornwallis in going eight miles to
camp at Tredyffrin. At Valley Forge they found a store of the rebels' supplies: "3800 Barrels of Flour, Soap and Candles, 25 Barrels of Horse
Shoes, several thousand tomahawks and Kettles and Intrenching Tools and
20 Hogsheads of Resin." On the 19th, when the rebels were making that
grueling twenty-nine-mile march, the British found halting "very necessary
for the men and particularly for our horses," though there was a small
shift of Cornwallis's column to another camp at the Bull's Head and
Mouth Tavern and a foraging party took 150 horses at New Town Square.
On the 20th a post was established at Valley Forge.[17]

Before Washington's army crossed at Parker's Ford on the 19th Anthony
Wayne's division, 1,500 men and four fieldpieces, was detached with orders
to lie in the neighborhood of the Warren Tavern so as to be in a position to
fall on the enemy's rear guard and baggage train. With every effort at
secrecy he took post in a wood on a hill about a mile north of that tavern
and two miles southwest of Paoli Tavern,[18] confident that his movement
and his place of lodgment were unknown to the enemy; but there were too
many Tories about, and some of them disclosed his secret to the British.[19]
Major General Grey, with the 40th, 42nd, 44th, and 55th regiments of
foot, the 2nd battalion of light infantry, and a handful of the 16th
Dragoons, was sent to surprise him.[20]

Grey ordered his men to march with unloaded muskets, those that could
not draw their loads to remove their flints, and set out at ten o'clock in the
evening of the 20th. He advanced by the road leading to the White Horse,
picking up every inhabitant as he went along to prevent an alarm. Near
the Warren Tavern, he came upon Wayne's outsentries, who fired and ran
off; but his van fell upon the pickets with the bayonet and killed most of
them.

The reports of the sentries' muskets alarmed the camp. Wayne ordered
his men formed for action, himself taking post with the artillery on the
right. Unfortunately his men were drawn up in the light of their campfires
and thus were clearly in view of the enemy. Grey ordered a charge with the
bayonet. The Americans met it with musketry but were overwhelmed by
the impetuosity of their opponents and swept into a confused retreat, followed by the stabbing bayonets. Wayne managed to draw off his guns and,
at some distance in the rear, re-formed such part of his fleeing men as
could be induced to stand. Satisfied with the execution effected, Grey
called off his troops and returned to the British camp, taking with him
seventy-one prisoners, of whom forty, badly wounded, were left at houses

along the road. He also took eight or ten loaded four-horse wagons. The next day a British detachment returned to the deserted field and gathered up and destroyed a thousand muskets abandoned by the fleeing Americans.

General Smallwood and Colonel Gist, with a force of Maryland militia, had been ordered to reenforce Wayne's post; but they were still on the road at the time of the attack. Within a half-mile of the scene they met a part of Grey's troops returning from the fray. At the sight of the enemy the militia fled in a panic.

It is impossible to make a certain estimate of the Americans' loss. The British claimed 300 killed or wounded and 70 to 80 taken prisoner; but their figures are probably exaggerations. The British loss was one officer and one or two privates killed, and four or five wounded.[21]

Wayne's defeat relieved Howe of all fear of attack from the rear; he was now able to move as he would. On the morning of September 21 he set out from Tredyffrin in a northerly direction, marched to Valley Forge, and encamped along the Schuylkill from the Forge to French Creek.[22] To Washington, who had been expecting a southward march towards one of the lower fords, this was a "perplexing manoeuvre." But this northward movement meant that they might turn his right, and it was in the direction of Reading Furnace. That spelled danger for his stores. He believed they had both objects in view.[23] "To frustrate those intentions," he decided to move north, too.

He first ordered Sullivan's division to "a Line between us and the Schuylkill, leaving a small Pickett at each Fording Place as a party of Observation." Then, "two hours before day" on the 22nd, he got his men afoot and marched them ten miles up the Reading road on his side of the Schuylkill. After rest and refreshment they went five miles farther and encamped near Pott's Grove [24] (now Pottstown). They were now well ahead of Howe towards Reading Furnace and well past danger of being outflanked on the right; also they were just where Howe wanted them to be.

He had intended neither the supposed flanking movement, nor yet the capture of the stores at the Furnace. What he did intend was disclosed by what he immediately did. He countermarched swiftly southward in the night to Fatland Ford and Gordon's Ford, blasted away a slimly held American militia post at Fatland with "a few cannon-shot," and sent the Guards, a battalion of light infantry and six guns, with twenty-five dragoons, across the river to hold the opposite end of the ford. Von Donop, with sixty jägers, twenty horse, and a hundred grenadiers cleared the way at Gordon's without difficulty and crossed there. That night "at the rising of the moon" the whole British army began crossing at Fatland. By eight the next morning all except Grant's brigade of British infantry, covering the baggage, artillery, and provision train, were on the east side of the river. The others soon followed, and the road to Philadelphia was clear before them.[25] Thus again Howe, with the greatest of ease, had outwitted the American commander in chief.

Washington got the news, doubtless from some of the expelled militia, while the enemy was still in the act of crossing. Here was an opportunity for an attack while they were in such a disabling condition. But the alertness of the Americans to the danger of being outflanked, and the effort they had made to prevent it, was now their undoing. They were nearly twenty miles from Fatland. With "Troops harrassed as ours had been with constant marching since the Battle of Brandywine" it was "in vain to think" of covering that distance in time to seize the opportunity. As strong a reason "against being able to make a forced March is the want of Shoes," so Washington wrote to the Congress that day. A council of war agreed with him that the best course was to stay where they were until rested and reenforced.[26]

Unopposed and unmolested, the British army continued its march "till three o'clock in the afternoon when it arrived at Norriton" and there encamped, but seventeen miles from Philadelphia, just half the distance of the American army from it.[27]

Washington lay at Pott's Grove for four days, resting his men and awaiting reenforcements. He had called on Putnam in the north for 2,500 Continentals, including McDougall's brigade; on Smallwood and Gist to bring their Maryland militia; on Wayne for his division; on Gates at Saratoga to send back Morgan's riflemen; on Philemon Dickinson for his New Jersey militia.[28] The men he already had were in a sad condition. They had marched 140 miles in the last eleven days. "While in almost continual motion, wading deep rivers and encountering every vicissitude of the season, they were without tents, nearly without shoes or winter clothes and often without food." [29] In the heat of the day and the heat of the battle at the Brandywine thousands of them had shed their blanket rolls and left them on the field. Washington had written to the Congress on the 15th begging for blankets. The Congress had "disguised its impotence" by again making him a "dictator" for a period of sixty days, with special authority "to take wherever he may be, all such provisions and articles as may be necessary for the comfortable subsistence of the army under his command, paying or giving certificates for the same." [30]

Washington accepted the job. He sent Alexander Hamilton to Philadelphia to "procure from the inhabitants, contributions of blankets, and Clothing and materials . . . with as much delicacy and discretion as the nature of the business demands." [31] But "the canny Quakers and the sly Tories 'hid their goods the moment the thing took wind' and the Whigs had already 'parted with all they could spare.' " [32] Washington tried the country districts, ordered Colonel Clement Biddle "to impress all the Blankets, Shoes, Stockings and other Articles of Cloathing . . . that can be spared by the Inhabitants of Bucks, Philadelphia and Northampton," [33] to be paid for with cash or promises, and gave similar orders for Lancaster, with small results from any place.

On the 26th the Americans marched from Pott's Grove to encamp at Pennybacker's Mill (now Schwenksville) on the Perkiomen; and on the same day Cornwallis, with two British and two Hessian grenadier battalions, two squadrons of the 16th Dragoons, and ten guns in his train, took possession of Philadelphia, "amidst the acclamation of some thousands of the inhabitants, mostly women and children," [34] while the major part of the army encamped at Germantown. The Congress had fled to Lancaster eight days before.

CHAPTER 33

Germantown

Reenforcements came to Washington—McDougall, with 900 Continentals from Peekskill, Smallwood with 1,000 Maryland militia, Forman with 600 militiamen from New Jersey, Maxwell's corps of 650 light infantry, and Wayne's division. It is hard to say how large the army then was. Washington informed the Congress on September 28 that he had 8,000 Continentals and 3,000 militia at Pennybacker's Mill,[1] yet Henry Knox declared that the army was "more numerous after the battle of Brandywine than before." [2] There was some thought of an attack on the British camp at Germantown at this time, but a council of war, voting ten to five against that, decided that it would be well to move closer, "within about 12 Miles of the Enemy," and await events.[3] On the 29th the army marched five miles to the Skippack Road, and on October 2, three miles down that road to encamp sixteen miles from Germantown.[4]

There the question of an attack was again considered. Three thousand of Howe's men had been sent down to escort supplies from Elkton, which, because of the obstructions and the forts in the Delaware River, he could not bring up by water. Cornwallis had two British and two Hessian grenadier battalions with him in Philadelphia, and he had just sent one of the British battalions and two regiments of foot across to New Jersey to capture the fort at Billingsport. Probably not more than 9,000 men were left with Howe at Germantown. A council of war decided that conditions were favorable.[5]

Germantown was a village consisting of a string of houses, each in its enclosure of rail fence, stretching for two miles along the Skippack Road,

362

which ran northwest from Philadelphia to Reading. At its center this main street was crossed at a right angle by a road called School House Lane west of the street, Mill Street on the east. At this crossing stood the market house. The village was approachable directly from the northwest by this Skippack (Reading) Road running over Chestnut Hill and Mount Airy and so to its center. There was another avenue of approach from the north by the Limekiln Road, east of the Skippack, which swung into the east end of Mill Street. East of that road the Old York Road came down from the northeast to a crossroad running past Luken's Mill and so into Mill Street. Far to the west, on the other side of the gorge of Wissahickon Creek, the Manatawny or Ridge Road met the west end of School House Lane where the creek empties into the Schuylkill.

The British camp was a little south of the Lane, extending east and west parallel to it and across the main street from the Schuylkill on the left (west) to a point beyond the Old York Road on the right. It had no definite center. Generals Grant and Matthew lay on the right of the main street, with the Guards, six British battalions, and two squadrons of dragoons. Generals Knyphausen, Stirn, Grey, and Agnew lay on the left, with seven British and three Hessian battalions. The mounted and dismounted jägers were on the far left, beside the Schuylkill and below the mouth of the Wissahickon. On the far right and somewhat in advance were the 1st Battalion of British light infantry and the Queen's Rangers. At Mount Airy, on the Skippack Road and about two miles north of the Lane, was an outpost held by Colonel Musgrave's 40th Regiment and the 2nd Light Infantry.[6] Howe's headquarters was in the Logan House at a short distance in the rear of the camp.

The plan of attack called for a division of the American army into four columns, each one operating on one of the four approaching roads above mentioned. Sullivan was to command the first column, composed of his division and Wayne's, flanked by Conway's brigade. Stirling, with Nash's and Maxwell's men, was to follow this column as a reserve. It was to enter the town by the Skippack Road and strike the British left.

Greene was to command the second column, his own and Stephen's divisions, flanked by McDougall's brigade. He was to approach by the Limekiln Road, take care of the light infantry and Rangers advanced on the extreme British right, enter the town by the Mill Street, and attack Grant and Matthews. As this part of the British force was esteemed the strongest, Greene had the strongest column, about two-thirds of the American army.

The third column, Maryland and New Jersey militia under Smallwood and Forman, was to march by the Old York Road, a mile or more east of Greene's route, and fall on the rear of the British right.

Far to the other side, farther still from the main battle, coming down the Manatawny or Ridge Road, Armstrong and his Pennsylvania militia were to cross the mouth of the Wissahickon at Vandeering's Mill and strike the rear of the British left.

All four columns were to arrive "within two miles of the enemy's pickets on their respective routs by two oClock and there halt till four in the morning." They were to make simultaneous attacks "precisely at five oClock with charged bayonets without firing." [7] In that order for a bayonet charge no consideration was given to the fact that the terrain was crossed by many stout rail fences which would repeatedly interrupt the proposed charge and make it practically impossible.

It will be seen that that was a plan for a great pincers movement, in which, while the British main force was to be smashed by Greene and Sullivan, Armstrong and Smallwood were to close in on its right and left wings and crumple the whole line in upon itself. It was to be somewhat like the attack on Trenton, including the element of surprise, but on a grander scale. As the attack was to be made before dawn, each soldier was to have a piece of white paper fixed in his hat to identify him to his comrades.

It was "one of the most carefully elaborated designs" that Washington ever evolved,[8] and it had classical authority. Hannibal had so planned and won the battle of Cannae, nearly two thousand years before. Scipio Africanus had, in like manner, gained a victory at Ilipa in Spain, annihilating 74,000 Carthaginians with 48,000 Romans. There was, however, in both those cases, a difference. Hannibal and Scipio had put their weakest forces in the center, their strongest in the crushing pincer jaws. Washington reversed this arrangement; his two jaws were made up entirely of militia, whom he had so often found to be unreliable.

There were, too, faults inherent in the character of the troops involved and in the terrain, the like of which the Carthaginians and Romans had not confronted. Green troops—even the Continentals were largely new recruits —led by relatively amateur officers, were to march in perfect concert sixteen miles in four columns over roads separated by six or seven miles of rough, broken country, with no means of communication among their several bodies, and arrive at the scene of action at the same moment of time, ready to fall with vigor and determination upon a not much smaller, compact army of professional soldiers led by competent officers. The failure of any one of the four elements of the attack meant the failure of the whole scheme. It was typically the kind of plan easily worked out at headquarters and looking perfect on paper, yet practically impossible of execution in the field. Yet it very nearly did succeed, though not as planned.

The march from Metuchen Hill on the Skippack Road began at seven in the evening of October 3, the several columns taking their respective roads. According to the plan, Sullivan's column, with Conway in advance, followed by Sullivan, Wayne, Stirling, Maxwell, and Nash, in that order, Washington marching with it, was to reach the British outpost at Mount Airy before dawn. But it was a long march on rough roads and a hard march for men so ill equipped, especially so ill shod, and so worn down by their incessant movements to and fro for months past. The column had to stop twice to rest and to bring up its rear. The sun was coming up when it reached Chestnut Hill.

At Mount Airy, Conway's advance brigade came upon the pickets of the first British outpost. Captain Allen McLane of Delaware, with his company of light horse, charged upon this picket, killed two men and, at the loss of one of his own, drove it back, but not before it had fired two fieldpieces as a signal to its support and an alarm for the whole British army.

To the rescue of the retreating pickets came the 2nd Light Infantry, and the real fighting began. They attacked Conway so viciously that he had to throw forward his entire brigade to meet them. The rest of the outpost, Colonel Musgrave and his 40th Regiment, came up. Conway was stopped in his tracks. Sullivan deployed his men in line of battle along a lane to the west of the main road. Musgrave, a courageous man and a fine officer, refused to give way. He led his men against Sullivan's too narrow front. Sullivan called up Wayne's division from the rear to his left and part of Conway's brigade to his right. Then with the bayonet he drove against Musgrave's line. Wayne's division, smarting under the recollection of the Paoli "massacre," fought bitterly. The British fell back, charged, and charged again. The Americans answered in kind and "took Ample Vengeance for that Night's work," striking down "many of the poor wretches who were Crying for Mercy, in spite of their officers' exertions to restrain them." At last a British bugle sounded a retreat.

But the British fell back doggedly, making a stand at every fence, wall, and ditch, firing and falling back again. Sullivan's troops followed, tearing down fences as they came to keep their line. For a full mile they drove Musgrave's regiment and the light infantry before them.

Howe had hurried to the front. He cried shame on the retreating men "Form! Form! I never saw you retreat before! It's only a scouting party.

To the delight of the men he chid, a burst of grape from the American guns rattled in the leaves of a chestnut tree under which he sat on his horse, and showed it was no mere scouting party.

It had been misty at sunrise. The mist thickened into fog; the fog grew more dense, so dense that Musgrave was able to slip aside and throw six weak companies of his regiment into a great, square stone house on the east of the main road, the house of Chief Justice Benjamin Chew. He closed the thick shutters, barricaded the doors, and posted his 120 men at the windows of the second story, whence they delivered a continuous and deadly fire upon Sullivan's and Wayne's men passing on either side of the house.

Now, what to do? The reserve was held up, except Nash's North Carolinians, who pushed on after Sullivan and fought most bravely throughout the battle. Washington and his generals consulted. Some of them were for leaving a regiment to immobilize the garrison in the house and going on. But Henry Knox, deeply imbued with the lessons he had learned while studying the military classics in his bookshop, said "No!" While penetrating an enemy's country, you must not leave an occupied castle in your rear. Washington, always respectful of Knox's larger store of military science, as he was of Greene's military genius, agreed. The "castle" must be summoned in due form. An officer, sent with a flag to demand surrender, was fired upon and killed. So much for classical warfare!

Knox turned his artillery upon the stronghold. His six-pounders blew in the front door and smashed windows, but the balls rebounded from the thick, stone walls; and a barricade of furniture in the hallway, backed by bayonets, denied entry. Burn it, then. The Americans tried, but a would-be incendiary was shot down. In spite of that, two spirited young fellows, Colonel John Laurens of South Carolina and the Chevalier de Mauduit du Plessis from France, volunteered to try again. Laurens got straw from the stables. Mauduit forced the shutters of a window, mounted the sill. A single British officer, pistol in hand, demanded to know what the Frenchman was doing there. "I'm only taking a walk." "Surrender, sir!" Before Mauduit could answer, a British soldier came into the room, took a shot at him, but only hit the British officer. He escaped unharmed. Laurens got a bullet in his shoulder. The artillery resumed its futile bombardment, in which Maxwell's musketry joined uselessly.

But where was Greene, with two-thirds of the American army, all this time? He had four miles longer to march and had also been led astray by his guide, so that his column was an hour late when it drew near. Without orders from Greene, Stephen on hearing the gunfire swung his division off

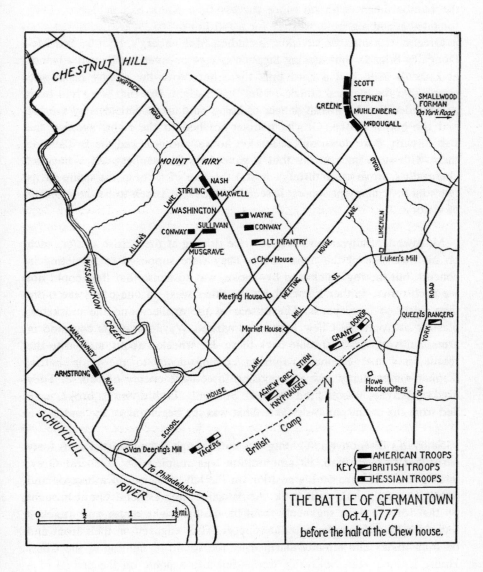

CHESTNUT HILL

SKIPPACK ROAD

SCOTT
STEPHEN
GREENE
MUHLENBERG
McDOUGALL

SMALLWOOD
FORMAN
On York Road

MOUNT AIRY

NASH
STIRLING MAXWELL
WASHINGTON
CONWAY SULLIVAN
MUSGRAVE

WAYNE
CONWAY
LT. INFANTRY

Chew House

LANE

ALLEN'S

WISSAHICKON CREEK

Luken's Mill

LIMEKILN LANE

HOUSE LANE

Meeting House

MILL ST.

MEETING ST.

YORK ROAD

QUEEN'S RANGERS

Market House

GRANT DONOP

AGNEW GREY STIRN
KNYPHAUSEN

Howe
Headquarters

OLD

MANATAWNEY ROAD

ARMSTRONG

HOUSE LANE

N

SCHOOL LANE

Van Deering's Mill

YAGERS

British Camp

To Philadelphia

SCHUYLKILL RIVER

0   ½   1   1½ mi.

KEY
■ AMERICAN TROOPS
◣ BRITISH TROOPS
◨ HESSIAN TROOPS

THE BATTLE OF GERMANTOWN
Oct. 4, 1777
before the halt at the Chew house.

to the right away from the column and made for the Chew House, thus departing from the plan. Woodford's artillery of Stephen's division joined in the bombardment with no more success than Knox had achieved. They fought that impregnable "castle" for a full hour.

Greene with his own division, including Muhlenberg's, Scott's, and Mc-Dougall's brigades but lacking Stephen's, kept on, met the British advance at Luken's Mill, had a hard time there but drove the enemy back, and swung into the planned attack on the British right. But that wing had been so extended that he was in danger of being outflanked. Shielded by the fog and the battle smoke, Greene countermarched to the right, avoided the British wing, bore down on the market house, and attacked the British line there with such impetuosity that it gave way. Muhlenberg led a bayonet charge that drove clear through it and the line of tents in the camp in its rear and took many prisoners. It seemed to Greene's men to be the moment of victory.

Meanwhile, Sullivan and Wayne were driving at the British center, each on his own side of the main street. They were supposed to be acting in concert, but the fog, thickened by smoke, was so dense that they could not see each other; neither knew where the other was; no one could see more than thirty or forty yards. The uproar of the artillery and the musketry, blasting away at the Chew House, convinced Wayne that his comrade in arms, Sullivan, was in trouble back there. He wheeled about, started to the rescue, and met Stephen's division coming down to the main battle. Stephen's men dimly saw an opposing force—the enemy of course. They fired on Wayne; Wayne fired on them. Suddenly, both divisions broke, each fled from the other, panic-stricken. That was the beginning of the end.

Sullivan's division was fighting on, but, though it had started with forty cartridges to each man, its ammunition was running low. General Grey, finding little pressure on his position on the left, wheeled up a brigade and threw it on Sullivan's right flank. At the same time General Grant brought up the 5th and 45th regiments from the British right center and attacked Sullivan's left, which was without support. Thus engaged on their front and on both flanks and already alarmed by the sound of fighting at the Chew House in their rear, Sullivan's troops fell into a panic on the arrival of a light horseman crying that they were surrounded. A part of them broke, and then the rest. Their officers tried in vain to rally them. "With as much precipitation as they had before advanced," they turned and ran.[9]

Greene had no support, right or left. The British and Hessians who had been fighting Sullivan let his men run without pursuit and swung to the center against Greene. He was caught on both sides. Muhlenberg was far off, more than a thousand yards in the rear of the enemy, far behind their camp. But he turned his bayonets back against the encircling British line, charged through it and joined Greene with all of his regiments but one.

Colonel Matthews, with the 9th Virginia, had been conspicuously daring and successful. He had led Greene's advance, crushed the resistance at Luken's Mill as the division swung in from the Limekiln Road, and fought all the way to the market house, driving the enemy before him and taking a hundred prisoners. He tried to draw them off by Luken's Mill, but a breastwork there had been manned again. The British right wing enveloped him. He lost his captives, and he himself, with his 400 men, was taken. That was the regiment missing from Muhlenberg's brigade.

Now Greene, with Muhlenberg, Scott, and McDougall, faced the divisions of Grey, Grant, and Agnew drawn together to oppose him. The Americans were worn out by their long march and the strain of the battle. There was little fight left in them, but they did fight as they withdrew through the village, using fences, walls, and houses in a delaying rear-guard action. Greene drew off his guns. When the wheels of one were shattered, he got it into a wagon, and it went on. Muhlenberg rode in the rear of his retiring men. His tired horse refused a fence. While his men were pulling it down, the exhausted general fell asleep in his saddle. He was awakened by the whistle of a ball past his ear and by the cries of the oncoming enemy.

Washington tried to check the retreat, to rally the fugitives, "exposing himself to the hottest fire." But his efforts could not avail. Entirely out of hand, the whole army swept on in full retreat, the men holding up their empty cartridge boxes to show him why they ran. Greene and Wayne in the rear did their best to hold back the pursuers, even bringing their artillery, all of which they kept, into play more than once. But it was no orderly withdrawal. It was a confused mass, "past the powers of description; sadness and consternation expressed in every countenance," that swarmed up the Skippack Road. Pulaski's small cavalry contingent, hovering in the rear, was attacked by British dragoons, fled, and, in their flight, rode into and through Greene's men, who thought they were British and scattered in every direction. Greene nearly had to abandon his guns, but got together enough men to save them. The celebrated Thomas Paine, who was on Greene's staff, said: "The retreat was extraordinary. Nobody hurried themselves." With good reason, it was all those tired men could do to tramp wearily onward.

Cornwallis led three fresh battalions, brought up from Philadelphia, after them for eight miles, apparently with as little haste. "The enemy kept a civil distance behind," says Paine, "sending every now and then a shot after us and receiving the same from us," then gave over the pursuit. Some of the American officers would have stopped at that distance, but Washington drove them on, not only to their last camping ground, sixteen miles from Germantown, but clear back to their former camp at Pennybacker's Mill, eight miles farther. All of them had marched that sixteen miles, some of them as much as twenty, the night before. They had fought fully two and a half hours and now they were trudging twenty-four miles more. "Here we old soldiers had marched forty miles," wrote Captain Anderson of the Delaware Regiment. "We eat nothing and drank nothing but water on the tour."

But what of Armstrong and his Pennsylvania militia, Smallwood and the militia from Maryland and New Jersey—the jaws of the pincers, the claws of the crab? Nothing had been heard or seen of them. Well, Armstrong did march his men down the Manatawny Road clear to the point where they were to cross the Wissahickon at Vandeering's Mill. There they found the Hessian jägers, the extreme left of the British line, trained their four guns on them, and drove them back from the bridge. The Hessians retired to a hill and replied with musket fire. Instead of crossing the bridge and charging on the Hessians, Armstrong continued his cannonading until nine o'clock, when the Hessians charged across the bridge and drove him from an opposite height. He and his men retreated three miles, pursued by the same Lieutenant Colonel von Wurmb who had fought Maxwell at Cooch's Bridge. This pursuit relaxing, Armstrong came on a casual detachment of the enemy, was overcome, and made a final, complete evasion. He did not even know what had happened in the main battle. When Smallwood's force, the other pincer jaw, arrived at the scene of action, it was too late for it to do anything but join in the retreat.

Yet, in spite of the failure of the pincers to operate, the battle had been nearly won by the Americans. While Sullivan and Wayne and Greene were still in the fight and Muhlenberg was piercing the enemy's line, victory was within their grasp. It is said that at that time the British were actually appointing Chester as the place of rendezvous after the expected defeat. If Stirling and Maxwell, the reserve, had not been held up at the Chew House, or if Stephen had not disobeyed orders and taken his division away from Greene, or if Wayne had not turned back thinking to help Sullivan and so collided with Stephen, or if Sullivan's ammunition had not been all shot away, or if Armstrong and Smallwood had not failed to attack the British left and right with vigor and determination—if any one or two of these miscarriages had not happened, the Americans might have won. For with all the misadventures it was a near thing, a very near thing. But they all did happen. The whole affair was a tragedy of errors.

The British losses, as officially reported, were 4 officers and 66 men killed, 30 officers and 420 men wounded. The Americans were reported by the Board of War to have lost 152 killed, 521 wounded, and upwards of 400 captured. General Nash of the Americans and General Agnew and Colonel Bird of the British were among the slain. The disastrous siege of the Chew House laid 53 Americans dead on its lawn, 4 on its very doorsteps.

A sad incident of the battle was the discovery of General Stephen, a brave and generally competent officer, helplessly intoxicated, lying in a fence corner. It resulted in his being cashiered. Lafayette, who had been appointed a major general without command, got Stephen's division. In Stephen's defense it might be urged that his condition was the result of overstimulation to combat extreme fatigue; for Conway, a magnificently brave soldier, was found asleep in a barn on the retreat, and Pulaski, whose merit is undeniable, was found asleep in a farmhouse. The exhaustion of those mounted officers casts a revealing light on the wonderful stamina of their foot soldiers, who endured far greater hardship and fatigue in that heartbreaking retreat.

It was unquestionably a defeat for the Americans; but, as has happened more than once in warfare, that fact was of small consequence in comparison with its ulterior effects. In its larger aspects it was of "great and enduring service to the American cause." Trevelyan says: "Eminent generals and statesmen of sagacity, in every European court, were profoundly impressed by learning that a new army, raised within the year, and undaunted by a series of recent disasters, had assailed a victorious enemy in its own quarters and had only been repulsed after a sharp and dubious conflict. . . . The French government, in making up its mind on the question whether the Americans would prove to be efficient allies, was influenced almost as much by the battle of Germantown as by the surrender of Burgoyne." [10] It is doubtful, however, that Germantown had so much effect at the French court.

CHAPTER 34

The Forts on the Delaware

"This morning 36 Sail of the Enemies Ships went past this Town up the Bay and this Evening 47 more were seen from the light House Standing in for the Cape." So, on October 5, 1777, William Peery, captain of the "independent company of 100 men on the Continental establishment" on guard at Cape Henlopen,[1] wrote to Caesar Rodney.

It was a part of Admiral Lord Howe's fleet, which now, more than a month out from the Head of Elk, was about to ascend the Delaware without difficulty, as it might have done two months before, except for the dissuasion of Captain Hamond of the *Roebuck*. The admiral himself, with twelve vessels, had preceded this part of his fleet by three or four days.[2]

The ships went on up the bay and the river, past Bombay Hook on the 9th, past New Castle on the 11th, where General Howe's army might have disembarked on, say, the 9th of August instead of at Head of Elk on the 25th and been nearer Philadelphia than it was on that day. On the 12th, the flagship was off Chester; but that was about as far as it dared try to go, for above that point began the obstructions of the channel and the fortifications of which Captain Hamond had warned the Howes. The main fleet was then anchored in the river from Reedy Island up to New Castle.[3] But it was necessary that the river should be opened to shipping if the British were to continue to hold Philadelphia.

While the enemy army lay in that city Washington's army was active in cutting off its supplies from the back country. The British had to be supported and supplied by the ships. The way from Head of Elk to Philadelphia by land was too difficult, too liable to interruption by the Americans. Therefore water communication was vital to the continuance of the occupation of the rebel capital.

Washington understood that. If the river's defenses, he wrote, "can be maintained General Howe's situation will not be the most agreeable; for if his supplies can be stopped by water, it may easily be done by land . . . the acquisition of Philadelphia may, instead of his good fortune, prove his ruin." [4]

The first obstacle was at Billingsport—a double line of chevaux-de-frise that extended from the Jersey shore across the channel to Billings Island. These were cratelike structures made of heavy timbers, loaded with stones and sunk in the water. They were mounted with wooden beams, shod at the upper end with iron points, slanting upwards to within four feet of the surface of the river at low tides and pointing downstream. They were capable of ripping open the bottom of any ship that tried to pass over them. This line was protected by a small redoubt on the Jersey shore. [5]

That redoubt, however, was a slight affair, unfinished and lightly held. On October 2 Howe sent against it the 42nd Regiment and part of the 71st, under Colonel Sterling. When they landed below the fort and attacked it in the rear, the garrison spiked its guns, set fire to the barracks, and fled. Captain Hamond cut through the chevaux and opened a passage through which six ships passed. [6]

The next obstacle was thirty chevaux strung in a triple line from Mud Island, a little below the mouth of the Schuylkill, across the channel to Red Bank on the Jersey side. This line was guarded by a fort at either end. [7] Above this lay the American fleet, comprising the frigate *Montgomery*, a brig, a schooner, two xebecs, thirteen row-galleys, two floating batteries, fourteen fire ships, and several fire rafts. [8] The best vessel, the frigate *Delaware* of thirty-two guns, had run aground September 7 on the Jersey shore, where it had been set on fire by shots from British batteries and had surrendered. [9]

The first attempt against the forts was made on October 21 by Colonel von Donop with three Hessian grenadier battalions, a regiment of foot, four companies of jägers, and some artillery, about 2,000 men in all. [10] It was directed against Fort Mercer at Red Bank. Washington had garrisoned it with a Rhode Island Continental regiment under Colonel Christopher Greene, and had called on New Jersey for militia to strengthen that force and to cover the rear of the works on the outside, but had met with no response. He had therefore added to the garrison another Rhode Island Continental regiment under Colonel Israel Angell, making a total force of about 400 rank and file. The Chevalier de Mauduit du Plessis, a young

French engineer, had also been sent to assist Greene in strengthening the fort. He found that the Americans, "little practised in the art of fortification," had overbuilt the works to an extent "beyond their strength" to hold. He reduced them by drawing a wall across an extension along the river side "which transformed them into a large redoubt nearly of a pentagonal form." [11] The walls were of earth, guarded without by a ditch and an abatis and mounting fourteen guns.

The attacking troops crossed the Delaware at Philadelphia and marched to Haddonfield, where they encamped for the night. They were again afoot at three o'clock in the morning, but were delayed by having to make a detour where a bridge had been taken up, so that they did not arrive at the fort until noon. Their preparations seem to have been very leisurely; it was half-past four when they made their demand for surrender.

A Hessian officer, with flag and drum, then advanced. "The King of England," said he, "orders his rebellious subjects to lay down their arms and they are warned that if they stand the battle, no quarters whatever will be given." That this summons should be made by one of the hated Hessians added insult to the arrogance of his language. "It only served to irritate the garrison and inspire them with more resolution." [12] Greene replied that he accepted the challenge, and that there would be no quarter on either side.

Von Donop opened fire from a battery he had erected in the rear of the fort. The attack was made in two columns, one against the northern wing of the works, the part that had been cut off and abandoned. The other, led by von Donop, was against the redoubt. Like a torrent the first flowed over the breastworks, the men shouting, "Vittoria!" and waving their hats in air, only to find themselves faced by the new wall forming one side of the redoubt. At the same time, with equal confidence, von Donop's column approached the redoubt. Meeting no fire, they penetrated the abatis, crossed the ditch, and reached the berm, the space between the ditch and the parapet. There they were checked; they had no scaling ladders. Then, and not until then, Greene gave the order to fire—to fire at the broad belts of the Hessians as he had before instructed his men. Such an avalanche of grapeshot and bullets fell upon the Hessians of both columns in front and in flank, from the projecting corner of the redoubt, as had been seldom heard and felt. They went down in rows and heaps. "It may well be doubted," says Trevelyan, "whether so few men in so small a space of time had ever delivered a deadlier fire." [13] The officers, von Donop conspicuous among them, tried to rally their men. Their leader was too conspicuous by his dress, as well as by his efforts. He fell, mortally wounded, and his men

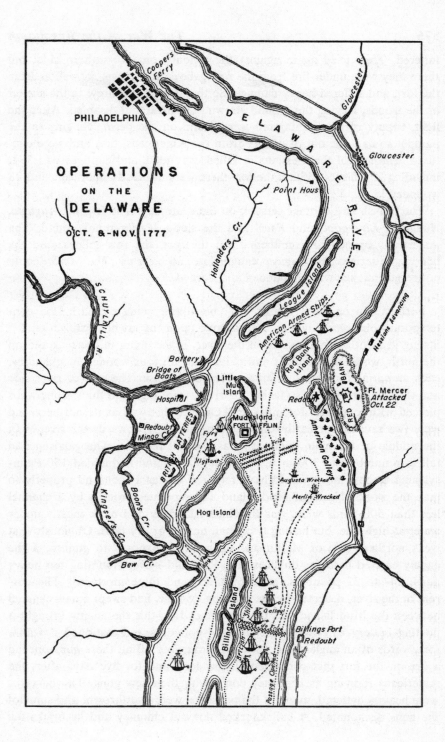

PHILADELPHIA

Coopers Ferry

DELAWARE

Gloucester R.

Gloucester

OPERATIONS
ON THE
DELAWARE
OCT. & NOV. 1777

Point Hous

Hollanders Cr.

SCHUYLKILL R.

DELAWARE RIVER

League Island

American Armed Ships

Hessians Advancing

Battery
Bridge of Boats

Hospital

Little
Mud
Island

Redoubt
Mingo Cr.

BRITISH BATTERIES

Mud Island
FORT MIFFLIN

Fyrs

Red Bank
Island

RED BANK

Ft. Mercer
Attacked
Oct. 22

Redoubt

Vigilant

Chevaux de Frise

American Galleys

Augusta Wrecked

Merlin Wrecked

Kingsel's Cr.

Boon's Cr.

Hog Island

Bew Cr.

Billings Island

Galley

Chevaux de Frise

Billings Fort

Redoubt

Passage Opened

faltered. They tried again against the redoubt on its southern side; but there they were under fire from the row-galleys in the river as well as from the fort, and suffered heavy damage. So they finally withdrew to the shelter of the woods, leaving the ground strewn with dead and disabled. After the fight, twenty of them uninjured were found on the berm, clinging to the parapet so as to be out of danger from the Americans' fire, and were captured. The loss of the Hessians in killed, wounded, and captives was 371, including 22 officers. Within the fort there were 14 dead Americans and 23 wounded.[14]

The British had another setback on the same day. The frigates *Augusta, Roebuck, Liverpool,* and *Pearl* and the sloop *Merlin* ran aground. The Americans opened fire on them from the fort, the row-galleys, and the floating batteries. The *Augusta* caught fire and blew up. The *Merlin* could not be got off; she was abandoned and burned.[15]

Fort Mifflin on Mud Island was "unskillfully constructed." One contemporary observer called it "a Burlesque upon the art of Fortification." [16] Strong in front against vessels on the river, it was weak in the rear and on the north, where only ditches and palisades with four wooden blockhouses, each mounting four guns, offered means of defense. The east or river side and the southern side, also facing the river, were high and thick stone walls pierced with loopholes for musketry. Outside this wall at its northern end were two ravelins, or earthworks forming an angle, towards the river.[17] In the middle of the main enclosure was a small redoubt. The garrison had fallen in numbers to 300 men, to which Washington had added 150 Pennsylvania troops; but it would have required nearer a thousand properly to man the works. North of Mud Island and separated from it by a channel less than 500 yards wide, was Province Island, a mud bank mostly under water at high tide, but having two small humps of dry land. Obviously that weak northern side of Mifflin was dangerously exposed to gunfire, if the enemy erected batteries on Province. They did—five, mounting ten heavy guns, 24- to 32-pounders, two howitzers, and three mortars.[18] The current of the river, deflected by the chevaux-de-frise, had swept a new channel between the Mud Island and the mainland. Into this the enemy brought a floating battery carrying twenty-two 24-pounders and stationed it within forty yards of an angle of the fort. On November 10 all these guns opened a fire on the fort that continued all day long and for five days after, the Americans replying as best they could with their few guns. The barracks were heavily battered, many of the palisades were overthrown, and some of the guns dismounted. A ball knocked down a chimney and its bricks fell on Lieutenant Colonel Samuel Smith, injuring him so severely that he had to be evacuated to Red Bank, Major Simeon Thayer of Rhode Island taking over the command. During those five days many of the garrison were killed or disabled.[19]

On the 15th, the British brought their ships into play. The ship of the line *Somerset*, 64 guns, the *Isis*, 50 guns, the *Roebuck*, 44, the *Pearl*, 32. the *Liverpool* frigate, with 32 guns, moved into position within range of the fort, while the *Vigilant*, 16 guns, and a hulk with 3 reenforced the floating battery in the new channel. The garrison had only two guns that had not been already dismounted by the cannonading of the previous days.

The rain of cannon balls from the ships and the shore batteries was terrific. It was estimated that over a thousand shot were fired every twenty minutes.[20] Within an hour the last two guns were overthrown. The ships were so near that marines in their maintops shot down every man that showed himself in the fort. By night the palisades were gone, the blockhouses destroyed, the whole parapet overthrown. Fort Mifflin was only a name. In the darkness Major Thayer and his surviving men crossed the river to Red Bank, after having set fire to whatever was inflammable.[21]

The defense of Fort Mifflin was one of the most gallant and obstinate of any in the war. Two hundred and fifty of the garrison were killed or wounded during the bombardment, their number having been made up by reliefs sent from time to time. They had had no assistance from the American fleet. Its commander, Commodore Hazelwood, having perhaps the safety of his ships too much in mind, had failed to respond to calls for assistance. The loss on the British side was but seven killed and five wounded.[22]

With the fall of Mifflin, Mercer was doomed. Cornwallis took 2,000 men across the river to storm it. Washington had sent General Greene around by Burlington to reenforce it, but Greene found himself so greatly outnumbered by the approaching force that he wisely refrained from attempting to hold it. Colonel Christopher Greene, seeing that his position was hopeless, evacuated it. The idle American fleet was abandoned and burned.[23] The Delaware from the Capes to Philadelphia was now altogether in the hands of the enemy.

For two months after the retreat from Germantown to the campground on the Perkiomen, the Americans engaged in no aggressive military operations. The time was spent in resting the men; combing the countryside for blankets, shoes, and clothing; and drawing troops from the north, from Putnam and Gates,[24] Burgoyne's surrender having permitted such withdrawals. Varnum's Rhode Island brigade, 1,200 men, came, and about a thousand others from Pennsylvania, Maryland, and Virginia. Gates sent down Patterson's and Glover's brigades and Morgan's invaluable rifle corps. By October 29 the army numbered 8,313 Continentals and 2,717 militia rank and file.[25] But the terms of enlistment of many of the Maryland and Virginia troops were about to expire.[26] The army was, as usual, in a state of incipient dissolution. The distress of the men for want of blankets, shoes, and clothing was "amazingly great."

Washington hardened his heart in his search for his army's necessities. "Buy, if you can," was his policy; if not, take, especially from the Tories. He wrote to George Read of Delaware, "You are to take care, that the unfriendly Quakers and others notoriously disaffected to the cause of American Liberty do not escape your Vigilance." "Obtaining these things from the Quakers and disaffected inhabitants is recommended, but at all events get them." [27] The returns from anywhere were never enough. To meet the appalling need for foot covering, Washington offered "a reward of *Ten Dollars*" to the person who should produce the best "substitute for shoes, made of raw hides." [28]

During those two months he was changing his camps restlessly and, except in one instance, with no apparent purpose. On October 8 he marched from the Perkiomen eight miles to a position in Towamencin Township. On the 16th the men "struck tents and marched to the Skippack Road and Encamped on the Same Ground we were at on the 3rd instant." [29] The purpose this time was "to divert the Enemy's attention and force them from the Forts," [30] but the enemy took no notice. On the 20th, the Americans again broke camp and marched to a new one in Whippany Township. On November 2 they made their last shift for the time being; "Cross'd Whissahickon Creek on Skippack Road, march'd to the left & encamped on the brow of an hill on ye North Wales Road White Marsh Township." [31] They remained there nearly six weeks.

The only bright spot in this dull period of marches to and fro was the announcement on October 18, in general orders, of Burgoyne's surrender. Washington expressed his own happiness and adjured his men, "Let every face brighten and every heart expand with grateful Joy and praise to the supreme disposer of all events who has granted us this signal success." A salute by "*Thirteen* pieces of cannon" to be followed by a "*feu-de-joy* with blank cartridges or powder by every brigade and corps of the army" was ordered. To add to the gayety of the celebration, the chaplains were directed to deliver to their several corps or brigades "short discources suited to the joyful occasion." [32]

Other than that, there is little of interest in the records of Washington's army of that period, save such as can be gleaned from the usual, dreary routine of courts-martial for various offenses. Drunkenness was common, desertion frequent. Cowardice was charged against not a few officers; most of them were acquitted, a few cashiered. On conviction of the privates, sentences of reprimand, of lashes on the bare back, of running the gantlet between files of fifty, one hundred, two hundred men, of death for desertion, were imposed. Disobedience usually drew thirty-nine lashes; drunkenness, the same. Sometimes noncommissioned officers were reduced to the ranks.

On October 19 Howe withdrew his troops from Germantown and concentrated his whole force in Philadelphia. He established a chain of fourteen redoubts, connected by a strong stockade and extending from the Upper Ferry on the Schuylkill to the shore of the Delaware above the town.[33]

Washington's army with its recent additions felt its strength. The near-success at Germantown had made it confident of its fighting ability, and Saratoga had aroused a spirit of emulation. On November 25, a council of war discussed the advisability of an attack on Philadelphia. Stirling had a prettily complicated plan for it; [34] Wayne was eager to try it. But eleven of the fifteen officers in attendance, including Greene, Knox, Sullivan, de Kalb, Smallwood, du Portail, and Maxwell, prudently voted against it. An open town, like Germantown, with only a part of the enemy's force to defend it, was one thing; a fortified city, garrisoned by such troops as held Philadelphia, was quite another thing. Disaster would certainly have resulted from such an attempt.

But the mere presence of the American army so near at hand was a continuous menace to the British. Howe decided to try once more to bring on a battle. At midnight of December 4 he set out from Philadelphia, with almost his entire force, to surprise the American camp at Whitemarsh. But that vigilant leader of American partisan troops Captain Allen McLane, who had been constantly scouting between the lines, discovered the enemy's intentions and reported them to Washington. Dispositions to receive the attack were made accordingly, one of them being the dispatch of McLane, with a hundred picked horsemen, to observe the enemy's movements.[35]

The British were advancing in two columns on the Manatawny and Skippack roads. At Three Mile Run on the Skippack Road, McLane, not content with mere observation, attacked the British van with "brilliant cavalry rushes" and with such effect that the front division was obliged "to change its line of march." [36] After that he hovered on the enemy's front and flank, "galling them severely."

At three o'clock in the morning of the 5th the British encamped on Chestnut Hill. When day dawned they "had a fine View of the Rebel Encampment about 3 miles distant on a Ridge of hills lying North of Whitemarsh," the "smoke and huts being plainly in view." [37] Before the British arrived the Americans had "increased their fires lighting many large ones in straight and deep lines, so that it looked as if fifty thousand men were encamped there. By day we could see this was merely a trick to deceive us," [38] says the Hessian Major Baurmeister.

Washington's camp was well defended. "Both wings were fortified by strong abatis; the center approaches were completely covered by several batteries; the whole position was strongly fortified by fifty-two heavy pieces." [39] There was no point in leaving such defenses and attacking the enemy in the open ground. If Howe wanted to bring on a battle, let him assault the American works.

Washington did, however, take the precaution of striking his tents in the early morning and sending his heavy baggage to the rear.[40] At eleven o'clock he sent Brigadier General James Irvine, with 600 Pennsylvania militia, to feel out the enemy. Irvine attacked an advance post held by the 2nd Battalion of British light infantry and supported by British and Hessian grenadiers. There was a heavy fire from both sides, and several men fell in either party. Irvine himself was wounded and captured. His force was driven back, broke, and ran away.[41]

The two armies held their respective positions until one o'clock in the morning of December 7, when the British marched from Chestnut Hill to Edge Hill, within a mile of the American left wing. Their line then was formed in a curve, threatening both the American wings. Washington moved Morgan's riflemen and Webb's Continental regiment, together with Brigadier General James Potter's brigade of Pennsylvania militia, all to the right.[42]

Howe then decided to try again his old Long Island and Brandywine trick. His army moved at ten o'clock that night in one column to Jenkintown. Grey was detached with the Hessian jägers, Simcoe's Tory Queen's Rangers, the light infantry, and the 3rd brigade and sent towards Tyson's Tavern on the Limekiln Road, "where he was to drive in a Post of the Enemy and draw up in view of their camp," says Major André. "While they presumed an attack impending from that quarter, Sir William Howe with the *Elite* and main army was to have made the real attack" on Washington's left.[43]

On the Limekiln Road, Grey's troops were received with a burst of fire from a woody ridge held by Morgan's riflemen and Gist's Maryland militia.

The jägers and Simcoe's Rangers advanced on the right and left, "with great activity and ardor." Outflanked on both wings, the Americans retreated. There were inconsiderable losses on both sides in this engagement, but, as usual, the account of the casualties varies with the side giving it.[44]

On the American left Potter's Pennsylvania militia and Webb's Continentals, with whom were General John Cadwalader and General Joseph Reed as observers, had taken post in a wood in Cheltenham Township. Grey's column attacked them. At the first fire Reed's horse was shot, and he fell to the ground. The British charged; the Americans gave way and fled in confusion. Some of the foe ran to bayonet Reed where he lay, but the ubiquitous McLane was at hand. He and his men charged, drove back the bayoneteers and rescued the injured general.[45] The Americans lost about 50 men.

The main body of the British army now occupied the position which had been held by Potter and Webb. But, says Major André, "the fullest information being procured of the Enemy's position, most people thought an attack upon ground of such difficult access would be a very arduous undertaking; nor was it judged that any decisive advantage could be obtained, as the Enemy had reserved the most easy and obvious retreat. Probably for these reasons the Commander in Chief determined to return to Philadelphia." [46] So both columns started back home.

Grey's column was unlucky in the weight of its artillery and the insufficiency of its horses. A body of American light infantry and some horsemen pursued it, "pressed on the rearmost parties and drove them in." The jägers were drawn up to oppose the attack. The Americans "formed at a fence and delivered a very brisk fire." The Hessians brought their fieldpieces into play and finally drove off their assailants. And so ended the abortive Battle of Whitemarsh.[47]

Washington decided to move his camp again, for what purpose does not appear. Early in the morning of December 11 the Americans left Whitemarsh, intending to cross to the west side of the Schuylkill at Matson's Ford by a bridge "consisting of 36 waggons, with a bridge of Rails between each." [48] Sullivan's division and half of another were across when a body of British soldiery appeared on the opposite hill. It developed as the van of a force of 3,500 led by Cornwallis on a foraging expedition. The Americans were in an awkward position, astride the river with a rickety bridge between the two parts. Washington recalled Sullivan and the others with him and broke the bridge. The two forces were then aligned in battle formation face to face with a river between, which neither dared to cross.

But Potter and his militia, who had been operating on the other side, had not been able to get back before the bridge was broken. Cornwallis scattered them and went on with his foraging. Washington returned to Whitemarsh.[49]

It was getting cold now; snow had already fallen, "though not to lay." It was time to plan for the coming winter. Should the Americans continue their campaign, as they had done throughout the last wintry season, or go into winter quarters in the approved military manner? Washington knew the answer, knew that his worn, half-fed, half-frozen, half-naked men simply could not endure the rigors of a winter campaign. When a committee of the Congress, now a bobtail organization of a score or so of mediocre gentlemen, most of whose names have all but passed into oblivion, came to him to confer on the means of carrying on a "Winter's Campaign with vigor and success," he gave them an earful, plenty of reasons why it could not be done. The committee seemed to be convinced.[50]

Winter quarters, then, but where? Some of the officers proposed a chain of posts from Lancaster to Reading; but such a scattering of a none-too-cohesive army would only result in its disintegration. Wilmington in Delaware was proposed. Greene favored it, and so did Joseph Reed, Lafayette, Armstrong, Smallwood, Wayne, and Scott. Cadwalader urged it. If this step were not taken, he said, the enemy might take over that town and so secure "the lower counties on the Eastern Shore" of the Chesapeake. Besides, gondolas based on that "strong post" could annoy the British shipping.[51] Washington favored the idea, looking for mild weather there and facilities for securing supplies by the river. But Pennsylvania had to be heard from. It raised an outcry.

The Pennsylvania Council and Assembly drew up a hot remonstrance and sent it to the Congress at York. It cried aloud against letting the army go into winter quarters anywhere. Pennsylvania and New Jersey would be ravaged. The inhabitants would be obliged to fly or to submit to such terms as the enemy might prescribe—regardless of the fact that the Philadelphians were already submitting and having rather a better time, on the whole, than Washington's hungry and cold troops.

The Congress submissively sent the document to Washington, and the gentlemen from Pennsylvania got an answer that burned their ears. Who had told them whether he intended to hibernate or to fight all winter? Assuredly, he had not. They were reprobating the idea of winter quarters "as if they thought the Men were made of stocks and stones and equally insensible to frost and Snow," as if they thought the army, in such condition as it was in, could hold "a superior one, in all respects well appointed

. . . within the city of Philadelphia and cover from depredation and waste the States of Pennsylvania and New Jersey." It amazed him still more that these very gentlemen, who, knowing the nakedness of his soldiers, had asked him to postpone his plan of commandeering clothes "under strong assurances that an ample supply would be collected in ten days . . . not one Article of which, by the bye, is yet come to hand"—that these same gentlemen should think "a Winter's Campaign and the covering of these States from the Invasion of an Enemy, so easy and practicable a business. I can assure these Gentlemen, that it is a much easier and less distressing thing to draw remonstrances in a comfortable room by a good fireside, than to occupy a cold, bleak hill and sleep under frost and Snow without Cloaths or Blankets; however, although they seem to have little feeling for the naked and distressed Soldiers, I feel superabundantly for them and, from my Soul, I pity those miseries, which it is neither in my power to relieve or prevent." [52] If the gentlemen of the Pennsylvania Council and Assembly did not curl up under that lash, they certainly had rhinoceros skins.

Washington was already at Valley Forge when he wrote to the state Assembly. That place, selected as a compromise between campaigning and wintering in Wilmington, was suggested by Wayne, a Pennsylvanian, "to cover this Country against the Horrid rapine and Devastation of a Wanton Enemy." [53] Like most compromises, it was not a good solution of the problem—"a most unwise one," indeed. Chester County had been so stripped by both armies that it was "doubtful if any location could have been secured where supplies were more difficult to secure than Valley Forge." [54]

De Kalb expressed himself forcibly against that location for the camp, writing: "The idea of wintering in this desert can only have been put into the head of the commanding general by an interested speculator or a disaffected man." [55] Varnum was even more emphatic: "I have from the beginning viewed this situation with horror! It is unparalleled in the history of mankind to establish winter-quarters in a country wasted and without a single magazine." [56] Nevertheless, the choice was made, and on those bleak and barren hills the army settled down for a winter of torture and heroism.

With this, our narrative will turn back six months to the army on Lake Champlain.

CHAPTER 35

Valcour Island

"Our Army at Crown Point is an object of wretchedness to fill a humane mind with horrour; disgraced, defeated, discontented, diseased, naked, undisciplined, eaten up with vermin; no clothes, beds, blankets, no medicines; no victuals, but salt pork and flour." [1] In those words, which for clearness, force, and accuracy could not be bettered, John Adams described the condition of the American troops who, after the disasters at Quebec and Trois Rivières, retreated from Canada in June, 1776.

Three thousand of them, afflicted with smallpox, dysentery, malarial fevers, and all sorts of camp diseases, were in hospital; that is to say, they were lying in tents and huts with no proper care or treatment. Surgeons were few, medicines almost entirely lacking. For food they had almost rancid salt pork and flour, nothing else. [2] "I can truly say," wrote Colonel Trumbull, "that I did not look into a tent that did not contain a dead or dying man." [3] Five thousand were supposed to be fit for duty, but they seemed mere "walking apparitions." Five thousand men had been lost in the whole Canadian venture. [4]

Schuyler at Albany was in command. Sullivan, his second, was with the troops. But on June 17 the Congress, having news of the disaster at Trois Rivières and of the retreat, had resolved that "an experienced general be immediately sent into Canada" and directed Washington to order Major General Horatio Gates "to take command of the forces in that province." [5]

Washington sent Gates his orders, with the comment, "The Command is important." John Adams wrote him, "We have ordered you to the Post of Honour and made you Dictator in Canada for Six Months or at least until the first of October." [6] To Gates this naturally meant that he was to take over the chief command from Schuyler. But Schuyler thought that only Sullivan was displaced, and that he himself still held the dominant position, pointing out, with some logic, that, while the order gave Gates chief command of the troops in Canada, there were, in fact, no longer any troops whatever in Canada. On July 8 the Congress gave Schuyler support by declaring that its intention was to give Gates "command of the troops whilst in Canada," with no purpose of giving him "a superior command to General Schuyler, whilst the troops should be on this side Canada." It also recommended to both generals that they "carry on the military operations with harmony." [7] So Gates had to accept the inferior position, which, to give him due credit, he did with good grace.

Gates arrived at Crown Point along with Schuyler on July 5. A council of war was held, in which Schuyler, Gates, Sullivan, Arnold, and the Prussian general Baron de Woedtke took part. They unanimously agreed that Crown Point was not tenable, that they should retire to Ticonderoga, sending all the sick to Fort George, and that "a naval armament of gondolas, row-galleys, armed batteaus &c" should be provided. [8]

Some of the field officers were not content with this intention to retreat further. Twenty-one of them signed a remonstrance and delivered it to Schuyler. There was discontent also in higher quarters. Washington was inclined to the view of the malcontents. He wrote to Schuyler that, while he did not wish to encourage inferior officers in setting up their opinions against their superiors' decisions, yet he felt as they did and stated his reasons at length. Indeed, he said, nothing but a belief that, by the time he had news of the intended move, the works had been demolished and the withdrawal already made, plus a fear of encouraging such remonstrances, had prevented him from ordering the retention of the post at Crown Point. [9]

Schuyler defended the decision to withdraw with reasons that were cogent, [10] but not so briefly and briskly stated as were Gates's. "Your Excellency Speaks of Works to be Destroyed at Crown Point," Gates wrote to Washington on July 29. "Time & the Bad Construction of those Works had Compleatly Effected that business before General Schuyler came with me to Crown Point. The Ramparts are Tumbled down, the casements are Fallen in, the Barracks Burnt, and the whole so perfect a Ruin that it would take Five times the Number of Our Army for several Summers to put Those Works in Denfensible [*sic*] Repair." [11]

Under these conditions, no other course was possible, and so the sick were sent on to Fort George, and the rest of the army moved to Ticonderoga. The remnant of their salt pork had become utterly rancid and was

thrown away. They had nothing to eat but flour, boiled to a gruel or baked
into thin cakes on flat stones. They had no attention except what less than a
dozen surgeons could give to 2,000 desperately sick men. Nature and
Death took care of them. Some recovered, some did not. By the middle of
August, they were down to a thousand.[12]

Three thousand "effectives" were now at Ticonderoga. The 6th Pennsylvania, under Lieutenant Colonel Thomas Hartley, had been left to establish an outpost at Crown Point—one not to be held against the enemy
appearing in force.[13] A reenforcement, consisting of the 1st and 2nd Pennsylvania and three companies of the 4th, arrived at Ticonderoga on July 9,
without shoes or stockings and almost in rags, "in miserable plight from
the fatigue and sickness they had undergone," but, compared with the rest,
"robust and healthy." [14]

The army was now divided into four brigades. The 1st, commanded by
Arnold, comprised Bond's, Greaton's, and Porter's Massachusetts Con-
tinentals, and Burrell's Connecticut. The 2nd, under Colonel James Reed,
was composed of his own, Poor's, and Bedel's from New Hampshire and
Patterson's from Massachusetts. The 3rd commanded by Colonel John
Stark, was made up of his own New Hampshires, Wind's and Maxwell's
New Jerseymen, and Wynkoop's New Yorkers. The 4th, General Arthur
St. Clair's, had his own, De Haas's, Wayne's, and Hartley's commands, all
Pennsylvanians.[15]

The first three brigades were encamped on Mount Independence, on the
east side of the lake, to keep them away from St. Clair's Pennsylvanians,
encamped on the Ticonderoga side. The intense jealousy and ill feeling between the "southern" troops and those of New England and the consequent
disorder had made this separation necessary.[16]

When Ethan Allen and Benedict Arnold took Ticonderoga from the
British in May, 1775, it was well supplied with ordnance and ordnance
stores; but Knox took most of the heavy cannon to the army at Boston.
There were left, however, 120 guns of various sizes from 3-pounders to
one 32. But there were not enough carriages to mount more than 43 of
them, and there was a great lack of all their equipment, sponges, ram-
mers, and so on. Powder was, as always, deficient, also lead, flints, and
cartridge paper, for all which Gates now called on the Congress. He got
them at last, on October 6.[17]

More men were needed to man these extensive works. Two emotions,
prevalent throughout the northern states, affected the supply of such reenforcements. One was fear of the British invasion, which prompted the
militia to come forward. The other was dread of the smallpox in the camp,

which deterred them. The first was, however, the stronger. Militiamen from the neighborhood and from the New England states began to come late in July. By August they were coming in considerable numbers, though for the most part they were so ill provided and so worn down by the fatigue and hardships of their march that they were more of a burden to the garrison than a help. But three Continental regiments from Massachusetts really strengthened the army in July.[18]

By August 24 the returns showed twenty regiments in five brigades, a total of 9,157 rank and file, but only 4,899 present and fit for duty, besides 1,500 effectives at Crown Point, Fort George, and Skenesboro.[19]

The Americans had a flotilla on the lake, the schooner *Royal Savage,* captured the year before by Montgomery at St. Johns, the sloop *Enterprise,* which Arnold had taken when Ticonderoga fell, the schooner *Liberty,* taken at Skenesboro by Herrick at the same time, and the schooner *Revenge,* built at Ticonderoga. Arnold, whom Gates adjudged to be "perfectly skilled in naval affairs," had "most nobly undertaken to command" this fleet.[20] But Carleton was building boats at the other end of the lake, and Arnold wanted more than those four. He wanted auxiliary craft, gondolas, row-galleys, gunboats. They had to be built. But how could they be built?

There was plenty of standing timber, but it must first be felled, then hewn into keels and ribs and sawn into planks. Felling axes were scarce. Of broadaxes, adzes, crosscut saws, hammers, grindstones, chisels, augers, and all sorts of necessary hand tools, there were none. There were, to be sure, three sawmills in the neighborhood—one at Ticonderoga, another at Crown Point, a third near Skenesboro. Though disuse and neglect had left them in bad shape, they could be repaired. Planks could be got out in them. But how could those necessary tools be had in that wilderness? Where were bolts and nails, oakum and other naval stores, hawsers and anchors, paint, iron, ropes and blocks for rigging, canvas for sails, and all the hundred and one necessary articles and things for equipment to be procured?[21]

And, if you had all those, who was to use them? Who was to build and rig the vessels? Ship carpenters, sailmakers, and riggers were few in that army. The shipyards and sail lofts along the seacoast were humming with work for shipmasters and privateersmen. Few mechanics were fools enough to join a naked, starved, diseased army, when plenty of work with good pay was to be had at home. Nevertheless, those boats had to be built, and they were built.

Felling axes came first, in quantity, 1,500 from Schuyler at Albany, a thousand more from Governor Trumbull of Connecticut.[22] The soldiers were put to work in the forest. A few ship carpenters, so improvident as to have enlisted, were combed out of the army, a few house carpenters also. These were sent to Skenesboro, where the boatyard was established; Schuyler sent thirty more from Albany.[23] But these were not enough, not nearly enough. The coastal towns were called on.

In four companies of fifty each, bringing their own tools, ship carpenters came on from Massachusetts, Connecticut, Rhode Island, and even from far-off Philadelphia. Not for nothing, however, and not for soldiers' pay. They demanded and they got "prodegious wages," as much as five dollars a day, hard money, it was rumored. Blacksmiths also came and oarmakers and riggers and sailmakers, on similar terms.[24] Brigadier General David Waterbury, Jr., of Connecticut took charge of the work. Arnold came to Skenesboro from time to time, "to give Life & Spirit to Our Dock Yards," as Gates put it.[25] His energy and drive were contagious among the workers, and Waterbury's constant attention kept things going. Hard as it was to get them, spikes and nails being especially scarce, the necessary supplies and equipment came in.

Two types of craft were built—row-galleys and gondolas. The row-galleys were the larger, 70 to 80 feet long and 18 feet beam. They had round bottoms with keels, quarterdecks, and cabins, and were of "Spanish construction" as to their rigging; that is to say, they had two short masts, equipped with lateen sails that gave them an exotic appearance on that lake but made them easy even for landlubbers to handle.[26] Their armament was a 12- and an 18-pounder in the bow, two 9-pounders in the stern, and from four to six 6-pounders in broadside. Their complement was eighty men each.

The gondolas were flat-bottomed, but had keels. They were about forty-five feet long, rigged with one mast and two square sails and carried forty-five men each. They were slower and less handy than the galleys and could sail only before the wind while the galleys could beat to windward. Their armament was one 12-pounder and two 9-pounders.[27]

The schooner and the sloop were not so heavily armed as the galleys. The *Royal Savage* carried four 6-pounders and eight 4-pounders; the *Enterprise*, twelve 4-pounders; the *Revenge*, four 4-pounders and two 2-pounders; the *Liberty*, the same. All the craft also mounted on their bulwarks several light swivel guns. Both galleys and gondolas were equipped with oars, the galley with thirty-six.[28]

While the boats were building, the army was cheered and refreshed by the arrival of beef on the hoof, twenty head a week, and plenty of bread. To those who could afford to pay, sutlers offered vegetables, sugar, butter, cheese, chocolate, rum, and wine. The condition of the troops was much improved.[29] On July 28 General St. Clair read the Declaration of Independence to the troops. They "manifested their joy with three cheers." "It was remarkably pleasing to see the spirits of the soldiers so raised after all their calamities; the language of every man's countenance was, Now we are a people; we have a name among the States of the world." [30]

Carleton had halted his pursuit of Sullivan's retreating army at St. Johns. But he had no intention of remaining there long. He was receiving large reenforcements from Britain, and he intended, if possible, to march to Albany and cooperate with Howe. The plan to isolate New England by occupying the Lake Champlain and Hudson River passageway, attempted in 1777, was to be executed, if feasible. As indicated above, the Americans were alarmed because of the threat of Carleton's army. At St. Johns, Carleton proceeded to assemble and construct a fleet of vessels for the lake, because he could not advance without commanding its waters. There were on the St. Lawrence a three-masted ship, the *Inflexible*, and two schooners, the *Maria* and the *Carleton*; but, because of the ten-mile-long rapids between Chambly and St. Johns, they could not be brought up the Richelieu. He tried to bring them around the falls on rollers, but the ground was too soft to bear their weight; he had to take them apart and carry them up in pieces. From England a frigate had brought him ten gunboats knocked down. These were brought to St. Johns to be reconstructed. A thirty-ton gondola, thirty longboats, and four hundred bateaux were also brought up, either overland or by dragging them through the rapids. The longboats and bateaux were to transport troops and baggage up the lake.[31]

Carleton had little difficulty in securing workmen, materials, tools, and supplies. There were the fleet in the St. Lawrence and the towns along that river to furnish them to his full requirement. The work was swiftly carried on. For instance, the *Inflexible* was rebuilt and equipped within twenty-eight days of the time the keel was laid. With equal dispatch, he rebuilt the others and constructed ten more gunboats and an extraordinary thing called a *radeau*. It was a huge, flat-bottomed affair, with two masts carrying square sails, but it was more like a raft than any other sort of vessel, having very low bulwarks. It was to be manned by three hundred men, and was armed with the heaviest ordnance, six 24-pounders, six 12-pounders, and two howitzers. It was, indeed, a sort of floating fortress. Its name was *Thunderer*.[32]

By October 4 Carleton's fighting fleet was complete and ready to sail. In it were the *Inflexible*, armed with eighteen 12-pounders, the *Maria*, with fourteen 6-pounders, the *Carleton* with twelve of the same, the gondola *Loyal Convert* with seven 9-pounders, the giant *Thunderer*, and twenty gunboats having bow-guns ranging from 9-pounders to 24-pounders.[33]

The British army in Canada had been reenforced by the arrival, in June, of the Regiment Hesse Hanau, 660 in number, and in September by a second installment of Hessians and Brunswickers, making up a total force of 5,000 German mercenaries under command of Major General Baron von Riedesel. Carleton's whole army now numbered about 13,000 rank and file.[34]

On September 10 operations against the Americans on the lake began. General William Philips with two regiments, part of a third, and some artillery was posted at St. Johns. Another regiment held Chambly. Lieutenant Colonel Carleton, a younger brother of the general, started up the Richelieu with 400 Indians in canoes, to be strengthened shortly afterwards by the addition of 100 Canadian volunteers under Captain Fraser. And 1,300 German troops embarked in eighty-two boats and moved up the river.[35]

General Simon Fraser with the light infantry, the grenadiers, and the 24th British regiment took post on the river about five miles above the New York State line. Burgoyne with the 9th, 21st, 31st, and 47th British regiments, the Hessian Regiment Riedesel, and the Hanau Regiment, moved up to Ile aux Noix, which had been possessed by the British in August and had been fortified and equipped as a base of supplies with magazines, block-houses, and barracks.[36]

But it was not until October 14 that Burgoyne and Fraser, having left the 20th and 61st to hold Ile aux Noix, embarked for the final advance against the Americans. All the German troops were left in Canada, except the Hanau artillery, which was with Carleton's fleet on board the *Thunderer*.[37]

Arnold's preparations to meet the enemy had been pushed with such success that, by August 20, the schooners *Royal Savage* and *Revenge*, the sloop *Enterprise* and the gondolas *Boston, New Haven, Providence, New York, Connecticut,* and *Spitfire*, the cutter *Lee*, and the sloop *Liberty* were ready. On the 24th he set sail at Crown Point. At Willsborough, halfway down the lake, a hard storm, with heavy rain, overtook him and nearly foundered the *Spitfire*. The whole fleet had to weigh anchor and run before the wind up to Buttonmould Bay, where, for three days without intermission, it was lashed by the gale. On September 1 the anchors were again

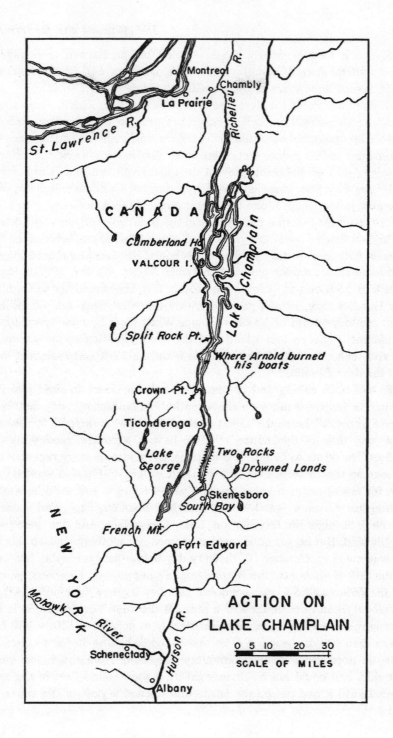

ACTION ON
LAKE CHAMPLAIN

0 5 10 20 30
SCALE OF MILES

lifted, and a fresh southerly breeze carried the fleet down to Schuyler's Island and then to Windmill Point at the northern end of the lake and within two or three miles of the Canadian border.[38]

At Windmill Point the fleet was joined by the *Lee,* which, sloop-rigged but with oars, might be called either a cutter or a row-galley, and the gondola *Jersey.* Arnold moored his vessels in a line across the lake and sent men ashore to fell spruce trees and make fascines for lining the sides of his galleys and gondolas "to prevent the enemy's boarding and to keep off small shot." [39] They were attacked by some of Carleton's Indians, who were now in the woods along the shore; three of the Americans were killed and six wounded before a few shot from the fleet drove off the assailants.

The lake is narrow at this point, and Arnold feared the erection of batteries on both sides to rake the line of his boats. He therefore retired to good anchorage in a broader part beside Ile la Motte. On the 19th he again shifted his position to a point farther south, Bay St. Amand above Cumberland Head, a long, curved promontory on the New York side of the lake about ten miles north of Valcour Island. While there he took soundings of the channel between that island and the shore. Finding it "an exceeding fine and secure harbour," he retired to it on the 23rd and remained there until the day of battle.[40]

He had been calling and continued to call on Gates to send him 200 sailors. His force was made up almost entirely of landsmen, "very indifferent men in general," he said. "Great part of those who shipped for seamen know very little of the matter." [41] "We have a wretched, motley crew in the fleet," he wrote to Gates, "the marines, the refuse of every regiment and the seamen few of them ever wet with salt water." [42] He also wanted gunners, for few of his men knew anything about laying a gun. And he wanted clothing for his men, watch coats, breeches, blankets, caps, and shoes. It was cold at night in October on Lake Champlain, and the men were scantily clad. But he got none, neither seamen nor clothing. Indeed, his last call was made on October 10, the very day before battle. He did, however, get the rest of his boats: the *Washington, Trumbull,* and *Congress,* galleys, and the *Jersey* and *Success,* gondolas, came on as they were finished.[43]

Valcour Island lies about half a mile off the New York shore. It is two miles long and half as wide, and rises steeply to heights of 120 to 180 feet. It was then heavily wooded. The vessels lying behind it were concealed from the north by a small promontory projecting from the island on its west side, and could not be discovered by a southbound fleet in the main channel until it had passed the island and opened a view of the water behind it.[44]

Arnold moored his fleet—two schooners, one sloop, eight gondolas, and four row-galleys—in a curved line, a "half-moon," between the island and the mainland, keeping the vessels as near together as practicable. He made the galley *Congress* his flagship, taking a position in the middle of the line. General Waterbury on the *Washington* galley commanded the right wing, and Colonel Edward Wigglesworth of Massachusetts on the *Trumbull* galley, the left. The entire force on the fleet was about 800 men.

Carleton sailed from St. Johns on October 4. His fleet consisted of the square-rigged ship *Inflexible*, the schooners *Maria* and *Carleton*, the great radeau *Thunderer*, the gondola *Loyal Convert*, twenty gunboats, four long-boats with fieldpieces in their bows, and twenty-four longboats for provisions and stores. The fleet was manned by 670 seamen from the British transports on the St. Lawrence, and each of the four larger vessels carried a company of the 29th Regiment acting as marines. Captain Thomas Pringle was in command.[45]

The fire power which this fleet could bring into action at one time was fifty-three guns, though in the approaching battle it was only forty-two, because neither the *Thunderer* nor the *Loyal Convert* was engaged. On the American side, the number was thirty-two.[46] The weight of metal which the British could throw in one complete discharge was perhaps 500 pounds, not counting the swivels, against the American 265.

The British fleet proceeded up the lake slowly and with apparent caution, yet really, at the last, incautiously. It first came to anchor below Ile la Motte and lay there until the 9th, while scouts went ahead looking for the Americans, without success. On the 10th it went on to an anchorage between Grand and Long islands. Here Carleton got news that the American fleet had been seen in the vicinity.

Getting under way the next morning, it stood up the lake before a strong northerly wind, rounded Cumberland Head, and passed Valcour Island. It was in mid-channel, about two miles beyond the southern end of Valcour, when the American fleet opened to its view.

Then the incaution of its proceeding was made plain. No scout boats had been sent ahead, which might have found the Americans before it had put itself to the disadvantage of having to attack from the leeward, that is to say, against the wind.

The Americans had been on the alert. The *Revenge* had been scouting to the north and had seen the British ships coming around Cumberland Head. On receiving this news Waterbury had urged Arnold "to come to sail and fight them on a retreat in [the] main lake as they were so much superior to us in number and strength and we being in such a disadvantageous harbour." But Arnold persisted in his plan to fight where he was.[47]

When the British discovered the American vessels, they hauled up for them. Arnold ordered the *Royal Savage* and the four galleys to get under way and commence the attack. He himself was on board the *Congress* galley. But when he got out into open water and saw the full strength of the enemy he signaled for a return to the line behind the island. The enemy, who by this time had made some headway in beating against the wind, opened fire at long range on the schooner and the galleys, to which the Americans replied with all the guns they could bring to bear.

The *Royal Savage*, either by misadventure or, as Arnold claimed, by mismanagement, fell to leeward while drawing under the lee of the island. Three shots in quick succession hit her, damaging one of her masts and cutting her rigging. She came up into the wind, but failed to go about on the other tack, hung in the eye of the wind for a long moment, fell off on the same tack as before, and grounded on the island shore. But her crew continued to fire her guns.

Neither the *Inflexible* nor the *Maria* had been able to beat back into close range. They anchored at long gunshot distance, and the *Inflexible* brought her heavy guns to bear on her enemy. Neither the *Thunderer* nor the *Loyal Convert* was engaged.

The schooner *Carleton*, boring into the fight, was caught by a flaw of wind and brought up opposite the middle of the American line. Lieutenant Dacres, her commander, anchored her, with a spring on her cable, broadside to the American fleet. Seventeen of the British gunboats came up into line with her. With no more than 350 yards distance between the two lines, the real battle began about noon.

"A tremendous cannonade was opened on both sides," wrote Baron von Riedesel. To the storm of shot and shell that fell upon the American fleet was added musketry from Captain Fraser's Indians and Canadians, who had landed from their canoes on the island and on the mainland west of the vessels. The crew of the *Royal Savage* was forced to abandon her. She was boarded by a boat's crew from the *Thunderer*, who turned her guns on her former friends. But they were soon driven off by the American fire. Another boat's crew, from the *Maria*, set her afire, and she blew up.

Meanwhile, the Americans' guns converged on the *Carleton*, Arnold himself sighting the guns of the *Congress*. She was hit time and again. Dacres was knocked senseless; another officer lost an arm. Edward Pellew, only a midshipman, a lad of nineteen, assumed command. After hours of fighting, the spring on her cable was shot away. Under the wind, she swung at her anchor, bows on to the enemy and, having no bow guns, hung there silenced, to be raked by every shot. Pringle on the *Maria* signaled her to withdraw, but she could not catch the wind so as to pay off on the right tack. Pellew climbed out on her bowsprit, under heavy musket fire, and tried to throw the jib over to make it draw, but without success. Two boats came to her assistance. Pellew, holding his position on the bowsprit in spite of a rain of musket-bullets, threw them a line, and the *Carleton* was towed away. She had been hulled several times, there was two feet of water in her hold, and half of her crew had been killed or wounded. Pellew further distinguished himself in later years, rising to the rank of admiral, and was honored with the title Viscount Exmouth.

Towards evening the *Inflexible* got within point-blank range and discharged five heavy broadsides against the American line, completely silencing its fire. But about five o'clock she dropped back to a distance of 700 yards from the Americans. The gunboats withdrew, and the whole British fleet anchored in a line across the southern end of the passage between Valcour and the mainland, keeping up a desultory fire until darkness fell.

The Americans took account of their injuries. The *Congress* had been hulled twelve times. She had two holes in her side between wind and water. Her mainmast was hit in two places. The *Washington* had also been severely punished and had one shot through her mainmast. The hull of the *Philadelphia* had been so damaged that she sank about an hour after the battle. All the sails of the fleet had been torn to tatters, and the rigging hung in tangles. The loss among the personnel was grievous; 60 had been either killed or wounded. Their store of ammunition was three-fourths gone. It was not possible to contemplate a renewal of the conflict on the morrow. It seemed that they were trapped and must surrender. But Arnold had another thought—to attempt an escape under the cover of night.

The night was dark. A heavy fog enshrouded the two fleets. A lantern, so hooded as to show a light only directly behind, was fixed in the stern of each vessel. At seven o'clock, the *Trumbull* galley got under way before a light northerly wind. The others fell in line at practicable intervals. The *Congress* and the *Washington* brought up the rear. And so, noiselessly, the whole line crept past the left of the British fleet, the fog so thick that none of the enemy's vessels could be seen. When they were beyond hearing distance the oars were got out, and the crews labored at them and at the pumps all through the night.

By dawn the *Trumbull* galley, with the *Revenge* and *Enterprise,* the *Lee* galley, and the gondolas *Boston, New Haven, Connecticut, Spitfire,* and *Success* had got ahead of the rest. The *Congress* and *Washington* galleys, the gondolas *Providence, New York,* and *Jersey,* which had made only eight miles, put in at Schuyler's Island. There the *New York* and *Providence* were found to be so badly damaged that their equipment was removed and they were sunk. The *Jersey* had run aground and, with the weight of water in her, could not be moved. The other two set out again early in the afternoon.

On discovering the escape of the Americans the next morning, Carleton immediately started after them. But, so upset was he by his surprise and rage, he forgot to give orders to his land forces. When within sight of Schuyler's Island he had to turn back to remedy his oversight.

The wind had shifted to the south, and, although Arnold put his men to the oars again, his battered galleys made little progress. By morning, after sixteen hours rowing, they had covered only six miles, and the pursuing British fleet, favored by a fresh northerly wind, which had not reached the Americans, was in sight in the rear. Also in sight, in front, were four American gondolas, which had been unable to keep up with the *Trumbull* and the others.

The *Inflexible,* the *Carleton,* and the *Maria* came on rapidly, the *Maria* ahead. At eleven o'clock, Arnold opened fire on her from his stern 9- and 12-pounders. But at Split Rock the pursuers caught up, and poured broadsides of grape and round shot upon the fleeing vessels. The *Washington* was overwhelmed by this fire. Waterbury struck her flag. In the course of the retreat, the *Lee,* like the *Jersey,* ran ashore and was abandoned; both were taken by the British.

But the *Congress* and the four gondolas kept on under the favoring wind, which had now caught up with them. For five glasses, two hours and a half, this unequal combat raged. The three British vessels, one on her broadside and two astern of her, concentrated their fire on the *Congress.* Her hull was shattered, her sails and rigging shot to rags, but there was no hint of surrender. Instead, Arnold signaled to the galleys to turn to windward so that the British sailing vessels could not follow, and to run for the east shore.

In Buttonmould Bay he beached his wrecks and set fire to them. He drew his men up on the shore and held them there until he was sure that his boats would blow up with their flags still flying, while the enemy stood off, keeping up a constant cannonade. The remains of his men, 200 in number—46 only of the *Congress* out of a crew of 73—started on a bridle path for Crown Point, ten miles away. They escaped an Indian ambush and reached the Point after dark, finding what was left of their fleet, the *Trumbull,* the *Enterprise,* the *Revenge,* the *Liberty,* and one gondola.

There was no stopping at Crown Point. Lieutenant Colonel Hartley and his garrison of the 6th Pennsylvania Regiment, together with Arnold's survivors, could not attempt to hold it. They burned all the buildings and retreated to Ticonderoga.[48]

A singular occurrence took place immediately upon their reaching that fort. A number of British rowboats came up under a flag of truce and delivered up General Waterbury and the entire crew of the *Washington*, 110 in number. Carleton had paroled them. This generous treatment made such an impression on the captives, and they were so loud in their praise of him, that it was thought dangerous to allow them to mingle with the others. They were immediately sent off on their way home.

Arnold had been utterly defeated, losing eleven of his sixteen vessels and 80 of his men; but his gallantry and theirs was not unrewarded. Indeed, the greatest American victories in the war thereafter were made possible by that desperate fight. The sequence of events is closely connected.

Carleton had been so delayed by the necessity of building a fleet to meet Arnold's, by his subsequent necessarily cautious maneuvering, and by the battle that he reconsidered his decision to attack Ticonderoga and withdrew all his army and his fleet from the lake to St. Johns. He felt that Ticonderoga was too strong to be carried by storm, and the season was too far advanced to allow siege operations. If he should be held up in the attack even for a short time he could not follow through to the Hudson in the winter and of course could not establish communication with Howe. If he could have reached Albany, the effect upon the American cause might have been disastrous. If he could have wintered at Ticonderoga and made it his base of supplies so as to start for the Hudson in the early spring, the British campaign might not have met with disaster in the next year at Saratoga. It was Saratoga that gave the needed encouragement to the French to send land and naval forces to aid the Americans. And those forces ensured the surrender at Yorktown and finished the war. Valcour Island was no defeat, therefore. "It was the American cause that was saved that day." [49]

Captain Alfred Thayer Mahan, the distinguished authority on naval affairs, has endorsed this view: "That the Americans were strong enough to impose the capitulation of Saratoga was due to the invaluable year of delay secured to them in 1776 by their little navy on Lake Champlain, created by the indomitable energy, and handled with the indomitable courage of the traitor, Benedict Arnold." [50]

Burgoyne's Expedition

Canada in the winter of 1776–1777 had no attractions for Major General John Burgoyne. After the retirement of the British army in October, 1776, following the battle with Arnold at Valcour, there would be no more military operations in the North until the spring, which was not to be expected before May. A prospect of six months of idleness in Quebec or Montreal had little appeal to such a restless and ambitious spirit. He could look forward to active service at the end of that period; but the plans for that would not be made in Quebec, nor would commands be allotted there. London was headquarters.

This was his second visit to America. His first had been to Boston in 1775. There he had been subordinate to Gage, Howe, and Clinton and he had not relished that position. He wrote to Lord Rochford after Bunker Hill: "The inferiority of my station as youngest Major-General upon the staff left me almost a useless spectator. . . . My rank only serves to place me in a motionless, drowsy, irksome medium, or rather vacuum, too low for the honour of command, too high for that of execution." So he had gone home in December of that year.[1]

He came back in the spring of 1776, but again as a subordinate, second in command to Carleton. It was Carleton, not he, that had won the victory at Valcour. It might be Carleton that would lead the King's forces in Canada in the coming campaign of 1777. Plainly, something should be done about it. So he went home again.[2]

In London he found conditions favorable to his ambition. Carleton was definitely out of favor. The King had been disappointed and vexed at his failure to press on after Valcour and take Ticonderoga. So had the country in general, including Lord George Germain, colonial secretary, responsible for the conduct of the war in America.

At first Germain was inclined to couple Burgoyne with Carleton as blameworthy for that failure. But there was another element in Germain's feelings toward Carleton, a bitter personal animosity antedating Valcour. He was glad to put all the blame on him, eager, indeed, when he observed the King's attitude towards Burgoyne.[3]

The King had shown a friendly face to the general. "Yesterday morning," announced the *Morning Chronicle* early in January, "his Majesty took an outing on horseback in Hyde Park upwards of an hour, attended by General Burgoyne." [4] Indeed, his Majesty had already indicated to Lord North his pleasure that Burgoyne should command operations from Canada in the spring.

So everything was going smoothly, and Burgoyne did nothing to cause friction. He did not intrigue against Carleton, criticized him not at all—indeed he defended him—and so aroused no opposition among that general's friends. To aid his own cause, he wrote and submitted to the King a paper entitled "Thoughts for Conducting the War from the Side of Canada," which, because of its results, was a very important document of the Revolution.

Burgoyne's plan assumed a strong American force at Ticonderoga, perhaps as many as 12,000 men. It called for a British army of 8,000 regulars, with a sufficient equipment of artillery, supplemented by "a corps of watermen," 2,000 Canadians, and "1000 or more savages." Of this force, he would leave 3,000 to hold Canada. He proposed, after establishing magazines at Crown Point, to embark the rest upon Lake Champlain. Ticonderoga was to be attacked and reduced "early in the summer."

After that, the advance should proceed, preferably by way of Lake George and the Hudson, to Albany. Or, if the enemy should be found on that route in too great force, it should go to Albany by the lower end of Champlain, through Skenesboro and the Hudson. In either case, a chain of posts should be established along the route of the expedition to secure its communications. From Albany, after the end of the campaign, Burgoyne was to establish contact with Howe. He did not expect Howe to send forces northward during the campaign to support him. He would have sufficient strength to reach Albany and to maintain himself there.

Burgoyne also proposed an auxiliary expedition to the same objective, but by way of Lake Ontario, Oswego, and the Mohawk River, which empties into the Hudson near Albany. He did not enlarge upon the advantages of his scheme, nor even specifically suggest its strategic purpose; but an already prevailing idea among the British high command was that holding the Hudson, and thus separating the New England colonies from the rest, was a matter of the first importance to the success of the King's arms in America.

Burgoyne was tactfully silent as to the command of the expedition, except by an indirect reference to it. This business, he said, would depend for its success upon the cooperation of the governor of Canada; to wit, Carleton. His "peremptory powers, warm zeal and consonant opinion" must be had, else "plausible obstructions . . . will be sufficient to crush such exertions as an officer of a sanguine temper, entrusted with the future conduct of the campaign and whose personal interest and fame therefore consequently depend upon a timely out-set, would be led to make." Clearly, Carleton was not suggested for the leadership.[5]

The King liked the plan. Its outlines, he said, seemed to be "on a proper foundation." The Mohawk River diversion, he also approved. Germain issued the necessary orders in a letter to Carleton. He was to remain in Canada and guard that province with 3,770 men of specified British and German regiments, including McLean's Royal Highland Emigrants, and detach Burgoyne with the remainder of the troops, 7,173 in number, "to proceed with all possible expedition to join General Howe and put himself under his command." He was also to furnish Lieutenant Colonel Barry St. Leger with 675 men, "together with a sufficient number of Canadians and Indians," for the Mohawk expedition.[6]

"I shall write to Sir William Howe," Germain went on, "from hence by the first packet." But Carleton, Burgoyne, and St. Leger were also to inform Howe of the plan, so that they might receive instructions from him.[7]

Germain's letter to Carleton was long and insultingly specific in its details. Not only so, but it also charged Carleton with "supineness" in his failure to attack Ticonderoga, and even blamed him for the defeat of the Hessians at Trenton, because that failure had set free American troops to act with Washington against the Jersey outpost.[8]

Such a letter was enough to anger Carleton, and it did. He wrote a spirited reply, defending his actions in forcible language. But, magnanimous man that he was, he added that, in spite of the "Slight, Disregard and Censure" visited upon him, he would give Burgoyne all possible assistance.[9] And he did.

Looking backward, one observes the weaknesses, indeed the stupidity, of Burgoyne's plan. There was little to be gained by a march from Canada to Albany. The cutting of communications between New England and the other colonies, if it had been possible, could have had important results only after the passage of time. And it was necessary that the war be won before Britain's financial resources should be overstrained, and before France should take advantage of the American situation to win revenge for the many defeats Britain had inflicted upon her. The troops set aside for Burgoyne's expedition could have given Howe useful added strength, even strength perhaps sufficient for a final destruction of Washington's army. Further, Burgoyne's army under the plan was to cooperate with Howe's only *after* the end of the campaign. It was to reach Albany unsupported from the south; and Howe was authorized by Lord Germain to move against Philadelphia by sea, leaving only a garrison force in New York. Burgoyne was to travel through the woods to Albany, with an ever lengthening line of communications and with no assurance of help even at Albany, should he need it. Germain finally saw this defect in the plan, perhaps not too clearly, and got off a letter to Howe suggesting that he cooperate with Burgoyne during the campaign. But Howe received Germain's letter in August while he was en route by sea to Chesapeake Bay, and he could hardly act to help Burgoyne at such a late time—at least he could not without completely disrupting his own plan of operation. He did make a gesture toward assisting Burgoyne by asking Clinton, who was in command of the garrison at New York, to do what he could to help his fellow general.[10]

Burgoyne arrived at Quebec on May 6, 1777. Spring had just come; the ice in the river had broken up, "with a most astonishing noise," one week before. He found the troops, after a mild winter, in good condition, except their clothing. New uniforms to replace those worn in last year's campaign had not come from England. To patch the old ones, the tails of the coats of the British regiments had been cut off. They all now wore short jackets, like the regulation coats of the light infantry. Their cocked hats had been cut down into caps. But these alterations were all for the better in forest warfare.[11]

The Brunswickers, too, were far from smart in their appearance. Their duke, in his prudent care for his own purse, had sent them out in worn uniforms and old shoes, and Canada had not afforded complete replacements. But all such matters were merely surface. The substance was sound.

There was one difference in uniforms, however, between the British and German contingents that was important. While the British uniforms had been modeled after those of the army of Germany and were too heavy, too awkward, too tight, and too elaborate for rough campaigning in America, those of these Brunswickers were far worse in all of these respects. Their dragoons, who had come without horses and were to serve dismounted to the end of the campaign, were most preposterously equipped for such service. Their great cocked hats, ornamented with a long plume, their hair worn in a long, stiff queue, their tight, thick coats, their stiff leather breeches, their huge leather gauntlets almost elbow-length, their great jack boots reaching to mid-thigh, weighing twelve pounds a pair without the long brass spurs always worn even on the march, made up as unsuitable an outfit for marching and fighting in a forested wilderness in an American midsummer as could have been devised by the most ingenious. Add to that a long, straight broadsword to trail at the thigh and a short heavy carbine, and one could have no feeling but pity for a Brunswick dragoon.[12]

So much for the main force of British and German regulars; they were fit and ready to go. The same could not be said for the irregular auxiliaries included in the plan. After all, they were French; and, however willing they had been in Montcalm's time to fight for their flag, this war meant little or nothing to them. Instead of the desired 2,000, Burgoyne could round up only 150. The Tories were also backward; only 100 enlisted. With the Indians he had somewhat better luck. He got 400 of the 1,000 he wanted. They were collected and led by La Corne St. Luc and Charles de Langlade.[13]

For his navy, he had the *Inflexible,* the *Maria,* the *Carleton,* the *Loyal Convert,* and the *Thunderer* of last year's fleet. To these were added the *Washington,* the *Jersey,* and the *Lee,* taken from Arnold after Valcour, another ship-rigged vessel, built that winter at St. Johns, the *Royal George,* and twenty-eight of last year's gunboats. Of bateaux for the transport of troops, there was an ample number.[14]

In his artillery section there were 138 guns, ranging from little 4.4-inch mortars and light 3-pounders to heavy 24-pounders. But many of these were mounted in the vessels, others were to be left at St. Johns, others at Ticonderoga and Fort George after they were taken. His field train for the whole expedition was to consist of 42 guns, large and small.[15]

The British advance corps was composed of the 24th regiment, the light infantry, and the grenadiers, including not only those of the expeditionary regiments, but also the flank companies of the 29th, 31st, and 24th, whose "battalion companies" remained in Canada.[16] This corps was under Brigadier General Simon Fraser. The 1st Brigade, the 9th, 47th, and 53rd regiments, was under Brigadier General Powell; the 2nd brigade, the 20th, 21st, and 62nd regiments, under Brigadier General Hamilton. This division constituted the right wing of the army and was under command of Major General William Phillips.

The German advance corps consisted of grenadiers and light infantry, including a company of forty jägers and forty "marksmen" selected from the different British regiments. This whole corps was commanded by Lieutenant Colonel Breymann. The 1st brigade, the Riedesel, Specht, and Rhetz regiments, was under Brigadier Specht; the 2nd brigade, the Prince Frederick and Hesse Hanau regiments, was under Brigadier Gall. This division was the left wing, commanded by Major General von Riedesel.[17]

The British infantry division numbered 3,724 rank and file, the German 3,016. The guns were to be divided between the two and served by 245 regular British artillerymen, 150 men drawn from the infantry, and 78 of the Hesse Hanau artillery company. The Canadian and Tory volunteers were to cover the British right wing, the Indians to cover the German left wing. The Brunswick dismounted dragoons were to act as reserves. In all the army numbered 7,213 rank and file.[18]

It was not a large army, but it was, for its size, a strong fighting force composed of trained, disciplined, and experienced men, under capable officers. Burgoyne, though not a military leader of the first or even second class, was an active, resolute, courageous soldier, well versed in the arts of war and, what is very important in such an extensive expedition as was about to be undertaken, he had the trust and confidence of his men. General Phillips, second in command, had served for twenty years in the British army. He was a distinguished artillerist and an exceptionally able strategist. Fraser was a scion of the noble Scotch house of Lovat. He, too, had had long experience as a soldier, had served with Wolfe at Louisburg and Quebec, and had acquired a high reputation for energy, activity, and good judgment coupled with cool daring. Hamilton had attained his command solely because of his professional merits and accomplishments. Kingston, the adjutant general, had served with distinction under Burgoyne in Portugal. Major the Earl of Balcarres, commanding the light infantry, and Major Acland of the grenadiers were officers of high professional attainments and undoubted courage.[19]

Of the Germans, Baron von Riedesel was the most distinguished. He had been a soldier in the Hessian and Brunswick armies for more than twenty years. At the outbreak of the Seven Years' War he was attached to the staff of the Duke of Brunswick and was employed by him in special duties which called for the use of delicate tact, good judgment, and personal courage. His reputation for intrepidity thus established was later confirmed by his conduct in many dangerous enterprises. He possessed the essential qualities of a good soldier; he was cool and discreet in danger, swift in action. His clear understanding had been studiously applied to the principles of his profession, and now, at the age of thirty-eight, he was at the height of his mental and physical powers. He was of medium height, strongly built, vigorous and hardy. His florid face was full and round, his features regular, his blue eyes notably large and clear. His amiable disposition was displayed in his care for the comfort and well-being of his men.[20] Under his leadership, backed by such experienced professional soldiers as his subordinate officers, the German contingent in Burgoyne's army was bound to give a good account of itself.

Burgoyne's troops were first assembled at St. Johns. There, on June 13, was enacted a bit of pageantry strange to that wilderness. On the *Thunderer*, moored in the river, there was erected the royal standard of Britain, bravely displaying on its embroidered silken fabric the golden lions of England, the red lion of Scotland, the harp of Ireland and, somewhat reminiscently, the fleur-de-lis of France. This symbol of Britain's might was then saluted by a discharge of all the guns of the fleet and in the fort.[21]

Still further to impress the Americans with the majesty of the laws they flouted, Burgoyne a week later issued a proclamation, in language which, according to a contemporary pamphleteer, was characterized by "the tinsel splendor of enlightened absurdity." It was Burgoyne the dramatist at his worst, at his almost unbelievable worst. It is difficult for one reading it now to realize that it is not a parody of some less bombastic manifesto.

Among other emotional appeals, it called upon "the suffering thousands," that is to say, the Tories, in the colonies to declare whether they were not subject to "the completest system of Tyranny that ever God in his displeasure suffer'd for a time to be exercised over a froward and stubborn Generation." It declared that "persecution and torture, unprecedented in the inquisitions of the Romish Church, are among the palpable enormities that verify the affirmative." To consummate this tyranny, it said, "the profanation of Religion is added to the most profligate prostitution of common sense." And so it went on to offer encouragement and protection to all who would take part in "the glorious task of redeeming their Countrymen from dungeons" and reestablishing the rule of the King.

The writer gave warning to those who persisted in this "unnatural Rebellion," that he had but "to give stretch" to his Indian auxiliaries, "and they amount to thousands," to overtake such recalcitrants "wherever they may lurk," for which vengeance upon those persisting in "the phrenzy of hostility" he would "stand acquitted in the Eyes of God and Men." There was a final warning uttered in "Consciousness of Christianity," that "devastation, famine and every concomitant horror that a reluctant but indispensable prosecution of military duty must occasion" awaited the impenitent.[22]

Instead of frightening the rebellious Americans, it first made them angry, then made them laugh. Parodies by the dozen appeared, notably an excellent one by Francis Hopkinson.[23] In England, there was a similar reaction. Horace Walpole called its author "the vaporing Burgoyne," "Pomposo," and "Hurlothrumbo," and remarked upon one who with "consciousness of Christianity" could "reconcile the scalping knife with the Gospel." [24]

A few days after the issuance of that rodomontade, Burgoyne addressed a council of his Indian auxiliaries in equally high-flown language. "Warriors, you are free—go forth in might and valor of your cause—strike at the common enemies of Great Britain and America—disturbers of public order, peace and happiness, destroyers of commerce, parricides of state," and so on at length, an incitement to the usual methods of savage warfare, if ever there was one, it seemed. But no, not that. "I positively forbid bloodshed, when you are not opposed in arms. Aged men, women, children and prisoners must be held sacred from the knife or hatchet, even in actual conflict." After that speech, the savage instincts of the Indians were tamed and subdued, their excitable natures sobered by a distribution of rum and by a "war-dance, in which they threw themselves in various postures, every now and then making most hideous yells." [25]

Again Burgoyne, a good soldier afflicted with a mania for the pen, exposed himself to ridicule. Walpole called it "still more supernatural" than his proclamation. Edmund Burke blasted it in the House of Commons. He supposed a riot on Tower Hill, where the royal menagerie was kept. "What would the Keeper of His Majesty's lions do? Would he not fling open the dens of the wild beasts and then address them thus? 'My gentle lions—my humane bears—my tender-hearted hyenas, go forth! But I exhort you, as you are Christians and members of civilized society, to take care not to hurt any man, woman or child!' " And Lord North, who had sanctioned the employment of the Indians, laughed until the tears ran down his cheeks.[26]

Ticonderoga, familiar name to British and Americans alike by 1777, is a bold, squarish, blunt-nosed promontory a mile long and three-quarters of a mile wide, that juts out from the western side of Lake Champlain, whose waters wash its base on the north, east, and south. At the foot of its southwest shoulder a very narrow gorge extends westward a mile or more, through which the waters of Lake George are poured into Champlain. The highest elevation on the promontory is about seventy feet above the lake.

From the east side of Champlain, another headland, a rocky bluff thirty to fifty feet high called Mount Independence, is thrust out towards the southeast corner of Ticonderoga. The points of the two narrow the lake to a width of about a quarter of a mile. This is the gateway from the upper lake to the lower, also to Lake George. Having passed through it one may go on by water directly south into the narrow, upper end of Champlain, and from its extremity up Wood Creek to within a few miles of the upper reaches of the Hudson. Or one may turn aside at Ticonderoga into Lake George and follow it to a point as near the Hudson.

About two miles to the northwest of the nose of Ticonderoga, Mount Hope commands the road to Lake George. A mile to the southwest, another hill, called Sugar Loaf from its conical appearance as seen from the east— but renamed Mount Defiance by the British after its capture—rises 750 feet above the water. At this time both shores of the lake and all the mentioned heights, except where Ticonderoga had been cleared for its fortification, were densely forested.

As has been hereinbefore stated, the French had built a star-shaped stone fort, with five bastions, on Ticonderoga in 1755. When it was attacked by Jeffrey Amherst in 1759 its retreating garrison blew up a large part of it. The British rebuilt it in less substantial fashion; but after the Peace of Paris, in 1763, it was allowed to fall into decay, though a considerable part of it, facing the lake, was still in serviceable condition in 1777.

While the French held it, they had constructed lines, extending in a curve across the promontory, about three-quarters of a mile behind the fort. These were built of logs heaped upon one another to a height of eight feet, covered with earth and faced with an abatis.

After the evacuation of Crown Point in July, 1776, and the concentration of the American troops at Ticonderoga, vigorous efforts were made to strengthen its defenses. The remains of the old fort were to some extent repaired. Blockhouses were built to protect the flanks and rear of the old French lines, which had been enlarged. Other blockhouses, also breastworks and small redoubts, defended the lower slopes on the north and south and various other points.

On Mount Hope a new barbette battery was built in a position covering the slope down to the outlet of Lake George and the road which ran south along its shore.

Across the lake Mount Independence showed a high, rugged, precipitous face. Its rear was protected naturally by a creek and a wide and deep morass, artificially by batteries and a strong, stone breastwork cleverly designed to take advantage of the irregularities of the ground. On its summit, an eight-pointed star redoubt, enclosing barracks, was the citadel of that position.

To close the water gateway, a boom of heavy logs, strung together on a massive iron chain, was stretched across from the northern point of Independence to the southern corner of Ticonderoga. Behind it, for communication between the two, was a bridge.

The plan of these works was suggested by Colonel John Trumbull; they were designed by the Polish engineer, Colonel Thaddeus Kosciuszko. Trumbull had proposed fortifying Sugar Loaf, but Gates had declared that it was an entirely inaccessible height and could therefore neither be fortified by him, nor be possessed by the enemy. Although Trumbull, Wayne, and game-legged Arnold climbed its steepest face, the eastern side, to the top, and although the northwest side was much less steep and difficult, Gates adhered to his decision not to try to fortify it.

A return of the troops at this post, dated June 28, 1777, showed ten Continental and two militia regiments, but they were slim regiments, ranging in number from 45 rank and file, present and fit, to 265, the average being 160. There were also Benjamin Whitcomb's little corps of 19 scouts, Thomas Lee's Rangers numbering 23, 124 artificers, and 250 in the artillery section. In all, including officers, the garrison might be estimated at 2,500.[27] The outside lines around Mount Independence plus the old French lines behind Ticonderoga were over 2,000 yards long. Even distributed along them in one thin line, with no reserves, no allowance for a force to hold Mount Hope, the blockhouses, and other works, there would have been one man for each yard, a mere skeleton defense. To man the works properly, at least five times the number of that garrison were necessary.

In chief command was Major General Arthur St. Clair. Born in Scotland, he had served in the British army in the French and Indian War, earning distinction at the siege of Louisburg and the capture of Quebec. Having married an American lady of wealth, he left the British service and established a home in Pennsylvania. He took the side of the rebels and was commissioned colonel of the 2nd Pennsylvania battalion in January, 1776. He was creditably concerned in the retreat across the Jerseys and the battles of Trenton and Princeton, as well as in the disaster at Trois Rivières. In February, 1777, the Congress appointed him a major general. He had been selected by Gates to command at Ticonderoga and had arrived at that post on June 12, 1777.

He was now past his fortieth year, tall, well built, and handsome in figure. His features were regular, his blue-gray eyes clear and intelligent, his hair reddish brown.[28] His manners were easy and graceful. Though his service during the war was competent to a degree, it cannot be said that he showed the capacity, the military ability, that would have justified his appointment as major general. A brigadier's rank would have been more suitable to his qualifications.

Serving under St. Clair at that post were three brigadier generals, the Frenchman Matthias Alexis Roche de Fermoy, John Paterson of Massachusetts, and Enoch Poor of New Hampshire, none of whom achieved distinction in the war.

The condition of internal affairs at Ticonderoga was far from satisfactory. There were not only too few men, there was too little of everything—arms, equipment, ammunition, supplies, and even food and clothing.[29] Schuyler came up from Albany and held a council of war with the four Ticonderoga generals on June 20. They agreed that there were too few troops to hold the whole works; that, nevertheless, they should hold on as long as possible and then concentrate all their force on Independence, which they might be able to hold as long as their food lasted; that bateaux should be kept ready for a final retreat.[30]

How they expected to get the troops safely across to Independence in the face of an enemy force that had beaten them out of Ticonderoga, how they expected to preserve that fleet of bateaux and to make that retreat, after the enemy held Ticonderoga and possessed the water gate, seem not to have been considered. But those questions are, after all, merely academic. They never had to be answered.

Two days before that council was held Burgoyne's entire force had assembled at Cumberland Head. It was there that he issued his great manifesto. From that point, the progress of the fleet and army was smooth and deliberate at the rate of eighteen to twenty miles a day.

Twenty or more great canoes, each holding twenty Indians, with another fleet bearing the Canadians and Tories dressed—or undressed—like Indians, formed the vanguard. Then came the gunboats and the bateaux of the British advance, the 24th regiment, the light infantry, and the grenadiers. The fleet was next in line, the tall-masted, square-sailed *Inflexible* and *Royal George*; the two schooners *Carleton* and *Maria*; the gondola *Loyal Convert*; the huge, unwieldy, absurd radeau *Thunderer*, that would "neither row nor sail" [31] but had to be got along somehow; the captives of last year's encounter, the galley *Washington*, the cutter *Lee*, and the gondola *Jersey*; and the gunboats, twenty-four of them.

After the fleet came the bateaux of the 1st British brigade "in the greatest order and regularity," [32] and then Burgoyne and his two major generals, Riedesel and Phillips, each in his own pinnace. The British 2nd brigade was followed by the two German brigades. Ignominiously, the tail of the procession was a motley fleet of boats of all kinds carrying the sutlers, the women, and all the raggle-taggle of camp followers that hung on the rear of the armies of that day.[33]

Against a setting of the blue waters of the lake and the dark green background of its forested shores, the painted faces and bodies of hundreds of Indians and their make-believe savage companions, the masses of British scarlet and of German dark blue, the green of the jägers and the light blue of the dragoons, with their regimental facings of every hue, the shining brass of the tall hats of the Hessian grenadiers, the glinting of the sunlight upon polished musket barrels and bayonets, the flashing of thousands of wet paddles and oars made up a spectacular pageant, brilliant in its color, light, and motion, thrilling in its purpose and intention.

On the 26th General Fraser's advance corps left Crown Point, where the army had by that time been concentrated, and pushed on ahead with the Indians, Canadians, and Tories. On July 1, "the weather being fine," the main army divided, the British taking the west side of the lake, the Germans the east side. The whole expanse of the lake, a mile wide, was "cover'd with Boats or Batteaux's"; as Lieutenant Hadden wrote, "some of the Armed Vessels accompanied us, the Music and Drums of the different Regiments were continually playing and contributed to make the Scene and passage extremely pleasant." [34] Three miles above Ticonderoga, the British landed and encamped on their side, the Germans opposite them. Fraser was a mile in advance. Early the next day the operations against the forts began.[35]

General Phillips, commanding Fraser's advance strengthened by one British brigade, started for Mount Hope. Its garrison set the works on fire, ran down the steep, rear slope and fled to the old French lines, a sensible proceeding proving the folly of the occupation of that outpost so far from the main defenses. A quick movement by the British might have cut off the retreating Americans; but not until one o'clock did they occupy the abandoned position and send Captain Fraser with his Indians and British marksmen on a circuit around the hill for that purpose. Finding no one to cut off, they went on towards the old French lines, drove in a picket of sixty men, approached within less than a hundred yards of the lines, took cover in the woods, and opened fire. St. Clair, thinking that this was a prelude to an assault at that point, ordered its defenders to sit down on the fire steps, keep under cover, and hold their fire. But, when tempted by the very near approach of one of the British marksmen, Lieutenant Colonel James Wilkinson ordered a sergeant to take a shot at him.

At the sound of that single discharge, the entire force within the old

French lines jumped to their feet, mounted the fire steps, and loosed a volley, then another and another. The artillery joined in the fusillade. When at last the officers had succeeded in stopping these unauthorized pyrotechnics and the smoke had cleared away, it was seen that the enemy had retreated to 300 yards' distance, leaving but one man lying on the field, the man Wilkinson had ordered shot. But when a corporal's guard went on to fetch him in and bury him, he was found to be unhurt. He was merely drunk. At least 3,000 musket shots had been fired and eight pieces of artillery had been discharged; yet only one man of 500—all within 80 to 100 yards—had been killed and two wounded.[36]

In the meantime, Riedesel's division had advanced close to the creek behind Independence and had been fired on. But darkness fell before any nearer hostile move could be made. The next day, Mount Hope was occupied in force by the British, and there was a certain amount of cannonading of little avail to either side. But something less noisy, that was to prove immediately decisive of the contest, was on foot.

Burgyone sent Lieutenant Twiss, his chief engineer, to take a look at that neglected Sugar Loaf. Twiss climbed its northwest flank, came back, and reported that it commanded Ticonderoga at 1,400 yards and Independence at 1,500. He could open a road and have guns up there within twenty-four hours. Burgoyne gave the orders. Phillips took charge. "Where a goat can go," said he, "a man can go and where a man can go he can drag a gun." [37] On July 4 the engineers were at work on the road.

St. Clair had been strengthened by the arrival of 900 fresh militiamen. He was looking for an assault on some part of his works, but there seemed to be little enemy activity. Yet there were movements. Burgoyne took Gall's brigade from Riedesel and moved it to the Ticonderoga side, giving him in exchange Fraser's Indians, Canadians, Tories, and British "marksmen." Riedesel was to move to the south around Independence and close the way of retreat by the road on that side of the lake, the guns on Sugar Loaf being expected to prevent any embarkation for retreat by water. But Riedesel had not yet begun his circuitous move.[38]

On the morning of July 5, St. Clair took a good look at something moving on the top of Sugar Loaf. Were there men up there? There were and something else, two guns, 12-pounders, not yet mounted, but on the way to be. He turned to his adjutant, Wilkinson. "We must away from this," said he, "for our situation has become a desperate one." [39] At least, that is the way Wilkinson reports his speech. Doubtless St. Clair was more brief and less stilted.

A council of war, immediately held, promptly and unanimously voted to give up the forts and retreat. But the withdrawal could not be begun by day, in full sight of the enemy. The night promised concealment. There would be a new moon, setting early and leaving comforting darkness.[40]

The relics of Arnold's Valcour fleet, the *Trumbull* and *Gates* galleys, the schooners *Liberty* and *Revenge,* and the sloop *Enterprise*, had been anchored in line across the narrow water behind the bridge. More than two hundred bateaux and other small craft lay beyond these. It was decided to use all these vessels to transport, up the lake to Skenesboro, the invalids and as much of the artillery and stores as could be got away. The main force would march from the east side by a road that ran from behind Independence southeast to Hubbardton, thence around Lake Bomoseen to Castleton and thence west to Skenesboro.

To drown the noise of the preparations for departure and divert the enemy's attention, the heavy guns in the forts and the various batteries opened fire as darkness fell. When it was quite dark, the embarkation of the invalids and stores began. Colonel Pierce Long of New Hampshire, with four or five hundred effectives, was in charge of the boats. The work of loading them was toilsome, and its progress slow, because everything that was got away had to be carried on men's backs from the forts to the spot where the boats were moored.

The cannonade was continuous and thunderous throughout the evening. What the enemy thought of this apparently senseless waste of powder does not appear. One might have supposed that it would lead them to suspect just what was actually in progress. Another signal was a fierce burst of flame from the Independence fort. General Roche de Fermoy had adopted the "scorched earth" policy by setting his headquarters ablaze rather inopportunely. Indeed, some of the enemy were moved to speculate whether the Americans "were meditating an attack or . . . were retreating." [41] But it was not until about daybreak that General Fraser had definite information of the retreat, from three American deserters.

Fraser's headquarters were on the Ticonderoga side, a mile and a half from the bridge. Hurrying to it with his troops, he found that it was partially destroyed, also that several fieldpieces at the farther end were trained down its length. Four men had been left there to fire one blast at the enemy attempting to cross, and then to retire.

But when Fraser's men made a tentative approach nothing happened. They pushed on to find all four gunners lying dead drunk beside a cask of

Madeira. Only one of the guns was fired, by an Indian who picked up a lighted slow match and carelessly dropped a spark upon its priming. Fortunately for those on the bridge, the gun was elevated to such a degree that it fired over their heads.[42]

Burgoyne ordered Fraser's light infantry and grenadiers to pursue the main force of the Americans retreating by land, and directed Riedesel, with his own regiment and Breymann's grenadiers and light troops, to follow in support. The 62nd British regiment was put in charge of Ticonderoga, and Prince Frederick's Brunswickers of Independence. The British fleet was to go on up the lake after the American boats.[43]

It was along but a pretense of a road that St. Clair led his troops towards Hubbardton, a mere wagon track, new, rough, rutted, and spotted with stumps of trees. It ran up hill and down across a broken country, "a continuous succession of steep and woody hills," [44] interspersed with ponds, swamps, and streams. The day, July 6, became hotter and hotter as it wore on. Over that road, shut in on both sides by dense forest walls, there were no cooling breezes, and the men sweltered in the overpowering heat. But there was no stopping until they had gone twenty-four miles and, through a high notch in a line of hills, had come down into Hubbardton, a hamlet of two houses. Even then they did not rest long. Six miles more would bring them to Castleton, where they would be within thirteen or fourteen miles of Skenesboro. St. Clair pushed his men on to that point before night.

Colonel Seth Warner of Vermont was left at Hubbardton with 150 men, under orders to wait until the rear guard came up and then follow closely after the main body. But Colonel Warner, brave and patriotic though he was, lacked discipline. He had been a Green Mountain Boy, accustomed to acting on his own and taking orders from nobody. Instead of bringing on the rear guard, he and Colonel Francis, its commander, agreed to spend the night at Hubbardton. So three regiments, Warner's Vermonters, Francis's 11th Massachusetts, Colonel Hale's 2nd New Hampshires, and a number of stragglers from the main body bivouacked there.[45]

Fraser lost no more time than St. Clair. Starting at four o'clock in the morning, his men marched along the same road until one in the afternoon. Riedesel, behind them, was equally vigorous. When Fraser paused for breath at one o'clock Riedesel himself, with a company of jägers and about 80 grenadiers, came up. He and Fraser decided to go a few miles farther, rest for the night, and go on at three the next morning. They camped within a short distance at Hubbardton.[46]

The careless Americans had thrown out no pickets. They were all together around their campfires cooking breakfast when Fraser and Riedesel, whose Indians had scouted the American camp the night before, marched unobserved through the notch north of the camp. Close to the camp, they deployed their 750 men and charged upon the nearest body, Hale's New Hampshires.

The surprise was complete. Hale and his men fled in disorder, each man for himself. Warner and Francis had but a few minutes to get into fighting order, but they stood their ground and gave the enemy a volley that struck down 21 men. Major Grant of the 24th was killed, the Earl of Balcarres wounded. This was the opening of a bitter fight.[47]

The ground was all forest, covered with standing trees, fallen trees, and underbrush. For the Americans, it was the best of cover. For the British and Germans it was a tangle in which there could be no orderly fighting. Warner's men held the left of an irregular American line, with an extremely steep hill, called Zion, on their left. Francis had the right upon a smaller rise of ground. The whole line extended about half a mile.

Fraser moved to turn the American left, drawing men from his own left to strengthen his right. When he was ready he ordered his grenadiers to go over Zion Hill. It was an almost precipitous ascent. The grenadiers had to sling their muskets, grasp tree branches, bushes, and rocks, and scramble up on all fours. They made it and took a position behind Francis and astride the road to Castleton.[48]

But Francis had adopted Fraser's tactics in reverse. He edged towards the weakened British left. Some of Hale's men were now coming back to fight. The firing was heavy. Major Acland commanding the British grenadiers had been wounded. That movement of the grenadiers around Francis had yielded no good results. The situation for the British was worse than unpromising. In his desperation Fraser was about to order a bayonet charge when there broke on the ears of all the combatants a surprising sound of fifes and hautboys, trumpets and drums playing a German hymn, and of hundreds of lusty German voices singing it. It was the equivalent of the Scottish pipes at Lucknow. The Brunswicks were coming![49]

Riedesel had heard the firing and had come on with the same advance guard as on the day before. The rest of his troops were following. At Castleton, St. Clair also had heard it. Two of his militia regiments, with their customary freedom from restraint, had dropped away from his marching men the night before and had encamped only two miles from Hubbardton. He sent them orders to go to the aid of Warner and Francis. They refused and hurried on to Castleton.[50]

Without waiting for the rest of his men, Riedesel sent his jägers straight against the American right. The grenadiers, he ordered to try to turn that flank. The jägers, with a band ahead playing as if on parade, marched boldly forward. Francis's troops held their ground for ten minutes, firing as fast as they could in reply to the Brunswickers' volleys. But the turning movement had begun to envelop their right. Francis was shot down, and when Fraser's bayonet charge developed, the Massachusetts men broke and disappeared in the woods. Warner and his Vermonters had been doing well, but when their companions retreated, they could hold out no longer. Warner gave the order, "Scatter and meet me at Manchester." His force at once evaporated. Twelve guns were taken by the enemy.[51]

There had been sharp fighting in that little forty-minute battle. The enemy lost 15 officers and 183 men, killed or wounded.[52] The American casualties, including those captured, were 12 officers and 312 men, out of a force which after Hale's defection did not much exceed 600 fighting men. Hale and about 70 of his men were captured in their retreat. Though of miniature dimensions, that battle was, in proportion to the numbers engaged, as bloody as Waterloo.

In the meantime, the American fleet was pursuing a leisurely course up the lake for Skenesboro. There was no hurry. There was behind them that boom of great logs strung along a massive chain made of inch-and-a-half iron bars. This was backed by a bridge supported by twenty-two piers of timber. Between these piers were floats fifty feet long and thirteen feet wide made of logs "fastened together by rivetted bolts and double chains." It would take some time to cut through that. Colonel Long, in command of the boats, was sure he had a day's start, so he wasted no effort on trying to block the extremely narrow and, in places, tortuous channel.[53]

But he was mistaken in his confidence in the boom. Immediately on the discovery of the retreat from Ticonderoga, British gunboats were brought up, "a few well directed cannon-shots broke in two the collossal chain upon which so many hopes had hung." [54] The bridge piers were cut through. Within a few hours after Long's boats had started, the British fleet was running before a northerly wind up the lake after them. Long's men had landed at Skenesboro at one o'clock. At three o'clock Burgoyne was within three miles of them.

He landed three regiments with orders to get across Wood Creek, a small stream on which Skenesboro was situated and a part of the water road to the south, flowing into the extreme upper end of Champlain just above the mouth of South Bay. They were also to occupy the road to Fort Ann, the only other avenue of retreat to the south. After waiting awhile to give time for this operation, Burgoyne went on with his fleet to attack Skenesboro.

Long, however, had wisely decided that the weak stockaded fort at that place was not tenable against the strong force of the enemy and had sent his invalids and women up the creek, with enough sound men to row the boats. With the rest, he set about destroying the fort. The stockade, the barracks, and other buildings were set on fire. Burgoyne arrived in time to capture the *Trumbull* galley and the schooner *Revenge*, but the *Enterprise*, the *Liberty*, and the *Gates* and everything else combustible that had been brought from Ticonderoga went up in flames. What would not burn was abandoned, and Long, with the remains of his soldiers, about 150, hurried away down the Fort Ann road.[55]

Assuming that the three regiments already sent forward had gained their desired positions to intercept Long's retreat, Burgoyne dispatched Lieutenant Colonel Hill with the 9th Regiment after him early the next morning. But the three regiments were so delayed in getting over a thickly forested ridge that Long got to Fort Ann without interruption. Hill, however, pushed on after him.[56]

The road was in dreadful condition, and its bridges had been broken down. Hill made only ten miles that day. He lay that night within a mile of the fort. Early the next morning an American came to the camp, announced himself as a deserter, and told Hill there was a garrison of a thousand in the fort. Hill had but 190 of all ranks. He sent to Burgoyne for reinforcements.

The "deserter" got away secretly and told Long of Hill's weakness. Long had, indeed, received an addition, 400 New York militiamen under Colonel Henry Van Rensselaer. He now turned on Hill, whose force lay in a narrow, heavily wooded space between Wood Creek and a steep, almost precipitous, rugged ridge.

There was no possibility of regular battle formation on either side. Parties of the Americans crossed the creek and fired on Hill's left, crossed it again, and gained his rear. Although their voices were audible, they were invisible. All he knew was that he seemed to be surrounded. He ordered his men up the steep slope that hemmed them in. With great difficulty they got up, faced about, and held the ridge for about two hours of fairly heavy fire on both sides. Hill's ammunition was running low. Nothing had been heard from Burgoyne. He was about at the end of his tether, when from the woods to the north he heard an Indian war whoop.[57]

The Americans heard it too. It meant to them the arrival of British reinforcements from Skenesboro, and they started for Fort Edward. But they were deceived: there were no Indians behind that war whoop, and only one Englishman, Captain Money. He had been sent ahead with a party of

Indians, who "either stood still or advanced very slow." He had therefore run ahead and tried his luck with that one wild outcry.[58]

When St. Clair, with his main force at Castleton, got word of the disasters at Skenesboro and Hubbardton, there was nothing to do but try to save the remains of his army. He turned to the east and, unmolested, took a straight road to Rutland. Thence, by a circuitous route, he got to Fort Edward on the 12th.[59]

Bennington

While his advance troops under Fraser, Riedesel, and Hill were engaged with the Americans at Hubbardton and near Fort Ann, Burgoyne at Skenesboro was preparing to continue his-southward march. He had the choice of two routes. He could return to Ticonderoga, get his boats over into Lake George, and march his army to Fort George at the head of that lake. Thence he could march by a tolerable road ten miles to the Hudson at a point a little above Fort Edward. This way, in his "Thoughts" on the war delivered to the King in February, he had declared to be "the most expeditious and commodious route to Albany."

The other way was up Wood Creek from Skenesboro to Fort Ann, thence by road sixteen miles to Edward. This route he had predicted would offer "considerable difficulties, the narrow parts of the river may be easily choked up and rendered impassable; and, at best, there will be necessity for a great deal of land-carriage for the artillery, provisions &c." [1] Yet he now chose that route.

The principal reason he gave for this choice was his fear of the harmful impression which "a retrograde motion is apt to make upon the minds both of enemies and friends." [2] But it is thought that his decision may have been the result of the advice of Philip Skene.

Skene, formerly an officer in the British army, had obtained grants of 34,000 acres of land at the head of Lake Champlain, had founded a colony there, Skenesboro, and engaged in divers industries, operating limekilns, forges, sawmills, and a shipyard, with much success. In 1775, when Ticonderoga was taken by Allen and Arnold and he was dispossessed, he man-

417

aged to get to Canada. Now with Burgoyne, he acted as a general adviser on the state of the country, with which he was so well acquainted. Under such conditions, coupled with his personal characteristics—he was "a large, fine-looking person, with a pleasant countenance and affable deportment" [3] —he had much influence with the general. His reason for using his influence in favor of the Skenesboro route is believed to have been the fact that it would require the cutting of a road from his colony to the Hudson, which would be of very great value in the event of the recovery of his property after the war. At all events, for this reason or another, Burgoyne so decided.

He did, however, also decide to send his gunboats, his artillery, and his heavy stores in boats by way of Lake George to its head.[4] That lake being more than 200 feet higher than Champlain, its waters descended through the narrow gorge that connected the two in a series of falls and rapids against which boats could hardly be propelled. It was necessary to carry his bateaux and barges around by land about three miles, a difficult and slow operation.

From the 9th of July until the 25th, Burgoyne's right wing, his British troops, lay on the heights at Skenesboro; his left, the Germans under Riedesel, about ten miles away at Castleton, with Fraser's corps between.[5] The disposition of the German troops was intended to confuse the Americans as to the next move, whether down the Hudson or east to the Connecticut River country. The long delay at this time was caused by the activities of the Americans on the road to Fort Ann and so to Fort Edward.

Schuyler, in general command of the American northern army, had come up from Albany to Fort Edward; and thence on the 8th, as has been said, he had sent Van Rensselaer and his 400 New York volunteers to reinforce Long at Fort Ann. He had at his own post six or seven hundred Continentals and about 1,400 militia. With this puny force, he could not hope to cope with Burgoyne's army, more than three times as large and many more times as strong in fighting quality, equipment, and supplies.

The fort itself was a miserable affair, a dilapidated relic of the French and Indian War.[6] Schuyler wrote to Washington that he had often jumped his horse over the remains of its ramparts. It had some guns, but they lay about on the ground; there were no carriages to mount them. Its garrison, 100 men, was in a sad condition. Not only small, but discouraged by defeat, it was out of hand that its members committed "the most scandalous depredations" [7] on the countryside. It was so short of ammunition that there were but five musket cartridges for each man. If Burgoyne had sent

Fraser's light troops forward, without the encumbrance of artillery or wagon trains, he could easily have taken that pretense of a fort. The Americans had only one circumstance in their favor, the character of the country through which Burgoyne had to march, between Skenesboro and Fort Edward, and through which the British supplies and stores had to be carried, between Fort George, at the head of Lake George, and Fort Edward.

The roads connecting those points were mere traces cut through a primeval forest of enormous pines and hemlocks. They seldom ran straight for any considerable distance. Innumerable huge, fallen trees, "as plenty as lamp-posts upon a highway about London," [8] interrupted their course, and the roads swung around them in a succession of zigzags. The way from Skenesboro to Fort Edward ran in the valley of Wood Creek and, for the most part, close beside the stream. It crossed no fewer than forty deep ravines over which high and long bridges had been built. There were also numerous bogs and swamps. The spring had been unusually wet, and the rains still fell, so that the soil was saturated and the morasses were deep and wide. At one place, if the artillery and wagons were to be got through, it would be necessary to build a causeway or corduroy road two miles long. Such a country afforded opportunity for the creation of almost insurmountable impediments, and Schuyler started to create them.

He put a thousand axmen to work. They destroyed every bridge and dug ditches to carry water from the bogs so as to create new swamps. They felled trees along the Skenesboro road and the creek so that the trunks crossed them both from each side, the tops coming together in a stiff entanglement. The creek itself was choked by great rocks rolled down from its bordering hillsides.[9] He sent out other men to warn the few inhabitants to drive their cattle out of reach of the invaders, to remove or conceal their foodstuffs. They were even induced to burn their unharvested grain. The whole country within reach of the roads was reduced to desolation.

Even without this extraordinary destruction, the passage of the British army, its guns, and its wagons over the roads would have been most difficult. It was sadly short of draught cattle. Of the 1,500 horses Burgoyne had asked for in Canada, no more than 500 had been furnished. On his way, he had managed to commandeer 50 teams of oxen, an insufficient supplement.[10] And the Canadian country carts which he had were ramshackle affairs built of green wood and likely to fall apart under any heavy strain. Under these conditions, the roads in their usual state, and the frail bridges, would have been bad enough to daunt an invader. Now, and until all Schuyler's work had been undone, progress was impossible. But Burgoyne was not stopped.

Into that jungle of obstructions he sent hundreds of his men, expert Canadian axmen among them. Working under the most difficult conditions, tormented by millions of "moschetoes" and gnats—"punkies," the natives call them—in the stifling, sultry heat of the close woods, they hacked away at the trees, drained the bogs, rebuilt the bridges, and made that two-mile causeway. By July 25 he was able to leave Skenesboro and advance to Fort Ann. Four days he lay there while his men worked on the road ahead of him. At last on the 29th, three weeks from the day he landed at Skenesboro twenty-three miles away, he came to Fort Edward.[11]

In the meantime, Schuyler had been reinforced. The remains of St. Clair's force had come in on July 12, as has been stated. Long's detachment, from Ticonderoga, had arrived. Brigadier General John Nixon with 600 Continentals had come on from Peekskill. There were now nearly 2,900 Continental rank and file and more than 1,600 militia, present and fit, in and about the fort.[12] To support the general, who was disliked and distrusted by the New England troops, Washington had sent two Yankee major generals, Benedict Arnold of Connecticut and Benjamin Lincoln of Massachusetts. But even with these acquisitions Schuyler and his generals knew they could not hold that dilapidated fort. Leaving a small rear guard to take care of it until the enemy came, he fell back down the Hudson, first about five miles to Moses Creek, then to Saratoga; at last, on August 3, he reached Stillwater, twelve miles farther. Here Kosciuszko laid out the works of a defensive position, and entrenchment was begun. But within a few days Schuyler again withdrew twelve miles down the river to the mouth of the Mohawk.

The morale of the Connecticut troops was now at its lowest ebb. Continued retreats in the face of a continually advancing enemy, and their sad physical condition, were enough to undermine their confidence in themselves as well as in their leaders; but more active causes of discouragement were working among them. There was a growing belief, now really a full-grown belief, that both Schuyler and St. Clair were not merely incompetent, but actually traitorous.

The most ridiculous of the stories bandied about in the camp was that Burgoyne had bought both generals by firing into Ticonderoga "silver balls," which had been gathered up by St. Clair and sent down to Schuyler: that explained the surrender of Ticonderoga and the subsequent evacuations and retreats. Absurd as the story was, the New Englanders, in their dislike of Schuyler as a New York aristocrat, seem to have believed it, or at least affected to do so. The plague of desertion, to which the American troops, especially the militia, were so subject throughout the war, became an epidemic. Two hundred men were missing between the 20th and 24th of July. By the 4th of August as many more had gone. Of the remaining 4,000, fully a third were Negroes, boys, or old men. And at that time Burgoyne was only a long day's march, twenty-four miles, from Stillwater.

After their slow and enormously difficult march from Skenesboro, the British troops were in high spirits. That terrible wilderness was behind them. Before them the Hudson, a sweetly flowing river, led to their grand objective, Albany. "They considered their toils to be nearly at an end; Albany to be within their grasp, and the adjacent provinces certainly reduced." [13] That they had to wait at Fort Edward for the big guns, the munitions and supplies, and the boats to be brought down from the head of Lake George meant nothing. For the rank and file the delay was a welcome vacation. For Burgoyne, however, this was a period of some anxiety. He was not so certain that his troubles were over. And he knew by August 3 that he could expect no help from Howe, unless Washington attempted to help Schuyler. Howe had written to him on July 17: "My intention is for Pennsylvania, where I expect to meet Washington, but if he goes to the northward contrary to my expectations, and you can keep him at bay, be assured I shall soon be after him to relieve you. . . . Success be ever with you." [14] The day that letter was written, Howe's troops were already aboard their transports bound for the Chesapeake. By the time Burgoyne received it, the fleet was south of the Delaware capes.

Burgoyne did not know that, of course; but one thing he did know—that Howe was carrying out the original plan and that Howe was not coming up the Hudson. There would be no meeting of the two forces at Albany during the campaign. In view of the obstacles still to be faced, might it not be wise to abandon the advance, turn about, and march back to Ticonderoga? It might be done safely enough, no doubt. But no. His orders were to march to Albany, and march he would. He put Howe's letter away, told no one about it, not even Riedesel. [15]

Major General Baron von Riedesel had for a long time been worrying about his horseless dragoons. [16] They were not proper foot soldiers. Their costume was sufficient evidence of that. Yet here they were in their stiff leather breeches, [17] their enormous cocked hats, clumping along day after day in their great, clumsy boots over the miscalled roads of this God-forsaken wilderness in a hell of heat, their spurs catching in the underbrush, the ends of their long broadswords clattering over the stones, their heavy carbines, that might have been slung on their saddles, borne on their shoulders. Something had to be done about it.

All along he had been urging Burgoyne to find mounts for them. He was sure horses were to be had over in the Connecticut River valley. At Skenesboro he had proposed an expedition into that country by the dragoons and the Tories of the army. Burgoyne had approved the plan, but had been too busy with his arrangements for pushing on southward to do anything about it. Now, at Fort Edward, the matter came up again, and Burgoyne and Riedesel drew up the orders for the expedition. These were very specific and very elaborate.

Lieutenant Colonel Baum, who could not "utter one word of English," was to lead the foray—a most unsuitable leader of an enterprise that was to penetrate enemy country and enlist the services of English-speaking people. Its objects and purposes were manifold. Baum was "to try the affections of the people, to disconcert the councils of the enemy, to mount Riedesel's dragoons, to compleat Peters's corps [of Tories] and to obtain large supplies of cattle, horses and carriages," specifically 1,300 horses, besides those for the dragoons. They were to be "tied together by strings of ten each, in order that one man may lead ten horses." To get this loot, he was to impose taxes in kind upon the several districts and to hold "the most respectable people" as hostages for their delivery. He was also to make prisoners of "all persons acting in committees, or any officers acting under the directions of Congress, whether civil or military." [18]

The country to be subjected to this drastic treatment extended from Manchester in the north through Arlington to Bennington in the south, and as far east as the Connecticut River. The whole process was to be effected by a force of 650 rank and file, made up of 170 dismounted Brunswick dragoons, 100 German grenadiers and light infantry, 300 Tories, Canadians, and Indians, 50 of Fraser's British "marksmen," and a few artillerymen with two small fieldpieces. [19] In the orders, it was called "a secret expedition." To help to preserve its secrecy, a German band of musicians was included in the outfit. It seems not to have occurred to Burgoyne that sending such a force upon such an expedition was likely to result in another retreat from Concord.

To assist Baum with advice and to help him "distinguish the good subjects from the bad," [20] Burgoyne added Colonel Philip Skene to the party. His advice, given at a crucial moment, had much to do with the outcome of the excursion.

Burgoyne knew that the remains of Colonel Seth Warner's regiment had gathered at Manchester in obedience to their commander's last order at Hubbardton; but he thought it "highly probable" that they would retreat before Baum. If they did not, he left it to Baum's discretion whether he should fight them or not, "always bearing in mind that your corps is too valuable to let any considerable loss be hazarded." But, besides Warner's men, there were others of whom the British and German generals were ignorant.

The country lying west of New Hampshire had long been claimed by that colony and by New York. It had been settled under grants of land made by the governor of New Hampshire and was therefore called the New Hampshire Grants. Its settlers, the Green Mountain Boys, had long defended their land titles against New York's pretensions. Now, in 1777, it had declared itself the independent State of Vermont and organized a Council of Safety as a preliminary to establishing a regular government. Threatened with invasion by Burgoyne, its council called on New Hampshire and Massachusetts for help.[21]

New Hampshire had already taken notice of the impending danger to itself and had proposed to raise troops for its own defense; but it was thinly settled and poor, so that the problem of the expense of an armed force seemed difficult of solution. It was solved by John Langdon, the speaker of the General Court. "I have," said he, "three thousand dollars in hard money. I will pledge my plate for three thousand more. I have seventy hogsheads of Tobago rum, which shall be sold for the most it will bring. These are at the service of the State. If we succeed in defending our homes, I may be remunerated; if we do not, the property will be of no value to me. Our old friend Stark, who so nobly sustained the honour of our State at Bunker's Hill, may be safely entrusted with the conduct of the enterprise, and we will check the progress of Burgoyne." [22] So goes an old, if not true, story.

John Stark had served in the French and Indian War as a captain in the famous Rogers' Rangers. He had instantly responded to the Lexington alarm, raising a regiment with which he gallantly and successfully defended the American left wing at Bunker's Hill. He had led a regiment to Canada in May, 1776, as a part of the force sent by Washington to succor the defeated American army. In the battles of Trenton and Princeton, he had fought courageously and effectively. He was a brave, a gallant soldier, experienced in warfare, and a great leader of men, with a colonel's commission dated January 1, 1776. Yet, when the politicians in the Congress, in April, 1777, appointed new brigadier generals, they jumped certain junior colonels over his head, as over Arnold's. A proud man, tenacious of his rights and jealous of his honor as a soldier, Stark then resigned his commission and retired to his farm in New Hampshire. But now, at the call of his state, he came forward.

Tall, straight, and sinewy as an Indian, his figure was that of a fighting man. His strong nose, high cheekbones, weathered countenance lit up by steady and piercing light blue eyes, the straight, set line of his thin lips all indicated a character in keeping with his figure. They indicated also that unyielding spirit which in his New England is sometimes characterized as "cantankerous." [23]

Yes, he would take command of the proposed new brigade, but on one condition; it was to be a New Hampshire brigade pure and simple, independent of the Congress and of the Continental army, accountable only to the General Court of the state. The Congress he heartily disliked. Schuyler, he both disliked and distrusted. He would have nothing to do with either. Those were his terms. It was a case of take him or leave him. They took him, commissioned him a brigadier general, and gave him power to direct his operations according to his own judgment.

The response of his fellow citizens to his call was immediate and beyond expectation. On July 18, the day after his commission was signed, 221 men enlisted; the next day, although it was Sunday, the rolls bore the names of 419. Within less than a week, the brigade numbered 1,492 officers and men, 10 per cent of all the enrolled voters in the state, old and young. They had no uniforms and brought their own muskets or fowling pieces.[24]

By July 30, Stark had his command sufficiently organized and equipped to march it to Charleston on the east side of the Connecticut River. In the first week of August, he crossed the river and took post at Manchester, Vermont, where Seth Warner's scattered Vermonters had come together again. Here he had his first and his decisive clash with Schuyler, that disliked and distrusted New York general.

Schuyler was willing that Warner's regiment should remain in Vermont while it was uncertain whether Burgoyne would go south by the Hudson or turn east into the Connecticut valley. He even reinforced Warner with some New England militia and sent Major General Lincoln over there to command them, but he wanted this new brigade of Stark's to strengthen his own weak army. Through Lincoln, he directed Stark to join him.[25]

Stark's reply was prompt and definite. He was, he said, a New Hampshire brigadier, responsible only to its General Court, and by it he had been given a free hand in the conduct of his brigade. No, he would not go to the Hudson on order of Schuyler or anyone else except the General Court of New Hampshire.[26] Lincoln reported this insubordination to the Congress, and it resolved to inform New Hampshire that its orders to Stark were "destructive of military subordination" and to request it to instruct Stark "to conform himself to the same rules which other general officers of the militia are subject to, whenever they are called out at the expence of the United States." [27] But, before that resolution reached New Hampshire, certain events had occurred that caused the Congress to pass other resolutions of a different tone.

On August 8, Stark marched his men twenty miles south to Bennington, where an important depot of American military supplies was situated, leaving Warner at Manchester with the remains of his regiment and 200 rangers whom he had gathered in since Hubbardton.

Three days later Baum's expedition started from Fort Miller, seven miles down the Hudson from Fort Edward.[28] Just as he was leaving, Burgoyne changed his orders. Instead of Manchester, his first objective was to be Bennington, of whose treasures in the way of supplies, cattle, and horses, Burgoyne had just received an exaggerated report.[29] He had also heard that the place was held only by three or four hundred militia. All this was very promising for the success of the enterprise.

After a march of four miles Baum camped on the Batten Kill, a little tributary of the Hudson. There 50 Brunswick jägers came up to be added to his force. On the 13th he marched through a notch in the ridge between Batten Kill and the Hoosic River and down to the village of Cambridge on the Owl Kill.

He had much trouble with his Indians. Preceding the main body, they ran wild, looting and destroying property, killing cows for the sake of their bells and so alarming the country that the inhabitants drove off their horses and cattle instead of leaving them where Baum might have picked them up. There were several light skirmishes with small parties of the local militia, but at Sancoick's—or Van Schaick's—mill on Owl Kill he had his first contact with the American organized troops.

Stark, hearing of the Indian depredations, had sent Colonel Gregg, with 200 men, against them. Gregg was now in posession of the mill.[30] At Baum's approach, the Americans fired one volley and retreated. Baum pursued them. They broke down a bridge, delaying the Germans and ensuring their own escape. Baum had learned that a force stronger than a few militia was at Bennington. He sent a letter back to Burgoyne, announcing the capture of flour, wheat, and potash at the mill, and telling him that fifteen to eighteen hundred rebels were in Bennington, but were "supposed to leave at our approach." He would "fall on the enemy to-morrow early." [31]

Stark, in the meantime, had heard that a strong enemy force was following the Indians, and had set out to rescue Gregg, having first called on Warner at Manchester to join him. About four miles west of Bennington, the opposing forces sighted each other and halted. Between them were the Walloomsac River and a bridge.[32] Baum did not seem disposed to attack, and so Stark withdrew two or three miles towards Bennington. Baum took a position on a height above the river.[33] Both forces bivouacked on the night of the 14th.

The 15th was rainy, and no move was made by either side, except that Baum disposed his troops to meet an expected attack. Stark, however, was reinforced by 400 Vermont militia, also a party from Berkshire County, Massachusetts, and some Stockbridge Indians. He had then about 2,000 men. Baum was strengthened by the arrival of 90 Tories under "Colonel" Pfister, a retired British lieutenant.[34] His force then numbered about 800.

The German dragoons and half of Fraser's contingent were posted on the steep hill where they had encamped, which looked down from a height of 300 feet upon the bridge half a mile away. Trees were felled to make breastworks and one of the two 3-pounders was mounted there. In some log cabins on both sides of the bridge the Canadians were stationed. On the hither side of the bridge the other half of Fraser's force and about 50 German infantrymen, with the other gun, took their stand. In a field southwest of the principal position 50 German foot soldiers and some Tories were supposed to guard the rear of that group. About 250 yards to the south and beyond the bridge 150 Tories were posted and threw up a breastwork. Southeast of the hilltop the 50 jägers were placed. The Indians were grouped on a plateau behind the main position. Having thus scattered his men as effectively as possible all over the landscape—some of the little detachments more than a half-mile from the others—Baum awaited Stark's move.

That move was concerted between Stark and Warner, who had come from Manchester in advance of his regiment. They made a rather elaborate plan. It involved complete encirclement of Baum's main position and simultaneous attacks on his front, rear, and flanks. It was carried out without a flaw.

About noon on the 16th, the rain having ceased, Colonel Moses Nichols with 200 New Hampshire men started on a long circuit to get around Baum's left. Colonel Samuel Herrick led 300 men, Vermont Rangers and Bennington militia, similarly to turn the German right. Colonel David Hobart and Colonel Thomas Stickney, with 200 men, were to go against the Tory position south of the bridge. A hundred more were to demonstrate against the front of the main position to divert Baum's attention. Stark was to hold the remaining twelve or thirteen hundred for the principal frontal attack, the signal for which was to be the first fire by Nichols and Herrick.[35]

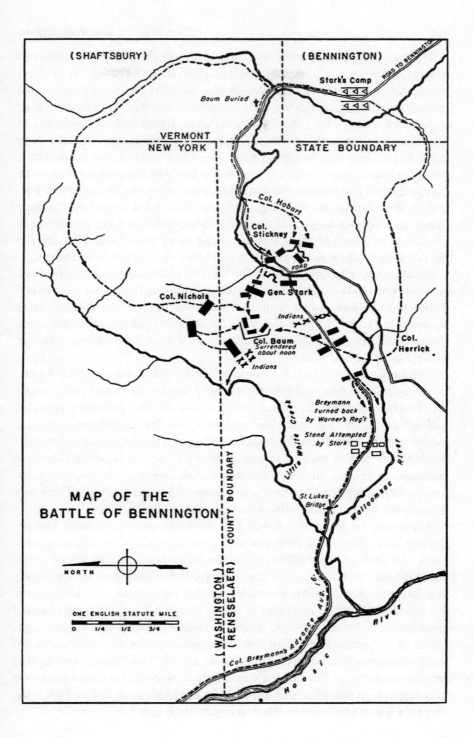

(SHAFTSBURY)   (BENNINGTON)

ROAD TO BENNINGTON

Stark's Camp

Baum Buried †

VERMONT
NEW YORK   STATE BOUNDARY

Col. Hobart

Col. Stickney

FORD

Col. Nichols   Gen. Stark

Indians

Col. Baum
Surrendered
about noon   Col.
Indians   Herrick

Little White Creek

Breymann
turned back
by Warner's Reg't

Stand Attempted
by Stark

Walloomsac River

St. Lukes
Bridge

MAP OF THE
BATTLE OF BENNINGTON

NORTH

ONE ENGLISH STATUTE MILE
0   1/4   1/2   3/4   1

(WASHINGTON)
(RENSSELAER)   COUNTY BOUNDARY

Col. Breymann's Advance Aug. 16.

Hoosic River

The two encircling detachments made their way through the thick woods without discovery until they had nearly reached Baum's rear. Then the Germans saw several small, irregular bodies of shirt-sleeved farmers, with muskets or fowling pieces on their shoulders, but with no other military appearance, coming up behind them. At once, Baum bethought himself of the valuable advice which Skene, now absent from the camp, had been delegated to give him and had given him. The inhabitants of that countryside, Skene had said, were Tories five to one. On the march to Bennington, small groups dressed like these newcomers, had sifted in among Baum's men, protesting their loyalty to the King, and had been kindly received.[36] These others now approaching must also be friends, either seeking protection in his rear or prepared to assist him. He made no effort to keep them off. On the contrary he drew in his pickets so that they should not be molested.

By three o'clock Nichols and Herrick had gained satisfactory positions. Nichols opened fire, followed by Herrick. On hearing this signal Hobart and Stickney went into action against the Tories beyond the bridge. Stark mounted his horse and gave the order for the principal frontal attack. "See there, men!" he cried. "There they are! We'll beat them before night, or Molly Stark will be a widow." [37]

The Tories beyond the river put up a fight for a few minutes. The Americans waited until one volley had been fired against them and then, before the Tories could reload, rushed the breastworks. Its defenders retreated pellmell down into the little river and across it. The Canadians in the log cabins and the Indians on the plateau, yelling and jangling their stolen cowbells, simply fled at the first sound of the musketry. St. Luc La Corne, in command of the Indians, and Charles de Lanaudière, his son-in-law, in command of the Canadians led their contingents in headlong retreat. There was nothing left but the main position on that steep and high hill.

The attack on that position was fiercely made and stoutly met. The defenders, those Brunswick dragoons with their heavy rifles, the British marksmen, and such of the fugitives from the other posts as had joined them, stood off the encircling foes in the open ground in their rear with a steady fire. In front, the assailants scrambled up that high, steep hill, taking cover behind rocks and trees and firing at will so fast that their gun barrels burned their hands. Some of the New Hampshire militia crept up to within a dozen yards of the artillery and shot down the gunners. For two hours this hot fight went on—"the hottest I ever saw in my life" said Stark, and he had been through many. Then Baum's fire began to slacken; his ammunition was running low. When what was left of it, in a wagon, took fire and blew up, the fight seemed to be over. But it was not quite ended.

Though the rest of his command broke and fled, Baum's dragoons still stood by him. He called for their swords. They drew those fearful weapons to cut their way through their enemies. The Americans had no bayonets to oppose them. The dragoons made a steady, if lumbering, progress through the swarming Americans, the shirt-sleeved farmers who circled around, closed in, fell back, and closed in again; but when Baum fell, fatally wounded, his men gave up the fight.[38]

Now it seemed that nothing remained but to comb the woods for more prisoners and loot the German camp. But there was yet other work to be done. Baum had sent Burgoyne a second note on the evening of the 14th asking for reinforcements,[39] and Burgoyne had ordered Lieutenant Colonel Breymann, with 642 men and two fieldpieces, to march to Baum's support. They set out at eight o'clock in the morning of the 15th. The roads were deep with mud, and a hard rain was falling. The heavily uniformed and equipped Germans were notoriously slow in movement. They had twenty-five miles to go. In rigid, regular formation, halting frequently to re-dress their ranks, they progressed at the rate of half a mile an hour,[40] making only eight miles that day. A courier was sent forward to tell Baum that they were coming, and they bivouacked for the night.

The next day, the day of the battle, they crawled on at the same rate, to reach Sancoick's mill at half-past four, with six miles yet to go. There Breymann received vague and confused reports of the fight. A little later, Stark had word of Breymann's coming.

He had promised his men the spoils of victory, and they were scattered widely among the various enemy positions gathering up their plunder. He rallied as many as he could and sent them back along the road to delay Breymann.

Breymann, pushing on from Sancoick's mill, met the first party of Americans within a mile. It was merely a disorganized body of shirt-sleeved men carrying guns. Skene, who had gone back to meet Breymann, assured him that they were friendly Tories. But when they took a position behind a rail fence on a height by the road and fired a ragged volley, killing Breymann's horse, he had his doubts. He sent a detachment to dislodge them.[41]

From that time on, there was a series of such skirmishes. Three times the Americans took positions on the high ground north of the road, fired into the solid German column, and retreated when hard-pushed. But the Germans moved steadily, if slowly, forward.

Stark was in a bad way. His men were still scattered, still busy looting, and he could assemble only a small part of them. It seemed that he would have to give way and leave the field to the enemy. But Warner encouraged him to hold on.[42] Help was coming from Manchester. Before sunset it arrived.

The rest of Warner's regiment, 130 men led by Lieutenant Colonel Samuel Safford, and 200 rangers, had made a long day's march until midnight. They came on the next day, but slowly, halting to dry their muskets when the rain stopped, again to draw ammunition at Bennington, again to put aside their coats and knapsacks, again to receive a ration of rum, again to quench their thirst with water. But they came to the battlefield at last and went on to meet Breymann a mile or so beyond it.

By this time Stark had collected a good number of his men. He joined Warner. At first they took an unfortunate position in low, swampy ground devoid of cover; but after a few shots they withdrew to a wooded hill north of the road. Breymann attacked. He tried a flanking movement to turn the American right and began to gain ground. But half of Warner's men outflanked and checked the flankers. Meanwhile the rest of Warner's men, with Stark's troops, stretched out to threaten the Germans' right. The fight then went on face to face.

Breymann's two 6-pounders were active. The musketry was continuous and heavy. About sunset his men, who had carried forty rounds,[43] had almost exhausted their ammunition; but the American fire was still sustained. Breymann gave up, ordered a retreat. Many of the artillery horses had been shot. The rest were exhausted. The Germans abandoned their guns, and started west along the road in good order. Those that still had cartridges answered the shots of pursuing Americans. But their pace was slow. The enemy was on their flanks and at their heels, still relentlessly firing. The ordered ranks became confused in the haste to get away, broke up into a pushing, shoving disorder. In the gathering dusk, the retreat became a rout.

Some of the Germans threw down their muskets and ran. Others held them out, as if to surrender them. They dropped out, kneeled down, and cried for mercy. Breymann's drums beat a parley, a call to a conference for a surrender. But the untutored Americans did not know its meaning. To them it was just drums beating. They kept on shooting.

Breymann had been hit in a leg, and there were five bullet holes in his coat, but he held together a small rear guard, himself the last man, and so kept his men going in the increasing darkness. When it was quite dark, Stark called off the pursuit. Breymann, with less than two-thirds of his men, got away. "Had day lasted an hour longer," said Stark, "we should have taken the whole body of them."[44]

It was a notable little battle in that a body of farmers, for the most part entirely inexperienced in warfare, had so decisively beaten two forces of trained, professional soldiers. It is true that in the first fight Stark outnumbered Baum more than two to one; but that was not an overwhelming advantage when the experience and training of the Germans is considered. In the second the preponderance of the Americans in number was much less. Their lack of organization and their fatigue after hours of fighting reduced their advantage practically to zero.

Of the Germans, 207 were left dead on the field; about 700, including 30 officers, were captured. The spoils were rich: four brass fieldpieces, twelve drums, two hundred fifty broadswords, four ammunition wagons, and several hundred muskets and rifles. The Americans lost about 30 killed and 40 wounded.[45]

On October 4 the Congress unanimously voted its thanks to Stark and his men, and appointed him a brigadier general in the Continental army.[46]

Notes

CHAPTER 1

The best general accounts of the Anglo-American crises, 1763–1775, are to be found in Channing, III, Van Tyne, *C,* and Miller, *O.* Miller, *T,* is the most recent account of the period of the Revolutionary War.

1. Belcher, I, 134.
2. Frothingham, *S,* 6.
3. *Massachusetts Spy,* May 19, 1774. Frothingham, *S,* 6. A Boston Tory wrote to a friend in London: "You nor your friends must not imagine there was any honesty in those marks of joy these Bostonians showed the General on this occasion—no sir, it was hypocrisy all" (Force, 4, I, 299 n.).
4. For Gage's personality and career see Alden, *passim.*
5. For a brief discussion of the Sugar Act see Lecky, 55–58.
6. Bancroft, III, 77.
7. For the Stamp Act see MacDonald, 122–131.
8. Bancroft, III, 245.
9. Bancroft, III, 238.
10. MacDonald, 107.
11. Fiske, I, 82.
12. Frothingham, 299.
13. Grahame, IV, 328.
14. Ramsay, I, 129.
15. Frothingham, 305.

CHAPTER 2

1. Frothingham, *S,* 37; Bancroft, IV, 19; Force, 4, I, 669.
2. Gage was astonished at the support given the Bostonians indicating the solidarity of the colonies. "I find," he wrote in September, "they have some warm friends in New York and Philadelphia . . . that the people of Charleston are as mad as they are. . . . This province is supported and abetted by others beyond the conception of most people, and foreseen by none."
3. Bancroft, IV, 95.
4. Force, 4, I, 768. Cf. Trevelyan, I, 317.

5. Frothingham, *S*, 113; Stiles, I, 510–511.
6. Adams, *J*, 31.
7. Percy, 46; Barker, 12; Stiles, I, 503; Force, 4, I, 1041–1043, 1054; Gordon, I, 422.
8. Frothingham, *S*, 48; Stiles, I, 523; Gordon, I, 470.
9. Trevelyan, I, 258.
10. Force, 4, III, 1330.

<h2 style="text-align:center">CHAPTER 3</h2>

Fortescue and Curtis are very useful upon the make-up of the British army; French, *C*, and French, *F*, upon that of the American forces.

1. Stiles, I, 515; Barker, 13; Force, 4, II, 441; Frothingham, *S*, 46, 55; Murdock, *B*, 5; French, *F*, 89. Belcher, I, 151, mentions two other regiments, the 29th and 40th, but indicates in a table of the services of the various regiments that the 29th had its first service with Burgoyne in 1777, and the 40th at Long Island in 1776.
2. The regiments so raised bore the name of the colonel up to 1751, when George II gave them numbers. In 1782 they received the names of counties. Thus one such regiment was originally Greville's, then the 10th, then the Lincolnshire Regiment.
3. Smollett in *Humphry Clinker* pictures an officer who, having purchased an ensigncy, had risen in thirty years' service only to the rank of lieutenant, because he had no money to buy promotions.
4. Frothingham, *F*, 99, 102–103; Belcher, I, 249–252, 259. Belcher states that three British regiments were made up entirely of men who had been in prison.
5. Sydney, 346.
6. Belcher, I, 251–252.
7. Belcher, I, 281–282.
8. Belcher, I, 322–325; Lefferts, 148–168. Lefferts's plates show crossbelts, but Fortescue, III, 542, says that it was not until after the return of the army from America that the waist belt was transferred to the right shoulder, thus originating the crossbelt, and Belcher, I, facing 323, shows the infantryman before 1783 with one shoulder belt and after that date the crossbelts.
9. Fortescue, III, 543; Sawyer, 93.
10. Sawyer, 100.
11. Trevelyan, I, 211.
12. Sawyer, 98–100; French, *C*, 28 n.
13. French, *C*, 32–35, citing Bland's *Treatise on Military Discipline* (London, 1753), the British manual of 1764, and Timothy Pickering's *Easy Plan of Discipline for a Militia* (Salem, 1775).
14. French, *F*, 34.
15. For the history of Massachusetts militia and the minutemen see French, *F*, 32–46, and the numerous citations; also *D.A.H.*, III, 413, and French, *C*, 17. The term "minutemen" goes back at least to 1756, when a company of Massachusetts soldiers called themselves "Minnit men." French, *F*, 33.
16. French, *F*, 41 and note, telling of the participation of the alarm companies in the fight at Concord.
17. Adams, *J*, 65–66. A recent apologist (Anderson, 76) for General Howe's conduct of the war attributes the lack of success of his frontal attack at Bunker Hill to the fact that "the men who lined the parapet . . . carried rifles, for the most part, instead of muskets . . . the rifle was vastly superior to the musket in precision. The men who used it on this occasion had acquired their proficiency in the hunting field." Which, he says, "the British command apparently failed to realize." The "fact" was not realized, because it was not a fact. There were no riflemen in the American troops in Massachusetts at that time, nor were there any until July–August, 1775, when 1,400 of them from Pennsylvania, Maryland, and Virginia, under Thompson, Cresap, and Morgan, joined Washington at Cambridge. Before that time, it is quite possible that there was not one rifle in

all Massachusetts (French, *C*, 28). The lack of rifles in New England could be deduced from the fact that, although between 1600 and 1800 many gunsmiths were making muskets in that territory, a single rifle maker is known to have been north of Pennsylvania prior to 1783 (Sawyer, 153–157, 216–219).
18. Sawyer, 132–136.

CHAPTER 4

This account of the affair at Lexington has been drawn from the many sources individually cited below. A complete reconciliation of discrepancies has been impossible—for instance, between the blindly patriotic Coburn and the more broad-minded French and Murdock, and between the monographs of Elias Phinney and Ezra Ripley, champions respectively of Lexington and Concord in the great dispute between the two towns in 1825 for the honor of having been the scene of the first "battle" of the war. In that contest the affidavits of many survivors of April 19, 1775, taken at a later time were marshaled, their recollections differing in many respects from the statements of the ninety-eight survivors of the day whose affidavits were taken by the Provincial Congress within the week following the 19th. These may be found in Force, 4, I, 486–501. The truth is often not easily found.

1. French, *C*, 39.
2. Trevelyan, I, 331–333.
3. Barker, 27–28; French, *C*, 41.
4. French, *C*, 51–52; Coburn, 15.
5. Barker, 29.
6. French, *C*, 65.
7. French, *C*, 66.
8. French, *C*, 75.
9. Coburn, 17; Stedman, I, 119; Frothingham, *S*, 59.
10. Phinney, 15; Ripley, 11; Coburn, 18.
11. Coburn, 22–24; French, *C*, 77–80. The lanterns were seen by British soldiers in Boston. They found the sexton of the church and arrested him, but let him go when he denied all knowledge as to who had displayed them. Pulling, disguised as a sailor, escaped from Boston in a fishing boat to Nantucket and was careful not to return until the British had left (Coburn).
12. French, *C*, 69–70; Murdock, 22. Why a major of marines was detailed to lead a detachment of infantry is a mystery. It is said, without definite authority, that it was because he was familiar with the roads to Concord and had studied the town in disguise. (French, *C*, 70.)
13. Stiles, I, 575, says 600 officers and men; Barker, 31, says "about 600"; Evelyn, 53, says "near 700"; Gordon, I, 477, says 800, "the flower of the army." According to French, *C*, 73, the last is generally accepted by American historians; but Murdock, 48 n., thinks 600 the proper number.
14. French, *C*, 100–101; Coburn, 19; Barker, 31–32; Force, 4, I, 360–364. It seems probable that the march from Lechmere began at one o'clock, to give time to reach Lexington at sunrise (Murdock, 50).
15. Coburn, 30–31; French, *C*, 90–91; Phinney, 16.
16. Coburn, 24–29; French, *C*, 91–94.
17. Coburn, 47–57; French, *C*, 102.
18. Coburn, 60; French, *C*, 95–96.
19. Coburn, 61; French, *C*, 97.
20. French, *C*, 107.
21. French, *C*, 95–99. Heath, 6, says: "This company standing so near to the road, after they had certain notice of the advancing of the British in force, was but a too much braving of danger; for they were sure to meet with insult, or injury which they could not repel. Bravery, when called to action, should always take the strong ground on the basis of reason."
22. Coburn, 63. As to the weather see Murdock, 55, quoting a contemporary diary

23. Stiles, I, 604–650. Lieut. Barker, who was with Pitcairn, says (p. 32) the Americans "fired one or two shots, upon which our Men without any orders rushed in upon them, fired and put 'em to flight."
24. Barker, 32; Murdock, 24, 39.
25. Stiles, I, 604–605.
26. Murdock, 22.
27. Murdock, 37.

CHAPTER 5

In the main, the story of Lexington and Concord follows two excellently documented accounts. Coburn's *The Battle of April 19, 1775,* is an exhaustive study of both original and secondary materials. It is full of detail and is copiously annotated. French's *The Day of Concord and Lexington* is more discursive, less intimately factual, but is very valuable for its more impartial and less chauvinistic viewpoint. Besides these, the journals and letters of Stiles, Barker, Evelyn, Mackenzie, and Percy, the accounts of Ripley, Phinney, and Reynolds, Frothingham's *History of the Siege of Boston,* and the affidavits and letters, especially the letter of Rev. William Gordon, published in Force, 4, II, have been carefully studied. Murdock's *The Nineteenth of April, 1775,* is an illuminating discussion of the day's events, viewed with detachment and a healthy incredulity as to many generally accepted beliefs concerning certain aspects of the conflict, although his arguments seem at times to be rather casuistic.

1. Coburn, 32–46.
2. French, *C,* 149–151, 156. Rev. William Emerson was the grandfather of Ralph Waldo Emerson and the builder of Hawthorne's Old Manse.
3. Ripley, 21; Frothingham, *C,* 179.
4. French, *C,* 152, map.
5. French, *C,* 156–158.
6. French, *C,* 161.
7. Barker, 32; Stedman, I, 117.
8. French, *C,* 163. Emerson's diary is owned by the Emerson family. French obtained a copy of it; the quotations herein are drawn from his book.
9. French, *C,* 164; Reynolds, 17; Coburn, 75; Ripley, 16.
10. French, *C,* 164–165; Ripley, 17.
11. French, *C,* 177; Coburn, 77; Ripley, 19.
12. French, *C,* 167–182; Coburn, 77; Ripley, 19–20.
13. French, *C,* 186–187; Coburn, 81; Ripley, 18.
14. Coburn, 82–83; French, 187–190.
15. Barker, 34.
16. Barker, 34.
17. French, *C,* 191, 201 n.; Coburn, 84–85; Barker, 35.
18. French, *C,* 207–209; Coburn, 85, 88; Ripley, 28.
19. Coburn, 93; French, *C,* 217. At the bridge, after the fight, occurred one of the most lamentable incidents of the day. A half-grown boy, armed only with a hatchet, hastening after the Americans, found a severely wounded British soldier struggling to his knees. Conceiving it to be his duty to kill the enemy, the boy sank the hatchet in the skull of the wounded man. When Parsons's men came that way from Barrett's place, they found the dead man, his head covered with blood, and reported that he had been scalped and his ears cut off. The story spread; Gage published it; it got to England; and, though the true story was soon made known, the false one persisted. Stedman in his history (I, 119), published in 1794, wrote: 'Several of Smith's party were scalped by the Americans." In 1841, Adolphus in his history wrote that "several were scalped or had their ears cut off by the Americans" (French, *C,* 211–214). And even as late as 1911 Fortescue (III, 153) wrote that "a few of the dead and wounded had been scalped by some rough Americans at the bridge."

20. Coburn, 96–97, Supplement, 14–38.
21. Coburn, 98; French, *C*, 219.
22. French, *C*, 219.
23. Force, 4, II, 359.
24. Barker, 35. A British soldier wrote to his family, "They did not fight us like a regular army, only like savages" (Force, 4, I, 440).
25. French, *C*, 222; Coburn, 107. The pistols are preserved by the Lexington Historical Society.
26. Barker, 35.
27. French, *C*, 224.
28. French, *C*, 224.
29. Coburn, 114.
30. French, *C*, 226–227.
31. Percy, 49; Mackenzie, I, 19. Murdock, 47 n., thinks they were not more than 900.
32. French, *C*, 229 n. Percy had a low opinion of the colonials. He wrote home (Percy, 31, 35, 52): "The people here are a set of sly, artful, hypocritical rascalls, cruel & cowards. . . . I cannot but despise them completely. . . . Such a set of timid creatures I never did see." A similar opinion was general among the British officers in America before Bunker Hill. Captain Glanville Evelyn about this time wrote to his father that he believed "there does not exist so great a set of rascals and poltroons" (Evelyn, 27).
33. Coburn, 116–120; French, *C*, 230.
34. Percy, 50.
35. Mackenzie, I, 19.
36. Barker, 35.
37. Stedman, I, 118.
38. Mackenzie, I, 20.
39. Percy, 50.
40. Coburn, 133–134; Trevelyan, I, 335.
41. Barker, 36. On p. 39 Barker states that the British soldiers on the 19th, "tho' they shew'd no want of courage, yet were so wild and irregular, that there was no keeping 'em in order . . . the plundering was shamefull; many hardly thought of anything else; what was worse they were encouraged by some Officers." Mackenzie, I, 21–22, confirms the forcing of houses, killing, and plundering, but says the officers tried to stop the looting.
42. Heath, 7–8, says he did form one regiment in Lexington, "which had been broken by the shot from the British field-pieces"; but there seems to be little or no evidence that they continued to operate as a unit.
43. Coburn, 150–154; Mackenzie, I, 21. Lieutenant Barker, 36, says of the change in route that it threw the colonials off the scent.
44. Percy, 50; French, *C*, 255 n.; Coburn, 157–160.
45. Heath, 11.
46. Percy, 53.
47. Barker, 37.
48. Evelyn, 53.

CHAPTER 6

1. Force, 4, II, 363–370; French, *F*, 23–24; Jones, I, 39–40. Gage sent a ship to England with the news of Lexington and Concord. Within a week after the battle the Committee of Safety gathered the depositions of ninety-two Americans, one British officer, and two privates, prisoners, all of whom had taken part in the hostilities. The gist of the affidavits was that the British had fired first at both places (the officer could not say who had begun it at Lexington, but admitted the charge as to Concord). A letter was written to "The Inhabitants of Great Britain," giving the story of the day, briefly describing "the ravages of the Troops," protesting against the measures pursued by the British government, but declaring that "they have not yet detached us from our Royal Sovereign." This,

438   *The War of the Revolution*

with the depositions, was dispatched in a light, fast vessel belonging to Richard
Derby of Salem and commanded by his son John. Although it sailed four days
after Gage's ship, it carried only ballast and it reached England twelve days
sooner.

The news flew about London. The King refused to believe "an American
newspaper," the *Essex Gazette*, which went along with the other papers. The
ministry announced that there was no such official news. Nevertheless, the
American report obtained wide credence, and though Gage's dispatches, when
they arrived, minimized the affair as much as possible all England knew that a
war was on, and that it would take more than Gage's little army to fight it.
(Force, 4, III, 437–438; 489–501, 945; French, *F*, 131, 313–316.)

2. Bancroft, IV, 170; French, *F*, 83. Romantic though this story about Putnam be,
   it is generally accepted by other historians, of cooler blood than Bancroft. For
   the disturbance in New York, see Jones, I, 39–41.
3. Bancroft, IV, 170.
4. French, *F*, 31, 50, 52, 62; Bancroft, IV, 170; Force, 4, II, 378–379, 384, 446–447.
5. Force, 4, II, 765; Heath, 11.
6. Force, 4, II, 1145; French, *F*, 77–78.
7. Force, 4, II, 655; Bancroft, IV, 174.
8. Force, 4, II, 411; Bancroft, IV, 174–175; French, *F*, 85.
9. French, *F*, 66, 72.
10. Frothingham, *S*, 99; French, *F*, 86.
11. Gordon, I, 492; Force, 4, II, 1122, 1142.
12. Gordon, I, 492; Force, 4, II, 820; French, *F*, 179–182.
13. French, *F*, 184; Barker, 50–52.
14. Heath, 10; French, *F*, 183; Barker, 50–52.
15. Force, 4, II, 370–814. French, *F*, 123–124; Frothingham, *S*, 93–96; Barker, 38,
    44; Stiles, I, 541.
16. Lushington, 50, 52; Barker, 38. Burgoyne wrote that the fresh provisions
    smuggled into the town "were of great consequence to the health and spirits both
    of army and inhabitants; the former live entirely on salt meat, and I hardly dare
    to guess how some of the latter live at all" (Fonblanque, 151).
17. French, *F*, 188–189; Barker, 48–49; Frothingham, *S*, 108; Barker, 49.
18. French, *F*, 190–191; Frothingham, *S*, 109.
19. Force, 4, II, 719; French, *F*, 191–193; Frothingham, *S*, 109–110; Barker, 50–53.
20. Barker, 38–41; French, *F*, 163–166; Harris, 51.
21. This enumeration of regiments may not be exactly correct. There has not been
    found a complete list of an official character. This one has been made up by
    comparing statements in Fortescue, Belcher, Murdock, *B*, Drake, Swett, Clarke,
    and others. Swett includes the 14th Regiment, but without support elsewhere
    except that Drake mentions "One officer of that regt a volunteer" as having been
    killed at Bunker Hill and one wounded who may have been on detached service.
    There were but three companies of the 18th and six companies of the 65th.
    These were combined into an Incorporated Corps. Careful calculations in
    Murdock, *B*, 7, and French, *F*, 737–739, seem to fix the number correctly between
    6,340 and 6,716, not including officers.
22. Partridge, *passim*; Wilkin, 6–24; French, *F*, 195–198; Trevelyan, I, 308. Anderson,
    T, *passim*, gives a more favorable estimate of Howe's military ability.
23. Wilkin, 46–73; French, *F*, 198–199.
24. Hudleston, *passim*; French, *F*, 199–200; Fonblanque, 136–159.
25. Force, 4, II, 968–970.
26. French, *F*, 204, quoting London *Evening Post*, July 18, 1775.

CHAPTER 7

The material for a story of the capture of Ticonderoga and Crown Point is to be
found mainly in original documents printed in Force's *American Archives*, 4th
Series, Vol. II, and in *Conn. Hist. Soc. Colls.*, Vol. I. Allen French's *The First Year of*

the *Revolution* and *The Taking of Ticonderoga in 1775* give well supported accounts of the expedition and its results. Arnold's *Life of Benedict Arnold* and Pell's *Ethan Allen* are valuable secondary sources.

1. Greene, FV, 101; French, *F*, 143.
2. *D.A.H.*, V, 268; Pell, 74.
3. Force, 4, II, 243–244; French, *F*, 145–146; Pell, 72. Carleton had in Canada only two regiments of infantry and two companies of artillery; these were widely scattered. French, *F*, 147 n.
4. Pell, *passim; D.A.B.*, I, 185; Lossing, I, 180; Tyler, II, 229; French, *F*, 148–149; Irving, 1, 442–443.
5. Arnold, 36.
6. French, *F*, 149–150.
7. Force, 4, II, 450.
8. Force, 4, II, 485, 750.
9. Van Doren, 145–150; Arnold, 17–29.
10. *Conn. Hist. Soc. Colls.* I, 165–169, 181; Chittenden, 100; Force, 4, II, 556, 557; Dawson, I, 32. The committee says they had 70 men from Massachusetts and 140 from the New Hampshire Grants. Other reports make the force 40–50 and 100; but Mott's letter to the Massachusetts Provincial Congress indicates that there were 170 in all.
11. Philip Skene, an officer in Amherst's army of 1759, had obtained a grant of 30,000 acres at the head of navigation of Lake Champlain and had established there a considerable settlement, with a great stone house, mills, docks, and stores (Pell, 90–91).
12. Pell, 79–80; Force, 4, II, 558; *Conn. Hist. Soc. Colls.*, I, 119, 179.
13. Dawson, I, 23; Lossing, I, 124; *Conn. Hist. Soc. Colls.*, I, 171–172.
14. Force, 4, II, 558; *Conn. Hist. Soc. Colls.*, I, 172.
15. Force, 4, II, 557, 734; *Conn. Hist. Soc. Colls.*, I, 165 ff.; Pell, 81; Gordon, II, 12. Allen French (French, I, 28), who has made a special study of this expedition, is inclined to believe that Arnold did secure joint command with Allen.
16. Pell, 82; Force, 4, II, 1086. French, *T*, 151, says there were nearly 300 men at the cove.
17. Pell, 83; Dawson, I, 34. A different report as to what happened after they landed on the beach may be found in two letters to newspapers that are re-printed in Force, 4, II, 1086–1087. James Easton in the first letter described the affair without even mentioning Arnold's name. "Veritas" wrote to another paper that, instead of two boats, there was but one, in which "Colonel Arnold with much difficulty persuaded 40 men to embark with him"; then he sent it back for "near 50" others. When they landed "some gentleman" proposed "to wait open day. This Colonel Arnold strenuously opposed and urged to storm the fort immediately, declaring he would enter it alone, if no man had courage to follow him. This had the desired effect. . . . Colonel Arnold was the first that entered the fort." Pell (p. 104) thinks "Veritas" was Benedict Arnold himself.
18. Pell, 83–84.
19. Pell, 84–85; Force, 4, II, 623, 624–625.
20. Lossing, I, 125. It is interesting to note that Allen's words have been taken as evidence of his orthodox theological beliefs, whereas, in fact, he was a confirmed deist. Did he use them?
21. Force, 4, II, 556. Pell, 90, preserves the original spelling.
22. Force, 4, II, 557.
23. Pell, 92–93; Force, 4, II, 584.
24. Force, 4, II, 584, 645, 686, 734; Pell, 95–96; French, *F*, 153.
25. Force, 4, II, 645, 693, 734, 839, 840; Pell, 96–99.
26. Force, 4, II, 693, 714–715.
27. Force, 4, II, 892.
28. *Journals*, II, 55–56.
29. Force, 4, II, 732–735. 847. 892, 1066; French, *F*, 154.

30. Force, 4, II, 605–606, 623–624, 705, 706, 711, 713, 715, 719, 720, 721, 730, 735–737, 808, 869, 944, 1382; *Journals*, II, 74.
31. Force, 4, II, 1539, 1593, 1596, 1598, 1649.
32. Force, 4, II, 646.

CHAPTER 8

1. Frothingham, *S*, 114 n. "Elbow-Room" clung to him as a nickname. When he came to Boston as a prisoner after Saratoga, it is said, an old woman in the crowd cried out: "Make way! Make way! The General's coming! Give him elbow-room!"
2. Dawson, I, 66–68.
3. Force, 4, II, 1354; Frothingham, *S*, 116.
4. Frothingham, *C*, 14–15; Frothingham, *S*, 119–120; Ellis, 12; Swett, 16.
5. Ellis, 17; Frothingham, *C*, 10; Martyn, 117–119. Swett (p. 15) gives a graphic picture of this council, which he describes as "Gen. Putnam's statement to his son." He represents Ward and Warren as objecting because "the enterprize would lead to a general engagement." To which Putnam answered that they would risk only 2,000 men and "defend ourselves as long as possible, and, if driven to retreat, . . . every stone wall shall be lined with their dead, and at the worst, suppose us surrounded and no retreat, we will set our country an example of which it shall not be ashamed." Warren, it seems, "walked the floor, leaned on his chair, 'Almost thou persuadest me, Gen. Putnam,' said he, 'but I still think the project rash.' " Pomeroy, to the objection as to the lack of powder, answered that he "would fight the enemy with but five cartridges apiece." Putnam said of him that he was used to going out with three charges of powder and bringing home "two and sometimes three deer." Putnam and Pomeroy were much alike in their disregard of all the basic rules of warfare.
6. Martyn, 91; French, *F*, 49, 83.
7. Tarbox, 320–322; Field, 221–222; *D.A.B.*, XI, 281; Humphreys, *passim*; French, *F*, 214.
8. Swett, 19; Frothingham, *S*, 167; Martyn, 119.
9. Frothingham, *W*, *passim*; Bancroft, IV, 230; French, *F*, 120.
10. Frothingham, *S*, 121–122; Frothingham, *C*, 16–17; Swett, 15–16; Dawson, I, 71.
11. Swett, 16; Ellis, 22; Frothingham, *S*, 122; Dawson, I, 51, 71.
12. Frederic Kidder, *The History of New Ipswich* (1852), 95.
13. Dawson, I, 52; Frothingham, *S*, 122–123; Coffin, 31.
14. Frothingham, *S*, 123, 393–395; Ellis, 23; Swett, 20. The Committee of Safety afterwards stated that Breed's Hill was fortified "by some mistake," which was certainly not the case. It was the deliberate choice of the officers.
15. Frothingham, *S*, 135; Swett, 20.
16. Swett, 21; Ellis, 26; Frothingham, *S*, 124–125.
17. Frothingham, *S*, 125; Ellis, 27–28; Heath, 12; Force, 4, II, 1093.
18. French, *F*, 216; Coffin, 9.
19. Swett, 22; Murdock, *B*, 3, 12–14.
20. Stiles, I, 595; Frothingham, *S*, 126; Ellis, 28.
21. French, *F*, 217.
22. Frothingham, *S*, 127; Swett, 23.
23. Trevelyan, I, 353; French, *F*, 219; Ellis, 23; Swett, 22.
24. Frothingham, *S*, 128; Swett, 24–25; Ellis, 31.
25. Swett, 28; French, *F*, 217–218; Ellis, 31; Heath, 11; Frothingham, *S*, 130 n.
26. Murdock, *B*, 10–11; French, *F*, 220–221; Swett, 23; Ellis, 29–30; Fortescue, III, 158; Trevelyan, I, 353.
27. Murdock, *B*, 11–12; French, *F*, 222.
28. French, *F*, 222.
29. Murdock, *B*, 15–17; French, *F*, 740. Stedman, I, 128, says they carried three days' provisions.

30. Frothingham, *S*, 131; Force, 4, II, 1093; Trevelyan, I, 352.
31. Ellis, 33; Frothingham, *S*, 131.
32. French, *F*, 225; Ellis, 34.
33. Coffin, 16; Swett, 26; Ellis, 31; Dearborn, 16.
34. French, *F*, 225–226; Frothingham, *S*, 132; Dearborn, 17; Frothingham, *C*, 33.
35. Frothingham, *S*, 134, 390; French, *F*, 219; Drake, 17; Coffin, 17; Swett, 26–27; Force, 4, II, 1094.
36. Frothingham, *S*, 134–135; Coffin, 11, 17; French, *F*, 227.
37. French, *F*, 227–228, 741–742.
38. This disposition of the forces in the various parts of the defense is made by Frothingham, *S*, 135–136. He admits that there is no certainty as to its correctness. Some of the troops mentioned may have arrived on the field after the action began. Some regiments were dispersed in companies or smaller parties in all parts of the defenses. The disposition here shown can be only a more or less close approximation of the facts.
39. Frothingham, *S*, 136.
40. Irving, I, 475; Ellis, 38; French, *F*, 225; Frothingham, *S*, 133.
41. Ellis, 37; French, *F*, 229; Frothingham, *S*, 133.
42. Murdock, *B*, 21; French, *F*, 231.
43. Murdock, *B*, 22–23; Force, 4, II, 1089; French, *F*, 231. Landing parties also set fire to some of the houses. Force, 4, II, 1376.
44. French, *F*, 234.
45. Frothingham, *S*, 137.
46. Frothingham, *S*, 138–140; French, *F*, 234; Swett, 290.
47. French, *F*, 233–234; Murdock, *B*, 24–26; Belcher, I, 196.
48. French, *F*, 234–235; Murdock, 27. Stedman, I, 128, says the British carried 125 pounds per man.
49. Murdock, *B*, 27.
50. Dawson, I, 66–67, quoting Burgoyne's letter of June 25, 1775, to Lord Stanley. Fonblanque, 155, contains a letter to Stanley much the same in substance but strikingly different throughout.
51. Force, 4, II, 1098; Belcher, I, 196–197.
52. French, *F*, 237; Coffin, 12; Drake, 32.
53. French, *F*, 238; Belcher, I, 174; Frothingham, *S*, 141.
54. Frothingham, *S*, 142–143.
55. French, *F*, 239.
56. Frothingham, *S*, 146.
57. Frothingham, *S*, 389–391.
58. Frothingham, *S*, 147; French, *F*, 244.
59. Force, 4, II, 1662.
60. French, *F*, 243.
61. French, *F*, 243.
62. French, *F*, 247.
63. Drake, 28.
64. Frothingham, *S*, 150; French, *F*, 249; Drake, 28.
65. Frothingham, *S*, 150–151.
66. French, *F*, 250.
67. Coffin, 13, 14, 19, 30.
68. French, *F*, 252; Frothingham, *S*, 152.
69. Frothingham, *S*, 153, 210; French, *F*, 255.
70. Clarke, 5 n.; Frothingham, *S*, 152; French, *F*, 261.
71. Clarke, 13; Percy, 56; Trevelyan, I, 359; Force, 4, II, 1098.
72. Frothingham, *S*, 193; French, *F*, 263.
73. Fonblanque, 157; French, *F*, 218, 240; Frothingham, *S*, 138, 146, 152, 185; Swett, 36. Reports as to the number of guns vary between two small brass and six iron fieldpieces; five cannon and six swivel guns; six fieldpieces. The last is probably correct.

74. Force, 4, II, 1097.
75. Frothingham, S, 154.

CHAPTER 9

1. Journals, II, 79, 84, 85, 89, 91.
2. Adams, L, 65; Adams, J, II, 415.
3. Fitzpatrick, III, 292–293.
4. Journals, II, 97, 103.
5. Journals, II, 100–101.
6. Adams, L, 59, 70.
7. Jones, I, 55–57; Force, 4, II, 1318.
8. Force, 4, II, 1084–1085; Fitzpatrick, III, 302–304.
9. Fitzpatrick, III, 320.
10. See notes of contemporaneous references to assumption of command in French, F, 299.
11. Force, 4, II, 1472–1473.
12. Fitzpatrick, III, 371, 374.
13. French, F, 300.
14. Reed, I, 243.
15. Graydon, 147–148.
16. Fitzpatrick, III, 339, 357, 362.
17. French, F, 300.
18. Fitzpatrick, III, 325, 387, 389, 404, 415, 422, 445, 511; Frothingham, S, 891; Conn. Hist. Soc. Colls., II, 254.
19. Fitzpatrick, III, 308; Force, 4, II, 1625, 1629.
20. Fitzpatrick, III, 355–356.
21. French, F, 301.
22. This survey of the early commissariat has been derived from the study of it by Victor L. Johnson.
23. Journals, II, 100.
24. Fitzpatrick, III, 324, 409.
25. Fitzpatrick, V, 192.
26. Journals, II, 89, 104, 173; Bancroft, IV, 247–248; Pennsylvania, I, 3–5.
27. Thacher, 31; Gordon, II, 68; Frothingham, S, 228 n. Their shirts are variously described as white, ash-colored, and brown.
28. Sawyer, 34–37, 80, 144–153.
29. Fitzpatrick, III, 367; Reed, I, 117.
30. Pennsylvania, I, 9–10.
31. French, F, 472.
32. See letters to Congress and the colonies in Fitzpatrick, III and IV, especially IV, 288; Reed, I, 118, 119.
33. French, F, 272 n.; Trevelyan, I, 406.
34. French, F, 321.
35. Frothingham, S, 316, 331.
36. Frothingham, S, 224–230; Pennsylvania, I, 21.
37. Frothingham, S, 226–227, 230–231.
38. Fitzpatrick, III, 453.
39. Frothingham, S, 234; French, F, 481; Pennsylvania, I, 6.
40. French, F, 482–483; Frothingham, S, 265, 267; Fitzpatrick, IV, 118; Barker, 66; Evelyn, 74–75; Moore, I, 166–167.
41. Trevelyan, I, 408.
42. Sparks, L, I, 156.
43. Fitzpatrick, III, 483–484.
44. Fitzpatrick, III, 511; Force, 4, III, 767–768.
45. Journals, III, 273–274.
46. Force, 4, III, 1153; Frothingham, S, 257.
47. Fitzpatrick, III, 505–513.

48. *Journals*, III, 265–266.
49. *Journals*, III, 321–323.
50. French, *F*, 365–366; Force, 4, III, 263–266, 354; *Journals*, II, 189.
51. French, *F*, 364, 370; Force, 4, II, 1118.
52. Force, 4, III, 1416; Fitzpatrick, III, 467.
53. French, *F*, 371–375; *Journals*, III, 278–279, 486.
54. Frothingham, *S*, 261, 269, 272, 289, 308; French, *F*, 370–372, 497; Evelyn, 72–73. For particulars of many captures, see the index to Fitzpatrick, IV, under the names of captains.
55. Trevelyan, I, 385.
56. French, *F*, 533–534.
57. Evelyn, 67.
58. Trevelyan, I, 386.
59. Frothingham, *S*, 281–282; French, *F*, 534–535.
60. French, *F*, 533, 536; Frothingham, *S*, 280, 287.
61. Trevelyan, I, 386; Frothingham, *S*, 294.
62. French, *F*, 332.
63. Fonblanque, 148.
64. Force, 4, III, 927.
65. Force, 4, III, 7.
66. Force, 4, III, 642.
67. Force, 4, III, 642, 1671.
68. Trevelyan, I, 396–397; Frothingham, *S*, 293.
69. Frothingham, *S*, 275.
70. *Journals*, III, 321–324; Fitzpatrick, III, 390.
71. Fitzpatrick, III, 391.
72. Fitzpatrick, IV, 77; French, *F*, 510.
73. *Journals*, II, 220, III, 322, 393; Force, 4, IV, 1245.
74. Frothingham, *S*, 276.
75. Fitzpatrick, IV, 60.
76. French, *F*, 520.
77. Fitzpatrick, IV, 208.
78. Force, 4, III, 1666–1667.
79. Fitzpatrick, IV, 137, 142, 146; Sullivan, I, 29–30; Frothingham, *S*, 273.
80. *Conn. Hist. Soc. Colls.*, VII, 128.
81. Fitzpatrick, IV, 124, 240.
82. Sullivan, I, 130.
83. Fitzpatrick, IV, 156–157, 138 n.
84. Fitzpatrick, IV, 211; Heath, 28.
85. Fitzpatrick, IV, 202, 210.
86. Stephenson, I, 339.
87. French, *F*, 630.
88. Fitzpatrick, IV, 122.
89. Fitzpatrick, IV, 238, 242.
90. Fitzpatrick, IV, 241–242.
91. Force, 4, IV, 699.
92. Fitzpatrick, IV, 319, 243–244; Frothingham, *S*, 287–288 and n.
93. Duer, 124–125.
94. Brooks, *passim*; Fitzpatrick, IV, 74.
95. Fitzpatrick, IV, 93.
96. Sparks, *C*, I, 94–95; French, *F*, 525–526, 655–656; Brooks, 38–44; Heath, 30; Greene, *GW*, III, 94.

CHAPTER 10

1. Fitzpatrick, IV, 336.
2. Fitzpatrick, IV, 314; Dawson, I, 87 n.
3. Force, 4, IV, 1539, 1636.

4. Fitzpatrick, IV, 335; Frothingham, *S*, 290; Dawson, I, 86.
5. Dawson, I, 85–87.
6. Fitzpatrick, IV, 348.
7. See map in Sparks, *W*, III, facing p. 26.
8. French, *F*, 656; Heath, 32–33.
9. Fitzpatrick, IV, 373; Frothingham, *S*, 297; Greene, FV, 19; Gordon, II, 190.
10. Barker, 69.
11. Fitzpatrick, IV, 370; Gordon, II, 191–192; Frothingham, *S*, 297.
12. Gordon, II, 193; French, *F*, 660; Frothingham, *S*, 298; Heath, 32.
13. Gordon, II, 193.
14. Dawson, I, 94.
15. Robertson, 74.
16. Frothingham, *S*, 298.
17. Fitzpatrick, IV, 375; Frothingham, *S*, 298–299.
18. *Orderly Book at Charlestown, Boston, and Halifax, June 17, 1775 to 1776, 26 May* (London, 1890), 71, 313.
19. Gordon, II, 195.
20. Frothingham, *S*, 299; Heath, 33.
21. *Mass. Hist. Soc. Colls.*, 4, I, 261.
22. Heath, 33.
23. Gordon, II, 196; Fitzpatrick, IV, 380.
24. *Orderly Book at Charlestown, Boston, and Halifax, June 17, 1775 to 1776, 26 May* (London, 1890), 313; Robertson, 74.
25. Fitzpatrick, IV, 371–377; Frothingham, *S*, 303–304.
26. Frothingham, *S*, 305; Heath, 34.
27. Frothingham, *S*, 302 n.
28. Trevelyan, I, 435.
29. Fitzpatrick, IV, 444; Frothingham, *S*, 302.
30. Robertson, 79.
31. Fitzpatrick, IV, 448.
32. Robertson, 75.
33. Gordon, II, 197; Frothingham, *S*, 307 n.; French, *F*, 666–667.
34. Fitzpatrick, IV, 449.
35. French, *F*, 665.
36. Barker, 72.
37. Robertson, 79.
38. Robertson, 81; Fitzpatrick, IV, 403.
39. *Mass. Hist. Soc. Proc.*, XIV, 284.
40. Fitzpatrick, IV, 415, 430.
41. Fitzpatrick, IV, 401, 407, 410.
42. Frothingham, *S*, 311.
43. French, *F*, 345.
44. French, *F*, 356.
45. Fonblanque, 196–197.
46. French, *F*, 540. Howe wrote to Lord George Germain, secretary of state for the colonies, that the expedition "was concerted by the General and Admiral for the destruction of Cape Ann [Gloucester] and Falmouth, two seaport towns, that were distinguished for their opposition to government." But, in reply to Germain's inquiry as to the reasons for destroying Falmouth, Howe wrote some time later that Gage's orders to the soldiers were only to assist Mowat "in annoying and destroying all ships belonging to rebels on the coast and in the harbours to the eastward of Boston." Sparks, *W*, III, 520–521. It would seem that the orders of Graves to the sailors and of Gage to the soldiers differed from each other, and that Mowat acted according to the admiral's directions as to what was to be destroyed.
47. French, *F*, 539–544.

CHAPTER 11

1. Smith, JH, I, 37.
2. This description of the inhabitants of Canada and the effects upon them of the Quebec Act is derived chiefly from French, *F*, 395–399, and Metzger, *passim*. While French estimates the number of Old Subjects at "more than 600," Smith, JH, I, 48, apparently on good authority, says "some 2,000."
3. *Journals*, II, 68–70.
4. *Journals*, II, 68–70.
5. Force, 4, II, 230.
6. *Journals*, I, 82–90.
7. Force, 4, II, 231.
8. *Journals*, II, 75.
9. Force, 4, II, 734.
10. *Journals*, II, 55–56.
11. Force, 4, II, 732.
12. Force, 4, II, 892.
13. *Journals*, II, 105, 123.
14. *Journals*, II, 109–110.
15. This description of Schuyler is derived chiefly from Smith, JH, I, 244–265, and Lossing, *S, passim*. It is possibly too favorable to Schuyler. For interesting materials on Schuyler's patriotism, see Van Doren, 45–47, 51–58, 231, 239–240, 391, 394–395.
16. Smith, JH, I, 320–321, 367–370, 610; Lossing *S*, 393–394; Bancroft, IV, 292, 308. The first news Montgomery's young wife had of his commission and his acceptance of it was conveyed to her when he asked her to make a cockade for his hat. Observing that she wept while she worked on it, he tried to turn her thoughts from danger to glory by saying, "You shall never blush for your Montgomery"—a remark so exactly in accord with the manner of speech of the period that it might have appeared in the pages of Richardson's *Sir Charles Grandison* or *Pamela*. Stilted though it sounds to modern ears, it was a sincere and touching expression of his pride in himself and his affection for her. She never did have to blush for him.
17. Smith, JH, II, 112; Bancroft, IV, 308. Heitman's *Historical Register* accredits Macpherson to Delaware. He had, in fact, been appointed major in Haslet's Delaware Continental regiment in Jan., 1776, before the fact of his death on Dec. 31, 1775, was made known in the colony.
18. Fitzpatrick, III, 302–303.
19. *D.A.H.*, III, 1–4, II, 280; Bancroft, IV, 448–449.
20. *D.A.H.*, I, 1; Reed, I, 119; Smith, JH, I, 275.
21. Smith, JH, I, 177.
22. Force, 4, II, 914, 1670, III, 301.
23. Smith, JH, I, 356.
24. Force, 4, II, 661, 665, 842–843.
25. Force, 4, II, 1140, 669, 1666; Lossing, *S*, 349, 353–356.
26. Force, 4, II, 244.
27. Force, 4, II, 939.
28. Force, 4, II, 1319.
29. Force, 4, II, 1594–1595.
30. Force, 4, II, 1735.
31. Force, 4, III, 26.
32. *Journals*, II, 178–183. The Speech likened the King to a father, the ministry to his servants, and the colonies to his son, carrying a little pack. The "proud and ill-natured servants [become] displeased to see the boy so alert and walk so nimbly with his pack." They advise the father to "enlarge the child's pack." This being done, "the child takes it up again . . . speaks but few words—those very small—for he was loth to offend his father . . . but the proud and wicked

servants . . . laughed to see the boy sweat and stagger under his increased load." They prevail on the father to double the load, saying, "He is a cross child —correct him, if he complains any more." The load is doubled amid "the tears and entreaties of the child," who staggers under the weight, "ready to fall at any moment. . . . He entreats the father once more, though so faint he could only lisp out his last humble supplication—waits a while—no voice returns . . . He gives one more struggle and throws off the pack. . . . The servants are very wroth. . . . They bring a great cudgel to the father, asking him to take it in his hand and strike the child." Thus persuasively were the great issues of the American Revolution described for the Indians.

33. Force, 4, III, 473–496. At a preliminary meeting an Oneida sachem had, toward the end of the day, blandly suggested that "as this day is far spent . . . [and] we are weary from having sat long in council, we think it time for a little drink."
34. Lossing, *S*, 387.
35. Force, 4, III, 1275–1276.
36. Force 4, II, 611; French, *F*, 758.
37. Force, 4, III, 339.
38. Force, 4, II, 714.
39. Smith, JH, I, 603. Later in the war, in 1777, Captain Allen McLane had a number of Oneida Indians in his partisan corps operating between Valley Forge and Philadelphia.
40. Lossing, *S*, 345–346, 352, 358.
41. Force, 4, II, 1685–1686, 1702.
42. Lossing, *S*, 343, 358.
43. Force, 4, II, 1606.
44. Force, 4, II, 1646.
45. Force, 4, II, 1702.
46. Smith, JH, I, 190; Force, 4, II, 1685.
47. Force, 4, II, 1605–1606.
48. Heitman, 291.
49. Force, 4, II, 1667.
50. Force, 4, II, 760, III, 17–18; Pell, 112.
51. Force, 4, III, 95.
52. Force, 4, II, 1535, 1606.
53. French, *F*, 386–387
54. Force, 4, II, 1729, 1734, 1735, 1759, III, 141, 242, 243. Facing a lack of gun-smiths in New York, the Provincial Congress appointed a committee "to write to Great Britain for four complete sets of Lock-Smiths to make Gun-Locks and . . . to pay the passage of Smiths from Britain to America."
55. Force, 4, II, 1704, 1735; Smith, JH, I, 255.
56. Force, 4, III, 135.
57. Force, 4, II, 1730.
58. Force, 4, III, 447, 452; Smith, JH, I, 256.
59. *Journals*, I, 186.
60. Lossing, *S*, 332, 381, 392.
61. Force, 4, III, 18, 126.
62. Force, 4, III, 47.
63. Force, 4, III, 263.
64. Smith, JH, I, 94–103.
65. Force, 4, II, 243, 1729; Smith, JH, I, 93–96, 99–103.
66. Force, 4, III, 135–136.
67. Force, 4, III, 18–19.
68. Force, 4, III, 50, 135, 442.
69. Force, 4, III, 468.
70. Lossing, *S*, 393.
71. Force, 4, III, 442; Smith, JH, I, 317.

CHAPTER 12

1. French, *F*, 381.
2. Force, 4, III, 467; Smith, JH, I, 321.
3. Smith, JH, I, 397, 323.
4. Force, 4, III, 669, 738; Smith, JH, I, 323–324.
5. Force, 4, III, 671, 669; Smith, JH, I, 324.
6. Force, 4, III, 669; Smith, JH, I, 328.
7. Force, 4, III, 669–670, 757; Smith, JH, I, 328–329, 331.
8. Force, 4, III, 752.
9. Force, 4, III, 672.
10. Smith, JH, I, 330.
11. Force, 4, III, 767; Smith, JH, I, 332.
12. Smith, JH, I, 332; French, *F*, 418; Burnett, *L*, I, 143.
13. Force, 4, III, 738–740.
14. Force, 4, III, 738.
15. Force, 4, III, 741–742, 923–924.
16. Force, 4, III, 723–724, 741–742, 923–924; Smith, JH, I, 333–334; French, *F*, 418–419.
17. Smith, JH, I, 334.
18. Force, 4, III, 723–724, 741–742, 923–924.
19. Force, 4, III, 738, 742.
20. Smith, JH, I, 335.
21. Force, 4, III, 697, 739, 753.
22. Smith, JH, I, 345–346.
23. Fortescue, III, 155.
24. Force, 4, III, 925–926; Smith, JH, I, 343–344.
25. Force, 4, III, 726.
26. Force, 4, III, 926; Smith, JH, I, 347–352.
27. Force, 4, III, 779, 797, 923, 980; Lossing, I, 412–414.
28. Force, 4, III, 754; Lossing, I, 415.
29. Force, 4, III, 952, 799, 953; Smith, JH, I, 380–390; French, *F*, 422–424; Allen, 14.
30. Force, 4, III, 951, 963; Smith, JH, I, 410.
31. Force, 4, III, 1124.
32. Smith, JH, I, 445.
33. Force, 4, III, 954, 839, 951.
34. Smith, JH, I, 418.
35. Force, 4, III, 1097–1098.
36. Force, 4, III, 796.
37. Force, 4, III, 459.
38. Force, 4, III, 1093–1094.
39. Force, 4, III, 1107–1108.
40. Force, 4, III, 1131.
41. Force, 4, III, 1095, 1096, 1098.
42. Force, 4, III, 1133–1134.
43. Force, 4, III, 1132.
44. Force, 4, III, 1342, 1392, 1185, 1395.
45. Force, 4, III, 1344, 1391–1394.
46. Force, 4, III, 1343–1344; Smith, JH, I, 464–465; Lamb, 116.
47. Force, 4, III, 1394, for terms of capitulation.
48. Force, 4, III, 1603.
49. Force, 4, III, 1603.
50. Force, 4, III, 1597, IV, 290, V, 1234; Smith, JH, I, 475–477, 483.
51. Smith, JH, I, 490.

CHAPTER 13

The basic material for a narrative of Arnold's march is to be found in the many journals, diaries, and letters written by those who took part in it. Probably no other expedition of similar length made by so few men has produced so many contemporary records. Arnold's journal tells the tale to October 30, where it breaks off abruptly. There may have been more, but no more has been discovered. He also wrote many letters. No fewer than nineteen other accounts by participants are to be found, written by Dearborn, Senter, Meigs, Thayer, Topham, Humphrey, Wild, Ware, Henry, Stocking, Morison, Melvin, Pierce, Tolman, Kimball, Haskell, Fobes, Squier, and one anonymous person. They are of uneven value, as some were compiled from others, and some were written long after the expedition. Many of them are individually printed, but the most convenient access to them may be had in *March to Quebec*, in which Kenneth Roberts has annotated Arnold's journal and letters and twelve of the other more important accounts, as well as Montresor's journal and Enos's defense. In his novel *Arundel*, Roberts follows closely the actual events of the march and illuminates it with his remarkably vivid imagination, re-creating as truly as the novelist can its scenes and characters.

Among the strictly historical accounts, *Arnold's March from Cambridge to Quebec* and *Our Struggle for the Fourteenth Colony* both by Justin H. Smith, are complete, discriminating, and scholarly. *Arnold's Expedition to Quebec*, by John Codman, is more readable but not so accurate in detail. Allen French's account in *The First Year of the American Revolution* is not so full as Smith's, but is equally reliable. Graham's *Life of General Daniel Morgan*, Parton's *Life and Times of Aaron Burr*, Arnold's *Life of Benedict Arnold*, and Gordon's *History of the Rise, Progress and Establishment of the Independence of America* contain valuable material.

To limit the following notes to a reasonable compass, many references to Smith's and Codman's and French's books and to the journals and letters have been omitted.

1. Smith, J, 10.
2. Smith, JH, I, 498.
3. Fitzpatrick, III, 436. Montresor's journey, on which his map was based, had been made in a canoe, not in a bateau, in June and in the opposite direction from the one now proposed. Moreover, much of the most difficult part had been made at night, when he could not see difficulties which he fortunately escaped.
4. Smith, J, 75–76.
5. Fitzpatrick, III, 471.
6. Fitzpatrick, III, 472–473.
7. Parton, *passim*. French, *F*, 433, says of Burr: "Romance and tradition connect his name with that of an Indian girl, Jacataqua, who is said to have followed the expedition, but the historical foundation of the tale is so slight that the girl is not even mentioned by the best modern student of the march."
8. Greene, GW, III, 94–101; Bancroft, IV, 287–288; Henry, 12.
9. Fitzpatrick, III, 491–496.
10. Morison, 13. Humphrey, 8, says the delay was for the purpose of filling up the ranks of the companies.
11. Stocking, 10. Fobes, 10, says the vessels were "dirty schooners and fishing-boats."
12. Force, 4, III, 960.
13. Force, 4, III, 960–961. Whether Natanis was actually in Carleton's pay and inimical to the Americans, or whether he was merely trying to prevent the expedition from intruding on his hunting grounds, is uncertain. His subsequent conduct indicated no unfriendliness to the expedition. On the other hand, he may simply have inclined toward whichever party was, at the moment, the more useful to him.
14. Henry, 23.

15. Arnold had appointed Greene to lead the riflemen; but Morgan, Smith, and Hendricks, especially Morgan, refused to take orders from anyone but himself, nor would the other two willingly subordinate themselves to Morgan. Arnold yielded and gave Morgan a sort of leadership of the others, rather than official command of them. While he did lead them, Smith and Hendricks showed much independence at various times. Washington gently reproved Morgan for taking such an attitude. Fitzpatrick, IV, 2.
16. Force, 4, III, 960.
17. Smith, J, 468.
18. Dearborn, 6.
19. Senter, 8.
20. Smith, J, 469.
21. Smith, JH, I, 537.
22. Dearborn, 9.
23. Senter, 11.
24. Senter, 11–12; Force, 4, III, 1061.
25. Smith, J, 125.
26. Smith, JH, I, 547.
27. Henry, 46.
28. Smith, J, 472.
29. Smith, J, 131.
30. Smith, JH, I, 554.
31. Smith, J, 474.
32. Melvin (Roberts, 439) says that Morgan's men let Greene's division pass them so that they might have a chance to steal some of the provisions, which they succeeded in doing. Hence Greene's unexpected shortage.
33. Senter, 15. It has been said that this was a West Indian hurricane, following the the same course as that of September 22, 1938, and with similar devastating results.
34. Henry, 52.
35. Morison, 25.
36. Smith, J, 478; Force, 4, III, 1610, 1634.
37. Senter, 16–17. On his return to Cambridge, Enos was court-martialed "for quitting his commanding officer without leave." The only witnesses were his own officers, who had retreated with him. They testified that the return was necessary because of lack of provisions, and Enos was acquitted. But within a month he left the army; and he "never survived the stigma of having done a disreputable act." (Henry, 59–63; Force, 4, III, 1701–1721.)

   Yet there is something to be said for Enos. Though to the rest of the expedition, who went on in spite of hardship and starvation, his departure seemed a base and cowardly act, he had a case. One of his descendants, Rev. Horace E. Hayden, has defended him in a rather convincing manner, for which see Roberts, 631–648.
38. Senter, 18.
39. Smith, JH, I, 586. There were two women in the expedition. One was the wife of Sergeant Grier, "a large virtuous and respectable woman." The other, "beautiful though coarse in manner, was the wife of James Warner, a rifleman, young, handsome in appearance . . . athletic and . . . [such as] seemed to surpass in bodily strength." These two "appeared to be much interested in each other's welfare and unwilling to be separated." In the march up Dead River, Warner gave out, seated himself at the foot of a tree, and "said he was determined to die." His wife "attended him for several days, urging him to march forward," but he could not. Stocking says she "tarryed with him until he died, while the rest of the company proceeded on their way." Being unable to bury him, "she covered him with leaves and then took his gun and other implements and left him with a heavy heart. After traveling twenty miles she came up with us." Henry says she stayed until she found her ministrations unable to save him,

then placed her own share of food and a canteen of water at his feet and left him. In either event, she survived the journey and arrived at the St. Lawrence with the others. (Henry, 61, 64–65; Stocking, 21.)

40. Smith, J, 482.
41. Smith, JH, I, 591; Morison, 28.
42. Senter, 23.
43. Henry, 73.
44. Stocking, 34.
45. Morison, 34.
46. Henry, 73–74.
47. The quotation is from Stocking, 23–24. Exactly how many men had survived that march is uncertain. With the volunteers and Colburn's artificers added to the original draft, about 1,100 started. The defection of Enos subtracted possibly 300. A considerable number of invalids were sent back, and with them went sound men to take care of them. Morison, one of the diarists, figures the total loss on this account at 200, which seems excessive. He says that 510 reached the St. Lawrence; hence he concludes that 70 or 80 had been lost on the way. His estimate has been questioned by Justin H. Smith (Smith, J, 233), who reckons the survivors at 675, that being the number of men for whom Arnold drew clothing from Montgomery on December 5. If that be correct and Enos's men are added, making a total of 975, it would appear that no more than 125 all told were lost by death, sickness, desertion, and as able-bodied caretakers of the invalids. As we know that about 70 invalids were sent back from the Dead River alone, in two parties, it seems incredible that no more than 55 were lost otherwise. It seems probable that the arrivals were not much more in number than half of the original party.
48. Joseph Warren wrote to Samuel Adams: "Arnold has made a march that may be compared to Hannibal's or Xenophon's." Thomas Jefferson also thought it equaled Xenophon's retreat. Murray, the English historian, wrote: "The march of Col. Arnold and his troops is one of the greatest exploits recorded in the annals of nations." A letter from Quebec dated November 9 states: "There are about 500 Provincials arrived at Point Levi . . . by way of Chaudiere, across the woods. Surely a miracle must have been wrought in their favour. It is an undertaking above the common race of men." (Force, 4, III, 1420.)

CHAPTER 14

1. Force, 4, III, 1633–1636.
2. Ogden, 24.
3. Morison, 26; Humphrey, 19.
4. Force, 4, III, 1635–1636; Morison, 36; Henry, 81; Senter, 27; Humphrey, 20.
5. Morison, 36; Henry, 82; Force, 4, III, 1724.
6. The estimates of Carleton's force vary slightly. See Force, 4, III, 1697, 1724–1725, IV, 175. But 1,200 seems to be a proper figure.
7. Smith, JH, II, 16 n.
8. Force, 4, III, 1697.
9. Fobes, 17.
10. Dearborn, 13.
11. Ogden, 29.
12. Fobes, 18.
13. Stocking, 26.
14. Humphrey, 24.
15. Henry, 94.
16. Stocking, 26.
17. Henry, 94.
18. Force, 4, IV, 188–193. The archaic sense of "pretty" as defined by *The Concise Oxford Dictionary of Current English*: "fine, stout, as *a pretty fellow*."

19. Justin H. Smith (Smith, JH, II, 90) seems to have supposed that the clothes brought by Montgomery were the conventional uniforms of the British army, scarlet coats and white breeches, for he describes the troops marching back to Quebec as "drawing a long red mark across the snow." Pierce in his journal (Roberts, 689) tells of drawing "red Coats." These may have been undercoats or waistcoats (Smith, JH, II, 90). However, the journal of Captain Pausch of the Brunswickers, who came with Burgoyne (Pausch, 93–94), describes in detail, as given in the text, the uniforms issued to Burgoyne's army for winter service in Canada. Lefferts, p. 160, pl. XXXIII, also describes and pictures them. Henry in his *Account of Arnold's Campaign*, p. 103, mentions his "fine white blanket coat" and his "cap or *bonnet rough*," which exactly accords with the descriptions of Pausch and Lefferts. Pausch tells of these uniforms being made in Montreal, not brought from England. So they were no new thing for Canada; indeed, they were of proper Canadian fashion. As Montgomery had captured a full year's supply of uniforms of the 7th and 26th regiments, they must have included these winter garments. The sealskin moccasins are also described by Henry. They were made "large, and according to the usage of the country, stuffed with hay or leaves to keep the feet dry and warm." These were, doubtless, also a part of the British equipment, for Burgoyne's entire army was taught how to use snowshoes" (Lefferts, 160). It would not have been possible with ordinary shoes or boots. The Americans were not all equipped with these new warm garments until Dec. 29, when final distribution—delayed perhaps by difficulties of transporting all Montgomery's supplies—was made (Humphrey, 24, 26).
20. Force, 4, III, 1595.
21. Sparks, *C*, I, 95.
22. Fitzpatrick, IV, 147.
23. Fitzpatrick, IV, 231.
24. Force, 4, III, 1638.
25. Force, 4, IV, 288.
26. Force, 4, IV, 289; Stocking, 26–27.
27. Force, 4, IV, 289.
28. Force, 4, III, 1638–1639.
29. Stocking, 27.
30. Force, 4, IV, 464.
31. Force, 4, IV, 464; Smith, JH, II, 117.
32. Dearborn, 18.
33. Stocking, 27.
34. Force, 4, IV, 289.
35. Henry, 105.
36. Leake, 127.
37. Force, 4, IV, 706.
38. Senter, 107.
39. Stocking, 29.
40. Henry, 108.
41. Graham, 102.
42. Dearborn, 21.
43. Dearborn, 23; Lossing, I, 200; Force, 4, IV, 656.
44. *Journals*, IV, 70, 78.
45. Smith, JH, II, 352.
46. Smith, JH, II, 406.
47. *Journals*, IV, 394.
48. Fitzpatrick, V, 78–79.
49. Stillé, 31.
50. Force, 4, VI, 1103–1104.
51. Arnold, 94.
52. Smith, JH, II, 434.
53. Smith, JH, II, 441.

CHAPTER 15

1. Fitzpatrick, IV, 407–408, 440, 442, 444, 462, 467; Heath, 32.
2. *Journals*, II, 207, 225.
3. *Journals*, III, 270.
4. *Journals*, III, 321–325.
5. Fitzpatrick, IV, 121.
6. Fitzpatrick, IV, 299–301.
7. Fitzpatrick, IV, 316.
8. *Journals*, III, 285.
9. *Journals*, II, 107, III, 291, 337, 418, IV, 59. These calls on the various colonies are to be found in *Journals*, III, 285, 291, 387, 418, IV, 59, 235, 237, 331, 347, 355, 357, V, 461, 466, 487, 607, 666. The call on Maryland mentions only two regiments, but four regiments and seven independent companies were actually raised. New York raised thirteen, New Jersey three, Pennsylvania twelve including the riflemen, Massachusetts eleven, Connecticut thirteen. Those mentioned in the text include only such as were specifically called for by resolutions of the Congress passed between October 9, 1775, and July 24, 1776. The absence of a call on Connecticut, except for one more regiment (*Journals*, IV, 360), is probably accounted for by the fact that the troops of that colony at Boston were taken into the army at its adoption in 1775. The text, therefore, is not to be taken as enumerating the whole number of regiments included in the army at the time of the Battle of Long Island, but rather the slow steps by which it was built up to become a real Continental army.
10. *Journals*, IV, 412; Lundin, 122–134.
11. *Journals*, III, 322.
12. *Journals*, V, 631.
13. Lefferts, 26. A Hessian officer who saw the regiment on Long Island remarked on their "most beautiful English muskets and bayonets" (Field, 438, Lowell, 67–68).
14. Johnston, *C*, Pt. I, 123.
15. Fitzpatrick, IV, 395, 397, 399, 414.
16. Sparks, *C*, I, 152.
17. Trevelyan, Pt. II, Vol. I, 179.
18. Field, 525.
19. Trevelyan, Pt. II, Vol. I, 179; Duer, *passim*
20. Johnston, *C*, Pt. I, 63; Irving, II, 300.
21. Johnston, *C*, Pt. I, 126–132.
22. Trevelyan, Pt. II, Vol. I, 32–34.
23. Lowell, 299–300. Lecky, 244, says the hiring of the German mercenaries "made reconciliation hopeless and the Declaration of Independence inevitable. It was idle for the Americans to have any further scruples about calling in foreigners [the French] to assist them when England had herself set the example."

    Before the Germans were hired the British government had tried to get Russians; but the other European governments, "which feared, or hated, or envied Britain," besieged Empress Catherine with "warnings and expostulations" and wrecked the negotiations. The smaller German states were next solicited, successfully (Trevelyan, Pt. II, Vol. I, 42–45). They were willing to furnish thousands of men, at a price. The Duke of Brunswick, for example, agreed to furnish 4,300 men. He was to receive an annual payment of £11,517 17s. 1½d., while his troops were in the British service, and twice as much each year for two years thereafter. He was also to get "head money" at the rate of £7 4s. 4½d. for each man furnished, and, for each one killed, the same sum additional. "According to custom three wounded men shall be reckoned as one killed": so ran the treaty. All this was to go into the Duke's own pocket, the wounded men and the dead men's families not receiving even the extra halfpenny (Lowell, 17–18). In all, during the war six German states sent out to America 29,875 men, of whom 12,562 never returned to Germany, about 5,000 deserting and remaining in America. (Lowell, 20, 300.)

24. Ambrose Serle, who was aboard Lord Howe's flagship as secretary to his lordship, described their arrival in his journal (Serle, 28): "We were saluted by all the Ships of War in the Harbour, by the Cheers of the Sailors all along the Ships and by those of the Sailors on the Shore. A finer Scene could not be exhibited, both of Country, Ships and men, all heightened by one of the brightest Days that can be imagined."
25. Van Tyne, 243.
26. Stedman, I, 198; Kemble, 80; Serle, 28.
27. Fitzpatrick, V, 444.
28. Johnston, *C*, Pt. I, 99–100; Greene, FV, 34; Serle, 67.

CHAPTER 16

The most fully detailed story of the Battle of Long Island and the subsequent retreat is to be found in Henry P. Johnston's *The Campaign of 1776.* Although he fails to cite authority for most of the statements in his narrative, his sources are not hard to trace, especially as he reprints the greater part of the contemporary source material in Part II of his book. Another full account is in *The Battle of Long Island,* by T. W. Field. This also lacks specific citation in the text but has a supplement in which much of the source matter is printed. Field's text, however, is less reliable than Johnston's. His fervor, excitability, and one-sidedness, apparently due to excessive patriotism, and his superabundance of adjectives disqualify him as a reliable historian. In substance and style his account is very much like the Fourth of July orations of eighty or ninety years ago.

Force, Fitzpatrick, Kemble, Serle, Read, Reed, Robertson, Gordon, Ramsay, and the original documents printed in Johnston, Field, and Dawson form the major part of the contemporary or near contemporary authorities. They are supplemented by Carrington, Dawson, Johnston, Bancroft, Trevelyan, Anderson, and other writers.

1. Kemble, I, 84–85; Johnston, *C*, Pt. I, 139–140.
2. Kemble, I, 84–85; Serle, 71; Carrington, 200; Johnston, *C*, Pt. I, 140–141; Dawson, I, 154. A Hessian officer made the following comment in his diary (Lowell, 60): "Not a soul opposed our landing. This was the second blunder of the rebels. . . . Their first mistake was when we disembarked on Staten Island, for they might have destroyed a good many of our people with two six-pounders, and now they might have made it very nasty for us." The officer, however, seems to have forgotten the much heavier guns on the frigates covering the landing, which would have made it even more "nasty" for the Americans attempting opposition.

    Ambrose Serle in his journal (Serle, 73–74) describes the scene of the landing: "The Disembarkation of about 15,000 Troops upon a fine Beach, their forming upon the adjacent Plain, a Fleet of above 300 Ships & Vessels with their Sails spread open to dry, the Sun shining clear upon them, the green Hills and Meadows after the Rain, and the calm Surface of the Water upon the contiguous Sea and up the Sound, exhibited one of the finest & most picturesque Scenes that the Imagination can fancy or the Eye behold."
3. Lowell, 58.
4. Trevelyan, Pt. II, Vol. I, 271.
5. Serle, 71.
6. *Pennsylvania,* I, 306.
7. Lowell, 80; Dawson, I, 154; Kemble, I, 85; Johnston, *C*, Pt. I, 141.
8. Carrington, 201.
9. Johnston, *C*, Pt. I, 142–143.
10. Johnston, *C*, Pt. I, 142.

11. Johnston, *C*, Pt. I, 148–150.
12. Graydon, 179, describes "the celebrated General Putnam, riding with a hanger belted across his brawny shoulders, over a waistcoat without sleeves (his summer costume) . . . much fitter to head a band of sickle-men or ditchers, than musketeers."

    Trevelyan, Pt. II, Vol. I, 275, describes him as "a shrewd, genial, New England uncle . . . well fitted for infusing an extra dose of hopefulness and enthusiasm into soldiers, who, just then, would have been better for a little self-distrust, but he did not possess either the training or the temperament indispensable for the leader of a regular army."
13. Johnston, *C*, Pt. I, 143.
14. Field, 146.
15. Fitzpatrick, V, 485.
16. Johnston, *C*, Pt. I, 148. The lack of intelligence service at this time is in strong contrast with the espionage which Washington organized after his retreat across the Jerseys, and which made possible his subsequent success at Trenton.
17. Lowell, 60–61; Johnston, *C*, Pt. I, 202; Field, 429–430.
18. Carrington, 202; Dawson, I, 153; Force, 5, I, 1255; Stedman, I, 193–194.
19. Fitzpatrick, V, 491.
20. Read, 17; Johnston, *C*, Pt. I, 154; Dawson, I, 152.
21. Johnston, *C*, Pt. I, 155–157.

CHAPTER 17

1. *Pennsylvania*, I, 307.
2. Greene, FV, 37.
3. Johnston, *C*, Pt. I, 175–176; Force, 5, I, 1256; Carrington, 202; Dawson, I, 154; Kemble, I, 85.
4. Serle, 77; Johnston, *C*, Pt. I, 176–177.
5. *Pennsylvania*, I, 310; Johnston, *C*, Pt. I, 160–161, Pt. II, 48.
6. Dawson, I, 151, 152.
7. Irving, II, 319.
8. Bancroft, V, 31.
9. Dawson, I, 151.
10. Field, 353; Johnston, *C*, Pt. II, 33.
11. Johnston, *C*, Pt. I, 164–166; Dawson, I, 151.
12. Field, 354; Johnston, *C*, Pt. I, 166.
13. Field, 488.
14. Dawson, I, 152.
15. Field, 354; Dawson, I, 151.
16. Field, 355.
17. Field, 356.
18. Duer, 162 n.
19. Dawson, I, 151; Serle, 78; Johnston, *C*, Pt. I, 167.
20. Field, 450.
21. Johnston, *C*, Pt. I, 173.
22. Johnston, *C*, Pt. II, 62.
23. Field, 159–160.
24. Read, 172; Johnston, *C*, Pt. I, 182–185; Dawson, I, 155.
25. Johnston, *C*, Pt. I, 183–184.
26. Dawson, I, 155. The Hessian jägers, also commonly called "chasseurs," were an element in the German forces in America, few in number—perhaps about 600—but active and efficient in combat. Their functions were like those of the British light infantry. Most of them had been foresters or gamekeepers in civil life and were therefore used to acting individually and thoroughly accustomed to the conditions of bush fighting. They were armed with short, heavy rifles of large bore, which carried no bayonets. These German rifles were the model from which

the early Pennsylvania gunsmiths, most of them German immigrants, had developed the American long-barreled, small-bore weapon.

27. Lowell, 62–63; Kemble, I, 85.
28. Trevelyan, Pt. II, Vol. I, 279. A Hessian officer in his diary (Lowell, 64) wrote: "Our Hessians marched like Hessians; they marched incorrigibly."
29. Field, 352.
30. Trevelyan, Pt. II, Vol. I, 280.
31. Onderdonk, 152. From a letter of Lieut. Col. Bedford (Read, 173) it appears that three Hessians had been picked up somewhere and were taken to the camp along with these British prisoners. It is amusing to note that the Delawares were accused of unmilitary duplicity in counterfeiting Hessian uniforms to deceive their foe, although, at the time the Delaware uniform was adopted, probably few of them had even heard of Hessians and certainly none had ever seen one in uniform.
32. Bancroft, V, 32.
33. *Pennsylvania*, I, 307.
34. Dawson, I, 147, 151; Johnston, *C*, Pt. I, 137–139; Greene, FV, 38–40.
35. Field, 489.
36. Moore, I, 296.
37. Field, 389, 511; Read, 175; *Archives*, III, 1341.
38. Field, 378. Kemble, I, 86, reports 349 casualties.
39. Dawson, I, 156.
40. Johnston, *C*, Pt. II, 64.
41. Johnston, *C*, Pt. I, 193.
42. Bancroft, V, 33.
43. Fitzpatrick, V, 489.
44. Greene, FV, 40.
45. Greene, FV, 41.
46. Irving, II, 327.
47. Adams, CF, 60.
48. Graydon, 156–157.
49. Fitzpatrick, V, 240.
50. Trevelyan, Pt. II, Vol. I, 203–204.
51. Frothingham, 134.
52. Van Tyne, 25.
53. Fisher, I, 493; Marshall, I, 109.
54. Fitzpatrick, VI, 4–7.
55. Van Tyne, 251.
56. Fortescue, III, 409.
57. Van Tyne, 251.
58. Fortescue, III, 409.

CHAPTER 18

1. Field, 452; Stedman, I, 193.
2. Johnston, *C*, Pt. I, 208.
3. Fitzpatrick, V, 497. Serle, 80, says that on the 28th "the Firing was very continual & very hot and lasted till dark night."
4. Trevelyan, Pt. II, Vol. I, 287.
5. Johnston, *C*, Pt. II, 43.
6. Graydon, 165, speaking for Shee's regiment. There were some tents, but not more than half enough for all.
7. Goldwin Smith, 85–94, has written, "Howe . . . though brave, was torpid; probably he was not only torpid but half-hearted. Had he followed up his victory [on Long Island] there probably would have been an end of the Continental army, whatever local resistance might have survived. . . . His subsequent conduct seems to have been marked with a sluggishness and irresolution which the

energy of his lieutenant, Cornwallis, could not redeem. Washington was allowed to pluck victory and reputation out of the jaws of defeat."

8. Trevelyan. Pt. II, Vol. I, 286.
9. Johnston. C. Pt. I, 218.
10. Force, 5. I. 1230, 1246.
11. Johnston. C, Pt. II, 30.
12. Dawson, I, 152.
13. Reed, I, 227; Johnston, C, Pt. I, 223. Of this premature withdrawal Graydon (167–168) wrote as follows: "We received orders to retire. We were formed without delay and had marched near halfway to the river, when it was announced that the British light horse were at our heels. Improbable as was the circumstance, it was yet so strenuously insisted upon that we halted and formed, the front rank kneeling with presented pikes . . . to receive the charge of the supposed assailants." None appearing, "we again took up the line of march and had proceeded but a short distance . . . when we were informed that we had come off too soon and were compelled to return to our post. This was a trying business for young soldiers; it was nevertheless strictly complied with."
14. Heath, 49.
15. Irving, II, 329.
16. Trevelyan, Pt. II, Vol. I, 290. Kemble (I, 86) says, "In the Morning, to our Astonishment found they had Evacuated all their Works . . . without a shot being fired at them."
17. Stedman, I, 193; Irving, II, 335; Trevelyan, Pt. II, Vol. I, 292; Frothingham, 137; Greene, FV, 44.
18. Johnston, C, Pt. I, 199–201.
19. Greene, GW, I, 212.
20. Fitzpatrick, VI, 4–7.
21. *Journals*, V, 762.

CHAPTER 19

1. Whitton, 143.
2. Fitzpatrick, VI, 16, 25.
3. Rodney, C, 112.
4. Johnston, C, Pt. I, 227 n.
5. Fitzpatrick, VI, 5.
6. Fitzpatrick, VI, 32.
7. Fitzpatrick, VI, 4; Johnston, C, Pt. I, 126–131.
8. Force, 5, II, 182–183.
9. Reed, I, 213, 235 n.; Force, 5, II, 120–121; Trevelyan, Pt. II, Vol. I, 294.
10. Fitzpatrick, VI, 6; *Journals*, V, 733.
11. Fitzpatrick, VI, 28–29.
12. Greene, FV, 45.
13. Fortescue, III, 189.
14. Fitzpatrick, VI, 30.
15. *Journals*, V, 749.
16. Force, 5, I, 326–327.
17. Force, 5, I, 329–330.
18. Fitzpatrick, VI, 53.
19. Mackenzie, I, 39.
20. Mackenzie, I, 37–38.
21. Heath, 50; Serle, 90–91, 99–100, 103; Mackenzie, I, 45; Robertson, 97; Force, 5, I, 443.
22. Evelyn, 84.
23. Serle, 103.
24. Johnston, C, Pt. II, 81.
25. Evelyn, 85. Trevelyan (Pt. II, Vol. I, 297) says: "It was an imposing spectacle.

The amazing fire from the shipping, the soldiers in scarlet clambering up the steep rocks, and the river covered with boats full of armed men . . . forming one of the grandest and most sublime stage-effects that had ever been exhibited."

26. Fitzpatrick, VI, 58.
27. Johnston, *H*, 34.
28. Johnston, *H*, 35.
29. Johnston, *C*, Pt. II, 83, Martin's narrative.
30. Heath, 52; Gordon, II, 327; Graydon, 174; Irving, II, 353; Rodney, C, 122; Force, 5, II, 1013; Johnston, *C*, Pt. II, 86.
31. Johnston, *C*, Pt. II, 83.
32. Irving, II, 343.
33. Johnston, *C*, Pt. I, 237. Trevelyan (Pt. II, Vol. I, 298) says: "Not one of the retreating battalions would ever have reached the American lines in military order, and with half its full numbers, if Howe had promptly pushed his troops athwart the peninsula [island] which here was less than 3000 yards wide."
34. Stephenson, I, 365. "The Rebels left a great quantity of Cannon, Ammunition, Stores, provisions, tents &c.&c. behind them" (Mackenzie, I, 50).
35. Johnston, *C*, Pt. I, 238–239. Colonel Humphrey (quoted in *ibid.*, 89) tells of Putnam, "for the purpose of issuing orders and encouraging the troops, flying, on his horse, covered with foam, wherever his presence was most necessary. Without his extraordinary exertions . . . it is probable the entire corps would have been cut to pieces."
36. Trevelyan, Pt. II, Vol. I, 298.
37. Van Tyne, 255 n.
38. Johnston, *C*, Pt. II, 90.

CHAPTER 20

The best account of this affair is Henry P. Johnston's *The Battle of Harlem Heights*. It is especially valuable for the considerable collection of contemporary letters, reports, and other documents to be found on pp. 125–234. E. C. Benedict's monograph of the same name is of very little value, being chiefly controversial on unimportant details and apparently generally erroneous in its conclusions. Carrington and Dawson add hardly at all to Johnston's account; nor is there much additional to be found elsewhere.

1. Johnston, *H*, 49–50, map.
2. Force, 5, II, 450–451; Johnston, *H*, 65.
3. Johnston, *H*, 65.
4. Johnston, *H*, maps facing 50, 70.
5. Johnston, *H*, 44–47; map facing 50.
6. Fitzpatrick, VI, 59.
7. Johnston, *H*, 52–55. One of the Ranger captains was Nathan Hale, but he was at this time on duty as a spy within the British lines in New York, a duty in which he risked and forfeited his life.
8. Johnston, *H*, 61–62.
9. Reed, I, 237. Johnston, *H*, 67, quotes from a favorite song of the British light infantry the following stanza:

> Hark! Hark! The bugle's lofty sound
> Which makes the woods and rocks around
> Repeat the martial strain,
> Proclaims the British light-armed troops
> Advance. Behold! Rebellion droops.
> She hears the sound with pain.

10. Johnston, *C*, Pt. I, 251–252; Irving, II, 359.
11. Fitzpatrick, VI, 68.

12. Johnston, *H*, 82–83, 143.
13. Lushington, 79.
14. Reed, I, 238; Johnston, *H*, 177.
15. Johnston, *H*, 204. Lieut. Col. Kemble of Howe's army said that 14 were killed, and that 11 officers, 5 sergeants, 3 drummers, and 138 privates were wounded. (Kemble, I, 89.)
16. Johnston, *H*, 226.
17. Fitzpatrick, VI, 96.
18. Johnston, *H*, 87.
19. Fitzpatrick, VI, 96.
20. Rodney, C, 129.
21. Johnston, *H*, 154, 177.
22. Reed, I, 238. Howe claimed a victory for his side in this affair. As the British held the ground and the Americans retreated, it was technically their success. But Gen. Sir Henry Clinton admitted that the British had been "in a scrape," and Col. von Donop reported that, but for the arrival of his jägers, "two regiments of Highlanders and the British infantry would have all, perhaps, been captured." The improvement in the behavior of the Americans engaged has caused some American historians to regard this little battle "as a turning point in the uphill progress of their national military efficiency." (Trevelyan, Pt. II, Vol. I, 304.)

CHAPTER 21

1. Heath, 53.
2. Fitzpatrick, VI, 96.
3. Fitzpatrick, VI, 96, 138.
4. Reed, I, 240.
5. Fitzpatrick, VI, 91. One ensign was caught leading 20 men "all loaded with plunder, such as house-furniture, tableware, linen and kitchen utensils, china and delf ware," as well as some women's clothing.
6. Fitzpatrick, VI, 117–118.
7. Fitzpatrick, VI, 112.
8. *Journals*, V, 762.
9. Heath, 62–63; Hufeland, 111–112; Force, 5, III, 471, 921–922; Rodney, C, 139; Irving, II, 377–378; Trevelyan, Pt. II, Vol. I, 312; Bancroft, V, 69.
10. *Journals*, VI, 866.
11. Sparks, *W*, IV, 155 n.; Hufeland, 114–115; Heath, 63.
12. Hufeland, 116.
13. Force, 5, II, 1188–1189; Hufeland, 118–122; Heath, 65.
14. Hufeland, 124. The Americans claimed to have shot down "140 or 150" (Stiles, II, 91). Other estimates ran as high as 800 to 1,000, absurd exaggerations, of course. The Americans lost Col. Shephard; the British lost Capt. W. G. Evelyn, a young soldier of great promise (Evelyn, 11).
15. McDonald, Part I, 21.
16. Reed, I, 245.
17. Heath, 66. The principal facts in this account of the affair at Mamaroneck have been derived from McDonald's narrative. See also *Archives*, II, 1030, for an account by Haslet.

CHAPTER 22

1. Force, 5, II, 607.
2. Hufeland, 135–136, map on 130.
3. Kemble, I, 94–95.
4. Trevelyan, Pt. II, Vol. I, 312.
5. Mackenzie, I, 82; Serle, 26; Force, 5, II, 1158; Lowell, 75.
6. Force, 5, III, 473, 725–726.

7. Force, 5, III, 725–726; Hufeland, 134–137; Johnston, *C*, Pt. II, 56; Tallmadge, 17.
8. Hufeland, 136–137.
9. Hufeland, 137.
10. Rodney, C, 142.
11. Hufeland, 137–138.
12. Heath, 70.
13. Hufeland, 140.
14. Rodney, C, 142.
15. Lowell, 77; Rodney, C, 142; Irving, II, 392.
16. Lowell, 75; Hufeland, 141–142.
17. Rodney, C, 143.
18. McDonald, I, 50.
19. McDonald, I, 53.
20. Rodney, C, 143.
21. Heath, 70.
22. Trevelyan, Pt. II, Vol. I, 314–315.
23. Heath, 7. Hufeland comments (p. 143) on the discipline the British and Hessian troops displayed at this point: "All of these men had waded through the cold waters of the Bronx and had fought a bloody battle in their wet clothing on a day late in October, in which hundreds of their comrades were left on the field and yet they formed and dressed their lines before being permitted to build fires to dry their clothing." He compares this "perfect military machine" with Washington's "poorly armed, ill-supplied and inexperienced army."
24. Bancroft, V, 74; Irving, II, 393; Whitton, 149; Hufeland, 144.
25. Greene, FV, 53.

CHAPTER 23

The most complete account of the battle at Fort Washington is to be found in Edward F. De Lancey's monograph *The Capture of Mount Washington*, a pamphlet published in a very small edition in 1877 after first appearing in the *Magazine of American History* for Feb. of that year. The author fortifies his statements by numerous references to original sources, and his story may be relied upon, in general. The best contemporary account by a witness is in the *Diary* of Lieut. Frederick Mackenzie, of the Welch Fusileers, I, 104–110. The *Memoirs* of Captain Graydon give interesting details, as also does the diary of Archibald Robertson. Vols. II and III of Force's *American Archives*, 5th Series, contain much valuable material, notably Howe's dispatches and his full return of casualties, prisoners taken, etc. Heath's *Memoirs* yield some material. From these and the other sources, such as Kemble, George W. Greene, Hufeland, Carrington, and Dawson, the account herein has been compiled. The individual references below are confined chiefly to the sources of quotations.

1. Anderson, 25; Read, 210–211.
2. Hufeland, 148; Greene, FV, 53; Heath, 72–73.
3. Heath, 75.
4. Force, 5, III, 521.
5. Fitzpatrick, VI, 248–249.
6. Force, 5, III, 543–544.
7. De Lancey, 6–7.
8. De Lancey, 9.
9. Graydon, 186.
10. Bancroft, V, 74.
11. Force, 5, III, 619. Graydon says (p. 186) of Magaw: "He had heard of sieges being protracted for months and even years . . . as the place he had to defend was called a Fort and had cannon in it, he thought the deuce was in it, if he could not hold out for a few weeks."

12. Force, 5, III, 619.
13. Fitzpatrick, VI, 257–258.
14. Fitzpatrick, XVI, 150–152.
15. Force, 5, III, 1294.
16. Force, 5, III, 519.
17. *Pennsylvania*, I, 106.
18. Force, 5, II, 330.
19. Graydon, 94–95; Dawson, I, 89; Johnston, *C*, Pt. I, 277.
20. Fortescue, III, 194 n
21. Force, 5, III, 921–925.
22. Sparks, *W*, IV, 179 n.
23. Kemble, I, 99.
24. Robertson, 111.
25. Force, 5, III, 1058.
26. Force, 5, III, 1059.

CHAPTER 24

1. Force, 5, III, 831.
2. Force, 5, III, 822, 833.
3. Mackenzie, I, 114.
4. Mackenzie, I, 97–98.
5. Force, 5, III, 822.
6. Trevelyan, Pt. II, Vol. II, 18–19.
7. Fitzpatrick, VI, 265.
8. Force, 5, III, 634, 639.
9. Force, 5, III, 708, 764; Fitzpatrick, VI, 287, 293.
10. Mackenzie, I, 112; Gordon, II, 352; Greene, GW, I, 276.
11. Force, 5, III, 861, 1058; Greene, GW, I, 276–278; Serle, 144.
12. Kemble, I, 101.
13. Force, 5, III, 828; Greene, GW, I, 277.
14. Fitzpatrick, VI, 266.
15. Force, 5, III, 779; Fitzpatrick, VI, 295 n.
16. Fitzpatrick, VI, 298.
17. Force, 5, III, 792.
18. Reed, I, 255–257.
19. Reed, I, 257–258
20. Fitzpatrick, VI, 298.
21. Force, 5, III, 790.
22. Gordon, II, 354.
23. Fitzpatrick, VI, 303.
24. Fitzpatrick, VI, 305–306.
25. Bancroft, V, 82.
26. Force, 5, III, 926; Trevelyan, Pt. II, Vol. II, 20.
27. Fitzpatrick, VI, 303.
28. Force, 5, III, 1082.
29. Fitzpatrick, VI, 314.
30. Fitzpatrick, VI, 320.
31. Fitzpatrick, VI, 313.
32. Fitzpatrick, VI, 320–322.
33. Fitzpatrick, VI, 325, 397.
34. Trevelyan, Pt. II, Vol. II, 20.
35. Anderson, 27.
36. Fitzpatrick, VI, 33; Stryker, *TP*, 20.
37. Fitzpatrick, VI, 333.
38. Fitpatrick, VI, 331.
39. Force, 5, III, 1316.

40. Fitzpatrick, VI, 336.
41. Anderson, 28.
42. Lundin, 147.
43. Fitzpatrick, VI, 339.

CHAPTER 25

1. *Archives,* III, 1358.
2. Thacher, 67
3. Anderson, 28.
4. Fitzpatrick, VI, 346, 355, 381.
5. Fitzpatrick, VI, 355.
6. Fitzpatrick, VI, 398.
7. Force, 5, III, 927–928.
8. Fitzpatrick, VI, 397–398.
9. Force, 5, III, 1199, 1434; Marshall, C, 105–107.
10. Force, 5, III, 1434.
11. Read, 253–254.
12. Force, 5, III, 1290.
13. Force, 5, III, 1180; *Journals,* VI, 1027; Bancroft, V, 89.
14. Trevelyan, Pt. II, Vol. II, 63, 67–69.
15. Force, 5, III, 794, 795, 834; Heath, 79–86.
16. Force, 5, III, 1121, 1138.
17. Fitzpatrick, VI, 398.
18. Force, 5, III, 1201.
19. Fitzpatrick, VI, 347.
20. Stryker, *TP,* 59–60.
21. Force, 5, III, 1201.

CHAPTER 26

William S. Stryker's book, *The Battles of Trenton and Princeton,* contains the fullest account of the campaign in the Jerseys from Dec. 26, 1776, to Jan. 5, 1777. It is supported by the inclusion, in Part II, of more than a hundred contemporaneous letters and other documents, many of them otherwise not readily accessible. It has not been thought necessary to refer to this material in the footnotes, except in a few instances. Capt. Thomas Rodney's diary is of great value in its full details and in the sidelights it throws on the activities of the army. Force, 5, III, contains much relevant material, as also does Fitzpatrick. Lundin's *Cockpit of the Revolution* covers all the operations of the war in New Jersey in a comprehensive manner. Carrington's and Dawson's accounts are helpful.

1. Stryker, *TP,* 48 n.
2. Force, 5, III, 1317.
3. Force, 5, III, 1401–1402.
4. Force, 5, III, 1317.
5. Fitzpatrick, VI, 366, 372, 373.
6. Irving, II, 469.
7. Force, 5, III, 1376. Fitzpatrick, VII, 427 n., doubts the authenticity of this letter and does not include it in his collection. Whether authentic or not, it well describes the situation.
8. Dunbar, I, 282.
9. Rodney, C, 150–151.
10. Stryker, *TP,* 362.
11. Stryker, *TP,* 137.
12. Force, 5, III, 1443, 1445–1446.
13. Trevelyan, Pt. II, Vol. II, 113.

14. Rodney, T, 23.
15. Force, 5, III, 1441.
16. Force, 5, III, 1429.
17. Rodney, C, 150.
18. Rodney, T, 24.
19. Fitzpatrick, VI, 440.
20. Stryker, *TP*, 213.
21. Force, 5, III, 1462.
22. Irving, II, 500.
23. Stephenson, I, 383.
24. *Journals*, VI, 1045.

CHAPTER 27

The most recent account of events before and after the battle of Princeton is to be found in Alfred H. Bill, *The Campaign of Princeton, 1776–1777* (Princeton, N. J., 1948).

1. Force, 5, III, 1429.
2. Reed, I, 278.
3. Fitzpatrick, VI, 445–446.
4. Irving, II, 494.
5. Reed, I, 278–280.
6. Rodney, T, 25.
7. Reed, I, 281; Fitzpatrick, VI, 447–450.
8. It is usually stated that the extension of time was for six weeks, though Washington wrote to the Congress that it was a month (Fitzpatrick, VI, 45).
9. Fitzpatrick, VI, 457–458. Besides this call for bounty money, Washington asked Morris for more the next day. "We have the greatest occasion at present for hard money to pay a certain set of people, who are of particular use to us. If you could possibly collect a sum, if it were but one hundred or one hundred and fifty pounds, it would be of great service." These people were his spies in New Jersey. His intelligence service was very good at this time, in strong contrast to the lack of it at Long Island and in the Pennsylvania campaign of 1777. Paper money might do for the bounty to the troops, but these gentlemen required real money.
    No more revealing light could be thrown on the financial condition of the time than that of the list of hard moneys collected by Morris by scraping Philadelphia: "410 Spanish milled dollars @ 7s. 6d., 2 English crowns, 72 French crowns, 1072 English shillings" (Force, 5, III, 1486).
10. Stephenson, I, 386.
11. Stryker, *TP*, 259.
12. Stryker, *TP*, 271–272; Fischer, I, 566; Bancroft, V, 105; Irving, II, 504; Frothingham, 173; Lundin, 206; Carrington, 286. G. W. Greene, in *The Life of Nathanael Greene*, says: "Each course had its advocates, when a voice was heard, saying, "Better than either of these, let us take the new road through the woods, and get in the enemy's rear by a march upon Princetown, and, if possible, on Brunswick even.' From whom did this bold suggestion come? St. Clair claimed it as his, and why should the positive assertion of an honorable man be lightly called in question?" But it has been questioned, by Bancroft elaborately, as a tale "written in extreme old age . . . self-laudatory." He gives the credit to Washington, as do Irving, Frothingham, Lundin, Carrington, and Trevelyan. Stryker thinks it more probably originated with General Philemon Dickinson of the New Jersey militia or Reed, because thev knew the country.
13. Reed, I, 288.
14. Rodney, T, 32–33.
15. Stryker, *TP*, 276.
16. Rodney, T, 32.

17. Rodney, T, 33.
18. Rodney, T, 34.
19. Trevelyan, Pt. II, Vol. II, 135: "Colonel Haslet dropped with a bullet through his brain. In his pocket was an order directing him to go home on recruiting service, which he had divulged to no one and had silently disobeyed."
20. Rodney, T, 34.
21. Rodney, T, 36.
22. Rodney, T, 36.
23. Fitzpatrick, VI, 469.
24. Fortescue, III, 205, says, "The whole cause of the rebellion in America was saved by Washington's very bold and skilful action." Nicholas Cresswell, a young Englishman adrift in America, wrote in his *Journal* (pp. 179–180) that the news of Trenton and Princeton "is confirmed. The minds of the people are much altered. A few days ago they had given up the cause for lost. Their late successes have turned the scale and now they are all liberty mad again. Their Recruiting Parties could not get a man (except he bought him from his master) no longer since than last week, and now the men are coming in by companies. . . . They have recovered their panic and it will not be an easy matter to throw them into confusion again."
25. Fitzpatrick, VI, 470.
26. The details of the operations after Princeton have been derived chiefly from Thomas Rodney's *Diary*.

CHAPTER 28

1. Irving, III, 4–5; Lundin, 20; Stephenson, I, 394; Stedman, I, 239; Greene, GW, I, 309; Greene, FV, 75.
2. Fitzpatrick, VI, 472; Irving, II, 4.
3. Fitzpatrick, VII, 29.
4. Fitzpatrick, VII, 288.
5. Gordon, II, 422.
6. Fitzpatrick, VII, 350. Alexander Graydon, a visitor at the camp, wrote in his *Memoirs* (p. 277): "I had been extremely anxious to see the army. Here it was, but I could see nothing which deserved the name . . . the motley, shabby covering of the men."
7. Fitzpatrick, VII, 189.
8. Fitzpatrick, VI, 496–497.
9. Fitzpatrick, VII, 38.
10. Fitzpatrick, VI, 473, and VII, 128, 129, 230; Lundin, 234–235; Trevelyan, III, 56–57.
11. Fitzpatrick, VII, 288. Inoculation, at that time "rarely practised" in America, was the forerunner of vaccination. The patient was infected in such a way that a mild form of the disease was induced. Trevelyan, III, 80–82, gives a full account of the process.
12. *Journals*, VI, 1045. The Additional Battalions were not allotted among the states as the original eighty-eight battalions had been. They could be recruited anywhere, and officers could be appointed without regard to state lines.
13. *Journals*, V, 763.
14. Fitzpatrick, VII, 86.
15. Fitzpatrick, VII, 139 n.
16. *Journals*, VI, 1093.
17. Fitzpatrick, VII, 89; also 91, 120, 133, 138, and especially 349.
18. Fitzpatrick, VII, 66. Washington repeated his call for "companies or half Companies" on Feb. 23 and again on Mar. 6 (*ibid.*, 194, 254).
19. *Journals*, VII, 211. Washington (see Fitzpatrick, VII, 208) had written on Feb. 28, "Nothing distresses me more than the Universal Call . . . from all Quarters for fire Arms. which I am totally unable to supply." Trevelyan (III, 39) says

that the manufacturing capabilities of America were so limited that contracts could seldom be made for more than 100 muskets at a time.

20. Jones, I, 71; Trevelyan, Pt. II, Vol. II, 153; Lundin, 221; Kemble, I, 107.
21. Lundin, 222; Sullivan, I, 310; Stedman, I, 240.
22. Stedman, I, 240.
23. Frothingham, 189. Thomas Jones, a judge of the Supreme Court of New York and an ardent Loyalist, in his *History of New York During the Revolutionary War* caustically comments on a New York incident of March, 1777: "This month was remarkable for the investiture of General Howe with the Order of the Bath; a reward for *Evacuating* Boston, for *lying indolent* upon Staten Island for near two months, for *suffering* the whole rebel army to escape him upon Long Island, and *again* at the White Plains, *for not putting an end to rebellion* in 1776, when so often in his power, for making such *injudicious cantonments* of his troops in Jersey as he did, for *suffering* 10,000 veterans under experienced generals to be cooped up in Brunswick and Amboy by about 6,000 militia under the command of an inexperienced general." Of Howe's "cooped up" condition in Amboy and New Brunswick he says, "Not a stick of wood, a spear of grass or a kernel of corn could the troops in New Jersey procure without fighting for it." (Jones, I, 177, 171.)
24. Hufeland, 209–213; Fitzpatrick, VII, 328 n.; Stedman, I, 278; Jones, I, 177.
25. Jones, I, 180–181; Gordon, II, 468; *Journals*, VII, 579.

CHAPTER 29

The most useful account of Howe's maneuvers described in this chapter is to be found in Troyer S. Anderson, *The Command of the Howe Brothers During the American Revolution.* Anderson is always helpful on the plans and thought of the Howes. He is perhaps too gentle in his treatment of them.

1. Marshall, I, 170; Stedman, I, 283; Irving, III, 73; Lundin, 313; Greene, FV, 80.
2. Sullivan, I, 354.
3. Greene, FV, 81.
4. Montresor, 421; Frothingham, 193.
5. Montresor, 421–422; Marshall, I, 173.
6. Sullivan, I, 383.
7. Trevelyan, III, 61, writes: "To the surprise and amusement of the American officers . . . [Howe] placidly and deliberately began to entrench his camp, as if he had come into their neighborhood to spend a quiet Summer."
8. Stedman, I, 284; Lundin, 317; Sullivan, I, 393; Gordon, II, 470; Fitzpatrick, VIII, 261.
9. Fitzpatrick, VIII, 353; Lundin, 317–318.
10. Lundin, 319.
11. Stedman, I, 284; Montresor, 123; Kemble, I, 121; Fitzpatrick, VIII, 270, 276; Irving, III, 81.
12. Greene, GW, I, 394; Fitzpatrick, VIII, 281–282; Gordon, II, 471.
13. Cresswell, 242.
14. Fitzpatrick, VIII, 298.
15. Stedman, I, 285.
16. Gordon, II, 474.
17. Kemble, I, 123; Lundin, 323–324; André, 34. Trevelyan, III, 63, writes: "Stirling, who was still something of a military pedant, neglected the rare advantages which the locality presented, and drew up his command in parade-ground order; while Cornwallis made no mistakes and gave full play to the indignant valour of his followers."
18. Fitzpatrick, VIII, 307; Montresor, 429; Lundin, 323; Marshall, I, 175–176; Gordon, II, 473–474; André, 33.
19. Stedman, I, 286.

20. Montresor, 426.
21. Irving, III, 74, 85; Lundin, 312; Marshall, I, 176.
22. Fitzpatrick, VIII, 355; Whitton, 179–180.
23. Fitzpatrick, VIII, 336.
24. Fitzpatrick, VIII, 364, 365, 366.
25. Irving, III, 104; Fitzpatrick, VIII, 365; Kirkwood, 104.
26. Stedman, I, 289; André, 34; Serle, 239.
27. Fitzpatrick, VIII, 376, 407.
28. Fitzpatrick, VIII, 386, 414, 454.
29. Montresor, 429; Serle, 241; Baurmeister, 2.
30. Fitzpatrick, VIII, 460–468.
31. Fitzpatrick, VIII, 496, 497, 499. On July 30 Washington wrote to Gates: "Gen'l. Howe's in a manner abandoning Genl. Burgoyne is so unaccountable a matter, that till I am fully assured it is so, I cannot help casting my Eyes continually behind me."
32. *Pennsylvania Archives*, V, 415.
33. Fitzpatrick, VIII, 503, 505, and IX, 5.
34. *Archives*, III, 1380–1381.
35. Fitzpatrick, VIII, 1–5.
36. Fitzpatrick, IX, 37, 45; Kirkwood, 130.
37. Fitzpatrick, IX, 57.
38. Fitzpatrick, IX, 107, 110 n., 113, 114.
39. Fitzpatrick, IX, 115–116.
40. Stedman, I, 290; Fortescue, III, 214.
41. Wilkin, 238.
42. Carrington, 364.
43. Carrington, 364.
44. Fitzpatrick, IX, 119.

CHAPTER 30

There is a wealth of information concerning the movements of the British army on the way to the Brandywine in the journals of Captain John Montresor, Archibald Robertson (an engineer), Ambrose Serle (secretary to Admiral Howe), Major John André, and the letters of the Hessian Major Baurmeister. On the American side, Washington's letters and orders are the chief sources. Edward W. Cooch's *Battle of Cooch's Bridge* is very helpful.

1. Hughes, III, 149.
2. Fitzpatrick, IX, 125–127.
3. Adams, J, 298. The number of men in Washington's army is in doubt. A committee of the Congress, which visited the camp about August 1, reported 17,949 privates, exclusive of certain contingents; including officers, 16,920 were fit for duty, of whom 14,089 were privates. The number of men in September is more generally reckoned at 11,000. See Greene, GW, I, 443; Irving, III, 148, writes: "The disaffected, who had been taught to believe the American forces much less than they were in reality, were astonished as they gazed on the lengthening procession of a host, which to their unpractised eyes, appeared innumerable; while the Whigs, gaining fresh hope and animation from the sight, cheered the patriot squadrons as they passed." See also Fitzpatrick, IX, 127–128.
4. Graydon, 291.
5. Fitzpatrick, IX, 129, 130–135.
6. Fitzpatrick, IX, 128, 147; *Journals*, VIII, 667.
7. Irving, III, 194; Fitzpatrick, IX, 451–452; Stephenson, II, 20; Greene, GW, I, 444; Hughes, II, 150.
8. Montresor, 442; André, 36; Serle, 245; Robertson, 142.
9. André, 37; Serle, 245; Montresor, 442; Baurmeister, 3–4; Robertson, 143.

10. Montresor, 443; André, 38; Robertson, 143; Baurmeister, 4. Lieut. William J. Hale of the 45th British regiment wrote: "We found a great part of the stores remaining in the Town, though they had employed several of the preceding days in removing them to Wilmington. 100 butts of Porter were left in one cellar, Madeira, Rum, Melasses, Tobacco, Yams, Flower etc; a number of Sloops loaded with shoes, stockings and rum . . . fell into our hands."
11. Marshall, I, 182; Irving, III, 198; Montresor, 444; Baurmeister, 7; André, 38.
12. Montresor, 444; Baurmeister, 8; André, 41.
13. Baurmeister, 6; André, 41; Robertson, 144.
14. André, 41–42.
15. Montresor, 443.
16. Fitzpatrick, IX, 146–147, 148.
17. Baurmeister, 8–9, notes that the army's wagon train "consisted of 276 waggons loaded with rum, flour and salt-meat."
18. Montresor, 445.
19. This account of the affair at Cooch's Bridge is based on the accounts of Montresor, 445–446; André, 42–43; Baurmeister, 9; Robertson, 144–145; Irving, III, 198–199; and Cooch, *passim*.
20. Montresor says the Americans left 20 dead on the field. Baurmeister says 30, including five officers. Marshall reckons 40 killed and wounded in Maxwell's corps. On the other side Montresor admits only 3 killed and 20 wounded. Robertson says 30 killed and wounded. Washington wrote to the Congress that a woman said she had seen nine wagonloads of British wounded.

    Montresor says that Maxwell's force consisted of 720 Continentals, "together with 1,000 militia and Philadelphia Light Horse." No other account mentions any horsemen. Marshall says that there were 900 cavalry with Washington's army, who were "employed principally on the lines in watching the enemy, gaining intelligence and picking up stragglers." It is pretty safe to say that there were none at Cooch's Bridge. It is also very improbable that there were any militia in important numbers with Maxwell. They were concentrated elsewhere. Sergeant Thomas Sullivan of the British 49th regiment in an account of the fight (*Pa. Mag. of Hist.*, XXXI, 410) calls Maxwell's men "a chosen corps of 1000 men." He says the British had "3 men killed; 2 officers and 19 men wounded," and claims Maxwell's loss was "the commanding officer . . . and other officers killed and wounded, besides 50 men killed and many more wounded." Maxwell was certainly not killed.
21. Montresor, 446; Robertson, 145.
22. André, 43; Montresor, 446–448.
23. Fitzpatrick, IX, 140.
24. Fitzpatrick, IX, 179.
25. Montresor, 448.
26. Fitzpatrick, IX, 197. Montresor, 449, says: "The Army moved . . . through an amazingly strong country, being a succession of large hills, rather sudden with narrow vales . . . not a shot fired. . . . Rebel Light Horse about, but fled."

CHAPTER 31

1. MacElree, 132–133.
2. Bowen, 7–8; MacElree, 131–133; Lossing, II, 171 n. Some confusion as to these fords has arisen from the fact that change of ownership of the adjacent farms resulted in change of name of some of the fords. Painter's was also known as Jones's, Wistar's as Shunk's, Buffington's as Brinton's, confusing it with the truce Brinton's next above Chad's. To make matters worse some of the actors in the drama miscalled certain fords. Washington called Jefferis's Ford Jones's; and, as if that common name stuck in everybody's mind, Sullivan gave it to Wistar's Ford. In this narrative "Jones's" has been voided, the distinctive alternative name being used in each case.

3. Carrington, 368; Bowen, 10; Fitzpatrick, IX, 425 n.
4. Carrington, 368; Bowen, 7; MacElree, 134.
5. Bowen, 8; Hughes, III, 157–158; MacElree, 136; Lee, 89.
6. Baurmeister, 12. One of the many anecdotes clustering about this battle tells of an English Quakeress, who ran out of her house and implored Knyphausen not to go on to the Ford. "Dear man," she cried, "George Washington is on the other side and he has all the men in this world with him. To which the General replied: "Never mind, madam. I have all the men in the other world with me."
7. Baurmeister, 13; Carrington, 369–370; Bowen, 9.
8. Baurmeister, 13.
9. Baurmeister, 13.
10. Greene, GW, I, 447.
11. Fitzpatrick, IX, 205.
12. Bowen, 10; Carrington, 370; Lossing, II, 174.
13. Sparks, W, V, 459.
14. Muhlenberg, 492. It seems strange that Washington should have regarded Howe's division of the British army as "a terrible blunder" after his own action at the Battle of Trenton.
15. Hughes, III, 159; Lossing, II, 174; Bowen, 10, 30. Fortescue (III, 216) regards it as fortunate for Washington that he did not persist in his plan to cross and attack Knyphausen. "For Knyphausen was an able commander, his troops were far superior to Washington's in training and discipline, and, by Howe's fore-thought, he had been supplied with plenty of guns, so that he would certainly have held his own until Cornwallis came up in the enemy's rear and destroyed the Americans utterly."
16. Sparks, W, V, 459.
17. Hughes, III, 161–162; Bowen, 10.
18. Carrington, 342; MacElree, 141. It is impossible to be certain as to the order in which the conflicting messages were sent and received, and the authorities differ. Marshall mentions only Ross's dispatch received at eleven o'clock. Irving speaks only of "an express from Sullivan," giving no time, but states that Washington immediately sent Bland to reconnoiter and then resolved to cross and attack Knyphausen. Bowen sends Bland out first and states that he reported the enemy on the Valley Road and the dust arising there, which was afterwards confirmed by Ross, yet it appears that Bland's dispatch about the dust was dated 2 P.M., while Ross reported at 11 A.M. Carrington puts Bland's message at "between nine and ten o'clock," states that similar news came from Hazen, fixes Ross's dispatch at 11 A.M. and omits reference to Washington's order to Bland. Lossing puts Bland's message first and has it confirmed by Ross and by Hazen. Greene, GW, mentions only a message from Sullivan that the enemy was marching to the upper fords, follows this by Washington's order to cross, then Sullivan's con-tradicting message and finally Cheyney's arrival. Hughes gives Ross first place, with news of the enemy on the road, makes Washington then order the attack, but send Bland out to scout; after that he brings in the Ross message and then Spear's contradiction. Unfortunately, Washington's order to Bland was dated "11 September, 1777, 20 minutes after   o'clock," so that it cannot be placed in time.

In the text an effort has been made to sort out the times of the messages and arrange them in their proper order. The result may not be in accord with the facts, but it certainly seems to fit in with the known circumstances and the apparently proper relations between the several messages. The questions raised may not be of the first importance, but it is annoying not to be able to be sure of their answers.

19. Montresor, 449; Dawson, I, 281. There is some uncertainty as to the strength of Cornwallis's column. In the American histories it is usually reckoned at 10,000 men. Montresor puts it at "about 7,000." Howe had reported 13,799 privates on embarkation. He had lost some through sickness, a few by capture, but pretty

certainly still had twelve to thirteen thousand. Of these there were about 5,000
with Knyphausen. That would leave Cornwallis perhaps 8,000 rank and file,
which is the way an army's strength is usually computed.

20. Townsend, 21–25.
21. Carrington, 376; Marshall, I, 185; Irving, III, 204; Sullivan, I, 463, 472; Greene,
    GW, I, 418.
22. Sullivan, I, 463, 472–473.
23. Montresor, 449; Lossing, II, 175; MacElree, 144; Irving, III, 185.
24. Bowen, 11.
25. Montresor, 450; André, 46; Dawson, I, 282.
26. Bowen, 11; MacElree, 144; Townsend, 24; Lossing, II, 175; Dawson, I, 276.
27. Montresor, 450.
28. Sullivan, I, 463–464, 476, 555.
29. Fitzpatrick, IX, 206–207.
30. Hughes, III, 164; Greene, GW, I, 449.
31. Greene, GW, I, 449; Gordon, II, 511; Hughes, III, 163–164.
32. Anderson, 36–37.
33. Dawson, I, 282.
34. Bowen, 12.
35. Greene, GW, I, 451–453; Irving, III, 207–208; Montresor, 450.
36. Dawson, I, 282.
37. Baurmeister, 14–15.
38. Dawson, I, 282. Most histories dismiss the fight at the Ford in a paragraph or
    two, as if there were only a brief resistance by the troops under Wayne, Maxwell,
    and Proctor, followed by a quick retreat. The account sent by Major Baurmeister
    of the Regiment von Mirbach, a participant in the action, to his superior officer
    in Hesse-Kassel, on which the description in the text is based, shows clearly that
    the Americans put up a stiff and prolonged defense. This may be accepted, if
    for no other reason, because it began at half past four o'clock and lasted until
    dark.
39. Bancroft, V, 179.
40. Dawson, I, 282.
41. Montresor, 451; Bancroft, V, 179.

CHAPTER 32

1. Stedman, I, 293; Gordon, II, 513.
2. Fitzpatrick, IX, 207–208.
3. *Journals*, VIII, 735–738; Fitzpatrick, IX, 212.
4. Fitzpatrick, IX, 229, 215, 258.
5. Montresor, 452–453; Baurmeister, 18.
6. Marshall, I, 188.
7. Hughes, III, 181.
8. Baurmeister, 18.
9. Baurmeister, 18; Montresor, 453.
10. Greene, GW, I, 462, gives Pickering credit, on his own statement, for suggesting
    this move.
11. Baurmeister, 18–19; Montresor, 451–453.
12. Marshall, I, 188; Greene, GW, I, 462; Irving, III, 212; Belcher, II, 269; Brooks,
    105.
13. Fitzpatrick, IX, 238–239.
14. Kirkwood, 175; Greene, GW, I, 462; Irving, III, 214.
15. Fitzpatrick, IX, 238.
16. Kirkwood, 175.
17. Montresor, 454–456.
18. Lossing, II, 163.
19. Marshall, I, 189.

20. Montresor, 455; André, 49; Baurmeister, 19.
21. Gordon, II, 516–517; Montresor, 455; Marshall, I, 89; Irving, III, 215; Stedman, I, 294; Lossing, II, 163; Baurmeister, 19; André, 49. This was the celebrated "Paoli Massacre," commonly described as a butchery of defenseless men, fleeing from the dreaded bayonet and stabbed to death while crying for mercy. The commander of the British troops was dubbed "No-Flint Grey" and execrated as a brutal murderer. Lossing says that he "marched stealthily" (an infamous practice in surprise attacks, of course), that he gave "his usual order to rush upon the patriots with fixed bayonets without firing a shot" (another indefensible proceeding), and that his men were *"to give no quarters"*—a statement for which there seems to be no basis in fact. Trevelyan (III, 234) attributes the infamy heaped upon Grey to the dread of the bayonet, which was undoubtedly prevalent among the Americans: "Men always attach the idea of cruelty to modes of warfare in which they are not proficient; and Americans liked the bayonet as little as Englishmen approved of taking deliberate aim at individual officers," against which American practice there was frequent outcry from the British, especially the officers. The dread of unaccustomed weapons and the horror of them as brutal appears also in the white man's objections to the Indian tomahawk, which is certainly, in itself, no more cruel or barbarous than the sword or the bayonet.

    Against the charge that "quarter had been refused and that the wounded were stabbed to death where they lay," Trevelyan urges the fact that only 53 dead were found on the ground the next day—a statement supported by Lossing, II, 164. It should be noted, also, that many wounded, including 40 badly injured, were actually carried away by the British.

    The fact seems to be that the ascription of brutal slaughter to the British was based upon a published letter, said to have been written by a Hessian participant, in which the Americans were described as "running about barefoot and half clothed," while "we killed three hundred" of them with the bayonet. "I struck them myself like so many pigs, one after another, until the blood ran out of the touch-hole of my musket." A sufficient answer to this sanguinary narration is the fact that there were no Hessians in Grey's force. That letter was probably American propaganda.

    Wayne was ordered before a court-martial on a charge of having had notice of the enemy's intention to attack and failing to make "a Disposition till it was too late." He was acquitted "with the highest honor."
22. Montresor, 356; André, 51; Baurmeister, 20–21; Robertson, 149–150; Gordon, II, 517.
23. Fitzpatrick, IX, 257, 259.
24. Kirkwood, 177.
25. Montresor, 456–457; André, 31–32; Baurmeister, 20–21; Robertson, 149–151; Gordon, II, 517.
26. Fitzpatrick, IX, 257–259, 262.
27. Baurmeister, 21; Montresor, 457; André, 52; Robertson, 149–150; Gordon, II, 517.
28. Fitzpatrick, IX, 232–253.
29. Marshall, I, 191.
30. *Journals*, VIII, 752; Bancroft, V, 181.
31. Fitzpatrick, IX, 248–249.
32. Stephenson, II, 31; Fitzpatrick, IX, 275.
33. Fitzpatrick, IX, 269, 270.
34. Montresor, 458; André, 26; Baurmeister, 21.

CHAPTER 33

    This account of the Battle of Germantown has been drawn from so many sources that it would unduly laden the notes to assign particular authority to each of its several elements. General reference is made to Fitzpatrick, IX, *passim*; Gordon, II, 522;

Stedman, I, 291; Ramsay, II, 15; Kemble, I, 137; Baurmeister, 24–25; Greene, GW, I, 474–481; Marshall, I, 197; Lossing, II, 110–111; Hughes, III, 187–206; Bancroft, V, 193–195; Greene, FV, 91–92; Sullivan, I, 542–547; Anderson, 44–46; Carrington, 382–391; Dawson, 318–331; André, 54–57; Irving, III, 280–287; Lee, 95; Lowell, 201–203; Trevelyan, III, 237–251.

1. Fitzpatrick, IX, 278.
2. Hughes, III, 185.
3. Fitzpatrick, IX, 279.
4. Kirkwood, 188.
5. Fitzpatrick, IX, 308.
6. Carrington, 384; Greene, FV, 92, map; Dawson, I, 330.
7. Fitzpatrick, IX, 309; Greene, FV, 90; Greene, GW, I, 473; Sullivan, I, 542–543.
8. Dawson, I, 324. Fortescue, III, 223, justly criticizes the plan as "too intricate for inexperienced officers and imperfectly disciplined troops." Chastellux, 106, calls it "absolutely chimerical" and criticizes it in detail.
9. Trevelyan, III, 245, has this to say about the break-up of Sullivan's division: "They had travelled through the night. They had been fighting for nearly three hours. They had fired away all their ammunition. Their flank was unprotected. Their reserves stopped behind to help, or to hinder, the attack upon Musgrave's garrison. . . . The roar of the American batteries around the Chew mansion told upon the nerves of Sullivan's exhausted soldiers. A rumor arose and spread that they were being assailed in the rear by a hostile force; and, to the surprise of the officers who commanded them, they broke their ranks and retired from the field in hurry and confusion."
10. Trevelyan, III, 249.

CHAPTER 34

1. Rodney, C, 240.
2. Serle, 253–256.
3. Gordon, II, 519; Stedman, I, 297.
4. Fitzpatrick, IX, 259.
5. Stedman, I, 296; Ramsay, II, 17; Lossing, II, 86.
6. Robertson, 151.
7. Stedman, I, 296.
8. Lossing, II, 293.
9. Montresor, 459.
10. Eelking, 117; Dawson, I, 356.
11. Chastellux, 124.
12. Chastellux, 125.
13. Trevelyan, III, 258.
14. Dawson, I, 355; Stedman, I, 302; Lossing, II, 87–88, 208.
15. Stedman, I, 303–304; Trevelyan, III, 256–260.
16. Waldo, 301.
17. Lossing, II, 90.
18. Lossing, II, 91.
19. Montresor, 474–476.
20. Fisher, II, 50.
21. Montresor, 474–476.
22. Dawson, I, 336.
23. Lossing, II, 93.
24. Fitzpatrick, IX, 266–268.
25. Carrington, 296; Frothingham, 330–331.
26. Fitzpatrick, IX, 462.
27. Fitzpatrick, IX, 318, and X, 19, 20.
28. Fitzpatrick, IX, 318, 319, 351, 358, 375, and X, 19, 24.

29. Kirkwood, 211.
30. Fitzpatrick, IX, 382.
31. Kirkwood, 226.
32. Fitzpatrick, IX, 390–391.
33. Stedman, I, 302; Trevelyan, III, 266.
34. Sparks, *W*, V, 168 n.
35. Marshall, I, 215; Irving, III, 328.
36. Marshall, I, 215.
37. Robertson, 159; André, 57.
38. Baurmeister, 36.
39. Baurmeister, 36.
40. Kirkwood, 265.
41. André, 67; Robertson, 159–160.
42. André, 68.
43. André, 68.
44. André, 69; Robertson, 160; Simcoe, 31; Marshall, I, 215–216. André says one of Simcoe's men was killed and 9 chasseurs killed or wounded, while 20 to 30 Americans fell and 15 were taken. Robertson says a single British officer was killed, 2 were wounded, and about 40 rank and file were killed or wounded. Simcoe, a rather boastful person, claims "near a hundred" American casualties, "little or none" among the King's troops. Marshall admits one officer of Morgan's corps killed and 27 of his men killed or wounded, besides "a small loss" among the militia.
45. Reed, I, 351 n.
46. André, 70.
47. Marshall, I, 217–218; Reed, I, 354; Fitzpatrick, X, 156; Baurmeister, 39; Robertson, 161.
48. Waldo, 305.
49. Marshall, I, 217–218; Reed, I, 354; Fitzpatrick, X, 156; Baurmeister, 39; Robertson, 161.
50. *Journals*, IX, 1029–1030.
51. Fitzpatrick, X, 133 n., 134 n.; Reed, I, 348 n.
52. Fitzpatrick, X, 195–196.
53. Stillé, 112.
54. Hughes, III, 231.
55. Kapp, 137.
56. Sparks, *W*, V, 241 n.

CHAPTER 35

Original sources of information as to Arnold's Champlain battle are to be found in Force's *American Archives*, 4th Series, Vol. IV, and 5th Series, where many letters from and to Arnold, Schuyler, Gates, Hartley, and others appear. Other contemporary sources are Riedesel's and Wilkinson's memoirs, the journals of Wells, Hadden, and Pausch. Secondary sources of much value are Mahan's *Major Operations*, Jones's *Conquest of Canada*, Allen's *Naval History*, Lowell's *Hessians*, and Patterson's *Horatio Gates*. Kenneth Roberts has told the story, in great detail and with historical accuracy, in his novel *Rabble in Arms*.

1. Force, 5, I, 103.
2. Force, 5, I, 232, 238.
3. Jones, CH, 97.
4. Force, 5, I, 339, 376.
5. *Journals*, V, 448; Force, 5, II, 637.
6. Patterson, 69.
7. *Journals*, V, 526.
8. Force, 5, I, 233, 238.

9. Force, 5, I, 390, 445, 450, 650.
10. Force, 5, I, 559, 794.
11. Patterson, 85.
12. Jones, CH, 105–106.
13. Force, 5, I, 474, and II, 204. Hartley commanded the 6th Pennsylvania after Col. Irvine's capture at Trois Rivières.
14. Jones, CH, 107.
15. Jones, CH, 111–112.
16. Force, 5, I, 390; Jones, CH, 112.
17. Jones, CH, 125.
18. Force, 5, I, 125, 512, 582, 797, 826, 872, 987.
19. Force, 5, I, 1199.
20. Force, 5, I, 649.
21. Force, 5, I, 745–746.
22. Force, 5, I, 350, 399, 400, 620, 623, 624, 932.
23. Force, 5, I, 209.
24. Force, 5, I, 145, 163, 194, 303, 474, 549, 563, 630, 649, 682.
25. Force, 5, I, 340, 512, 649.
26. This description was supplied by Kenneth Roberts, who secured from the British Admiralty drawings of the *Washington* galley made by a British naval officer after her capture. Before this discovery, no description of the galleys had been obtainable, except the meager account in "a letter from Skenesborough, dated August 16, 1776," printed in Force, 5, I, 988, which merely noted that they were "from sixty to seventy feet in keel and eighteen feet in beam" and gave no description of their shape or their rigging.
27. Force, 5, I, 1123, 1201, and II, 1039.
28. Force, 5, I, 988, and II, 1039.
29. Force, 5, I, 969; Jones, CH, 116.
30. Force, 5, I, 630.
31. Force, 5, II, 1179.
32. Force, 5, II, 1178–1179; Pausch, 75 n.
33. Force, 5, II, 1178. The gondola had been taken from the Americans the day the siege of Quebec was raised. Hence its new name, *Loyal Convert.*
34. Lowell, 109.
35. Riedesel, I, 65.
36. Force, 5, I, 626, 799.
37. Pausch, 74–76; Riedesel, I, 59; Jones, CH, 144, 157–159.
38. Force, 5, I, 1266, and II, 969, 1166, 1201, 1266; Jones, CH, 143–144.
39. Force, 5, II, 223. Kenneth Roberts states that these fascines were made by tying small hemlock trees, each into a bundle, and that they were fixed, butts upward, along the bulwarks of the gondolas and galleys.
40. Force, 5, II, 251, 265, 440, 933.
41. Force, 5, II, 224.
42. Force, 5, II, 481.
43. Force, 5, II, 982. The usual lists of Arnold's fleet in the battle total 15, omitting the *Success;* but Wells notes its arrival on September 11, making 16. It may be noted that Riedesel (I, 73) lists 16 vessels in the American fleet, but does not name them all. The *Liberty* galley was away from the fleet, on command, on the day of the battle. The *Gates* galley had not been finished.
44. Force, 5, II, 591.
45. Force, 5, II, 1179. The description there of the longboats puts one gun in each bow. Riedesel, I, 70, gives them "three cannons each," but Hadden, 23, says one.
46. Mahan, 17–18.
47. Force, 5, II, 224. Mahan, 19, emphasized Arnold's "sounder judgment": "A retreat before square-rigged sailing vessels having a fair wind, by a heterogeneous force like his own, of unequal speeds and batteries, could result only in disaster. . . . Better trust to a steady, well-ordered position, developing the utmost

fire . . . The correctness of Arnold's decision not to chance a retreat was shown in the [results of his] retreat of two days later."
48. Force, 5, II, 1040.
49. Van Tyne, 373–374. Riedesel, I, 83, wrote, "If we could have begun our last expedition four weeks earlier, I am satisfied that everything would have ended this year." Four weeks was exactly the time consumed in building the *Inflexible*. That it was the intention of the British command, if feasible, to join Howe on the Hudson that year is indicated by an extract from a contemporary English paper (Almon, IV, 291) of Sept. 6, 1776: "The design was that the two armies commanded by Generals Howe and Burgoyne should cooperate; that they should both be on the Hudson River at the same time; that they should join about Albany, and thereby cut off all communication between the northern and southern Colonies."
50. Mahan, 25.

CHAPTER 36

1. Hudleston, 69.
2. Fonblanque, 226.
3. Fonblanque, 227; Hudleston, 110; Nickerson, 8.
4. Nickerson, 81.
5. Burgoyne, Appendix, iii; Fonblanque, Appendix C; Nickerson, 83–89. Trevelyan III, 71, attributed the conception of this plan to Germain, but every indication seems to point to Burgoyne's authorship of it. He certainly wrote the paper that the King read and approved.
6. Nickerson, 89–90.
7. Nickerson, 91–94.
8. Nickerson, 94.
9. Hudleston, 114.
10. The best analysis of the plan, and of all others in which Howe was concerned, is in Anderson, *passim*.
11. Hadden, 43; Burgoyne, 9; Anburey, I, 121.
12. Nickerson, 110.
13. Burgoyne, 10. Luc de Chapt de la Corne Saint-Luc, commonly called La Corne St. Luc or even La Corne or St. Luc, was a Frenchman who had seen much service as a leader of Indian bands in King George's War and the French and Indian War. He had entered into the spirit and adopted the methods of Indian warfare with so little compunction and with such great success as to evidence an identity of taste and temperament with his savage followers. He had, consequently, great influence among them. Though past sixty-five at the expulsion of the Americans from Canada, he had been active in raising Indian recruits for Burgoyne and, with physical stamina and hardihood unimpaired, had undertaken their leadership in active service. The Americans feared him even more than they hated him. One described him as "that arch devil incarnate, who has butchered hundreds, men, women and children of our colonies . . . in the most inhuman manner." There seems to be no doubt that he was of a brutal, bloody and pitiless nature, cruel and remorseless in his methods of warfare. Charles de Langlade, a French officer associated with him in command of the Indians, had seen service in the French and Indian War. He is sometimes said to have planned and executed the ambush which resulted in Braddock's defeat.
14. Hadden, 34, 44, 53.
15. Burgoyne, 13.
16. Hadden, 49.
17. Hadden, 44–45; Riedesel, 105–107.
18. Burgoyne, 10–17. Fonblanque, 488, gives the total force as 7,902, presumably including officers.
19. Fonblanque, 240–241; Jones, CH, 158, 181; Nickerson, 116.

20. Riedesel, I, 2–17; Nickerson, 117–118.
21. Hadden, 52; Nickerson, 104–105.
22. Nickerson, 120–122; Anburey, I, 184.
23. Hudleston, 148–151.
24. Walpole, X, 188.
25. Burgoyne, Appendix, xxi; Anburey, I, 168, 174.
26. Walpole, X, 188.
27. Wilkinson, I, 155 ff.
28. Nickerson, 182–183.
29. Wilkinson, I, 169 n.
30. Wilkinson, I, 174–176.
31. Hadden, 54.
32. Lamb, 135.
33. Anburey, I, 182.
34. Hadden, 82.
35. Wilkinson, I, 181.
36. Hadden, 82; Wilkinson, I, 180; Nickerson, 41–42.
37. Burgoyne, Appendix, xxviii, xxxix; Anburey, I, 190.
38. Hadden, 84.
39. Wilkinson, I, 184.
40. Wilkinson, I, 184–185 n.; *The Royal Kalendar* for 1777.
41. Anburey, I, 192.
42. Anburey, I, 193.
43. Burgoyne, Appendix, xxi; Riedesel, I, 113–114.
44. Anburey, I, 194.
45. Wilkinson, I, 186–187.
46. Hadden, 92; Wilkinson, I, 186.
47. Wilkinson, I, 188.
48. Anburey, I, 195.
49. Anburey, I, 196.
50. Wilkinson, I, 187.
51. Riedesel, I, 115–116; Hadden, 85–86; Burgoyne, Appendix, xxxii.
52. Wilkinson, I, 187–188 n.; Hadden, Appendix 15. Hadden, 88, gives the enemy losses as 17 officers and 109 men killed or wounded.
53. Burgoyne, Appendix, xxv; Lamb, 146. Hadden, 89, says the lake was "so narrow that the Ships Yards almost touched the Precipes which overhung them."
54. Riedesel, I, 117.
55. Wilkinson, I, 186, 190.
56. Burgoyne, Appendix, xxxi.
57. Burgoyne, Appendix, xxxiv.
58. Lamb, 142.
59. Wilkinson, I, 189.

CHAPTER 37

Among the original sources of information for this chapter and the next following are Burgoyne's *State of the Expedition*, Hadden's *Journal*, Anburey's *Travels*, Wilkinson's *Memoirs*, Riedesel's *Memoirs*, Lamb's *Memoirs*, Digby's journal, and the letters of Schuyler. Secondary sources of value are Coburn's *Centennial History*, Hall's *Battle of Bennington*, Dawson's *Battles*, Lowell's *Hessians*, Lossing's *Pictorial Field Book*, Fonblanque's *Political and Military Episodes*, Hudleston's *Gentleman Johnny Burgoyne*, Patterson's *Horatio Gates*, Neilson's *Original Account of Burgoyne's Campaign*, Stone's *Campaign of Lieut. Gen. John Burgoyne*, Gordon's *History* and Stedman's. Nickerson's *Turning Point of the Revolution*, a large book devoted entirely to Burgoyne's campaign, is the fullest account. Its value to succeeding historians is definitely and considerably less than it might be, because the author has not provided a single footnote or specific reference by which the verity of any statement in it or the validity of any of his conclusions or opinions may be tested.

1. Burgoyne, Appendix, vi.
2. Burgoyne, 17.
3. Hadden, Appendix I.
4. Hadden, 100; Burgoyne, Appendix, xxxvi.
5. Hadden, 91–96; Burgoyne, Appendix, xxxv.
6. Hadden, 109.
7. Nickerson, 186; Wilkinson, I, 192, 200; Sparks, *C*, I, 397–399.
8. Trevelyan, III, 120.
9. Stedman, I, 327; Hadden, 94.
10. Burgoyne, Appendix, xi, xxxvi.
11. Hadden, 95, 97.
12. Wilkinson, Appendix B.
13. Nickerson, 18, gives this quotation with no indication of its source.
14. Burgoyne, Appendix, xii, xlvi, xlix.
15. Riedesel, I, 125–126; Burgoyne, 51.
16. Burgoyne, 137, Appendix, xiv.
17. Riedesel, I, 101, states that, before the southward march of Burgoyne's force began, in June, 1777, he had ordered for the dragoons "long linen trousers, striped with white and blue, and similar to those worn by the inhabitants during summer." That these were actually provided and displaced the leather breeches does not appear.
18. Burgoyne, Appendix, lxiii; Hadden, 111–117.
19. Burgoyne, Appendix, xii; Lamb, 151.
20. Burgoyne, Appendix, lxiii.
21. Coburn, B, 22–23.
22. Lossing, I, 393.
23. Stryker, *TP*, 350.
24. Coburn, B, 31.
25. Lossing, I, 394; Sparks, *C*, I, 397, 423.
26. Lossing, I, 394.
27. *Journals*, VIII, 656–657.
28. Riedesel, I, 128.
29. Burgoyne, Appendix, xi.
30. Dawson, I, 260.
31. Burgoyne, Appendix, lxx.
32. Lossing, I, 395, says there was no bridge there at that time, but only a ford. He calls the river Walloomscoick.
33. Dawson, I, 260.
34. Coburn, B, 40.
35. Dawson, I, 260.
36. Riedesel, I, 130; Lamb, I, 153. Burgoyne, Appendix, xiii, says many of these Americans took the oath of allegiance and were afterwards the first to fire on Baum.
37. Lossing, I, 397 n. This historic order is reported by the historians generally, with slight differences in verbiage.
38. Riedesel, I, 131.
39. Hadden, 118; Riedesel, I, 129–130.
40. Dawson, I, 264; Anburey, I, 233. Burgoyne (Appendix, xiv) wrote to Germain on August 20: "Could Mr. Breyman have marched at the rate of two miles an hour, any given twelve hours out of the two and thirty, success would probably have ensued."
41. Dawson, I, 264; Riedesel, I, 131.
42. Coburn, B, 55.
43. Dawson, I, 264.
44. Dawson, I, 260.
45. The various estimates of losses on both sides differ, as usual. The statement in the text seems to be approximately correct.
46. *Journals*, IX, 770.

CHAPTER 38

Stanwix and Oriskany

It will be remembered that there was a third element in Burgoyne's plan for the conquest of the Hudson: an expedition from Canada by way of Lake Ontario, Oswego, and the Mohawk River to meet Burgoyne at Albany. Its purpose was also the occupation of the extensive and important Mohawk valley, the gateway to the great western country and to the territory of the powerful Six Nations of Indians, whose support in the war Great Britain was seeking. We must now turn to that valley.

The American border settlements in the West were not left undisturbed during the War of Independence. Rather the war was waged there with the ferocity and cruelty characteristic of the chief components of the British forces in that section, that is to say the Indians enlisted with them, not to mention their Tory allies. A ruthlessness, one regrets to say, that was matched at last by the great American punitive expedition finally sent against the Indian towns in that section.

Tryon County in New York was one of the chief seats of the conflict in the West. It was a vast tract, comprising the land west and northwest of Schenectady and extending to Lake Ontario. Through it ran the Mohawk River in a beautiful and fertile valley. Its great area was sparsely settled, harboring perhaps 5,000 people. They were of diverse nationalities. A numerous element of Germans from the Rhenish Palatinate, indicated by the name of one of the chief settlements, German Flats, lived chiefly along the upper reaches of the river. In its lower reaches the population was largely of Dutch extraction. Everywhere there were people of English descent. The Irish were well represented, also the Scotch-Irish. Scottish Highlanders were numerous, particularly in the neighborhood of Johnstown.

As in the South under similar conditions, the political sentiments of the people were divided, in part along lines of nationality, in part by individual or family preferences. The Germans and many of the Dutch were inclined to favor the royal government; the Highlanders were as loyal to the King as their kinsmen in the Carolinas. The whole county was generally regarded as a Tory stronghold. One historian says that "the loyalists in that [Mohawk] valley were probably more numerous, in proportion to the whole . . . population, than in almost any other section of the northern states." [1] And yet the fact that the course of the war forced so many of them, including the most powerful and influential, to flee to Canada would seem to prove the existence of a majority of patriots, unless as elsewhere they were merely better organized and more vigorous in their activities.

To the west of Tryon County was the seat of the great Iroquois League, the Six Nations, the Mohawks, Onondagas, Cayugas, Senecas, Oneidas, and Tuscaroras. Their towns and their "castles," the headquarters of the various tribes or of their component clans, were numerous over a wide extent of country.

The ruling family in the county were the Johnsons, headed by Sir William, the British Superintendent of Indian Affairs, until his death in 1774 and after that by his son, Sir John, and his son-in-law, Colonel Guy Johnson, who was his successor in office. The Johnsons were strongly and unitedly Tory. Sir William had been the greatest landholder and the wealthiest man in the county. His handsome mansion house at Johnstown was the center of governmental relations with the Indians, the symbol of the wealth and power of the great nation he officially represented. While his influence was strong in determining the attitude of many of the whites toward the conflict between Britain and the colonists, it was predominant among the Indians.

This influence over the Indians was based not only on his official position, but also on a lifelong, sympathetic study of their ways, habits, and dispositions. It was also powerfully backed by his left-handed family relationship with two of their great chieftains. After the death of his first wife, a German, he took to himself, successively, two Indian mistresses, Caroline, the daughter of Hendrick, the famous Mohawk "King," and Molly, sister of Joseph Brant, also called Thayendanegea, chief war leader of the Mohawks and as such of the whole Iroquois League. Molly, indeed, may have been actually married to Sir William in Indian fashion; at all events she had a recognized position as the head of his household. She was a woman of considerable mental ability and great shrewdness, and her influence among the Indians was freely exerted and very potent.

Her brother, Joseph Brant, was a figure of distinction, a remarkable man.

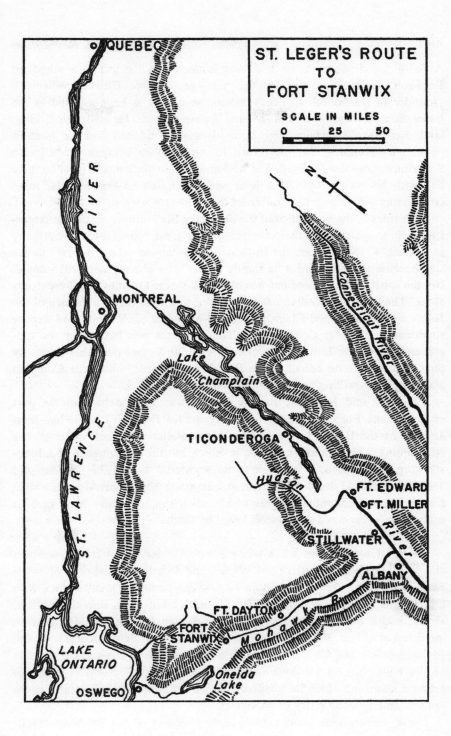

ST. LEGER'S ROUTE
TO
FORT STANWIX

SCALE IN MILES
0   25   50

A full-blooded Mohawk, he had been educated in English at a school in Lebanon, Connecticut, under the tutelage of Dr. Eleazar Wheelock (founder of Dartmouth College), where he is said to have assisted in the translation of religious books into the Indian tongue. He had visited England, had been entertained by James Boswell, and had had his portrait painted by Romney. On his return to America he became secretary to Superintendent Guy Johnson. Yet he remained an Indian. He went back to live with his own people and distinguished himself as one of their most courageous warriors and undoubtedly their ablest strategist.

Both sides in the war solicited the aid of the Six Nations or, on the American side, sought at least their neutrality. The great "council-fire" at Albany in August, 1775, at which the Indians agreed "not to take any part" in the war because they deemed it "a family affair," has already been mentioned. But the spirit of that agreement was observed by the Oneidas and Tuscaroras alone. The other four Indian nations yielded to the powerful influence of the Johnsons and of Daniel Claus, also a son-in-law of Sir William and deputy superintendent under Colonel Guy. This influence was backed by the munificent gifts to the Indians of arms, clothing, and other desirable things by Sir Guy Carleton on behalf of the British government, which the Congress was possibly unwilling and certainly unable to match.

It must be said, however, that the alliance was not unnatural on the part of the Indians. For more than a hundred years the Iroquois League had been assisted by the British forces in their long conflict with their enemies, the Algonquins. This new alliance was, in effect, but the continuance of a long-standing cooperation. It is rather to be wondered at that the Oneidas and Tuscaroras should decide to adhere, at least passively, to the American side; for this much credit must be given to Samuel Kirkland, a missionary in their midst, much respected and indeed loved by them.

Colonel Guy Johnson left his home with Colonel John Butler, an outstanding Tory leader, Butler's son Walter, and Joseph Brant shortly after the news of Bunker's Hill reached him. At Oswego he held a great council with the Indians. Thence he departed for Canada, taking with him the Butlers, Brant, and a numerous delegation of his Indian friends. At Montreal an interview with Sir Guy Carleton strengthened the determination of the Mohawks, Senecas, Cayugas, and Onondagas to join in the war on the side of the King. Sir John Johnson, however, remained at Johnson Hall, his father's mansion, which he fortified. He was guarded by 150 armed Highlanders and a strong party of Mohawks.

These preparations seemed to indicate "designs of the most dangerous tendency to the rights, liberties, property and even lives" of the patriots, as General Schuyler wrote to Sir John in January, 1776. He ordered out the county militia under General Herkimer, to the number of more than 3,000, and marched to a point near Johnson Hall, where he met Sir John. At the meeting Sir John agreed to surrender all his armament and submitted to being taken prisoner. He was soon thereafter liberated upon his parole not to engage in hostilities against the Americans. Within four months from the time of his agreement, he broke his parole and, with a large number of his tenants and other Tories, took to the woods on his way to Montreal, where he arrived after a journey of great hardship lasting nearly three weeks.

By the departure of the Johnsons, the Butlers, Brant, and their adherents, Tryon County was relieved of the most powerful members of its Tory element; but the dangers to its peace and the welfare of its patriot inhabitants were thereby increased rather than lessened. Their Tory enemies were now in touch with the British forces in Canada and thus able to concert measures for hostile operations with more facility and greater effectiveness than if they had remained in the midst of their former neighbors, where they could have been observed and more readily suppressed. This was soon made evident when Sir John received a commission as colonel in the British service and raised a Tory regiment of two battalions, entitled the Royal Greens from the color of their coats, which conformed to the customary uniforms of the Loyalist troops attached to the British army. Colonel John Butler also raised a corps of Tory Rangers, similarly clad.[2]

Hostile invasion of the county was not, however, immediately begun. Two years were to elapse before Johnson and Butler appeared in arms against their former neighbors. That was in August, 1777, when their troops formed a part of the British expedition auxiliary to Burgoyne's plan for the conquest of the Hudson.

The principal defensive post in the Mohawk valley was Fort Stanwix, built in 1758 to hold the portage, the Great Carrying Place, between the river and Wood Creek, which runs into Lake Ontario. Originally a strong fortification with bomb-proof bastions, a glacis, a covered way, and a well picketed ditch, it had, as usual, been allowed to decay. When in April, 1777, Colonel Peter Gansevoort with the 3rd New York Continental regiment took over its command, he found it "not only indefensible, but untenable."[3] Gansevoort, energetic and resolute, a competent soldier, was a young officer, no more than twenty-eight years old. He was ably seconded by his courageous, enterprising lieutenant colonel, Marinus Willett, spirited and active. They put their men to work on the old fort, and before its day of supreme trial it was restored to a defensible condition. Standing athwart the way from Oswego to Albany, it must first be reduced before invaders from the west could proceed to the Hudson. The task of reducing it fell to Barry St. Leger, who was appointed by Burgoyne to lead the auxiliary expedition forward from Oswego.

Barry St. Leger was an experienced soldier; more than half of his forty years had been spent in the King's service. He had taken part in the siege of Louisburg and in the capture of Quebec. His regular and permanent rank was lieutenant colonel of the 34th Foot; but temporarily and locally he had the title of brigadier general.

The force allotted to St. Leger was made up of detachments of 100 men each from the 8th and the 34th regiments, a regiment of 133 Tories of Sir John Johnson's "Royal Greens," a company of Tory Rangers under Colonel John Butler, and about 350 Hanau jägers. Forty artillerists were equipped with two 6-pounders, two 3-pounders, and four very small mortars, called "cohorns" or "royals." Some Canadian irregulars, a large number of axmen, and other noncombatants were added.[4] As he started with only one company of the jägers, about 100 men, the rest being delayed, his force of white men numbered about 875 of all ranks. The Indian contingent, under Joseph Brant, between 800 and 1,000 strong, met him at Oswego on his arrival July 25. The next day he started for Fort Stanwix, which he had been led to believe was in a ruinous condition and garrisoned by only 60 men.

Thomas Spencer, a half-breed chief of the Oneidas, was present at a council of the Six Nations where Daniel Claus urged the Indians to join St. Leger, and he brought word of this to the inhabitants of the valley. The result was unfortunate for the American cause: the Tories became bolder and more active. The less courageous and the uncertain patriots either professed neutrality or secretly allied themselves with the Tories. There was a general paralysis of the patriot effort throughout the valley.

To counteract this sad effect was the task of Nicholas Herkimer, brigadier general of the county militia. The son of a Palatine German immigrant named Ergheimer who had secured large grants of land along the river, he was now, in his fiftieth year, a moderately wealthy man. He had fought in the French and Indian War. He has been described as "short, slender, of dark complexion, with black hair and bright eyes."[5] Like many of the people of the valley, he was better acquainted with the tongue of his ancestors than with the English language.

On July 17 Herkimer issued a brief but vigorous and stirring proclamation calling on all able-bodied men between the ages of sixteen and sixty to prepare for mobilization; all invalids and old men were to be ready to defend their homes, and all Tories and slackers were to be arrested and confined. This appeal, powerfully backed by the dread prospect of an Indian invasion, had the desired effect. The fighting spirit of the rebels of Tryon County was fully aroused.

St. Leger's march was conducted with much caution, with great regularity, and in excellent formation. Five single-file columns of Indians, widely spaced, preceded the advance guard of soldiers by about a quarter of a mile. A middle single file, its members ten paces apart, followed these soldiers, to ensure communication with the main body. The regulars' advance guard, 60 marksmen of the Royal Greens, marched in two columns a hundred yards ahead of the British regulars, whose two detachments marched side by side. Indian flankers covered both sides of the main body, and a guard of regulars brought up the rear. All the columns were in single file. Though St. Leger moved cautiously, he moved swiftly. His force marched ten miles a day, excellent progress in a wilderness of forests, streams, and swamps.

But he wished for an even swifter movement to surprise the fort and cut off its communications with the lower country, and especially to intercept a convoy of provisions and supplies on the way to it. Accordingly, he pushed forward a detachment of 30 regulars of the 8th Regiment under Lieutenant Bird, and 200 Indians led by Brant. They reached Stanwix on the 2nd, just too late to cut off the convoy of five bateaux and a reenforcement of 200 men, which got safely into the fort, although one of several bateaumen lingering about the boats was killed. Two others were wounded, and the captain of the boats was captured. The next day St. Leger and his full force arrived.

His first move was an attempt to intimidate the garrison by a review of his troops in plain sight of the palisaded earthwork. The varied uniforms, scarlet for the British, blue for the Germans, green for the jägers, the rangers, and Johnson's Tories, made a gay display; but the naked bodies of a thousand savages were more impressive. Impressive, however, in a way contrary to St. Leger's intentions. They were visible indications of the cruel fate of the men of the garrison and of their families in the settlements behind them, if the fort were not held against the invaders. And so that parade stiffened the determination of the 750 defenders not to let the savages and their allies pass.

St. Leger's second move was to send a proclamation, under a flag, into the fort. It rivaled Burgoyne's similar effort in pomposity. Indeed, most of it was a copy of that sample of "enlightened absurdity." It received no answer.

Perceiving that the fort was too strong and too strongly held to yield to an assault, St. Leger disposed his force to besiege it. It stood on a slight elevation on the north side of the river and close to the road from Wood Creek to the Lower Landing on the Hudson, being the important portage or Great Carrying Place. Behind it there was a somewhat higher elevation on which he established the camp of his regular troops. At the Lower Landing, most of the Canadians, Tories, and Indians were posted. Another detachment of Tories held a position on Wood Creek to the west of the fort. Little groups of Indians were strung along from that place to the Lower Landing. Thus the fort was surrounded. But it was not closely invested, for the circuit of the investment was nearly three miles long and there was heavily wooded and swampy ground on the southwest, which could not be tightly held.

St. Leger's next thought was for his communications with Lake Ontario. A road sixteen miles long through the forest had to be cut before he could bring up his artillery and heavy supplies. Also Wood Creek had to be cleared of the trees that Gansevoort had felled to obstruct it. Besides his Canadian axmen and other noncombatants, he put so many of his men to work at that job that on August 5, when he had news of a relieving force on its way to the fort, he had in camp fewer than 250 regular troops to oppose it.

In the meantime, the Indians along with their friends, the German jägers, had been enjoying a safe kind of warfare. Taking cover as near the fort as possible, they fired at the Americans who were piling sods on the parapet to increase its height, and wounded several of them. To reply, marksmen were posted at different parts of the works; and a brisk, though desultory, fire was kept up throughout the 4th and 5th.

On July 30 Herkimer, having news of St. Leger's advance, summoned his militia to rendezvous at Fort Dayton on the Mohawk about thirty miles below Stanwix. They turned out in satisfactory numbers, about 800 of them, and marched on August 4. Although encumbered by a train of oxcarts,[6] they made good progress, about twenty-two miles in two days. On the way, they were joined by 60 Oneida Indians, who were to act as scouts.

Herkimer sent forward four runners to inform Gansevoort of his approach. In reply Gansevoort was to fire three cannon shots, acknowledging receipt of the news and signaling his readiness to make a sortie when the relief column was near, then to engage the enemy about the fort and prevent them from concentrating on Herkimer's troops.

On the morning of the 6th Herkimer held a council of war. No gunshots from the fort had been heard. The question was whether the relieving force should, nevertheless, immediately advance or await the expected signal. Herkimer was for waiting; but in that opinion he stood almost alone. His subordinate officers were for going on, regardless of the lack of reply by Gansevoort.

The matter was debated with acerbity which developed into hot anger on the part of those urging an immediate advance. Herkimer seems to have kept his temper, but stubbornly held to his opinion. The others charged him with cowardice, called him a Tory at heart, brought up the fact that one of his brothers was an officer in a Tory company under St. Leger. At last he could no longer withstand their urgency, coupled with accusations of poltroonery. He yielded and gave the order.

The Oneida scouts went ahead. Herkimer, conspicuously mounted on a white horse, showed that he was no coward by taking the lead of his men. After him, 600 marched in double file. Then came the wagon train, followed by a rear guard of 200.

At the news of the advance of Herkimer's men St. Leger prepared to receive them before they got to the fort. Six miles short of Stanwix, and near Oriskany village, the road crossed a wide ravine, fifty feet deep with steep sides. Through it ran a small stream bordered by a morass. Across that bottom, the road was corduroyed with loose logs, offering a difficult and a narrow passage. Here St. Leger proposed to check, indeed to annihilate, Herkimer's force. To this work he detailed a part of his Royal Greens, a detachment of Butler's Rangers, and the whole force of Indians under Joseph Brant.

The plan was to post the white men on the west of the ravine and the savages in hiding along its western margin in a curve almost encircling it, but leave the eastern side open for Herkimer's troops to enter the trap. When the middle of the column was deep in the ravine, the Tories and Rangers were to check its head, and the Indians were to close the circle around the rear on the east. Thus Herkimer would be completely surrounded by enemies under cover of rocks and trees, their fire converging on his trapped column. It was a well conceived scheme, admirably fitted to the character of those who were to execute it and likely to be successful.

It is difficult to understand why the Oneida scouts did not discover some signs of that ambuscade; but they did not. If the Americans had thrown out any flankers, they must have stumbled upon some of the ambushed Indians and given the alarm. It seems probable that no such precautions were taken, that the long thin column was confined to the narrow road.

The main body, led by Herkimer, had made its way down into the ravine and up the other side, and the groaning, creaking supply train of oxcarts was negotiating the difficult passage when the trap was sprung. The Indians east of the ravine leaped from their cover, delivered their fire, and rushed in with whoops and yells to close the circle—rushed in a little too soon for complete encirclement, for they closed upon the rear of the wagon train, between it and the rear guard. Cut off from the main body, the guard fled along the road, pursued by some of the savages.

Herkimer, at the head of the column, heard the firing in the rear, turned his horse, and hurried to investigate the situation. As he did so, the Tories and Indians on the west of the ravine pushed forward and began shooting. On the western slope of the ravine, his horse fell dead; his own leg was wounded.

The circle was now complete. Hemmed in on every side, the Americans broke from their ordered line. Singly or in groups they took cover behind trees. There was no front to this fight. Behind a tree, a man was not covered from the bullets of the enemy in his rear. And the Indians were coming closer on every side, ready to charge upon the disorganized mass with tomahawk and knife.

To protect their rear, groups of the Americans formed little circles, facing out from behind trees. Herkimer was carried into their midst. His saddle was brought. Astride it, his back against a tree, he lit his pipe and with great coolness directed his men to form one great circle and thus oppose their fire to all those around them.

But it was not a compact circle after the manner of a British square. It was irregular and widely spaced. The attack was irregular, too, and there was much hand-to-hand fighting, Indian tomahawks and knives and Tory bayonets against clubbed muskets. At this work, the Indians were experts. As soon as an American had fired, an Indian would rush in upon him and cut him down with a tomahawk before he could reload.

But after three-quarters of an hour of this desperate conflict there was a sudden and complete cessation of fire on both sides. The lowering clouds of that hot, sultry day had broken and discharged a downpour that wet the priming of the flintlocks. No gun could be discharged. For a full hour, this armistice lasted. Then the sun came out and the fight began again, but with a slight difference. Herkimer had ordered his men to take cover by twos, so that, when one had fired and was reloading, the other would be ready to shoot any of the savages that attempted their favorite trick.

The Indians had been suffering severely and had begun to lose interest in such a well contested struggle. Their fire slackened; they showed signs of uneasiness. At this juncture Major Watts came up with a second detachment of Royal Greens. He had them turn their coats inside out, so that their uni-

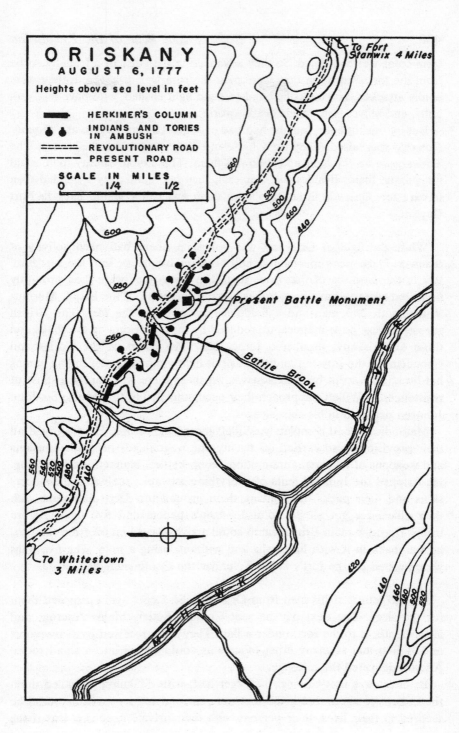

ORISKANY
AUGUST 6, 1777
Heights above sea level in feet

■■■■ HERKIMER'S COLUMN
●● INDIANS AND TORIES
    IN AMBUSH
====== REVOLUTIONARY ROAD
------ PRESENT ROAD

SCALE IN MILES
0   1/4   1/2

To Fort
Stanwix 4 Miles

Present Battle Monument

Battle Brook

MOHAWK

To Whitestown
3 Miles

form color was concealed. So they advanced in the guise of a friendly sortie from the fort. But when they were near the ruse was discovered; they were boldly attacked, and a terrific hand-to-hand fight ensued, with bayonets, gun butts, and knives doing their deadly work.

But by this time the Indians had had enough. The cry of retreat, *"Oonah! Oonah!"* was raised. They drew back and disappeared into the woods. The Tories gave up the fight and followed them. The Tryon County men could not pursue them. Besides their general, they had some fifty wounded men to care for. On rude litters they bore them away in a march back to Fort Dayton.

While the fight at Oriskany was going on, there had been activity at Stanwix. Herkimer's messengers had been unable to get into the fort until late in the morning of that same day. The three guns were then promptly fired, but seem to have been unheard amid the noise of the battle. Marinus Willett with 250 men and a fieldpiece issued from the fort. The British regular troops in the main camp, reduced by those working on the roads and those at Oriskany, numbered rather less. The camp of the Tories and Canadians at the Lower Landing was but lightly guarded, the Indian camps hardly at all, except by their squaws. At these there was hardly a show of resistance. At Willett's approach their occupants fled to the woods; Sir John Johnson departed in his shirt sleeves.

Methodically and completely, Willett looted the camps. He destroyed all their provisions, and carried off twenty-one wagonloads of spoils, muskets and weapons of all sorts, ammunition, camp kettles, blankets, and clothing. He stripped the Indians' tents of everything movable, including their deerskins and their packs, thus giving them ground for deep discontent with their allies. He got all Sir John Johnson's papers and five flags. Before troops from the main British camp could arrive to cut him off from the fort, he was back in it with his spoils and without losing a man. The five flags were hoisted on the fort's flagstaff "under the Continental flag." [7]

On the return of his men from Oriskany, St. Leger again disposed them for the siege. The next day he sent Colonel Butler, Major Ancron, and another officer to the fort, under a flag. They were received by Gansevoort and Willett and as many other officers as could crowd into a small room. Ancron delivered the message.

Its effect was that Colonel St. Leger had, with difficulty, prevailed upon the Indians to agree that if the fort were surrendered its garrison would be secured in their lives, their persons, and their private property. But if the fort had to be taken by force he could not restrain his savage allies from an indiscriminate massacre of its defenders. Indeed, he went on, the Indians were so provoked by their recent losses of several favorite chiefs that they threatened to march down the valley and destroy all the settlements and their inhabitants, men, women, and children; and he could not prevent it.

Willett answered for the garrison: "Do I understand you, sir? I think you say you come from a British Colonel, who is commander of the army that invests this fort; and by your uniform you appear to be an officer in the British service. . . . You come from a British colonel to the commandant of this garrison to tell him that, if he does not deliver up the garrison . . . he will send his Indians to murder our women and children." With blistering scorn, Willett told Ancron that he had brought a message degrading for any British officer to send and disreputable for any British officer to carry. No, they would not surrender.[8]

St. Leger set about building new redoubts more closely to invest the fort and establishing batteries to bombard it. But his guns were too light to have any effect on its sod-covered walls. He then began digging trenches, regular approaches by parallels, which would allow him to undermine the walls of the fort and breach them.

While this was going on, Willett and one companion undertook to penetrate the enemy's lines with an appeal to the militia of Tryon County for help. Working their way by night through the swamps and across the streams in the ground held by the Indians, they got to Fort Dayton in two days and there learned that a relieving force of Continental troops was already on its way.

Schuyler at Stillwater had received news of the investment of Stanwix. He called a council of war and proposed to send a detachment to relieve it. Most of his officers opposed this as weakening the army already too weak to resist Burgoyne. They muttered among themselves that it was an intentional weakening. The insinuation was in line with the charges of cowardice and even of treason, which had been leveled against the general on account of his successive retreats. Schuyler, who was pacing the room in agitation at the opposition to his plan for succor, overheard the remarks. In his anger he bit the stem of his clay pipe in two. Casting away the fragments, he stopped and looked the council in the face. "Gentlemen," he said, "I shall take the responsibility upon myself. Fort Stanwix and the Mohawk Valley shall be saved! Where is the brigadier who will command the relief? I shall beat up for volunteers to-morrow."[9]

Benedict Arnold, angry at the false imputations cast upon Schuyler and ever ready for action in the field, instantly offered his services. Although a major general, second in command to Schuyler, he was more than willing to take up the duties of a brigadier. Volunteers to the number of 950 were eager to follow a leader whom they admired and trusted. Brigadier General Ebenezer Learned of Massachusetts took the second command.

At Fort Dayton, on the 21st, they were joined by a hundred Tryon County militia and were informed that St. Leger had 1,700 men to oppose them. It seemed even to Arnold, that fighting man, that prudence called for reinforcements. Yet, the next day, hearing that St. Leger's approaches were very near their objective, and that the fort was in grave danger, Arnold decided to go forward with what men he had. On the 23rd he started, with a part of his force, on a forced march up the Mohawk. He had gone but ten miles when he got word that a ruse he had employed had been successful.

A Mohawk Valley German, Hon Yost Schuyler, had been sentenced to death for trying to recruit men for the British cause. He was generally esteemed a half-idiot, and was therefore regarded by the Indians with the respect and awe that they always accorded to the insane. Yet he was both cunning and shrewd. Arnold promised him a pardon if he would go to St. Leger's camp and spread a report of the approach of a relief force overwhelming in numbers.

Hon Yost took off his coat and had it shot through by several bullets. With an Oneida Indian as assistant, he started for Stanwix. Entering the Indians' camp alone, he said he had narrowly escaped from Arnold's force, and showed the bullet holes as proof. He had come, he said, to warn his red brothers that they were in danger. Thousands of troops were about to attack them. To St. Leger he told a circumstantial story of his escape while on the way to the gallows.

The Oneida assistant came in to tell *his* red brothers of their danger, repeating the story the other had told. The Indians took alarm, began to pack up for immediate departure. St. Leger's attempts to quiet them had no effect. Rumors that Arnold was coming with 3,000 men, that he was only two miles away, ran through the camp. He was feared by the white soldiers and the red warriors alike as was no other American officer. A panic ensued. The Indians rioted, seized the officers' supplies of liquor and even their clothing. They became, as St. Leger said, "more formidable than the enemy!" Two hundred of them fled to the woods. The chiefs of those remaining insisted on an immediate retreat. St. Leger gave the order.

Leaving their tents standing, their artillery, ammunition, and supplies, the whole force started for their boats on Wood Creek, with only such baggage as they could carry on their backs. So they made their way back to Oswego.

That was the story Arnold got from the crazy Hon Yost, who slipped away and came back to meet him. There was nothing now to do but push on to Stanwix and be received by its garrison with cheers and a salute from the artillery.

The losses on both sides at Oriskany were never accurately ascertained. It was as bloody a battle in proportion to the numbers engaged as any in the war. Fought at close quarters with unusual ferocity, the usual relative proportions of killed and wounded were reversed. Perhaps as good a guess as any is that the Tryon militia had 150 to 200 killed and 50 wounded, while of the Indians and Tories 150 may have fallen. Herkimer died shortly after his wounded leg was amputated.

But one thing was certain. Part of Burgoyne's plan had been knocked into a cocked hat. St. Leger had been beaten back. There would be no one to meet Burgoyne at Albany. He had to see it through alone.

CHAPTER 39

Danbury

Before the narrative of the movements of the two armies towards their final meeting at Saratoga, two incidents that occurred previously must have their place here, for, though they were slight in proportion to the magnitude of the Hudson River campaign, both had important effects upon it.

The first of these occurred in April, 1777. General Howe directed William Tryon, royal governor of New York, lately commissioned a major general, to destroy a magazine of American stores and provisions at Danbury in Connecticut. Detachments of 250 men each were drawn from the 4th, 15th, 23rd, 27th, 44th, and 64th British infantry regiments, and of 300 from Brown's Tory regiment. A few light dragoons and some fieldpieces were added. Generals Agnew and Erskine were appointed to commands under Tryon. Convoyed by two frigates, the expedition sailed from New York on the 23rd and landed near Norwalk in the evening of the 25th.

The march to Danbury was unopposed. Its garrison of 150 Continentals removed a small part of the stores before they retired on Tryon's approach. About three o'clock in the afternoon of the 26th the work of destruction was begun; and it was continued until the next morning. Nineteen dwelling houses and twenty-two storehouses and barns, as well as great quantities of pork, beef, flour, wheat, clothing, and tents were burned. At ten o'clock the next morning the return march to the ships was begun.

In New Haven, Brigadier General Benedict Arnold, the Achilles of the American army, was sulking in his tent, that is to say in the house of his sister. Despite his brilliant services in the war, five brigadiers, all junior to him in rank and one a mere militia general, had been made major generals

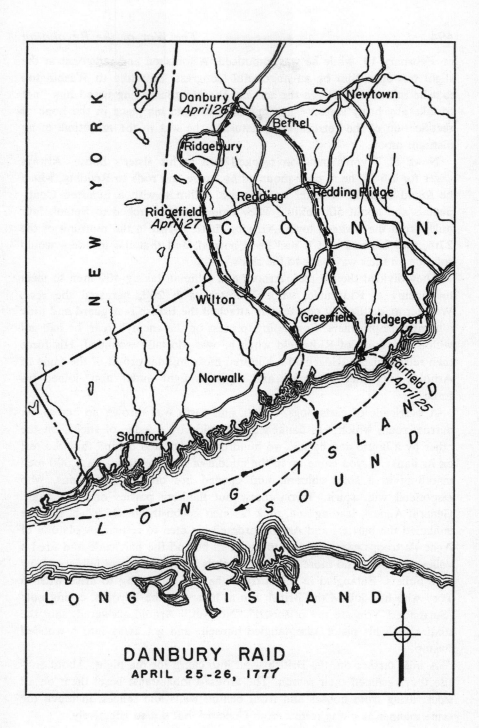

DANBURY RAID
APRIL 25-26, 1777

on February 19, while he was unnoticed. Astonished and indignant at the slight put upon him by an ungrateful Congress, he wrote to Washington that he intended to resign the service. Washington having urged him "not to take any hasty steps," [1] he consented to hold his place in the hope of rectification of the "error." But, naturally, he was in the meantime in no pleasant mood.

News of Tryon's invasion reached him at his sister's house. Always eager for a fight, he at once mounted his horse and rode to Redding, where he found General Wooster and General Silliman with a hundred Continentals and about 500 militia. They immediately marched to Bethel, four miles from the ravaged town. Arriving there at two in the morning of the 27th, they learned that it had been burned, and that the invaders would soon be on their way back to the ships.

They divided their forces, Arnold and Silliman taking 400 men to meet the enemy at Ridgefield, while Wooster, with 200, harassed the rear. Wooster made the first contact. He attacked the British rear guard and took a number of prisoners. Continuing to press on the enemy's rear, he had got within two miles of Ridgefield when he was mortally wounded. His force then retreated. At Ridgefield a hundred more militia, proud of the fame of Arnold, a Connecticut man, and eager to fight under him, joined his force.

A barricade of carts, logs, stones, and earth was thrown up across the narrow road, which was flanked on one side by a ledge of rocks, on the other by a house and barn. Two hundred were posted behind this, the rest on its flanks. Tryon came up in the middle of the afternoon, his 2,000 men marching in a solid column, and opened fire on the Americans, who responded with spirit. Tryon threw out flanking parties on both sides. General Agnew, leading one, took his men up on the rocky ledge. His fire enfiladed the barrier, and Arnold ordered his men to retreat. A platoon of Agnew's troops came down into the road behind the barricade and fired a volley at Arnold, no more than thirty yards away. His horse fell, struck by nine bullets. Entangled in the stirrups, he was struggling to arise when a Tory who had joined the British ran at him with the bayonet, crying out: "Surrender! You are my prisoner!" "Not yet!" Arnold answered, shot the soldier with his pistol, disentangled himself, and got away into a wooded swamp.

A mile farther on, the British went into camp for the night. About sunrise they resumed their march. The aroused inhabitants beset them on all sides, firing from houses and from behind walls and fences, in much the same manner as in the retreat from Concord, but not so effectively.

In the meantime, Arnold had collected his men and secured three field-pieces with their appropriate companies of artillerists. He posted his force so as to command both of two roads by which Tryon might gain the water-side where his ships awaited him. But a Tory guide showed Tryon a cir-cuitous way around Arnold's position to Compo Hill near the landing place. There the British stood on the defensive. The Americans formed in two columns for the attack. But before it could be launched, General Erskine led 400 of his men in a bayonet charge, which despite the valiant efforts of Colonel John Lamb's artillery to check it, broke the American ranks, and Tryon was enabled to embark his men.

Howe admitted no greater loss than 60 killed and wounded, but Sted-man, the English historian, figured their casualties at "near two hundred men, including ten officers." The Americans lost perhaps 20 killed and 40 wounded.[2]

The results of this expedition reflected no credit upon the Connecticut people, who allowed the British to make a leisurely march through their country without opposition until its objects had been accomplished, and failed to remove the precious stores from Danbury before they could be taken and destroyed. The contrast between such pusillanimous behavior and that of the men of Massachusetts on a similar occasion is painful to contemplate.

Lamb and Wooster, however, and especially Arnold, deserved much praise. Of Arnold's services the Congress took notice immediately. Within a week, it made him a major general and shortly afterward ordered the gift of a horse "properly caparisoned as a token of . . . approbation of his gallant conduct . . . in the late enterprize to Danbury."[3] This was balm to Arnold's injured feelings, yet not a complete assuagement of his resent-ment, for he was still junior to the five major generals who had been pro-moted over his head. He still sought for the restoration of his proper rank, but in vain. Again he offered his resignation, driven to it, he said, by a sense of injustice. "Honor is a sacrifice no man ought to make," said he. "As I received, so I wish to transmit it to posterity."[4]

But on the very day that his letter was presented to the Congress, that body received a letter from Washington suggesting the sending of Arnold, "an active, spirited officer . . . judicious and brave," to the northern army opposing Burgoyne. "I am persuaded his presence and activity will animate the militia greatly."[5] This praise from his chief calmed Arnold. He asked leave to suspend his resignation and even agreed to serve "faithfully" under St. Clair, one of the juniors who had been promoted over his head. So it came about that Arnold had a part in the affairs at Saratoga.

The second incident was a tragedy, in which a woman played the leading part. Jane McCrea was the daughter of a Presbyterian minister of New Jersey. On the death of her mother and her father's marriage to a second wife, she went to live with her brother, who had settled in the Hudson valley about halfway between Fort Edward and Saratoga. At the time of Burgoyne's invasion, her brother, a colonel in the militia, decided to move to Albany. But she was engaged to marry David Jones, who had fled to Canada and become an officer in one of the Tory contingents then on the march with Burgoyne.

Jane refused to go with her brother, went instead up to Fort Edward, evidently hoping to greet her lover on his arrival. In one of two or three cabins near the fort lived a cousin of the British General Fraser, an old woman, Mrs. McNeil, who received her as a guest.

On July 27, two days before Burgoyne's army took over the abandoned fort, a group of his Indian forerunners came to it. They seized Mrs. McNeil and Jane and started back towards the British army at Fort Ann. They had not gone far when two of them "disputed who should be her guard," [6] and one shot her, scalped her, and stripped the clothing from her body.

They took Mrs. McNeil and Jane's scalp to the British camp, where General Fraser received his cousin and, it is said, David Jones recognized his fiancée's hair. Burgoyne ordered the arrest of the murderer and proposed to execute him, but St. Luc La Corne advised him that if this were done all the Indians would desert the army. Burgoyne pardoned the culprit, who is said to have borne the suitable name of Wyandot Panther.

That is the story of Jane McCrea as related by the most credible historians. In itself, it was but a minor incident in the list of Indian atrocities on that march. There was, for example, the slaughter of the whole family of John Allen—himself, his wife, three children, and three Negroes—on the day when Jane was killed. No one ever hears of them, yet not a history of the war fails to tell of Jane McCrea's murder. The difference lies in the results of the two outrages. The massacre of the Allen family was but one of a familiar type that had happened all along the frontier ever since the white man came to America; but Jane McCrea's murder was different, and for propaganda purposes it was made to measure.

She was young, twenty-three years of age, beautiful, "tall and noted for her long lustrous hair, which could reach to the floor when she stood up and let it down." [7] Or at least, if "not lovely in beauty of face," she was "so lovely in disposition, so graceful in manners and so intelligent in features, that she was a favorite of all who knew her." And her hair, an important element even if it did not reach to the ground, "was of extraordinary length and beauty, measuring a yard and a quarter . . . darker than a raven's wing," [8] says one authority; but another sees her locks, not as long and dark, but as "clustering curls of soft blonde hair." [9] Still another says "she was finely formed, dark hair, and uncommonly beautiful." [10] Another description makes her "a beauty in her bridal dress, hastening to her lover." [11] These descriptions are all from reputable histories. It matters not that James Wilkinson, who must have seen her, describes her as simply "a country girl of honest family in circumstances of mediocrity, without either beauty or accomplishments." [12]

The beautiful Jenny McCrea of the general run of the historians is the Jenny McCrea that was important, and she was very important. To the Americans she became more real than the real Jenny had ever been—a martyred saint in the patriotic hierarchy. Gates was the one most responsible for her prompt canonization. He had lately received a letter from Burgoyne complaining of the treatment of some of the prisoners taken by Stark at Bennington. To that he replied:

That the savages of America should in their warfare mangle and scalp the unhappy prisoners who fall into their hands is neither new nor extraordinary; but that the famous Lieutenant General Burgoyne, in whom the fine gentleman is united with the soldier and the scholar, should hire the savages of America to scalp Europeans and the descendants of Europeans, nay more, that he should pay a price for each scalp so barbarously taken, is more than will be believed in England until authenticated facts shall in every gazette convince mankind of the truth of this horrid tale. Miss McCrae, a young lady lovely to the sight, of virtuous character and amiable disposition, engaged to be married to an officer of your army was, with other women and children, taken out of a house near Fort Edward, carried into the woods, and there scalped and mangled in the most shocking manner. . . . The miserable fate of Miss McCrae was partly aggravated by her being dressed to receive her promised husband; but met her murderers employed by you.[13]

Gates was proud of that letter. He showed it to Lincoln and to Wilkinson. When they suggested it was rather personal, he exclaimed, "By God! I don't believe either of you can mend it." And he had a right to be proud. It was a prize bit of propaganda, and it worked. That letter was printed and reprinted in newspapers all over New England.

The story got about. It was "told at every village fireside and no detail of pathos or horror was forgotten. The name of Jenny McCrea became a watchword." [14] "It seems to have been the one thing needed to inflame the patriot imagination." [15] Washington added fuel to the flame when he wrote urging the brigadiers of militia in Massachusetts and Connecticut to "repel an enemy from your borders, who not content with hiring mercenaries to lay waste your country, have now brought savages, with the avowed and expressed intention of adding murder to desolation." [16] A general statement; but in the common mind it was Jenny McCrea he was writing about.

Trevelyan says that the men of New England were "determined that the story of Jane MacCrea should not be repeated in their own villages. They arrived at the very sound conclusion that, in order to protect their families from the Wyandot Panther and his brother warriors, the shooting must be done, not from the windows of farm-houses . . . but in the line of battle outside the borders of New England. Before the middle of August, a sixth of the militia of several counties marched off to reinforce the Northern army." [17] They came to it, says John Fiske, "inflamed with such wrath as had not filled their bosoms since the day when all New England had rushed to besiege the enemy in Boston." [18] They were also encouraged to come by the fact that Gates, whom they trusted, was now in command.

A few days after the murder of Jenny McCrea another important incident occurred—Gates was chosen commander of the northern American army. A tug of war in the Congress between the friends of Schuyler (that is to say, the delegates from New York and the more southerly colonies) and the friends of Gates (the New Englanders) had been won temporarily by the Schuyler men when on May 22 their favorite was ordered to the command of the northern army; [19] but since that time the fortunes of war had run against him.

The precipitate evacuation of Ticonderoga, that famous fortress which had bulked so large in the imagination of the Americans, had caused astonishment and spread dismay throughout the country. For this St. Clair might be held primarily responsible; but Schuyler, as chief commander of the northern army, must also bear the blame. Added to that, the continuous series of retreats was certainly Schuyler's work. Moreover his reports to Congress were tinged with defeatism. New England raged against him, with the result that he was displaced from his command, and on August 4 Gates was elected "by the vote of eleven States." Subsequently both Schuyler and St. Clair were "called down" to face a committee of the Congress appointed to conduct an inquiry into their conduct "at the time of surrendering Ticonderoga and Mount Independence." [20]

Horatio Gates, English-born, was the son of an upper servant in the family of the Duke of Leeds. Although his membership in the servant class apparently debarred him from elevation in the aristocratic military profession, he succeeded in obtaining a captaincy at the age of twenty-seven in a provincial regiment in Nova Scotia. He saw service in Braddock's expedition and in the capture of Martinique, and achieved the rank of major. In 1772, resigning from the British army, he crossed the Atlantic and settled in Virginia on an estate of modest dimensions. There he renewed an acquaintance with George Washington which had begun in the Braddock affair, and in 1775 he enthusiastically threw himself into the American cause.

Gates was one of the few American generals who had seen service in a regular army. Probably at Washington's suggestion the Congress, in 1775, made him adjutant general of the army with the rank of brigadier.[21] In that position, so especially important in the organization of a new army, Gates rendered excellent service. He was acquainted, as were few of the American officers, with military paper work and seems to have been indefatigable in the performance of his duties. He had undoubted ability as an administrator, and he was not without talent in the field.

In May, 1776, Gates was raised to the rank of major general and, in the next month, after the disaster at Trois Rivières, was ordered to the command of the American forces in Canada. How that order failed to take effect, because all the American troops had been driven out of Canada, and how he obtained only a subordinate command under Schuyler, have been already noted in this narrative. Gates, always ambitious, was disappointed. With the support of New Englanders in Congress who admired him and despised Schuyler he succeeded in displacing Schuyler to his own advantage, only to lose out two months later when his rival was reinstated. Now he had again achieved the high command.

It is not proposed here to follow his subsequent career. It is enough to say that he was more at home and more effective in the lobby of the Congress, that source of promotion and preferment, than on the field of battle. What seems to be an example of Gates's preference of intrigue to combat is furnished by his conduct in December, 1776. Washington was then, with a sadly deficient force, trying to hold the Delaware River in the neighborhood of Trenton against any attempted crossing by Howe's army on the way to Philadelphia. Schuyler ordered Gates to march with certain regiments to reenforce Washington. Gates's regiments arrived a few days before that Christmas Day on which Washington planned to attack the Hessian troops at Trenton. In expectation of his coming, Washington had allotted to him the command of the right wing of the attacking force. Gates did not fancy committing himself to so desperate an enterprise, and he seems not to have had the courage to present his excuses to Washington in person. He sent a letter by Wilkinson, his aide-de-camp, begging off on the plea of illness. He wished to go to Philadelphia to recover his health. What he actually did was immediately to go on to Baltimore, where the Congress was in session after its flight from Philadelphia. There he busied himself in an effort to secure the command of the northern army.

In person, Gates was of medium height, his body not muscular, his shoulders somewhat stooped. He seemed older than fifty, his age at that time. His face was rather long, his features heavy, especially his aquiline nose with its drooping tip and his long chin. His eyes were somewhat hooded by heavy lids. In the excellent portrait of him by Gilbert Stuart, his face wears a shrewdly calculating expression, the eyes as if watching an opponent narrowly, the slightly smiling lips confident, as if he had an ace up his sleeve.[22]

Gates, whatever his faults, was jolly and kindly.

Gates arrived in the camp at the mouth of the Mohawk on August 19. There he found an army of about 4,500 rank and file, less one brigade posted about five miles up the Mohawk. Arnold had not yet returned from Stanwix. Lincoln, with about 500 militia, was in Vermont ready to act against Burgoyne's rear. Stark and his brigade still lingered at Bennington.

Arnold, having left a garrison of 700 men at Stanwix, brought 1,200 men to the camp in the first week of September. About the same time came a contingent, sent by Washington, which, though small, added vastly to Gates's strength. It was a corps of Pennsylvania, Maryland, and Virginia riflemen led by that redoubtable warrior Daniel Morgan numbering 331 effectives, with 36 on the sick-list. To strengthen it, 250 "vigorous young men" [23] equipped with muskets and bayonets were selected from the army. Major Henry Dearborn, a veteran of Arnold's march to Quebec, was assigned to their command under Morgan.

Gates wanted to add Stark's brigade to the main force. Lincoln again undertook to induce that difficult soldier to take his men over to the Hudson, but Stark would not give up his independent position. To be sure, his brigade was enlisted for only two months, its term expiring in the middle of September; but there was still need for his men in the army, even for so short a time. And, with the fateful conflict with Burgoyne so imminent, Stark should have been able to induce them to extend their time. But his ingrained cantankerousness had the upper hand of his patriotism. He felt that he and his men had been "slighted" in the report of the Bennington battle made by Lincoln. He made various excuses: his men had the "meazels," he himself was ill, he had only 800 men, too few to march so close to Burgoyne, and so on.[24] At last, in the morning of September 18, he appeared. At noon, he and all his troops departed. Their time was up. The very next day the Americans were locked in combat with the enemy.

The effect of Bennington on Burgoyne's army had been immediate and severe. In general orders he said that Baum's expedition to procure stocks of food, which "might have enabled the Army to proceed without waiting for the arrival of the Magazines" from the north, having failed "thro the chances of War, the Troops must necessarily halt some days, for bringing forward the Transport of Provisions." [25] So they remained in camp at the so-called Fort Miller a short distance above the Batten Kill and about four miles above Saratoga.

The shortage of provisions was not the only cause for concern on the part of Burgoyne. Bennington had deprived him of more than 800 men, of whom nearly 450 were regulars. Severe restrictions which he had imposed on the independent operations of his Indians, in consequence of the McCrea murder, had disgruntled his savage allies, and the Bennington affair had not encouraged them. They held a council and decided to go home. Soon there were left to him no more than 80 out of his original 500.

The Tories in his ranks were few and unreliable. "I have about 400 (but not half of them armed), who may be depended upon," he wrote to Germain after Bennington. "The rest are trimmers merely actuated by interest." [26] His belief in a prevailing mood of loyalism in Tryon County and in Vermont had been shattered. He could not rely on any uprisings to assist him.

He had begun to doubt, more than doubt, the success of his expedition with only his present force. "Had I a latitude in my orders," he wrote to Germain, "I should think it my duty to wait in this position, or perhaps as far back as Fort Edward, where my communication with Lake George would be perfectly secure, till some event happened to assist my movement forward; but my orders being positive to 'force a junction with Sir William Howe,' I apprehend I am not at liberty to remain inactive longer than shall be necessary to collect twenty-five days' provision" and to receive the reenforcement of certain new German auxiliaries coming down from Canada. But he added, "I yet do not despond." If he could get to Albany, he would fortify it and wait for Howe to get in touch with him.[27]

Gates's army had been built up to about 6,000 rank and file, say 7,000 in all. The Mohawk, since the Stanwix affair, was no longer a threat in his rear. His position at its mouth offered no satisfactory ground for the

American style of fighting, being rather fit for the British regular formations. He decided to move north to a more suitable and more easily defensible terrain. On September 9 he was at Stillwater again, and his chief
engineer, Kosciuszko, began to lay out defenses; but it was not a good
choice. The wide river meadows offered too favorable an opportunity for
turning the chosen position. He therefore moved again, on the 12th, about
three miles north to a point where the river ran through a narrow defile
dominated on the west by bluffs rising steeply more than a hundred feet,
called Bemis Heights from the name of the owner of a tavern by the
riverside.[28]

The plateau above the bluffs rose again in steep slopes to greater heights,
200 to 300 feet above the river. These heights were irregularly shaped
and were separated from one another by ravines, in which small streams
flowed down to the Hudson. One of the ravines, that of Mill Creek, reached
through the bluffs northwestwardly, in front of the position taken by the
American army, and thence northerly to the final position of the British.
Another, the widest and deepest, called the Great Ravine, started somewhat farther north and reached northwestwardly behind the ground on
which the British army was first deployed. On the bluffs and the plateau
were thick woods of pine, maple, and oak, interspersed with a few small
clearings. Certain roads, or rather wagon tracks, ran from the main river
road up the sides of the ravines and interlaced on the plateau above in a
complicated and irregular pattern.

At the southern end of this area, on a 200-foot elevation south of the
Mill Creek ravine, the American position was taken. It is said to have been
selected by Arnold and Kosciuszko, who laid out plans for its fortification.
Beginning at the river's edge, near Bemis's tavern, an entrenchment was
drawn across the main river road; and at its eastern end a battery was
erected. From this point a bridge of boats was swung across the Hudson.

Connected with this, trenches were dug; and breastworks of logs and
earth were erected in a line running at a right angle with the river up the
bluff to the higher level of the main fortification. This was constructed of
the same materials in the form of three sides of a square about three-
quarters of a mile on each side. The rear, which was somewhat protected
by a ravine, was left open. A small redoubt, mounting artillery, was built at
the middle of each of the three fortified sides. At the northwest angle there
was a house belonging to one Neilson. A log barn near by was stockaded
and named Fort Neilson.[29]

The ground was well chosen to oppose Burgoyne's advance down the
west side of the river, except in one respect. To the west and not far distant

was a greater height, which dominated the fortification. If it should be occupied with artillery in sufficient force, the American stronghold would be in a precarious situation. This point had been incompletely entrenched and was not occupied by the Americans when Burgoyne pushed forward in force, on September 19.

Gates established his headquarters in "a small hovel, not ten feet square" [30] in the side of a slope near the rear end of the western side of the fortification and awaited the arrival of the enemy.

CHAPTER 40

Freeman's Farm

For his southward march from Fort Miller, Burgoyne had a choice between the road on the east side of the Hudson, where he was, and that on the west. Gates had blocked the west road at Bemis Heights and held a position dominating it; the east road was open. But Albany, Burgoyne's objective, was on the west side. If he marched down the east side, he would find the Hudson at Albany greatly increased in volume and width by the inflow of the Mohawk, and the American army would certainly have moved down to oppose him. The crossing there would be difficult and hazardous.

On the other hand, if he now crossed to the west side and took that road he would have to fight his way past his enemy. In either case, he would have to cut his already too long and too tenuous communications with Lake Champlain and Canada. Choice was difficult, but it had to be made promptly: he could not winter where he was, having no proper shelter for his troops, nor any certainty of food even from Canada after Champlain froze over—a supply sufficient for thirty days already brought down was all he could rely upon.[1] Unless he retreated, Albany was his only hope for the winter. He boldly chose the west road and a fight at Bemis Heights.

Strengthened by the arrival of the guns from Fort George and by a new draft of 300 regulars from Canada, Burgoyne threw a bridge of boats across the river; and his right wing, the British troops, crossed to Saratoga on the 13th, followed shortly after by the Germans. On the 15th the bridge was dismantled, and the whole army resumed its southward march in three columns: the right wing taking the right of the road; the left wing the meadows between the road and the river; the artillery, the road itself. The supplies and baggage were committed to the bateaux. So they proceeded about three miles to a farm called Dovecote—or "Dovegat." Two days later they made another three miles and camped about the house of one Sword.[2] Up to this time, although he was now within four miles of Gates's position, Burgoyne seems to have had no definite idea of his enemy's whereabouts. His intelligence had formerly been derived from his Indian scouts, of whom few were left to him. But now he heard of the Americans.

A small party of British soldiers and some women went out to dig potatoes on an abandoned farm. An American patrol surprised them, fired on them, killed several, and took 20 prisoners.[3] So Burgoyne knew that the Americans were close at hand. He soon ascertained their exact position and made his dispositions to attack them.

The right wing, under General Fraser, was made up of the light infantry companies of the 9th, 20th, 21st, 24th, 29th, 31st, 34th, 47th, 53rd, and 62nd British regiments, under command of Major the Earl of Balcarres; the grenadiers of the same regiments, commanded by Major John Dyke Acland; also the battalion companies of the 24th Regiment, Lieutenant Colonel Breymann's Brunswick riflemen, and an artillery brigade of four 6-pounders and four 3's. Being the advance corps, it received the few remaining Indians (about 50), the 70 to 80 Canadians, the Tories (perhaps 150), and 50 of the British "marksmen." All told, there were about 2,000 in this wing.

The center, under command of General Hamilton, included battalion companies of the 20th, 21st, and 62nd British regiments, with the 9th regiment in reserve. It had six light fieldpieces, 6's and 3's under Captain Jones. General Burgoyne was to accompany this section.

The left, led by General Phillips and General Riedesel, comprised the Brunswick infantry regiments of Riedesel, Specht, and Rhetz, and Captain Pausch's Hesse Hanau artillery, six 6-pounders and two 3's. Six battalion companies of the British 47th were detailed to guard the 200 bateaux containing the provisions and supplies. The wheeled carriages for the rest of the baggage were to be protected by the Hesse Hanau infantry. The center and left wings numbered about 1,100 each, rank and file. Fifty Brunswick dragoons, the relics of Baum's expedition, "shabbily mounted, attended (occasionally)" General Burgoyne. All in all, the British army now numbered only about 6,000 rank and file.[4]

On the morning of September 19, the sun rose bright and clear; the air was cool and bracing, and hoarfrost whitened the grass.[5] The British army prepared for its advance, but it was not until some time after ten o'clock that the discharge of a gun called for a simultaneous movement of the three divisions.⁶ Led by a party of the "shabbily mounted" dragoons and a hundred light infantry, Riedesel's division, accompanied by a detachment of pioneers and followed by the heavy artillery and the baggage, took its way in two columns down the road that ran under the bluffs and through the alluvial meadows by the riverside. Bridges, destroyed by the Americans, had to be replaced and guarded. Dispositions of troops on the heights above the road to protect the workers had to be made at each halt. Thus the progress of the division was much delayed. By one o'clock it reached a point about a quarter-mile below Wilbur's Basin, the farthest south that any part of Burgoyne's army ever penetrated.⁷

Meanwhile, Fraser's division had left the riverside by a rough road running west from Sword's house. Crossing the head of the Great Ravine, it marched nearly three miles until it met a crossroad on which it swung to the left, then south for a short distance to take a position on a height of land west of Freeman's Farm.⁸

The center division followed the right for about a mile, took a southward road for a half-mile, crossed the stream in the bottom of the Great Ravine on a bridge that the Americans had failed to destroy, and halted at noon for an hour on the south side of the ravine to give Fraser time to make his more circuitous march.

In the American camp, the right wing was composed chiefly of the Continental troops of Brigadier General John Glover, Colonel John Nixon and Brigadier General John Paterson. It occupied the heights near the river and the narrow level ground below them, under personal command of Gates.

The left wing, commanded by Arnold, included the New Hampshire regulars of Colonels Joseph Cilley, Nathan Hale,⁹ and Alexander Scammell; Colonel Philip Van Cortlandt's and Colonel Henry Livingston's New Yorkers; the Connecticut militia under Colonel Jonathan Lattimer and Colonel Thaddeus Cook; Colonel Daniel Morgan's riflemen; and Lieutenant Colonel Henry Dearborn's light infantry.

The center was held by Brigadier General Ebenezer Learned's Continental brigade, the Massachusetts Continental regiments of Colonel John Bailey, Colonel Henry Jackson, and Colonel James Wesson, and Colonel James Livingston's New Yorkers. The total number of effectives in Gates's army was about the same as that in Burgoyne's, perhaps a thousand more.¹⁰

Burgoyne's army, divided into three widely spaced parts, its communications so difficult because of the broken terrain, was really in a pre-

carious condition. It would seem, for example, that a swift attack in substantial force down the slope and upon Riedesel's division, in its narrow
space by the waterside, might have routed it before it could have help from
the right or center, Fraser or Burgoyne. Or that a strong detachment might
have turned either the right or the left of the British center division and
fought it successfully in the woods, in which neither its artillery nor its
bayonets would have been of much use. But Gates undertook no such
bold enterprises. To be sure, the defense would probably be less costly, and
time then seemed to be on the American side.

Gates is said to have been subject to "the fatal attraction which the
apparent security of a fortress has so often exercised upon the mind of a
timid and incompetent general." It is argued that he proposed to concentrate his army either altogether within his fort or in that and on the
narrow ground between it and the river, in "the insensate belief that his
adversaries would run their heads, wantonly and obstinately, against his
impenetrable bulwarks." [11] But it is asserted only by Gates's enemies,
friends of Schuyler and Arnold, with whom he was now on bad terms, that
he was not properly concerned about his left flank and the possibility that
it might be turned.

Burgoyne planned an attack. Phillips and Riedesel were to advance along
the river road and engage the American right. Burgoyne and Hamilton,
with their four regiments, were to attack in the center, while Fraser's light
infantry and grenadiers, the 24th British regiment, and his mixed auxiliary
force of Tories, Canadians, and Indians swept around the American left
and occupied that undefended higher ground to the west of the fort. From
it Fraser could bring his guns to bear on the entrenchments, enfilade their
front lines, and finally assault them in flank and rear, in the hope of pushing the Americans down the slope and into the river.[12] It was a bold plan,
yet not unfeasible.

The movements of the British army into its chosen positions could not
be concealed from the American scouts perched in treetops. The brilliant
colors of the uniforms and the flash of sunlight reflected from their polished
steel gave notice for three hours of its continuing advance; yet Gates gave
not a single order to meet the developing emergency. Arnold was not so
complacent. He could not have known what Burgoyne planned. Indeed, he
seems to have been at fault in permitting that western dominating height
to remain partly fortified and entirely undefended; or, at least, if he could
not induce Gates to occupy it, in making no protest. But he did argue with
his superior against remaining on the defensive in and about the fortifications. Letting Burgoyne approach the fort unopposed would permit him to

bring up his heavy guns to bombard it. And if the camp were stormed successfully there would be no natural rallying place for the defeated Americans, no chosen position to which they could withdraw. But if the fight were made in the woods—where their superior marksmanship would tell and the British could not fight in close ranks with orderly volleys and finally with the bayonet—and they were beaten off they could still retire to the fort and defend themselves.[13]

Arnold was vehement in his argument and, according to a bitter enemy of Gates, "urged, begged and entreated" [14] permission to attack with his division. Whether or not he had any influence upon Gates is not clear. Gates did send Morgan's riflemen and Dearborn's light infantry to cover his left and to meet the enemy's flanking move, Arnold's division to be called on for support when needed.

It was after one o'clock when Burgoyne in his temporary position on the southern side of the Great Ravine concluded, or was informed, that Fraser had gained his appointed post. As a signal for the advance, three guns were fired; and Burgoyne's division marched west along a road towards Freeman's Farm.[15]

In the meantime, Morgan's riflemen, seconded by Dearborn's light infantry, had set out from the American left wing through the woods towards Freeman's Farm. The riflemen divided into parties to comb the woods and deployed in a long irregular line, Morgan taking his accustomed place close behind its center, where he could best observe and control his men. In a ravine south of Freeman's Farm, the riflemen came upon a picket of Fraser's irregulars, Canadians, Indians, and Tories. Under a crackling, deadly fire from the riflemen, every officer of the picket and many of its men fell, dead or wounded. The rest fled.

With too great impetuosity and in no order at all, Morgan's riflemen rushed after the fleeing enemy. From Fraser's position, Major Forbes led out a strong detachment of Tories and struck the disorganized Americans with such force that they were dispersed and scattered through the woods, leaving Morgan almost alone. He stood there, tears of chagrin and anger on his face, sounding the turkey call, an instrument used to decoy wild turkeys, which he most appropriately substituted for trumpet or drum. His men soon responded and began to gather about him.[16]

In the meantime Cilley's and Scammell's New Hampshire Continentals in Arnold's division came out. They went to the left of Morgan's and Dearborn's reorganized line, extending beyond Fraser's right, which they

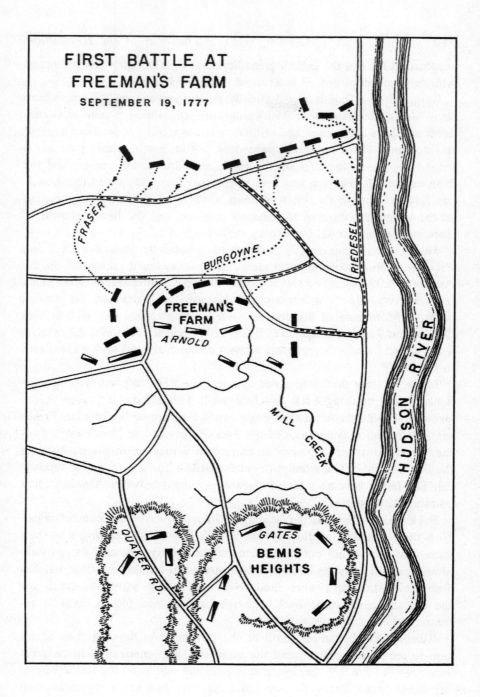

FIRST BATTLE AT
FREEMAN'S FARM
SEPTEMBER 19, 1777

FRASER

BURGOYNE

RIEDESEL

FREEMAN'S
FARM
ARNOLD

MILL CREEK

HUDSON RIVER

QUAKER RD.

GATES
BEMIS
HEIGHTS

sought to turn. But the British grenadiers and light infantry met the thrust with "a tremendous fire" [17] and forced them to withdraw.

Burgoyne and Hamilton had already arrived at Freeman's Farm, where there was a clearing about 350 yards long, containing fifteen or twenty acres around a log house. The artillery was posted in the northern edge of this opening. Three regiments were deployed in line in a thin pine wood behind the guns—the 21st on the right, the 62nd in the center, and the 20th on the left. The 9th was held in reserve. Thus they faced the American fortified lines to the south of them, about a mile distant, but, because of the irregular nature of the ground between and the heavy growth of trees, neither side could be seen by the other.[18]

There was a considerable interval of ground between the 21st and Fraser's position. Arnold, who seems to have assumed command on the American left, thought he saw a chance to strike at this and cut the enemy force in two. He "countermarched" his men and attacked the British center.[19] More men of his division were coming to his aid; Hale's, Van Cortlandt's, James Livingston's, Bailey's, Wesson's, Jackson's, Marshall's, Cook's, and Lattimer's regiments arrived successively and took their places in the line.[20]

In the clearing the fighting was furious. The 21st, to prevent being outflanked, had to swing back and face west. This created a salient in the British line, with the 62nd at its angle exposed to fire on both flanks. Fraser sent the battalion companies of the 24th Regiment and Breymann's riflemen to aid Burgoyne. Otherwise he remained inactive in his position on the British right.[21] The attempt to cut the British line in two was unsuccessful. The battle became a face-to-face engagement between Arnold's force and the British center.

Back and forth across the clearing in alternate waves, the combat raged. Now the Americans would push the British into the woods and take their guns. But they could not turn them on the enemy, because the gunners always carried away the linstocks, the instruments holding the slow matches with which the guns were fired. Nor could they withdraw them, for the British always came back with the bayonet and forced them to retreat.

Riflemen climbed trees south of the clearing and devoted their attention to the British officers and the gunners. The Americans had "a great superiority of fire." [22] "Senior officers who had witnessed the hardest fighting of the Seven Years' War declared that they had never experienced so long and hot a fire." [23] The 62nd British regiment was punished with especial severity. It almost broke. Once it tried a bayonet charge, but carried it too far beyond its supporting regiments and lost 25 men as prisoners.[24]

General Phillips had ridden up from his and Riedesel's division, to see what was going on in the center. He found a deplorable condition.[25] Every officer of the British artillery in the center save one and 36 out of 48 gunners and matrosses had been shot down. The guns had been silenced. Phillips called on Riedesel for four more. They came, but were soon also out of action for want of ammunition.[26]

In person, Phillips led the 20th out into the clearing in a bayonet charge to rescue the 62nd, enable it to withdraw and re-form.[27] Yet, for all he could do and for all Burgoyne and Hamilton could do, repeatedly exposing themselves to the American fire,[28] the center remained in a desperate situation.

Arnold believed that only a little more force was needed to break through and throw the enemy's line into complete confusion; but his entire division was already engaged—he wanted more men. He applied for a reenforcement.

Gates "deemed it prudent not to weaken" his lines.[29] Late in the afternoon he sent General Learned's brigade. Instead of striking at the British center, Learned led his men in a futile attack on Fraser's wing and was beaten off. All other aid, Gates refused.

But Riedesel down by the river was not so "prudent." When he had word of the precarious condition of the British line he ordered his own regiment to follow two companies of the Rhetz regiment which he led through the woods a mile and a half to a height where he could see the field of battle. The fight was "raging at its fiercest." "The three brave English regiments had been, by the steady fire of fresh relays of the enemy, thinned down to one-half and now formed a small band surrounded by heaps of dead and wounded." Without waiting for the support of his own regiment, he called on the two companies to charge. "With drums beating and his men shouting 'Hurrah!' he attacked the enemy on the double-quick." [30]

This sudden and unexpected attack on the flank drove the Americans back into the woods. Captain Pausch of the Hesse Hanau artillery was coming up with two 6-pounders. Officers and privates of the British regiments and some of the Brunswick jägers seized the dragropes and hauled the guns up the steeps and through the forest into position in the British line. They opened fire on the Americans with grape, "within good pistol-shot distance." [31] Riedesel's own regiment came up and fired a volley of musketry. That was about the end. It was growing dark. Hopeless of achieving a decisive victory, the Americans ceased firing and withdrew. The British bivouacked on the field.

The British loss was extraordinarily heavy. With as many as 2,500 men on the field, only three of the four regiments in the center—about 800 men—were deeply and continuously engaged. Yet the casualties of the whole British force amounted to about 600 killed, wounded, or captured. Of these, 350 were in the three regiments, the 20th, 21st, and 62nd. The 62nd was reduced from about 350 to scarcely 60 men.[32]

Of the Americans, 8 officers and 57 noncoms and privates were killed, 21 officers and 197 noncoms and privates were wounded; 36 others were reported missing.[33]

The incapacity of Gates as commander of a fighting force was convincingly demonstrated that day. If Arnold's persistent importunity had not forced his hand, the battle would have been fought on Burgoyne's own terms, in accordance with his plan, with the Americans trying to hold their works under a heavy, enfilading fire from that undefended western height. All the advantages which the Americans enjoyed in woods fighting, where marksmanship counted for so much and where the artillery and the bayonets of the British were of little avail, would have been lost.

Again, his failure to send to Arnold, at the crucial moment of the battle, a substantial reenforcement prevented the Americans from achieving a complete victory. Sir John Fortescue, the English military historian, says, "Had Gates sent to Arnold the reinforcements for which he asked, Arnold must certainly have broken the British centre, which, even as things were, could barely hold its own."

There was also open to Gates an opportunity to act on his own in a decisive manner. When Riedesel withdrew his own regiment, the two Rhetz companies, and Pausch's guns to go to Burgoyne's aid, there were left on the low ground by the riverside to protect all the baggage, provisions, and supplies of the entire British army only the 47th British regiment, the regiment of Specht, the Hesse Hanau infantry, and the rest of the Rhetz, perhaps eight or nine hundred in all. Gates had at least 4,000 on the height above. A swift descent by half of these could hardly have failed to capture and destroy all the British bateaux and land carriages with all their contents, leaving Burgoyne, bereft of food and supplies of every kind, to surrender or starve.[34]

CHAPTER 41

Fort Clinton and Fort Montgomery

From the day after the fight at Freeman's Farm until the 7th day of October, the opposing forces lay in their respective positions, facing each other at a distance of little more than a mile, without any hostile move except frequent little affairs of outposts and continual sniping. But, in that interval, there occurred a conflict at a place somewhat distant, yet closely related to the principal contest between Burgoyne and Gates. This must be described before returning to the major scene.

It will be remembered that Burgoyne received a letter dated July 17 in which General Howe announced his intention of going south to Pennsylvania instead of up the Hudson to Albany, writing, "Sir Henry Clinton remains in command here and will act as occurrences direct." This unpromising reference gave no assurance that Clinton would move northward; nor did Howe give Clinton any orders in that respect.

Certain letters to Clinton vaguely referred to the possibility of Clinton's "acting offensively"; and on July 30 Howe had written, "If you can make any diversion in favor of General Burgoyne's approaching Albany, I need not point out the utility of such a measure." [1] Clinton accepted this merely permissive, casual suggestion at its face value. He later wrote to General Hervey, "I have not heard from Howe for six weeks and have no orders to co-operate with Burgoyne." [2]

Howe had left in New York no more than 7,000 troops, including 3,000 Tories, with whom Clinton had to hold Manhattan Island and the various outposts on Long Island, Staten Island, and Paulus Hook. This was not a force sufficient to be divided for offensive operations elsewhere. But Clinton was expecting reenforcements from England, and when he heard that Burgoyne was no farther advanced than Saratoga on September 12 he wrote a reassuring message: "You know my good will and are not ignorant of my poverty. If you think 2000 men can assist you effectually, I will make a push at [Fort] Montgomery in about ten days." [3] Burgoyne got this on the 21st and immediately dispatched a message urging Clinton to hasten his advance. The messenger failed to arrive. Another messenger, sent on the 27th, was so long delayed by the difficulties of travel and of escaping American patrols that he did not find Clinton until October 8, the day after Burgoyne's surrender at Saratoga. But Clinton had not awaited an answer. His reenforcements came in on September 24 or thereabouts, bringing his force of regulars up to nearly 7,000 men—2,700 British and 4,200 Germans. He at once began preparations for the projected advance.

Sir Henry Clinton was by now in his fortieth year. Behind him were one signal failure, his repulse at Fort Moultrie, and one signal success, his part as commander of the flanking column in the Battle of Long Island. He had been too often hindered by an abundance of caution, as at Kip's Bay and at White Plains and on the whole had scarcely distinguished himself. He was, however, competent and hard-working, apt to the burdens of administration and thoroughly reliable, a man normal in every respect save one; namely, his curious *idée fixe* that General Howe had slighted and wronged him. Troyer Anderson concludes from a perusal of Clinton's papers that he was "almost mentally unbalanced on this subject." Perhaps because of this unfortunate (and completely unjustified) prepossession, or perhaps through less partisan judgment, he had opposed Howe's move southward and had urged a junction with Burgoyne. He had no fondness for Burgoyne; indeed, he seems to have been disappointed that he himself had not received the Canadian command. But he was strong in force, temporarily unrestrained by Howe's presence, and in every way perfectly situated for a vigorous stroke.[4]

Though he "never showed that he possessed the tactical ability" [5] of Howe, Clinton was a skillful soldier, especially in such an enterprise as he was now about to embark upon, capable of striking hard and effectively. He conducted his operation "with more energy than most of the military operations that took place in America." [6] He was not handicapped in his activities by Howe's sloth, nor by such dissipated habits as characterized both Howe and Burgoyne.

Clinton's immediate objectives were two forts about forty miles above New York in the Highlands of the Hudson. A lofty height of land, a huge massif about fifteen miles wide, extends like a great wall across the course of the Hudson, which flows through a narrow cleft in it. On both sides of the river steep, rocky eminences arise to heights of a thousand feet or more, the southernmost on the west side being Dunderberg. Next above that is Bear Mountain, which slopes sharply downward on its northern side to a deep ravine through which little Popolopen Kill flows into the Hudson. On the northeast shoulder of Bear Mountain, about 120 feet above the water, stood Fort Clinton. Across the ravine was Fort Montgomery, on a similar, somewhat lower, shoulder a half-mile distant. These guarded the half-mile width of the river, which was blocked by a chevaux-de-frise of heavy timbers, strengthened by a log boom and a great iron chain extending to Anthony's Nose on the opposite side. Montgomery was the larger and the more elaborately planned of the forts but was yet unfinished, so that Clinton was the stronger. Both had been planned especially for offense and defense on the waterside to hold this narrow gateway to the upper Hudson. The approaches on the land side were through narrow, steep, and rugged defiles extremely difficult to penetrate and very easy to defend.

The two forts were under the command of Brigadier General George Clinton, who was also governor of New York. His brother, Brigadier General James Clinton, was in particular charge of Fort Montgomery. They were garrisoned by a few regulars, a number of militia from the surrounding country, many of them unarmed, and a company of Colonel John Lamb's 2nd Continental Artillery, a force "not a tenth part enough to defend them." [7] In the river above the boom a little American flotilla of two frigates, the *Congress* and the *Montgomery*, a sloop, and two galleys rode at anchor.

On the other side of the Hudson, in and about Peekskill, Major General Putnam had been posted in May with a strong force to cooperate with the forts in guarding the Highlands. But that force had been reduced, by drafts in aid of Gates and Washington, to 1,200 Continentals and 300 incompletely armed militia.

Sir Henry Clinton did not expect to be able to fight his way through to Albany. To create a diversion in Gates's rear, in the hope of relieving the pressure on Burgoyne, was as much as he considered feasible. Indeed, he regarded even so much as "a desperate attempt on a desperate occasion." [8] For this purpose, he detached 4,000 men, including some of his Tory regiments.

The first contingent, 1,100 men, embarked in flatboats and bateaux at

Spuyten Duyvil Creek in the evening of October 3 and reached Tarrytown on the Hudson, about halfway to Peekskill, at daybreak. There it was joined by a second division of equal strength, which had marched overland from Kingsbridge. The third division embarked on the 4th in transports, convoyed by the frigates *Preston, Mercury,* and *Tartar* under the command of Commodore William Hotham, and arrived off Tarrytown on the same day. In the evening of the 5th, the convoy of transports, flatboats, bateaux, and galleys carrying the entire force proceeded up the river to Verplanck's Point, where there was a little breastwork mounting two guns. There 400 men were landed, and the small force of Americans holding the point retired without any resistance.

This concentration of attention upon the east side of the river was intended to make the Americans think that the expedition was against Putnam at Peekskill, and it succeeded. Putnam hastily withdrew to the hills four miles inland and sent a message to George Clinton asking for all the troops he could spare from the forts, and actually obtained some of them. Having accomplished this initial purpose of deception, Sir Henry proceeded vigorously and without delay against his real objective.

Leaving a thousand of his men, chiefly Tories, to hold Verplanck's Point against Putnam, he carried the rest early in the morning of the 6th, under cover of a thick fog, across the river to Stony Point, whence a rugged road ran west for two miles and then turned to the north behind Dunderberg and towards the forts. The British column took this northern road under the guidance of Brom Springster, a Tory. The advance was led by Lieutenant Colonel Campbell, with the 27th and 52nd British regiments, Colonel Andreas von Emmerich's Hessian jägers, and 400 of Colonel Beverley Robinson's Loyal Americans (Tories), a force of 900 in all. General Sir John Vaughan followed with the main body, the light infantry, the Koehle and Anspach grenadiers, the 26th and 63rd British regiments, a company of the 71st, a troop of dismounted men of the 17th Light Dragoons, and a number of Hessian jägers, making up 1,200 rank and file. General Tryon brought up the rear, with the 7th British and the Trumbach Hessian regiments. Sir Henry marched with the main body.

The road soon degenerated into a wagon track so narrow that the troops could march only three abreast. After three miles, it came to a 500-foot, almost precipitous ascent to a notch called the Timp. Up this, for three-quarters of a mile, scrambled the heavily laden men—the British carrying sixty pounds of equipment each, the Germans even more. A handful of determined opponents posted at the top of the acclivity could have held them off; but the road was not guarded, not even picketed.

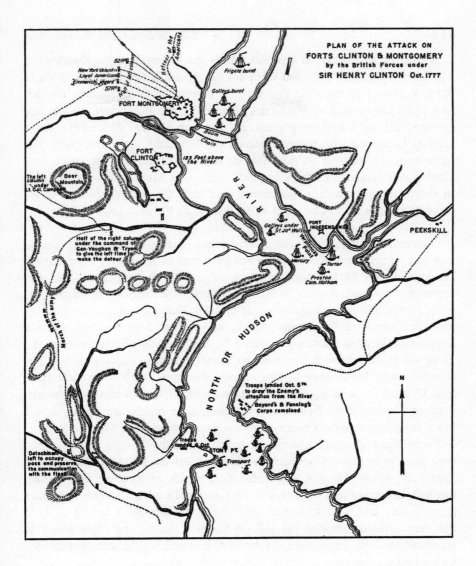

PLAN OF THE ATTACK ON
FORTS CLINTON & MONTGOMERY
by the British Forces under
SIR HENRY CLINTON Oct. 1777

A mile or so farther, at Doodletown in the valley between Dunderberg and Bear Mountain, the road forked. The right-hand branch led down to the low ground by the river and then up directly to Fort Clinton. The left fork passed around Bear Mountain, came down the Popolopen ravine, and emerged behind Fort Montgomery. At this fork Clinton divided his army, sending Campbell with the advance on the left-hand, circuitous path. The main body was to time its march along the other road so as to reach Fort Clinton simultaneously with Campbell's arrival at Montgomery. Tryon was to secure the pass with a detachment and hold the rest of his men in reserve to cover a retreat or assist either attack, as the case might require.

General George Clinton was in attendance upon a session of the legislature at Esopus (now Kingston) when he heard of Sir Henry's expedition. He immediately hastened to the forts, calling out the militia on the way, and took command. A party of 30 under Lieutenant Jackson was dispatched from Fort Clinton to reconnoiter. It met Sir Henry's advance at Doodletown, exchanged a few shots with it, and retreated to the fort. Clinton hoped for aid from Putnam, to whom he had sent an urgent message. To delay the enemy, he sent Lieutenant Colonel Jacobus Bruyn with 50 Continentals, and Lieutenant Colonel James McLarey with 50 militia from Fort Clinton, back along the Doodletown road. From Montgomery he dispatched Captain John Fenno with 60 men, later reenforced by 40, and a brass fieldpiece to meet Campbell in the pass behind Bear Mountain.

Bruyn and McLarey had little success. Though they fought courageously, they were promptly driven back to their fort, at the point of the bayonet. Fenno did better. He posted his men on the side of a ravine and opened fire with musketry and his one gun on Campbell's advance. The American fire was hot and well sustained, and checked Campbell's troops at first; but they divided, climbed the hill on Fenno's flanks, and were about to surround his little force when it retreated, first spiking the gun, but leaving its captain a prisoner.

Captain Lamb had brought out a 12-pounder and placed it in a commanding position. To it Fenno's men rallied, but from it they were again driven, leaving it, spiked, to the enemy. That was the end of resistance outside the forts.

Although Sir Henry's force had left its landing early in the morning and had reached Doodletown by ten o'clock, it was half past four when the divisions were in position before their respective forts. A summons to surrender having been refused by General George Clinton, simultaneous attacks were begun.

Sir Henry sent the 63rd Regiment around Fort Clinton to attack it on the northwest. The rest he formed for an assault on the southern side, the flank companies of the 7th and 26th British regiments and a company of Anspach grenadiers in the van, backed by the battalion companies of the 26th, the dragoons, and some Hessian jägers, with a Hessian battalion and the battalion companies of the British 7th in the rear. Between a small lake and the river there was a space no wider than 400 yards. It was blocked by an abatis and commanded by ten of the fort's guns. Through this space Sir Henry sent his men with orders to fire no shot, but to assault the works with the bayonet alone.

In the face of all the fire the insufficient garrison could bring to bear on them, the British regulars gallantly pressed forward. The defenders were too few—a few Continentals and 600 militia divided between the two forts —but their fire was deadly. The attackers fell by tens and twenties; but unfalteringly the rest came on. They reached the fort, pushed and pulled one another up through its embrasures, and swept into the works. The defenders immediately threw down their arms.

At Montgomery, Campbell had placed his German jägers in the center, his two British regiments on the right, and Robinson's Tories on the left. Thus he led them to the assault, only to be shot down before he reached the works. Colonel Robinson took command, and, with gallantry equal to that of Sir Henry's men, the fort was stormed successfully. The two forts fell almost at the same time.

It was now late in the day. Under cover of darkness General George and General James Clinton escaped with the greater part of their troops, some taking to the woods, others crossing the river in boats.

The American loss was heavy. Of the 600-odd men in the two garrisons, 250 were reported killed, wounded, or missing.[9] Also lost were sixty-seven guns and a considerable amount of stores.

The British lost about 40 killed and 150 wounded.[10] Whether these figures include the Hessian casualties, not usually included in the British returns, is uncertain.

The American vessels in the river tried to get away, but they were insufficiently manned, and the wind was against them. One of the sloops was captured, and one of the frigates went aground. They were all burned. "As every sail was set, the vessels soon became magnificent pyramids of fire." The loaded guns were set off by the heat in succession until the fire reached the magazines and "the whole was sublimely terminated by the explosions that left all to darkness." [11]

The next day, Sir Henry cut through the river barrier, chevaux de frise, boom and chain, and sent a flag, with a demand for surrender, to little Fort Constitution on an island opposite West Point. The tiny garrison fired on the flag, but set fire to the works and fled the following day on the approach of the enemy.

The two American Clintons, bringing Lamb's artillery company and some others that had escaped from the forts, joined Putnam at New Windsor. General George Clinton tried to arouse him to active measures; but he was gloomy. He thought he saw Sir Henry pushing on vigorously to a junction with Burgoyne, and did not see how he could be stopped. He was for standing on the defensive where he was. [12]

But Sir Henry Clinton had no intention of going farther. He had carried out a diversion, and he believed he could do no more. Beyond sending Vaughan to burn Esopus, some barracks at Continental Village, and residences of conspicuous rebels, he engaged in no further hostilities. He garrisoned the forts and returned to New York. But first he wrote a short note from Fort Montgomery on the 8th to cheer and encourage Burgoyne: *"Nous y voici* and nothing now between us and Gates; I sincerely hope this little success of ours may facilitate your operations. . . . I heartily wish you success." But Burgoyne did not derive from the debonair epistle the encouragement intended. The messenger, having been captured by the Americans, tried the silver bullet trick; it was recovered in the usual manner, and its bearer met the prescribed fate. In any event, the encouragement, such as it was, would have been too late. The day before it was written, Burgoyne had finally put his fortunes on the wheel and had lost everything.

CHAPTER 42

Bemis Heights

Burgoyne was of a mind to attack Gates in full force on the day after the Battle of Freeman's Farm. Had he done so, it is quite possible that he would have won. The ill organized American army was in confusion. Though heartened and inspirited by their demonstrated ability to cope with the British and German regulars, the men who had fought through that long afternoon of the 19th were tired out and in no condition to fight again the next day. So were the British, especially the three regiments that had borne the brunt of the battle; but there is a greater resilience in the regular soldier than in the militiaman. Accustomed to checks, which doubtless they longed to avenge, the British regulars, well disciplined to obey orders to the utmost of their strength, would have gone forward with the same dogged courage that had characterized the repeated attacks on Bunker Hill. Fraser, however, was opposed to immediate action. He said his grenadiers and light infantry who were to make the first move, against the American left wing, would do better after a day's rest. So Burgoyne decided to wait a day.

On the 21st his army was drawn up in battle array and an attack seemed imminent; but Burgoyne was digesting the contents of a dispatch received from Sir Henry Clinton early that morning. It was that note, dated September 12, in which Clinton had written that he expected to "make a push" against the two forts, Montgomery and Clinton, "in about ten days." That "push" might be the turning point of the campaign; it might draw men from Gates and leave him too weak to defend his position. So Burgoyne canceled the orders for the attack; he would await the outcome of Clinton's move. And by that decision he lost the last chance for success in his enterprise, the last chance even for a safe retreat, for from that time onward the American army gained strength by the continued arrival of reenforcements, while under the usual attrition of sickness and desertions the British force grew steadily weaker.

To hold his position while awaiting good news from Clinton, Burgoyne at once began to entrench. From Freeman's Farm on the right, the lines were run across the British front to the bluffs at the riverside. They began, on the right, with a short entrenchment facing west, then turned at an angle to face south and ran eastward to their end on the river bluffs. Redoubts strengthened the angle and the extremities of the line. One of considerable size in a horseshoe shape was erected well in the rear of the right end of the lines, facing north to prevent that wing from being outflanked. "A deep, muddy ditch" [1] covered the entire front and ran in a curve around the angle at the right. All trees within a hundred yards of the front of the lines were felled. Fraser's corps of light infantry and grenadiers held its old position on the extreme right, beyond the angle and outside the ditch. The Earl of Balcarres held the angle with more of the British light infantry. Breymann's corps was posted in the horseshoe, which was separated from Balcarres by an interval defended only by two stockaded log cabins held by some Canadians. The rest of the army manned the lines to the river bluff.[2]

On the bluffs by the riverside redoubts were built to protect the boats and baggage. A floating bridge spanning the Hudson was contrived. The Hesse Hanau regiment, the British 47th, and a corps of Tories were encamped in the meadows by the stream. "An abundance of artillery" [3] was distributed along the lines. These positions were held until the final battle.

There was no change in the American lines, except that the western height outside them, which had been Burgoyne's objective in the first battle, was occupied and fortified. But within the camp there was enough discord in the high command to wreck an army.

Ill feeling had existed for some time between Gates and Arnold. After Freeman's Farm, Gates was angered because friends of Schuyler and Arnold in the army gave the whole credit in that affair to Arnold. He did not even mention Arnold's name in his report to Congress on the engagement. Arnold wrote to him protesting and asking for a pass for himself and two aides to Philadelphia. Gates responded by offering a letter to the president of Congress. But Arnold was unsatisfied with this document, technically not what he had requested. He called at headquarters to protest.

Gates laughed at Arnold's pretensions; expressed the view that he did not consider him a major general since he had submitted his resignation to the Congress, that he had in fact never received any command in that army, that he was of little consequence anyhow, and that the command of the left wing was to be given to General Lincoln; and wound up by saying that he would gladly give Arnold a pass to Philadelphia whenever he wanted it.[4]

Arnold was enraged, and there was a bitter quarrel with high words on both sides. Following that there was an exchange of foolish, quibbling letters. "Gates was irritating, arrogant and vulgar; Arnold indiscreet, haughty and passionate." [5] Finally came an order relieving Arnold of all command and excluding him from headquarters. Brockholst Livingston, one of Gates's enemies, wrote that most of the other officers and many of the men "had lost all confidence in Gates and had the highest opinion of Arnold"; and he declared that all the general officers except Lincoln signed a letter urging Arnold to remain, "for another battle seemed imminent." [6] In any case Arnold stayed, an idle hanger-on in the camp waiting for that coming fight.

General Benjamin Lincoln had been sent in July by Schuyler at Washington's suggestion to encourage and to command the militia in Vermont; and he had remained in that territory ever since. He had collected 2,000 men whom he held inactive as a menace to Burgoyne's flank and rear until the middle of September. Then he sent three detachments of 500 men each, under Colonel Woodbridge, Colonel Johnson, and Colonel John Brown, against Skenesboro and Ticonderoga.

Skenesboro had been abandoned by the British, and Woodbridge occupied it without opposition. But Brigadier General Powell still held Ticonderoga and its outposts with the 53rd British regiment and some Canadians, also Mount Independence with the Prince Frederick Regiment of Brunswickers—in all, about 900 rank and file.

Brown rushed the Lake George landing place at daybreak on September 18, occupied Mount Defiance (Sugar Loaf Hill), captured 300 of the enemy, 200 bateaux, a sloop, and some gunboats, drove all the rest of the garrison into the fort, and released a hundred American prisoners. Johnson, coming a little later in the day, kept the Germans on Independence busy under a continuous fire. But the main defenses were too strong to invite an assault, and both forces withdrew. Johnson went back to Lincoln's camp Brown sailed up Lake George in the captured British boats, tried to surprise two companies of the British 47th, under Captain Aubrey on Diamond Island; but he was expected and was beaten off.[7]

This was a minor affair; but such an operation in Burgoyne's rear encouraged the army at Bemis Heights, which celebrated it by prolonged cheering and a salute of thirteen guns. To Burgoyne, the news brought no comfort.

Gates now called on Lincoln to bring his men over to the main army. Between the 22nd and the 29th they arrived, and this was not the only addition to the army. Aroused by the story of Jennie McCrea—which had been published throughout the country—encouraged by the news of Burgoyne's plight, and eager to serve under Gates as they had not been to serve under Schuyler, the militia of New England and New York were flocking to Bemis Heights. They came singly, in groups, in companies, armed men looking nothing like soldiers, but each with his musket or fowling piece and as much powder and lead as he owned. They were ready and fit to take their places in the ranks. They could shoot from behind a tree better than the best of their enemies. By October 4 Gates had more than 7,000 men— about 2,700 Continentals, the rest militia—and they were still coming. By the 7th he had 11,000. His slender store of ammunition had been replenished by Schuyler from Albany. His men were well fed; they rejoiced in their gathering strength; and they were ready, eager, to try conclusions with the redcoats and the bluecoats again.

In Burgoyne's camp the case was far otherwise. Three months in the bushes and brambles of the wilderness had reduced their uniforms, the pride of the regulars, to tatters. Their food was salt pork and flour, and even that was running out. On October 3 their rations were reduced by one-third.[8] The grass in the meadows had been very soon eaten by their horses. There was no more forage to be had, and many horses died of starvation. Of the 8,000 rank and file with whom Burgoyne had appeared before Ticonderoga, there were perhaps fewer than 5,000 now in the camp; and even this number was continually sapped by desertions. It was easy enough to slip off into the surrounding forest. Every man in the British camp must have known that the invasion had been stopped, and that even a retreat was hardly possible.

To those discouraged men the Americans gave no rest. Day after day and night after night their outposts were under fire so close to their camp that the sleep of the men within the lines was disturbed. Burgoyne described this continual harassment:

From the 20th of September to the 7th of October, the armies were so near, that not a night passed without firing, and sometimes concerted attacks, on our advanced picquets; no foraging party could be made without great detachments to cover it; it was the plan of the enemy to harrass the army by constant alarms and their superiority of numbers enabled them to attempt it without fatigue to themselves. . . . I do not believe that either officer or soldier ever slept during that interval without his cloaths, or that any general officer, or commander of a regiment, passed a single night without being upon his legs occasionally at different hours and constantly an hour before daylight." [9]

On the 4th of October, Burgoyne called Riedesel, Phillips, and Fraser into a council of war and proposed action. His plan was to leave 800 men to defend the low ground by the river where were the boats and the army's store of supplies, and to march with all the rest against the American left wing in an effort to flank it and get to its rear.

It was an audacious plan; it was, indeed, a foolhardy plan, as the other generals more than intimated. In the first place, none of them knew anything about the American position. Time after time parties had been sent out on reconaissance, but had not succeeded in approaching near enough to get more than the sketchiest idea of the position and shape of the lines, hidden as they were by the dense forest.[10] In the second place, leaving so few men to guard the boats and supplies would amount to an urgent invitation to the Americans to attack them. While the main force was making a slow and difficult march around the American left, the Americans could capture the whole store of provision and ammunition and destroy the bridges across two streams running into the Hudson above and below the riverside defenses, and thus cut the British army off from its only means of retreat and leave it to starve and surrender. To clinch this argument, an inspection of the British works by the riverside was proposed and made. They were found to be badly placed for protection of the supplies, and the plan was abandoned.[11]

Riedesel now proposed a retreat to their old position at the mouth of Batten Kill, where communication with Lake George might be reopened and the hoped-for arrival of Sir Henry Clinton's force could be awaited. Fraser seconded him. Phillips declined to give any opinion.

Burgoyne refused to agree to a retreat before he had made one more attempt to find out whether there was not a way through or around the Americans.[12] He presented another plan, a "reconnoisance in force" to discover the American position and find out its weak point. There was that much discussed height on the American left, the objective of the attempted movement of September 19: it might be seized, fortified, and armed with artillery to fire down into the American works. He evidently did not know that since September 19th it had been strongly occupied by the Americans.[13]

His plan was to draw out 1,500 regulars and some of his irregular auxiliaries and approach near enough to learn whether the American left was vulnerable. If it were, an attack in force could be made on the following day. If not, a retreat to Batten Kill would be in order. That was the final decision. To hearten the troops for the adventure, twelve barrels of rum were broken out of the stores and distributed.

In the morning of the 7th the reconnoitering party was made up. The British light infantry, led by Lord Balcarres, composed the right. The 24th Regiment, a detachment of Brunswickers chosen from all their regiments and from Breymann's jägers, made up the center, commanded by Riedesel. The left was composed of the British grenadiers under Major Acland.[14] First having sent out Captain Fraser with his rangers and 600 Canadian and Indian auxiliaries on a long circuit to westward to divert the Americans and keep them in check, the expedition moved southwest from Freeman's Farm in three columns, supported by six 6-pounders, two 12's, and two howitzers.[15] When they had gone about three-quarters of a mile they halted in a wheat field on a low ridge, deployed into line, and sat down to wait while foragers cut the wheat for its straw. At the same time the generals, mounted on the roof of a log cabin, strained their eyes to see through their glasses something of the American position and saw absolutely nothing. As a reconnaissance, the expedition was a complete fiasco. As an invitation to attack, it could hardly have been better. As a preparation for defeat, it was an outstanding success.

The British line extended about a thousand yards with only two men to hold every three yards. Though its front was cleared of trees and was a good field for artillery practice or for a bayonet charge, its flanks rested on thick woods, which gave cover for the kind of fighting favored by the Americans. So they sat there, discovering nothing, doing nothing, a "meaningless and objectless military expedition which, on Burgoyne's part, was a counsel of despair." [16]

The first news of this movement of the enemy came to Gates from an outpost on Mill Creek. He sent Major James Wilkinson out to investigate. Receiving an account of the enemy's disposition, he ordered Morgan "to begin the game." Morgan suggested that his men should attack the British right. Gates agreed, and directed that Poor's brigade should go against the flank of the enemy's left. The two detachments were to move secretly through the dense forest, so as to strike by surprise at the same moment.

To secure a proper position from which to launch his attack, Morgan had to make a wide circuit. Poor's march was much shorter. His brigade, comprising Scammell's, Hale's, and Cilley's New Hampshire Continental regiments, Van Cortlandt's and Livingston's New Yorkers and Cook's and

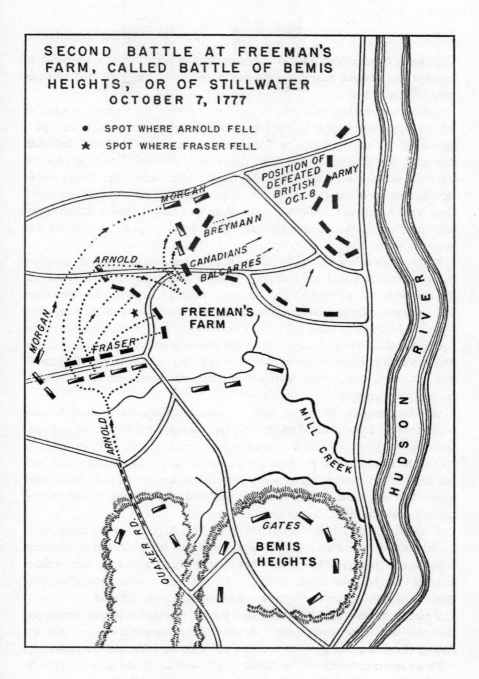

SECOND BATTLE AT FREEMAN'S
FARM, CALLED BATTLE OF BEMIS
HEIGHTS, OR OF STILLWATER
OCTOBER 7, 1777

● SPOT WHERE ARNOLD FELL
★ SPOT WHERE FRASER FELL

POSITION OF DEFEATED BRITISH ARMY OCT. 8

MORGAN

BREYMANN

ARNOLD

CANADIANS

BALCARRES

MORGAN

FREEMAN'S FARM

FRASER

ARNOLD

HUDSON RIVER

MILL CREEK

QUAKER RD.

GATES

BEMIS HEIGHTS

Lattimer's Connecticut militia—perhaps 800 in all [17]—by "a sudden and rapid" [18] movement gained the desired point about half past two and immediately attacked.

Acland's grenadiers occupied an elevated position. Poor's men, advancing up the slope, received a heavy fire of grape and musketry; but most of it flew high, cutting the leaves and branches of the trees. They reserved their fire until this first volley had been discharged. Acland then called for the bayonet, but the Americans loosed a deadly blast before the charge could develop. Many of the grenadiers fell. Acland himself was shot through both legs. The Americans, shouting, rushed the position, seized a 12-pounder, and turned it on the enemy. The grenadiers were swept away. Acland was taken prisoner.

By this time Morgan was in action. His riflemen, in the face of "a severe fire of grape-shot and small arms," "poured down like a torrent" on the flank and the rear of the British right, posted behind a rail fence.[19] Balcarres tried to change front to receive them, but Dearborn's light infantry, coming up after Morgan, poured in a close fire, leaped the fence, and drove the enemy in disorder. Balcarres rallied his force behind a second fence, but Morgan's and Dearborn's men came on with fierce impetuosity that could not be denied. His troops retired in disorder to the shelter of their lines, leaving their guns to the Americans.[20]

At this juncture Burgoyne sent his aide-de-camp, Sir Francis Clarke, with an order for a general retirement; but Clarke was shot down and captured before he could deliver the order.

The Brunswickers in the center were left without support. Learned with his brigade was advancing to meet them when a new figure, a small man dressed in a general's uniform and mounted on a great, brown horse, flashed onto the field. It was Benedict Arnold.

Ever since Gates had displaced him, he had lingered in the camp, with no command, no status at all in the army, eating his heart out in enforced idleness and disgrace. Now, with a battle raging before his very eyes, neither the lack of orders nor consideration for his irregular condition could restrain him. He had put spurs to his horse and dashed into the conflict.

Fearing that he "might do some rash thing," Gates sent Major Armstrong to order him back to the camp. Arnold saw Armstrong and spurred the faster. He first came up with one of Poor's Connecticut militia regiments. "Whose regiment is that?" he shouted. "Colonel Lattimer's, sir." "Ah!" he cried. "My old Norwich and New London friends. God bless you! I'm glad to see you." [21] They gave their old general a hearty cheer as he swept on to overtake the head of Learned's brigade.

Three regiments were in advance. Arnold called on them to follow him. They responded with shouts and cheers, charged across Mill Creek and up the opposite slope full upon Riedesel's Brunswickers, commanded by Colonel Specht. But these had been strengthened by detachments of the Rhetz and Hesse Hanau regiments and manfully withstood the shock. The Americans were repulsed.

Specht's right was uncovered when Balcarres's light infantry were driven back to the lines, and the Americans came back. Though exposed to fire on three sides, the Germans fought bravely until, when about to be surrounded, they were ordered to retreat to the works.

General Fraser had been conspicuous throughout the fight, riding to and fro and encouraging his troops. Now he tried, with the British 24th and the light infantry, to form a second line. Arnold saw him and said to Morgan, "That man on the gray horse is a host in himself and must be disposed of." Morgan called on one of his riflemen, Tim Murphy, an old Indian fighter and a noted marksman.

Murphy climbed a tree and took aim with his double-barreled rifle. His first shot cut the crupper of Fraser's horse. The second went through the horse's mane. One of Fraser's aides told his chief that he was the object of dangerous personal attention and urged him to withdraw. Fraser answered that his duty compelled him to remain there. The third shot passed through his body, wounding him mortally.[22]

At this point Brigadier General Abraham Ten Broeck, with his brigade of 3,000 New York militia lately arrived in camp, appeared on the field; but they were not needed. At Fraser's fall the last hope of British resistance had died. The whole line gave way and retreated to the shelter of the breastworks, just fifty minutes from the time the first shot was fired.

The fighting seemed to be over, and if Gates had commanded in the field it would have been over; but Arnold was of different stuff. He was not content with driving the enemy from the field; he wanted a smashing victory. "With true military instinct, [he] seized the opportunity for a general attack upon the British entrenchments." [23]

With a part of the brigades of Patterson and Glover he assaulted that part of the works held by Balcarres and his light infantry, and drove through the abatis. But though Arnold, raging with the ardor of battle, exposing himself to the rain of grapeshot and musketry, animated his men to the last degree of courage, the defense was too strong. They were driven back, and the fight settled down to continued hot firing at musket range.

While this was going on, Learned's brigade appeared off to the left, marching toward the extreme British right. Arnold clapped spurs to his horse and galloped straight across the line of fire, exposing himself to what seemed certain death. With his complete disregard of all military conventions he took charge of Learned's men and led them past Balcarres's right and against the two stockaded log cabins between Balcarres and Breymann's horseshoe redoubt. They had been and were still held by a weak force of unreliable Canadian irregulars. The Americans swept them away.

Now Breymann was exposed on all sides. His force had been reduced from 500 to 200 by drafts for the British line of battle. Arnold took over two regiments, Wesson's and Livingston's, and Morgan's riflemen, who had made a complete circuit of the British right, and ordered them forward. At the head of Brooks's Massachusetts regiment, just then coming up, he swung to the left and attacked Breymann's redoubt. "His impetuous onset carried everything before it." [24] He rode around the redoubt and entered the sally port. There his horse was shot down, and he himself received a bullet in his leg that fractured his thigh bone. It was the same leg that had been wounded at Quebec. It is said that the shot was fired by a wounded German, and that Arnold called out, "Don't hurt him! He's a fine fellow. He only did his duty." [25] Here at last Armstrong caught up with the man who had successfully avoided him up to this time. There was no need to deliver Gates's order to return to the camp. Arnold went willingly enough on a litter, with the glory of that mad afternoon coruscating about him.

Breymann had been mortally wounded in the attack, and his small force had given up the redoubt. Burgoyne's main position was thus open to the Americans, both on the right and in the rear. But it was growing dark, and, besides, they had no Arnold to lead them. Colonel Specht with a small force of Brunswickers made an attempt to recover the redoubt; but they were easily driven off, and he himself taken prisoner. That ended the battle.

The losses of the British army amounted to about 600 killed, wounded, and captured. They also lost every one of the ten guns they brought into the action. The Americans suffered about 150 casualties.

From the time when Arnold had come onto the field, he was never for a moment idle. Exercising command without warrant, but most effectively, over whatever brigade, regiment, or company he came across, he was incessantly active wherever the fighting was heaviest. He seemed to be endowed with the headlong energy of a madman,[26] exposing himself to the enemy's fire with the utmost temerity, flourishing his sword, shouting encouragement to the troops, and inspiring them with his own intrepidity and dash. He was exactly the sort of leader needed by the untrained militia and by the half-trained Continentals as well. The British were, of course, heavily outnumbered, and their defeat was in the cards before ever Arnold injected himself into the battle; but that it would have been so quickly and so completely accomplished without him is more than doubtful. Certainly to him and to Morgan belongs the credit for the victory.

Gates, on the other hand, was never on the field of battle at any time during the fighting. He remained in his headquarters, about three-quarters of a mile behind the front line of the American entrenchments and fully two miles from the scene of action. From there he could not even see what was going on; and, except for that first order to Morgan to attack and the subsequent sending out of other detachments, he exercised no control over the conduct of his troops nor over the tactics of the battle.

It may have been Gates's idea that a general commander should remain in a safe place, where reports of the progress of the fight could be brought to him and where he would be safe from injury. That is doubtless the correct principle in warfare, where enormous numbers have to be guided by a master-mind, but it was not the principle generally observed in the battles of the Revolution. Howe at Bunker Hill did not disdain to lead his men to the attack in person and to share their dangers. Washington exposed himself fearlessly at Kip's Bay and at Princeton; so did Burgoyne and Phillips and Riedesel at Bemis Heights; so did Arnold and Montgomery at Quebec. Someone has said that Gates never once heard the whistle of an enemy's bullet through his whole term of command of the northern army.[27]

That to Arnold is due the credit for the victory at Bemis Heights is the considered opinion of a distinguished military historian, Sir John W. Fortescue:

> In natural military genius neither Washington nor Greene are to my mind comparable with Benedict Arnold. The man was, of course, shallow, fickle, unprincipled and unstable in character, but he possessed all the gifts of a great commander. To boundless energy and enterprise he united quick insight into a situation, sound strategic instinct, audacity of movement, wealth of resource, a swift and unerring eye in action, great personal daring and true magic of leadership. It was he and no other who beat Burgoyne at Saratoga and, with Daniel Morgan to command the militia, Benedict Arnold was the most formidable opponent that could be matched against the British in America.[28]

The opinions of some others regarding Arnold's behavior before Saratoga are not so favorable.

CHAPTER 43

Saratoga

The loss of Breymann's redoubt threw the British wide open to attack in flank and in the rear, so that Burgoyne's position was no longer tenable. During the night of October 7 he withdrew his army in good order to a position north of the Great Ravine, on the riverside bluffs where strong redoubts had been erected to protect the train of artillery, the provisions, the bateaux, and the hospital. The next day, the Americans took over his old campground.[1] Lincoln occupied the bluff and the river meadows nearby, threatening an attack, of which Burgoyne was apprehensive. He wrote afterward that he had offered battle,[2] but that his position was too strong for the Americans to risk it. There was, however, "a great deal of cannonading"[3] of the enemy's camp and some skirmishing between the outposts, in which Lincoln was wounded.

That same morning Gates dispatched Brigadier General John Fellows and his brigade of 1,300 Massachusetts militia up the east side of the Hudson to the mouth of the Batten Kill, with orders to cross the river and entrench a position on the west side at Saratoga. Brigadier General Jacob Bayley, with 2,000 New Hampshire militia, was already posted on a height north of Fort Edward. Thus Burgoyne was menaced both in the front and in the rear; but Fellows in the rear was too weak to offer effective opposition.[4]

Anticipating the necessity of further retreat, Burgoyne sent Lieutenant Colonel Sutherland with the 9th and 47th British regiments to reconnoiter the road up to Fort Edward.

The movement of Fellows's troops had been observed by the British.

Burgoyne interpreted it as a preliminary to an attack on his rear. To obviate that, he decided to withdraw at once to the heights of Saratoga.

The retreat began about nine o'clock in the evening of the 8th. Captain Fraser's Rangers and the few remaining Tories and Indians led the van, followed by the Brunswickers, the heavy artillery, and the baggage train. The British regiments under Balcarres, marching in two columns, Burgoyne with them, closed the rear. While they were on the march Sutherland's detachment returned and fell in behind the Brunswickers.[5] The bateaux were laboriously rowed upstream alongside the marching men. The hospital, with more than 300 sick and wounded men, was left, in the care of a surgeon, to the mercy of the Americans.[6]

The progress of the British army was slow beyond belief, not more than a mile an hour. At Dovecote—now Coveville—a halt was ordered at two o'clock in the morning to let the bateaux carrying the provisions catch up. The march was not resumed until four o'clock in the afternoon. It was a dolorous march. Rain was falling heavily. The road, bad enough before, was now a bog. The tired men could hardly drag their feet out of the mud. The wagons stuck fast and were unable to go on.[7] The tents and baggage were therefore left behind. Parties of Americans hung on the rear of the retreating army, waylaying the bateaux, many of which were captured and looted. It was late in the evening of the 9th when the beaten army reached the mouth of the Fish Kill, forded the stream, and found itself in its desired position on the heights of Saratoga—where Schuylerville is today, near Saratoga Springs on the north. Wet to the skin and almost dead-beat, the men "had not strength or inclination to cut wood and make fires, but rather sought sleep in their wet cloaths and on the wet ground, under a heavy rain that still continued"; so says one that was with them.[8]

From that place Burgoyne sent Sutherland, with the 9th and 47th, some Canadians, and a corps of artificers, up the river again to the neighborhood of Fort Edward to build a bridge by which the retreating army could cross the Hudson to the only practicable northward road, that on the east side.[9]

The position taken was favorable for a defensive stand. It was on a rise of ground north of Fish Kill, with much open ground before it, which would afford a field of fire for the artillery and permit of battle formation in the classic style and the free use of the bayonet, the favorite weapon of the British and Brunswick regulars. It had already been fortified by Burgoyne's troops when they lay there on September 13 and 14. These works were now strengthened. Fellows and his brigade, who were there before Burgoyne, forded the river on his approach and took a position on a height opposite the British camp.

Gates was slow in his pursuit, lingering in camp until after noon of the 10th; but his men marched faster than the British and came in sight of them by four o'clock.[10] Burgoyne had left the 20th, 21st, and 62nd British regiments south of Fish Kill as a guard for headquarters established in Schuyler's great house near the river. These were now withdrawn to the main position, and Schuyler's house, being in the way of artillery fire from the heights, was burned.

After all his seeming dilatoriness and lack of energy Gates now suddenly grew bold. The movement of Sutherland's detachment up the river had been reported to him, and he assumed that it was the main body of the British, and that he faced only the rear guard. Without any reconnaissance to determine the true state of affairs, he drew up orders for an attack at dawn the next day.[11]

At that season of the year a morning fog always overhangs the river country; and so it did on the morning of October 11 when Morgan advanced along the edge of the bluffs and the rest of the army moved up the road by the riverside. They were going blindly against a strong position strongly held and mounting twenty-seven guns of various calibers with a clear field of fire when, by mere chance, Brigadier General John Glover learned the truth. His men had picked up a lone British deserter, who told them that the whole British army was in the entrenchments they intended to attack, even Sutherland's two regiments having been recalled. Glover sent the news back to Gates and to Nixon, whose brigade had already crossed Fish Kill. He suggested a return. Nixon halted. At that moment the fog lifted, disclosing the British position. The enemy opened fire, and Nixon's men hurriedly withdrew to the south side of the Kill.[12]

Learned's brigade had meanwhile proceeded according to orders, and was advancing in the fog up the slope against the enemy when James Wilkinson, Gates's youthful aide, overtook them bringing news of the true situation. Learned, with some reluctance, ordered a withdrawal, which was made under fire. There can be little doubt that, if the attack had been made according to Gates's orders, it would have resulted in a defeat.[12]

Concentrating their attention on Burgoyne's fleet of bateaux, the Americans captured most of them that day. Morgan, who had remained north of Fish Kill, now took post to the west of the British position and was joined by Learned's brigade and some Pennsylvania regiments. Burgoyne was thus invested on three sides, but his way to the north was still open. For the first time in the campaign he called a council of war—always before he had made his own decisions without asking his generals' advice.

Riedesel proposed abandonment of the baggage and retreat up the west side of the river, to cross above Fort Edward and go on to Fort George. But Burgoyne would not agree.[13] The Americans established three batteries at Fellows's position on the opposite side of the river and opened fire on the British camp, and there was constant fighting of outposts.

In the afternoon of the 12th Burgoyne called another council, including Riedesel, Phillips, and the two brigadiers, Gall and Hamilton. He placed before it the situation of his army: It was facing 14,000 rebels equipped with "considerable artillery" and was threatened with attack by them; other forces were between the British position and Fort Edward; the bateaux were either ruined or captured; the way up the west side of the river was impracticable, except for "small parties of Indians"; to get the artillery away, bridges would have to be built across the affluents of the Hudson under the fire of the enemy and with Gates attacking their rear; nothing had been heard from Clinton. He now asked for opinions on five propositions: (1) to wait in this position for coming, fortunate events; (2) to attack the enemy; (3) to retreat, repair the bridges on the march and thus, with artillery and baggage, force the fords at Fort Edward; (4) to retreat by night, leaving the artillery and baggage behind, cross above Fort Edward or march round Lake George; (5) in case the enemy should move to the left, to force a passage to Albany.

The first, second, and third propositions were promptly rejected as impracticable. Burgoyne, Phillips, and Hamilton were inclined toward the fifth; but its execution depended on a foolish move by Gates, and he could not be relied upon to make it. Riedesel insisted on the adoption of the fourth, and it was approved, the march to begin that night "with the greatest secrecy and quietness," each soldier carrying his own provision for six days.[14]

At ten o'clock Riedesel sent word to headquarters that the rations had been distributed and asked for marching orders. The answer was: "The retreat is postponed; the reason why is not known." [15] So Burgoyne lost his last chance to get away, for by the next day he was entirely surrounded.[16] In the night American troops had crossed from the mouth of Batten Kill on the east side of the river and erected a battery on the west side. They were commanded by John Stark, that unpredictable person having arrived with 1,100 New Hampshire militia.

"Numerous parties of American militia . . . swarmed around the little adverse army like birds of prey," says Sergeant Lamb, who was there. "Roaring of cannon and whistling of bullets from their rifle pieces were heard constantly by day and night." [17] And according to Riedesel:

Every hour the position of the army grew more critical, and the prospect of salvation grew less and less. There was no place of safety for the baggage; and the ground was covered with dead horses that had either been killed by the enemy's bullets or by exhaustion, as there had been no forage for several days. . . . Even for the wounded, no spot could be found which could afford them a safe shelter—not even, indeed, for so long a time as might suffice for a surgeon to bind up their ghastly wounds. The whole camp was now a scene of constant fighting. The soldier could not lay down his arms day or night, except to exchange his gun for the spade when new entrenchments were thrown up. The sick and wounded would drag themselves along into a quiet corner of the woods and lie down to die on the damp ground. Nor even here were they longer safe, since every little while a ball would come crashing down among the trees.[18]

Small wonder it is that "order grew more and more lax."

On the 13th another council was assembled, including not only the general officers but also "the field-officers and captains commanding corps of the army." [19] Burgoyne presented the same five propositions, but added a statement of the increased difficulties. He also said that he believed that some of the officers were in favor of capitulation, but he would not consider that without the assent of those in the council. He asked three questions. (1) Could an army of 3,500 effective combatants enter into an agreement with the enemy without detriment to the national honor? They all answered "Yes." (2) Was this now the case for this army? They all agreed that it was. (3) Was this army's situation such as to make an honorable capitulation really detrimental? They replied in the negative.[20]

Burgoyne sent Gates a letter asking for a meeting with a staff officer "in order to negotiate matters of high importance to both armies," [21] and in the morning of the 14th Major Kingston met Wilkinson between the lines and was conducted to Gates's headquarters. Kingston said that his chief knew Gates's superiority of numbers and their disposition, which would render a retreat "a scene of carnage on both sides," [22] and proposed a cessation of hostilities to consider terms. To his surprise, Gates presented a paper already drawn up, containing his terms.

They included a surrender of the troops as prisoners of war, grounding their arms within the camp and marching out to such destination as should be directed. Other provisions allowed the officers and soldiers to keep their personal baggage, admitted the officers to parole, and required the delivery of all public stores, arms, ammunition "&c &c." [23] But the two terms first mentioned amounted to a demand for unconditional surrender, and Burgoyne's officers made violent objection. The terms were "inadmissible in any extremity. Sooner than this the army will ground their arms in their encampment, they will rush on the enemy, determined to take no quarter." [24] So Burgoyne replied to Gates.

In thus presenting his terms, Gates made a tactical error. It was customary to let the besieged propose terms, which the besiegers could modify or reject. Now Gates had either to stand on the terms he proposed and take the consequences, or to let Burgoyne do the revising and accept what he offered. Burgoyne sent back his terms, to which, he said, he would accept no amendment. His troops were to march out of the camp with the honors of war and ground their arms by the riverside at the command of their own officers. Moreover, they were not to be considered as prisoners of war, but were to be granted passage back to Great Britain from the port of Boston, on British transports "whenever General Howe shall so order," on condition of "not serving again in North America during the present contest." [25] They were to have rations at American expense while on the march to Boston and while quartered there. The officers were to retain their carriages and horses, and "no baggage was to be molested, General Burgoyne giving his honour that their are no public stores secreted therein." The Canadians were to be permitted to return to Canada, being supplied by the Americans on the march. There were other similarly generous provisions, but those mentioned constitute the gist of the proposal.

To the amazement of Burgoyne and his officers, Gates immediately accepted the proposal, with only one addition: the surrender was to take place at two o'clock in the afternoon of the following day. This precipitate abandonment of his former demands and acceptance of the extraordinary proposals of the enemy aroused Burgoyne's suspicions. He thought that Gates must have heard that Clinton was coming up to relieve his compatriots. To gain time he asked for a postponement of the ceremony. Gates agreed, and the articles were drawn up in form and signed by representatives of both armies.

Then Burgoyne asked one more concession. The agreement must not be called a "capitulation" but rather a "convention." Again Gates consented. His willingness to yield was indeed, as Burgoyne suspected, prompted by news of movements of Clinton's army.

Although Clinton himself had returned to New York after capturing the two forts, he had sent a detachment up the river as far as Esopus. From this fact Gates deduced an intention to push on to Burgoyne's relief. Burgoyne had also heard of this. Hopes that relief was coming burgeoned in his mind, and he began to regret his proposal to give up. He went so far as to ask his council whether, at this stage of the proceedings, he could honorably withdraw from the negotiations. The council voted that he could not, and that the advantageous terms agreed to by Gates should not be rejected. Still Burgoyne delayed signing. He called another council, but found his officers still of the same mind. Then he yielded and signed.[26]

In the afternoon of the 16th, Burgoyne and his staff in their "rich, royal uniforms" rode out to the American camp and met Gates in "a plain, blue frock." "The fortune of war, General Gates," said Burgoyne, "has made me your prisoner." To which Gates replied, "I shall ever be ready to testify that it has not been through any fault of your Excellency," and invited the party to dine with him.[27]

In the morning of the 17th, the British army marched out of its camp to the appointed place in the meadows by the river and, at the command of its own officers, piled its arms and emptied its cartridge boxes. In order that the conquered troops might be humiliated as little as possible, Gates had ordered his men to remain within their own lines. The British then marched through the American camp between two lines of troops drawn up in order, from whom they received not "the least disrespect, or even a taunting look, but all was mute astonishment and pity." [28]

One of the Brunswickers has described the appearance of the American troops:

Not one of them was properly uniformed, but each man had on the clothes in which he goes to the field, to church or to the tavern. But they stood like soldiers, erect, with a military bearing which was subject to little criticism. All their guns were provided with bayonets, and the riflemen had rifles. The people stood so still that we were greatly amazed. Not one fellow made a motion as if to speak to his neighbor; furthermore, nature had formed all the fellows who stood in rank and file, so slender, so handsome, so sinewy, that it was a pleasure to look at them and we were all surprised at the sight of such a finely built people. And their size! . . . The officers . . . wore very few uniforms and those they did wear were of their own invention. All colors of cloth . . . brown coats with sea-green facings, white linings and silver sword-knots; also gray coats with straw facings and yellow buttons were frequently seen. . . . The brigadiers and generals have special uniforms and ribbons which they wear like bands of orders over their vests . . . most colonels and other officers, on the other hand, were in their ordinary clothes.

He was amazed at the variety and size of the wigs worn by the older Americans "between their fiftieth and sixtieth year," who had "perhaps at this age followed the calfskin [drum] for the first time" and "cut a droll figure under arms"; yet "it is no joke to oppose them . . . they can cold-bloodedly draw a bead on anyone." He noted the variety of "standards with all manner of emblems and mottoes, some of which seemed to us very caustic. . . .

There was not a man among them who showed the slightest sign of mockery, malicious delight, hate or any other insult; it seemed rather as if they wished to do us honor." [29]

When the beaten army came to a large tent, Gates and Burgoyne emerged from it, turned and faced each other. Silently, Burgoyne drew his sword and tendered it to Gates, who received it with a bow and returned it. So the ceremonies of the "convention" were completed, and the British army set out on its march to Boston.

For the Americans it was a stupendous victory. Two lieutenant generals, two major generals, three brigadiers, with their staffs and aides, 299 other officers ranging from colonels to ensigns, chaplains and surgeons, 389 non-commissioned officers, 197 musicians, and 4,836 privates passed out of the armed forces of Great Britain in America. The matériel captured was of vast importance, including 27 guns of various calibers, 5,000 stand of small arms, great quantities of ammunition, and military stores and equipment of all kinds.[30]

Even more important were its psychological effects among the patriots. Coming close after Washington's defeats at Brandywine and Germantown, it was a needed restorative of confidence in the American cause; and it acted as such. The ill organized, ill disciplined, ill supplied American amateur soldiers had defeated the British and German regulars in two battles in the open field. To be sure, the enemy was greatly outnumbered; but that fact did not affect the rejoicing, nor did it reduce the newborn confidence in the American armies. They had a great store of men to draw upon and might again produce armies greater in numbers than their foes.

Upon the disposition of the British troops in America, Burgoyne's defeat had an immediate effect. Ticonderoga and Crown Point were evacuated, and their garrisons were withdrawn to Canada. Sir Henry Clinton recalled Vaughan's detachment, which had got within forty miles of Albany and withdrew the garrison he had left in Fort Clinton, thus abandoning his hold on the Highlands and retaining only the town and island of New York, with their outlying posts. Only there, in Rhode Island, and in Philadelphia had His Majesty's forces any hold upon the revolted colonies.

In England the news of Bennington had already called forth from the politicians and newspapers of the Opposition "croaking prophecies of disaster to Burgoyne." When Saratoga's news arrived the Opposition in Parliament received it with "a howl of insulting triumph." But upon the country in general it had a tonic effect. There was considerable apprehension that the defeat would bring France into the war on the side of America. It was evident that a greater army would be needed, in that case, to carry on the struggle. Towns and cities volunteered to raise regiments at their own expense. In Scotland a number of noblemen and wealthy gentlemen offered to enroll battalions, though not at their own expense. Thus 15,000 men were added to the royal army.[31]

In France the effect was more encouraging to the Americans. Although for a long time, secretly and by various subterfuges, that country had been supplying the Americans with great quantities of arms and war matériel, it had refrained from entering the conflict even to the extent of recognizing their national existence. Now it acted with almost dizzy haste. Within two days after the arrival of the news of Saratoga, the King of France signed a short note extending such recognition and virtually making his country the ally of the United States. On February 6, 1778, a formal treaty was signed. Upon its publication, in March, the British ambassador was recalled from Paris. France and England were now at war, and after a considerable delay Spain and then Holland came into the conflict on the American side. Saratoga thus fairly earned the epithet of Turning Point of the Revolution.

Although the subsequent treatment by the Congress of the troops surrendered at Saratoga is a political matter, not within the strict scope of this account of the military operations of the Revolution, it is so intimately connected with the war itself and is of such interest and importance that it should be briefly discussed.

While the victory was received with rejoicings, the terms granted to the defeated were thought by the Congress and by the people generally to be far too liberal. It was too plain to be overlooked that, though they were under engagement not to serve against the Americans in the war, there was nothing to prevent the government of Great Britain from employing them elsewhere and so releasing other troops that might be sent to America. The Congress was indisposed to give Britain this advantage by ratifying and carrying out the terms of the convention, if any subterfuge could be hit upon to justify refusal. "The public wished to have some pretence for detaining them." [32]

Having scanned the returns of the matériel surrendered, a committee of the Congress reported, on November 22, that they included only 648 cartridge boxes, a manifestly insufficient number for over 5,000 men. This evident failure to give them all up was esteemed to be a breach of the convention. Yet, at that time, the committee did not regard that state of facts as warranting delaying the embarkation.[33]

Unfortunately for the captive troops, Burgoyne himself furnished a reason deemed by the Congress sufficient to justify a refusal to carry out the agreement. Boston was already overcrowded with American troops when Burgoyne's soldiers arrived. There was a consequent delay in securing for the British officers quarters "according to their rank," as specified in the agreement. They were crowded together, without regard to rank, in huts made of boards, poorly built, and quite open to the wintry weather.[34] Burgoyne took offense and wrote a haughty letter to General Heath, in command there, charging that, by this failure in the matter of quarters, "the public faith is broke." [35]

Howe contributed his share to the difficulties of the situation. Instead of at once dispatching to Boston a fleet of transports to carry the British troops back to England, he delayed for months in an effort to change the plan so that the embarkation might be made in some port in British possession—Newport or New York. This meant, in the minds of the delegates to the Congress, that his real intention was to get Burgoyne's troops within the British lines and keep them as an addition to his own army.[36] But, chiefly, it was Burgoyne's words that were seized upon as an excuse for disregarding the agreement. "Congress had now obtained what they wanted, a plea for detaining the convention troops." [37]

On January 8, 1778, a committee of the Congress reported that "this charge of a breach of public faith is of a most serious nature, pregnant of alarming consequences," affording grounds for a belief that Burgoyne intended to rely upon such breach of faith to absolve himself and his army from the obligations of the contract, including the agreement that his troops should not serve again in America. The Congress, with this in mind, but falling back upon the missing cartridge boxes as a concrete breach, resolved that "the convention, on the part of the British, has not been strictly complied with." [38]

Yet it had not the resolution boldly to denounce the agreement as broken by the other side. It merely suspended the embarkation "till a distinct and explicit ratification of the convention of Saratoga shall be properly notified by the court of Great Britain to Congress." [39] When the British transports arrived off Boston, late in December, they were not admitted to the harbor.[40]

His Majesty sent orders to Clinton, Howe's successor, to signify his ratification of the convention. Clinton did so, whereupon the Congress was driven to declaring that it had "no evidence" that Clinton "had any orders from his King for the ratification of the Convention, that the whole might be, for what they knew, a forgery" and that "a responsible witness" must be produced "to swear he saw the King sign the order"; until then "they would not believe a word that he [Clinton] advanced," [41] which was surely as miserable a pretense of honorable dealing as was ever put forth.

Burgoyne and a few of his officers were allowed to go home, but the rest of his troops were marched down into Virginia and held as prisoners until the end of the war. The action of the Congress in this regard reflected great discredit upon the nation. The public faith had been broken without justifiable excuse or palliation. It was, indeed, a dirty business altogether.

CHAPTER 44

Valley Forge

Although the distance from Whitemarsh to Valley Forge is not more than thirteen miles, the American army under Washington was on the road to its new camp site for more than a week. It first marched north three miles to Gulph Mills and bivouacked. Its tents and baggage, sent from Whitemarsh at the time of the threatened attack on that position, were now at Trappe, eighteen miles to the northwest. For four days and nights of snow and sleet, the wretched, ill clad, tired soldiers huddled around campfires, trying to cook their meager provisions or to sleep, unsheltered and in wet clothes, thousands of them blanketless, on the snow-covered ground.[1] The night after the tents came up, the snowfall turned to rain; but before morning the temperature fell below freezing point, and the rutted, slush-covered roads were congealed in icy ridges. The army waited three days more for weather that would permit its barefoot men to march.

On December 19, 1777, its march was resumed. That oft-repeated story of bloody footprints was unimpeachably confirmed by Washington himself. Years later he told William Gordon, the historian, that "you might have tracked the army from White Marsh to Valley Forge by the blood of their feet." [2]

It is impossible to exaggerate the misery of the troops at this time. General Greene wrote: "One half of our troops are without breeches, shoes and stockings; and some thousands without blankets." A quarter of the whole number were reported unfit for duty, "because they are barefoot and otherwise naked." [3] The quartermaster's department, as well as the commissariat, had completely broken down. "While the army was suffering . . . for

543

want of shoes &c., hogsheads of shoes, stockings and clothing were at different places upon the road and in the woods, lying and perishing, for want of teams and proper management." [4]

Nevertheless, the army staggered on and came at last to Valley Forge, too tired, too hungry, and too weak to do more than huddle again around the campfires on its icy heights.

The place took its name from an ancient forge at the side of Valley Creek, which flows north into the Schuylkill, whose own course there is east-west, Valley Forge being on its southern side. From the creek the land rises steeply, over 250 feet in two-fifths of a mile, to an undulating plateau about two miles long and a mile and a quarter wide. The slopes on the west and on the north to the Schuylkill are less steep. This elevation was heavily forested with a variety of trees.

Along its southern edge was drawn an irregular line of entrenchments. Its western end was guarded by similar entrenchments and an abatis, running roughly north-south, also by certain redoubts and redans, forming a sort of inner stronghold. The western or creek side was thought to be sufficiently defended by the abruptness of approach from that quarter, and the north side by the width of the Schuylkill.

Throughout this space the various brigades were posted, each having its little village of huts drawn up in lines facing each other with streets between. Washington refused to seek other shelter for himself than that afforded by his marquee of coarse homespun linen, until his men were at least partly sheltered. He lived in it for a week, then established his headquarters at the western end of the camp in a large stone house. The general officers, although by the original plan each of them was to occupy a hut, soon distributed themselves in neighboring houses, mostly outside the camp.

The first requirement of the army on its arrival was shelter more suitable for winter than canvas tents. It was proposed that the troops build themselves log huts. Washington's general orders prescribed the plans and specifications. They were to be fourteen feet by sixteen in size, with log walls six and a half feet high, the interstices between the logs stopped with clay, the fireplaces and chimneys of clay-daubed wood, the steep-pitched roofs of planks or slabs. Twelve men were to occupy each hut. All this material had, of course, to be got out of standing timber.

Stirred to emulation by a prize of twelve dollars offered to the group which should finish its hut "in the quickest and most workmanlike manner," as well as driven by their necessities, the men went to work. Trees fell before their axes, were sawn into lengths, dragged through the snow by the men themselves, and notched to fit together at the corners of the huts. Others were split or sawn into rude boards for roofs and doors. Within two days the prize had been won by the most efficient group, but it was not until after Christmas that all the 9,000 men were housed. Even then their shelters were but apologies for dwelling places. They were far from weatherproof. The cold winter winds blew through their crevices. The ill designed fireplaces filled them with eye-stinging, throat-choking smoke. Few had wooden floors. For the most part the men lay on the damp earth, padded by a thin coating of scarce straw. Yet there was some warmth within them and shelter from snow and rain.

Shelter they had, of a sort; but in clothing there was a desperate lack. Lafayette wrote: "The unfortunate soldiers were in want of everything; they had neither coats, hats, shirts nor shoes; their feet and legs froze until they became black and it was often necessary to amputate them." [5] Dr. Albigence Waldo, surgeon of a Connecticut regiment, pictured a typical incident:

There comes a Soldier, his bare feet are seen thro' his worn-out shoes, his legs nearly naked from the tattered remains of an only pair of stockings, his Breeches not sufficient to cover his nakedness, his Shirt hanging in Strings, his hair dishevell'd, his face meagre; his whole appearance pictures a person forsaken & discouraged. He comes and crys with an air of wretchedness & despair, I am Sick, my feet lame, my legs are sore, my body covered with this tormenting Itch [a disease common in the camp].[6]

The lack of clothing was hardship enough; the lack of food was added torture. On December 20 General Varnum reported that his division had been two days without meat and three days without bread.[7] Three days later Washington informed the Congress that, the day before, lack of food had caused "a dangerous mutiny" which was suppressed with difficulty, and that there was in the camp "not a single hoof of any kind to slaughter and not more than twenty-five barrels of flour," nor did the commissary know when any more would arrive.[8] Salted beef and pork were almost as scarce as fresh meat. The lack was to some extent supplied by salted herring, which, however, were often found to be decayed when the barrels were opened. The common diet was flour-and-water paste baked in thin cakes on hot stones. "Fire-cake," the men called it. "Fire-cake and water for breakfast!" cried Dr. Waldo. "Fire-cake and water for dinner! Fire-cake and water for supper! The Lord send that our Commissary for Purchases may have to live on fire-cake and water!"

Even of water there was a lack. The high hills were barren of springs. Every drop the men got had to be carried in buckets from Valley Creek or the Schuylkill, or from a brook half a mile from the camp. "The warter we had to Drink," wrote one of them, "and to mix our flower with was out of a brook that run along by the Camps, and so many a dippin and washin it which maid it very Dirty and muddy." [9]

That in such conditions disease should be prevalent was to be expected. Smallpox was frequent, but not so frequent as the "putrid fever," typhus. There was no knowledge of the proper means of treating that dreadful ailment, or of preventing its spread; nor was there an adequate force of physicians, or a supply of even such medicines as they would have prescribed, or proper food for the men that came down with the fever that winter. A large hospital was established at Yellow Springs at which 1,300 cases were treated according to the limited knowledge and skill of the surgeons. Other cases were submitted to the care of the Adventist Sisters in their community at Ephrata, the Moravian Brethren at Bethlehem, and to "hospitals" in other near-by towns.

These hospitals were already crowded with sick and wounded men from the battlefields of Brandywine and Germantown—500 from Brandywine alone at Ephrata. Part of them had to be lodged in tents. Their beds were bundles of straw laid on the floors and used over and over again, without change, by successive invalids. Dr. William Smith said he had "known from four to five patients die on the same straw before it was changed." The typhus patients that came from Valley Forge were put in with the wounded men in the condition in which they arrived, not only ill with that contagious disease, but also "attired in rags swarming with vermin." That deadly fever became epidemic in the hospitals themselves. Doctors and nurses came down with it. At Bethlehem "not an orderly man or nurse escaped, and but a few of the surgeons." At Lititz there were 250 invalids cared for by two doctors. Both of them fell ill of typhus.[10] Of 1,500 patients received there, 500 died. Of 40 men of one Virginia regiment, only three survived. Those "hospitals" were but way stations on the road to the grave. It was not until spring that the spread of the disease abated at Valley Forge and the convalescents began to return to duty.

Foraging parties did what they could to supply food. Wayne harried New Jersey and secured some cattle, thereby earning the sobriquet of "The Drover." [11] Henry Lee (Light-Horse Harry) made forays into Delaware and brought up cattle that had been fattening on the marsh meadows along the river for the British army.[12] But Allen McLane was "the most dashing of all the raiders." [13] The whole territory outside the British lines was his playground. He foraged from the farmers, but had more joy in cutting off British expeditions and taking their cattle from them. Captain of an independent corps, now a small troop of horsemen, now a hundred men, mounted and on foot, including sometimes a contingent of Oneida Indians, he was at once forager, scout, and raider everywhere about Philadelphia and even, at times, in that city in disguise. "He became known to everybody as the constant hero of surprise and daring." [14]

To counteract Wayne's successful forays in New Jersey and to procure forage for their own army, the British sent similar parties into that state. One of these, commanded by Colonel Mawhood, the gallant leader of the British troops defeated at Princeton, was made up of the 17th, 27th, and 46th British regiments, the Queen's Rangers, a mixed force of 300 Tory foot and horse under Colonel John G. Simcoe, and the Tory New Jersey Volunteers. On March 12, 1778, it crossed the Delaware to Salem in New Jersey. There the 30 cavalrymen—"hussars"—of the Rangers "borrowed" horses from the inhabitants and mounted them.

About three miles southeast of Salem, Colonel Asher Holmes held Quintin's Bridge, spanning Alloway Creek, with a small force of New Jersey militia in some slight earthworks on the eastern side of the creek. For further security they had taken up the planks of the bridge. To mask this force and allow the foraging to proceed unmolested, another Colonel Holmes of the 17th British regiment with 70 men took post at a tavern on the west side. To strengthen this party Colonel Mawhood concealed the Rangers, part of them under Captain Stephenson in the tavern, part under Captain Saunders behind a fence in its rear, and the rest, with Simcoe, in the woods farther behind. The masking party of the 17th, in full view of the Americans, then began to retreat from the creek with apparent precipitation. Deceived, the Americans relaid the bridge planks and crossed the creek. Part of them took post on high ground near the bridge; the rest, 200 in number, pushed on in pursuit of the retreating British. Suddenly and unexpectedly they came upon the Rangers behind the fence. Their leader ordered a retreat. He was wounded and captured. The Rangers in the tavern issued forth and cut off the way to the bridge. Caught between two fires, the unfortunate militiamen broke and fled to the right to cross the stream above the bridge. "Captain Stephenson drove them across the fields. Captain Saunders pursued them, the Huzzars were let loose" upon them, "and afterwards the battalion, Colonel Mawhood leading them." Many of them were shot, others cut down by the hussars of the Rangers, and more were driven into the creek and drowned. There is no record of the American losses, but, though the party that had taken post on the high ground near the bridge appears to have escaped across it, the death toll was heavy. The British lost one hussar, mortally wounded.

In New Jersey this affair was called a massacre. It aroused strong feelings, particularly because of the presence of the New Jersey Tories and their participation in the ruthless pursuit and slaughter of fleeing men of their own state.[15]

Mawhood, after returning to Salem, decided to attack another party of American militia posted at Hancock's Bridge across Alloway Creek about five miles from Salem. He sent Simcoe with his Rangers and the New Jersey Volunteers in boats down the Delaware to a point below the mouth of the Alloway. Thence they marched two miles through knee-deep swamps before they reached fast ground near the bridge. At the same time, the 27th Regiment was approaching it in front, cooperating with Simcoe.

The attack was elaborately planned to entrap the 400 militia at the bridge, detachments being sent here and there to occupy different houses in the village, including Hancock's house near the bridge, which was supposed to be the headquarters of the militia.

But all except 20 of the 400 militia that had been holding the bridge had been withdrawn the day before. Simcoe's men approaching the village came first upon two sentries, whom they bayoneted. They then entered Hancock's house, in which the few remaining militia were sleeping. Aroused, these few made no opposition but, recognizing some of the New Jersey Volunteers, offered to shake hands with them. The answer was the bayonet. Every occupant of the house was killed, including Hancock and his brother, both Tories.

Meanwhile, a detachment of the Rangers had come upon a patrol of seven of the militia and shot down all but one. No prisoners were taken. This exploit, so typical of the ruthlessness of Simcoe's operations, most certainly was a "massacre," in the exact meaning of the word.[16]

To organize the effort to secure food and forage for the troops at Valley Forge and to push it to every extremity, Washington had appointed Nathanael Greene. A kind-hearted man, Greene undertook the "very disagreeable" job with reluctance; but, having undertaken it, he laid down rules for executing it which lacked nothing of thoroughness. His subordinates were to harden their hearts and "despatch the business as fast as possible." He bade them "search the country through and through," take all horses, cattle, sheep, hogs, all forage of every sort, all the wagons to carry it in. If distance or lack of wagons prevented the bringing of hay, corn, and such, they were to be burned; for an object secondary to feeding the Americans was starving the British. The motto was, "Forage the country naked!" [17] Receipts were given for the things taken, with promise of future payment.

But the country, he found, was already "very much drained." It was "strongly marked with poverty and distress." The cattle and horses had been largely taken into Philadelphia by the British. "The country has been so much gleaned that there is little left in it." [18] Not unnaturally, what was left was carefully concealed by the owners. All that Greene and his men could get was not enough.

Conditions in the camp grew steadily worse. The horses starved to death, 500 of them. For want of burial in the frozen ground their carcasses rotted about the camp in such numbers as to endanger the health of the men.[19] The soldiers themselves were not much better off than the horses. On February 16, 1778, Washington wrote: "For some days past there has been little less than a famine in the camp. A part of the army has been a week without any kind of flesh and the rest three or four days. Naked and starving as they are, we cannot enough admire the incomparable patience and fidelity of the soldiery, that they have not been ere this excited by their suffering to a general mutiny and dispersion." [20] Lafayette wrote in his memoirs, "The army frequently remained whole days without provisions, and the patient endurance of both soldiers and officers was a miracle which each moment seemed to renew." [21]

Fortunately, before the army could starve to death the combined efforts of Greene, now quartermaster general, and of Jeremiah Wadsworth of Connecticut, commissary general, gradually bettered conditions. Wadsworth applied himself to the collection of foodstuffs and clothing; Greene, to their transportation, gathering wagons and horses, repairing bridges, mending roads, organizing a corps of wagoners, so that much that once had had to be destroyed for want of transport could now be brought to the camp. By the arrival of spring there was a regular daily allowance to each man of a pound and a half of bread, a pound of beef or fish or pork and beans, and a gill of whisky. This was supplemented by fresh, sweet food that came to the army like manna from Heaven. The regular spring run of shad up the Schuylkill to spawn brought thousands upon thousands of those succulent fish to the nets of those accustomed to harvest them. The soldiers ate to repletion, and hundreds of barrels of the fat fish were salted down for future use.[22] "The cheeks of the young soldiers filled out, their arms recovered muscle and their step regained its spring; while the invalids who had survived the winter came back to the ranks by hundreds." [23]

But before the spring and its betterment of conditions there was a sad diminution of the army's strength. Not only death but desertion had reduced its numbers. Unable to endure the physical hardships, the weaker men, especially the foreign-born, went off "ten to fifty at a time." "In great numbers and even by companies," [24] they repaired to Philadelphia either to sell their arms for food or, in some cases, to seek service in the well fed, warmly clothed British army. Joseph Galloway, civilian governor of the town, whose duty it was to investigate the character of newcomers, testified that 2,300 of these deserters had reported to his office. Of these, one-half were Irish, one-fourth English or Scottish, the rest Americans.[25] The patriots were quoted as saying, "Our men depreciate as fast as our money." By these means, Washington's force was finally reduced to five or six thousand, of whom probably not more than half were really fit for duty. As the spring came on, efforts were made with some success to build up the enrollment by new enlistments; but it was hard to induce new men to submit themselves to the hardships of that sink of misery.

Yet more than restoration to health and increase of numbers was needed to turn that ragged horde into an army effective in the field. It had gone into camp a body of men experienced in a year, in many cases two years, of hard service. Its members knew how to shoot and how to stand being shot at—even, in a few cases, how to withstand the bayonet. But of the school of the soldier, of the manual of arms, of the facings, of forming column, of deploying in line of battle, of all the other military practices by which a soldier or a body of soldiers is exercised, moved, and maneuvered in camp, on the march, and on the field, they had only a slight and fumbling knowledge. Instruction in such practices was now the greatest need of the Americans, and it was miraculously supplied.

In February there came to the camp a forty-seven-year-old German soldier, a man of middle height, solidly built, heavy-featured, with a high forehead, a long nose, a strong chin, a full-lipped mouth, more often smiling than not. His light brown hair had somewhat thinned; but his brown-gray eyes, under heavy brows, were keenly alive, and his broad, full cheeks were ruddy with health.[26]

He called himself Frederick William Augustus Henry Ferdinand, Baron von Steuben. His letters of introduction to the Congress from Benjamin Franklin and Silas Deane in Paris stated that he had been a lieutenant general in the army of Frederick the Great and that monarch's aide-de-camp and quartermaster general. He himself spoke casually of his estate in Swabia. All that was simply eyewash. In fact, his Christian name was not Frederick William Augustus Henry Ferdinand, but something quite different; his family name was not Steuben, but Steube; he had no claim to the "von"; he had never been a lieutenant general, nor a general of any sort, in Frederick's army, nor his aide. His highest rank in Germany had been captain, and he had no estate in Swabia, nor anywhere else.[27]

He had, in fact, come to America a simple soldier of fortune looking for a job, and so closely resembled the typical specimen in fiction, with his easy disregard of truth in his accounts of himself, as to sound fictitious. But he was not a fiction, and all his fanciful fabrications were and are no matter at all. Baron von (or de, as he preferred it) Steuben deserves all the honor and praise he has since received from a grateful people. He was one of God's best gifts to America in its struggle for liberty.

Doubtless he was aware of the temper of the Congress towards foreign aspirants for office in the army and had sufficiently well justified confidence in his own ability to climb by his own merits, if he could only get a foot on the ladder of preferment, for he told a committee of the Congress that "he did not seek any rank or pay. He wished only to join the war as a volunteer and render such services as General Washington might think him capable of." [28] He would ask only that his necessary expenses while in the service should be defrayed. That seemed fair enough. The committee applauded his generosity, and the Congress accepted his services.[29]

Washington received him cordially, recognized his military ability, and asked him to serve as a volunteer acting inspector general in charge of the training of the troops. Steuben accepted the position and took a look at them. With his idea of an army, what he saw was shocking.

"The men," Steuben wrote, "were literally naked, some of them in the fullest extent of the word. The officers who had coats had them of every color and make. I saw officers . . . mounting guard in a sort of dressing-gown made of an old blanket or woollen bed-cover. With regard to military discipline, I may safely say no such thing existed. . . . There was no regular formation. A so-called regiment was found of three platoons, another of five, eight, nine and the Canadian regiment of twenty-one. The formation of the regiments was as varied as their mode of drill, which consisted only of the manual exercise. Each colonel had a system of his own, the one according to the English, the other according to the Prussian or the French style. . . . The greater part of the captains had no roll of their companies and had no idea how many men they had. . . . When I asked a colonel of the strength of his regiment, the usual reply was 'Something between two and three hundred men.' " He found one regiment of 30 men, one company consisting of one corporal. "The arms were in a horrible condition, covered with rust, half of them without bayonets, many from which a single shot could not be fired . . . muskets, carbines, fowling-pieces and rifles were seen in the same company." [30] The other equipment was equally varied.

Yet Steuben recognized the quality of the material he had to deal with, the fortitude of the soldiers, and their devotion to their cause. He told Washington that no European army would have held together under such deprivations of food, clothing, and shelter. [31]

The German officer's first task was to devise a uniform system of drill regulations. He based it on the Prussian system, with such adaptations as were required by American conditions. As he knew no English, but only French and German, he wrote it in French from which it was translated by his aide, Pierre Duponceau, and then polished by John Laurens and Alexander Hamilton. When the English version was presented to him he could not understand a word of it. He had to memorize the English form of each of its commands and rehearse them before his young American assistants. [32]

There was no printing press with the army. Hundreds of copies of the regulations had to be written in longhand for distribution to the officers and then copied into their orderly books. Speed was important as there was little time left before the year's campaign would open. Day by day the composition and translation of the original went on. The first lesson, written on a Monday night would be translated, copied, and in the hands of the drill-masters by Wednesday. [33]

Though, in accordance with the English practice, drilling the men in the American army had been left to the sergeants, Steuben would not have it that way. He would drill the men himself. His method was first to organize a model company of a hundred men selected from various regiments. When it was drawn up, he took from it a small squad and started at the beginning with "the position of the soldier." To explain that, he relied upon pantomime, himself assuming the proper attitude and calling on each man to imitate him, correcting each man's faults by indicating them. He taught them how to dress their line. He marched them forward in slow step, himself calling the time—over and over again. So he went on, teaching them to halt, to about-face, to march to the rear, and so on. [34]

While he drilled the squad the rest of the model company looked on, as did also hundreds of officers and thousands of men. He then split the whole company into similar squads and had an officer take over each one, while he watched and corrected errors. Then he drilled the company as a whole. This went on for three days, beginning always with the squads and ending with the full company, and always he exacted the strictest precision in their movements.[35]

Then Steuben took up the manual of arms, taught the men by his own example a simplified form of the Prussian manual, how to carry the musket, load it, fire it, how to fix the bayonet, and to charge. The men of the model company, all veterans, were interested and eager to acquire proficiency. They quickly learned the new movements, while the onlookers, practically the whole army, were instructed by observation.[36]

But his lack of English was a handicap. Once he gave an order which, because of his pronunciation, was misunderstood. Some of the men went one way, some another. He shouted it in French, then in German, but the model company was in complete confusion. He tried the sign language with no success. Then he blew up and cursed them vigorously in French and German, with an occasional "Goddam" for emphasis. Everybody laughed uproariously. A young American officer, Captain Benjamin Walker of New York, came to his aid, addressed him in French, and offered to interpret the command to the troops. Steuben said later that he was like an angel from heaven. The company was re-formed, the command given, and the maneuver executed. Steuben made Walker one of his permanent aides. It needed only such a bit of comedy, which was repeated more than once, to make the baron one of the most popular officers in the camp.[37]

A general drill program for the whole army was instituted on March 24. From that time on, the camp was busy. Each regiment was divided into squads of 20 men, to which the lessons were given in the same manner as to the original squad. The use of the bayonet was emphasized for the first time in the army of the Revolution. Under Steuben's instructions the men, who had shrunk from the bright steel of the British, became the "fierce bayonet fighters" that displayed their new ability a few weeks later at Monmouth and after that in the capture of Stony Point with that weapon alone and without firing a shot.[38]

The most important lesson the army learned was to march "in compact masses with steadiness and without losing distance." [39] Until then they had generally marched in Indian file, so that their column reached four times the distance needed for columns of fours, making it impossible to enforce discipline and prevent straggling as well as lengthening the time needed to form in line and front the enemy. This defect had been felt at Brandywine and at Germantown, where the heads of columns had arrived in time, but their tails came too late.[40] In April, Washington issued an order against marching in single file.[41]

Within a month Steuben "had the Satisfaction . . . to see not only a regular Step introduced in the Army, but I also made maneuvers with ten and twelve Battalions, with as much precision as the Evolution of a Single Company." He made a penetrating comment on the characteristics of the American in a letter to his friend Baron von Gaudy: "The genius of this nation is not in the least to be compared with that of the Prussians, Austrians or French. You say to your soldier 'Do this' and he doeth it; but I am obliged to say 'This is the reason why you ought to do that'; and then he does it." [42]

A letter from an officer at Valley Forge published in May said: "The Army grows stronger every day. It increases in numbers . . . and there is a spirit of discipline among the troops that is better than numbers. Each brigade is on parade almost every day for several hours. You would be charmed to see the regularity and exactness with which they march and perform their maneuvers. . . . Last year . . . it was almost impossible to advance or retire in the presence of the enemy without disordering the line and falling into confusion. That misfortune, I believe, will seldom happen again . . . for the troops are instructed in a new and so happy a method of marching that they soon will be able to advance with the utmost regularity, even without musick and on the roughest grounds." [43]

As they became more skilful, their soldierly pride increased and "a new morale, never more to be extinguished, soon pervaded the ranks of the Continental Army."

In May there was a grand review to celebrate the treaty of alliance with France. "The several brigades marched by their right to their posts in order of battle and the line was formed with admirable rapidity and precision." The artillery gave three salutes of thirteen guns each, and the troops fired a *feu de joie*, a fire of musketry commencing at the right of the front line and running, shot by shot, to its left and then back again along the second line to its right, which was "executed to perfection" and "gave a sensible pleasure to every one present." [44] Washington, in general orders, acknowledged "the highest satisfaction" with the spectacle. "The exactness and order with which their movements were performed," he wrote, "is a pleasing evidence of the progress they are making in Military Improvements." And he thanked "Baron Steuben & the gentlemen under him for their Indefatigable Exertions . . . the good effects of which are already so apparent." [45]

The Congress also took notice and on May 5, appointed Steuben inspector general of the army with the rank and pay of major general, the pay to commence from the time of his first joining the army.[46]

The exercises and training continued throughout May and until the middle of June, when the evacuation of Philadelphia called for active operations by the Americans. Then the troops took the field a real army at last, thanks in large part to the "baron."

Before the American army left the Forge, there occurred an affair very like those at Quintin's Bridge and Hancock's Bridge in March. General John Lacey with a body of Pennsylvania militia numbering 456 had been stationed at the Crooked Billet Tavern and village in Montgomery County, Pennsylvania. But the expiration of their terms of service had reduced their number by the end of April to 53 fit for duty, though some small reenforcements may have arrived. The purpose of this post was the interruption of supplies intended for Philadelphia.

Annoyed by this interference, Lieutenant Colonel Balfour sent Lieutenant Colonel Abercrombie with 400 light infantry, part of them mounted, a party of light dragoons, and Major Simcoe with 300 Queen's Rangers infantry, to attack Lacey. Abercrombie took a direct road; Simcoe made a circuit to get behind the Crooked Billet. By a night march on May 1 they enveloped Lacey in front and rear. A sentinel alarmed the camp, and Lacey marched his men towards a near-by wood, where they made a stand and exchanged fire with the enemy. Seeing that he was overpowered, he abandoned his baggage and retreated rapidly, keeping up his fire as best he could against the enemy on both his flanks and his rear during a two-mile retreat. Then he "made a sudden turn to the left, through a wood, which entirely extricated" him. He reported 30 of his men killed and 17 wounded, but changed this later to 26 killed and 8 or 10 severely wounded. The British had 9 wounded.[47]

CHAPTER 45

Barren Hill

This narrative must now revert to the middle of the period of greatest destitution, the winter at Valley Forge. When the fortunes of the American cause and the strength of its military forces were at almost their lowest ebb, the Board of War conceived and the Congress approved one of the maddest of all mad projects. It was nothing less than, as expressed in the Congressional resolution of January 22, 1778, "an irruption . . . into Canada." [1] In spite of the lessons which should have been learned from the fate of Arnold's and Montgomery's expeditions and from the defeat at Trois Rivières, the Board and the Congress lightheartedly proposed this new venture, to be undertaken by some force or other not yet provided nor even reasonably in prospect. No plan of possibly successful operations was devised. Apparently that was left entirely to the ingenuity of the officers selected to lead the expedition, of whom the chief was a twenty-year-old Frenchman, who had had the very slightest military experience, his only qualifications being his nationality and his religion, Roman Catholic, to whose standard the French Canadians were hopefully expected to flock on those two accounts in an uprising against the British government.

That French youth was Marie Joseph Paul Yves Roch Gilbert du Motier, Marquis de Lafayette. Although a scion of an ancient and noble family, a typical aristocrat, and a favorite of the French court, young Lafayette had developed, as he later said, "an ardent love of liberty." When therefore, in 1776, he heard of the rebellion in America, knowing as little as possible of that country and of the reasons and causes of its revolt, "my heart espoused warmly the cause of liberty and I thought of nothing but of adding also the aid of my banner." [2] Actually he did not become a republican until later,

556

His real reasons for joining the Americans were a youthful desire for glory and an equally youthful hatred of Britain.

He made no secret of his project of going to help the colonists. It was discussed by all Paris as the gallant idea of a romantic boy. "Of course," Madame du Deffand wrote to Horace Walpole, "it is a piece of folly; but it does him no discredit. He receives more praise than blame." It became known in London, too. "We talk chiefly," wrote Gibbon, the historian, "of the Marquis de la Fayette. He is about twenty, with 130,000 Livres a year. . . . The [French] Court *appears* to be angry with him." [3]

It was not really angry with him. Marie Antoinette herself favored his enterprise. But, being yet technically at peace with England, France had to preserve appearances. The Count de Broglie at first tried to dissuade him out of regard and affection for his family, but at last promised to help him and did so in one respect, that is, by introducing to him an experienced, able, and judicious soldier, a man of fifty years, the so-called Baron de Kalb, who was then seeking an engagement in the American army for himself and might, to some extent, act as guardian for the inexperienced, youthful enthusiast.

With his own money Lafayette purchased a ship and outfitted it. From Silas Deane, the American agent in Paris, he obtained a promise of major generals' commissions for himself and De Kalb and lesser offices for eleven other Frenchmen whom he proposed to take with him.[4] But at the last moment Viscount Stormont, the British ambassador, remonstrated strongly against such a breach of neutrality, and the French government, discouraged as to American prospects by Washington's successive defeats at Long Island, White Plains, and Fort Washington and his desperate retreat across the Jerseys,[5] intimated a purpose to arrest the young adventurer and wreck his plans. His own family, as well as the government, forbade his departure. Even Deane and Benjamin Franklin discouraged him.[6] But he persisted. Disguised as a postboy, he made his way to Bordeaux, where he found De Kalb and the others awaiting him and, on March 26, 1777, his ship, the *Victoire*, set sail. It was met in a Spanish port by two French officers with a *lettre de cachet* commanding him to return to France. Release from this entanglement was not effected until April 20, and even then only by Lafayette's audacious assumption that the government's failure to answer his request that it "relax in its determination" to stop him was "a tacit consent" to his departure. So again he set sail and landed, June 13, on an island off the South Carolina coast. Rowing to the mainland, he and some members of his party came at midnight to the house of Major Benjamin Huger, who received them with gracious hospitality.[7]

Carriages were procured, and Lafayette with six of his companions started on a journey of nine hundred miles through a country that impressed him with its "youth and majesty," to arrive in Philadelphia on July 27. His reception by the Congress was anything but gracious. In justice it must be observed that the Congress had been fairly overwhelmed by great numbers of adventurers seeking office in the American army. Silas Deane had been responsible for many reckless promises of commissions to men who, when commissioned, proved to be entirely unfit. In the case of Philippe du Coudray the demand was for the rank of major general, second in command of the whole army under Washington, and commander in chief of the artillery, the position already held by Henry Knox. This demand had resulted in threats to resign not only by Knox, but also by Greene and Sullivan. Coudray got the commission he asked for, but was not made second in command, nor chief of the artillery.

Lafayette's group was looked upon with disfavor. An appointment was made to meet them at the door of the State House. There, on the sidewalk, they were confronted by James Lovell, a delegate from Massachusetts and one of the few congressmen that could speak French. He very curtly asked for their credentials and complained to them of the quality of the French officers that had preceded them. "It seems," he said, "that French officers have a great fancy to enter our service without being invited. It is true we were in need of officers last year, but now we have experienced men and plenty of them." "It would be impossible," wrote Buysson, one of the group, "for anyone to be more stupefied than we were at such a reception." [8]

But Lafayette was not to be gainsaid by this representative of the Congress. He asked him to return to that body and read to it a short note: "After the sacrifices I have made, I have the right to expect two favours; one is to serve at my own expense,—the other is to serve, at first, as volunteer," that is to say, without a command. [9]

No pay, no command, merely the honor of a commission—those were novel terms. The Congress sent a second embassy to the applicants on the sidewalk, Lovell with another, "more skilful as well as more polite," says Buysson. The result of that conference was a resolution, adopted on July 31, recognizing Lafayette's "great zeal to the cause of liberty," accepting his services, and making him a major general on his own terms. [10] But the others of his party were yet uncared for and in an uncomfortable position.

De Kalb, a veteran soldier, was especially chagrined that so young a man as Lafayette, with practically no military experience, should be taken while he was left. He wrote a sharp and bitter letter to the Congress, setting forth his claims and inveighing against Deane's making engagements that the Congress would not fulfill. He closed by asking either the promised appointment or reimbursement of his expense in coming to America.[11] The Congress, on September 8, thanked him and the Viscount de Mornay, "with the officers that accompany them, for their zeal," declined their services, and ordered that "their expences to this continent and on their way home be paid." [12]

De Kalb, with Buysson and two others, was on a leisurely excursion to Bethlehem preparatory to departure from a southern port when he was overtaken by a messenger from the Congress, who informed him that he had been commissioned a major general. Buysson was later made a lieutenant colonel. Six others of Lafayette's party of eleven were also commissioned in accordance with Deane's agreement.[13]

Lafayette's first contact with Washington occurred at a dinner in Philadelphia. He was impressed by the "majestic figure and deportment" of the commander in chief and no less by "the noble affability of his manner." [14] Washington seems to have taken to the tall, slender, handsome, blond youth from the first. In him he saw the gentleman, as well as the ardent young seeker of glory. Gentility was always grateful to the Virginia aristocrat. He invited the boy to become one of his own military "family"—his staff—and there grew up between them an affectionate relationship which, Lafayette wrote to his wife, was like that of "attached brothers, with mutual confidence and cordiality," [15] but which would be more accurately described as that existing between father and son. Perhaps the childless Washington saw in this lad a son such as he would have liked to have.

The youth, accustomed to the uniform appearance of the pipe-clayed European armies, was less favorably impressed by the army in its camp on the Neshaminy. That army of "about eleven thousand men, ill armed and still worse clothed," he wrote in his memoirs, "presented a strange spectacle to the eye of the young Frenchman; their clothes were parti-colored, and many of them were almost naked; the best clad wore *hunting-shirts*, large grey linen coats." Their military tactics, too, were strange to him, awkward, and ill managed. Yet he thought "the soldiers were fine and their officers zealous; virtue stood in place of science and each day added to both experience and discipline." [16]

To this inexperienced though gallant young man the sapient Board of War and the compliant Congress confided the leadership of the proposed

March-hare "irruption" into Canada, naming as second in command Major
General Thomas Conway.

Conway, a French Irishman, a capable, experienced soldier, was brave in
battle, but of a discontented disposition. His name was given to the probably
mythical "Conway Cabal." The other members, it has been said, were
Horatio Gates, Richard Henry Lee and Francis Lightfoot Lee of Virginia,
Benjamin Rush and Thomas Mifflin of Pennsylvania, Samuel Adams, John
Adams, and James Lovell of Massachusetts; their object, the displacement
of Washington and the succession of Gates in the chief command of the
army.

That there was actually a conspiracy among those men, an organized
effort worthy the appellation of "cabal" is very unlikely. Certainly no
sufficient evidence of its existence has ever been discovered. But just as
certainly some of them at least, notably Lovell, Conway, and Mifflin, were
bitterly hostile to Washington as a military leader and laudatory of Gates,
the conqueror of Burgoyne.[17]

The actual existence of such a conspiracy is of little importance in comparison with the general belief in its existence, which prevailed among
Washington's friends in the army and elsewhere. Lafayette asserted it was
a fact. When the Board of War, then composed of Gates as president,
Mifflin, William Duer, Francis Lightfoot Lee, and Richard Peters (three of
them reputed to be members of the supposed Cabal it will be observed)
proposed this new Canadian expedition, and the Congress authorized it,
the action was taken without consulting the commander in chief, without
even giving him notice of it. With the same disregard of him, the officers to
conduct the "irruption" were named by the Congress, Lafayette, Conway,
and John Stark.[18] The first knowledge Washington had of it was conveyed
in a letter from Gates advising him that the scheme had been adopted, asking him to spare Hazen's regiment as a part of the force to be sent, and enclosing instructions to be handed to Lafayette. Washington swallowed the
insult, ordered Hazen's regiment detached for the purpose, and gave Lafayette the letter of instructions. But that high-spirited youth, though desirous
of a command and a chance to win glory in the field, thought he saw in the
proposal a scheme "to intoxicate" him with a prospect of military fame and
thus to seduce him from his allegiance to Washington. He understood the
offer to be of a command independent of the commander in chief, thus be-
littling Washington and weakening his position. Moreover, he objected to
Conway, the conspirator, as his second in command. Although he regarded
him as "a very brave and very good officer," yet he considered him as "an
ambitious and dangerous man." He had already written to Washington that

Conway had "done all in his power, by cunning manoeuvres, to take off my confidence and affection for you." [19] He, therefore, wrote to the Congress that he must decline the commission, unless it was understood that he should remain subject to Washington's orders and report directly to him. He also went to York, where the Congress was in session and, as Henry Laurens, its president, put it, "discovered a noble resentment for the affront offered to his Commander Genl. Washington" and "said he would not go without a General Officer of the Rank of Major General in whom he could put confidence and therefore demanded Genl. McDougal or Baron Kalb and that their appointment should be through his General."

When the Congress and the Board of War hesitated to comply with these demands, Lafayette threatened to return to France and take all the foreign officers with him. "A good deal of struggle," says Laurens, "was made to elude the Marquis's demands, [but] he was firm and succeeded." [20] He also succeeded in obtaining from a now completely submissive Congress commissions for six of his fellow travelers from France, who should go with him to Canada. He went back to obtain Washington's orders detaching either McDougall or Kalb for the expedition.

The young commander's instructions called for the assemblage of a force of 2,500 rank and file, including Nixon's brigade, five other regiments, and "Capt. Whitcomb's Rangers." At Albany he was to be provided with ammunition, provisions, stores, and woolen clothing for the troops. If unable to raise a general revolt of the Canadians he was merely to destroy the works and vessels at St. Johns, Chambly, and Ile aux Noix and then retire to the Hudson River country; but if the Canadians responded to his seductions he was to invite them to send delegates to the Congress, and then he was to take Montreal.[21]

Lafayette undertook this mad project in good faith and with an enthusiasm that carried him uncomplainingly through the difficult journey of four hundred miles to Albany on horseback in midwinter. But there he was promptly disillusioned. Instead of the promised 2,500 men he found only 1,200 fit for duty; and the "most part of those very men are naked, even for a summer's campaign." Their pay was far in arrears, and all of them, quite naturally, "disgusted and reluctant to the last degree to begin a winter campaign in a so cold country." He had been assured by Gates that Stark would have cleared the way for him by burning the British fleet on the Lake "before your arrival." He found that Stark had not even been informed "what number of men, from whence, for what time, for what rendezvous I desire him to raise." He found that Conway, who had preceded him, had received letters from Schuyler, Lincoln, and Arnold, men who knew what they were talking about, declaring "in the most expressive terms that, in our present circumstances, there was no possibility to begin now an enterprise into Canada." The deputy quartermaster, the deputy commissary, and the deputy clothier-general, who were to have furnished the supplies and the warm clothing for the troops, were "entirely of the same opinion." The one who was "most desirous of getting there," Hazen, the Canadian, confessed that they were "not strong enough to think of the expedition at this moment." Everybody whom Lafayette consulted told him "it would be madness to undertake this operation." [22]

The ambitious young commander was chagrined at the failure of his enterprise before it had even begun, chagrined and angry. "I have been deceived by the board of War," he wrote to Washington. He was concerned about his reputation. He saw himself in a "distressing, ridiculous, foolish and indeed, nameless situation. . . . I am sure I will be very ridiculous and laughed at." [23] But the thing was plainly impossible. It was a fraud and a foreordained fiasco from the beginning. Even the Congress at last realized its absurdity. On March 2 it ordered that the "intended irruption be suspended for the present," at the same time recognizing the "prudence, activity and zeal" of its leader, being "persuaded nothing has or would have been wanting on his part." And belatedly, on March 13, it called the whole thing off by authorizing Washington to recall him and De Kalb.[24]

Lafayette had not long been established again in the camp at Valley Forge, and had, perhaps, not yet recovered from his chagrin on account of the Canadian fiasco, when he entered upon another adventure that came within a hairbreadth of plunging him into far deeper humiliataion, indeed of ruining his military career, and not only that but also placing the entire American army in dire jeopardy.

On May 18 Washington issued an order placing under Lafayette's command a division of about 2,200 men, one-third of the whole then much diminished American army,[25] and directing him to "march towards the enemy's lines" for the purpose of "being a security to this camp and a cover to the country between the Delaware and the Schuylkill, to obstruct the incursions of the enemy's parties and to obtain intelligence of their motions and designs. This last a matter of very interesting moment and ought to claim your particular attention." At the same time, he should remember that his detachment "is a very valuable one and that any accident happening to it would be a very severe blow to this army." He should therefore use every precaution "to guard against a surprise." [26]

That this expedition was as useless as it was perilous is manifest. The

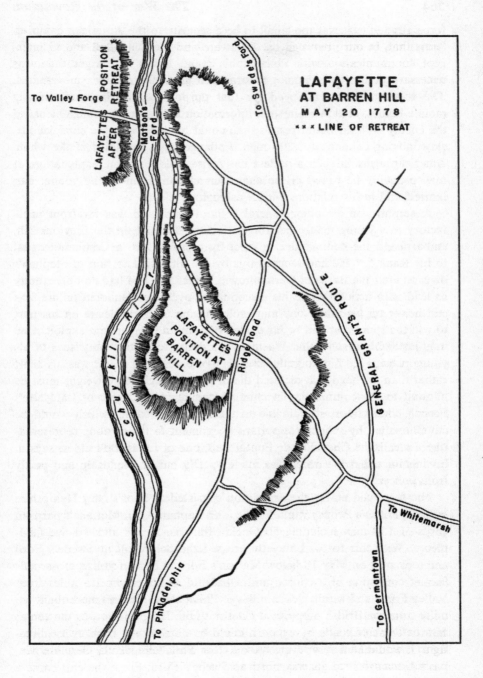

LAFAYETTE
AT BARREN HILL
MAY 20 1778
×××LINE OF RETREAT

To Valley Forge

LAFAYETTE'S POSITION AFTER RETREAT

Matson's Ford

To Swede's Ford

Schuylkill River

LAFAYETTE'S POSITION AT BARREN HILL

Ridge Road

GENERAL GRANT'S ROUTE

To Whitemarsh

To Philadelphia

To Germantown

force allotted to it was too small to be a security to the American camp, to "cover the country between the Delaware and the Schuylkill and to interrupt communication with Philadelphia"; and it was far larger than was necessary or useful in gaining information as to the enemy's movements. The scouts already employed for that purpose, acting in small, swiftly mobile bodies, could obtain such information and watch the movements of the enemy with far better results than could be achieved by a conspicuous, slow-moving column of 2,200 men. Endangering a full third of the whole American army in such a useless enterprise calls for some explanation. It may probably be found in the character and ambition of the young man himself and in his relations with Washington.

A commission as major general without command was far from satisfactory to a young man eager for distinction. He had, in the previous fall, embarrassed the commander in chief by pressing for "a Command equal to his Rank." [27] He had secured this by the allotment to him of Stephen's division after the Battle of Germantown, but, so far, had had no opportunity to lead it in action. While his discomfiture over the Canadian failure was still heavy on his mind, one may well imagine a strong desire on his part to win the spurs that had so far eluded him, in an independent exploit. One may justifiably assume that Washington's desire to gratify the wishes of his young protégé led him to authorize this new enterprise, that it was his heart rather than his head that dictated the order, although some weight must be allowed to the commander in chief's estimate of the value of Lafayette's French connections, so valuable to the American cause, which would be complimented by such an important assignment to their young representative. Indeed, the Chevalier de Pontgibaud, one of Lafayette's aides, says in his memoirs that the order was made "partly out of friendship and partly from policy." [28]

The force chosen for the expedition consisted of Poor's New Hampshire brigade, Potter's Pennsylvania Militia, and Captain Allen McLane's partisan corps of 150 men including 50 Oneida Indians. It was allowed five fieldpieces. With this force, Lafayette crossed the Schuylkill at Swede's Ford and took post on May 18 below Matson's Ford at Barren Hill, a crossroads hamlet consisting of a church and a handful of houses twelve miles from Valley Forge and within eleven miles of Philadelphia, but no more than two miles from the British outposts at Chestnut Hill. His position was the center of a network of roads by which it could be approached from every direction. The Manatawny or Ridge Road from Philadelphia, via Germantown, passed through it on its way north to Swede's Ford. From the east came a road from Whitemarsh and Chestnut Hill to cross that other in the village, and still another led from Germantown to cross the first at a point a mile or so north of the Hill and run finally to Matson's Ford.[29]

Lafayette disposed Poor's brigade in a good position on a small elevation south of the church. The line faced the south, its right defended by the steep declivity to the Schuylkill, its left resting on two or three stout stone houses. In advance of the line he placed his five guns. Potter's 600 Pennsylvanians were detached to take post, at a distance, on the road from Whitemarsh to guard against surprise from that quarter. McLane's irregulars were stationed about a mile to the south on the Ridge Road and pickets were thrown out a mile farther on that road. Thus apparently secure from surprise, Lafayette rested that night.[30]

Of course the movement of such a column could be no secret. Clinton, who was about to supersede Howe in command in Philadelphia, knew about it immediately. To him it seemed simply a wonderful opportunity to capture the young Frenchman and so humiliate him and his country, America's new ally by a treaty made in February. He regarded it as a sure thing. Howe invited a party for dinner on the next night "to meet the Marquis de La Fayette." To make good this boast, he turned out almost the whole British army.[31]

General Grant, with 5,000 men and fifteen guns, marched from Philadelphia at half past ten in the evening of the 19th, taking a circuitous route which would bring him to that point where the road from Whitemarsh crossed the Ridge Road about a mile and a half north of Barren Hill. There he could cut the Americans off from a retreat by the Ridge Road to either Matson's or Swede's Ford and so to Valley Forge.

Grey was to lead another column, of 2,000 grenadiers and a small troop of dragoons, by way of Germantown on the road direct to the Hill with intent to attack Lafayette's left flank. Clinton, accompanied by Howe, was to bring a strong force up the Ridge Road from the south and establish himself not far below the American front. Thus the Americans would be boxed in on three sides, and the river was the fourth; and in the face of such overwhelming numbers, they could only surrender. The trap was to be sprung the next morning.[32]

Grant made good progress along the Whitemarsh road. Potter and his Pennsylvania militia, who had been ordered to hold that road, seem to have disappeared without trace. Lafayette says Potter had "thought proper to retire" from his post.[33] At all events, he offered no hindrance to Grant, who gained his desired position; nor did he give any warning to Lafayette. Grey got to his post on Lafayette's left flank. But the case of Clinton and Howe, coming up the Ridge Road, was different.

Captain Allen McLane, "a vigilant partisan of great merit," was on duty
there. "In the course of the night," says John Marshall, "he fell in with two
British grenadiers at Three Mile Run" and, presumably, captured them.
They "informed him of the movement made by Grant and also that a large
body of Germans was getting ready to march up the Schuylkill." That
would be Clinton's column. McLane guessed what was afoot. He detached
Captain Parr with a company of riflemen to meet Clinton's force and to
"oppose and retard" it, while he hurried to the camp. He got there at daybreak and told Lafayette about Grant and Clinton. His news was confirmed
by the sound of shots from Parr's company and by the arrival of a local
patriot who had seen redcoats on the Whitemarsh road.[34]

The situation seemed desperate. Grant and Clinton, in great force, held
the roads to the nearest fords, Swede's, Bevin's, and Matson's. It was a test
for the young general, but he met it fairly. He put his men in a posture of
defense and sent out scouts in all directions. One brought him good news;
there was another road from the Hill to Matson's Ford by which Grant
could be eluded, although his post was actually nearer the ford than was
Lafayette's. It ran from Barren Hill down the steep ground to the riverside
and then along it to the ford. It dropped down so suddenly and was so concealed by the height above that a marching army would be immediately
out of sight from Grant's position and from Grey's as well.[35]

Lafayette arranged for a small rear guard to make demonstrations about
the church and to throw out false heads of columns towards the north, so as
to make it appear to Grant that he was about to be attacked. Grant's attention was arrested, and he prepared to oppose this apparent advance. While
he was thus amused Lafayette sent Poor and the rest of his brigade down
the sloping path. He himself remained behind to carry off the rear guard.
The whole force reached and crossed the ford, with all its guns, before
Grant was aware of the evasion. On some heights on the west side of the
river, Lafayette drew up his men to contest the passage of the enemy; but
no such crossing was attempted.[36]

Clinton, marching against the abandoned American post, was disgusted
at meeting some of Grant's column coming down from the north and finding no Americans anywhere in sight. Without any further effort, the whole
British force marched back to Philadelphia "much fatigued, and ashamed
and . . . laughed at for their ill success," as Lafayette exultantly says in
his memoirs.[37]

A ludicrous incident of the affair occurred when Clinton's dragoons, in
advance of his column, came suddenly upon McLane's Indians, who were
on picket duty on the Ridge Road. The Oneidas, unused to mounted troops,

sprang up with such terrified and terrifying whoops and yells as to frighten the horses and the dragoons themselves. Both parties fled the scene in equal disorder and in opposite directions.[38]

McLane and his men got much honor for their service and were officially thanked for their "vigilancy," which had enabled the marquis to make "a glorious retreat as well as a safe one." [39]

At Howe's own request, preferred as early as the middle of November, 1777, the King graciously allowed him to resign his command in February, 1778. On May 8 Sir Henry Clinton came to Philadelphia from New York, with orders to take over from Howe, and more besides—no less than an order that the long sought, much desired, dearly bought capital of the rebels should be immediately evacuated.[40]

The truth is that Howe's entire campaign, from its beginning when he first proposed to himself the capture of Philadelphia, had been a sheer waste of time, of money, and of men. His thought all along had been to wear down American resistance by occupying places and winning battles without too great expenditure of man power. He had never thought it advisable to take large risks for decisive victories. His policy would have required large numbers of men and much time. Certainly the taking of Philadelphia could never have destroyed American resistance. In the countries of Europe, where not only the administrative and executive functions, including the nerve centers of the military forces, but also a large part of the commercial and industrial operations were concentrated in the capital cities, the capture of one of these would result both in a loss of prestige and usually also in a sort of paralysis of all national functions; wherefore the government would be compelled to ask for terms of peace. Philadelphia was in no degree such a capital. The governmental machinery did not center there, for the very good reason that the Americans had little governmental machinery; they had nothing but a Congress, which could sit in Baltimore or in York—or not sit at all, for that matter—without fatal harm to the country. The nerve center of the military forces, if the Board of War might be called that, could operate as well, or as badly, in any town as in Philadelphia. It is plain that, by capturing Philadelphia, Howe got nothing at all, and that the only result from Clinton's keeping it would be the strain of dividing his forces, maintaining a garrison there as well as in New York and keeping open the communications with New York across the contested territory of New Jersey or over more than 300 miles of river and ocean. The evacuation was a tardy confession of the costly error of its acquisition.

But all that afforded no consolation to thousands of Philadelphians, to whom the news of the intended evacuation was but little less terrible than a death sentence. The avowed Loyalists, who had fled to New York when the town was held by the American army, had hurried home on Howe's arrival. Other Tories, theretofore secret, had come out into the open. The Quakers, pacifists, nonresisters, had been more than suspected of aiding the royal cause. What was going to happen to all these when the American army came back to the city? They did not know, but they feared mightily.

Conspicuous among the repatriated Tories were the Allens, Andrew, John, and William; and even more conspicuous, dreadfully more so, Joseph Galloway. Widely enough known before, he had attained a peak of notoriety by personally guiding Howe's army along the road to those unguarded fords above the Forks of the Brandywine. No one in all the American army would ever forget that, nor could Galloway.

When the news of the intended evacuation was released, Galloway called on Ambrose Serle, secretary to Admiral Howe, with whom he had been on confidential terms for the last three months. He was filled "with Horror & melancholy," says Serle, "on the view of his deplorable Situation; exposed to the Rage of his bitter Enemies, deprived of a Fortune of about £70,000, and now left to wander like Cain upon the Earth, without Home & without Property. Many others are involved in the like dismal Case." [41]

Though not in the same kind of "deplorable Situation," certain gentlemen from England, arriving soon after the news became current, were almost equally disgusted. The British government, faced by the Franco-American alliance, had suddenly resolved to attempt conciliation of the rebellious colonies. It had proposed and carried through measures repealing the tea tax, the Boston Port Act, the restraints on the fisheries and on trade with Britain, and so on, wiped out practically every law that had been objected to by the colonists, and offered to give them a large measure of self-government, with free pardon to all the individual rebels. The Earl of Carlisle, William Eden, and George Johnstone, together with the two Howes, were appointed as a royal commission to settle details in America. [42]

The three commissioners from England landed in Philadelphia on the 8th of June to open negotiations with the Congress. They were horrified to find that their victorious army was in the midst of hurried preparations for the evacuation of the conquered capital, was, in fact, about to scuttle back to New York. The attempted reconciliation came to nothing; the Congress would not treat for peace unless the King would first acknowledge complete American independence or withdraw his troops from the country. [43] Later Congress refused to deal with the commission, partly because Johnstone tried to bribe influential Americans.

The officers of the British army were loath to lose General Howe. He had glaring faults, but when he set his mind to the business and stirred his sluggish disposition to activity, he was a strategist of great ability, a skillful tactician, and a bold and resourceful fighter in the field. They gave him a farewell party that outshone every celebration ever before seen in America. It was "a fantastic exhibition of sham chivalry," called the *Mischianza,* combining a tournament in which the Knights of the Burning Mountain and the Knights of the Blended Rose contended for the favor of the ladies, a ball, a banquet, a show of fireworks—all on a ridiculously elaborate and expensive scale.

CHAPTER 46

The Race Across the Jerseys

Washington's intelligence service informed him late in May that the British were "preparing for a general movement" of some sort. He was apprehensive that it might be "of an offensive kind,"[1] perhaps against the post at Wilmington in Delaware, which had been held all winter by Smallwood's brigade of Maryland and Delaware regiments. On the other hand, it might be of an entirely different character: the evacuation of Philadelphia, of which there had been rumors, and a march across the Jerseys to New York. To provide for that contingency, he called on General Philemon Dickinson to arouse the New Jersey militia, and sent Maxwell's New Jersey Continental brigade to Mount Holly in that state. These two forces were to be ready to "give the Enemy some annoyance" by cutting away bridges and obstructing roads.[2]

But if Clinton evacuated the capital he might go by water, and go on up the Hudson to possess that important valley. To be ready for that, Washington laid out in full detail an "Arrangement of Army and Route to March to the North River." When even with "the most diligent pains" he could not find out which way Clinton was going or whether he was going at all, he came to believe that lack of transport vessels would compel him to go by land across the Jerseys.[3] To plan his own movements and to prepare for a possible attack on Clinton in New Jersey, he studied a map.[4]

He saw that the most direct route to New York from Gloucester in New Jersey, opposite Philadelphia, would be by way of Haddonfield, Mount Holly, Crosswicks, Allentown, Cranbury, New Brunswick, and Staten Island. It would be through country offering no important natural defensive

positions until the enemy got to Cranbury; but in the hills above that village
there was a position that might easily block further progress.

He hardly needed to study the map to lay out his own course; it was all
too familiar to him. From Valley Forge he could cross the Schuylkill at
Swede's Ford, go on eastward to the Crooked Billet Tavern (now Hatboro),
turn north to Doylestown, then east and across the Delaware at Coryell's
Ferry. After that, by way of Hopewell and Kingston, he would come to
Cranbury. Could he wait until Clinton had actually started and then beat
him to that point? The distance was against him; it would be seven or eight
miles, a good half-day's march, longer for him than for Clinton. But Clinton
would be dragging an immensely heavy baggage train, while his own would
necessarily be very light, and the road from Coryell's Ferry was somewhat
better than that from Gloucester. It looked like a fair race.

By June 16 Washington's guess as to Clinton's plan seemed good, for on
that day all the redoubts about Philadelphia having been stripped of their
artillery before daybreak, several British and Hessian regiments passed over
the Delaware at Cooper's Point.[5] That evacuation was a ticklish business.
It involved the withdrawal of vast quantities of provisions and supplies,
wagons, horses, and artillery, as well as 10,000 men [6] under the eyes of an
enemy, now strengthened, refreshed, and drilled into a real army, a trained
and disciplined fighting force. A vigorous attack, while Clinton's army was
astride of the river, would probably result in a catastrophic defeat for him.

There was also another element to be considered. Three thousand
Loyalists, men, women, and children, dared not remain in Philadelphia and
submit themselves to the mercies of the incoming Americans. They and
their portable possessions had to be carried away in ships, using cargo space
that might have taken in a considerable part of the baggage that must now
be carried overland. To evacuate that town was no light task, but it was successfully accomplished.

On the 18th the rest of the army left Philadelphia,[7] marched four miles
to Gloucester Point and crossed to Gloucester in flat-bottomed boats, after
which the last of the war vessels and the fleet of transports dropped down
the river. "No shot was fired, nor did an Enemy appear until the whole were
on the opposite shore," says André [8]—which is not exactly true.

In the interval between the withdrawal of the last defenders from the line
of redoubts and the complete evacuation of the town, Allen McLane and
his corps went in "by way of Bush Hill . . . between the 9th and 10th
redoubts." At Second Street they came upon "the last patrol" and, having
exchanged shots with it, cut off and captured a captain, a provost marshal,
a guide, and 30 privates, with no loss on their own part.[9]

In the next night "the gallant Captain McLane" crossed the river and, in disguise, made his way through the British camp at Haddonfield.[10] The next day he reported his observations to General Benedict Arnold, who had been appointed to the command of the evacuated town.

A certain George Roberts had hastened to Valley Forge, and, at half past eleven of the morning of the 18th, told Washington that the evacuation was complete. This was confirmed by a courier coming immediately after from McLane with the same news.[11] Washington at once put his army in motion for Coryell's Ferry. Charles Lee had been released from captivity by exchange in March, had come to Valley Forge in May, and been reinstated in command of a division of three brigades: Hunterdon's, Poor's and Varnum's. It was immediately on its way. Wayne, in command of Mifflin's 2nd Division, composed of the 1st and 2nd Pennsylvania brigades and Conway's, got away at three in the afternoon. Lafayette's, De Kalb's, and Stirling's divisions, with the artillery, were to start at five the next morning. However, a rearrangement of the troops for the march across New Jersey was proposed. Lee was to command the right wing, six brigades, and Lafayette the second column, made up of the 1st and 2nd Maryland brigades and Weedon's and Muhlenberg's divisions.[12]

The number of men in Washington's army at this time has been variously estimated. The official returns on June 12 showed that the army had been increased—miraculously, it must seem—to a total of 13,503 officers and men. There were perhaps 1,300 in Maxwell's brigade at Mount Holly and 800 New Jersey militiamen under Philemon Dickinson also in that state. There may have been, on the march from Valley Forge from 11,000 to 12,000 of all ranks—a large force for that war, in excellent condition. The good work of Nathanael Greene as quartermaster general and of Jeremiah Wadsworth as commissary general showed in the clothing and equipment of the men and in their improved physical condition. Steuben's efforts had been so effective that they now performed "manoeuvres with great exactness and dispatch" and were "well disciplined." [13]

By the 23rd the entire army had crossed the Delaware at Coryell's Ferry, and the next night it was encamped at Hopewell, about fifteen miles west of Cranbury. The British army was then in camp at Allentown, about fifteen miles southeast of the Americans and ten miles south of Cranbury.[14] This was satisfactory progress for Washington's troops. But what use were they going to make of their effort?

On June 17, before leaving Valley Forge, Washington had called a council of war and told it that he believed Clinton would evacuate Philadelphia with a force of about 10,000; that he himself had about 11,000 fit for duty and there were 800 in New Jersey (which does not seem to take into account either Maxwell's or Dickinson's troops); that he wanted advice as to the conduct of the campaign in the immediate future. Two members of the council were for attacking the British on their march, if they crossed New Jersey, in order to make an "impression." Six were for following and annoying them, without bringing on a general action. The rest seem to have agreed with Charles Lee that it was advisable to let them get away. Now, at Hopewell, another council was called: Should they now "hazard a general action"? If not, what? Lee was "passionately opposed to strong measures." He said it would be "criminal" to hazard an engagement. Let Clinton get on to New York and good riddance to him. The majority, "still under Lee's spell," voted with him.[15] What then? Why, strengthen the troops hanging on Clinton's left flank, Maxwell's and Dickinson's, and keep the main army in hand until the situation developed further.

Maxwell with his 1,300 Continentals, and Dickinson with his 800 New Jersey militia, had been obeying their original orders, advancing before Clinton's left flank, destroying bridges and obstructing roads. John Cadwalader with about 300 Continentals and a few militia was hanging on the British rear. Now Morgan was detached with 600 riflemen to annoy the enemy's right flank, and Scott, with "a very respectable Body of Troops" was to hang on their rear and left flank. All this contemplated no more than annoyance and harassment of Clinton's march, with no idea of a general engagement.[16]

At Allentown the British army was nearer the key town of Cranbury than the Americans were. On paper Clinton could win a race to it; but not in reality. All the way from Philadelphia his army had been subject to an alternation of burning sun and soaking rain. Heavily clothed as his troops were, especially the Hessians, they were drenched first with sweat, then with rain. They either trudged through ankle-deep dry sand or slopped through puddles of water. The bridges were demolished; new ones had to be built. The roads were obstructed with felled trees; they had to be cleaned. Causeways had to be built over bogs so that the heavy artillery and wagons could get across. They had 1,500 wagons in their train, subject to all the delays and accidents that happen to wagons in a rough country. Because of these circumstances and perhaps because Clinton was in no hurry anyway, they had taken six days to make the thirty-four miles to Allentown. The heat and the rain bore heavily on the Americans too; but their clothing was light, very light, and the packs they carried weighed almost nothing compared with those of the British and the Hessians—60 to 100 pounds of clothing and equipment.[17] Their bridges and roads had been left unmolested; their wagon train was small and light. In the same six days they had made forty-seven miles.[18] Clinton would not be at Cranbury before Washington.

And if Clinton were now to follow the road he was on, leading to New Brunswick and Staten Island, Washington, being several miles nearer New Brunswick, might reach that place first and fall upon him while he was crossing the Raritan. Worse still, perhaps, would be an attack in force on his left flank, while he was dragging his heavy column between swamps and streams on the way to New Brunswick. That might result in a crushing defeat. As he had no knowledge of the Americans' intention not to attack him in full force, he had to act on the assumption that they would. It was time now for him again to consult a map.

Yes, there was a way to avoid the New Brunswick route. At Allentown a road forked to the right from the one he was following. It ran in a north-easterly direction past Monmouth Court House to Sandy Hook, whence his army might be carried in ships to New York. And it would take his army constantly farther from the Americans instead of always nearer, like the road to New Brunswick. He decided to take it, for it was most important to get his army to New York—far more important than a victory over the Americans, unless it should be a crushing one.

For this new route a complete rearrangement of the British army was necessary. Hitherto it had been able to move for the most part in two columns on parallel roads, thus keeping a compact, strong formation. But from Allentown to Sandy Hook there was only a single road. Clinton divided his army into two bodies and put Knyphausen in advance with one. After it came the baggage train, twelve miles long, and then the second half of the army with Cornwallis in immediate command, Clinton over him. Early in the morning of June 25 this interminable serpent of soldiery, guns, horses, wagons, and camp followers set out on a march of nineteen miles to Monmouth Court House.[19]

The road was deep with sand, the atmosphere heavily humid, and the heat terrific—exceeding 100° in the sun. On the march nearly a third of the Hessians, struggling along under clothing and equipment enough for three times as many men, were overcome by the heat and fell by the roadside. Many of the troops died of sunstroke.[20] In the afternoon of the 26th they went into camp at Monmouth Court House, and all that night a furious thunderstorm poured upon them. The exhaustion of the men and the continued intense heat made it impossible to go on, the next day.[21]

On the 25th Washington, leaving his tents and heavy baggage at Hopewell, moved his army about seven miles to Rocky Hill and Kingston. He was not too well satisfied with the cautious decision of the last council of war. He rather inclined to the opinion held by Greene and Wayne and Lafayette, favoring an attack by a strong force on the enemy's rear. In anticipation of such action, he had detached Wayne, with Poor's New Hampshire Continental brigade, 1,000 men, to join the advance guards under Scott, Maxwell, Morgan, Dickinson, and the others. The advance contingent was thus built up to the respectable total of more than 4,000.[22] But it needed unified command.

Charles Lee, who as the senior major general had first claim to this separate command, declared when Washington offered it to him that it was "a more proper business of a young volunteering general, than of the second in command of the army," thereby pointing directly at Lafayette, who was eager for it. Washington gave it to Lafayette, and he set out to take the job.[23] Then Lee learned that the advance force was to include nearly half the army and asked for the command.

The shift of command from Lafayette to Lee was the fundamental error of the campaign. It is, or should be, a military axiom that the execution of any intended operation should never be committed to an officer that disapproves of the plan. "That," says Jomini in his *Art of War*, "is to employ but one-third of the man; his heart and his head are against you; you have command only of his hands. . . . An unwilling commander is half beaten before the battle begins." [24] Lafayette, strongly in favor of attack, should have been left to carry it out.

When the commander in chief, with his unaccountably persistent blindness to Lee's real character, consented to his superseding Lafayette he arranged the transfer with as little injury to Lafayette's feelings as possible.[25] With Lee went Varnum's brigade and the rest of Scott's, bringing the force under his command up to more than 5,000 men. If Morgan's 600 riflemen and Dickinson's 800 militia, both properly subject to Lee's orders, be added, his available force should be 6,400.[26] Morgan actually was operating independently. Lafayette had been ordered to Englishtown, about five miles west of Monmouth Court House. Lee joined him there and took command of all the advance troops, including Dickinson's men, who were on the left flank of the British army. Morgan was on the right.

On the night of the 25th Washington marched the rest of his men from Kingston to Cranbury. There he was halted by a heavy rainstorm followed by intense heat, but at sunrise he pushed on along the Cranbury road within five miles of his advance at Englishtown. The British army still lay in a good defensive position, centering on Monmouth. Such was the situation of the two armies in the evening of June 27, 1778.[27]

CHAPTER 47

Monmouth

In spite of the reluctance of the council of war at Valley Forge to advise any sort of attack upon the retreating British army, Washington decided upon an attack in some force. On June 27 he called Lee to his headquarters and, in the presence of Lafayette, Wayne, Maxwell, and Scott, told him his intention and directed him to carry it out by engaging Cornwallis's grand division as soon as it was in motion the next morning, promising to support him, if necessary, with the rest of the army. He prescribed no particular plan, but requested Lee to call together that afternoon the general officers of his division and arrange the details of the attack. He also asked the other generals to waive their respective claims to precedence of rank, to submit themselves to Lee's orders and to fight wherever he directed them.

Lee appointed a conference at five o'clock. When the generals attended he merely said that, as the numbers and exact situation of the enemy were not definitely known and the terrain had not been carefully examined, he would make no plan, but would move cautiously and rely upon his officers and men to act according to circumstances. During that night he made no effort to secure the information, the lack of which he had urged as preventing the adoption of a plan.

Late that evening Washington sent an order, directing Lee to detach a party of observation to lie near the enemy's camp and give notice of its moving off or of any movement that might portend a night attack. The order was received about one o'clock in the morning; but it was six o'clock before a detachment of 600 men, composed of Grayson's Virginia regiment, Scott's brigade, and part of Varnum's, with four guns, all under command of Colonel William Grayson, started from Englishtown, five miles from the British camp.

To an understanding of the extraordinarily confused and confusing battle now imminent, a clear comprehension of its terrain is essential. The road from Englishtown to Monmouth Court House came first to Freehold Meeting House. Thence it continued in a southeasterly direction to the Court House, where it stopped at a right angle against a road which ran northeast to Middletown and Sandy Hook and was the route of the British retreat. Another road from the Court House ran north to Amboy. The principal points otherwise to be noted are three "ravines." The first of these, the west "ravine," a morass through which ran a branch of Wemrock Brook, was crossed by a bridge on the Freehold-Monmouth road about two and a half miles from the Meeting House. A mile to the southeast on that road was the middle ravine, another morass through which ran the main stream of Wemrock Brook. A causeway crossed it. These morasses, it must be noted, were on the road by which the American troops advanced to Monmouth. The third morass, the east "ravine," was parallel to the road from Monmouth to Middletown and Sandy Hook and some distance west of that road. No road crossed it, but it played a part early in the battle.

The camp of the British army stretched in a line along the road from Allentown, which continued past Monmouth through Middletown to Sandy Hook. It therefore formed a right angle with the road from Englishtown to Monmouth by which the Americans were advancing.

Clinton was convinced that Washington's purpose was not simply to capture the British baggage train. He therefore started Knyphausen, with a part of the army and the wagons, forward on the Middletown road at four o'clock the next morning, while he himself and Cornwallis, with a larger force, prepared to follow. Cornwallis's command was composed of the 3rd, 4th, and 5th British infantry brigades, the 1st and 2nd battalions of British grenadiers, all the Hessian grenadiers, the British Guards, the 1st and 2nd battalions of British light infantry, the 16th Light Dragoons, and Simcoe's Tory Queen's Rangers, all together comprising the élite of the British army.

General Dickinson with his New Jersey militia had been on the alert all through the previous night. He discovered the movement of Knyphausen's grand division and sent word of it to Lee and to Washington. He was then on a hill just east of the west ravine. There he came into contact with a party of the enemy with whom he exchanged fire. Thinking that it was the advance guard of the second division of the British army, he retreated across the ravine, just as an American detachment came up. It was, in fact, merely a flanking party thrown out by Cornwallis, and when the Americans advanced across the bridge over the ravine, it withdrew. This was the first skirmish of the battle.

On receiving Dickinson's message, Washington is reported to have sent word to Lee that he "desired he would bring on an engagement, or attack the enemy as soon as possible, unless some very powerful circumstance forbid it, and that he would very soon be up to his aid." He is also reported to have ordered Lee to attack so as to make an impression upon the enemy, but to be careful not to be drawn into a scrape.

Lee's column moved from Englishtown about seven o'clock in the morning, Colonel Richard Butler with 200 men in the van, followed by Colonel Henry Jackson with an equal number, then part of General Woodford's brigade, 600 men with two guns, then General Varnum's, about as many with two guns, General Wayne's command of 1,000 men and four guns, General Scott's "detachment" of 1,400 with four guns, and General Maxwell's 1,000 men and two guns.

At some time after eight, before he arrived at the Meeting House, Lee halted the column for half an hour. There was some excuse for this delay, because Captain Benjamin Walker, aide to Steuben, had come up with word that the British had not yet marched. This of course referred to Cornwallis's division, Knyphausen's then being well on its way. When Dickinson came up Lee, petulant as ever, accused him of sending false information, to which Dickinson replied with spirit. This altercation was not calculated to steady the mind of so unstable a man as Charles Lee.

There was another halt in this march—the column's advance seems to have been marked by a spirit of hesitation—and Lee sent Wayne forward to take over command of the advanced detachment, which had been under Colonel Grayson.

This advance guard came into contact with the enemy when it met a small body of cavalry and infantry, a covering party sent out by Clinton. It was attacked, and retreated. This was the "second skirmish."

From that time onwards the conduct and disposition of the various elements of Lee's force, their movements to and fro, before Washington came up and the real battle began, make this preliminary part of the affair "the most confusing in its movements and the most difficult to present or follow in detail of any of the battles of the Revolutionary War." [1] In broad terms, it may be stated that Lee's troops were brought into the part of the field that lay between the east ravine and the road to Middletown, facing that road.

They were not drawn up in formal line of battle. The various brigades and detachments were, in general, disposed in an irregular pattern and shifted about in kaleidoscopic arrangements and rearrangements. There were skirmishes here and skirmishes there, advances and withdrawals, shifts of this and that brigade or regiment to this point and that. Orders were given and promptly countermanded. Lee certainly had no plan and no grasp of the situation as a whole. He gave orders, and so did Wayne and the other generals; the field officers gave orders to one another, and those to whom orders were given obeyed or disobeyed as they pleased. The field must have looked like a great anthill, with those bodies of soldiery hurrying hither and thither and back again. It would serve no useful purpose to describe it all in detail, as no clear understanding of so many simultaneous movements could be conveyed in words; nor is it important that they should be. The one fact that emerges clearly from that welter of maneuvers is that Lee had no plan of attack.

Clinton had started to follow Knyphausen about eight o'clock, leaving a rear guard or covering party at Monmouth. Lee conceived the idea of cutting off this covering party and had even sent word to Washington that "the rear of the enemy was composed of 1,500 or 2,000 men; that he expected to fall in with them and had great certainty of cutting them off." One of his aides, imbued with his general's confidence, said to Lafayette, "The rear guard of the enemy is ours," and Lee himself made a similar statement. He began to move his troops with that in view, but without telling any of his officers what his plan was, nor how these movements contributed to it. Having no idea of what they were doing, and receiving, in most cases, only brief orders in general terms, the officers made ineffective and uncoordinated dispositions of their men.

But there had been some hot fighting between various individual elements of the Americans and the British rear guard, with successes and repulses about evenly divided. Clinton saw that they were not merely such attacks as were to be expected from Dickinson and Morgan, but seemed to be the preliminaries of an attack in force. He therefore sent for a brigade of British foot and the 17th Light Dragoons from Knyphausen's division, to cover his right flank, then faced about and marched back to the scene of action. There he disposed his troops in line facing the Americans and prepared to receive their attack. Lee saw his plan of cutting off the rear guard fade into impossibility.

He ordered Lafayette, with three regiments of Wayne's detachment and some artillery, to march against and attack the British left. Lafayette, having gained a proper position for that purpose, believed that he could not attack, indeed that his troops were exposed to a British thrust. He began to move to a new position. Scott and Maxwell observed his movement. To them it looked like a retreat that would leave them cut off from the main body. They therefore fell back. So did Colonels Grayson and Jackson with other troops. Lafayette also began to pull back, probably without orders. Then came an order from Lee for him to retire. Similar orders were given and were not given to others. And that is how the retreat began.

It became general. By regiments in good order, by disorganized regiments in no order at all, the retreating mass swelled until it included Lee's entire division. In sweltering heat—the thermometer stood at 96° in the shade—5,000 weary, sweating, thirsty men tramped along the road back towards Englishtown, and Lee rode along with them. He seemed altogether self-possessed. The descriptions of his conduct by some officers would lead one to believe that he was enjoying a quiet satisfaction in the defeat of an attempt that he had disapproved and voted against, a sort of I-told-you-so satisfaction. Other officers later said the retrograde movement was carried out in good order, that Lee covered it with rear-guard actions, and that the movement was necessary to avert a crushing blow from Clinton.

Washington, with the main army, a little larger than Lee's advance force, had been on the march to his support ever since he got word of Clinton's movement from Monmouth. He stopped at a house on the way for a late breakfast, while his men went on. He had received Lee's message about cutting off Clinton's rear guard. Comparing the number of Lee's troops with Lee's estimate of the size of the Brititsh rear guard, he had no reason to doubt that all was going well with the advance. He was therefore incredulous of news given him by a gentleman of the vicinity that Lee's force was retreating. His informant said he had got this from an American fifer, who was then at hand. Washington indignantly ordered the fifer under arrest for spreading false alarms. He was again on his way when he met several other men who told the same story. Still he would not believe it.

Pushing on, he met an indubitably retreating party, then a whole regiment in disorder, the men apparently exhausted with the heat, then another regiment and another, then Maxwell's brigade, and Ogden's regiment. Why were they retreating? Maxwell didn't know. They were just going along until he got further orders. Ogden said angrily they were all flying from a shadow. At last Washington met Lee.

Of what happened then there are half a dozen different accounts. Washington certainly challenged him with some such question as "I desire to

know, sir, what is the reason—whence arises this disorder and confusion."
Disconcerted by his chief's angry manner, Lee stammered out, "Sir? Sir?"
"What's all this confusion for?" Washington demanded. "And what is the
cause of this retreat?" Of the rest of the interview, there are several versions.
Washington Irving offers a full page of dubious dialogue. Lafayette, who
was not on the spot, said many years later that Washingtton called Lee "a
damned poltroon" and ordered him to the rear. Others report his language
as "strongly expletive," as "a terrific eloquence of unprintable scorn." But
the most thoroughly satisfying, though probably apocryphal, account came
from General Scott in reply to the question whether he had ever heard
Washington swear. "Yes, sir, he did once; it was at Monmouth and on a
day that would have made any man swear. Yes, sir, he swore that day till
the leaves shook on the trees. Charming! Delightful! Never have I enjoyed
such swearing before or since. Sir, on that memorable day he swore like
an angel from heaven!" But whatever turn the conversation took, whatever
Lee's answer was, one thing is certain, the retreat was stopped.

Washington, who as an equestrian was always impressive, was mounted
on a great white horse, a gift that day from Governor William Livingston
of New Jersey. Lafayette described the effect of his arrival upon the tired,
discouraged men: "His presence stopped the retreat . . . his fine appearance on horseback, his calm courage, roused to animation by the vexations
of the morning, gave him the air best calculated to excite enthusiasm."
Lafayette also recalled how, later, he rode "all along the lines amid the
shouts of the soldiers, cheering them by his voice and example and restoring to our standard the fortunes of the fight. I thought then, as now,
that never had I beheld so superb a man." [2]

The retreat having been halted and the troops turned back towards the
scene of action, Washington galloped along the road to Monmouth Court
House. He had crossed the bridge over the west ravine when he met Colonel
Walter Stewart's 13th Pennsylvania Regiment and Lieutenant Colonel
Nathaniel Ramsay, with the 3rd Maryland. They were the last in the retreat, with the British coming after them and not more than 200 yards in
their rear. Washington called on them to face about and hold the enemy
back until he could form a new line behind them. Wayne was at hand; he
undertook to form these two regiments on the north side of the road, while
Washington went about organizing the new line.

The two regiments were immediately attacked by a party of Light
Dragoons. Stewart was badly wounded and was carried off the field, Lieutenant Colonel Lewis Farmer taking his place. The heavy pressure of the

dragoons was strongly resisted, but the Marylanders were slowly driven back. Ramsay, the last to withdraw, was wounded in a hand-to-hand fight with one of the dragoons, overpowered and taken prisoner.

Washington sent Varnum's brigade and Lieutenant Colonel Eleazer Oswald, with six guns, to reenforce the two hard-pressed regiments. Four more guns were soon after brought up, and Knox took charge of the artillery. Colonel Henry Beekman Livingston's 4th New York Regiment was added to the defenders. In all these movements while under sharp attack, there was much confusion. There was confusion also on the road to the west, along which many men, not having been checked by any orders, were still in full retreat. But there was heavy fighting between the now stationary American defenders and an attacking force of dragoons and grenadiers.

Meanwhile, Washington was drawing up his fresh force on a rise of ground just west of the westerly ravine. Greene's division was on the right, Washington in the center, Stirling's division on the left. Lafayette commanded the second line. Artillery was well posted on both wings, particularly well on the right, where it was so placed on Comb's Hill as to enfilade an attacking force. Varnum's brigade, which had been heavily engaged, was withdrawn to the rear to be refreshed. Wayne, with the 3rd, 7th, and 13th Pennsylvania Continentals, the 3rd Maryland, and one regiment from Virginia, was posted along a hedge by an orchard in front of the American center.

A British attack was aimed at Stirling's wing. The British light infantry, the 42nd Foot, and the famous Black Watch pressed forward and were met by a heavy fire from the guns of Lieutenant Colonel Edward Carrington's battery. British fieldpieces were brought up, and a smart artillery duel ensued. Volley after volley of musketry came from both sides. Stirling, with Washington and Steuben, passed along the American line, encouraging the men. For nearly an hour the guns on both sides pounded their opponents, the muskets rained lead without cessation. The fighting was terrific. The American regiments in that line had been brought up to their positions under the eye of Steuben. Under fire they had wheeled into line "with as much precision as on an ordinary parade and with the coolness and intrepidity of veteran troops." Alexander Hamilton afterwards said that never, until he saw those troops deploy and fight as they did, had he "known or conceived the value of military discipline." [3] It was Steuben's reward to see those results of his teaching.

The pressure on Stirling's wing was relieved when the 1st and 3rd New Hampshire regiments and the 1st Virginia moved out to the left through

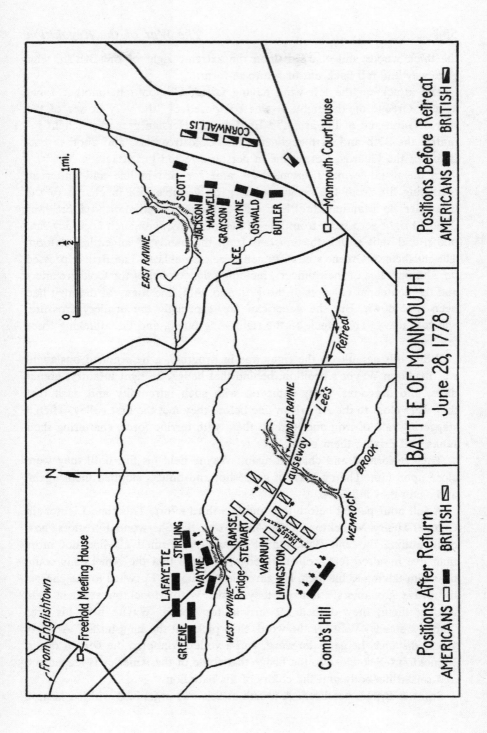

BATTLE OF MONMOUTH
June 28, 1778

Positions Before Retreat
AMERICANS ▭   BRITISH ▬

Positions After Return
AMERICANS ▭   BRITISH ▭

CORNWALLIS

SCOTT
JACKSON
MAXWELL
GRAYSON
LEE WAYNE
OSWALD
BUTLER

EAST RAVINE

Monmouth Court House

Retreat

Lee's

MIDDLE RAVINE

Causeway

WEMROCK

BROOK

N

From Englishtown

Freehold Meeting House

LAFAYETTE
STIRLING
WAYNE
GREENE

RAMSEY
STEWART

Bridge
WEST RAVINE

VARNUM

LIVINGSTON

Comb's Hill

1 mi.

1
½
0

the thick woods and charged upon the extreme right of the British, who gave way and fell back out of fire to re-form.

The attack on the left wing having failed, Clinton sent another force against Greene on the right. It was composed of "the very flower of the rear division and of the army," [4] English and Hessian grenadiers, light infantry, the 37th and 44th regiments, the Coldstreamers, and another battalion of the Guards. Cornwallis in person directed the attack.

In the usual formal fashion, they came forward in line and under an enfilading fire from the six-gun battery on Comb's Hill in charge of the Chevalier de Mauduit du Plessis, Knox's brigade adjutant. Its fire was directed right across the front line of the attackers, with such accuracy that one round shot struck the muskets from the hands of an entire platoon. The muskets of Greene's infantrymen were also ablaze. The British pressed on, although five of their officers, including the colonel of the Coldstreamers and the lieutenant colonels of the 37th and 44th, and many of the men had been shot down. But the American fire, especially the artillery crossfire, was too heavy. The attack on the right wing failed, and the attacking force fell back.

While this assault on the right was in progress, a determined onslaught was made on Wayne's position, behind that hedge, by light infantry, grenadiers, and dragoons. They came on with such intrepidity and dash that they were close to the American line before they met the first volley. Then a staggering rain of iron and lead hit them with terrific force, shattering their ranks and driving them back.

They re-formed and charged again. Wayne held his fire until they were close upon him. Then a blast of grapeshot and bullets stopped them again, and again they fell back.

A full hour passed before they made a third effort. This time Lieutenant Colonel Henry Monckton of the 45th Foot, the Sherwood Foresters, now commanding the 2nd Battalion of grenadiers, formed his line not more than five hundred feet from the hedge, so close that the Americans could hear him talking to his men. He gave the command "Forward to the charge, my brave grenadiers!" and on they came. With Monckton at their right leading them, they dashed forward at top speed. Wayne held his fire: "Steady, steady! Wait for the word, then pick out the king-birds!" At forty yards' distance, he gave the word, and a volley crumpled the British ranks. Monckton fell so close to the hedge that some of the Americans leaped out and seized his body and the colors of his battalion.

Still the British persisted. A fourth attack was organized with so large a body of troops that the line along the hedge was outflanked on both ends. No further resistance was possible. Wayne drew off his men in good order. They had served their purpose well, for the principal American line, from Greene to Stirling, was now too firmly posted to be endangered by the withdrawal. There was no further attempt to take the position by assault. Cannonading on both sides continued for a while, until the British withdrew about six o'clock to a strong position east of the middle ravine.

But Washington was not satisfied with having beaten off these attacks; he wanted a victory. Fresh troops—if any troops that had borne the burden and heat of that day could be called "fresh"—were brought forward, General Woodford's Virginians, Colonel Thomas Clark's North Carolina Continentals. They were to attack the British on both flanks simultaneously. But by the time they were organized and had got within striking distance of the enemy, it was too dark to risk an engagement.

The Americans lay on their arms that night, Washington beneath the branches of an oak with his cloak for covering, Lafayette beside him. Every man was ready to renew the fight in the morning, but when morning came there was no enemy to fight. As noiselessly as Washington had slipped away from Cornwallis at Trenton, now Clinton had eluded Washington. Having started at midnight, he caught up with Knyphausen's division by daybreak and was in Middletown by ten o'clock. On the 30th his whole army was at Sandy Hook, and by July 5 it was in New York.

The casualties reported by the Americans were 8 officers and 61 privates killed, 19 officers and 142 privates wounded, 130 privates missing. The British admitted 4 officers and 61 enlisted men killed, 15 officers and 155 men wounded, 64 missing; and then there is an unusual entry, "3 sergeants, 56 rank and file died with fatigue." That means, of course, by sunstroke or heat prostration, to which may also be ascribed the deaths of at least 37 of the "missing" Americans.[5] The British had also lost 136 men by desertion while on the march from Philadelphia; and the Hessians, 440.

Monmouth might be claimed as a victory by both sides with equal justice. Both sides occupied the field, which is the usual criterion of victory. Clinton did not want the field; he wanted to get to New York, which he did. The Americans had repulsed all the attacks on their main position, but that was only a matter of defense, while their real intention was offensive. On the whole, one can see little gained by that toilsome march across New Jersey in pursuit of the British army, except the kudos of having fought a drawn battle with the formidable professional soldiers of England and Germany. The battle is, however, notable for the courage displayed by both armies, as well as for the fact that it was the longest of the whole war and the last important engagement in the North.

But for General Charles Lee it had the most serious consequences. He had been publicly rebuked on the battlefield by the commander in chief, and the talk of some in the camp was bitter against him; he writhed under the double injury to his self-respect. On the 29th he wrote Washington a letter which began mildly enough, but grew bitter as it went on to accuse him of "an act of cruel injustice" and to "demand some reparation." With this Lee coupled a threat of resigning "from a service, at the head of which is placed a man capable of offering such injuries." He was confident, he said, of justifying himself, "to the Army, to the Congress, to America and to the World in general."

Washington replied that he would soon have an opportunity of justifying himself or of being found guilty of a breach of orders, of misbehavior before the army, and of "making an unnecessary disorderly and shameful retreat." To this Lee replied in equally strong terms and asked for a court martial. It was granted; he was found guilty of disobedience of orders, making "an unnecessary and, in some few instances, a disorderly retreat," and disrespect for the commander in chief, and sentenced to be suspended from the army for twelve months. This verdict went to the Congress for its approval, and was approved by a close vote. Many months later Lee wrote an insulting letter to the Congress, and it finished the affair by resolving that it had "no further occasion for his services in the army of the United States." [6]

CHAPTER 48

Newport

The American army lay at Englishtown two days for rest and refreshment. On the second day the men were under orders "to wash themselves this afternoon and appear as decent as possible," so that at seven o'clock in the evening they might, in seemly fashion, "publickly unite in thanksgiving to the supreme Disposer of human Events for the Victory which was obtained on Sunday over the Flower of the British Troops." [1]

On the 1st of July they began a series of marches northward through New Brunswick, Scotch Plains, Aquackanock, and so on, that familiar road so often trod by them either in retreat or in advance, through Paramus (now Ridgewood) and Kakiat (now West New Hempstead) to Haverstraw, where they encamped on July 15.[2] On that day Washington called on the Commissary Department for "Fifty of your best Bullocks and . . . two hundred Sheep, if to be procured, and a quantity of poultry" to be presented to Charles Henri Théodat, Comte d'Estaing, "Admiral of the French Fleet now laying off Sandy Hook," [3] for the French had come. The treaty of alliance had blossomed and borne fruit. Twelve ships of the line and four frigates, mounting 834 guns and carrying 4,000 soldiers, had arrived at the Delaware capes on July 8, just ten days too late to catch Admiral Howe's fleet, retreating from Philadelphia, and bottle him up in Delaware Bay. D'Estaing had then turned northward to Sandy Hook, across which he could see the English fleet at anchor in the bight formed by the Hook and the Jersey shore. Howe had only nine ships of the line to d'Estaing's twelve and only 534 guns to the Frenchman's 834.[4] D'Estaing had but to get across the bar, extending from Staten Island to the Hook, to get at the British fleet, and the odds against Howe would do the rest.

But he could not cross the bar; the water was too shallow for the deep-draft French ships. Try as he would, using pilots sent by Washington, offering 50,000 crowns to anyone that would take him over, he could not get at the Britishers. He lay in that tantalizing position for eleven days, then gave it up and, in agreement with Washington,[5] sailed north to Rhode Island, where Newport had been held by the British ever since Howe had sent Clinton with 6,000 men and many ships to occupy it in December, 1776. It was now under the command of Sir Robert Pigot with 3,000 men.

General John Sullivan had been in command at Providence with a force of about 1,000 Continentals since the middle of March. Anticipating d'Estaing's movement, Washington had directed Sullivan to apply "in the most urgent manner" to the states of Rhode Island, Massachusetts, and Connecticut to raise "a Body of 5,000 men inclusive of what you already have," also to collect boats, engage pilots and in general get ready for a descent on Newport in conjunction with the French fleet and troops.[6] Six thousand of the New England militia had turned out, with Major General John Hancock at their head. Washington had sent Lafayette to Providence, with two of the best brigades in the army, Varnum's Rhode Islanders and Glover's from Marblehead. He also sent Greene to assist Sullivan in the enterprise. Sullivan's force was thus raised to 10,000 men.[7]

The part of Rhode Island occupied by the British was that island cut off from the mainland by Seaconnet Passage on the east, Middle or Narragansett Passage on the west, and narrow straits on the north. Newport was at its southern end, from which two roads, the east and west, ran to the island's northern extremity.

D'Estaing's fleet arrived off Point Judith, close to Newport, on July 29, but Sullivan's army was not collected and ready for cooperation until August 5. It had been agreed that d'Estaing should send troops up the Middle Passage and land them on the west side of the island, while Sullivan's men were to come down from Providence, cross over by the ferry at Tiverton, and so possess the east side.[8]

In accordance with this arrangement, d'Estaing sent two ships of the line up the Middle Passage and two frigates up the Seaconnet Passage.[9] The British frigate *Cerberus*, 32 guns, lying on the western side of the island, tried to get down into Newport harbor, but ran aground, and was set on fire by her captain and blown up. The frigates *Juno*, *Orpheus*, and *Lark*, each carrying 32 guns, the *Kingfisher*, 16, and the *Pigot* galley met a like ignominious fate. The *Flora*, 32 guns, and the *Falcon*, of 18, also

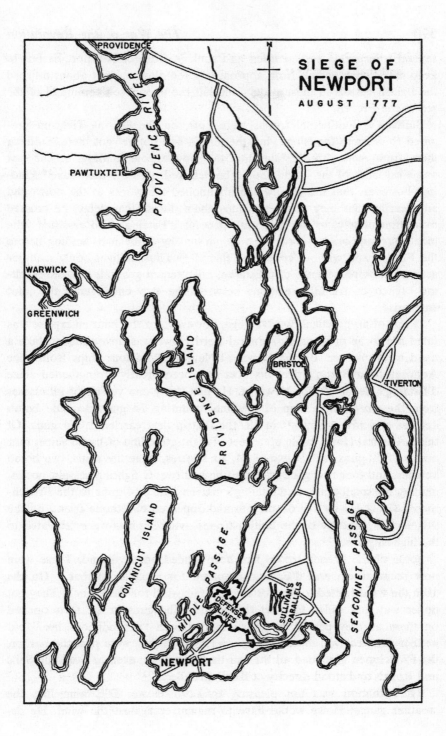

PROVIDENCE

PROVIDENCE RIVER

PAWTUXTET

WARWICK

GREENWICH

BRISTOL

TIVERTON

PROVIDENCE ISLAND

CONANICUT ISLAND

MIDDLE PASSAGE

SEACONNET PASSAGE

DEFENSE LINES

SULLIVAN'S PARALLELS

NEWPORT

N

SIEGE OF
NEWPORT
AUGUST 1777

several transports, were scuttled and sunk in front of Newport harbor to keep the French vessels from approaching too close.[10] That about finished the British vessels in those waters and left the unopposed command of the sea to the French.

Sullivan's Continental troops were now, on the 8th, at Tiverton prepared to cross to the island; but the militia had not yet got there. Sullivan therefore agreed with d'Estaing that the simultaneous landings on the east and west sides of the island should be deferred until the next day.[11] Finding, however, that the enemy had abandoned the works at the north end and fearing that they might reoccupy them during that delay, he crossed over immediately, to the disgruntlement of d'Estaing, who resented "the indelicacy supposed to have been committed by Sullivan in landing before the French and without consulting them." [12] Thus Sullivan, only a major general, took precedence of d'Estaing, a lieutenant general; and the resulting breach of friendly relations between the two endangered the joint enterprise.

It was of no practical disadvantage, however, for the joint enterprise was fated not to be prosecuted; Admiral Lord Howe was now about to take a hand in the matter. By the arrival at New York of four ships from Vice Admiral John Byron's fleet his fleet had been greatly strengthened since d'Estaing's departure for Newport. He had thirty-one vessels of all classes from the *Cornwall*, a ship of the line mounting 74 guns, to little bomb ketches and row galleys; [13] in all, the British fleet carried 1,064 guns. Of these Admiral Howe made up a fleet of eight great line-of-battle ships, four others of 50 guns each,[14] two of 44, six frigates, three fire ships, two bomb ketches, and four row galleys; [15] thus he had twenty fighting vessels, not including his small craft, to d'Estaing's sixteen, and 914 guns to the Frenchman's 834.[16] He set sail on the 6th and appeared off Rhode Island on the 9th, to the great joy of the British troops, whose spirits were "elevated to the highest pitch." [17]

Some of the French troops had been landed on the island. These were now reembarked, and d'Estaing prepared for a naval combat.[18] On the 10th the wind shifted to the northeast, a fair wind for the French. They got under way and sailed to meet the British. The guns in the forts opened on them as they passed out; they replied with "a prodigious fire," but neither side received much damage. As soon as they were past the harbor, the Frenchmen "crouded all the sail they could set, even to Studding Sails and Royals and stood directly at the British fleet." [19]

The situation was not pleasing to Lord Howe. D'Estaing had the weather gauge; Howe would have to maneuver against the wind. He de-

clined the offered engagement and stood off to the southward, hoping for a
turn of the wind that would give him the windward position.[20] For two
days the fleets maneuvered within sight of each other, and then Nature
intervened. A great gale blew up and scattered both fleets. A result of
this dispersal was the meeting of single ships in combat. The French line-of-
battle ship *Languedoc*, 84 guns, engaged the British *Renown*, 50 guns, in a
brief battle, without decisive result. The French *Marseillais*, 80 guns, met
the British *Preston* of 50 and fought until darkness put an end to the conflict, again without result. The French *César*, 74 guns, encountered the
British *Isis*, 50, and was somewhat worsted, but not put out of action.[21]
But the ships of both nations had been much damaged by the storm. The
British frigate *Apollo* was dismasted and most of the rest were in unsea-
worthy condition. Howe's fleet bore away for New York to refit, the
French returned to Rhode Island.

In the meantime, on the 15th, Sullivan with about 10,000 men including the lately arrived militia, though unsupported by his allies, had moved
down towards the enemy. General Pigot withdrew his outposts into the
lines about Newport and set about strengthening them with a new breastwork and an abatis.[22] Sullivan broke ground for entrenchments, mounted
two batteries, and began a line of approach by parallels. There was heavy
cannonading by both sides with no substantial damage to either.[23] The
British were surprised that he confined his works to the eastern side of the
island and made no move against their western flank, whereby he might
have compelled Pigot to defend two fronts at once;[24] but the western side
appears to have been left, out of politeness, for the French to care for in
accordance with the original agreement. Both sides kept on with their labors
on the offensive and defensive works until the 20th, when d'Estaing's fleet
reappeared.

Sullivan then applied to d'Estaing for the promised aid. But that thin-
skinned gentleman was still nursing his injured pride and was in no way
mollified by Sullivan's forwardness since his departure. He said that the
orders of his King and the advice of his officers constrained him to retire
to Boston at once for refitment of his vessels. Sullivan and Lafayette joined
in a personal appeal for only two days cooperation, within which time they
were sure Newport could be taken.[25] D'Estaing was obdurate. At midnight
of the 21st he sailed away, taking his 4,000 troops.

Discouraged by the defection of the allies in whom they had placed their
greatest trust, the militia deserted in droves; 5,000 went off within a few
days,[26] so weakening Sullivan's force that there was no more thought of
attacking Pigot. Sullivan's job now was to get out with a whole army.

During the night of the 28th the retreat began. Pigot followed, sending General Prescott with the 38th and 54th British regiments against Sullivan's left, General Smith with the 22nd and 43rd regiments and the flank companies of the 38th and 54th up the east road of the island, also against Sullivan's left, and General Baron von Lossberg with Hessian jägers and two Anspach battalions up the west road.[27] Sullivan had posted his light infantry under Colonel Henry B. Livingston on the east road and Colonel John Laurens on the west, each being about three miles in advance. Both made contact with their respective opponents, but were too few to withstand them. Both were reenforced and repulsed the enemy.

Pigot then sent the 54th Regiment and Brown's Provincial corps, Tories, to Smith, and Huyne's Hessians and Fanning's New York Provincials to Lossberg. The Americans were driven back. Sullivan drew up his men in two lines. Smith's corps attempted the American left, but was repulsed by General John Glover's brigade and retired to a piece of high ground.[28] Lossberg took two small redoubts and set up batteries from which he cannonaded the American right. Sullivan's artillery replied.[29] The *Sphynx* and *Vigilant*, sloops of war, the *Spitfire* galley, and the brig *Privateer* came up close to that wing and brought their guns to bear on it. Aided by this fire, Smith sought to turn the Americans' right; but it was reenforced, and after he had made three assaults its musketry broke the British ranks and sent them back in confusion.[30] Though only 1,500 of Sullivan's men had ever been under fire, their spirit and resolution were without fault. A newly raised Rhode Island all-Negro regiment under Colonel Christopher Greene especially distinguished itself by "desperate valor," repelling three successive "furious onsets" of the Hessians.[31]

The cannonading from both sides was heavy for an hour; that of the Americans so discouraged Pigot's troops that they failed to come to grips with Sullivan's. Desultory musketry continued between the two sides for six hours until it faded out at dark. In the night Sullivan resumed his retreat as secretly as possible. John Glover's amphibious Marblehead regiment again proved its special worth in carrying the army across Howland's ferry to Tiverton, where it was landed safely with its guns and baggage by the next morning. Sullivan dismissed the remaining militia and took his Continentals back to Providence where they remained throughout the winter.[32]

In these various encounters the Americans are reported to have lost 30 killed, 137 wounded, and 44 missing, the British 38 killed, 210 wounded, and 12 missing.[33]

It was a most fortunate escape, for the very next day a British fleet brought to Newport eight regiments, a battalion of grenadiers, and one of

light infantry, 5,000 men under command of Sir Henry Clinton and Major
General Grey, who would, without fail, have demolished Sullivan's force,
if it had not withdrawn.[34] Having nothing to do at Newport, Grey conducted an expedition along the Massachusetts coast in the course of which
he burned a number of privateers and merchant vessels, also a part of the
towns of New Bedford and Fairhaven.[35]

Success in this enterprise against Newport had been confidently expected throughout the country. Anticipations of brilliant results in the capture of the British garrison had been universal. The disappointment of these
expectations was equally great and widespread, and the blame for the
failure was generally laid at d'Estaing's door. In general orders Sullivan indiscreetly censured the Frenchman for not having remained to help the
Americans. This was resented by the French officers. D'Estaing explained
and justified his movements to the Congress in a letter in which "his
chagrin and irritation" at the censure "were but ill-conceived." [36]

Washington was disturbed by the situation. Writing that it had given him
"very singular uneasiness," he reminded Sullivan that the French were "a
people old in war, very strict in military etiquette and apt to take fire
where others are scarcely warmed." He recommended, "in the most particular manner, the cultivation of harmony and good agreement and your
endeavors to destroy that ill humour which may have got into the officers"
and urged that "the misunderstandings" be kept from the soldiers. He
addressed similar letters to Greene, Heath, and other persons of prominence
in New England.[37]

But "the discontent in New England generally, and in Boston particularly, was so great as to inspire fears that the means of repairing the
French ships would not be supplied" [38] at Boston. Hancock and Lafayette
exerted themselves to allay it. The Congress resolved that "Count d'Estaing
hath behaved as a brave and wise officer and that his Excellency and the
officers and men under his command have rendered every benefit to these
states, which the circumstances and nature of the service would admit of
and are fully entitled to the regards of the friends of America." [39] Thus
d'Estaing was appeased, and harmony was restored. His ships were refitted,
and in due course he sailed away to Martinique, taking his 4,000 troops.

While these futile operations were being carried on, Washington had
moved his army from Haverstraw to King's Ferry, thence across the Hudson and down to White Plains. He was pleased by the fact that "after two
years of Manoeuvring and undergoing the strangest vicissitudes" he was
now again at the place from which he had been driven after the retreat

from Long Island, and that his enemy, then on the offensive, was now in New York "reduced to the use of the spade and pick axe for defence." [40]

The inactivity of Clinton's army puzzled Washington; he did not know whether it stayed quiet in New York from choice. The fact, of course, was that the war between Britain and France had developed into a conflict whose field was the high seas, its seat being the West Indies; the war in America had become a subsidiary element of that larger war. When Clinton took over the command of the British armies in America, in May, it had already been decided to desist from offensive operations in the North.[41] In November, besides sending General Grant and 5,000 men to St. Lucia, Clinton dispatched Lieutenant Colonel Archibald Campbell of the 71st Regiment with a force of 3,500 made up of British, Hessians, and New York Tories to Georgia. Under such conditions, he was satisfied to rest for the time being in his strongholds at New York and Newport.

During the summer of 1778 Washington's army was "the largest body of regular troops ever assembled under the American banner." [42] A return made in July showed 16,782 rank and file fit for duty; of these between 11,000 and 12,000 were in and about White Plains.[43] In September the army was rearranged; Putnam, Gates, Stirling, Lincoln, De Kalb, and McDougall each commanded a division.[44] Putnam was sent to West Point, De Kalb to Fredericksburg (now Patterson), New York, Gates and McDougall to Danbury, Connecticut, Stirling to a point between Fredericksburg and West Point.[45]

There was good news in October: a large shipment of clothing and shoes had arrived from France. The waistcoats and breeches were all alike, but some of the coats were blue, others brown, both kinds faced with red. They were assigned to the different states by lot: North Carolina, Maryland, New Jersey, and New York drew the blue; Virginia, Delaware, Pennsylvania, Massachusetts, New Hampshire, and Hazen's Canadians got the brown. But, as there were more of the blue than were needed for the first four states a second drawing was made, by which Massachusetts, Virginia, and Delaware got in the blue.[46] This was the first time that anything like uniform dress for the whole army had been possible.

In November the army went into winter quarters at several different places. At Middlebrook, Elizabeth, and Ramapo, New Jersey, at West Point and Fishkill, New York, and at Danbury, Connecticut, camps were established; thus a semicircle with a forty-mile radius was drawn about New York, and the vital points of the Hudson Highlands, through which the more southerly states communicated with New England, were guarded.[47]

The soldiers were to be sheltered that winter in log cabins like those built at Valley Forge; these they were, of course, to build for themselves. While building them they lived in canvas tents, and, although the winter was "remarkably mild and temperate" they "suffered extremely from exposure to cold and storms." [48] They were "better clad" than they had been at Valley Forge, but "exceedingly deficient in the articles of Blankets and Hats and soon will be of Shoes," said Washington, "as the call for them is incessant." There was almost always "a scarcity of food and forage." [49]

The difficulty was not a shortage of money; there was plenty of that, bushels of it, to be had of the Congress for the asking, plenty of Continental paper money. The trouble was that there was too much of it. It had sunk steadily during the past two years in real value, in purchasing power; and it was still sinking, faster and faster, month by month all that winter. By April, 1779, it was so depressed that, as Washington wrote, "a waggon load of money will scarcely purchase a waggon load of provision." [50] Nobody wanted to exchange good beef for vanishing paper.

CHAPTER 49

Stony Point

There were no military operations in the north during the winter of 1778, nor in the spring of 1779. Both armies lay in their winter quarters until summer was almost at hand. Then Clinton made the first move. On May 28 he assembled at Kingsbridge 6,000 of his best troops, British and Hessian grenadiers, light infantry, dragoons, Hessian jägers, and Provincial (that is to say, Tory) regiments including Simcoe's Queen's Rangers and Ferguson's corps, a very formidable force. On the 30th they embarked in a fleet of seventy sailing vessels and one hundred and fifty flat-bottomed boats, and on June 1 they landed on both sides of the Hudson, at Stony Point and Verplanck's Point, just below Peekskill.[1]

Washington had been apprehensive of a movement up the Hudson for the capture of West Point, and had ordered St. Clair's division up to Springfield, Stirling's and De Kalb's divisions to Pompton. McDougall was already posted in the Highlands with five brigades of Continental troops and two North Carolina regiments.[2]

There was a small, unfinished fort on Stony Point, occupied by a handful of Americans; on Verplanck's Point, across the river, was Fort Lafayette, held by a captain and seventy North Carolinians. Stony Point was taken by the British without opposition, the garrison having burnt a blockhouse before fleeing at the approach of the enemy. Fort Lafayette was a small but complete work, palisaded and surrounded by a double ditch and an abatis; suffering because of heavy cannon fire from Stony Point and from the ships, and surrounded by British troops on the land side, it was forced to surrender.[3] The British at once set about completing the works on Stony Point, a strong natural position.

Washington interposed his army between Stony Point and West Point, and Clinton made no further move up the Hudson. The principal position of the Americans was in Smith's Clove on "a fine level plain of rich land situated at the foot of the high mountains on the west side of Hudson river." [4] Though West Point seemed to be adequately protected for the moment, Stony Point and the opposite headland, Verplanck's, formed the gateway to the Hudson. Washington Irving likens them to the Pillars of Hercules, the gateway to the Mediterranean, Stony Point being the Gibraltar. Their possession by the enemy menaced West Point, "the key to the Continent." [5] They also effectively commanded King's Ferry, which ran from one point to the other and was a link in the principal highway from the New England states to the south.

Stony Point was "a defiant promontory" thrust out into the Hudson more than half a mile and rising 150 feet from the water, which washed three-fourths of its perimeter. To the river it presented a bold front, steep, rugged, and rocky. On the westerly, or inland, side it fell off irregularly to a wide and deep morass, which curved around from the river above to the river below. At high tide, this marsh was drowned and could be crossed on dry feet only by a bridge and a causeway from which ran a road to the King's Ferry landing on the northerly side of the Point, and another road to the fort.[6] Thus, for military purposes, the Point was virtually an island.

Clinton erected there two series of works. On the summit of the Point seven or eight detached batteries, connected in part by trenches, made a sort of semienclosed fort. To the west of it, but still on the height, a curved line of abatis was swung around from one side of the Point to the other. Farther down the landward slope were three small works protected by another line of abatis, also stretching from shore to shore; and all the woods thereabout had been felled. The garrison established there consisted of the 17th British regiment, the grenadier company of the 71st (or Fraser's Highlanders), a body of Loyal Americans, and certain detachments of artillerymen, something over 600 men in all, commanded by Lieutenant Colonel Henry Johnson.[7]

Washington had been much disturbed by the loss of the two points to the British, but felt that "an attempt to dislodge them, from the natural strength of the positions, would require a greater force and apparatus than we are masters of. All we can do is to lament what we cannot remedy." But after a little while he began to hope for the accomplishment of that difficult task.[8]

On June 28 he wrote to Anthony Wayne asking him to employ a trust-worthy and intelligent man to go into the British works, if possible, or other-wise to find out their nature and the strength of their garrison.[9] Allen McLane's partisan corps had, shortly before that, been detached from the Delaware Regiment and attached to Henry Lee's corps of similar troops,[10] which was operating in the country near Washington's camp. The task set by Washington was given to Lee's "most active officer," McLane, an astute and experienced scout.

On July 2, in company with a Mrs. Smith who wished to see her sons, presumably members of the garrison, he approached the fort with a flag of truce and was admitted. Wearing a hunting shirt and assuming the air of a simple countryman, he was allowed to look about the fort and obtain the desired information. He noted particularly that the entrenchments intended to connect the several batteries of the inner fort were incomplete.[11]

Covered by McLane's men, Washington himself spent a day in examining the vicinity. Colonel Rufus Putnam, Major Henry Lee, and Major Thomas Posey made reconnaissances under similar protection. On the basis of McLane's report and these other examinations, Washington made a plan for the attack and gave it to Wayne. Lee was ordered to patrol the region about the Point, and for nearly two weeks his men were scattered around, spying out all the approaches to the Point. McLane and his company were especially active, lying in the woods at night and picking up information by day from British deserters and the farmers that carried food to the fort.[12]

The force to be employed was the brigade of light infantry recently organized under the command of Wayne. This was made up of hardy and active veterans chosen for alertness, daring, and military efficiency from all the regiments in Washington's army. It was composed of four regiments of two battalions each.

Lieutenant Colonel Christian Febiger, a Dane from Virginia, commanded the 1st Regiment, made up of Virginians and Pennsylvanians, his battalion leaders being Lieutenant Colonel Francois Louis de Fleury, a distinguished French soldier, and Major Thomas Posey of Virginia. Colonel Richard Butler of Pennsylvania led the 2nd Regiment, with Lieutenant Colonel Samuel Hay of Pennsylvania and Major John Stewart of Maryland as bat-talion commanders. This regiment comprised men from Pennsylvania, Delaware, and Maryland. The 3rd Regiment, all Connecticut men, was led by Colonel Return Jonathan Meigs of that state, with Lieutenant Colonel Isaac Sherman and Captain Henry Champion. The 4th was but partially organized. It comprised men from Massachusetts and North Carolina under

Major William Hull of the former state and Major Hardy Murfree of the other. Captain James Pendleton of Virginia and Captain Thomas Barr, with 24 gunners, were to go along taking two small fieldpieces, more for ornament than for use, the plan of attack having no place for artillery. The whole force numbered about 1,350 of all ranks.[13]

In the morning of July 15, Wayne's men were drawn up at Sandy Beach, five miles below West Point, presenting themselves by command, in accordance with his customary attention to their appearance, "fresh shaved and well powdered." At noon they set out on a thirteen-mile march by a circuitous route "over rugged roads, across mountains, morasses and narrow defiles in the skirts of Dunderberg, where frequently it was necessary to proceed in single file."[14] At eight o'clock they arrived a mile and a half back of the Point where they were out of sight of the enemy. Up to this time none of the enlisted men and few of the officers had been informed of their objective, though most of them must have guessed it.

Here Wayne gave them their instructions. They were to form two columns: on the right, Febiger's regiment followed by that of Meigs and by Hull's battalion; on the left, Butler's regiment, Murfree's battalion following it. In advance of the right column, Fleury was to lead 150 "determined and picked men"; in advance of the left, a similar body was to be led by Stewart. These two detachments were to sling their muskets and carry axes to cut through the abatis. But accompanying each body of axmen there was to be a forlorn hope (in modern language, a "suicide squad"), an officer and 20 daredevils to rush through the openings they made and engage hand to hand with the enemy; Lieutenant George Knox was to lead the group on the right, Lieutenant James Gibbons that on the left. Each man of the whole force was to wear a piece of white paper in his hat, as was customary in night attacks, to distinguish him from the enemy.

Except in Major Murfree's battalion, not a musket was loaded; the bayonet was to be the only weapon. They were all to march to the attack with their pieces shouldered and in solid ranks. Any soldier that took his musket from his shoulder on the march or attempted to fire it or to "begin the Battle until ordered by his proper officer," and any one "so lost to every feeling of Honor as to attempt to Retreat one single foot or Skulk in the face of danger," was to be "instantly put to Death by his proper Officer." The strictest silence was to be observed on the march; but when they entered the works they were to shout and keep on shouting, "The fort's our own!" Rewards ranging from $500 to $100 were to be given the first five successively entering the works.

The two columns were to attack at different points; the right, which was

the stronger, to make the main attack on the southerly side; the left, on the
northerly. Murfree's men, with their loaded muskets, were to diverge from
the route of the left column and approach the center of the outside abatis.
As soon as they heard the sound of the attack on the right, "they were to
begin and keep up a perpetual and gauling fire" to make the garrison believe
the real attack was on front.[15]

At half past eleven the two columns advanced. The right column was to
pass around the morass at its lower end, where a sand bar offered a fair
crossing at lower tides. But the tide was high, and the bar was covered with
water waist-deep. Keeping their close-ranked formation, the men started to
wade across. At that moment the enemy's pickets discovered them, opened
fire, and gave the general alarm. From the fort's guns and the garrison's
muskets, round shot, grape, and bullets poured down upon them. There
was no response from the Americans. Inspired by the courage and dash of
Fleury and Knox, leaders of the van, they pressed forward the faster,
reached solid ground and then the first abatis. The axmen swung at it.
Their swift, biting strokes made an opening. The forlorn hope scrambled
through. The main body followed, clambering over tree trunks, formed
again, and pushed up the rough ascent towards the fort, now all alive with
defenders and ablaze with gunfire. Wayne was struck down by a bullet that
made a flesh wound in his head. He was stunned, but soon revived and continued to direct the assault. Captain Selden was hit; Captain Phelps, Lieutenant Palmer, and Ensign Hale fell. Men were dropping all around, but
the column kept on. At the second abatis the axmen were already at work.

Meanwhile, off to the left, the other column was doing as well. Lieutenant Colonel Hay was wounded. Colonel Febiger received a slight wound.
Lieutenant Colonel Hall's hat was shot through, his boots pierced. Many a
man felt the impact of the bullets that rained upon their ranks as they
pressed on to the fort. Signaled by the sound of the axes, Murfree's men,
midway between two attacking forces, were keeping up a continuous fire.

The left column was through the second abatis now, Major Stewart at
its head. He turned Lieutenant Gibbons and his forlorn hope off to the
right towards the main works. Gibbons, his clothes "muddy to the neck"
from crossing the morass and "almost torn to rags" by the sharp branches
of the abatis, attacked the fort. Of his 20 men, 17 were shot down.

The right column had reached the fort first, near the flag bastion, and
rushed through the sally port or climbed over the parapet. Fleury was the
first man in. He tore down the flag. Behind him came Knox, then Sergeant
Baker of Virginia, already four times wounded, then two other sergeants,
Spencer of Virginia and Donlop of Pennsylvania, who earned the fourth

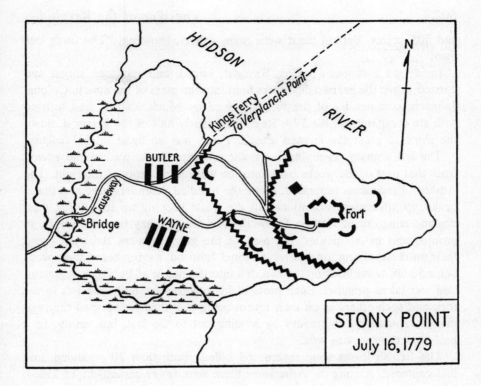

STONY POINT
July 16, 1779

and fifth prizes. Behind them were many others, shouting, "The fort's our own!"

Inside the fort was a mêlée. Bayonet, sword, and spontoon thrust and parried, while the harried defenders fired into the mass of the attack. Colonel Johnson, commander of the fort, deceived by Murfree's fire, had hurried with six companies of the 17th Regiment, nearly half of the garrison, down the slope to meet the feigned attack. There was no head to the defense.

The left column, sweeping in on the northern flank, pushed the enemy from that part of the works back into the welcoming arms of the right. The American regiments separated, drove the huddled defenders here and there, broke up attempted formations, all the while keeping up the din of their disconcerting cry of victory. Inside the fort was a crazy turmoil. Singly, in groups, and in companies, the men of the garrison were throwing down their muskets, crying for quarter. Colonel Johnson, having heard the uproar behind him, came back on the run, fell into the hands of Febiger's regiment, and was taken prisoner. Such parts of his regiment as had been left in the fort, and such others as on their return could join them, supported the regiment's reputation for bravery by holding out to the last, but vainly. In a half-hour the fort was won.

The British losses were severe: 63 killed, more than 70 wounded, and 543 captured. Among the Americans there were fewer casualties: 15 killed, 80 wounded, most of these in the right column. Fifteen pieces of artillery and a great quantity of military equipment and stores were taken.

As soon as the fort was taken its guns were turned on Fort Lafayette on Verplanck's Point and upon the sloop of war *Vulture*, anchored in the river. The sloop dropped downstream. The commander of the Verplanck fort, receiving, in the language of Clinton, "the heavy fire of the Enemy," did not deign "to return a single shot, being sensible that it would have been of no material effect." [16]—of no more effect than the fire from Stony Point, which seems to have been no effect at all.

An attack on Fort Lafayette had been planned to follow the capture of the other, but whether as a determined effort to take it or merely as a distracting feint there is some doubt. At all events the attack was not made, owing to the failure of some of the troops detailed for that purpose to appear.

Washington inspected the captured fort and concluded that "it would require more men to maintain it than we can afford." He therefore ordered the removal of its guns and stores and the destruction of the works. Clinton reoccupied the Point, rebuilt the works, and installed a stronger garrison.

The American light infantry brigade was soon after disestablished, and its members returned to their proper regiments.[17]

No military advantage was gained by this exploit, beyond the capture of so many of the enemy and the guns and stores; but it had an inspiriting effect upon the American army and upon the people in general. A successful attack upon British regulars in a fortified position, with the bayonet alone, was an achievement unparalleled up to that time. The Congress hailed the news with enthusiasm, unanimously thanked Wayne for "his brave, prudent and soldierly conduct" and gave him a gold medal, commended Fleury and Stewart for their "personal achievements" and gave them silver medals. It praised Gibbons and Knox for "their cool determined spirit," and made them captains by brevet. It also ordered the captured military stores valued, and an equivalent sum of money divided among the troops.[18]

That the capture of Stony Point was a signal achievement, ably planned and gallantly executed, has been universally recognized. Charles Stedman, the English historian, wrote, "It was an enterprise of difficulty and danger, and the American general, Wayne, who conducted it, deserved great praise for his gallantry . . . as did the troops . . . for their bravery." [19] A gratifying element of the reports by the British officers is their recognition of the clemency displayed by the Americans towards their foes. General Pattison wrote that it must be allowed to Wayne's credit, "as well as to all acting under his orders, that no instance of Inhumanity was shown to any of the unhappy Captives. No one was unnecessarily put to the sword or wantonly wounded." Commodore George Collier wrote: "The laws of war gave a right to the assailants of putting all to death who are found in arms. . . . The rebels had made the attack with a bravery never before exhibited, and they showed at this moment a generosity and clemency, which during the course of the rebellion had no parallel." [20]

CHAPTER 50

Paulus Hook

Major Henry Lee, Jr., was an active and daring officer, high-spirited and mettlesome. His sobriquet, Light-Horse Harry, has in it more than a suggestion of the romantic kind of valor that is also implied in the nickname of his colleague, Mad Anthony Wayne, and neither of them was averse to public recognition of his own gallantry and dash. Now, in July, 1779, Mad Anthony was basking in the glory of his achievement at Stony Point—in which Lee and his corps had been unnoticed and inactive participants in the reserve—with the thanks of the Congress ringing in his ears and, what was more important, in the ears of everyone else. Light-Horse Harry took notice; "Stony Point had piqued his emulation." [1]

While scouting in the country west of the Hudson he had observed an outlying British post at Paulus—or Powles—Hook. It was not in such a romantic position as that other perched on its rugged eminence, but in many respects it was not unlike Wayne's prize. Here then was an opportunity to match his rival. He suggested to Washington an enterprise against it. [2]

After some hesitation, on the score of the number of men proposed by Lee to be risked and of the advisability of a plan of attack differing in some respects from Lee's, Washington approved the scheme. [3]

Paulus Hook was a low-lying, blunt point of sandy land projecting into the Hudson directly opposite New York City; it is now a part of Jersey City. It was backed by wide boggy salt meadows, across which ran a single marshy road from the fast land beyond. A creek, fordable in only two places, cut it off from the main, and a deep ditch that ran entirely across

604

the peninsula made it an island. This could be crossed only at low tide; access to the works was by a drawbridge across the ditch, closed on the land side by a heavy gate. Beyond the ditch a double row of abatis extended from the water above the Hook to the water below; this formed the wall of the position on the land side. The water side was defended by a continuation of the abatis and by certain breastworks. It was thus, except for its low-lying position, a sort of second edition of Stony Point.

On a slight elevation in the middle of the enclosure was a circular redoubt, about 150 feet in diameter, surrounded by a ditch and a line of abatis; it mounted six heavy guns. Near it, to the northeast, was another redoubt oblong in plan, 250 feet long, 150 wide, mounting three 12-pounders and one 18. The entrance to the works, by the drawbridge, was well defended by a substantial blockhouse and breastworks. There was another blockhouse by the riverside, and scattered about were barracks and other buildings. Its natural position and these artificial works made Paulus Hook a position of considerable strength.[4]

The garrison had been composed of a part of the 64th British infantry, a part of the Invalid Battalion, a regiment of Skinner's Provincials, and a detachment of Van Buskirk's New Jersey Volunteers; but Van Buskirk's men went out on a marauding expedition in the morning of July 28, and were replaced by a company of 48 Hessians and Captain Dundas's light infantry company, making its total strength on the night of the attack something over 200 rank and file. There were also within the works a number of artificers and other noncombatants. Major William Sutherland was in command.[5]

McLane and his company had been scouting all up and down the country from Stony Point to the Hook for two months, traveling light, fast, and incessantly and sending information to Lee's headquarters near Paramus. As the time for the attack on the Hook drew near, McLane concentrated his attention on its near neighborhood. From a deserter, he obtained precise information as to its garrison. He arranged a rendezvous with Lee "in order to conduct him to attack Powles Hook." [6]

The attacking force was to consist of 100 men from Woodford's Virginia brigade under Major Jonathan Clark; these were to form the right; two Maryland companies commanded by Captain Levin Handy were to compose the center; 100 of Muhlenberg's Virginians and McLane's troop of dismounted dragoons were to make up the left, which was to be led by Lee in person. After the fashion of the Stony Point enterprise, there were three forlorn hopes, "desperadoes led by officers of distinguished merit," to lead the van and cut through the abatis. Their leaders were Lieutenant Mark

Vanduval of the 1st Virginia on the right, Lieutenant Philip Reid of the 5th Maryland in the center, and Lieutenant James Armstrong of Lee's dragoons on the left. There was also a reserve under Captain Nathan Reid of the 10th Virginia.[7] But this arrangement became somewhat disordered and had to be altered to meet certain exigencies before the attack was actually begun, as will appear.

At half past ten in the morning of August 18, Lee left Paramus with Handy's two Maryland companies, taking a number of wagons to make the enemy think this was an ordinary foraging party. At the New Bridge across the Hackensack he met the Virginia contingent and McLane's troop. He was then fourteen miles from the Hook and should have been able to reach it by half an hour after midnight, the time set for the assault; but a number of delaying difficulties soon arose.

From the New Bridge the combined forces set out at four o'clock on the direct Bergen road; but when they came near some enemy outposts they filed off on a road to the left. Their principal guide, either from timidity or from treachery, misled them, and what should have been a short march was prolonged to three hours. "By this means the troops were exceedingly harassed." To regain the right way, they had to penetrate the "deep mountainous woods." [8]

Dissatisfaction rent the party. Major Clark was aggrieved at having been put under the command of Major Lee, whose commission was of later date than his own, and had some words with him about it. Perhaps because of that or perhaps because of disgust with the conduct of the enterprise, discontent spread through the ranks of the Virginians; and half of them abandoned the expedition. Thus Lee lost a substantial part of his force and, although Clark stayed with him and "exerted himself," the efforts of the rest of the Virginians "to second his endeavours were not the most vigorous." [9]

In spite of this defection, in spite of the fact that he could now rely only upon the Marylanders, half of the Virginians, and McLane's troop for the necessary vigor and élan of the assault, Lee pushed on; but it was four o'clock in the morning when he came to the edge of the marshy meadows behind the Hook. The coming dawn menaced his success, and a rising tide would soon make the ditch impassable.

Undiscovered by the enemy's sentries, Lee sent Lieutenant Michael Rudulph of McLane's troop forward to reconnoiter the approaches. He reported all quiet within the works and the ditch still fordable. The troops were then set in motion.[10]

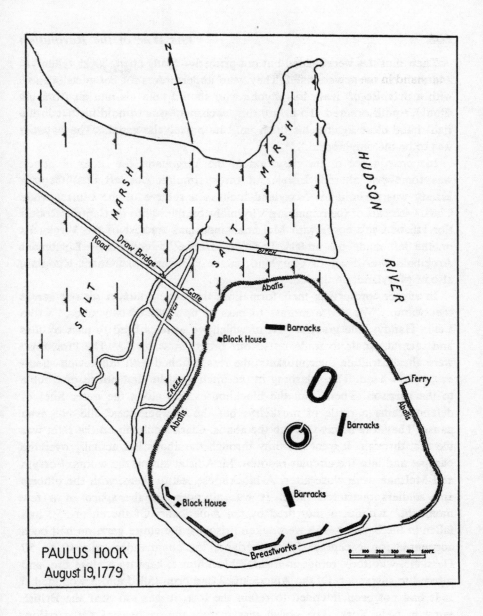

PAULUS HOOK
August 19, 1779

Their muskets were loaded but not primed—"pans open, cocks fallen"—and their bayonets were fixed. They were under orders for complete silence, with a promise of death for anyone who should take his musket from his shoulder until ordered. To insure this, each man was to hold his hat in his right hand close against his thigh until he passed the canal. "The bayonet was to be the only appeal." [11]

In consequence of the desertion of the Virginians, the order of attack was somewhat altered. Instead of three simultaneous assaults, Captain Handy was to hold his Maryland men as a reserve in the center, while Clark with part of the remaining Virginians on the right and Captain Robert Forsyth of Lee's corps with McLane's men and the rest of the Virginians on the left made the attack. The "desperadoes" were led by Lieutenant Archibald McAllister of Maryland on the right and Lieutenant Rudulph, also of Maryland, on the left.[12]

In silence, preserving their formation, the three columns set out across the swamp. "We had a morass to pass of upwards of two miles," wrote Levin Handy, "the greatest part of which we were obliged to pass by files and several canals to wade up to our breast in water." [13] The "forlorns" were ahead, trailing their muskets; the rest marched with musket on shoulder, hat in hand. The splashing in the ditch was the first notice of trouble to the garrison. Then from the blockhouses and along the outer lines of defence came a rattle of musketry; but the "desperadoes" did not even pause. They tore a way through the abatis. Clark's column on the right was the first through. It went not only through the abatis but actually over the parapet and into the circular redoubt. McAllister struck the colors. Forsyth and McLane were close after. A blockhouse fell to them, with the officers and soldiers quartered there. It was all over "in the space of a few moments," without a shot fired by the Americans. Of the enemy 50 had fallen to the bayonet, 158 were taken prisoner; the entire garrison had been accounted for, except Major Sutherland, the commander, and 40 or 50 Hessians, who took refuge in a small blockhouse, kept up a close fire, and refused to surrender. Of the Americans 2 had been killed and 3 wounded.[14]

It had not been intended to retain the fort; it was too near the British army in New York. The object was merely the capture of the garrison. That done, it behooved the Americans to make haste back to their camp with their prisoners before the enemy could cross over from New York, cut off their retreat to the north, and hem them in the narrow strip of land between the Hudson and the Hackensack. Already the alarm guns in New York were arousing the British. There was no time to take Sutherland and his Hessians in the blockhouse, no time, as it seems, even to spike the guns, not to mention packing up any booty. Lee had intended to burn the barracks, but, learning that there were a number of sick soldiers, women, and children in them, he forbore. Without delay the columns were re-formed, and the retreat began.

It is probable that only then did Lee realize the precariousness of his situation. He had arranged to have boats collected at Douwc's Ferry across the Hackensack below New Bridge and nearer the Hook. Stirling was holding 300 men at the bridge as a covering party. But Lee's troops were greatly fatigued; all their ammunition had been wet when they crossed the ditch, and Colonel Van Buskirk's strong foraging party might be coming back to the Hook by this time. An attack by them would probably result in disaster to the Americans. The situation was hazardous indeed. Lee detached Forsyth with a party of the least fatigued men to occupy Bergen Heights behind the Hook and cover the retreat. With the rest he made the best speed he could, hampered as he was by his reluctant prisoners, who obviously hung back in hope of a rescue.

The tired men pushed on to the rendezvous with the boats—and found no boats there. Captain Henry Peyton, with the first company of Lee's Legion, had been entrusted with that important element of the enterprise. He had expected the expedition to arrive hours earlier. When it did not he assumed that the enterprise had been abandoned and so took the boats back to Newark. Lee's men had marched thirty miles "through mountains, swamps and deep morasses, without the least refreshment," fought a battle, and now were fourteen miles from the New Bridge and without a single dry cartridge. Their situation was worse than hazardous; it was desperate.

Lee took it in hand. He ordered his troops "to regain the Bergen road and shove on to the New Bridge," and sent an express to Stirling to come down to meet him. At a point opposite Weehawken, he split his force in three, sending Handy with one part on the road over the hills. Clark with another along the Bergen road. With the rest he himself took "the centre route." The prisoners were divided among the three detachments. At that moment Captain Thomas Catlett and 50 of the recalcitrant Virginians appeared, equipped with dry ammunition. Lee gave some of them to each column to act as rear guards. Not long afterwards, Colonel Ball arrived with a detachment from Stirling, and none too soon, for just before the column reached the Liberty Pole (Englewood) Van Buskirk and his raiders fell on its right flank. Lee's rear guard faced about, Rudulph threw a party of the Legion into a stone house—and Van Buskirk retired. So, at one o'clock in the afternoon of the 19th, the entire command forgathered at the New Bridge, all safe and with all their prisoners.[15]

This enterprise, like that against Stony Point, had no military value except the prisoners taken and the inspiration derived by the army in general. But to Lee it was valuable indeed: "The country resounded with his praise." The Congress responded with a vote of thanks and a gold medal to match Wayne's. McAllister and Rudulph were brevetted captains. The sum of $15,000—Continental paper, of course—was appropriated to be divided among the soldiery. Another resolution commending the conduct of Clark, Handy, Reed, McLane, and half a dozen others was rejected, even though it carried no appropriation.[16]

But there was an unpleasant aftermath for Lee. The difficulty with the Virginians blossomed into charges against him of various minor acts of misconduct, chiefly based on his having taken precedence over senior officers in the expedition—which he had done by direct command of Washington. He was tried by court-martial and acquitted with honor.

Paulus Hook ended the active military operations of the armies of Washington and Clinton for the year 1779. Washington kept his men busy fortifying West Point and drilling under Steuben. Clinton, anticipating an intensification of the British effort in the south, abandoned Newport. Cornwallis arrived from England with reinforcements. These, added to the troops from Newport, brought the New York garrison up to 28,756 men, of whom 13,848 were British regulars, 10,836 were Hessians, and 4,072 Provincials.[17]

Washington's "whole force including *all sorts of troops*" amounted, in November, on paper to 27,099; but it had been dwindling, and it continued to dwindle. Only 14,998 were enlisted for three years or the duration of the war; the terms of the rest were expiring month by month. Also, as Washington wrote to the Congress on November 18, it could not be "supposed that the whole of the Troops borne on the Muster Rolls, were either in service, or really in existence, for it will ever be found for obvious reasons, that the amount of an army on Paper will greatly exceed its real strength." [18] But all the ordinary allowances were not enough to account for the diminution of the American forces, which actually occurred during the following winter. By April, 1780, the whole army under Washington's command amounted to no more than 10,400 rank and file, again on paper, of whom 2,800 were to complete their term of service in May.[19]

CHAPTER 51

The Hard Winter at Morristown

Washington kept his army about West Point until November in the hope that, in combination with the French fleet under d'Estaing "something important and interesting, if not decisive might have been attempted against the Enemy in this Quarter, with a good prospect of success." [1] But d'Estaing had taken his thirty-seven ships, his 2,000 guns, and his 4,000 men to besiege Savannah, Georgia. When his final attack there was beaten off he raised the siege, sent some of his ships to the West Indies, and, with the rest, sailed for France—on the same day that Washington wrote to Lafayette, "we have been in hourly expectation, for the last fifteen days, of seeing Count d'Estaing off Sandy Hook." A month later, he received this disappointing news.[2]

He immediately began to arrange for retirement of his troops into winter quarters. Poor's brigade was ordered to Danbury, Connecticut, to have "an eye to the Sound towards Norwalk, Fairfield &ca," all the cavalry to be quartered near by. Four Massachusetts brigades were to remain at West Point. The North Carolina brigade and Pawling's New York State corps were sent to a point in New Jersey near Suffern. Lee's Legion was posted at Monmouth in the same state. For the main army's cantonment, Morristown was again chosen.[3]

The movement of the army to Morristown exposed it to great hardships. De Kalb, for example, marched his division of two brigades of Maryland and Delaware troops, 2,030 in all, in six days to the new camp. It was a toilsome march. He wrote: "Our march lasted six days and traversed a country almost entirely unpeopled; it proved fatal to many of the soldiers, in consequence of the cold, the bad weather, the horrid roads, the necessity of spending the night in the open air and our want of protection from snow and rain." [4]

James Thacher, a surgeon in the army, was marching down from Danbury about the same time. His journal is eloquent of similar hardships, without baggage or tentage:

It snowed all the afternoon and we took shelter in the woods. . . .

Marched the next day through deep snow . . . marched again early . . . twenty miles it being late at night before our men could all find accomodations in the scattering houses and barns along the road . . . on the 14th reached this wilderness, about three miles from Morristown, where we are to build log-huts for winter-quarters. Our baggage is left in the rear for want of wagons to transport it. The snow on the ground is about two feet deep and the weather extremely cold; the soldiers are destitute of both tents and blankets and some of them are actually barefooted and almost naked. Our only defence against the inclemency of the weather consists of brushwood thrown together. Our lodging the last night was on the frozen ground. [5]

The huts and barracks were then to be got out of standing timber, chiefly oak and walnut. They were weeks at this hard work. On February 1, 1780, one of the Connecticut officers wrote, "Completed our Hutts which destroyed our cloathing still more & we had to my certain knowledge not more than Fifty Men in the Reg[ts] return[d] fit for duty." [6]

The winter before, at Middlebrook, had been "remarkably mild and moderate." [7] This one was of another sort. It has been described truthfully as the worst during the war: "Though Valley Forge is fixed forever in the popular imagination, it deserves forgetfulness in comparison with the second stay at Morristown. . . . Very early that winter the cold came. And such cold! There had been nothing like it in the memory of the oldest inhabitant. Roads disappeared under snow four feet deep. New York harbor was frozen over." [8]

In January the men were still under canvas, "a miserable security from storms of rain and snow." Thacher relates that on the 3rd tents were torn asunder in

one of the most tremendous snowstorms ever remembered: no man could endure its violence many minutes without danger to his life. . . . Some of the soldiers were actually covered while in their tents and buried like sheep under the snow. . . . The sufferings of the poor wretches can scarcely be described, while on duty they are unavoidably exposed to all the inclemency of storms and severe cold; at night they now have but a bed of straw on the ground and a single blanket to each man; they are badly clad and some are destitute of shoes. . . . The snow is now from four to six feet deep. [9]

In February, De Kalb wrote: "It is so cold that the ink freezes on my pen, while I am sitting close to the fire. The roads are piled with snow until, at some places they are elevated twelve feet above their ordinary level." And all through March this "most severe and distressing weather" continued; "an immense body of snow" still lay on the ground.[10]

It was not only the piercing, petrifying cold, the four-foot snow, the nights of shelterless misery that the half-clad army at Morristown had to endure; there were the pangs of hunger as well. On December 18 Washington wrote to the governors of several neighboring states:

> The situation of the army in respect to supplies is beyond description alarming. It has been five or six weeks past on half allowance and we have not more than three days bread at a Third allowance on hand, nor any where within reach. . . . Our magazines are absolutely empty everywhere and our commissaries entirely destitute of money or credit to replenish them. We have never experienced a like extremity at any period of the war. . . . Unless some extraordinary and immediate exertions are made by the States from which we draw our supplies, there is every appearance that the army will infallibly disband in a fortnight.[11]

Major Patten of the Delaware Regiment wrote on January 17, "The Army has been reduced to the most Extreme want of provisions, having subsist[d] five days on half a pound of salt Beef and half a pint of Rice without any other kind of support whatever." [12]

Whatever supplies were furnished by the states appealed to, they were not enough. In the three weeks after Washington's appeal the situation grew steadily worse. By the first week in January, the army was "almost perishing." The soldiers then took the matter into their own hands. Washington wrote on January 9:

> They have borne their distress . . . with as much fortitude as human nature is capable of; but they have been at last brought to such dreadful extremity that no authority or influence of the officers could any longer restrain them from obeying the dictates of their own sufferings. The Soldiery have in several instances plundered the neighbouring Inhabitants even of their necessary subsistence.[13]

The state of affairs was unbearable. When Washington wrote that letter, he had already planned a stern remedy. He divided the state of New Jersey into eleven districts, fixed a contribution of grain and cattle to be supplied by each, allotted an officer to each district, and gave orders to go and get it. Bergen County, for example, was to supply 600 bushels of grain and 200 beef cattle, and Colonel Matthias Ogden was sent after them. Other counties were to furnish less or more, in accordance with their circumstances.

Major Henry Lee was to take care of Salem, Cumberland, and Cape May—750 bushels and 200 cattle from Salem, while Cape May was let off with only 50 head of horned beasts.

The officers were first to apply to the magistrates of their respective districts and solicit their aid. "You will at the same Time delicately let them know that you are instructed, in case they do not take up the business immediately, to begin to impress the Articles called for. . . . This you will do with as much tenderness as possible to the Inhabitants." The provisions seized were to be valued, to be paid for at some indefinite future time.[14]

The scheme was effective. By January 27 Washington could write to the Congress, "The situation of the Army for the present is, and has been for some days past, comfortable and easy on the score of provisions." It is pleasant to read in the same letter that the Jerseymen "gave the earliest and most chearful attention to my requisitions and exerted themselves for the Army's relief in a manner that did them the highest honour. They more than complied with the requisitions in many instances." [15]

But 10,000 half-starved men can eat a large quantity of bread and meat. By the first days of March the Board of War was writing to the states the same story of empty magazines of provisions and predicting the disbanding of the army if relief were not afforded.[16] The difficulty was not the lack of food in the country; it was the lack of money with which to buy it, the lack of money that had unquestioned purchasing power.

The value of the Continental paper dollar had been sinking during three years past, as steadily and as irresistibly as the passage of time itself. In March, 1777, it was but a little below par. In March, 1779, it took $1,000 Continental to buy $100 in specie. In May, 1780, De Kalb, for "a bad supper and grog" and a night's lodging for himself, three others, and three servants, without breakfast, paid $850. "An ordinary horse is worth $20,000; I say twenty thousand dollars!" [17] At that time the pay and subsistence for a captain of one certain regiment, $480, was worth about $13, and a lieutenant's $126.60 was worth about $3.30. In January, 1781, the paper dollar was rated at 75 for one of hard money. In that month Allen McLane paid $600 for a pair of boots, $900 for six yards of chintz; and none too soon did he make his purchases, for within three months the paper dollar was quoted at zero.[18]

There was very little diversion, in active duty, for the army during that dreary winter. In January, Stirling carried 2,500 men in five hundred sleighs over the snow and across the ice to Staten Island for a surprise attack on the enemy's camp. But the enemy were not surprised; they retired to their strongholds, and nothing came of the effort beyond the capture of a handful of prisoners, some tents, arms, and other loot. Against that profit, he had to charge a loss of 6 men killed and 500 "slightly frozen." [19] There were a few other unimportant forays on both sides, which accomplished nothing of consequence. In the spring of 1780 the war in the north was practically at an end. The south had become and continued to be the nation's principal battlefield.

C H A P T E R 5 2

Some Minor Conflicts in the North, 1778-1781

Although Monmouth was the last important battle in the north, it will be well for the sake of clarity to pursue the other minor operations of the war in that sector, some occurring before and some long after the opening of the major conflict in the south.

The first of these took place in September, 1778. Early in that month it appeared to Washington that preparations were being made in New York for some major activities. He thought these might be intended either against the Highlands or against the French fleet then being refitted in Boston. As it finally appeared, there was nothing more serious afoot than two foraging expeditions, one on each side of the Hudson; but they were both conducted in considerable force. Cornwallis with 5,000 men was out on the west side of the river; Knyphausen with 3,000, in Westchester County on the east side.

Recognizing their purpose, Washington did not attempt to meet them in force. He merely sent small bodies of his troops to annoy them and check their movements as far as possible. One of these, composed of New Jersey militia and Lieutenant Colonel George Baylor's 3rd Continental Light Dragoons (otherwise known as "Mrs. Washington's Guards") under command of Wayne, took a position in front of Cornwallis. The militia under General William Winds were posted at New Tappan, in Rockland County, New York, the light horse at Old Tappan two and a half miles from the others. Cornwallis proposed to himself to cut them off.

The 71st Regiment and Simcoe's Queen's Rangers were detached from Knyphausen and ordered, under Lieutenant Colonel Campbell, across the

Hudson to go against Wayne at New Tappan. General Grey of Paoli fame, with the 2nd Light Infantry, the 2nd Grenadiers, the 33rd and 64th regiments, was sent against Baylor at Old Tappan.

But the boats for Campbell's contingent failed to arrive, and that part of the entreprise was abandoned. General Winds, having learned of the proposed attack on his troops, withdrew from his post without notifying Baylor. Grey approached Old Tappan at night unobserved until he met a sergeant's guard of a dozen men posted near Baylor's headquarters. They were all bayoneted. He then silently surrounded three barns in which Baylor's dragoons were asleep, fell upon them, and bayoneted 36 of the defenseless men, capturing 40 more. Only 37 managed to escape. Baylor was wounded and captured; his major, Alexander Clough, was mortally wounded. The escape from death of the 40 prisoners, the whole 4th Troop, has been attributed to the intervention of one of Grey's captains to save them.[1]

This savage exploit was soon followed by another of like character. The American privateers had been giving British ships a good deal of trouble. One of their favorite ports was Little Egg Harbor in New Jersey. In October, 1778, the British sloops of war *Zebra*, *Vigilant*, and *Nautilus*, two row galleys, and four small armed vessels were sent against that place, while Captain Patrick Ferguson with 300 men of the 70th Regiment and the Tory 3rd New Jersey Volunteers also marched against it.

Several privateers had left that port a few days before, but ten large vessels were caught and, with a dozen houses and several magazines of stores, were burned. A deserter—a French captain in Count Casimir Pulaski's Legion, an independent corps—told Ferguson that the Legion, consisting of three incomplete companies of light infantry, three troops of light dragoons, and a company of artillery, with one fieldpiece, which had been sent to cover Little Egg Harbor, was encamped eight or ten miles distant.

Late in the evening of October 14, Ferguson embarked 250 of his men in small boats, in which they rowed ten miles to Mincock Island. Leaving 50 men to occupy a defile through which Pulaski's post was approachable, Ferguson marched to a spot where the Americans, infantry of the Legion, were cantoned in three houses; and, at a little after four in the morning, he surprised them. The bayonet again did its deadly work. Fifty of the Legion were killed, including Lieutenant Colonel the Baron de Boze and Lieutenant de La Borderie, French officers. Pulaski had, on the first alarm, brought up his dragoons and, with the aid of the surviving infantry, drove Ferguson from the scene of slaughter. By taking up the planks of a bridge, Ferguson stopped the dragoons and escaped to his boats in much confusion. Pulaski's infantry followed, firing upon the retreating men and taking a few prisoners.

Ferguson made no bones of having been merciless in his murder of the unarmed men in the houses. "It being a night attack," he reported to Clinton, "little quarter could, of course, be given, so that there are only five prisoners." He also said he learned from the French deserter that Pulaski had "lately directed no quarter to be given and it was therefore with particular satisfaction that the detachment marched against a man capable of issuing an order so unworthy of a gentleman and a soldier"—as pretty a piece of self-indictment as one could hope to find.[2]

In the village of Poundridge, twenty miles northeast of White Plains, dwelt Major Ebenezer Lockwood, an active patriot, for whose arrest the British command had offered a reward. Colonel Elisha Sheldon with 90 of the 2nd Continental Dragoons was encamped in that vicinity. Lieutenant Colonel Banastre Tarleton undertook the double task of arresting Lockwood and defeating Sheldon. He took with him 70 of the 17th light Light Dragoons, part of his own Legion of foot and horse, all mounted, Simcoe's Queen's Rangers, a detachment of hussars, and some mounted jägers, about 360 in all. His approach was discovered by an American spy, and Lockwood and Sheldon were informed of it.

Sheldon formed his men a little above Poundridge church. Tarleton advanced in a narrow column because of the nature of the ground. His dragoons, in the van, drove Sheldon's small force from its position. Tarleton followed him for two miles, pressing heavily on his rear, both parties keeping up a scattering fire. But the militia of the neighborhood turned out and, from fences and farm buildings, began to fire on Tarleton's flanks. He took warning of his danger, faced about, and retreated, Sheldon and the gathering militia pursuing him. Part of his force, left at Poundridge, burned the church and several dwellings, Lockwood's among them. They also found in one of the houses Sheldon's colors and some officers' baggage and carried them off.

Tarleton made his escape, having lost only one man killed and one wounded. In his report to Clinton he gloried in the rather inglorious capture of Sheldon's standard and the baggage. The Americans' loss was 10 wounded, 8 missing.[3]

It was, as in the Little Egg Harbor case, the annoyance of small vessels and whaleboats that had been attacking British commerce in Long Island

Sound, as well as the activity of the Connecticut people in supplying the Continental army, that prompted Clinton to undertake a punitive incursion in that state. On July 3, 1779, a fleet of transports, to be convoyed by the frigate *Camilla,* the sloop of war *Scorpion,* the brig *Halifax,* and the row galley *Hussar,* was assembled at Whitestone, and the troops for the expedition embarked. They comprised the 54th Regiment, a regiment of fusiliers, the flank companies of the Guards, and a detachment of jägers, as a first division, under Brigadier General Garth, also the 23rd, or Royal Welch Fusiliers, the Landgrave's Regiment of Hessians, and the "King's Americans," a Tory regiment, as a second division under General William Tryon, former royal governor of New York—about 2,600 men in all.

Early in the morning of the 5th, the fleet anchored off West Haven, in New Haven harbor. The first division, accompanied by four fieldpieces, landed and marched against New Haven. There was little opposition. Twenty-five young men stood against them for a brief space of time and drove the Guards' light infantry back upon the main body, but without greatly delaying the advance. The planks of a bridge across West River were taken up, and two guns were mounted in some slight earthworks there. A skirmish ensued, and the invaders were forced to turn to another bridge. The militia opposed them in the usual style, firing from behind fences and buildings and causing some loss.

In the meantime, the second division had landed at East Haven, overcoming some opposition. These were joined the next day by Garth's detachment. Garth had expressed an intention of burning New Haven, but contented himself with general plunder of its inhabitants and with carrying off thirty or forty prisoners when on the 6th he reembarked all his troops and proceeded to Fairfield. Landing there on the 8th, the British force occupied the village. Its inhabitants having fled, there was no resistance to the plundering of their houses and the burning of two churches, eighty-three dwellings, fifty-four barns, forty-seven storehouses, two schoolhouses, the jail, and the courthouse. From that place, private property of great value was carried off. The next outrage was perpetrated upon the village of Green's Farms, where the church, fourteen dwellings, thirteen barns, and a store were burned and much valuable property was looted.

On the 11th, Norwalk was attacked. A body of fifty militia opposed the invaders for several hours with fire from houses but was, of course, unable to do more than delay them. Looting was general, to the value of over $150,000, and fire consumed the saltworks, some magazines, two churches, one hundred thirty dwellings, eighty-seven barns, twenty-two stores, seventeen shops, four mills, and five vessels.

The loss of life in these barbaric attacks was slight on both sides. The result was chiefly the arousing of intense indignation throughout the country and the strengthening of opposition to a government whose emissaries would so ravage undefended towns and so wantonly pillage the effects of their unresisting inhabitants.[4]

In February, 1780, an American force was posted in and about "Young's House," a dwelling in the town of Mount Pleasant in the turbulent county of Westchester, New York. It consisted of five companies of Connecticut troops under Lieutenant Colonel Joseph Thompson of Massachusetts, Captain Abraham Watson's company of the 3rd Massachusetts, Captain Moses Roberts's company of the 15th Massachusetts, Captain-Lieutenant Michael Farley's company of the 9th Massachusetts, and Captain James Cooper's of the 14th Massachusetts, perhaps 450 men in all.

In the night of February 2 a British force composed of the four flank companies of the 1st and 2nd regiments of the Guards, a hundred Hessians, a party of jägers, some of them mounted, and 40 mounted Westchester Tories of Colonel James De Lancey's regiment, 450 foot soldiers and 100 horsemen in all, commanded by Colonel Norton of the Guards, set out from near Fort Knyphausen (formerly Fort Washington) to attack the post at Young's House. An American sergeant's guard on picket duty fired upon the van of the enemy, but were all captured. Colonel Thompson, having been advised of the enemy's approach, formed his own force in front of the house to withstand them, placing the four other companies on his flanks. When the British came within gunshot, there was a hot exchange of fire for about fifteen minutes. But Norton flanked the American left and occupied an orchard behind the house. Thus surrounded, the Americans gave way; some took refuge in the house; the rest retreated, pursued by the mounted Tories. The grenadiers of the Guards forced the house, killed or captured all its occupants, and burned it.

The American loss was 14 killed, among whom was Captain Roberts, 37 wounded, and 76 taken prisoner, including Joseph Young, the owner of the house, Colonel Thompson, Captain Watson and Captain-Lieutenant Farley, two lieutenants, and two ensigns. The British lost but 5 killed and 18 wounded.[5]

The spring of 1780 was for the Americans one of the most doubtful seasons of the whole war; for the British it was one of the most hopeful. They were convinced that the American cause was on the verge of collapse. And that was not far from the truth, especially in New Jersey. Several causes operated to bring about this state of affairs. By the expiration of enlistments and the lag in recruiting new men, Washington's army, still in camp at Morristown, had been reduced to fewer than 4,000 men fit for duty; and the pay of this remainder was five months in arrears. Even if the arrears were made up, the soldiers knew that the paper money they would receive would be almost valueless. Meanwhile, on less than half-rations, they were always hungry.

The depreciation of the Continental currency struck a hard blow at the morale of the New Jersey civilians, too. Throughout that state, food had been taken from them upon promises to pay. But they knew that, if and when payment was made, it would be in worthless paper.

These causes created, among both soldiery and civilians, discontent, discouragement, and doubt as to the success of the cause. Among the soldiers, the feelings culminated on May 25 in open mutiny. Two regiments of the Connecticut line assembled, under arms, on parade at beat of drum and declared their intention of going home, "or, at best, to gain subsistence at the point of the bayonet." It was with the greatest difficulty that they were persuaded by their officers to return to their huts.

Under such conditions it is not surprising that Clinton thought that, by a demonstration of British strength, he could prevail upon the American soldiers to desert in large numbers, and upon the civilian population of the state to return to allegiance to the King. Accordingly, he assembled a force of 5,000 men under command of General Knyphausen and Brigadiers Mathews, Tryon, and Sterling, and sent it over from Staten Island to Elizabethtown. Washington was too weak to attack them in force, but the militia turned out to disappoint the enemy in the belief that the people were completely disaffected from the American cause. Twelve of them dared oppose the British advance, firing upon it and wounding General Sterling, who led the van. They were of course swept aside without difficulty, and the invaders marched on to the village of Connecticut Farms, being "annoyed by parties of militia the whole way." While passing through Connecticut Farms, one of the British soldiers fired through a window of the house of the Reverend James Caldwell and killed Mrs. Caldwell, who was sitting with her small children about her. Her body was removed from the house, and it was fired. The church and every other house in the village, save one, were also burned after they had been looted of everything portable. General William Tryon is said to have given the incendiary orders.

The American militia assembled, with a few Continental troops, at Springfield near by. On the way to that town Knyphausen was checked at a bridge across the Rahway River "by a detachment from that army which was represented to be mutinous . . . drawn up in force, ready to dispute his passage." Other detachments of the Continental army arrived from Morristown and took up a threatening position in support of the men at the bridge.

Knyphausen now perceived that "the information upon which the expedition had been undertaken was not to be depended upon." He therefore faced about and returned to Elizabethtown. But, upon reflection, he concluded "for the credit of the British arms" he would "remain some days longer in New Jersey, lest their precipitate retreat should be represented as a flight."

On June 23, he marched back toward Springfield, harassed on the way by a body of militia under General Maxwell. General Greene, with 1,000 Continentals and a force of militia under General Philemon Dickinson, proceeded from Morristown to Springfield, having detached Major Henry Lee and Colonel Elias Dayton with small parties of Continentals to delay the British advance. Greene and Dickinson posted their men behind the bridge at Springfield.

Approaching that town, Knyphausen divided his force into two columns. General Mathews, with half of the troops, went forward on the direct road to the town to amuse Greene, while the other column went to the right towards Vauxhall bridge, with intent to turn the American left and gain its rear.

Greene sent Henry Lee's cavalry and a Continental regiment to the Vauxhall bridge. They made a good stand there, inflicting "very considerable injury" on Mathews's troops, but were driven back towards Greene's force and made a new stand, still on the Vauxhall road. Knyphausen then attacked the main position, coming first upon Colonel Israel Angell's Rhode Island Regiment, which offered a spirited resistance for forty minutes, then fell back to a new position with Colonel William Shreve's New Jersey militia. Greene recalled both of them to the main body. Being so outnumbered, his left flank threatened with encirclement, Greene withdrew all his troops to certain heights in his rear. His force being now concentrated and holding a good position, he sent Colonel Henry Jackson's Massachusetts Continental regiment and Colonel Webb's of Connecticut to support Lee's contingent on the Vauxhall road. There the British right column was stopped.

Knyphausen hesitated to attack Greene in his new position. He realized that "every mile of his future march . . . through a country naturally difficult . . . would be no less obstinately resisted." He, therefore, decided to abandon his enterprise. He set fire to nearly fifty dwellings in Springfield, leaving only four unburnt, then took the road back to Elizabethtown, pursued by Captain Davis with a small party of Continentals and a number of militia, who fired on his flanks and rear and inflicted considerable damage.

The loss of the British in this expedition seems not to have been reported. Of the Americans, 13 were killed, 61 wounded, and 9 were missing. The success of Greene with a thousand Continentals, and of Dickinson with his untrained militia, in checking the advance of 5,000 enemy infantry supported by several guns and a substantial number of horsemen, and turning them back from Morristown, was highly creditable. The barbarous incendiarism, with the wanton murder of Mrs. Caldwell, increased the animosity of the Jerseymen and instilled a new spirit of resistance in the American troops. There was no further attempt at hostile operations by the enemy in that state.[6]

A little before Knyphausen's incursion into New Jersey, Clinton had embarked some troops on transports and made a feint of ascending the Hudson. To counter this threat, Washington had started the greater part of his troops north towards Ramapo and the Clove, leaving Greene in command at Morristown, with two Continental brigades and the Jersey militia. He continued to move north, to Peekskill and finally to West Point, of which post Benedict Arnold was in command.

On September 22 an affair that shocked the army and the American people as nothing had done since the beginning of the war, culminated at West Point. It was the effort of Benedict Arnold to deliver that post to the enemy. The well known story of Arnold's treason has been fully and so ably covered in Carl Van Doren's *Secret History of the American Revolution*, and no effort will be made to tell it in this narrative, which seeks to confine itself to a description of the armed conflicts between the British and American land forces. We therefore proceed to the next and to the last engagement of the war in the North.

In the fall of 1780 a party of Tory refugees from Rhode Island was established in St. George's manor house in the town of Brookhaven on Long Island, which had been turned into a sort of fort.

To this enemy post Major Benjamin Tallmadge of the 2nd Continental Dragoons turned his attention. With two companies of dismounted dragoons, about eighty men, he embarked in eight boats at Fairfield, Connecticut, in the afternoon of November 21, 1780. Having landed on Long Island at nine o'clock in the evening, he detailed Captain Sutton, with twenty men, to guard the boats and started across the island with the rest of his force. But so heavy a storm of wind and rain blew up that he realized he could not recross the Sound that night. He therefore returned to the boats and lay hid until it abated in the evening of the 22nd, when he again set out.

The fort, though small, was formidable. The original house was protected by two strong stockades, twelve feet high, diverging at angles to its front, on its right and left. That on the right terminated at a strongly barricaded house; that on the left at a strong little fort close to the shore, surrounded by a deep ditch and an abatis. It mounted two guns. Another line of stockade connected the extremities of the other two, making the whole a triangle.

Tallmadge divided his men into three parties, so as to move against all sides of the triangle at the same time. Their muskets were unloaded, their bayonets fixed. At dawn his own party approached the east front of the fort, undiscovered by the enemy until they had got within forty yards of the stockade. When a sentinel fired on them, all three parties rushed to the attack. Tallmadge's pioneers cut through the stockade on the east front. The others scaled their respective sides, shouting "Washington and Glory!" The manor house was carried "with the bayonet in less than ten minutes." But a part of the garrison took refuge in the other house, from which it directed its fire upon the attackers. It was answered, and the house was stormed. A door was burst in, and the occupants were seized and thrown out the windows. The entire garrison was captured, and the works with a quantity of stores were destroyed.

Tallmadge got back to his boats, having as his only casualty one man wounded. Of the Tories seven were killed or wounded, and fifty-four officers and privates, "with a host of others in the garrison," presumably noncombatants, were captured. The whole party reached Fairfield in safety that night. For this exploit Major Tallmadge was thanked by Washington and by a resolution of the Congress.[7]

During the winter of 1780–1781 Washington's army was cantoned at various points from Morristown through the Hudson Highlands to Connecticut. Its physical condition was, as in its former winter camps, distressing in the extreme. Food was lacking, shelter was inadequate, clothing was scanty, and pay was always in arrears.

The soldiers of the Pennsylvania line had an additional reason for discontent. Their enlistment papers bound them to serve "for three years or during the war." They construed this as limiting their service to whichever event should first ensue, either the expiration of three years or the end of the war. As the three-year period had expired, they claimed their discharge; but the military authorities held that they must serve to the war's end, even if it was postponed beyond three years. That dubious statement in the enlistment papers, capable of either interpretation, was a cause of trouble in other cases also; but, coupled with their physical hardships at this time, it aroused strong resentment among Wayne's brigade of Pennsylvanians now in camp near Morristown.

In the evening of January 1, 1781, there was a deal of disorder in their camp. The men, who should have been in their huts, were out on the parade ground, muskets in hand, running about, shouting to one another, and occasionally firing their muskets. The officers strove to quiet the tumult and get the men back into their huts. The efforts were partially successful for a time, but at midnight the men again broke out. Shots were fired here and there. One officer was killed, and two were wounded. The mutineers took possession of the artillery park, killing a soldier on guard there.

Wayne, Colonel Walter Stewart, and Colonel Richard Butler attempted to control the situation; but Sergeant William Bouzar, the ringleader, boldly demanded payment of the arrears in pay and discharges for all that had served three years, saying the men were determined to present their grievances to the Congress in Philadelphia. Wayne faced them intrepidly, but without avail. At beat of drum six regiments formed in column in good order, under command of their sergeants, and set off on the road to Trenton.

Unable to control them, Wayne, Stewart, and Butler followed. The men bivouacked first at Vealtown, then at Middlebrook, and finally at Princeton on January 3. Appeals to the Congress had been sent ahead, and at Princeton they awaited a reply. Lafayette and St. Clair, of whose division the Pennsylvanians were a part, met them there; but the mutineers ordered them out of the camp, saying that they would deal only with Wayne, Stewart, Butler, and the Congress.

In Philadelphia there was the greatest consternation, and it was even proposed that the Congress should leave town to avoid meeting the mutineers; but better advice prevailed. Joseph Reed, President of the Congress, with a committee of its members went to Princeton and, after protracted negotiations, obtained an agreement. Arrears of pay, with allowance for depreciation in value, were to be made up as soon as possible; certain articles of clothing, to which the men were entitled, were to be furnished; and every soldier that had enlisted "for three years or during the war," and had served three years, was to be discharged. If the enlistment papers could not be found, each man's oath was to determine his right to discharge. Nearly all of them were discharged, but a large proportion of them reenlisted. It was a complete victory for the mutineers, and one result was the encouragement of a similar revolt.

Three New Jersey regiments at Pompton marched off towards Trenton on January 20. But Washington was ready now to adopt sterner measures. He sent Major General Robert Howe of North Carolina with a detachment of New England Continentals, "to compel the mutineers to unconditional submission" and "instantly [to] execute a few of the most active and incendiary leaders." Howe surrounded the mutineers' camp at Pompton—to which place they had returned—and ordered them to assemble, without arms, which they did. He then selected one man from each of the three regiments, the most forward in the matter according to the officers' reports, and tried them by court martial. Having been found guilty, two of them were hanged; the third, not so vicious as the others, was reprieved. That broke the revolt. The body of mutineers submitted and returned to duty.

While the negotiations for settlement of the Pennsylvania revolt were in progress, Clinton, thinking he saw an opportunity to demoralize the American army, sent two Tory emissaries, James Ogden and John Mason, to Princeton with an offer to take the mutineers under his protection, give them free pardons and pay them what was due. The mutineers seized the two messengers and turned them over to Wayne. They were tried, condemned as spies, and hanged. Wayne offered a reward in gold to the mutineers for this indication of their fidelity. It was declined by Bouzar, their leader, who said his men agreed that they were not entitled "to any other reward but the love of our country." [8]

As a part of the reward for his treason Benedict Arnold received a commission as brigadier general in the British army, and was sent in December, 1780, on an incursion into Virginia, to be more fully described hereinafter. By June, 1781, he was back in New York. There he devised a plan for an expedition against Connecticut in the hope of diverting the attention of some part of Washington's army from the campaign in Virginia.

The troops assembled for this purpose were in two divisions. The first included the 40th and 54th British regiments, the 3rd battalion of New Jersey Volunteers, Tories, a detachment of Hessian jägers, and some artillery, Lieutenant Colonel Eyre in command. The second, led by Arnold in person, was made up of the 38th British regiment, two Tory battalions, called the Loyal Americans also the American Legion, a detachment of jägers, and some guns, about 1,700 in all.

New London, where a very considerable quantity of military stores had been accumulated by the Americans, was chosen for the first attack. It was defended by two forts, Trumbull and Griswold. Trumbull, on the west bank of the Thames River, was built to defend the harbor and was weak on the land side. Griswold was a square fortification. Its stone walls, twelve feet high, were surrounded by a ditch. It was fraised with pointed pickets and supported by outside earthworks. Trumbull's garrison was Captain Adam Shapley's company of 24 Connecticut State troops. Griswold contained about 140 militia under Lieutenant Colonel William Ledyard.

At nine o'clock in the morning of September 6, 1781, Arnold's force landed, one division on each side of the harbor. Arnold's corps marched towards the town, but four companies of the 38th, under Captain Millett, were detached against Fort Trumbull. On the way, Millett's troops were strengthened by the addition of a Tory company under Captain Frink. Shapley's tiny force could not hope to hold the fort. It fired a single volley of grape and musket bullets upon the invaders, striking down four or five of them, spiked the fort's guns, and retreated to Griswold.

Arnold, meanwhile, had gone on to take a small redoubt on Town Hill, commonly called "Fort Nonsense." It was held only by a small party of the townsmen, but they offered resistance with "a brisk fire" which inflicted some damage. Then Arnold formed his men for an assault, and the civilian garrison abandoned the redoubt. Arnold now ordered Eyre with his division to attack Griswold, leading his own corps on towards the town. A few of the citizenry with an old, iron six-pounder fired on him and fled. Eyre approached Griswold and summoned it to surrender. Shapley, its commander, knowing his garrison was too weak to resist successfully, was inclined to comply, but Colonel Nathan Gallup urged him not to do so, promising him a reinforcement of two or three hundred militia if he would hold out. Shapley then refused the demand. But Gallup was unable to bring in the promised aid.

Eyre divided his men into two parties and attacked two sides of the fort simultaneously. The garrison met them with a heavy fire. Eyre was mortally wounded, and his men were repulsed. They came on again, made a lodgment in the ditch and succeeded in tearing down a part of the fraising, but were again repulsed. A third attack was successful. Mounting on one another's shoulders, they swarmed over the parapet or climbed through the embrasures, in spite of an enfilading fire from a 9-pounder in the fort. The garrison offered a stubborn resistance. Major Montgomery was killed by a bayonet thrust at the hands of Captain Shapley. An ensign of the 40th was killed. Three officers of the 54th were wounded. But the works had been forced, and Ledyard offered to surrender. He tendered his sword to Lieutenant Colonel Van Buskirk of the New Jersey Volunteers, who received it and instantly plunged it into Ledyard's body. Some of the attackers finished him off with their bayonets.

Then began an indiscriminate slaughter of the garrison. Tories, Hessians, and British regulars alike joined in the butchery with musket shot and bayonet. They pursued men that had fled into the barracks and the magazine or crept under the gun platforms, shot them, cut them down with swords, bayoneted them without mercy, killing wounded men as they lay on the ground. The fort was a bloody shambles. Only 6 of the garrison had been killed while defending it and no more than 18 were wounded, but when the massacre ceased 85 lay dead in the fort and 60 wounded, many of them mortally. The remaining few were taken captive.

In the meantime Arnold's division entered the town and began its destruction. The torch was applied to building after building by detachments that proceeded systematically. The courthouse, the jail, churches, stores, shops, dwelling houses, warehouses, wharves, shipyards, and a dozen vessels small and large were burned. The little town of Groton met the same fate. In the two towns more than 140 buildings were consumed by fire.

The loss of the British in this expedition was more than might be expected, 48 killed and 145 wounded. The Americans lost, in all, about 240 killed, wounded, or taken captive. In matériel, their loss was heavy, including 71 cannon of various sizes and many muskets, besides a great quantity of stores of food.

Having thus visited upon the unoffending civil population of his own state this punishment for devotion to the cause that he himself had so long and so well defended and then so basely betrayed, General Arnold embarked his gallant troops and returned to New York. This was the last engagement of the war in the north.[9]

CHAPTER 53

Wyoming

One of the more important operations of the war on the northern border took place not in Tryon County, but in a somewhat remote sector, the Wyoming Valley in Pennsylvania.

That valley was a particular part of the great valley of the north branch of the Susquehanna River, the greater part of it being in Luzerne County. Its length was about twenty-five miles; its width about three. Two ranges of hills, rising to a height of 800 to 1,000 feet, hemmed it in. Between them the valley was diversified by hill and dale, upland and lowland; its broad levels bordering the river to a width of one to two miles were conspicuous for beauty and fertility. In all its aspects it was a land formed by nature as a garden spot of peaceful fruitfulness as well as a delight to the eye. And yet, although its first settlers in 1742, Moravians led by Count Zinzendorf, enjoyed for a few years untroubled peace and plenty, it soon became and continued for thirty years to be a scene of tumultuous conflict between rival claimants. Pennsylvania claimed the Wyoming Valley as a part of Penn's grant from the King. Connecticut claimed the Valley as lying between lines extended westward from its own northern and southern boundaries, on the ground that its territory beyond New Jersey extended "from sea to sea," from the Atlantic Ocean to the Pacific.

Rival land companies were chartered by those two colonies that fought bloody battles for the Wyoming Valley, and each tried to dispossess the other's settlers. At the outbreak of the Revolution, Connecticut was in the ascendant, the inhabitants generally recognizing the authority of that state in all their affairs.

For protection from the Indians of the surrounding country the settlers had built a number of "forts," stockaded and entrenched blockhouses. Of these the most important were Fort Durkee on the left bank of the Susquehanna a little below the borough of Wilkes-Barre; Fort Wyoming in the borough; Ogden's Fort on the left bank three or more miles up the river; Forty Fort opposite Ogden's on the other bank; the Pittstown Redoubts five miles farther up on the left bank; Wintermoot's Fort opposite Pittstown; and Fort Jenkins a mile above Wintermoot's. These were, as usual in the border country, intended as places of refuge for the inhabitants in case of Indian attacks, rather than as permanent military posts. Although there were of course differences of political opinion among the settlers, the Tories seem to have been largely outnumbered by the patriots. Many of the Tories left the Valley and joined the forces of Sir Guy Johnson. The remaining patriots enrolled their militia to the number of 1,100, of whom 300 left to join the regular American army.

The headquarters of the Tory forces of Johnson and Colonel John Butler in the spring of 1778 was at Fort Niagara on Lake Ontario. At that time a decision was taken to launch an expedition against Wyoming. Colonel Butler set out near the end of June with 400 white men, including his Rangers, a detachment of Johnson's Royal Greens, and a miscellaneous contingent of unattached Tories from New York, Pennsylvania, and New Jersey, also perhaps 500 Indians, chiefly Senecas, the most ferocious of the Six Nations.

At Tioga Point on the river they embarked in canoes and bateaux and on rafts, to land about twenty miles above Wyoming; and they entered the Valley on June 30 through a notch in the mountains on the west. Their first contact with the settlers was with a party of seven men and a boy working in the fields near Fort Jenkins. Four of these were killed, three captured; the boy escaped. A little "fort" near by, called Exeter, occupied chiefly by Tories, surrendered without resistance. Fort Jenkins was also promptly surrendered, its tiny garrison having been weakened by loss of the seven mentioned. Wintermoot succumbed without fighting. It must be understood that the "garrisons" of those little places consisted of a few men in each, with the women and children of their families, who had taken refuge therein.

In the meantime, a very different Butler, the patriot Colonel Zebulon Butler, had taken command of the available armed forces of the Valley—a company of about 60 men, so-called "regulars," which had been authorized by the Congress to be enlisted for its defense; he had also assembled two or three hundred of the militia. These had been concentrated at Forty Fort. By the decision of a council of war the patriots marched against the invaders on July 3, intending to take them by surprise. Approaching Wintermoot, where John Butler maintained his headquarters, they were discovered by an Indian who gave the alarm. The Tory commander promptly took a position in a plain covered by trees and undergrowth and deployed his men in line of battle. His left, composed of his Rangers, rested on the fort; the Royal Greens held the center; and the Indians, the right.

Zebulon Butler's line was formed with militia on the right and left and the "regulars" in the center. At two hundred yards his men opened fire, continuing to advance until they were within half that distance. For half an hour the two sides kept up a heavy fire. Then a body of Indians gained unperceived a position on the Americans' left flank and opened fire which threw that wing into confusion. Its commander, Colonel Nathan Denison, ordered one company to wheel so as to face this flank attack. Some of his untrained men took the order for a command to retreat, and the whole wing was disordered. The savages seized the opportunity. Throwing down their muskets and yelling like madmen, they fell upon the confused mass with their tomahawks and knives. In a hand-to-hand encounter the Americans fought back; but the whole line was broken and was soon in full flight pursued by their savage enemies, who had regained their muskets and now shot down or tomahawked those they could come up with. The Americans, cut off from retreat to their fort, scattered to seek safety by swimming the river or fleeing to the mountains. Their losses were great; no more than 60 of the whole force escaped death or capture. Of those taken, many were subjected by the Indians to systematic torture ended only by lingering death after agonizing sufferings. John Butler said that 227 scalps were harvested in that fight. He reported his losses as one Indian and two Rangers killed, eight Indians wounded.

Colonel Denison with a few of his men succeeded in getting back to Forty Fort. Colonel Zebulon Butler, with such of the "regulars" as he could gather together, retired to Fort Wyoming and thence withdrew from the Valley. Both forts were surrendered under a promise by John Butler that the lives and property of the people should be preserved. But the promise was not made good. In spite of his orders, it is said, the whole Valley was given over to plunder and destruction and was soon entirely laid waste. Houses and mills were burned. John Butler reported 1,000 houses and "all their mills" so destroyed. Included in these was every house in Wilkes-Barre. A thousand horned cattle and countless sheep and swine were driven away. Personal property of all sorts was carried away or destroyed. The families of the inhabitants were broken up and individually dispersed in the mountain wilderness and in the great swamp in the Poconos, thereafter called "The Shades of Death," where they died of exhaustion and starvation. Many were carried into captivity by the Indians. Depopulated and devastated, the beautiful Wyoming Valley had become a scene of ruin and desolation.[1]

CHAPTER 54

Mohawk Valley

German Flats, a village on the Mohawk River in perhaps the most fertile and beautiful part of the valley—where now stands the town of Herkimer—was the next to fall victim to the fury of the Indians. It contained sixty or seventy houses on both sides of the river, several mills, a massively built stone church, and the large stone mansion house of General Herkimer, which had been stockaded and was generally known as Fort Herkimer. There was also another small defensive work, a dilapidated blockhouse called Fort Dayton.

Late in August, 1778, Joseph Brant was at Unadilla, an Indian town about fifty miles southwest of the Flats. At the head of 300 Tories and 150 Indians, he marched against the ill-fated village early in September.[1] Its inhabitants had suspected an attack and had sent out four scouts towards Unadilla. They were met by Brant's Indians, and three of them were killed. The fourth got back to the town and spread the alarm.

Having this warning, the inhabitants gathered up their most valuable portable possessions and took refuge in the two forts and the church. Brant's marauders reached the Flats in the stormy night of September 12. At dawn, they swept into the town. Without making even a demonstration against the three little strongholds, they set fire to every house and barn. When the entire town was in flames, they collected all the horses, cattle, and sheep and drove them back to Unadilla. No lives were lost; but the prosperous little town was but a heap of ashes and its people were entirely bereft of their only livelihood.

In revenge the Americans struck at Unadilla. From Schoharie, early in

October, came Lieutenant Colonel William Butler. (The chronicles of the time are as full of Butlers as of Clintons; but William was no kin of Zebulon, nor of John, nor were they related to each other.) With him were his 4th Pennsylvania Continental regiment, a detachment of Morgan's riflemen, and a small corps of "rangers." On October 8 they entered the town without opposition, "the enemy having that day left it in the greatest confusion, leaving behind a large quantity of corn, their dogs, some cattle and a great part of their household furniture." Butler's troops "fared sumptuously, having poultry and vegetables in great abundance." [2]

Unadilla was not a savage village of huts and wigwams. It was a well built town of stone and frame houses, with brick chimneys and glazed windows. The troops first burned an outlying part consisting of "ten good frame houses, with a quantity of corn," then "set fire to all the town . . . burned all the houses" except one. They also reduced to ashes "a saw-mill and grist mill, the latter the only one in the country." [3] Having revenged German Flats, they marched back to Schoharie.

As German Flats had been followed by Unadilla, so now Unadilla invited reprisal. Cherry Valley was a village in Tryon County about fifty miles west of Albany. Its people were of more intelligence and a higher grade of morality than was common in these border settlements, scrupulous in the observance of their religious duties and industrious in a civilized manner. In the spring of 1778 Lafayette, then at Albany preparing for his "irruption" into Canada which never came off, visited the Mohawk Valley and directed the building of a fort at Cherry Valley, considering it as an important military outpost in its relation to Albany through the intermediate post at Schoharie. It appears to have been built in the form of a heavy stockade surrounding the village meetinghouse.

Apprehensive of an attack, the villagers called on the Continental army for aid. Colonel Peter Gansevoort, who had so well defended Fort Stanwix, solicited the command of the force to be sent; but his application was denied, and Colonel Ichabod Alden with the 7th Massachusetts Regiment, 250 men, was sent—unfortunately because neither he nor his men had had any experience in Indian warfare.

From Chemung, near Tioga, Captain Walter Butler, son of Colonel John, with 200 of his father's Rangers, set out late in October on a 150-mile march down the Chemung River to the Susquehanna, up that river to Otsego Lake, and so on toward Cherry Valley—a march not only long and toilsome, but also, as November drew on, of great hardship from cold weather and heavy rains and snows. At some point on the way, he met Joseph

Brant, with 500 Indians then on the way from the Susquehanna country to winter quarters at Fort Niagara, and induced him to join in the enterprise.

On November 8 Alden had word from Fort Stanwix (Fort Schuyler) that his post was in danger of attack. The people of the village were properly alarmed and asked permission to remove themselves and their valuables into the fort; but Alden refused their request, assuring them that he and his men would be vigilant against surprise and strong in defense.

On the 9th he dispatched scouts along two roads from the enemy country but, in his ignorance, overlooked an old Indian trail leading to the village. He was so careless as to permit his officers to quarter themselves in houses outside the fort. He himself and Lieutenant Colonel William Stacey lodged in the house of Robert Wells.

Captain Walter Butler approached the town in the early morning of November 11 by the unwatched trail, unseen in a heavy fog, and scattered his men in parties to attack the houses. One of the first was the Wells house. Alden and Stacey tried to escape to the fort; but Alden was overtaken, shot or tomahawked, and scalped, and Stacey was captured. The savage intruders burst into the house and massacred Wells, his mother, wife, brother, sister, three sons, and a daughter as well as the sixteen soldiers billeted there as a sort of headquarters company. Other houses were similarly attacked, and their inmates murdered or taken prisoners. In all more than 30 of the noncombatant inhabitants of the village were slaughtered. Many escaped into the surrounding forests.

Having no artillery, Butler could make no impression on the fort. He kept up a heavy musket fire upon it for several hours, but made no attempt to take it by assault. The town was given over to plunder and the torch. Every dwelling house, barn, and building in it was burned, and all the livestock were collected and driven off. With thirty to forty prisoners in his train, he marched away. But he had not gone far when he decided to release all the captive women and children except two women and their children, whom he retained as a punishment to their husbands, who had been especially active against the Tories and Indians. His motive for this apparently humane action was the desire to secure the release of his own mother, some of her young children, and some other members of his family, who had been detained in Albany when he and his father fled to Canada. General James Clinton agreed to the exchange.[4]

Although the towns in the border country were never free from casual attack and many of them suffered from the desire of the Indians for plunder and scalps, the next real battle in Tryon County did not come until the summer of 1779, when the Tories and Indians attacked Minisink, a village on the Neversink River in the Shawangunk Mountains. Count Pulaski and his cavalry command had been stationed there in the winter of 1778–1779, but were ordered south in February to join Benjamin Lincoln's army.

In July, Joseph Brant saw his chance. He detached 60 Indian warriors and 27 Tories disguised as Indians from a much larger body, which he left in the mountains between Minisink and the Delaware River, and stole into the sleeping town during the night of the 19th. Its inhabitants were awakened by the sound of crackling flames and the smell of smoke to find several of their houses already afire. The intruders seem to have been bent on plunder and destruction rather than on taking scalps, for few of the inhabitants were actually shot down as they attempted to escape, though many were taken prisoners. Then houses and twelve barns, a paltry stockade-fort, and two mills were plundered and burned before the invaders marched away with all the cattle, their other booty, and their captives, to Grassy Bank on the Delaware, where the main body lay.

When news of this outrage reached Goshen, Dr. Benjamin Tusten, lieutenant colonel of the militia, called on his regiment to repair at once to Minisink. On the next day 149 of the militiamen and volunteers met him there; and, in spite of his prudent reluctance to venture on a battle against so astute and subtle a warrior as Brant and in spite of the fact that Brant's strength was unknown, a majority voted to pursue the intruders. Major Meeker brought matters to a head by mounting his horse, flourishing his sword, and crying: "Let all the brave men follow me. The cowards may stay behind!" Everybody followed him.

That day they traveled seventeen miles and encamped. The next morning they were joined by a militia colonel, John Hathorn, with a few men. Hathorn, outranking Tusten, took command. The next day they came upon the camp occupied by Brant's force the night before. By the extent of it and the number of fires, it seemed that the enemy greatly outnumbered the pursuers. A second "council" outvoted the more prudent officers, including Tusten and Hathorn, and decided to go on.

A small scouting party, sent ahead, fell into an ambush, and its leader was shot down. Nevertheless, the whole body pushed recklessly onward until, at the edge of the Delaware River, near where Port Jervis now stands, they descried the Indians and Tories making towards a ford. Hathorn led his men to the right to intercept the enemy before they got to the ford, thus losing sight of them. Brant turned his course also to the right and took a position in the rear of Hathorn's party. Finding no Indians at the ford or on the road to it, the patriots turned back, met their enemies, and the firing began.

By "an ingenious movement" Brant contrived to cut off about 50 of his foes from their main body. The rest took a position on a hill, formed a square and, from the cover of its rocks and trees, engaged the Indians and Tories who surrounded them. It was then about ten o'clock in the morning; and from that time until late in the afternoon a battle of musketry was kept up. Then Brant saw that one man, holding a corner of the square behind a rock, had been shot down. He led his men in a charge through the opening and poured a deadly fire on all sides upon the patriots around him. Hathorn's little force was greatly outnumbered; the square was burst apart and a general flight ensued. The Indians followed the flying men and shot them down or tomahawked them relentlessly. Tusten had gathered 17 of those wounded in the battle in a sheltered place and was caring for them when the Indians found him. He and all of the wounded were massacred. Of those in the fight, 45 were killed in action. Of the whole number, including the 50 earlier separated from the rest, only 30 survived.

Brant went on his way and destroyed another small village in the Mohawk Valley. Other small towns in Pennsylvania near the New York boundary were ravaged by the Tories and Indians within the next few days.[5]

CHAPTER 55

Sullivan's Expedition

Petitions from the inhabitants of the frontiers in Pennsylvania and New York stirred the Congress to activity in their behalf. On February 25, 1779, it directed Washington to take effectual measures for their protection and for the "chastisement of the savages." [1] Washington had had the matter in mind long before that. In January he had considered an expedition against Fort Niagara, the British base on Lake Ontario, which he decided to lay "entirely aside for the present and content ourselves with some operation in a smaller scale against the savages," to be prosecuted in the spring.[2]

In February, Washington had sent to Schuyler and others for information as to the number of men needed for an expedition against the Six Nations and their British and Tory allies, the character of their country, the roads leading to it, and so on.[3] When he received the congressional resolution in March, he was able to reply that a plan for the purpose had been "some time since determined upon and preparations are making." [4] He immediately offered the leadership of the enterprise to Gates, at the same time writing to Major General John Sullivan that he wished him to take it if Gates declined. Gates did decline, prudently, on the ground that he had not the "youth and strength" requisite for such service; [5] and Sullivan accepted.

The country of the Six Nations extended from Lake Ontario on the north to the Susquehanna River in Pennsylvania and from the Catskill Mountains on the east to Lake Erie. These Indians had achieved a high degree of civilization, measured by their establishment of a constitution regulating their affairs, by their permanent settlements, and by their cultivation of the soil. The men were hunters and warriors, but the women were agriculturists

638

of merit. Their villages and towns were composed of substantial log cabins or houses framed with hewn timbers, covered with bark or with sawn boards that were painted. A few of the houses were stoutly built of stone, and many had fireplaces, brick or stone chimneys, and glazed windows. Surrounding the villages were extensive fields and gardens which grew an abundance of corn, peas, beans, pumpkins, and other vegetables in wide variety. Most notable, as evidence of a culture of long standing and promised permanence, were the orchards of apple, pear, and peach trees of great extent and rich fruitfulness.

Washington's purposes, as communicated to Sullivan, were two, "the total destruction and devastation of their settlements and the capture of as many prisoners of every age and sex as possible" to be held as hostages—"the only kind of security to be depended on" for the good behavior of the Six Nations. The country, he wrote, was not to be "merely *overrun* but *destroyed*." [6] The first purpose, destruction and devastation, Sullivan achieved to his complete satisfaction; the second, seizure of hostages, Sullivan completely failed to achieve.

The plan of operations was twofold. Sullivan's grand division of the forces to be employed was to rendezvous at Easton in Pennsylvania and march north by Wyoming to meet at Tioga Brigadier General James Clinton's division coming from Canajoharie by Otsego Lake and the Susquehanna to that point, whence the combined forces were to march north into the Indian country.[7]

Sullivan's division was composed of three brigades. The first brigade, under General William Maxwell, comprised the 1st and 2nd New Jersey Continental regiments and Oliver Spencer's Regiment—one of the sixteen Additional Continental regiments. The second, under General Enoch Poor, consisted of the 1st, 2nd, and 3rd New Hampshire Continentals and the 7th Massachusetts. The third brigade, under General Edward Hand, included the 4th and 11th Pennsylvania Continentals, the "German Regiment" from Pennsylvania and Maryland, Colonel Thomas Proctor's 4th Artillery Regiment with four 3-pounders, two 6's, and two howitzers, a detachment of Morgan's Riflemen under Major James Parr, Captain Anthony Selin's Independent Rifle Company, and a corps of Wyoming militia. This division had, in all, 2,312 rank and file. Clinton's division was in one brigade, made up of the 2nd, 3rd, 4th, and 5th New York Continentals and a company of Lamb's 2nd Artillery, about 1,400 in all, with two small guns.[8]

Sullivan arrived at Easton on May 7,[9] and found part of his force already there, the rest on the way. He lingered for what seemed to Washington and

Clinton an unduly long time; but he himself laid the delay to the failure of
the quartermaster's department and the commissariat to furnish the necessary supplies and clothing for his men, also to the fact that he had to cut
twenty-three miles of road for the passage of his artillery, his pack-horses,
and his herd of beef cattle to Wyoming.[10] He reached that place on June 23.
Again there was a long delay while he waited for new provisions and
ammunition, to replace what had been spoiled on the way, and for boats.

Meanwhile, Clinton at Canajoharie had been more expeditious. When he
received his first instructions from Sullivan his preparations were well under
way. More than two hundred bateaux were ready and a three months'
supply of provisions was stored at Fort Stanwix (Schuyler). By June 17 the
portage of his boats and supplies across the twenty miles of exceedingly
bad, hilly roads between the Mohawk River and Otsego Lake was begun.
Four horses were required to draw each boat. On June 30 he wrote Sullivan
that his entire force, boats, and supplies were on Otsego Lake awaiting
orders.[11] Sullivan was tarrying at Wyoming.

Washington was filled "with inexpressable concern" by the extent of
Clinton's preparations in provisions and bateaux. He had expected him "to
move rapidly . . . quite light" with provisions only to serve until he met
Sullivan at Tioga. By such preparations, he wrote to Sullivan, "instead of
having his design concealed till the moment of execution, and forming his
junction with you in a manner by surprize, the design is announced; the
enemy watching him and in place of moving light and rapidly, and as it
were undiscovered, he goes incumbered with useless supplies" and "has
his defence weakened by the attention he must pay to his convoy." [12]

Sullivan answered that he himself had not "the most Distant prospect of
keeping that part of the Army which is with me from Starving Long Enough
to Compleat the Expedition," so that it was necessary for Clinton to bring
full supplies for his own division for the whole period.[13] Washington accepted the explanation, merely urging Sullivan to lighten his troops "to the
greatest possible degree" and hasten his operations.[14]

It is difficult to understand how Washington could have expected Clinton
to march 1,400 men through the Indian country, even traveling light and
with a minimum of provisions and boats, and at the same time conceal his
design and surprise the watchful savages ever on the alert and spying upon
him every step of the way. Certainly Clinton entertained no delusions as to
the possibility of preserving secrecy. On July 4, at Otsego Lake, he celebrated the day with a salute of thirteen guns and a *feu de joie* of "three
Volleys of musketry one after another," which meant that thirteen cannon
and more than four thousand muskets resounded through the forest. Sulli-

van was equally unconcerned about secrecy. When at last he moved from Wyoming his departure was signaled by cannon fire; and every morning on the march the sunrise gun gave the enemy notice of his position.

Clinton at the lower end of Otsego Lake impatiently awaited Sullivan's orders for seven weeks. He used some of the time in damming the outlet, thus raising the level of the lake two feet and storing water to give him good depth in the stream below when his boats should be on their way. At last, on July 31, Sullivan left Wyoming; 120 boats carried his artillery and stores, 1,200 pack-horses transported the baggage of the army, and 700 beef cattle promised it food. On August 11 he reached Tioga.[15]

Sullivan had not waited, however, for a junction with Clinton before beginning the devastation of the Indian villages. On the second day of his march he detached General Hand, with the light troops, and General Poor's brigade to take positions west and east of the town of Chemung, while Colonel Reid with two New Hampshire companies approached another side and the rest of the army yet another, so as to "prevent an Escape" of its inhabitants. But "the Enemy's Precaution defeated the intention of a Surprize,"[16] which is hardly to be wondered at, since "a few cannon" had been fired the night before and the army had marched in style—"drums were beating, fifes playing and colors flying."[17] All the inhabitants had left Chemung.

The town consisted of "between 30 & 40 Houses, some of them large and neatly finish'd; particularly a Chapel and Council House." Sullivan ordered it burned; he also "caus'd their Fields of Corn, which were of a considerable extent and all their gardens, which were replete with Herbage, to be destroy'd." "We had a glorious Bonfire of upwards of 30 Buildings at once," wrote Major James Norris in his journal.[18]

Clinton left Otsego Lake on August 9, his more than two hundred boats riding grandly on the flood caused by breaking down the dam. On the 22nd he met Sullivan at Tioga and was greeted by a salute of "13 Pieces of Cannon,"[19] which contributed little more to the preservation of secrecy and surprise. Meanwhile, on August 14 the town of Onaquaga, "one of the Neatest of the Indian towns on the Susquehana . . . with good Log houses with Stone Chimneys and glass windows" and a "Church" had been burned and "a great number of apple trees" either girdled or cut down; on the 18th, another of twenty houses, with "plenty of Cucombars, Squashes, Turnips &c" was similarly destroyed.

On the 26th the combined forces, having left most of their heavy baggage and 250 men to hold Tioga, moved up the Chemung River with proper caution, light infantry well in advance and strong bodies of flankers thrown out on both sides of the main body. But William Rogers, the chaplain of Hand's Brigade, though not a military man, or perhaps because he was not a military man, expressed an opinion in his journal that "the great parade and regularity, which is observed, must unavoidably in the end . . . greatly defeat the purpose of the expedition"—the capture of Indians to be held as hostages—"considering the coyness and subtilty of the Indians." [20] The other purpose, however, was in part effected by the destruction of a hundred acres of "beans, cucumbers, Simblens, watermelons and pumpkins," also corn "such as cannot be equalled in Jersey." [21] In the course of the expedition one officer who kept a diary marveled at an ear of corn eighteen inches long; another measured an ear an inch short of two feet from butt to tip.

So far the enterprise had had only a slight brush with a party of Indians near Chemung. The Indians had abandoned their towns and had fled as the troops advanced. But on the 29th they made a stand on the left bank of the Chemung River, about six miles southeast of the present city of Elmira and close to the Indian village of Newtown.

On a height parallel with the river and not far back from its edge, the Iroquois and their British allies had erected a long breastwork of logs that they artfully concealed by planting green bushes along the front. Between it and the river was the trail Sullivan's troops were following. The breastwork was evidently intended as an ambuscade, rather than as a defensible position, the expectation being that an unexpected fire upon the flank of an unwary marching column would throw it into confusion. This was to be followed by attacks on its front and rear from both ends of the breastwork that would cause a panic among the men, a stampede of the horses and cattle, and a complete rout of the invaders. The position was held by Captain Walter N. Butler with two battalions of the Rangers, a small detachment of the 8th British regiment, and perhaps 200 Tories, and by Joseph Brant with about 500 Indians.

Fortunately for the Americans, their advance was led by Major James Parr with three companies of Morgan's riflemen who discovered the ambuscade before being endangered by it. The column was halted, and a plan for an attack was made. The artillery was posted on a height whence its fire could "enfilade the breastwork and sweep the ground in its rear." General Poor's brigade of three New Hampshire regiments and Alden's Massachusetts men, together with the riflemen, supported by Clinton's New Yorkers, were to make a circuit of the enemy's left and attack it in flank and rear, thus cutting off its retreat.

With considerable difficulty Poor's brigade mounted a steep hill covered by thick underbrush. He was opposed by "a loose scattering fire" from the

Indians on that side; but a bayonet charge forced them back, and he gained the top just as the artillery began its bombardment of the works. At this the enemy abandoned the breastwork and attacked the right of Poor's line, Colonel John Reid's 2nd New Hampshire, swarming about it in a half-circle of superior numbers. The 3rd New Hampshires under Colonel Henry Dearborn, who had gone ahead, turned at command and moved to the aid of the endangered regiment. Two regiments of Clinton's New Yorkers also came up from the support. There was a short but sharp conflict, the British regulars, Brant's Indians, and Butler's Greens fighting bravely. Meanwhile, Colonel Hand's Pennsylvanians and Colonel Ogden's New Jerseymen had worked their way along the river to the enemy's right. Thus menaced on all sides, Butler and Brant gave up the fight. The "retreat halloo" was sounded, and the defenders fled around Poor's right, "leaving their dead behind (amounting to eleven or twelve) which were scalped immediately." The light troops pursued them for a mile or two and took prisoners—one white man and one Negro, hardly important enough to serve as hostages. In this fight the Americans lost 3 killed and 39 wounded.[22]

Here was added to the chronicles of the expedition a pleasing touch. The bodies of two dead Indians were found after the battle and "skinned . . . from their hips down for boot legs; one pair for the Major the other for myself," says Lieutenant William Barton of the 1st New Jersey in his journal.[23]

The American army remained on the ground, sending the wounded and the heavier guns back to Tioga and destroying a near-by village and "150 acres of the best corn that Ever I saw (some of the stalks grew 16 feet high) besides great quantities of Beans, Potatoes, Pumpkins, Cucumbers, Squashes & Watermellons," says Lieutenant Beatty. Newtown was the next to go. "Good buildings of English construction" were burned there.[24] On the 31st Catherine's Town, thirty houses, another village of eight, and a third of twenty, with their cornfields and orchards, were destroyed.[25] Appletown was burned on the 4th of September, and Kindaia's thirty "neatly built & finished" houses made a fine bonfire on the 5th, while the army was employed in "destroying corn & fruit" trees, of which there was a great abundance. "Many of the trees appeared to be of great age." Two days later, one detachment burned the chief town of the Senecas, Kanadaseagea, eighty houses, and destroyed "a great number of fruit trees"; another put an end to Schoyere. Canandaigua, "a very pretty town," "very Compact & Neatly built" with thirty houses "much better built than any I have seen before" went up in flames.[26] Honeoye and Kanagha followed.

On the 13th Lieutenant Thomas Boyd of Morgan's rifles met with disaster. Sent out with a small party to reconnoiter Genesee, he was ambushed; 22 of his men were killed, and he was captured along with Sergeant Parker. Taken to Little Beard's town, they were subjected to the most ingeniously hideous tortures before being decapitated.

Genesee, an ancient town of 128 houses, "mostly very large and elegant," says Sullivan, was the next victim. The surrounding fields of corn and "every kind of vegetable that can be conceived" engaged the whole army in their destruction. The corn was cut and stuffed into the houses before they were set on fire.[27]

The expedition went no farther; but on the way back it mopped up what it had overlooked before. The towns around Cayuga Lake, including about a hundred "exceedingly large and well built" houses with two hundred acres of "excellent corn, [and] a number of orchards, one of which had in it 1500 fruit trees," were destroyed.[28] A squaw "so old as not to be able to be brought off" and an Indian boy "decrepid to such a degree that he could not walk" were captured. One house was left standing for them to stay in, but some practical jokers, soldiers of the army, fastened the door on the outside and set the house afire. The old squaw and the crippled boy were burned to death in it.[29]

By September 30 the expedition was at Wyoming, and by October 15 at Easton. Sullivan summed up his achievements in a letter from Wyoming to John Jay, President of the Congress: "The number of Towns destroyed amounts to 40, besides scattering houses. The quantity of Corn destroyed . . . must amount to 160,000 bushels, with a vast quantity of vegetables of every kind. . . . Except one Town . . . about 80 miles from Genesee, there is not a single Town left in the Country of the five nations." He was congratulated by Washington on the success of his expedition, and the Congress voted its thanks to him.[30]

Although he had brought back no hostages, he had achieved "the total destruction and devastation" of the Indian towns. And yet there have been hostile criticisms of the whole affair. One historian calls it the "ruthless destruction of the greatest advance in civilization that the red men in this country have ever attained." Another declares: "A greater degree of barbarity than Pontiac or Brant ever exercised—putting even Wyoming to the blush—was seen in the savage mutilation of the bodies of the fallen enemy, by scalping them and by flaying them for boot-tops; in the destruction without mercy of the growing crops and orchards which surrounded the dwellings; in the burning of cabins, [one] with the helpless and decrepit who had sought refuge therein." [31] The destruction of the growing crops and especially the orchards, which was never before practiced by the Indians, has been especially disapproved. Against such destruction it is said that General Hand and Colonel Dearborn protested without avail.[32]

Entirely apart from such excesses, the expedition may be criticized on the ground that it failed to accomplish its real purpose, the protection of the border settlements from further ravages. The Indian and Tory forces were not destroyed, nor even crippled. True, they were driven from their towns, but only to be thrown back upon the British at Niagara for shelter and food during the terrible winter of 1779–1780 and thus welded more firmly than ever to the King's cause. From Niagara they returned, exasperated and revengeful to ravage the borders with even greater malignity than before. The enterprise may seem as futile as it was barbarous. Yet the Iroquois must have been daunted by the sight of the Americans marching through their country. A heavy blow had been dealt to their military prestige, which was fast diminishing.

In July, Washington had authorized a similar expedition, on a smaller scale, against the Mingos, Munsees, and Senecas in the Allegheny River valley.[33] On August 11 the 8th Pennsylvania Continentals under Colonel Daniel Brodhead accompanied by a number of militia and volunteers, in all about 600 men, set out up the river. On the 15th a party of 30 to 40 Indians coming down in canoes, after a sharp brush, were defeated with a loss of five dead on the ground and others carried away. The Indian town of Cannawago was found deserted and was destroyed, as were several others. In all, several hundred houses were burned and five hundred acros of corn were destroyed, without opposition and without loss, in a journey of four hundred miles, going and returning.[41] Brodhead also received the thanks of the Congress and the commendation of the commander in chief.[34] This expedition is subject to the same comment as Sullivan's.

CHAPTER 56

The Indians Strike Back

Washington wrote to Lafayette on October 20, 1779, that he was well pleased with "the entire destruction of the Country of the Six Nations" and was convinced that the Indians were exceedingly "disconcerted" and "humbled." [1] But the Iroquois were not yet utterly helpless. In the following year the savages, aided by their British and Tory allies, struck back with a vigor increased and a ferocity intensified by their exasperation.

The prelude to these new operations was on a minor scale. In April, Brant led a small force of Indians and Tories against the little village of Harpersfield, which he surprised and destroyed, killing a few people and taking 19 prisoners. He intended to follow this by an attack on one of the Schoharie forts, but, being falsely informed that the fort had been reinforced by 300 Continental troops, he abandoned that enterprise and marched back to Fort Niagara. Other sporadic attacks, particularly upon the Dutch settlements along the base of the Catskill Mountains and farther north, with the usual tale of houses burned, people killed and captured, indicated that the borderers were not immune from further depredations; but all these were trifling compared with the foray which Sir John Johnson organized.

In May, 1780, Johnson sailed up Lake Champlain to Crown Point at the head of 400 of his Royal Greens and Butler's Rangers and 200 Indians. Thence he marched to the Sacandaga River and came entirely undiscovered in the night of May 21 to the Johnstown settlements, where he divided his force. Half of it swept westward up the Mohawk to the Dutch village of Caughnawaga, burning on the way "the houses and barns of the inhabitants, putting to death every male capable of bearing arms," [2] and finally laying the village in ashes.

With the remaining half, Sir John occupied Johnstown and then marched to the mouth of the Cayadutta, burning houses and killing or capturing the inhabitants, and to a junction with the other part of his force at Caughnawaga. He continued up the Mohawk valley for several miles, burning every house not owned by a Tory, slaughtering the cattle and sheep, and carrying off the horses. A number of persons were killed, and many prisoners were taken. Back at Johnstown, the invaders applied the torch to all its houses before they started on their return march.

Governor Clinton assembled the available militia and attempted to intercept Johnson at Ticonderoga; but Johnson got safely to his boats at Crown Point and so to St. Johns, with 40 prisoners. After that there was a lull in the hostilities until August, when Canajoharie felt the blows of the revengeful Indians and Tories.

The Canajoharie settlements were defended by Fort Plain, Fort Clyde, and Fort Plank. Plain, the most important, at the point where Oquaga Creek flows into the Mohawk, was an irregular quadrangle of earth and logs surrounding a three-story blockhouse of heavy hewn timbers. The upper stories were pierced for musketry, the lower one for three or four cannon. Smaller blockhouses strengthened the four bastions at the corners of the fort. Clyde was about two miles southwest of Plain; and Plank, an equal distance northwest.[3] There were lesser fortifications near these, simple stockades surrounding houses.

At the head of about 500 Indians and Tories, Brant approached Fort Plain on August 2. Disregarding the fort, into which most of the neighboring settlers had fled for protection, he burned the neighboring church, fifty-three dwelling houses, as many barns, and a gristmill. Sixteen persons were slain and fifty or sixty made captive. Three hundred cattle and horses were killed or driven away. Taking a leaf from Sullivan's book, the invaders burned the ripe grainfields. Thus, in one day, this fair settlement was reduced to ashes and left a desolation.

The Schoharie valley was next. Its main points of defense were Upper Fort, Middle, and Lower—stockades of logs and earth drawn around strong stone houses, the Lower Fort also enclosing a stone church.

In September, Sir John Johnson collected at Lachine, near Montreal, three companies of his Greens, a company of British regulars, a company of Hessian jägers, and 200 of Butler's Rangers, with two mortars and a "grasshopper." He ascended the St. Lawrence to Lake Ontario and Oswego and marched thence across country to Unadilla on the Susquehanna, where he was joined by Brant and a famous Seneca chief, Cornplanter, with a large body of Indians. The united forces have been variously estimated at 800 to 1,500 men. The plan of Johnson and Brant was to march along the east branch of the Susquehanna, thence to the head of Schoharie valley and sweep it from end to end clear down to Schenectady. They passed the Upper Fort in the night of October 15 without being observed and approached the Middle Fort early in the morning, setting fire to the intervening houses as they went along.

The Middle Fort was held by 150 state troops, "three months' men," and about 50 militia—all under command of Major Melanchthon Woolsey of the state troops. He sent out 40 men to reconnoiter; they were driven back by Johnson's advance guard. The invaders then completely invested the fort and sent a flag with a demand for surrender.

In the garrison was Tim Murphy, who had shot General Simon Fraser at Bemis Heights, as has been told. Murphy was a frontiersman and Indian fighter of note, and his remarkable double-barreled rifle had accounted for 40 of his pet foes. He knew that the Indians had kept a score against him and was sure that, no matter what promises of protection might be given the garrison upon its surrender, he would be marked by the Indians for vengeance. Moreover, he had no confidence in the steadfastness of Major Woolsey, who seems to have been generally regarded as a bit of a coward. He therefore decided to prevent negotiations for a surrender.

As the flag approached the fort, Murphy took a shot at it. He did not hit its bearer, who immediately retired to the enemy's lines. Sir John then opened on the fort with artillery and musketry, to little effect. In the middle of the morning another flag appeared, and Murphy prepared to receive it as before. Woolsey objected, drawing his sword and threatening to run him through if he attempted to fire. But the militia rallied about the rifleman, supporting his statement that Woolsey was a coward and intended to surrender. Murphy took another shot at the flag-bearer, fortunately without hitting him; the flag retreated, and the firing on the fort was resumed. The farce of the flag was enacted a third time, Murphy playing the same part as before.

Woolsey then ordered a white flag to be raised, but Murphy, backed by Captain Reghtmeyer of the militia, threatened to shoot anyone who tried to obey the order. Sir John then decided to raise the siege from a fort which he could not batter down. He drew off his forces and marched down the valley.

The Lower Fort was attacked in a feeble way, without success, and again the invaders went on down the valley, burning all the patriots' houses, barns, and standing crops and killing or carrying off all the domestic animals.

No buildings were left standing except those known to belong to Tories. On these the patriots later visited their vengeance by burning them.

Johnson then called at Caughnawaga again and destroyed the houses erected since his last visit. Marching up the Mohawk valley, he continued his ravages with torch and tomahawk on both sides of the river; everything combustible was burned.

Fort Paris, in the village of Stone Arabia, was held by Colonel John Brown, who will be remembered for his activities in connection with the capture of Saratoga by Ethan Allen and Benedict Arnold and in the Quebec campaign. He had only 130 men, all militia. General Robert Van Rensselaer, who had mustered a force of militia and marched to Caughnawaga, ordered Brown to sally out and attack the enemy, promising to fall upon their rear. Brown, a good soldier, obeyed, and marched his 130 men against Johnson's force, perhaps ten times as many. They met and engaged the enemy near an old ruined earthwork, Fort Keyser; but Van Rensselaer failed to come up. Outnumbered perhaps ten to one, Brown's men fought until a third of them, including the intrepid leader, had been killed. Not until then did the rest abandon the fight.

Stone Arabia was destroyed. After that Johnson sent out small bands to pillage and burn all the country for miles around. Having reassembled his men in the evening of October 19, he marched to Klock's Field on the north side of the Mohawk. Van Rensselaer with 1,500 men, including a number of Oneidas, followed him along the south side. While delayed in a search for a ford, Van Rensselaer received and accepted an invitation to dine with Governor Clinton at Fort Plain, some distance away. His departure at this critical moment angered his officers, the Oneida chief boldly denouncing him as a coward and a Tory. While he was gone, the baggage wagons were driven into the river in a line to serve as a sort of bridge, by the help of which the troops crossed in single file.

Johnson accepted the challenge and drew up his men in battle formation behind a hastily contrived breastwork. The British regulars, the Greens, and the Rangers held this, while Brant's Indians, supported by the Hessian jägers, were posted on the left in a concealing growth of shrub oaks. Van Rensselaer, on his return from the dinner, deployed his force in line, Colonel DuBois commanding the right, Colonel Cuyler the left, and Colonel Morgan Lewis the advance. Captain Robert McKean and his Oneidas were in the right wing. Thus arrayed, the whole line advanced upon the enemy. DuBois's wing charged upon Brant's Indians with such impetuosity that they broke and fled. Sir John is said to have left with them. The rest of Johnson's troops, however, stood fast, and there was a spirited encounter. The flight of the

Indians encouraged the attackers and greatly weakened Johnson's force. The Americans were eager to pursue the fugitives and to assault the feeble breastwork, but Van Rensselaer, with a decisive victory in sight, failed to push his advantage. He withdrew his troops three miles to a place suitable for a bivouac.

In the morning the Oneida chief Louis with his warriors and Captain McKean with his volunteers broke away from Van Rensselaer's command and started after Johnson's retreating men. Van Rensselaer and his main force followed as far as German Flats. Van Rensselaer then ordered McKean and Louis to push ahead, promising support. The advance party, the next day, came upon Johnson's camp-ground and found his fires still burning; but Louis, distrusting the general, refused to go any farther until assured of the promised support. He was proved to be right by the arrival of a messenger announcing that Van Rensselaer had given over the pursuit and was already on his return march. It seems to be certain that only his irresolution stood in the way of a complete victory, either in the battle or on the retreat. Johnson escaped to Canada by way of Oswego.

There was comparative peace in the valley for some two months. In January, 1781, Brant again took the warpath. The Oneida villages had been destroyed in 1780 by an expedition sent down from Canada by Sir Frederick Haldimand as a punishment for their adhesion to the American cause. Their inhabitants had been forced to flee to the white settlements near Schnectady for shelter and food. Even the slender barrier they had interposed between the marauders and the settlers in the valley was gone. Brant's Indians now dared openly to visit German Flats in small parties and carry on their work of destruction. In March fifteen men from Colonel Philip Van Cortlandt's 2nd New York Continentals convoying provisions for Fort Stanwix were cut off and captured. In April a similar party was taken.

To add to the terrors of the population, continually menaced by Indians and Tories, Fort Stanwix, the key post in the valley, was abandoned in May. It had been partly damaged by floods. Then it caught fire and was destroyed. When the garrison removed to Fort Dayton and Fort Plain the valley was struck by the deepest gloom. Its few remaining "forts" were feebly garrisoned and ill supplied with provisions and ammunition. The despondency was so great that Schuyler and General Clinton were apprehensive that in case of another invasion there would be wholesale defections among the troops, which were unable to defend the homes of the inhabitants of the border, and which seemed hopeless of final success.

In his trouble General Clinton appealed to Colonel Marinus Willett, who had so signally distinguished himself in the siege of Stanwix and upon other occasions and was then in command of the 5th New York Continental regiment, soliciting him to take command of the militia and state troops to be raised for the summer campaign. Willett accepted, and confidence in him revived the spirits of the people. He established headquarters at Fort Rensselaer (Canajoharie) and collected the remains of the companies engaged in the previous year's campaign—no more than 380 men. These were divided among German Flats, Schoharie, and other settlements. They soon found work to do.

On June 30, 1781, several hundred Indians and a few Tories led by Doxstader, a Tory, attacked Currytown, on the river below Canajoharie, killed several of its people, took others captive, and looted and burned the houses. Seeing the smoke, Willett at Fort Plain gathered 150 men and set out in the night against the invaders. Doxstader's force had taken a strong position for his camp. At six in the morning Willett approached it. He sent Lieutenant Jacob Sammons with ten men to give the enemy one fire and then retreat. The Indians were thus drawn from their position. Leaping forward, they pursued Sammons until they came upon the main force, which they attacked furiously. But a heavy fire drove them back. Willett called for bayonets and soon they were in full flight, leaving 40 dead on the field. The patriots' loss was 5 killed and 9 wounded or missing.

Willet was successful in giving some measure of protection to the settlers in the lower part of the valley; but the upper valley was still harassed. Shell's Bush, five miles north of Herkimer village, was attacked in August by a Scottish refugee from Johnstown, Donald McDonald, with 60 Indians and Tories. Shell's house was stockaded, and after most of the inhabitants of the settlement had fled to Fort Dayton he undertook, with two or three of his sons, to defend it. The attackers tried to fire it and then to force its door; but Shell and his boys, supplied with loaded muskets by Mrs. Shell, held them off for several hours, killing 11 and wounding 6. They finally gave up and withdrew.

A similar incursion that summer by Captain Caldwell of Butler's Rangers and 400 Indians and Tories from Niagara was repelled by Colonel Albert Pawling with a force of state troops and militia, with considerable enemy losses.

In October there was an invasion in force. Four companies of the Royal Greens, Butler's Rangers commanded by Colonel John's son Walter, and 200 Indians—in all, 1,000 men, under command of Major Ross—marched from Oswego. From the lower end of Oneida Lake they struck through the forest and, on October 24, came upon the village of Warrensbush, where

Schoharie Kill emptied into the Mohawk. Their coming was unobserved; they struck it "as suddenly as though they had sprung from the earth," [4] and committed the usual outrages, killing people, destroying property and burning houses. Willett was twenty miles away at his headquarters when he got the news. He marched all night with 400 men and found Ross's force at Johnstown, where great damage had been done. He sent Colonel Aaron Rowley with a body of state troops and militia to attack Ross on the flank and in the rear, and led his main body against the enemy's front, driving them back from an open field into the woods. There was a stubborn fight for some time, Willett's single fieldpiece being taken and retaken. In spite of the discrepancy in numbers, Willett seemed to be in a fair way to overcome Ross when his militia were seized with an unaccountable panic and the whole right wing turned and fled. Ross might then have had a complete victory; but as his men were confused in an effort to take prisoners and scalps, Rowley fell upon them in the rear and pressed the attack with vigor. Willett, with what men he could collect, kept up the fight in front, and the broken and tangled battle lasted until dark. The enemy then retreated precipitately to a height six miles distant. The loss was 40 killed on each side; but Willett's men took 50 prisoners.

In the morning Willett pushed the pursuit to Stone Arabia, whence he sent a detachment to destroy Ross's boats on Oneida Lake. This effort failed, but at German Flats he learned that the enemy had taken a northerly course. With 400 of his best men and 60 Oneidas who had joined him, he marched all day in a driving snowstorm and encamped in a wood in the Royal Grant. Jacob Sammons, sent forward with some Indians to reconnoiter, found the enemy's camp; but a night attack was deemed inadvisable.

The next day Willett overtook his quarry at Jerseyfield on Canada Creek, and the two forces engaged in a fight across the creek. After Walter Butler was shot down by an Oneida, the Indians broke and fled, followed by the rest of Ross's men. Willett kept after them until they were entirely routed and dispersed in the forest. He then led his troops in triumph back to Fort Dayton, having lost only one man in the pursuit and fight. The loss on the other side was never known. This expedition of Ross and Butler was the last invasion of the New York border during the war. Negotiations for peace were under way, and hostilities on the border ceased.

The War in the South

CHAPTER 57

The Seat of War in the South

The war in the South may be considered under two heads: the campaigns in Virginia, and those in the Carolinas and the northern fringe of Georgia. Most of the earlier battles were fought in the more southern country and the later and final campaigns were conducted in Virginia, so that they may be taken up separately in that order. As the physical characteristics of the Carolinas' terrain and the racial characteristics of their inhabitants largely determined the military operations there, these may profitably be first considered.

The coastal region of the Carolinas extends, in general, eighty to one hundred miles inland—a level, sandy plain "without a hill and almost without a stone, but gradually rising, as you advance, to 190 feet above the level of the coast. Sixty miles of sandhills follow, with hollows between, like the waves of a stormy sea. . . . A fertile tract of highlands succeeds . . . beyond which . . . extends a region of hills and dales, well watered and well wooded." Back of all these rise the Blue Ridge Mountains, forming the western border of North Carolina and touching South Carolina on its northwestern corner.

The lower lands are in considerable part sandy pine barrens, monotonous and desolate, although healthy and valuable for their timber. Here and there in the barrens are treeless savannas, "vast natural lawns" of tall grasses affording pasture for cattle, sometimes surrounded by swamps. Along the rivers and at their mouths are swamps in which grow cypress, bay trees and loblolly pines. Interspersed in the low country and predominant in the higher back country are red earth, oak and hickory lands, fit for orchards, corn, small grains, tobacco, indigo, and other crops. The low lands have produced rice in abundance.

Most important in the two states are their river systems. Rising in the high hinterland, the principal rivers flow roughly parallel southeast to the sea, dividing the country into long, narrow districts. From north to south, important in this narrative because they were so influential over the military campaigns, the rivers begin with the Dan, which crosses into Virginia and empties into the Roanoke. South of that two small streams, Troublesome Creek and Reedy Fork, unite to form the Haw, which receives the Alamance and unites with the Deep River to form the Cape Fear River.

Southwest of that again is the Yadkin, which also changes its name about midway in its course to Pee Dee. This habit of name changing reaches its height in the next great river. It begins in the North Carolina mountains as the Catawba; below Camden, in South Carolina, it becomes the Wateree; after it receives the Congaree, which begins at the junction of the Broad and the Saluda, the Wateree becomes the Santee; and under that name it flows onward to the ocean.

South of the Wateree-Santee system are the little Edisto and the Combahee. Finally, there is the great Savannah River, the boundary between South Carolina and Georgia. All of which is highly confusing. The principal facts important to remember are that the river systems dividing the terrain into long, narrow districts were mostly bordered by swamps; that they were almost entirely unbridged and passable only at a few fords except by boats; that they were subject to sudden, high rises from unpredictable, torrential rains, which rendered crossing difficult, hazardous, or impossible; that they, therefore, largely controlled the movements of the contending armies and often determined the outcome of campaigns in that country.

In the two states there was only one considerable city, Charleston. This, one of the four principal American seaports, had fewer than 14,000 people, of whom more than a third were Negro slaves. Hillsboro and Salisbury, in North Carolina, had perhaps sixty to seventy houses each; Charlotte was but a village.[1]

The population of the Carolinas was most diverse in origin, race, and religious belief. The earliest settlers were English, coming largely after the restoration of the monarchy—Roundheads in flight from the new régime and Cavaliers seeking to mend broken fortunes. After the Revocation of the Edict of Nantes in 1685 French Huguenots flowed in. Dutchmen, dissatisfied with life in New Amsterdam after it became New York, Scotch-Irish, Scottish Highlanders, Catholic Irish, Swiss led by their compatriot John Peter Pury, foreign Protestants of various nations induced by bounties

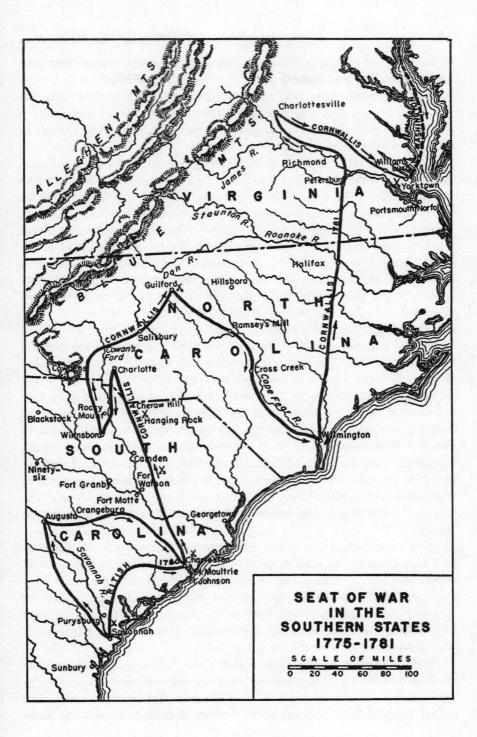

SEAT OF WAR
IN THE
SOUTHERN STATES
1775-1781

SCALE OF MILES

0   20   40   60   80   100

of land offered by South Carolina, thousands of mixed settlers from the
northern colonies who came down after 1740—all these made up a mélange
of races, national origins, and religions hardly to be matched in America.
And the tendency of all was to segregate themselves in distinct communities,
for the most part along the great rivers.[2] Among them, racial and religious
differences bred political differences.

The Scottish Highlanders constituted an important and a disturbing element. Some of these settled in South Carolina before 1685; others came to
Georgia in the 1730's. After the termination of the Seven Years' War, in
1763, large numbers of men of the Highland regiments in the British army
were rewarded for their service by grants of land in Georgia and North
Carolina, and emigrated to those provinces. The major part settled in the
Cape Fear River country of North Carolina. Their reports of the fertility
of the land, and especially the lure of free ownership, brought thousands
of their people from the isles of Rasay and Skye to join them. By that immigration and by natural increase, they became a numerous people.

They brought their own language, habits, and customs, their plaids and
kilts, their bagpipes and their peculiar weapons, the broadsword and the
skean dhu, or dirk. They brought also their own spirit of loyalty. The only
civic tie formerly known in the Highlands was personal devotion by the
members of each clan to its chieftain. Later there was imposed upon that
devotion to the Stuart king. After the forced abdication of James II, as
long as the Old Pretender and the Young Pretender actively sought to
establish their house again on the British throne, they remained stanch
Jacobites. When the Battle of Culloden, in 1746, ended all hope of such re-
establishment and the clans were broken up, their allegiance was perforce
transferred to the Hanoverian King, George II, even though his son, the
Duke of Cumberland, had ruthlessly butchered their kinsmen after that
battle.

Their natural clannishness and solidarity was excited in North Carolina
to a high pitch by the arrival, in 1774, of Allan Macdonald and his wife
Flora, who, after Culloden, had rescued Prince Charles Edward, the Young
Pretender, from his pursuers and got him safely away to France. She, so
fervently then a Jacobite, was now as stanchly loyal to George III, and
there was hardly a man in all the thousands of these American Highlanders
who would not follow where she led.

In the upper North Carolina country, west of Raleigh, was another
group of people linked together not by a common national origin, though
the majority were Scotch-Irish, but by common circumstances and grievances. Most of them had come down from western Pennsylvania. Their

contacts in trade and otherwise were with that province; they had few relationships with the Carolinians to the east and south, whom they grew to dislike and distrust. Their particular grievance was the impositions upon them of illegal fees and excessive taxes by dishonest court officials, sheriffs, and collectors of taxes appointed by the governor. This resulted in a group hatred of all the machinery of the law, which was displayed in many acts of violence by which they prevented the holding of courts in their district. They called themselves Regulators.

William Tryon, the royal governor, undertook to put down this inchoate rebellion. He gathered a force of 1,018 militia infantry and 30 light horse and marched against them, ravaging and looting their farms and homes. At the Alamance River, he found about 2,000 of them, only half armed and completely unorganized. On May 16, 1771, there was a battle. Though Tryon's force was completely equipped and provided with artillery, the Regulators held their ground for two hours before they were dispersed with a loss of 20 killed and a great many wounded, the attacking force having 9 killed and 61 wounded. On trial, 12 of the prisoners taken by Tryon were found guilty of treason; 6 were hanged.

Thousands left the now hated province, crossed the mountains and sought new homes in the valley of the upper Tennessee River, where they set up "a state, independent of the authority" of the British King. Most of these emigrants became patriots.

To 6,400 who remained, Tryon administered a British oath of allegiance; they swore "never to bear arms against the King, but to take up arms for him, if called upon." This oath, taken under circumstances amounting to duress, probably did not rest heavily upon their consciences. Because they hated the people of the low country who supported Tryon, and who became patriots, many of the regulators were Loyalists in the American struggle for independence, and could not be moved from their position even by the adjurations of their own Presbyterian ministers.

The Germans and the Scotch Irish, largely settled in the back country where there was no political organization, no representation in the legislature, no courts, had no use for stamps and did not drink tea; nor had they any interest in the abstract principles of the rights of men to be governed and taxed only by their own elected representatives. Quite comfortable under British rule, they were often passively, if not actively, disaffected to the American cause. In South Carolina the two groups made the area between the Broad and Saluda rivers, where they were especially strong, a territory inimical to the revolutionary movement.

Those are but samples of the wide and deep cleavages of sentiment toward the Revolution, splitting section from section, race from race, one family from another, and even dividing the individual persons in the same family. Nowhere else in the American colonies were the different opinions so often, so continuously, and so ferociously expressed in action.[3]

The bitterness of feeling between the two factions was carried to extremes beyond anything ever experienced in the northern colonies, except possibly in Tryon County, New York. In Massachusetts, for example, and pretty much in all the northern colonies, the revolutionists were in the majority or, at least, were so much better organized that the Loyalists were unable to make headway and were effectively oppressed and repressed. They wore tar and feathers, rode on rails; their farms and houses were ravaged, with occasional burning or complete wreckage of their buildings; and ordinarily in the North they were unable to retaliate. In the Carolinas there were barbarous outrages and bloody murders, shootings and hangings, and they were not all on one side. The Tories were strong enough and bitter enough to hold up their end in this kind of warfare, and the patriots responded in kind.

The country was mostly wild, and its inhabitants, outside the few towns, were largely lawless men, accustomed to asserting their own rights and avenging their own wrongs without intervention of law, and to carrying on their feuds with deadly weapons and ruthlessly. The encounters between Tories and patriots were therefore violent without restraint, to the extent of downright savagery on both sides.

Before the war began, the three most southern colonies had the usual militia regiments; but the militiamen were so divided in their political opinions that they could not be relied upon to act in favor of the cause of the Revolution. In August, 1775, the legislature of North Carolina responded to the request of the Continental Congress by authorizing the enlistment of two regiments; James Moore and Robert Howe were commissioned as colonels. In April, 1776, four additional regiments were raised, and Moore and Howe were appointed brigadier generals. Four more regiments were raised later. In 1775 South Carolina first raised two infantry battalions to serve principally in the eastern section of the state and one of Rangers, or mounted infantry, for the western part. In the next year a regiment of artillery and a regiment of riflemen were added. Georgia, though much smaller in population than either of the others, responded to the call of the Congress by raising three regiments in 1776. The colonels were Lachlan McIntosh, Samuel Elbert, and James Screven. In the next year a fourth was raised, Colonel John White commanding.

These regiments were supposed to conform in numbers to the Continental standard fixed by the Congress in November, 1775—eight companies of 91 men each, officers included; but their ranks were of course, not always full. For instance, in March, 1776, McIntosh's Georgia regiment numbered only 236 men and had only 100 present for duty.

But with such a background and with passions so rampant, organized partisan warfare flourished as nowhere else in the Thirteen States. Nowhere else did this war show its true character as a civil war so plainly. Among the leaders of partisan bands on the side of the revolutionaries, three were pre-eminent. Their names became household words throughout the country and they typified the racial diversification of the people. Francis Marion was of French Huguenot stock, Thomas Sumter's parents were English-Welsh, Andrew Pickens was born of Irish parents. These three were of such outstanding importance in the southern conflict that they deserve individual notice.

Francis Marion was forty-three years old at the outbreak of the Revolution. He entered the war as a captain in one of South Carolina's first regiments in 1775, but became colonel of his own partisan regiment, a legion of combined horse and foot. Still later he had the title of brigadier general of state troops, but continued to act as a partisan leader. He was small of stature, healthy, hardy, and vigorous, brave in action but not foolhardy. His countenance, notably handsome in all its features, was impassive. He was sparing of words, abstemious in his habits, a strict disciplinarian, ever vigilant and active, fertile of stratagems and expedients that justified his nickname of Swamp Fox, quick in conception and equally swift in execution, unrelenting in the pursuit of his purposes, yet void of ruthlessness or cruelty to his victims. Henry Lee said of him that "calumny itself never charged him with violating the rights of person, property or humanity." [4] He was in all respects unexcelled as a partisan leader.

Thomas Sumter was forty-one years old in 1775, the year in which he entered the regular service as a captain in one of the South Carolina regiments, the Rangers. Later he commanded his own corps of irregulars as a brigadier general. He has been variously described: by one authority as "tall" and "vigorous"; by another as "a man of large frame, well fitted in strength of body to the toils of war"; and by a third as a small man possessed of great strength and agility.[5] In any case it is certain that he was dauntless and resolute. His bold, imperious countenance signified the arrogance of his decisions, the tenacity of his prejudices, his persistence in the execution of his own plans, and his unwillingness to subject himself to the control of another. Less scrupulous than Marion in the use of military force, "he was apt to make considerable allowances for a state of war. . . . He did not occupy his mind with a critical examination of the equity of his measures, but indiscriminately pressed forward to his end—the destruction of the enemy and the liberation of his country." [6] Not so cautious as Marion, not so much of a strategist, he was more inclined to take risks and trust to boldness of attack and the sheer fighting ability of his men. Lee likened him to "Ajax, relying more upon the fierceness of his courage than upon the results of unrelaxing vigilance and nicely adjusted combination." His fighting spirit and personal intrepidity gained for him the sobriquet of "Carolina Game Cock." [7]

Andrew Pickens was five years younger than Marion. Beginning as a captain he became a colonel and finally a brigadier general of South Carolina militia. His command, like those of the others, was always chiefly engaged in irregular operations. He was of medium height, lean, and healthy. His long, narrow face, with strongly marked features, was indicative of his strict religious character; he was an elder of the Presbyterian Church, devoted to its observances. It also indicated his rather dour habit of mind—it is said that he seldom smiled and never laughed. He was extremely guarded in conservation; "he would first take the words out of his mouth, between his fingers, and examine them before he uttered them." [8] His exploits were less spectacular than those of the other two, but his work as a partisan was not less vigorous, nor less successful.

The troops under command of these three varied from time to time. Now they were numbered in hundreds, horse and foot; now, but a dozen bold and hardy followers, white and black; sometimes they were all dragoons, fully armed and uniformed as such; sometimes they wore nondescript, even ragged, clothing and were haphazardly armed. At times they acted in concert with the Continental regulars, at others independently. They were always ready to attack a British outpost, cut off an enemy detachment, a foraging party or wagon train. If defeated, they scattered, took refuge in the swamps or forests, only to reassemble and carry on the fight as occasion served. It was such men as these that harassed the British and the Tories, encouraged the patriots, and kept the flame of resistance to tyranny alight in the South during the darkest days of the Revolution.

Among the Regulators and especially among the Highlanders, Josiah Martin, who had become governor of North Carolina after Tryon's transfer to New York, thought he saw excellent material for a force to resist the rebellious colonists and to assist an expedition under Sir Henry Clinton and Sir Peter Parker then on its way south. He obtained from the Earl of Dunmore a thousand stand of arms, which had been intended for Dunmore's proposed Indian and Ethiopian allies. On January 10, 1776, Martin issued from the sloop of war *Scorpion*, in which he had taken refuge, a flamboyant proclamation referring to the "most daring, horrid and unnatural Rebellion . . . exerted in the Province . . . by the base and insidious artifice of certain traitorous, wicked and designing men." To suppress it he proposed "to erect His Majesty's Royal standard," and did "hereby exhort, require and command . . . all His Majesty's faithful subjects . . . forthwith to repair" to it, pronouncing "all such Rebels as will not join the Royal banner, Rebels and Traitors, their lives and properties to be forfeited." [9]

On the same day he addressed a warrant to Allan Macdonald, Donald McDonald, and half a dozen McLeods, McLeans, Stewarts, Campbells, McArthurs, and sundry others not bearing Celtic names and living in the middle part of the province and in Rowan County, including former Regulators. It called on them to raise a force of Loyalists to resist the rebels and apprehend them. They were to assemble at Brunswick, opposite Wilmington, on February 15. Donald McDonald was named as brigadier general, Donald McLeod second in command. On February 5 McDonald called on all Loyalists to assemble immediately at Cross Creek (now Fayetteville) in the Scottish country, in accordance with Martin's command. All the nine Scots named in Martin's manifesto promptly appeared at Cross Creek, but only four of the 17 others. About 1,500, mostly Scots, also repaired to the standard. On the 18th they encamped four miles below Cross Creek. [10]

James Moore, colonel of the 1st North Carolina regiment, had brought his troops with five fieldpieces and a few militia to Rockfish, seven miles below Cross Creek, and entrenched his camp there. On the 18th he was joined by Colonel John Lillington, with 150 minutemen, Colonel Kennon with 200, and Colonel John Ashe with 100 volunteer rangers, making up a force of about 1,100. [11]

There ensued an odd exchange of communications. McDonald sent a flag with a copy of Martin's proclamation to Moore and called on the rebels "to join the royal standard." Moore replied with a copy of the patriots' Test Oath which, if signed by McDonald's men, would entitle them to join the Continental army. Neither accepted the other's invitation. [12]

Lieutenant Colonel Alexander Martin of the 2nd North Carolina and Lieutenant Colonel James Thackston of the 4th were on their way to join Moore. He sent them orders to possess Cross Creek, in the rear of McDonald's force. To Colonel Richard Caswell and his 800 Partisan Rangers, also on the march, he sent Lillington and Ashe as a reinforcement, with orders to hold Moore's Creek Bridge while he endeavored to circumvent the Scots and fall on their rear. [13]

There followed a series of small-scale movements complicated by the necessity of crossing several streams, the Loyalists trying to get through to the coast, the patriots trying to hold them back. On the 25th Lillington posted his men at the east end of Moore's Creek Bridge, for which the Tories were heading. The next day Caswell arrived on the west bank and threw up a small breastwork which he soon abandoned, joining the others on the east side. Lillington then took up the planks of the bridge, leaving only the log stringpieces. These two forces amounted to 1,000 men.

The Tories had decided not to avoid their opponents any longer, but to cut through them. Before dawn on February 27, they marched to the attack. General Donald McDonald had fallen ill, and Colonel Donald McLeod was in command. A picked company of 80 Scots under Captain John Campbell led the van, followed by about 1,400, and 300 riflemen brought up the rear. The Highlanders, many in plaids and kilts and others wearing homespun, were armed with rifles, broadswords, and dirks. The rifles were for the first fires, and were then to be thrown aside. The broadswords were to take the place of bayonets in the charge.

Coming to the bridge over the narrow but deep, stream, they discovered its almost impassable condition. Nevertheless, they attacked. Drums beat, bagpipes skirled, and Campbell shouted the battle-cry, "King George and the Broadswords!" Flinging away their useless rifles, grasping their swords, the vanguard started to cross. The stringers were round and slippery—the Scots afterwards said they had been greased—and many fell into the water. Others were struck down by the fire of the riflemen in the entrenchment. Campbell, McLeod, and some others got across, but the two officers and many of their followers were killed. The hot fire from the breastwork, bullets from the rifles and grape from the guns, stopped the oncoming columns. The rebels charged down the slope, some of them carrying the bridge planks, which they relaid, and started across. The Tories turned and fled in utter confusion. The next day Allan Mcdonald, some other officers, and 850 soldiers were captured. The chief officers were confined, the privates disarmed and dismissed. The wagon train, 1,500 rifles, 350 muskets, and 150 swords became the spoil of the victors.[14]

In this short fight no more than 30 of the Scots were killed or wounded and only 2 of the other side. It was a small affair, but important in that it prevented a considerable reenforcement from joining the 900 men General Clinton had landed in Brunswick County, and forced him to retire from the state. Also, it broke up the strongest united groups of Tories and forced him to at least temporary inactivity.

CHAPTER 58

Charleston

When Lord William Campbell, newly appointed royal governor of South Carolina, landed in Charleston on June 18, 1775, he was politely received, but not cordially welcomed. The militia were drawn up in formal order, but the customary *feu de joie* was lacking. When his commission was read to the populace there were no loyal cheers, nor any handclapping. "The citizens for the most part preserved a sullen silence . . . no private gentleman awaited his Excellency's landing, nor attended his parade along the streets." [1] His escort did not exceed fifteen persons, comprising his own officers and a few placemen. It was altogether a chilly affair.

His stay in Charleston lasted for three uncomfortable months, during which he had the dissatisfaction of observing continuous preparations for armed resistance to the government, the enlistment of new provincial troops, the arming of a provincial sloop, and its capture of a vessel with a cargo of gunpowder. A crisis was reached when the Council of Safety effected the seizure of Fort Johnson, on an island at the mouth of the harbor, and even discussed the capture of the governor himself. He thereupon, on September 15, took refuge on the sloop of war *Tamar,* and never again set foot on Carolina soil.

Josiah Martin, who underwent a similar mortification in North Carolina, culminating in a similar escape to the *Scorpion,* wrote from the gubernatorial mansion to the British ministry: "The people of South Carolina forget entirely their own weakness and are blustering treason; while Charleston, that is the head and heart of their boasted province, might be destroyed by a single frigate. In charity to them and in duty to my king and country,

I give it as my sincere opinion that the rod of correction cannot be spared." [2]
A little later Lord William made a similar suggestion. Now, aboard his ship
of refuge, he wrote: "Let it not be entirely forgot that the king has dominions
in this part of America. What defence can they make? Three regiments, a
proper detachment of artillery, with a couple of good frigates, some small
craft, and a bombketch, would do the whole business here." [3]

That suggestion was unnecessary, for the King himself showed before its
arrival that he had not forgot the southern provinces, and, "in charity to
them," was preparing the appropriate "rod of correction."

On January 8, 1776, Washington in Cambridge had "undoubted Intelligence of the fitting out of a Fleet at Boston and of the Imbarkation of
Troops from thence, which from the Season of the year and other Circumstances, must be destined for a Southern Expedition," very probably for
New York, though "some say Virginia but all in conjecture." [4] He, therefore, directed Major General Charles Lee—whom he esteemed to be "the
first Officer in Military knowledge and experience we have in the whole
Army" [5]—to repair to New York and "put that City into the best Posture
of Defence, which the Season and Circumstances will admit of" and disarm
such of the inhabitants of New York and Long Island as were "not only
Inemical to the Rights and Liberties of America" but also disposed to aid
"in the reduction of that Colony to Ministerial Tyranny." [6]

Charles Lee has already bulked large in our narratives. He was born in
England, probably in 1731, of a family in good social standing, his father
an officer in the army, his mother the daughter of a baronet. He was an
ensign at the age of sixteen, a captain at twenty-four, a major at thirty. He
was brevetted lieutenant colonel in 1772. He served with credit in America
in the French and Indian War under Abercromby and Amherst. In the same
conflict in Europe, the Seven Years' War, he performed a brilliant feat of
arms on October 5, 1762, when he led a night attack on a Spanish post in
Portugal, crossing the Tagus River and carrying his objective at the point
of the bayonet, with the assistance of a charge of dragoons. He was the
recipient of testimonials of bravery and good conduct from his commander
in chief, the Count de la Lippe, and from the King of Portugal.

At the close of that war he retired from the army on half-pay. Seeking
service elsewhere, he was well received by Frederick the Great and became
aide-de-camp to Stanislaus, King of Poland, in whose army he attained the
rank of major general. With the Russian army he fought the Turks in 1769.
For several years he led a restless life, wandering about Europe and becoming more and more cynical and irascible. His liberal predilections, including

an unconcealed hatred of King George III and his friends, played a part in his failure to secure advancement in the British army; and this added to the violence of his criticism of the King.

In 1773 Lee returned to America, visited various parts of the country, and vented his spleen against the ministry, taking the part of the colonists in the political agitations then prevalent. His clever wit, his caustic tongue, and his pungent oral and written attacks upon the British government gained him much favor among the American politicians. But, more especially, his military reputation was highly regarded. Military commanders of wide experience were scarce among the American opponents of the British government; indeed, there was none other than he. When the Congress on June 17 1775, appointed major generals for the army around Boston, it could not overlook the claims of Artemas Ward, in full command there until the arrival of Washington as commander in chief, and it made him first major general; then quite naturally it named Charles Lee as the second. By the resignation of Ward less than a year later, Lee obtained command next under Washington.

In person Lee was above middle height and very thin. A well known caricature of him, which depicts him in the extremest tenuity possible in a human being, is said to be the best likeness available. His countenance was not prepossessing. He had an enormous aquiline nose, a mouth whose drawn-down corners indicated a satirical, cynical, sarcastic disposition. His manner of speaking was positive and dogmatic. In the character of an experienced professional soldier amid the amateur Continental officers, he strutted unchallenged as the one general who knew what it was all about. His arrogance and pedantry in the constant use of technical military terms, of which his associates did not even know the meaning, put them all to the blush. He was careless, even slovenly, in his dress. It may be said that he was egotistic, vain, petulant, captious, ill mannered, profane, violently changeable in his opinions, excitable almost to the verge of madness, and ambitious. At this time and for long after, his adherence to the Cause was almost universally thought to be "a prodigious acquisition." [7]

Sir Henry Clinton had in fact sailed from Boston on January 20 in the 20-gun frigate *Mercury* accompanied by a transport carrying two companies of light infantry and "a few Highlanders." [8] When Lee reached New York on February 4, he found that this enemy force had come into the harbor less than two hours before, and had thrown the town "into such a convulsion as it never knew before." [9] The alarm and confusion were "truly distressing." "It is imbossable to Describ the Convusen that this City was in . . . pepel moving as fas as posseble . . . as if it was the Last Day," wrote Garish Harsin to a friend. Rev. Mr. Shewkirk noted in his diary: "There was nothing but Comotion & Confusion. Trade & publick business was at a stand. . . . A Panic & Fear seized the People." Wagons were hurriedly sought to evacuate the women and children. But Clinton assured the mayor that he did not intend to land a single soldier, that he was there merely to have a talk with Governor William Tryon, who had formerly been governor of North Carolina. He sailed on the 11th, taking with him Governors Campbell and Martin, who had in the meantime come north from their respective posts. The alarm and confusion subsided somewhat.[10]

Having now for the first time in the War of Independence a separate command, Lee entered upon his novel duties with characteristic gusto. On his way through Connecticut he had persuaded Governor Trumbull to allot to him two regiments of that province's troops, 1,200 men; and he brought them with him, much to the alarm of the would-be peaceful inhabitants of New York. They feared that such an incursion of armed men portended an attack on the British vessels then in the harbor that would provoke a general conflict, for which New York was unprepared in ammunition and defensive fortifications. Its Council of Safety, by letter to Lee then on his way, protested against the proposed intrusion.[11]

Lee assured the committee that he had no intention of attacking the British. "If the ships-of-war are quiet, I shall be quiet." He promised to leave the main body of his troops "on the western frontiers of Connecticut" and to bring into New York "a force just strong enough to secure it against any designs of the enemy" until the Continental Congress should "take measures for its permanent security." [12]

This matter having been amicably adjusted, Lee made his entrance into the town on the 4th of February, as has been stated. Acting in harmony with the committee, he planned and began to put into execution an elaborate series of defensive works on Long Island as well as Manhattan. He made a full and really excellent report to the Congress on fortifying the town and its environs, in which he took into account the difficulty, if not the actual impossibility, of permanently holding a post "almost environ'd by navigable waters . . . against a powerful sea armament" and promised no more than making it "a most advantageous field of Battle." [13] If the Congress had apprehended the full meaning of that report, and had not tried so soon after to do the impossible, one of the great disasters of the war would have been averted.

But Lee was not to complete the work thus begun. The Congress, after directing him on February 17 to repair to Canada and relieve Schuyler of his command, changed its mind and ordered him to take command of the newly erected Southern Department, comprising Virginia, the Carolinas, and Georgia.[14] His selection to take on the defense of the southern colonies, now seen to be menaced by Clinton, was generally approved; but he predicted the direst consequences for New York unless the Congress or Washington acted decisively: "The instant I leave it," he wrote to Washington, "I conclude the Provincial Congress and the inhabitants will relapse into their former hystericks; the men-of-war, and Mr. Tryon, will return to their old stations at the wharves, and the first regiments who arrive from England will take quiet possession of the town and Long-Island." [15]

On March 7, Lee left New York for Charleston. En route he stopped in the governor's palace at Williamsburg, Virginia, where he learned that Clinton had put in at Norfolk and was holding conferences with Dunmore, the evicted governor. Soon he learned also that Clinton's little force was not the "rod of correction" which the King had directed to be prepared for his recalcitrant subjects in the southern provinces, that it was to be a much bigger stick indeed.

The revelation came through an intercepted letter.

Captain James Barron, commanding a vessel fitted out at Hampton to prey upon enemy commerce in the Chesapeake, found in the mails aboard a seized vessel a letter dated December 23, 1775, from Lord George Germain to Governor Robert Eden of Maryland. It appeared that His Majesty, "being determined, in concurrence with Parliament, to pursue the most vigorous measures for reducing his rebellious subjects in North America to obedience," had organized "an armament, consisting of seven regiments and a fleet of frigates and small ships," which was at that time "in readiness to proceed to the Southern Colonies . . . in the first place to North Carolina, and from thence either to South Carolina or Virginia as circumstances . . . shall permit." [16]

As a result of this discovery "the curtain" was, in the words of Lee, "in a great measure, drawn up." Yet not altogether, for, while the destination of the hostile fleet was North Carolina and, without doubt, that colony's principal harbor, the mouth of the Cape Fear River, the point of actual attack was not disclosed. It might be in any one of the three southern provinces. This uncertainty held him momentarily at Williamsburg, since Virginia might be the objective.[17]

Although the intercepted letter said that the expedition was "in readiness to proceed," it did not actually proceed for almost two months. On February 13, 1776, an impressive armada put out from Cork under command of

Admiral Sir Peter Parker. It comprised the 50-gun flagship *Bristol*, the 28-gun frigates *Active*, *Actaeon*, *Solebay*, and *Syren*, the frigate *Sphynx* carrying 20 guns, the *Friendship* with 22, the sloop *Ranger* with 8, the schooner *St. Lawrence* with 6, and the bomb ketch *Thunder* mounting 6 guns and 2 mortars.[18] It convoyed a fleet of more than thirty transports carrying about 2,500 troops—the 15th, 28th, 33rd, 37th, 54th, and 57th regiments and seven companies of the 46th—besides the usual complement of marines and seamen. General Lord Cornwallis commanded the military. Five days out from Cork, the fleet met violent adverse gales and was scattered. Some of the vessels were driven back to Cork, others found refuge at Plymouth and Portsmouth. The first vessels arrived at Cape Fear on April 18, and it was not until May 3 that the whole fleet, minus a few of the smaller vessels, reassembled there.[19]

Then began a discussion as to the point of attack. The original purpose seems to have been to invade North Carolina, set up the King's standard at Cross Creek, invite the Loyalists of that region to repair to it, and reestablish the royal government there. But the decisive defeat of the North Carolina Tories at Moore's Creek Bridge on February 27 had so diminished their ardor that no reliance could be placed on them.[20] Governor Dunmore had pleaded with Clinton to recover Virginia for him, and Clinton was so inclined. But Governor Campbell was equally insistent that South Carolina deserved the honor. Charleston was the most important port south of Philadelphia. Its commerce was of great aid to the American cause in the South. Its defensive works were unfinished. These arguments prevailed, and on May 30 the fleet again put to sea.[21]

Meanwhile, Lee had left Williamsburg for Wilmington, North Carolina. From that town he wrote on June 1 that the fleet had sailed—whether northward or southward, he could not tell. The people in Wilmington were "all of the opinion that Charlestown was their object; for my own part I do not see on what they ground their opinion." He would set out for that town on the morrow, "but at the same time [I] confess I know not whether I shall go to or from the enemy." [22] On his arrival at Charleston early in June, he learned that he had come in the right direction. The fleet dropped anchor almost simultaneously a short distance off Charleston bar. Lee's "presence gave us great spirits," says Colonel William Moultrie in his memoirs, "as he was known to be an able, brave, and experienced officer, though hasty and rough in his manners, which the officers could not reconcile themselves to at first: it was thought by many that his coming among us was equal to a reinforcement of 1000 men, and I believe it was." [23]

Low, sandy islands fringe the South Carolina coast, separated from the mainland and from each other by narrow inlets or creeks lined with swamps which are interlaced with other small creeks. In 1776 they were largely covered with palmetto trees, thickets of myrtle and other low shrubs, interspersed with occasional live oaks. Between James Island on the south and Sullivan's on the north was the entrance to Charleston harbor, the city being about six miles within the entrance. On James Island was Fort Johnson, which had been seized by the troops of the province in September and held against the royal governor ever since. It mounted twenty guns, 18- and 25-pounders. On the same island, nearer the town, was a battery of twelve heavy guns.

Sullivan's Island was about four miles long; and at high tide, when the wide swamps towards the mainland were under water, the fast ground was less than a mile wide. North of it lay Long Island, and between them was a narrow inlet called the Breach. Long Island was not fortified; but a small battery had been set up at Haddrell's Point, on the mainland below the south end of Sullivan's Island.

There were other fortifications about the town—batteries, flèches, and "bastions," distributed along and behind the waterfront—which had no part in the battle and hence need not be particularly described. In the town stores and warehouses along the wharves were torn down to clear the way for the fire from some of the earthworks in their rear.

Near the southern end of Sullivan's Island, where it swung around parallel with the curving shore of the mainland, was the principal fortification guarding the entrance to the harbor. Fort Sullivan had been planned, and construction had been begun, in January; but it was yet no more than half built.

The plan was for a square redoubt with a long, pointed bastion at each angle. So far as it was completed, it was built of two parallel walls of palmetto logs laid upon one another, the two rows tied together at intervals with logs dovetailed and bolted at each end. The space between the lines of logs, sixteen feet wide, was filled with sand. There were proper embrasures for cannon all along its sides and in its bastions, the merlons, or spaces between them, being especially strengthened. Inside, platforms for the guns were supported on brick pillars, the walls rising ten feet above them.

At the time of the attack upon it, only the front wall, toward the sea, its two bastions, and the wall on the southerly side, with the gun platforms, had been finished. The other two walls and the two rear bastions had been built to a height of no more than seven feet. Thus it was practically open and undefended in the rear and on the northerly side.

Along the front were mounted six 24-pounders and three 18-pounders. Along the southerly side were six guns, 9- and 12-pounders. In each bastion were five guns, ranging from 9 to 26 pounds.

Somewhat to protect its undefended rear, a traverse—that is to say, a simple line of earthen breastworks—was drawn across from one side of the enclosure to the other, and epaulements, or similar earthworks, had been hastily erected outside the fort, extending from the rear bastions to right and left. Three 12-pounders were mounted in each of these. Thus the front, including the two breastworks and excluding four guns on the inner side of each bastion, showed twenty-one guns to an enemy directly before it, while the southerly side showed only nine—six in the wall and three in the breastwork on that side.

To hold these outer defenses and the town itself, there were certain regiments of provincial troops. These had been first raised in 1775 to give the province a force independent of the militia—who, as has been said, were so divided in their attitude towards the British government as to be unreliable in case of conflict with the King's troops. The new regiments were to be "officered by gentlemen"; the rank and file, "enlisted for hire." At this time, there were six such regiments: the 1st Regiment of Foot under Colonel Christopher Gadsden and Lieutenant Colonel Charles Cotesworth Pinckney; the 2nd under Colonel William Moultrie, Lieutenant Colonel Isaac Motte, and Major Francis Marion; the 3rd under Lieutenant Colonel William Thompson; a regiment of artillery commanded by Lieutenant Owen Roberts; the 1st Rifle Regiment under Colonel Isaac Huger, and the 2nd under Lieutenant Colonel Thomas Sumter. Three volunteer artillery companies, not on the regular establishment, served during the coming battle. In all these numbered about 2,000 men.[24]

To them were added three Continental regiments: two from North Carolina numbering 1,400 rank and file, and one of 500 from Virginia which had been ordered down by Lee. The Virginians were commanded by that gallant fighting man, Colonel Peter Muhlenberg. The Charleston militia numbered 700. The rural militia responded to a call by Governor John Rutledge to the number of nearly 2,000, making a total defensive force of more than 6,500. However, but a few hundreds had any part in the coming fight.

The principal defense, the redoubt known as Fort Sullivan, was manned by Colonel Moultrie's 2nd South Carolina Regiment, 413 men, and the 4th Artillery, 22 men. The 1st South Carolina, 380 men under Colonel Gadsden, and a small detachment of artillerists held Fort Johnson. In the other battery on James Island, Captain Thomas Pinckney with a company from Gadsden's regiment was stationed. The positions of the rest, except the 3rd South Carolina and certain other troops, need not be described as they were mere onlookers of the conflict.

Of all these troops, only those from Virginia and North Carolina were in the Continental army, and therefore rightly under Lee. The South Carolina regiments were commanded only by Governor John Rutledge until the following September, when they were taken into the Continental line. Lee immediately assumed command of all of them, and began to issue orders or requests. A difficult situation at once developed, for some South Carolinians refused to follow his directions. It might have had serious consequences had not the governor at once issued a general order vesting the command of "the Regular forces and Militia of this Colony . . . in Major General Lee, orders issued by him are to be obeyed." [25]

The British fleet arrived off Charleston on the 4th of June, but many days elapsed before it could go into action. It was first necessary to take soundings, and to find a channel past the bar and buoy it. By the 7th the frigates and most of the transports had got across and anchored in good ground at Five Fathom Hole. On the 9th Clinton landed 500 men on Long Island, menacing Sullivan's Island. Lee detached Lieutenant Colonel Thompson's 3rd Regiment of South Carolina Rangers (300 in number), about 200 North Carolina Continentals under Lieutenant Colonel Thomas Clark, 200 South Carolinians under Captain Daniel Horry, the Raccoon Company of 50 riflemen, and a small corps of militia—780 in all—and directed them to proceed to Long Island and attack. Soon afterward, however, he withdrew the order to attack. In the course of the battle Thompson was reenforced by Muhlenberg's Virginians.[26]

The Breach was a peculiar body of water. When in the course of the battle the 15th Regiment, the light infantry, and the grenadiers tried to cross it their boats ran aground on shallows only a foot and a half deep: but in wading they plumped into great holes seven feet deep. There was simply no practicable way for troops to get from Long Island to Sullivan's. So, though the British force on land had been increased on the 10th to upwards of 2,500 men, they could not get at Thompson, and Thompson could not get at them, except for a sporadic interchange of harmless gunfire between a battery of palmetto logs, erected by the Americans and armed with an 18-pounder and a 6-pounder fieldpiece, and two small British earthworks, one for mortars and the other for guns. These two forces simply held each other in check and had no other part in the battle. Clinton perforce left to Parker "the glory of being defeated alone." [27]

For more than two weeks, Admira Parker was busy in getting his warships over the bar. He had to lighten the *Bristol* and another 50-gun ship. the *Experiment,* which had joined him, by removing their guns, before they could be got across. At last, on the 26th, they were all inside the bar and ready for action.[28]

On the morning of the 28th the bomb ketch *Thunder,* covered by the 22-gun *Friendship,* anchored a mile and a half from the fort and opened fire. The *Active,* the *Solebay,* the *Bristol,* and the *Experiment* came within four hundred yards of the shore opposite the fort and dropped anchor with springs on their cables, in line broadside to the fort, at wide intervals. Behind them in a second line, spaced opposite the intervals in the first, the *Syren,* the *Actaeon,* and the *Sphynx* were anchored. As each came into position, it began to fire. When all were at their stations more than a hundred guns poured their metal upon the half-built fort of palmetto logs and sand, while the *Thunder* rained 10-inch shells upon it. Twenty-one guns responded to that "furious and incessant cannonade." [29] There was but little powder in the fort, not more than thirty-five rounds for each of the twenty-one guns that could be brought to bear on the ships. The artillerists laid their guns with care and without haste, striving for accuracy of aim and economy of ammunition. "Their artillery was surprisingly well served," wrote a surgeon in the fleet. The fire "was slow, but decisive indeed; they were very cool and took care not to fire except their guns were exceedingly well directed." [30]

For an hour the terrific thunder of great guns and small in this unequal combat was unabated. Then the second line, the *Actaeon, Syren,* and *Sphynx,* lifted anchor and drew around the lower end of the island towards a position whence they could enfilade the gun platforms along the seaward face of the fort, and at the same time bring their guns to bear upon the Cove behind that end of the island across which was the garrison's only line of retreat. To escape the fort's guns in this maneuver, they stood away to the south towards a shoal, the Middle Ground. Their circuit was too wide, and all three ran aground. The *Actaeon* and the *Sphynx* fouled each other, the *Sphynx* losing her bowsprit. The *Syren* and the *Sphynx* finally got off and had to withdraw for repairs. The *Actaeon* was immovable.

Meanwhile, the bombardment continued, all through the afternoon. The *Thunder,* trying to fire effectively at too long range, overcharged her mortars and shattered their beds. She had to pull away, but her companion the *Friendship* joined the fighting line, and the *Syren* again went into action.

The amount of metal thrown against that flimsy fort apparently should have been enough to blast it to pieces; and it would have done so had the

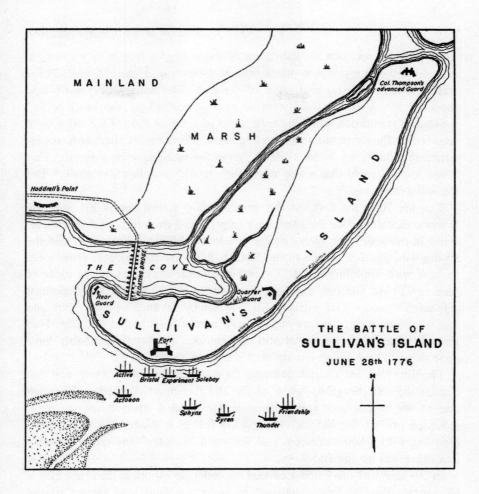

MAINLAND

MARSH

Haddrell's Point

THE   COVE

Rear
Guard

FLOATING BRIDGE

Quarter
Guard

SULLIVAN'S

ISLAND

Col. Thompson's
advanced Guard

Fort

Active

Bristol   Experiment Soleboy

Actaeon

Sphynx

Syren

Thunder

Friendship

THE BATTLE OF
SULLIVAN'S ISLAND
JUNE 28th 1776

N

walls been of oak. But the substance of the palmetto tree is so porous, so soft, and so spongy that it offers little resistance to a cannon ball. There was no splintering, no shattering of the logs. The balls simply sank into them as into a sponge, and were as gently received by the sand behind the logs. Yet at times, when the broadsides of three or four of the ships were received at the same moment, the combined blows shook the whole super-structure. According to Moultrie, it "gave the merlons such a tremor, that I was apprehensive that a few more such would tumble them down." But the walls stood fast.[31]

The fire from the fort, on the contrary, did almost incredible damage. It was concentrated on the two larger ships, the *Bristol* and the *Experiment*. Early in the action the spring on the *Bristol*'s cable was shot away, and she swung with the tide end on to the fort. Its guns raked her decks from stern to bow with appalling effect. Twice her quarter-deck was swept clear of men except the admiral, and he was wounded.[32] The top of her mainmast was carried away. Her mizzenmast was hit by seven 32-pound shot and had to be cut away. Seventy of the fort's cannonballs hulled the ship. Had the sea been rough instead of still and smooth, she would probably have gone down. The *Experiment* suffered almost as much.

The fort did not escape damage. Its flagstaff was shot away and fell outside the wall. Sergeant Jasper of the 2nd Regiment climbed out through one of the embrasures and rescued it. He fixed it upon a sponge staff, mounted one of the bastions, and set it firmly in place. Once more the blue flag with a white crescent and the word "Liberty" showed the enemy that there was no surrender.[33]

In the midst of the battle Lee sent an order to Moultrie directing him if his ammunition became exhausted to spike his guns and retreat to the mainland. The ammunition was running low. After three o'clock Moultrie reduced the fire of his guns to ten-minute intervals. Gradually it dwindled to silence, and for more than an hour no shot was fired. Then Lee sent 700 pounds of powder to him, and a slow but steady fire was resumed.

Lee came over to see how things were going. He afterwards wrote: "The behaviour of the garrison, both men and officers, with Colonel Moultrie at their head, I confess astonished me. It was brave to the last degree. I had no idea that so much coolness and intrepidity could be displayed by a collec-tion of raw recruits." [34]

The bombardment of the fort continued until sunset, when it slackened. At half past nine the fire ceased on both sides. At eleven the ships "began to steal away—they made no piping, nor waited to heave up their anchors, but slipped their cables." [35] They anchored again at the Five Fathom Hole.

The morning found the *Actaeon* still aground. She was set afire by her crew, who rowed away to rejoin the fleet.

The losses in the British fleet were heavy, 64 men killed and 131 wounded. Of these casualties, 111 occurred on the *Bristol* and 79 on the *Experiment,* indicating the concentration of the Americans' fire on those two capital ships. Among the officers, Captain John Morris of the *Bristol* was killed, and Captain Alexander Scott of the *Experiment* lost his right arm. Lord William Campbell, who had volunteered to fight some of the *Bristol*'s guns, received a wound from which he died two years later. Among the Americans, 12 were killed, 5 died of their wounds, and 20 others were wounded. The weight of the fire from the fleet is indicated by the fact that 7,000 cannon balls were gathered on the island after the engagement. The British had expended 34,000 pounds of powder, the Americans 4,766 pounds.[36]

Clinton's troops lingered in their camp on Long Island for three weeks, entirely inactive, before they were embarked in transports for New York under the convoy of the *Solebay.* The rest of the fighting ships remained some time longer at anchor, repairing their damages.

From the first, Lee had been firmly of the opinion that the fort on Sullivan's Island was untenable. He declared that "it could not hold out half an hour and that the [gun] platform was but a slaughtering stage." He wanted to abandon the island entirely, and establish his main defenses on the mainland at Haddrell's Point. This would have left little Fort Johnson on James Island as the only defense against a close approach to the town by the ships, which, once it was silenced, could have taken a position close to that island, within half a mile of the town, and a full mile from Haddrell's Point. As Lee himself declared that four hundred yards was the maximum effective range for his guns, the ships would have then been quite safe from the Haddrell battery. He nevertheless would have effected the abandonment of Sullivan's Island if Governor Rutledge and his advisers had not insisted upon defending it.[37]

Lee had tried to provide a means of retreat from the fort to Haddrell's Point. He wanted a bridge built across the Cove between the two. As the Cove was a mile wide, there was neither time nor material to build such a bridge. Nevertheless, he stretched across the Cove a double line of planks, supported by boats and empty hogsheads. Two hundred men started to cross on it. It sank under them when they were halfway over. He was then obliged to rely on boats as a means of retreat.[38]

The stubborn insistence of Governor Rutledge and Colonel Moultrie upon holding the fort was responsible for the battle and the victory. Yet it must be said that Lee's judgment was not at fault, and that the governor and the colonel were probably in the wrong. No one could possibly have foreseen the accident that enabled the Americans to win—the grounding of the *Actaeon*, the *Syren*, and the *Sphynx* on the Middle Ground. There was plenty of water between that shoal and the southern end of Sullivan's Island to permit the three vessels to come to anchor in the undefended rear of the fort and then to blast the garrison out of its defenses. But for that accident, the whole tide of the battle might have been turned against the Americans. But that is the way with battles. In any case, the Americans had won a victory of the first importance that freed the entire lower south from the King's troops for more than two years. The credit belongs particularly to Rutledge, to Moultrie, and to Lee, who exhibited great energy in a situation where energy was badly needed. He saw to it that Fort Sullivan was in readiness. Had the British taken it, they would have had no easy task in capturing Charleston, for he was prepared to make an obstinate defense of the city.

While the fleet battered uselessly at Fort Sullivan the British were losing allies in the south, the Cherokee warriors. The Cherokees entered the war in 1776 because of long-standing grievances against the colonists. But their attacks on the frontiers of the Carolinas, injurious though they were, were not synchronized with British movements and had little bearing on the war in the south in general. Virginia, the Carolinas, and Georgia promptly sent militia and rangers into their country, which was laid waste. When the Cherokees resumed hostilities in 1779 their principal towns were again put to the torch. The Cherokees remained vexatious until the end of the war, but their power, weakened in the Cherokee War of 1760–1761, was now broken. Since the Catawba tribe aided the Americans, and since the warlike Creeks were mostly neutral until the last years of the war, the southern frontier did not suffer so much as Kentucky. When the Creeks did finally ally themselves with the British they were able to do little, especially since the appearance of the Spanish in strength at Mobile and Pensacola gave them much to think about. The forces of Bernardo de Gálvez on the shores of the Gulf of Mexico probably relieved the pressure upon the frontiers of Georgia and South Carolina in 1780 and thereafter. The entrance of Spain into the war in 1779 no doubt gave large indirect benefits to the American cause in the south.

CHAPTER 59

Georgia

The gallant defense of Charleston, ending in a brilliant victory for the Americans, so discouraged the British government that no further serious military operations were attempted in the south until after the British reverses in the north of 1777–1778. Thirty-four Continental regiments, in all, were raised in the four southern states; many of them went north, joined Washington, and were of great service in the operations around Philadelphia. But the failure of the British efforts of 1777 and 1778 in the north to produce results that promised finality and permanence turned the attention of the government again to the south. When Clinton evacuated Philadelphia in June, 1778, he was under orders to discontinue offensive operations in the north, send 3,000 men to Georgia or Florida, and, in the following winter, to attempt the conquest of South Carolina, which would be "comparatively easy." [1]

On November 27, 1778, Lieutenant Colonel Archibald Campbell set sail from Sandy Hook with a fleet of transports convoyed by a squadron of war vessels under command of Commodore Hyde Parker; and on December 23 he arrived at Tybee Island at the mouth of the Savannah River, fifteen miles below the town of Savannah. General Augustine Prevost, commanding the British forces in East Florida, had orders to join in the reduction of the town; but he had not come up, and so Campbell undertook the task alone.

General Robert Howe, in command of an American southern army, was then at Sunbury, about thirty miles from Savannah. With 700 Continentals and 150 militia he marched to oppose the invaders.

Campbell brought his transports, guarded by the man-of-war *Vigilant,* the *Comet* galley, the armed brig *Keppel,* and the sloop of war *Greenwich* up the river to Girardeau's plantation, the first hard ground. He was opposed by fire from two small American galleys, but a single shot from the *Vigilant* drove them away, and he made an unopposed landing. His force comprised the 71st Regiment, the Hessian regiments of Woellwarth and Wissenbach, four Tory battalions, and a detachment of artillery—about 3,500 rank and file in all.

From the landing place a narrow causeway led through rice swamps to Girardeau's house and the main road to Savannah. Howe posted Captain John Carraway Smith with 50 South Carolina Continentals to oppose Campbell at that point. The British advance was led by Captain Cameron, with the light infantry, the New York Volunteers, and the first battalion of the 71st. Smith's men opened a smart fire of muskets, killing Cameron and two privates of the 71st and wounding five others; but the onward rush of the enemy's van drove them back, and they retired to the main American force.

Savannah had been fortified some twenty years before, but the defenses had fallen in ruins and were not tenable. Howe therefore stationed his troops on the road from Girardeau's, a half-mile east of the town. His right, composed of two South Carolina Continental regiments, the 1st Rifles under Colonel Isaac Huger, and the 3rd Rangers under Lieutenant Colonel William Thompson, extended from the road to a wooded swamp. It was supported by a hundred Georgia riflemen, militia, under Colonel George Walton in some buildings, and by one fieldpiece. The left was composed entirely of Georgia militia under Colonel Samuel Elbert. Its flank also rested on a swamp, and it had one fieldpiece. In the center, on the road, two guns were placed. A trench was dug across the road in front of the American line from one swamp to the other.

With the flanks of the line thus protected by swamps, it seemed that the British would have to make a frontal attack. But Campbell had picked up an aged Negro, one Quamino Dolly, and learned from him that there was a "private way" through the swamp on the American right by which its rear could be gained. He advanced to a point on the road where an intervening slight rise of the ground concealed his force from the Americans. He then proceeded to demonstrate against their left in a feint to cover his real purpose, which was to send Sir James Baird with his light infantry, followed by Turnbull's New York Volunteers, around their right by the way through the swamp.

Meanwhile the American artillery had been firing upon Campbell's main force, but had provoked no reply. The Americans learned of the enemy's intentions when Baird's force fell upon the rear of the Georgia militia on their extreme right and routed them. At the sound of the fire in that quarter Campbell ran his guns up on the concealing rise of ground and opened fire on Huger and Thompson. This was immediately followed by a charge of the whole British force. Attacked in front and rear, the American line broke and fled in confusion under heavy fire. The right managed to get away in large part over a causeway through the swamp, but the Georgia militia on the left had no such means of escape. Taking to the rice-swamp, they had to cross a deep creek, in which many were drowned.

The British pressed on into the town. Commodore Parker brought the *Comet* galley up to it and took possession of three ships, three brigs, and eight smaller vessels at its wharves. The houses of those regarded as rebels were looted, and many of the owners were captured. The American loss in this affair was heavy: 83 killed in the battle or drowned in the retreat; 453 captured, along with 48 cannon, 23 mortars, and 94 barrels of powder. On the British side only 3 were killed and 10 wounded.

The remains of Howe's disorganized force retreated eight miles to Cherokee Hill, and thence to South Carolina, leaving Georgia to its fate. Prevost, coming up from Florida, took the town of Sunbury, and Campbell took Augusta with little difficulty early in January. Between Campbell and Prevost, the state of Georgia was then in almost complete subjection. Campbell "acted with great policy, in securing the submission of the inhabitants." [2] They "flocked by hundreds to the King's officers, and made their peace at the expense of their patriotism." [3] "He not only extirpated military opposition, but subverted for some time every trace of republican government, and paved the way for the re-establishment of a royal legislature. Georgia . . . was the only state of the union, in which after the declaration of independence, a legislative body was convened under the authority of the crown of Great-Britain." [4] It "soon became one of the most loyal of His Majesty's possessions." [5]

Howe was greatly blamed for this defeat. It was charged that not only might he have made a successful stand on the bluff at Girardeau's plantation against the landing of the enemy, but he knew of that circumventing road through the swamp and neglected to guard it. A court of inquiry absolved him of blame, but "his military reputation never recovered from the shadow cast upon it by the loss of the capital of Georgia." [6]

Major General Benjamin Lincoln of Massachusetts had been appointed by the Congress in September, 1778, to command the Southern Department and had taken post at Purysburg on the South Carolina side of the Savannah River about fifteen miles above Savannah. Having been joined by the remains of Howe's force, he had 3,639 men, but only 1,121 were Continental troops; the rest were "inexperienced, undisciplined and restless militia." Even among the Continentals few had seen service. Of his whole force only 2,428 were reported fit for duty. Across the river, in Georgia, General Prevost had perhaps 3,000 troops, besides an unknown number of Tory irregulars.

Both sides desired to cross the river, but it was so wide and deep and was bordered by such extensive swamps that neither dared attempt a crossing in force. With the aid of the navy, however, Prevost succeeded in sending Major Gardiner across with two companies of the 20th and one of the 16th, about 200 men, to take possession of Port Royal Island at the mouth of the Broad River, about thirty miles behind Purysburg. Lincoln sent General William Moultrie to arouse the militia in that district.

Moultrie was successful in his endeavor. With 300 of the Charleston militia, 10 Continentals, and three fieldpieces, he occupied the town of Beaufort on the island, on February 3, 1779. He formed his troops on both sides of the road by which Gardiner was advancing, and their single gun opened on Gardiner's troops with considerable effect. Although the British had some shelter in a wood, while the American troops were on open ground, the militia behaved well. The enemy's only gun, a howitzer, was hit and dismounted early in the action, giving Moultrie an advantage. For three-quarters of an hour the two forces fought a hot little battle. Then the Americans' ammunition gave out, and Moultrie ordered a withdrawal, only to discover that Gardiner's force was already in retreat. A small body of American light horse pursued it and took a few prisoners.

The Americans lost 8 killed and 22 wounded. The British loss was unascertained, but was comparatively heavy. A captured British lieutenant was quoted as saying that it was not less than half of their whole number, which is very improbable. This little affair sufficed for Prevost; he made no further attempt upon South Carolina at the time.[7]

The complete subjection of Georgia had aroused the Tories in the back country of that state and of South Carolina. Many were inclined to join Campbell at Augusta. To stimulate such interest, he sent Lieutenant Colonel John Hamilton with 200 mounted Tory partisans, to the back country of Georgia. Hamilton was a man of worth, wealth, and high social position, a typical Scottish Highlander and a veteran of Culloden, very influential among his own people, yet highly respected by his opponents. Aroused by his progress, in spite of well meant but ineffectual opposition, Colonel Boyd, a North Carolina Tory, raised a force of 700 adherents to the crown, chiefly Scotsmen, and started for Georgia to join him.

Boyd's men committed depredations upon the inhabitants of the country he passed through; "their general complexion was that of a plundering bandetti, more solicitous for booty than for the honour and interest of their royal master." [8] Colonel Andrew Pickens of South Carolina assembled a force of militia of that state and was joined by Captain John Dooley with a number of Georgians, making up about 300 men. They crossed into Georgia, leaving Captain Anderson with a small party at Cherokee Ford to oppose Boyd's crossing there.

Anderson was driven back, and Boyd's force crossed the river. Pickens thereupon set out in pursuit and took Boyd unawares at Kettle Creek, where his men were engaged in slaughtering a herd of stolen cattle. Their horses were turned out to graze, and their camp was in disorder when Pickens, having deployed his men in line, himself in the center, Dooley on the right, and Lieutenant Colonel Thomas Clark on the left, swept down upon it. The two wings swung around the camp and attacked it simultaneously with the center.

Boyd was an able soldier. He pulled his men together and fell back, disputing the approach with much obstinacy for nearly an hour. But, after he had been mortally wounded, more than 40 of his men killed, many more wounded, and 75 captured, his force broke and scattered—300 joining Campbell at Augusta and the rest fleeing to their homes. The patriots lost 9 killed and 23 wounded.

The prisoners were carried to South Carolina. There, they were tried on charges of treason, and 70 were condemned to death. All except five were pardoned, but these, deemed to be ringleaders, "to the shame of Southern justice and the horror of mankind, were hung." [9]

Beaufort and Kettle Creek raised the spirits of the rebels in the same degree as the conquest of Georgia had elevated those of the Tories. The militia flocked to Lincoln's camp at Purysburg in such numbers that his force was doubled, and he was emboldened to try to recover the lost state. For this purpose he sent General Andrew Williamson of Georgia with 1,200 men to the eastern bank of the Savannah River opposite Augusta, General Griffith Rutherford with 800 to the Black Swamp, and General John Ashe with 1,400 North Carolina militia and about 100 Georgia continentals, under Colonel Elbert, to Briar Creek in Georgia, south of Augusta.

When Ashe neared Williamson's post Campbell evacuated Augusta and

started with its garrison towards Savannah. Ashe crossed the Savannah
River and pursued the retreating enemy, but Campbell crossed Briar Creek
and destroyed the bridge ahead of him. Ashe reached that stream on February 27, his force having been increased by 200 light-horse militia, and
started to rebuild the bridge. General Prevost, disturbed by this incursion,
devised a plan to defeat it.

He sent Major Macpherson with the 1st battalion of the 71st Regiment,
some Tory irregulars, and two fieldpieces to the south bank of the creek
facing the rebels, while Lieutenant Colonel Mark Prevost with the 2nd
battalian of the 71st, Baird's light infantry, three companies of grenadiers
of the 60th Regiment, a troop of Provincial light horse, and 150 Tory
militia—about 900 in all—made a circuit of fifty miles to cross the creek
above Ashe's camp and attack it in the rear.

Although reconnoitering parties of the enemy had been seen in the
afternoon of March 2 and in the following morning, Ashe took no steps to
meet the attack, except to form his troops in column with Colonel Elbert's
Continentals in front. At Lieutenant Colonel Prevost's approach, Elbert
advanced a hundred yards and opened fire. At this alarm, the militia faced
about and ran without firing a shot. The Continentals continued firing for
a few minutes. Then, finding themselves deserted, they also broke and fled
in disorder. Most of the fugitives threw down their arms and plunged into
the swamp. In trying to cross the river, many were drowned.

Between 150 and 200 having lost their lives, either in the brief action or
by drowning, the catastrophe was completed by the capture of 11 officers
including Elbert, and 162 noncommissioned officers and privates. Of those
who escaped, not more than 450 rejoined the army; the rest returned to
their homes.[10] Seven cannon, almost all the small-arms, the Americans'
colors and all their ammunition and baggage were taken by General
Prevost. The British lost 5 killed and 11 wounded. "This brilliant action
by the British destroyed the possibility of recovering Georgia at that time."

The possession of Georgia by the British, and General Prevost's hostile
activities, aroused apprehensions of imminent danger among the South
Carolinians. Governor Rutledge received almost dictatorial power. He
called out the militia in greater numbers than ever before. General Moultrie,
now in command at Purysburg and the Black Swamp, was strengthened to
1,000 men. Lincoln's main army was also reenforced; he had in all about
4,000 men, besides those with Moultrie. With this force, he felt able to
take the offensive.

On April 23, 1779, Lincoln crossed the Savannah River and marched towards Augusta. To counter this movement, Prevost crossed the river on April 29 into South Carolina, at Purysburg, with 2,500 men. Lieutenant Colonel Alexander McIntosh held that post with the 2nd and 5th South Carolina Continentals, about 220 men. At Prevost's approach he retired to join Moultrie at the Black Swamp. Prevost pursued him. Moultrie had withdrawn from the Swamp to Coosahatchie Bridge, a few miles in his rear. Thence, followed by Prevost, he retreated by successive stages marked by rear-guard skirmishes, to Charleston, where "he was received with open arms by the terrified inhabitants." [11] A number of militia from Orangeburg came in, and 300 light infantry sent back in haste by Lincoln were added to Moultrie's force, also the infantry of Pulaski's Legion, 80 men, while Lincoln, having occupied evacuated Augusta, was coming on with his main army by forced marches.

Prevost's plan had been merely to draw Lincoln back from Georgia, but now, encouraged by Moultrie's retreat and by the general panic among the inhabitants along his route, he decided to push on for Charleston. Leaving the larger part of his troops on the south side of the Ashley River, he crossed that stream and approached the town with 900 men.

Count Pulaski sallied out to meet him. Posting his men behind some slight earthworks, he rode forward to where a party of light horse was skirmishing with Prevost's advance. His intent was to draw the British van within range of his ambuscade. But his men, too eager for combat, left their works and followed him. The British van attacked them and drove them back into the town.

The neck of land between Charleston and the mainland, hitherto undefended, had been hastily but rather effectively fortified while Prevost was pursuing Moultrie, and all the houses that would afford cover for an attack on that side had been burnt. This presented an unexpected obstacle to Prevost, and he hesitated to attack. To gain time for Lincoln's army to arrive, Moultrie entered into correspondence with the British general, discussing terms for surrender, but, after two days' delay, notified him that he had decided to fight.

Prevost had intercepted a letter from Lincoln telling of his return to South Carolina. Fearful of being caught between two fires, he withdraw his troops in the night of May 12 to James Island, about two miles south of the town, then to the adjoining Johns Island. On the mainland at Stono Ferry, he erected fortifications—three strong redoubts with a heavy abatis in front. In their rear a bridge of boats connected the works with the island. Then, oddly enough, on June 16, he began to withdraw his troops in boats to Savannah, finally leaving only one battalion of the 71st, the Hessian von

Trumbach Regiment, a detachment of artillery, and some Tory militia, 900 in all, Lieutenant Colonel Maitland in command.

Lincoln had between 6,000 and 7,000 men in Charleston. He quite naturally saw his opportunity for a stroke. After midnight of the morning of June 20, with 1,200 men, he advanced against the enemy's lines. General Jethro Sumner commanded the right wing made up of North and South Carolina militia, with two fieldpieces; General Isaac Huger commanded the left, Continental troops with four guns; Colonel the Marquis de Malmedy and Lieutenant Colonel John Henderson with two companies of light infantry covered the flanks; and a force of Virginia militia with two guns was the reserve. Certain detachments of horsemen on the Virginian's right guarded the rear.

Advancing in line through a dense growth of pine saplings, the right wing was delayed, and Henderson's light infantry, covering the left wing, made the first contact with the enemy, two companies of the 71st Highlanders posted in advance of the British lines. Though greatly inferior in numbers, the Scotsmen stood fast. Henderson attacked with the bayonet, and a furious hand-to-hand fight ensued. With obstinate bravery the intrepid Highlanders maintained their ground until all but 11 of them had fallen.

Three hundred yards from the British lines, the main body of the Americans halted and for an hour exchanged cannon and musket fire with their opponents. The Hessian regiment gave way, and the Americans then pressed forward against the abatis. There their left was stopped by a shift of part of the 71st to that side. The Hessians were rallied and brought into action. Now Moultrie had word of British reenforcements coming over from Johns Island and thought it best to retire. The retreat, though pursued by the enemy, was made in good order, Colonel Andrew Pickens with some light infantry effectively covering the rear.

The American loss was heavy, 146 killed or wounded, and 155 missing. The British lost 3 officers and 23 men killed, 10 officers and 93 men wounded, one man missing. The extraordinary number of missing Americans suggests heavy desertions among the militia, for it does not appear that the British took any prisoners.

This affair reflected little credit upon Moultrie's generalship. To take only 1,200 men, largely militia, against 900 British and Hessian regulars strongly entrenched, when he had five or six times that number available, was certainly poor judgment. It did, however, hasten the departure of the British from the state. They withdrew in boats to Port Royal Island within a few days.

Prevost's incursion into South Carolina gave him no profit in a military sense, except that it drew Lincoln back from Georgia. But it is averred that, in another sense it was highly profitable to his force. Looting was widespread. The houses along the route were pillaged of valuables of every sort. Slaves in great numbers flocked to the invaders and disclosed to them the places where their owners had concealed their valuables. They were well received by the redcoats, but not so well treated. "It is supposed that the British carried out of the state about 3,000 slaves, many of whom were shipped off and sold in the West Indies." [12]

CHAPTER 60

Savannah

The summer of 1779 was a period of quiet in the south. After the affair at Stono Ferry, the British were content to hold their positions in Georgia and on Port Royal Island, and the Americans made no move against them. Port Royal was safe from attack as long as the British commanded the sea. But if such command could be overcome the separation of the British force between that post and Savannah would render both of them vulnerable, thought Governor Rutledge and General Moultrie.

With that in view, they sent messengers to Admiral Comte d'Estaing, whose fleet was operating in the West Indies, asking his aid. He accepted the invitation and sent two ships of the line and three frigates to Charleston to announce the coming of his fleet. With twenty ships of the line, two others of 50 guns, eleven frigates, and a number of transports carrying 6,000 soldiers, he arrived off Tybee Island at the mouth of the Savannah River on September 8, having first fallen in with and taken the British ship *Experiment* of 50 guns, the frigate *Ariel,* and two storeships conveying a large sum of money for the payment of troops in Georgia, also a quantity of naval stores.

The large ships of the fleet, which could not cross the bar, were anchored outside. The frigates *Truite* and *Chimère,* two armed American galleys, and the armed storeship *Bricole* were brought up into the river. The fleet had been sighted by the British frigate *Rose,* five days before it arrived, and a fast-sailing brig had been dispatched to New York to call on Clinton and Admiral Marriot Arbuthnot for aid. Prevost requested Maitland to bring his troops from Port Royal, and Lieutenant Colonel John Harris Cruger with a battalion of De Lancey's New Yorkers was called in from Sunbury. The war vessels *Vigilant, Fowey, Rose, Keppel,* and *Germain* had been stationed outside the harbor, but they retired up the river upon the approach of the French.

Savannah, as has been said, was surrounded only by indefensible ruined earthworks. The city stood on a bluff on the right or west bank of the river. On the north a broad, wooded morass extending to the river offered some protection, but on the south and west the land dropped from the bluff and there was open ground. Prevost set about rebuilding the old defenses, and erecting new ones.

Four or five hundred Negroes were brought in from neighboring plantations to aid the garrison and the town dwellers in this effort. A curved line of earthworks, faced with a ditch and an abatis, was drawn around the town from the river below to the swamps above. On the north, or right, side three redoubts were built. The one on the left was the Spring Hill Redoubt. At the extreme right, beyond the first, or more northerly, redoubt, the Sailors' Battery of 9-pounders was erected, and another was placed between the second and third redoubts.

On the south side of the town two strong redoubts were framed of heavy logs, the spaces between the logs being filled with sand. The first redoubt on the north was held by a part of the King's Rangers, a Tory battalion under Captains Samuel Roworth and Alexander Wylly; the second was held by two companies of Georgia Tory militia and a regiment of the Tory North Carolina Volunteers, under Lieutenant Colonel John Hamilton; the third, the Spring Hill Redoubt, was commanded by Captain Tawes, who had a detachment of dismounted dragoons, with a South Carolina Tory regiment in support. The most northerly battery was manned by a company from the British Legion, a Tory corps, under Captain Patrick Stewart; the second battery was held by Captain Manby with the grenadiers of the 60th British regiment and marines from the British ships.

The great redoubts to the south were garrisoned, one by a body of the Georgia Volunteers under Major Sir James Wright, the royal governor of that state, the other by the 1st battalion of De Lancey's New Yorkers under Cruger. Both were supported by a battalion of the 71st Regiment, the 3rd battalion of Lieutenant Colonel Isaac Allen's New Jersey Volunteers, and detachments of Georgia militia.

A strong picket of British regulars, with a large body of armed Negroes, was stationed in the center, west of the town. Within the lines were stationed, in order from south to north, the 1st battalion of the 71st Regiment under Major McArthur, the Hessian Regiment von Trumbach, the 2nd

battalion of De Lancey's New Yorkers, the British light infantry under
Major Graham of the 16th Regiment, the Hessian Regiment Wissenbach,
the 2nd battalion of the 71st under Major McDonald, the 2nd battalion of
the 71st, the grenadiers of the 60th and a company of marines, under Lieutenant Colonel Glasier, and a body of North Carolina Royalists. Exclusive
of the Negroes, Prevost's force numbered 2,360 rank and file. It will be
noticed that the great majority of the garrison was made up of American
Loyalists, a fact emphasizing the character of the conflict in the South as a
civil.war.

To obstruct the river approach, the frigate *Rose*, the armed vessel
Savannah, four transports, and several smaller vessels were sunk in the
channel. To prevent the passage of fire rafts from the north down the river,
a boom of logs was strung across it above the town. The armed brig *Germain*
was stationed in the river off Yamacraw swamp.

On September 12, 1779, d'Estaing transferred 3,500 of his troops to small
vessels which carried them up the river to Beaulieu plantation, about eight
miles south of Savannah, and thence marched against that town. On the 15th
Pulaski's Legion joined him, and on the 16th he summoned the garrison,
in a rather flamboyant proclamation, to surrender "to the arms of the King
of France." Prevost, in order to gain time for the arrival of Maitland's
troops, applied Moultrie's method at Charleston: he asked a truce for
twenty-four hours in which to consider the demand, and it was granted.
Prevost used this interval in further strengthening his works.

Maitland's march from Port Royal has received the highest praise. Unable
to proceed by sea because of the French fleet or by land because of Lincoln's
intervening army, he was fortunate enough to discover a sort of inside
channel through the swamps and, though himself ill of malaria, took his
troops through a country that might have been deemed impassable. Wading
waist-deep, they dragged their boats two miles through swamps, launched
them again in creeks and rivers and so made their way to the Savannah
River. Under cover of a fog they crossed it to the town, thus adding 800 men
of the best fighting quality to Prevost's 2,400. Maitland himself was a most
important acquisition for Prevost, who on his arrival replied to d'Estaing
that he would defend the town.

Lincoln's army had left Charleston on September 8 and, after a tedious
march delayed by broken bridges, joined d'Estaing on the 16th. He had only
600 Continental troops and 750 militia. The combined attacking force now
numbered nearly 5,000 against the defenders' 3,200, but the garrison was
strongly entrenched. If d'Estaing had attacked immediately upon landing,
there is little doubt that he could have taken the town without difficulty—

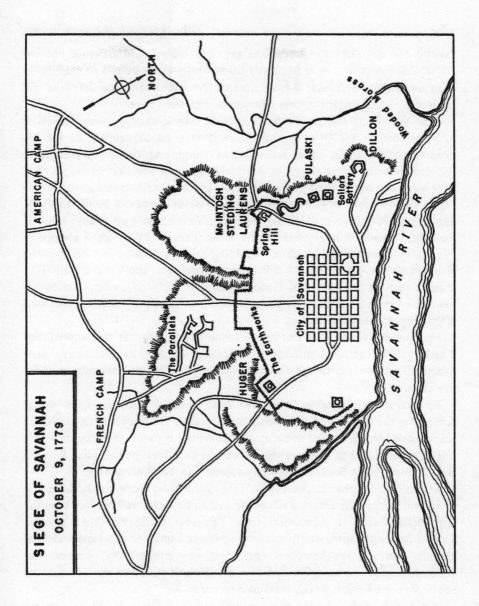

SIEGE OF SAVANNAH
OCTOBER 9, 1779

NORTH

AMERICAN CAMP

FRENCH CAMP

The Parallels

The Earthworks

HUGER

McINTOSH
STEDING
LAURENS

Spring
Hill

City of Savannah

Sailor's
Battery

PULASKI

DILLON

Wooded Morass

SAVANNAH RIVER

"within ten minutes and without the aid of artillery," said a British officer,[1] for at that time there were not more than twenty-three guns mounted on its then incomplete defenses. By the time of the final attack the defenses had been completed, and more than a hundred guns were in position.

The Americans and the French established their camps behind the town at a distance of 1,200 yards and broke ground on September 23 for approaches by parallels. There was delay in bringing up the heavy guns from the fleet because of shortage of draft animals and wheeled carriages. But they were in place in their proper batteries by October 3. Early in the morning of the 4th nine large mortars and thirty-seven pieces of heavy artillery, together with sixteen guns of the frigate *Truite* and the two galleys lying in the river, opened a heavy fire on the town. Prevost asked for a chance to remove the women and children, including his own family, to vessels in the river under the protection of d'Estaing. A previous application from Lincoln to remove the family of General Lachlan McIntosh, who were in the town, having been refused by Prevost, it is not surprising that Lincoln and d'Estaing refused this request.

Fortunately, there were not many casualties among the noncombatants. The houses in the town suffered considerable damage; but the works were practically unhurt, although the cannonade was kept up intermittently for five days.

By that time d'Estaing, who had been assured that ten days would suffice for the capture of the town, grew restive. His fleet was in the open sea, exposed to the danger of being driven ashore by southeast storms which might be expected at that season, as well as to attack by Admiral Byron's British West India fleet, which was supposed to be approaching.

Before the bombardment began, two sorties had been made from the town to interrupt the erection of the American batteries and the work on the approaches, without substantial result. Prevost made no other attempt against his opponents, wisely conserving his strength for the expected final assault. Nor did the besiegers engage in any preliminary personal encounters, except to send Captain Pierre L'Enfant with five men to fire the abatis. Made of green wood, it refused to burn.

D'Estaing's disinclination to wait until the approaches could be brought up to the enemy's works, which his engineers told him would take ten days more, resulted in a decision to storm the fortifications. Four o'clock in the morning of the 9th was the time fixed for the attack, and 3,500 French soldiers, 600 Continentals, 250 Charleston militia, and Pulaski's 200 horse were ordered to parade at one o'clock. They were formed in columns—the French in three, the first to be led by General Count Dillon, the second under Baron de Steding, a Swede in the French army, and the third a reserve under Colonel the Viscount de Noailles. The Americans were in two columns; the first being composed of the 2nd South Carolina Continentals and the 1st battalion of Charleston militia under Colonel John Laurens, and the second of the 1st and 5th South Carolina Continentals and some from Georgia, under General McIntosh.

Dillon's column was to march to the left and, by a hollow way between the bluff on the west side and the swamp, was to try, unobserved and hidden from the enemy's fire, to turn the British right between the Sailors' Battery and the town and so enter it. General Huger with an independent force of 500 militia was to proceed to the right against the east side of the enemy's works as a mask or feint to draw attention from the main attack and, if opportunity offered, to penetrate the defenses on that side.

The main attack was to be made by the forces of Laurens, Steding, and McIntosh, led by d'Estaing and Lincoln, against the Spring Hill Redoubt. Pulaski's cavalry was to precede Laurens's column, incline to the left, and enter the works when a breach should be made in the abatis on the left of the Spring Hill Redoubt.

Unfortunately, the discussion of the plan was overheard by Sergeant Major James Curry of the Charleston Grenadiers. He deserted to the enemy and informed them of the point of the main attack. A battalion of the 71st, one of the 60th, and a company of marines were added to its defenders, and that very able soldier Lieutenant Colonel Maitland was put in command of it.

As so often happened in these projected night attacks, the forward movement of the attacking force was delayed beyond the hour fixed. It was daylight before it began. Another misfortune occurred when Dillon's troops lost their way in the swamps west of the town and came out in the open instead of approaching secretly by the hollow way. They were discovered and were subjected to such a heavy fire that they never reached the enemy lines at all. Dillon ordered a retreat to the camp, and that was the end of that movement.

Huger on the right, after leading his men through some rice swamps, met such a heavy fire that he also withdrew. But the main force went on against the Spring Hill Redoubt. Laurens's force was the first to attack it. It climbed the bluff, crossed the ditch, cut through the abatis, and assaulted the redoubt with the utmost determination, in the face of a murderous fire of muskets and a devastating crossfire from adjoining batteries, which mowed them down rank by rank. The 2nd South Carolina Continentals, led by Lieutenant Colonel Francis Marion, reached the parapet first. Lieutenant John Bush and Lieutenant Homes planted the French standard and their regimental colors on it and were instantly shot down. Lieutenant Henry Gray replaced them and also fell. Sergeant Jasper, of Fort Sullivan fame, raised them again and was mortally wounded. But the parapet was too high to scale. The gallant South Carolinians were crowded together on the berm and in the ditch. They were forced back into and beyond the ditch just as McIntosh's troops came to their aid. Then Maitland turned loose the grenadiers of the 60th and a body of marines under Major Glasier.

The British left the redoubt and fell upon the mass of men in front of it with terrific effect in a hand-to-hand encounter, using bullets, bayonets, swords, pikes, feet, and fists. Captain Tawes, the former commander of the redoubt, himself killed three of the attackers with his sword before he was struck down. The fight at that point raged with unremitting fury for nearly an hour; but the crowded and confused allies were at last driven back, and retreated to their camp, leaving 80 dead in the ditch and 93 between it and the abatis.

While they were still fighting there, Pulaski, with his 200 horse, was attempting to force a passage between the Spring Hill Redoubt and the works west of it. At the abatis he encountered a crossfire which threw his men into confusion. He was hit in the body by a canister shot and mortally wounded. His men desisted from any further attempt and bore him from the field.

So the assault was beaten off at every point. The allies lost 16 officers and 228 men killed, 63 officers and 521 men wounded—a fifth of the whole number engaged and perhaps nearly half of those actually in the fight at the Spring Hill Redoubt. The British lost 40 killed, 63 wounded, and 52 missing. It had been the most severe fight of the war since Bunker's Hill—a magnificent attack and a superb defense.

After the battle Lincoln wanted to continue the siege operations; but d'Estaing would remain no longer. He returned his troops to their ships and sailed away. Lincoln marched back to Charleston. The south was sadly disheartened by this defeat, and much feeling against the French was aroused. Their defection at Newport in the previous year was remembered, and confidence in their value as allies was severely shaken. Throughout the country there was a great depression of spirits, and a corresponding depression in the already nearly worthless Continental money. Among the British and their American friends there was much elation. The southern Tories were emboldened to become more openly active against the American cause.

CHAPTER 61

Charleston Again

When Sir Henry Clinton heard of d'Estaing's arrival at the mouth of the Savannah River in September, 1779, he recalled to New York the 3,000 men that had been uselessly stationed at Newport for three years. When the French and Americans were defeated in their attempt upon Savannah and d'Estaing sailed away, leaving Georgia in the hands of the British, it seemed to Clinton that the time had arrived to attempt the subjugation of the southern states by a campaign that should begin in South Carolina and move through North Carolina into Virginia. He rather hoped that he could arouse the numerous Loyalists in the Carolinas, that they would flock to the King's standard and so reenforce him that he would be irresistible in his march to complete victory over the rebel forces in the south and that thus that great section would be restored to the crown. His plan was first to capture that most important city Charleston and establish a base there, and then to proceed inland.

Every circumstance seemed favorable to the project. Clinton's own army approximated 25,000 men, so that he could well spare a strong body of troops for this expedition. Washington's army, wintering in New Jersey, was so few in numbers that there seemed to be little prospect of his being able to send aid to the South. Lincoln's garrison in Charleston was desperately weak. The Carolinians generally were disheartened by the defeat at Savannah and the disappearance of the French. They were discouraged, moreover, by the fact that they had been left alone to oppose the enemy, with no aid from the North. Indeed, their forces had been drawn upon to help the North when, in 1777, all the Virginia and North Carolina Continentals had been sent up to reenforce Washington's army. The Tories had been so animated by the success of the British at Savannah that they might be expected to rise in numbers to aid the royal army. Then, too, the season was favorable. While operations in the north were extremely difficult in the winter, that was the best time for campaigning in the south. Altogether, Clinton's prospects were rosy.

On December 26, 1779, he turned over the command in New York to Knyphausen and sailed south with Cornwallis as second in command. His fleet of ninety transports carried eight British infantry regiments, five of Hessians, and five corps of Tories, besides detachments of artillery and cavalry—8,500 rank and file in all. It was convoyed by five ships of the line and nine frigates, with 650 guns, under command of Admiral Arbuthnot. The crews of all these vessels numbered about 5,000.

The voyage was stormy. Off Hatteras heavy gales came near to wrecking the expedition. Most of the cavalry and artillery horses perished; the stores were badly damaged; and the fleet was dispersed far and wide. One transport loaded with Hessians was driven clear across the Atlantic and went ashore on the coast of Cornwall. Thirty days had elapsed when the ships began to arrive off Tybee Island at the mouth of the Savannah River. After repairs to the rigging they sailed for Charleston on February 10, entered North Edisto Inlet on the 11th, and landed the troops on Johns Island, thirty miles south of Charleston.

The city of Charleston occupied the southern end of a narrow peninsula between the Ashley River on the west and the Cooper River on the east. Those two streams met at the tip of the peninsula and flowed into Charleston harbor, which was bounded on the south by James Island and Morris Island, on the north by the mainland and Sullivan's Island. Its defenses on the ocean side were two forts, Moultrie (formerly known as Sullivan's) on Sullivan's Island and Johnson on James Island. Moultrie, which had withstood the attack by Clinton and Admiral Parker in 1776, then being only partly built, had been allowed to fall into disrepair and was not now tenable. Johnson was in ruins. There was no defense against the intrusion of the enemy ships into the harbor.

On the land side Charleston was vulnerable. The broader part of the peninsula, on which the city was situated, was connected with the mainland by a long and narrow isthmus known as the Neck. It had been partially fortified in 1779, but these defenses were quite insufficient to repel a strong attack.

Immediately upon landing on Johns Island, Clinton sent part of his fleet to blockade the harbor; but after that he moved with the leisureliness which so often marked the operations of the British army in the war and so often seemed inexplicable. He first seized Stono Ferry connecting Johns Island with the adjoining James Island; then he occupied James Island itself and bridged the creek or strait called Wappoo Cut that separated it from the mainland. Not until March 7 did he cross the Cut and erect batteries on the west bank of the Ashley opposite the town. March 29 had arrived before he crossed the Ashley, seven weeks after his landing on Johns Island.

His delay was deemed at the time to be a great advantage to the Americans, because it gave them time to strengthen their defenses. But it proved in the end to be their undoing, because, with reenforced defenses, they felt themselves strong enough "to hazard their lives and fortunes upon the event of a siege," [1] and this false sense of security induced Lincoln to draw all available troops into a town that was doomed to be captured and with it the whole American army in South Carolina—an event that any competent military man should have foreseen.

The legislature having invested Governor Rutledge with dictatorial powers, he impressed 600 slaves for work on the fortifications. The Neck was cut across by a ditch or small canal filled with water. Behind it were erected stout breastworks and redoubts well fraised and covered by a double abatis. One of the redoubts, a "horn-work" built of stone, stood in the center of the lines upon the main road to the north. It was known as the Citadel and was a work of considerable strength. On these lines, sixty-six guns were mounted, and a number of mortars.

At the town's southern extremity, a redoubt mounting sixteen guns was erected. Along the Ashley River side was strung a line of six small "forts," each mounting four to nine guns. On the Cooper River side there were seven of these little works, each mounting from three to seven guns. Fort Moultrie and Fort Johnson were repaired and armed.

To aid in the defense of the waterfront, there was a little fleet of armed vessels, several of which had been bought from d'Estaing. They were the *Bricole*, 44 guns, *Providence* and *Boston*, 32 guns each, *Queen of France*, 28, *Aventure* and *Truite*, 26 each, *Ranger* and *General Lincoln*, 20 each, and *Notre Dame*, 16. These were commanded by Commodore Whipple.

Within the town Lincoln had, at first, all 800 South Carolina Continentals, 400 Virginia Continentals, Horry's dragoons, the remains of Pulaski's Legion numbering about 380, and about 2,000 militia of both Carolinas. But in December, Washington had ordered south the Virginia and North Carolina Continentals that had been with him in the north.

Clinton had left 2,500 troops in Georgia, bringing 6,000 to Charleston. Feeling that he needed more men to take the town, he sent some of his transports to New York for reenforcements. He also called on General Patterson to bring up the Savannah garrison. In the middle of March, Patterson arrived with the 71st Regiment of Highlanders, the light infantry, the infantry of Tarleton's Tory British Legion, Ferguson's American Volunteers, Tory riflemen, and other Tory corps including Turnbull's New York Volunteers, Innes's South Carolina Royalists, and Hamilton's North Carolina Royalists, also a number of dragoons—in all about 1,500 men. In the middle of April, Lord Rawdon came from New York with 2,500 men. These additions brought the British force up to 10,000 men, exclusive of the 5,000 seamen.

To the aid of the garrison, Governor Rutledge called the South Carolina militia; but they failed to respond, declaring that they feared an outbreak of smallpox if they were cooped up in Charleston, which had indeed suffered from an epidemic of a peculiarly fatal character a few years before. He sent an emissary to Havana to ask for a Spanish fleet and an army to cooperate in the town's defense, Spain having lately declared war on Britain. But the Spaniards declined the invitation.

The reenforcements from the north did, however, arrive. On March 3 General James Hogun with 700 North Carolina Continentals finished a most arduous march of nearly three months through heavy snows and extreme cold. On April 6 General William Woodford appeared with 750 Virginia Continentals, who had marched five hundred miles in twenty-eight days.

To hold the fords of the Cooper River and keep open his communications with the northern part of the state, thus affording a way of retreat up the east bank, Lincoln stationed General Isaac Huger with about 500 men— Horry's horse, Pulaski's dragoons, Bland's, Baylor's and Moylan's horse, and about 100 men under Lieutenant Colonel William Washington—at Monck's Corner near the head of the Cooper and thirty miles north of Charleston. Thus, in the town, there were left about 2,650 Continentals and 2,500 militia to hold a circuit of about three miles of fortified lines.

In the meantime Clinton had been closing in. On March 20 there were indications of an intention to bring the warships into the harbor. The little American fleet could find no position there that offered a possibility of preventing or even delaying the entrance of the enemy vessels. It was therefore withdrawn into the mouth of the Cooper River, in the main channel between the town and the small island called Shute's Folly. Its guns were removed and four of the frigates with several merchant ships were sunk there and

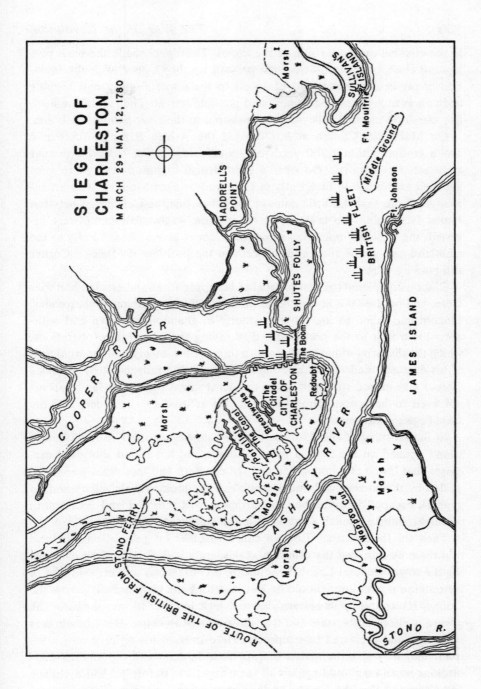

SIEGE OF CHARLESTON
MARCH 29 - MAY 12, 1780

SULLIVAN'S ISLAND

Marsh

Ft. Moultrie

Middle Ground

BRITISH FLEET

Ft. Johnson

HADDRELL'S POINT

SHUTE'S FOLLY

The Boom

Redoubt

The Citadel

Breastworks

CITY OF CHARLESTON

The Canal

Parallels

Marsh

COOPER RIVER

Marsh

Marsh

ASHLEY RIVER

JAMES ISLAND

Marsh

Wappoo Cut

Marsh

STONO FERRY

ROUTE OF THE BRITISH FROM STONO FERRY

STONO R.

in the channel on the far side of the island. They were made the basis of a
log-and-chain boom to obstruct the passage up the Cooper, with the intention of preserving that means of access to the upper country and keeping
open an avenue for reenforcement and possible retreat. The rest of the fleet,
five warships and five galleys, were anchored in the river behind the boom.

On March 29 Clinton at last crossed the Ashley River in force and
broke ground within 1,800 yards of the defenses on the Neck for regular
approaches by parallels. On April 8 eight British frigates carrying 216 guns
left their anchorage in Five Fathom Hole, ran by Fort Moultrie with an exchange of fire that did little damage on either side, and anchored between
James Island and the town. Now Charleston was almost completely invested; the only way open was across the Cooper above Shute's Folly to the
mainland east of the river and so north to the position at Monck's Corner
still held by Huger.

Clinton completed the first parallel of his approaches and erected batteries
there, and on the 10th he and Arbuthnot joined in a summons to surrender.
Lincoln had failed to use his opportunity to abandon the town and withdraw his troops to the northward, thus saving them for future operations,
which the disparity of his numbers with those of the enemy and the weakness
of his defenses made advisable. The way for such a movement by Monck's
Corner was indeed still open, risky though it might be, but so far he seems
not even to have considered taking it. He refused to surrender, and the
siege began in earnest.

In the morning of the 13th the enemy batteries on the Neck and James
Island opened on the town a rain of bombs, red-hot round shot, and carcasses that lasted two hours. Fires broke out here and there that were controlled by the citizens with much trouble. They took to their cellars and, in
general, escaped injury. The bombardment was renewed and lasted until
midnight, inflicting much damage upon the buildings.

Then for the first time Lincoln called together his general officers, and
told them he regarded the situation as desperate and contemplated evacuating the town. General Lachlan McIntosh, a courageous soldier, said that in
his opinion not an hour should be lost in getting the Continentals across the
Cooper River and up its eastern side to safety, in order to save them for the
general welfare of the state and the whole American cause. But Lincoln was
irresolute and preferred to temporize. He dismissed his officers with a request that they give the matter mature consideration and report their conclusions when he should again call them together. Before he had a chance
to call upon them the chance of such an evasion was lost. His northward

communications were severed by the destruction of the post at Monck's Corner.

The dragoons in Clinton's army were commanded by Lieutenant Colonel Banastre Tarleton, who was destined to achieve fame and merited obloquy in the south. Entering the British service at the outbreak of the war in America, he had proved himself an able soldier in Cornwallis's command throughout all the campaigns in the north, gaining some personal distinction. He was at this time twenty-six years old. In person he was short, stout and strongly built, muscular, and active. His countenance was handsome in feature, bold, insolent, and domineering in expression, revealing notable resolution, bravery, and pertinacity. In action, he was shrewd, sudden, and swift to strike. As a leader of cavalry, he was unmatched on either side for alertness and rapidity of movement, dash, daring, and vigor of attack. As a man, he was cold-hearted, vindictive, and utterly ruthless. He wrote his name in letters of blood all across the history of the war in the South. His command was the British Legion, made up of American Tories, a force of horse and foot, his infantry being usually mounted.

On the voyage of the British transports to Tybee, all his horses perished. He replaced them with horses impressed in the neighborhood, little tackies not strong enough for the heavy work of dragoons. His first desire was for better mounts, and he got a few in his first contact with the Americans, on February 23—a skirmish with a small body of militia, of whom he killed ten and took four prisoners. Three days later he encountered Lieutenant Colonel William Washington in command of the remains of Bland's, Baylor's, and Moylan's Virginia regiments of horse, who, as has been said, had been posted at Monck's Corner under General Huger, but were then operating along the Ashley. Washington drove Tarleton back and took several prisoners. But on April 14 Tarleton had his revenge.

His legion, reenforced by Major Patrick Ferguson's American Volunteers, a corps of riflemen, struck Huger's force at three o'clock in the morning, drove in the vedettes on the main road and followed them into their camp, charging upon the American cavalry with such suddenness and force that he routed it completely. His infantry instantly attacked with the bayonet a meetinghouse where Huger's militia was quartered, and dispersed all that were not cut down.

The Americans suffered heavy losses. Major Peter Vernie of Pulaski's Legion, four other officers, and fifteen privates were killed or wounded; seven officers and sixty men were captured. The rest, including General

Huger and Colonel Washington, fled to the swamps and escaped. In addition to forty-two loaded wagons, one hundred and two wagon horses and eighty-three dragoon horses were taken, affording qualified remounts for Tarleton's dragoons. The British lost only two men.

Lieutenant Colonel James Webster, with the 33rd and 64th British regiments, joined Tarleton the next day. Together with subsequent reenforcements, they possessed all the country east of the Cooper River and down to within six miles of Charleston, cutting that town's communications with the north and leaving Lincoln without a way of retreat.

By the 19th of April, Clinton's approaches were within two hundred and fifty yards of the lines on the Neck. At last convinced of the hopelessness of his situation, Lincoln called a council of war; and the possibility of evacuation and retreat or capitulation on favorable terms was discussed. Lieutenant Governor Christopher Gadsden was, somewhat irregularly, admitted to the council and strongly opposed the abandonment of the town. This dispute between the civil authorities and the military, who were convinced of the necessity of giving up the fight, caused an adjournment of the council to the next day. When it reconvened, Gadsden brought in the rest of the members of the Governor's Council, who stood with him against the evident intention of the officers to discontinue opposition to the enemy. One of the councillors even went so far as to say that, if the Continentals showed any sign of withdrawing, the townspeople would burn their boats, open the gates to the enemy, and assist them in attacking the American troops before they could get away. Gadsden and his supporters carried the day in the council of war, but on the 21st Lincoln took matters into his own hands. He proposed a capitulation on terms allowing the withdrawal of his force with the honors of war and with their arms and baggage and an unmolested march up the east side of the Cooper River to whatever destination they chose, also the unmolested withdrawal of the American ships. Clinton, of course, instantly and curtly refused the proposal. So the fight, such as it was, went on.

A sortie of 200 men with the bayonet only attacked the British lines on the Neck. A few of the enemy were killed, and a few captured. The British took a small work on Haddrell's Point on the mainland across the Cooper River opposite the town. Arbuthnot landed a body of seamen and marines on Sullivan's Island to take Fort Moultrie. The garrison, 200 men, surrendered without resistance. Tarleton attacked the remains of Huger's cavalry at Lenud's Ferry on the Santee, killed or captured 30 or 40 of them and dispersed the rest. By May 8 Clinton's approaches were close to the American lines, and a sap had drained the ditch across the Neck. All was in readiness for an assault when the British again demanded surrender.

Lincoln could not get away if he tried. He was hemmed in on every side by 14,000 of the enemy, including sailors from the fleet who had been landed to work the siege guns. But he still temporized, asking for a truce while terms were discussed. This was granted, and a correspondence with Clinton was prolonged until the evening of May 9. The two points on which agreement could not be reached were Lincoln's demand that the militia in the town should not be held as prisoners of war, and that upon surrender the garrison should march out with the honors of war, colors unfurled and drums beating a British march. Clinton and Arbuthnot denied both demands. They would not release the militia, nor would they allow the Continentals to march out with colors unfurled to the beating of either a British or an American march.

At eight o'clock in the evening of the 9th of May hostilities were renewed. The garrison fired the first gun, and then all the guns on the fortifications began a tremendous cannonade. Nearly 200 pieces of artillery were fired simultaneously, mortars threw shells in air that crossed one another and burst like meteors; "it appeared as if the stars were falling to the earth." [2] said Moultrie. The whole thing was aimless, a mere outburst of sound and fury, relieving the feelings of the garrison, but effecting nothing, yet it was kept up all night. The enemy, replying with everything they had, set many houses on fire. It was a night of horror that broke the spirit of the townsmen, who until now had resisted submission, and they petitioned for a surrender.

Lincoln then accepted Cornwallis's terms. The Continental troops were to be prisoners of war. The militia were to be allowed to go to their homes, being regarded with the armed citizens as prisoners on parole. At eleven o'clock in the morning of May 12, all the Continentals marched out,[3] with colors cased and drums beating a Turkish march, and piled their arms beside the Citadel. The militia followed them later in the day and also gave up their arms. So Clinton took the town, 5,466 Continentals, militia, and armed citizens, 391 guns, 5,916 muskets, 15 regimental colors, 33,000 rounds of small-arms ammunition, over 8,000 round shot, 376 barrels of powder, all the remaining American vessels, and a great quantity of military stores, at a cost of only 76 men killed and 189 wounded. The American losses were also light, 89 Continentals killed and 138 wounded. Among the militia there were not more than a dozen casualties. The surrender was one of the greatest disasters suffered by the Americans during the whole war.

CHAPTER 62

Civil War in the South

Charleston having been captured, Clinton's next effort was to reduce the interior parts of the Carolinas to subjection to the crown. He sent out a series of detachments composed almost wholly of Tories, and for the next three months the Carolinas were the scene of the most furious and ferocious partisan warfare. Within that period, there were five engagements between the militia of the states favoring the American cause and their Tory opponents. British regulars had little part in any of them. It was a civil war, and it was marked by bitterness, violence, and malevolence such as only civil wars can engender.

Cornwallis proceeded first to occupy the interior parts of South Carolina. He sent Lord Rawdon with the 23rd and 33rd British regiments, the Volunteers of Ireland, a Tory corps raised by him in Philadelphia, Tarleton's Legion, Browne's and Hamilton's corps of Tories, and a detachment of artillery, about 2,500 men in all, to establish the principal post at Camden. Major McArthur with two battalions of the 71st Highlanders advanced to Cheraw to cover the country between Camden and Georgetown, where a Tory corps was posted. To connect Camden with Ninety-six, Lieutenant Colonel Turnbull with the New York Volunteers and some Tory militia was stationed at Rocky Mount. The remote post at Ninety-six was held by three battalions of Royal Provincials and some light infantry under Lieutenant Colonel Balfour. Lieutenant Colonel Browne with his own Florida Rangers and certain other detachments was posted at Augusta, Georgia. Major Ferguson with his American Volunteers was assigned to the country between the Catawba and the Saluda. The rest of the British troops were stationed at Charleston, Beaufort, and Savannah. Thus from Cheraw in the

extreme northeast a strongly held line of posts ran across the northern part
of the state through Camden to Ninety-six, while the posts at Georgetown,
Charleston, Beaufort, and Savannah held the seacoast.

This unopposed occupation of such an extensive territory is eloquent evidence of the complete subjection of South Carolina at the time. After Lincoln's army had been captured there were no troops left in the state to
oppose the enemy. The few small bodies of patriot militia coming to the
relief of the besieged town had precipitately retreated to their homes to melt
into the civil population as inconspicuously as possible.

A regiment of 350 Virginia Continentals and a small party of William
Washington's horse led by Colonel Abraham Buford had advanced as far
as Lenud's Ferry on the Santee, not more than forty miles from Charleston,
when the town was surrendered. Huger sent them orders to retire to Hillsboro, North Carolina. Cornwallis sent Tarleton after them with 40 of the
17th British Dragoons, 130 of the cavalry of the British Legion, Tarleton's
Tories, and 100 mounted infantry of the same corps. Both forces moved
with great rapidity, and not until May 29 at the Waxhaws, a district near the
North Carolina border now in Lancaster County, was Buford overtaken,
after a march of 154 miles in fifty-four hours in which some of Tarleton's
horses fell dead from the heat and were replaced by others taken from the
inhabitants. Tarleton sent forward a flag, representing that he had 700 men,
cavalry, infantry, and artillery, and that Cornwallis was close behind with
nine British battalions. Under these falsely stated conditions, which made
resistance seem vain, he called on Buford to surrender on the same terms as
had been granted to the garrison at Charleston. Buford took counsel of
his officers and decided to march on, maintaining the best rearguard action
that was possible. He accordingly refused the offered terms and began to
march.

But, in this short interval of truce, Tarleton had prepared for action. His
right wing was composed of 60 of his own dragoons and as many of his
mounted infantry, now on foot; his centre, of the 17th British dragoons and
part of the Legion horse; his left, of 30 chosen horsemen and some infantry.

Immediately upon receiving the refusal of his terms, Tarleton's bugles
sounded and his force swept down upon Buford's rear guard. They were cut
down to a man. Buford, surprised by the suddenness of the attack, disposed
his men to receive it; but, instead of throwing his wagons into a line across
his front as a barricade peculiarly advantageous in opposing a cavalry
attack, he drew the men up in open ground. He made another mistake in
holding his fire until the enemy were within thirty feet of his line. That delay
was fatal to him.

The shock of his volley came upon the enemy's horse too late to stop or even to confuse them. The impetus of their charge carried them against the Americans, broke their line, swept around both flanks, and left them a huddled defenseless mass. Buford hoisted a white flag and ordered his men to ground their arms. But Tarleton would not stay his troops. They fell upon the unarmed Americans with sword and bayonet. Cries for quarter were answered with slashing and stabbing steel. Men who had fallen wounded were bayoneted. Across the field and back the ferocious Tories raged seeking half-dead men to kill. Where one man lay on top of another, he was stabbed and then thrown off to expose the man underneath. The affair was a savage slaughter of helpless men.

A hundred of Buford's infantry, who had been in advance on the march, managed to get away. Buford himself with a few other mounted men escaped. Of the rest 113 were killed; 150 were so badly wounded that they could not be moved; 53, mostly wounded, were taken prisoners. Tarleton lost 5 killed and 12 wounded. Three regimental colors, four guns, a quantity of ammunition, and twenty-six wagons loaded with clothing and military stores fell into his hands. From that time on, "Tarleton's quarter" became a byword to describe relentless slaughter of surrendered men.

This little affair extinguished the last flickering flame of resistance in South Carolina. The British power throughout the state was thoroughly established. Clinton went back to New York with about a third of his troops, leaving Cornwallis and a mixed force of six British, one Hessian, and six Tory regiments, about 8,300 rank and file, in the South.[1]

With South Carolina and Georgia well under control, North Carolina was Cornwallis's next field for action. Its Loyalists gave glowing accounts of their strength and urged him to come over and conquer; but the extreme heat of the summer and the scarcity of provisions inclined him to remain in his camps until later in the year. There were, however, plenty of restless Tories in the Old North State who were disinclined to delay. One of these, John Moore of Ramsour's Mills, returning from service under Cornwallis early in June in a tattered suit of Provincial regimentals with a sword at his side, announced himself as lieutenant colonel of Hamilton's North Carolina Tory regiment. He raised a force of 200 Tories and encamped. Others flocked to his standard until, by June 20, he had 1,300 men, three-quarters of them armed.

In the meantime the North Carolina patriots were preparing to resist invasion. General Griffith Rutherford called on the militia, who responded to the number of 800 at a plantation near Charlotte. They were organized in three divisions: a body of 65 horse equipped as dragoons, under Major

William R. Davie; a battalion of 300 light infantry, under Colonel William L. Davidson, a Continental officer; and the remainder, infantry, under Rutherford. With this force, he decided to attack Moore's Tories. Colonel Francis Locke gathered another body of 400 patriot militia at Mountain Creek, not far from Ramsour's Mills, and also decided to go after Moore. With three small companies of mounted men in the van and the rest, an unorganized crowd of inexperienced, undisciplined, armed civilians, following in double file, Locke set out on June 19 to surprise Moore.

The Tories, equally irregular in organization and discipline, were encamped on a hill, with a picket guard of 12 men thrown out six hundred yards in front. At the approach of Locke's horse, this guard fired and fled to the camp, throwing it into confusion. The horsemen galloped after them up the hill, outstripping their own infantry. The unarmed Tories took flight, but the rest, seeing only the patriot horsemen, opened fire and drove them back down the hill until Locke's foot came in sight, formed a line at the foot of the slope, and opened fire. Responding to it, the Tories fell back to the top of the hill and over its brow. Their fire was renewed; and they came forward again, but when a small party of patriots gained their right flank and another their left, they again retreated to the hilltop. There was no concert in the movements of Locke's militia, no central command. Each captain led his men as he deemed proper at the moment. The simultaneous flanking of the Tories was purely accidental.

But Locke's force had, by these haphazard movements, gained the rear of the Tories and now fell upon them at close quarters. Neither side had any bayonets. Muskets were clubbed and fell upon heads vengefully. The Tories had green twigs in their hats; the rebels had pieces of white paper. These were the only distinctive equipment, and they lost their virtue when the hats fell off in the struggle and both forces were commingled. Doubtless many a patriot musket fell upon a patriot head, and many a Tory was struck down by a companion. For a while the combat was equal; but the Tories finally began to get the worst of it, broke through, and fled down the far side of the hill to a creek and across it, where they halted.

Thinking that his foe was about to renew the fight, Locke tried to re-form his men on the hilltop. Only 110 of the original 400 could be assembled, and he sent word to Rutherford, who was on the march, to hurry. But there was no fight left in Moore's men. They sent a flag to Locke asking for a truce to collect their wounded and bury their dead. While he was considering it, they ran off singly or in small parties. Moore got away with 30 men and joined Rawdon at Camden.

The affair sounds like a comic opera encounter, but it was far from playful. Of Locke's 400, not more than 250 were in the fight. Of these more than 150 were killed or wounded. Of the Tories, about 700 were engaged; and their casualties were equal in number to those of the patriots. The fight on the hilltop was a desperate hand-to-hand struggle, the crudity of the weapons equaled by the ferocity with which they were employed. The result was the crushing of the Tory element in that part of North Carolina.[2]

The downfall of Charleston and the activity of the British thereafter encouraged the South Carolina Tories to organize and join in repressing the rebels. On May 29 a party of Tories near Winnsboro was defeated and dispersed by Colonel William Bratton and Captain John McClure, leading a party of patriot militia. A similar group near Fishing Creek was similarly dealt with. To counteract these patriot successes, Lieutenant Colonel Turnbull, in camp at Rocky Mount, South Carolina, detached Captain Christian Houk (or Huck) with 30 or 40 dragoons, 20 mounted infantry of the New York Volunteers, and about 60 Tory militia, with orders to "collect all the royal militia on his march" and "push the rebels as far as he deemed convenient." Houk succeeded in increasing his force to about 400. With these he visited the house of Captain McClure, where Mrs. McClure, her son James, and her son-in-law Edward Martin were molding bullets. He plundered the house and took the two men prisoners, announcing that he would hang them the next day. Colonel Bratton's house was also looted, but no prisoners were taken. Houk then went on to Williamson's plantation, adjoining Bratton's, and camped for the night.

Bratton and McClure were thirty miles distant in camp with General Thomas Sumter's militia force when Mary McClure brought the news to her father. They led 150 mounted volunteers against Houk, and were joined by Captain Edward Lacey, Jr., Colonel William Hill, and Colonel Thomas Neal, militia officers, with 350 other volunteers. It was an entirely irregular force with no organization, led by officers with no authority. Every move was decided by vote of all the volunteers. In consequence, there was such misunderstanding of orders that 150 rode away from the rest and never stopped until they had reached Charlotte, North Carolina, forty miles distant. The remaining 350 went on to find Houk.

The division of sentiment in South Carolina is illustrated by an incident on this march. The little army had to pass the house of Edward Lacey, Sr., who was as much a Tory as his son was a patriot. To prevent him from alarming Houk, Captain Lacey set a guard about the house. But the old gentleman escaped and was on his way to Houk's camp, two miles distant, when he was recaptured and, by his son's orders, tied up in his bed.

By the time the patriots came near Williamson's plantation, 90 of them had fallen away. The remainder were divided into two parties to attack Houk's camp simultaneously on two sides. At dawn of July 12, they advanced from both directions, got between the camp and the picketed horses of the enemy, and opened fire from behind fences. Houk's force attempted resistance, but was overwhelmed by the fire from the fences. When Houk was shot from his horse and fell dead the patriots leaped the fences and charged upon the camp. The Tories threw down their arms and fled. They were pursued a dozen miles, and many were shot down in this pursuit. In all, Houk's force lost 30 to 40 killed and about 50 wounded. The rebels had one man killed. The two young men condemned to death were found tied up in a corncrib, and were of course released.[3]

Emboldened by the successful attack on Houk's force, many men in the neighborhood joined Sumter at Mecklenburg, in North Carolina about 35 miles north of the South Carolina line, building his force up to nearly 600. Sumter then decided to strike at Turnbull's post at Rocky Mount, the origin of Houk's expedition.

It was a strong position by nature and had been reenforced by art. On a high hill on the west bank of the Catawba, three log houses, perforated with loopholes and encircled by an open wood, were surrounded by a ditch and an abatis. They were garrisoned by 150 New York Volunteers and a detachment of South Carolina Loyalists. Sumter's attacking force consisted of Colonel Hill's and Colonel Lacey's South Carolina militia and Colonel John Irwin's Mecklenburgers, an unknown number. Turnbull had learned of their advance and was prepared to receive them.

"With all the impetuosity which characterized the movements of this gallant officer," Sumter attacked, but was repulsed three separate times by fire from the log houses. He then ordered an assault. Colonel Thomas Neal led the forlorn hope, which got through the abatis; but he and five of his men were killed in the attempt and many others were mortally wounded. Despairing of success, Sumter drew off his men and retired to Land's Ford on the Catawba. The Americans lost 14 men killed or wounded, the enemy about the same number.[4]

The actions at the Waxhaws, Ramsour's Mills, Williamson's plantation, and Rocky Mount were affairs of short duration, irregularly fought by small numbers of combatants. The next encounter between the patriots and Tories in South Carolina assumed the form and proportions of a real battle.

At Hanging Rock, twelve miles from Rocky Mount, Major Carden, with a detachment of infantry from the British Legion, Colonel Morgan Bryan's regiment of North Carolina Loyalists, a detachment from the Prince of Wales Loyal American Volunteers, and part of Colonel Thomas Browne's regiment of Rangers—in all, about 500 men—held a strong position on a high, rolling plain, its front covered by a deep ravine and a creek. Sumter, with 500 North Carolina militia under Colonel Irwin and Major William Davie, and 300 South Carolinians under Colonel Lacey and Colonel Hill, all being mounted infantry, marched from Land's Ford on the Catawba in the evening of August 5 to attack Carden.

In Carden's camp the Prince of Wales Loyal Americans were posted on the right, the Legionaries and Browne's Rangers held the center, and Bryan's Loyalists the left, which was separated from the others by a wood. Approaching the camp, Sumter split his force into three divisions: Major Davie on the right with his "dragoons" and a mixed corps of militia from both states, Irwin in the center with his Mecklenburg men, and Hill on the left with the South Carolinians. They were to ride to a point near the enemy's center and dismount. Then each division was to attack the corresponding part of the enemy's force. Misled by their guides, all three were brought opposite the enemy's left. Having dismounted, the entire corps fell upon Bryan's Loyalists. Attacked in front and on their flank, they were routed and with heavy losses fled in confusion to the center.

Pressing on, Sumter's men were met by a heavy fire from the Legionaries and the Rangers, and their advance was checked. Twice their opponents charged with the bayonet. While this part of the battle was being hotly fought, Carden took his Prince of Wales Loyalists on a circuit and gained the wood between his center and his left, thus bringing them down on Sumter's flank just as the Legionaries and the Rangers broke and retreated from their camp. This unexpected attack on their flank might have routed Sumter's men, confused as they were in the fight with the Legion and the Rangers. But they faced their new foes and, from behind trees, opened such a deadly fire that almost every officer was shot down and so many of the men fell that the rest threw down their arms and surrendered.

The camp was now open to plunder and, in great disorder, the victors seized their opportunity. The commissary's stores were ransacked. Liquor was found and disposed of on the spot. No thought was given to the still existing though scattered forces of the enemy, while an orgy of looting and drinking occupied the attention of nearly all the triumphant militiamen. In this state of affairs Carden saw a chance to retrieve his fortunes. A number of his Tories were got together near the center and formed into a hollow square. A larger body was collected in the wood. Sumter and his officers did their utmost to organize a new attack, but only about 200 men could be induced to leave their plundering and join Davie's dragoons for more fighting. These opened fire on the square, which was supported by two fieldpieces, but without much effect. Davie did, however, succeed in routing the other body in the wood.

A new danger now threatened Sumter in the shape of two companies of cavalry of the British Legion, which came into view. Davie's "dragoons" charged them and drove them into the woods. In this situation, Sumter decided that a retreat was necessary. Loaded with plunder, the disorganized militiamen, many of them intoxicated, left the scene of action, Davie's dragoons bringing up the rear and herding the stragglers forward.

The contest had lasted nearly four hours and had been fought with obstinacy and determination on both sides. Of the 500 Tories in the camp more than 200 were killed or wounded. The Prince of Wales detachment was wiped out, only nine escaping death or capture. The losses of the attacking party were never ascertained. It is noteworthy that the battle was fought entirely by Americans—patriots and Tories—not a single British soldier being present.[5]

De Kalb Marches Southward

As has been said, Washington in November, 1779, sent the North Carolina and Virginia Continentals south to reenforce Lincoln in Charleston. But when, in April, 1780, he learned that Rawdon was about to take 2,500 men down to join Clinton's army in South Carolina, he decided to "put the Maryland line and the Delaware Regiment, with the 1st Artillery of 18 field-pieces, under marching Orders immediately" to give "further succour to the Southern States." [1] Of these troops and this movement a military historian of the war has said: "It is just here that one fact in the struggle for American Independence should have specific notice. From 1776 before Boston and through the entire war, the states of Maryland and Delaware were represented on nearly every battlefield. Although their troops were few in numbers, they were distinguished for valor." [2] The Baron de Kalb was placed in command of the force sent southward.

Major General the Baron de Kalb was, in some particulars, a close parallel to General Steuben. Like Steuben a soldier of fortune, he also availed himself of fiction to support his pretensions to command in the American army. He called himself "Baron de Kalb," but he was not a baron nor had he a right to use the aristocratic particle "de." His name was simply Johann or Hans Kalb. He was the son of a Bavarian peasant. In 1737, at the age of sixteen, he left home. Nothing is known of his career until 1743, when he reappears as Jean de Kalb, a lieutenant in a French infantry regiment. The change in his Christian name and the assumption of "de" were intended to secure practical advantages. In the European armies of that period no commoner might hope for a commission; all such advancement was reserved for the aristocracy. Hans Kalb's merit as a soldier would have availed him not at all. Jean de Kalb might and did rise from the ranks.

For four years the young lieutenant fought in the European wars with credit. In 1747 he was a captain and regimental adjutant. At the outbreak of the Seven Years' War he was a major. Before long he became a lieutenant colonel. After the peace, in 1763, he married Anne van Robais, daughter of a wealthy French manufacturer. On the death of her parents four years later, she inherited the family homestead at Courbevoye, and with it a tidy fortune.

In 1767 the Duc de Choiseul sent De Kalb to America to "inquire into the intentions of the inhabitants," to report on their resources, "their plan of revolt," their strength and leadership—all, of course, to determine whether France should assist them in obtaining independence and thus injure Britain. De Kalb made an extended tour of the colonies and brought back a full report, but found Choiseul more interested in European than in American affairs. De Kalb remained inactive in civil life until 1776, when it became clear that a real war was on in America, and that there was a field for the military activities that he longed for. The Duc de Broglie recommended him to the American agent in Paris, Silas Deane, who engaged him, with a promise of a major general's commission. How he came to America with Lafayette and how he got his commission have already been told.

In person De Kalb had distinction. His aide-de-camp, Nicholas Rogers of Baltimore, described him as "a perfect Ariovistus, more than six feet tall." His countenance was engaging; he had a high forehead, keen hazel eyes, aquiline nose, strong chin, and an expression of good nature mixed with shrewdness. His physical endurance was extraordinary; he often made twenty to thirty miles in a day on foot, preferring "that exercise to riding." His "temperance, sobriety and prudence" were noteworthy. He would arise before day, work until nine, then take a slice of dry bread with a glass of water. After performing his morning duties, he partook of soup and a bit of meat, washed down with water, his only drink. His supper was as frugal as his breakfast. He bore the hardships of war with "patience, long-suffering, strength of constitution, endurance of hunger and thirst and a cheerful submission to every inconvenience in lodging," and would "arrange his portmanteau as a pillow and, wrapping his great horseman's cloak around him, stretch himself before the fire" and sleep soundly. Though ambitious for advancement in his calling, he was single-hearted and honest; energetic and enterprising, he yet tempered his actions with caution and common sense.

Brave to the point of temerity, he was an ideal leader of a combat force in action.[3]

There was some delay in getting started. When the quartermaster general reported that he was unable to make provision for the march Washington was disturbed; he wrote, on April 13, 1780: "How they will get on for want of Provisions, Transportation &ca., Heaven alone can tell, I cannot."[4] But the detachment broke camp at Morristown on the 16th, set out on its long journey, and somehow did get on. It numbered about 1,400 of all ranks.[5] The first brigade was composed of the 1st, 3rd, 5th, and 7th Maryland regiments under Brigadier General William Smallwood; the second, of the 2nd, 4th, and 6th Marylanders and the regiment of Delaware under Brigadier General Mordecai Gist. Their route was through Philadelphia to the Head of Elk in Maryland and thence by water to Petersburg, Virginia, the artillery following by land. De Kalb himself lingered in Philadelphia in an effort to procure wagons, of which he got only enough to carry his tentage; the soldiers were obliged "notwithstanding the heat of the season, to carry their own baggage."[6]

From Petersburg they marched at the rate of fifteen to eighteen miles a day into North Carolina.[7] Having news of the fall of Charleston, to the aid of which he was marching, De Kalb was somewhat at a loss as to his next move.[8] He held his men in camp at the plantation of General Parsons in Granville County on the border of that state. It had been Washington's idea that these Continentals would serve as a nucleus around which the patriot militia of the southern states could gather, making up a force sufficient "to check the progress of the British troops and prevent their getting intire possession" of South Carolina, also to encourage the rebels and depress the Tories.[9] De Kalb, accordingly, hoped for reenforcements while holding his troops in Granville County.

Reenforcements were disappointingly slow and few. There were no accessions of any importance. So he had to go on with his own troops. They marched on June 21, and arrived on the 22nd at Hillsboro,[10] thirty-five miles to the southwest. It was a hard journey. The soldiers, carrying all their baggage on their backs, suffered from the heat and from "the most voracious of insects of every hue and form," especially the ticks. "My whole body is covered with these stings," De Kalb wrote to his wife in France.[11]

At Hillsboro they rested a week, and then went on. With every mile they marched, their difficulties increased. North Carolina had been relied upon for provisions and transportation within its borders; but nothing was prepared. De Kalb sent requisitions and remonstrances to its governor without the slightest result.[12] Still they struggled forward for three days to Chatham Court House, thirty miles. There they rested three days; then on again one day to Deep River where they had to stop again, for they had no food at all.[13]

They had been living on the country, foraging as they went. The inhabitants had about exhausted the last year's crop of corn, and the new crop was not yet ripe. The foraging parties scraped the bottoms of the farmers' granaries and got little. For meat, they had only the lean, half-starved cattle that ran wild in the woods. They themselves were as lean as the cattle. One of them wrote of their hardships: "We marched from Hillsborough about the first of July, without an ounce of provision being laid up at any one point, often fasting for several days together, and subsisting frequently upon green apples and peaches; sometimes by detaching parties, we thought ourselves feasted, when by violence we seized a little fresh beef and cut and threshed out a little wheat; yet, under all these difficulties, we had to go forward." [14] But at Buffalo Ford on Deep River there was no going any farther. They lay there for two weeks.

Major General Richard Caswell was in the field with a numerous force of North Carolina militia. De Kalb had reason to believe that the state was taking care of its own, and that a junction with Caswell would not only strengthen his army but also relieve its wants. He called on Caswell to join him; but that gentleman preferred the personal distinction of an independent command and the glory of harrying Tories who had fled to the woods and swamps. He offered excuses and held aloof.[15]

Brigadier General Edward Stevens with some Virginia militia was supposed to join De Kalb, and Lieutenant Colonel Porterfield with a hundred other Virginians was somewhere about. But neither of these came to De Kalb's camp. With his unaided and uncared-for alien Continentals, many of them ill with dysentery induced by unwholesome food, and Colonel Charles Armand's Legion, formerly Pulaski's, of 60 horse and 60 foot, which had joined him, De Kalb was lying at Buffalo Ford when he received news of action of the Congress concerning the southern campaign.

Lincoln, formerly in command of the Southern Department, was in captivity. As De Kalb was the senior officer in the department, that command had devolved upon him. But he was a foreigner, and, though a thorough and widely experienced soldier and an officer of proved ability, he was little known in Philadelphia and had no influential friends or patrons to urge his merits upon the Congress. His continuance in the chief command was hardly considered.[16]

Washington's choice for the position was Nathanael Greene, undoubtedly the ablest of his major generals.[17] But the Congress had its own man in view, none other than Horatio Gates, the victor at Saratoga, about whose head hung an aureole of glory. Congress loved him; so "with almost unbecoming haste" and without asking Washington's advice, "though not ignorant of his opinion," it ordered Gates "to repair to and take command of the southern department." [18]

CHAPTER 64

Gates Takes Command

Gates got word of his preferment at his plantation in Virginia and gladly accepted it. He received a sardonic warning from his friend and neighbor, Charles Lee: "Take care lest your Northern laurels turn to Southern willows." De Kalb received the news with no regrets. He wrote on July 16 that he was "happy to hear of Gates's coming." He also mentioned the difficulties he had encountered and his present condition: "Altho I have put the troops on short allowance for bread, we cannot get even that . . . no assistance from the legislature or executive power. . . . The design I had to move nearer the enemy to drive them from the Pedee River, a plentiful country, has been defeated by the impossibility of subsisting on the road. . . . I could hardly depend on any but the Maryland and Delaware regiments of my division and Col. Armand's legion and all those very much reduced by sickness, discharge and desertion." [1] He had been obliged to leave four pieces of artillery at the Roanoke River and six at Hillsboro for want of horses to draw them. He had now only eight guns. He intended to move up Deep River and join the recalcitrant Caswell, who had a considerable force of North Carolina militia.

De Kalb had marched to "Hollinsworth's Farm on Deep River" before Gates arrived on July 25. The meeting of the two generals was marked by proper ceremonies, including a salute of thirteen guns. Gates was polite; De Kalb was courteous and cheerful. While assuming command of the whole Southern Department, Gates confirmed De Kalb in command of his own division of "the grand army" (Gates's phrase); namely the Maryland and

717

Delaware troops. The rest of "the grand army" was but Armand's 120 and three small companies of artillery.[2]

Gates had now "an army without strength, a military chest without money." [3] Of the population around him, the patriots were depressed, the Tories elated and swarming everywhere. He faced a victorious enemy, strong, strongly posted, and planning to spread its conquests wider and wider. He might have been dismayed by the situation of affairs.

He took hold at once with all the vigor and decision to be expected from a great military genius. It had been De Kalb's intention to move southwest by way of Salisbury and Charlotte and so around to Camden, a circuitous route. But the forthright Gates would have none of that. The Grand Army must go at once, and by the most direct road, to Camden.[4]

Although the road De Kalb had intended to take was more circuitous, the country it traversed was fruitful, and the people were well affected towards the Revolution. Rowan and Mecklenburg counties, in which Salisbury and Charlotte lay, were chiefly inhabited by patriotic Scotch-Irish, and magazines of supplies and hospitals could be provided there. From Charlotte he could strike directly south to Camden and make an attempt upon it, with the comforting assurance of a friendly country behind his army in case of retreat.[5]

On the other hand the road Gates proposed to take, while fifty miles shorter, ran through thinly peopled and infertile pine barrens, a kind of wilderness in which deep sand alternated with swamps, presenting obstacles to the passage of the artillery and the few baggage wagons. Moreover, it was crossed by many watercourses, liable to be impassably swollen by a few hours' rain. More important was the fact that the scanty stores of food and forage had long since been gathered by the enemy. In addition to these disadvantages, the road traversed the Cross Creek country, the region of all the South most unfriendly to the American cause.[6]

When Gates gave the order to take this direct road "men and officers looked at each other with blank amazement." That they should march so precipitately, "with only a half-ration for today and not even a half-ration for tomorrow" [7] seemed hardship enough. But that they should be compelled to take the hard and hungry way was simply foolishly cruel.

Colonel Otho Holland Williams of the Maryland line was urged by De Kalb to persuade Gates to shift to the other road. Williams told the General about its advantages in the way of food and friendly inhabitants and that it was the old trading road from Philadelphia to Charleston, by which supplies from the north could reach the army. He pointed out, also, that they could increase their force by additions of the militia of the two well disposed counties, and advised orders to Caswell to join the army on the way, at the mouth of Rocky River on the Pee Dee.[8] To fortify his remonstrance, he presented a paper signed by the leading officers, advising the proposed change of plan. Gates listened, and promised to call a council of officers to discuss the matter, but never did call it. The order to march stood, and on July 27 the army set out by the hard way.

Day by day, the distress of the marching men grew more severe. Food was worse than scarce; there was none in the wagons. The men lived on green corn plucked from the few cultivated fields, and on peaches, with the usual physical results. Of pigs from farmers' pens, of chickens from their roosts, there were none. There were not even any farmers; they had fled and taken everything edible with them. Now and then stray cows were found running wild, miserable lean creatures; they were devoured. The officers made soup and thickened it with their hair powder. So they struggled on, plodding through deep sand, wading through swamps.[9]

At setting out on this journey Gates had tried to silence objections as to the lack of provender by asserting that there would soon be plenty, particularly rum; wagonloads were on the way and would catch up with them within two days at the latest.[10] Unless he had information that such wagons were coming from heaven, loaded with manna, there was, to put it mildly, no basis in fact for his statement; no wagons came, nor were there any on the way.

Having ceased to look behind with hope for these wagons, the men were told to look ahead: there was an abundance of corn growing on the banks of the Pee Dee. It was there, when they came to it, beautiful to see, but green, still green. They ate it ravenously, with the same results as before.[11]

Up to this time they had gathered no new adherents. Colonel Anthony White and Lieutenant William Washington, with the remains of Lincoln's cavalry, had retired into North Carolina after their disastrous experiences at Monck's Corner and Lenud's Ferry. They now solicited the aid of Gates's authority in their efforts to recruit their corps and offered to join him. He gave them no assistance. Indeed, "he did not conceal . . . that he held cavalry in no estimation in the southern field." [12] That, in the face of Tarleton's repeated successes, is a measure of Gates's military ability. By this neglect to aid Washington and White, he deprived himself of potential additions of great value to his army.

At the crossing of the Pee Dee, on August 3, Lieutenant Colonel Charles Porterfield, who as a captain of Virginia Continentals had fought so valiantly at Brandywine, joined Gates with a hundred Virginia state troops, a much needed reenforcement.[13]

Half starved, half sick, fatigued almost to exhaustion, still the men had to go on; and they did, seventeen or eighteen miles a day, though with no good grace. There were sullen murmurs among them, ominous glances at one another, black looks for the commander; mutiny seemed imminent and doubtless was, for they had almost reached the limit of their endurance. But the regimental and company officers went among them, praised them for their fortitude, reminded them of their past good conduct, showed them their own empty canteens and haversacks, and quieted them, at least for the time.[14] Sergeant Major William Seymour of the Delawares tells of their privations in his Journal: "At this time we were so much distressed for want of provisions, that we were fourteen days and drew but one half pound of flour. Sometimes we drew half a pound of beef per man and that so miserably poor that scarce any mortal could make use of it—living chiefly on green apples and peaches, which rendered our situation truly miserable, being in a weak and sickly condition, and surrounded on all sides by our enemies the Tories." [15]

At last, at Deep Creek, some beef and a little corn were brought in. The troops ground the corn in their little hand mills, making enough meal to give each man half a pound. The officers saw to it that the privates got their mush and their johnnycakes first.[16]

In the afternoon of August 5 came a letter from Caswell; he was going to attack an enemy post. Fearing that an injudicious action might result in the destruction of Caswell's force, upon which he relied to strengthen his own, Gates ordered his men forward to join the others. Discontent, arising from acute suffering, still prevailed in the ranks, and only the personal appeals of their officers induced the men to obey. They had marched five miles the next morning when another dispatch came from Caswell: instead of attacking the enemy, he was about to be attacked by Rawdon; he wanted help and wanted it at once.[17] Gates halted his men while he and Otho Williams pushed on to Caswell's camp for more information. They found the camp in the most complete confusion and disorder. But there seemed to be no lack of food; Caswell's table was furnished with "wine and other delicacies," such as the visitors had not seen for many a day.[18] North Carolina seemed to have cared for its own.

Rawdon made no attack. On the contrary, he intended to retire before the oncoming Americans; he had made a feint to scare Caswell and had then withdrawn from Lynch's Creek to Little Lynch's Creek, within a mile of Camden. The next day Gates joined Caswell, thus adding 2,100 North Carolina militia [19] to his "grand army," but greatly weakening it as the event proved. The combined forces then marched to Lynch's Creek.

What to do next might have puzzled an abler general than Horatio Gates.

He could not stay where he was; there was no food there. If he turned to the left, Camden would be in his rear, cutting off any help from the north. If he turned to the right, to the flourishing settlements of the Waxhaws, a two or three days' march, he would seem to be retreating and the North Carolina militia would desert him. So, without any plan or purpose, he went blindly straight ahead. He apprehended his insecurity sufficiently to order his heavy baggage, "as well as a part of the women and children following the camp" sent back to Charlotte. A futile order; there was no sufficient transport for the baggage, and "the women and children clung to their protectors." [20]

On the 11th he came to Little Lynch's Creek and found Rawdon at the other side of the stream on a commanding height, the approaches to which were difficult if not impossible in the face of a hostile force. The only road across the creek was by way of a wooden bridge, and even to reach that the attacking force would have to traverse a broad marsh in full view of the enemy.[21] But, difficult as the situation appeared to be, a really capable captain might have ordered a forced night march up the creek, crossed it above, flanked Rawdon, circumvented him, and entered Camden in his rear, almost unopposed, and thus taken the baggage, provisions, ammunition, and stores held there under a weak guard.[22] De Kalb is said to have advised such a movement, but Gates's sublime self-sufficiency was proof against all advice.

Yet he had to go on somehow, to some other place, so he turned to the right from the direct road he had been so persistently following, and marched away in broad daylight. Rawdon saw him go; he called in the small garrison at Rugeley's Mill, on Gates's route, and withdrew his own force to Logtown, a mile in advance of Camden, a position offering better opportunity for resistance than Camden itself.[23]

At Rugeley's, also called Clermont, on the 14th, Gates was joined by General Edward Stevens, with 700 Virginia militia.[24] He lay there two days.

CHAPTER 65

Camden

On the same day that Stevens added 700 men to the army, Sumter subtracted 400. He informed Gates that a number of South Carolina militia had joined him, and that he proposed to attack a British wagon train carrying clothing, ammunition, and other military stores from Charleston to Camden. He wanted reenforcements. The acquisition of such supplies would have gratified the Americans, but Gates's true objective was the destruction of Rawdon's force and the occupation of Camden. Those purposes accomplished, the wagon train would have fallen into his hands without much further effort. For their accomplishment he needed every man and every musket in his command and even more. The reasonable thing was to send for Sumter and add his troops to the main army. But Gates did the unreasonable thing. He detached a company of artillery, with two fieldpieces, 300 North Carolina militia, and, worst of all, 100 Maryland Continentals, and sent them to Sumter, under command of Lieutenant Colonel Thomas Woolford of the 5th Maryland.[1] For lack of horses, De Kalb had been obliged to deplete his artillery by leaving several pieces at the Roanoke and others at Hillsboro, as has been stated. The eight remaining were now reduced to six.[2]

In the meantime Cornwallis, disturbed by the approach of the Americans, whose numbers rumor multiplied by two, had hastened from Charleston to join Rawdon. Four companies of light infantry had also come to Camden from Ninety-six. There were now in the force opposing Gates a detachment of 17 men of the Royal Artillery, three companies of the 23rd Regiment (Royal Welch Fusiliers), numbering 282 rank and file, the 33rd (West

Riding) Regiment, 283 men, five companies of the 71st (Fraser's High-landers), 237 men, Tarleton's British Legion of horse and foot, 289 men, the Royal North Carolina (Tory) Regiment, 247 men, the Volunteers of Ireland, composed entirely of Irish deserters from the American army, 287 men, a company of 26 Pioneers, and more than 300 volunteer militiamen. The rank and file numbered 1,944, the total of all ranks being 2,239.[3]

Gates had the Maryland and Delaware Continentals, reduced by the wear and tear of their long and difficult marches, by sickness, by desertion, and by the subtraction of the hundred sent to Sumter, to hardly more than 900 rank and file, Armand's 120 horse and foot, Porterfield's 100 Virginia light infantry, and the Virginia and North Carolina militia of Stevens and Caswell, nearly 2,800, Colonel Harrison's three companies of artillery, 100 men and six guns, and about 70 volunteer horsemen—4,100 rank and file in all, of whom 3,052 were reckoned fit for duty. Gates, therefore, outnumbered his enemy by 50 per cent, but, of the Americans, only the 900 Maryland and Delaware troops were disciplined and veteran regulars, while the British rank and file of regulars, including the Volunteers of Ireland, counted about 1,400 rank and file.[4]

Gates decided to march to a point on Sanders Creek about seven miles from Camden. He called his principal officers together and read to them his definite orders prescribing in detail the order of a night march. He did not ask for their advice as to the proposed move. The orders were simply read to them, "and all opinion seemed suppressed by the very positive and decisive terms in which they were expressed." Consequently, no one ventured to oppose them. But they "were no sooner promulgated than they became the subject of animadversion" among all the officers, who could not imagine "how it could be conceived that an army consisting of more than two-thirds militia and which had never been once exercised in arms together, could form columns and perform other manoeuvres in the night and in the face of an enemy." [5]

It had become apparent in the council of the officers that Gates counted his force at 7,000 men. Otho Williams, his deputy adjutant general, knew this was a gross error. He called on the regimental officers for instant returns of their strength; it proved to amount to 3,052 present and fit for duty. He showed the figures to Gates. But Gates wanted neither advice nor this information. "Sir," said he, "there are enough for our purpose." [6] Terse, epigrammatic, confident, that reply might have had a place in history along with Farragut's "Damn the torpedoes! Full speed ahead!" if only Gates had not been merely Gates.

The orders stood. They called for a march at ten o'clock that night.

Armand's horse were to lead the van with Porterfield's Virginians and Major John Armstrong's North Carolinians, both acting as light infantry, in Indian file on their right and left flanks, each two hundred yards from the road. Then an advance guard of infantry was to be followed by the 1st and 2nd Continental brigades, Caswell's North Carolina militia, Stevens's Virginians, and a rear guard of the volunteer horsemen flanking the baggage train. There were elaborate provisions for action, if attacked on the way, and for rearrangement, if necessary for any reason, and an injunction of the strictest silence on the march. Armand protested against placing the cavalry in the van for night service, because of the impossibility of its approaching the enemy unheard; Gates declined to see the point.[7] He was confident of victory. "I will breakfast to-morrow in Camden with Lord Cornwallis at my table," an incredible tradition makes him say.[8] He very nearly did, though as a guest of Cornwallis, instead of as host.

Some meat and corn meal had been secured and a full ration was served out to the men. Instead of the promised rum, the usual heart warmer and even more necessary stimulant for unusual exertion, Gates had the happy thought of issuing to each man a gill of molasses from the hospital store, brought down by Stevens from Virginia; it proved to be a medicine indeed, an untimely physic.[9] The men ate voraciously of half-cooked meat and half-baked bread with a dessert of corn meal mush mixed with the molasses. "Instead of enlivening our spirits," says Sergeant Major Seymour, it "served to purge us as well as if we had taken jallap."[10] On the march, Otho Williams tells us, the men were of necessity "breaking the ranks all night and were certainly much debilitated before the action commenced in the morning."[11]

So the already tired, worn-down men, now more than half sick, started at ten o'clock of the night of August 15 on a dreary, bewildering march. There was no moon. The air was sultry with the heat and humidity of a Carolina August. Starlight made the road dimly visible to the main column; but the way of the flanking parties, difficult enough to keep through the pine woods two hundred yards from the silently marching men on the road, was obscured by the trees. So for more than four weary hours they trudged through the deep sand and the frequent swamps to nobody knew what.[12]

Then, suddenly, the silence of the night was shattered by the rattle of musketry ahead. Without the least warning they had met the enemy. By an extraordinary coincidence, Cornwallis and Rawdon, intent on surprising Gates, had marched from Camden at exactly the same hour that he had chosen for his advance from Rugeley's Mills. To the astonishment of both, they had met. The fresh British soldiers had marched more than twice as far as the weary Americans, and the advance troops of Tarleton's British and Armand's American Legion had simultaneously opened fire.[13]

Tarleton immediately charged upon Armand's men; they fell back upon the infantry vanguard and then upon the 1st Continental Brigade, throwing it into confusion and spreading consternation throughout the whole American army. But Porterfield, ever stanch, and Armstrong threw in their flankers and poured upon Tarleton's men such a heavy fire that they in turn gave way.[14] The 23rd and 33rd British infantry deployed in line across the road and checked this attack. The Americans, somewhat recovered from the first shock of surprise, also hastily formed, and for fifteen minutes or so musket fire was kept up by both sides. Then, as if by common consent, the firing ceased. Neither side wanted to fight in the dark.[15]

There were a number of casualties. The greatest loss to the Americans was gallant Porterfield, who was mortally wounded in this first encounter.[16] Prisoners were taken by both sides, and from them each learned of the composition of the other. Gates's astonishment could not be concealed when he learned that both Cornwallis and Rawdon, with 3,000 men, lay opposite him at a distance of 600 yards.[17] He at once called together his general and regimental officers. There was still time to withdraw, and De Kalb thought that should be done. When Otho Williams summoned him to the conference, he disclosed his opinion by asking, "Well, has the General given you orders to retreat the army?" [18]

The council met. "You know our situation, gentlemen," said Gates. "What is best to be done?" Each man looked at the others, those who favored a retreat being naturally reluctant to be the first to suggest it. Then "the brave, but headlong" Stevens broke the painful silence: "We must fight! It is now too late to retreat. We can do nothing else. We must fight!" The other officers looked at him, at Gates, at each other, but no one spoke. "We must fight, then," said Gates. "To your commands, gentlemen." [19]

The two armies had met in an open forest of pines, thinly set—a narrow space flanked on both sides by wide swamps. Somewhat narrower where the British were, it widened behind the Americans. Thus, if they were driven back, their wings would be out of touch with the swamps and would be open to flank attacks. Otherwise, they had a slight advantage in that they were on higher ground with a clear way of retreat, while the British had the creek, two hundred feet wide, in their rear, a trap in case of defeat.[20]

The American line was formed before daybreak: Gist's 2nd brigade, composed of one Delaware and three Maryland regiments, on the right;

Caswell's North Carolina militia in the center; and Stevens's Virginians on the left, with Armand's corps on its left flank. Smallwood's 1st Maryland Brigade was held in reserve in the rear. The artillery was posted in front of the center. De Kalb, in command of the right wing, took his post with it in the line. Gates and his staff took a position six hundred yards back of the line.[21]

When the British line was formed its left, facing Gist's brigade and part of the American center, was composed of the Volunteers of Ireland, Tarleton's infantry, the Royal North Carolina Regiment, and Colonel Bryan's North Carolina Tory volunteers; Rawdon commanded that wing. The right wing comprised the 33rd Regiment, three companies of the 23rd, and a body of light infantry, Lieutenant Colonel James Webster commanding. There was a second line composed of the Highlanders, with two 6-pounders. Tarleton's British Legion cavalry was held in column behind the second line. Two 6-pounders and two 3's were in front of the British center. The flanks of both armies rested on the swamps.[22]

There had been desultory skirmishing during the night, with little effect except to prevent the militia from getting any sleep. In the gray dawn, Colonel Williams descried the British advance. They were coming on in columns. He hurried to Captain Anthony Singleton of the artillery.

"Yes," said Singleton. "I can distinguish the grounds of their uniforms. They're not more than two hundred yards off."

"Open on them at once!" replied Williams, and galloped away to report to Gates.[23] Singleton opened fire; the enemy's guns answered. The smoke settled in the hazy atmosphere, which was soon completely befogged. The British advanced steadily and began to deploy.

Williams found Gates at his post in the rear. "The enemy are deploying on the right, sir. There's a good chance for Stevens to attack before they're formed."

"Sir, that's right. Let it be done," said Gates, and that was the last order he gave in that battle or in any other to the end of the war.

Williams hurried to Stevens and gave the order to advance. The Virginians moved raggedly and reluctantly forward. But, even if they had moved with alacrity, it would have been too late for the intended purpose; the British were already in line.

While Stevens's men hung back, Williams called for volunteers to go forward with him and draw the enemy's fire. Forty or fifty responded and ran forward within forty yards of the British line.

"Take trees, men!" shouted Williams. "Choose your trees and give them an Indian charge!"[24]

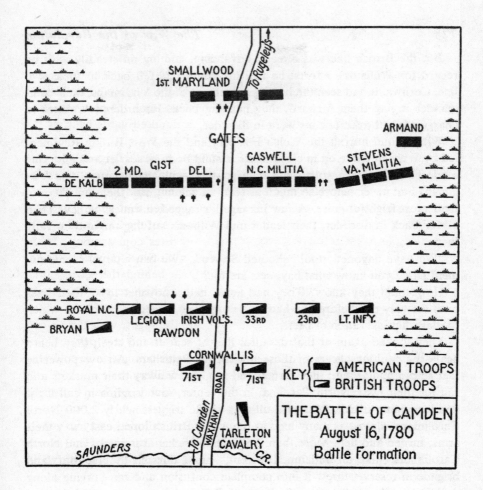

SMALLWOOD
1ST. MARYLAND

To Rugeley's

GATES

ARMAND

2 MD. GIST DEL.   CASWELL   STEVENS
                       N.C. MILITIA   VA. MILITIA
DE KALB

ROYAL N.C.

BRYAN

LEGION   IRISH VOL'S.   33RD   23RD   LT. INFY.
RAWDON

CORNWALLIS

71ST   71ST   KEY { AMERICAN TROOPS
                                           BRITISH TROOPS

To Camden   WAXHAW ROAD

TARLETON
CAVALRY

SAUNDERS   CR.

THE BATTLE OF CAMDEN
August 16, 1780
Battle Formation

But the British line was already advancing, coming on steadily with no regard for Williams's efforts; he and his volunteers fell back to their own line. Cornwallis had seen the halting movement of the Virginians, their commander urging them forward, they hanging back. He ordered Webster to charge while the Americans were in disorder.

With a loud hurrah the Welch Fusiliers and the West Riding Regiment led by Webster came on in close ranks, a solid body of scarlet and glittering steel. They fired one volley and then charged with the bayonet. The Virginians had never before so much as seen an enemy; now they saw them in their most frightful guise. A few managed a ragged, harmless volley. Then all fell back in disorder, their leader and Williams striving mightily to rally them.

"We have bayonets, too!" shouted Stevens. "We can charge! Come on, men! Don't you know what bayonets are for?"

How could they know? They had never had a bayonet in all their lives until the very day before and had never used one, except as a spit on which to roast that last ration of beef.

They looked again at that dreadful line of scarlet and steel; they heard again the exulting cheers of those murderous Britishers. An overpowering fear seized upon them; they turned and ran, threw away their muskets and ran for their lives. North Carolina, in the center, saw Virginia in full flight and was panic-struck. Without pulling a single trigger, nearly 2,000 North Carolinians, almost as many men as the whole British force, cast away their arms, turned and fled. More than 2,500 fear-stricken Virginians and North Carolinians, "like an undamned torrent," burst through the 1st Maryland brigade in reserve, threw it into complete confusion and ran "raving along the roads and bypaths towards the north." One regiment alone, Lieutenant Colonel Henry Dixon's North Carolina, posted next to the steady ranks of the Marylands and Delawares on its right, was held by the power of example in its place.[25]

Now both the center and the left were gone, hopelessly gone. The right wing of Marylands and Delawares, under General Mordecai Gist and dauntless De Kalb, its own left wide open to the enemy, alone held the field against Rawdon's repeated attacks.

De Kalb called for the reserve, the 1st Maryland brigade. It had recovered from its confusion, but had so far had little part in the battle. His aide sought its commander, to give him the message; but Smallwood was not with his troops—he had, in fact, left the field.[26] Otho Williams took charge and brought the brigade forward in line with the American right wing. It was immediately hotly engaged. Williams tried to bring it up to the left of the

2nd Brigade, but the British were between them. In spite of his efforts, the enemy held open a gap of six hundred feet between the two.

Cornwallis saw his chance. He swung Webster's regulars against the front and flank of the 1st Maryland Brigade. The Marylanders gave ground, rallied, were driven back, rallied again, but at last were overcome and routed.[27]

Now there were only Gist's Marylands and Delawares left to fight or fly. They fought. "Firm as a rock the phalanx of de Kalb and Gist remained." [28] They had stood off Rawdon's Volunteers of Ireland, the Legion infantry, the Royal North Carolina Regiment, and Bryan's Tory volunteers, more than 1,000 men against their possibly 600—not only had held them off, but had driven them back. With one bayonet charge, they had broken through the ranks of their attackers and taken 50 prisoners. Then their left was turned, and they were forced back. De Kalb and Gist re-formed them. Again they charged, and again they were driven back. Yet once more they attacked.

It was at this point that their companion brigade was broken and swept away. The smoke and dust hung in clouds in the air, so thick that one could see but a little distance. De Kalb and Gist knew nothing of the retreat of the other brigade, were not aware of the fact that they and their few men stood alone on the field. They knew that *they* were winning their fight and thought the battle was going as well for the rest of the Americans; otherwise they would have seen that a further contest was hopeless and would have retreated as best they could, with no further sacrifice of their men. They had had no orders from Gates to retire. So they fought on, and "never did troops show greater courage than those men of Maryland and Delaware." [29] "With the same unflinching obstinacy, which they had shown at the Gowanus and on Chatterton's Hill, in 1776, the Delaware and Maryland troops contended with the superior force of the enemy for nearly an hour." [30]

De Kalb's horse was shot under him. "Long after the battle was lost in every other quarter, the gigantic form of De Kalb, unhorsed and fighting on foot, was seen directing the movements of his brave Maryland and Delaware troops." [31] His head had been laid open by a saber stroke. Captain Peter Jaquett, adjutant of the Delawares, fighting by his side, hastily bandaged the wound and begged him to retire. But no orders had come from Gates, now miles away in full flight. De Kalb still thought victory was in sight; he refused.[32]

The fighting was hand-to-hand, terrific in its fierceness. Sabers flashed and struck, bayonets lunged and found their meat, clubbed musket fell on cracked skulls. But Cornwallis, as vigilant as Gates was not, had now thrown his entire force on these last remaining foemen, 2,000 men on no more than 600.

Overwhelmed by numbers that almost entirely surrounded him, De Kalb called for the bayonet again. All together his men answered. De Kalb at their head, they crashed through the enemy's ranks, wheeled, and smote them from the rear. But ball after ball had struck their heroic leader. Blood was pouring from him; yet the old lion had it in him to cut down a British soldier, whose bayonet was at his breast. That was his last stroke. Bleeding from eleven wounds, he fell.[33]

The brigade had lost its leader, yet the worse than decimated ranks closed, advanced once more, repelled another charge—but that was all. Tarleton's cavalry, returned from pursuit of the fugitives, swept down upon them, broke their ranks, and the battle was over.

Major Archibald Anderson of Maryland rallied a few men of different companies of the Continentals; Colonel John Gunby, Lieutenant Colonel John Eager Howard, Captain Henry Dobson, all of Maryland, and Captain Robert Kirkwood of Delaware collected about 60 men. All these preserved a compact body in the retreat. Such of the rest as had not fallen or been captured scattered and fled to the swamps.[34]

Prostrate in the field lay De Kalb. It was only when the Chevalier du Buysson, his aide, threw himself on his general's body, crying out his name and rank, that the thirsty bayonets were withheld from further thrusts into his body.[35] Some of the enemy, British or Tory, carried him off and propped him against a wagon so that they might more easily appropriate his gold-laced coat. There he stood, gripping the wagon with both hands, his head in weakness bowed on his chest, bleeding to death from all his wounds, when Cornwallis came riding by, rescued him from the despoilers, and caused him to be cared for by the British surgeons. His great bodily vigor kept the life in him for three days before he died in Camden.

But where was Gates? From the time he gave that first order to Stevens, not a word of any sort had come from him to his fighting men. He had been "swept away" in that torrent of fleeing militia in the very first minutes of the battle, as some of the historians kindly describe his flight. "Swept away," he was—on the fastest horse in the army, a noted racer, "the son of Colonel Baylor's Fearnaught, own brother to His Grace of Kingston's famous Careless," [36] a fit charger for General Gates. And that gallant steed never stopped sweeping him away until he landed his master at Charlotte, sixty miles from the field of honor. There Gates slept that night.

CHAPTER 66

After Camden

"Never was victory more complete, or a defeat more total." It has been described as "the most disastrous defeat ever inflicted on an American army." [1] In the wildest disorder the beaten men were scattered everywhere; few could find their officers, who were as widely dispersed. In the swamps and the forests where their pursuers could not find them, but which separated them the more widely from one another, the fugitives found temporary refuge.

Colonel Tarleton and his horsemen pursued the fleeing Americans that kept to the road, picking up many prisoners, including General Rutherford of the North Carolina militia. At Rugeley's Mills be found Colonel Armand, with several other officers apparently trying to save and send off the baggage train, which, despite Gates's orders, had not left that camp; in fact, Americans were busy looting it.[2] They offered some resistance to Tarleton's horsemen on their approach, but were soon captured or driven away.

This chase went on for more than twenty miles; more and more of the fugitives were captured. Twenty ammunition wagons, and the entire baggage, stores, and camp equipage of the Americans, were taken. It was only when the British horses were too fatigued that Tarleton gave over the chase.[3]

Scattered in small groups or singly, looking vainly for their comrades and for leadership, the beaten men, though clear of their military foe, found themselves in a country swarming with civilian enemies. Most of them had thrown away or lost their arms and were unable to resist the Tories, "every day picking them up, taking everything from them which was of value." [4]

They had had no orders where to assemble in case of defeat. Those few
that had retreated in more orderly fashion and escaped Tarleton, went on
to Charlotte. The remains of Armand's horse and a few others also gathered
there; Gist came in with only two or three men; Smallwood arrived with a
handful. There was little food and no hope of defense in that open village,
so they went on to Salisbury. Otho Williams has given an account of the
miseries of the march to Salisbury of that "wretched remnant of the Southern army," followed by "a great number of distressed Whig families," 300
friendly Catawba Indians, wounded men from Buford's late "unfortunate
affair . . . some in wagons, some in litters and some on horseback—their
sufferings were indescribable . . . the disorder of the whole line of
march . . . Compound wretchedness, care, anxiety, pain, poverty, hurry,
confusion, humiliation and dejection would be characteristic traits in the
mortifying picture." [5]

Sergeant Major Seymour of the Delawares wrote in his Journal, "We
assembled at Salisbury the few that were left . . . this being the first place
we made any halt. . . . From here we marched on the 24th under the
command of Genl. Smallwood, directing our route for Hillsborough, which
we reached with much difficulty on the 6th of September, 200 miles from
Campden." [6]

Gates was already there. He had stopped only overnight at Charlotte on
the 16th, the day of the battle, and had pushed on, the following morning,
to Hillsboro as fast as fresh horses could carry him, arriving on the 19th,
two hundred miles in three and a half days, a good record even for such a
fast rider.[7]

"The fugitives from Camden came in daily, but in a deplorable condition,
hungry, fatigued and almost naked" until about 700 had assembled, the
meager relics of Gates's army of 4,000 men. There they must rest until they
could be "completely refitted with clothes, tents and blankets"—also, most
of them, with arms.[8]

The British army's casualties in the battle amounted to 324 of all ranks:
2 officers and 66 men killed, 18 officers and 227 wounded, 11 men missing.[9]
Of the American loss there is no accurate record. It has been estimated that
650 of the Continentals were killed or captured, the wounded falling into
the hands of the enemy. About 100 of the North Carolina militia were killed
or wounded, and 300 were captured. Only 3 of the Virginians were
wounded,[10] which proves the advantage of their more prompt departure
from the scene. A heavy toll of Continental officers was taken in that battle:
3 were killed and 20 wounded, 14 of whom were captured—in all, 30 offi-

cers were taken. In this respect, the Delawares suffered most severely. Their commanding officer, a lieutenant colonel, their major, and 8 other officers were taken.

Gates's first job was to reorganize his shattered army. The North Carolina militia gave him no trouble; the survivors had "fled different ways as their hopes led or their fears drove them," and were so pursued and harried by the Tories that few, if any, turned up at Hillsboro. Many of the agile Virginians did appear at the camp, but their term of enlistment had so nearly expired that "all who had not deserted were soon afterward discharged." [11] It was only the Continentals that remained for reorganization.

The two brigades were compressed into one regiment of two battalions. The 1st, 3rd, 5th, and 7th Marylands became the 1st Battalion under command of Major Archibald Anderson of Maryland. The 2nd, 4th, and 6th Marylands and the Delawares became the 2nd Battalion under Major Henry Hardman of the same State. Colonel Otho Williams and Lieutenant Colonel John Eager Howard, both of Maryland, commanded the regiment. [12] In this rearrangement the Delaware Regiment became two companies of 96 men each of all ranks, under the two senior captains, Robert Kirkwood and Peter Jaquett. [13] The cavalry was embodied in one troop under Lieutenant Colonel William Washington of Virginia. The two brass fieldpieces left at Hillsboro, with a few iron pieces, composed the artillery. [14]

The initial losses of the army had been somewhat diminished by a gallant exploit of Colonel Francis Marion and 16 of his daredevils. On August 20 they fell upon a detachment of British and Tory troops escorting 160 American prisoners to Charleston. Rushing upon the guard at daybreak, before they had time to form, Marion took them all captive and released their prisoners, of whom fewer than half returned to the army. The rest were too much discouraged by their overwhelming defeat to continue in the service and left for their homes. [15]

There had been another momentary gleam of light on the otherwise dark horizon. Sumter with 300 of his own men and the 100 Continentals and 300 militia lent him by Gates, had made good his proposal to capture that British wagon train. On the 15th he took 100 British soldiers, 50 Tory militiamen, and 40 wagons laden with stores. But that gleam was quickly extinguished.

Hearing of Gates's defeat, Sumter began a retreat with his captives and wagons up the Wateree. At high noon of the 18th, while in camp on Fishing Creek, with all his arms stacked, some of his men bathing, others sleeping, himself asleep under a wagon, he was surprised by Tarleton, with 160 men. Charging on the unguarded camp, Tarleton cut Sumter's men off from their arms and routed them completely, killing 150 and capturing more than 300. All the recently taken British and Tory prisoners were released, and the wagon train recovered. In the little resistance the Americans were able to offer, one British officer was killed and 15 men either killed or wounded. Sumter himself escaped and rode into Charlotte two days later "without hat or saddle." [16]

Gates got news of this catastrophe while on his flight to Hillsboro, and it must have added gall and wormwood to his already bitter cup. Now he knew he was a hopelessly beaten man.

The reorganized American force at Hillsboro received some additions to its numbers. Colonel Abraham Buford, whose Virginia contingent had been cut to pieces by Tarleton's Legion at the Waxhaws in May, brought in its few remains and 200 new recruits. About 50 of Porterfield's light infantry also arrived. These were added to Buford's force, and they, with Colonel Otho Williams's newly formed regiment of Continentals, made up a brigade under General Smallwood, who was soon after superseded by Williams,[17] of whom some particular notice should now be taken.

He was a native of Maryland, thirty-one years old. His first military service had been with Captain Michael Cresap's Maryland Riflemen as ensign in 1775, marching with it to join Washington's army before Boston. In June, 1776, he became a major in a regiment of Maryland and Virginia riflemen which took part in the defense of Fort Washington, and he, with the rest of the garrison, was taken prisoner. Having been exchanged in January, 1778, he was appointed colonel of the 6th Maryland Continental Regiment, which became a part of De Kalb's division on his march to the south. His services in the Camden battle have been noted.

In person he was tall and "elegantly formed . . . his manner such as made friends of all who knew him." As a soldier and a man, he was highly valued by his companions in arms. His education was superior to that of most of his fellow officers.

On October 7 Gates made a new arrangement of his troops. Selected men were drawn from the Maryland and Delaware Continentals and from Buford's corps and made into three companies of light infantry. Those drafted from Buford made up the 1st Company, under Captain Peter Bruin of Virginia. The 2nd Company came from the lately formed 1st Battalion of Marylanders and was commanded by Captain Benjamin Brookes of that state. The 3rd was composed chiefly of Delawareans, with some addition of Marylanders; Captain Kirkwood of Delaware took command. To these were added 70 horsemen under Lieutenant Colonel Washington and Major Rose, also 60 Virginia riflemen. The infantry of this new *corps d'élite* were commanded by Lieutenant Colonel Howard of Maryland.[18]

Robert Kirkwood was born in New Castle County, Delaware, was educated at Newark Academy, and was engaged in farming when the war began. He was commissioned a lieutenant in Haslet's Delaware Regiment in January, 1776, and served in it until it was mustered out in December. He was a captain in Hall's regiment from its organization to the end of the war. His services in the southern campaigns will be described hereafter. Of the value of those services and his character as a soldier no better, more unbiased, more sincere estimate could be penned than the eulogium Henry Lee, a comrade in arms, included in his memoirs:

The remnant of that corps . . . from the Battle of Camden, was commanded by Captain Kirkwood who passed through the war with high reputation; and yet, as the line of Delaware consisted but of one regiment and that regiment was reduced to a captain's command, Kirkwood could never be promoted in regular routine. . . . The sequel is singularly hard. Kirkwood retired upon peace, a captain, and when the army under St. Clair was raised to defend the West from the Indian enemy, this veteran resumed his sword as the eldest captain in the oldest regiment.

In the decisive defeat on the 4th November [1791, the Battle of Miami] the gallant Kirkwood fell, bravely sustaining his point in the action. It was the thirty-third time he had risked his life for his country; and he died as he had lived, the brave, meritorious, unrewarded Kirkwood.

That gallant soldier Daniel Morgan, who had achieved fame by his splendid services at Quebec under Montgomery in 1776, and who, with his light troops, had contributed so much to the defeat of Burgoyne, had been neglected by the Congress. He had seen junior officers promoted over his head while his infinitely greater claim to rank as a general remained unrecognized. In justifiable resentment, he had resigned his colonel's commission in 1779 and retired to his home in Virginia.[19]

In June, 1780, the Congress "ordered" that he be called into service and "employed in the southern army as Major General Gates shall direct." No suggestion of even restoring him to his relative rank having accompanied the call, he declined to obey it. But after the Camden catastrophe he put aside his personal grievances and hastened to join Gates at Hillsboro, arriving late in September. On October 2 he was given general command of the newly formed corps of light infantry, and on the 13th the Congress belatedly gave him the deserved rank of brigadier general.[20]

The presence of a disorganized body of hungry soldiers made trouble in Hillsboro. The peaceful citizens complained to Gates, and he withdrew his men to a camp in the woodlands of an abandoned farm. Having no tents, they built wigwams of fence rails and poles thatched with brush and cornstalks. Some food—not much, but more than they had had on their long march from Camden—was obtained, and gradually order was restored and discipline reestablished.[21]

But it was no picnic. Lieutenant Caleb Bennett of the Delawares wrote long afterward, "We found ourselves in a most deplorable situation, without arms, ammunition, baggage and [with] very little sustenance and for some time our situation was unenviable." [22] The light infantry corps fared somewhat better than the rest of the army. The state of North Carolina, though its resources were well-nigh exhausted, managed "to collect a suit of comfortable clothing for each one of Morgan's command before they entered upon the severe and active duties before them." Each man got one new shirt, a short coat, a pair of woolen overalls or trousers, a pair of shoes, and a hat or cap. The state also "supplied the other troops, but not so comfortably as Morgan's." [23] There were not enough blankets to go around; what could be got were distributed to each regiment in proportion to its numbers.

CHAPTER 67

King's Mountain

Sir Henry Clinton in New York was commander in chief of all His Majesty's forces in America. He had instructed Cornwallis to make the security of South Carolina, with its important port of Charleston, his main object, aiming to hold fast to what was won and not to risk it by bold and hazardous adventure. He had in mind as his next possible move the occupation of Delaware, perhaps during the following summer, with the considerable Tory element to render his army's subsistence there easy. But, even if this were not undertaken, he felt that, holding New York, South Carolina, and Georgia, he could carry on a war of attrition until the rebels were worn out and save for Britain at least a considerable part of her colonies, if not all.

After the destruction of Gates's army at Camden, Cornwallis was in practically undisputed possession of South Carolina and Georgia; a period of mere holding on to what he had would have fulfilled his duty to his superior. Clinton had, however, guardedly suggested that the conquest of North Carolina would be acceptable, provided that it could be accomplished without jeopardizing his hold on the other two states.

This suggestion gave Cornwallis a chance to do what he wanted; he was all for an aggressive war. Unless North Carolina were conquered and possessed, he said, it would endanger his posts to the southward; he might be compelled to abandon all he had gained and take refuge within the fortifications of Charleston. After North Carolina, he saw himself taking Virginia; then the rest of the south up to Pennsylvania "would fall without much resistance and be retained without much difficulty." [1] He had arranged with

Clinton to send his reports directly to the Ministry in London as well as to New York, thus in effect short-circuiting Clinton. The home government was induced to believe in his plans and later instructed Clinton to fall in with them. Now, it seemed to Cornwallis, was the opportune time to carry them out.

Cornwallis had concentrated his forces at Camden after Gates's defeat. There he had been reenforced by the arrival of the 7th British regiment (Royal Fusiliers) from Charleston and by some additions to his Tory regiments. From that point he now moved north in two divisions. The principal one, led by himself, comprised the 7th, 23rd, 33rd, and 71st regiments of infantry, the Volunteers of Ireland, Hamilton's and Bryan's North Carolina Tory regiments, and a detachment of horse, with four guns. It marched, on September 8, north up the left (east) side of the Wateree towards the Waxhaws. A secondary force led by Tarleton, comprising the British Legion cavalry and infantry and an additional detachment of light infantry with one small fieldpiece, marched parallel with the other up the right side of the river. At the Waxhaws, Cornwallis encamped on the left side of the river, there called the Catawba, its course at that point being from west to east. Tarleton's force made its camp on the right side at Wahab's plantation some distance away.

The American Colonel William Davie was in the neighborhood with 80 dragoons and two small companies of riflemen, commanded by Major George Davidson, the only regularly armed body of patriot troops in the whole state. Early in the morning of September 21, Davie approached Wahab's plantation. He found the cavalry of the Legion already in their saddles in a body near the house. He sent Davidson with most of the riflemen around through a cornfield, which would conceal their approach, to take the house in the rear. Leading his horsemen and the rest of the riflemen, he charged up the lane towards the front with such ardor and such a shouting that the whole enemy force gave way at once and fled, only to meet a sharp fire from Davidson's riflemen by which 60 were killed or wounded. Davie collected 96 fully equipped horses and 120 stand of arms and hastily retired to his camp at Providence before troops sent by Cornwallis could arrive on the scene. His loss was one man wounded. It may be noted that Tarleton himself at this time was ill and absent from his command.[2]

On September 25 Cornwallis resumed his northward march from the Waxhaws towards Charlotte in North Carolina, with Tarleton's Legion and light infantry in advance of the main body. Davie, with 20 horsemen, Davidson's two companies of riflemen, and a small body of Mecklenburg militia under Major Joseph Graham, was in Charlotte, a village of twenty dwelling houses and a courthouse, when Cornwallis's van approached.

Davie posted his 20 dragoons behind a stone wall near the courthouse, the rest of his men behind fences on both sides of the road to it. The infantry of the British Legion, commanded by Major George Hanger, and the light infantry deployed in line across that road and moved slowly up towards the courthouse, to be received with a close fire from the men behind the fences. From this they recoiled, though Cornwallis himself urged them on. Hanger ordered the Legion cavalry to dislodge Davie's dragoons behind the stone wall. They charged, but were stopped by the fire of the 20 men, and would not again go forward. As Stedman says, "The whole of the British army was actually kept at bay for some minutes by a few mounted Americans, not exceeding twenty in number."

Davidson's and Graham's troops abandoned their fences and joined the dragoons. Under the repeated orders of Cornwallis, the Legion infantry and the light infantry again attacked and succeeded in turning Davie's right flank. He ordered a retreat. He was pursued for several miles and lost 30 killed, wounded, or captured. The British lost 15 killed or wounded.[3]

It may be remembered that, in June, when Cornwallis was sending various expeditions to occupy posts throughout South Carolina, he had detached Major Patrick Ferguson with his American Volunteer regiment to cover the country between the Catawba and Saluda rivers. Ferguson went on to join Lieutenant Colonel Balfour, who was holding the post at Ninety-six. Thence he moved a few miles east and established his camp on Little River. It became a rallying post for large numbers of South Carolina Tories, whom he organized into seven regiments, about 4,000 men. With this strong force, Ferguson held the district of Ninety-six—the "upcountry"—in complete subjection, sending detachments in every direction to harass and plunder the rebels and making every effort to encourage the Tories to join the King's army.

At the time Cornwallis marched north from Camden, he sent orders to Ferguson to move from Ninety-six into North Carolina to spread the gospel of loyalism there and finally to join the main army at Charlotte.

Late in September, Ferguson was at Gilberttown in what is now Rutherford County, North Carolina. He had in mind the interception of a force of Carolinians and Georgians under Colonel Elijah Clark, which had made an unsuccessful attempt upon Augusta in Georgia, had been beaten off, and was now, with 300 men and 400 women and children, endeavoring to avoid the British forces in South Carolina and escape into the Old North State. But trouble was brewing for Ferguson behind the mountains to the westward.

Patrick Ferguson was a remarkable man. The son of a Scottish judge, he entered the British army as a cornet of horse at the age of fifteen and served in the wars on the continent of Europe until, as a captain, he came to America. He was ingenious enough to invent a breech-loading rifle which could be fired five or six times a minute, at least twenty-five times as fast as a muzzle-loading rifle when its barrel became fouled. It also used a pointed, instead of a spherical, bullet. A few such rifles were manufactured and were used with effect by the men in the British rifle corps he commanded at the Battle of the Brandywine; but for the most part his men were equipped with the muzzle-loader.

When Clinton sent the expedition south in 1779, Ferguson was allowed to raise his own corps of riflemen, American Tories, called the American Volunteers, of which he made effective use in independent operations until his death. He was a soldier of great merit, "a fit associate for Tarleton in hardy, scrambling, partisan enterprise; equally intrepid and determined, but cooler and more open to impulses of humanity." [4] Less bloodthirsty than the more famous Tarleton, he was yet a bitter foe of the rebels, whose homes he mercilessly plundered and destroyed.

Ferguson was at this time in the prime of life, thirty-six years of age, of "middle stature, slender make and possessing a serious countenance, yet it was his peculiar characteristic to gain the affections of the men under his command." [5] Though of slight build, he was strong and athletic. He was a dead shot with rifle and pistol, and, though his right arm had been disabled in battle, he was a formidable antagonist with the sword, wielded in his left hand.[6]

Beyond the mountains on the west, in what is now Tennessee, were the Watauga settlements inhabited by a hardy breed of frontiersmen, mostly Scotch-Irish, hunters, Indian fighters, expert shots with their long-barreled Deckhard rifles, weapons of precision. Their only other equipment was a horse, a blanket, a hunting knife, and a bag of ground, parched corn sweetened with maple syrup. When this gave out, they lived on the game that the country afforded. They were not only rebels, but bitter enemies of Ferguson himself, whose merciless plundering in the Carolinas had made his name infamous. To them he audaciously sent word that if they did not desist from opposition to the king he would march over the mountains, hang their leaders, and lay waste their country with fire and sword. This message was not well received.

The Watauga men had an idea that, if any fighting was to be done, it ought to be in the enemy's country rather than among their farms and homes and women and children. Colonel Isaac Shelby of Virginia and Colonel John Sevier accepted the challenge. They called on Colonel William Campbell of Virginia to join them. Campbell summoned Colonel Benjamin Cleveland of North Carolina. To Sycamore Flats on the Watauga River, by September 25, Colonel Charles McDowell of North Carolina brought 160 men, Sevier brought 240 "over-mountain men," Shelby brought 240 of the same, Campbell brought 400 Virginians. They were mostly mounted but, with their long rifles, would fight on foot. Ferguson called on Cornwallis for reenforcements; the over-mountain men called on Heaven, the Rev. Samuel Doak being their mouthpiece. In a service of prayer before they set out, he asked for the aid of "the sword of the Lord and of Gideon."

Ferguson started south towards Ninety-six. The "backwatermen," as Ferguson called them, followed. At the Catawba River Colonel Cleveland joined them with 350 North Carolinians. Ferguson eluded his pursuers, who thought he was for Ninety-six, by turning east towards King's Mountain. They came to the Cowpens, west and somewhat south of the mountain, on October 6. There Colonel James Williams with 100 North Carolinians and Colonel William Graham with 60 joined them, making their total force over 1,400. Having news of Ferguson's real route, they decided that 900 of the best mounted men should push after him as rapidly as possible, the rest to follow. On October 7 the forerunners came to the mountain on which Ferguson had established himself, with the announcement that "he defied God Almighty and all the rebels out of Hell to overcome him."

King's Mountain afforded a position of extraordinary natural strength. Its level summit was about 500 yards long and 70 to 80 yards wide, but broadened to 120 yards at its northeast end, where Ferguson had fixed his camp. Its steep, rocky, heavily wooded sides rose about 60 feet from the plain below. He had about 100 Rangers, picked men from the King's American Rangers, the New Jersey Volunteers, and the Queen's Rangers, also 1,000 Tory militia. The Rangers were men of a good class. The second in command was Captain Abraham de Peyster of New York. Another captain was Samuel Ryerson of New Jersey. The adjutant was Anthony Allaire of New York, and the surgeon was Dr. Uzal Johnson of New Jersey. These men were as well trained and experienced as regular soldiers. They were equipped with bayonets and well drilled in their use. The local Tory auxiliaries were provided with long blades to be fitted into the muzzles of their rifles or muskets and used as bayonets. It is a remarkable fact that Ferguson was the only British soldier in the ensuing battle, one of the most important of the war. On both sides, all the rest were Americans.

The patriots reached the mountain about noon of October 7, 1780, dismounted, fastened their blankets and coats to their saddles, tied their horses, and took positions in a line around its broader end and along the sides of its narrower part nearly to its southwestern extremity, Campbell's troops at the southwest end of the line on one side, Shelby's on the other. These two forces were to begin the attack, swarming up their respective sides and meeting so as to enclose Ferguson's at the broad end. A war whoop signaled the attack. The drums in the camp called their men to arms.

Shelby met the first fire. He restrained his men from replying until they had got nearer the top. Campbell could be heard shouting, as his men climbed the mountain: "Here they are, boys! Shout like hell and fight like devils!" Shelby's men were driven back by a bayonet charge part way down the height. Having no bayonets, they could only take trees and fire up at their enemy; and they did this with deadly effect.

Meanwhile, the rest of the rebels around the broad end of the mountain were climbing, taking cover, and firing. Cleveland's men gained the top, and Ferguson sent his bayonets at them, driving them back as he had driven Shelby's; but they, too, kept up their fire. Campbell and Shelby had again come on, and again Ferguson's bayonets repelled them. But Sevier's corps was now on the summit, and he had to turn to them. The bayonet was only a temporary resource. It might drive the attackers before it; it could not stop the bullets from the Deckhard rifles, aimed by dead-shot frontiersmen. All the rebel contingents came into the fight with unrestrained fury. Everywhere the Tories were surrounded by men, not in solid bodies to be attacked with the bayonet and driven back, but fighting each man on his own behind the trees fringing the open plateau. From every side came a hail of bullets.

The position of the Tories was hopeless, but Ferguson would not give up. He was everywhere on the field animating his men. Twice, when white flags were raised, he cut them down with his sword. To an officer who begged that the carnage might cease, he replied that he "would never surrender to such banditti." But at last he had to admit that the battle was lost. With a few others he tried to cut a way through the ring of his enemies. A rifle bullet stopped him. He fell from his horse and died with one foot caught in his stirrup.

His men, in terrified disorder, crowded behind their wagons and tried to keep up the fight. Cleveland brought up his force behind them. Completely surrounded, they fled to a hollow place. But there was no shelter there. They stood like a herd of deer in a corral, while the infuriated Whigs shot them down, crying, "Buford! Buford! Tarleton's quarter!" One of them rode out of the press showing a white flag. His saddle was emptied. Another met the

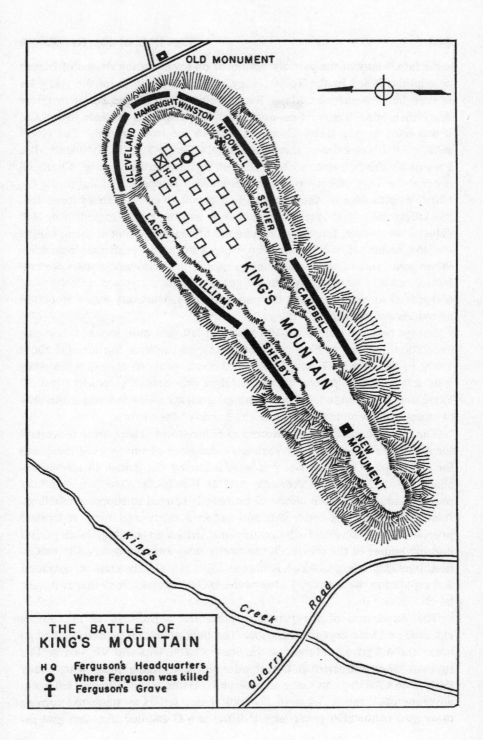

OLD MONUMENT

HAMBRIGHT WINSTON

CLEVELAND

McDOWELL

H.Q.

SEVIER

LACEY

WILLIAMS

KING'S MOUNTAIN

CAMPBELL

SHELBY

NEW MONUMENT

King's

Creek Road

Quarry

THE BATTLE OF
KING'S MOUNTAIN

H Q   Ferguson's Headquarters
○   Where Ferguson was killed
✝   Ferguson's Grave

same fate. Many of the patriots were bent on avenging the deaths of friends or relations killed by the Tories. They would not desist from the slaughter of their helpless enemies. Major Evan Shelby called on the Tories to throw down their arms. They did so, and he implored his men to cease firing. But it was hard to stop them. Campbell rode to the front crying: "For God's sake, quit! It's murder to shoot any more!" De Peyster, in command after Ferguson's death, protested to Campbell against further killing. Campbell ordered the Tory officers to separate from their troops and called to the defeated men to take off their hats and sit down. Even after this submission, the killing did not altogether cease; but at last the rebels ceased firing and gathered in a circle, four deep, around the prisoners, glaring at them, calling out the names of individuals who were known for particular atrocities. When some sort of order was finally restored the prisoners' arms were collected, and they were confined under guard. Ferguson's personal effects were divided, as souvenirs, among the patriot officers. His body was wrapped in an oxhide and buried.

Except one body of about 200 who had left that morning on a foraging expedition, not one of Ferguson's men escaped death or capture. Of about 1,000 in the fight, 157 were killed, 163 were wounded so badly that they were left on the field, and 698 were taken prisoners. The patriots lost 28 killed and 62 wounded. Fifteen hundred muskets and rifles and a quantity of stores and ammunition fell into the hands of the victors.

The rebels marched their prisoners to Gilberttown. There arose a demand for retaliation upon them for Tarleton's slaughter of surrendered men, and for execution of forty patriot prisoners taken by the British in former encounters, at Camden, at Augusta, and at Ninety-six. One patriot officer present had recently seen eleven of his friends hanged to suppress rebellion. A sort of court was convened, and between thirty and forty individual prisoners were convicted of assisting the British in raiding, looting, and burning houses of the rebels. Of the twelve who were condemned to execution, nine, including Colonal Ambrose Mills, an elderly man of character and reputation, were hanged. One of the twelve escaped; the other two were let off.

The disposition of the prisoners presented a problem to the hastily gathered and little organized patriots. The over-mountain men wanted to go home and did go, as did most of the South Carolinians and Virginians. The captives were entrusted to Cleveland's North Carolina men, who finally decided to take them to Gates at Hillsboro. Gates asked Thomas Jefferson, governor of Virginia, what to do with them. Jefferson suggested turning them over to the civil governments of the two Carolinas. But such governments hardly existed. In this impasse they were loosely guarded and within a few months all but sixty escaped.[7]

The effect of the victory at King's Mountain was instantaneous and of great importance. It turned the tide of the war in the south. On receipt of Ferguson's appeal for help, the very day of the battle, Cornwallis had sent Tarleton. Tarleton heard of the disaster on the way and returned in all haste to Cornwallis at Charlotte with the news. Rumor magnified the numbers of rebels to 3,000, and the British commander feared they would sweep around him into South Carolina and capture Ninety-six and Camden. Though the fear was baseless, it was true that the patriots of Mecklenburg and Rowan counties had been aroused and the partisan corps of Marion, Sumter, and Pickens were increasing in numbers and were more and more active. They did present an immediate danger to the British.

Cornwallis abandoned at once his project for the subjugation of North Carolina and, on October 14, started his troops on a hurried retreat. The rainy season had set in, and for several days rain fell incessantly. The roads were deep with mud, the swampy parts almost impassable. There was a lack of provision; for one five-day period the soldiers lived on corn gathered from the fields. Lacking tents, they spent the nights in the open, lying on wet ground. And always they were harassed by the American militia, hanging on their rear and cutting off baggage wagons. There was much sickness; Cornwallis himself, stricken with fever, lay in one of the wagons. After fifteen days of this wretched flight they reached Winnsboro, between Ninety-six and Camden, and encamped.[8]

For some time the two armies lay in camp, the Americans at Hillsboro, North Carolina, the British at Winnsboro, South Carolina. Morgan's newly organized light troops made an expedition to Salisbury and down into Mecklenburg County to cooperate with the local militia, but nothing "of consequence" happened.[9] Then, having heard of a Tory outpost at Rugeley's Mills, South Carolina, William Washington's horsemen marched against it.

Colonel Rugeley with 100 Tories occupied a log barn surrounded by an abatis. It was impregnable to bullets, the horsemen could do nothing with it, and Washington had no artillery. He fashioned a log into the semblance of a gun and propped it up on the stubs of three of its limbs. This "Quaker gun" was pushed boldly to the front by some of his dismounted men. The garrison was summoned to surrender or have their fortress blown to pieces. They surrendered, and Washington led the colonel, a major, and 107 privates back to Morgan's camp at New Providence, where Gates with his main force also came and established his camp.

Though there was no major activity on the part of the two armies at this time, Marion's irregulars were busy in South Carolina between the Pee Dee and the Santee River, arousing the people to revolt against the British, threatening the enemy's communications between Camden and Charleston, and cutting off supply trains. Cornwallis sent Tarleton after him. The Swamp Fox successfully eluded Tarleton's stronger force.

Sumter was active in the same country. Against him Cornwallis sent Major Wemyss with a part of the 63rd Regiment mounted and 40 of the British Legion horse. At Fish Dam Ford in what is now Chester County, Wemyss came upon Sumter's camp on November 9 and attempted a surprise; but he was on guard, and when Wemyss dashed upon the American pickets he was received with a volley. Two bullets hit and disabled him. His second in command pushed on, but Sumter from behind a fence poured upon the enemy such a fire that 28 of them were shot down. Further attempts were fruitless. Wemyss was captured, as were 25 of his men, and the rest retreated.[10]

Sumter then crossed the Broad River and, having received considerable additions to his force, threatened Ninety-six. Cornwallis was alarmed. He recalled Tarleton from his pursuit of Marion and ordered him to go after Sumter, taking the men of the 63rd who had been with Wemyss, along with his own Legion. Sumter was apprised of his danger by a British deserter. He crossed the Enoree River and marched to Blackstock's plantation on the south side of the Tiger. Tarleton followed so rapidly that his foot soldiers could not keep up. He pushed on with 170 of the Legion horse and 80 mounted men of the 63rd, leaving the footmen to follow.

Blackstock's was on high ground, the slope of the hill being quite abrupt and covered with brush and thickets. The Tiger River swung around the American rear and right flank. A road led past the buildings of the plantation, a house and a log barn, and Sumter posted part of his men in these, the rest along fences skirting the road. His whole force numbered 420 men.

Tarleton saw the strength of the American position and paused at the foot of the hill for his foot soldiers to come up, meanwhile dismounting the infantry of the 63rd to fight on foot. Sumter took advantage of the division of his enemy's force. He directed Colonel Elijah Clark with 100 men to pass Tarleton's flank and get between him and the infantry he was expecting. Sumter led a corps against the men of the 63rd. Under heavy fire, the British charged up the steep hill and drove Sumter back, Tarleton's horse following in support. But near the buildings they met a concentrated fire from the men posted in them and had to retire. Tarleton tried again, without success. He was finally obliged to retreat.

The Americans claimed that Tarleton's casualties amounted to 92 killed and 100 wounded, an impossible number if, as he claimed, only 250 of his men were actually in the fight. He admitted a loss of 51 killed and wounded. Of the Americans, 3 were killed and 4 wounded, one of them Sumter, who was shot in the right shoulder.

Sumter, fearing another attack by the 71st Regiment and the rest of the 63rd, who had been sent in support of Tarleton, withdrew across the Tiger River. This withdrawal seems to have been the basis of Tarleton's extraordinary claim of success in his attempt, in which he said 100 Americans had been killed and wounded and 50 captured. The prisoners appear to have been civilians picked up on his withdrawal to Winnsboro, one of whom he hanged. The only advantage actually gained by Tarleton was the temporary disablement of Sumter.[11]

CHAPTER 68

Before Cowpens

The Congress had been unfortunate in the selection of commanders in the South. It had chosen Robert Howe, and he had lost Savannah and all Georgia. It had chosen Benjamin Lincoln, and he had lost Charleston and all South Carolina. It had chosen Horatio Gates, and he had lost all the rest of the south and his army. When his successor was to be chosen the Congress decided to entrust the choice to Washington. On October 5 it resolved "that the Commander-in-Chief be and is hereby directed to appoint an officer to command the southern army, in the room of Major General Gates." [1]

Washington delayed not at all in making his selection. On the day after he received a copy of the resolution, he wrote to Nathanael Greene at West Point, "It is my wish to appoint You." The Congress approved the appointment, gave Greene command over all troops from Delaware to Georgia with extraordinarily full powers, "subject to the control of the Commander-in-Chief"—Gates had reported to Congress only—and adopted Washington's suggestion that Steuben go south with Greene.[2] From the very beginning of the war, Greene had been Washington's right arm and had displayed indefatigable industry and strength and breadth of intelligence. Indeed, in the opinion of some well qualified judges he was Washington's superior, both as strategist and as tactician.

Whether his appointment was a misfortune, Greene was in doubt. Certainly, in the state of affairs in the south, there was little promise of an easy task or of a successful result of the best efforts he could put forth. Nevertheless, he was not "altogether without hopes of prescribing some bounds to

748

the ravages of the enemy." ³ With that modest program he accepted the appointment and was soon on his way to his new command.

Henry Knox had promised him a company of artillery with four field-pieces and two light howitzers, and Quartermaster General Timothy Pickering was to send him two companies of artificers. In Philadelphia he asked Joseph Reed, president of Pennsylvania, for four or five thousand stand of arms. All Reed and the Board of War could furnish was fifteen hundred. He called on the Congress for clothing, but they had none to give him. He tried to get the Philadelphia merchants to furnish five thousand suits and take bills on France in payment, but they excused themselves. Reed promised him 100 "road-wagons"; and Pickering, 40 "covered wagons." From the Congress he got $180,000 in Continental currency, which was worth practically nothing in real money. Having begged Washington "to urge unceasingly the necessity of forwarding supplies for the southern army, as it will be impossible to carry on a winter campaign without clothing," ⁴ he went on his way.

At Annapolis, Greene pleaded with the Maryland Board of War for clothing; and he wrote to Caesar Rodney, president of Delaware, for "speedy reinforcements of men and supplies of every kind." He left General Mordecai Gist in Baltimore to arrange for forwarding whatever he could get from Maryland and Delaware, and Steuben in Richmond for a similar purpose. In Virginia, Governor Thomas Jefferson told him "The situation as to clothing is desperate." By letter, Greene called again and again on the Congress and everyone else he could think of for clothing. He got assurances of good will everywhere, but very little else. Virginia and Maryland pleaded poverty so great that they could not even furnish forage for his horses. Neither Delaware nor North Carolina took "any measures for giving effectual aid" to him.⁵

On November 27 he was at Hillsboro; and on December 2, at Charlotte. There he met Gates "with respectful sympathy and Gates, whose manners were those of a man of the world, returned his greeting with dignified politeness." Otho Williams wrote that their conduct was "an elegant lesson of propriety exhibited on a most delicate and interesting occasion." ⁶ On the next day, Gates issued his last orders, announcing the change of officers, and Greene found himself in command of the "grand army" of the Southern Department of the United States of America. It consisted of 90 cavalrymen, 60 artillerists, and 2,307 infantrymen on paper, of whom 1,482 were present and fit for duty. Only 949 of the paper infantry were Continentals; the rest were militia. And, for a final summing up, fewer than 800 of the whole force were properly clothed and equipped.⁷ Greene wrote to Joseph Reed on January 9, 1781: "The appearance of the troops was wretched beyond description, and their distress, on account of [lack of] provisions was little less than their suffering for want of clothing and other necessaries."

The first task of the new commander was the establishment of order. The troops, he wrote to Reed, had lost "all their discipline" and were "so addicted to plundering that they were a terror to the inhabitants." He saw that it was necessary to establish "a camp of repose, for the purpose of repairing our wagons, recruiting our horses and disciplining the troops." [8]

There were but three days' provisions on hand when he arrived in Charlotte, and no promise of any more. The country round about had been stripped clean by the army and, more especially, by the North Carolina militia, who had ravaged it without any compensating military service.[9] It was plain that another place must be found for the camp of repose.

Greene sent General Thaddeus Kosciuszko, a Pole on whose sound judgment and engineering ability he greatly relied, on an exploring trip. Kosciuszko reported that on the Pee Dee River near Cheraw Hill, just south of the border between the Carolinas, there was a suitable location. To that point Greene decided to go.[10] But there was a still more important decision to be made; and, in making it, Greene determined the whole course of the ensuing campaign.

With such troops as he had, in such a wretched condition, Greene could not hope to offer battle to Cornwallis. He must wait until they were refitted and reenforced. Yet he must not appear to retreat before the expected advance of his opponent from Winnsboro, lest he increase the confidence of his enemy, lower the spirits of his own men, and dishearten the people of the country, who looked to him for defense and would be valuable to him if they believed in him. But, as Cheraw Hill was more distant from the enemy than Charlotte, a removal to that point would look like a retreat and hence have the undesirable effect he wished to avoid. He must carry on some encouraging operations that would not incur the danger of a general engagement. Such operations must, in short, be partisan in nature, threatening Cornwallis's flanks, interrupting his communications, cutting off his supplies, and at the same time animating Marion, Sumter, and Pickens with their partisan bands to similar enterprises.[11]

To meet the situation, Greene made a daring decision; he decided to divide his already insufficient army. The decision was opposed to the classic rules of warfare: to divide an inferior force in the face of a superior enemy was to invite that enemy to destroy first one and then the other of the parts. There had been examples enough of the impropriety of such a division in this very war: Washington splitting his army at New York and Long Island in August, 1776; Howe scattering his Hessians in New Jersey in December, 1776; Burgoyne sending his Hessians to defeat at Bennington in August, 1777; Washington allowing Lafayette to take post at Barren Hill in May, 1778. The most recent example was Ferguson at King's Mountain. Every one of these, except Barren Hill, had resulted in disaster; and Lafayette had escaped from Barren Hill only by the skin of his teeth. To divide so vastly inferior a force as Greene's at Charlotte might seem to be suicidal.[12]

On the other hand, there were excellent reasons, even compelling reasons, to disregard the classic rule and fit the strategy of the moment to the inescapable actual conditions. The ability to do that is the hallmark of a really great general.

Greene saw that, by separating his army into two parts, he made it easier for both to subsist on the country, living on the very regions from which the British drew their supplies; and that if Cornwallis later should take the natural route back into South Carolina he would find a fighting force on each of his flanks. If he turned against the left-hand American force, that on the right might attack Charleston; if against the right-hand force, Ninety-six and Augusta would be exposed to that on the left. If he made no movement, the intended harassment of his army could be better effected. As to the danger of either division being attacked and defeated, Greene relied upon the mobility of the Americans to escape from the more encumbered, slower British. So, with all those reasons to justify him, he carried out his plan, "the most audacious and ingenious piece of military strategy of the war." [13] The proof of its validity was that it worked.

Greene had confirmed Morgan in the command of the light infantry, now composed of 320 Maryland and Delaware Continentals, 200 Virginia riflemen under Captains Triplett and Tate, and "from 60 to 100" light dragoons under Lieutenant Colonel Washington, Major Howard being still in command of the infantry. This was to be one of the two divisions. The second division, about 1,100 Continentals and militia, was entrusted to General Isaac Huger of South Carolina, Greene remaining with it.[14]

Three great rivers traversed the country in which Greene expected to operate. A knowledge of the fords and ferries and of the roads leading to them was indispensable to his safety and success. He accordingly sent Lieutenant Colonel Edward Carrington, his quartermaster, to explore and map the Dan River, and Edward Stevens, major general of Virginia militia, and General Kosciuszko to the Yadkin and the Catawba for the same purpose. They were also to collect or build flatboats to be carried on wheels or in wagons from one river to another.[15] These precautionary measures proved to be of the utmost importance in the ensuing campaign.

On December 16 Greene directed Morgan to cross the Catawba to its western side, join the North Carolina militia under General William Davidson, and operate between the Broad and the Pacolet rivers, "either offensively or defensively, as your own prudence and discretion may direct—acting with caution and avoiding surprises by every possible precaution." The main objects of the detachment were to protect the people, to annoy the enemy, and to collect and store provisions and forage. If Cornwallis moved in force towards Greene's proposed camp at Cheraw Hill, Morgan was to rejoin the main army or to fall upon the enemy's flank and rear, as occasion served.[16]

An excessive rainfall that inundated the lowlands delayed Greene's departure; but on the 20th he was on his way. The march of his army was a desperate affair: the roads were deep with mud, the horses were too weak for want of food to drag the wagons without frequent halts, and the men were not much better off. But on the 26th he arrived at his destination, Cheraw Hill, and established the camp of badly needed repose.[17] There, with his 650 Continentals, 303 Virginia and 157 Maryland militia, he was in a position to support Marion or to threaten Camden, and he was nearer than Cornwallis to Charleston.[18] It was not a bad situation, though it was 140 miles from Morgan across the Catawba.

Morgan left Charlotte the day after Greene, "marched to Biggon Ferry on Catawba River, crossed the ferry," and marched, marched, marched, under the same hardships as the other part of the army. On Christmas Day he went into camp on the Pacolet River, after fifty-eight miles in all of "very difficult marching in crossing deep swamps and very steep hills which rendered our march very unpleasant." [19] While in this camp he was further reenforced by Davidson with 120 men, and by Major Joseph McDowell with 190 North Carolina riflemen.[20]

Two days after his arrival at the Pacolet, Morgan detached William Washington with his dragoons and 200 mounted militia and sent him against a party of 250 Tories who were ravaging the country along Fairfort Creek. They rode forty miles the next day, found their enemy near Ninety-six, killed or wounded 150 of them, and took 40 prisoners, without any loss to themselves.[21]

The two divisions of the army lay in their respective camps, with only routine activity, for three weeks. To Greene in this period came a desirable reenforcement. Lieutenant Colonel Henry Lee's Legion, sent down by

Washington, arrived on January 13. It comprised 100 horse and 180 foot. About the same time Colonel John Green of Virginia brought in 400 militia. The men of Lee's Legion were worth far more to Greene than their numbers would seem to indicate. They were "the most thoroughly disciplined and best equipped scouts and raiders in the Revolution" and one of the few corps of American troops that were maintained in uniform. Their short, green coats closely resembled those of Tarleton's men. Lee was "horse-proud," and the mounts of his horsemen were "powerful, well bred and kept in high condition." On the march, the horsemen frequently took up the foot soldiers behind them and thus expedited their progress.[22] Greene sent the Legion to Marion to assist him in a stroke against Georgetown. They had a brush with the garrison there and captured its commander by surprise, but, for want of artillery, were unable to breach the "fort," in which the rest had taken refuge. They paroled the captive officer and retired.[23]

Meanwhile, Cornwallis had rested at Winnsboro, with a secure hold on South Carolina and Georgia. He too had been reenforced. His dispatches and reports to London had convinced Germain that his plan for the conduct of the war should displace Clinton's; and Clinton had taken a decision to send substantial reinforcements to the south. He had accordingly sent Major General Leslie down with 2,500 men; 1,500 of these joined Cornwallis at Winnsboro, and the others remained at Wilmington. Cornwallis then had in his army a brigade of the Guards, the 7th or Royal Fusiliers Regiment, three companies of the 16th Regiment, the 23rd or Royal Welch Fusiliers, the 33rd, the 2nd battalion of the 71st or Fraser's Highlanders, the Hessian Regiment von Bose, 600 Hessian jägers, Tarleton's Legion, and 700 Provincials or Tories, a total of about 4,000 men.[24] It was a force so much greater in numbers, so much better trained, armed and equipped than Greene's whole army of 3,000 tatterdemalions that one would have supposed Cornwallis secure in his position and confident of the future. In fact, he was much disturbed in mind.

Greene's splitting of his army had astonished him, shocked his sense of the proprieties of warfare; it seemed to him audacious to the verge of recklessness. Tarleton could not believe Greene would have done it if he had known of Leslie's addition to the British army. It offered such a good opportunity for an advance from Winnsboro, "which, if executed with tolerable rapidity, might separate the two divisions of the American army and endanger their being totally dispersed or destroyed." [25] But Cornwallis saw the situation more clearly.

He saw what Greene had seen: that if he attacked Huger's force Morgan might strike at Ninety-six and Augusta; if he went for Morgan the way to Charleston would be open to Greene. He therefore saw he could only follow the unorthodox example of his opponent and divide his own army—not into two parts, but into three.[26]

He sent Leslie to hold Camden against an attack by Huger's division. He directed Tarleton to find and crush Morgan, while he himself, with his main army, moved cautiously and slowly up into North Carolina to intercept and destroy the remains of Morgan's force after its expected defeat by Tarleton.[27]

His orders to Tarleton, then posted at Ninety-six, were set forth, on January 2, in these terms: "If Morgan is still at Williams' or anywhere within your reach, I should wish you to push him to the utmost. . . . No time is to be lost." To which Tarleton replied: "I must either destroy Morgan's corps or push it before me over Broad river towards King's Mountain." Cornwallis answered that Tarleton had understood his intentions "perfectly." [28]

CHAPTER 69

Cowpens

Tarleton's force comprised his own Legion, 550 horse and foot; a battalion of the 7th (Royal Fusiliers) Regiment numbering 200; a battalion of the 71st (Highlanders) Regiment, 200 men; 50 of the 17th Light Dragoons; a small detachment of the Royal Artillery, and a party of Tory militia of unknown number. The whole numbered about 1,100 rank and file, with two light fieldpieces, 3-pounders called "grasshoppers." [1] Morgan's corps, as has been noted, consisted of 320 Continentals, 200 Virginia militia riflemen, about 80 of Washington's dragoons, and Davidson's 140 and McDowell's 200 North Carolina and Georgia militia riflemen. [2] On the march, he was joined by Lieutenant Colonel James McCall with 30 mounted South Carolina and Georgia militia, [3] making his total force up to about 1,040, nearly equal in numbers to Tarleton's corps. In trained regulars Tarleton outnumbered him more than three to one.

Tarleton's first move was made on January 15, north across the Enoree and Tiger rivers towards Morgan, then on the south side of the Pacolet. Having news of this advance, Morgan crossed the Pacolet with the intention of defending the ford; but Tarleton, on the 16th, crossed the river six miles below him. Morgan then withdrew precipitately to Thicketty Creek, his adversary occupying the ground, on which he had lain the night before, a few hours after it had been vacated. [4] Early in the morning of the 17th, Tarleton resumed his pursuit of the Americans, who retired to the Cowpens, where "a certain prosperous Loyalist, named Saunders" [5] used to roundup his ranging cattle. At this place Morgan decided to stand.

His choice of battleground has been severely criticized. It was in "a wide

plain covered with primeval pines, chestnut and oak," free from undergrowth
and therefore open to Tarleton's horsemen, three times as many as his own
and of the best quality. There were no swamps or thickets upon which to
rest the flanks of a battle line or to offer a refuge from cavalry. At a short
distance in the rear and around the left of such a line drawn up to face
Tarleton's advance, the Broad River curved, cutting off a retreat to the north
or east towards Greene and Huger.[6] Henry Lee has pointed out that beyond
the Broad, near King's Mountain, there was a position disadvantageous to
cavalry, convenient for riflemen, and affording means of retreat. The Cowpens position was a most unlikely place for a small force to choose for
battle, presenting every opportunity for its wings to be turned and for complete destruction in case of defeat. Yet Morgan chose it and afterwards
stoutly defended his decision:

> I would not have had a swamp in view of my militia on any consideration;
> they would have made for it, and nothing could have detained them from it.
> And, as to covering my wings, I knew my adversary, and was perfectly sure I
> should have nothing but downright fighting. As to retreat, it was the very thing
> I wished to cut off all hope of. I would have thanked Tarleton had he surrounded
> me with his cavalry. It would have been better than placing my own men in the
> rear to shoot down those who broke from the ranks. When men are forced to
> fight they will sell their lives dearly and I knew that the dread of Tarleton's
> cavalry would give due weight to the protection of my bayonets and keep my
> troops from breaking as Buford's regiment did. Had I crossed the river, one half
> of my militia would immediately have abandoned me.[7]

The argument seems labored, to excuse an unmilitary decision. The truth
seems to be that Morgan, a fighter by nature, was irked by being obliged to
retreat before Tarleton, and turned on his foe because he wanted to give
battle, disregarding the weakness of his position. Henry Lee thought that
his choice of that field grew out of "irritation of temper" which "overruled
his sound and discriminating judgment," and that "confiding in his long-
tried fortune, conscious of his personal superiority in soldiership and relying on the skill and courage of his troops," [8] he simply decided to stop his
backward movement and fight it out where he happened to be.

Whatever may be said of his choice of ground, there is no criticism of the
disposition of his troops for the battle. It was novel, ingenious, and masterly.

Having been joined by Pickens with 70 North Carolina riflemen the evening before the battle, Morgan, who, though a general, was far from being a
"brass hat," visited the campfires, talking and joking with his men in their
own language, his voice cheerful, his manner confident and reassuring. He
told them that "the Old Wagoner" (his nickname) would crack the whip

over Ban Tarleton in the morning as sure as he lived. "Just hold up your heads, boys," he said to the militia, "give them two fires and you're free." They had a good night's rest and a full breakfast the next morning.[9]

After breakfast Morgan formed his battle line. Behind and to the north of the ground where his men had bivouacked was a slight eminence, rising gradually for about three hundred and fifty yards and then sloping northward into a swale. Behind that the ground ran to a lesser eminence, which in turn sloped northward to a plain, beyond which ran the river. The whole terrain was covered by an open wood.

His disposition of his men was as unorthodox as Greene's division of his army. On the southern and higher elevation, he formed his main line. Howard's light infantry of Maryland and Delaware Continentals held the center. On their right were Tate's Virginia militia and a small company of Georgians, and on their left Triplett's Virginians. These militiamen were mostly old Continental soldiers who had served their terms of enlistment and rejoined as volunteers. This line contained in all about 450 men. Howard commanded it.

About one hundred and fifty yards in front, 300 North and South Carolinia militia under Pickens were posted in open order in a thin line three hundred yards long. In front of them, at a similar interval, 150 picked riflemen, Georgians and North Carolinians under Major John Cunningham of Georgia and Major Charles McDowell of North Carolina were thrown out in line as sharpshooters. Back of all these, and behind the lesser rear eminence, Morgan posted as a reserve 80 of William Washington's dragoons and 45 of Lieutenant Colonel James McCall's Georgia mounted infantry armed with sabers to operate as cavalry.[10]

The formation was unusual in that it put the weakest contingents so far in front of the battle line to receive the first shock of the attack without immediate support from the regulars. But Morgan's plan was well considered as suitable to the character of his own troops and of his enemy, as was disclosed by his orders for the conduct of the battle.

The sharpshooters in the front line in irregular formation were to take cover behind trees. They were to withhold their fire until the advance of the enemy was within fifty yards, and then to take careful aim at "the men with the epaulets." After two volleys they were to retire slowly, firing at will, and fall into the spaces in the second line of militia.

The second line, thus reenforced, was to fire "low and deliberately," was not on any account to break, but, when too hard pressed, was to retire to the left and so around to the rear of the main formation, where they would, Morgan told them, be perfectly safe. There they were to rally, re-form, and be held in reserve. Those orders were not given to the officers only; every man was informed of the plan of action, and all in the second line were especially cautioned not to be alarmed by the falling back and apparent defeat of the men in front of them; it was all a part of the plan.[11] The baggage had been sent under suitable escort a few miles to the rear, and the horses of the militiamen in the first two lines (they were all mounted) were tied to trees behind the cavalry reserve, an arrangement very consoling to their owners as affording a means of swift retreat in case of disaster.

This disposition having been made, the men were told to "ease their joints"—that is, to sit down—until the enemy was sighted, but not break their formation. Morgan then rode along the lines, encouraging the men with homely exhortations. The disposition had been made without haste and in a confident and assured manner. As a consequence, the men were in good spirits and ready for a fight.

Tarleton, eager to fulfill his promise to destroy Morgan's corps or push it back towards King's Mountain, where Cornwallis would finish it off, had allowed his men little rest that night. At three in the morning they were afoot. For five hours, mostly in the dark, they marched on muddy roads, through swamps and creeks and over broken ground, covering eight very long miles, before they came in sight of the Americans.[12]

When he first perceived his enemies Tarleton, with a small party, rode forward to reconnoiter their position. A sight of the first line of riflemen checked him before he was near enough to observe satisfactorily the main battleline. He at once ordered his Legion cavalry forward to dislodge the sharpshooters. As the horsemen came on, they received a volley that emptied fifteen saddles. They recoiled, so convinced of the marksmanship of the always dreaded riflemen that they could not be induced afterwards to charge upon the Americans. The front-line men, still firing at will, then retired and took their places in the second line.

Tarleton thereupon deployed his troops in battle formation, his light infantry on the right, the infantry of the Legion in the center, and the 7th Regiment on the left, with 50 dragoons flanking each wing. The Highlanders and 200 cavalry formed the reserve. The "grasshoppers" were placed in the center and on the left. This disposition had hardly been effected when the impetuous Tarleton opened the battle with his guns and immediately sent his whole line forward.

The second line of the Americans, under Pickens, waited until the enemy were "within killing distance." Then, taking careful aim, they delivered their fire, reloaded, and fired again with deadly accuracy. A large proportion of

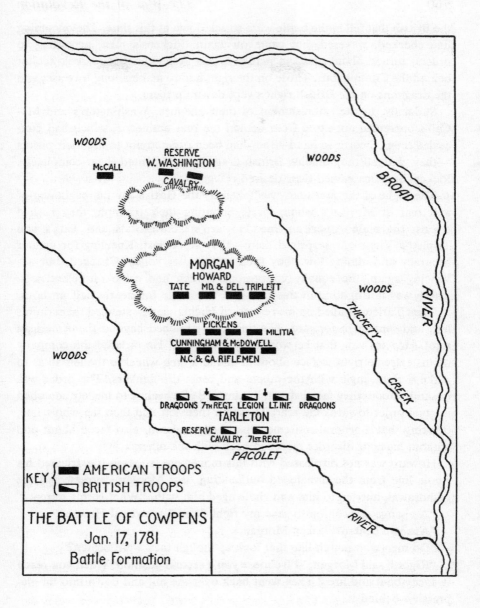

WOODS

McCALL

RESERVE
W. WASHINGTON

CAVALRY

WOODS

BROAD

RIVER

MORGAN
HOWARD

TATE   MD. & DEL.   TRIPLETT

WOODS

THICKETY

PICKENS

MILITIA

CUNNINGHAM & McDOWELL

N.C. & GA. RIFLEMEN

WOODS

CREEK

DRAGOONS   7TH REGT.   LEGION   LT. INF.   DRAGOONS

TARLETON

RESERVE

CAVALRY   71ST. REGT.

PACOLET

KEY {   ■ AMERICAN TROOPS
        ◣ BRITISH TROOPS

RIVER

THE BATTLE OF COWPENS
Jan. 17, 1781
Battle Formation

the British that fell in the battle were struck down at this time. The oncoming line checked, wavered, but came on again. Pickens's men, according to orders, turned about and ran across to the American left to seek shelter behind the Continentals. Those on the right had to make a long traverse, and the dragoons on the British right swept down on them.

Suddenly, to the astonishment of their enemies, Washington's and McCall's horsemen appeared from behind the rear eminence, which had concealed them. Swords in hand—they had been ordered not to fire their pistols —they charged the pursuing British dragoons and routed them completely. Pickens's troops gained their desired refuge.

The flight of the first lines was taken by the British for the beginning of a retreat of Morgan's whole force. Shouting their triumph, they rushed against the main American line. Howard's Continentals and Tate's and Triplett's Virginians surprised them—they stood fast. Kneeling for greater accuracy and aiming low, they fired volley after volley. Checked, but advancing again, the equally courageous British line came on relentlessly. There was hot fighting in this phase of the battle for nearly half an hour.

Then Tarleton called on his reserve of Highlanders, extended them on his left, and sent them forward. His line now stretched beyond the American right. Howard saw that he would be outflanked. He ordered the company on his extreme right to face about in line and then wheel to the left so as to make a right angle with the others and repel the flankers. The order was misunderstood; they faced about, but instead of wheeling to the left, marched in good order towards the rear. Those on their left and then the whole line, thinking that a general retirement had been ordered, also faced about and without haste or disorder marched back with the others.

Howard was not displeased with this movement, because it extricated his whole line from the threatened outflanking. But Morgan, surprised at the withdrawal, hurried to him and challenged him with, "What is this retreat?"

"A change of position to save my right flank," answered Howard.

"Are you beaten?" asked Morgan.

"Do men who march like that look as though they were beaten?"

"Right!" said Morgan. "I'll choose you a second position. When you reach it, face about and fire." They went back over the hill and down into the depression behind it.

Seeing this withdrawal, Tarleton was sure of his victory. He ordered up his Legion cavalry and threw everything he had against the Americans. His men, each eager to outstrip the others, broke ranks and ran forward in tumultuous disorder. Washington, pursuing the British dragoons, had got in advance of the American line and seen the confusion in the British ranks, not visible to the others behind the hill. He sent word to Morgan: "They're coming on like a mob. Give them one fire, and I'll charge them."

Morgan received the message just as Pickens's riflemen, having made a complete circuit of the field, came up on his right. He gave the order to the Continentals: "Face about, give them one fire and the day is ours!" The British had followed the Americans over the hill first occupied. Coming down its rear slope in a mad rush, they were within fifty yards of their enemy when Morgan's order was obeyed. The whole line faced about and blazed with gunfire. The Americans fired from the hip, holding their muskets with bayonets ready. The shock was terrific. Howard seized the moment for the final order: "Give them the bayonet!" Into the tangled ranks of Tarleton's infantry and the Royal Fusiliers, the Maryland and Delaware Continentals drove with irresistible force. At the same time, Washington and McCall struck them on the flank and in the rear. Bayonet and saber split the throng of redcoats and tore it apart.

"Throw down your arms and we'll give you good quarter!" shouted Howard. Muskets clattered on the ground; some of the British ran, others stood, crying for mercy. The American officers were put to it to hold their men from giving the beaten foe what they called "Tarleton's quarters," which meant the bayonet to disarmed men, but they succeeded.

In the center the battle was over; but on the American right the High-landers held out, and the British dragoons from their left wing were still active. Pickens's riflemen, re-formed and ready, opened upon these with such a destructive fire that the dragoons fled; but the stubborn Highlanders fought on. Not until the whole weight of the Americans fell upon them did they yield. Then their commander, Major McArthur, gave up his sword to Colonel Pickens.

Meanwhile Tarleton had been urging his reserve of 200 dragoons to go forward from their post in the rear. They refused to move. He tried to protect and remove his artillery. Washington attacked him and drove his men from the field, but the British artillerists stood to their guns. They were the last to be overcome; they never did surrender. Almost to a man they were struck down at their posts.

Washington followed Tarleton, who, with a few officers and about 140 horsemen, was in full retreat. In the ardor of the chase, Washington got well ahead of his troop. Seeing that, Tarleton and two of his officers turned and attacked him. One of them aimed a stroke at him; but an American sergeant who had come up caught the blow on his saber and wounded the assailant in the arm. Another officer was about to cut Washington down when a four-teen-year-old bugler shot him with his pistol. Tarleton thrust at the American colonel; when the blow was parried he fired, wounding Washington's horse, and galloped away. Washington kept up pursuit of the fugitive infantry and took many prisoners. The British baggage guard cut the horses loose, mounted them, abandoned the wagons, and got away.

The victory was complete in every particular. The British lost 100 killed, among them 39 officers. Prisoners were taken to the number of 229 wounded and 600 unhurt. In all, nearly nine-tenths of the entire British force were killed or captured. Of the Americans only 12 were killed and 60 wounded. The two British guns, 800 muskets, two stand of colors of the 7th Regiment, 35 baggage wagons, 100 dragoon horses, 60 Negro slaves, and a quantity of ammunition fell into American hands.[13]

News of the victory at Cowpens was received with delight throughout the country. In Greene's camp at Cheraw it was celebrated by a *feu de joie*. South Carolina made Pickens a brigadier. Virginia gave Morgan a horse and a sword. The Congress, in an enthusiastic resolution, praised and thanked him and his troops for obtaining "a complete and important victory" over Tarleton's "select and well appointed detachment," and gave him a gold medal. To William Washington and Howard it awarded silver medals and swords and to Pickens a sword. This battle again proved the value of militia properly handled. Also it gave a deathblow to Tarleton's reputation as a military leader.

It had other far more important results. Though "small in scale" it was "momentous in result." [14] In the opinion of John Marshall, "Seldom has a battle, in which greater numbers were not engaged, been so important in its consequences as that of Cowpens." [15] It gave Greene his chance to exercise his strategical genius in the conduct of a campaign of "dazzling shiftiness" that led his opponent by "an unbroken chain of consequences to the catastrophe at Yorktown which finally separated America from the British crown." [16]

Cornwallis Pursues Morgan

In the moment of his victory the cool-headed Morgan did not forget that his position was still precarious. Cornwallis's much greater army was in the field and might be near at hand. The British general had agreed with Tarleton to march his men to King's Mountain to cut off Morgan's retreat; but he seems to have been apprehensive of danger to his right flank from the army of Greene and Huger. He moved only a few miles from Camden and then waited a week, until Leslie, on the way to join him, had crossed the Wateree. On the day of the battle, instead of being at King's Mountain in Morgan's rear, he was twenty-five miles to the south.[1]

Nevertheless, he endangered Morgan. In five or six hours after the battle, Tarleton's fleeing cavalry would bring him news of the catastrophe at Cowpens; and, marching light and with speed, he might yet intercept Morgan's column, encumbered with a mass of prisoners nearly two-thirds of its own number. Moreover, the road Morgan had to travel to escape to the north met at Ramsour's Mills the road Cornwallis would take to cut him off, and the distance to that point from Cowpens was about the same as the distance from Turkey Creek, where Cornwallis had halted and still held his army. Even if the British general detached only a thousand infantry with a few pieces of light artillery, and sent them posthaste to Ramsour's Mills, he could without doubt hold Morgan until the rest came up to finish him off. It was plain that only the utmost expedition on Morgan's part would suffice, not only to save the fruits of his victory, but also to avoid disaster.[2]

Morgan's first duty was to his wounded men and to those of the enemy. He detached Pickens and a number of mounted militia to gather them up

763

and care for them as best they could; after that they were to bury the dead. Of the enemy's baggage, he prepared to carry off as much as he could that might be useful, especially tents, of which he had none, and ammunition. The abandoned muskets were also collected. Though the battle was not over until about ten o'clock, the retreat was under way towards the east by a little after noon. Between Morgan and Greene ran four rivers: the Broad, the Catawba, Lynch's Creek, and the Pee Dee. Marching six miles, Morgan crossed the Broad and encamped. Pickens, having set up tents for the wounded on the battlefield and having left them in care of the surgeons under a flag of truce, joined him the next day.[3]

Early in the morning of the 18th, after sending out patrols to secure information as to the movements of Cornwallis's army, Morgan pushed on towards the fords of the Catawba. At Gilberttown he detached Pickens with the greater part of the militia and an escort of Washington's cavalry to conduct all the prisoners towards Island Ford on a branch of the Catawba, while he himself took the Continentals and the rest of the militia to Sherrill's Ford on the main stream.[4]

On the evening after the battle Cornwallis, in his camp at Turkey Creek twenty-five miles away, was still awaiting Leslie's reenforcement when a hard-riding courier on a well lathered horse brought him the news of Tarleton's defeat. Since he had been confident of the overthrow of Morgan, "it is not difficult to conceive of his embarrassment and mortification," says Fortescue. "He was now in exactly the same position as after Ferguson's defeat at King's Mountain, when, with Rawdon at his side, he had declared that the invasion of North Carolina must be abandoned." [5]

But now he was hopelessly committed to the projected invasion by the destruction of the fortifications of Charleston which he had ordered, and by his having brought up, under Leslie's escort, the whole matériel for the campaign. "Deeply as his lordship was affected with the weight of this misfortune, and greatly as he saw his difficulties increased by it, he was nevertheless resolved to prosecute the original plan . . . as the only means of maintaining the British interest in the southern colonies." However, perhaps necessarily in making preparations, he delayed his departure from Turkey Creek until the 19th, and thereby let his prey escape.[6]

Even when he did start, he went in the wrong direction. Thinking that Morgan, dazzled by his success, would hold his ground near the Broad River or perhaps make an attempt on Ninety-six, Cornwallis marched northwestward toward the Little Broad River to cut him off. But Morgan, as has been said, had headed straight for Sherrill's Ford by way of Ramsour's Mills, where Cornwallis by marching due north with equal celerity might have met and destroyed his depleted and much inferior army.[7] Having learned of Morgan's actual movement, Cornwallis shifted his march towards the north and arrived at Ramsour's Mills on the 25th, to find that the Americans had not only passed that point two days before, but had now crossed the Catawba, thus putting two rivers between themselves and him.[8]

In contrast to the slow movement of the British army was the rapidity of Morgan's march. In less than five whole days he crossed two rivers and covered one hundred miles, under conditions that were not particularly favorable. Seymour's restrained statement, "On our way thither we had very difficult marching, being very mountainous," [9] hardly even suggests the hardships they endured, duplicated soon after by those of Huger's division on the march to join Morgan.

At Ramsour's Mills, Cornwallis again paused. If he was to catch up with the fast-moving Americans he must travel even more rapidly than they did. He had lost all his light troops at Cowpens; now, therefore, he must transform his whole force into light troops by relieving it of its cumbersome impedimenta.

He spent two days in destroying his superfluous baggage. He set an example to his men by drastically reducing his own, and his officers did likewise. Except the wagons needed to carry ammunition, salt, and hospital stores and four others for the transport of the sick and wounded, every wagon and all its contents were burned. All the tents went into the fire; all the store of provisions, except as much as the men could carry in their haversacks, went up in smoke. And last, the greatest sacrifice of all, the rum casks were stove in and the precious liquor was poured out on the ground. "The men," says Trevelyan, "looked on sadly, but passively." They could not do otherwise, of course; but it may have been largely because of this disheartening and ill-boding destruction that during those two days at Ramsour's many Hessians and some few British soldiers deserted, perhaps 250 in all. It was a magnificent gesture, but in the event it proved to be "vain and useless and finally fatal" to Cornwallis and his army.[10]

Meanwhile, on the east side of the Catawba, Morgan was resting and refreshing his troops while he waited the return of the detachment he had sent off with the captives. Pickens, having delivered them to a commissary for prisoners at Island Ford to be sent into Virginia, crossed the stream there and rejoined Morgan at his camp, where the whole command lay until February 1. [11]

For a whole week after the battle Greene and Huger, with their division, waited at Cheraw for news of Morgan; on the 25th it came. Overjoyed though he was, Greene could not fail to see that the situation of Morgan and the best of the American army was precarious and might soon become desperate; he took measures accordingly. He sent orders to the commissaries at Salisbury and Hillsboro to get ready to move their prisoners and their stores to Virginia. He directed Carrington, his quartermaster general, to assemble boats on the Dan River at the boundary between North Carolina and Virginia, against the possible necessity of a retreat, and he ordered Huger to get his division ready to march and ultimately join forces with Morgan. Then, with a guide, one aide, and a sergeant's guard of dragoons, he set out on the 28th to ride through a country infested with Tories the hundred and twenty-five miles that lay between the Cheraw and Morgan's camp on the Catawba. It was an imprudent act, its only justification being success; he arrived in a little over two days.[12]

Huger's orders were to march up the Pee Dee and the Yadkin (really the same river) to Salisbury, North Carolina, whither Greene expected to direct Morgan's force. Huger sent off the least necessary baggage, the poorest horses, and the worst wagons to Hillsboro, and on the 28th started a march of one hundred and twenty-five miles to Salisbury. It was a hard march. His men were sometimes without meat, often without flour, always without rum. It was cold; they had little clothing, few blankets, no tents. Every day they had to ford deep creeks of icy water and march on until the heat of their bodies dried their rags. Rain fell on them. The roads froze in rough ruts at night and were slippery with mud by noonday. Over them many marched on naked feet. Yet, in all that march, Huger lost not even "a single sentinel" by desertion.[13]

Greene reached Morgan's camp on the 30th. In conference, a difference of opinion arose. Morgan was for a quick retreat into the western mountains beyond probable, or even possible, pursuit—a prudent move if nothing but the army's safety were desired. But Greene had larger, more far-reaching plans. As soon as he heard from Morgan that Cornwallis had destroyed his baggage and seemed resolved to march on towards the north, he exclaimed, "Then, he is ours!" He immediately wrote to Huger that he hoped to ruin Cornwallis, if he persisted in the "mad scheme of pushing through the country," and urged him to effect a junction of the two divisions as soon as possible; also to recall Lee's Legion from Marion at Georgetown. "Here is a fine field and great glory ahead." [14]

Greene's plan was to retreat due north—not into the mountains, difficult if not inaccessible to Cornwallis's army, but through a country where the

British general not only could but would follow. Day by day, he would keep just far enough ahead of his pursuer to avoid being caught, but near enough to keep alive in Cornwallis a hope, even an expectation, of bringing him to battle. He would tease his opponent along farther and farther from his supply bases, while he himself would be drawing nearer and nearer his own in Virginia and the north. It was a bold, a hazardous plan, subject to all the accidents of such a march, which might force him to stop and give battle under difficult conditions. Morgan saw in it the danger of disaster and opposed it, declaring that he would not be answerable for the consequences if it were tried. "Neither will you, for I shall take the measure upon myself," Greene replied, and issued orders accordingly.[15]

On the 28th Cornwallis, having completed the destruction of his baggage, marched towards Beattie's Ford on the Catawba, beyond which was Morgan's camp. Finding the river so swollen by rains that it could not be passed, he halted within four miles of the ford and waited two full days for the flood to subside.[16]

General William Davidson had called on the North Carolina militia to guard the fords in the neighborhood of Morgan's camp. He had collected 800, including 56 mounted riflemen, and posted them on the eastern bank at four crossings along thirty miles of the river, the largest number, about 300, at Beattie's Ford.[17]

The river having fallen to a practicable depth by January 31, Cornwallis moved to cross it. He had left Rawdon with 700 men to hold Camden, and now had nearly 3,000. His plan was his favorite, an outflanking movement. One division of his army under Lieutenant Colonel Webster, comprising the 33rd Regiment, the 2nd battalion of the 71st, the Royal North Carolina Regiment of Tories, the Hessian jägers, the artillery, and the wagons, was to approach Beattie's Ford as if to cross there. This movement was made at one o'clock in the morning of February 1. It was, however, merely a feint. Cornwallis himself and General O'Hara, with the brigade of Guards, the Hessian Regiment von Bose, the Royal Welch Fusiliers, 200 cavalry, and two light fieldpieces, started at the same time for Cowan's—or Mc-Cowan's—private ford six miles below Beattie's.[18] This was the real movement, a crossing which, without the opposition expected from Morgan at Beattie's, would outflank the Americans.

Cowan's Ford was about five hundred yards wide, with a rocky bottom over which the river was still three to four feet deep, running with swift turbulence. The ford had a certain peculiarity; about halfway across it split in two. The straight course, used by wagons, was deeper and rougher. That which diverged to the right was longer but shallower and had a smoother bottom; it was more used by horsemen. It reached the east bank about a quarter of a mile below the other. At its point of emergence, Davidson had posted most of his guard, leaving only a picket of 25 men at the wagon ford.[19]

It was near dawn of a dark and rainy morning when O'Hara's division reached the west end of the ford and saw the fires of the militia on the opposite bank. He formed the Guards in column of fours and ordered them to cross. With cartridge boxes high on their shoulders and bayonets fixed on unloaded muskets, they marched into the waist-deep water led by a Tory guide; the rest of the division followed. The roaring of the water drowned the sound of their approach, and it was too dark for the American sentinel on the opposite bank to see them before the head of the column was a hundred yards advanced in the river. Then he gave the alarm, and the small body of militia opened fire. The first three ranks were visibly thinned by the rifle bullets. The column halted, only to come on again, the men and horses struggling against the current, stumbling over rocks, losing their footing, and being swept downstream, but nevertheless steadily advancing.

In mid-stream the guide took fright and got away, without telling the officer leading the advance that he should break off to the right and take the horse ford to its landing below. So the column kept on, straight across on the wagon ford. In its rougher, deeper waters, men and horses were swept off their feet. Colonel Hall's horse was shot under him and he sank under the water, but was caught and saved from drowning. Cornwallis's own horse was shot, but did not fall until it reached the other bank. General O'Hara and General Leslie were both overthrown and so were many of the cavalry. But still the column pressed forward.

General Davidson down at the horse ford had heard the firing and hurried his men up to the scene of action. Before he got there the light infantry of the Guards had reached the bank, loaded their muskets, and opened fire, driving back the few riflemen and covering the landing of the rest of the British. Davidson withdrew his men from the river's edge and tried to beat back the oncoming enemy, who formed, as soon as they were out of the water, loaded, and fired. A bullet struck him in the left breast; he fell dead, and his men broke and scattered. Colonel Hall, who had so courageously led the British across, was shot dead just after he set foot on the bank.

This brave exploit accomplished nothing save the crossing of one contingent. Morgan was not outflanked; his troops had left their camp the evening before. General Webster with the other division of the British crossed at Beattie's Ford later in the day without opposition. By the time Cornwallis's whole force was across, Morgan's troops, who had marched all night and part of the next day, were thirty miles away on the road to Trading Ford on the Yadkin, the next river. Their march, says Seymour, was "very unpleasant . . . it having rained incessantly all night, which rendered the roads almost inaccessible." [20]

Morgan and his men had departed, but Greene with two or three aides had stayed behind to arrange for Davidson's militia to rendezvous at a certain point and to join Morgan's force, after their duty at the fords was done. His aides were sent here and there on this business. Greene went on alone and narrowly escaped capture. He was but a few miles beyond Tarrant's Tavern, where many of Davidson's militia had assembled, when Tarleton's cavalry came clattering up in pursuit of them. The militiamen delivered a hasty fire, ran to their horses, and made off with some loss. [21]

At the point of rendezvous Greene waited vainly for the militia until midnight. Then came a messenger to tell him that Davidson was dead, the militia dispersed, and Cornwallis across the river. He rode on alone to Salisbury. At Steele's Tavern in that village he dismounted, stiff and sore, to be greeted by a friend. "What? Alone, Greene?" "Yes," he answered, "alone, tired, hungry and penniless." Mrs. Steele heard him. After getting him a breakfast she brought two little bags of hard money and gave them to him. "You need them more than I do," she said. [22] The contents of those two little bags constituted the entire military chest of the Grand Army of the Southern Department of the United States of America.

CHAPTER 71

The Retreat to the Dan

With the crossing of the Catawba by both armies began the famous Retreat to the Dan, "one of the most memorable in the annals of war." [1] From the numbers of men engaged in it—about 2,000 in the American army and less than 3,000 in the British—it may seem to have been a trifling affair; but its consequences were great. It led—indeed, forced— Cornwallis to Yorktown, where the power of Britain in the American states was shattered.

There had been four unbridged rivers, besides innumerable tributaries, after Morgan had passed the Broad. One, the Catawba, was now behind both, but there yet remained the Yadkin, the Deep River, and finally the Dan. At any of these, the mischance of high water at the fords or lack of boats elsewhere might stop either army, forcing the pursued to stand and fight or balking the pursuer of his quarry.

The Dan was the ultimate goal of the Americans. Once across it and in Virginia, Greene could call on reenforcements and supplies; there was safety. It could be crossed on its upper reaches at fords; lower, ferriage in boats would be necessary. These had been provided for the Americans by the foresight of Greene and the skill and energy of Carrington. Towards them Greene must make his way, but in such manner as to deceive his opponent into believing that he was for the fords above. That was the strategic problem which Greene solved in such masterly fashion as to extort from Tarleton the admission that "every measure of the Americans during their march from the Catawba to Virginia was judiciously planned and vigourously executed." [2]

Greene wrote to General Washington [3] that "heavy rains, deep creeks, bad roads, poor horses and broken harriers, as well as delays for want of provisions," had prevented Huger's division from reaching Salisbury in time to join him and Morgan there. With Cornwallis at his heels he knew he could not await Huger's arrival. So, from Steele's Tavern that night, he sent a message to Huger to change course to the northeastward and meet Morgan's column at Guilford Court House. He then rode on to catch up with Morgan.

Morgan had passed through Salisbury and reached Trading Ford on the Yadkin, about seven miles east of the town. It was usually a good fording place, but the long continued rains had raised it above fording depth. Boats were necessary, and, by Greene's foresight and Kosciuszko's energy, they were there. In the night of the 2nd and 3rd of February, the cavalry swam their horses across, the infantry took to the boats.

After passing the Catawba, the two temporary divisions of the British army had joined on the road to Salisbury. Cornwallis had then added O'Hara's mounted infantry to his own cavalry and sent the combined force to catch Greene before he crossed the Yadkin, while he himself burned more baggage so as to double his teams and get the few remaining wagons out of the mud, in which they were sunk to the hubs.

The Americans had been followed by many of the country people fleeing from the British advance. A few of their wagons, guarded by some of the militia, were still on the west bank of the Yadkin when O'Hara's van came up. There was an exchange of shots before the guard was dispersed. O'Hara got the wagons, but nothing more. The American army was on the other side, and so were all the boats. O'Hara could not cross.[4]

Despite the continued rain and the almost impassable roads Cornwallis, by doubling his teams, succeeded in reaching Salisbury by three o'clock in the afternoon of February 3. He was then only seven miles from Trading Ford, beyond which were the Americans. O'Hara had sent his cavalry back from the ford to Salisbury, but held his infantry on high ground overlooking the river. Cornwallis sent him some fieldpieces, and he attempted to bombard Greene's camp across the river. Greene had sent away with his prisoners his only artillery, the two little "grasshoppers" captured at Cowpens, and could not reply. But his camp was behind a high, rocky ridge that paralleled the stream, and the bombardment did no damage, except to knock the roof off a cabin in which he was busy with correspondence.[5]

The river was still rising and was now too deep even for horses; but Shallow Ford, ten miles up the river, was always passable. Taking it involved a wide swing to the west from Greene; but Cornwallis was encouraged to make this departure by the receipt of information that the lower fords on the Dan were impassable at this season of the year, and that there were not enough boats at the ferries to take the Americans across within a reasonable time. He was therefore convinced that Greene would have to use the upper fords. A swing to the west would give the British army a shorter road to them. Accordingly he gave up trying to catch Greene and Morgan before they could join with Huger, and decided to intercept their combined forces before they could reach the upper fords. With this in view, he lay at Salisbury four days, collecting food. On the 8th he crossed the Yadkin at Shallow Ford.[6]

Greene and Morgan marched from Trading Ford on the evening of February 4 in a northerly direction, which must have confirmed Cornwallis's belief as to their destination. They halted at Abbott's Creek, a few miles from the Moravian settlement at Salem, to obtain definite information as to Cornwallis's course and then turned due east to Guilford Court House, which they reached on the 6th. In forty-eight hours, including all hours of rest, they marched forty-seven miles.[7] Considering the weather, continuously rainy, the state of the roads, the shortage of food, and the condition of the men, that was excellent progress. Seymour describes Huger's division, which met them there. The men were "in a most dismal condition for the want of clothing, especially shoes, being obliged to march, the chief part of them, barefoot from Chiraw Hills. Here, ho ever, the men were supplied with some shoes, but not half enough."[8]

By this time Cornwallis had reached Salem, twenty-five miles west of Guilford, and had encamped. Greene's primary purpose had been to draw him farther and farther from his base of supplies, to wear down his army and to add to his own force enough militia to turn on his pursuer at the proper time and give him a battle, which would be decisive. Retreating as far as the Dan and into Virginia was the alternative to that major purpose, to be adopted only if necessary. Now, at Guilford, he considered whether it was not time to stand and invite his opponent to fight. He studied the ground; it seemed to offer a good defensive position. Lee's Legion had joined him. He had called for the militia and sent to Hillsboro for a supply of ammunition. He expected reenforcements from Virginia. If the new troops and supplies would come, a stand at this point seemed possible.

But only 200 militia from the neighborhood joined him. The expected Virginia reenforcements and the ammunition failed to arrive. His whole army numbered only 2,036 men, of whom no more than 1,426 were reliable Continentals. Cornwallis had from 2,500 to 3,000 excellent troops. The addition of 1,500 militia would probably have decided the question in favor of fighting, because Greene dreaded continued retreat for its depression of the militia and its encouragement of the Tories to rise. A council of war decided against making a stand, and arrangements were made accordingly.[9]

Pickens was sent back to try to arouse the militia to intercept the British foragers and to cut off their intelligence service. Greene then detached 700 of the élite of his army, including all the cavalry, 240 men under William Washington, a battalion of 280 of the Continental infantry under Colonel Howard, the infantry of Lee's Legion, and 60 Virginia riflemen under Major Campbell. They were to act as a light corps covering the retreat of the main army, interposing themselves between it and the British, keeping as near the pursuers as possible, breaking down bridges and in every way harassing and delaying them, and leading them towards the upper fords of the Dan, while Greene and Huger made for Boyd's and Irwin's ferries on its lower reach.

The command of this corps was offered to Morgan; but he was so ill with ague and rheumatism that he was unable to continue in the campaign. It was then given to Colonel Otho Holland Williams of Maryland, and Morgan retired to his home in Virginia, to appear in arms no more.[10]

The stage was now set for a contest between Greene and Cornwallis, the result of which would be of vast importance to the American cause. If Greene's little army were overtaken and destroyed, Cornwallis would find his way open to join forces with the British in Virginia. He would be able to release all the Burgoyne prisoners and those recently taken at Cowpens, fortify Richmond, and establish strong posts at Hillsboro and elsewhere in the Carolinas. In short, the war in the south would virtually be at an end; except for partisan operations, the whole region would be completely and perhaps finally subjugated and permanently held by the British crown. So far as the four great southern states were concerned, the fate of the war hung in large part upon this contest.

For a month or more Americans throughout the country had realized how much was at stake, and had watched with fearful concern the movements of these two armies. Never since Burgoyne's invasion had their feelings been so wrought up; and in France as well as Britain interest in this fateful game was at a high pitch.[11]

In the evening of February 8 the light troops under Williams left Guilford and turned west towards Salem to take a road running north between the British army and the roads on which respectively the main American force was traveling. Two days later Greene and Huger, with the main army, started directly to the Dan's lower crossings.[12] Cornwallis, in an effort to alarm

Greene for the safety of his stores at Hillsboro and thus cause him to turn still farther east, made a demonstration towards the Americans with a part of his troops. But becoming aware of the intervening light troops, which he took to be the advance guard of the whole American army, he desisted and directed his march towards the upper fords of the Dan, thus, as he thought, fending off Greene from his objective.[13]

The race for the Dan was now on. The distance from Guilford was only seventy miles, but the season was still midwinter; it still rained and snowed intermittently. The roads, in a red-clay country, were frozen into a rough and broken surface at night, but by day softened into deep mud that clung to the wheels of the wagons, the hooves of the horses, and the feet of the men, so that yard after yard was gained only by an exhausting struggle.[14]

Williams and Cornwallis were on parallel roads, not far apart. At one time, when the British army had stretched out to the dangerous length of four miles, Cornwallis halted his van to bring up his rear and then pushed on with all possible speed, moving at times thirty miles a day, an almost inconceivable speed under the existing conditions. Williams had to travel as fast to keep ahead of the British. To guard against Cornwallis's making a detour and getting between the light troops and Greene's army, as well as to protect his own force from surprise, Williams had to send out such numerous patrols and establish such strong pickets that half of his force was always on night duty. He halted for only six hours each night; each man got only six hours rest in every forty-eight. They never set up a tent. "The heat of the fires was the only protection from rain and sometimes snow." [15] They started each day at three in the morning and hastened forward to gain a distance ahead of their pursuers that would give them time for breakfast— breakfast, dinner, and supper in one, because this was their only meal for the day. Cornwallis came on with equal speed.

In the afternoon of the 13th Cornwallis diverged from his line of march, taking a causeway that led him into the road that Williams's troops were following. According to custom, they had made their early morning march and were trying to roast their meat and bake their corn bread at fires dampened by the falling rain, when a countryman on a jaded, little pony came to tell them that the enemy was right behind, only four miles away.

Lee's Legion formed the rear guard of the light troops. Williams sent Lee back along the road to verify this information. The result was a clash with a troop of Tarleton's horse, in which eighteen of the enemy were slain and the rest put to flight. In this affair Lee's bugler, a lad of fourteen years, was cut down and killed in a manner that seems to have been wanton. In reprisal he declared his intention of hanging one of his prisoners, Captain

Miller, and was deterred only by the near approach of the British van, which compelled him to hasten to rejoin Williams.

But Williams had decided that by now the British had been sufficiently misled as to the route taken by the main American army, and that Greene and Huger had had time to reach the Dan. Therefore, while Lee was engaging Tarleton's troop, he had taken a right-hand road leading to Irwin's Ferry, where he expected to find the main army. Lee's men, having missed their one meal of the day, took a byroad that would lead them to Williams and meanwhile give time to refresh themselves at a farmhouse. The byway was somewhat obscure, and Lee felt safe from immediate pursuit; but while the men and his horses were in the midst of their meal they heard shots in their rear. Cornwallis had discovered the short cut, and Lee's vedettes were signaling the near approach of the enemy's van.

Horses were hastily saddled. The infantry were sent on the run to cross a bridge over a swollen creek, while Lee, with the horse, rode back to support his vedettes. He checked the British advance long enough for the foot soldiers to cross the bridge, and then turned and galloped after them. The enemy's cavalry followed fast, but Lee's horses were superior. They got over the bridge, and there was a hot chase across a mile-wide plain before the fugitives gained a height along which ran the Irwin's Ferry road, and the pursuit ceased.

Cornwallis still hoped to catch them before they crossed the Dan. He followed fast. More than once O'Hara in the van was within musket shot of Lee's rear guard. More than once it seemed that the light troops must stand and fight. When they came to a creek or a ravine, the British cavalry would rush forward to attack them in the confusion of crossing, but they always got across in time. At last Lee caught up with Williams. It was growing dark, and the Americans hoped that the enemy would halt for the night; but Cornwallis still came on, determined to run them down. Night fell and they could not see the rough and rutted road they traveled; it was hard going for the weary men.

Williams put his horsemen in front to hurry the pace of the infantry. Then, suddenly, they came in sight of a line of fires—campfires. It was Greene's camp beyond a doubt! He had not got away, and the enemy were close upon him! When this thought flashed through their minds, they were heartbroken. All their struggles, all their hardships had been for naught. Now there was only one thing to do; they must face their pursuers and fight to give the main army a chance to get away.

But Williams had had a dispatch from Greene: "It is very evident that the enemy intend to push us over the river. . . . I sent off the baggage and

stores with orders to cross as fast as they got to the river. The North Carolina militia have all deserted us, except about 80 men. . . . You have the
flower of the army, don't expose the men too much, lest our situation grow
more critical."

The date of the dispatch, February 13, and the place from which it was
sent made him sure that Greene would, by this time, be farther on the way.
He reassured his men and led them on to find that the fires were burning
where Greene had camped two days before. Friendly hands had kept them
alight for the benefit of the light troops.

But they could not stop to enjoy them. They kept on until news arrived
from the rear that the British had halted. Then they paused for two or
three hours, still a long distance from the river.

At midnight they were again afoot. In the morning came another dispatch
from Greene, sent the same day as the last: "4 o'clock. Follow our route. I
have not slept four hours since you left me, so great has been my solicitude
to prepare for the worst."

They halted for an hour's rest and a hasty meal, started again, slogged
through the mud, the enemy at their heels, and were still doggedly pushing
on at noon when a courier met them, found Williams, gave him a note dated
the night before: "Irwin's ferry, 12 past 5 o'clock. All our troops are over
and the stage is clear. . . . I am ready to receive you and give you a
hearty welcome." [16]

Williams gave out the news. The word ran back through the column, and
cheer after cheer followed it. They shouted so loud that O'Hara's van heard
them and knew that the game was up.

The reaction among the men was instantaneous. Their hearts were lifted,
their strength renewed. For three hours more they hurried forward. They
were now within fourteen miles of the river. Williams again detached Lee's
cavalry to delay the enemy, while he took the rest of his command on to
Irwin's Ferry. They got there before sunset, found the boats, and were
ferried across. They had marched forty of the hardest miles that ever man
traveled in about sixteen hours.

At dark, Lee's horsemen started after the others. Between eight and nine
o'clock they got to the ferry, just as the boats returned from transporting
Williams's troops. The men took to the boats; the horses swam. By midnight
they were all across. They had hardly landed when the British van arrived at
the river.[17]

Cornwallis got the news in the course of the evening. The river was too
high to cross without boats, and every boat was on the farther shore.
Greene had won the race.

CHAPTER 72

Greene Returns to North Carolina

Cornwallis had lost the race, but he had chased Greene out of the Carolinas. From Virginia to Florida there was no organized American army in the field; the southern states were possessed by the King. So much he had accomplished, and it seemed to be a great deal. But what was he to do next? He could not follow the American army into Virginia; he had no boats to cross the Dan, nor the Roanoke, if he moved eastward. He dared not try the upper fords, for Greene could anticipate the attempt and be there to oppose the crossing. Even if he should get across, Greene could again retreat to join Steuben, who had been enlisting Continentals in Virginia, and he would then be outnumbered: he had lost 250 men by sickness and desertion on this march. There was no feasible way to go forward.

Yet he could not stay where he was, for his base was two hundred and thirty miles behind; he could not get fresh supplies to replace those so rashly destroyed at Ramsour's Mills. The depredations of his army had aroused the country about him in enmity; supplies were not to be looked for there. Pickens, with 700 newly raised militia, was threatening his left flank. Caswell had a force not too far away on his right. To turn back would be to confess the failure of his expedition and would dishearten the Tory population, which had been encouraged by his pursuit of Greene. But there was no practicable alternative. He rested his army one day, then by easy marches took it back to Hillsboro.[1]

There he put the best face he could on his situation. He erected the royal standard and issued a proclamation:

777

"Whereas it has pleased the Divine Providence to prosper the operations of His Majesty's arms, in driving the rebel army out of this province; and whereas it is His Majesty's most gracious wish to rescue his faithful and loyal subjects from the cruel tyranny under which they have groaned for many years," he invited all the oppressed to repair "with their arms and ten days provisions to the royal standard." [2]

Greene's strategy in plan and in execution had been masterly. He had saved his army and rejoiced the hearts of the patriots throughout America. So much he had done, and it was not little. But after all it was a retreat; though armies may be saved, campaigns are not often won by retreating. Behind him lay the south, still completely dominated by the enemy. He had dragged Cornwallis away from his base and worn down his army. He could turn on him now and destroy him—if only he had the expected recruits from Virginia. But they had not come—not a man had come to him. And most of his militia, their time expired, had left him.

Greene still hoped for reenforcements, expected them in fact. He knew that both North Carolina and Virginia were arousing their militia again, though they were being sent anywhere else than to him. Steuben, who had been enlisting Continentals in Virginia, and was supposed to be on the way to him, had not yet come; he was days, maybe weeks, away. And now, right now, was the time for action. The Dan was falling rapidly; there were many fords near him. Cornwallis might cross and attack him in his weakness, or might slip away, and the chance he had worked for, to catch his enemy in a weakened condition, would be lost. When he got news of the withdrawal of the British, he knew the chance was lost. Now he must make new plans, and they must involve a return to North Carolina. They were soon made and soon in operation.[3]

Greene's first care was for the safety of his heavy baggage. He sent 345 Maryland and Delaware Continentals with it to Halifax Court House. They marched on February 15 and returned on the 17th.[4]

On February 18 he dispatched Lee's Legion and two companies of Marylanders under Captain Oldham, all under command of Pickens (who had by this time joined the army with a body of South Carolina militia) across the river again, with orders to approach Cornwallis as nearly as possible, cut off his foraging parties, annoy him generally, and suppress Tory uprisings.[5] With this force Pickens attempted to surprise Tarleton, who was out on one of his usual troublesome expeditions. Failing to come up with him, Pickens heard of a company of 400 Tory mounted infantry under Colonel John Pyle who were on the way to join Tarleton. They were now on the same road as his own detachment, and not far ahead. Two countrymen whom the Americans picked up thought Lee was Tarleton, since both his and Lee's horsemen wore short green coats. Lee sent one of them ahead to Pyle, with Colonel Tarleton's compliments. Would he kindly draw up his men in a line along the road, so that Colonel Tarleton's men might pass with ease and expedition?

Colonel Pyle readily complied and himself took his post at the right of his line, farthest from the advancing force. Lee's cavalry, with drawn swords, came on in single file past the Tory line, the Maryland foot soldiers in the rear following on and being more or less concealed by the thick woods through which the road ran. When Lee at the head of his men came up to Pyle he halted his troop to shake hands with the other commander. According to his own story, he intended to undeceive Pyle as to his own identity, advise him to disband his men and send them home, and promise that no harm would come to them if they took his advice; but, just as he was about to deliver the message, some of Pyle's men at the far end of the line descried Pickens and his infantry in the rear and fired on them.

Immediately Lee's troops wheeled their horses to the right to face Pyle's men and fell upon them. Sabers slashed them; pistols blazed in their faces. The Tories had only rifles and fowling pieces carried over their shoulders, and the lines were too close for them to use those weapons even if they had had a chance. There was no fight; it was simply a massacre. Of the 400 Tories, 90 were killed, and most of the rest wounded; those fled who could. Not a man in Lee's troop was injured.[6]

Greene and his main army might have stayed in safety north of the Dan until Steuben's Continental recruits and other reenforcements joined him and so strengthened him that he could seek out Cornwallis and attack him. Besides the considerations already mentioned as moving him to return to North Carolina, there was the fact that an abject acceptance of his having been pushed out of that state would inspirit the Tories there to join the British army and make it stronger than it now was. Also, the terms of enlistment of his own militia were short. It was necessary to display belligerent activity.

He had few men, perhaps no more than 1,500. The weather was cold, his thinly clad soldiers were suffering severely; a full quarter of the Maryland line were sick in hospital. His Delaware Continentals were "the admiration of the army and their leader, Kirkwood, was the American Diomed. Like the Marylanders, they had enlisted for the war and, like the veterans of that brigade, were not excelled by any troops in America, perhaps in the world." [7] But, though valiant, they were few. Nevertheless, Greene had to go forward again and without delay.

He sent Otho Williams, with the same light troops that he had led in the retreat, back across the Dan on February 20, instructing him to approach the enemy, watch their movements, retard them as much as possible, and attack them on the march if they withdrew towards Wilmington, but always to keep his force between the British and the main army of the Americans.[8] Three days later, having been reenforced by General Edward Stevens and 600 Virginia riflemen, Greene himself crossed the Dan. His plan now was to wear down Cornwallis's troops by desultory minor actions and to discourage Tory accretions, while his own army was built up by the expected reenforcements. For this service he relied chiefly upon the light troops. His main army he directed towards Hillsboro, Cornwallis's camp.[9]

At that place Cornwallis was in an uncomfortable position. The country round about had been nearly exhausted of provisions. Beef cattle could not be found. Although he had promised the farmers that their draft oxen would be spared, his commissary found it necessary to kill some. This aroused ill feeling among the owners. It was increased by house-to-house forcible requisitions of foodstuffs, which greatly distressed the people.[10] The activities of Lee's Legion, especially in the affair with Pyle, and of Williams's light infantry had chilled the ardor of the Tories, who had been flocking to the King's standard; recruiting suddenly ceased, and many who were on their way to join turned about and went home.[11] At Hillsboro, Cornwallis was, as he wrote to Germain in London, "amongst timid friends and adjoining to inveterate rebels," [12] the friends growing fewer, the rebels increasing day by day. He decided to move to more salubrious quarters.

On February 27 he marched southwest, across the Haw River, and encamped in a favorable position on the south side of Alamance Creek, a tributary, at the junction of roads leading east to Hillsboro, west to Guilford and Salisbury, and downriver to Cross Creek and Wilmington, this last being an avenue of escape, if needed.[13] On the same day Williams gathered to himself Pickens's corps, including Lee's Legion, William Washington's cavalry, and a corps of 300 mountaineer riflemen under Colonel William Preston of Virginia, which had lately joined Pickens.[14] They crossed the Haw that night and took up a position on the north side of the Alamance, within a few miles of Cornwallis's camp on the south side. Greene and Huger came along the next morning, crossed the Haw above Buffalo Creek and encamped between Troublesome Creek, the northernmost tributary of the Haw, and Reedy Fork farther down the river. This camp was about fifteen miles above the British on the Alamance. The American headquarters were alternatively at Speedwell Ironworks on Reedy and Boyd's Mill on Troublesome.[15]

The American position was not especially advantageous, nor was it long held. During the next ten days Greene was constantly on the move, shifting his camp from one place to another, now nearer Cornwallis, now farther away, his design being to keep the British general guessing as to his whereabouts and his purposes and so to lessen the chances of a sudden attack while his reenforcements were assembling.[16] Williams with the light troops was equally restless. Within a little more than two weeks after recrossing the Dan, they marched two hundred and thirty miles, making sixty miles in one period of two days.[17] Tarleton was moving about in much the same way for similar purposes.

Tired of profitless inactivity and annoyed by the restlessness of the American light troops, Cornwallis made a sudden hostile move at three o'clock in the morning of March 6. He crossed the Alamance under cover of a heavy fog and pushed on towards High Rock Ford on Reedy Fork. Williams's corps lay on another road also leading to that ford. Cornwallis intended to surprise him and, if possible, draw Greene to his aid, thus bringing on a general engagement while Greene's army was still few in numbers.[18] But the surprise did not come off.

It happened that late in the night of the 5th Williams had sent a small party under cover of the same fog to carry off another small party of the enemy from a mill about a mile from the main British camp. Arriving there, it learned that Cornwallis had marched. When this news reached Williams the British were within two miles of the left of his corps—the Virginia militia under Colonel William Campbell, who had recently joined Lee, relieving General Pickens. Williams sent Lee and Washington to support Campbell, while the rest of the corps retreated towards the ford across Reedy Fork at Wetzell's Mills. Lee, Washington, and Campbell slowed the advance of the British somewhat, but there was an exciting race between Williams and Cornwallis's advance, led by Tarleton's cavalry and Colonel Webster's light infantry, on parallel roads to the ford at the mills. Both parties traveled at their utmost speed, patrols and scouts from each side watching the progress of the other and reporting it. Williams got there first, just as the enemy appeared on rising ground in his rear, and threw out a covering party of Virginia militia riflemen under Colonel William Preston to protect the crossing. He got his men over safely and was joined by Lee, Washington, and Campbell, closely pursued by the British van.

Several near-by fords above and below exposed him to a flank attack. Having decided to retreat, he ordered Lee, Washington, and Campbell to hold the pass as long as possible, without hazarding serious injury, and withdrew the rest of his men. Lee posted a company of Preston's Virginians at the ford by the mill and drew up the rest of his infantry in a line along the stream. Campbell's and the rest of Preston's riflemen were concealed in a thick copse on the right. The cavalry was placed in the rear.

Having arrived at the stream, Cornwallis ordered Webster's brigade—composed of the Royal Welch Fusiliers, the 33rd British Regiment, and Fraser's Highlanders, with a light company of the Guards and the Hessian jägers—to form a line and attack while the rest of his army remained in column. Webster's detachment started for the ford, the Guards in the lead. As they entered the water they were met by a heavy and well directed fire, and fell back in disorder. Webster, disgusted by their hesitancy, rode up, called them to account, and plunged into the stream. His men followed.

When they gained the opposite shore, which lay under a high bank, the flanks of the American line drew in and formed behind the cavalry in the rear, while the center kept up a fire upon Webster's men clambering up from the water's edge; but there was no stopping them. The Americans retreated under heavy fire, and rear-guard action continued for about five miles until the pursuit ceased. Williams then encamped, and Cornwallis returned to his former ground on the Alamance. Greene, having had news of the advance of his enemy, had withdrawn from Reedy Fork and encamped at the ironworks on Troublesome. In the affair at Wetzell's Mill, the Americans lost about twenty killed or wounded. Tarleton admits a loss of twenty-one on his side.

A strange fact of this engagement was Webster's escape from death. Lee had posted twenty-five expert riflemen in a little log schoolhouse at the right of the ford. They all had participated in the King's Mountain affair and were reputed to be dead shots, and they had orders to concentrate their fire on the enemy's officers. Every one of them drew a bead on Webster, conspicuous as he was, and fired. Eight or nine of them tried a second shot, yet not a bullet touched him.[19]

Both armies rested for the next ten days, the British at Bell's Mills on Deep River, Greene at the ironworks on Troublesome. Meanwhile, Greene was considerably strengthened. Steuben in Virginia had raised 2,600 militia and 400 new Continentals and started them south; but, having been informed that Cornwallis was retreating to Wilmington and Greene was pursuing him with a superior force, he halted the militia and sent forward only the Continentals under Colonel Richard Campbell. From North Carolina came two brigades of militia, numbering 1,060, under Brigadier General John Butler and Colonel Pinketham Eaton. Virginia militia, 1,693 of them, also arrived and, with those already in camp, were organized in two brigades under Brigadiers Robert Lawson and Edward Stevens.[20]

Williams' light troops having rejoined the main army, that corps was dissolved "with the highest and best merited encomiums on the spirit and ability with which it had discharged its laborious and important duties." [21] Its various elements were returned to their respective regiments, except that Captain Kirkwood's Delaware company and Colonel Charles Lynch's Virginia riflemen were ordered to join William Washington's cavalry and thus form a legion.[22]

Greene was as strong as he could expect to be. From now on, the lapse of time would only waste his strength, through the usual depletion caused by sickness and desertion and by the expiration of the terms of service of the militia enlisted for no more than six weeks. Also he had just about exhausted the food supplies of the country in which he had been maneuvering for the last two weeks. Now was the time to fight, if he was going to fight at all. Cornwallis was ready, had been for some time. All that was needed was to choose his ground and make a stand on it.

Greene knew where it was; he had studied it six weeks before, on his way north. On April 14 he went into camp near Guilford Court House.

CHAPTER 73

Guilford Court House

On the day that Greene's army went into camp near Guilford Court House, it was composed of the following elements: Otho Williams's brigade of the 1st and 5th Maryland regiments, including the Delaware Continental infantry, commanded by Colonels John Gunby and Benjamin Ford, having 630 rank and file present and fit for duty; Brigadier General Isaac Huger's 4th and 5th Virginia Continental regiments commanded by Colonels John Green and Samuel Hawes, comprising 778 present and fit; the infantry of Lee's Legion, 82 men, and Kirkwood's light infantry company, making a total of about 1,600 regular infantry. There were four brigades of militia: two of about 500 men each from North Carolina under Brigadier Generals Pinketham Eaton and John Butler; two of about 600 Virginians each, commanded by Brigadier Generals Robert Lawson and Edward Stevens. There were two corps of riflemen, 200 in each, under Colonels Charles Lynch and Richard Campbell. These militia and volunteer infantry numbered in all 2,600. Of cavalry, Greene had the 75 horsemen of Lee's Legion and 86 of William Washington's light dragoons. His artillery consisted of four 6-pounders, served by 60 artillerists and matrosses under Captains Anthony Singleton and Samuel Finley.[1] The grand total was, therefore, over 4,400 rank and file.

Although 1,490 of the infantry were rated as of the Continental line, only those 630 weather-beaten, travel-toughened, war-hardened veterans of Maryland and Delaware had ever before been in battle. It was impossible to predict how the untried Virginia Continentals would stand the test of bullet and bayonet. Of the militia, those from Virginia were regarded as good; not much confidence was placed in the North Carolinians. The 400 riflemen of Lynch and Campbell were all volunteers; bound for no stated time, they could leave at a moment's notice.[2] Still, it was as large as any American army ever assembled in the south up to this time, and it greatly outnumbered Cornwallis's army. Although there has been some controversy as to the number of his force, different reckonings varying by two or three hundred, it is probable that 1,900 is about correct.[3]

The battleground chosen by Greene was approachable from the west along a road through a narrow defile shouldered by rising ground on both sides and lined with dense copses. The undulating ground towards the east, beyond the defile, spread out about half a mile on both sides of the road, which ran a little north of east and was the spine of the formation of each army. The whole area, except two cleared portions to be described, was well wooded. Passing north of east from the defile through an enclosed clearing about a quarter-mile square, the road held its course through an oak woods for half a mile to a considerable area of high cleared ground above a rather steep slope. On this height stood the courthouse. There was a wooded elevation about a quarter-mile to the right, or south, of the road midway between the defile and the courthouse. This was the highest point of the field and had the steepest approach.[4]

When Greene marched to Guilford, Cornwallis lay at New Garden, also known as Quaker Meeting House, not more than twelve miles to the southwest. Greene's move amounted to throwing a hat into the ring—a challenge Cornwallis could neither ignore nor refuse. In fact, it gave him the chance he had been so ardently seeking for two months. To be sure, he was not so avid for battle as he had been before his losses at Cowpens and on that hard march to the Dan. On the other hand, scarcity of supplies now compelled him either to fight or to retreat toward the seacoast; and as between those alternatives he had no hesitation.

In the evening of March 14 Cornwallis sent off what was left of his heavy baggage with the sick and wounded under guard of Hamilton's Tory regiment, 100 regular infantrymen, and 20 of Tarleton's horse to Bell's Mills on Deep River. At dawn of the 15th, without pausing to give his men a breakfast, he started for Guilford.[5]

Greene had sent Lee's Legion, horse and foot, with a detachment of riflemen under Campbell along the road to New Garden to observe the enemy. Three or four miles from Guilford, Lee met Tarleton leading the British van—the cavalry, the Hessian jägers, and the light infantry of the

Guards. He drew back, Tarleton pressing on him, until, in an embanked, narrow lane, his horsemen whirled about and charged, overthrowing Tarleton's first section and driving back the rest. They were pursued until the Americans came upon the head of the main British army. Here there was a hot skirmish for some little time before Lee "retired precipitately" to notify Greene of the coming of the enemy.[6]

Not long before, Morgan had written to Greene about the next battle and the "great number of militia" on the American side: "If they fight, you beat Cornwallis, if not, he will beat you." He advised flanking the lines of militia with riflemen under enterprising officers. "Put the . . . militia in the centre with some picked troops in their rear to shoot down the first man that runs." [7]

Greene followed this advice. His first line, composed of Butler's and Eaton's North Carolina militia, was established across the main road along the edge of the enclosed clearing and behind a zigzag rail fence, so that the enemy emerging from the defile would have to cross five hundred yards of open ground in order to reach the fence and the militia. This line was supported on its right flank by the infantry of Washington's Legion—that is to say, by Kirkwood's light infantry and Lynch's Virginia riflemen—formed at an obtuse angle so that their fire would enfilade the attacking ranks when they came near the fence. Washington's cavalry was in their rear on the far right. The left wing was similarly supported by Lee's Legion infantry, Campbell's riflemen, and Lee's cavalry.

About three hundred yards behind the first line was the second, Virginia militia under Stevens and Lawson. Sentinels were posted behind this at intervals for the purpose suggested in Morgan's letter. It was altogether in the forest and stretched an equal distance on each side of the road.

The third and principal line was drawn up in a curve along the brow of the courthouse hill and about five hundred and fifty yards behind the second. The main road, on which the first and second lines were posted, swerved slightly to the right, or southeast, so that this hill was on its left or north side. This line was, therefore, out of alignment with the others. An enemy force would have to swing to the left from the road in order to make a frontal attack on the third line.

From right to left, as this line faced, it was made up of the two regiments of Virginia Continentals and the two Maryland regiments, including Captain Jaquett's Delaware company. Two guns were in the center of the first line, under Singleton, and two under Finley were in the center of the third. During the battle Greene was with the Continentals. His first line was a full half-mile away and, because of the woods, that and the second were out of his sight. There was no reserve whatever; the entire army was in the lines.[8]

About midday the Americans, looking down the narrow avenue from the battlefield, saw the head of the British column approaching. It was a cold, cloudless spring day, and, though the nearest of the enemy were yet a mile away, the color of their uniforms and the reflection of the sun from their well burnished arms were plainly visible.[9]

As soon as the van was within range, Singleton opened on it with his pair of 6-pounders. Lieutenant MacLeod of the British pushed three guns forward along the road and replied. This duel was kept up, with little effect on either side, for about half an hour while the British were emerging from the defile, company after company at the double, and very smartly deploying right and left into a line facing the American first line at the distance of about a quarter-mile, that is to say a little short of the clearing in front of the Americans.

The right of the British line, under General Leslie, consisted of the Hessian Regiment von Bose and Fraser's Highlanders, with the 1st battalion of the Guards in support. Colonel Webster commanded the 23rd (Welch Fusiliers) and 33rd regiments in the left wing, with the grenadiers and 2nd battalion of the Guards under O'Hara in support. The guns were in the center, a small force of jägers and the light infantry being stationed beside them and behind the left wing. Tarleton's dragoons were held in column in the rear.[10]

When Greene had formed his troops, he walked along the front of the North Carolina militia in the first line asking as Morgan had asked his first line at Cowpens, for just two rounds of fire before they quit the battle. "Two rounds, my boys, and then you may fall back." [11]

About half-past one the battle began with the advance of the British center into the clearing in front of the North Carolinians, the enemy's wings being in the woods to the right and left. Singleton had withdrawn his guns to the second line; those of the British were necessarily silent. There was no martial sound, except the beating of the drums and the squealing of the fifes, as that broad, red line marched forward as if on parade, crossed the first fence, and traversed more than two-thirds of the open space. Then a thousand rifles spoke. Men fell all along the red line; there were gaps in it; but it came steadily forward.

Within musket shot of the zigzag fence the line halted, and delivered a volley; then at the command of Colonel Webster it charged. But it halted again in a straggling line fifty yards from the fence because, says Sergeant

Lamb of the Welch Fusiliers, it was perceived that the Americans' "whole force had their arms presented and resting on a rail-fence . . . they were taking aim with nice precision. . . . At this awful period, a general pause took place, both parties surveyed each other a moment with anxious suspense. Colonel Webster then rode forward in front of the 23rd regiment and said, with more than his usual commanding voice . . . 'Come on, my brave Fusiliers.' These words operated like an inspiring voice. They rushed forward amidst the enemy's fire. Dreadful was the havoc on both sides." [12]

The North Carolinians had now delivered their two fires as ordered. There was no time to reload, even if they had the inclination to do so. Without a moment's hesitation they turned and ran, pell-mell, helter-skelter, back through the woods, through the second line and so to safety.[13] After all, they had done everything they had been asked to do, and they had Greene's permission to leave the field.

The British were now up to the second fence with no opponent visible. But there was a steady and "most destructive fire" [14] upon both their flanks, enfilading their line, so that, if a bullet missed the nearest man, it had an excellent chance to hit another down the line. This fire came from Kirkwood's company and Lynch's riflemen on the British left, and from Lee's infantry and Campbell's riflemen on the right. They still held their ground, although the line they supported had vanished. These oblique lines had to be met by the attackers face to face. On the British left the jägers and the 33rd Regiment wheeled to the left to front Kirkwood and Lynch; on the other end the Regiment von Bose and the Highlanders swung to the right to meet Lee's and Campbell's troops. To fill the gap opened in the center by these maneuvers, the grenadiers and 2nd battalion of the Guards came up from their position in support of the left wing.

The cleared ground was left behind; it was woods fighting now. The Americans on both wings took cover, retired from tree to tree. Lynch and Kirkwood, covered by Washington's cavalry, at last took an oblique position on the right of the second line, the Virginia militia, and held it. On the American left, Campbell and Lee had been joined by one company of North Carolinians, under Captain Forbes, which had not fled the field. It had been Campbell's intention to fall back, as Kirkwood and Lynch had done, and take a position on the left of the Virginia line; but he was delayed by having to engage the 1st battalion of Guards, while the Regiment von Bose struck across his front and cut him off from the Virginians. Now he and Lee and Forbes were being forced farther and farther to their left, away from the rest of the Americans and finally up on to the height of ground already mentioned as being to the south of the main battlefield. The

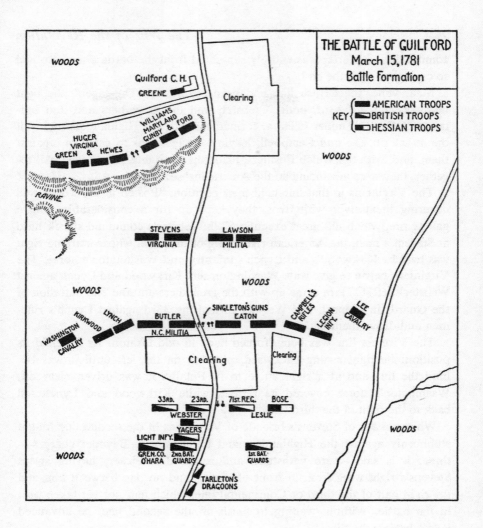

THE BATTLE OF GUILFORD
March 15, 1781
Battle Formation

KEY
■ AMERICAN TROOPS
▨ BRITISH TROOPS
□ HESSIAN TROOPS

WOODS

Guilford C. H.
GREENE

Clearing

WOODS

WILLIAMS
MARYLAND
GUNBY & FORD

HUGER
VIRGINIA
GREEN & HEWES

RAVINE

STEVENS
VIRGINIA

LAWSON
MILITIA

WOODS

WOODS

KIRKWOOD   LYNCH

WASHINGTON
CAVALRY

BUTLER

N.C. MILITIA

SINGLETON'S GUNS
EATON

CAMPBELL'S
RIFLES

LEGION
INF'Y.

LEE
CAVALRY

Clearing

Clearing

WOODS

33RD.   23RD.

WEBSTER

71ST. REG.

BOSE

LESLIE

YAGERS

LIGHT INF'Y.

WOODS

GREN. CO.
O'HARA

2ND. BAT.
GUARDS

1ST. BAT.
GUARDS

TARLETON'S
DRAGOONS

combat in this quarter was entirely separated from the battle elsewhere and so continued until the end.

Meanwhile, the British line had been readjusted. The jägers, the light infantry, and the 33rd, under Webster, and the grenadiers and 2nd battalion of Guards, under O'Hara, formed the left; the Highlanders had quit the attack on Lee and Campbell, leaving the Hessians to carry on against them, and, with the Welch Fusiliers, made up the right under Leslie. All together, they were advancing on the Americans' second line.

The Virginians in that line held their position. "Posted in the woods and covering themselves with trees, they kept up for a considerable time a galling fire, which did great execution." [15] Webster's command struck hard at Stevens's men, the American right wing of that line, whose extreme right was held by Kirkwood's and Lynch's infantry and Washington's horse. The Virginians began to give way. Washington sent Kirkwood and Lynch against Webster's left. O'Hara came up with the grenadiers and the 2nd battalion of the Guards in support, and Webster turned the 33rd against Lynch's riflemen and drove them back.

The Virginia line was being forced back in odd fashion. Its left held its position; its right swung backward, pivoting on the left until it was behind the line and at a right angle to it. Finally, it was driven clear off. Washington's horse covered its retreat, while Kirkwood and Lynch fell back to the right of the third line.

What was left of Stevens's brigade of Virginians in the second line fought stubbornly against the Highlanders and the Fusiliers. Bayonet charges— three, it is said—were withstood and repulsed. Webster, having swept Stevens's right wing from in front of him, found no one between him and the right half of the third or Continental line, which had not yet taken part in the battle. Without waiting to finish off the second line, he advanced boldly against the third.

Gunby's 1st Maryland, including Jaquett's Delaware company, Colonel Hawes's Virginia Continental regiment, and Kirkwood's light infantry, faced Webster at a distance of two hundred yards. Against them he sent the jägers, his light infantry, and the 33rd in a bayonet charge. The Americans waited until the oncoming enemy were within a hundred feet and then loosed a withering blast of fire that brought the enemy to a standstill. Immediately Gunby called for the bayonets. His 1st Maryland and Kirkwood's company sprang forward and drove the British back, down into a ravine and up the farther side in great disorder.[16]

Now was the critical moment of the battle. The Hessians were still engaged with Campbell's riflemen and Lee's Legion on the wooded height far to the south of the main battle. Stevens's Virginians were still holding Leslie's Fusiliers and Highlanders, now drawing back from the bayonet, now advancing from tree to tree to fire. And Webster's troops were beaten and confused. If the cavalry of Washington and Lee had been thrown on the disordered ranks of the enemy, and the whole line of Continentals had charged upon Leslie and O'Hara, as they had charged at Cowpens, the battle might have ended in the destruction of Cornwallis's army. But that was not in accordance with Greene's plans. Morgan had been able to risk his whole detachment in such an all-out attack—even if he should be defeated, Greene would still have the main force. But on this day such a move would risk the entire army; a defeat would mean the loss of the south. So Web-ster had time to recover while Gunby and Kirkwood returned to their former positions.

While a restoration of the lines was being effected O'Hara, who had been wounded, turned over his command of the grenadiers and the 2nd battalion of the Guards to Lieutenant Colonel Stuart. As the resistance of the Virginians in the second line was weakening, Leslie drew off the Welch Fusiliers and the Highlanders, leaving only the 1st battalion of the Guards to care for the Virginians. The Hessians were still struggling with Campbell and Lee in the woods. But for those two contingents so engaged, the whole British army was now free to give its attention to the Continentals in the third line.

Colonel Gunby having been unhorsed, Lieutenant Colonel Howard was leading the 1st Maryland and Kirkwood back to their old position in the line when Stuart, with his grenadiers and Guards, swept around the curve of the courthouse hill and attacked the 5th Maryland in its position supported by two guns. It was largely a new regiment, made up of recruits now in their first battle. The sight of the scarlet and steel was too much for their nerves. Without firing a shot, they turned and ran. Stuart followed, taking the guns as he went. Washington, witnessing this inglorious retreat, called on two small troops of volunteer cavalry to join his horse. All together, they dashed upon the rear of the Guards and rode right through them, slashing right and left. Stuart was killed in this encounter.

Meanwhile Howard had wheeled the 1st Maryland and Kirkwood's company to the right. Washington had just swept clear of the Guards when Howard charged them full in their left flank. But the Guards and the grenadiers were soldiers of the first order. O'Hara, in spite of his wound, rallied them; the Fusiliers and Highlanders came up on their flanks. They stood their ground. So did the Americans, and the fighting was close and bloody.

The British were getting the worst of it when Cornwallis resorted to a desperate remedy. He ordered MacLeod to open fire with grapeshot over the heads of the British between, and full upon the melee of Americans, Guards, and grenadiers. Grape cannot be fired with the accuracy of a rifle bullet, and it is no respecter of persons. The effect of such fire on the British in the fight, as well as on the Americans, was bound to be deadly. It is said that O'Hara, lying on the roadside by the guns, begged Cornwallis not to shoot down his own men. But Cornwallis persisted with bloody results to both armies. The effect was, however, that the Americans withdrew to their former line, and the British had a chance to re-form.

Webster, on the left, was the first to get his men in order. He recrossed the ravine beyond which he had been driven, and charged upon all that was left of the Americans' third line, the 1st Maryland, Huger's two Virginia Continental regiments, Kirkwood's light infantry, and Lynch's riflemen. There was no "give" to that line; it stood fast and, with a concentrated fire, drove Webster back.

Now there was a pause while both sides licked their wounds and prepared to renew the fight. The American militia was gone, the 5th Maryland irretrievably broken. Stevens's Virginia militia in the second line, their colonel wounded, had given way and fled to the woods. Away off to the left of the Americans, out of sight, Campbell's riflemen and Lee's infantry were still engaged with the Regiment von Bose in backwoods fashion. Only that remnant of the third line still held the field. If Greene had known how badly Cornwallis was crippled he might have won a victory in a fight to a finish; but, true to his resolution not to risk destruction of his whole army, he decided at half-past three to retreat.

He had first to stop the fight still going on between the American Continentals and Webster on his right. He ordered the Americans to withdraw, throwing in behind them Colonel John Green's Virginia Continental regiment, which had been held out of the fighting for that purpose. So the retreat began and was soon under way all along the line. Under heavy fire Green's regiment stood firm until all the rest of the American had left the field; then it too retired. "A general retreat took place; but it was conducted with order and regularity," says Stedman, the English historian, who was in the battle. The artillery horses having been killed, the Americans had to abandon their guns. The Welch Fusiliers and Highlanders, with some cavalry, started to follow, but were soon recalled. Greene halted after crossing Reedy Fork about three miles from Guilford, to collect his stragglers, and then went on to his old ground at the ironworks on Troublesome, marching all night.

After Greene had drawn off his men the bush-fighting between Lee and Campbell and the Hessians ceased—but not until Tarleton had been sent in to bring out the Hessians by chasing away the riflemen, with a charge on their flank and rear.

Cornwallis held the field. He had a victory to write home about, but he had paid a price for it. Of about 1,900 men who went into the battle on the British side, more than a fourth were casualties: 93 dead and 439 wounded, many of them mortally. The Guards were sadly reduced: 19 officers, 11 were killed or wounded; among 462 rank and file there were 206 casualties. In all, 29 British and Hessian officers were killed or wounded. General O'Hara and General Howard had suffered injuries; Lieutenant Colonel Webster was mortally wounded.

Not counting the militia who ran clear away and were returned "missing," Greene's casualties were 78 killed and 183 wounded.[17]

In this battle, on both sides the most admirable military qualities were displayed. Of the Americans, the 1st Maryland, Stevens's Virginia militia, and Kirkwood's light infantry bore the palm; but Lynch's riflemen, the Virginia Continentals, Campbell's riflemen, Lee's Legion infantry, and Washington's horse all gave proof of a high degree of valor and steadfastness.

On the whole, however, the laurels for military achievement must be awarded to the British. Starting hungry, they marched twelve hard miles, immediately went into battle against an enemy of greater numbers (even disregarding the North Carolina militia, it was more than 3,000 Americans against 1,900 British) who had been refreshed by a night's sleep and a breakfast. That enemy force was so posted as to have every advantage of its skill in woodcraft and marksmanship and of the superiority of the rifle over the musket. But the British faltered not at all in advancing across a quarter-mile of open ground against two rifle volleys precisely aimed. When the 33rd and the Guards were shattered—the Guards, indeed, torn to pieces —they rallied, re-formed, and attacked with no less vigor for their punishment. Fortescue, the historian of the British army, surveying its whole history from Crecy and Agincourt to the middle of the nineteenth century, says, "Never, perhaps, has the prowess of the British soldier been seen to greater advantage than in this obstinate and bloody combat." The merits and achievements of the Americans in this battle are enhanced, in the judgment of history, in proportion to the military ability of these opponents.

General Francis Vinton Greene estimates the importance and results of Greene's southern campaign up to this time in the following words: "The retreat to the Dan and the battle of Guilford were to the South what the retreat across New Jersey and the battles of Trenton and Princeton were to

the North. They turned the tide; and each attracted equal attention in
Europe. Greene lost the battle, but he won the campaign, and the first step
towards Yorktown was taken."

Henry Lee refers to Cornwallis's superiority in disciplined veteran troops:
"General Greene's veteran infantry being only the 1st Regiment of Maryland, the company of Delaware under Kirkwood (to whom none could be
superior) and the Legion infantry, altogether making on that day not more
than five hundred rank and file."

CHAPTER 74

Cornwallis Abandons the Carolinas

The battlefield at Guilford Court House on the night of March 15 was a sad place. The firing had hardly ceased when the weather broke, and rain began to fall in torrents. The night was unusually dark. The wounded lay scattered about over a wide area. The search for them was prosecuted as best it could be by the tired, hungry British soldiers, but not very successfully, for when day broke 50 men whose wounds were not in themselves mortal were found dead. Those that were gathered up suffered hardly less, for there were no proper surgical stores to meet their needs. There was not even any food. From the time they had their suppers in the evening of March 14, the British troops were entirely without food for forty-eight hours. What each man, sick, wounded, or well, got at the end of that starvation period was four ounces of flour and four ounces of lean beef.[1]

These facts alone are enough to prove that all the military sagacity exercised by the leaders, all the soldierly valor and endurance of hardship displayed by the men of the British army in the last six months had been exercised and displayed in vain. After all that and after the battle just won, Cornwallis found himself almost completely destitute of supplies. His nearest magazine of food was at Wilmington, two hundred miles away. As for securing provision from the country around him, his army was, in effect, the garrison of a besieged town. No foraging party could safely go abroad. No provisions could come unmolested by road or river. He had lost the campaign, and there was no hope of recovery; his army was too weak to fight another battle. If it should try and should lose as many men as in this last one, the patriot countrymen would rise and tear the rest of it to pieces.

All he could hope for now was a swift, safe retreat to a place of refuge and a store of food.

Cornwallis stayed at Guilford, resting his men, for two days. During that time the wounded of both armies were given equal attention by the British surgeons and by American army surgeons who had been sent back to the field by Greene under a flag of truce. Cornwallis left about seventy of his own worst wounded men at the Quaker Meeting House at New Garden, with a request that the American general do what he could for them.[2]

Greene, having retired to his old ground on Troublesome Creek, detached Lee's Legion and a corps of riflemen under Campbell to hang on the rear of the British army, now in full retreat, but more particularly to show the countryside that the American army had not been put out of action and to discourage any inclination to join Cornwallis.[3] With the rest of his army, he followed on the 20th.

At Ramsey's Mill on the Deep River where it joins with the Haw to form the Cape Fear River, Cornwallis built a bridge while his army was momentarily resting to facilitate his retreat. Greene sent Lee by a roundabout way to destroy the bridge; but it was found to be too strongly guarded, and the project was abandoned. Greene came up to that point on the 28th, to find that the British army had just crossed the bridge and was on its way down the Cape Fear.[4]

Cornwallis was making for Cross Creek, the settlement of loyal Scottish Highlanders, on the Cape Fear River. He hoped for a plentiful supply of provisions and for the care and refreshment of his sick and wounded in that friendly place. He expected also to arrange for the shipment of supplies up the river from Wilmington. In these hopes and expectations he was disappointed. Provisions for both man and beast were scarce at Cross Creek. The narrow river ran, for a part of its course, through hostile country, and no boats could be got through to him. The Cross Creek settlers did what they could for him, but he could not stay there. He had to push a hundred miles farther to Wilmington.[5]

It was to Cornwallis a distressing march in every respect. His soldierly pride was wounded by this lame-dog finish to his campaign, and he had to stop more than once to bury by the roadside some valued officer who had died of his wounds. Colonel Webster, lamented by the whole army, an officer who "united all the virtues of civil life to the gallantry and professional knowledge of a soldier," [6] was one of these. Two captains of the Guards and two officers of the Regiment von Bose were others. General O'Hara, General Howard, and several other officers of lesser rank, so badly wounded that they could not ride their horses, endured the painful journey in horse litters. On April 7 the melancholy procession reached Wilmington.[7]

After resting and refitting his army, now reduced to 1,435 fit rank and file, Cornwallis had to plan his next move. It was a difficult job. He could not be idle in Wilmington, simply maintain a garrison there; such supine conduct would emphasize to the Carolinians that he had been driven out of the rest of their state and would indicate that he was unable to recover the lost ground. Patriot uprisings throughout the state would be many, and their results bloody. He could not go back to meet Greene again, with any reasonable hope of overcoming him, which would be the only real solution of his problem.

While Cornwallis was studying the problem he got news that added to his perplexity. Greene had marched south from Ramsey's Mill. It seemed evident that he was bound for South Carolina to try conclusions with Rawdon at Camden. Rawdon might need help, but could Cornwallis get it to him in time? He saw obstacles: Camden was a long way off; the intervening country was too poor to support his army on the march; crossing the Pee Dee, if opposed by the enemy, would be hazardous, perhaps fatal; he might be caught between two great rivers and forced to fight without an avenue of retreat; if he were as badly used as at Guilford, it would be all up with his whole army. It was altogether too dangerous an experiment. He decided that he could not get to Camden before Greene; that if Rawdon were already defeated he could do nothing to help him, and that if Greene were defeated he would not be needed. But what should be his active purpose? [8]

Cornwallis concluded that, if Britain was to keep what she had already gained in the South, "a serious attempt upon Virginia would be the most solid plan, because successful operations might not only be attended with important consequences there, but would tend to the security of South Carolina and ultimately to the submission of North Carolina." He therefore "resolved to take advantage of General Greene's having left the back part of Virginia open and march immediately into the province, to attempt a junction with General Phillips." [9] There could be no more eloquent, no more convincing evidence of the complete success of Greene's campaign against Cornwallis than that sentence. The picture of His Majesty's army bottled up in Wilmington until Greene drew off his forces, and then scuttling in haste to enter Virginia by the back door is pathetic in its ignominy.

As early as March 29, the day following his arrival at Ramsey's Mill, Greene had written to General Washington, "I am determined to carry the war immediately into South Carolina." [10] There was plenty to be done in that state and in Georgia. Besides their main positions in Charleston and Savannah, the enemy had outposts, with garrisons of from 120 to 630 each, in South Carolina at Ninety-six, Fort Granby, Orangeburg, Fort Motte, Fort Watson, and Georgetown, a chain that must be broken up if the state was to be redeemed. In the two states the British forces totaled about 8,000.[11]

To Greene there were available scattered commands that might be either drawn upon or reenforced to act independently. Sumter was on the Broad River in western North Carolina, recruiting. Pickens was in western South Carolina, his familiar ground. Marion was hiding in the swamps along the Pee Dee, awaiting his opportunity. Greene sent messengers to them, telling of his intended activities and asking their help. He then proposed to move southward.

First, he had to deal with his North Carolina and Virginia militia. They had been enlisted for only six weeks—a short-term engagement that began for each man when he signed up and ended when he got home again, travel both ways being counted as part of his term. So, though they had been with the army only twenty-three days, their time was up; he had to let them go. His army then consisted of the 1st and 5th Maryland Continental regiments (the 1st including Jaquett's Delaware company), the 1st and 2nd Virginia Continentals, Lee's Legion of horse and foot, Kirkwood's light infantry, and William Washington's dragoons, perhaps 1,400 in all. By a resolution of the "Council Extraordinary" of North Carolina it was provided after Guilford that "every man who abandoned his post in the late action should be enrolled in the Continental army for twelve months." A few hundred such men were eventually rounded up and sent to Greene; they are said to have behaved well.[12]

In the Carolinas and at Augusta, Georgia, Lieutenant Colonel Francis Rawdon, known by the courtesy title of Lord Rawdon, had been in general command since Cornwallis had gone north in pursuit of Greene. He was a young man, but an able soldier. He had entered the British army at the age of seventeen and had been in the American war from its beginning at Lexington. At Bunker's Hill, as a lieutenant, he had greatly distinguished himself by leading the grenadiers of his company after his captain had fallen. Burgoyne said he had that day "stamped his fame for life." He had seen active service in the principal battles in the north from Long Island to Monmouth and in the south from the siege of Charleston to Camden. In person he was tall and dark, and was said to be "the ugliest man in England"; but his bearing was stately and dignified. His manner was genial, and it was said of him that "no man possessed in a higher degree the happy, but rare, faculty of attracting to him all who came within the sphere of his influence." [13] Now at the age of twenty-six, he was to meet in battle a man twelve years his senior, as fully experienced as he in warfare, with a growing reputation as the wisest strategist in the American army, who would, at the time of their meeting, have 1,400 men to his 900.

On April 6 Greene detached Lee's Legion and Captain Oldham's company of Maryland Continentals with one gun to join Marion on the Pee Dee. He directed them first, however, to proceed down the Cape Fear River towards Cross Creek, to mislead the enemy into thinking that the destination of the whole army was Wilmington. Lee's objective after joining Marion was to be Fort Watson on the Santee below Camden.[14]

Word was sent to Pickens suggesting that he invest Ninety-six if he felt able, or, at all events, that he prevent a reenforcement of Camden from that post. To Sumter, Greene sent a request for a junction of their two forces at Camden. On April 7 he broke camp at Ramsey's Mill and took the road down the Cape Fear, as if intending for Wilmington. The next day he changed his course to the west, across the Little River, the Yadkin, the Rocky River, and so on, the days' marches averaging about eighteen miles. His men had plenty of food now and of rum; it was late spring, instead of midwinter, and they suffered a minimum of hardship.

On the 17th they were in camp on Lynch's Creek. The invalids, spare arms, and heavy baggage were sent off to Salisbury under guard. Orders were given that "the women who have children and all those unable to march on foot must also be sent off, as none will be permitted to ride on wagons or horses, on any pretext whatever." [15]

While Greene was on the march, Lee found Marion. Together they proceeded against Fort Watson. It was a small but stout stockade, surrounded by three rows of abatis and perched upon an ancient tumulus about thirty feet high, which stood upon a bare level plain. It was held by 80 regulars and 40 Tory militiamen commanded by Lieutenant McKay.[16] Lee and Marion invested this little fortress on April 14. They had no artillery, no entrenching tools. Colonel Watson, a British regular officer, who had originally held that post, was on his way to find and fight Marion and might return at any time, so that there was no time for a protracted siege.

Colonel Hezekiah Maham of South Carolina had a plan to meet the situation. In the near-by woods trees were felled, trimmed into logs, and notched to suit their purpose; this took five days. On the night of the 22nd these timbers were carried within rifle shot of the fort and there erected to form a rectangular structure high enough to overlook the stockade. A rough platform was laid on top, with a low parapet of logs. At dawn, from this height, a company of riflemen opened fire upon the fort; their bullets searched every part of the stockade. At the same time two parties attacked the abatis. The men in the garrison were unable to repel them without exposing themselves to the marksmen on the tower. They promptly surrendered. With a loss of 2 killed and 6 wounded, Marion and Lee took 114 prisoners. This made the first gap in Rawdon's communications with Charleston. The device used in the siege was given the name "Maham Tower" and was subsequently used in similar cases.[17]

Greene had hoped—overoptimistically, it would seem—that he might surprise Rawdon. But news of the American army's approach reached Camden long before April 19, when he actually arrived in the neighborhood. Halting for the night four miles from the town, Greene sent Kirkwood's light infantry ahead to try for possession of Logtown, a group of six or eight cabins in a rather extensive clearing on a slight elevation less than a mile north of the town.

Kirkwood marched at eight o'clock in the evening and arrived at Logtown between nine and ten. He had a smart fight with a picket guard posted there. By midnight he had driven it out and established his own men in the little village. Through the night there were desultory attacks, and at sunrise a smart skirmish; but the Americans held the place until an hour or two later, when Greene's advance came up. The American force took possession, and Greene considered his next move.[18]

The town of Camden occupied a strong military position. It was covered on the south and southwest by the Wateree River, which curved around it at a distance of less than a mile, and on the east by Pine Tree Creek, a considerable tributary. The north and west were protected by a series of five or six independent redoubts strung around the central fortification, which was a strong stockade.[19] The garrison, numbering about 900 in all, consisted of the 63rd Regiment of regulars and three bodies of Tory troops—the New York Volunteers, the King's American Regiment (also called Fanning's, from the man who had raised it in New York in 1776), and the Volunteers of Ireland, Rawdon's own regiment. There were also 60 Provincial dragoons and a small party of militia. Colonel Watson had taken 500 other Tory troops to look for Marion.[20]

Greene realized that his force was not sufficient to take the town by assault. He hoped that Sumter would soon bring him a substantial addition, and he expected Lee and Marion to join him as soon as they had reduced

Fort Watson. Meanwhile, he decided to withdraw to Hobkirk's Hill about a mile in his rear, which offered a good position.[21]

The next day, he sent Colonel Washington's horse and Kirkwood's light troops on a foraging expedition. They "went Westerly round Camden, Burn't a House in one of the Enemy's Redoubts . . . took 40 horses and 50 Head of cattle & returned to Camp." [22]

On the 21st, tidings were brought to Greene of the imminent arrival of Colonel Watson and his party of 500 and of their intention to enter Camden, reenforcing Rawdon. To intercept the party, it was thought best to take a position on the east side of the town, Watson being expected from that quarter. This made it necessary to cross Pine Tree Creek and its deep and difficult swampy borders, impassable by artillery and baggage wagons. The impedimenta were sent back twenty miles to Lynch's Creek, and the army shifted its position. But after one night on the new ground more reassuring information as to Watson's movements was received, and Greene moved back to Hobkirk's Hill and sent for the artillery and the baggage.[23]

Up to this time Greene seems to have had no plan except to wait for Sumter, Marion, and Lee; and it may be said at once that Sumter, with his usual rather arrogant independence, had no intention of coming and never did, while the others were too busy trying to catch Watson in the Santee country to give a thought to Greene's predicament.

A deserting drummer of the Maryland line brought Rawdon news about the condition of Greene's force, told him that the artillery had been sent away, and gave him a correct description of the disposition of the troops on the hill. Rawdon promptly relieved Greene of the necessity of making a plan by making one of his own.[24]

Hobkirk's Hill

Hobkirk's Hill was a narrow, sandy ridge of no great height about a mile and a half north of Camden, extending from east to west. It was covered by a dense pine forest. At its eastern end it sloped gradually down to meet the edge of a wide and deep swamp bordering Pine Tree Creek and extending south past the defensive works of Camden. At its southern base the plain was covered by thickets which extended to a space of cleared ground north of the Logtown hill. South of Logtown an extensive clearing reached down to Camden. The main road from that town to the Waxhaws ran almost due north through Logtown and across the middle of Hobkirk's Hill. Because of the forest and of the shape of the hill, there was no clear view from the summit of the approaches.[1]

Greene's troops were encamped in a curved line around the eastern and southeastern end of the top of the hill, in positions corresponding to those the different regiments would take in order of battle, if attacked from that quarter. To guard against surprise, the southern and western sides of the hill were patrolled. On the plain below the southeast side two strong picket guards under Captain Perry Benson of Maryland and Captain Simon Morgan of Virginia were posted, supported by Kirkwood's light troops a little distance in their rear.[2]

Early in the morning of April 25, Colonel Carrington, Greene's quartermaster, arrived in the camp bringing "a comfortable supply of provisions" anticipated in the orders of the day before, which had promised two days' rations of food and a gill of rum to each man. On their arrival, just after the morning drill at daybreak, the men's arms were stacked and the desired distribution was made. Although the rum had not yet come, the provisions were eagerly received, and the men made haste to cook them. Those who had eaten first repaired to a brook running down the northeast side of the hill to wash their clothes. This was the peaceful scene upon which broke, at about ten o'clock, the report of a musket and then another and then many more. As the startled men sprang from their various occupations, the drums in the camp beat to arms.[3]

The attack had come on the picket guards, against whom Rawdon's van pressed forward, his whole force following. The pickets answered this first fire and fell back slowly. "Meanwhile, Kirkwood had hastened to the support of the pickets, and the quick, sharp volleys from the woods told how bravely he was bearing up against the weight of the British army." [4]

The pickets and the light infantry put up a stubborn resistance. Retreating slowly from tree to tree, they obstinately contested Rawdon's advance and so delayed it that the lines on the hill had time to form and even to obey an order to "ease their joints," which meant to sit down, while this preliminary skirmish was being fought in their hearing but out of their sight.[5] "The beautiful example . . . exhibited by Kirkwood, as he deliberately retired firing . . . contributed to produce upon the army an effect from which everything was to be hoped for." [6] Not until Rawdon had brought upon them the weight of his whole force did the light infantry and the pickets retreat to the army awaiting them on the hill.

The American line was disposed in a curve following the contours of the hill. The 4th Virginia Continental Regiment, under Lieutenant Colonel Richard Campbell, was on the extreme right of the first line; next was the 5th Virginia under Lieutenant Colonel Samuel Hawes. This wing was commanded by General Huger. Towards the left was Colonel John Gunby's 1st Maryland, and then Lieutenant Colonel Benjamin Ford's 5th Maryland. Colonel Otho Williams commanded that wing. The North Carolina militia, about 250 under Colonel Jesse Read, formed the second, or reserve, line; thus the formation was the reverse of those at Cowpens and Guilford, where the militia were in the first lines. William Washington's cavalry was also held in reserve behind the left wing, with whom presumably Kirkwood's light infantry took their place on their retirement from the front, since they had been lately attached to Washington's dragoons. The artillery, which had just come back from Lynch's Creek, three 6-pounders under Colonel Charles Harrison of Virginia, was posted in the center on the road running over the hill and behind the first line; it was thus concealed from the enemy. There were about 250 men in the militia reserve, 1,174 Continentals, 87 in Washington's cavalry, but only 56 of them mounted, and 40 in the artillery contingent.[7]

Rawdon had made his way to the field of action by a wide detour from Camden towards the east and close to the edge of the Pine Tree Creek swamps, so as to approach the hill on its southeast side, where the ascent was easier. When he had driven in the pickets and their support, he deployed in line of battle: the New York Volunteers in the center, the 63rd British Regiment and the King's American Regiment right and left, the Volunteers of Ireland in support of the right wing, and a corps of "convalescents" under Captain Robertson behind the left. The South Carolina Provincial Regiment and the New York Dragoons were held in reserve, while picked Tory riflemen were sprinkled in the woods on the right and left to snipe at American officers.[8]

Greene watched the display of the enemy and saw that it presented a narrow front, much less extensive than his own line. In this discrepancy he saw his chance. Instead of awaiting an assault by Rawdon's force, now advancing steadily and in good order, he would attack in such manner as to secure a quick and crushing victory. He gave orders accordingly.

Preceded by a discharge of the artillery, the whole first line of the patriots was to charge down the hill upon the advancing foe. While the 5th Virginia under Hawes and Gunby's 1st Maryland crashed into Rawdon's front with the bayonet and without firing, the American right and left wings, Campbell's 4th Virginia and Ford's 5th Maryland, were to wheel upon the enemy's flanks, thus folding their whole line in a deadly embrace. At the same time Washington's dragoons would start on a swift circuit of the combat and fall upon the British rear.

The battle began when the American center stepped a few paces to right and left, disclosing the guns, which at once opened fire with grape and threw the surprised enemy into momentary confusion. Then the Americans started down the slope.

But Rawdon was quick to see the error of his formation and as quick to correct it. He called his supports into his front line, the volunteers of Ireland on the right and Robertson's corps on the left. This extended his front so that it outflanked the Americans and would subject them to an enfilading fire. Nevertheless, they hurried on to the conflict.

At first, despite the alteration of the British line, the attack seemed to be successful. The American right, led by Greene and Huger, gained ground. Hawes's Virginians and Gunby's Marylanders were coming on gallantly with the bayonet. The flanking regiments were hotly engaged. The artillery was still firing grape, and Washington's horse were sweeping around to get at the British rear. Then came the first break in the plan.

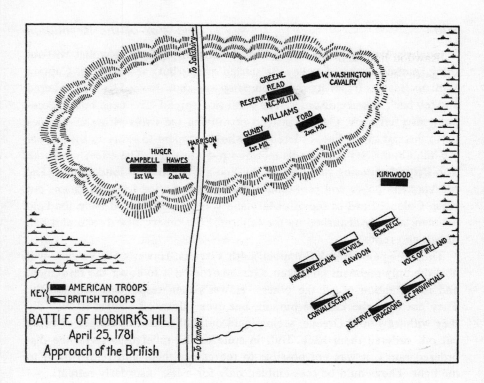

To Salisbury

GREENE
READ
RESERVE N.C. MILITIA
W. WASHINGTON
CAVALRY
WILLIAMS
GUNBY
1ST. MD.
FORD
2ND. MD.
HARRISON
HUGER
CAMPBELL HAWES
1ST VA.   2ND. VA.

KIRKWOOD

6TH. REGT.
KINGS AMERICANS
N.Y. VOLS.
RAWDON
VOLS. OF IRELAND
CONVALESCENTS
RESERVE DRAGOONS S.C. PROVINCIALS

KEY
AMERICAN TROOPS
BRITISH TROOPS

BATTLE OF HOBKIRK'S HILL
April 25, 1781
Approach of the British

To Camden

Gunby's 1st Maryland, instead of pushing on with the bayonet without firing, paused to fire a volley. It started again; but, as it did so, Captain William Beatty, Jr., of its right company was shot down. His men faltered and fell back in some disorder. The confusion spread. The neighboring company also fell back. Gunby, instead of rallying the two retiring companies up to the rest of the line, ordered the whole regiment to retire to the foot of the hill, about sixty yards in its rear and re-form there. The effect was fatal. The British opposing that part of the line advanced with loud shouts. The Marylanders broke and ran. Gunby and Williams tried to check them; but when Colonel Ford of the 5th Maryland was hit and carried from the field his men, already disturbed by the failure of the others, also broke and had to halt and retire.

The same panic struck Campbell's 4th Virginia. Hawes's 5th Virginia was now the only regiment unbroken. Greene ordered it to cover the retirement and re-formation of all the others. Hawes's men responded handsomely. They not only checked the pursuit, but even advanced against it. Nor did they withdraw until Greene, seeing them outflanked and in danger of being cut off, ordered them back. But, in spite of the relief thus given the disordered ranks, it was not possible to reorganize them and return them to the fight. They could be reassembled only for a less disorderly retreat.

Meanwhile the guns were in imminent danger of capture. The matrosses, who had been heaving at the dragropes, heard the shouts of the enemy coming up the hill and were leaving their posts. Greene sent Captain James Smith with a company of light infantry to defend and secure the three pieces. These were all young Irishmen drawn from the Maryland line, forty-five of them, none over thirty years of age. Seizing the abandoned ropes with one hand, holding their muskets with the other, they started for the rear; but the British dragoons led by Captain Coffin came galloping up the road. Smith's men dropped the ropes and made ready to receive the charge. Their fire was deadly. The dragoons wheeled and retired, but rallied, came on again, only to be driven back once more. So they fought, back and forth, while the British infantry was coming up through the woods. A sharp fire burst upon the little corps. Smith was wounded, all but fourteen of his men were shot down. Then Coffin made a final charge and not a man escaped; every one was either killed or captured.

Meanwhile Greene himself had rallied the matrosses, and they were drawing off the guns. He dismounted, held his bridle with one hand, and tugged with the other at the ropes. But when Smith's gallant band had been destroyed, the guns seemed hopelessly lost. They would have been, if just then Washington's dragoons had not returned from their errand of encirclement. They charged the enemy impetuously, dispersing them. Horses were hitched to the guns, and they were got away.

But what had Washington been doing all the time? The answer to this question discovers one of the several causes of the defeat. He had made a grand circuit of the field as had been ordered. The thick undergrowth and the tangle of trees, felled to clear the space between Logtown and the hill, had compelled such a long detour that he had emerged in the open far behind the enemy's fighting line. There he came upon a horde of noncombatants, surgeons, commissaries, quartermasters, "all the loose trumpery of the army," who had come out of Camden to watch the battle. Instead of disregarding them and galloping on to strike the rear of the fighting men, he began to take prisoners right and left. He had assembled two hundred when he heard of the American retreat. He mounted fifty of them behind his men and hastily took the parole of the officers he had to leave. Encumbered by reluctant passengers, his men could not fight; and so the intended attack on the enemy's rear was abandoned, and they swung around the circuit again on their way back to the hill. Having arrived, Washington heard the firing in the fight for the guns, dumped his captives by the roadside, and charged.

Greene assembled his men, his wagons, his guns, and the fifty prisoners and retreated in good order. He was followed for two or three miles, but his rear guard effectively discouraged the pursuit. When the enemy desisted from it, he halted to rest his men and await the stragglers.

Washington's dragoons and Kirkwood's light infantry were sent back to the field of action to bring off the wounded, collect stragglers, and pick up prisoners. There they again met Coffin's horsemen, attacked them, and drove them clear off. The rest of Rawdon's army had withdrawn into the town; Washington and Kirkwood had a clear field and were able to gather up all the wounded Americans and take them back to the army. Care of the wounded is much thought of by the survivors of any battle, who can picture the sufferings they themselves would have to undergo, if left helpless in the field. The recovery of these injured men was consoling to all the others. From their temporary halting place, the army marched on to Sanders Creek, the scene of Gates's disastrous defeat.

The American casualties, as reported by the adjutant-general, were one officer and 18 men killed, 7 officers and 108 men wounded, 136 men missing. Tarleton figured the British losses in killed, wounded, and missing at 258, of whom 38 were killed, including one officer; 13 officers were wounded.

Greene was sadly disappointed by the outcome of the battle. The signal

808   The War of the Revolution

failure of the 1st Maryland, the pride of his eye, to meet the test of the first encounter, followed by its inability to recover and return to the fight, was shocking to him. However, he blamed the men less than he did their commander. He felt that, when the first two companies had broken, Gunby should have rallied them to the rest of the regiment in the still advancing line, instead of ordering the whole regiment to the rear to re-form, thus precipitating a general withdrawal and finally a panic. He wrote to Joseph Reed, "We should have had Lord Rawdon and his whole command prisoners in three minutes, if Colonel Gunby had not ordered his regiment to retire, the greatest part of which were advancing rapidly at the time they were ordered off. I was almost frantic with vexation at the disappointment." [9]

A court of inquiry held at Gunby's request confirmed this opinion. Though it found his "spirit and activity unexceptionable," it also found that "his order for the regiment to retire, which broke the line, was extremely improper and unmilitary and, in all probability, the only cause why we did not obtain a complete victory." [10]

Rawdon won the day; but the price he paid was, like that of Cornwallis at Guilford, too high to profit him, as will appear. Greene expressed the sentiments of himself and his men when he wrote to the French envoy, the Chevalier de La Luzerne, "We fight, get beat, rise and fight again."

CHAPTER 76

Mopping Up the Carolinas

Greene and his army lay at Sanders Creek until the second day after the battle and then marched up to Rugeley's Mills, where he thought there was a better chance of "recruiting the cattle," that is to say refreshing the horses.[1] Marion and Lee were operating in the vicinity of the confluence of the Congaree and the Wateree in an effort to intercept Watson's force on its way to join Rawdon in Camden. Greene decided to assist them. He broke camp at Rugeley's on May 3, marched to the Wateree, crossed it, and established his army in a naturally strong position behind Twenty-five Mile Creek where it would interfere with Watson's getting into Camden from the south.[2] He believed that if Watson succeeded Rawdon would promptly attempt to engage the Americans. On May 7, having eluded Marion and Lee, Watson did get into Camden; and that same night Rawdon acted as Greene had foreseen. He crossed the Wateree at Camden Ferry, proposing "to turn the flank and attack the rear of Greene's army."[3]

Greene, however, had heard of Watson's arrival and had withdrawn on the same day five miles up the river to Sandy's—or Sawney's—Creek and then four miles farther to a better position on Colonel's Creek, leaving Washington's horse and Kirkwood's light troops as a corps of observation at Sandy's.[4] Rawdon mistook this corps for a picket guard of the main army, which he supposed lay in force close behind this outpost. As he afterward reported to Cornwallis, he found the situation too strong to be forced "without suffering such loss as would have crippled my force for any future enterprize." He returned to Camden. Washington and Kirkwood then marched to rejoin the army.[5]

For a long time Greene had been calling for reenforcements. He had counted on 1,500 to 2,000 men from Virginia and on the 1,000 Carolinians under Sumter. With these additions he could have taken the field, blockaded Rawdon in Camden until hunger compelled surrender, mastered the posts on the Santee and the Congaree, and opened the way to take Ninety-six and Augusta; in a word, he would have certainly reconquered most of the south.[6] Although he had sent several appeals to Sumter, that independent gentleman preferred to act alone, to carry on "rambling, predatory excursions unconnected with the operations of the army." [7] So the 1,000 Carolinians did not come to Greene's aid. Nor did the others. "The 2,000 Virginia militia I have been expecting to join us," he wrote to the Congress on May 5, "have not come out, nor can I learn that they will. . . . Maryland has neglected us altogether; not a man has joined us from that State since I have been in this department. Delaware has not answered my letters. . . . North Carolina has got next to no men in the field and few militia and those the worst in the world." [8]

The troops Greene had were too few for a regular battle. "You see," he said to Colonel William Davie of North Carolina, on his staff, "that we must again resume the partisan war. . . . You observe our dangerous and critical situation. The regular troops are now reduced to a handful and I am without militia to perform the convoy or detachment service. . . . Congress seems to have lost sight of the Southern States and have abandoned them to their fate, so much so that I am even as much distressed for ammunition as for men." He expected Rawdon to resume active operations and "push the Americans back to the mountains." [9]

Yet, in spite of the discouraging outlook after Hobkirk's Hill, Greene was now on the eve of sweeping the enemy from every foothold in the Carolinas, excepting only Charleston, for Rawdon was in worse case than he. Though not visibly beleaguered, Rawdon was cut off from food and forage by the activity of the partisan bands. Also mutiny was brewing among his men, for a rather odd reason.

Among the prisoners taken by the Americans at Hobkirk's Hill, were several deserters from the American army who had joined the British. On May 1, five were executed by hanging.[10] This incident disturbed the minds of many of the men in the Camden garrison, "which was composed very much of deserters" from the American army. The outlook for them, in case of capture by the Americans, was not pleasant; hence the growing unrest.

Under these conditions, Rawdon made up his mind to the drastic step of evacuating Camden and abandoning two other important posts. Immediately after his return on May 8 from the unsuccessful attempt to force Greene to fight, he sent orders to Lieutenant Colonel Cruger to leave Ninety-six and join Browne at Augusta, and to Major Maxwell to abandon Fort Granby and fall back on Orangeburg; both dispatches were intercepted, though Rawdon did not know it. He prepared for the evacuation of Camden, and his preparation was thorough, though hurried. On May 9 he burned the jail, the mills, and several private houses, leaving the town "little better than a heap of rubbish," [11] and destroyed all the stores he could not carry away. The next day he departed, taking with him four or five hundred Negro slaves and "all the most obnoxious loyalists." [12] He left behind 31 American privates and 3 British officers and 58 men, all of whom were too badly wounded to be moved.

Picking up on his route "all the well-affected neighbours . . . together with the wives, children, Negroes and baggage of almost all of them," Rawdon reached Nelson's Ferry on the Santee on the 13th. He had hoped to be in time to relieve Fort Motte, besieged by Marion and Lee, but was too late, as will appear. He had been joined by Major McArthur with about 380 dragoons, and failing succor for Fort Motte he designed to attack Greene, then on his way south, at McCord's Ferry on the Congaree. But Greene had already crossed, and so he finally came to rest at Monck's Corner on the Cooper Run, about forty miles north of Charleston.[13] There we may allow him to remain while we review the activities of Greene's army and the American partisan forces.

Kirkwood's light infantry, a detachment from the Maryland line, and a party of Washington's horse had been sent out from Greene's camp on Colonel's Creek in the evening of May 10, for the night surprise of a party of Tories. They marched eighteen miles without finding their quarry, but did discover that Rawdon had left Camden. Whereupon they turned that way and made eleven miles more by morning, when they entered the town.[14] Greene immediately brought down the rest of his army and destroyed the works, but tarried only one day. Correctly surmising that Rawdon's next move would be to relieve Fort Motte, he set out at once to interpose his force between Rawdon and the besiegers of Motte.[15]

The process of mopping up the Carolinas had begun before the evacuation of Camden. After the fall of that town, the successive steps occurred with almost bewildering rapidity. The first step had been taken by Sumter. Refusing to join Greene, he had been conducting an independent operation, which included a demonstration against Fort Granby (on the site later occupied by the town of Columbia). Finding it too strong to take, he withdrew and marched against Orangeburg, fifty miles to the south on the North Edisto River. Although its garrison was small, consisting of 15 British regulars and 70 Tory militia, it was a strong post. However, "by his address . . . in the disposition of his artillery and troops," he induced a prompt surrender on May 11 without the loss of a man and secured "great quantities of provision and some other stores." [16]

On May 8 Marion and Lee had approached Fort Motte, the principal depot of convoys from Charleston to Camden, on the southern bank of the Congaree a little above its confluence with the Wateree. It was a large and handsome mansion owned by Mrs. Rebecca Motte, who occupied a farmhouse near by since the British had ousted her from it. It had been strongly fortified with a stockade, a deep ditch, and an abatis, and was garrisoned by 150 infantry under Lieutenant McPherson, and a small detachment of cavalry. The Americans invested it and began approaches by parallels. But after two days of that work there appeared "beacon-fires on the distant hills," signals of Rawdon's coming to relieve the beleaguered garrison. It was plain that there would be no time to carry on regular siege operations before his arrival with a force greatly outnumbering the besiegers. With great regret, because the owner and all her family were stanch patriots, it was resolved to burn the fort, if it could be ignited.

When this resolution was made known to Mrs. Motte, she received it with "a smile of complacency," and herself furnished the means of setting it afire, a bow and arrows to be tipped with "combustible matter." Two days later the approaches had been dug to within bowshot of the house. The first arrow, launched by one of Marion's men with the appropriate name of Savage, struck the roof and ignited the shingles; two others were equally well aimed. The garrison started to knock off the shingles, but a few shots from a fieldpiece raked the attic and drove the soldiers from it. A white flag soon appeared, and the garrison surrendered. The British officers were paroled and invited, along with the American officers, to sit down to "a sumptuous dinner" provided by Mrs. Motte, whose "deportment and demeanor" as she conversed with "ease, vivacity and good sense" gave "a zest to the pleasures of the table." [17] It is pleasant to know that the fire was put out, and the house saved from destruction.

Greene, with a small escort, had hurried ahead of the army. He reached Motte shortly after the surrender, and, having ordered the prisoners to a place of security, directed Marion to proceed against Georgetown and Lee against Fort Granby, to which the army was also to march. The paroled British officers were allowed to join Rawdon, then engaged in crossing the

Santee at Nelson's Ferry, as has been stated. Receiving news of the fall of Motte, Rawdon ordered the post at that ferry abandoned.[18]

On May 13 Lee started for Granby, at Friday's Ferry on the Congaree, which he reached the next day. It was held by Major Maxwell, a Maryland Tory, with 352 men, chiefly Tory militia. The "fort" was a strongly built, two-story frame building, surrounded by a parapet with bastions mounting guns, a ditch, and the usual abatis—a strong post not to be taken without difficulty. But what force would have been slow to accomplish, guile quickly effected.

Lee had been told that Maxwell was ruled by cupidity, and that he and his men had gathered a considerable quantity of plunder. After two or three discharges of artillery and a brave show of infantry, he sent a flag to Maxwell and offered to allow all the private property on the premises to be taken away by its possessors, without inquiry as to their title to it, and carried to Charleston, to which place all the garrison were to go as prisoners of war until exchanged. The surrender was promptly arranged on those terms, Maxwell being allowed two wagons to transport his personal plunder. A considerable quantity of ammunition, some salt and liquor, the fort's guns, the garrison's weapons, and a number of horses were thus secured.[19]

Meanwhile Greene's army had been marching steadily southward. On the day Fort Granby surrendered, it was but a few miles distant. As usual, he was on the spot himself and viewed the work of Lee with satisfaction. Exactly twenty days had elapsed since his defeat at Hobkirk's Hill. In that short time, the enemy's imposing chain of posts in the Carolinas was broken by the loss of Camden, Watson, Motte, Granby, Nelson's Ferry, and Orangeburg. Besides Charleston and Savannah, only Georgetown and Ninety-six in South Carolina and Augusta in Georgia remained to the British. Greene had been beaten in every battle; he had barely saved his battered army from annihilation in the grueling retreat to the Dan; it had been reduced in numbers to an apparently almost negligible force; yet now he had swept two states, covering an enormous territory, almost clear of the enemy—almost, but not quite. There was more still to be done.

Georgetown had been assigned to Marion. Lee's Legion with some North Carolina militia under Major Pinketham Eaton was now to help Pickens in an attack on Augusta, while Greene with his army went on to Ninety-six.

Georgetown was no trouble at all: on the night after Marion's men had begun to break ground for approaches to it, the garrison evacuated the works and retreated to Charleston.[20] Lee moved against Augusta with his customary speed. He started from Granby a few hours after its surrender and made thirteen miles that evening. Haste was desirable because Greene was apprehensive that Cruger, hearing of Rawdon's retreat, might withdraw his garrison from Ninety-six and join Browne at Augusta, as indeed Rawdon's intercepted message from Camden had desired him to do. However, Lee learned on his march that Cruger was busily strengthening his fortifications to stand a siege.

The rapidity of Lee's march was made possible by his practice of occasionally dismounting his dragoons and mounting his foot-weary infantry on their horses. By this means, he was nearing Augusta on the third day when he learned that the annual King's present to his loyal Indians, a mass of material not to be overlooked or disregarded, had been temporarily deposited at Fort Galphin (Dreadnought), twelve miles below Augusta. Leaving Eaton with his militia and the artillery to follow on, he mounted his own infantry behind his dragoons for a forced march to the place of deposit.

In the next morning, May 21, he reached the little fort, a stockaded farmhouse garrisoned by two companies of Tory militia. There he detached a part of his force, which had been reenforced by parts of two regiments of Georgia and South Carolina militia, to make a sham attack on one side of the fort. At sight of these men, the major part of the garrison made a sortie. The attackers ran and the garrison pursued, while the main body of the Legion with its auxiliaries rushed the fort with little opposition. A considerable store of blankets, clothing, small arms, ammunition, rum, salt, medicines, and other articles, all most useful to the Americans, was taken. Lee then reassembled his troops and joined Pickens at Augusta.

In the center of that town was a strong fortification, Fort Cornwallis, held by the Tory Lieutenant Colonel Thomas Browne with 250 Tory militia and 300 Creek Indians. About half a mile distant there was another, smaller work, Fort Grierson, held by a Tory colonel of that name with 80 Georgia militia and two pieces of artillery.

The first attack was made on the smaller fort. Pickens and Lieutenant Colonel Elijah Clark of Georgia with their militia were posted on its north and west sides, Major Eaton and his North Carolinians on the south. Lee's infantry and artillery were also on the south side in support of Eaton. Major Joseph Egleston with Lee's cavalry was interposed between the two forts. The three detachments of infantry advanced against the fort simultaneously. There was little resistance. Without formally surrendering, the garrison attempted to escape to the other fort, but Clarke's force intercepted them, fell upon them with the ferocity habitual in those southern conflicts between rebel and Tory, and killed 30. All the rest were captured, including Grierson, who was shot while a prisoner by one of the Georgians, to whom he was "greatly obnoxious" because of the outrages he had visited upon them. The Americans lost a few, but one of them was Major Eaton, who was killed.

Fort Cornwallis was not so easily overcome. It was invested, and the usual approaches by parallels were begun, but were carried on with difficulty because of Browne's vigilance and activity. Twice a heavy detachment of the garrison sallied out and, after driving the men from the trenches in fierce, hand-to-hand fighting in which the bayonet was freely employed, was itself driven back to the fort.

The besiegers then began to erect a Maham tower. Browne turned two of his heaviest guns upon it; but it was completed, and the fire from it dismounted the two enemy guns and raked almost every part of the fort. Again there were sorties from the fort, two of them, and bitter fighting with the bayonet ensued. A pretended deserter from the fort, sent out to burn the tower, was discovered and taken prisoner.

A wooden house near the fort seemed to offer a vantage point for a party of riflemen to cover the proposed assault. They were about to occupy it when a violent explosion blew it to pieces. Browne had left it standing for a trap, had run a sap under it and mined it, but the mine had been prematurely set off.

In the morning of June 4 the besiegers were arrayed in columns ready for the assault, when it was decided again to summon the fort. The offered terms were accepted and on the 6th the garrison marched out and piled their arms. Browne was closely guarded to prevent assassination by the revengeful Georgians. The loss of the Americans in this affair was about 40 men killed or wounded. Except as to the 300 taken prisoners, the enemy's casualties are unknown. The day after the surrender, Lee set out to join Greene at Ninety-six, the only one of all the posts in the interior of Georgia and the Carolinas now held by the enemy.[21]

Ninety-six

When Greene left Camden on May 12 his thought was to interpose his army between the troops commanded by Marion and Lee, attacking Fort Motte, and Rawdon, who, he feared, might go to the relief of that post. The news of its surrender on the day he had left Camden relieved him of that apprehension; he turned west and was within a few miles of Granby when that post fell on the 15th. The way was now clear for him to proceed to his grand objective, Ninety-six. The army crossed the Broad River on the 18th, the Saluda on the 21st at Island Ford.

Ninety-six was so called because it was believed to be that number of miles from the old frontier fort of Prince George on the Keowee River. It was an important link in the chain of posts by which the British had held the Carolinas, because it served to protect the Tory element in its neighborhood, to hold in check the patriots in the settlements to the west of it, and to maintain communication with the Indian tribes that favored the British.[1]

For many years it had been stockaded. But that was insufficient defense against attack by a fully equipped army, and it was now much more strongly fortified. Since the fall of Camden and the other British posts the threat of an attack by Greene had caused still further elaboration and strengthening of its defenses.

The rectangular stockade surrounding the village was now protected by a deep ditch with an abatis, the earth from its excavation having been thrown up to form a high bank on the outside. At the easterly corner of the stockade, connected with it but lying wholly outside that enclosure, was a strong redoubt, the Star, of considerable size, roughly circular but with sixteen salient and reentering angles. This was also ditched about and abatised.

West of the main stockade was a large spring from which a rivulet ran down a little ravine. This was the only water supply for the villagers and the garrison. To protect it, the jail, which was within the stockade near the western corner, had been fortified; and upon the western bank of the ravine a small but strong palisaded fort containing two blockhouses had been built. This seems to have been called Holmes's Fort. A covered way led from the main stockade to the stream. The new works had been planned by Lieutenant Haldane, an engineer officer of the British army.[2]

The garrison of the fort was composed entirely of Tory troops. There were 150 of the 2nd battalion of the Loyalists of New York, a brigade raised by General Oliver De Lancey, a gentleman of wealth and high social position, 200 of the 2nd battalion of the New Jersey Volunteers, and 200 South Carolina Tory militia. Lieutenant Colonel John Harris Cruger, De Lancey's son-in-law, was in command of the whole. Cruger was a gentleman of spirit and courage, able and energetic far beyond the usual run of Tory leaders, and his men, "constantly employed in active service since the year 1776," were now "perhaps equal to any troops." He had also a considerable number of Tory civilians, who had taken refuge in the fort, and a noncombatant force of many Negro slaves, a sort of labor battalion.[3] Although he was well furnished with provisions his only artillery was three 3-pounder pieces mounted on wheel-carriages.[4]

Against this fortress Greene led fewer than a thousand regular troops and a few raw militia. Specifically, his army consisted of the two regiments of Maryland and Delaware Continentals—427 rank and file fit for duty—the Virginia brigade numbering 431, a North Carolina battalion of 66, and Kirkwood's 60 light infantry.[5]

Greene's advance arrived at Ninety-six on May 21, the main army coming the next day. The patriots made four camps in the woods, at the corners of an imaginary rectangle enclosing the fort, all within cannon shot of the stockade. Then Greene surveyed the situation. He saw "a very respectable work . . . so well furnished that our success is very doubtful." His force was not strong enough to invest the place completely, and he had no battering cannon. He decided that he must operate against it in the classic manner, by parallel approaches, and that they should be directed against the Star redoubt, since it commanded the main stockade.[6]

Without delay, without even first summoning the garrison to surrender, Kosciuszko, the chief engineer, began operations within two hundred feet of the Star, which was most discourteous as well as indiscreet. "Had he been acting against a raw and undisciplined militia, his temerity might have been excusable"—his impoliteness in omitting the usual preliminary formal summons might not even have been recognized as such, nor might the beginning of the approaches so rashly near the fort have been regarded as an insult. "But both the British commander and his garrison had seen too much service not to take advantage of so rash a proceeding and to teach him to his cost to shew them a little more respect." "Stung with this indignity," Cruger acted promptly. He mounted his three guns on a platform in the salient of the Star nearest the approach begun by the insolent besiegers. Under cover of a brisk fire from these guns and from some riflemen, a party of 30 under Lieutenant Roney sallied out, attacked the working party, put them all to the bayonet, destroyed their work, "loaded several Negroes with the intrenching tools," and returned to the fort before a rescue party from the American camp could reach the scene. Roney was the only casualty in the attacking force; he was mortally wounded.[7]

Having been taught this salutary lesson, Kosciuszko began again at a respectful distance, twelve hundred feet from the Star. The work was interrupted by frequent sallies from the fort but was pushed so expeditiously that the second parallel was complete by June 3. Then the previously omitted formality was gone through: the garrison was summoned. Cruger made the customary reply denying the request.[8]

From the nearest point in the approaches Greene then directed his artillery in a heavy cross fire, which enfiladed the enemy's works. Under cover of this, the digging was continued energetically night and day, and a sap was pushed forward. Meanwhile the timbers for a Maham tower were prepared. On the completion of the third parallel it was erected to a height of forty feet, within thirty-five yards of the abatis around the Star. It so overtopped that redoubt that the riflemen on its summit silenced the guns in the Star. Cruger answered by piling sandbags to raise the parapet, with loopholes which allowed his riflemen to reply effectively. He also tried to burn the tower by firing hot shot into it, but, lacking the proper furnaces, could not heat the balls sufficiently to ignite the timbers. Greene replied by trying to repeat the incendiarism that had been so successful at Fort Motte. Arrows whose butts were wrapped to fit closely in a musket barrel had points tipped with blazing tow, and then were fired at the barrack roofs. Cruger had the roofs torn off all the buildings, whereby the garrison was exposed "to all the pernicious effects of the night air." [9]

Lee and his Legion arrived on June 8, and Pickens with his militia came soon after. Lee immediately suggested that the approaches had been begun on the wrong side of the fort, the strongest side, while its most vulnerable

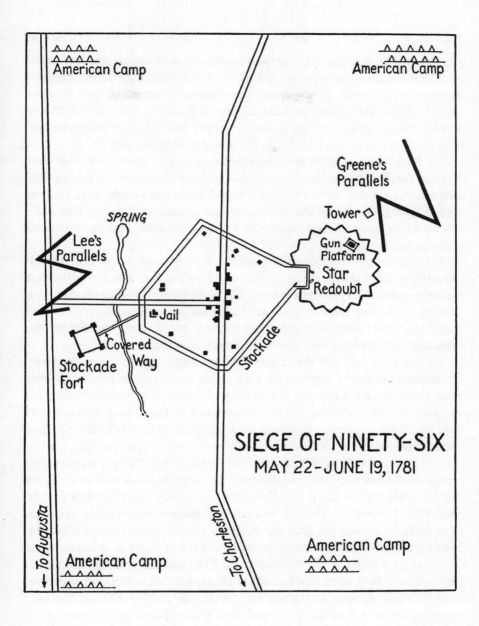

American Camp

American Camp

Greene's Parallels

Tower

SPRING

Lee's Parallels

Gun Platform

Star Redoubt

Jail

Stockade

Covered Way

Stockade Fort

To Augusta

American Camp

To Charleston

American Camp

SIEGE OF NINETY-SIX
MAY 22–JUNE 19, 1781

quarter had been neglected. The water supply was obviously the fort's vital spot and was the least strongly defended; if that were cut off, the garrison must inevitably soon give up. He was directed to attack it, and at once began approaches toward the little outside stockade on that side, erecting a battery of one gun to cover the work. Cruger made nightly sallies on one side or the other, which resulted in fierce and bloody combats.[10]

On June 11 a dispatch from Sumter brought bad news. A British fleet bearing reenforcements for Rawdon had arrived at Charleston on the 3rd, and he was already on the way to relieve Ninety-six. Greene sent Pickens and Washington with all the cavalry, to join Sumter in delaying Rawdon's advance. He also called on Marion to come up from the lower country and assist in this work.

It was plain that the operations against the fort must be pushed with all possible speed if they were to be successful before Rawdon arrived with a superior force. Fire was again tried. On a dark night a sergeant and nine men of the Legion infantry approached the stockade with a supply of combustibles. They were discovered before they could apply the fire to the palisades, and six were shot down, the others escaping.[11]

By this time Lee had made access to the water so precarious that only by sending out naked Negroes on dark nights could any be got. A well was dug inside the stockade, but no water was found. The weather being extremely hot, the suffering of the garrison and of the civilian refugees was intense. Without doubt it would have resulted in a surrender, if long protracted.[12]

It was now the 17th of June. A countryman came riding along the lines south of the town. Many people from the neighborhood had been in the habit of visiting the camp out of curiosity, and little attention was paid to him while he rode by, chatting in a friendly manner with officers and men. But when he neared the gate on the main road through the town he suddenly put spurs to his horse and galloped straight towards it, shouting aloud and waving a paper in his upraised hand. The besiegers fired upon him, but the gate was flung open, and he rode through unharmed. The cries of delight and the sound of a *feu de joie* told the Americans that the news of Rawdon's approach with a relieving force had been received and the courage of the garrison strengthened to withstand all hardships until the relief arrived.[13]

Rawdon had lain at Monck's Corner no more than ten days when, on June 3, he got word of the arrival of the fleet from Cork with his longed-for reenforcements. He hastened to Charleston and arranged for the expedition to succor Ninety-six. By the 7th he was on the way with a column made up of flank companies—light infantry and grenadiers—of the 3rd, 19th, and 30th British regiments. At Monck's Corner he picked up his own troops. He had now a force of 2,000 experienced men, including 150 horsemen.[14]

In spite of the excessive heat the rescue force proceeded by forced marches on its journey of nearly two hundred miles to the beleaguered fort. By swinging wide to the right, Rawdon avoided Sumter and the others that had been sent to delay him. At the time when the artful messenger got the good news into the fort the relief force was not more than thirty miles away.

Now there was not even a shadow of doubt that Greene must immediately make his choice among three possible courses of action: march to meet and fight Rawdon before he got to Ninety-six and then return to take the town; storm the fort before Rawdon arrived; give over the siege and retire. He was somewhat inclined to follow the example of Julius Caesar at Alesia and adopt the first course; but, as his force of regulars was only a little more than half Rawdon's, he decided to storm the fort.[15]

His plan for the attack called for two simultaneous assaults—one on the east side, one on the west. Lieutenant Colonel Campbell of the 1st Virginia Regiment with a detachment of the Maryland and Virginia Continentals was charged with the attack on the easterly side, of which the Star was a part. The third parallel of the approaches on that side had been completed, and two trenches had almost reached the ditch around the fort. Fascines were to be ready to fill the ditch, also long poles with iron hooks on their ends to pull the sandbags down from the parapet. A forlorn hope was chosen and was put under command of Lieutenants Duval of Maryland and Seldon of Virginia. The van of this contingent was to be composed of axmen who would cut through the abatis. The hookmen were to follow, and then the main assaulting force for that quarter was to come out of the trenches and swarm over the stockade.

On the west side, the smaller stockade—Holmes's Fort—which guarded the water supply, was to be the first objective. This was assigned to Lee's Legion infantry and Kirkwood's light troops. Captain Rudolph of the Legion was to lead the forlorn hope in that quarter.[16]

The firing of a second gun at noon on the 18th was the signal for the onslaught. On the west, Rudulph led his men swiftly against their objective. They gained the ditch, with the rest of the column close on their heels, and soon opened their "way into the fort from which the enemy, giving their last fire, precipitately retreated." Having so established themselves, Lee's detachment awaited news of the progress of the assault on the other side before following up the blow by passing the rivulet, entering the town, and forcing the fortified prison, which they intended to use as a base for operations that would divide Cruger's efforts to defend his post.[17]

Meanwhile, on the side of the Star, there was a bitter and bloody conflict. At the signal, Greene's little battery began a sustained bombardment of the fort, while the infantry fired by platoons, and the riflemen on the tower opened a continuous fire at the parapet of the Star. At the same moment the forlorn hopes led by Duval and Seldon leapt from the third parallel and ran to attack the abatis at two different points. The axmen soon cut their way through and entered the ditch. The hook men were close after them. The parapet bristled with pikes and bayonets; but they could not reach the men in the ditch, nor could the defenders fire down on them, without exposing themselves to the deadly aim of the riflemen on the tower.

The hook men went to work on the sandbags, pulling them down into the ditch. If the parapet could be stripped of them for a space, Campbell's men could clamber over and fight it out hand to hand. Major Green of De Lancey's regiment commanded the 150 men in the Star. He watched the bags falling into the ditch and saw that the garrison could not rely on musket fire to stop this breach in the defenses. Immediate and direct action was necessary. He issued the orders.

Two parties of 30 men each, led by Captain French of De Lancey's and Captain Campbell of the Jerseymen, issued from a sallyport in the rear of the Star, turned in opposite directions, and rushed upon the axmen and the hook men with the bayonet. There was hard fighting in little space and "the carnage was great"; [18] but when both Duval and Seldon were struck down their surviving men fell back to their support in the approaches.

The attempt had failed, and the failure had been costly. There was little hope of success in another effort, nor was there time to organize another; Rawdon was too near. Greene ordered a withdrawal and sent a flag to Cruger proposing a truce for the purpose of burying the dead. Cruger refused it, reserving that honor for the victor, whoever it might be. Greene then prepared to leave. The retreat began on the 20th, and Rawdon arrived on the 21st. The American losses were 57 killed, 70 wounded, and 20 missing. Cruger lost 27 killed and 58 wounded.[19]

Eutaw Springs

Greene's destination now was Charlotte, North Carolina; his course, therefore, was northeastward. He crossed the Saluda on his first day's march, picking up the baggage and the invalids he had sent off the day before the attack on Ninety-six. He organized a rear guard, consisting of all his cavalry, the infantry of Lee's Legion, and Kirkwood's company, and pushed on, expecting pursuit by Rawdon, who had started after him on the evening of his arrival at Ninety-six. The British van was within sight of the American rear guard before it reached the next river, the Enoree. The Americans retired slowly and crossed the river without being attacked. Rawdon's long and rapid march in the midsummer heat had told heavily upon his troops, and he lay overnight to rest them and then turned about and retraced his steps to Ninety-six.

Greene went on, crossing the Tiger River and the Broad on June 24. Then, finding he was no longer pursued, he detached his rear guard and sent it to watch the enemy and keep the main army informed of their movements.

Rawdon, meanwhile, had regained the fort and ordered its evacuation. He sent orders to Lieutenant Colonel Stuart at Charleston to proceed with his regiment to Friday's Ferry to a meeting on the Congaree. Then he divided his force, leaving a part of it with Cruger to protect the retreat of the garrison and the loyal refugees from the fort, by a more southerly route to Orangeburg.

With 800 infantry and 60 cavalry, Rawdon marched to meet Stuart. The heavy woolen clothing of the British troops burdened them excessively. They could hardly endure the scorching sun and the heavy humidity; 50

died of sunstroke or exhaustion on the march. Tarleton describes their hardships: "During a renewed succession of forced marches under the rage of a burning sun, and in a climate, at this season peculiarly inimical to man, they were frequently, when sinking under the most excessive fatigue, not only destitute of every comfort, but almost of every necessary which seems essential to his existence. During the greater part of the time, they were totally destitute of bread, and the country afforded no vegetables for a substitute. Salt, at length, failed; and their only resources were water and the wild cattle which they found in the woods." [1]

Greene had supposed that the division of Rawdon's force meant that the part left behind was, with Cruger's men, intended to hold Ninety-six. But he was soon informed of the preparations for evacuation. He halted his northward march and turned south towards the Congaree.

Stuart had marched from Charleston to Friday's Ferry in accordance with instructions, but was recalled to Charleston. Greene, learning of this, directed Lee and Kirkwood to try to gain Rawdon's front at that ferry and to join with Sumter and Marion, whom also he ordered to that point. They crossed the Congaree and encamped a mile in front of Rawdon to await Marion and Sumter.

Rawdon, disappointed by Stuart's recall, decided to move south to Orangeburg, and pushed back Lee and Kirkwood. He did not halt until nine o'clock in the evening. Lee and Kirkwood bedded their men a few miles in front of him, only to have them disturbed at dawn by the renewed advance of the British. All that day, they fell back, and Rawdon came on. They crossed Beaver Creek with Rawdon close behind them. Then they gave up trying to keep in front of that fast-moving column, turned aside, and left Rawdon a clear road to Orangeburg.

Sumter, Marion, and Washington's horse at last came up, and on July 10, Greene's whole force was reassembled near Beaver Creek.

Rawdon arrived at Orangeburg and was joined by Stuart and the 3rd Regiment, the famous Buffs. He had then about 1,600 infantry and artillery. A reconnaissance of the British position by Greene and several of his officers convinced them of its strength; there were several buildings in the town that would serve as citadels. The Americans had a strong force of cavalry; the British, none; but the ground was such that this arm could not operate. Cruger was on the way with about 1,400 men. So Greene decided not to attack, though his troops outnumbered Rawdon's.

The Americans, as well as the British, had suffered much from the extreme heat, the incessant marching, and the lack of food. Kirkwood's journal shows that the light troops, from the time they left Ninety-six until they came to Orangeburg, had covered 323 miles in twenty-two days, marching every day with no intervals for rest. Their food had been miserably scanty: "Rice furnished our substitute for bread. . . . Of meat we had literally none. . . . Frogs abounded . . . and on them chiefly did the light troops subsist. Even alligator was used by a few." They were sadly debilitated.[2]

The High Hills of Santee are a long, irregular chain on the east bank of the Wateree about twenty miles north of its confluence with the Congaree. Huge masses of sand and clay, twenty-four miles long, they rise two hundred feet above the river bank to plateaus one to five miles wide and fruitful in cotton and grain. They offered the Americans a salubrious campsite, free from the malaria so prevalent in the country in which they had been operating. On them Greene established his army, and there it remained for six weeks while the wounded recovered, the sick were restored to health, and everyone was invigorated by the pure air, the clear water, and the friendly hospitality of the inhabitants.[3]

Not all the American troops were so favored, however. Rawdon left Stuart in command at Orangeburg, and with 500 men set out for Charleston. Marion, Sumter, and Lee's cavalry were ordered to move in that direction, break up a post at Dorchester, and dislodge the 9th Regiment from Monck's Corner. Although not wholly successful, the American detachment forced the evacuation of Monck's Corner, took 150 prisoners, and captured 200 horses and a number of wagons before Lee rejoined the army on the High Hills, while Sumter held Friday's Ferry and Marion held Nelson's.[4]

Kirkwood's corps was also kept in motion. With Washington's horse it operated two weeks more along the Congaree, but without noteworthy result. On August 5 this detachment joined the army on the High Hills for a period of rest.

Rawdon, broken in health by the hardships of the campaign, sailed for home; but his ship was taken by the French fleet under Admiral de Grasse and he was carried to Brest a prisoner of war. Soon afterwards he was exchanged and returned to England.[5]

By the end of the third week of August, the American army was recuperated sufficiently to permit a renewal of active operations. During the interval reenforcements from various sources had been promised to Greene; but, as usual, few of them arrived. His command was, however, built up to about 2,000 men; with these he decided to move.

Stuart, now in command of the British forces in active operation in the

Carolinas, had taken a position on the west side of the Congaree near the point where it merges with the Wateree to make the Santee. He was but sixteen miles from Greene's camp; but the two great rivers between them were now so flooded as to appear to be lakes, and all the lowlands were under water, so that there was no possibility of a direct movement against Stuart. A wide circuit was necessary.[6]

On August 22 the Americans broke camp and marched twenty miles up the east side of the Wateree. The next day they traveled eighteen miles farther, to Camden, where they crossed the river. Following a southerly course, they crossed the Congaree and, on September 7, were within seven miles of Eutaw Springs, where Stuart and his army were encamped. On that day Marion and his men joined them. Brigadier General Jethro Sumner with a brigade of North Carolina Continentals had joined Greene at the High Hills. Pickens with his militia, and Lieutenant Colonel John Henderson with a small body of South Carolina state infantry, had come up with the main army at the crossing of the Congaree.[7]

Greene's army now consisted of 1,256 Continentals, 73 South Carolina state infantry, 72 state cavalry, 150 North Carolina militia, 307 South Carolinians under Sumter and Pickens, Marion's 40 horse and 200 foot, and about 300 of Lee's and Washington's horse—a total of 2,400. Of these, 200 were withdrawn to guard the baggage, which had been left behind at Howell's Ferry on the Congaree, only two wagons of ammunition, hospital stores and rum having been brought along. Greene's artillery comprised two 4-pounders and two 6's.[8]

Stuart seems to have had the battalion companies of the 3rd British regiment, the six flank companies, grenadiers and light infantry, of the 3rd, the 19th, and the 30th regiments, commanded by Major Marjoribanks of the 19th, the remains of the 63rd and 64th regiments, much reduced by their long service throughout the war, and the garrison of Ninety-six—that is to say a battalion of De Lancey's Loyalists of New York, a battalion of the New Jersey Volunteers, and one of the New York Volunteers. He had also a cavalry regiment of South Carolinians under Major John Coffin, a Boston Tory. The total number of Stuart's men was about 2,000. He had also three fieldpieces—two 6-pounders and a 4.[9]

It will be observed that, unlike the forces of Ferguson at King's Mountain, Tarleton at Cowpens, and Cruger at Ninety-six, which had been composed entirely of American Tories, Stuart's army was largely composed of British regulars. It should also be noted that a large proportion of his Tory troops were deserters from American Continental regiments, of whom it has been said that British discipline had been added to their American training as marksmen, making them, in action, the equals of the Continental troops. On the American side, many of the Continentals were deserters from the British army. To such an extent had this interchange of men taken place that Greene was wont to say: "At the close of the war, we fought the enemy with British soldiers; and they fought us with those of America." [10] There was little to choose between the two armies in the quality and experience of their men; and in numbers they were about equal. Perhaps in no other battle of the war were the two opposing forces so fairly matched.

Stuart had moved from Center Swamp to Eutaw Springs in order to meet a convoy of provisions coming up from Charleston. Otherwise he would have had to detach at least 400 men to meet and guard it, "which, at the time," he wrote later, "I could ill afford, the army being much weakened by sickness." [11]

The two Eutaw springs were really the first and second appearances above ground of a subterranean stream of considerable volume. From the lower of the two basins the water flowed in a winding stream, Eutaw Creek, between steep, heavily thicketed banks to the Santee. Close by the head of the creek, between it and the main highway, which ran east and west and sent off a branch road to Charleston, there was a large brick mansion of two stories and a garret. In front of it was a cleared area, an oblong of about eight acres surrounded by a palisade and divided into halves by the main road. On the side towards the creek and close beside the house was a palisaded garden. All about was a rather sparse woods. In the enclosed clearing the British camp was pitched. [12]

Stuart was comfortably established there, but he was unfortunate in one respect. "Notwithstanding every exertion being made to gain intelligence of the enemy's situation," he wrote to Cornwallis after the battle, "they rendered it impossible, by waylaying the bye-paths and passes through the different swamps." [13] So secure from immediate attack was he, in his own mind, that he sent out at daybreak of September 8, on the very road by which Greene was then advancing, a party of 100 unarmed men attended only by a small guard, a "rooting party" to gather sweet potatoes. At six o'clock two deserters from the North Carolina troops came to tell him that Greene was already on the march. He refused to believe them and ordered them confined. He did, however, dispatch Major Coffin with 140 foot and 50 horse to scout along the road. [14]

Greene had bivouacked on the night of the 7th at Burdell's plantation, seven miles from Stuart's camp. At dawn his army marched in four successive columns. The first was led by Lieutenant Colonel Henderson; it consisted of Lee's Legion and the South Carolina state infantry. Marion commanded the second, made up of the North Carolina militia under Colonel the Marquis de Malmedy and the South Carolina militia under Pickens. The third column was composed of the Continentals under General Jethro Sumner. The rear was closed by Washington's horse and Kirkwood's light troops. This arrangement was made to conform to the proposed deployment into line of battle. The army moved slowly and cautiously in the hope of surprising pickets and patrols of the enemy.[15]

The Americans were within four miles of Stuart's camp about eight o'clock, when Major John Armstrong, who had been reconnoitering ahead with a party of North Carolinians, fell back with the news that he had sighted a body of the enemy. That was Coffin's detachment. Henderson halted his column and drew it up across the road with Lee's Legion in the woods on the right, the South Carolina state troops in the woods on the left.

Hot on Armstrong's heels came Coffin. "With a degree of recklessness which indicated either his ignorance of its strength and the presence of the main body or his contempt for the service," Coffin charged on the American van. He met a shower of bullets. Major Egleston with the Legion cavalry circled around to Coffin's rear, while the infantry of the Legion charged with the bayonet. Coffin's infantry was "destroyed, several killed and about 40 taken with their captain." [16] His cavalry escaped by precipitate flight. The sound of the firing drew the rooting party to the scene, and they were all captured.

Stuart was apprised of Greene's advance by the fleeing cavalrymen. He sent a detachment of infantry down the road to delay the Americans and gain time for him to form his line. Greene had regaled his men with a ration of rum and was about a mile from the enemy's camp when this new opposition was met. It opened on Lee's Legion with one gun. Otho Williams sent Captain William Gaines of Virginia up from the third column at full gallop with two guns to return the fire, while Lee and Henderson on the right and left fired obliquely upon the enemy and drove them back.[17]

Meanwhile, Stuart was arranging his line of battle. He drew his troops out of their camp into the woods in front and formed them in a single line obliquely across the road along which the Americans were advancing. The 3rd Regiment was on the right of the line, its flank resting on the steep bank of Eutaw Creek. On that side it was supported by the six companies of grenadiers and light infantry—about 300 men—under Major Marjoribanks placed at some little distance, somewhat in advance and at an

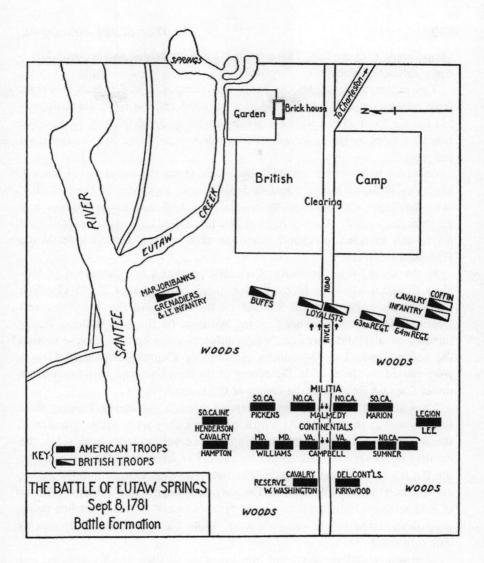

SPRINGS

Garden · Brick house

To Charleston →

N

British

Camp

Clearing

ROAD

RIVER

EUTAW CREEK

SANTEE

MARJORIBANKS

GRENADIERS & LT. INFANTRY

BUFFS

LOYALISTS

63rd. REGT.

64th. REGT.

CAVALRY INFANTRY · COFFIN

WOODS

WOODS

MILITIA

SO. CA. PICKENS

NO. CA.

MALMEDY

NO. CA.

SO. CA. MARION

LEGION LEE

SO. CA. INF. HENDERSON

CONTINENTALS

CAVALRY HAMPTON

MD. MD. WILLIAMS

VA. VA. CAMPBELL

NO. CA. SUMNER

KEY ▬ AMERICAN TROOPS ◣ BRITISH TROOPS

CAVALRY W. WASHINGTON · RESERVE

DEL. CONT'LS. KIRKWOOD

WOODS

THE BATTLE OF EUTAW SPRINGS
Sept. 8, 1781
Battle Formation

WOODS

obtuse angle with the line. This contingent was concealed and protected by a dense thicket of blackjack.

The center, lying across the road, was composed of Cruger's Loyalists from Ninety-six. The left was held by the 63rd and the 64th. Its flank was "in the air," but Coffin with his cavalry and a body of infantry was posted behind a thick hedge in its rear. The artillery was placed in the center, on the road.[18]

Greene's army came up into two lines from the columns of march. Malmedy with the North Carolina militia took the center of the first line, with the South Carolina militia on his right and left, under Marion and Pickens respectively. On the right of this line Lee's Legion was posted, and on its left Henderson's South Carolina state troops and Colonel Wade Hampton's cavalry.

In the second line Lieutenant Colonel Campbell's two battalions of Virginia Continentals were in the center, three battalions of North Carolina Continentals under General Sumner on the right, and the Maryland and Delaware Continentals under Colonel Williams on the left. William Washington's cavalry and Kirkwood's light infantry were held in reserve behind the second line. Two 3-pounder guns under Captain-Lieutenant Gaines were posted on the road in the center of the first line, and two 6-pounders under Captain Browne in the center of the second.[19]

Thus arrayed, the Americans advanced through the woods, keeping their lines as well as they could. At a little past nine, they were within gunshot of the enemy, and the battle began with repeated volleys from both sides, the artillery being served to advantage by each. The advance continued steadily, the British line holding its place. The musketry was extraordinarily heavy, and the conflict was obstinate and bloody. The enemy had rather the better of it in artillery, both the Americans' "grasshoppers" in the front line being soon dismounted by the enemy's guns, while the British had only one of theirs disabled.

The militia in Greene's front line stood up to their work manfully, advancing without hesitation and firing steadily, although they were receiving the fire of the whole British line, double their number. Greene said their "conduct would have graced the veterans of the great King of Prussia." [20] They fired seventeen rounds before they showed any sign of weakening. At that time Lee's Legion, in an effort to outflank the British left, was hotly engaged with the 63rd Regiment. Stuart sent the 64th and Cruger's Loyalists forward against the American center, Malmedy's North Carolina militia. The attack was sudden, unexpected, and heavy. The North Carolinians broke. Pickens's and Marion's men on the flanks of the broken center gave way. The whole American front line was gone, except its two extremities, Lee's Legion on the right, Henderson's infantry and Hampton's cavalry on the left. They were now fighting separate battles with the 63rd and the 3rd.

Greene acted promptly. He swung Sumner's North Carolina Continentals into the first-line center. They came up with alacrity and precision and reestablished the line. They not only withstood a renewed attack but even drove the enemy back to his first position, and the battle raged as furiously as before.

Signs of weakness now appeared in the British line; it was drawing back before the American attack. Stuart brought up on his left the detachment of infantry and Coffin's cavalry, which had been held in reserve behind his left flank. About the same time Henderson was wounded, and his South Carolina state troops, on the American left, faltered; but Hampton rallied them, and they stood fast against the fire of Marjoribanks's corps in the thicket on the British right.

The situation of the two armies was extraordinary in that, although the battle had been under way for so long and was so bitterly contested, with the whole British army active, the strongest elements of the American army had not been engaged: the Maryland, Delaware, and Virginia Continentals, Kirkwood's light infantry, and Washington's cavalry were mere spectators. But their time for action was at hand.

Sumner's North Carolina Continentals, bearing the brunt of the battle, now heavier than ever by the weight of the reenforced enemy line, could not stand the strain; they gave way and retreated. The British, shouting their triumph, rushed forward with disordered ranks. It was Greene's moment. He ordered the Continentals of the second line to charge. Williams and Campbell led them. At a distance of forty yards they fired a volley, and then, trailing their muskets and shouting defiantly, they sprang forward to a bayonet charge, while Captain Michael Rudulph with Lee's infantry wheeled upon the British left and poured in an enfilading fire. Howard, leading a part of the Marylanders, met the British right, the Buffs, in such close combat that the officers fought with their swords and men on both sides fell mutually transfixed by each other's bayonets.

It was too much for the British line. "Assailed on front and flank," it was driven back "in utter confusion"—first the left, then the center, and finally the right—the Buffs, though a recently raised regiment, holding out longest. The whole line, except Marjoribanks's detachment, "fell back in disorder into the clearing where the camp stood." [21]

Stuart called on Marjoribanks, and Greene countered with his reserve. Washington, attempting a charge upon Marjoribanks, found that his horses

could not penetrate the blackjack thicket. He saw an open space in his
enemy's rear. Wheeling by sections to gain that opening, his corps rode
right across Marjoribanks's murderous fire. Men and horses rolled on the
ground. Washington's own horse was shot down. He became entangled in
the stirrups, received a bayonet wound, and was captured. His second in
command and two of his lieutenants fell. A third was wounded and dismounted, and not a single man of his section escaped death or wounds. A
full half of Washington's whole corps were killed or wounded. Hampton
and his horsemen had come up. With the aid of Lieutenant John Gordon
and Cornet Simmons, both of Washington's cavalry, Hampton rallied the
survivors of that corps and led another charge upon Marjoribanks, without
success.

But Kirkwood's troops were coming on at the double to succor their
companions in the cavalry. Wasting no time in firing, they charged into the
thicket, and "rushed furiously" upon Marjoribanks with the bayonet.[22]
Backward, down into a ravine, they drove their opponents and up the
farther bank; but in a strong position there Marjoribanks stood and held
his ground, forming a new line with his rear to the creek, his left against the
palisaded garden.

Meanwhile the rest of the British were in full retreat through their own
camp and along the Charleston road, the Americans after them. In this rout
300 prisoners and two guns were taken. There was nothing left for the
Americans to do but consolidate their gains, sweep away Marjoribanks and
go after Stuart, who was trying to rally his soldiers on the Charleston road,
and then cut off Major Sheridan of Cruger's force, who was making for the
brick house. But in that moment of almost complete victory the discipline
of the Maryland and Virginia Continentals blew up and vanished. They and
the militia halted in the British camp and fell upon the spoils of a victory
not yet fully achieved. In utter disorder, complete confusion, they looted
the stores, ate the food they found, and drank the liquor until many were
drunk. No efforts of their officers sufficed to bring them back to their duty.

Sheridan had gained the brick house and was firing from it upon the disorderly rabble in the camp. Others were flocking to join him. Only the
infantry of Lee's Legion, a part of the Marylanders under Howard, and
Kirkwood's troops held themselves free from the disorder in the camp.
Though fatigued by their former exertions and "far spent for want of
water," they still fought for the prize of complete victory. Lee's infantry and
Kirkwood's struggled for entrance at the very door of the house and were
saved from Sheridan's fire only by grabbing prisoners and holding them as
shields while they retired. Greene ordered up his guns to breach the wall of

the house, but with swivel guns and muskets its garrison shot down the gunners.

Coffin's cavalry were still in the field. Greene, strangely unaware of the disorder in the camp, ordered Lee's horse to attack him. Egleston, leading the Legion horsemen, turned the head of the ravine, across which Kirkwood had driven Marjoribanks, swept across the field, and charged on Coffin, but was repulsed. Hampton then tried; there was a sharp fight at close quarters, and Coffin was driven back. But, in following him, Hampton exposed his own men to a close fire from Marjoribanks. It was so severe that Colonel Thomas Polk of Hampton's horse "thought every man was killed but himself."

The gallant Marjoribanks then added to his laurels of that day, his last on earth. Abandoning his protected position, he sallied out into the field, captured the American guns brought up to batter the house, and drew them back under its walls. Howard, with Oldham's Maryland company, met Marjoribanks, was wounded, and his troops fell back. Marjoribanks went on, swept down upon the rabble in the camp, and drove them into the woods.

Meanwhile, Stuart had rallied his men. He brought them back to the house. But by this time, after three hours of this grueling battle in the heat of a Carolina summer, both armies had had enough.[23]

Greene's battalions were in confusion, his cavalry was shattered, his guns lost, and many of his best officers wounded; only two of his Continental regimental commanders, Lee and Williams, had come through unscathed. One-fourth of his men were killed or wounded, and the rest were physically exhausted. Stuart's losses, including the prisoners taken by the Americans, amounted to more than two-fifths of his strength. There was no more fight left in either army. Greene drew his men back into the shelter of the woods and collected his wounded, all but those too near the house still in possession of the enemy. Stuart held the field that night, but retired towards Monck's Corner the next day, having destroyed a quantity of stores and left 70 of his more seriously wounded men to the care of the Americans. Marjoribanks, the hero of the day on the British side, had been badly wounded in the last encounter of the battle. He died on the way and was buried by the roadside.

Kirkwood's men and a party of Virginia Continentals under Colonel Thomas Edmunds were not only the last to leave the field but also the only ones to capture and carry off one of the British guns. "Major Edmund of the Virginians, with a Small party of men joined me in the British Encampment," Kirkwood wrote in his journal, "keeping up the fire for A small space of time. Found our army had withdrawn from the Field, made it necessary for us Likewise to withdraw. We brought off one of the Enemy's three Pounders, which with much difficulty was performed through a thick wood for near four miles without the assistance of but one Horse." [24]

"So ended the very bloody and desperate action of Eutaw Springs." [25] "Such was the heat of the action that officers on each side fought hand to hand and sword to sword." [26] Greene said it was by far the most obstinate fight he ever saw. In proportion to the numbers engaged, the losses on both sides were very great. The American casualties as published by the Congress amounted to 522 of all ranks: 139 killed, including 17 officers, 375 wounded, including 43 officers, and 8 missing.[27] The British losses were even more severe, 866 in all, more than two-fifths of the force: 85 killed, 351 wounded, and 430 missing.[28]

Both sides claimed the victory. As the British held the field, it was technically theirs. But the inability of both sides to carry on the fight after the Americans withdrew into the woods gives it the appearance of a drawn battle. As in all Greene's battles in the South, the results were distinctly favorable to his side, though he failed to gain a victory. This one drove the enemy back to the vicinity of Charleston. Except in and about that town and Savannah, the British held no territory in the South. The state governments in Georgia and the Carolinas were reestablished and were able to function without molestation to the end of the war. There was no serious fighting in any of the three states after Eutaw Springs.[29]

The Congress voiced the feeling of the American people when, on October 29, it thanked Greene for obtaining a most signal victory and "the Maryland and Virginia brigades and Delaware battalion of continental troops for the unparalleled bravery and heroism by them displayed in advancing to the enemy through an incessant fire and charging them with an impetuosity and ardor that could not be resisted." A British standard and a gold medal were presented to Greene.[30]

CHAPTER 79

After Eutaw Springs

When Greene withdrew his troops from the field of battle at Eutaw Springs he expected to remain close to Stuart until he could refresh them, and then to attack once more. But there was one bodily need that mere cessation of activity could not supply: the need for water. More than three hours of battle in the excessive heat of that day had generated a thirst that could not be denied. The men's lips were black, their mouths foul from the bitten cartridges, their tongues parched, their whole bodies drained of moisture. "The cry for water was universal." Every canteen had long since been emptied, and there was neither a spring nor a rivulet near them that was not in the possession of the enemy.[1] They had to retire to their position of the night before, Burdell's plantation, leaving Hampton and a strong picket guard to watch the enemy. But Greene did not abandon his intentions against Stuart.

The next day, September 9, he sent Marion and Lee to turn the enemy's left and to take a position between Eutaw Springs and Charleston, so as to hold Stuart where he was and to intercept any reenforcements from his base. But Stuart had hurried his preparations, and McArthur was already on the march from Charleston. Their junction was imminent by the time Marion and Lee gained the desired position, and the American troops were too few to fight the combined enemy forces. The junction of Stuart and McArthur was effected, and together they retired to Monck's Corner.[2]

Greene had hurried, too. Having arranged to send his wounded to the High Hills, he had taken the road after Stuart on the 10th. But the continued intense heat slowed his army; Stuart had a long start, and Greene could not catch him. Twelve miles from Monck's Corner, he halted and encamped. After one day he marched back to Eutaw and did what he could to ease the wounded of both armies left there because they were too severely injured to be moved. Then, by easy stages, the army returned to the High Hills.[3]

Recuperation of the patriots was imperative. Their exertions in the heat and the sultry humidity of the day and their exposure to the chill of the heavy dew at night had exhausted them. "Never," says Henry Lee, "had we experienced so much sickness at any one time as we did now." It "affected every corps, even those most inured to military life, and most accustomed to the climate. Nearly one-half of the army was disabled by wounds or fever." The High Hills offered rest, good air, pure water, accommodation for the wounded, restoration for the sick, and "a plentiful supply of wholesome provision"—but, as before, not for all of them.

The country along the southern bank of the Congaree was open to predatory excursions. On the way back from their pursuit of Stuart, Kirkwood's troops were detached from the main army and sent towards that district. On the fourth day after that, September 19, they came up with their old companions in arms, Washington's cavalry. It does not appear that they encountered any of the enemy; but they were constantly on the move looking for them, and they were in poor health. Kirkwood himself "took the Ague and fever" and was obliged to rest at a friendly plantation for nearly a month. His men were so debilitated that at times there were "scarce men enough to mount two small guards." [4]

In the salubrious camp of the main force, conditions were not much better. The army dwindled. Pickens, Marion, and Hampton were detached to cover various districts. Almost all the militia left; only 100 of North Carolina remained, and their time was nearly up. The camp was simply a hospital, where 350 American and 250 British wounded men, who had been brought in boats up the Santee and the Wateree, had to be cared for by the few sound Continentals and militia. Malaria was prevalent. Ten days after the battle, Greene had not a thousand men fit for duty.[5] On October 25 he wrote to General Washington, "Our troops have been exceedingly sickly, and our distress and difficulties have been not a little increased for want of medicines and hospital stores. . . . We can attempt nothing further except in the partisan way. . . . I look forward with pain to December, when the whole Virginia line will leave us. I hope measures will be taken before that period to reinforce us." [6] At that time, he wrote of his troubles to Colonel William Davie also: "An army which has received no pay for more than two years, distressed for want of clothes, subsisted without spirits, and often short in the usual allowances of meat and bread, will mutiny, if we fail in the article of salt." [7] And mutiny they did, or came so near it that the use of the word is a minor exaggeration.

Unrest spread through the Maryland Continentals. They petitioned Greene several times, complaining of lack of clothing; they called attention to the fact that there were but 200 survivors of the seven regiments. They "left off their usual sports" and gathered in sullen groups discussing their grievances. In the evening of October 21 a number of them "went privately out of camp with their arms." The officers were alarmed and ordered a roll call. The defection was only an experiment to see what would happen; the seceders crept back secretly and answered to their names. But the situation was definitely threatening. While the rolls were being called, Timothy Griffin, of the only South Carolina company still remaining in the camp, came on the parade drunk. Some of the officers were admonishing their men for their irregularities. Timothy cried out: "Stand to it, boys! Damn my blood if I would give an inch!" Captain Samuel McPherson of the Marylands knocked him down. He was arrested, court-martialed for encouraging mutiny and desertion, convicted, and shot the next afternoon, in the presence of the whole army. "No example was ever more effectual." [8]

On October 19 Cornwallis surrendered his army at Yorktown. Historians usually regard that surrender as the end of the war; but at the time it was not generally so regarded. Lord North may have taken the news "as he would have taken a ball in the breast" and exclaimed, "Oh God! It is all over!" as Lord George Germain said he did; [9] but that was not known in America. In fact, the capitulation at Yorktown was the surrender of only one of the three British armies in America, and that the weakest. New York was still held as strongly as ever; Wilmington in North Carolina and Savannah in Georgia were still in British hands, and Charleston, the capital city of the south and its most important strategic position. Yorktown was not everything.[10] In fact, peace was yet more than a year away; and during that time, though no important battle was fought, the troops in the south had to continue their exertions and undergo much hardship.

Although men were released by the fall of Yorktown to reenforce Greene and were soon on their way to him, two months elapsed before they arrived. Meanwhile, Stuart, incapacitated by a wound at Eutaw, had turned over his command to Major John Doyle, who had resumed hostilities. Hector McNeill, an active and daring Tory, with 300 men had marched from Wilmington to Hillsboro, North Carolina, the rebel capital, captured Governor Thomas Burke, some members of his Council, and every Continental and militia officer in the town, and carried them back to Wilmington.[11]

This exploit aroused the Tories throughout the state; especially along the Pee Dee River, they renewed their activities in harassing the patriots and ravaging their homes. Though Greene was weak it was incumbent upon him to quell these new uprisings.

On November 8 the American army struck the tents in the High Hills camp and went down into the South Carolina low country. It had been strengthened by a body of mountaineer riflemen under Colonel John Sevier of North Carolina and Colonel Isaac Shelby of Virginia. Greene had sent them to Marion to help in holding back Doyle, but he got word on the march that the freeborn mountaineers had gone home. Fortunately, as his little army advanced, Doyle fell back to Goose Creek Bridge, and no conflict with him was necessary. This evidence of a disinclination on Doyle's part to meet him, induced Greene to try to push him farther back.

Within fifteen miles of the chief British position at Charleston lay the village of Dorchester, held by 850 of the enemy. Greene decided to try to cut them off. He took 200 of Lee's, Washington's, and Sumter's cavalry and an equal number of Maryland and Virginia Continental infantry. Leaving the rest of his army under command of Otho Williams, he led that detachment against Dorchester. There were skirmishes between his advance and a reconnoitering party from the town, and between the opposing cavalry forces; but, Greene himself being recognized, the town's commander thought the whole American army was upon him. He destroyed his stores, threw his guns into the Ashley River, and fled to a post within five miles of Charleston, where Stuart, who now returned to the field, joined him. The British in South Carolina now held only Charleston and its immediate vicinity; they had 3,300 men in the garrison of the town besides a considerable body of Loyalists. There was "wild alarm" throughout the town, caused by rumors exaggerating Greene's strength, and "the most active Negroes were called to arms and enrolled." [12]

In the meantime, Williams had marched the rest of the army from the High Hills to the singularly named Round O, between the Edisto and the Ashepoo River and about forty miles from Charleston, and encamped there. Greene joined him on December 9. It was a pleasant place at that season of the year. Rice was abundant and, although not so palatable as cornmeal or wheat flour to the troops from the more northerly states, it was food. Game was plentiful in the woods and swamps, fish in the waters, and wild fowl on them. [13]

General Arthur St. Clair with 2,000 Pennsylvania, Maryland, and Delaware Continentals, including Anthony Wayne, painfully made the long and toilsome southward march from Yorktown. Rains were frequent; the roads were alternately frozen and "sloppy." For subsistence his men drove a herd of 400 beef cattle, which did not increase their speed. There were streams to be forded, and, though "the frogs in the swamps sang very sweetly," the swamps had to be crossed in "mud up to our knees." Yet they traveled about fifteen miles a day and arrived at Round O on January 4, 1782.[14]

Kirkwood and his fellow officers of the Delaware Continentals were relieved from duty after six years' continuous service and went home. The two Delaware companies, including new recruits, were then attached to Washington's cavalry to constitute the infantry section of his Legion. Soon afterward they participated in an attempt upon Johns Island, an extensive piece of land close to Charleston, on which cattle for the support of the British army were pastured. On the approach of St. Clair's force from the north, Major Craig in command of the British garrison in Wilmington had prudently evacuated that town and taken his men down to Charleston. With some additional infantry and cavalry, he was now occupying Johns Island.[15]

Lee and Marion had been working down the opposite side of the Ashley. They were now encamped near Charleston. Greene had brought the main army down from Round O and posted it at Ponpon on the Stono River, across from Johns Island. Lee had reconnoitered the island and concluded that an attack was feasible. The project was committed to him and Colonel John Laurens. To make up the necessary force, certain detachments from the Pennsylvania, Maryland, and Virginia Continentals were joined to Lee's Legion and the Delaware companies; this force amounted to about 700 men.[16]

The water separating the island from the mainland was passable only at low tide. Lee evolved an elaborate plan, the success of which depended upon crossing at night, at dead low water, in two columns. The first, led by Lee, passed over safely. The second, under Major James Hamilton, lost its way in the darkness and arrived too late to cross. Those who had crossed had to be recalled, as the tide was rising; they got back with difficulty through breast-deep water. The attempt was abandoned.[17]

The day after that, Greene moved to a position between Charleston and Jacksonboro, where the South Carolina legislature sat under protection of the army. Meanwhile Anthony Wayne had been sent into Georgia with 100 of Moylan's dragoons, commanded by Colonel Anthony White of New Jersey, and a detachment of field artillery. He crossed the Savannah River on January 12 and was soon joined by Colonel Wade Hampton with 300 of Sumter's mounted infantry and by 170 of Jackson's and McCoy's Georgia volunteers. The purpose was "to reinstate as far as might be possible the authority of the Union within the limits of Georgia." [18]

Wayne actively and successfully suppressed Tory partisan bands, prevented Indian reenforcement of the garrison in Savannah, and invested that town so far as to cut off its supplies. Among his encounters with the enemy was one hot fight with a strong band of Creek Indians and a detachment of British soldiers that attacked his camp; he succeeded in routing them. He continued his work until July 11, when the British evacuated Savannah, and he took possession of the town. Then he returned and rejoined Greene in South Carolina. Now, in all the three southern states only Charleston was held by the enemy.[19]

During these months there was little activity in South Carolina, except by Washington's and Lee's legions, who were "constantly kept on the alert, never stationary," continually "marching and countermarching, seldom, if ever, remaining two nights on the same ground, making frequent excursions on the British lines, often falling in with the enemy, when skirmishing would frequently ensue." Little of importance was accomplished, but the incessant activity was fatiguing. Seymour records a total of 117 miles of marching in one period of six days. This was kept up from February until the middle of June.[20]

The men were enduring great hardships. In March, Greene wrote to Washington that he had 600 men "so naked as to be unfit for duty. . . . Not a rag of clothing has arrived to us this Winter. It is true we get meat and rice, but no rum or spirits. Men and officers without pay cannot be kept in temper long." And he wrote later: "For upwards of two months, more than a third of our men were entirely naked, with nothing but a breech-cloth about them, and never came out of their tents; and the rest were as ragged as wolves." Their food was bad, too; the beef was simply carrion. By July he succeeded in procuring "materials for a check shirt, a pair of overalls and a coatee" for each of his men.[21]

Presumably these hardships excused a plot for a mutinous uprising, which was brewing in the camp in April. It began among the Pennsylvania troops, whose mutiny in Washington's camp at Morristown eighteen months before had secured for them the arrears of pay that they demanded. But this new plot, says Lee, "was grounded on the breach of allegiance and reared in the foulness of perfidy. Greene himself was to be seized and delivered to the enemy." It was discovered in time; the ringleader, a Pennsylvania sergeant, was convicted of the crime and executed.[22]

Charleston, the only post in all the South still held by the British, was surrounded on the land side. No supplies could be had for its garrison without penetrating the American lines, and they were tight. Major General

Leslie proposed to Greene a cessation of hostilities and an arrangement permitting the British to buy food and take it through the American lines. Greene referred the proposal to the Congress and refused to enter into such an engagement meanwhile. Leslie thereupon gave notice that he would resume hostile incursions into the surrounding country to take provisions by force.[23]

Greene then organized a force to combat the expected British operations. It was composed of infantry of Lee's Legion, the Delaware troops, 100 infantrymen from the other Continental regiments, and the dismounted dragoons of the 3rd Virginia, all under command of Colonel John Laurens; also the cavalry of Lee's Legion and of the 3rd and 4th Virginia regiments, under Colonel George Baylor of that state. General Mordecai Gist of Maryland was put in command of this light brigade.[24]

This corps took a position at Stono Bridge, in advance of the main army, to oppose Leslie's foraging fleet of small vessels on the Combahee River. They lay there for a month with little activity except foraging, but with no advantage to the health of the soldiers. "At this time," says Seymour, "the men were taken sick very fast, so that there were scarce any left to mount the necessary guards about the camp." On August 23 they were ordered to Combahee Ferry to oppose an enemy force that lay on the other side of the river and had a fleet of "two row-gallies, some topsail schooners and other small craft, the whole amounting to eighteen sail and three hundred regular troops and two hundred refugees [Tories]." [25] Gist dug an entrenchment and mounted a howitzer with a few artillerymen under Captain Smith at Cheraw Point about twelve miles below the ferry, to cut off the retreat of the vessels. The British force had found little rice on the south side of the river, and Gist prevented them from foraging on the north side. They therefore decided to withdraw, dropping down the river at night. Gist was informed of their intention and ordered Laurens, with the Delaware battalion, to hasten to the entrenchments at the Point and reenforce the few artillerymen there; the rest of the brigade was to follow.

Laurens pushed ahead with speed, but the British had landed three hundred men on the north side above the Point and placed them in ambush in the tall grass. The Americans were met by a sudden unexpected volley. Laurens was killed, and a number of his men were also shot down. The rest fell back upon Gist's advancing corps. The enemy followed and drew up in line in a wood. Gist tried to dislodge them, but they were too well protected by piles of logs and thickets of brush for the cavalry to get at them, and they were too strong for the infantry alone to attack them They got away without loss. Besides Laurens, the Americans lost one man killed and nineteen wounded. Captain Smith, his artillerymen, and their howitzer were captured and carried off.[26]

The enemy continued their foraging activities, penetrating the Broad River country and carrying off provisions and cattle to Beaufort. To oppose them Gist got more men and a 6-pounder, crossed the Combahee, and pushed down to Port Royal Ferry, where were two armed galleys. There was a brisk encounter, in which one of the galleys was captured, the other driven off. Gist's corps then rejoined the main army.[27]

These minor operations are noteworthy chiefly because they resulted in the death of Colonel John Laurens, one of the bravest and most gallant of the American officers. He was the son of Henry Laurens, President of the Continental Congress during a most important and eventful period of its existence. Born in 1755, John Laurens was educated in Geneva and in London. At the age of twenty-two he entered the Continental service and became an aide to Washington. At the Battle of Germantown, as has been said, he distinguished himself by a feat of daring. At Monmouth his services were notable, as also in Rhode Island, in the siege of Savannah, and in the defense of Charleston. He became a lieutenant colonel at the age of twenty-three. The Congress sent him on a special mission to France when he was twenty-five. On his return he again distinguished himself as an aide to Washington in the Yorktown siege, and represented the American army in the discussion of the terms of capitulation. After the surrender, he hastened back to his native state, joined Greene's army, and lost his life at the age of twenty-seven in an insignificant skirmish—an untimely end of a career of brilliant performance and of the greatest promise.[28]

There were a number of unimportant skirmishes arising out of foraging expeditions before it became certain that the enemy was preparing to give up his last hold on South Carolina by evacuating Charleston. During this interval the American army's condition was most miserable. Half naked, ill fed, sick with dysentery (which was often fatal), it barely survived as an army until the British fleet arrived on September 6 to carry away the Charleston garrison. Even then it had to hang on for three months more before, on December 14, the embarkation of the enemy was accomplished, three hundred ships sailing out of the harbor with the British troops, a horde of 3,800 Loyalists, and more than 5,000 of their Negro slaves. And so ended the war in the south.

The campaigns of Greene and his army in the south, which brought about the overthrow of British power in Georgia and the Carolinas, have been ably summarized and brilliantly characterized by three historians of note—one an American, the other two Englishmen. Major General Francis Vinton Greene writes: *

The eleven months campaign—January to December, 1781, from the Catawba to the Dan and from the Dan back to Charleston and Augusta—received at the time the enthusiastic commendation of Washington and his comrades on the one hand and of Tarleton and Stedman on the other. It has always been considered one of the most brilliant in American annals, and it has been quite as much praised by English as by American writers. Though the numbers on each side were small, yet from the military standpoint it is full of interest and instruction and well repays examination in all its details. The marches, the manoeuvres, the sieges, the raids and scouting by both Lee and Tarleton, the improvised pontoon-trains, the proper use of the topography of the country for defence and offence—were all admirable. There was but little artillery on either side, but it was well handled. The four battles were fiercely contested and the percentage of loss on both sides was large. The British had the advantage of well-trained and well-armed troops, but this was more than counter-balanced by the superiority of American generalship. In only one respect can Greene be criticised, and whether the criticism is just or unjust it is hard to say. He lost every battle. Morgan, under similar circumstances, gained a great victory. If Greene had possessed the same temperament as Morgan or Wayne [or, it may be said, as Benedict Arnold] he would probably, both at Guilford and at Eutaw, have made one more effort and risked everything on the result of it. If unsuccessful, he would have been destroyed; if successful, he would have hastened by a few months what he finally accomplished. The general opinion is, and it is probably well founded, that the circumstances did not justify the risk, and that his prudence—in saving his little army while there was yet time and after he had, in each case, inflicted such loss on his adversary as to compel the adversary's retreat—was not the least of the many exhibitions of good judgment which characterized the whole campaign.[29]

Sir George Otto Trevelyan in his history of the Revolution presents this appreciation of Greene's services and the services of his men:

Nathanael Greene, while he was securing those great and decisive results, had depended mainly on his own resources, and had taken all his measures entirely on his own responsibility. So far as any combined action between the Northern and Southern armies was concerned, they might just as well have been operating in two different hemispheres. The intervening spaces were so enormous, and the obstacles to free and rapid communication so formidable, that news of victory or defeat did not arrive at Washington's headquarters in New Jersey until three or four weeks after a battle had been fought in South Carolina; and Washington's letters of advice and criticism, even if he had been unwise enough to write them, would have taken as long, and longer still, to find Greene in one of his shifting bivouacs on the banks of the Santee or the Catawba.

* *The Revolutionary War and the Military Policy of the United States* by Francis Vinton Greene. Copyright, 1911, by Charles Scribner's Sons. Used by permission.

Greene's handful of Continental troops had performed wonders. . . . Between April, 1780, and April, 1781, they had marched above two thousand six hundred miles, besides being engaged in many skirmishes and two pitched battles. They had passed through, or over, a score of streams many of which . . . would have been reckoned large rivers in any other country in the world. Shoeless and in rags, and laden with their heavy firelocks, they plodded through the wilderness for month after month of a never-ending campaign without showing any perceptible diminution of their martial ardor. After a lost battle—which was a familiar experience to them—they almost instantaneously recovered their self-confidence and their self-complacency, with the invariable elasticity of the American soldier. . . .

At Eutaw Springs many of the Continental infantry, the cloth of whose coats had long ago rotted off them in fragments, "fought with pieces of [Spanish] moss tied on the shoulder and flank to keep the musket and the cartridge-box from galling." They sometimes got nothing for ten or twelve days running except half a pound of flour and a morsel of beef "so miserably poor that scarce any mortal could make use of it" and were fain to live upon green corn and unripe apples and peaches. During the pursuit of Cornwallis, after Guilford Court House, many of them fainted on the road for lack of food.[30]

Of Greene himself, Sir John Fortescue has this to say:

Greene's reputation stands firmly on his campaign in the Carolinas, his luring Cornwallis into a false position, and his prompt return upon Camden after the retreat of Cornwallis to Wilmington. His keen insight into the heart of Cornwallis's blunders and his skilful use of his guerilla troops are the most notable features of his work, and stamp him as a general of patience, resolution and profound common sense, qualities which go far towards making a great general. One gift he seems to have lacked, namely, the faculty of leadership, to which, as well as to bad luck must be ascribed the fact that he was never victorious in a general action. . . . Saving this one small matter, Greene, who was a very noble character, seems to me to stand little if at all lower than Washington as a general in the field.[31]

The Dunmore Raids

John Murray, Earl of Dunmore in the peerage of Scotland, was the royal governor of Virginia at the beginning of the War of Independence. An evil-tempered man, rapacious, irascible, tyrannical, and violent, he took a strong stand against the rising spirit of resistance to the encroachments upon the economic freedom of the colonies. When in March, 1775, the Convention of Virginia resolved to put the colony in "a posture of defence" by embodying and arming a force of militia, he countered, on April 21, by sending a body of marines to seize the province's store of powder at Williamsburg.[1] The town rose, drums were beaten, the militia company assembled in arms and demanded the return of the powder. In a passionate outburst, Dunmore swore, "By the living God, if any insult is offered to me, or those who have obeyed my orders, I will declare freedom to the slaves and lay the town in ashes!" All Virginia was aroused; there were threats from every quarter to assemble the militia and march against him. He declared that if they did he would "consider the whole country in rebellion" and would "not hesitate at reducing houses to ashes and spreading devastation wherever I can reach." To the British government he wrote that he could raise "such a force from among Indians, negroes and other persons, as would reduce the refractory people of this colony to obedience." [2]

But the Virginians, stirred by the news from Lexington and Concord were refractory beyond his expectations. Patrick Henry assembled the militia company of Hanover on May 2 and marched, gathering many adherents on the way. Dunmore was alarmed. He issued a proclamation declaring that he had seized the powder because he apprehended an insurrection of the slaves, "who had been seen in large numbers in the night time about the Magazine," and calling on "all His Majesty's liege subjects" to suppress the spirit of faction and obey the laws. Henry's march was not stayed until May 4, when a messenger from Dunmore paid the insurgents £330, the estimated value of the powder, whereupon he took his men back home.[3]

Emboldened by the withdrawal of the threatening troops, Dunmore issued another proclamation on May 6, stating that whereas he had "been informed from undoubted authority that a certain Patrick Henry and a number of deluded followers" had "put themselves in a posture of war . . . to the great terror of all His Majesty's faithful subjects" and had extorted from the Receiver General £330, he, the governor, now charged all persons not "to aid, abet or give countenance to the said Patrick Henry" and his companions, but to oppose them, lest the colony be involved "in the most direful calamity, as they will call for the vengeance of offended majesty and the insulted laws." In spite of this direful fulmination, various Virginia counties voted thanks to the insurgents, and the resistance was in no way lessened.[4]

It was Dunmore himself, and not the Virginians, that first took fright. He had heard from Gage that Samuel Adams and John Hancock would be excepted from the general offer of pardon to be issued on June 12. Fearing that he might be seized and held as a hostage for these proscribed men, Dunmore left his house secretly in the night of June 8 and took refuge on the *Fowey* man-of-war at Yorktown, while Virginia went on with her warlike preparations.[5] The governor himself also began to gather strength.

At Hampton in October, an armed British sloop was driven ashore in a gale. The colonists seized it, looted it, and set it afire. Dunmore, who had three warships and various other craft, blockaded the town. Its inhabitants called to their aid a company of Virginia regulars, another of minutemen, and a body of the militia. The noble Dunmore had but one answer: burn the town. A landing party attempting this on October 26 was driven off. Another the next day was answered by the accurate fire of a company of Culpeper riflemen, and several in the boats were killed or wounded. One of the tenders with seven sailors was captured without loss of any Virginian.[6]

Dartmouth had written on August 2 to Dunmore approving his purpose of raising "among the Indians, negroes and other persons, a force sufficient, if not to subdue rebellion, at least to defend Government." Dunmore issued another proclamation on November 7 declaring martial law throughout the colony, and requiring "every person capable of bearing arms to resort to

His Majesty's standard or be looked upon as traitors," subject to "forfeiture of life, confiscation of lands, &C., &C.," also declaring all the rebels' indented servants and slaves, "that are able and willing to bear arms," free upon their joining His Majesty's troops.[7]

The tidewater planters had many Negro slaves and many indentured servants, chiefly convicts serving terms of years. Dunmore hoped to alarm the rebellious Virginians by this call for an uprising of the subject peoples, and send them back to their homes to safeguard their families and property. He also called for a small detachment of British regulars stationed in the Illinois country, and authorized John Connolly to raise a regiment in the backwoods of Pennsylvania and Virginia, and one McKee to raise a force of Indians, all of them to march to Alexandria. He himself undertook to raise a regiment of whites, to be called "the Queen's Own Loyal Virginians," and another of Negroes, under the name of "Lord Dunmore's Ethiopians." [8]

Connolly went to Gage in Boston and received authority to engage Indians from about Detroit, with whom he was to take Fort Pitt and then march to Alexandria and join Dunmore. He came back to the south in November and started up the Potomac with two companions, Allan Cameron and Dr. John Smith. The Virginians sent men into the Indian country who arrested the three near Hagerstown with written plans including a letter from Dunmore to the Indian chief White Eyes. At the order of the Continental Congress they were taken to Philadelphia and confined in jail. McKee seems to have faded out of history without achieving any results.[9]

Dunmore got together two or three hundred Ethiopians and a number of candidates for the Queen's Own making a total, with his small force of regulars, of about 1,200 men. Against this mongrel force at Norfolk, Colonel William Woodford marched one of Virginia's two regular regiments (with John Marshall, afterwards chief justice of the United States, as a lieutenant of minutemen) and about 200 volunteer riflemen.

Dunmore sent a detachment to hold Great Bridge, about nine miles south of Norfolk and in Woodford's way. The bridge, crossing the Elizabeth River, was of considerable length, extending from one marshy shore across two islands to the other shore. It was approached at each end by a causeway. On the eastern side, Dunmore's men erected a substantial fortification with seven guns. Woodford's men threw up a semicircular breastwork on the other side, posted a guard of 25 men in it, and encamped in a near-by church. There for several days they faced each other.[10]

At length, to induce an attack on his fortification, Woodford arranged with a Negro to "desert" and inform Dunmore that there were only 300 "shirtmen" (riflemen) opposing him, and that they had but little ammunition. On December 8 the governor sent against Woodford Captain Samuel Leslie of the 14th Regiment with 200 regulars, a party of marines and sailors, a company of the Queen's Own, and enough Ethiopians to make up 600 men. Two fieldpieces accompanied them.[11]

At reveille on the 9th the artillery opened fire with a few shots. Then the regulars, including 60 grenadiers under Captain Fordyce, marched to the attack in column along the narrow causeway, six abreast. Lieutenant Edward Travis, commanding the guard in the breastwork, now reenforced to a total of 90 men, held his fire until the enemy were within fifty yards, when a withering blast struck down the van. Fordyce, with admirable bravery, urged on his men. They rallied "like true-born Englishmen," but a second fire blighted the attempt. Fordyce fell dead, with fourteen bullets in his body; many of his grenadiers were slain; his lieutenant and many others were wounded. The rest fled across the bridge.[12]

Leslie had held 230 of his Loyalists and Ethiopians in his works. He now rallied the remnant of his regulars and reopened fire with his guns. But Woodford had brought his main force down from the church. Colonel Edward Stevens with the Culpeper battalion crossed the bridge, flanked the enemy, and drove all of them into their fort, which they evacuated that night, returning to Norfolk. Leslie's force had lost 60 killed or wounded. He left on the field 12 dead and 17 wounded, three being lieutenants. The only casualty among the Americans was one man slightly injured by a grapeshot. Five days later, Woodford entered Norfolk, and took possession. Colonel Robert Howe with a North Carolina regiment joined him, and assumed command of all the American troops there.[13]

Norfolk, with 6,000 inhabitants, was one of the principal Virginia seaports and did a heavy trade in tobacco. Its business was largely in the hands of Scottish merchants of Glasgow. Their resident factors and clerks, also Scots, were the principal inhabitants, Loyalists almost to a man. The arrival of the dreaded riflemen created consternation among them, and they fled with their families to the ships in the harbor. Among these were the frigate *Eilbeck* with Dunmore aboard, the *Liverpool*, 28 guns, the *Otter*, 16 guns, the *Kingfisher*, 18 guns, an 8-gun sloop, and six or seven small tenders.[14]

Crowded with their crews, the soldiers, the Norfolk refugees, the Queen's Own, and such of the Ethiopians as had not been left to their fate ashore, the ships were not a comfortable refuge. Food was scarce. Dunmore asked for regular supplies of fresh provision, which were refused. Foraging parties, sent ashore, were cut off or driven back under fire. Hunger and disease took toll of the crowded ships, and bodies were thrown over-board daily. The undisciplined riflemen made targets of the vessels. Dunmore gave notice that, on the first day of January, he would burn the town.[15]

At four o'clock in the morning of New Year's Day, 1776, the bombardment began. Red-hot shot and carcasses from sixty guns rained on the town for seven hours without intermission. Landing parties fired buildings on the waterside. The riflemen joined in the sport by making sure that buildings known to belong to refugee Tories did not escape. The conflagration raged for two days and until four-fifths of the town "lay in ashes"—Dunmore's favorite phrase. Some weeks later, on order of the American military authorities, the rest of the houses were valued for compensation to their owners and destroyed to prevent them from sheltering the enemy. The most flourishing town in Virginia was reduced to a mere name on a map.[16]

Dunmore, having left Norfolk in February, lingered in Virginia waters until "the closeness and filth of the small vessels, in which the fugitives were crowded, the badness and scarcity of water and provisions, produced the pestilential fever, which made great havock, especially among the negroes, many of whom were swept away." He had to burn several of the smaller vessels. The rest, between forty and fifty, with the refugees aboard, he sent to Florida and the West Indies, where "a great number of negroes" were sold into slavery. He himself joined the British fleet off Staten Island in August. He soon after returned to England, where he was rewarded for his eminent services in America by being appointed governor of the Bahamas.[17]

The burning of Norfolk failed to intimidate the colonists; instead, it gave an impetus to the growing demand for complete independence, felt by Washington. "A few more such flaming arguments, as were exhibited at Falmouth and Norfolk . . . will not leave numbers at a loss to decide upon the propriety of a separation," he wrote to Joseph Reed on January 21.[18]

George Rogers Clark and the West

Although there was no fighting in the old settled parts of Virginia after the departure of Lord Dunmore and his bobtail forces until the closing period of the war, there was much and bitter fighting upon lands west of the Appalachians owned, or at least claimed, by the Old Dominion. At this point, therefore, a brief account of the war in the Ohio valley will break the narrative of the closing years of the Revolution in the south.

The British asked the assistance of the Indian nations between the Ohio River and the Great Lakes as they sought help from the Iroquois, Cherokees, and Creeks—with some success. From the British post at Detroit they carried on a ceaseless propaganda campaign among the tribes of the Old Northwest to inspire attacks upon the border settlements of Pennsylvania and Virginia (including, of course, Kentucky). They also freely supplied weapons, ammunition, and liquor. Many of the savages responded readily, for they had old grudges against the American frontiersmen, and British officials before the war had been their friends and protectors against exploitation. The thousands of Shawnee, Delaware, Miami, and Ottawa warriors therefore became a menace to the American cause.

Although Dunmore's plan for an attack upon Virginia from the West was not executed, the frontiersmen in the region of Pittsburgh continued to fear assaults by Indians and Tories. Rumors of savages advancing from the Ohio country led on several occasions to almost complete evacuation of western Pennsylvania by backwoods families who retreated to the older settlements. Lieutenant Colonel Henry Hamilton, the well known British agent at Detroit, vigorously attempted to mount a large-scale offensive in the upper Ohio valley that never quite came to pass. However, small parties of red men with muskets and tomahawks quite frequently moved in the direction of Pittsburgh from Detroit, and from other posts under British control north of the Beautiful River. The Indians in the Ohio region, urged by American emissaries to remain neutral, often promised to keep bright the chain of friendship with their backwoods neighbors. But they did not always keep their pledges, and indeed were sometimes provoked by American attacks.

The frontier about Pittsburgh was troubled, but the settlers of Kentucky suffered far more. The first settlers began to occupy the Dark and Bloody Ground immediately before the outbreak of Anglo-American hostilities. Their coming deeply angered the Cherokees and Shawnees, who claimed at least parts of Kentucky as hunting ground. Nor were the tribes appeased because the whites had purchased and extorted from them their claims to the territory. Moreover, other Indian nations, angered by the continuing westward advance of the pioneers, sympathized with the Shawnees and Cherokees. The settlers in Kentucky were under attack even before the shooting at Lexington and Concord; and the breaking out of the Anglo-American war merely intensified the assaults of the Indians. The years 1775, 1776, and 1777 were dark ones for the whites living below the Ohio. The tomahawk and the scalping knife were busy at their ugly work. All the horrors of Indian warfare were heaped upon the Long Knives, who fought back stubbornly and clung desperately to their homes in what seemed to many of them a new Eden surrounded by devils. Fortunately for the Kentuckians, Virginia soon effectively asserted its dominion over the region and sent men and ammunition. Kentucky staggered under the weight of continued Indian forays from the north; but the American grip upon it was only shaken, and the riflemen exacted a heavy toll from their red tormenters. George Rogers Clark, one of their leaders, depicts in miniature the sufferings of the Kentuckians in diary entries made in June, 1777:

5 Harrod & Elliott went to meet Col. Bowman & C°
Glen & Laird arrᵈ from Cumbᵈ Danˡ Lyons who parted with them on Green River we suppose was killed going into Logans Fort
Jnº Peters & Elisha Bathy we expect were killed coming home from Cumbᵈ
13 Burr Harrison died of his wounds recᵈ the 30ᵗʰ of May
22 Ben. Linn & Samˡ Moore arrᵈ from Illenois
Barney Stagner senʳ killed beheaded ½ Mile from the Fort
a few Guns fired at Boon[e]s[borough] [1]

The situation in Kentucky, and on the upper Ohio, too, seemed grave in 1777 for the Americans. There was a sure remedy for it, the capture of

Detroit, which would deprive many of the Indians of weapons, ammunition, and rum. Very early in the war astute American observers began to urge an expedition against that place. But nothing had been done either by the Continental Congress or by the states to execute such a project. George Morgan, a veteran in Indian affairs who served for a time as the American agent for such matters in the Ohio valley and who ardently championed it, finally resigned his office in disgust. In the spring of 1777 the Congress did send Brigadier General Edward Hand to assume command at Fort Pitt and to lead a punitive expedition into the Ohio country. However, the simultaneous murder by American troops of Cornstalk, chief of the Shawnees, a hostage, goaded the Shawnees to savage reprisal. Hundreds of Indians swept down to and across the Ohio. Hand was unable to take the aggressive for many months. In August and September the Indians defeated several parties of frontiersmen on the south shore of the river in the vicinity of Fort Henry, near the mouth of Wheeling Creek. More than forty whites were slain in skirmishes about that post. In February, 1778, after receiving orders from Congress permitting him to take the offensive if opportunity offered, even against Detroit, Hand set out with 500 men, mostly militia, to attack Sandusky, a forward British base. But melting snow and rain swelled the rivers and forced him to abandon his march. The failure of this expedition, commonly known as the "Squaw Campaign," discouraged the general, although he was not at fault, and he resigned his command.

In 1778 the Continental Congress again planned offensive operations from Pittsburgh, with Detroit as the ultimate objective, sending the southern general Lachlan McIntosh, 500 Continentals, and money for the purpose. McIntosh advanced nearly a hundred miles from Pittsburgh, but lack of supplies and expiration of the enlistment period of some militia who accompanied him forced him to halt. He accomplished relatively little and was relieved at his own request, being succeeded early in 1779 by General Daniel Brodhead, an experienced frontier fighter. Brodhead promptly began to prepare for offensive action. Before he could move, however, the military situation in the Ohio valley was greatly altered in favor of the Americans—and in a most unexpected way. The doughty George Rogers Clark had entered upon his major role in history.

George Rogers Clark, older brother of the almost equally famous William of the Lewis and Clark expedition, was born near Charlottesville, Virginia, in 1752. His formal education was somewhat limited, partly perhaps because of an aversion to academic learning. Like Washington he became a surveyor as a very young man. A lover of Nature and her keen student, he soon appeared as a frontier fighter, serving under Dunmore against the

Shawnees in 1774 and in Kentucky in the early part of the War of Independence. One of his biographers states that he had sandy hair and blue eyes; another, possibly more reliable, declares that he had red hair and black eyes.² They agree that he was tall, sturdy, shrewd, courageous, and bold, a born leader of men. He was, like Ulysses S. Grant, fond of liquor; like Grant, he did not let his drinking interfere with military business. He was Virginia's military commander in Kentucky throughout the war.

Doing his share of the fighting in Kentucky in 1777, Clark had an idea—to strike at the British in the Illinois country. This region, lying between the Wabash and Miami rivers on the east, the Mississippi on the west, the Ohio on the south, and the Illinois River on the north, was under British control, and was largely guarded by militia and Indian allies of the crown. From it came some of the attacks upon Kentucky. Clark concluded that the region could be subdued. Such a conquest would relieve the pressure upon Kentucky and would loosen the hold of the British everywhere north of the Ohio. He was particularly hopeful because the white inhabitants of the area, a few hundred families, were overwhelmingly of French origin. Most of these lived at Kaskaskia, near the mouth of the river of the same name, at Prairie du Rocher, about seventeen miles to the north, at Cahokia, some forty-odd miles farther north on the bank of the Mississippi, and at Vincennes, located on the east bank of the Wabash about one hundred and fifty miles from its mouth. Clark saw these Frenchmen as potential allies.

Clark received favorable reports from Benjamin Linn and Samuel Moore, whom he sent as spies into the Illinois territory in the spring of 1777. He was told that Kaskaskia actually had no garrison. In the summer or early fall he wrote to Patrick Henry, then governor of Virginia, urging an attack upon that town. Its capture would establish American control of the Ohio, open up a communication with the Spanish across the Mississippi, block the British upon the great river, give a valuable fur trade to the Americans, cut off an occasional source of food for Detroit, and frighten the Indians of the Wabash valley into neutrality or submission. Clark was ready to lead an expedition against the town; he needed help.³ To get that help he made his way back to Virginia in the fall of 1777.

There were many reasons why Virginia should not support Clark's seemingly rash proposal. But she claimed the Old Northwest as her own; and Clark's venture, if successful, would bring vast benefits to her and to the United States. Thomas Jefferson, George Mason, and Richard Henry Lee gave their approval, and they persuaded Governor Henry to support the scheme. These men also persuaded the Virginia assembly to authorize Clark to march, without telling most of the members *where* he intended to go. Clark received £1,200 for expenses, permission to draw for further funds upon somebody or other, and authority to procure boats, ammunition, and other supplies at Pittsburgh. He was authorized to raise seven companies of troops. According to public instructions, which he was to exhibit, he was to use these men in defending Kentucky. In secret orders he was commanded to attack Kaskaskia and, if feasible, Detroit.[4]

Clark moved rapidly. He hurried off Major W. P. Smith to the Holston River settlements to enlist riflemen with orders to meet him at the Falls of the Ohio (the site of Louisville). Early in 1778 he himself proceeded to Pittsburgh. En route he appointed as captains Joseph Bowman, Leonard Helm, and William Harrod. He and his aides were able to persuade only 150 frontiersmen to accompany them down the Ohio in May—perhaps he would not have started without Major Smith's assurance of the services of 200 men, or four companies, from the Holston. Reaching the Falls on May 27, Clark was joined not by four companies of Holston riflemen, but by a part of a company. A few recruits from Kentucky also were obtained. In addition he secured the services of a fourth captain, John Montgomery.

Establishing his camp on an island in the rapids so as to discourage desertion, Clark now told his men of the real purpose of his expedition. The news that France was about to enter the war had reached the camp. Aid from the French inhabitants in the Illinois region could therefore be expected with some assurance. Clark's proposals were nevertheless seemingly rash. Some of the Holston men promptly deserted, several being recaptured and forced to serve. But most of Clark's men, responding to his magnetic personality, promised their loyal support. Leaving a few of his troops to defend supplies in a blockhouse on the island, he set out for Kaskaskia with about 175 men on June 26 in a flotilla of flatboats. Shooting the rapids while the sun was in total eclipse—a happy augury, as Clark saw it—the little army floated and rowed down to old Fort Massac, about ten miles below the mouth of the Tennessee River. There, instead of proceeding by water, Clark hid his boats. He knew surprise was impossible if he went up the Mississippi. He therefore set out overland for Kaskaskia, about 120 miles distant.

Across level prairies and through trackless forests, with their commissariat on their backs, Clark and his men moved rapidly toward Kaskaskia. Their chief guide, John Saunders, lost his way. He found it again, after he was threatened with death. In the evening of July 4 they reached the Kaskaskia River three miles above the town. They had not eaten for two days, but they were determined to take the town or die in the attempt. About dusk they quietly marched down the river to a point about a mile above

Kaskaskia and on the opposite side of the river. At a farmhouse they learned that the Chevalier de Rocheblave, a veteran French officer who had entered British service, and who commanded at Kaskaskia, had had a report of their coming. He had called the local militia to arms and had sent out spies to confirm the report; but they had failed to find any trace of Clark. He had therefore disbanded the militia. Taking advantage of this happy circumstance, Clark procured boats and quickly crossed the river. He sent one division of his troops to surround the town; another, he led through an open fort gate. He himself marched to Rocheblave's house. The townsmen and the commander were completely surprised. Rocheblave promptly surrendered. Not a shot was fired, and Kaskaskia was in American hands in fifteen minutes. Captain Bowman was immediately sent with thirty men to demand the surrender of Prairie du Rocher and Cahokia, and these towns also quickly submitted to American rule without resistance.

Vincennes likewise came under American control without the firing of a shot. Clark treated the French inhabitants generously, in particular assuring them of religious freedom. However, he sent off Rocheblave, who assumed a defiant attitude, as a prisoner of war to Virginia. His generosity and his determination impressed the Frenchmen, and many of them enthusiastically promised their support to the American cause. Indeed, Father Pierre Gibault of Kaskaskia undertook to secure the surrender of Vincennes and its stronghold, Fort Sackville. Gibault and other Frenchmen left Kaskaskia for Vincennes on July 14, carrying letters to the French inhabitants of Vincennes. There were no British regulars in Vincennes. The letters and the persuasion of Gibault and his companions had the desired effect. Early in August the embassy returned home, announcing that Vincennes and its fort could be entered without resistance. A detachment led by Captain Helm promptly marched. Helm occupied the town and fort, and assumed command of the French militia.

In complete control of the French towns in the Illinois region Clark's position remained desperate. There was grave danger that the Indians in the Old Northwest would come against him in force. But Clark, like his younger brother William, was a master of the arts of Indian diplomacy. In conferences at Cahokia in August and September with the Chippewas, Ottawas, Miamis, Foxes, and other tribesmen—conferences attended by thousands of chiefs and warriors—he flattered, cajoled, and threatened the savages into promises of good behavior, pledges which were kept for many months. Another sore problem was the need for supplies. He solved it largely by calling upon Oliver Pollock for help. Pollock, an American merchant at New Orleans, responded wholeheartedly. Straining his personal credit to the utmost, he sent up the Mississippi the supplies which enabled Clark to keep the field.

The greatest danger for Clark was a British counterattack from Detroit, and the British soon moved. Lieutenant Colonel Hamilton learned early in August of Clark's impudent advance across the Ohio and quickly laid plans to deal with him. There is some dispute whether Hamilton, called the Hair Buyer by American frontiersmen, really bought American scalps from Britain's Indian allies. If he did, the fact is hardly surprising, for the British, French, and Americans all had long been accustomed to paying their red allies for such trophies.[5] The use of Indian allies inevitably brought forth this barbarity and others far more cruel and revolting. In any case, Hamilton was not without courage and enterprise. He realized that Clark's presence in the Illinois country imperiled even the British hold on Detroit. Gathering about 175 white troops, mostly Frenchmen, and 60 Indians, he set out for Vincennes on October 7. Traveling by boat, the force moved along the Maumee-Wabash portage route. Winter came, but Hamilton pushed on, acquiring additional Indian allies as he went until he had at least 500 men under his command. Captain Helm, hearing rumors of his approach, sent out a reconnoitering party. But Hamilton captured this party and another sent to warn Clark. On December 17 he marched into Vincennes. The French militia refused to fight, leaving Helm with one American soldier to defend Fort Sackville. Called upon to surrender the post, he bowed to the inevitable. The French inhabitants of Vincennes immediately resumed their allegiance to Britain.

Hamilton had great plans for dealing with Clark; but he did not move forward from Vincennes at once, probably in large part because of a lack of supplies. Had he done so, Clark would have been in the direst straits: expiration of enlistments had reduced him to about a hundred riflemen, and the French at Kaskaskia and Cahokia were panic-stricken. But Hamilton did not advance. The intrepid Virginian moved instead. With the help of Father Gibault he restored the enthusiasm of the French and mounted an offensive against Vincennes. On February 5 he sent the *Willing*, an armed row-galley with two 4-pounders, four swivel guns, and a crew of forty up the Ohio and the Wabash to cut off any retreat by the British to the Mississippi. Lieutenant John Rogers commanded this craft. On February 6, leading an army of 127 men, nearly half of whom were French, Clark began a bold march overland to Vincennes.

Vincennes was approximately 180 miles by trail from Kaskaskia. To attempt this march in midwinter with the idea of attacking Hamilton in Fort Sackville now seems extraordinarily rash. But the very audacity of

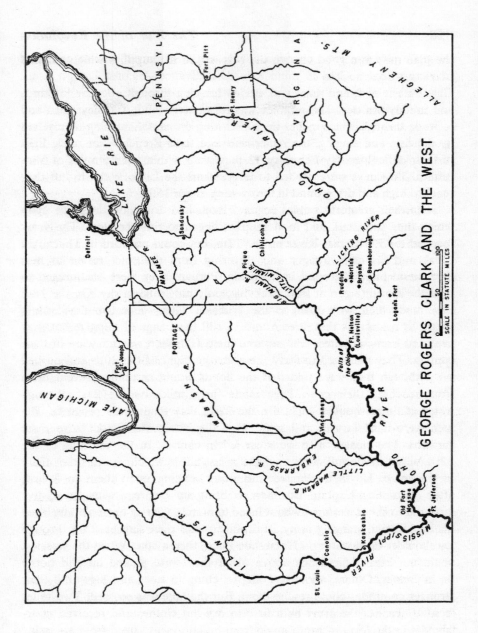

GEORGE ROGERS CLARK AND THE WEST

SCALE IN STATUTE MILES

0   50   100

the plan gave it a good chance of success. Clark himself was so confident of victory that he had in mind a further advance—against Detroit itself. Gay, determined, and masterful, he led his men through swampy lowlands and muddy prairies. The weather was fortunately mild, but they often had to wade through water inches deep. Feasting on game, amusing themselves by dancing and singing, the Americans and their French allies made light of their difficulties. By February 13 they were within twenty miles of Vincennes. Two days were needed to ferry across the Little Wabash, but they reached high and dry ground in the evening of the 15th.

Then their greatest troubles began. Floods had driven off the game upon which they subsisted, and food supplies began to run very low. The army reached the Embarrass River on the 17th, but could not ford it. That night Clark and his men, hungry and shivering from the cold, rested as best they could on wet ground in a drizzle. Perhaps they were encouraged to hear the morning gun at Fort Sackville, only nine miles away. On the 18th they made their way down to the Wabash. They spent two days vainly trying to get across that stream and to still the pangs of hunger; but they captured French hunters who assured them Hamilton was unaware of their coming. They managed to ferry the river the night of the 20th and pushed on, although they were told that the floods would certainly prevent them from reaching their goal. They made three miles on the 21st, through water at times shoulder-high. On the 22nd they made little progress. The men were half starved, and some were dispirited; but Clark drove them forward. The weaker men were carried in canoes. In the morning of the 23rd he urged his followers to make a last effort which would bring them to the town. He then plunged into water, calling upon them to follow, after instructing Captain Bowman to bring up the rear with twenty-five men and to shoot any man who refused to march. Clark's example inspirited his half-frozen, starving army, and officers and men staggered on through icy shoulder-deep water on Horseshoe Plain, then a lake. When the weariest could not keep their heads above water they were picked up and borne on in canoes. Others, about to collapse, clung to trees and logs until their stronger comrades could rescue them. But the lake was crossed. Two miles from Vincennes the army built fires to dry out clothes and received nourishment in the form of broth made from buffalo meat seized from a passing squaw. A Frenchman taken prisoner told Clark his presence was still unknown in the town. He also asserted that 200 Indians had just joined Hamilton.

There could be no turning back, even though the army had exhausted almost all its ammunition. Fortunately, Clark seemed to thrive upon disaster. He had carefully concealed the scanty number of his force from his French informant. Deciding to attempt to frighten into surrender an enemy he could not expect to subdue, he sent the Frenchman into town with a message to his fellow citizens: He intended to capture the fort that night; he did not wish to surprise the townsmen; those who were friends to the United States should go to their homes and remain in them; and those who desired to assist the British should join Hamilton in the fort! At sunset Clark ordered his men forward into the town in two major divisions, marching them to and fro in such a fashion as to give the impression that he had a thousand men. His message and his tactics quickly brought results. The townsmen, some of them secretly and stoutly pro-American, failed to join the British. The Indian allies of the British fled to the woods, after one of their chiefs had vainly offered the services of one hundred warriors to Clark. Some townsmen brought forth ammunition which they had secreted from Hamilton and presented it to the American army as it made its way into the town. With drums beating and the inhabitants cheering, Clark's force paraded up the main street and promptly began an attack on the fort. Not until a number of shots were fired did Hamilton realize that the American army was in Vincennes.

Fort Sackville was a solidly constructed wooden fort near the bank of the Wabash. Its walls, enclosing a space of about three acres, were eleven feet high. At each corner a bastion extended twelve feet above the wall, and there were three pieces of artillery on every bastion. The fort was well stocked with ammunition; and there was food within the walls. It might have been held indefinitely, although the garrison under Hamilton numbered fewer than 100 men—luckily for Clark, the British commander had sent part of his force up the Wabash to hurry in additional supplies.

The Americans and their French allies quickly put Hamilton to the test. During the night they threw up an intrenchment two hundred yards from the main gate. Using the cover of houses and hurriedly built breastworks they even penetrated within thirty yards of the fort. The British responded with cannon and small arms, but the cannon shot flew harmlessly over the heads of the attackers, who responded with rifle fire aimed at the portholes. So accurate was the aim of the Long Rifles that many British gunners were killed and wounded and the cannon silenced by early morning. Sometime after dawn one man in the American army was wounded.

About nine o'clock in the morning on the 24th, while his men were having their first decent meal in several days, Clark sent Hamilton a demand for his surrender. The British commander answered that the garrison was "not disposed to be awed into action unworthy of British subjects." [6] The shooting resumed; but the garrison ceased firing about eleven o'clock, and Hamilton sent out Captain Helm with an offer to surrender upon honorable terms. Clark asked complete surrender within thirty minutes. He told Hamilton he could hardly restrain his men from storming the fort. The British commander then suggested a three-day truce. Clark flatly refused and insisted upon unconditional surrender, but agreed to confer with Hamilton:

Colonel Clarks Compliments to M[r]. Hamilton and begs leave to inform him that Col. Clark will not agree to any other terms than that of M[r]. Hamilton's Surrendering himself and Garrison, Prisoners at Discretion———
If M[r]. Hamilton is Desirous of a Conferance with Col. Clark he will meet him at the Church with Capt[n] Helm[7]

To punctuate this demand Clark dealt sternly with five Indians who had been surprised and captured as they entered Vincennes carrying American scalps. They were tomahawked in sight of the garrison.

At last Hamilton, his subordinate Major Hay, Clark, Helm, and Captain Bowman met at the French church. Hamilton tried to persuade the American leader to moderate his terms but met with a flat refusal. Before nightfall he signed a capitulation by which he and his men became prisoners and the fort and all its contents became American property. The following morning Hamilton and his 79 men formally turned over the fort and gave up their arms. Shortly afterward Clark's victory was augmented by Captain Helm, who moved up the Wabash and captured the detachment of 40 men that had been sent out to bring up supplies. The two captures brought rich prizes in the form of goods used in the trade with the Indians. These were largely distributed among Clark's men as a reward for their devotion.

Clark was embarrassed by the number of his prisoners, almost as great as his own force. He sent Hamilton and others under guard to Virginia. Hamilton was held as a prisoner in the Old Dominion for many months, since Thomas Jefferson, Henry's successor as governor, firmly refused to permit his exchange and ordered him closely confined. No doubt he was fortunate not to lose his life.

Clark now had complete control of the Illinois country—control maintained to the end of the war; but he was not satisfied with his magnificent achievement. He began to plan an advance against Detroit, garrisoned by only 100 men under Captain Richard Lernoult, he was informed. His "very soul was wrapt" in this plan, he later declared.[8] To further it he released all the Frenchmen who had served under Hamilton upon their promise of neutrality for the future. He even gave them arms, food, and boats so that they could return to their homes. He assured some of them going to Detroit that he would be at that place almost as soon as they would. Thus he secured friends and even spies at Detroit. And he wrote to Captain Lernoult, "I learn . . . that you were very busy making new works, I am glad to hear it, as it saves the Americans some expences in building." [9]

The capture of Fort Sackville and Clark's confident and menacing attitude cast fear among the British and their Indian allies alike. Captain Lernoult was alarmed for the safety of Detroit. But at the moment Clark did not have either the men or the supplies to move against the main British base in the Old Northwest. He therefore laid plans for an expedition against that place in 1779. The government of Virginia promised him 500 men, and he hoped to obtain several hundred additional riflemen from Kentucky. His plans could not, however, be carried out. Virginia sent only 150 men under Colonel John Montgomery. Moreover, the Kentucky riflemen, after engaging in a fruitless expedition against the Shawnee town of Chillicothe, displayed no eagerness for an attack on Detroit; only 30 joined Clark. With no more than 350 troops the American commander was again forced to postpone his great project. He accomplished little in 1779. An American force under Daniel Brodhead advanced from Pittsburgh into the country of the Senecas and wrought great destruction among their towns. This success was counterbalanced in part by an exploit of the notorious Simon Girty. As Colonel David Rogers with 70 Americans was moving up the Ohio in October with blankets and munitions obtained at New Orleans, Girty and a band of Indians made a surprise attack. It was extraordinarily successful, only 13 Americans escaping slaughter.

Clark planned a march against Detroit for 1780 also, but was unable to carry it into effect, although the American position on the Ohio was strengthened by the entrance of Spain into the war. But the British were pouring money and goods into Detroit to strengthen their Indian alliances, and their efforts had an effect. They were even able to mount an assault in May against the Spanish post at St. Louis. Fortunately for both the Spanish and the Americans, they were beaten off. They were also able to send out of Detroit the redoubtable partisan leader Colonel Henry Bird with 150 whites and 1,000 Indians toward the upper Ohio. Bird assailed and captured two small American stockaded posts, Ruddle's and Martin's, in the Licking River valley. He carried away more than a hundred prisoners, many of whom were tomahawked on the journey to Detroit, in spite of his efforts to restrain his brutal allies. Clark promptly countered by leading nearly a thousand Kentucky riflemen toward the towns of the Shawnees and Delawares, the bitterest enemies of the American frontiersman. In

August this expedition destroyed Chillicothe, the Shawnee "capital," and moved forward against Piqua, another important Shawnee town on the Big Miami River. At Piqua the Shawnees and other Ohio tribesmen gathered to meet him. Simon Girty assisted them. There was fierce fighting near and in the town. An attempt to surround the Indians failed, but they suffered heavy losses and were finally driven into the woods. Small cannon transported on horseback by the Americans had an important part in this American victory. Piqua was given to the torch. Although it was not possible to move on into the country of the Delawares, Clark had won another important campaign. Meanwhile Fort Jefferson, which he had established as an American base at the mouth of the Ohio, was besieged for six days by British-led Chickasaws and Choctaws; but its defenders beat off all assaults.

The campaign of 1781 west of the Alleghenies began, oddly enough, with a surprise attack upon the British Fort St. Joseph in southwestern Michigan by a Spanish force of about 60 militia and 60 Indians led by Captain Eugenio Pourré. Pourré managed to reach the fort from St. Louis in midwinter and also to catch the British unprepared. The garrison promptly surrendered, in January, 1781. Pourré's feat was strikingly like Clark's capture of Fort Sackville. However, the Spanish commander evacuated Fort St. Joseph within twenty-four hours, remaining only long enough to permit Spain to claim the valleys of the St. Joseph and Illinois rivers at the end of the war—by right of conquest![10] The Spanish were far more active in 1781 on the shores of the Gulf of Mexico. Bernardo de Gálvez, the energetic governor of Louisiana, had laid plans to capture Pensacola, Mobile, and other smaller British posts on the Gulf coast; and he executed his plans with complete success.

For 1781 the American goal was still the capture of Detroit. Clark made his way to Richmond before the end of 1780 to consult Thomas Jefferson, then governor of Virginia. Arrangements were made to send him with 2,000 men against the British stronghold early in the spring. Jefferson hoped that "an extensive and fertile country" could thus be added to the "Empire of Liberty." The expedition was to be largely a Virginia affair, but was to be supported by Congress. Clark was made brigadier general by Jefferson early in 1781 and promptly set to work. But he encountered mountainous difficulties in securing both supplies and men. Finally, after resorting to a draft, he collected 400 men at Pittsburgh and moved down the Ohio, in August. But he had already modified his plans, for it had become apparent that a march on Detroit could hardly succeed. The British and their Indian allies were once more moving toward the Ohio, and Clark was compelled to deal with them. He decided to attack the Indians, then, if possible, to move against Detroit. His decision was confirmed by an exploit of Captain Joseph Brant. A force of 107 Pennsylvania militia under Colonel Archibald Lochay going down the Ohio to join Clark was surprised by Brant and 100 Tories and Indians near the mouth of the Big Miami River and was wiped out, a third being slain immediately. The rest were led off to captivity or a crueler fate. Brant then joined Captain Andrew Thompson and Alexander McKee, who were leading 100 British rangers and 300 Indians toward the Ohio in the hope of waylaying Clark himself. The combined British-Indian forces followed Clark to the Falls of the Ohio, but the Indians refused to join in an assault upon him. Nor were the rangers eager for a fight with Clark. They hurried back to Detroit.

Nevertheless, the situation on the lower Ohio and in the Illinois country was ugly for the Americans. It had been found necessary to evacuate Fort Jefferson in June, and dozens of Kentucky pioneers had fallen victims of Indian rage in preceding months. Fortunately, Fort Nelson, erected at the Falls of the Ohio as the result of Clark's orders, had been completed, a truly commanding position. To restore the situation Clark proposed to march up the Wabash with all available men and to engage the northwestern Indians in a fight to the finish. A victory might still open the way to Detroit. But civil officials of Kentucky and settlers alike urged a defensive policy, and he was again forced to postpone his dream of conquest.

The news of Yorktown did not end the war west of the mountains. Indeed, the British and their Indian allies south of the Great Lakes were more active than ever, partly because of an American massacre of 90 peaceful Delaware Indians of the Moravian towns in Ohio. The Indians, especially the Delaware tribe, sought vengeance, and they obtained it. When Colonel William Crawford, an old friend of Washington, led over 300 troops from Fort Pitt in an attempt to surprise the Wyandots and Shawnees on the upper Sandusky River, he met disaster. His plan was known before he marched, and Colonel Arent S. De Peyster, commandant at Detroit, sent reenforcements to his own allies. On June 4 Captain William Caldwell, a British officer, with 100 whites and 200 Indians encountered Crawford and his men in Sandusky valley. A battle began early in the afternoon and was continued the following day, when 140 Shawnees came to Caldwell's assistance. The Americans then decided to retreat. They cut their way through their encircling enemies. Hotly pursued, they fled helter-skelter for five miles. Reorganized by their officers, they then withstood a final attack and were able to continue their retreat without further molestation. But they had had 50 killed, and several, including Colonel Crawford and

Dr. Knight, a surgeon, were taken prisoner. Most of the prisoners were promptly slaughtered by the Indians. Crawford was tortured horribly and vainly begged Simon Girty to shoot him in order to end his sufferings. Knight, reserved for similar torments at the next town, was guarded en route by only one Indian. The Indian ordered him to gather wood for a fire. Knight found a "chunk," felled his guard, and escaped, finally reaching Fort Pitt with his sad tale.

The Crawford disaster led the raging savages to ravages of the frontier even to the east of Pittsburgh. General William Irvine began to organize a second force at Pittsburgh, hoping to make a more successful attack upon the Sandusky towns. He was never able to move.

Meanwhile 1,100 Indians, no doubt the greatest number ever collected in one body in the war, moved toward Wheeling in July. Luckily, most of these soon returned home for fear of Clark; but 300, with a few Loyalists under Caldwell, McKee, and Girty, crossed the Ohio and appeared at Bryan's Station, a small palisaded fort near Lexington, Kentucky, on the night of August 15. There were in the post forty cabins, occupied by 90 men, women, and children. Males in the garrison numbered 44. An attempt to surprise the fort failed. Irregular firing continued throughout the 17th. An American relieving force of forty-odd men led by Colonel Levi Todd was driven off, but 17 of Todd's men, who were mounted, were able to join the garrison. The garrison refused to surrender. In the morning of the 18th the British and Indians withdrew, moving deliberately and without any effort to hide their march. Girty and his gang hoped to gain an advantage over militia sure to pursue them, and they did.

The Kentucky frontiersmen soon began to gather, over 200 being ready to pursue the marauders within a few hours after the end of the siege of Bryan's. More were on the march, but the officers of the 200, refusing to listen to Daniel Boone's advice to wait for reenforcements, insisted upon an immediate advance. The morning of August 19 brought the opposing forces together on the Lower Blue Licks. Prudent American leaders counseled against fighting, but Major Hugh McGary stampeded the riflemen into battle, calling upon all those who were not cowards to follow him into battle. Colonel Boone, on the left wing of the Americans, drove back the Indians and their allies, but the enemy outflanked the American right wing and center. In five minutes the riflemen fled in a mad panic. Crossing the river in retreat they suffered heavy losses, many being tomahawked as they swam. More lives would have been lost, had it not been for the courage and leadership of Benjamin Netherland. One of the first across the stream, he rallied a covering party which finally forced the red men and their white friends to withdraw and enabled the surviving riflemen to get away. About 70 Kentuckians were slain, and 20 more were captured or badly wounded. Only 7 of the Girty gang were killed, and 10 wounded, and they retreated northward without further hindrance.

The disaster on the Little Blue Licks was followed by other savage forays on the Kentucky frontier. Clark was bitterly criticized as a result, since he was still in command for Virginia beyond the mountains. His response was to the point. He arranged with Irvine for a simultaneous attack upon the Ohio Indians, Irvine to march into the Sandusky valley while Clark struck again at the Shawnees. Irvine did not actually move, for he was informed by Washington that hostilities between Britain and America had ceased; but fear of his forces prevented the Indians from collecting all their forces to deal with Clark. On November 4 Clark led 1,050 mounted riflemen from the mouth of the Licking River toward Chillicothe. He also had some artillery. Six days later the Americans approached Chillicothe. They had hoped for a surprise, but the Shawnee townsmen learned of their approach and fled. Only 10 were killed and 10 wounded. However, Clark burnt Chillicothe and five other Shawnee towns, and destroyed large quantities of corn and other provisions belonging to the Indians. He dealt a blow which the Shawnees would not soon forget.

Clark's punitive expedition against the Shawnees was one of the last actions of the war. Already the diplomats of the United States and Britain had come to an agreement upon peace terms. These included recognition by Britain of American boundaries which gave not only Kentucky but also the whole of the Old Northwest to the United States. To what extent the acquisition of this magnificent domain was due to George Rogers Clark is disputed. At the end of the War of Independence the Americans did not hold Detroit. But they still controlled the Illinois country; and the region between the Illinois country, the Ohio, and Lake Erie was not firmly under the military control of the British. Clark's name may not have been mentioned by the diplomats, but his exploits can hardly be said to have weakened American claims. He was assuredly one of the greatest American frontier figures, an architect of the United States.

CHAPTER 82

The Ravaging of Virginia

During the fall of 1780, the succeeding winter, and the spring of 1781, while Greene was waging an apparently unsuccessful war in the south, the rest of the country was depressed almost to the point of giving up the struggle for independence. For two years, because of its small numbers and its inability to obtain proper supplies, Washington's army had perforce lain idle in the Highlands of the Hudson. On October 5, 1780, he wrote to General John Cadwalader: "We have been half our time without provision and are like to continue so. We have no Magazines, nor money to form them and in a little time we shall have no men [even] if we had money to pay them. We have lived upon expedients till we can live no longer." In December he had not even enough money to pay an express rider for a journey of a few miles, "neither money nor credit adequate to the purchase of a few boards for Doors for our Log huts." [1]

It was with difficulty that the main American army was maintained in strength sufficient to hold its positions in and about Peekskill. The Continental currency had depreciated to the vanishing point. The Virginia Assembly passed a law in April, 1781, fixing the price of cavalry horses, worth $150 in hard money, at $150,000 Continental; and they could not be bought even at that price. [2] The Congress was bankrupt. The people generally began to believe that the war was about over. Washington wrote: "We seem to be verging so fast on destruction that I am filled with sensations to which I have been a stranger till within these three months." And yet the war had already begun to blaze afresh in a new field where, within ten months, the American cause would be finally and lastingly triumphant. That field was the state of Virginia.

For the three years that followed the burning of Norfolk on January 1, 1776, the Old Dominion east of the mountains was unvexed by war; but Virginia and her stores of wealth were a prize too valuable to be forever disregarded by the British. The vast quantities of tobacco she raised strongly supported the credit of the Congress among foreign nations, and the salt provisions she produced helped feed the American army. It would have been well for the British to occupy the state permanently. Clinton did not feel strong enough to detach from New York a force sufficient to do that. In 1779, however, he was able to strike a blow toward destroying its usefulness to the Americans; he organized a large-scale raid.

On May 5, 1779, twenty-two transports heavily convoyed by war vessels under Vice Admiral Sir George Collier sailed from Sandy Hook with the grenadiers and light infantry of the Guards, the 42nd Regiment, the Hessian Regiment Prince Charles, the Tory Royal Volunteers of Ireland, and a detachment of artillery—1,800 men in all, commanded by Major General Matthews. On May 10 they landed at Portsmouth and took possession of that unfortified town without opposition. Detachments pushed on and captured Suffolk, Gosport, and other small towns, also without opposition except in Gosport, where a garrison of 100 in a rather strong little redoubt, Fort Nelson, resisted with a brief and ineffectual cannonade before abandoning the works. In Gosport there were a shipyard, ropewalks, and a very considerable store of ship timbers and naval stores. The Americans burned a nearly completed war vessel on the ways, also two French ships loaded with tobacco and other merchandise; the British did the rest. They sacked and burned all the towns, looted the neighboring plantations, destroyed or carried off 130 vessels and 3,000 hogsheads of tobacco, inflicting a loss estimated at £2,000,000, and sailed away, loaded with plunder of every sort, without the loss of a single man.[3]

Cornwallis was convinced that the conquest of Virginia would be followed by the control of all America. He even proposed the abandonment of New York and the concentration of all the royal forces in the Chesapeake to effect this great result.[4] Clinton would not consent to such a drastic change in the disposition of his army. He did, however, send a large detachment under Benedict Arnold to Virginia in 1780 and order all his subordinates there to cooperate with Cornwallis when that general had begun his march thither from Wilmington in April, 1781.[5]

Benedict Arnold, as a part of his purchase price, had received the rank of brigadier general in the British army. Lacking confidence in Arnold's stability, Clinton attached to his force two experienced and reliable officers, Colonels Dundas and Simcoe, "by whose advice he was to be guided in every important measure." [6] The corps under Arnold consisted of the 18th British regiment, Simcoe's Queen's Rangers, a detachment of New York Volunteers under Colonel Althouse, and Captain Thomas's Pennsylvania Volunteers from Bucks County, about 1,600 in all.[7] The principal purposes of the expedition were the destruction of military stores in Virginia, the prevention of reenforcements for Greene from that state, and the rallying of the Tories.

The expedition sailed from Sandy Hook on December 20 but was scattered by a violent gale on the 26th and 27th. One war vessel and three transports, carrying 400 men, failed to rejoin it when it reassembled off the Chesapeake capes.[8] The rest reached Hampton Roads on the 30th. There the 1,200 remaining troops were transferred to small vessels taken from the Americans. Convoyed by the armed vessels *Hope* and *Swift*, they sailed up the James River, arriving in the evening of January 3 at Hood's Point, where about 50 militia manned a battery of three 18-pounders, one 24, and a brass howitzer.[9] The Americans opened fire, but did no damage to the invaders. The vessels passed the battery; and, about a mile above it, Arnold put Simcoe's Rangers and the light infantry and grenadiers of the 18th Regiment ashore the next morning to attack it from the rear. The defenders had, however, evacuated the battery during the night. The guns were spiked, the howitzer carried off as a prize, and the expedition proceeded up the river to Westover, about twenty-five miles below Richmond, where the men were disembarked.[10]

Although Washington had written several times to Governor Jefferson of the probable invasion of his state,[11] adequate preparations had not been made for its defense when the enemy fleet was sighted off the Chesapeake capes. Then Jefferson sent General Thomas Nelson, Jr., of the Virginia state troops down to the coastal region ("the lower country") to call up the militia in that quarter, "but waited further intelligence before we would call for militia from the middle or upper country." [12] The response to the call was feeble. Years of freedom from attack had resulted in an apathy in Virginia which even the presence of invaders, at the very threshold of her capital, could not dispel. The only force in being was about 200 Continentals newly recruited by Steuben, and it was employed in removing military stores from Petersburg beyond the reach of the enemy.

Henry Lee explains this apathy partly by Matthews's devastation of the towns in 1779, and by the fact that the efforts of Virginia to support

Greene's army in the Carolinas had further exhausted her resources. "Yet," he says, "she possessed enough, more than enough, to have sustained the struggle for their restoration and to have crushed any predatory adventure like that conducted by Arnold." He lays the blame for the supineness of the state upon the government headed by Thomas Jefferson, "a gentleman . . . highly respected for his literary accomplishments and as highly esteemed for his amiability and modesty," who failed to heed Washington's warning and to make any preparations to meet the invasion, with the result that he had left "the archives of the State, its reputation and all the military stores deposited in the magazines of the metropolis at the mercy of a small corps conduced by a traitor." [13] To be sure, Light-Horse Harry and Jefferson were enemies, and the cavalryman could hardly be expected to lavish praise upon the governor. Perhaps Jefferson did all that he could.

Arnold marched his men from Westover, entirely unopposed, against Richmond and entered that town on January 5. About 200 militia under Colonel John Nicholas occupied the heights of Richmond Hill. Simcoe's Rangers were ordered to dislodge them; they fled without firing a shot. A small body of cavalry near the capitol also departed without resistance. The town was thus bloodlessly taken.[14] Arnold then sent Simcoe with his Rangers and the flank companies of the 18th Regiment six miles up the river to Westham, where there was an iron foundry, a "laboratory" (powder factory), and machine shops. These were destroyed with their contents, including five or six tons of gunpowder.[15]

He sent a letter to Jefferson offering to spare the capital if the British vessels were permitted to come up the river unopposed and carry away the tobacco from the warehouses. Although it seems that no effective opposition to the approach of the vessels could have been offered, Jefferson refused to make the bargain.[16] The work of destruction was then begun; buildings, public and private, were burned; other public and private property was destroyed, including state papers. Weapons of various sorts and military stores were carried off on the return march to Portsmouth on the 6th, which was accomplished without a whiff of gunpowder.[17] At Portsmouth, Arnold entrenched and encamped for the winter.

Meanwhile he had sent a scouting party of forty-two of the Queen's Rangers, horsemen, under Simcoe towards Long Bridge. Hearing of the presence of a body of one hundred and fifty of Nelson's militia under Colonel Dudley at Charles City Court House, Simcoe resolved to attack them. He sent his buglers to the right to sound a charge while the rest of his small party advanced on the left. Then, in a loud voice, he ordered his light infantry—of which he had none—to charge. Believing themselves about to be caught in the jaws of a pincers attack, the militia took fright, gave a confused and scattering fire, and started to disperse. Simcoe's horsemen drove into their bewildered opponents, killed twenty, and captured eight. He then returned to join Arnold at Westover, having lost one man killed and three wounded.[18]

Washington had his eye on Arnold in his isolated position in Virginia. To capture that traitor and bring him to a deserved end was worth an effort. It would be, he wrote, "an event particularly agreeable to this country." He solicited the aid of the French fleet and army at Newport in Rhode Island, blockaded by a stronger British fleet.[19] At the same time he ordered Lafayette with three regiments of light infantry—1,200 rank and file, drawn from the New England and New Jersey Continental regiments—to march southward and cooperate with the expected French force. These regiments were commanded by Colonel Joseph Vose of Massachusetts, Lieutenant Colonel de Gimat, a French officer, and Lieutenant Colonel Francis Barber of New Jersey.[20]

A timely storm struck the British blockaders off Rhode Island on January 22, 1781, wrecking several of the largest ships and so scattering the fleet that Admiral Destouches was able to send out the 64-gun ship *Eveille* and two frigates under command of Le Bardeur de Tilly to destroy Arnold's vessels and leave him without naval support. Arnold had, however, withdrawn his vessels up the Elizabeth River to Portsmouth, to which place Tilly's larger ships were unable to follow them. The French vessels therefore returned to Newport on February 24.[21]

Lieutenant General de Rochambeau, in command of the French army, and Admiral Destouches then agreed to send the whole French fleet and 1,200 soldiers to operate with Lafayette against Arnold. Lafayette promptly marched from Peekskill and arrived on March 3 at the Head of Elk, where he embarked his men in small vessels that carried them to Annapolis. On March 8 Destouches, with eight ships of the line and three frigates carrying the promised 1,200 troops, set sail from Newport. The British Admiral Arbuthnot, with an almost exactly equal force, put to sea from Gardiner's Bay on the 10th and overtook the Frenchmen at the entrance of the Chesapeake on the 16th. In the ensuing encounter Destouches was worsted and forced to return to Newport.[22] Lafayette's little army was thus left with little support to face not only Arnold's larger force but also Major General William Phillips, who had been sent by Clinton with 2,600 men to join Arnold and supersede him in command, and who had arrived at Portsmouth on March 26. [23] To assist Lafayette, there were only Steuben's small newly enlisted force of Virginia Continentals and such untrained militia as Generals Muhlenberg, Weedon, and Nelson were able to raise.

Arnold made the first move. On April 18, while Lafayette was on his southward march from Baltimore, the light infantry of the 76th and 80th British regiments, the Queen's Rangers, the American Legion, and a detachment of Hessian jägers, about 2,500 in all, embarked at Portsmouth under Arnold's command, sailed down to Hampton Roads and thence up the James, landing at various points and destroying whatever they came upon. On the 24th the whole force disembarked at City Point and marched towards Petersburg, where great supplies of tobacco and military stores were guarded by General Muhlenberg with about a thousand militia. The town was unfortified, and its approaches were merely picketed by small bodies. Muhlenberg's men were drawn up on an elevation east of Blandford, a village about a mile east of Petersburg. Arnold divided his force into two columns, sending the main body under Lieutenant Colonel Abercrombie directly towards his enemy, and the Queen's Rangers with one battalion of light infantry on a circuitous route around Muhlenberg's right flank. The American guns, firing grapeshot, were brought to bear on Abercrombie's column and for a considerable length of time held it off. But Abercrombie brought up four fieldpieces to a hill on the American right and so battered it that Muhlenberg decided to withdraw across the Appomattox by a neighboring bridge. The withdrawal was accomplished in good order, and the bridge was destroyed. Thence the retreat was continued to Chesterfield Court House, and Petersburg was left open to the enemy. Four thousand hogsheads of tobacco and several small vessels were burned, but the buildings seem to have escaped destruction.[24]

The success of these marauding expeditions and the lack of effective opposition encouraged Phillips to continue them. He repaired the bridge and marched on April 27, with the light infantry and detachments of jägers and of the Queen's Rangers horsemen, to Chesterfield Court House, where he burned a great range of barracks and 300 barrels of flour, with other stores. No defense was offered by the Virginians. At the same time Arnold, with the 76th and 80th British regiments, the American Legion, and some of the jägers and of the Queen's Rangers, set out for Osborne's, a small village on the James about fifteen miles below Richmond. There the Americans had assembled a considerable naval force, intended for cooperation with the French fleet in an enterprise against Portsmouth. Arnold used every precaution for surprise and succeeded in coming upon the ships without their crews' being aware of his approach. He sent a flag of truce with an offer to leave half of the cargoes unmolested, if they would surrender the other half. The offer was refused. He then brought to bear on the *Tempest*, a 20-gun frigate, two 3-pounders and two 6's. He also sent up a party of the jägers to fire on the crew. The *Tempest*, the *Renown*, 26 guns, and the 14-gun *Jefferson*, as well as a body of militia on the northern bank of the river, replied. But the *Tempest*'s cable having been cut by a shot, she swung around and exposed herself to a raking fire from Arnold's artillery, whereupon her crew took to their boats and escaped under musket fire from the jägers. The incident produced a panic in the other vessels, and the crews gave up the fight, scuttling some of the vessels, setting fire to others, and fleeing from them all.

The result was the burning or sinking of four ships, five brigs, and several smaller vessels, and the capture of two ships, three brigantines, two schooners, and five sloops, all laden with tobacco, flour, naval stores, and other merchandise. More than 2,000 hogsheads of tobacco and the rest of their cargoes were burned. The British suffered no losses. The casualties among the Americans are unknown.[25]

The two British forces, having joined, marched to Manchester and took and burned 1,200 hogsheads of tobacco. At Warwick they destroyed 500 barrels of flour, the flouring mills, several warehouses, more tobacco, and five vessels. Thence, by various stages, between April 30 and May 10, they proceeded to Petersburg, where they surprised and captured ten American officers.

Lafayette with his 1,200 Continentals arrived at Richmond on April 29 to defend that city.[26] Phillips was then on the opposite side of the James, but he made no attempt against this American army, which his own greatly outnumbered. He fell down the river to Jamestown Island with the intention of meeting Cornwallis on his expected arrival at Petersburg. On May 20 Cornwallis arrived with a brigade of the Guards, the 22nd, 33rd, and 71st British regiments, the light infantry of the 82nd, the Hessian Regiment von Bose, Tarleton's Legion, and Hamilton's Tories—about 1,500 men in all [27] —and the two British forces were united. A few days later another force of 1,500 sent by Clinton—two new British regiments and two battalions of Anspachers—brought the British army's numbers up to 7,200 rank and file. Meanwhile Lafayette had received additions to his original force of 2,000 Virginia militia and 40 dragoons, the relics of Armand's Legion. He had now about 3,000 men to oppose the 7,200 British.[28] He could not hope to meet his enemy in the field. "Were I to fight a battle," he wrote to Washington on May 24, "I should be cut to pieces, the militia dispersed and the arms lost. Were I to decline fighting, the country would think itself given up. I am therefore determined to skirmish, but not to engage too far, and particularly to take care against their immense and excellent body of horse, whom the militia fear as they would so many wild beasts. . . . Were I anyways equal to the enemy, I should be extremely happy in my present command, but I am not strong enough even to get beaten." [29]

Cornwallis, on the other hand, was confident of his strength. He wrote to Clinton on May 26, "I shall now proceed to dislodge LaFayette from Richmond, and with my light troops to destroy any magazines or stores in the neighbourhood." He would then move to the Neck at Williamsburg and keep himself disengaged from operations that might interfere with the plan for the campaign, until he heard from Clinton. "The boy cannot escape me," he is said also to have written.[30]

Cornwallis marched from Petersburg on the 24th of May, crossed the James to Westover, and encamped on June 1 at Hanover Junction, whence he sent Tarleton's and Simcoe's corps to scout the position of Lafayette's force, which had been encamped at Winston's Bridge eight miles north of Richmond.

Lafayette had left on May 28, retreating rapidly westward to Dandridge's on the South Anna River to wait the arrival of Steuben's Continentals and of Wayne's detachment of 800 men drawn from the Pennsylvania Continentals. This had been ordered south by Washington in February, but difficulties in organization and in procurement of supplies had prevented it from marching from York, Pennsylvania, until May 20.[31] Meanwhile Lafayette's plan was to keep his force intact and to avoid any engagement with the enemy.

With this in view and to prevent Cornwallis's interposing his army between him and the oncoming force of Wayne, he conducted his men by a series of rapid marches northward to Ely's Ford on the Rapidan twenty miles above Fredericksburg. Cornwallis followed as far as the North Anna River, but could not get between him and Wayne, nor even come up with him and force him to fight. So the British general turned to other objectives.

On June 1 Cornwallis sent Simcoe with his Rangers and the 2nd battalion of the 71st Regiment, 500 men, to Point of Fork, where the Fluvanna and Rivanna rivers join to form the James, and where Steuben with his now five or six hundred Continental recruits was guarding the main depot of American military stores. Simcoe found that Steuben had withdrawn his stores across the Fluvanna and was following them with his whole force. He captured a lingering group of thirty of Steuben's men, but could not pursue the main body for lack of boats.[32] He then employed an artifice. Displaying his small force widely along the river bank, he lighted many campfires and thus produced an appearance of such great numbers that Steuben believed that it was the advance of the whole British army and abandoned his stores and retreated rapidly southward to Cole's Ferry. Simcoe sent some men across the river in canoes and destroyed the stores.[33]

On June 4 Cornwallis dispatched Tarleton with 180 of the Legion's cavalry and 70 mounted infantry against Charlottesville, where the Virginia legislature was in session. On the way Tarleton fell in with a train of twelve wagons carrying much-needed clothing for Greene's army, took it, and burned it. At Charlottesville the legislature, notified of his coming, had adjourned; but he captured several of their number. Governor Jefferson had a narrow escape, avoiding capture by a flight to the mountains. A quantity of powder and of tobacco, a thousand muskets, and some clothing intended for Greene's army were taken and destroyed. Tarleton and Simcoe then rejoined Cornwallis.[34] About this time Arnold was recalled to New York and appeared no more on the southern scene of action. He had rendered genuine service to the British in Virginia, and he might have been useful to Cornwallis.

On June 10 Wayne, with three Pennsylvania regiments under Colonels Richard Butler, Walter Stewart, and Richard Humpton, and the 4th Continental Artillery under Lieutenant Colonel Thomas Forrest—about 800 men in all and six guns—joined Lafayette.[35] Lafayette now felt strong enough to make some effort to protect the remaining American magazines from destruction. He marched south towards the enemy. At Mechunk Creek on the 13th, he was further reinforced by 600 back country riflemen under General William Campbell of Virginia.[36]

Two days later Cornwallis broke his camp at Elk Hill a few miles below Point of Fork, where he had lain since June 7, and took the road towards Richmond. This retrograde movement encouraged the Americans, who regarded it as a confession of inability to continue the destruction of the American magazines and as a sign of a disinclination to engage Lafayette's increased army; but Cornwallis was merely shifting his ground towards the Chesapeake to get in closer relations with his superior, Clinton in New York.

Lafayette followed him at a distance of about twenty miles. When Cornwallis entered Richmond on June 16, the Americans were at Dandridge's on the South Anna. On the 20th Cornwallis resumed his eastward march, Lafayette still hanging on his rear. At that time the American army was composed of Lafayette's original force of light infantry, 800 men and Wayne's 750 Pennsylvanians, all seasoned Continental troops; three Virginia militia brigades under Generals Edward Stevens, Robert Lawson, and William Campbell, 2,100 in all; the 425 new Virginia Continentals raised by Steuben and now commanded by Colonel Christian Febiger; 200 of the 2nd and 4th Continental Artillery regiments with eight or ten guns; 60 regular cavalrymen; and as many volunteer dragoons. The total was about 4,500 rank and file.[37] He scattered these forces on different roads; they encamped separately, but sufficiently near one another to concentrate rapidly. Thus he created an impression of greater numbers than he actually had and made it more difficult for spies and deserters to convey certain intelligence of his numbers to Cornwallis. On June 26 he had his first encounter with the enemy.

Simcoe's Rangers and a party of jägers had been sent on the 23rd to forage and to destroy American stores on the Chickahominy River west of Williamsburg, where the British army was in camp. Lafayette detached Colonel Richard Butler with his Pennsylvania regiment, Majors Call and Willis with a corps of riflemen, and Major William McPherson with 120 horsemen to intercept Simcoe on his return to Williamsburg. They marched all night of the 25th and in the morning came upon the British refreshing themselves at Spencer's Ordinary. McPherson charged upon Simcoe's jägers and threw them into confusion; but the Rangers quickly deployed and came to their comrades' assistance, charging upon McPherson and driving him back. Call and Willis brought up their riflemen and there was a sharp conflict between them and Simcoe's infantry, before the Rangers' horsemen fell upon their flank and pushed them back upon Butler's Continentals. A confused fight ensued, in which Simcoe's men had the advantage. But as soon as he was sufficiently free of his assailants Simcoe, leaving his wounded in the tavern, drew off his force on the road to Williamsburg. He was not pursued, because of the dangerous propinquity of Cornwallis's main force.

Lafayette claimed a success in this fight, asserting that the enemy had lost 60 killed and 100 wounded; but Cornwallis acknowledged only 33 casualties. The American losses were 9 killed, 14 wounded, 14 missing.[38] During the following week there was little activity on either side. Cornwallis remained in his camp at Williamsburg. Lafayette hovered in the neighborhood of the British, changing his position almost daily, the various sections of his army encamping separately as before. His enemy's intentions were unfathomable to him; he could only await their disclosure. The next movement of the British was dictated by Clinton.

New York was threatened by the armies of Washington and Rochambeau. Clinton called on Cornwallis for 3,000 of his men. They had to embark at Portsmouth, and Cornwallis on July 4 started from Williamsburg for that port. In this movement Lafayette thought he saw his opportunity. He would strike while the British were crossing the James, fall upon their rear while the river divided them.

The crossing began at Jamestown Ford on July 5. On the 6th Lafayette detached Wayne with Stewart's Pennsylvania Continental regiment, certain other small parties under Mercer, McPherson, Galvan, Call, and Willis, 500 in all, to march to Greenspring Farm within half a mile of the British outposts; the rest of the army, exclusive of the militia, who were left under Steuben's command at Bird's Tavern, twelve miles in the rear, was held in reserve. At that time Lafayette and Wayne believed that the major part of the enemy had crossed the river, and that only the rear guard was left for them to engage. But Cornwallis had shrewdly calculated that just such an attack would be made and had sent across only Simcoe's Rangers and the army's baggage. The main body of his army lay in wait.

Wayne's contingent advanced across a broad morass, with Armand's and Mercer's cavalry in front, supported by the riflemen on both flanks, and Stewart's Pennsylvanians in reserve. They first met and engaged the patrols of Tarleton's Legion, which was thrown out in front of the main body of the British. Under a hot fire from the Americans, the Legion fell back into a wood, as ordered by Cornwallis to make the Americans believe that they had to contend with his rear guard only. Supported by a part of the 76th Regiment, Tarleton's men stood fast in the wood and stoutly resisted the Americans' advance, while screening from them the British army immediately behind the wood. In this part of the fight, the American riflemen took heavy toll of the British officers.

Wayne, ignorant of the proximity of the whole British army, had no idea of the hazard of his position. On the other hand, Cornwallis was uncertain as to what support the Americans then engaged had in their immediate rear. He could easily have beaten Wayne, but preferred to wait until he could be sure that the rest of Lafayette's army was at hand to offer him a prize worth taking.

About five o'clock Lafayette brought up his original force of light infantry and the rest of the Pennsylvania Continentals, his whole army except the militia who had been left under Steuben's command at Bird's Tavern. Having some doubt as to what part of Cornwallis's army was yet on the near side of the river, he sent across the morass to Wayne only the rest of the Pennsylvanians and a battalion of light infantry, under Major John Wyllys of Connecticut, with two fieldpieces. The fire of these two guns seems to have convinced Cornwallis that the whole American army was at last before him. He ordered an attack.

Cornwallis's army was formed in two lines, the light infantry on the right of the front line, the 43rd, 76th, and 80th regiments on the left. In the second line were the Guards, the 23rd, 33rd, and 71st regiments, the Hessian Regiment von Bose, and Tarleton's Legion. Wayne with his reenforcements was then also preparing to attack. In the center of his line were Stewart's Pennsylvanians, with Butler's and Humpton's on the right and left, Wyllys's Connecticut light infantry extending the line to the right. The American riflemen were holding a ditch behind a rail fence, which they had occupied in the first encounter. Against Wayne's line of 900 men the whole British army advanced. The riflemen bore the first attack with considerable fortitude, maintaining their fire for a short time before they were driven from their post. Wyllys's light infantry, somewhat in advance, were also forced to retire to the American line. Wayne, perceiving that he had taken on the whole British army, and that his small force was in peril of being outflanked on both sides, might well have ordered a retreat, but feared to do so lest it develop into a rout. If he could first check the British advance, he might have a chance to withdraw in order. He therefore ordered a charge with the bayonet upon the British left wing, its right being engaged in driving back Wyllys's troops and the riflemen.

Wayne's troops responded nobly, springing forward under a strong fire of grapeshot and musketry, but, within two hundred feet of the enemy they were brought to a stand. For a quarter of an hour, at this close range, the battle was sharply and destructively contested. But the British right, having beaten back Wyllys and the riflemen, now threatened to swing in upon and envelop the American left. The pressure of overwhelming numbers on Wayne's men was also too heavy to bear. He ordered a retreat. It was successfully accomplished without pursuit, though with the loss of the two guns, and the army was reassembled at Greenspring. The Americans lost in killed and wounded 133, besides 12 missing; the British casualties were 75.[39]

Cornwallis's failure to follow up his success saved Lafayette's army from destruction, but there was some excuse for the failure in that a very dark night had fallen by the time the Americans retreated. "One hour more of daylight must have produced the most disastrous conclusion," says Henry Lee. Cornwallis himself wrote to Clinton that half an hour more of light "would have probably given us the greatest part of the [American] corps." [40] As it was, he resumed his march, crossed the river, and went on his way to Suffolk and thence to Portsmouth. Tarleton was then dispatched to destroy American stores in Bedford County. Wayne and Morgan were sent by Lafayette to counteract his efforts. He accomplished little, except burning more tobacco, and rejoined Cornwallis at Suffolk after an exhausting tour of 400 miles in fifteen days. From Suffolk, Cornwallis sent to Portsmouth the 3,000 men called for by Clinton. Lafayette held his men in camp on Malvern Hill, between Richmond and Westover, awaiting developments.

Throughout this whole campaign, Cornwallis had been harassed by the conduct of his superiors, Germain in London and Clinton in New York. Germain, who has been harshly described as "probably the most incompetent official that ever held an important post at a critical moment," [41] as Secretary of State for the Colonies was charged with the general conduct of the war. He tried to direct it in some detail by letters that took four weeks to three months to reach his generals in America, by which time in most cases the circumstances on which he based his directions had entirely changed.

Clinton was in command of all the King's forces in America. His correspondence with Cornwallis, back and forth, took eight days or more to reach its destination. His directions therefore arrived often too late to be of use. Moreover, he did not quite give Cornwallis a free hand nor give him positive orders. As the two had conflicting views as to the proper conduct of the war, and as the orders Clinton gave usually had a saving clause to the effect that if Cornwallis had other plans he should disregard them, the result was a complete confusion of the intentions and purposes of both parties and discontent in Clinton with what Cornwallis did, expressed in almost every letter. This condition was to have a most important bearing on the outcome of the campaign. It was exemplified in orders Cornwallis received on July 8 to send the 3,000 troops to Philadelphia instead of to New York, on January 12 to dispatch them immediately to New York, then on July 20 and later not to send them at all but to hold them and occupy Old Point Comfort, also Yorktown if possible.[42]

Cornwallis visited Old Point with a corps of engineers and concluded that it was not suitable as a defensive point to command a harbor for the King's ships, which was Clinton's purpose. He thereupon seized Yorktown, and Gloucester across the York River, and proceeded to fortify them. Clinton tacitly acquiesced in this arrangement.[43]

CHAPTER 83

Washington Resumes Operations

While the war was raging in the Carolinas and the minor operations were carried on in Virginia, Washington's army in the north was inactive. But on May 22, 1781, he learned that the French were sending Admiral de Grasse with a new fleet to the West Indies and thence to the American coast to cooperate under his direction with Rochambeau's army (in Newport), and it seemed to be time for the American army to resume offensive operations.[1]

It was indeed time that something should be done in the north lest the American cause die of inanition. The people were tired of the war. Its long continuance had bred apathy as to its outcome. Few men could be induced to enlist for its duration or even for any definitely long term of service. The farmers wanted to be on their farms in seedtime and harvest time. The town dwellers were convinced that somehow or other, without much further effort on their part, a peace would be achieved. There was no capable central authority. The Congress had little real power beyond persuasion of the states to follow its guidance. The financial system was a wreck.

In the army itself there was little coherence, and no prospect of combined operation. At and about West Point, Washington had scarcely 3,500 Continentals, chiefly from New England. The regiments from New York were scattered along its western frontier. New Jersey was guarding its own territory. The best of the Pennsylvanians were in Virginia with Wayne and Lafayette. The Continentals of the more southerly states were with

Greene in the Carolinas. The allied French, about 4,000, were at Newport, Rhode Island, under Rochambeau.

For any of these, for all of these, except the French, there was little better prospect than practical destitution. The few and scattered magazines contained small supplies. The military chests were empty, and the credit of the army was exhausted. The impressment of food had soured the temper of the people.[2] "Instead of having the prospect of a glorious offensive campaign before us," wrote Washington in his journal on May 1, 1781, "we have a bewildered and gloomy defensive one, unless we receive a powerful aid of ships, land troops and money from our generous allies."

In contrast to this was the condition of the invaders. Besides Cornwallis's army of more than 5,000 well supplied veterans in Virginia, Clinton had 14,500 equally well or better supplied in New York. Yet it was against that post that Washington and his generals, upon hearing of the coming of Grasse, in a meeting at Wethersfield, Connecticut, concerted with Rochambeau for an attack.[3] A part of the French fleet, with 700 recruits for the French army in Newport, had arrived with word that more would come in July or August. But it was not until the first week in July that Rochambeau with four regiments of infantry, a battalion of artillery, and the Duc de Lauzan's Legion of horse and foot joined Washington on the Hudson. Meanwhile, Washington had been preparing his army, brigading it anew, drilling his men, calling in outlying detachments to his camp at Peekskill, and in general getting ready for the adventure.[4]

The enterprise against New York was to begin with an attempt against the British forts on the north end of Manhattan Island by General Benjamin Lincoln, commanding two regiments of light infantry and a detachment of artillery, 800 in all, brought down in the night of July 1 from Peekskill in boats and landed secretly on the New York shore under the height on which stood Fort Knyphausen—formerly Fort Washington. The plan was no less ambitious than an effort to take by surprise Fort Knyphausen, Fort Tryon, Fort George on Laurel Hill, the works on Cox Hill at the mouth of Spuyten Duyvil, and those at Kingsbridge. Washington was to arrive early the next day with the main army at Valentine's Hill, four miles above Kingsbridge. There was also a secondary purpose to be effected in case circumstances prevented fulfillment of the first: cooperation with a force led by the Duc de Lauzun in the capture or at least the defeat of De Lancey's corps of Tory horse and foot, then at Morrisania. According to the alternative plan Lincoln was to land above Spuyten Duyvil, march to the high ground in front of Kingsbridge, lie concealed until the beginning of Lauzun's attack, and then prevent De Lancey from turning Lauzun's right while he was cutting off the escape of the Tories over the bridge. It was all very prettily planned, but it did not work.[5]

Lincoln, viewing the ground from Fort Lee on the opposite shore, found it occupied by a considerable British force just returned from foraging in New Jersey. Also, a ship of war lay in the river between. He abandoned the principal attempt and landed his troops above Spuyten Duyvil for the secondary effort. This also failed. He was discovered by another British foraging party stronger than his own and was attacked. Lauzun with his Legion, Sheldon's dragoons, and a detachment of Connecticut state troops under General David Waterbury arrived after a hot and fatiguing forced march, only to find the intended surprise of De Lancey impossible. He gave support to Lincoln, and Washington hastened down from Valentine's Hill. The British took to their boats and escaped.[6] Washington spent the rest of the day in reconnoitering the ground about Kingsbridge, with a view to later operations. The next day his army fell back to Dobbs Ferry, where on the 6th the French army joined it in camp.[7]

Having still in mind an attack on New York, he prepared for a thorough reconnaissance in force. During the four days from the 21st to the 24th of July, screened by 5,000 troops interposed between them and the enemy, and guarded by 150 Continentals, he, Rochambeau, and two other French generals made a thorough examination of the British positions. They seem to have agreed that an attack upon them could not succeed—which, indeed, was undoubtedly true.

Rochambeau had four regiments, the Bourbonnois, Soissonois, Saintonge, and Royal Deux-Ponts, having now an effective strength of perhaps 930 each, besides Lauzun's Legion, the artillery, and engineers. This entire force numbered 4,796.[8] Washington had about as many. Clinton with 14,000 good troops held fortified lines that could not be reached without crossing one river or another held by British war vessels. The situation seems to have been too plain for argument. The wonder is that an attack should have been seriously considered.

Washington now turned his thoughts toward the south. It might be that Clinton would feel obliged to reenforce Cornwallis in Virginia and so weaken his New York garrison. Or he might call on Cornwallis for part of his troops—as he actually did, although he countermanded the order. In such an event, however, Washington might march south to help Lafayette clean up the weakened British force. Or he might go still farther, join Greene in South Carolina, and besiege Charleston.[9] While he was considering these cloudy matters, a letter from Grasse came to Rochambeau—a clear, concise, and definite letter that cleared the air, resolved all doubts, and determined the course of the war.

Grasse would embark the regiments Gatinois, Agenois, and Touraine, 3,000 in all, 100 dragoons, 100 artillerists, 10 field pieces, and a number of siege cannon and mortars, in twenty-five to twenty-nine war vessels. He would sail on August 13 from Santo Domingo directly to the Chesapeake, where he would remain until October 15 and then return with his troops to the West Indies.[10]

That was a time table explicit and definite, of which the Americans were wise to take notice. Washington did so without delay. Grasse's letter was received on August 14. On the 15th Washington wrote to Lafayette directing him so to dispose his troops as to prevent Cornwallis from retreating to North Carolina; to Heath on the 19th to take command of about half of the American army to be left in the Highlands—seventeen thin battalions of New England troops, Sheldon's horse, and some others.[11] He sent General Duportail, on the 17th, to Grasse with a letter saying that Rochambeau's French army and as large a part of the American army as could be spared would meet him in the Chesapeake, suggesting alternative plans for their combined operations according to circumstances, either in Virginia or at Charleston, and asking that frigates and transports be sent up to the Head of Elk to carry the troops down the Chesapeake.[12]

On the 21st the allied armies were started southward. The problem was to conduct their march in such a fashion that Clinton might be left in ignorance of their intentions. This was accomplished by crossing the Hudson by King's Ferry to Stony Point, then marching behind the Palisades and so through Newark and New Brunswick. In New Jersey they paused, established an extensive and apparently permanent encampment as if intended as a base from which to attack Staten Island, thus allowing Clinton to believe that the purpose was still against New York.[13] The true intent had been kept a secret even from the troops. James Thacher, a surgeon in the American army, wrote in his journal on the 15th, "The real object of the allied armies [in] the present campaign has become a subject of much speculation. Ostensibly an investment of the city of New York is in contemplation." From the circumstances of the encampment in New Jersey "we are left to conclude that a part of our besieging force is to occupy that ground. But," he sagely observed, "General Washington possesses a capacious mind, full of resource, and he resolves and matures his great plans and designs under an impenetrable secrecy, and, while we repose the fullest confidence in our chief, our own opinions must be founded only on doubtful conjectures."[14]

Secrecy was of vital importance, for this grand movement southward was a hazardous enterprise which had been, in a measure, forced upon Washington by Grasse's very definite plans. There was danger of an attack while the army was on the march. Moreover, Heath with half of the Americans, perhaps fewer than 2,500, was being left to hold the Hudson Highlands. Clinton, who had just been reenforced by 2,500 Hessians, had nearly 17,000 men in and about New York.[15] A swift attack on Heath would have ruined that half of the American army and left the British in control of the Hudson; and, in the event of failure of the Virginia expedition, New England would have been hopelessly cut off from the south. Then, whatever happened in the Carolinas and Georgia, the Revolution might have collapsed.

Yet the plan was definitely as wise as it was necessary. Unless some great advantage were achieved by the Americans somewhere, the cause might possibly have died of inanition; and nowhere else than in Virginia was there hope of such advantage. As was the case when Washington hazarded all on the daring attack at Trenton, this was a time when audacity would serve; and again Washington was equal to the occasion, although his hand was in some degree forced by Grasse. After three years of dreary inactivity he was ready and able to seize his opportunity and act with the boldness of high courage and the skill of a great captain.

This essential secrecy had been maintained in the most important quarter. It was not until September 2 that Clinton could say, "By intelligence which I have this day received, it would seem that Mr. Washington is moving an army to the southward, with an appearance of haste and gives out that he expects the co-operation of a considerable French armament." [16] By that time the allied armies, having lingered in the camp near Staten Island but a day or two, had passed through Princeton and Trenton, crossed the Delaware, and, for the most part, had reached Philadelphia, at which point concealment of its ultimate destination was neither useful nor possible.

The American army on this march was not a strong force. It comprised two New Jersey Continental regiments, Colonel Alexander Scammell's Continental light infantry, the Rhode Island Regiment, Hazen's "Canadian Regiment," otherwise called "Congress's Own," two regiments of New York Continentals, certain detachments of light infantry drawn from Connecticut and New York State troops, Colonel John Lamb's artillery regiment, and a small corps of engineers, sappers, and miners—about 2,000 in all.[17] Nor can it be said that it was a contented or even a willing army. "The soldiers being mostly from the eastern and middle States, marched with reluctance to the southward, and showed strong symptoms of discontent when they passed through Philadelphia." [18] They wanted a month's pay in hard money. Washington called on Robert Morris, the American superintendent of finance. Morris's only recourse was to Rochambeau's military chest, from which he borrowed $20,000 in specie to satisfy the men's demand.[19]

Philadelphia, always ready to welcome such visitors, British or American, whichever was at the moment in the ascendant, greeted the American soldiers with universal acclaim, although "the streets being extremely dirty and the weather warm and dry, we raised a dust like a smothering snowstorm." Even more gratifying to the populace was the sight of the French army, which followed the others, "dressed in complete uniforms of white broadcloth, faced with green, and . . . furnished with a complete band of music," a contrast to the Continentals' meager array of drums and fifes. The Congress reviewed these elegant allies, and one of their regiments "went through the exercise of fire-arms" before twenty thousand spectators, who were "surprised and enraptured by the rapidity of military evolutions, the soldierly appearance of the troops . . . and the exactness of their motions." They were particularly pleased by the French runners employed to carry orders from one command to another. Dressed in "his short, tight-bodied coat, his rich waistcoat, with a silver fringe, his rose-colored shoes, his cap adorned with a coat-of-arms and his cane with an enormous head," such a fellow was taken by "the common people" to be no less than a general and admired accordingly.[20]

But there was no delay. The armies pushed on to Head of Elk, where the Americans arrived on the 6th, having covered the two hundred miles from their starting point in fifteen days; the French came up two days later. There had been a period of uncertainty as to Grasse's arrival with the French fleet, no news having come since the admiral's letter from Santo Domingo dated July 8. But at Chester, on September 4, a letter from General Gist gave news of the arrival of the fleet in the Chesapeake. By September 18 the allies were all embarked—their advance in light transports at Head of Elk, the main body in frigates at Baltimore and Annapolis —and headed down the bay for landings on the James near Williamsburg, where, by the 26th, all were put ashore.

Meanwhile Lafayette had disposed his forces to prevent Cornwallis from escaping into North Carolina. He had moved his own division from its camp on the Pamunkey to a position near Williamsburg in Cornwallis's rear, while Wayne's force was posted at Cabin Point on the James.[21]

Grasse with a fleet of 24 ships of the line and six frigates had arrived outside Hampton Roads on August 30. His flagship, the *Ville de Paris,* 110 guns, was the greatest warship afloat on all the seas. The others ranged from 64 to 80 guns, most of them 74's.[22] Admiral de Barras, who had succeeded Destouches in command, had sailed from Newport with eight ships of the line. The British admirals Hood and Graves (the senior), with a combined fleet including nineteen ships of the line and seven frigates, left New York for the Chesapeake with intent to intercept Barras's smaller fleet and prevent its junction with Grasse, or at least to block Grasse's entrance into the bay, not being aware of the greater strength of the French fleet. They arrived too late to defend the bay. Grasse not only had entered it, but on September 5, the day the British fleet arrived off the Chesapeake, had disembarked his 3,000 troops under the Marquis Saint-Simon and added them to Lafayette's force.[23]

The British admirals discovered Grasse's fleet at anchor inside the mouth of the bay, off Cape Henry. At sight of his enemy, Grasse slipped his cables and stood out to meet them. The opposing forces were ill matched. Grasse had twenty-four great ships, carrying 1,700 guns and manned by 19,000 seamen, against the British nineteen sail, 1,400 guns and 13,000 men. The action, which began about four o'clock in the afternoon and lasted more than two hours, was inconclusive. The British had the advantage in their position to windward, but their ships seem to have been handled by Graves rather confusedly and the heavier metal of the French so greatly damaged five of them that, when Grasse hauled off at half past six, Hood and Graves were in no condition to renew the action. They maneuvered off the capes for several days, while Grasse reentered the bay. Barras having succeeded in joining him, the French strength was too great to allow the British any hope in further combat. They sailed back to New York, leaving Cornwallis to his doom,[24] because for one reason and another the British fleet could not be brought back to Chesapeake Bay in force and in time to rescue him.

CHAPTER 84

The Siege of Yorktown

The allied forces that marched from Williamsburg presented an impressive appearance of military strength. The American wing, under Washington's command, was composed of Lamb's 2nd Continental Artillery Regiment, with two companies of the 1st and 5th, 310 in all; Moylan's 4th Dragoons and Armand's horse, 100 men; Lafayette's light infantry, two brigades under General Muhlenberg and General Hazen, chiefly New England and New York troops, but including Hazen's "Canadian Regiment," about 1,500 rank and file; General Lincoln's Continental infantry division, two brigades, the first consisting of the 1st and 2nd New York under General James Clinton, the second of the combined 1st and 2nd New Jersey and the Rhode Island Regiment, under Colonel Elias Dayton, numbering 1,725 in all; Steuben's division of two brigades, the first Wayne's 1st and 2nd Pennsylvania battalions and one from Virginia, a total of 900, the second under General Mordecai Gist comprising the 3rd and 4th Maryland regiments, 1,000 men; General Thomas Nelson's three brigades of Virginia militia, under Generals Weedon, Lawson, and Stevens, 3,000 men; 200 of the Virginia state regiment under Lieutenant Colonel Charles Dabney and, finally, a corps of 110 sappers and miners, making a grand total of 8,845 rank and file.[1]

The French wing, commanded by Lieutenant General de Rochambeau, comprised 600 artillery, 600 of Lauzun's cavalry, the Brigade Bourbonnois consisting of the Regiments Bourbonnois and Royal Deux-Ponts under Colonel de Laval and Colonel de Deux-Ponts, 1,800 men; the Brigade Soissonois, two regiments under Colonel de St. Maime and Colonel de

Castine, 1,800 men; and the Brigade Agenois of three regiments under Colonel d'Audechamp, Colonel de Rostaing, and Colonel de Pondeux, 3,000 men. The French had a grand total of 7,800 rank and file, somewhat fewer than the Americans. They were certainly far better equipped, armed, and disciplined than the 3,000 militia that made up more than a third of the American force.[2]

To defend Yorktown, Cornwallis had 193 of the Royal Artillery; Simcoe's and Tarleton's 440 horse; a brigade of the Guards, 467 rank and file under General O'Hara; Abercrombie's 600 light infantry; Yorke's brigade of infantry, comprising the 17th, 23rd, 33rd, and 71st British regiments, about 900 men; Dundas's brigade, composed of the 43rd, 76th, and 80th British regiments, about 1,500; the two Anspach regiments of Colonel de Voit and de Seybothen, 950 men; the Hessian regiments Prince Hereditaire and von Bose, 700 men; 68 jägers; Lieutenant Colonel John Hamilton's 114 North Carolina Tories; and 33 pioneers. The grand total was about 6,000.[3]

At daybreak on September 28, a fine, clear day, the allied troops set out from Williamsburg in light marching order, with various detachments on parallel course. They encountered no opposition until close to Yorktown, where they came upon Abercrombie's light infantry pickets covering the British right, and Tarleton's Legion on the left. A few cannon shot caused these outposts to withdraw at sunset. The allies then formed a camp that extended from the York River above the town in a great curve through woods and fields to the Wormley Creek below, a line over six miles long interrupted only about its middle where the branches of Beaverdam Creek and the bordering marshes intervened and rendered occupation impossible and unnecessary. The French held the left above the creek, the Americans the right, below it. That night they lay on their arms.[4]

Yorktown was on a bluff on the south side of the York River about eleven miles from its mouth. The river in its main course was about two miles wide; but, opposite the town, the point of land projecting from the opposite side on which was the village of Gloucester narrowed it to about half a mile. In its rear, the town was almost encircled by two deep ravines which nearly met at their heads. For a long time after its founding in 1705 it vied with Williamsburg as the capital city of the province and therefore contained several public buildings besides about sixty dwelling houses.[5]

The fortifications erected by the British army extended in a curve around the town and consisted of seven redoubts and six batteries connected by intrenchments. There was also a line of batteries on the river side, one of which, the Grand Battery, mounted eleven heavy guns commanding the narrows between the town and Gloucester Point. These main fortifications were supported by certain outworks, three small redoubts along the edge of the ravine southwest of the town, two on the east side near the river, another, the Fusiliers' Redoubt, on the extreme northwest, also close to the river, and a battery to the eastward beside the road to Hampton. Gloucester was defended by a line of intrenchments drawn across the Point in the rear of the village. In the river off the town lay two frigates, the *Charon* and the *Guadeloupe,* 44 guns each, and three large transports.[6]

Cornwallis had garrisoned Gloucester with 700 men under Lieutenant Colonel Dundas, and Tarleton's Legion. To immobilize that force Lauzun's Legion, 800 marines from Barras's ships, and Weedon's brigade of 1,500 Virginia militia, all under command of General de Choisy, had been sent to take a position beyond the fortified line.

On the morning of September 30 the allies had a pleasant surprise. During the night Cornwallis had quietly abandoned the outlying redoubts southwest of the town and the battery by the Hampton road, drawing their garrisons into the town, but still holding the Fusiliers' Redoubt and the two close to the river on the east side of the town.

The surrender was thought by the American and French officers to be an unmilitary act, as the outlying positions could have been held for some time, delaying the close investment of the town. Clinton afterwards criticized it. But Cornwallis had a reason. He had received from Clinton, the day before, a dispatch dated September 24 saying, "It is determined that above five thousand men, rank and file, shall be embarked on board the King's ships and the joint exertions of the navy and army made in a few days to relieve you."[7] Expecting this succor, he felt that he could best hold out by concentrating his force within the main works and so notified Clinton.

As all these abandoned works except the battery were enclosed, they were immediately useful against the town and were promptly occupied by the allies. The battery was worked upon that night to turn it into an enclosure; and a new redoubt in line with the others was begun. In the same morning the French light infantry attacked the pickets in front of the Fusiliers' Redoubt and drove them in; but the redoubt was held. The Americans suffered a signal loss that day in the fall of Colonel Alexander Scammell, a brave and much loved officer. He and a small party were reconnoitering the abandoned works, when they met a detachment of Tarleton's Legionaries and were forced to surrender. After they were taken captive, it is said, Scammell was shot in the back by one of Tarleton's troopers and mortally wounded.

The abandoned redoubts were subjected to a heavy fire from the guns in the main fortifications; but the work of transforming the battery and constructing the new redoubt was carried on without interruption and with few casualties.

The first week of October was devoted by the allies to preparations for the advancement of the siege. Twelve hundred Americans were detailed to make thousands of stakes, also fascines, gabions, and saucissons—various forms of wicker basketwork needed for the intended approaches by parallels. Bringing up the heavy siege guns from the landing on the James, six miles distant, was difficult because of lack of horses; but the task was finally accomplished. In the meantime there was some excitement on the Gloucester side of the river.

On October 3 Choisy started to move his force nearer to the British fortification. That morning Dundas with nearly all his men came out of the works on a grand forage. The wagons loaded with corn were on their way back, covered by Simcoe's Rangers and Tarleton's Legion, when Choisy's van, entering one end of a lane, came upon this rear guard leaving the other end. Tarleton turned back to meet them. Lauzun's dragoons charged upon him, and there was a hot little encounter in which Tarleton and Lauzun came near meeting hand to hand. Just before they met, Tarleton's horse was overthrown. The rest of the British horse came up, and in the confusion, Tarleton secured another mount, sounded a retreat, and re-formed his men behind a company of infantry. The French pushed on, and a company of Virginia militia under Lieutenant Colonel John Mercer opened fire on the enemy, checking an attempt by Tarleton to renew the combat. The British retired to their lines with the loss of twelve men and one officer. Choisy established his camp close to the lines and held that position until the end of the siege.

By the evening of October 6 the preparations for the siege were completed; the heavy guns were at hand, and the first parallel was begun at six hundred yards' distance. Because of the ravine in front of the upper end of the town, the approaches were directed against the lower end. Fifteen hundred men were at work with the digging, while twenty-eight hundred guarded them. They worked all night, and the trenches were dug sufficiently deep by morning, with an embankment on the side toward the town, to cover the men from the enemy's fire. During the night the French

Regiment Touraine carried out a diversion against the Fusiliers' Redoubt. The redoubt was defended with "uncommon gallantry," as Cornwallis reported, and the French lost fifteen or twenty men.

The digging was continued without cessation, though under constant fire. To protect the approaches against sorties, four palisaded redoubts and five batteries were erected at intervals along the first parallel. There was considerable illness, the French especially suffering from ague. Similar disorders attacked the British, who were equally busy strengthening their defenses, as many as a thousand of them being reported on the sick list. Steuben, one of the few American officers who had had experience in sieges, was busy with advice as to the best methods of defending the approaches against sorties. Henry Knox, commanding the American artillery, was busily engaged in placing his guns and instructing his artillerists. By the 9th a sufficient number of batteries were in place to begin an effective bombardment of the town. The first to fire was the French battery on the extreme left opposite the Fusiliers' Redoubt. Four 12-pounders and six howitzers and mortars drove the frigate *Guadeloupe* from its station to the Gloucester side. An American battery on the extreme right brought six 18- and 24-pounders, four mortars, and two howitzers to bear on the works at the end, Washington himself firing the first shot.

On the 10th two other batteries opened; the Grand French Battery at the end of the approaches, with ten heavy guns and two mortars, and an American battery of four 18-pounders and two mortars. A red-hot ball fired by the French set the *Charon* on fire and in a vast sheet of flame it burned to the water's edge. Two transports were similarly destroyed. The next day, the first parallel having been extended to two thousand yards' length, the second was opened at three hundred yards from the defenses. Fifty-two guns were now in play, and the fire from the town was nearly silenced. At this time, Cornwallis wrote to Clinton, "We have lost about seventy of our men and many of our works are considerably damaged; with such works on disadvantageous ground, against so powerful an attack we cannot hope to make a very long resistance. P.S. 5 P.M. Since my letter was written (at 12 M.) we have lost thirty men. . . . We continue to lose men very fast." [8]

During the night of the 11th, seven hundred fifty yards of the new parallel were completed, a ditch three and a half feet deep and seven feet wide, a work of "amazing rapidity," in spite of "very heavy fire of the enemy's shot and shell going over our heads in a continual blaze the whole night. The sight was beautifully tremendous," wrote one of the officers in his journal. [9]

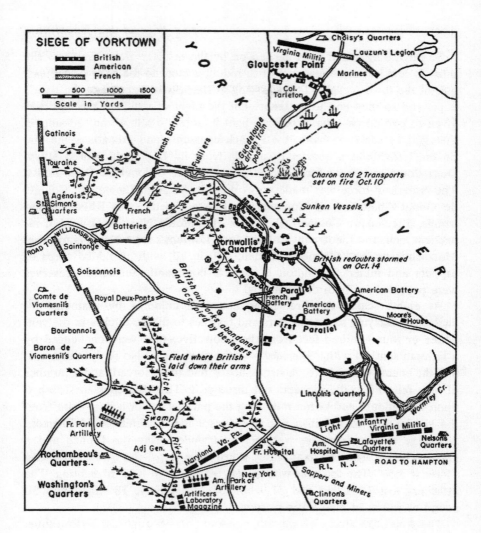

SIEGE OF YORKTOWN

British
American
French

0   500   1000   1500
Scale in Yards

YORK

Choisy's Quarters
Virginia Militia
Lauzun's Legion
Gloucester Point
Marines
Col. Tarleton

Gatinois
Touraine

French Battery

Fusiliers

Guadeloupe driven post from

Charon and 2 Transports set on fire Oct. 10

Agénois
St. Simon's Quarters

French Batteries

Sunken Vessels

RIVER

ROAD TO WILLIAMSBURG
Saintonge

Cornwallis' Quarters

British redoubts stormed on Oct. 14

Soissonnois

Second Parallel

American Battery

Comte de Viomesnil's Quarters

Royal Deux-Ponts

French Battery

American Battery

Moore's House

Bourbonnois

British outworks abandoned and occupied by besiegers

First Parallel

Baron de Viomesnil's Quarters

Field where British laid down their arms

Warwick

Wormley Cr.

Lincoln's Quarters

Fr. Park of Artillery

Swamp

River

Light Infantry
Virginia Militia

Nelson's Quarters

Rochambeau's Quarters

Adj. Gen.

Maryland Va. Pa.

Fr. Hospital

Am. Hospital

Lafayette's Quarters

R.I.   N.J.

ROAD TO HAMPTON

Washington's Quarters

Am. Park of Artillery

New York

Sappers and Miners

Artificers
Laboratory
Magazine

Clinton's Quarters

So far the fight had been carried on by the artillery alone; but now the infantry had its part. The two British redoubts close to the river on the east side of the town prevented the carrying of the second parallel to the river's edge, and so they had to be taken. On the night of the 14th the task was given to two corps—the American light infantry to attack the redoubt on the right by the river bank, the French chasseurs and grenadiers the one on the left, about a quarter of a mile from it. The Gatinois and Royal Deux-Ponts regiments furnished 400 men under Colonel de Deux-Ponts. The American force was made up of men drawn from Lieutenant Colonel de Gimat's battalion of Connecticut, Massachusetts, and Rhode Island troops, Lieutenant Colonel Alexander Hamilton's New York and Connecticut men, and Lieutenant Colonel John Laurens's from New Hampshire, Massachusetts, and Connecticut men, 400 in all, with an added corps of sappers and miners, Hamilton in general command. Substantial reserves were provided for both detachments.

At eight o'clock the French advanced in columns by platoons, 58 chasseurs, carrying scaling ladders and fascines to fill the ditches in the van. Three or four hundred feet from their objective, they were challenged by a Hessian sentinel with, *"Wer da?"*—Who goes there? No reply was made, and the enemy opened fire. A strong abatis had to be forced, and a number of men fell before the pioneers cut through it. Then the chasseurs dashed upon the redoubt and began mounting the parapet under a heavy fire from the garrison of 120 British and Hessians under Lieutenant McPherson. A charge by the defenders was met by a volley from the French and a countercharge. The Hessians threw down their arms, the French shouting *"Vive le Roi!"* The fort was won in less than half an hour of fighting. The attackers lost 15 killed and 77 wounded; the enemy, 18 killed and 50 sound or wounded men taken prisoners.

The American attack on the other redoubt was begun at the same time. This work, the smaller of the two, was held by 70 men under Major Campbell. The Americans advanced with unloaded muskets and fixed bayonets. Led by a forlorn hope of 20 men of the 4th Connecticut under Lieutenant John Mansfield, they crashed through the abatis without waiting for the sappers to cut it away, crossed the ditch, and swarmed over the parapets in spite of the bayonets of the garrison. In ten minutes they overcame all resistance, with a loss of 9 killed and 31 wounded, including Gimat and several other officers.

Immediately upon the taking of the two redoubts fatigue parties set to work extending the second parallel. By morning they had pushed it on to include the captured works. The next day Cornwallis wrote to Clinton:

"My situation now becomes very critical; we dare not show a gun to their old batteries, and I expect that their new ones will open to-morrow morning. . . . The safety of the place is, therefore, so precarious that I cannot recommend that the fleet and army should run great risque in endeavouring to save us." [10]

Cornwallis was facing the inevitable end, but was not yet ready to give up. He organized a sortie to cripple the two new batteries in the second parallel, "against the fire of which, it was foreseen that the British works on the left, already half ruined, could not stand many hours." [11] Lieutenant Colonel Abercrombie was to lead 350 men in two parties: one made up of men from the Guards with a company of grenadiers commanded by Lieutenant Colonel Lake of the Guards; the other, of light infantry under Major Armstrong. Just before daybreak of the 16th, they gallantly dashed upon the batteries, drove off the French guards in one of them, and spiked four guns by driving bayonet points into their touchholes and breaking them off. The other battery, held by Americans, was also forced, and its three guns similarly disabled. But the Comte de Noailles brought up his grenadiers and attacked the intruders, killing 8 and taking 12 prisoners, with a loss of 20 of the French. The rest of the British retreated to their works. It was a brave effort, but it was without any good result. Even the disabled guns were in service again within a few hours.

Still Cornwallis would not give up. There was a bare possibility of saving his army by a retreat, such as Washington had so successfully made after the Battle of Long Island. If he could get his men across the river to Gloucester, pick up the part of his army there, and overcome Choisy's small force holding that position, he might proceed by forced marches through Maryland, Pennsylvania, and New Jersey, where there were no substantial organized American forces to oppose him, and reach Clinton in New York. The Americans and French on the south side of the river would be put to it to cross in time to overtake him. He counted on taking the 600 horses of Lauzun's Legion in Choisy's command and picking up others on the way to mount as many as possible of his infantry. Traveling without baggage, his progress would be swift. "Undoubtedly," says Stedman, "the attempt was beyond calculation hazardous, and the issue totally precarious; but, if it afforded even a glimpse of hope, it was preferable to an immediate surrender."

Before midnight of the 16th Cornwallis embarked the greater part of the Guards, the light infantry, and part of the 23rd Regiment in small boats and landed them on the Gloucester side. But a violent storm arose and not only prevented a return of the boats, but also drove them a long way down the river. That ended all chance of escape. The boats did return the next day and brought back the troops that had been carried across, but that availed nothing.

In the morning the allies opened on the doomed town with all their guns. "By the force of the enemy's cannonade," says Stedman, "the British works were tumbling into ruin; not a gun could be fired from them." Anyhow, their ammunition was exhausted. So, in the morning of the 17th a red-coated drummer mounted the parapet and began to beat a parley. No one could hear him in the din of the cannonading; but he was seen, and his message was understood. The fire of the American guns ceased. An officer bearing a white handkerchief advanced from the town. He was blindfolded and led to the rear of the allies. Being presented to Washington, he asked for a twenty-four-hour armistice and the appointment of commissioners to discuss terms of surrender. Washington allowed two hours within which to receive proposals in writing. Within that time Cornwallis submitted his terms, which included a condition that his troops be returned to England on parole not to serve against France or America during the war or until exchanged. Washington refused and demanded a complete surrender of the enemy as prisoners of war. To this Cornwallis perforce agreed.

On the 18th commissioners from both sides met and drew up the articles, which were signed the next day. At two in the afternoon, the garrison marched out, spick-and-span in new uniforms, their colors cased and their bands playing an old British march entitled "The World Turned Upside Down." The allies were paraded in two lines. The French, resplendent in their white broadcloth uniforms, "displayed a martial and noble appearance. . . . The Americans, though not all in uniform, nor their dress so neat, yet exhibited an erect, soldierly air and every countenance beamed satisfaction." [12]

Between these lines the defeated army passed. Cornwallis did not march. Excusing himself on account of illness, he left the command to General O'Hara, who tendered Cornwallis's sword to the American general. Washington referred him to General Lincoln who accepted the token of surrender and immediately returned it to O'Hara.

In a field behind the approaches a squadron of French hussars formed a circle into which the British and Hessian regiments successively marched, piling their arms. The defeated troops at Gloucester were surrendered to Choisy by Tarleton, who had succeeded in Dundas in command. Tarleton, having in mind his evil reputation, had told Choisy that he feared for his life if he were left to the mercies of the American militia. Choisy therefore had only Lauzun's Legion and Mercer's Virginians drawn up for the ceremony, keeping the rest in the camp. No violence was offered to Tarleton.

The main body of prisoners was marched off to prison camps in Virginia and Maryland, under guard of militia. Cornwallis and his principal officers were paroled and allowed to go to New York, after being dined for several days at the tables of Washington, Rochambeau, and other American and French officers.

The prisoners taken by the allies numbered 7,247 of all ranks and 840 seamen. Eighteen German regimental standards and six British were captured, as well as 244 pieces of artillery, thousands of small arms, and considerable quantities of military stores and equipment. The casualties on both sides during the siege were comparatively light, the Americans losing 20 killed and 56 wounded, the French 52 killed and 134 wounded, the British 156 killed and 326 wounded.

Although Cornwallis's position had been hopeless from the first, the outcome of the siege was a near thing after all, for by October 5 Clinton had actually assembled 7,000 troops in New York to go to his aid. The fleet, twenty-five ships of the line, two of 50 guns, and eight frigates, did not sail until October 19, the day of the surrender. It arrived off the Chesapeake capes on the 24th. Its arrival a week sooner might have saved the British army.

News of the event was carried to the Congress by Lieutenant Colonel Tench Tilghman. Riding posthaste, he reached Philadelphia at three o'clock in the morning of the 22nd and delivered the glad tidings to President Thomas McKean. A watchman who conducted Tilghman to McKean's house then began to cry through the streets, "Past three o'clock and Cornwallis is taken!" On receipt of Washington's official dispatches two days later the Congress went in procession to the Lutheran church for services of thanksgiving. As it spread throughout the country, the news was hailed with rejoicing and celebrations, in the well grounded belief that the war was about over.

It was received in England on November 25. Lord George Germain communicated it to Lord North, who received it "as he would have taken a ball in his breast," crying out wildly as he paced to and fro, "Oh God! It is all over!" which he "repeated many times, under emotions of the deepest agitation and distress." [13] The King was also shocked, but he soon after expressed himself as determined to carry on the war "though the mode of it may require alterations." [14] But opinion in Parliament did not uphold this view, and early in 1782 the Commons voted to authorize the King to make peace with America, declaring on March 4 that it "would consider as enemies to his Majesty and the Country all those who should advise or by any means attempt the further prosecution of offensive war on the Continent of North America, for the purpose of reducing the revolted Colonies to obedience by force."

Commissioners were appointed by both sides. On November 30, 1782, they signed provisional articles, but not until September 3, 1783, was the definitive treaty acknowledging the independence of the United States of America formally signed.

Notes

CHAPTER 38

There is a dearth of original material for an account of the Siege of Fort Stanwix and the Battle of Oriskany. The chief sources are Marinus Willett's report to Governor Trumbull, his *Narrative,* published in 1831, and St. Leger's report to Burgoyne, both appearing in Dawson, I, 250–252. For detailed secondary accounts recourse may be had to Nickerson, Lossing, and Dawson, among others. Stone's *The Campaign of Lieut. Gen. John Burgoyne and the Expedition of Lieut. Col. Barry St. Leger* contains the fullest story and perhaps the best. These are the principal sources of the narrative.

1. Stone, *B,* I, 37.
2. The uniforms of the Rangers consisted of green coats and waistcoats, faced and lined with scarlet, and either buckskin Indian leggings reaching from the ankle to the waist, or leather overalls. They wore skullcaps of black leather, with a brass plate in front marked "G R" and "Butler's Rangers." Buff leather crossbelts were similarly marked on a brass plate at their intersection.
3. Dawson, I, 237. The fort, renamed Schuyler at the beginning of the Revolution, is often referred to by that name. It is better known by its original name, which is retained in this narrative.
4. Neilson, 18, says 2,000 axmen, certainly a great exaggeration.
5. Nickerson, 197.
6. Nickerson, 203, says the wagon train comprised "four hundred heavy ox-carts." The source of this information is not given. That there were anywhere near so many is incredible. Burgoyne's train, to transport the heavy baggage of 7,500 men on a long journey, was drawn by 500 horses and 50 ox teams. Certainly, 800 shirt-sleeved farmers on a two-day march would require no such preposterous procession as 400 carts. Nickerson, 204, estimates the full length of Herkimer's column, including the oxcarts, at three-quarters of a mile to a mile. With twenty feet for each cart in the train, which would be a nose-to-tailboard crowding, 400 carts alone would extend a mile and a half. Spaced out to give practicable room and allow for the marching men in a close-up formation, the column would have extended at least three miles.
7. It has been claimed that at Stanwix was first displayed in battle the Stars and Stripes. It appears to be quite certain that the homemade flag hoisted on its

897

ramparts showed thirteen stripes, alternately red and white, but that in its canton or field (the upper inside corner), it bore the cross of St. George superimposed on the cross of St. Andrew, instead of the stars of the United States flag adopted by the Congress in June, 1777. Indeed, it satisfactorily appears that the Stars and Stripes flag so adopted was not intended for the American army, but only for ships. Thruston is probably the best authority on the flag. See also Quaife, 62, on the flag at Fort Stanwix.

8. The conference between St. Leger's and Gansevoort's officers is fully reported in Willett's *Narrative,* 55–58.
9. Arnold, 153–154.

CHAPTER 39

1. Fitzpatrick, VII, 352.
2. Stedman, I, 279; Gordon, II, 466; Dawson, I, 212–217.
3. *Journals,* VII, 323, 379.
4. Arnold, 133–138.
5. Fitzpatrick, VIII, 377.
6. Hudleston, 165.
7. Nickerson, 183.
8. Lossing, I, 99 n.
9. Hudleston, 166.
10. Neilson, 78.
11. Van Tyne, 403.
12. Wilkinson, I, 231.
13. Hudleston, 163–164.
14. Fiske, I, 290.
15. Fisher, II, 86.
16. Fitzpatrick, VIII, 430.
17. Trevelyan, III, 148–150.
18. Fiske, I, 290. There is another version of the story of Jane McCrea; namely, that she was killed, not by an Indian, but accidentally by a bullet from the musket of a member of a party of Americans pursuing her captors. It appears that Mrs. McNeil told this to her granddaughter from whom Benson Lossing (I, 97–99) got it in 1848. The question has been elaborately discussed, e.g., by Nickerson, 470–472; but historically it is of little importance whether she was killed in one way or the other, of as little importance as it was to the girl herself. The only significance to be attached to her death arises out of the effect the story had upon the minds of her countrymen in exciting them to join the army. The story they heard is the real thing. That the Wyandot Panther shot and scalped Jane McCrea is just as certain as that Hamlet stabbed Polonius.
19. *Journals,* VIII, 375.
20. *Journals,* VIII, 604, and IX, 787.
21. *Journals,* II, 97.
22. Patterson, *passim.*
23. Wilkinson, I, 229.
24. Nickerson, 286–288. Stark's conduct at this time seems to have been motivated by that spirit of localism, of jealousy between the various colonies that, for so long, made them unwilling to cooperate as an united nation. New Hampshire and New York had fought over their conflicting claims of jurisdiction over the territory that became Vermont. There was bad blood between them. Stark, with his New Hampshire brigade, had defended Vermont at Bennington without help from New York. Now he let New York defend itself at Saratoga without calling on New Hampshire. That seems to be the explanation of his misbehavior.
25. Hadden, 119.
26. Fonblanque, 274.
27. Fonblanque, 275–276.
28. Wilkinson, I, 233.

29. Lossing, I, 45; Wilkinson, I, 234–238. This description is also derived from maps in Greene, FV, Arnold, Trevelyan, Nickerson, and others.
30. Patterson, 153.

CHAPTER 40

The original authorities for this battle are rather copious. Eelking's *Memoirs of Major General Riedesel*, Lamb's *Memoirs*, Pausch's *Journal*, Hadden's *Journal*, Anburey's *Travels*, and Burgoyne's *State of the Expedition*, present first-hand accounts by participants on the British side. On the American side are Wilkinson's *Memoirs*, interesting, but not very reliable. The secondary sources chiefly studied for this narrative include Lossing's *Pictorial Field Book*, Dawson's well documented *Battles*, Neilson's *Original Account of Burgoyne's Campaign*, Arnold's *Life of Benedict Arnold*, Stone's *Campaign of Lieut. Gen. John Burgoyne*, Fortescue's *History of the British Army*, Nickerson's *Turning Point of the Revolution*, Hudleston's *Gentleman Johnny Burgoyne*, Patterson's *Horatio Gates*, Lowell's *Hessians in the Revolutionary War*, and Irving's *Life of George Washington*.

1. Dawson, I, 305.
2. Dawson, I, 285; Anburey, I, 240–241; Wilkinson, I, 234.
3. Anburey, I, 242.
4. Lamb, 158; Hadden, 155–160; Trevelyan, III, 157; Dawson, I, 285–286; Burgoyne, 69; Anburey, I, 242.
5. Arnold, 170.
6. Riedesel, I, 145.
7. Riedesel, I, 145; Pausch, 133–134; Dawson, I, 305; Wilkinson, I, 435.
8. Dawson, I, 305; Burgoyne, 69.
9. Hale was not present, having been captured at Hubbardton.
10. Lossing, I, 51.
11. Trevelyan, III, 162.
12. Lossing, I, 51; Arnold, 170–171; Trevelyan, III, 162.
13. Nickerson, 307–308; Lossing, I, 51.
14. Arnold, 179.
15. Anburey, I, 242; Lamb, 159.
16. Wilkinson, I, 237.
17. Lamb, 159.
18. Wilkinson, I, 236.
19. Lamb, 159; Burgoyne, Appendix, lxxxvi.
20. Dawson, I, 288; Wilkinson, I, 239.
21. Anburey, I, 243. Fraser's inactivity throughout the battle is hard to understand. He had almost twice as many men as were in the center. He was nearer than Riedesel to the center, with less difficult ground separating him from it. Yet he sent no aid, except this once and then only temporarily. His immobility is not explainable except on the theory that his position on the right was too valuable to be hazarded. But Riedesel hazarded a more important element of the situation, the baggage provisions and supplies, when he went to aid the center.
22. Anburey, I, 245.
23. Trevelyan, III, 165.
24. Hadden, 165.
25. Lamb, 160.
26. Riedesel, I, 149.
27. Hadden, 166.
28. Lamb, 161, says that Burgoyne "behaved with great personal bravery; he shunned no danger; his presence and conduct animated the troops; he delivered his orders with precision and coolness."
29. Lossing, I, 52.
30. Riedesel, I, 149; Lamb, 160.
31. Pausch, 137–138.

32. Fortescue, III, 235–236; Stedman, I, 337; Hadden, 165; Dawson, I, 289; Burgoyne, 104.
33. Dawson, I, 289.
34. The judgments rendered here upon Arnold and Gates may seem too favorable to the former and too harsh toward the latter. Channing, III, 276–277, contends that on the evidence available to him Gates and Morgan deserve credit for the American success, such as it was, in this struggle; and that Arnold's share in the battle has probably been greatly overemphasized. Patterson, 153–155, takes much the same view.

CHAPTER 41

The principal original sources of information concerning Sir Henry Clinton's enterprise against the two forts are the dispatches of General George Clinton and General Putnam to Washington, and the dispatches of Sir Henry Clinton and Commodore Hotham to Howe. These are reprinted in Dawson, I, 341–346. Secondary accounts of value are to be found in Dawson, Carrington, Leake, Stedman, Gordon, and Irving. Nickerson presents an especially detailed account. It has not been thought desirable to make specific references as to particular events, except where direct quotations occur. Stedman and Irving afford excellent maps.

1. Nickerson, 339–346.
2. Fonblanque, 280 n.
3. Nickerson, 320.
4. Anderson, T, 254, 258, 265–266.
5. Wilkin, 72.
6. Stedman, I, 358.
7. Leake, 173.
8. Nickerson, 341.
9. Marshall, I, 245.
10. Dawson, I, 346.
11. Stedman, I, 364.
12. Putnam's failure to offer any resistance to the enemy outraged the feelings of the people of the vicinity.

CHAPTER 42

1. Riedesel, I, 152.
2. See maps in Greene, FV, Walworth, Fonblanque, and Burgoyne.
3. Riedesel, I, 155.
4. Irving, III, 234–235; Wilkinson, I, 253–260; Arnold, 191.
5. Arnold, 194.
6. Arnold, 178.
7. Gordon, III, 546; Nickerson, 323–326.
8. Burgoyne, Appendix, lxxxviii.
9. Burgoyne, 166.
10. Riedesel, I, 159–162.
11. Riedesel, I, 161–163.
12 Riedesel, I, 162.
13. Riedesel, I, 162.
14. Anburey, I, 257.
15. Dawson, I, 292.
16. Trevelyan, III, 177.
17. Dawson, I, 292.
18. Riedesel, I, 163; Burgoyne, Appendix, xc.
19. Anburey, I, 261; Wilkinson, I, 267.
20. Wilkinson, I, 268.
21. Arnold, 204.
22. Arnold, 200.
23. Fortescue, III, 240.

24. Trevelyan, III, 164–165.
25. Stone, W, 66.
26. Trevelyan, III, 163–164. Arnold's enemies said afterwards, accounting for his reck-lessness, that he was drunk that day. No liquor was needed to intoxicate Arnold while a battle was on. The smell of gunpowder smoke was quite enough. If he was in liquor, Gates might well have asked the question Abraham Lincoln is said to have put when U. S. Grant was accused of drunkenness: "What kind of whisky does he drink? I'd like to get some for my other generals."
27. Wilkinson, Gates's aide, who tells many stories hardly believable, tells a pretty one about his chief. Sir Francis Clarke, Burgoyne's aide-de-camp, having been wounded and captured, was carried to Gates's headquarters and laid upon a bed. Gates engaged in an effort to convince him, by argument, of the merits of the American cause. Clarke, suffering the agonies of a mortal wound, declined to agree. Gates lost his temper and left the room, calling to Wilkinson to come with him. As they went out, Gates testily asked him, "Did you ever hear so impudent a son of a bitch?" Clarke died that night. It should be recalled that Wilkinson became a bitter enemy of Gates, and that his memoirs are not to be trusted.
28. Fortescue, III, 410.

CHAPTER 43

1. Riedesel, I, 166; Burgoyne, 43; Wilkinson, I, 279.
2. Burgoyne, Appendix, xci; Lamb, 165.
3. Burgoyne, 107.
4. Nickerson, 370; Wilkinson, I, 280.
5. Lamb, 165; Anburey, I, 268.
6. Wilkinson, I, 282; Anburey, I, 269. Riedesel, I, 167, says 800 were left in the hospitals.
7. Riedesel, I, 170.
8. Anburey, I, 268; Burgoyne, 73, Appendix, xci.
9. Riedesel, I, 171.
10. Wilkinson, I, 284.
11. Wilkinson, I, 285–289.
12. Wilkinson, I, 287.
13. Riedesel, I, 173.
14. Riedesel, I, 175–178.
15. Riedesel, I, 178.
16. Riedesel, I, 179.
17. Lamb, 166.
18. Riedesel, I, 174.
19. Burgoyne, Appendix, xciii.
20. Riedesel, I, 179–180.
21. Riedesel, I, 181.
22. Burgoyne, Appendix, ciii.
23. Stedman, I, 346–347.
24. Stedman, I, 347; Fonblanque, 307.
25. Stedman, I, 349–350.
26. Riedesel, I, 183.
27. Nickerson, 399.
28. Anburey, II, 2.
29. Pettengill, 110.
30. Dawson, I, 299–300.
31. Fortescue, III, 245–247.
32. Gordon, III, 45.
33. *Journals*, IX, 950.
34. Riedesel, I, 218; Lamb, 191.
35. Heath, 134.
36. Jones, I, 212.

37. Gordon, III, 48.
38. *Journals*, X, 29–34
39. *Journals*, X, 35.
40. Riedesel, I, 227.
41. Jones, I, 210–214.

CHAPTER 44

1. Gordon, III, 10.
2. Gordon, III, 11–12.
3. Fitzpatrick, X, 195.
4. Gordon, III, 13–14.
5. Lafayette, 35.
6. Waldo, 307.
7. Sparks, *W*, V, 193 n.
8. Fitzpatrick, X, 193.
9. H. E. Wildes, *Valley Forge* (New York, 1938), 179.
10. Duncan, 219–227.
11. Greene, GW, I, 557, 561; Baurmeister, 58; Trevelyan, III, 321.
12. Lee, 18.
13. Hughes, III.
14. Watson, II, 322; Fitzpatrick, VII, 327 n., and X, 97, 117, 118.
15. The principal contemporary sources of material for the narrative of the Quintin's Bridge affair are Simcoe and Stedman. Dawson, I, 379–382, presents a full account, well documented.
16. Simcoe again furnishes a first-hand account of this affair, and Stedman is to be relied upon. Dawson's account, as usual, is full and is well supported by citations.
17. Greene, GW, I, 552.
18. Greene, GW, I, 553–554.
19. Hughes, III, 265–266.
20. Fitzpatrick, XI, 469.
21. Lafayette, 35.
22. Wildes, *op. cit.*, 174–175.
23. Trevelyan, III, 324.
24. Stedman, I, 308, 310.
25. Van Tyne, *L*, 157.
26. Palmer, 31; Fiske, II, 48 (portrait).
27. Palmer, 3–4, 9, 13, 14.
28. Palmer, 124.
29. *Journals*, X, 50.
30. Tower, I, 322.
31. Palmer, 137.
32. Palmer, 140.
33. Palmer, 141.
34. Palmer, 142, 144.
35. Palmer, 145.
36. Palmer, 146.
37. Palmer, 147–148.
38. Palmer, 152.
39. Palmer, 156.
40. Palmer, 156.
41. Fitzpatrick, XI, 233.
42. Palmer, 157.
43. Palmer, 160.
44. Palmer, 164.
45. Fitzpatrick, XI, 360–363
46. *Journals*, XI, 465.
47. Dawson, I, 388.

CHAPTER 45

There is an excellent brief account of the Barren Hill affair in Gottschalk's *Lafayette Joins the American Army,* 185–193. Gottschalk's biography of Lafayette largely supersedes Tower's work. Nolan's *Lafayette in America Day by Day* is also useful.

1. *Journals,* X, 84.
2. Lafayette, 4, 6.
3. Trevelyan, III, 219–220.
4. Tower, I, 34.
5. Lafayette, 9.
6. Trevelyan, III, 219–220.
7. Lafayette, 14–15. Lafayette was doubtless correct in his assumption that his government did not wish to stop him, but merely to pretend so.
8. Tower, I, 180.
9. Lafayette, 17.
10. Tower, I, 183.
11. Tower, I, 186.
12. *Journals,* VIII, 721–722, 743–744.
13. Tower, I, 188–189.
14. Lafayette, 8.
15. Lafayette, 105.
16. Lafayette, 19.
17. Knollenberg, *passim.*
18. *Journals,* X, 87.
19. Lafayette, 35, 137. Knollenberg, Chap. 8, "Conway and Lafayette."
20. Burnett, 292–293.
21. Tower, I, 272–274.
22. Tower, I, 283–285.
23. Lafayette, 159.
24. *Journals,* X, 217, 253–254.
25. Stedman, I, 379.
26. Fitzpatrick, XI, 418–419.
27. Fitzpatrick, IX, 480.
28. Pontgibaud, 74.
29. Greene, FV, 146, map.
30. Tower, I, 329; Marshall, I, 288; Irving, III, 405–406.
31. Tower, I, 331.
32. Tower, I, 331–332.
33. Lafayette, 47.
34. Marshall, I, 289.
35. Tower, I, 334.
36. Tower, I, 335; Marshall, I, 288–291; Stedman, I, 376–379.
37. Lafayette, 78.
38. Tower, I, 336.
39. Marshall, I, 289 n.
40. Trevelyan, III, 284, 366–367.
41. Serle, 295. For the best account of Galloway's career, see Boyd, *Anglo-American Union.*
42. Trevelyan, III, 358–361; Irving, III, 409–410; Gordon, III, 129; Bancroft, V, 247–248.
43. Trevelyan, III, 365; Irving, III, 413; Van Doren, 95.

CHAPTER 46

1. Fitzpatrick, XI, 435.
2. Fitzpatrick, XI, 445, 448. On British strategy, 1778, see Willcox, S.
3. Fitzpatrick, XI, 465, 471, 483.

4. The map Washington used, which bears many notes in his handwriting, is preserved among the Washington Papers in the Library of Congress. A reproduction appears as Plate 14 in *The George Washington Atlas* (Washington, 1932), edited by Lawrence Martin and issued by the George Washington Bicentennial Commission.

5. There are at least four contemporary accounts of this beginning of the evacuation, all written by men in the British army who were on the ground, and no two of them agree as to the make-up of this first contingent. André, who was adjutant general of the army and should have known, says (p. 74) it comprised the 5th Brigade, the 46th and 55th regiments, Simcoe's Rangers, and Stirn's Hessians. Montresor, who was the army's chief engineer, says (p. 499) the 16th and 17th dragoons, the Hessians, and the Hessian grenadiers went across that day. Lieut. Gen. Archibald Robertson says (p. 173) it was the 5th Brigade and all the Hessians. Maj. Baurmeister says (p. 87) the 16th and 17th dragoons and the artillery. He puts Stirn's and Loos's Hessians over on the 15th, the Hessian grenadiers, Simcoe's corps, and the jägers over on the 17th. It is a matter of the least possible importance, except as showing how little confidence can be placed upon the details in even the apparently most reliable contemporary statements. We really know nothing more than that all those brigades and regiments got across at about that time, which is enough.

6. Frothingham, 251. Fortescue, III, 265, says there were but 15,000 on the march. Possibly some thousands went in the ships.

7. Montresor, 499.

8. André, 74.

9. Marshall, I, 292; Stryker, *M*, 58. Baurmeister, 67, describes this exploit, not naming McLane, of course, and calls the party "one enemy patrol."

10. Stryker, *M*, 64.

11. Stryker, *M*, 58; Fitzpatrick, XII, 82–83.

12. Fitzpatrick, XII, 107.

13. Stryker, *M*, 38, 42.

14. Fitzpatrick, XII, 110; André, 77; *Atlas*, pl. 38.

15. Dawson, I, 396; Stephenson, II, 74; Fitzpatrick, XII, 38, 75 n.

16. Fitzpatrick, XII, 113, 116; Marshall, I, 294.

17. Belcher, I, 324.

18. Greene, FV, 142; Lowell, 142; Irving, III, 420; Fisher, II, 179.

19. André, 77–78; Dawson, I, 415–416; Greene, FV, 143.

20. Lowell, 213.

21. Stephenson, II, 79; Marshall, I, 296; André, 78.

22. Stryker, *M*, 80.

23. Marshall, I, 294; Hughes, III, 348; Irving, III, 422; Stryker, *M*, 80.

24. Quoted in Stryker, *M*, 102.

25. Stryker, *M*, 100–101; Marshall, I, 295.

26. Stryker, *M*, 115–116.

27. Stryker, *M*, 95–98.

CHAPTER 47

This account of the Battle of Monmouth is based chiefly on William S. Stryker's book *The Battle of Monmouth* (edited by William S. Myers), an exhaustive monograph. No attempt is made to describe all the details, the unmeaning marches and countermarches of the various brigades and regiments in the first part of the battle, the shifting here and there of this or that contingent. An attempt is made to present the essential features of the conflict, avoiding unnecessary and confusing detail. Other authorities examined include the contemporary accounts in André, 74–81; Robertson, 177; Stedman; Fitzpatrick, XII, 74–130; Lafayette, 50–53; also the extended studies in Carrington, 412–415, and Dawson, I, 394–417, including Clinton's report; also such descriptions as are given in Greene, FV, 142–148; Hughes, III, 357–381; Tower, I,

347–393; Irving, III, 420–443; Marshall, I, 292–300; Duer, 195–197; Lossing, II, 148–158; and Gottschalk, *Lafayette Joins the American Army*, 204–233.

1. Tower, I, 366.
2. Quoted in Stryker, *M*, 185.
3. Stryker, *M*, 209.
4. Stryker, *M*, 212.
5. Stryker, *M*, 293–294.
6. *Journals*, XVI, 33.

CHAPTER 48

There is ample available documentation of the enterprise against Rhode Island. The diary of Lieutenant Frederick Mackenzie of the Royal Welch Fusiliers tells the story from the British side in the most remarkable detail. On the same side, other contemporary accounts are to be found in Stedman and in Pigot's dispatch to Clinton, quoted in Dawson, I, 442–444. On the American side, the contemporary accounts are in Gordon, Marshall, Fitzpatrick, and in the letters of Sullivan and other American and French officers in Volume II of the *Letters and Papers of Major-General John Sullivan*.

1. Fitzpatrick, XII, 131.
2. Fitzpatrick, XII, 146, 147, 165, 182. On the march from Englishtown many of the men, exhausted by the heat, had to be carried in the wagons (Bolton, 204).
3. Fitzpatrick, XII, 182.
4. Greene, FV, 149.
5. Fitzpatrick, XII, 208; Sparks, *C*, II, 160, 171; Sparks, *W*, VI, 12 n.
6. Fitzpatrick, XII, 184.
7. Fitzpatrick, XII, 195, 202, 204.
8. Marshall, I, 306; Dawson, I, 433.
9. Stedman, II, 28; Dawson, I, 433.
10. James, 102; Mackenzie, II, 330, 340.
11. Gordon, III, 158–159.
12. Marshall, I, 307.
13. Mackenzie, II, 332.
14. Mackenzie, II, 344.
15. Stedman, I, 29.
16. Stedman, II, 29; Mackenzie, II, 332. Mackenzie, II, 341, says there were thirty-five vessels in the British fleet. Mackenzie, II, 342, says there were in the French fleet twelve ships of the line and four frigates. The French fleet was actually the stronger because it was more powerful in ships of the line. Mahan, 71.
17. Mackenzie, II, 342.
18. Mackenzie, II, 346.
19. Mackenzie, II, 345.
20. James, 104; Stedman, II, 30.
21. James, 106.
22. Gordon, III, 161–164; Dawson, I, 435.
23. Dawson, I, 443.
24. Mackenzie, II, 357–360.
25. Marshall, I, 309–310; Gordon, III, 161–164.
26. Amory, 85.
27. Mackenzie, II, 381; Dawson, I, 437.
28. Gordon, III, 166.
29. Mackenzie, II, 383.
30. Gordon, III, 167; Sullivan, II, 283.
31. Amory, 82.
32. Amory, 96.
33. Greene, FV, 154.

34. Mackenzie, II, 389.
35. Gordon, III, 169; Marshall, I, 315–316.
36. Marshall, I, 313.
37. Fitzpatrick, XII, 385.
38. Marshall, I, 315.
39. *Journals*, XII, 1021.
40. Fitzpatrick, XII, 343.
41. Sparks, *W*, V, 548.
42. Hughes, III, 410.
43. Fitzpatrick, XIII, 230.
44. Fitzpatrick, XII, 409.
45. Fitzpatrick, XII, 460.
46. Fitzpatrick, XIII, 53, 78, 82, 173, and XIV, 184.
47. Greene, FV, 155–156.
48. Thacher, 158, 161.
49. Fitzpatrick, XIII, 352, 489, 466.
50. Fitzpatrick, XIII, 437.

CHAPTER 49

The fullest account of the taking of Stony Point is to be found in Henry P. Johnston's *The Storming of Stony Point*, a completely documented monograph. Where not otherwise specifically noted, reference is made to that work. The official reports of Wayne and Clinton are printed in Dawson, I, 524–527. Other contemporary accounts are in Stedman, Gordon, *The Literary Diary of Ezra Stiles*, II, 364, and the "authorities" reprinted in Johnston's book.

1. Kemble, I, 179; Robertson, 193–194; Fitzpatrick, XV, 223, 234–235.
2. Fitzpatrick, XV, 176, 195, 202, 210, 213, 221, 225.
3. Stedman, II, 141; Robertson, 194.
4. Thacher, 164.
5. Irving, III, 497; Fitzpatrick, XV, 243; Johnston, *S*, 41.
6. Irving, III, 502; Johnston, *S*, 83–84; Marshall, I, 363; Greene, FV, 158, map.
7. Johnston, *S*, 64.
8. Fitzpatrick, XV, 260, 261, 280, 292, 313.
9. Fitzpatrick, XV, 339.
10. Fitzpatrick, XV, 297, 345; *Journals*, XIV, 823.
11. Garden, III, 74.
12. Johnston, *S*, 62–63.
13. Johnston, *S*, 69–71.
14. Irving, III, 504.
15. Johnston, *S*, 158–160.
16. Johnston, *S*, 124.
17. Johnston, *S*, 91, 101.
18. *Journals*, XIV, 886, 891. Captain Archer, who carried the news of the victory to the Congress, rode at speed, 46 miles one day, 63 miles the next. "I came into the City with colors flying," he wrote to Wayne, "trumpets sounding and heart elated, drew crowds to the doors and windows and made not a little parade, I assure you. These were Baron Steuben's instructions and I pursued them literally, although I could not help thinking it had a little the appearance of a puppet-show." (Reed, II, 115.)
19. Stedman, II, 145.
20. Johnston, *S*, 131, 135.

CHAPTER 50

Contemporary sources of material for Paulus Hook comprise Lee's report to Washington, a British account in Gaine's New York *Gazette and Weekly Mercury*, both in Dawson, I, 549–553; letters by sundry participants in Reed, II, 125–127; Stedman, II,

153; Gordon, III, 283–284; Marshall, I, 368–370; and the Allen McLane Papers, New-York Historical Society. Dawson's account is full and well documented. W. H. Richardson's monograph *Washington and the Enterprise Against Powle's Hook* gives many details, but is unfortunately not annotated.

1. Irving, III, 513.
2. Irving, III, 515. Hughes, III, 474, citing no authority, attributes to Washington the initiation of the enterprise: "Encouraged perhaps by the public rejoicing over the brief exploit against Sandy Hook, Washington cast about for another dramatic blow. His eyes fell on . . . Paulus Hook. . . . He talked with Major Henry Lee and asked him to look into the matter." Washington's first letter to Lee on the matter, dated August 10, although it begins with an acknowledgment of receipt from Lee of a plan to attack the Hook, refers to "the idea I had of the matter" with respect to the number of men required; and a letter of August 12 to Stirling says, "I have had in contemplation an attempt to surprise the enemy's Post at Powlus Hook." But nothing in either letter necessarily contradicts Irving's statement—concurred in by Greene, FV, 159, and definitely endorsed by Frothingham, 296—that Lee originated the scheme. Marshall, I, 368, definitely attributes the scheme to Lee. Moreover, on July 28 one of Washington's aides wrote to Lee asking him to come to see Washington "on the very subject you mentioned in y^r letter of this date . . . in order that the scheme you propose may be adopted." Lee's letter seems not to be extant; its subject, therefore, is not known, but it is highly probable that the "scheme" was none other than the enterprise against the Hook.
3. Fitzpatrick, XVI, 72.
4. The description has been derived from Dawson, I, 543–544; Irving, III, 513; Richardson, map facing p. 4; Lossing, II, 622 n., with plan; Marshall, I, 368.
5. Richardson, 59.
6. McLane MS. journal in New-York Historical Society.
7. Richardson, 15; Irving, III, 514; Dawson, I, 545.
8. Dawson, I, 545, 549.
9. Reed, II, 127; Dawson, I, 546.
10. Dawson, I, 546, 549.
11. Richardson, 15–16.
12. Dawson, I, 546, 549.
13. Reed, II, 126.
14. Dawson, I, 547, 549. Stedman, II, 153, says that Lee's troops approaching the Hook were mistaken by a sentinel for Van Buskirk's foraging party returning and were "suffered to pass." Robert E. Lee's "Life of General Henry Lee" prefacing Henry Lee's *Memoirs,* says eight or ten soldiers disguised as countrymen carrying provisions for sale "procured the gate to be opened by the sentinel and held it until the rest of the party, concealed near, rushed in." Neither statement is supported by Henry Lee's dispatch, or by any other contemporary account.
15. Dawson, I, 548–549.
16. *Journals,* XV, 1100.
17. Sparks, *W,* V, 543.
18. Fitzpatrick, XVII, 126.
19. Fitzpatrick, XVIII, 198.

CHAPTER 51

1. Fitzpatrick, XVII, 105.
2. Fitzpatrick, XVI, 491, and XVII, 105.
3. Fitzpatrick, XVII, 210.
4. Kapp, 179–180.
5. Thacher, 180.
6. Hughes, III, 495.
7. Thacher, 161.

8. Stephenson, II, 121.
9. Thacher, 185.
10. Kapp, 182–183; Thacher, 190–191.
11. Rodney, C, 344–345.
12. Rodney, C, 334.
13. Fitzpatrick, XVII, 366.
14. Fitzpatrick, XVII, 273.
15. Fitzpatrick, XVII, 449–450.
16. Rodney, C, 338.
17. Kapp, 184.
18. Lossing, I, 319 n.
19. Thacher, 188. Major Patten of the Delaware Regiment was rather scornful of Stirling's adventure. He wrote to Caesar Rodney: "Their Intention was to *sweep* the Island. Why they did not do it I am not at present able to tell you. . . . We hear that they drew up in the face of the Enemy and remain^d there for some Hours without firing a single shot. . . . Rivington's Royal Gazette will no doubt . . . give us a Pompous description of this adventure of his Lordship." (Rodney, C, 334.)

CHAPTER 52

1. *Simcoe's Military Journal*, Marshall's *Washington*, Gordon's and Ramsay's histories, Wayne's letter to Hartley and Cornwallis's dispatch to Clinton, in Dawson, I, 452, 453, and Gaine's New York *Gazette and Weekly Mercury*, of Oct. 5 and 19, 1778, in Dawson, I, 453, present the principal contemporaneous accounts of this affair. Irving, III, 471–473, is a good secondary source.
2. Pulaski's report to the Congress and Ferguson's report to Clinton, in Dawson, I, 459–460, Gaine's New York *Gazette and Weekly Mercury* of Oct. 26, 1778, Stedman, Gordon, and Marshall are the contemporary authorities for this affair.
3. Tarleton's dispatch to Clinton, in Dawson, I, 506, and Heath's *Memoirs* are the principal contemporary sources. Dawson's account is full and well documented.
4. This invasion of Connecticut is well covered by Tryon's report to Clinton and Collier's letter to the Admiralty and an article in the *Connecticut Journal* of July 7, 1778, printed in Dawson, I, 512–514, 516, and by Lamb, Gordon, and Stedman. There are good secondary accounts in Barber and Hinman.
5. Heath's letter to Washington, Feb. 10, 1780, in Sparks, C, II, 395–398, gives a good account of this affair. Heath's *Memoirs* and Thacher's *Military Journal* are other contemporary sources.
6. For the affairs at Connecticut Farms and Springfield reference is made to Marshall, Stedman, Washington's letters to the Congress of closely subsequent dates, Greene's letter to Washington of June 23, 1780, in Sparks, C, III, 6, Gordon, and Johnson's *Greene*, I, 192.
7. A first-hand account of this affair, with a plan of the fort, is in Tallmadge, 59–63.
8. In *Pennsylvania*, II, 632–674, may be found a "Diary of the Revolt of the Pennsylvania Line," giving in full all letters and documents pertaining to the mutiny. Cf. also Van Doren, M, *passim*.
9. Heath, Marshall, Stedman, and Arnold's dispatch of Sept. 8 to Clinton in Arnold, 348–352, contain the chief contemporary accounts of this invasion. Dawson, I, 721–732, presents a detailed narrative, well supported by citations of authorities.

   In this report to Clinton, Arnold attributed the destruction of New London to an explosion of gunpowder in one of the storehouses, which had been fired. This, he said, "communicated the flames to a part of the town, which was, notwithstanding every effort to prevent it, unfortunately destroyed." This does not account for the burning of Groton. The contemporary historian Gordon (IV, 179) rejects the excuse: "The burning of the town was intentional and not accidental." Caulkins's *History of New London* presents a detailed and circumstantial account of the deliberate and systematic application of the torch to one street after another.

CHAPTER 53

1. The chief sources for the Wyoming Valley battle are Stone, *B*, and Dawson's account, appended to which are Zebulon Butler's report to the Board of War and John Butler's relation. Swiggett's *War Out of Niagara* and Chapman's account in an appendix to Campbell's *Annals of Tryon County* have been helpful.

CHAPTER 54

1. Lossing, I, 255.
2. *Pennsylvania*, I, 485.
3. *Pennsylvania*, I, 485.
4. These narratives of the ravishment of German Flats, Unadilla, and Cherry Valley are based on the accounts in Dawson, I, 464–471; Stone, *B*, I, 331–334, 338–345; Lossing, I, 253–255, 268–269, 296–298; and Swiggett, 138–157.
5. The story of Minisink and the succeeding fight is based upon the authorities cited in the preceding note.

CHAPTER 55

The materials for a story of Sullivan's Expedition are full and authentic. Of the officers and men engaged in it no fewer than 28 kept journals or afterward wrote accounts of it. Of the journals 17 are printed in full in the *Journals of the Military Expedition of Maj. Gen. John Sullivan Against the Six Nations of Indians,* published by the State of New York in 1887. These have been supplemented by examination of secondary accounts, Stone, *B*, Campbell, Dawson, Lossing, and other obvious sources.

1. *Journals*, XIII, 252.
2. Fitzpatrick, XIV, 3, 18, 75.
3. Fitzpatrick, XIV, 94, 168, 314.
4. Fitzpatrick, XIV, 180.
5. Patterson, 287.
6. Fitzpatrick, XV, 189.
7. Fitzpatrick, XV, 190.
8. Winsor, VI, 639, 667 n.
9. Sullivan, III, 4.
10. Sullivan, III, 20, 47; Amory, 107; Gordon, III, 308.
11. Stone, *B*, II, 10, 12.
12. Fitzpatrick, XV, 348–349.
13. Sullivan, III, 75.
14. Fitzpatrick, XVI, 1.
15. Sullivan, *J*, 194–195.
16. Sullivan, III, 96.
17. Sullivan, *J*, 260.
18. Sullivan, III, 197; Sullivan, *J*, 229.
19. Sullivan, *J*, 25.
20. Sullivan, *J*, 265.
21. Sullivan, *J*, 44.
22. Sullivan, *J*, 8, 27; Sullivan, III, 111.
23. Sullivan, *J*, 27.
24. Sullivan, *J*, 186.
25. Sullivan, III, 127.
26. Sullivan, III, 126, 128; Sullivan, *J*, 31, 234.
27. Sullivan, III, 131.
28. Sullivan, III, 134.
29. Sullivan, *J*, 13.
30. Sullivan, III, 134; Fitzpatrick, XVI, 437; *Journals*, XV, 1170.

31. Fisher, II, 245; Dawson, I, 541.
32. Stone, *B*, II, 26.
33. Fitzpatrick, XV, 302, 418.
34. Stone, *B*, II, 42–43; *Journals*, XV, 1212; Fitzpatrick, XVI, 485.

CHAPTER 56

The material for this chapter has been gathered chiefly from secondary sources, including Stone, *B*, Campbell, Swiggett, and Lossing. Specific references are deemed unnecessary in most cases.

1. Fitzpatrick, XVI, 492.
2. Swiggett, 214.
3. Lossing, I, 261–262.
4. Stone, *B*, 168.

CHAPTER 57

1. This description of the Carolinas is largely based on Ramsay, *R*, I, 2–3, and Greene, GW, III, 1–10, citing Morse's *American Universal Geography*, edition of 1793.
2. Greene, GW, III, 10–11; Irving, IV, 26, 86; Ramsay, *R*, I, 3–5.
3. McCrady, R, I, 33–35.
4. Lee, 174–175.
5. Greene, GW, III, 122; McCrady, *R*, I, 566; A. K. Gregorie, in *Dictionary of American Biography*, XVIII, 221.
6. McCrady, *R*, I, 566.
7. The descriptions of Marion and Sumter are drawn from Greene, GW, III, 122–127, and Irving, IV, 89, 196, and Lee, 174–175.
8. *Dictionary of American Biography*, XIV, 559.
9. Force, 4, IV, 981–982; Bancroft, IV, 320.
10. Force, 4, IV, 982–983; Dawson, I, 129.
11. Dawson, I, 131; Bancroft, IV, 387.
12. Dawson, I, 129; Force, 4, V, 63–65.
13. Dawson, I, 133.
14. Dawson, I, 130–132; Force, 4, V, 59 et seq., 170–171.

CHAPTER 58

The principal original authorities for this first battle of Charleston are John Drayton's *Memoirs of the American Revolution* (Charleston, 1821), William Moultrie's work of the same name, and Force's *American Archives*—a treasure house of contemporary letters and documents. McCrady's *The History of South Carolina in the Revolution, 1775–1780* is a very full and detailed account, based chiefly on Drayton and Moultrie. Gordon's and Stedman's histories are of value as contemporary relations, while Dawson and Carrington give excellent accounts.

1. McCrady, *R*, I, 6.
2. Bancroft, IV, 382.
3. Bancroft, IV, 383.
4. Fitzpatrick, IV, 221, 267, 271, 273.
5. Fitzpatrick, IV, 451.
6. Fitpatrick, IV, 221–223.
7. Trevelyan, Pt. II, Vol. II, 41–49; Bancroft, IV, 232–234, and V, 66–67; Irving, I, 413–419.
8. Force, 4, IV, 812; Bancroft, IV, 484.
9. Gordon, IV, 275.
10. Force, 4, IV, 1153; McCrady, *R*, I, 132–135; Gordon, II, 175.
11. Force, 4, IV, 807, 1062.

12. Force, 4, IV, 830.
13. Force, 4, IV, 1538; *Journals*, IV, 201–204.
14. *Journals*, IV, 157, 206, 174.
15. Force, 4, IV, 1537.
16. Force, 4, IV, 733, and V, 928, 1517.
17. Force, 4, V, 80, 981.
18. James, 430.
19. Dawson, I, 135; Gordon, II, 279; Stedman, I, 183.
20. McCrady, R, I, 132, citing *Annual Register*, XIX, 157; Stedman, I, 183; Force, 4, V, 981; Gordon, II, 279.
21. Stedman, I, 184.
22. Force, 4, V, 1220, and VI, 720.
23. Moultrie, I, 141.
24. McCrady, R, I, 13, 126–127.
25. Force, 4, VI, 1188.
26. McCrady, R, I, 145; Dawson, I, 140; Moultrie, I, 142.
27. Force, 4, VI, 1206; Stedman, I, 186; Bancroft, IV, 405; Carrington, 188.
28. Gordon, II, 280.
29. Gordon, II, 282; Moultrie, I, 174.
30. Force, 4, VI, 1210.
31. Moultrie, I, 178.
32. Force, 4, VI, 1210; Moultrie, I, 175.
33. Bancroft, IV, 403.
34. Force, 4, VI, 1129; Moultrie, I, 176.
35. Force, 4, VI, 206.
36. Gordon, II, 284–286; Ramsay, R, I, 147; Dawson, I, 140; McCrady, R, I, 159.
37. McCrady, R, I, 144; Moultrie, I, 141.
38. Moultrie, I, 142.

CHAPTER 59

1. Sparks, W, V, 549.
2. Ramsay, II, 130.
3. Dawson, I, 476.
4. Ramsay, II, 130–131.
5. Dawson, I, 476.
6. Jones, C, II, 323. The best original authority for this Battle of Savannah is Campbell's very fully detailed dispatch to Germain in Dawson, I, 477–479. Dawson, as usual, gives a good account, as also do Ramsay, Jones, C, and Henry Lee.
7. The affair at Beaufort is fully covered by Moultrie's dispatch to Lincoln and a letter from an American officer, in Dawson, I, 482–484.
8. Ramsay, R, II, 14.
9. Garden, II, Appendix, xvi. Contemporary accounts of the Kettle Creek encounter are to be found in Stedman, Ramsay, R, Marshall, and Garden. Detailed secondary accounts are in McCrady, R, I, Jones, C, and Dawson.
10. Contemporary accounts of the action at Briar Creek are to be found in Dawson, I, 492–494, also in Stedman, Lee, Gordon, Lamb, and Ramsay, R.
11. Dawson, I, 497.
12. Ramsay, R, II, 32. First-hand accounts of this affair may be found in Dawson, I, 501–503. Other contemporary accounts are in Ramsay, R, Marshall, Lee, Gordon, Stedman.

CHAPTER 60

1. Jones, C, II, 384. Contemporary accounts of the siege of Savannah are to be found in Stedman, Ramsay, R, Marshall, Gordon, Lee, Lincoln's diary, Moultrie's memoirs, and the dispatches of various officers, cited in Dawson, I, 562–569.

CHAPTER 61

Contemporary accounts of the siege of Charleston are to be found in Ramsay, *R,* Tarleton, Lee, Gordon, Stedman, Marshall, Moultrie's memoirs, and the various dispatches cited in Dawson, also in Uhlendorf.

1. McCrady, *R,* I, 431.
2. McCrady, *R,* I, 500.
3. Moultrie's memoirs say that only 1,500 to 1,600 Continentals marched out, 500 being in hospital, but careful calculations in McCrady, *R,* I, 507–510, show that there were 2,650 Continentals in the garrison.

CHAPTER 62

1. Contemporary accounts of the affair at the Waxhaws are in Marshall, Ramsay, *R,* Gordon, Lee, Stedman, Moultrie, Tarleton, and in various letters cited in Dawson. The English Stedman, II, 193, gives Tarleton's troops credit for activity and ardor, but admits that "the virtue of humanity was totally forgot."
2. The best contemporary account of the engagement at Ramsour's Mills was written for Gen. Joseph Graham—first published in the *Catawba Journal,* Charlotte, N.C., in 1825 and reprinted in full in Schenck, 51–62. Other such accounts are in the works cited in note 1.
3. The story of the encounter at Williamson's plantation in Dawson, I, 601–603, differs in details (particularly as to the numbers engaged) from the much fuller account in McCrady, *R,* I, 594–599, which has been followed in this narrative.
4. Gordon, Ramsay, *R,* Stedman, Lee, and Tarleton are the contemporary sources for the skirmish at Rocky Mount.
5. Tarleton, Lee, Gordon, and Stedman furnish contemporary accounts of the Hanging Rock affair. Davie's narrative is copiously cited in Dawson.

CHAPTER 63

1. Fitzpatrick, XVIII, 197–198.
2. Carrington, 491.
3. Kapp, *passim.*
4. Fitzpatrick, XVIII, 226–227, 243, 257–258.
5. Gordon, III, 390; Carrington, 514; Winsor, VI, 475.
6. Kapp, 179, 198.
7. Kirkwood, 9.
8. Kapp, 198–199.
9. Fitzpatrick, XVIII, 265.
10. Kirkwood, 10.
11. Kapp, 200.
12. Kapp, 203; Bancroft, V, 384. North Carolina was "solely occupied with" providing for "her own militia" (Johnson, I, 485).
13. Kirkwood, 10.
14. Moore, II, 310.
15. Kapp, 202; Gordon, III, 390.
16. Kapp, 203; Gordon, III, 391.
17. Fiske, II, 190; Bancroft, V, 384.
18. Kapp, 203; Bancroft, V, 384; *Journals,* XVII, 508.

CHAPTER 64

1. Kapp, 205.
2. Gordon, III, 392; Kapp, 207.
3. Lossing, II, 462.

4. Schneck, 86.
5. Greene, GW, III, 17–18; Fiske, II, 192; McCrady, *R*, I, 658; Johnson, I, 294.
6. McCrady, *R*, I, 659.
7. Greene, GW, III, 18–19; Johnson, I, 294.
8. Kapp, 207–208; Gordon, III, 429–430; Johnson, I, 487.
9. Gordon, III, 430–431; Kapp, 212; Greene, GW, III, 19–20; Johnson, I, 487.
10. Kapp, 209; Irving, III, 92; Johnson, I, 294, 486.
11. Greene, GW, III, 20.
12. Johnson, I, 506; McCrady, *R*, I, 659.
13. McCrady, *R*, I, 657; Greene, GW, III, 21; Gordon, III, 430. The number of men in Porterfield's force is variously stated. McCrady, *R*, I, 520, 837, says 400. Gordon, III, 430, says 100. Lossing, II, 464, says 100. Dawson, I, 613, says there were 800 Virginians in all. This includes Stevens's 700. Colonel Otho Williams calls it "a small detachment" (Johnson, I, 488).
14. Greene, GW, III, 22; Johnson, I, 295, 488.
15. Seymour, 4.
16. Greene, GW, III, 22; Kapp, 215; Gordon, III, 432; Johnson, I, 488.
17. Greene, GW, III, 23; Kapp, 216–217; Gordon, III, 431.
18. Greene, GW, III, 23; Kapp, 217; Winsor, VI, 476; Johnson, I, 489.
19. Though Caswell's force had been figured at 1,200 originally, Dawson computes it at 2,100 at this time, by deducting the strength of the other contingents from the known total strength of Gates's army. There may have been additions bringing up his original number to this figure.
20. Greene, GW, III, 25–26; Kapp, 219; Johnson, I, 491. One finds it difficult to realize that, in the eighteenth century, all armies had their trains of camp followers, even of women and children. Many of the women were wives of the men in the ranks; others had more temporary and more promiscuous attachments. They played their part in the camps, washing the soldiers' clothes, cooking their food, and so on. They were so customary and usual that the historians take them for granted and seldom mention them except on occasions such as this, when they were sent away.
21. Kapp, 219.
22. Kapp, 219–220; Tarleton, 102, comments on this failure of Gates to use his opportunity: "He had not sufficient penetration to conceive that by a forced march up the creek, he could have passed Lord Rawdon's flank and reached Camden which would have been an easy conquest and a fatal blow to the British."
23. Kapp, 220; Gordon, III, 433; Tarleton, 104.
24. Kapp, 220; Greene, GW, III, 25; Gordon, III, 434.

CHAPTER 65

The original sources for the Battle of Camden are Otho Williams's narrative, in Johnson, I, 485–510; Gates's dispatch to the Congress, in Tarleton, 148–151; Tarleton, 107–111; Cornwallis's dispatch to Germain in Tarleton, 132–137; Lamb, 302–305. Other contemporaneous accounts are in Gordon, III, 432–442; Lee, 182–185; and Ramsay, *R*, II, 146–149. Later full descriptions are in Dawson, I, 613–619; Carrington, 514–518; and McCrady, *R*, I, 666–680.

1. Gordon, III, 433; Kapp, 220; Lee, 180; Johnson, I, 492.
2. Kapp, 205.
3. Tarleton, 139.
4. Gordon, III, 436. Carrington, 514, makes the Continentals 1,400, but he evidently overlooked natural wastage of the original number.
5. Johnson, I, 487–493.
6. Johnson, I, 493.
7. Johnson, I, 493. Lee, 182 n., comments on the fact that Armand's corps was

made up chiefly of deserters from the British army. "It was the last corps in the army which ought to have been intrusted with the van post."

8. Greene, GW, III, 26; Kapp, 224. That he actually so boasted is doubtful. His intention seems to have been to advance no farther than Sanders Creek, not to Camden and attack it in the morning.
9. Johnson, I, 495; Kapp, 221; Greene, GW, III, 26–27.
10. Seymour, 5.
11. Johnson, I, 494.
12. Greene, GW, III, 27; Kapp, 226; Lossing, II, 465.
13. Johnson, I, 297, 494; Kapp, 226; Greene, GW, III, 27.
14. Tarleton, 107; Johnson, I, 297, 494.
15. Tarleton, 107; Kapp, 227; Greene, GW, III, 27; Gordon, III, 437; Lee, 182.
16. Heitman, 448.
17. Johnson, I, 494; Kapp, 227.
18. Johnson, I, 495; Greene, GW, III, 27; Kapp, 227.
19. Greene, GW, III, 28; Kapp, 227–228; Gordon, III, 438.
20. Kapp, 226, 229; Carrington, 516.
21. Johnson, I, 495, quoting Otho Williams's narrative. Kapp, 230, says the American artillery was divided, two guns in Gist's right wing, two on the center, and two on the left. But Williams ought to have known.
22. Tarleton, 108–109, 135; Dawson, I, 616.
23. Johnson, I, 495; Greene, GW, III, 28–29; Kapp, 231; Gordon, III, 439.
24. Carrington, 516.
25. Johnson, I, 497; Kapp, 231; Greene, GW, III, 28; Gordon, III, 440; Carrington, 516–517; Dawson, I, 617; Schenck, 89. Colonel Dixon had seen service in the Continental army under Washington. To his experience and firmness Lee, 187, ascribes much of the merit of his regiment. "Yet praise," he says, "is nevertheless due to the troops. Dixon's regiment held its ground for some time, even beat back the enemy, but was swept away before the final debacle."
26. Bancroft, V, 388; Schenck, 88; Greene, GW, III, 20. Gordon, III, 446, writes: "Smallwood had been separated from the first Maryland brigade, after the men had been engaged a while and finding it impractical to rejoin them, as well as apprehending they must be overpowered and could not retreat, rode off for personal safety."
27. Bancroft, V, 388; Dawson, I, 617; Carrington, 517; Kapp, 232; Greene, GW, III, 30; Gordon, III, 440.
28. Lossing, II, 467.
29. Bancroft, V, 388.
30. Dawson, I, 618.
31. Fiske, II, 196.
32. Kapp, 235.
33. Gordon, III, 443; Lee, 186; Lossing, II, 467; Kapp, 234; Dawson, I, 618.
34. Johnson, I, 497; Dawson, I, 618; Tarleton, 111.
35. Gordon, III, 443; Kapp, 236.
36. Moore, 312 n.

CHAPTER 66

1. Marshall, I, 405; Fiske, II, 197.
2. Seymour, 6.
3. Tarleton, 111–112; Johnson, I, 498.
4. Seymour, 7.
5. Johnson, I, 501.
6. Seymour, 7.
7. Schenck, 99.
8. Schenck, 99, 100; Greene, FV, 220.
9. Tarleton, 140–141.
10. Dawson, I, 619.

11. Gordon, III, 442–443.
12. Gordon, III, 459; Seymour, 7; Lee, 208.
13. *Archives*, III, 1343; Bennett, 459.
14. Lee, 208; Schenck, 184.
15. Gibbes, I, 12; Gordon, III, 455.
16. Bancroft, V, 390; Tarleton, 114–119; Gordon, III, 447; Seymour, 7.
17. Gordon, III, 459, 469. Schenck, 183, says Buford brought "the mangled remnant of his regiment and 200 recruits." Gordon, 460, says his regiment was recruited "to about 200 men." The words "cut to pieces" are advisedly used. Bancroft, V, 378, says that Buford and about 100 men "saved themselves by flight. The rest, making no resistance, vainly sued for quarter. . . . A hundred and thirteen were killed on the spot; a hundred and fifty were too badly hacked to be moved; fifty-three only could be brought to Camden as prisoners."
18. Seymour, 8; Kirkwood, 11. Gordon, III, 461, Bancroft, V, 477, and Schenck, 184, say that there were four companies of light infantry, but do not name the commanders. It may be that they regarded the Virginia riflemen as the fourth company.
19. Fiske, II, 260–261; Bancroft, V, 476.
20. *Journals*, XVII, 319, and XVIII, 921.
21. Gordon, III, 459; Greene, GW, III, 32.
22. Bennett, 456. Otho Williams reports (Johnson, I, 501) on the behavior of the Continentals in their difficult situation at Hillsboro: "Absolutely without pay; almost destitute of clothing; often with only a half-ration and never with a whole one . . . not a soldier was heard to murmur after the third or fourth day of their being encamped . . . they filled up the intervals from duty with manly exercises and field-sports." Inducements to desert were offered—rum in particular, of which "most desirable refreshment" they had none—but without effect. On the contrary, they brought "some of the most bold and importunate incendiaries" to their officers for punishment.
23. Johnson, I, 508.

CHAPTER 67

1. Fisher, II, 337–338.
2. Tarleton, 153. Marshall, Stedman, Lee, and Lamb give contemporary accounts of the affair at Wahab's Plantation. McCrady has a good secondary account.
3. Lee, Stedman, Tarleton, and Lamb give contemporary accounts of the affair at Charlotte. Schenck's narrative is full of detail.
4. Irving, IV, 51.
5. Schenck, 119.
6. A good account of Ferguson is in Wilkin, 152–171. Lamb, 308–309, has a sympathetic description.
7. Lee, Marshall, Ramsay, Tarleton, Moultrie, and Gordon give contemporary accounts of King's Mountain, but the very full and authenticated story in Draper supersedes all others.
8. Bancroft, V, 401; Lee, 201–203; Schenck, 178–182.
9. Seymour, 8.
10. Tarleton, Stedman, Marshall, Ramsay, and Gordon have contemporary accounts of this affair. McCrady, *R*, I, 820–823, gives a full account.
11. Contemporary accounts of the affair at Blackstock's may be found in Ramsay, Lee, Tarleton, Stedman, and a more detailed secondary account in McCrady, *R*, I, 824–829.

CHAPTER 68

1. *Journals*, XVIII, 906. The resolution also directed Washington to order a court of inquiry into the conduct of Gates in his late campaign, and the tenure of office of the new general to be appointed was limited in time "until such enquiry

be made." It never was made, and Greene continued to hold his place without special limitation.

2. Fitzpatrick, XX, 181–182; *Journals*, XVIII, 994–996.
3. Greene, GW, III, 35–36.
4. Greene, GW, III, 39–47.
5. Greene, GW, III, 48–64.
6. Johnson, I, 510.
7. Greene, GW, III, 68–70.
8. Reed, II, 344, 346.
9. Sparks, C, III, 189; Gordon, IV, 30.
10. Sparks, C, III, 189.
11. Gordon, IV, 30; Greene, FV, 226.
12. Fisher, II, 378.
13. Fisher, II, 377.
14. Johnson, I, 346; Lee, 222; Greene, FV, 226.
15. Greene, FV, 226; Fisher, II, 380.
16. Johnson, I, 346.
17. Greene, GW, III, 91.
18. Johnson, I, 50; Gordon, IV, 32.
19. Kirkwood, 13; Seymour, 11–12.
20. Gordon, IV, 31; Schenck, 200.
21. Gordon, IV, 31; Greene, GW, III, 135; Seymour, 12.
22. Lee, 222; Schenck, 199; Greene, GW, III, 133.
23. Lee, 224.
24. Greene, FV, 228; Fortescue, III, 365. There is doubt as to the number of men Leslie brought to Winnsboro. Some accounts give him 3,000 when he left New York, others 2,500. Some historians imply that he brought his whole force to Winnsboro; but this is obviously not so, else Cornwallis would have had more than 4,000 men there. The truth seems to be that he actually added 1,500, leaving the rest at Wilmington. See Greene, GW, III, 137; Stedman, II, 317; McCrady, R, II, 17. Tarleton, 216, says 1,530.
25. Tarleton, 214.
26. Fortescue, III, 366; Greene, FV, 228.
27. Fortescue, III, 366; Greene, GW, III, 138.
28. Tarleton, 250, 252.

CHAPTER 69

This account of the Battle of Cowpens is based on contemporary accounts in Tarleton, Lee, Gordon, Stedman, Ramsay, supplemented by McCrady and by Dawson's very full, annotated description.

1. Dawson, I, 647; Greene, GW, III, 138; Gordon, IV, 33; Schenck, 205. The 3-pounders were not mounted on wheeled carriages but propped up on legs, hence the resemblance to a grasshopper. On the march, they were carried on horseback.
2. McCrady, R, II, 30–31.
3. McCrady, R, II, 23, 32.
4. Stedman, II, 320; McCrady, R, II, 30.
5. Fisher, II, 353.
6. McCrady, R, II, 35; Dawson, II, 648; Lossing, II, 430.
7. Johnson, I, 576.
8. Lee, 226.
9. Greene, GW, III, 140, 144.
10. Johnson, I, 377; Schenck, 209; Lossing, II, 433–434.
11. Johnson, I, 377–379; Dawson, 649; Marshall, I, 471; Schenck, 211–212; Greene, GW, III, 142.
12. Stedman, II, 320; Dawson, I, 648.

13. The accounts of casualties on both sides are, as usual, conflicting. The numbers stated in the text are taken from Greene, FV, 230, after comparison with the various contemporary narratives.
14. Fortescue, III, 368.
15. Marshall, I, 368.
16. Trevelyan, VI, 154–155.

CHAPTER 70

1. Greene, FV, 231.
2. Johnson, I, 385.
3. Johnson, I, 386–387.
4. Seymour, 15; Kirkwood, 13; Schenck, 228; Johnson, I, 386.
5. Schenck, 227; Fortescue, III, 370.
6. Fortescue, III, 371; Stedman, II, 325; Johnson, I, 387.
7. Fortescue, III, 376; Stedman, II, 325.
8. Fortescue, III, 370; Johnson, I, 388.
9. Seymour, 15.
10. Johnson, I, 389; Stedman, II, 326; Fortescue, III, 371; Trevelyan, VI, 156; Gordon, IV, 37; Schenck, 234; Lee, 232.
11. Schenck, 230.
12. Fortescue, III, 371; Stedman, II, 327; Lee, 233; Sparks, C, III, 225.
13. Gordon, IV, 41–42.
14. Greene, GW, III, 154, 158; Gordon, IV, 38–39; Johnson, I, 404.
15. Gordon, IV, 38–39; Johnson, I, 407.
16. Fortescue, III, 371; Stedman, II, 326; Schenck, 234, 237.
17. Schenck, 236–237.
18. Tarleton, 230; Dawson, I, 655; Stedman, II, 327.
19. Schenck, 238–239.
20. Schenck, 238; Stedman, II, 327–328; Sparks, C, III, 226; Lee, 233–234; Fortescue, III, 371–372; Dawson, I, 655–656; Greene, GW, III, 155–157; Kirkwood, 13; Seymour, 15–16.
21. Schenck, 251. Tarleton, 270, modest as usual, acknowledges that he "with excellent conduct and great spirit attacked" the militia at Tarrant's Tavern "instantly and totally routed them." Against this huddle of militia, whose rifles had been wet by the rain so that few of them would fire, and who had emerged from the tavern wishing only to get away, he "resolved to hazard one charge . . . he desired his soldiers to advance and *remember the Cowpens.* Animated by this reproach, a furious contest ensued. They broke through the centre with irresistible velocity, killing near fifty on the spot, wounded many in the pursuit and dispersed near five hundred of the enemy." According to Irving, IV, 251, there were about a hundred in this party of militia. Greene, GW, III, 157, says three hundred, and a British officer who rode over the ground soon after the attack, saw only ten dead bodies on the ground (Stedman, II, 329 n.).
22. Schenck, 252. Greene, GW, III, 259, tells of a tradition that a portrait of George III hung over the fireplace when General Greene received this gift. He turned its face to the wall and wrote on the back of it, "Hide thy face, George, and blush."

CHAPTER 71

1. Greene, FV, 232.
2. Tarleton, 236.
3. Sparks, C, III, 226.
4. Fortescue, III, 371–372; Stedman, II, 330; Schenck, 253.
5. Johnson, I, 419; Schenck, 253.
6. Stedman, II, 331; Fortescue, III, 372; Tarleton, 271.
7. Kirkwood, 13.

8. Seymour, 16.
9. Johnson, I, 425–426; Stedman, II, 331; Gordon, IV, 42–43; Lee, 236; Marshall, I, 475.
10. Johnson, I, 427, 429; Sparks, *C*, III, 227, 234; Stedman, II, 331; Lee, 236–237.
11. Johnson, I, 429–430.
12. Kirkwood, 13; Seymour, 16; Greene, GW, III, 168.
13. Johnson, I, 430.
14. Greene, GW, III, 165
15. Lee, 248 n.
16. Gordon, IV, 44–45.
17. Lee, 237–247.

CHAPTER 72

1. Greene, FV, 236.
2. Tarleton, 263. Seymour, 17, says: "A vast number of the inhabitants joined them [the British], taking the oath of allegiance, and many more they compelled to do the same, forcing them away from their wives and children."
3. Johnson, I, 433–434.
4. Kirkwood, 13; Johnson, I, 433–434.
5. Lee, 253.
6. Lee, 256–258. Lee's story of his amicable intentions towards Pyle's men is hard to credit; it has too much the air of an afterthought to palliate a piece of strategy fully matured and intentionally executed, whose outcome shocked its author. Stedman, II, 334, says that Pyle's men cried for mercy, "but no quarter was granted; and between two and three hundred were inhumanly butchered, while in the act of begging for mercy. Humanity shudders at the recital of such a massacre." The bloody results of the attack are, in themselves, sufficient proof of its relentless ferocity.
7. Johnson, I, 443.
8. Johnson, I, 449.
9. Gordon, IV, 50; Johnson, I, 444.
10. Stedman, II, 337. Stedman himself was the commissary that slaughtered the oxen and made the requisitions.
11. Gordon, IV, 49; Johnson, I, 448.
12. Tarleton, 273.
13. Fortescue, III, 373.
14. Lee, 259; Gordon, IV, 49.
15. Gordon, IV, 49; Lossing, II, 399; Greene, GW, III, 184–185; Johnson, I, 461.
16. Lee, 264; Lossing, II, 399; Greene, GW, III, 185.
17. Kirkwood, 15–16; Greene, GW, III, 186–187.
18. Lee, 264; Greene, GW, III, 188.
19. Lee, 266–267; Stedman, II, 336; Tarleton, 242–243; Gordon, IV, 51–52; Johnson, I, 463.
20. Johnson, I, 438; Lee, 269; Greene, GW, III, 189.
21. Johnson, I, 472.
22. Kirkwood, 14. Kirkwood says merely "one [company] from Virginia"; but as in the battle at Guilford Court House, Washington's horse, Kirkwood's company, and Lynch's riflemen were posted in one group it seems fairly certain that the identification in the text is correct.

CHAPTER 73

1. Johnson, II, 2–3; Gordon, IV, 54.
2. Johnson, II, 3.
3. Fortescue, III, 374 n.
4. Fortescue, III, 375; Schenck, 316–317. There are maps in Stedman, II, 342; Schenck, 320; Greene, FV, 238.

5. Johnson, II, 4; Schenck, 328; Stedman, II, 337.
6. Lee, 272–275; Stedman, II, 337; Johnson, II, 4; Tarleton, 278.
7. Schenck, 321–322.
8. Schenck, 322–328; Johnson, II, 4–6.
9. Lossing, II, 402.
10. Fortescue, III, 375; Greene, FV, 238; Schenck, 330.
11. Schenck, 335–345.
12. Lamb, 361.
13. They ran because they could not face the enemy bayonets, having none of their own. They had no time to reload their rifles. It took three minutes to do that. They ran fast, because that was the sensible thing to do; in disorder, because they were not trained soldiers, but a mere collection of individuals having no formation.
14. Fortescue, III, 376.
15. Stedman, II, 339. Stedman was in this battle.
16. Seymour, 20–21.
17. This account of the battle is partly based on accounts of participants: Lee, 272–285; Tarleton, 276–286; Stedman, II, 337–347; Lamb, 345–357; and Seymour 20–21. The contemporary account in Marshall, I, 480–487, has been consulted, and also later accounts in Johnson, II, 1–15; Schenck, 320–372; Fortescue, III, 374–380; Greene, FV, 338–342; and Greene, GW, III, 190–202.

CHAPTER 74

1. Trevelyan, VI, 166.
2. Tarleton, 286; Lee, 286–287; Johnson, II, 26.
3. Lee, 287.
4. Lee, 289; Johnson, II, 27.
5. Stedman, II, 352.
6. Tarleton, 289.
7. Stedman, II, 352.
8. Stedman, II, 354; Tarleton, 291, 334–335, 337–338.
9. Tarleton, 333, 334–335. On Cornwallis's decision to march into Virginia see Willcox, 11–14.
10. Sparks, C, III, 378.
11. Greene, FV, 244.
12. Schenck, 394.
13. Wilkin, 74–83.
14. Greene, GW, III, 233–234; Lee, 325; Schenck, 399.
15. Schenck, 399–400; Lee, 325; Johnson, II, 44; Greene, GW, III, 231–235.
16. Greene, GW, III, 233.
17. Lossing, II, 500; Stedman, II, 360.
18. Lee, 332; Lossing, II, 500; Stedman, II, 360.
19. Kirkwood, 16; Seymour, 24.
20. Greene, GW, III, 271–272.
21. Stedman, II, 356; Fortescue, III, 386; Schenck, 400.
22. Greene, GW, III, 241.
23. Kirkwood, 16. Seymour, 24, says they "brought away 350 horses and cattle."
24. Lee, 334, 335; Greene, GW, III, 242, 243; Seymour, 24.

CHAPTER 75

This account of the battle is largely based on the contemporary and later accounts, in Stedman, II, 355–358; Tarleton, 474–485; Lee, 334–341; Seymour, 24–26; Gordon, IV, 81–85; Ramsay, R, II, 230–231; Greene, GW, III, 243–251; Johnson, II, 76–85; McCrady, R, II, 188–198; Schenck, 400–412.

1. Greene, GW, III, 243; Schenck, 402; Lee, 336.
2. Johnson, II, 77; Schenck, 403; Lee, 336.
3. Lee, 336; Greene, GW, III, 245.
4. Greene, GW, III, 245.
5. Greene, GW, III, 245.
6. Johnson, II, 77.
7. Greene, GW, III, 244; Schenck, 403–404; Greene, FV, 246; Johnson, II, 77.
8. Fortescue, III, 386; Johnson, II, 79; Schenck, 404.
9. Greene, GW, III, 252.
10. Greene, GW, III, 253.

CHAPTER 76

1. Greene, GW, III, 257, 262; Johnson, II, 83; Lee, 342.
2. Lee, 342, 344; Greene, GW, III, 267; Kirkwood, 17; Seymour, 26.
3. Tarleton, 492; Greene, GW, III, 271, 276; Lee, 344; Gordon, IV, 88.
4. Greene, GW, III, 271, 276; Lee, 344; Kirkwood, 17.
5. Tarleton, 492; Lee, 344; Greene, GW, III, 276.
6. Greene, GW, III, 254; Reed, II, 353.
7. Greene, GW, III, 265.
8. Greene, GW, III, 264–265; Gordon, IV, 87–88; Reed, II, 351–353.
9. Greene, GW, III, 265.
10. Gordon, III, 89; Kirkwood, 17; Seymour, 26.
11. Greene, GW, III, 277.
12. Lee, 345.
13. Sparks, *C*, III, 510; Tarleton, 490–494; Lee, 344–345; Greene, GW, III, 277; Gordon, IV, 89; Lossing, II, 475.
14. Kirkwood, 17; Seymour, 27.
15. Lee, 345.
16. Sparks, *C*, III, 310.
17. Dawson, I, 689–692; Lossing, II, 683; Lee, 345–349; Gordon, IV, 89–90; Greene, GW, III, 278–279.
18. Lee, 349; Greene, GW, III, 280.
19. Lee, 349–352.
20. Ramsay, II, 318; Schenck, 415.
21. Lee, 353–358, 360–371; Gordon, IV, 91; Dawson, I, 673–679.

CHAPTER 77

1. Lossing, II, 483–484.
2. Dawson, I, 692; Johnson, II, 140; Lossing, II, 485.
3. Stedman, II, 366; Lossing, II, 484; Johnson, II, 139.
4. Johnson, II, 140–141.
5. Lossing, II, 485 n.
6. Johnson, II, 141; Stedman, II, 367.
7. Stedman, II, 367; Dawson, I, 693; Lossing, II, 485.
8. Stedman, II, 368; Dawson, I, 693.
9. Stedman, II, 368, 369.
10. Lee, 371–372.
11. Lee, 373–374; Lossing, II, 486.
12. Stedman, II, 370.
13. Johnson, II, 148; Lossing, II, 486; Lee, 374.
14. Fortescue, III, 388–389; Stedman, II, 371.
15. Lee, 375.
16. Greene, GW, III, 312; Lee, 376; Johnson, II, 149.
17. Lee, 377; Greene, GW, III, 313–314; Kirkwood, 19; Seymour, 28.
18. Lee, 376–378; Johnson, II, 149–150.
19. Stedman, II, 373; Greene, FV, 252.

CHAPTER 78

1. Tarleton, 523.
2. The narrative of the American army's movements after Ninety-six has been derived chiefly from Lee, 377–386; Stedman, II, 374–375; Greene, GW, III, 318–322; Johnson, II, 152–165; Lossing, II, 488–489; McCrady, *R*, II, 300–440. The quotations about food and the condition of the army are from Lee, 385.
3. Greene, III, 334; Lee, 448.
4. Greene, III, 332–334; Lee, 386–394.
5. Wilkin, 86–89.
6. Johnson, II, 208, 216; Greene, GW, III, 385.
7. Lossing, II, 491.
8. Johnson, II, 218; Greene, GW, III, 386. These are Johnson's figures. Greene, FV, 254, gives a total of 2,300, 1,254 being Continentals. Lee, 465, gives a total of 2,300, of which 1,600 were Continentals, horse, foot, and artillery.
9. Johnson, II, 230; Greene, FV, 254. Fortescue, III, 380, allows Stuart "fewer than 1,600 effective men." On the other hand, Lossing, II, 491, states that, when they left the High Hills only 1,600 Americans "were fit for active duty."
10. Johnson, II, 220.
11. Tarleton, 524; Stedman, II, 377.
12. Lossing, II, 492; Johnson, II, 224.
13. Tarleton, 524.
14. Tarleton, 525; Stedman, II, 378; Fortescue, III, 389; Johnson, II, 222; Lee, 466. The number in the rooting party and its fate are left in doubt by the conflicting statements of the authorities. According to Stedman there were 400, and they "fell an easy prey to Greene's army"; "a few straggling horsemen escaped" and brought the news to Stuart. Johnson says there were 100, and they were captured. Lee says there were 200 or 300, and they escaped. Fortescue says there were 100, and all were captured except the cavalry guard. Stuart's report to Cornwallis (quoted in Tarleton, 525) makes the number 400.
15. Dawson, I, 713; Lossing, II, 484; Johnson, II, 220.
16. Lee, 466.
17. Greene, GW, III, 393; Lee, 466; Johnson, II, 222.
18. Lee, 467; Stedman, II, 378; Lossing, II, 495; Fortescue, III, 390; Carrington, 379–381.
19. Lee, 467; Lossing, II, 495; Johnson, II, 223.
20. Johnson, II, 225.
21. Fortescue, III, 390.
22. McCrady, *R*, II, 454.
23. Fortescue, III, 392.
24. Kirkwood, 23. This account of the battle has been derived from Lee, 475–478; Stedman, II, 377–381; Gordon, IV, 167–172; Greene, GW, III, 384–402; Lossing, II, 492–499; Schenck, 444–459; Fortescue, III, 389–392; McCrady, *R*, II, 442–463.
25. Fortescue, III, 392.
26. Gordon, IV, 171.
27. Tarleton, 533.
28. Greene, FV, 257. Stuart reported to Cornwallis 525 casualties, including 247 missing. As the prisoners taken by the Americans numbered well over 400, this report is plainly incorrect.
29. Greene, FV, 257.
30. *Journals*, XXI, 1084–1085.

CHAPTER 79

1. Lee, 474.
2. Lee, 475.
3. Lee, 475; Kirkwood, 25; Seymour, 31–32.

4. Kirkwood, 25–26; Seymour, 25–26, 32.
5. Johnson, II, 242.
6. Sparks, *C*, III, 430.
7. Greene, GW, III, 408.
8. Gordon, IV, 173–174.
9. Wraxall, II, 238.
10. Fisher, II, 504.
11. Stedman, II, 406; McCrady, *R*, II, 465–466.
12. Greene, GW, III, 421; Gordon, IV, 176.
13. Johnson, II, 268; Kirkwood, 27.
14. *Pennsylvania*, II, 703–705.
15. Bennett, 459; Lee, 524–525.
16. Seymour, 33; Lee, 525–526.
17. Lee, 529–536; Seymour, 33; Greene, GW, III, 431.
18. Jones, C, 505.
19. Jones, C, 505–520; Stillé, 286–291.
20. Bennett, 459.
21. Sparks, *C*, III, 490, and IV, 524; Gordon, IV, 292.
22. Lee, 517, 548; Greene, GW, III, 450.
23. Lee, 549, 565.
24. Johnson, II, 329.
25. Seymour, 39; Johnson, II, 339.
26. Johnson, II, 340–341; Seymour, 39–40; Bennett, 461.
27. Johnson, II, 343; Seymour, 40; Bennett, 460.
28. McCrady, *R*, II, 646–649.
29. Greene, FV, 257–258.
30. Trevelyan, VI, 176–178.
31. Fortescue, III, 409.

CHAPTER 80

1. Force, 4, II, 477, 516, 526, 539–541, 711, 1023, 1103, 1191.
2. Bancroft, IV, 146–147.
3. Bancroft, IV, 179; Force, 4, II, 465–466; Gordon, II, 85–91.
4. Force, 4, II, 516.
5. Gordon, II, 85–91; Bancroft, IV, 202, 254.
6. Bancroft, IV, 317.
7. Force, 4, III, 6, 1385.
8. Bancroft, IV, 317–318.
9. Force, 4, III, 1047, 1543, 1660, 1714, and IV, 342, 508, 615, 616 n.; Gordon, II, 114–115; Andrews, 312–313; *Journals*, III, 394, 415, 445.
10. Dawson, I, 122, 346; Force, 4, IV, 349–350; Lossing, II, 329.
11. Gordon, II, 114; Dawson, I, 112.
12. Force, 4, IV, 224, 228 n., 538.
13. Dawson, I, 122–124, 125–126; French, *F*, 576–577; Lossing, II, 329–330; Force, 4, IV, 538–539; Gordon, II, 112–113.
14. Force, 4, III, 1191, and IV, 577; Trevelyan, I, 345–346.
15. Gordon, II, 206; Lossing, II, 333; Force, 4, IV, 293.
16. Force, 4, IV, 53; Gordon, II, 206–207; Dawson, I, 126; Lossing, II, 333–334.
17. Gordon, II, 298–299; Force, 4, IV, 946.
18. Fitzpatrick, IV, 297.

CHAPTER 81

For some unknown reason Mr. Ward's manuscript, when it came to the editor, did not include a description of the war in the Ohio valley. It was thought necessary to insert a brief account of it, emphasizing the George Rogers Clark expedition of 1778–1779.

Writings concerning the war in the region of Beautiful River are too numerous to cite. In the nineteenth century Justin Winsor, Theodore Roosevelt, Consul W. Butterfield, Burke A. Hinsdale, and others made major contributions. Reuben G. Thwaites, Louise Phelps Kellogg, and others have since added greatly. George Rogers Clark has also been a favorite subject. William H. English published a useful account of Clark's exploits in the Old Northwest in 1896, followed seven years later by one written by Thwaites. In 1926 appeared Temple Bodley's biography of Clark. In 1930 James A. James's *Life of George Rogers Clark*, the best biography, was published. His volume is the basis for much of this chapter. Professor James also edited the *George Rogers Clark Papers, 1771–1784*, a very useful and convenient compilation.

1. James, *CP*, 22.
2. Bodley, 8; James, *C*, 114–115.
3. James, *C*, 30–32.
4. James, *CP*, 34, 36, 115–116; James, *C*, 114–115.
5. American colonial assemblies frequently offered handsome rewards for enemy Indian scalps. It has not been shown that, in practice, a distinction was made between a French scalp and that of a hostile Indian.
6. James, *C*, 143–144.
7. There is a facsimile of this message in James, *C*, opp. p. 144.
8. James, *C*, 148.
9. James, *C*, 149.
10. F. J. Teggart, "The Capture of St. Joseph," *Miss. Vall. Hist. Rev.*, XIX (1918), 214–228; Lawrence Kinnaird, "The Spanish Expedition Against Fort St. Joseph in 1781: A New Interpretation," *Miss. Vall. Hist. Rev.*, XIX (1932), 173–191.

CHAPTER 82

The best account of Lafayette's maneuvers is to be found in Gottschalk, *Lafayette and the Close of the American Revolution*, 189–306.

1. Fitzpatrick, XX, 122, 458, 473.
2. Sparks, *C*, III, 298.
3. Gordon, III, 260–261; Lee, 135; Jones, I, 295–296; James, 163; Stedman, II, 137–139.
4. Clinton, II, 12.
5. Clinton, II, 58–59.
6. Irving, IV, 289.
7. Dawson, I, 641; Stedman, II, 382.
8. Dawson, I, 642.
9. Dawson, I, 642; Sparks, *C*, III, 200; Simcoe, 159.
10. Simcoe, 160; Sparks, *C*, III, 200; Lee, 299.
11. Fitzpatrick, XX, 31, 147, 190, and XXI, 21; Lee, 298.
12. Sparks, *C*, III, 200.
13. Lee, 298–300.
14. Simcoe, 161–163; Dawson, I, 643.
15. Simcoe, 163; Sparks, *C*, III, 201.
16. Dawson, I, 644.
17. Sparks, *C*, III, 201.
18. Lossing, II, 237–238; Simcoe, 165–167; Dawson, I, 645.
19. Fitzpatrick, XXI, 231, 229.
20. Johnston, *Y*, 34.
21. Tower, II, 222–226.
22. James, 270–275.
23. Wilkin, 66; Gordon, IV, 62.
24. Dawson, I, 684–687; Stedman, II, 383; Simcoe, 189–197.
25. Dawson, I, 687–689; Simcoe, 198; Lee, 200.
26. Tower, II, 293.

27. Clinton, II, 77.
28. Johnston, Y, 37.
29. Lafayette, I, 417.
30. Clinton, II, 79–81; Johnston, Y, 38.
31. Stillé, 264, 286.
32. Simcoe, 212–219; Palmer, 275.
33. Simcoe, 220; Stedman, II, 389; Palmer, 279.
34. Tarleton, 303–305; Lee, 424.
35. Johnston, Y, 45; Stillé, 266.
36. Johnston, Y, 52.
37. Johnston, Y, 52–55.
38. Dawson, I, 698–700; Lee, 299; Simcoe, 225–237.
39. Dawson, I, 701–704; Gordon, IV, 117; Simcoe, 239; Lee, 301–304; Lamb, 373.
40. Lee, 436; Clinton, II, 132.
41. Greene, FV, 264.
42. Clinton, II, 126, 141, 145, 146, 164.
43. Clinton, II, 174.

CHAPTER 83

On the events and the strategy which led to the siege of Yorktown, the most recent and the best writings are to be found in Gottschalk, *Lafayette and the Close of the American Revolution*, 189–306; Willcox, "The British Road to Yorktown: A Study in Divided Command"; and Adams, "A View of Cornwallis's Surrender at Yorktown." Among the contemporary accounts on the British side, those published in Stevens are of the greatest importance.

1. Fitzpatrick, XXII, 103.
2. Fitzpatrick, XXII, 21.
3. Fitzpatrick, XXII, 103–107.
4. Fitzpatrick, XXII, 136, 325.
5. Fitzpatrick, XXII, 301–304.
6. Johnston, Y, 82–83; Fitzpatrick, XXII, 329–330.
7. Fitzpatrick, XXII, 330.
8. Greene, FV, 269.
9. Fitzpatrick, XXII, 429–433.
10. Sparks, W, VIII, 522–523.
11. Fitzpatrick, XXII, 501, and XXIII, 20.
12. Fitzpatrick, XXIII, 7.
13. Johnston, Y, 88–89.
14. Thacher, 268.
15. Sparks, W, V, 545.
16. Clinton, II, 193.
17. Johnston, Y, 87–88.
18. Sparks, L, I, 366.
19. Fitzpatrick, XXIII, 12; Fisher, II, 489.
20. Thacher, 271–272.
21. Johnston, Y, 96.
22. James, 444–445.
23. James, 289.
24. James, 288–294.

CHAPTER 84

This account of the Siege of Yorktown is based upon contemporary sources—Marshall, Fitzpatrick, Gordon, Clinton, Lafayette, Thacher, Lee, Tarleton, and Simcoe—as well as upon the various histories and biographies of the participants. Reliance has been placed upon Henry P. Johnston's able, exhaustive, and well documented monograph, *The Yorktown Campaign.* The account in Gottschalk, *Lafayette and the Close of the American Revolution,* 307–328, is also valuable.

1. Johnston, *Y,* 112–115.
2. Johnston, *Y,* 116–117.
3. Johnston, *Y,* 118–119.
4. Johnston, *Y,* 119–120.
5. Lossing, II, 304.
6. Lossing, II, 304 n.
7. Clinton, II, 198.
8. Clinton, II, 204.
9. Johnston, *Y,* 141 n.
10. Clinton, II, 205.
11. Stedman, II, 48.
12. Thacher, 346.
13. Wraxall, II, 238.
14. Johnston, *Y,* 160.

Abatis A defense formed by placing felled trees lengthwise, one over another, with the branches toward the enemy's line.

Amuse To occupy or divert the attention of the enemy from the real point of attack.

Banquette A raised step along the inside of a parapet or bottom of a trench, upon which soldiers stand to fire at the enemy.

Bastion A pointed projecting part of a fortification thrust out from the face of the main line or at an angle at its corners.

Battalion A body of soldiers, consisting of several companies and being part of a regiment. In the Revolutionary War a full regiment was often called a battalion.

Battalion companies The companies left in a regiment after the grenadier and light infantry companies had been withdrawn from it.

Berm The narrow space between the ditch and the base of the parapet of a fortification.

Brigade A subdivision of an army composed of two or more regiments.

Canister Small round shot packed in a case fitting the bore of a cannon, which scatter on its discharge.

Carcass An iron shell packed with ignited combustibles and pierced with holes through which the flame blazes, for setting fire to buildings or ships.

Chandelier A wooden frame filled with fascines.

Chevaux-de-frise A framework of heavy timbers fitted with iron spikes on top used to check infantry, and also sunk in a channel to prevent the passage of ships.

Cohorn A small mortar for throwing grenades.

Column A formation of troops narrow laterally and deep from front to rear.

Counterscarp The outer wall or slope of the ditch surrounding a fortification.

Covered way A space about thirty feet broad extending around the counterscarp of the ditch, being covered by the parapet.

Curtain The part of the wall of a fortification connecting its bastions.

Demilune An outwork, like a curved bastion, to protect a bastion or curtain.

Deploy To spread troops out from a column into a line of battle.

Dragoon A mounted infantryman; but often used in the sense of cavalryman.

Embrasure An opening in a parapet to permit the firing of a gun.

Epaulement The shoulder of a bastion where it meets the curtain, or a simple outwork added to a fortification.

Fascine   A long, cylindrical bundle of brushwood or the like, firmly bound together, used to fill ditches, construct batteries, etc.

Fieldpiece   A light, portable cannon for use on a field of battle.

Flank   The side of a marching column or the end of a line of battle.

Flank companies   The companies of grenadiers and light infantry drawn from a regiment.

Flèche   A small earthwork, V-shaped and open at the rear.

Forlorn hope   A picked body of soldiers, detached to the front to begin the attack; a storming party.

Fraise   A palisade of pointed timbers planted in an upward slanting position.

Gabion   A cylindrical wicker basket open at both ends, to be filled with earth and used in fortifying a position or erecting a battery.

Glacis   The sloping approach to the parapet of a covered way.

Grapeshot   Small iron balls enclosed in an open frame fitting the bore of a gun, which scatter when the gun is discharged.

Grasshopper   A 3-pound cannon, so called because it was mounted on legs instead of a wheeled carriage.

Gun   Any firearm except a pistol, but usually a cannon of whatever caliber and not a musket or rifle.

Howitzer   A short, light gun to fire a heavy projectile at a high angle of elevation and low velocity.

Invalids   Soldiers disabled for active service.

Linstock   Instrument holding slow matches with which cannon were fired.

Mask   To hinder or hold from activity an enemy fortification or body of troops.

Matross   A soldier next in rank below an artilleryman, assisting with the guns.

Merlon   The part of a parapet between two embrasures.

Mortar   A short piece of ordnance with a large bore having trunnions on its breech to throw shells at high angles.

Ordnance   Heavy guns.

Parallels   Trenches approaching a fortification by a series of zigzags.

Parapet   The wall of a fortification.

Partisans   Irregular troops, guerrillas.

Picket   A small, detached body of troops set out in front of a camp to discover the approach of the enemy.

Platoon   A small body or squad of infantry acting as a unit, as when firing.

Pound   The rating of a gun by the weight of its projectile.

Provincials   Troops raised in the colonies on the side of Great Britain; Tory troops.

Quarter   Exemption from being put to death, granted to vanquished troops.

Rank and file   The common soldiers, privates.

Ravelin   An outwork of two faces forming a salient angle constructed outside the main ditch and in front of the curtain of a fortification.

Redan   A simple form of earthwork, not completely enclosed, with two faces forming a salient angle, like a flèche.

Redoubt   A small independent earthwork, usually square or polygonal, completely enclosed.

Regiment   A body of troops made up of companies and commanded by a colonel.

Royal   A small mortar.

Sally port   An opening in a fortification for the passage of troops.

Sap   A covered trench or tunnel for approaching or undermining a fortification.

Saucisson   A sausage-shaped fascine.

Spontoon   A pike or halberd carried by infantry officers.

Stand of colors   A complete set of colors.

Traverse   A barrier thrown across the approach to a fortification or across its interior to cut off a part.

A P P E N D I X   A

ETHAN ALLEN'S CAPTIVITY

After Ethan Allen's surrender, he was roughly treated by Brigadier General Prescott, whom he had to face in the city, an elegantly dressed soldier who looked with disdain upon this wild man wearing a deerskin jacket, rough breeches, hobnailed cowhide shoes, and a red woolen cap. On learning that this man had taken Ticonderoga, Prescott "put himself into a great fury," brandished his cane, and called him "hard names." Allen shook his fist at the general. "You'd better not cane me. I'm not used to it," he shouted. "Offer to strike and that's the beetle of mortality for you" (by which he probably meant his fist). The other officers interceded, and the general turned upon certain captive Canadians, ordering them to be bayoneted. Allen stepped between them and their captors. "I'm the one to blame," he cried, tearing open his shirt and offering his breast to the bayonets. Prescott was taken aback. After a moment of sullen silence, he said: "I'll not execute you now. But you shall grace a halter at Tyburn, God damn ye!" They handcuffed him, shackled his legs with thirty-pound irons attached to a bar eight feet long. He was confined on shipboard for a month in this uncomfortable equipment, sent to England, and lodged in Pendennis Castle. But the government did not know what to do with him. Reprisals might follow his gracing Tyburn Tree. So they shifted the problem to the other side of the water. He was ordered aboard the *Solebay* frigate to go back to America as a prisoner of war. There was a remarkable demonstration at Cork, when the vessel put in there. Irish sympathizers loaded him with gifts of money, delicate foods, fine clothes, including two silk suits and two beaver hats.

He reached Halifax in June, 1776. In October he was taken to New York and admitted to parole. Captain Alexander Graydon, who saw him there, described him in his *Memoirs* (p. 243):

"His figure was that of a robust, large-framed man, worn down by confinement and hard fare; but he was now recovering his flesh and spirits; and a suit of blue clothes, with a gold-laced hat, that had been presented to him by the gentlemen of Cork, enabled him to make a very passable appearance for a rebel colonel. . . . I have seldom met a man possessing, in my opinion a stronger mind, or whose mode of expression was more vehement and oratorical. His style was a singular compound of local barbarisms, scriptural phrases and oriental wildness; and, though unclassical and sometimes ungrammatical, it was highly animated and forcible. . . . Notwithstanding that Allen might have had something of the insubordinate, lawless, frontier spirit in his composition . . . he appeared to me to be a man of generosity and honor."

The British tried to bribe him, with a colonelcy in a regiment of Tories, a gift of money, and a promise of a large tract of land, to desert the American cause. He told the officer that tempted him that he "viewed the offer of land to be similar to that which the devil offered Jesus Christ . . . when, at the same time, the damned soul had not one foot of land upon earth." That closed the conversation.

His brother brought him money, so that he was able to live in comfort on Long Island until he was arrested and confined in jail in New York, on a charge of breaking parole, which he admitted was "partly true." After eight months there, he was exchanged and started at once for the American army at Valley Forge. Washington received him with kindness, and wrote that he had found "something in him that commands admiration." In the spring Allen returned to his beloved Vermont, just then so named. He never again had an active part in the war.

A P P E N D I X B

THE CASUALTIES AT LONG ISLAND

It may seem almost incredible that, in a fight lasting four hours, as between Stirling and Grant, during which time the firing on both sides, even though not continuous, was heavy enough to exhaust Grant's ammunition, so few of the Americans were hit. But, when certain facts are considered, the lack of results is easily understood.

First, the distance between the lines appears not to have been much less that 150 yards at the beginning and between 300 and 600 yards for the rest of the fight, until Grant made his final advance. Musketry at that time was utterly ineffective at such distances. The British musket's ultimate range, when fired from the shoulder horizontally, was no more than 125 yards, at which distance the ball fell to the ground.

In the second place, the British soldier, as has been remarked elsewhere, was no marksman. He was never taught to take aim at a single object, or even at the mass of the enemy. His instructions were to throw the gun to the shoulder in a horizontal position, "point it—not sight it—toward the enemy and, at the word of command, to pull the trigger." Its effect was "entirely entrusted to volley shooting at ranges not exceeding 100 yards." As Trevelyan puts it: "He was taught to point his weapon horizontally, brace himself for a vicious recoil and pull a ten-pound trigger till his gun went off: if, indeed, it did go off when the hammer fell."

The British really relied on cold steel, this ineffective volley firing being usually merely a prelude to a charge with the bayonet. Such an attack, carried out by a body of trained men, terrible in their brilliant uniforms, their compactness, their grim courage, was, time and again in this war, enough to put the untrained American militia, most of whom had no bayonets, to flight even before the charge fell upon them.

A third consideration is that Grant's orders were merely to menace Stirling's men, to hold them in their position, until Howe gave the two-gun signal of his presence in their rear. Ambrose Serle says, "Grant had been ordered to advance no further." He therefore kept up an ineffective fire at long range for that purpose. He may even have instructed his gunners to overshoot the enemy, lest too much execution drive them from their position and let them escape to their lines before Howe had them entrapped.

In military language it was Grant's duty to "amuse" Stirling's force and "divert its attention" from the flanking movement—though Stirling's men would probably have described the fire from the British muskets and fieldpieces as anything else than "amusing" or "diverting."

Nevertheless, Stirling's men, ignorant of the British strategy and believing that at any minute Grant's force might advance and attack at close quarters, are entitled to the praise they received for their courage and steadfastness.

After the battle, stories of a brutal massacre by the British and Hessians, particularly the Hessians, of unresisting Americans offering to surrender were widespread throughout the colonies. The Americans were so inflamed by them that, when Count Donop fell in the attack on Red Bank on the Delaware on October 22, 1777, his death was hailed as an example of "God's revenge against murder."

Field, who in 1869 wrote a book about the battle, says that "there is no incident of the battle better attested than the massacre." He tells in lurid language of "entire battalions of Hessians" charging on unarmed men and never pausing "while one of them remained alive," of Americans "bayoneted, while lying on the ground and begging for quarter," and states that thus "nearly two thousand Americans were pitilessly put to death"—this in spite of the fact that Washington reported the loss of only about 1,000 in all, including those captured, and that pretty certainly no more than 1,000 Americans were killed, wounded, or captured in the whole battle.

The more modern historians either ignore these reports or, like John Fiske, declare that "the stories of a wholesale butchery by the Hessians, which once were current, have been completely disproved." But this is certainly a too sweeping statement. There can be little doubt that a number of Americans, when surrounded, hesitated to surrender and were bayoneted while practically defenseless.

A P P E N D I X C

THE FEELING BETWEEN NORTHERN AND SOUTHERN TROOPS

At the outbreak of the Revolution, the inhabitants of the colonies below New York and those above knew little of each other. In spite of a considerable commerce between them, there had been, by and large, few personal contacts. Very few of the rank and file of Pennsylvanians, for instance, had ever wandered so far from home as Boston, and Massachusetts men were equally unfamiliar with Maryland. Even among the upper classes there was a similar lack of acquaintance with their distant fellow countrymen. Philadelphia was new to John Adams when he came down to the Congress of 1774. George Washington had been only briefly in New York and New England.

This common ignorance had bred mutual ill feeling among the troops from the several colonies when in the campaigns of 1776 they were for the first time brought together. The New England Yankees suspected and distrusted the "southern" soldiers. The southerners reciprocated with dislike and even contempt. This was first noticeable in the army in New York and on Long Island, the first contact of these discordant elements.

The better uniformed and equipped Continentals from Pennsylvania, Delaware, and Maryland, with aristocratic disdain, looked down upon the homespun rustics of New England. (Greene, GW, I, 209; Reed, I, 239.) Captain Graydon of Shee's Pennsylvanians, in his *Memoirs* (pp. 147–149), derides the officers of the "Eastern battalions" for trying "to preserve the existing blessing of equality" with their rank and file, excepting, however, the officers of Glover's Marblehead regiment, who "seemed to have mixed with the world, and to understand what belonged to their stations." Of the privates also, he had a low opinion. Even in Glover's regiment, he noted with disgust "a number of negroes, which, to persons unaccustomed to such associations, had a disagreeable, degrading effect."

After the headlong flight of the Connecticut militia from Kip's Bay, on September 15, 1776, this contempt of the Yankees was openly shown. Caesar Rodney wrote to his brother Thomas, "That the New-England men behaved in a most dastardly, cowardly and scandalous manner is most certain." In another letter he quoted a gentleman of his acquaintance as writing to him, "These were not Southern Troops." (Rodney, C, 129, 125.)

In the camps after that, the southern troops, proud of the distinction they

934

had achieved on Long Island, were free with their tongues. Graydon (p. 156) says, "In so contemptible a light were the New England men regarded that it was scarcely held possible to conceive a case which would be construed into a reprehensible disrespect of them."

The Yankees naturally resented being called cowards. The tension grew so great that Colonel John Haslet of Delaware thought it a most serious matter. "Some officers," he wrote, "have poured such contempt upon the Eastern Troops & great Animosity subsists just now among them—'tis true they are not like the Children of the South, this however between Ourselves, 'tis even got among the Soldiers, whose Officers I think much to blame, who have sown the seeds of Discord, & [I] have used my small Influence to discourage it . . . 'tis likely to have most Dangerous Consequences." (Rodney, C, 138.)

Commissary General Joseph Trumbull of Connecticut accused Adjutant General Joseph Reed of Pennsylvania of doing "more to raise and keep up a jealousy between the New England and other troops than all the men in the Army beside . . . his stinking pride . . . has gone so far that I expect every day to hear he is called to account by some officer or other." (Force, 5, III, 1498.)

A like condition existed in Schuyler's Northern Army on Lake Champlain. It has been noted in the text that all the Pennsylvania troops were brigaded together and encamped apart from the rest for the sake of peace. Here there was used, hardly for the first time, an expletive afterwards attached to the Union troops by the Confederates and which is still in general vogue in the South, though now with little malice. Charles Cushing of Massachusetts in a letter refers to the fact that "none of the 'damn'd Yankees' . . . as the Southern troops are pleased to call us," were in the disaster at Trois Rivières. (Force, 5, I, 130.)

A New England brigadier general described the animosity between the northern and southern troops: "It has already risen to such a height that the Pennsylvania and New England troops would as soon fight each other as the enemy. Officers of all ranks are indiscriminately treated in the most contemptible manner, and whole colonies traduced and vilified as cheats, knaves, cowards, poltroons, hypocrites and every term of reproach, for no other reason but because they are situated east of New York." (Jones, CH, 122.)

One of the chief causes of this discord was the objection of the southern officers to the "leveling principle," the extreme democracy, prevalent among their Yankee colleagues in their attitude toward the private soldiers. The southerners felt that this was derogatory to the standing of all of them as officers and gentlemen. When Colonel Asa Whitcomb of Massachusetts detailed one of his sons, a private in his regiment, to act as his servant and allowed another son, also a private, to set up a cobbler's bench in the colonel's quarters, Wayne's Pennsylvanians were highly incensed. They assaulted the colonel's quarters and even his person, threw out the bench and climaxed their protest by firing thirty or forty rounds at his men, driving them from their tents and barracks and wounding several of them. (Jones, CH, 122–123.)

Washington was much concerned about these internecine disorders and entreated Schuyler to use his exertions "to do away the unhappy, pernicious distinctions and jealousies between the troops of the different governments. . . .

I am persuaded, if the officers will but exert themselves, that these animosities and disorders will in a great measure subside."

These ill feelings and consequent disorders did finally subside, after the troops from both sections had marched and camped and fought side by side, had got used to each other, discovered each other's good qualities and made allowance for each other's differences and defects.

A P P E N D I X   D

GENERAL HOWE AND MRS. MURRAY

General Howe has been blamed for allowing the American troops south of Kip's Bay to escape capture after his landing. Trevelyan (Pt. II, Vol. I, 324) writes: "Howe's great chance had come. The garrison of New York—as well as the three brigades of infantry which had been stationed along the bank of the East River, south of the point where the British landed—might all be had for the taking . . . not one of the retreating battalions would ever have reached the American lines in military order, and with half its full numbers, if Howe had promptly pushed his troops athwart the peninsula [island], which here was less than three thousand yards wide." Similar observations have been made by Gordon, F. V. Greene, Fortsecue, T. G. Frothingham, Fisher, Fiske, Botta, and others.

It seems so obvious that the movement across the island would have had fatal results, at least to Putnam's division, if not also to those of Parsons, Wadsworth, and Scott, that one looks for the reason why it was not made. It is found, according to several historians, in a very pretty little story.

The story appeared first in Thacher's *Military Journal* (p. 58) and in Gordon's *History* (Vol. II, p. 328), and it has been rehearsed by later writers countless times. John Fiske's version (Vol. I, p. 225) closely follows the originals, but in somewhat more elegant language: "When Howe had reached the spot known as Murray Hill . . . Mrs. Lindley Murray * . . . well knowing the easy temper of the British commander, sent out a servant to invite him to stop and take luncheon. A general halt was ordered; and while Howe and his officers were gracefully entertained for more than two hours by their accomplished and subtle hostess, Putnam hastily marched his 4,000 men up the shore of the Hudson." Thacher adds the statement, "It has since become almost a common saying among our officers that Mrs. Murray saved this part of the American army."

The legend presents Mrs. Murray, a middle-aged Quaker lady, the mother of twelve children, in the light of a siren, a veritable Circe, "with feminine delaying wiles" (Frothingham, 145) beguiling "the gallant Britons . . . with smiles and pleasant conversation, and a profusion of cakes and wine" (Lossing, II, 611) while they "lingered over their wine, quaffing and laughing, and bantering

* Wrong first name. It was Mrs. Robert Murray.

their patriotic hostess about the ludicrous panic and discomfiture of her countrymen" (Irving, II, 355). It has been accepted as a historic fact, by Irving,
Lossing, Johnston, Gordon, Fortescue, Frothingham, Bancroft, Winsor, Trevelyan, Fiske, Bryant, and the *Dictionary of American Biography*, not only that
the "subtle" hostess served her guests cakes and wine, but that she actually
held up the whole British force for those two critical hours, during which, but
for that beguilement, it would have hastened to cut off Putnam and all his
men. General G. W. Cullum, writing about this affair in Winsor's *Narrative
and Critical History* (Vol. VI, p. 284), goes so far as to say, "Howe was in
close pursuit of this rear-guard [Putnam's] . . . but unexpectedly stopped for
nearly two hours" at Mrs. Murray's "to enjoy her old Madeira."

With such a wealth of authority behind it, who shall deny the lady her
heaped-up honors? Yet one must.

Not deny that the cakes and wine were served, no. Howe's first division
moved at once from the landing place to Murray Hill and halted there, at the
very door of Mrs. Murray's mansion. It was an excessively hot day. What
more natural, what more in accord with the polite customs of the time, than an
impulsive invitation from the good lady to Howe and Clinton and Cornwallis
and the other generals to enjoy the cool of her parlor and to refresh themselves
with her "old Madeira," instead of broiling in the sun? So much may be accepted
as probable. But that Howe was bamboozled into forgoing immediate, proper
military activity, that the whole British force was brought to a stand, not only
while but because, Howe and his generals enjoyed Mrs. Murray's hospitality, is
quite unbelievable.

The simple fact is that Howe's tactics, planned beforehand and exactly
carried out, had as their first objective only the possession of the Incleberg
height. On taking that commanding position, the first division was to wait until
the arrival of the rest of his force for any further major movement.

The first division numbered no more than 4,000 men, less than a third
of the whole force which was to come over from Long Island. Washington
had three or four times 4,000 men fit for duty. If Howe had thrown his troops
across the island at once, he would have exposed them to attack on two fronts,
by Putnam, Wadsworth, Parsons and the rest on the south and Washington on
the north, each American force greatly outnumbering the British. Good behavior by the Americans, under such conditions, might easily have resulted in a
complete defeat of Howe's first division long before all his second arrived.

That Howe planned the task of the first division exactly as it was accomplished, and was not diverted from his plans by the excellent Mrs. Murray,
is proved by Clinton's testimony on page 63 of his "Historical Detail" (cf.
Anderson, 177 ff.): "It happened unfortunately too that much time was
lost before the second embarkation landed (it being some hours after the first);
as by our striking immediately across the Island great numbers of the enemy
must have been taken prisoners; but my orders being to secure the Inclenberg,
I do not think myself at liberty to attempt it before Sir William Howe joined
us."

Clinton commanded that first division and led it immediately to the hill.
So say the *Diaries* of General Archibald Robertson (p. 98): "We then went

on to the heights of Inklenberg about a mile in front . . . where we halted. . . . About 2 General Howe came up and after the 2d Embarkation arrived about 4 we moved on." The *Diary* (p. 48) of Lieut. Frederick Mackenzie of the Royal Welch Fusiliers confirms this: "As soon as the troops were formed, they advanced to Murray's hill (or Ingleberg) an advantageous piece of ground . . . the whole of the Troops [the second division] . . . were landed at Kipp's Bay about 5 o'clock in the afternoon. General Howe [then] made a movement with the greatest part of the army towards Haerlem."

It was all according to plan. Whether Howe was too cautious in planning had no more to do with the question about Mrs. Murray's part in the affair than Mrs. Murray's undoubtedly sincere hospitality had to do with the delay at Incleberg—which was exactly nothing.

A P P E N D I X   E

THE TREACHERY OF WILLIAM DEMONT

On November 2, 1776, William Demont, an ensign in Magaw's 5th Pennsylvania and the regimental adjutant, deserted and carried to Lord Percy "the plans of Fort Washington." To the receipt of these papers Edward F. De Lancey, in his monograph on the capture of the fort, ascribes a change in Howe's plans—which, before that, he assumes, had intended an immediate crossing to New Jersey and a descent upon Philadelphia.

De Lancey's conclusion, that the attack upon the fort and its capture was attributable to Demont's treachery, seems hardly justifiable. His belief that Howe had planned to cross to New Jersey without first attacking the fort is a pure assumption, based on nothing more than the guess of Colonel Joseph Reed and "a great majority" of the American officers (Reed, I, 248, and De Lancey, 18). There is nothing other than this guess upon which to base such assumption.

The only evident change in Howe's plans was the abandonment of his attempt to get behind the American army and the consequent withdrawal of his forces from in front of the American lines at North Castle on November 4. That his intention then was immediately to withdraw from Manhattan Island leaving Fort Washington intact, and devote all his energies to the capture of Philadelphia, nobody knows, nor can know. Moreover, such an intention is inherently improbable.

That Howe himself regarded the fort as an important factor in his plans is clearly shown by a sentence in his letter of November 30 to George Germain (Force, 5, III, 924): "The importance of this post, which, with Fort Lee on the opposite shore of Jersey, kept the enemy in command of the navigation of the North River, while it barred the communication with York by land, made the possession of its absolutely necessary." That he should have intended to leave it standing, while he marched against Philadelphia, is incredible.

That Demont's plans of the fort disclosed so much not already known to the British as to cause them to undertake the reduction of the fort, which, otherwise they would not have attempted, is equally incredible. Although Graydon, fully conversant with the facts, says that Howe "might have been more thoroughly informed of everything desirable to be known" as to the fort by Demont, yet he might have acquired "a perfect knowledge of the ground we occupied . . . from hundreds in New York" (Graydon, 215). That pretty well disposes of the importance of Demont's treachery.

ARNOLD AT FREEMAN'S FARM

James Wilkinson, twenty years of age, was Gates's adjutant at the time of the battle of Freeman's Farm. He wrote on September 21 to St. Clair, "General Arnold was not out of camp during the whole action." In his *Memoirs,* published thirty-nine years later, he said: "It is worthy of remark, that not a single general officer was on the field of battle on the nineteenth of September, until the evening when General Learned was ordered out."

William Gordon, the contemporary historian (II, 551), wrote, "Arnold's division was out in the action, but he himself did not head them; he remained in the camp the whole time."

George Bancroft (V, 184) presumably relied on both Wilkinson and Gordon when he wrote (V, 184) that "on the American side not one" major general was on the field, "nor a brigadier till near its close"—evidently referring to General Learned's futile attack on Fraser's division.

These positive statements by historians deserve respectful consideration and an examination of countervailing evidence, if any there be, before they are disregarded.

There is evidence to the contrary. Colonel Richard Varick wrote on the 22nd to General Schuyler, "Arnold has all the credit of the action"; and after the surrender he wrote, "During Burgoyne's stay here he gave Arnold great credit for his bravery and his military abilities; especially in the action of the 19th" (Arnold, 179, 189).

Colonel Henry Brockholst Livingston, on the 22nd, wrote to Schuyler that some of the officers proposed an address to Arnold "returning thanks for his services and particularly for his conduct during the late action" (Arnold, 178). Again, on the 23rd, he wrote of Arnold, "Believe me, Sir, to him alone is due the honour of our late victory" (Arnold, 180).

Major Cochran wrote to the Vermont Council of Safety on the 21st: "General Arnold, with his division, attacked a division of Burgoyne, in which General Arnold gained the ground" (Arnold, 186).

Varick, Livingston, and Cochran were in the camp on the day of the battle. They offset Wilkinson.

Opposed to Gordon is Charles Stedman (I, 336–337), a contemporary English historian of high repute: "The enemy were led to battle by general Arnold, who distinguished himself in an extraordinary manner."

In 1844 Charles Neilson, whose father's house was within the American lines and who received much information from his parent as well as from surviving "old revolutionary officers and soldiers" of the vicinity, published an account of Burgoyne's campaign which is generally regarded as authoritative. On page 148 of that book he contradicts Wilkinson's statement.

Max von Eelking in his *Memoirs and Letters and Journals of Major General Riedesel* (I, 150), the material for which he derived from Riedesel says that deserters from the American army stated that "they were commanded on this occasion by General Arnold."

So much for the authorities. Considering the known facts of the affair, one might ask, Who directed the movements in that four- or five-hour battle if Arnold did not? Is it conceivable that the ten or more regiments engaged, each led by its own commander, with no general officer over them could have acted in unison and as coherently as they did act—in making that "countermarch" from Fraser's right to Burgoyne's center, for instance? No direction could have been given from the American camp, from which the battlefield was not visible. There must have been a leader on the field, and there has never been a suggestion of anyone in that capacity other than Arnold.

Again, consider the nature of the man, proud, ardent, impatient, brave, always eager for action in the thick of combat. It is not conceivable that he would have remained an idle spectator—not even a spectator, indeed, for from the camp he could not even have seen what was going on—while his own men fought through half a day.

One must conclude that John Marshall, Washington Irving, Botta, Lossing, Fiske, Woodrow Wilson, F. V. Greene, Fonblanque, S. G. Fisher, Hall, Trevelyan, Nickerson, Fortescue, Dawson, and Carrington are right in rejecting the statements of Wilkinson and Gordon and giving Arnold the honor of active participation in the battle as the directing head of the American troops.

Trevelyan (III, 186 n.) says that Wilkinson's "impudent falsehood has been judged worthy of refutation by several excellent historians. . . . One might as well demand evidence to prove that Nelson was in the sea-fight off Cape St. Vincent."

PRINCIPAL AUTHORITIES

WITH KEY WORDS USED IN THE NOTES

Abbatt, *P*   William Abbatt. *The Battle of Pell's Point.* New York, 1901.

Abbott   Wilbur C. Abbott. *New York in the American Revolution.* New York, 1929.

Adams   Randolph G. Adams. "A View of Cornwallis's Surrender at Yorktown," *American Historical Review*, XXXVII (Oct. 1931), 25–49.

Adams, CF   Charles Francis Adams. *Studies Military and Diplomatic, 1775–1865.* New York, 1911.

Adams, *J*   Charles Francis Adams, editor. *Familiar Letters of John Adams.* New York, 1876.

Adams, *L*   *Letters of John Adams, Addressed to His Wife* . . . 2 vols., Boston, 1841.

Alden   John Richard Alden. *General Gage in America.* Baton Rouge, La., 1948.

Allen   *Ethan Allen's Narrative of the Capture of Ticonderoga* . . . Burlington, Vt., 1849.

Allen, GW   Gardner W. Allen. *A Naval History of the American Revolution.* 2 vols., Boston, 1913.

Almon   John Almon, editor. *The Remembrancer.* 17 vols., 1775–1784.

Amory   Thomas C. Amory. *The Military Services and Public Life of Major-General John Sullivan.* Boston, 1868.

Anburey   Thomas Anburey. *Travels Through the Interior Parts of America.* 2 vols., Boston, 1923.

Anderson   Enoch Anderson. *Personal Recollections* . . . (*Papers of the Hist. Soc. of Del.*, No. XVI). Wilmington, 1896.

Anderson, T   Troyer S. Anderson. *The Command of the Howe Brothers During the American Revolution.* New York, 1936.

André   John André. *Major André's Journal* . . . Tarrytown, N.Y., 1930.

Andrews   Matthew P. Andrews. *History of Maryland* . . . New York, 1929.

Archives   *Delaware Archives.* 5 vols., Wilmington, 1911–1916.

Arnold   Isaac N. Arnold. *The Life of Benedict Arnold.* Chicago, 1880.

Ashburn   Percy M. Ashburn. *A History of the Medical Department of the United States Army.* Boston, 1929.

Atlas   Lawrence Martin, editor. *The George Washington Atlas.* United States George Washington Bicentennial Commission. Washington, 1932.

Bancroft   George Bancroft. *History of the United States* . . . 6 vols., New York, 1887.

Barber   John W. Barber. *History and Antiquities of New England* . . . New Haven, Conn., 1870.

Barker   John Barker. *The British in Boston* . . . Cambridge, Mass., 1924.

Baurmeister   Bernhard A. Uhlendorf and Edna Vosper, editors. *Letters from Major Baurmeister to Colonel von Jungkenn* . . . Philadelphia, 1937.

Belcher   Henry Belcher. *The First American Civil War* . . . 2 vols., London, 1911.

Benedict   Erastus C. Benedict. *The Battle of Harlem Heights* . . . New York, 1880.

Bennett   Caleb P. Bennett. "Narrative of . . . the Delaware Regiment . . ." *Pa. Mag. of Hist. and Biog.*, IX (1885), 451–462.

Bodley   Temple Bodley. *George Rogers Clark*. Boston, 1926.

Bolton   Charles K. Bolton. *The Private Soldier Under Washington.* New York, 1902.

Botta   Charles Botta. *History of the War of the Independence* . . . Edinburgh, 1844.

Boudinot   Elias Boudinot. *Journal or Historical Recollections* . . . Philadelphia, 1894.

Bowen   John S. Bowen and J. Smith Futhey. "A Sketch of the Battle of Brandywine," *Bulletin of the Hist. Soc. of Pa.*, Vol. I, No. 7 (Sept., 1846), pp. 3–13.

Boyd   Julian P. Boyd. *Anglo-American Union: Joseph Galloway's Plans to Preserve the British Empire, 1774–1788.* Philadelphia, 1941.

Brooks   Noah Brooks. *Henry Knox* . . . New York, 1900.

Bruce   Robert Bruce. *Brandywine* . . . Clinton, N.Y., 1922.

Burgoyne   John Burgoyne. *A State of the Expedition from Canada* . . . London, 1780.

Burgoyne, *OB*   *Orderly Book of Lieut. Gen. John Burgoyne* . . . Albany, N.Y., 1860.

Burnaby   Andrew Burnaby. *Travels Through North America.* New York, 1904.

Burnett   Edmund C. Burnett. *The Continental Congress.* New York, 1941.

Burnett, *L*   Edmund C. Burnett, editor. *Letters of Members of the Continental Congress.* 8 vols., Washington, 1921–1936.

Butcher   H. Borton Butcher. *The Battle of Trenton* . . . Princeton, 1934.

Campbell   William W. Campbell. *Annals of Tryon County* . . . Cherry Valley, N.Y., 1880.

Carrington   H. B. Carrington. *Battles of the American Revolution.* New York, 1888.

Caulkins   Frances M. Caulkins. *History of New London, Conn.* . . . New London, 1860.

Channing   Edward Channing. *History of the United States.* 6 vols., New York, 1905–1925.

Chastellux   Marquis de Chastellux. *Travels in North-America* . . . New York, 1828.

Chittenden   L. E. Chittenden. *The Capture of Ticonderoga.* Rutland, Vt., 1872.

Cincinnati   H. H. Bellas. *A History of the Delaware State Society of the Cincinnati . . . (Papers of the Hist. Soc. of Del.,* No. XIII). Wilmington, 1895.

Clarke   John Clarke. *An Impartial and Authentic Narrative of the Battle Fought . . . on Bunker's Hill . . .* New York, 1909.

Clinton   Sir Henry Clinton and Earl Cornwallis. I *Narrative of the Campaign in 1781 . . .* II *Answer to Sir Henry Clinton's Narrative . . .* III *Observations on Earl Cornwallis' Answer.* Philadelphia, 1865–1866.

Coburn   Frank W. Coburn. *The Battle of April 19, 1775 . . .* Lexington, Mass., 1912

Coburn, *B*   Frank W. Coburn. *The Centennial History of the Battle of Bennington . . .* Boston, 1877.

Codman   John Codman. *Arnold's Expedition to Quebec.* New York, 1902.

Coffin   Charles Coffin. *History of the Battle of Breed's Hill . . .* Portland, Me., 1835.

Cooch   Edward W. Cooch. *The Battle of Cooch's Bridge . . .* Wilmington, Del., 1940.

Cowpens   *The Battle of King's Mountain and the Battle of the Cowpens.* Washington, 1928.

Cresswell   *The Journal of Nicholas Cresswell, 1774–1777.* New York, 1924.

Curtis   Edward P. Curtis. *The Organization of the British Army in the Revolution.* New Haven, Conn., 1926.

D.A.B.   *Dictionary of American Biography.* 20 vols. and Index, New York, 1928–1937.

D.A.H.   James Truslow Adams, editor. *Dictionary of American History.* 5 vols. and Index, New York, 1940–1941.

Dawson   Henry B. Dawson. *Battles of the United States . . .* 2 vols., New York, 1858.

Dearborn   *Journal of Captain Henry Dearborn in the Quebec Expedition, 1775.* Cambridge, Mass., 1886.

Dearborn, *J*   *Journals of Henry Dearborn, 1776–1783.* Cambridge, Mass., 1887.

Dearborn, N   Henry Dearborn. "A Narrative of the Saratoga Campaign," *Fort Ticonderoga Museum Bulletin,* Vol. I, No. 5 (Jan., 1929), pp. 3–12.

De Lancey   E. F. De Lancey. *The Capture of Mount Washington . . .* New York, 1877.

Digby   *The British Invasion from the North . . . with the Journal of Lieut. William Digby . . .* Albany, N.Y., 1887.

Drake   Samuel A. Drake. *Bunker Hill.* Boston, 1875.

Draper   Lyman C. Draper. *King's Mountain and Its Heroes.* Cincinnati, 1881.

Duer   William A. Duer. *The Life of William Alexander, Earl of Stirling.* New York, 1847.

Dunbar   Seymour Dunbar. *A History of Travel in America.* 4 vols.,
                 Indianapolis, 1915.

Duncan   Louis C. Duncan. *Medical Men in the American Revolution,*
                 1775–1783. Carlisle, Pa., 1931.

Eelking   Max von Eelking. *The German Allied Troops* . . . Albany,
                 N.Y., 1893.

Ellis   George E. Ellis. *History of the Battle of Bunker's* (*Breed's*)
                 Hill. Boston, 1875.

Evelyn   W. G. Evelyn. *Memoirs and Letters* . . . *1774–1776.* Oxford,
                 1879.

Fellows   John Fellows. *The Veil Removed.* New York, 1843.

Field   Thomas W. Field. *The Battle of Long Island* (*Long Island Hist.*
                 Soc. Memoirs, Vol. II). Brooklyn, 1869.

Fisher   Sydney G. Fisher. *The Struggle for American Independence.*
                 2 vols., Philadelphia, 1908.

Fiske   John Fiske. *The American Reovlution.* 2 vols., Boston, 1901.

Fitzpatrick   John C. Fitzpatrick, editor. *The Writings of George Washing-*
                 ton. 39 vols., Washington, 1931–1944.

Fletcher   Ebenezer Fletcher. *The Narrative of* . . . New York, 1866.

Fobes   Simon Fobes. *Journal of a Member of Arnold's Expedition to*
                 Quebec. Tarrytown, N.Y., 1927.

Fonblanque   E. B. de Fonblanque. *Political and Military Episodes* . . . *De-*
                 rived from the Life and Correspondence of the Right Hon. J.
                 Burgoyne. London, 1876.

Force   Peter Force, editor. *American Archives,* Fourth and Fifth
                 Series. 6 vols. and 3 vols., Washington, 1837–1846, 1848–1853.

Fortescue   Sir John W. Fortescue. *A History of the British Army.* 13 vols.,
                 London, 1899–1930.

Fraser   Georgia Fraser. *The Stone House at Gowanus.* New York, 1909.

French, *B*   Allen French, editor. *A British Fusilier in Revolutionary Boston,*
                 by Frederick Mackenzie. Cambridge, Mass., 1926.

French, *C*   Allen French. *The Day of Concord and Lexington.* Boston,
                 1925.

French, *F*   Allen French. *The First Year of the American Revolution.*
                 Boston, 1934.

French, *G*   Allen French. *General Gage's Informers.* Ann Arbor, Mich.,
                 1932.

French, *T*   Allen French. *The Taking of Ticonderoga in 1775.* Cambridge,
                 Mass., 1928.

Frothingham   T. G. Frothingham. *Washington, Commander in Chief.* Boston,
                 1930.

Frothingham,   Richard Frothingham. *The Alarm on* . . . *April 18, 1775.*
  A   Boston, 1876.

Frothingham,   Richard Frothingham. *The Centennial.* Boston, 1875.
  C

Frothingham,   Richard Frothingham. *History of the Siege of Boston.* Boston,
  S   1851.

Frothingham, W	Richard Frothingham. *Life and Times of Joseph Warren.* Boston, 1865.
Fuller	J. F. C. Fuller. *Decisive Battles of the U.S.A.* New York, 1942.
Ganoe	William A. Ganoe. *The History of the United States Army.* New York, 1924.
Garden	Alexander Garden. *Anecdotes of the American Revolution.* 3 vols., Brooklyn, 1865.
Gibbes	R. W. Gibbes. *Documentary History of the American Revolution.* 3 vols., Columbia, S.C., and New York, 1853–1857.
Gilmore	James R. Gilmore. *The Rear-Guard of the Revolution.* New York, 1897.
Goolrick	J. T. Goolrick. *The Life of Gen. Hugh Mercer.* New York, 1906.
Gordon	William Gordon. *The History . . . of the United States of America.* 4 vols., London, 1788.
Gottschalk	Louis R. Gottschalk. *Lafayette Comes to America.* Chicago, 1935. *Lafayette Joins the American Army.* Chicago, 1937. *Lafayette and the Close of the American Revolution.* Chicago, 1942.
Graham	James Graham. *Life of General Daniel Morgan.* New York, 1856.
Grahame	James Grahame. *The History of the United States . . .* 4 vols., London, 1836.
Graydon	Alexander Graydon. *Memoirs of His Own Time.* Philadelphia, 1846.
Greene, FV	Francis Vinton Greene. *The Revolutionary War and the Military Policy of the United States.* New York, 1911.
Greene, GW	George W. Greene. *The Life of Nathanael Greene.* 3 vols., New York, 1867–1871.
Hadden	[James M.] *Hadden's Journal and Orderly Books.* Albany, N.Y., 1884.
Hall	Hiland Hall. *The Battle of Bennington.* Milford, Mass., 1877.
Hanger	*The Life, Adventures, and Opinions of Col. George Hanger . . .* 2 vols., London, 1801.
Hartley	Cecil B. Hartley. *Life of Major General Henry Lee . . .* Philadelphia, 1859.
Hatch	Louis C. Hatch. *The Administration of the American Revolutionary Army.* New York, 1904.
Heath	*Memoirs of Major-General William Heath . . .* New York, 1901.
Heitman	Francis B. Heitman. *Historical Register of Officers of the Continental Army . . .* Washington, 1914.
Henry	John J. Henry. *Account of Arnold's Campaign Against Quebec . . .* Albany, N.Y., 1877.
Hildreth	Richard Hildreth. *The History of the United States of America.* 6 vols., New York, 1880.

Hinman	Royal R. Hinman. *A Historical Collection, from Official Records, Files, etc., of the Part Sustained by Connecticut During the War of the Revolution.* Hartford, 1842.
Holbrook	Stewart H. Holbrook. *Ethan Allen.* New York, 1940.
Hollister	*The Journal of Josiah Hollister.* (Chicago, 1928?)
Honyman	*Colonial Panorama, 1775: Dr. Robert Honyman's Journal . . .* San Marino, Calif., 1939.
Hooton	F. C. Hooton. *Battle of Brandywine.* Harrisburg, Pa., 1900.
How	*Diary of David How.* Morrisania, N.Y., 1865.
Howard	George E. Howard. *Preliminaries of the Revolution, 1763–1775.* New York, 1905.
Hudleston	F. J. Hudleston. *Gentleman Johnny Burgoyne.* Indianapolis, 1927.
Hufeland	Otto Hufeland. *Westchester County During the American Revolution, 1775–1783.* New York, 1926.
Hughes	Rupert Hughes. *George Washington . . .* 3 vols., New York, 1926–1930.
Humphrey	*A Journal Kept by William Humphrey . . . on a March to Quebec . . .* Tarrytown, N.Y., 1931.
Humphreys	David Humphreys. *The Life and Heroic Exploits of Israel Putnam.* Hartford, Conn., 1847.
Huntington	*Letters Written by Ebenezer Huntington During the American Revolution.* New York, 1914.
Hutchinson	*The Diary and Letters of . . . Thomas Hutchinson.* 2 vols., London, 1883–1886.
Irving	Washington Irving. *Life of George Washington.* 5 vols., New York, 1855–1859.
James	W. M. James. *The British Navy in Adversity.* London, 1926.
James, C	James A. James. *The Life of George Rogers Clark.* Chicago, 1928.
James, CP	James A. James, editor. *George Rogers Clark Papers, 1771–1784 (Colls. of the Ill. State Hist. Lib., Virginia Series, III–IV).* 2 vols., Springfield, Ill., 1912–1926.
Johnson	William Johnson. *Sketches of the Life and Correspondence of Nathanael Greene.* 2 vols., Charleston, S.C., 1822.
Johnson, V	Victor L. Johnson. *The Administration of the American Commissariat During the Revolutionary War.* Philadelphia, 1941.
Johnston, C	Henry P. Johnston. *The Campaign of 1776 Around New York and Brooklyn (Long Island Hist. Soc. Memoirs, Vol. III).* Brooklyn, 1878.
Johnston, H	Henry P. Johnston. *The Battle of Harlem Heights.* New York, 1897.
Johnston, S	Henry P. Johnston. *The Storming of Stony Point.* New York, 1900.
Johnston, Y	Henry P. Johnston. *The Yorktown Campaign.* New York, 1881.
Jones	Thomas Jones. *History of New York During the Revolutionary War . . .* 2 vols., New York, 1879.

Jones, C	Charles C. Jones, Jr. *The History of Georgia.* 2 vols., Boston, 1883.
Jones, CH	C. H. Jones. *History of the Campaign for the Conquest of Canada* . . . Philadelphia, 1882.
Journals	*Journals of the Continental Congress, 1774–1789.* 34 vols., Washington, 1904–1937.
Kapp	Friedrich Kapp. *The Life of John Kalb.* New York, 1884.
Kemble	*The Kemble Papers (New-York Hist. Soc. Collections, 1883–1884.* 2 vols., New York, 1884–1885.
Kirkwood	*The Journal and Order Book of Capt. Robert Kirkwood (Papers of the Historical Society of Delaware,* No. XVI). Wilmington, 1910.
Knollenberg	Bernhard Knollenberg. *Washington and the Revolution.* New York, 1940.
Lafayette	*Memoirs, Correspondence and Manuscripts of Gen. Lafayette.* 3 vols., London, 1837.
Lamb	R. Lamb. *Memoirs of His Own Life* . . . Dublin, 1809.
Landers	H. L. Landers. *The Battle of Camden.* Washington, 1929.
Leake	Isaac Q. Leake. *Memoir* . . . *of General John Lamb.* Albany, N.Y., 1857.
Lecky	W. E. Hartpole Lecky. *The American Revolution, 1763–1783.* New York, 1898.
Lee	Henry Lee. *Memoirs of the War in the Southern Department* . . . New York, 1869.
Lefferts	Charles M. Lefferts. *Uniforms* . . . *in the War of the American Revolution, 1775–1783.* New York, 1926.
Lossing	Benson J. Lossing. *The Pictorial Field Book of the American Revolution.* 2 vols., New York, 1850–1852.
Lossing, S	Benson J. Lossing. *The Life and Times of Philip Schuyler.* New York, 1883.
Lowell	E. J. Lowell. *The Hessians* . . . *in the Revolutionary War.* New York, 1884.
Lundin	Leonard Lundin. *Cockpit of the American Revolution: The War for Independence in New Jersey.* Princeton, 1940.
Lushington	Stephen R. Lushington. *The Life and Services of General Lord Harris* . . . London, 1840.
McCrady, R,I	Edward McCrady. *The History of South Carolina in the Revolution, 1775–1780.* New York, 1901.
McCrady, R,II	Edward McCrady. *The History of South Carolina in the Revolution, 1780–1783.* New York, 1902.
McDonald	John M. McDonald. *The McDonald Papers,* Pt. I. White Plains, N.Y., 1926.
MacDonald	William MacDonald. *Documentary Source Book of American History.* New York, 1937.
MacElree	Wilmer W. MacElree. *Along the Western Brandywine.* West Chester, Pa., 1909.
Mackenzie	*Diary of Frederick Mackenzie.* 2 vols., Cambridge, Mass., 1930.

McMichael   "Diary of Lieut. James McMichael . . . 1776–1778," *Pa. Mag. of Hist. and Biog.*, XVI (1892), 129–159.

Mahan   Alfred T. Mahan. *The Major Operations of the Navies in the War of American Independence.* Boston, 1913.

Mahon   Philip H. Stanhope, Lord Mahon. *History of England from the Peace of Utrecht* . . . 7 vols., London, 1858.

Marshall   John Marshall. *The Life of George Washington.* 2 vols., New York, 1930.

Marshall, C   *Extracts from the Diary of Christopher Marshall 1774–1781.* Albany, N.Y., 1877.

Martyn   Charles Martyn. *The Life of Artemas Ward.* New York, 1921.

Mauduit   Israel Mauduit. *Observations upon the Conduct of S—r W—m H—e, at the White Plains.* Tarrytown, N.Y., 1927.

Metzger   Charles H. Metzger. *The Quebec Act.* New York, 1936.

Miller, O   John C. Miller. *Origins of the American Revolution.* Boston, 1943.

Miller, T   John C. Miller. *Triumph of Freedom, 1775–1783.* Boston, 1948.

Montresor   "Journals of Capt. John Montresor," *New-York Hist. Soc. Colls.*, 1881, pp. 113–520. New York, 1882.

Moore   Frank Moore. *Diary of the American Revolution.* 2 vols., New York, 1863.

Moore, GH   George H. Moore. *"Mr. Lee's Plan—March 29, 1777": The Treason of Charles Lee.* New York, 1860.

Morison   George Morison. *An Interesting Journal of Experience During the Expedition to Quebec* . . . Tarrytown, N.Y., 1916.

Moultrie   William Moultrie. *Memoirs of the American Revolution* . . . 2 vols., New York, 1802.

Muhlenberg   Henry A. Muhlenberg. *The Life of Major-General Peter Muhlenberg.* Philadelphia, 1849.

Murdock   Harold Murdock. *The Nineteenth of April, 1775.* Boston, 1923.

Murdock, B   Harold Murdock. *Bunker Hill.* Boston, 1927.

Neilson   Charles Neilson. *An Original . . . Account of Burgoyne's Campaign.* Bemis Heights, N.Y., 1926.

Nickerson   Hoffman Nickerson. *The Turning Point of the Revolution.* Boston, 1928.

Niles   H. Niles. *Principles and Acts of the Revolution in America.* Baltimore, 1822.

Nolan   J. Bennett Nolan. *Lafayette in America Day by Day.* Baltimore, 1934.

Ogden   "Journal of Maj. Matthias Ogden," *New Jersey Hist. Soc. Proc.*, New Ser. XIII, 17–30 (Jan., 1928).

Onderdonk   Henry Onderdonk. *Revolutionary Incidents of Suffolk and Kings Counties.* New York, 1849.

Palmer   John M. Palmer. *General von Steuben.* New Haven, Conn., 1937.

Parton   James Parton. *The Life and Times of Aaron Burr.* 2 vols. New York, 1858.

Partridge   Bellamy Partridge. *Sir Billy Howe.* New York, 1932.

Patterson   S. W. Patterson. *Horatio Gates.* New York, 1941.

Pausch   *Journal of Captain Georg Pausch* . . . Albany, N.Y., 1886.

Pell   John Pell. *Ethan Allen.* Boston, 1929.

Pennsylvania   *Pennsylvania in the War of the Revolution.* 2 vols., Harrisburg, 1880.

Pennsylvania   Samuel Hazard, editor. *Pennsylvania Archives,* First Series. 12
  Archives   vols. Philadelphia, 1852–1856.

Percy   *Letters of Hugh, Earl Percy* . . . *1774–1776.* Boston, 1902.

Pettengill   R. W. Pettengill, editor. *Letters from America, 1776–1779.* Boston, 1924.

Phinney   Elias Phinney. *History of the Battle at Lexington.* Boston, 1825.

Pitkin   Timothy Pitkin. *A Political and Civil History of the United States.* 2 vols., New Haven, Conn., 1828.

Pontgibaud   Chevalier de Pontgibaud. *A French Volunteer of the War of Independence.* Transl. from the French. New York, 1898.

Quaife   Milo M. Quaife. *The Flag of the United States.* New York, 1942.

Ramsay   David Ramsay. *The History of the American Revolution.* 2 vols., Trenton, N.J., 1811.

Ramsay, R   David Ramsay. *History of the Revolution of South-Carolina.* 2 vols., Trenton, N.J., 1785.

Read   William T. Read. *Life and Correspondence of George Read.* Philadelphia, 1870.

Reed   William B. Reed. *Life and Correspondence of Joseph Reed.* 2 vols., Philadelphia, 1847.

Reynolds   Grindall Reynolds. *The Concord Fight.* Boston, 1875.

Richardson   William H. Richardson. *Washington and "the Enterprise Against Powle's Hook."* Jersey City, 1938.

Riedesel   Max von Eelking. *Memoirs and Letters and Journals of Major General Riedesel During His Residence in America.* 2 vols., Albany, N.Y., 1868.

Riedesel, F   Friederike von Riedesel. *Letters and Journals* . . . Albany, N.Y., 1867.

Ripley   Ezra Ripley. *A History of the Fight at Concord.* Concord, Mass., 1827.

Roberts   Kenneth Roberts, editor. *March to Quebec.* New York, 1940.

Robertson   *Archibald Robertson* . . . *His Diaries and Sketches in America.* New York, 1930.

Rodney, C   *Letters to and from Caesar Rodney, 1756–1784.* Philadelphia, 1933.

Rodney, T   *Diary of Capt. Thomas Rodney, 1776–1777.* Wilmington, Del., 1888.

Sabine   Lorenzo Sabine. *The American Loyalists.* Boston, 1847.

Sawyer   Charles W. Sawyer. *Firearms in American History,* Vol. I. Boston, 1910.

Schenck   David Schenck. *North Carolina, 1780–81.* Raleigh, 1889.

Senter	*The Journal of Isaac Senter* . . . Philadelphia, 1846.
Serle	*The American Journal of Ambrose Serle.* San Marino, Calif., 1940.
Seymour	William Seymour. *A Journal of the Southern Expedition, 1780–1783 (Hist. and Biog. Papers of the Historical Society of Delaware,* Vol. II). Wilmington, 1896.
Shurtleff	N. B. Shurtleff. *A Topographical and Historical Description of Boston.* 1871.
Simcoe	J. G. Simcoe. *Simcoe's Military Journal* . . . New York, 1844.
Simms	W. Gilmore Simms. *The Life of Francis Marion.* New York, 1857.
Smith	Goldwin Smith. *The United States* . . . *1492–1871.* New York, 1893.
Smith, J	Justin H. Smith. *Arnold's March from Cambridge to Quebec.* New York, 1903.
Smith, JH	Justin H. Smith. *Our Struggle for the Fourteenth Colony.* 2 vols., New York, 1907.
Spargo	John Spargo. *The Bennington Battle Monument.* Rutland, Vt., 1925.
Sparks, *C*	Jared Sparks. *Correspondence of the American Revolution* . . . 4 vols., Boston, 1853.
Sparks, *L*	Jared Sparks. *The Life of George Washington.* 2 vols., London, 1839.
Sparks, *W*	Jared Sparks. *The Writings of George Washington.* 12 vols., Boston, 1858.
Squier	"The Diary of Ephraim Squier, of Arnold's Expedition to Quebec," *Mag. of Hist.* Vol. XL (1930), No. 4 (Extra No. 160), pp. 203–214.
Stedman	Charles Stedman. *The History* . . . *of the American War.* 2 vols., London, 1794.
Stephenson	N. W. Stephenson and W. H. Dunn. *George Washington.* 2 vols., New York, 1940.
Stevens	B. F. Stevens, editor. *The Campaign in Virginia, 1781.* 2 vols., London, 1888.
Stiles	*The Literary Diary of Ezra Stiles.* 3 vols., New York, 1901.
Stillé	C. J. Stillé. *Maj. Gen. Anthony Wayne* . . . Philadelphia, 1893.
Stocking	*An Interesting Journal of Abner Stocking* . . . Tarrytown, N.Y., 1921.
Stone	E. M. Stone. *Life* . . . *of John Howland.* Providence, R.I., 1837.
Stone, *B*	William L. Stone. *Border Wars of the American Revolution.* 2 vols., New York, 1864.
Stone, *W*	William L. Stone. *The Campaign of Lieut. Gen. John Burgoyne and the Expedition of Lieut. Col. Barry St. Leger.* Albany, N.Y., 1877.

Stryker, *F*   W. S. Stryker. *The Forts on the Delaware*. Trenton, N.J., 1901.

Stryker, *M*   W. S. Stryker. *The Battle of Monmouth*. Princeton, 1927.

Stryker, *TP*   W. S. Stryker. *The Battles of Trenton and Princeton*. Boston, 1898.

Sullivan   *Letters and Papers of Major-General John Sullivan* . . . 3 vols., Concord, N.H., 1930–1939.

Sullivan, *J*   *Journals of the Military Expedition of Maj. Gen. John Sullivan Against the Six Nations of Indians*. Auburn, N.Y., 1887.

Swett   S. Swett. *History of the Bunker Hill Battle*. Boston, 1827.

Swiggett   Howard Swiggett. *War Out of Niagara*. New York, 1933.

Sydney   William C. Sydney. *England and the English in the Eighteenth Century*. 2 vols., London, 1892.

Tallmadge   *Memoir of Colonel Benjamin Tallmadge*. Boston, 1876.

Tarbox   I. N. Tarbox. *Life of Israel Putnam*. Boston, 1876.

Tarleton   Banastre Tarleton. *A History of the Campaigns of 1780 and 1781* . . . Dublin, 1787.

Thacher   James Thacher. *Military Journal of the American Revolution* . . . Hartford, Conn., 1862.

Thruston   R. C. Ballard Thruston. *The Origin and Evolution of the United States Flag* (U. S. Pub. Docs., 69th Congress, 1st Sess., House Doc. 258). Washington, 1926.

Tower   Charlemagne Tower. *The Marquis de La Fayette in the American Revolution* . . . 2 vols., Philadelphia, 1895.

Townsend   Joseph Townsend. "Some Account of the British Army . . . and of the Battle of Brandywine," *Bulletin of the Hist. Soc. of Pa.,* Vol. I, No. 7 (Sept., 1846), pp. 17–29.

Trevelyan   George O. Trevelyan. *The American Revolution*. 6 vols. (including *George III and Charles Fox*, numbered V and VI), London, 1909–1914.

Tyler   Moses C. Tyler. *The Literary History of the American Revolution, 1763–1783*. 2 vols., New York, 1941.

Uhlendorf   Bernard Uhlendorf, editor. *The Siege of Charleston* . . . Ann Arbor, Mich., 1938.

Van Doren   Carl Van Doren. *Secret History of the American Revolution*. New York, 1941.

Van Doren, *M*   Carl Van Doren. *Mutiny in January*. New York, 1943.

Van Tyne   C. H. Van Tyne. *The War of Independence: American Phase* Boston, 1929.

Van Tyne, *C*   C. H. Van Tyne. *The Causes of the War of Independence*. Boston, 1922.

Van Tyne, *L*   C. H. Van Tyne. *The Loyalists in the American Revolution*. New York, 1902.

Waldo   "Valley Forge, 1777–1778: Diary of Surgeon Albigence Waldo," *Pa. Mag. of Hist. and Biog.,* XXI (1897), 299–323.

Walpole   Mrs. Paget Toynbee, editor. *The Letters of Horace Walpole*. 19 vols., Oxford, 1903–1925.

Walton   Joseph S. Walton. "George Washington in Chester County,"
                Chester Co. Hist. Soc. Bulletin, 1899–1900.

Walworth   Ellen H. Walworth. *Battles of Saratoga, 1777.* Albany, N.Y.,
                1891.

Watson, E   Elkanah Watson. *Men and Times of the Revolution.* New York,
                1856.

Watson, J   John F. Watson. *Annals of Philadelphia, and Pennsylvania.* 3
                vols., Philadelphia, 1927.

Weelen   Jean-Edmond Weelen. *Rochambeau.* New York, 1936.

Wells   "Journal of Bayze Wells . . ." *Conn. Hist. Soc. Colls.,* VII,
                239–296. Hartford, 1899.

Whitton   F. E. Whitton. *The American War of Independence.* New
                York, 1931.

Wildes   H. E. Wildes. *Anthony Wayne.* New York, 1941.

Wilkin   W. H. Wilkin. *Some British Soldiers in America.* London, 1914.

Wilkinson   James Wilkinson. *Memoirs of My Own Times.* 3 vols., Phila-
                delphia, 1816.

Willcox   William B. Willcox. "The British Road to Yorktown: A Study
                in Divided Command," *American Historical Review,* LII (Oct.,
                1946), 1–35.

Willcox, S   William B. Willcox. "British Strategy in America, 1778," *Jour-
                nal of Modern History,* XIX (June, 1947), 97–121.

Winsor   Justin Winsor. *Narrative and Critical History of America.* 8
                vols., Boston, 1884–1889.

Wirt   William Wirt. *Sketches of the Life and Character of Patrick
                Henry.* Philadelphia, 1818.

Wraxall   *The Historical and the Posthumous Memoirs of Sir Nathaniel
                W. Wraxall, 1772–1784.* 5 vols., London, 1884.

INDEX

955

350, 469, 785, 791; British use of, 29, 90, 93, 129, 315, 352, 358, 366, 486, 495, 510, 511, 518, 519, 528, 533, 548, 617, 627, 628, 694, 701, 706, 710, 728–730, 741, 742, 768, 790, 791, 818, 822, 831, 832, 892, 893, 932; lack of, in American army, 31, 205, 232, 273; Hessian use of, 223, 297, 300, 339, 414; American use of, 295, 323, 364, 365, 368, 369, 500, 538, 599, 603, 608, 624, 651, 686, 702, 729, 730, 756, 761, 790, 804, 806, 828, 831, 832, 877, 892; drilled in, 553
Beach, Gershom, 66
Beall, Gen. Reazin, 246, 250, 281
Bear Mountain, 515, 518
Beattie's Ford, 767, 768
Beatty, Lt., 643
Beatty, Capt. William, Jr., 806
Beaufort, 682, 683, 704, 705, 842
Beaulieu plantation, 690
Beaver Creek, 824
Beaverdam Creek, 887
Bedel, Col. Timothy, 147, 155, 156, 160, 198, 386
Bedford, Long Island, 43, 213–227 *passim*
Bedford County, 877
Beer, 85, 117; spruce, 106, 204
Belknap, Samuel, 44
Bell's Mills, 782, 785
Bemis Heights, 502, 504, 648; battle of, 524–531
Bemis's tavern, 502
Bennett, Lt. Caleb, 736
Bennington, 66, 333, 422, 497, 500, 501, 539; battle of, 425–430, 751
Benson, Capt. Perry, 802
Bergen road, 606, 609; Heights, 609; County, 613
Berks County militia, 214; riflemen, 214
Berkshire County, 426
Berkshires, 124
Bernier's Brook, 151
Berry, Samuel, 165, 169
Bethel, 494
Bethlehem, 546, 559
Beverly, 49
Bevin's Ford, 566
Biddle, Col. Clement, 361
Bigelow, Major Timothy, 168, 170, 175, 176, 193
Biggon Ferry, 752
Billerica, 40, 44
Billings Island, 373
Billingsport, 362, 373
Bird, Col., 371; Lt., 483

Bird, Col. Henry, 861
Bird's tavern, 876
Birmingham, 295, 296; meeting house, 347, 349, 351
Bissel, Israel, ride of, 52–53
Black Swamp, 683–685
Blackstock's plantation, 746
Blanchard, Luther, 43
Bland, Col. Theodorick, 329, 342, 346, 347
Blandford, 871
Bland's Virginia horse, 698, 701
Blankets, 277, 293, 316, 317, 340, 360, 361, 377, 392, 595, 740, 742, 814, 861; scarcity of, 275–286 *passim*, 357, 378, 383, 384, 543, 612, 732, 736, 766
Blockade, of Boston, 20, 133
"Blockade of Boston," burlesque, 113, 122
Bloomingdale, 244, 247
Blue Ridge Mountains, 655
Board of War, 371, 556, 559–562, 567, 614; Pennsylvania, 749; Maryland, 749
Bog Brook, 173
Bohemia Manor, 338
Bombay Hook, 372
Bombazee Rips, 172
Bomoseen, Lake, 411
Bond, American officer, 386
Bonhamton, 327
Boone, Col. Daniel, 864
Boonesborough, 851
Boot tavern, 356
Bordeaux, 557
Bordentown, 284–312 *passim*
de Borre, Gen. Prudhomme, 349, 350
von Bose Hessian regiment, 753, 767, 787, 788, 792, 796, 872, 877
Boston, 3, 15–20, 32–35, 37, 115, 127, 163, 195, 202, 236, 386, 398, 498, 537, 539, 541, 591, 593, 616, 847; Cadets, 3; Grenadier Corps, 3; Massacre, 5, 11; Tea Party, 13; port of, closed, 14–16; Neck, 19, 20, 33, 34, 47, 50, 58, 73–98 *passim*, 109, 126, 127, 132; blockade running, 20; unemployed in, 33; siege of, 52–62; refugees from, 56, 133; evacuation of, 116, 122, 129–133, 666, 667
Boston, American gondola, 390, 395; armed vessel, 697
Boswell, James, 480
Botta, Alexander, cited, 235
Boundbrook, 325
Bounty for military service, 118, 120, 203, 308, 320–321, 658
Bourlamaque, 63